HANDBOOK OF
U.S. LABOR
STATISTICS

HANDBOOK OF U.S. LABOR STATISTICS

Employment, Earnings, Prices, Productivity, and Other Labor Data

24th Edition
2021

Edited by Mary Meghan Ryan

Lanham • Boulder • New York • London

Published by Bernan Press
An imprint of The Rowman & Littlefield Publishing Group, Inc.
4501 Forbes Boulevard, Suite 200, Lanham, Maryland 20706
www.rowman.com
800-462-6420

86-90 Paul Street, London EC2A 4NE

ISBN: 978-1-63671-017-4
E-ISBN: 978-1-63671-018-1
ISSN: 1526-2553

CONTENTS

LIST OF TABLES

CHAPTER 1: POPULATION, LABOR FORCE, AND EMPLOYMENT STATUS

Population, Labor Force, and Employment Status

Employment

Unemployment

CHAPTER 5: PRODUCTIVITY AND COSTS

CHAPTER 6: COMPENSATION OF EMPLOYEES

Employment Cost Index (ECI)

Employer Costs for Employee Compensation (ECEC)

Employee Benefits Survey

CHAPTER 7: RECENT TRENDS IN THE LABOR MARKET

Local Area Unemployment Statistics

CHAPTER 12: AMERICAN TIME USE SURVEY

CHAPTER 13: INCOME DATA IN THE UNITED STATES (CENSUS BUREAU)

CHAPTER 14: OCCUPATIONAL SAFETY AND HEALTH

LIST OF FIGURES

PREFACE

Bernan Press is pleased to present a compilation of Bureau of Labor Statistics (BLS) data in this 24th edition of its award-winning *Handbook of U.S Labor Statistics: Employment, Earnings, Prices, Productivity, and Other Labor Data*. BLS and the U.S. Census Bureau provide a treasure trove of historical information about all aspects of labor and employment in the United States. The current edition maintains the content of previous editions and updates the text with additional data and new features. The data in this *Handbook* are excellent sources of information for analysts in both government and the private sector.

The *Handbook* addresses many of the issues that are being discussed across the United States, such as high unemployment, employment projections for the future, the decline in income, the rapidly increasing costs of health care services, and the dramatic aging of the labor force. In addition, this publication provides an abundance of data on topics such as prices, productivity, consumer expenditures, occupational safety and health, international labor comparisons, and much more. For the first time, the *Handbook* includes a chapter on green jobs, technologies, and practices.

The comprehensive and historical data presented in the *Handbook* allow the user to understand the background of current events and compare today's economy with previous years. Select data in this publication go back to 1913 and several tables have data going back to the 1940s.

FEATURES OF THIS PUBLICATION

- Approximately 220 tables that present authoritative data on labor market statistics, including employment and unemployment, mass layoffs, prices, productivity, and data from the American Time Use Survey (ATUS).

- Each chapter is preceded by a figure that calls attention to noteworthy trends in the data.

- In addition to the figures, the introductory material for to each chapter also contains highlights of other salient data.

- The tables in each section are also preceded by notes and definitions, which contain concise descriptions of the data sources, concepts, definitions, and methodology from which the data are derived.

- The introductory notes also include references to more comprehensive reports. These reports provide additional data

and more extensive descriptions of estimation methods, sampling, and reliability measures.

NEW IN THIS EDITION

The 24th edition includes a new chapter titled "The Impact of Coronavirus (COVID-19) on the Labor Force". This chapter examines the impact that COVID-19 had on the labor market throughout 2020. The chapter addresses the sharp decline in employment, the increase in unemployment, and the rise of telework. In addition, it provides information on how Americans planned to use their stimulus payments.

In addition, this edition includes updated employment projections through 2029.

SOURCES OF ADDITIONAL INFORMATION

BLS data are primarily derived from surveys conducted by the federal government or through federal-state cooperative arrangements. The comparability of data over time can be affected by changes in the surveys, which are essential for keeping pace with the current structure of economic institutions and for taking advantage of improved survey techniques. Revisions of current data are also periodically made as a result of the availability of new information.

More extensive methodological information, including further discussion of the sampling and estimation procedures used for each BLS program, is contained in the *BLS Handbook of Methods*. This publication is in the process of being updated, and completed chapters are available on the BLS Web site at <https://www.bls.gov>. Other relevant publications, including those from the Census Bureau, are noted in the notes and definitions in each chapter.

OTHER PUBLICATIONS BY BERNAN PRESS

Handbook of U.S Labor Statistics: Employment, Earnings, Prices, Productivity, and Other Labor Data is just one of a number of publications in Bernan Press's award-winning U.S. DataBook Series. Other titles include *The Almanac of American Education*; *Business Statistics of the United States: Patterns of Economic Change*; *Crime in the United States*; *Housing Statistics of the United States*; *States Profiles: The Population and Economy of Each U.S. State;* and *Vital Statistics of the United States: Births, Life Expectancy, Deaths, and Selected Health Data*. In addition, Bernan Press publishes *Employment, Hours, and Earnings: States and Areas* as a special edition of this *Handbook*. Each of these titles provides statistical information from official government sources.

CHAPTER 1: POPULATION, LABOR FORCE, AND EMPLOYMENT STATUS

HIGHLIGHTS

This chapter presents the detailed historical information collected in the Current Population Survey (CPS), a monthly survey of households that gathers data on the employment status of the population. Basic data on labor force, employment, and unemployment are shown for various characteristics of the population, including age, sex, race, Hispanic origin, and marital status.

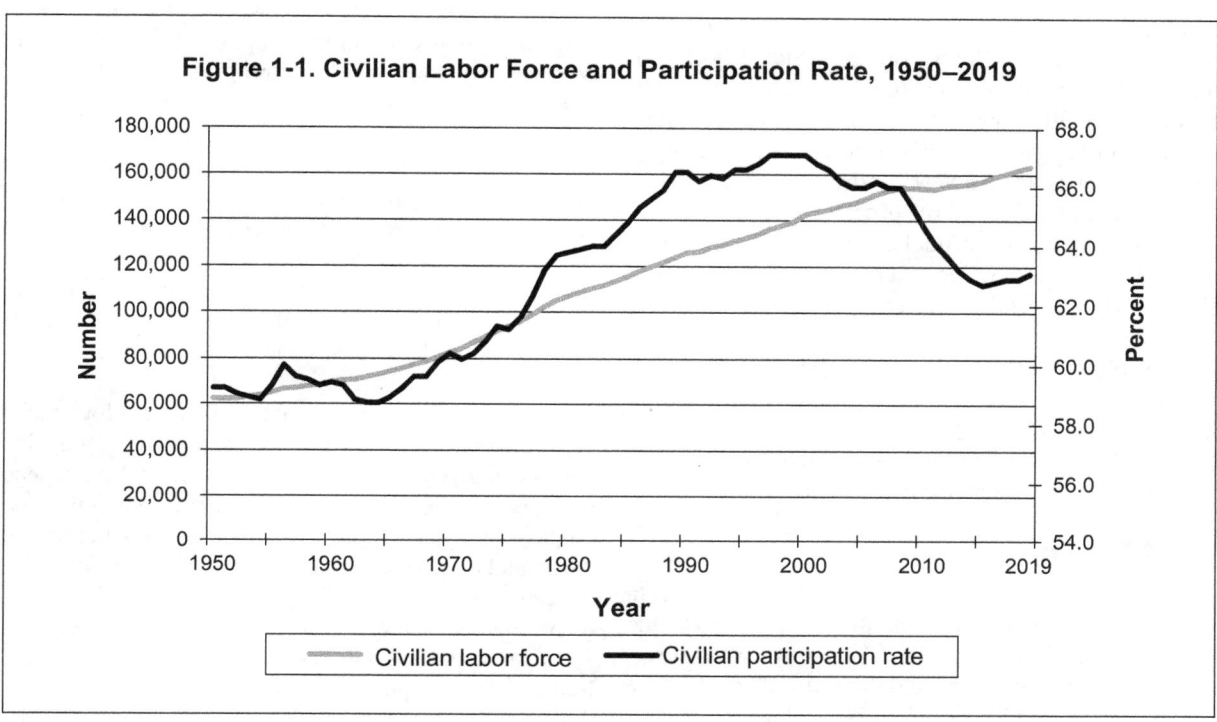

Figure 1-1. Civilian Labor Force and Participation Rate, 1950–2019

Over 163 million people were in the labor force in 2019 compared with 62 million in 1950. While the labor force has grown considerably, the labor force participation rate has grown much slower increasing from 59.2 percent in 1950 to 63.1 percent in 2019. The labor force participation rate increased slightly 2019 after remaining steady in 2018. In March 2020, as the global pandemic began to have a major impact on the labor market in the United States, unemployment increased sharply as the stay-at-home orders caused many businesses to close. (See Table 1-1.)

OTHER HIGHLIGHTS

- In 2019, employment increased 1.1 percent after increasing 1.6 percent in 2018. Employment decreased each year from 2008 to 2010 after increasing each year from 1992 through 2007 except for in 2002. The drop in employment was the steepest between 2008 and 2009 when it fell 3.8 percent. (See Table 1-1.)

- While the proportion of white men in the labor force declined significantly from 1985 to 2019, the proportion of black women in the labor force increased from 5.3 percent to over 6.6 percent. Additionally, Hispanic representation in the labor force also rose increasing from 6.7 percent in 1985 to 17.8 percent in 2019. (See Table 1-7.)

- The labor force participation rate increased for all age groups in 2019. Those aged 35-44 had the largest participation rate at 83.1 percent. Since 1999, the labor force participation rate has increased or remained steady each year, except in 2014, for those 65 years and over. (See Table 1-8.)

NOTES AND DEFINITIONS

CURRENT POPULATION SURVEY OF HOUSEHOLDS

Collection and Coverage

The Current Population Survey (CPS) is a monthly survey that analyzes and publishes statistics on the labor force, employment, and unemployment, and is classified by a variety of demographic, social, and economic characteristics. This survey is conducted by the Census Bureau for the Bureau of Labor Statistics (BLS). The CPS includes the civilian noninstitutional population age 16 years and older in the 50 states and DC. Respondents are interviewed to obtain information about the employment status of each household member age 16 years and over. Persons under 16 years of age are excluded from the official estimates because child labor laws, compulsory school attendance, and general social custom in the United States severely limit the types and amount of work that these children can do.

The inquiry relates to the household member's employment status during the calendar week, Sunday through Saturday that includes the 12th day of the month. This is known as the "reference week." Actual field interviewing is conducted during the following week (the week that contains the 19th day of the month).

Concepts and Definitions

The concepts and definitions underlying the labor force data have been modified—but not substantially altered—since the inception of the survey in 1940 when it began as a Work Projects Administration program. Current definitions of some of the major concepts used in the CPS are described below.

The civilian noninstitutional population includes persons 16 years of age and over who reside in the 50 states and the District of Columbia who are not inmates of institutions (such as penal and mental facilities and homes for the aged) and who are not on active duty in the armed forces.

An *employed person* is any person who, during the reference week: (1) did any work at all (at least one hour) as a paid employees in their own business, profession, or on their own farm, or who worked 15 hours or more as an unpaid worker in an enterprise operated by a member of the family; and (2) any person who was not working but who had a job or business from which he or she was temporarily absent due to vacation, illness, bad weather, childcare problems, maternity or paternity leave, labor-management disputes, job training, or other family or personal reasons, despite whether the employee was being paid for the time off or was seeking other jobs.

Each employed person is counted only once, even if he or she holds more than one job. For purposes of occupation and industry classification, multiple jobholders are counted as being in the job at which they worked the greatest number of hours during the reference week.

Included in the total are employed citizens of foreign countries who were temporarily in the United States but not living on the premises of an embassy. Excluded are persons whose only activity during the reference week consisted of work around their own house (painting, repairing, or own home housework) or volunteer work for religious, charitable, and similar organizations.

Unemployed persons are all persons who had no employment during the reference week, but who were available for work (except for temporary illness) and had made specific efforts to find employment some time during the four-week period ending with the reference week. Persons who were waiting to be recalled to a job from which they had been laid off need not have been looking for work to be classified as unemployed.

Reasons for unemployment are divided into four major groups: (1) job losers, defined as (a) persons on temporary layoff, who have been given a date to return to work or who expect to return to work within six months; (b) permanent job losers, whose employment ended involuntarily and who began looking for work; and (c) persons who completed a temporary job and began looking for work after the job ended; (2) job leavers, defined as persons who quit or otherwise terminated their employment voluntarily and immediately began looking for work; (3) reentrants, defined as persons who previously worked but were out of the labor force prior to beginning their job search; and (4) new entrants, defined as persons who had never worked but were currently searching for work.

Duration of unemployment represents the length of time (through the current reference week) that persons classified as unemployed had been looking for work. For persons on layoff, duration of unemployment represents the number of full weeks they had been on layoff. Mean duration of unemployment is the arithmetic average computed from single weeks of unemployment; median duration of unemployment is the midpoint of a distribution of weeks of unemployment.

A *spell of unemployment* is a continuous period of unemployment of at least one week's duration and is terminated by either employment or withdrawal from the labor force.

Extent of unemployment refers to the number of workers and proportion of the labor force that were unemployed at some time during the year. The number of weeks unemployed is the total number of weeks accumulated during the entire calendar year.

The *unemployment rate* is the number of unemployed persons as a percentage of the civilian labor force.

The *civilian labor force* comprises all civilians classified as employed or unemployed.

The *participation rate* represents the proportion of the civilian noninstitutional population currently in the labor force.

The *employment-population ratio* represents the proportion of the population that is currently employed.

Persons not in the labor force are all persons in the civilian noninstitutional population who are neither employed nor unemployed. Information is collected about their desire for and availability to take a job at the time of the CPS interview, job search activity during the prior year, and reason for not looking for work during the four-week period ending with the reference week. Persons not in the labor force who want and are available for a job and who have looked for work within the past 12 months (or since the end of their last job, if they had held one within the past 12 months), but who are not currently looking, are designated as *marginally attached to the labor force*. The marginally attached are divided into those not currently looking because they believe their search would be futile—so-called *discouraged workers*—and those not currently looking for other reasons, such as family responsibilities, ill health, or lack of transportation.

Discouraged workers are defined as persons not in the labor force who want and are available for a job and who have looked for work sometime in the past 12 months (or since the end of their last job, if they held one within the past 12 months), but who are not currently looking because they believe that there are no jobs available or there are none for which they would qualify. The reasons for not currently looking for work include a person's belief that no work is available in his or her line of work or area; he or she could not find any work; he or she lacks necessary schooling, training, skills, or experience; employers would think he or she is too young or too old; or he or she would encounter hiring discrimination.

Usual full- or part-time status refers to hours usually worked per week. Full-time workers are those who usually work 35 hours or more (at all jobs). This group includes some individuals who worked less than 35 hours during the reference week for economic or noneconomic reasons. Part-time workers are those who usually work less than 35 hours per week (at all jobs), regardless of the number of hours worked during the reference week. These concepts are used to differentiate a person's normal schedule from his or her specific activity during the reference week. Unemployed persons who are looking for full-time work or who are on layoff from full-time jobs are counted as part of the full-time labor force; unemployed persons who are seeking part-time work or who are on layoff from part-time jobs are counted as part of the part-time labor force.

Year-round, full-time workers are workers who primarily worked at full-time jobs for 50 weeks or more during the preceding calendar year. Part-year workers worked either full- or part-time for 1 to 49 weeks.

At work part-time for economic reasons, sometimes called involuntary part-time, refers to individuals who gave an economic reason for working 1 to 34 hours during the reference week. Economic reasons include slack work or unfavorable business conditions, inability to find full-time work, and seasonal declines in demand. Those who usually work part-time must also indicate that they want and are available to work full-time to be classified as working part-time for economic reasons.

At work part-time for noneconomic reasons refers to persons who usually work part-time and were at work 1 to 34 hours during the reference week for a noneconomic reason. Noneconomic reasons include illness or other medical limitations, childcare problems or other family or personal obligations, school or training, retirement or Social Security limits on earnings, and being in a job where full-time work is less than 35 hours. This also includes workers who gave an economic reason for usually working 1 to 34 hours but said they do not want to work full-time or were unavailable for full-time work.

Absences are defined as instances in which persons who usually work 35 or more hours a week worked less than that during the reference period for reasons of illness or family obligations. Excluded are situations in which work was missed for vacation, holidays, or other reasons. The estimates are based on one-fourth of the sample only.

Earnings are a remuneration of a worker or group of workers for services performed during a specific period of time.

Usual weekly earnings for wage and salary workers include any overtime pay, commissions, or tips usually received (at the main job in the case of multiple jobholders). Earnings reported on a basis other than weekly (such as annual, monthly, or hourly) are converted to weekly. The term "usual" is as perceived by the respondent. If the respondent asks for a definition of usual, interviewers are instructed to define the term as more than half the weeks worked during the past 4 or 5 months.

Minimum wage refers to the prevailing federal minimum wage which was $7.25 in 2019. It increased from $6.55 per hour to $7.25 per hour on July 24, 2009 and has remained at that level since. Data are for wage and salary workers who were paid hourly rates and refer to a person's earnings at the sole or principal job.

A *multiple jobholder* is an employed person who, during the reference week, had two or more jobs as a wage and salary worker, was self-employed and also held a wage and salary job, or worked as an unpaid family worker and also held a wage and salary job.

Self-employed persons with multiple businesses and persons with multiple jobs as unpaid family workers are excluded.

Occupation, industry, and class of worker for members of the employed population are determined by the job held during the reference week. Persons with two or more jobs are classified as being in the job at which they worked the greatest number of hours. The unemployed are classified according to their last job. Beginning with data published in 2003, the systems used to classify occupational and industry data changed. They are currently based on the Standard Occupational Classification (SOC) system and the North American Industry Classification System (NAICS). (See the following section on historical comparability for a discussion of previous classification systems used in the CPS.) The class-of-worker breakdown assigns workers to one of the following categories: private and government wage and salary workers, self-employed workers, and unpaid family workers. Wage and salary workers receive wages, salaries, commissions, tips, or pay in kind from a private employer or from a government unit. Self-employed workers are those who work for profit or fees in their own businesses, professions, trades, or on their own farms. Only the unincorporated self-employed are included in the self-employed category in the class-of-worker typology. Self-employed workers who respond that their businesses are incorporated are included among wage and salary workers, because they are technically paid employees of a corporation. An unpaid family worker is a person working without pay for 15 hours or more per week on a farm or in a business operated by a member of the household to whom he or she is related by birth or marriage.

Educational attainment refers to years of school completed in regular schools, which include graded public, private, and parochial elementary, and high schools, whether day or night school. Colleges, universities, and professional schools are also included.

Tenure refers to length of time a worker has been continuously employed by his or her current employer. These data are collected through a supplement to the CPS. All employed persons were asked how long they had been working continuously for their present employer and, if the length of time was one or two years, a follow-up question was asked about the exact number of months. The follow-up question was included for the first time in the February 1996 supplement to the CPS. CPS supplements that obtained information on tenure in the January of 1983, 1987, and 1991 did not include the follow-up question. Prior to 1983, the question on tenure was asked differently. Data prior to 1983 are thus not strictly comparable to data for subsequent years.

White, Black, and Asian are terms used to describe the race of persons. Persons in these categories are those who selected that race only. Persons in the remaining race categories—American Indian or Alaskan Native, Native Hawaiian or Other Pacific Islander, and persons who selected more than one race category—are included in the estimates of total employment and

unemployment but are not shown separately because the number of survey respondents is too small to develop estimates of sufficient quality for monthly publication.

Hispanic origin refers to persons who identified themselves in the enumeration process as being Spanish, Hispanic, or Latino. Persons of Hispanic or Latino origin may be of any race.

Single, never married; married, spouse present; and other marital status are the terms used to define the marital status of individuals at the time of the CPS interview. Married, spouse present, applies to a husband and wife if both were living in the same household, even though one may be temporarily absent on business, vacation, in a hospital, etc. Other marital status applies to persons who are married, spouse absent; widowed; or divorced. Married, spouse absent relates to persons who are separated due to marital problems, as well as husbands and wives living apart because one was employed elsewhere, on duty with the armed forces, or any other reason.

A *household* consists of all persons—related family members and all unrelated persons—who occupy a housing unit and have no other usual address. A house, an apartment, a group of rooms, or a single room is regarded as a housing unit when occupied or intended for occupancy as separate living quarters.

A *householder* is the person (or one of the persons) in whose name the housing unit is owned or rented. The term is not applied to either husbands or wives in married-couple families; it refers only to persons in families maintained by either men or women without a spouse.

A *family* is defined as a group of two or more persons residing together who are related by birth, marriage, or adoption. All such persons are considered as members of one family. Families are classified as either married-couple families or families maintained by women or men without spouses.

Children refer to "own" children of the husband, wife, or person maintaining the family, including sons and daughters, stepchildren, and adopted children. Excluded are other related children, such as grandchildren, nieces, nephews, cousins, and unrelated children.

Persons are referred to as *disabled* if they answer yes to the following questions: 1.) Are you deaf or do you have serious difficulty hearing? 2.) Are you blind or do you serious difficulty seeing even when wearing glasses? 3.) Because of a physical, mental, or emotional condition, do you have serious difficulty concentrating, remembering, or making decisions? 4.) Do you have serious difficulty walking or climbing stairs? 5.) Do you have difficulty dressing or bathing? 6.) Because of a physical, mental, or emotional condition, do you have difficulty doing errands alone such as visiting a doctor's office or shopping? Labor force measures are only tabulated for persons 16 years and over.

Veterans are men and women who previously served on active duty in the U.S. Armed Forces and who were civilians at the time they were surveyed.

Nonveterans are men and women who never served on active duty in the U.S. Armed Forces.

World War II, Korean War, Vietnam-era, and Gulf War-era veterans are men and women who served in the Armed Forces during these periods, regardless of where they served.

Veterans of other service periods are men and women who served in the Armed Forces at any time other than World War II, the Korean War, the Vietnam era, or the Gulf War era.

Veteran status is obtained from responses to the question, "Did you ever serve on active duty in the U.S. Armed Forces?"

Period of service is obtained from answers to the question asked of veterans, "When did you serve on active duty in the U.S. Armed Forces?" The following service periods are identified:

Gulf War era II — September 2001–present

Gulf War era I — August 1990–August 2001

Vietnam era — August 1964–April 1975

Korean War — July 1950–January 1955

World War II — December 1941–December 1946

Other service periods — All other time periods

Veterans who served in Iraq, Afghanistan, or both are individuals who served in Iraq at any time since March 2003, in Afghanistan at any time since October 2001, or in both locations.

Presence of service-connected disability is determined by answers to the question, "Has the Department of Veterans Affairs (VA) or Department of Defense (DoD) determined that you have a service-connected disability, that is, a health condition or impairment caused or made worse by any of your military service?"

Service-connected disability rating is based on answers to the question, "What is your current service connected disability rating?" Answers can range from 0 to 100 percent, in increments of 10 percentage points.

Displaced workers are wage and salary workers 20 years of age and older who lost or left jobs because their plant or company closed or moved, there was insufficient work for them to do, or their position or shift was abolished. Data are often presented for long-tenured displaced workers—those who had worked for their employer for 3 or more years at the time of displacement.

Historical Comparability

While the concepts and methods are very similar to those used for the inaugural survey in 1940, a number of changes have been made over the years to improve the accuracy and usefulness of the data. Only recent major changes are described here.

Major changes to the CPS, such as the complete redesign of the questionnaire and the use of computer-assisted interviewing for the entire survey, were introduced in 1994. In addition, there were revisions to some of the labor force concepts and definitions, including the implementation of changes recommended in 1979 by the National Commission on Employment and Unemployment Statistics (NCEUS, also known as the Levitan Commission). Some of the major changes to the survey at this time were:

1. The introduction of a redesigned and automated questionnaire. The CPS questionnaire was totally redesigned in order to obtain more accurate, comprehensive, and relevant information, and to take advantage of state-of-the-art computer interviewing techniques. Computer-assisted interviewing has important benefits most notably that it facilitates the use of a relatively complex questionnaire that incorporates complicated skip patterns and standardized follow-up questions. Additionally, certain questions are automatically tailored to the individual's situation to make them more understandable.

2. Official labor force measures were defined more precisely. While the labor force status of most people is straightforward, some persons are more difficult to classify correctly, especially if they are engaged in activities that are relatively informal or intermittent. Many of the changes to the questionnaire were made to deal with such cases. This was accomplished by rewording and adding questions to conform more precisely to the official definitions, making the questions easier to understand and answer, minimizing reliance on volunteered responses, revising response categories, and taking advantage of the benefits of an automated interview.

3. The amount of data available was expanded. The questionnaire redesign also made it possible to collect several types of data on topics such as multiple job holding and usual hours regularly for the first time.

4. Several labor definitions were modified. The most important definitional changes concerned discouraged workers. The Levitan Commission had criticized the former definition because it was based on a subjective desire for work and on somewhat arbitrary assumptions about an individual's availability to take a job. As a result of the redesign, two requirements were added: For persons to qualify as discouraged they must have engaged in some job search within the past year (or since they last worked, if they worked within the past year), and they must be currently available to take a job. (Formerly, availability was inferred from responses to

other questions; now, there is a direct question.) Also, beginning in January 1994, questions on this subject are asked of the full CPS sample, permitting estimates of the number of discouraged workers to be published monthly (rather than quarterly).

Beginning in January 2003, several other changes were introduced into the CPS. These changes included the following:

1. Population controls that reflected the results of the 2000 census were introduced into the monthly CPS estimation process. The new controls increased the size of the civilian noninstitutional population by about 3.5 million in May 2002. As a result, they also increased the estimated numbers of people unemployed and employed. Because the increases were roughly proportional, however, the overall unemployment rate did not change significantly. Data from January 2000 through December 2002 were revised to reflect these new controls. Over and above these revisions, the U.S. Census Bureau introduced another large upward adjustment to the controls as part of its annual update of population estimates for 2003. These updated population estimates were not available in time to incorporate them into the revised population controls for January 2000 to December 2002. Thus, the data on employment and unemployment levels for January 2003 (and beyond) are not strictly comparable with those for earlier months. The unemployment rate and other ratios, however, were not substantially affected by the 2003 population control revisions.

2. Questions on race and Hispanic origin were modified to comply with the new standards for maintaining, collecting, and presenting federal data on race and ethnicity for federal statistical agencies. The questions were reworded to indicate that individuals could select more than once race category and to convey more clearly that individuals should report their own perception of what race is. These changes had no impact on the overall civilian noninstitutional population and civilian labor force. However, they did reduce the population and labor force levels of Whites, Blacks, and Asians beginning in January 2003.

3. Improvements were introduced to both the second stage and composite weighting procedures. These changes adapted the weighting procedures to the new race/ethnic classification system and enhanced the stability over time for demographic groups. The second-stage weighting procedure substantially reduced the variability of estimates and corrected, to some extent, for CPS underreporting.

Changes in the Occupational and Industrial Classification System

In January 2003, the CPS adopted the 2002 census industry and occupational classification systems, which were derived, respectively, from the 2002 North American Industry Classification System (NAICS) and the 2000 Standard Occupational Classification (SOC) system. The 1990 Census occupational and industry classifications were replaced. The introduction of the new industry and occupational classification systems in 2003 created a complete break in comparability at all levels of industry and occupation aggregation. The composition of detailed occupations and industries changed substantially in the 2002 systems compared with the 1990 systems, as did the structure for aggregating them into major groups. Therefore, any comparisons of data on the different classifications are not possible without major adjustments.

Historical employment series on the 2002 Census classifications are available at broad levels of occupational and industry aggregation back to 1983. However, historical employment series at the detailed occupational and industry levels on the 2002 classifications are available back to 2000 only.

In 2009, BLS began using the 2007 Census industry classification system, which was derived from the 2007 NAICS series, and still uses it currently. The 2010 Census occupational classification was introduced with data for January 2011 and replaced an earlier version that was based on the 2000 SOC. As a result of the classification change, occupational data beginning with January 2011 are not strictly comparable with earlier years. Although the names of the broad- and intermediate-level occupational groups in the 2010 Census occupational classification remained the same, some detailed occupations were re-classified between broader groups, affecting comparability over time.

The Current Population Survey currently uses the 2010 Census occupational classification and, beginning with data for January 2014, the 2012 Census industry classification. These classifications were derived from the 2010 Standard Occupational Classification (SOC) and the 2012 North American Industry Classification System (NAICS), respectively, to meet the special classification needs of demographic household surveys.

Sources of Additional Information

A complete description of sampling and estimation procedures and further information on the impact of historical changes in the surveys can be found in the updated version of the *BLS Handbook of Methods*. This can be found on the BLS Web site at <http://www.bls.gov/opub/hom/>.

Table 1-1. Employment Status of the Civilian Noninstitutional Population, 1950–2019

(Thousands of people, percent.)

Year	Civilian noninstitutional population	Civilian labor force								Not in labor force
		Total	Participation rate	Employed				Unemployed		
				Total	Percent of population	Agriculture	Nonagricultural industries	Number	Unemploy-ment rate	
1950	104 995	62 208	59.2	58 918	56.1	7 160	51 758	3 288	5.3	42 787
1951	104 621	62 017	59.2	59 961	57.3	6 726	53 235	2 055	3.3	42 604
1952	105 231	62 138	59.0	60 250	57.3	6 500	53 749	1 883	3.0	43 093
1953	107 056	63 015	58.9	61 179	57.1	6 260	54 919	1 834	2.9	44 041
1954	108 321	63 643	58.8	60 109	55.5	6 205	53 904	3 532	5.5	44 678
1955	109 683	65 023	59.3	62 170	56.7	6 450	55 722	2 852	4.4	44 660
1956	110 954	66 552	60.0	63 799	57.5	6 283	57 514	2 750	4.1	44 402
1957	112 265	66 929	59.6	64 071	57.1	5 947	58 123	2 859	4.3	45 336
1958	113 727	67 639	59.5	63 036	55.4	5 586	57 450	4 602	6.8	46 088
1959	115 329	68 369	59.3	64 630	56.0	5 565	59 065	3 740	5.5	46 960
1960	117 245	69 628	59.4	65 778	56.1	5 458	60 318	3 852	5.5	47 617
1961	118 771	70 459	59.3	65 746	55.4	5 200	60 546	4 714	6.7	48 312
1962	120 153	70 614	58.8	66 702	55.5	4 944	61 759	3 911	5.5	49 539
1963	122 416	71 833	58.7	67 762	55.4	4 687	63 076	4 070	5.7	50 583
1964	124 485	73 091	58.7	69 305	55.7	4 523	64 782	3 786	5.2	51 394
1965	126 513	74 455	58.9	71 088	56.2	4 361	66 726	3 366	4.5	52 058
1966	128 058	75 770	59.2	72 895	56.9	3 979	68 915	2 875	3.8	52 288
1967	129 874	77 347	59.6	74 372	57.3	3 844	70 527	2 975	3.8	52 527
1968	132 028	78 737	59.6	75 920	57.5	3 817	72 103	2 817	3.6	53 291
1969	134 335	80 734	60.1	77 902	58.0	3 606	74 296	2 832	3.5	53 602
1970	137 085	82 771	60.4	78 678	57.4	3 463	75 215	4 093	4.9	54 315
1971	140 216	84 382	60.2	79 367	56.6	3 394	75 972	5 016	5.9	55 834
1972	144 126	87 034	60.4	82 153	57.0	3 484	78 669	4 882	5.6	57 091
1973	147 096	89 429	60.8	85 064	57.8	3 470	81 594	4 365	4.9	57 667
1974	150 120	91 949	61.3	86 794	57.8	3 515	83 279	5 156	5.6	58 171
1975	153 153	93 775	61.2	85 846	56.1	3 408	82 438	7 929	8.5	59 378
1976	156 150	96 158	61.6	88 752	56.8	3 331	85 421	7 406	7.7	59 991
1977	159 033	99 009	62.3	92 017	57.9	3 283	88 734	6 991	7.1	60 025
1978	161 910	102 251	63.2	96 048	59.3	3 387	92 661	6 202	6.1	59 659
1979	164 863	104 962	63.7	98 824	59.9	3 347	95 477	6 137	5.8	59 900
1980	167 745	106 940	63.8	99 303	59.2	3 364	95 938	7 637	7.1	60 806
1981	170 130	108 670	63.9	100 397	59.0	3 368	97 030	8 273	7.6	61 460
1982	172 271	110 204	64.0	99 526	57.8	3 401	96 125	10 678	9.7	62 067
1983	174 215	111 550	64.0	100 834	57.9	3 383	97 450	10 717	9.6	62 665
1984	176 383	113 544	64.4	105 005	59.5	3 321	101 685	8 539	7.5	62 839
1985	178 206	115 461	64.8	107 150	60.1	3 179	103 971	8 312	7.2	62 744
1986	180 587	117 834	65.3	109 597	60.7	3 163	106 434	8 237	7.0	62 752
1987	182 753	119 865	65.6	112 440	61.5	3 208	109 232	7 425	6.2	62 888
1988	184 613	121 669	65.9	114 968	62.3	3 169	111 800	6 701	5.5	62 944
1989	186 393	123 869	66.5	117 342	63.0	3 199	114 142	6 528	5.3	62 523
1990	189 164	125 840	66.5	118 793	62.8	3 223	115 570	7 047	5.6	63 324
1991	190 925	126 346	66.2	117 718	61.7	3 269	114 449	8 628	6.8	64 578
1992	192 805	128 105	66.4	118 492	61.5	3 247	115 245	9 613	7.5	64 700
1993	194 838	129 200	66.3	120 259	61.7	3 115	117 144	8 940	6.9	65 638
1994	196 814	131 056	66.6	123 060	62.5	3 409	119 651	7 996	6.1	65 758
1995	198 584	132 304	66.6	124 900	62.9	3 440	121 460	7 404	5.6	66 280
1996	200 591	133 943	66.8	126 708	63.2	3 443	123 264	7 236	5.4	66 647
1997	203 133	136 297	67.1	129 558	63.8	3 399	126 159	6 739	4.9	66 837
1998	205 220	137 673	67.1	131 463	64.1	3 378	128 085	6 210	4.5	67 547
1999	207 753	139 368	67.1	133 488	64.3	3 281	130 207	5 880	4.2	68 385
2000	212 577	142 583	67.1	136 891	64.4	2 464	134 427	5 692	4.0	69 994
2001	215 092	143 734	66.8	136 933	63.7	2 299	134 635	6 801	4.7	71 359
2002	217 570	144 863	66.6	136 485	62.7	2 311	134 174	8 378	5.8	72 707
2003	221 168	146 510	66.2	137 736	62.3	2 275	135 461	8 774	6.0	74 658
2004	223 357	147 401	66.0	139 252	62.3	2 232	137 020	8 149	5.5	75 956
2005	226 082	149 320	66.0	141 730	62.7	2 197	139 532	7 591	5.1	76 762
2006	228 815	151 428	66.2	144 427	63.1	2 206	142 221	7 001	4.6	77 387
2007	231 867	153 124	66.0	146 047	63.0	2 095	143 952	7 078	4.6	78 743
2008	233 788	154 287	66.0	145 362	62.2	2 168	143 194	8 924	5.8	79 501
2009	235 801	154 142	65.4	139 877	59.3	2 103	137 775	14 265	9.3	81 659
2010	237 830	153 889	64.7	139 064	58.5	2 206	136 858	14 825	9.6	83 941
2011	239 618	153 617	64.1	139 869	58.4	2 254	137 615	13 747	8.9	86 001
2012	243 284	154 975	63.7	142 469	58.6	2 186	140 283	12 506	8.1	88 310
2013	245 679	155 389	63.2	143 929	58.6	2 130	141 799	11 460	7.4	90 290
2014	247 947	155 922	62.9	146 305	59.0	2 237	144 068	9 617	6.2	92 025
2015	250 801	157 130	62.7	148 834	59.3	2 422	146 411	8 296	5.3	93 671
2016	253 538	159 187	62.8	151 436	59.7	2 460	148 976	7 751	4.9	94 351
2017	255 079	160 320	62.9	153 337	60.1	2 454	150 883	6 982	4.4	94 759
2018	257 791	162 075	62.9	155 761	60.4	2 425	153 336	6 314	3.9	95 716
2019	259 175	163 539	63.1	157 538	60.8	2 425	155 113	6 001	3.7	95 636

Table 1-2. Employment Status of the Civilian Noninstitutional Population, by Sex, 1980–2019

(Thousands of people, percent.)

Sex and year	Civilian noninstitutional population	Civilian labor force		Employed				Unemployed		Not in labor force
		Total	Participation rate	Total	Percent of population	Agriculture	Non-agricultural industries	Number	Unemployment rate	
Men										
1980	79 398	61 453	77.4	57 186	72.0	2 709	54 477	4 267	6.9	17 945
1981	80 511	61 974	77.0	57 397	71.3	2 700	54 697	4 577	7.4	18 537
1982	81 523	62 450	76.6	56 271	69.0	2 736	53 534	6 179	9.9	19 073
1983	82 531	63 047	76.4	56 787	68.8	2 704	54 083	6 260	9.9	19 484
1984	83 605	63 835	76.4	59 091	70.7	2 668	56 423	4 744	7.4	19 771
1985	84 469	64 411	76.3	59 891	70.9	2 535	57 356	4 521	7.0	20 058
1986	85 798	65 422	76.3	60 892	71.0	2 511	58 381	4 530	6.9	20 376
1987	86 899	66 207	76.2	62 107	71.5	2 543	59 564	4 101	6.2	20 692
1988	87 857	66 927	76.2	63 273	72.0	2 493	60 780	3 655	5.5	20 930
1989	88 762	67 840	76.4	64 315	72.5	2 513	61 802	3 525	5.2	20 923
1990	90 377	69 011	76.4	65 104	72.0	2 546	62 559	3 906	5.7	21 367
1991	91 278	69 168	75.8	64 223	70.4	2 589	61 634	4 946	7.2	22 110
1992	92 270	69 964	75.8	64 440	69.8	2 575	61 866	5 523	7.9	22 306
1993	93 332	70 404	75.4	65 349	70.0	2 478	62 871	5 055	7.2	22 927
1994	94 355	70 817	75.1	66 450	70.4	2 554	63 896	4 367	6.2	23 538
1995	95 178	71 360	75.0	67 377	70.8	2 559	64 818	3 983	5.6	23 818
1996	96 206	72 087	74.9	68 207	70.9	2 573	65 634	3 880	5.4	24 119
1997	97 715	73 261	75.0	69 685	71.3	2 552	67 133	3 577	4.9	24 454
1998	98 758	73 959	74.9	70 693	71.6	2 553	68 140	3 266	4.4	24 799
1999	99 722	74 512	74.7	71 446	71.6	2 432	69 014	3 066	4.1	25 210
2000	101 964	76 280	74.8	73 305	71.9	1 861	71 444	2 975	3.9	25 684
2001	103 282	76 886	74.4	73 196	70.9	1 708	71 488	3 690	4.8	26 396
2002	104 585	77 500	74.1	72 903	69.7	1 724	71 179	4 597	5.9	27 085
2003	106 435	78 238	73.5	73 332	68.9	1 695	71 636	4 906	6.3	28 197
2004	107 710	78 980	73.3	74 524	69.2	1 687	72 838	4 456	5.6	28 730
2005	109 151	80 033	73.3	75 973	69.6	1 654	74 319	4 059	5.1	29 119
2006	110 605	81 255	73.5	77 502	70.1	1 663	75 838	3 753	4.6	29 350
2007	112 173	82 136	73.2	78 254	69.8	1 604	76 650	3 882	4.7	30 036
2008	113 113	82 520	73.0	77 486	68.5	1 650	75 836	5 033	6.1	30 593
2009	114 136	82 123	72.0	73 670	64.5	1 607	72 062	8 453	10.3	32 013
2010	115 174	81 985	71.2	73 359	63.7	1 665	71 694	8 626	10.5	33 189
2011	116 317	81 975	70.5	74 290	63.9	1 698	72 592	7 684	9.4	34 343
2012	117 343	82 327	70.2	75 555	64.4	1 626	73 930	6 771	8.2	35 017
2013	118 555	82 667	69.7	76 353	64.4	1 611	74 742	6 314	7.6	35 889
2014	119 748	82 882	69.2	77 692	64.9	1 685	76 007	5 190	6.3	36 865
2015	121 101	83 620	69.1	79 131	65.3	1 826	77 305	4 490	5.4	37 481
2016	122 497	84 755	69.2	80 568	65.8	1 839	78 729	4 187	4.9	37 743
2017	123 275	85 145	69.1	81 402	66.0	1 843	79 559	3 743	4.4	38 130
2018	124 678	86 096	69.1	82 698	66.3	1 797	80 902	3 398	3.9	38 582
2019	125 353	86 687	69.2	83 460	66.6	1 790	81 670	3 227	3.7	38 667
Women										
1980	88 348	45 487	51.5	42 117	47.7	656	41 461	3 370	7.4	42 861
1981	89 618	46 696	52.1	43 000	48.0	667	42 333	3 696	7.9	42 922
1982	90 748	47 755	52.6	43 256	47.7	665	42 591	4 499	9.4	42 993
1983	91 684	48 503	52.9	44 047	48.0	680	43 367	4 457	9.2	43 181
1984	92 778	49 709	53.6	45 915	49.5	653	45 262	3 794	7.6	43 068
1985	93 736	51 050	54.5	47 259	50.4	644	46 615	3 791	7.4	42 686
1986	94 789	52 413	55.3	48 706	51.4	652	48 054	3 707	7.1	42 376
1987	95 853	53 658	56.0	50 334	52.5	666	49 668	3 324	6.2	42 195
1988	96 756	54 742	56.6	51 696	53.4	676	51 020	3 046	5.6	42 014
1989	97 630	56 030	57.4	53 027	54.3	687	52 341	3 003	5.4	41 601
1990	98 787	56 829	57.5	53 689	54.3	678	53 011	3 140	5.5	41 957
1991	99 646	57 178	57.4	53 496	53.7	680	52 815	3 683	6.4	42 468
1992	100 535	58 141	57.8	54 052	53.8	672	53 380	4 090	7.0	42 394
1993	101 506	58 795	57.9	54 910	54.1	637	54 273	3 885	6.6	42 711
1994	102 460	60 239	58.8	56 610	55.3	855	55 755	3 629	6.0	42 221
1995	103 406	60 944	58.9	57 523	55.6	881	56 642	3 421	5.6	42 462
1996	104 385	61 857	59.3	58 501	56.0	871	57 630	3 356	5.4	42 528
1997	105 418	63 036	59.8	59 873	56.8	847	59 026	3 162	5.0	42 382
1998	106 462	63 714	59.8	60 771	57.1	825	59 945	2 944	4.6	42 748
1999	108 031	64 855	60.0	62 042	57.4	849	61 193	2 814	4.3	43 175
2000	110 613	66 303	59.9	63 586	57.5	602	62 983	2 717	4.1	44 310
2001	111 811	66 848	59.8	63 737	57.0	591	63 147	3 111	4.7	44 962
2002	112 985	67 363	59.6	63 582	56.3	587	62 995	3 781	5.6	45 621
2003	114 733	68 272	59.5	64 404	56.1	580	63 824	3 868	5.7	46 461
2004	115 647	68 421	59.2	64 728	56.0	546	64 182	3 694	5.4	47 225
2005	116 931	69 288	59.3	65 757	56.2	544	65 213	3 531	5.1	47 643
2006	118 210	70 173	59.4	66 925	56.6	543	66 382	3 247	4.6	48 037
2007	119 694	70 988	59.3	67 792	56.6	490	67 302	3 196	4.5	48 707
2008	120 675	71 767	59.5	67 876	56.2	518	67 358	3 891	5.4	48 908
2009	121 665	72 019	59.2	66 208	54.4	496	65 712	5 811	8.1	49 646
2010	122 656	71 904	58.6	65 705	53.6	541	65 164	6 199	8.6	50 752
2011	123 300	71 642	58.1	65 579	53.2	556	65 023	6 063	8.5	51 658
2012	125 941	72 648	57.7	66 914	53.1	560	66 353	5 734	7.9	53 293
2013	127 124	72 722	57.2	67 577	53.2	519	67 058	5 146	7.1	54 401
2014	128 199	73 039	57.0	68 613	53.5	552	68 061	4 426	6.1	55 159
2015	129 700	73 510	56.7	69 703	53.7	597	69 106	3 807	5.2	56 190
2016	131 040	74 432	56.8	70 868	54.1	621	70 247	3 564	4.8	56 608
2017	131 804	75 175	57.0	71 936	54.6	611	71 324	3 239	4.3	56 629
2018	133 112	75 978	57.1	73 063	54.9	628	72 435	2 916	3.8	57 134
2019	133 822	76 852	57.4	74 078	55.4	635	73 443	2 774	3.6	56 970

Table 1-3. Employment Status of the Civilian Noninstitutional Population, by Sex, Age, Race, and Hispanic Origin, 1995–2019

(Thousands of people.)

Characteristic	1995	1996	1997	1998	1999	2000	2001	2002	2003	2004	2005	2006
ALL RACES												
Both Sexes												
Civilian noninstitutional population	198 584	200 591	203 133	205 220	207 753	212 577	215 092	217 570	221 168	223 357	226 082	228 815
Civilian labor force	132 304	133 943	136 297	137 673	139 368	142 583	143 734	144 863	146 510	147 401	149 320	151 428
Employed	124 900	126 708	129 558	131 463	133 488	136 891	136 933	136 485	137 736	139 252	141 730	144 427
Agriculture	3 440	3 443	3 399	3 378	3 281	2 464	2 299	2 311	2 275	2 232	2 197	2 206
Nonagricultural industries	121 460	123 264	126 159	128 085	130 207	134 427	134 635	134 174	135 461	137 020	139 532	142 221
Unemployed	7 404	7 236	6 739	6 210	5 880	5 692	6 801	8 378	8 774	8 149	7 591	7 001
Not in labor force	66 280	66 647	66 837	67 547	68 385	69 994	71 359	72 707	74 658	75 956	76 762	77 387
Men, 16 Years and Over												
Civilian noninstitutional population	95 178	96 206	97 715	98 758	99 722	101 964	103 282	104 585	106 435	107 710	109 151	110 605
Civilian labor force	71 360	72 087	73 261	73 959	74 512	76 280	76 886	77 500	78 238	78 980	80 033	81 255
Employed	67 377	68 207	69 685	70 693	71 446	73 305	73 196	72 903	73 332	74 524	75 973	77 502
Agriculture	2 559	2 573	2 552	2 553	2 432	1 861	1 708	1 724	1 695	1 688	1 654	1 663
Nonagricultural industries	64 818	65 634	67 133	68 140	69 014	71 444	71 488	71 179	71 636	72 836	74 319	75 838
Unemployed	3 983	3 880	3 577	3 266	3 066	2 975	3 690	4 597	4 906	4 456	4 059	3 753
Not in labor force	23 818	24 119	24 454	24 799	25 210	25 684	26 396	27 085	28 197	28 730	29 119	29 350
Men, 20 Years and Over												
Civilian noninstitutional population	87 811	88 606	89 879	90 790	91 555	93 875	95 181	96 439	98 272	99 476	100 835	102 145
Civilian labor force	67 324	68 044	69 166	69 715	70 194	72 010	72 816	73 630	74 623	75 364	76 443	77 562
Employed	64 085	64 897	66 284	67 135	67 761	69 634	69 776	69 734	70 415	71 572	73 050	74 431
Agriculture	2 335	2 356	2 356	2 350	2 244	1 756	1 613	1 629	1 614	1 596	1 577	1 579
Nonagricultural industries	61 750	62 541	63 927	64 785	65 517	67 878	68 163	68 104	68 801	69 976	71 473	72 852
Unemployed	3 239	3 146	2 882	2 580	2 433	2 376	3 040	3 896	4 209	3 791	3 392	3 131
Not in labor force	20 487	20 563	20 713	21 075	21 362	21 864	22 365	22 809	23 649	24 113	24 392	24 584
Women, 16 Years and Over												
Civilian noninstitutional population	103 406	104 385	105 418	106 462	108 031	110 613	111 811	112 985	114 733	115 647	116 931	118 210
Civilian labor force	60 944	61 857	63 036	63 714	64 855	66 303	66 848	67 363	68 272	68 421	69 288	70 173
Employed	57 523	58 501	59 873	60 771	62 042	63 586	63 737	63 582	64 404	64 728	65 757	66 925
Agriculture	881	871	847	825	849	602	591	587	580	547	544	543
Nonagricultural industries	56 642	57 630	59 026	59 945	61 193	62 983	63 147	62 995	63 824	64 181	65 213	66 382
Unemployed	3 421	3 356	3 162	2 944	2 814	2 717	3 111	3 781	3 868	3 694	3 531	3 247
Not in labor force	42 462	42 528	42 382	42 748	43 175	44 310	44 962	45 621	46 461	47 225	47 643	48 037
Women, 20 Years and Over												
Civilian noninstitutional population	96 262	97 050	97 889	98 786	100 158	102 790	103 983	105 136	106 800	107 658	108 850	109 992
Civilian labor force	57 215	58 094	59 198	59 702	60 840	62 301	63 016	63 648	64 716	64 923	65 714	66 585
Employed	54 396	55 311	56 613	57 278	58 555	60 067	60 417	60 420	61 402	61 773	62 702	63 834
Agriculture	830	827	798	768	803	567	558	557	550	515	519	520
Nonagricultural industries	53 566	54 484	55 815	56 510	57 752	59 500	59 860	59 863	60 852	61 258	62 182	63 315
Unemployed	2 819	2 783	2 585	2 424	2 285	2 235	2 599	3 228	3 314	3 150	3 013	2 751
Not in labor force	39 047	38 956	38 691	39 084	39 318	40 488	40 967	41 488	42 083	42 735	43 136	43 407
Both Sexes, 16 to 19 Years												
Civilian noninstitutional population	14 511	14 934	15 365	15 644	16 040	15 912	15 929	15 994	16 096	16 222	16 398	16 678
Civilian labor force	7 765	7 806	7 932	8 256	8 333	8 271	7 902	7 585	7 170	7 114	7 164	7 281
Employed	6 419	6 500	6 661	7 051	7 172	7 189	6 740	6 332	5 919	5 907	5 978	6 162
Agriculture	275	261	244	261	234	141	128	124	111	121	100	108
Nonagricultural industries	6 144	6 239	6 417	6 790	6 938	7 049	6 611	6 207	5 808	5 786	5 877	6 054
Unemployed	1 346	1 306	1 271	1 205	1 162	1 081	1 162	1 253	1 251	1 208	1 186	1 119
Not in labor force	6 746	7 128	7 433	7 388	7 706	7 642	8 027	8 409	8 926	9 108	9 234	9 397
WHITE[1]												
Both Sexes												
Civilian noninstitutional population	166 914	168 317	169 993	171 478	173 085	176 220	178 111	179 783	181 292	182 643	184 446	186 264
Civilian labor force	111 950	113 108	114 693	115 415	116 509	118 545	119 399	120 150	120 546	121 086	122 299	123 834
Employed	106 490	107 808	109 856	110 931	112 235	114 424	114 430	114 013	114 235	115 239	116 949	118 833
Agriculture	3 194	3 276	3 208	3 160	3 083	2 320	2 174	2 171	2 148	2 103	2 077	2 063
Nonagricultural industries	103 296	104 532	106 648	107 770	109 152	112 104	112 256	111 841	112 087	113 136	114 872	116 769
Unemployed	5 459	5 300	4 836	4 484	4 273	4 121	4 969	6 137	6 311	5 847	5 350	5 002
Not in labor force	54 965	55 209	55 301	56 064	56 577	57 675	58 713	59 633	60 746	61 558	62 148	62 429
Men, 16 Years and Over												
Civilian noninstitutional population	80 733	81 489	82 577	83 352	83 930	85 370	86 452	87 361	88 249	89 044	90 027	91 021
Civilian labor force	61 146	61 783	62 639	63 034	63 413	64 466	64 966	65 308	65 509	65 994	66 694	67 613
Employed	58 146	58 888	59 998	60 604	61 139	62 289	62 212	61 849	61 866	62 712	63 763	64 883
Agriculture	2 347	2 436	2 389	2 376	2 273	1 743	1 606	1 611	1 597	1 583	1 562	1 554
Nonagricultural industries	55 800	56 452	57 608	58 228	58 866	60 546	60 606	60 238	60 269	61 129	62 201	63 330
Unemployed	2 999	2 896	2 641	2 431	2 274	2 177	2 754	3 459	3 643	3 282	2 931	2 730
Not in labor force	19 587	19 706	19 938	20 317	20 517	20 905	21 486	22 053	22 740	23 050	23 334	23 408

[1]Beginning in 2003, persons who selected this race group only; persons who selected more than one race group are not included. Prior to 2003, persons who reported more than one race group were included in the group they identified as the main race.

Table 1-3. Employment Status of the Civilian Noninstitutional Population, by Sex, Age, Race, and Hispanic Origin, 1995–2019—*Continued*

(Thousands of people.)

Characteristic	2007	2008	2009	2010	2011	2012	2013	2014	2015	2016	2017	2018	2019
ALL RACES													
Both Sexes													
Civilian noninstitutional population	231 867	233 788	235 801	237 830	239 618	243 284	245 679	247 947	250 801	253 538	255 079	257 791	259 175
Civilian labor force	153 124	154 287	154 142	153 889	153 617	154 975	155 389	155 922	157 130	159 187	160 320	162 075	163 539
Employed	146 047	145 362	139 877	139 064	139 869	142 469	143 929	146 305	148 834	151 436	153 337	155 761	157 538
Agriculture	2 095	2 168	2 103	2 206	2 254	2 186	2 130	2 237	2 422	2 460	2 454	2 425	2 425
Nonagricultural industries	143 952	143 194	137 775	136 858	137 615	140 283	141 799	144 068	146 411	148 976	150 883	153 336	155 113
Unemployed	7 078	8 924	14 265	14 825	13 747	12 506	11 460	9 617	8 296	7 751	6 982	6 314	6 001
Not in labor force	78 743	79 501	81 659	83 941	86 001	88 310	90 290	92 025	93 671	94 351	94 759	95 716	95 636
Men, 16 Years and Over													
Civilian noninstitutional population	112 173	113 113	114 136	115 174	116 317	117 343	118 555	119 748	121 101	122 497	123 275	124 678	125 353
Civilian labor force	82 136	82 520	82 123	81 985	81 975	82 327	82 667	82 882	83 620	84 755	85 145	86 096	86 687
Employed	78 254	77 486	73 670	73 359	74 290	75 555	76 353	77 692	79 131	80 568	81 402	82 698	83 460
Agriculture	1 604	1 650	1 607	1 665	1 698	1 626	1 611	1 685	1 826	1 839	1 843	1 797	1 790
Nonagricultural industries	76 650	75 836	72 062	71 694	72 592	73 930	74 742	76 007	77 305	78 729	79 559	80 902	81 670
Unemployed	3 882	5 033	8 453	8 626	7 684	6 771	6 314	5 190	4 490	4 187	3 743	3 398	3 227
Not in labor force	30 036	30 593	32 013	33 189	34 343	35 017	35 889	36 865	37 481	37 743	38 130	38 582	38 667
Men, 20 Years and Over													
Civilian noninstitutional population	103 555	104 453	105 493	106 596	107 736	108 686	110 017	111 299	112 671	114 023	114 783	116 185	116 908
Civilian labor force	78 596	79 047	78 897	78 994	79 080	79 387	79 744	80 056	80 735	81 759	82 206	83 188	83 737
Employed	75 337	74 750	71 341	71 230	72 182	73 403	74 176	75 471	76 776	78 084	78 919	80 211	80 917
Agriculture	1 514	1 552	1 514	1 589	1 611	1 547	1 532	1 614	1 757	1 767	1 776	1 722	1 725
Nonagricultural industries	73 823	73 198	69 828	69 641	70 571	71 856	72 644	73 857	75 019	76 317	77 143	78 489	79 192
Unemployed	3 259	4 297	7 555	7 763	6 898	5 984	5 568	4 585	3 959	3 675	3 287	2 976	2 819
Not in labor force	24 959	25 406	26 596	27 603	28 656	29 299	30 273	31 243	31 936	32 263	32 577	32 997	33 172
Women, 16 Years and Over													
Civilian noninstitutional population	119 694	120 675	121 665	122 656	123 300	125 941	127 124	128 199	129 700	131 040	131 804	133 112	133 822
Civilian labor force	70 988	71 767	72 019	71 904	71 642	72 648	72 722	73 039	73 510	74 432	75 175	75 978	76 852
Employed	67 792	67 876	66 208	65 705	65 579	66 914	67 577	68 613	69 703	70 868	71 936	73 063	74 078
Agriculture	490	518	496	541	556	560	519	552	597	621	611	628	635
Nonagricultural industries	67 302	67 358	65 712	65 164	65 023	66 353	67 058	68 061	69 106	70 247	71 324	72 435	73 443
Unemployed	3 196	3 891	5 811	6 199	6 063	5 734	5 146	4 426	3 807	3 564	3 239	2 916	2 774
Not in labor force	48 707	48 908	49 646	50 752	51 658	53 293	54 401	55 159	56 190	56 608	56 629	57 134	56 970
Women, 20 Years and Over													
Civilian noninstitutional population	111 330	112 260	113 265	114 333	115 107	117 614	118 875	120 014	121 511	122 801	123 542	124 841	125 574
Civilian labor force	67 516	68 382	68 856	68 990	68 810	69 765	69 860	70 212	70 695	71 538	72 213	73 002	73 906
Employed	64 799	65 039	63 699	63 456	63 360	64 640	65 295	66 287	67 323	68 387	69 344	70 424	71 470
Agriculture	460	491	471	519	534	534	498	536	574	593	586	599	615
Nonagricultural industries	64 339	64 548	63 228	62 936	62 826	64 106	64 798	65 750	66 749	67 794	68 758	69 824	70 856
Unemployed	2 718	3 342	5 157	5 534	5 450	5 125	4 565	3 926	3 371	3 151	2 868	2 578	2 435
Not in labor force	43 814	43 878	44 409	45 343	46 297	47 849	49 015	49 802	50 816	51 263	51 330	51 839	51 668
Both Sexes, 16 to 19 Years													
Civilian noninstitutional population	16 982	17 075	17 043	16 901	16 774	16 984	16 787	16 633	16 619	16 714	16 754	16 765	16 693
Civilian labor force	7 012	6 858	6 390	5 906	5 727	5 823	5 785	5 654	5 700	5 889	5 901	5 885	5 896
Employed	5 911	5 573	4 837	4 378	4 327	4 426	4 458	4 548	4 734	4 965	5 074	5 126	5 150
Agriculture	121	125	119	98	109	105	100	86	91	100	92	103	85
Nonagricultural industries	5 790	5 448	4 719	4 281	4 218	4 321	4 358	4 462	4 643	4 865	4 982	5 023	5 065
Unemployed	1 101	1 285	1 552	1 528	1 400	1 397	1 327	1 106	966	925	827	759	746
Not in labor force	9 970	10 218	10 654	10 995	11 048	11 162	11 002	10 979	10 919	10 824	10 853	10 879	10 796
WHITE[1]													
Both Sexes													
Civilian noninstitutional population	188 253	189 540	190 902	192 075	193 077	193 204	194 333	195 498	196 868	198 215	198 942	200 221	200 827
Civilian labor force	124 935	125 635	125 644	125 084	124 579	123 684	123 412	123 327	123 607	124 658	124 941	125 815	126 600
Employed	119 792	119 126	114 996	114 168	114 690	114 769	115 379	116 788	117 944	119 313	120 176	121 461	122 441
Agriculture	1 953	2 021	1 968	2 071	2 134	2 033	1 975	2 093	2 262	2 309	2 267	2 251	2 254
Nonagricultural industries	117 839	117 104	113 028	112 098	112 556	112 735	113 404	114 695	115 682	117 004	117 909	119 210	120 187
Unemployed	5 143	6 509	10 648	10 916	9 889	8 915	8 033	6 540	5 662	5 345	4 765	4 354	4 159
Not in labor force	63 319	63 905	65 258	66 991	68 498	69 520	70 920	72 170	73 261	73 557	74 001	74 407	74 227
Men, 16 Years and Over													
Civilian noninstitutional population	92 073	92 725	93 433	94 082	94 801	94 266	94 865	95 513	96 147	96 861	97 225	97 933	98 220
Civilian labor force	68 158	68 351	68 051	67 728	67 551	66 921	66 842	66 680	67 018	67 564	67 592	68 082	68 367
Employed	65 289	64 624	61 630	61 252	71	61 990	62 322	63 108	63 892	64 612	65 000	65 702	66 100
Agriculture	1 501	1 539	1 499	1 557	1 602	1 515	1 495	1 571	1 701	1 725	1 694	1 670	1 649
Nonagricultural industries	63 788	63 085	60 131	59 695	60 318	60 476	60 827	61 537	62 192	62 887	63 306	64 031	64 452
Unemployed	2 869	3 727	6 421	6 476	5 631	4 931	4 520	3 572	3 126	2 952	2 592	2 380	2 266
Not in labor force	23 915	24 374	25 382	26 353	27 249	27 345	28 024	28 834	29 129	29 297	29 633	29 850	29 853

[1]Beginning in 2003, persons who selected this race group only; persons who selected more than one race group are not included. Prior to 2003, persons who reported more than one race group were included in the group they identified as the main race.

Table 1-3. Employment Status of the Civilian Noninstitutional Population, by Sex, Age, Race, and Hispanic Origin, 1995–2019—*Continued*

(Thousands of people.)

Characteristic	1995	1996	1997	1998	1999	2000	2001	2002	2003	2004	2005	2006
WHITE[1]												
Men, 20 Years and Over												
Civilian noninstitutional population	74 879	75 454	76 320	76 966	77 432	78 966	80 029	80 922	81 860	82 615	83 556	84 466
Civilian labor force	57 719	58 340	59 126	59 421	59 747	60 850	61 519	62 067	62 473	62 944	63 705	64 540
Employed	55 254	55 977	56 986	57 500	57 934	59 119	59 245	59 124	59 348	60 159	61 255	62 259
Agriculture	2 132	2 224	2 201	2 182	2 094	1 640	1 512	1 519	1 517	1 495	1 488	1 473
Nonagricultural industries	53 122	53 753	54 785	55 319	55 839	57 479	57 733	57 605	57 831	58 664	59 767	60 785
Unemployed	2 465	2 363	2 140	1 920	1 813	1 731	2 275	2 943	3 125	2 785	2 450	2 281
Not in labor force	17 161	17 114	17 194	17 545	17 685	18 116	18 510	18 855	19 386	19 671	19 851	19 927
Women, 16 Years and Over												
Civilian noninstitutional population	86 181	86 828	87 417	88 126	89 156	90 850	91 660	92 422	93 043	93 599	94 419	95 242
Civilian labor force	50 804	51 325	52 054	52 380	53 096	54 079	54 433	54 842	55 037	55 092	55 605	56 221
Employed	48 344	48 920	49 859	50 327	51 096	52 136	52 218	52 164	52 369	52 527	53 186	53 950
Agriculture	847	840	819	784	810	578	568	560	551	520	515	510
Nonagricultural industries	47 497	48 080	49 040	49 543	50 286	51 558	51 650	51 604	51 818	52 007	52 672	53 440
Unemployed	2 460	2 404	2 195	2 053	1 999	1 944	2 215	2 678	2 668	2 565	2 419	2 271
Not in labor force	35 377	35 503	35 363	35 746	36 060	36 770	37 227	37 581	38 006	38 508	38 814	39 021
Women, 20 Years and Over												
Civilian noninstitutional population	80 567	81 041	81 492	82 073	82 953	84 718	85 526	86 266	86 905	87 430	88 200	88 942
Civilian labor force	47 686	48 162	48 847	49 029	49 714	50 740	51 218	51 717	52 099	52 212	52 643	53 286
Employed	45 643	46 164	47 063	47 342	48 098	49 145	49 369	49 448	49 823	50 040	50 589	51 359
Agriculture	799	798	771	729	765	546	537	532	522	488	492	488
Nonagricultural industries	44 844	45 366	46 292	46 612	47 333	48 599	48 831	48 916	49 301	49 552	50 097	50 871
Unemployed	2 042	1 998	1 784	1 688	1 616	1 595	1 849	2 269	2 276	2 172	2 054	1 927
Not in labor force	32 881	32 879	32 645	33 044	33 239	33 978	34 308	34 548	34 806	35 218	35 557	35 656
Both Sexes, 16 to 19 Years												
Civilian noninstitutional population	11 468	11 822	12 181	12 439	12 700	12 535	12 556	12 596	12 527	12 599	12 690	12 856
Civilian labor force	6 545	6 607	6 720	6 965	7 048	6 955	6 661	6 366	5 973	5 929	5 950	6 009
Employed	5 593	5 667	5 807	6 089	6 204	6 160	5 817	5 441	5 064	5 039	5 105	5 215
Agriculture	262	254	236	250	224	135	125	121	109	116	97	102
Nonagricultural industries	5 331	5 413	5 571	5 839	5 980	6 025	5 692	5 320	4 955	4 923	5 008	5 113
Unemployed	952	939	912	876	844	795	845	925	909	890	845	794
Not in labor force	4 923	5 215	5 462	5 475	5 652	5 581	5 894	6 230	6 554	6 669	6 739	6 847
BLACK[1]												
Both Sexes												
Civilian noninstitutional population	23 246	23 604	24 003	24 373	24 855	24 902	25 138	25 578	25 686	26 065	26 517	27 007
Civilian labor force	14 817	15 134	15 529	15 982	16 365	16 397	16 421	16 565	16 526	16 638	17 013	17 314
Employed	13 279	13 542	13 969	14 556	15 056	15 156	15 006	14 872	14 739	14 909	15 313	15 765
Agriculture	101	98	117	138	117	77	62	69	63	50	51	60
Nonagricultural industries	13 178	13 444	13 852	14 417	14 939	15 079	14 944	14 804	14 676	14 859	15 261	15 705
Unemployed	1 538	1 592	1 560	1 426	1 309	1 241	1 416	1 693	1 787	1 729	1 700	1 549
Not in labor force	8 429	8 470	8 474	8 391	8 490	8 505	8 717	9 013	9 161	9 428	9 504	9 693
Men, 16 Years and Over												
Civilian noninstitutional population	10 411	10 575	10 763	10 927	11 143	11 129	11 172	11 391	11 454	11 656	11 882	12 130
Civilian labor force	7 183	7 264	7 354	7 542	7 652	7 702	7 647	7 794	7 711	7 773	7 998	8 128
Employed	6 422	6 456	6 607	6 871	7 027	7 082	6 938	6 959	6 820	6 912	7 155	7 354
Agriculture	93	86	103	118	99	67	56	63	52	43	43	51
Nonagricultural industries	6 329	6 371	6 504	6 752	6 952	7 015	6 882	6 896	6 768	6 869	7 111	7 303
Unemployed	762	808	747	671	671	620	709	835	891	860	844	774
Not in labor force	3 228	3 311	3 409	3 386	3 386	3 427	3 525	3 597	3 743	3 884	3 884	4 002
Men, 20 Years and Over												
Civilian noninstitutional population	9 280	9 414	9 575	9 727	9 926	9 952	9 993	10 196	10 278	11 656	10 659	10 864
Civilian labor force	6 730	6 806	6 910	7 053	7 182	7 240	7 200	7 347	7 346	7 773	7 600	7 720
Employed	6 137	6 167	6 325	6 530	6 702	6 741	6 627	6 652	6 586	6 912	6 901	7 079
Agriculture	89	83	101	112	96	67	55	62	51	274	43	49
Nonagricultural industries	6 048	6 084	6 224	6 418	6 606	6 675	55	6 591	6 535	6 638	6 858	7 030
Unemployed	593	639	585	524	480	499	573	695	760	860	699	640
Not in labor force	2 550	2 608	2 665	2 673	2 743	2 711	2 792	2 848	2 932	3 884	3 060	3 144
Women, 16 Years and Over												
Civilian noninstitutional population	12 835	13 029	13 241	13 446	13 711	13 772	13 966	14 187	14 232	14 409	14 635	14 877
Civilian labor force	7 634	7 869	8 175	8 441	8 713	8 695	8 774	8 772	8 815	8 865	9 014	9 186
Employed	6 857	7 086	7 362	7 685	8 029	8 073	8 068	7 914	7 919	7 997	8 158	8 410
Agriculture	8	13	14	20	18	10	6	6	11	7	8	9
Nonagricultural industries	6 849	7 073	7 348	7 665	8 011	8 064	8 062	7 907	7 908	7 990	8 150	8 402
Unemployed	777	784	813	756	684	621	706	858	895	868	856	775
Not in labor force	5 201	5 159	5 066	5 005	4 999	5 078	5 192	5 415	5 418	5 544	5 621	5 691

[1]Beginning in 2003, persons who selected this race group only; persons who selected more than one race group are not included. Prior to 2003, persons who reported more than one race group were included in the group they identified as the main race.

Table 1-3. Employment Status of the Civilian Noninstitutional Population, by Sex, Age, Race, and Hispanic Origin, 1995–2019—*Continued*

(Thousands of people.)

Characteristic	2007	2008	2009	2010	2011	2012	2013	2014	2015	2016	2017	2018	2019
WHITE[1]													
Men, 20 Years and Over													
Civilian noninstitutional population	85 420	86 056	86 789	87 502	88 191	87 780	88 474	89 193	89 865	90 572	90 941	91 662	91 993
Civilian labor force	65 214	65 483	65 372	65 265	65 165	64 540	64 505	64 430	64 710	65 169	65 296	65 812	66 037
Employed	62 806	62 304	59 626	59 438	60 118	60 193	60 511	61 289	61 959	62 575	63 009	63 719	64 070
Agriculture	1 417	1 447	1 410	1 483	1 518	1 438	1 418	1 504	1 638	1 658	1 629	1 600	1 587
Nonagricultural industries	61 389	60 857	58 216	57 955	58 600	58 755	59 093	59 785	60 321	60 917	61 380	62 118	62 483
Unemployed	2 408	3 179	5 746	5 828	5 046	4 347	3 994	3 141	2 751	2 594	2 288	2 094	1 967
Not in labor force	20 206	20 573	21 417	22 236	23 026	23 241	23 969	24 763	25 155	25 403	25 645	25 849	25 956
Women, 16 Years and Over													
Civilian noninstitutional population	96 180	96 814	97 469	97 993	98 276	98 938	99 467	99 984	100 720	101 354	101 717	102 289	102 607
Civilian labor force	56 777	57 284	57 593	57 356	57 028	56 763	56 571	56 648	56 589	57 095	57 349	57 732	58 233
Employed	54 503	54 501	53 366	52 916	52 770	52 779	53 057	53 680	54 052	54 701	55 176	55 759	56 341
Agriculture	452	482	469	513	532	519	480	522	562	585	573	581	605
Nonagricultural industries	54 050	54 019	52 897	52 402	52 238	52 260	52 577	53 158	53 490	54 117	54 603	55 178	55 735
Unemployed	2 274	2 782	4 227	4 440	4 257	3 985	3 513	2 968	2 537	2 393	2 173	1 973	1 893
Not in labor force	39 403	39 531	39 876	40 638	41 248	42 175	42 897	43 337	44 132	44 260	44 368	44 556	44 374
Women, 20 Years and Over													
Civilian noninstitutional population	89 790	90 400	91 078	91 683	92 068	92 766	93 360	93 928	94 680	95 301	95 661	96 242	96 587
Civilian labor force	53 925	54 508	54 976	54 957	54 700	54 475	54 299	54 421	54 410	54 871	55 103	55 426	55 968
Employed	51 996	52 124	51 231	50 997	50 881	50 911	51 198	51 798	52 161	52 771	53 179	53 682	54 304
Agriculture	423	457	444	492	511	493	460	507	540	557	549	553	587
Nonagricultural industries	51 572	51 667	50 787	50 505	50 371	50 418	50 737	51 291	51 621	52 214	52 630	53 129	53 718
Unemployed	1 930	2 384	3 745	3 960	3 818	3 564	3 102	2 623	2 249	2 100	1 923	1 743	1 664
Not in labor force	35 864	35 892	36 101	36 725	37 368	38 291	39 060	39 507	40 270	40 430	40 559	40 816	40 619
Both Sexes, 16 to 19 Years													
Civilian noninstitutional population	13 043	13 084	13 035	12 891	12 818	12 658	12 499	12 377	12 323	12 342	12 339	12 318	12 247
Civilian labor force	5 795	5 644	5 295	4 861	4 714	4 669	4 608	4 476	4 487	4 618	4 542	4 576	4 594
Employed	4 990	4 697	4 138	3 733	3 691	3 665	3 671	3 701	3 824	3 967	3 989	4 060	4 067
Agriculture	113	118	114	96	105	103	97	82	84	94	89	98	80
Nonagricultural industries	4 877	4 580	4 025	3 637	3 585	3 563	3 574	3 619	3 740	3 874	3 899	3 962	3 987
Unemployed	805	947	1 157	1 128	1 024	1 004	937	775	662	651	554	516	528
Not in labor force	7 248	7 440	7 740	8 030	8 103	7 988	7 891	7 901	7 836	7 724	7 797	7 741	7 653
BLACK[1]													
Both Sexes													
Civilian noninstitutional population	27 485	27 843	28 241	28 708	29 114	29 907	30 376	30 843	31 386	31 889	32 247	32 761	33 036
Civilian labor force	17 496	17 740	17 632	17 862	17 881	18 400	18 580	18 873	19 318	19 637	20 088	20 414	20 632
Employed	16 051	15 953	15 025	15 010	15 051	15 856	16 151	16 732	17 472	17 982	18 587	19 091	19 381
Agriculture	53	55	66	59	52	61	58	62	66	66	75	62	54
Nonagricultural industries	15 998	15 898	14 959	14 951	14 999	15 795	16 093	16 670	17 406	17 916	18 512	19 030	19 327
Unemployed	1 445	1 788	2 606	2 852	2 831	2 544	2 429	2 141	1 846	1 655	1 501	1 322	1 251
Not in labor force	9 989	10 103	10 609	10 846	11 233	11 508	11 797	11 970	12 068	12 252	12 159	12 347	12 404
Men, 16 Years and Over													
Civilian noninstitutional population	12 361	12 516	12 705	12 939	13 164	13 508	13 747	13 997	14 268	14 525	14 712	14 964	15 102
Civilian labor force	8 252	8 347	8 265	8 415	8 454	8 594	8 733	8 909	9 099	9 315	9 508	9 694	9 790
Employed	7 500	7 398	6 817	6 865	6 953	7 302	7 497	7 818	8 164	8 471	8 742	9 018	9 145
Agriculture	46	49	56	53	47	51	48	54	57	58	67	50	44
Nonagricultural industries	7 454	7 350	6 761	6 812	6 905	7 252	7 448	7 764	8 107	8 413	8 675	8 968	9 101
Unemployed	752	949	1 448	1 550	1 502	1 292	1 236	1 091	935	845	766	676	645
Not in labor force	4 110	4 169	4 441	4 524	4 710	4 913	5 014	5 089	5 169	5 209	5 204	5 270	5 312
Men, 20 Years and Over													
Civilian noninstitutional population	11 057	11 194	11 379	11 626	11 882	12 189	12 471	12 751	13 031	13 278	13 464	13 723	13 881
Civilian labor force	7 867	7 962	7 914	8 076	8 125	8 256	8 386	8 586	8 773	8 965	9 163	9 327	9 454
Employed	7 245	7 151	6 628	6 680	6 765	7 104	7 304	7 613	7 938	8 228	8 500	8 745	8 883
Agriculture	45	47	55	52	46	50	48	54	55	55	66	48	43
Nonagricultural industries	7 201	7 104	6 573	6 628	6 719	7 053	7 256	7 559	7 883	8 173	8 435	8 696	8 841
Unemployed	622	811	1 286	1 396	1 360	1 152	1 082	973	835	737	663	582	571
Not in labor force	3 189	3 232	3 465	3 550	17	3 932	4 084	4 165	4 258	4 313	4 301	4 396	4 426
Women, 16 Years and Over													
Civilian noninstitutional population	15 124	15 328	15 536	15 769	15 950	16 400	16 629	16 846	17 118	17 365	17 535	17 797	17 934
Civilian labor force	9 244	9 393	9 367	9 447	9 427	9 805	9 846	9 964	10 218	10 321	10 580	10 720	10 842
Employed	8 551	8 554	8 208	8 145	8 098	8 553	8 654	8 915	9 308	9 511	9 845	10 073	10 236
Agriculture	7	6	10	6	5	10	9	8	10	8	8	12	10
Nonagricultural industries	8 544	8 548	8 198	8 139	8 093	8 543	8 645	8 906	9 298	9 503	9 837	10 062	10 226
Unemployed	693	839	1 159	1 302	1 329	1 252	1 192	1 050	911	810	735	646	607
Not in labor force	5 879	5 934	6 169	6 322	6 523	6 595	6 783	6 881	6 899	7 043	6 955	7 077	7 092

[1]Beginning in 2003, persons who selected this race group only; persons who selected more than one race group are not included. Prior to 2003, persons who reported more than one race group were included in the group they identified as the main race.

Table 1-3. Employment Status of the Civilian Noninstitutional Population, by Sex, Age, Race, and Hispanic Origin, 1995–2019—*Continued*

(Thousands of people.)

Characteristic	1995	1996	1997	1998	1999	2000	2001	2002	2003	2004	2005	2006
BLACK[1]												
Women, 20 Years and Over												
Civilian noninstitutional population	11 682	11 833	12 016	12 023	12 451	12 561	12 758	12 966	13 026	14 409	13 377	13 578
Civilian labor force	7 175	7 405	7 686	7 912	8 224	8 215	8 323	8 348	8 409	8 865	8 610	8 723
Employed	6 556	6 762	7 013	7 290	7 663	7 703	7 741	7 610	7 636	7 997	7 876	8 068
Agriculture	7	12	13	19	17	9	6	5	10	7	7	7
Nonagricultural industries	6 548	6 749	7 000	7 272	7 646	7 694	7 735	7 604	7 626	7 701	7 868	8 060
Unemployed	620	643	673	622	561	512	582	738	772	868	734	656
Not in labor force	4 507	4 428	4 330	4 291	4 226	4 346	4 434	4 618	4 618	5 544	4 768	4 854
Both Sexes, 16 to 19 Years												
Civilian noninstitutional population	2 284	2 356	2 412	2 443	2 479	2 389	2 388	2 416	2 382	2 423	2 481	2 565
Civilian labor force	911	923	933	1 017	959	941	898	870	771	762	803	871
Employed	586	613	631	736	691	711	637	611	516	520	536	618
Agriculture	5	3	3	8	4	1	1	2	1	0	1	3
Nonagricultural industries	581	611	611	728	687	710	637	609	515	520	535	614
Unemployed	325	310	310	281	268	230	260	260	255	241	267	253
Not in labor force	1 372	1 434	1 434	1 427	1 520	1 448	1 490	1 546	1 611	1 661	1 677	1 694
HISPANIC[2]												
Both Sexes												
Civilian noninstitutional population	18 629	19 213	20 321	21 070	21 650	23 938	24 942	25 963	27 551	28 109	29 133	30 103
Civilian labor force	12 267	12 774	13 796	14 317	14 665	16 689	17 328	17 943	18 813	19 272	19 824	20 694
Employed	11 127	11 642	12 726	13 291	13 720	15 735	16 190	16 590	17 372	17 930	18 632	19 613
Agriculture	604	609	660	742	734	536	423	448	446	441	423	428
Nonagricultural industries	10 524	11 033	12 067	12 549	12 986	15 199	15 767	16 141	16 927	17 489	18 209	19 185
Unemployed	1 140	1 132	1 069	1 026	945	954	1 138	1 353	1 441	1 342	1 191	1 081
Not in labor force	6 362	6 439	6 526	6 753	6 985	7 249	7 614	8 020	8 738	8 837	9 310	9 409
Men, 16 Years and Over												
Civilian noninstitutional population	9 329	9 604	10 368	10 734	10 713	12 174	12 695	13 221	14 098	14 417	14 962	15 473
Civilian labor force	7 376	7 646	8 309	8 571	8 546	9 923	10 279	10 609	11 288	11 587	11 985	12 488
Employed	6 725	7 039	7 728	8 018	8 067	9 428	9 668	9 845	10 479	10 832	11 337	11 887
Agriculture	527	537	571	651	642	449	345	361	350	356	350	347
Nonagricultural industries	6 198	6 502	7 157	7 367	7 425	8 979	9 323	9 484	10 129	10 476	10 987	11 540
Unemployed	651	607	582	552	480	494	611	764	809	755	647	601
Not in labor force	1 952	1 957	2 059	2 164	2 167	2 252	2 416	2 613	2 810	2 831	2 977	2 985
Men, 20 Years and Over												
Civilian noninstitutional population	8 375	8 611	9 250	9 573	9 523	10 841	11 386	11 928	12 797	13 082	13 586	14 046
Civilian labor force	6 898	7 150	7 779	8 005	7 950	9 247	9 595	9 977	10 756	11 020	11 408	11 888
Employed	6 367	6 655	7 307	7 570	7 576	8 859	9 100	9 341	10 063	10 385	10 872	11 391
Agriculture	501	510	544	621	602	423	328	345	336	335	341	337
Nonagricultural industries	5 866	6 145	6 763	6 949	6 974	8 435	8 773	8 996	9 727	10 050	10 532	11 054
Unemployed	530	495	471	436	374	388	495	636	693	635	536	497
Not in labor force	1 477	1 461	1 471	1 568	1 573	1 595	1 791	1 951	2 041	2 061	2 177	2 157
Women, 16 Years and Over												
Civilian noninstitutional population	9 300	9 610	9 953	10 335	10 937	11 764	12 247	12 742	13 452	13 692	14 172	14 630
Civilian labor force	4 891	5 128	5 486	5 746	6 119	6 767	7 049	7 334	7 525	7 685	7 839	8 206
Employed	4 403	4 602	4 999	5 273	5 653	6 307	6 522	6 744	6 894	7 098	7 295	7 725
Agriculture	76	72	89	91	92	87	77	87	96	85	73	80
Nonagricultural industries	4 326	4 531	4 910	5 182	5 561	6 220	6 445	6 657	6 798	7 013	7 222	7 645
Unemployed	488	525	488	473	466	460	527	590	631	587	544	480
Not in labor force	4 409	4 482	4 466	4 589	4 819	4 997	5 198	5 408	5 928	6 007	6 333	6 424
Women, 20 Years and Over												
Civilian noninstitutional population	8 382	8 654	8 950	9 292	9 821	10 574	11 049	11 528	12 211	12 420	12 858	13 262
Civilian labor force	4 779	5 106	5 304	5 666	6 275	6 557	6 863	7 096	7 257	7 377	7 735
Employed	4 116	4 341	4 705	4 928	5 290	5 903	6 121	6 367	6 541	6 752	6 913	7 321
Agriculture	72	69	83	85	88	81	73	84	91	78	70	77
Nonagricultural industries	4 044	4 272	4 622	4 843	5 202	5 822	6 048	6 283	6 450	6 674	6 843	7 244
Unemployed	404	438	401	376	376	371	436	496	555	504	464	414
Not in labor force	3 863	3 875	3 845	3 988	4 155	4 299	4 492	4 666	5 114	5 163	5 481	5 527
Both Sexes, 16 to 19 Years												
Civilian noninstitutional population	1 872	1 948	2 121	2 204	2 307	2 523	2 508	2 507	2 543	2 608	2 689	2 796
Civilian labor force	850	845	911	1 007	1 049	1 168	1 176	1 103	960	995	1 038	1 071
Employed	645	646	714	793	854	973	969	882	768	792	847	900
Agriculture	31	29	33	36	45	31	22	19	19	25	13	14
Nonagricultural industries	614	617	682	757	809	942	947	863	749	767	834	887
Unemployed	205	199	197	214	196	194	208	221	192	203	191	170
Not in labor force	1 022	1 103	1 210	1 197	1 257	1 355	1 331	1 404	1 583	1 612	1 651	1 725

[1]Beginning in 2003, persons who selected this race group only; persons who selected more than one race group are not included. Prior to 2003, persons who reported more than one race group were included in the group they identified as the main race.
[2]May be of any race.

Table 1-3. Employment Status of the Civilian Noninstitutional Population, by Sex, Age, Race, and Hispanic Origin, 1995–2019—*Continued*

(Thousands of people.)

Characteristic	2007	2008	2009	2010	2011	2012	2013	2014	2015	2016	2017	2018	2019
BLACK[1]													
Women, 20 Years and Over													
Civilian noninstitutional population	13 788	13 974	14 178	14 425	14 638	15 076	15 340	15 584	15 863	16 102	16 272	16 539	16 693
Civilian labor force	8 828	8 991	8 988	9 110	9 110	9 433	9 476	9 606	9 843	9 943	10 171	10 324	10 437
Employed	8 240	8 260	7 956	7 944	7 906	8 313	8 408	8 663	9 032	9 219	9 514	9 751	9 910
Agriculture	7	6	10	6	5	10	9	8	10	8	8	12	9
Nonagricultural industries	8 233	8 254	7 946	7 938	7 901	8 303	8 399	8 655	9 022	9 211	9 506	9 739	9 900
Unemployed	588	732	1 032	1 165	1 204	1 119	1 069	943	811	724	657	573	527
Not in labor force	4 960	4 982	5 190	5 315	5 529	5 643	5 864	5 978	6 021	6 159	6 101	6 215	6 256
Both Sexes, 16 to 19 Years													
Civilian noninstitutional population	2 640	2 676	2 684	2 657	2 594	2 643	2 565	2 508	2 491	2 510	2 511	2 499	2 463
Civilian labor force	801	787	729	677	647	711	717	681	701	729	754	763	741
Employed	566	541	442	386	380	438	439	456	502	535	573	596	588
Agriculture	1	1	1	1	1	0	1	0	2	3	1	2	2
Nonagricultural industries	564	540	440	385	379	438	438	456	500	532	571	594	586
Unemployed	235	246	288	291	267	272	278	225	199	194	181	167	153
Not in labor force	1 839	1 889	1 954	1 980	1 947	1 932	1 848	1 827	1 790	1 781	1 758	1 736	1 722
HISPANIC[2]													
Both Sexes													
Civilian noninstitutional population	31 383	32 141	32 891	33 713	34 438	36 759	37 517	38 400	39 617	40 697	41 371	42 734	43 507
Civilian labor force	21 602	22 024	22 352	22 748	22 898	24 391	24 771	25 370	26 126	26 797	27 339	28 336	29 053
Employed	20 382	20 346	19 647	19 906	20 269	21 878	22 514	23 492	24 400	25 249	25 938	27 012	27 805
Agriculture	426	441	426	480	523	491	495	517	580	604	629	630	666
Nonagricultural industries	19 956	19 904	19 221	19 426	19 746	21 387	22 019	22 975	23 820	24 645	25 309	26 383	27 139
Unemployed	1 220	1 678	2 706	2 843	2 629	2 514	2 257	1 878	1 726	1 548	1 401	1 323	1 248
Not in labor force	9 781	10 116	10 539	10 964	11 540	12 368	12 746	13 030	13 491	13 900	14 032	14 398	14 454
Men, 16 Years and Over													
Civilian noninstitutional population	16 154	16 524	16 897	17 359	17 753	18 434	18 798	19 244	19 745	20 266	20 578	21 287	21 660
Civilian labor force	13 005	13 255	13 310	13 511	13 576	14 026	14 341	14 651	15 054	15 396	15 604	16 113	16 439
Employed	12 310	12 248	11 640	11 800	12 049	12 643	13 078	13 655	14 111	14 563	14 874	15 418	15 782
Agriculture	352	364	344	377	418	388	392	403	454	464	477	468	487
Nonagricultural industries	11 958	11 884	11 296	11 423	11 631	12 255	12 686	13 251	13 657	14 099	14 397	14 950	15 294
Unemployed	695	1 007	1 670	1 711	1 527	1 383	1 263	996	943	833	730	695	657
Not in labor force	3 149	3 270	3 588	3 849	4 177	4 408	4 457	4 593	4 691	4 870	4 974	5 174	5 221
Men, 20 Years and Over													
Civilian noninstitutional population	14 649	14 971	15 305	15 693	15 941	16 555	16 928	17 371	17 860	18 346	18 627	19 289	19 640
Civilian labor force	12 403	12 629	12 730	12 958	13 030	13 407	13 728	14 066	14 444	14 775	14 987	15 464	15 757
Employed	11 827	11 769	11 256	11 438	11 685	12 212	12 638	13 202	13 624	14 055	14 355	14 873	15 204
Agriculture	337	351	332	367	405	374	378	391	440	454	468	458	478
Nonagricultural industries	11 490	11 418	10 924	11 071	11 281	11 838	12 259	12 811	13 184	13 602	13 887	14 415	14 726
Unemployed	576	860	1 474	1 519	1 345	1 195	1 090	864	820	720	632	591	553
Not in labor force	2 246	2 342	2 575	2 735	2 911	3 149	3 200	3 305	3 416	3 571	3 640	3 825	3 883
Women, 16 Years and Over													
Civilian noninstitutional population	15 229	15 616	15 993	16 353	16 685	18 324	18 719	19 156	19 872	20 430	20 794	21 447	21 846
Civilian labor force	8 597	8 769	9 043	9 238	9 322	10 365	10 430	10 720	11 072	11 401	11 735	12 223	12 614
Employed	8 072	8 098	8 007	8 106	8 220	9 235	9 437	9 838	10 289	10 686	11 064	11 594	12 023
Agriculture	74	77	82	103	105	103	103	114	126	140	153	162	179
Nonagricultural industries	7 999	8 021	7 925	8 003	8 115	9 131	9 334	9 724	10 163	10 547	10 912	11 433	11 845
Unemployed	525	672	1 036	1 132	1 102	1 130	994	882	783	715	671	628	591
Not in labor force	6 632	6 847	6 951	7 116	7 363	7 959	8 289	8 437	8 800	9 029	9 058	9 224	9 232
Women, 20 Years and Over													
Civilian noninstitutional population	13 791	14 127	14 463	14 776	15 090	16 548	16 938	17 367	18 052	18 573	18 900	19 507	19 877
Civilian labor force	8 108	8 274	8 560	8 789	8 902	9 853	9 911	10 195	10 539	10 844	11 128	11 592	12 012
Employed	7 662	7 707	59	7 788	8 902	8 858	9 056	9 431	9 853	10 217	10 543	11 045	11 516
Agriculture	69	75	78	101	104	100	99	111	123	137	148	159	175
Nonagricultural industries	7 593	7 632	7 570	7 687	7 814	8 758	8 957	9 320	9 730	10 079	10 394	10 886	11 341
Unemployed	446	567	911	1 001	984	995	855	764	686	627	585	547	497
Not in labor force	5 682	5 853	5 903	5 987	6 187	6 695	7 028	7 172	7 513	7 729	7 773	7 915	7 865
Both Sexes, 16 to 19 Years													
Civilian noninstitutional population	2 944	3 042	3 123	3 243	3 407	3 656	3 651	3 662	3 705	3 777	3 844	3 938	3 989
Civilian labor force	1 091	1 121	1 063	1 002	965	1 131	1 133	1 109	1 144	1 178	1 225	1 280	1 283
Employed	894	870	742	680	665	808	821	859	922	977	1 041	1 094	1 085
Agriculture	20	15	16	12	14	17	18	15	17	13	13	13	14
Nonagricultural industries	874	855	726	668	651	791	803	844	906	964	1 027	1 081	1 072
Unemployed	197	251	321	322	300	324	312	250	221	201	184	186	198
Not in labor force	1 853	1 921	2 061	2 242	2 442	2 524	2 518	2 553	2 562	2 599	2 619	2 658	2 706

[1]Beginning in 2003, persons who selected this race group only; persons who selected more than one race group are not included. Prior to 2003, persons who reported more than one race group were included in the group they identified as the main race.
[2]May be of any race.

Table 1-4. Employment Status of the Civilian Noninstitutional Population, by Sex and Marital Status, 2000–2019

(Thousands of people.)

Race, marital status, and year	Men Civilian noninstitutional population	Men Civilian labor force Total	Men Employed	Men Unemployed	Women Civilian noninstitutional population	Women Civilian labor force Total	Women Employed	Women Unemployed
ALL RACES								
Single								
2000	29 887	22 002	20 339	1 663	25 920	17 849	16 628	1 221
2001	30 646	22 285	20 298	1 988	26 462	18 021	16 635	1 386
2002	31 072	22 289	19 983	2 306	26 999	18 203	16 583	1 621
2003	31 691	22 297	19 841	2 457	27 802	18 397	16 723	1 674
2004	32 422	22 776	20 395	2 381	28 228	18 616	16 995	1 621
2005	33 125	23 214	21 006	2 209	29 046	19 183	17 588	1 595
2006	33 931	23 974	21 907	2 067	29 624	19 474	17 978	1 496
2007	34 650	24 276	22 143	2 132	30 219	19 745	18 322	1 422
2008	35 274	24 643	21 938	2 705	30 980	20 231	18 513	1 717
2009	36 087	24 640	20 628	4 011	31 500	20 224	17 800	2 424
2010	37 137	24 985	20 850	4 135	32 548	20 592	17 950	2 642
2011	37 782	25 301	21 474	3 827	33 266	20 878	18 266	2 612
2012	38 180	25 494	22 002	3 492	34 267	21 506	18 973	2 533
2013	38 930	26 046	22 648	3 398	35 047	22 070	19 690	2 381
2014	39 676	26 456	23 535	2 921	35 506	22 320	20 222	2 098
2015	40 151	26 803	24 267	2 537	36 145	22 738	20 881	1 857
2016	40 928	27 545	25 217	2 328	36 800	23 321	21 606	1 715
2017	41 059	27 691	25 553	2 138	37 318	23 993	22 442	1 552
2018	41 958	28 394	26 442	1 952	38 079	24 556	23 124	1 432
2019	42 811	29 159	27 218	1 941	38 498	25 023	23 637	1 386
Married, Spouse Present								
2000	58 167	44 987	44 078	908	57 557	35 146	34 209	937
2001	58 448	45 233	44 007	1 226	57 610	35 236	34 153	1 083
2002	59 102	45 766	44 116	1 650	58 165	35 477	34 153	1 323
2003	60 063	46 404	44 653	1 751	59 069	36 046	34 695	1 352
2004	60 412	46 550	45 084	1 466	59 278	35 845	34 600	1 244
2005	60 545	46 771	45 483	1 287	59 205	35 941	34 773	1 168
2006	60 751	46 842	45 700	1 142	59 576	36 314	35 272	1 042
2007	61 760	47 520	46 314	1 206	60 474	36 881	35 832	1 049
2008	61 794	47 450	45 860	1 590	60 554	37 194	35 869	1 325
2009	61 773	47 114	43 998	3 115	60 675	37 264	35 207	2 057
2010	61 254	46 430	43 292	3 138	60 257	36 742	34 582	2 160
2011	61 358	45 954	43 283	2 671	60 061	36 141	34 110	2 031
2012	61 757	46 094	43 820	2 274	61 219	36 436	34 521	1 915
2013	61 932	45 971	43 978	1 993	61 386	36 137	34 484	1 653
2014	62 432	45 919	44 377	1 542	61 754	36 082	34 720	1 363
2015	62 975	46 248	44 938	1 310	62 203	36 135	34 997	1 138
2016	63 748	46 586	45 327	1 259	62 852	36 387	35 294	1 093
2017	64 184	46 818	45 705	1 113	63 178	36 776	35 782	994
2018	64 171	46 891	45 932	959	63 353	36 885	35 988	897
2019	64 112	46 794	45 937	857	63 486	37 214	36 378	836
Divorced, Widowed, or Separated								
2000	13 910	9 291	8 888	403	27 135	13 308	12 748	559
2001	14 188	9 367	8 892	476	27 738	13 592	12 949	642
2002	14 411	9 445	8 804	641	27 821	13 683	12 846	837
2003	14 680	9 537	8 838	699	27 862	13 828	12 986	842
2004	14 875	9 654	9 045	608	28 141	13 961	13 133	828
2005	15 481	10 048	9 484	563	28 680	14 163	13 396	768
2006	15 923	10 440	9 895	545	29 010	14 385	13 675	709
2007	15 763	10 341	9 797	544	29 001	14 362	13 638	724
2008	16 044	10 427	9 688	739	29 141	14 342	13 494	849
2009	16 275	10 370	9 043	1 326	29 490	14 531	13 201	1 330
2010	16 783	10 570	9 217	1 352	29 851	14 570	13 173	1 397
2011	17 177	10 719	9 533	1 186	29 974	14 623	13 203	1 420
2012	17 406	10 738	9 734	1 005	30 454	14 706	13 420	1 286
2013	17 694	10 649	9 726	923	30 691	14 515	13 403	1 112
2014	17 639	10 508	9 780	727	30 938	14 637	13 672	965
2015	17 975	10 569	9 926	643	31 352	14 637	13 825	812
2016	17 821	10 624	10 025	600	31 389	14 725	13 968	757
2017	18 032	10 636	10 144	492	31 308	14 405	13 712	693
2018	18 550	10 811	10 325	487	31 680	14 538	13 951	587
2019	18 431	10 734	10 306	429	31 838	14 615	14 063	552

Note: See notes and definitions for information on historical comparability.

Table 1-5. Employment Status of the Civilian Noninstitutional Population, by Region, Division, State, and Selected Territory, 2018–2019

(Thousands of people, percent.)

Region, division, and state	2018						2019					
	Civilian noninstitutional population	Civilian labor force					Civilian noninstitutional population	Civilian labor force				
		Total	Participation rate	Employed	Unemployed	Unemployment rate		Total	Participation rate	Employed	Unemployed	Unemployment rate
UNITED STATES[1]	257 791	162 075	62.9	155 761	6 314	3.9	259 175	163 539	63.1	157 538	6 001	3.7
Northeast	45 168	28 495	63.1	27 362	1 133	4.0	45 135	28 594	63.4	27 523	1 071	3.7
New England	12 110	8 073	66.7	7 793	280	3.5	12 132	8 095	66.7	7 844	251	3.1
Connecticut	2 883	1 905	66.1	1 827	78	4.1	2 884	1 914	66.4	1 842	71	3.7
Maine	1 104	699	63.3	675	24	3.4	1 110	693	62.4	672	21	3.0
Massachusetts	5 630	3 805	67.6	3 678	127	3.3	5 635	3 817	67.7	3 707	111	2.9
New Hampshire	1 114	762	68.4	743	19	2.5	1 121	774	69.0	754	20	2.5
Rhode Island	861	556	64.6	533	23	4.1	864	556	64.4	536	20	3.6
Vermont	519	346	66.7	337	9	2.7	518	342	66.0	334	8	2.4
Middle Atlantic	33 058	20 422	61.8	19 569	853	4.2	33 003	20 499	62.1	19 679	821	4.0
New Jersey	7 082	4 423	62.5	4 240	183	4.1	7 071	4 493	63.5	4 333	160	3.6
New York	15 705	9 575	61.0	9 181	394	4.1	15 656	9 514	60.8	9 138	377	4.0
Pennsylvania	10 271	6 424	62.5	6 149	276	4.3	10 277	6 492	63.2	6 208	284	4.4
Midwest	53 674	34 817	64.9	33 530	1 287	3.7	53 780	35 000	65.1	33 734	1 266	3.6
East North Central	37 072	23 642	63.8	22 687	955	4.0	37 112	23 679	63.8	22 766	912	3.9
Illinois	10 035	6 470	64.5	6 191	278	4.3	10 001	6 447	64.5	6 191	256	4.0
Indiana	5 208	3 382	64.9	3 266	116	3.4	5 246	3 387	64.6	3 275	112	3.3
Michigan	7 986	4 902	61.4	4 699	203	4.1	7 993	4 937	61.8	4 736	201	4.1
Ohio	9 229	5 755	62.4	5 492	263	4.6	9 239	5 802	62.8	5 564	239	4.1
Wisconsin	4 615	3 133	67.9	3 039	94	3.0	4 633	3 105	67.0	3 001	104	3.3
West North Central	16 602	11 176	67.3	10 843	332	3.0	16 668	11 321	67.9	10 968	353	3.1
Iowa	2 465	1 687	68.4	1 644	43	2.5	2 468	1 739	70.5	1 691	48	2.7
Kansas	2 222	1 482	66.7	1 432	50	3.4	2 229	1 487	66.7	1 440	47	3.2
Minnesota	4 395	3 070	69.9	2 981	89	2.9	4 424	3 110	70.3	3 009	100	3.2
Missouri	4 796	3 052	63.6	2 955	98	3.2	4 811	3 083	64.1	2 982	102	3.3
Nebraska	1 474	1 020	69.2	992	29	2.8	1 481	1 035	69.9	1 004	32	3.0
North Dakota	582	404	69.4	394	11	2.6	582	404	69.4	394	10	2.4
South Dakota	669	459	68.6	446	14	3.0	672	464	69.0	449	15	3.3
South	97 203	59 772	61.5	57 497	2 275	3.8	98 053	60 551	61.8	58 428	2 122	3.5
South Atlantic	51 681	31 846	61.6	30 670	1 176	3.7	52 147	32 271	61.9	31 191	1 080	3.3
Delaware	772	482	62.4	464	18	3.8	778	487	62.6	469	18	3.8
District of Columbia	575	405	70.4	382	22	5.6	577	410	71.1	387	22	5.5
Florida	17 233	10 235	59.4	9 870	365	3.6	17 410	10 337	59.4	10 016	321	3.1
Georgia	8 099	5 108	63.1	4 906	201	3.9	8 196	5 110	62.3	4 935	175	3.4
Maryland	4 755	3 197	67.2	3 072	125	3.9	4 761	3 261	68.5	3 144	117	3.6
North Carolina	8 141	4 982	61.2	4 787	195	3.9	8 243	5 080	61.6	4 884	197	3.9
South Carolina	4 004	2 323	58.0	2 244	80	3.4	4 063	2 376	58.5	2 308	68	2.8
Virginia	6 645	4 331	65.2	4 203	129	3.0	6 672	4 412	66.1	4 289	123	2.8
West Virginia	1 456	783	53.8	742	41	5.3	1 447	797	55.1	758	39	4.9
East South Central	14 958	8 781	58.7	8 431	350	4.0	15 023	8 935	59.5	8 596	339	3.8
Alabama	3 847	2 199	57.2	2 112	86	3.9	3 862	2 242	58.1	2 174	67	3.0
Kentucky	3 490	2 062	59.1	1 972	89	4.3	3 494	2 073	59.3	1 984	89	4.3
Mississippi	2 293	1 276	55.6	1 215	61	4.8	2 287	1 276	55.8	1 207	69	5.4
Tennessee	5 329	3 245	60.9	3 132	113	3.5	5 379	3 345	62.2	3 232	113	3.4
West South Central	30 563	19 145	62.6	18 396	749	3.9	30 883	19 345	62.6	18 641	704	3.6
Arkansas	2 336	1 351	57.8	1 301	50	3.7	2 343	1 363	58.2	1 314	48	3.5
Louisiana	3 582	2 103	58.7	2 001	103	4.9	3 577	2 095	58.6	1 994	101	4.8
Oklahoma	3 011	1 842	61.2	1 779	63	3.4	3 029	1 841	60.8	1 781	61	3.3
Texas	21 635	13 848	64.0	13 314	534	3.9	21 934	14 045	64.0	13 552	494	3.5
West	61 046	38 555	63.2	36 954	1 601	4.2	61 513	38 955	63.3	37 430	1 525	3.9
Mountain	19 028	12 224	64.2	11 736	487	4.0	19 341	12 512	64.7	12 056	456	3.6
Arizona	5 606	3 440	61.4	3 274	166	4.8	5 713	3 551	62.2	3 385	167	4.7
Colorado	4 477	3 096	69.2	2 995	102	3.3	4 545	3 149	69.3	3 062	87	2.8
Idaho	1 337	857	64.1	833	24	2.8	1 368	882	64.5	856	26	2.9
Montana	843	528	62.6	509	20	3.7	850	533	62.7	515	19	3.5
Nevada	2 382	1 500	63.0	1 432	68	4.6	2 424	1 542	63.6	1 482	60	3.9
New Mexico	1 633	940	57.6	894	47	4.9	1 640	955	58.2	908	46	4.9
Utah	2 303	1 572	68.3	1 523	49	3.1	2 351	1 608	68.4	1 566	42	2.6
Wyoming	448	290	64.7	278	12	4.1	450	292	64.9	282	11	3.6
Pacific	42 018	26 331	62.7	25 218	1 114	4.2	42 171	26 443	62.7	25 374	1 069	4.0
Alaska	547	357	65.3	333	24	6.6	545	348	63.9	326	21	6.1
California	31 063	19 398	62.4	18 583	815	4.2	31 107	19 412	62.4	18 627	784	4.0
Hawaii	1 092	679	62.2	662	17	2.4	1 091	665	61.0	647	18	2.7
Oregon	3 376	2 105	62.4	2 017	87	4.2	3 409	2 104	61.7	2 025	79	3.7
Washington	5 941	3 793	63.8	3 622	171	4.5	6 020	3 914	65.0	3 748	166	4.3

Note: Data refer to place of residence. Region and division data are derived from summing the component states. Sub-national data reflect revised population controls and model reestimation.

[1]Due to separate processing and weighing procedures, totals for the United States differ from the results obtained by aggregating data for regions, divisions, or states.

Table 1-6. Civilian Noninstitutional Population, by Age, Race, Sex, and Hispanic Origin, 1948–2019

(Thousands of people.)

Race, Hispanic origin, sex, and year	16 years and over	16 to 19 years			20 years and over						
		Total	16 to 17 years	18 to 19 years	Total	20 to 24 years	25 to 34 years	35 to 44 years	45 to 54 years	55 to 64 years	65 years and over
ALL RACES											
Both Sexes											
1948	103 068	8 449	4 265	4 185	94 618	11 530	22 610	20 097	16 771	12 885	10 720
1949	103 994	8 215	4 139	4 079	95 778	11 312	22 822	20 401	17 002	13 201	11 035
1950	104 995	8 143	4 076	4 068	96 851	11 080	23 013	20 681	17 240	13 469	11 363
1951	104 621	7 865	4 096	3 771	96 755	10 167	22 843	20 863	17 464	13 692	11 724
1952	105 231	7 922	4 234	3 689	97 305	9 389	23 044	21 137	17 716	13 889	12 126
1953	107 056	8 014	4 241	3 773	99 041	8 960	23 266	21 922	17 991	13 830	13 075
1954	108 321	8 224	4 336	3 889	100 095	8 885	23 304	22 135	18 305	14 085	13 375
1955	109 683	8 364	4 440	3 925	101 318	9 036	23 249	22 348	18 643	14 309	13 728
1956	110 954	8 434	4 482	3 953	102 518	9 271	23 072	22 567	19 012	14 516	14 075
1957	112 265	8 612	4 587	4 026	103 653	9 486	22 849	22 786	19 424	14 727	14 376
1958	113 727	8 986	4 872	4 114	104 737	9 733	22 563	23 025	19 832	14 923	14 657
1959	115 329	9 618	5 337	4 282	105 711	9 975	22 201	23 207	20 203	15 134	14 985
1960	117 245	10 187	5 573	4 615	107 056	10 273	21 998	23 437	20 601	15 409	15 336
1961	118 771	10 513	5 462	5 052	108 255	10 583	21 829	23 585	20 893	15 675	15 685
1962	120 153	10 652	5 503	5 150	109 500	10 852	21 503	23 797	20 916	15 874	16 554
1963	122 416	11 370	6 301	5 070	111 045	11 464	21 400	23 948	21 144	16 138	16 945
1964	124 485	12 111	6 974	5 139	112 372	12 017	21 367	23 940	21 452	16 442	17 150
1965	126 513	12 930	6 936	5 995	113 582	12 442	21 417	23 832	21 728	16 727	17 432
1966	128 058	13 592	6 914	6 679	114 463	12 638	21 543	23 579	21 977	17 007	17 715
1967	129 874	13 480	7 003	6 480	116 391	13 421	22 057	23 313	22 256	17 310	18 029
1968	132 028	13 698	7 200	6 499	118 328	13 891	22 912	23 036	22 534	17 614	18 338
1969	134 335	14 095	7 422	6 673	120 238	14 488	23 645	22 709	22 806	17 930	18 657
1970	137 085	14 519	7 643	6 876	122 566	15 323	24 435	22 489	23 059	18 250	19 007
1971	140 216	15 022	7 849	7 173	125 193	16 345	25 337	22 274	23 244	18 581	19 406
1972	144 126	15 510	8 076	7 435	128 614	17 143	26 740	22 358	23 338	19 007	20 023
1973	147 096	15 840	8 227	7 613	131 253	17 692	28 172	22 287	23 431	19 281	20 389
1974	150 120	16 180	8 373	7 809	133 938	17 994	29 439	22 461	23 578	19 517	20 945
1975	153 153	16 418	8 419	7 999	136 733	18 595	30 710	22 526	23 535	19 844	21 525
1976	156 150	16 614	8 442	8 171	139 536	19 109	31 953	22 796	23 409	20 185	22 083
1977	159 033	16 688	8 482	8 206	142 345	19 582	33 117	23 296	23 197	20 557	22 597
1978	161 910	16 695	8 484	8 211	145 216	20 007	34 091	24 099	22 977	20 875	23 166
1979	164 863	16 657	8 389	8 268	148 205	20 353	35 261	24 861	22 752	21 210	23 767
1980	167 745	16 543	8 279	8 264	151 202	20 635	36 558	25 578	22 563	21 520	24 350
1981	170 130	16 214	8 068	8 145	153 916	20 820	37 777	26 291	22 422	21 756	24 850
1982	172 271	15 763	7 714	8 049	156 508	20 845	38 492	27 611	22 264	21 909	25 387
1983	174 215	15 274	7 385	7 889	158 941	20 799	39 147	28 932	22 167	22 003	25 892
1984	176 383	14 735	7 196	7 538	161 648	20 688	39 999	30 251	22 226	22 052	26 433
1985	178 206	14 506	7 232	7 274	163 700	20 097	40 670	31 379	22 418	22 140	26 997
1986	180 587	14 496	7 386	7 110	166 091	19 569	41 731	32 550	22 732	22 011	27 497
1987	182 753	14 606	7 501	7 104	168 147	18 970	42 297	33 755	23 183	21 835	28 108
1988	184 613	14 527	7 284	7 243	170 085	18 434	42 611	34 784	24 004	21 641	28 612
1989	186 393	14 223	6 886	7 338	172 169	18 025	42 845	35 977	24 744	21 406	29 173
1990	189 164	14 520	6 893	7 626	174 644	18 902	42 976	37 719	25 081	20 719	29 247
1991	190 925	14 073	6 901	7 173	176 852	18 963	42 688	39 116	25 709	20 675	29 700
1992	192 805	13 840	6 907	6 933	178 965	18 846	42 278	39 852	27 206	20 604	30 179
1993	194 838	13 935	7 010	6 925	180 903	18 642	41 771	40 733	28 549	20 574	30 634
1994	196 814	14 196	7 245	6 951	182 619	18 353	41 306	41 534	29 778	20 635	31 012
1995	198 584	14 511	7 407	7 104	184 073	17 864	40 798	42 254	30 974	20 735	31 448
1996	200 591	14 934	7 678	7 256	185 656	17 409	40 252	43 086	32 167	20 990	31 751
1997	203 133	15 365	7 861	7 504	187 769	17 442	39 559	43 883	33 391	21 505	31 989
1998	205 220	15 644	7 895	7 749	189 576	17 593	38 778	44 299	34 373	22 296	32 237
1999	207 753	16 040	8 060	7 979	191 713	17 968	37 976	44 635	35 587	23 064	32 484
2000	212 577	15 912	7 978	7 934	196 664	18 311	38 703	44 312	37 642	24 230	33 466
2001	215 092	15 929	8 020	7 909	199 164	18 877	38 505	44 195	38 904	25 011	33 672
2002	217 570	15 994	8 099	7 895	201 576	19 348	38 472	43 894	39 711	26 343	33 808
2003	221 168	16 096	8 561	7 535	205 072	19 801	39 021	43 746	40 522	27 728	34 253
2004	223 357	16 222	8 574	7 648	207 134	20 197	38 939	43 226	41 245	28 919	34 609
2005	226 082	16 398	8 778	7 619	209 685	20 276	39 064	43 005	42 107	30 165	35 068
2006	228 815	16 678	9 089	7 589	212 137	20 265	39 230	42 753	42 901	31 375	35 613
2007	231 867	16 982	9 222	7 760	214 885	20 427	39 751	42 401	43 544	32 533	36 228
2008	233 788	17 075	9 133	7 942	216 713	20 409	39 993	41 699	43 960	33 491	37 161
2009	235 801	17 043	8 944	8 100	218 757	20 524	40 280	40 919	44 365	34 671	37 998
2010	237 830	16 901	8 943	7 957	220 929	21 047	40 903	40 090	44 297	35 885	38 706
2011	239 618	16 774	8 727	8 048	222 843	21 423	41 364	39 499	43 842	36 987	39 729
2012	243 284	16 984	8 891	8 093	226 300	21 799	40 975	39 642	43 697	38 318	41 869
2013	245 679	16 787	8 943	7 845	228 892	22 052	41 548	39 613	43 246	39 022	43 412
2014	247 947	16 633	8 898	7 735	231 314	22 079	42 131	39 565	42 815	39 764	44 959
2015	250 801	16 619	8 852	7 767	234 182	21 971	42 771	39 701	42 637	40 594	46 509
2016	253 538	16 714	8 994	7 720	236 824	21 721	43 547	39 817	42 397	41 308	48 035
2017	255 079	16 754	9 073	7 681	238 325	21 396	43 958	39 952	41 787	41 691	49 542
2018	257 791	16 765	8 917	7 848	241 026	21 239	44 581	40 569	41 240	42 114	51 283
2019	259 175	16 693	8 798	7 894	242 482	21 055	44 877	40 960	40 445	42 241	52 905

Table 1-6. Civilian Noninstitutional Population, by Age, Race, Sex, and Hispanic Origin, 1948–2019
—Continued

(Thousands of people.)

Race, Hispanic origin, sex, and year	16 years and over	16 to 19 years			20 years and over						
		Total	16 to 17 years	18 to 19 years	Total	20 to 24 years	25 to 34 years	35 to 44 years	45 to 54 years	55 to 64 years	65 years and over
ALL RACES											
Men											
1948	49 996	4 078	2 128	1 951	45 918	5 527	10 767	9 798	8 290	6 441	5 093
1949	50 321	3 946	2 062	1 884	46 378	5 405	10 871	9 926	8 379	6 568	5 226
1950	50 725	3 962	2 043	1 920	46 763	5 270	10 963	10 034	8 472	6 664	5 357
1951	49 727	3 725	2 039	1 687	46 001	4 451	10 709	10 049	8 551	6 737	5 503
1952	49 700	3 767	2 121	1 647	45 932	3 788	10 855	10 164	8 655	6 798	5 670
1953	50 750	3 823	2 122	1 701	46 927	3 482	11 020	10 632	8 878	6 798	6 119
1954	51 395	3 953	2 174	1 780	47 441	3 509	11 067	10 718	9 018	6 885	6 241
1955	52 109	4 022	2 225	1 798	48 086	3 708	11 068	10 804	9 164	6 960	6 380
1956	52 723	4 020	2 238	1 783	48 704	3 970	10 983	10 889	9 322	7 032	6 505
1957	53 315	4 083	2 284	1 800	49 231	4 166	10 889	10 965	9 499	7 109	6 602
1958	54 033	4 293	2 435	1 858	49 740	4 339	10 787	11 076	9 675	7 179	6 683
1959	54 793	4 652	2 681	1 971	50 140	4 488	10 625	11 149	9 832	7 259	6 785
1960	55 662	4 963	2 805	2 159	50 698	4 679	10 514	11 230	10 000	7 373	6 901
1961	56 286	5 112	2 742	2 371	51 173	4 844	10 440	11 286	10 112	7 483	7 006
1962	56 831	5 150	2 764	2 386	51 681	4 925	10 207	11 389	10 162	7 610	7 386
1963	57 921	5 496	3 162	2 334	52 425	5 240	10 165	11 476	10 274	7 740	7 526
1964	58 847	5 866	3 503	2 364	52 981	5 520	10 144	11 466	10 402	7 873	7 574
1965	59 782	6 318	3 488	2 831	53 463	5 701	10 182	11 427	10 512	7 990	7 649
1966	60 262	6 658	3 478	3 180	53 603	5 663	10 224	11 294	10 598	8 099	7 723
1967	60 905	6 537	3 528	3 010	54 367	5 977	10 495	11 161	10 705	8 218	7 809
1968	61 847	6 683	3 634	3 049	55 165	6 127	10 944	11 040	10 819	8 336	7 897
1969	62 898	6 928	3 741	3 187	55 969	6 379	11 309	10 890	10 935	8 464	7 990
1970	64 304	7 145	3 848	3 299	57 157	6 861	11 750	10 810	11 052	8 590	8 093
1971	65 942	7 430	3 954	3 477	58 511	7 511	12 227	10 721	11 129	8 711	8 208
1972	67 835	7 705	4 081	3 624	60 130	8 061	12 911	10 762	11 167	8 895	8 330
1973	69 292	7 855	4 152	3 703	61 436	8 429	13 641	10 746	11 202	8 990	8 426
1974	70 808	8 012	4 231	3 781	62 796	8 600	14 262	10 834	11 315	9 140	8 641
1975	72 291	8 134	4 252	3 882	64 158	8 950	14 899	10 874	11 298	9 286	8 852
1976	73 759	8 244	4 266	3 978	65 515	9 237	15 528	11 010	11 243	9 444	9 053
1977	75 193	8 288	4 290	4 000	66 904	9 477	16 108	11 260	11 144	9 616	9 297
1978	76 576	8 309	4 295	4 014	68 268	9 693	16 598	11 665	11 045	9 758	9 509
1979	78 020	8 310	4 251	4 060	69 709	9 873	17 193	12 046	10 944	9 907	9 746
1980	79 398	8 260	4 195	4 064	71 138	10 023	17 833	12 400	10 861	10 042	9 979
1981	80 511	8 092	4 087	4 005	72 419	10 116	18 427	12 758	10 797	10 151	10 170
1982	81 523	7 879	3 911	3 968	73 644	10 136	18 787	13 410	10 726	10 215	10 371
1983	82 531	7 659	3 750	3 908	74 872	10 140	19 143	14 067	10 689	10 261	10 573
1984	83 605	7 386	3 655	3 731	76 219	10 108	19 596	14 719	10 724	10 285	10 788
1985	84 469	7 275	3 689	3 586	77 195	9 746	19 864	15 265	10 844	10 392	11 084
1986	85 798	7 275	3 768	3 507	78 523	9 498	20 498	15 858	10 986	10 336	11 347
1987	86 899	7 335	3 824	3 510	79 565	9 195	20 781	16 475	11 215	10 267	11 632
1988	87 857	7 304	3 715	3 588	80 553	8 931	20 937	17 008	11 625	10 193	11 859
1989	88 762	7 143	3 524	3 619	81 619	8 743	21 080	17 590	11 981	10 092	12 134
1990	90 377	7 347	3 534	3 813	83 030	9 320	21 117	18 529	12 238	9 778	12 049
1991	91 278	7 134	3 548	3 586	84 144	9 367	20 977	19 213	12 554	9 780	12 254
1992	92 270	7 023	3 542	3 481	85 247	9 326	20 792	19 585	13 271	9 776	12 496
1993	93 332	7 076	3 595	3 481	86 256	9 216	20 569	20 037	13 944	9 773	12 717
1994	94 355	7 203	3 718	3 486	87 151	9 074	20 361	20 443	14 545	9 810	12 918
1995	95 178	7 367	3 794	3 573	87 811	8 835	20 079	20 800	15 111	9 856	13 130
1996	96 206	7 600	3 955	3 645	88 606	8 611	19 775	21 222	15 674	9 997	13 327
1997	97 715	7 836	4 053	3 783	89 879	8 706	19 478	21 669	16 276	10 282	13 469
1998	98 758	7 968	4 059	3 909	90 790	8 804	19 094	21 857	16 773	10 649	13 613
1999	99 722	8 167	4 143	4 024	91 555	8 899	18 565	21 969	17 335	11 008	13 779
2000	101 964	8 089	4 096	3 993	93 875	9 101	19 106	21 683	18 365	11 583	14 037
2001	103 282	8 101	4 102	3 999	95 181	9 368	19 056	21 643	18 987	11 972	14 155
2002	104 585	8 146	4 140	4 006	96 439	9 627	19 037	21 523	19 379	12 641	14 233
2003	106 435	8 163	4 365	3 797	98 272	9 878	19 347	21 463	19 784	13 305	14 496
2004	107 710	8 234	4 318	3 916	99 476	10 125	19 358	21 255	20 160	13 894	14 684
2005	109 151	8 317	4 481	3 836	100 835	10 181	19 446	21 177	20 585	14 502	14 944
2006	110 605	8 459	4 613	3 846	102 145	10 191	19 568	21 082	20 991	15 095	15 219
2007	112 173	8 618	4 658	3 960	103 555	10 291	19 858	20 910	21 313	15 658	15 525
2008	113 113	8 660	4 625	4 035	104 453	10 249	19 999	20 567	21 512	16 123	16 002
2009	114 136	8 643	4 548	4 095	105 493	10 284	20 167	20 199	21 731	16 698	16 414
2010	115 174	8 578	4 540	4 038	106 596	10 550	20 465	19 807	21 713	17 291	16 769
2011	116 317	8 582	4 486	4 095	107 736	10 844	20 711	19 446	21 451	17 810	17 474
2012	117 343	8 657	4 550	4 107	108 686	10 889	20 205	19 416	21 339	18 416	18 422
2013	118 555	8 539	4 532	4 006	110 017	11 038	20 511	19 388	21 125	18 751	19 189
2014	119 748	8 449	4 513	3 936	111 299	11 067	20 841	19 388	20 920	19 116	19 967
2015	121 101	8 430	4 509	3 920	112 671	11 012	21 142	19 444	20 839	19 518	20 717
2016	122 497	8 475	4 509	3 966	114 023	10 897	21 570	19 514	20 727	19 867	21 448
2017	123 275	8 493	4 587	3 906	114 783	10 726	21 819	19 597	20 435	20 054	22 151
2018	124 678	8 493	4 527	3 967	116 185	10 639	22 205	19 933	20 157	20 263	22 988
2019	125 353	8 445	4 456	3 989	116 908	10 530	22 386	20 143	19 774	20 335	23 740

Table 1-6. Civilian Noninstitutional Population, by Age, Race, Sex, and Hispanic Origin, 1948–2019
—*Continued*

(Thousands of people.)

Race, Hispanic origin, sex, and year	16 years and over	16 to 19 years			20 years and over						
		Total	16 to 17 years	18 to 19 years	Total	20 to 24 years	25 to 34 years	35 to 44 years	45 to 54 years	55 to 64 years	65 years and over
ALL RACES											
Women											
1948	53 071	4 371	2 137	2 234	48 700	6 003	11 843	10 299	8 481	6 444	5 627
1949	53 670	4 269	2 077	2 195	49 400	5 907	11 951	10 475	8 623	6 633	5 809
1950	54 270	4 181	2 033	2 148	50 088	5 810	12 050	10 647	8 768	6 805	6 006
1951	54 895	4 140	2 057	2 084	50 754	5 716	12 134	10 814	8 913	6 955	6 221
1952	55 529	4 155	2 113	2 042	51 373	5 601	12 189	10 973	9 061	7 091	6 456
1953	56 305	4 191	2 119	2 072	52 114	5 478	12 246	11 290	9 113	7 032	6 956
1954	56 925	4 271	2 162	2 109	52 654	5 376	12 237	11 417	9 287	7 200	7 134
1955	57 574	4 342	2 215	2 127	53 232	5 328	12 181	11 544	9 479	7 349	7 348
1956	58 228	4 414	2 244	2 170	53 814	5 301	12 089	11 678	9 690	7 484	7 570
1957	58 951	4 529	2 303	2 226	54 421	5 320	11 960	11 821	9 925	7 618	7 774
1958	59 690	4 693	2 437	2 256	54 997	5 394	11 776	11 949	10 157	7 744	7 974
1959	60 534	4 966	2 656	2 311	55 570	5 487	11 576	12 058	10 371	7 875	8 200
1960	61 582	5 224	2 768	2 456	56 358	5 594	11 484	12 207	10 601	8 036	8 435
1961	62 484	5 401	2 720	2 681	57 082	5 739	11 389	12 299	10 781	8 192	8 679
1962	63 321	5 502	2 739	2 764	57 819	5 927	11 296	12 408	10 754	8 264	9 168
1963	64 494	5 874	3 139	2 736	58 620	6 224	11 235	12 472	10 870	8 398	9 419
1964	65 637	6 245	3 471	2 775	59 391	6 497	11 223	12 474	11 050	8 569	9 576
1965	66 731	6 612	3 448	3 164	60 119	6 741	11 235	12 405	11 216	8 737	9 783
1966	67 795	6 934	3 436	3 499	60 860	6 975	11 319	12 285	11 379	8 908	9 992
1967	68 968	6 943	3 475	3 470	62 026	7 445	11 562	12 152	11 551	9 092	10 220
1968	70 179	7 015	3 566	3 450	63 164	7 764	11 968	11 996	11 715	9 278	10 441
1969	71 436	7 167	3 681	3 486	64 269	8 109	12 336	11 819	11 871	9 466	10 667
1970	72 782	7 373	3 796	3 578	65 408	8 462	12 684	11 679	12 008	9 659	10 914
1971	74 274	7 591	3 895	3 697	66 682	8 834	13 110	11 553	12 115	9 870	11 198
1972	76 290	7 805	3 994	3 811	68 484	9 082	13 829	11 597	12 171	10 113	11 693
1973	77 804	7 985	4 076	3 909	69 819	9 263	14 531	11 541	12 229	10 290	11 963
1974	79 312	8 168	4 142	4 028	71 144	9 393	15 177	11 627	12 263	10 377	12 304
1975	80 860	8 285	4 168	4 117	72 576	9 645	15 811	11 652	12 237	10 558	12 673
1976	82 390	8 370	4 176	4 194	74 020	9 872	16 425	11 786	12 166	10 742	13 030
1977	83 840	8 400	4 193	4 206	75 441	10 103	17 008	12 036	12 053	10 940	13 300
1978	85 334	8 386	4 189	4 197	76 948	10 315	17 493	12 435	11 932	11 118	13 658
1979	86 843	8 347	4 139	4 208	78 496	10 480	18 070	12 815	11 808	11 303	14 021
1980	88 348	8 283	4 083	4 200	80 065	10 612	18 725	13 177	11 701	11 478	14 372
1981	89 618	8 121	3 981	4 140	81 497	10 705	19 350	13 533	11 625	11 605	14 680
1982	90 748	7 884	3 804	4 081	82 864	10 709	19 705	14 201	11 538	11 694	15 017
1983	91 684	7 616	3 635	3 981	84 069	10 660	20 004	14 865	11 478	11 742	15 319
1984	92 778	7 349	3 542	3 807	85 429	10 580	20 403	15 532	11 501	11 768	15 645
1985	93 736	7 231	3 543	3 688	86 506	10 351	20 805	16 114	11 574	11 748	15 913
1986	94 789	7 221	3 618	3 603	87 567	10 072	21 233	16 692	11 746	11 675	16 150
1987	95 853	7 271	3 677	3 594	88 583	9 776	21 516	17 279	11 968	11 567	16 476
1988	96 756	7 224	3 569	3 655	89 532	9 503	21 674	17 776	12 378	11 448	16 753
1989	97 630	7 080	3 361	3 719	90 550	9 282	21 765	18 387	12 763	11 314	17 039
1990	98 787	7 173	3 359	3 813	91 614	9 582	21 859	19 190	12 843	10 941	17 198
1991	99 646	6 939	3 353	3 586	92 708	9 597	21 711	19 903	13 155	10 895	17 446
1992	100 535	6 818	3 366	3 452	93 718	9 520	21 486	20 267	13 935	10 828	17 682
1993	101 506	6 859	3 415	3 444	94 647	9 426	21 202	20 696	14 605	10 801	17 917
1994	102 460	6 993	3 528	3 465	95 467	9 279	20 945	21 091	15 233	10 825	18 094
1995	103 406	7 144	3 613	3 531	96 262	9 029	20 719	21 454	15 862	10 879	18 318
1996	104 385	7 335	3 723	3 612	97 050	8 798	20 477	21 865	16 493	10 993	18 424
1997	105 418	7 528	3 808	3 721	97 889	8 736	20 081	22 214	17 115	11 224	18 520
1998	106 462	7 676	3 835	3 840	98 786	8 790	19 683	22 442	17 600	11 646	18 625
1999	108 031	7 873	3 917	3 955	100 158	9 069	19 411	22 666	18 251	12 056	18 705
2000	110 613	7 823	3 882	3 941	102 790	9 211	19 597	22 628	19 276	12 647	19 430
2001	111 811	7 828	3 917	3 910	103 983	9 509	19 449	22 552	19 917	13 039	19 517
2002	112 985	7 848	3 959	3 889	105 136	9 721	19 435	22 371	20 332	13 703	19 575
2003	114 733	7 934	4 195	3 738	106 800	9 924	19 674	22 283	20 738	14 423	19 758
2004	115 647	7 989	4 257	3 732	107 658	10 072	19 581	21 970	21 085	15 025	19 925
2005	116 931	8 081	4 297	3 784	108 850	10 095	19 618	21 828	21 521	15 663	20 125
2006	118 210	8 218	4 476	3 742	109 992	10 074	19 662	21 671	21 910	16 280	20 394
2007	119 694	8 364	4 564	3 800	111 330	10 137	19 893	21 491	22 231	16 876	20 703
2008	120 675	8 415	4 508	3 907	112 260	10 160	19 994	21 132	22 448	17 367	21 160
2009	121 665	8 401	4 396	4 004	113 265	10 240	20 113	20 721	22 633	17 973	21 584
2010	122 656	8 323	4 403	3 919	114 333	10 497	20 438	20 283	22 584	18 594	21 937
2011	123 300	8 193	4 241	3 952	115 107	10 579	20 653	20 053	22 391	19 177	22 255
2012	125 941	8 327	4 341	3 986	117 614	10 910	20 770	20 226	22 358	19 902	23 447
2013	127 124	8 249	4 410	3 838	118 875	11 014	21 037	20 209	22 121	20 271	24 222
2014	128 199	8 184	4 385	3 799	120 014	11 012	21 290	20 178	21 894	20 648	24 992
2015	129 700	8 189	4 342	3 847	121 511	10 959	21 629	20 257	21 798	21 076	25 792
2016	131 040	8 239	4 485	3 754	122 801	10 823	21 976	20 303	21 670	21 441	26 587
2017	131 804	8 261	4 486	3 775	123 542	10 669	22 139	20 354	21 352	21 637	27 390
2018	133 112	8 272	4 390	3 882	124 841	10 600	22 376	20 637	21 083	21 851	28 295
2019	133 822	8 247	4 342	3 905	125 574	10 525	22 491	20 817	20 670	21 906	29 165

Table 1-6. Civilian Noninstitutional Population, by Age, Race, Sex, and Hispanic Origin, 1948–2019
—Continued

(Thousands of people.)

Race, Hispanic origin, sex, and year	16 years and over	16 to 19 years			20 years and over						
		Total	16 to 17 years	18 to 19 years	Total	20 to 24 years	25 to 34 years	35 to 44 years	45 to 54 years	55 to 64 years	65 years and over
WHITE											
Both Sexes											
1954	97 705	7 180	3 786	3 394	90 524	7 794	20 818	19 915	16 569	12 993	12 438
1955	98 880	7 292	3 874	3 419	91 586	7 912	20 742	20 110	16 869	13 169	12 785
1956	99 976	7 346	3 908	3 438	92 629	8 106	20 564	20 314	17 198	13 341	13 105
1957	101 119	7 505	4 007	3 498	93 612	8 293	20 342	20 514	17 562	13 518	13 383
1958	102 392	7 843	4 271	3 573	94 547	8 498	20 063	20 734	17 924	13 681	13 645
1959	103 803	8 430	4 707	3 725	95 370	8 697	19 715	20 893	18 257	13 858	13 951
1960	105 282	8 924	4 909	4 016	96 355	8 927	19 470	21 049	18 578	14 070	14 260
1961	106 604	9 211	4 785	4 427	97 390	9 203	19 289	21 169	18 845	14 304	14 581
1962	107 715	9 343	4 818	4 526	98 371	9 484	18 974	21 293	18 872	14 450	15 297
1963	109 705	9 978	5 549	4 430	99 725	10 069	18 867	21 398	19 082	14 681	15 629
1964	111 534	10 616	6 137	4 481	100 916	10 568	18 838	21 375	19 360	14 957	15 816
1965	113 284	11 319	6 049	5 271	101 963	10 935	18 882	21 258	19 604	15 215	16 070
1966	114 566	11 862	5 993	5 870	102 702	11 094	18 989	21 005	19 822	15 469	16 322
1967	116 100	11 682	6 051	5 632	104 417	11 797	19 464	20 745	20 067	15 745	16 602
1968	117 948	11 840	6 225	5 616	106 107	12 184	20 245	20 474	20 310	16 018	16 875
1969	119 913	12 179	6 418	5 761	107 733	12 677	20 892	20 156	20 546	16 305	17 156
1970	122 174	12 521	6 591	5 931	109 652	13 359	21 546	19 929	20 760	16 591	17 469
1971	124 758	12 937	6 750	6 189	111 821	14 208	22 295	19 694	20 907	16 884	17 833
1972	127 906	13 301	6 910	6 392	114 603	14 897	23 555	19 673	20 950	17 250	18 278
1973	130 097	13 533	7 021	6 512	116 563	15 264	24 685	19 532	20 991	17 484	18 607
1974	132 417	13 784	7 114	6 671	118 632	15 502	25 711	19 628	21 061	17 645	19 085
1975	134 790	13 941	7 132	6 808	120 849	15 980	26 746	19 641	20 981	17 918	19 587
1976	137 106	14 055	7 125	6 930	123 050	16 368	27 757	19 827	20 816	18 220	20 064
1977	139 380	14 095	7 150	6 944	125 285	16 728	28 703	20 231	20 575	18 540	20 508
1978	141 612	14 060	7 132	6 928	127 552	17 038	29 453	20 932	20 322	18 799	21 007
1979	143 894	13 994	7 029	6 964	129 900	17 284	30 371	21 579	20 058	19 071	21 538
1980	146 122	13 854	6 912	6 943	132 268	17 484	31 407	22 174	19 837	19 316	22 050
1981	147 908	13 516	6 704	6 813	134 392	17 609	32 367	22 778	19 666	19 485	22 487
1982	149 441	13 076	6 383	6 693	136 366	17 579	32 863	23 910	19 478	19 591	22 945
1983	150 805	12 623	6 089	6 534	138 183	17 492	33 286	25 027	19 349	19 625	23 403
1984	152 347	12 147	5 918	6 228	140 200	17 304	33 889	26 124	19 348	19 629	23 906
1985	153 679	11 900	5 922	5 978	141 780	16 853	34 450	27 100	19 405	19 620	24 352
1986	155 432	11 879	6 036	5 843	143 553	16 353	35 293	28 062	19 587	19 477	24 780
1987	156 958	11 939	6 110	5 829	145 020	15 808	35 667	29 036	19 965	19 242	25 301
1988	158 194	11 838	5 893	5 945	146 357	15 276	35 876	29 818	20 652	18 996	25 739
1989	159 338	11 530	5 506	6 023	147 809	14 879	35 951	30 774	21 287	18 743	26 175
1990	160 625	11 630	5 464	6 166	148 996	15 538	35 661	31 739	21 535	18 204	26 319
1991	161 759	11 200	5 451	5 749	150 558	15 516	35 342	32 854	22 052	18 074	26 721
1992	162 972	11 004	5 478	5 526	151 968	15 354	34 885	33 305	23 364	17 951	27 108
1993	164 289	11 078	5 562	5 516	153 210	15 087	34 365	33 919	24 456	17 892	27 493
1994	165 555	11 264	5 710	5 554	154 291	14 708	33 865	34 582	25 435	17 924	27 776
1995	166 914	11 468	5 822	5 646	155 446	14 313	33 355	35 222	26 418	17 986	28 153
1996	168 317	11 822	6 026	5 796	156 495	13 907	32 852	35 810	27 403	18 136	28 387
1997	169 993	12 181	6 213	5 968	157 812	13 983	32 091	36 325	28 388	18 511	28 514
1998	171 478	12 439	6 264	6 176	159 039	14 138	31 286	36 610	29 132	19 231	28 642
1999	173 085	12 700	6 342	6 358	160 385	14 394	30 516	36 755	30 048	19 855	28 818
2000	176 220	12 535	6 264	6 271	163 685	14 552	30 948	36 261	31 550	20 757	29 617
2001	178 111	12 556	6 291	6 265	165 556	15 001	30 770	36 113	32 475	21 434	29 762
2002	179 783	12 596	6 346	6 250	167 187	15 360	30 676	35 750	33 012	22 540	29 849
2003	181 292	12 527	6 629	5 898	168 765	15 536	30 789	35 352	33 466	23 589	30 033
2004	182 643	12 599	6 561	6 038	170 045	15 817	30 585	34 845	34 005	24 549	30 245
2005	184 446	12 690	6 768	5 921	171 757	15 871	30 592	34 554	34 649	25 534	30 556
2006	186 264	12 856	6 981	5 875	173 408	15 848	30 661	34 217	35 228	26 486	30 968
2007	188 253	13 043	7 026	6 018	175 210	15 945	31 011	33 770	35 665	27 392	31 426
2008	189 540	13 084	6 962	6 122	176 456	15 914	31 234	33 093	35 941	28 109	32 165
2009	190 902	13 035	6 775	6 261	177 867	15 963	31 471	32 378	36 166	29 022	32 867
2010	192 075	12 891	6 799	6 091	179 184	16 280	31 813	31 647	36 064	29 983	33 396
2011	193 077	12 818	6 673	6 145	180 259	16 562	32 136	31 030	35 526	30 799	34 206
2012	193 204	12 658	6 617	6 040	180 547	16 289	31 242	30 597	34 935	31 511	35 973
2013	194 333	12 499	6 690	5 809	181 834	16 357	31 488	30 427	34 413	31 954	37 194
2014	195 498	12 377	6 650	5 727	183 121	16 329	31 782	30 254	33 948	32 450	38 358
2015	196 868	12 323	6 538	5 784	184 545	16 171	32 036	30 186	33 633	33 005	39 513
2016	198 215	12 342	6 639	5 703	185 873	15 947	32 384	30 116	33 266	33 478	40 662
2017	198 942	12 339	6 687	5 652	186 603	15 701	32 541	30 182	32 668	33 709	41 803
2018	200 221	12 318	6 564	5 754	187 904	15 557	32 770	30 538	32 046	33 900	43 094
2019	200 827	12 247	6 419	5 828	188 580	15 427	32 817	30 770	31 306	33 915	44 346

Table 1-6. Civilian Noninstitutional Population, by Age, Race, Sex, and Hispanic Origin, 1948–2019
—*Continued*

(Thousands of people.)

Race, Hispanic origin, sex, and year	16 years and over	16 to 19 years			20 years and over						
		Total	16 to 17 years	18 to 19 years	Total	20 to 24 years	25 to 34 years	35 to 44 years	45 to 54 years	55 to 64 years	65 years and over
WHITE											
Men											
1954	46 462	3 455	1 902	1 553	43 007	3 074	9 948	9 688	8 172	6 341	5 787
1955	47 076	3 507	1 945	1 563	43 569	3 241	9 936	9 768	8 303	6 398	5 923
1956	47 602	3 500	1 955	1 546	44 102	3 464	9 851	9 848	8 446	6 455	6 038
1957	48 119	3 556	2 000	1 557	44 563	3 638	9 758	9 917	8 605	6 518	6 127
1958	48 745	3 747	2 140	1 607	44 998	3 783	9 656	10 018	8 765	6 574	6 203
1959	49 408	4 079	2 370	1 710	45 329	3 903	9 499	10 081	8 909	6 639	6 298
1960	50 065	4 349	2 476	1 874	45 716	4 054	9 373	10 131	9 042	6 721	6 395
1961	50 608	4 479	2 407	2 073	46 129	4 204	9 290	10 178	9 148	6 819	6 490
1962	51 054	4 520	2 426	2 094	46 534	4 306	9 080	10 239	9 191	6 917	6 801
1963	52 031	4 827	2 792	2 036	47 204	4 610	9 039	10 309	9 297	7 031	6 919
1964	52 869	5 148	3 090	2 059	47 721	4 862	9 024	10 301	9 417	7 153	6 963
1965	53 681	5 541	3 050	2 492	48 140	5 017	9 056	10 262	9 516	7 261	7 028
1966	54 061	5 820	3 023	2 798	48 241	4 974	9 085	10 136	9 592	7 362	7 092
1967	54 608	5 671	3 058	2 613	48 937	5 257	9 339	10 013	9 688	7 474	7 167
1968	55 434	5 787	3 153	2 635	49 647	5 376	9 752	9 902	9 790	7 585	7 242
1969	56 348	6 005	3 246	2 759	50 343	5 589	10 074	9 760	9 895	7 705	7 320
1970	57 516	6 179	3 329	2 851	51 336	5 988	10 441	9 678	9 999	7 822	7 409
1971	58 900	6 420	3 412	3 008	52 481	6 546	10 841	9 578	10 066	7 933	7 517
1972	60 473	6 627	3 503	3 125	53 845	7 042	11 495	9 568	10 078	8 089	7 573
1973	61 577	6 737	3 555	3 182	54 842	7 312	12 075	9 514	10 099	8 178	7 664
1974	62 791	6 851	3 604	3 247	55 942	7 476	12 599	9 564	10 165	8 288	7 849
1975	63 981	6 929	3 609	3 320	57 052	7 766	13 131	9 578	10 134	8 413	8 031
1976	65 132	6 993	3 609	3 384	58 138	7 987	13 655	9 674	10 063	8 556	8 203
1977	66 301	7 024	3 625	3 399	59 278	8 175	14 139	9 880	9 957	8 708	8 420
1978	67 401	7 022	3 619	3 404	60 378	8 335	14 528	10 236	9 845	8 826	8 608
1979	68 547	7 007	3 568	3 439	61 540	8 470	15 008	10 563	9 730	8 949	8 820
1980	69 634	6 941	3 508	3 433	62 694	8 581	15 529	10 863	9 636	9 059	9 027
1981	70 480	6 764	3 401	3 363	63 715	8 644	16 005	11 171	9 560	9 139	9 195
1982	71 211	6 556	3 249	3 307	64 655	8 621	16 260	11 756	9 463	9 188	9 367
1983	71 922	6 340	3 098	3 242	65 581	8 597	16 499	12 314	9 408	9 208	9 556
1984	72 723	6 113	3 019	3 094	66 610	8 522	16 816	12 853	9 434	9 217	9 768
1985	73 373	5 987	3 026	2 961	67 386	8 246	17 042	13 337	9 488	9 262	10 010
1986	74 390	5 977	3 084	2 894	68 413	8 002	17 564	13 840	9 578	9 201	10 229
1987	75 189	6 015	3 125	2 890	69 175	7 729	17 754	14 338	9 771	9 101	10 481
1988	75 855	5 968	3 015	2 953	69 887	7 473	17 867	14 743	10 114	9 001	10 688
1989	76 468	5 813	2 817	2 996	70 654	7 279	17 908	15 237	10 434	8 900	10 897
1990	77 369	5 913	2 809	3 103	71 457	7 764	17 766	15 770	10 598	8 680	10 879
1991	77 977	5 704	2 805	2 899	72 274	7 748	17 615	16 340	10 856	8 640	11 074
1992	78 651	5 611	2 819	2 792	73 040	7 676	17 403	16 579	11 513	8 602	11 268
1993	79 371	5 650	2 862	2 788	73 721	7 545	17 158	16 900	12 058	8 590	11 470
1994	80 059	5 748	2 938	2 810	74 311	7 357	16 915	17 247	12 545	8 618	11 629
1995	80 733	5 854	2 995	2 859	74 879	7 163	16 653	17 567	13 028	8 653	11 815
1996	81 489	6 035	3 099	2 936	75 454	6 971	16 395	17 868	13 518	8 734	11 968
1997	82 577	6 257	3 209	3 048	76 320	7 087	16 043	18 163	14 030	8 929	12 067
1998	83 352	6 386	3 233	3 153	76 966	7 170	15 644	18 310	14 400	9 286	12 155
1999	83 930	6 498	3 266	3 232	77 432	7 244	15 150	18 340	14 834	9 581	12 283
2000	85 370	6 404	3 224	3 181	78 966	7 329	15 528	18 003	15 578	10 028	12 501
2001	86 452	6 422	3 229	3 194	80 029	7 564	15 486	17 960	16 047	10 369	12 604
2002	87 361	6 439	3 251	3 189	80 922	7 750	15 470	17 792	16 317	10 918	12 676
2003	88 249	6 390	3 378	3 012	81 860	7 856	15 569	17 620	16 555	11 442	12 818
2004	89 044	6 429	3 301	3 129	82 615	8 024	15 486	17 404	16 834	11 922	12 946
2005	90 027	6 471	3 464	3 006	83 556	8 057	15 507	17 286	17 169	12 415	13 123
2006	91 021	6 555	3 551	3 004	84 466	8 052	15 567	17 143	17 467	12 891	13 346
2007	92 073	6 653	3 567	3 086	85 420	8 113	15 762	16 927	17 686	13 341	13 591
2008	92 725	6 669	3 550	3 120	86 056	8 072	15 884	16 599	17 830	13 698	13 972
2009	93 433	6 644	3 469	3 175	86 789	8 076	16 011	16 260	17 956	14 154	14 332
2010	94 082	6 580	3 473	3 107	87 502	8 240	16 174	15 920	17 919	14 634	14 615
2011	94 801	6 610	3 496	3 114	88 191	8 485	16 332	15 540	17 602	15 018	15 213
2012	94 266	6 486	3 387	3 099	87 780	8 211	15 691	15 263	17 287	15 333	15 995
2013	94 865	6 391	3 413	2 978	88 474	8 256	15 824	15 185	17 043	15 547	16 619
2014	95 513	6 321	3 370	2 950	89 193	8 250	15 992	15 110	16 823	15 794	17 224
2015	96 147	6 282	3 328	2 955	89 865	8 164	16 087	15 067	16 677	16 067	17 802
2016	96 861	6 289	3 346	2 943	90 572	8 057	16 280	15 055	16 507	16 300	18 373
2017	97 225	6 284	3 398	2 886	90 941	7 925	16 374	15 088	16 220	16 413	18 922
2018	97 933	6 271	3 374	2 897	91 662	7 848	16 536	15 288	15 920	16 515	19 554
2019	98 220	6 227	3 265	2 962	91 993	7 769	16 567	15 412	15 559	16 532	20 153

Table 1-6. Civilian Noninstitutional Population, by Age, Race, Sex, and Hispanic Origin, 1948–2019
—Continued

(Thousands of people.)

Race, Hispanic origin, sex, and year	16 years and over	16 to 19 years			20 years and over						
		Total	16 to 17 years	18 to 19 years	Total	20 to 24 years	25 to 34 years	35 to 44 years	45 to 54 years	55 to 64 years	65 years and over
WHITE											
Women											
1954	51 242	3 725	1 884	1 841	47 517	4 720	10 870	10 227	8 397	6 652	6 651
1955	51 802	3 785	1 929	1 856	48 017	4 671	10 806	10 342	8 566	6 771	6 862
1956	52 373	3 846	1 953	1 892	48 527	4 642	10 713	10 466	8 752	6 886	7 067
1957	52 998	3 949	2 007	1 941	49 049	4 655	10 584	10 597	8 957	7 000	7 256
1958	53 645	4 096	2 131	1 966	49 549	4 715	10 407	10 716	9 159	7 107	7 442
1959	54 392	4 351	2 337	2 015	50 041	4 794	10 216	10 812	9 348	7 219	7 653
1960	55 214	4 575	2 433	2 142	50 639	4 873	10 097	10 918	9 536	7 349	7 865
1961	55 993	4 732	2 378	2 354	51 261	4 999	9 999	10 991	9 697	7 485	8 091
1962	56 660	4 823	2 392	2 432	51 837	5 178	9 894	11 054	9 681	7 533	8 496
1963	57 672	5 151	2 757	2 394	52 521	5 459	9 828	11 089	9 785	7 650	8 710
1964	58 663	5 468	3 047	2 422	53 195	5 706	9 814	11 074	9 943	7 804	8 853
1965	59 601	5 778	2 999	2 779	53 823	5 918	9 826	10 996	10 088	7 954	9 042
1966	60 503	6 042	2 970	3 072	54 461	6 120	9 904	10 869	10 230	8 107	9 230
1967	61 491	6 011	2 993	3 019	55 480	6 540	10 125	10 732	10 379	8 271	9 435
1968	62 512	6 053	3 072	2 981	56 460	6 809	10 493	10 572	10 520	8 433	9 633
1969	63 563	6 174	3 172	3 002	57 390	7 089	10 818	10 396	10 651	8 600	9 836
1970	64 656	6 342	3 262	3 080	58 315	7 370	11 105	10 251	10 761	8 769	10 060
1971	65 857	6 518	3 338	3 180	59 340	7 662	11 454	10 117	10 841	8 951	10 315
1972	67 431	6 673	3 407	3 267	60 758	7 855	12 060	10 105	10 872	9 161	10 705
1973	68 517	6 796	3 466	3 331	61 721	7 951	12 610	10 018	10 891	9 306	10 943
1974	69 623	6 933	3 510	3 424	62 690	8 026	13 112	10 064	10 896	9 356	11 236
1975	70 810	7 011	3 523	3 488	63 798	8 214	13 615	10 063	10 847	9 505	11 556
1976	71 974	7 062	3 516	3 546	64 912	8 381	14 102	10 153	10 752	9 664	11 860
1977	73 077	7 071	3 525	3 545	66 007	8 553	14 564	10 351	10 618	9 832	12 088
1978	74 213	7 038	3 513	3 524	67 174	8 704	14 926	10 696	10 476	9 974	12 399
1979	75 347	6 987	3 460	3 527	68 360	8 815	15 363	11 017	10 327	10 122	12 717
1980	76 489	6 914	3 403	3 511	69 575	8 904	15 878	11 313	10 201	10 256	13 022
1981	77 428	6 752	3 303	3 449	70 677	8 965	16 362	11 606	10 106	10 346	13 292
1982	78 230	6 519	3 134	3 385	71 711	8 959	16 603	12 154	10 015	10 402	13 579
1983	78 884	6 282	2 991	3 292	72 601	8 895	16 788	12 714	9 941	10 418	13 847
1984	79 624	6 034	2 899	3 135	73 590	8 782	17 073	13 271	9 914	10 412	14 138
1985	80 306	5 912	2 895	3 017	74 394	8 607	17 409	13 762	9 917	10 358	14 342
1986	81 042	5 902	2 953	2 949	75 140	8 351	17 728	14 223	10 009	10 277	14 551
1987	81 769	5 924	2 985	2 939	75 845	8 079	17 913	14 698	10 194	10 141	14 820
1988	82 340	5 869	2 878	2 991	76 470	7 804	18 009	15 074	10 537	9 994	15 052
1989	82 871	5 716	2 690	3 027	77 154	7 600	18 043	15 537	10 853	9 843	15 278
1990	83 256	5 717	2 654	3 063	77 539	7 774	17 895	15 969	10 937	9 524	15 440
1991	83 781	5 497	2 646	2 850	78 285	7 768	17 726	16 514	11 196	9 435	15 647
1992	84 321	5 393	2 659	2 734	78 928	7 678	17 482	16 727	11 851	9 350	15 841
1993	84 918	5 428	2 700	2 728	79 490	7 542	17 206	17 019	12 398	9 302	16 023
1994	85 496	5 516	2 772	2 744	79 980	7 351	16 950	17 335	12 890	9 306	16 148
1995	86 181	5 614	2 827	2 787	80 567	7 150	16 702	17 654	13 390	9 333	16 337
1996	86 828	5 787	2 927	2 860	81 041	6 936	16 457	17 943	13 884	9 402	16 419
1997	87 417	5 924	3 004	2 920	81 492	6 896	16 047	18 162	14 357	9 582	16 447
1998	88 126	6 053	3 031	3 023	82 073	6 969	15 642	18 300	14 732	9 944	16 486
1999	89 156	6 202	3 076	3 127	82 953	7 150	15 366	18 415	15 214	10 274	16 536
2000	90 850	6 131	3 041	3 090	84 718	7 223	15 420	18 258	15 972	10 729	17 116
2001	91 660	6 134	3 062	3 071	85 526	7 438	15 284	18 153	16 428	11 065	17 158
2002	92 422	6 157	3 096	3 061	86 266	7 611	15 207	17 958	16 695	11 622	17 173
2003	93 043	6 137	3 251	2 886	86 905	7 680	15 220	17 731	16 911	12 147	17 216
2004	93 599	6 169	3 260	2 909	87 430	7 794	15 099	17 441	17 170	12 627	17 299
2005	94 419	6 219	3 304	2 915	88 200	7 814	15 086	17 268	17 480	13 119	17 433
2006	95 242	6 301	3 429	2 871	88 942	7 796	15 094	17 074	17 760	13 596	17 623
2007	96 180	6 390	3 458	2 932	89 790	7 832	15 249	16 843	17 979	14 051	17 835
2008	96 814	6 414	3 412	3 003	90 400	7 842	15 349	16 493	18 111	14 411	18 193
2009	97 469	6 391	3 306	3 086	91 078	7 887	15 460	16 118	18 210	14 868	18 535
2010	97 993	6 311	3 327	2 984	91 683	8 040	15 640	15 727	18 146	15 349	18 781
2011	98 276	6 208	3 177	3 031	92 068	8 077	15 803	15 490	17 925	15 781	18 992
2012	98 938	6 172	3 230	2 942	92 766	8 078	15 550	15 334	17 648	16 179	19 978
2013	99 467	6 107	3 277	2 830	93 360	8 101	15 664	15 242	17 370	16 408	20 575
2014	99 984	6 056	3 280	2 777	93 928	8 079	15 790	15 144	17 125	16 656	21 134
2015	100 720	6 040	3 211	2 829	94 680	8 007	15 950	15 119	16 956	16 938	21 711
2016	101 354	6 053	3 293	2 760	95 301	7 890	16 104	15 082	16 758	17 178	22 289
2017	101 717	6 055	3 289	2 767	95 661	7 776	16 168	15 094	16 448	17 296	22 881
2018	102 289	6 047	3 189	2 857	96 242	7 709	16 234	15 250	16 126	17 384	23 540
2019	102 607	6 020	3 154	2 865	96 587	7 658	16 249	15 359	15 747	17 382	24 193

Table 1-6. Civilian Noninstitutional Population, by Age, Race, Sex, and Hispanic Origin, 1948–2019
—*Continued*

(Thousands of people.)

Race, Hispanic origin, sex, and year	16 years and over	16 to 19 years			20 years and over						
		Total	16 to 17 years	18 to 19 years	Total	20 to 24 years	25 to 34 years	35 to 44 years	45 to 54 years	55 to 64 years	65 years and over
BLACK											
Both Sexes											
1985	19 664	2 160	1 083	1 077	17 504	2 649	4 873	3 290	2 372	2 060	2 259
1986	19 989	2 137	1 090	1 048	17 852	2 625	5 026	3 410	2 413	2 079	2 298
1987	20 352	2 163	1 123	1 040	18 189	2 578	5 139	3 563	2 460	2 097	2 352
1988	20 692	2 179	1 130	1 049	18 513	2 527	5 234	3 716	2 524	2 110	2 402
1989	21 021	2 176	1 116	1 060	18 846	2 479	5 308	3 900	2 587	2 118	2 454
1990	21 477	2 238	1 101	1 138	19 239	2 554	5 407	4 328	2 618	1 970	2 362
1991	21 799	2 187	1 085	1 102	19 612	2 585	5 419	4 538	2 682	1 985	2 403
1992	22 147	2 155	1 086	1 069	19 992	2 615	5 404	4 722	2 809	1 996	2 446
1993	22 521	2 181	1 113	1 069	20 339	2 600	5 409	4 886	2 941	2 016	2 487
1994	22 879	2 211	1 168	1 044	20 668	2 616	5 362	5 038	3 084	2 045	2 524
1995	23 246	2 284	1 198	1 086	20 962	2 554	5 337	5 178	3 244	2 079	2 571
1996	23 604	2 356	1 238	1 118	21 248	2 519	5 311	5 290	3 408	2 110	2 609
1997	24 003	2 412	1 255	1 158	21 591	2 515	5 279	5 410	3 571	2 164	2 653
1998	24 373	2 443	1 241	1 202	21 930	2 546	5 221	5 510	3 735	2 224	2 695
1999	24 855	2 479	1 250	1 229	22 376	2 615	5 197	5 609	3 919	2 295	2 741
2000	24 902	2 389	1 205	1 183	22 513	2 611	5 089	5 488	4 168	2 407	2 750
2001	25 138	2 388	1 212	1 176	22 750	2 686	5 003	5 467	4 343	2 478	2 775
2002	25 578	2 416	1 235	1 181	23 162	2 779	5 015	5 460	4 513	2 571	2 823
2003	25 686	2 382	1 309	1 074	23 304	2 773	4 978	5 387	4 628	2 692	2 846
2004	26 065	2 423	1 350	1 072	23 643	2 821	5 020	5 335	4 739	2 827	2 899
2005	26 517	2 481	1 341	1 140	24 036	2 835	5 075	5 311	4 869	2 980	2 967
2006	27 007	2 565	1 408	1 157	24 442	2 851	5 133	5 302	4 992	3 137	3 027
2007	27 485	2 640	1 497	1 143	24 845	2 891	5 210	5 271	5 110	3 284	3 080
2008	27 843	2 676	1 459	1 217	25 168	2 914	5 262	5 198	5 183	3 429	3 182
2009	28 241	2 684	1 462	1 221	25 557	2 973	5 349	5 109	5 290	3 596	3 239
2010	28 708	2 657	1 438	1 219	26 051	3 097	5 491	5 031	5 322	3 773	3 337
2011	29 114	2 594	1 353	1 240	26 520	3 168	5 606	4 995	5 357	3 955	3 440
2012	29 907	2 643	1 381	1 262	27 265	3 326	5 455	5 107	5 446	4 281	3 650
2013	30 376	2 565	1 344	1 221	27 811	3 425	5 585	5 131	5 429	4 430	3 811
2014	30 843	2 508	1 345	1 163	28 335	3 460	5 742	5 168	5 377	4 573	4 015
2015	31 386	2 491	1 343	1 148	28 895	3 425	5 929	5 232	5 383	4 718	4 207
2016	31 889	2 510	1 377	1 132	29 380	3 338	6 138	5 273	5 380	4 840	4 409
2017	32 247	2 511	1 352	1 159	29 736	3 239	6 308	5 311	5 335	4 934	4 610
2018	32 761	2 499	1 280	1 218	30 262	3 172	6 502	5 408	5 295	5 037	4 848
2019	33 036	2 463	1 308	1 155	30 573	3 104	6 636	5 474	5 207	5 095	5 058
Men											
1985	8 790	1 059	543	517	7 731	1 202	2 180	1 462	1 060	924	902
1986	8 956	1 049	548	503	7 907	1 195	2 264	1 517	1 072	934	924
1987	9 128	1 065	566	499	8 063	1 173	2 320	1 587	1 092	944	947
1988	9 289	1 074	569	505	8 215	1 151	2 367	1 656	1 121	951	970
1989	9 439	1 075	575	501	8 364	1 128	2 403	1 741	1 145	956	989
1990	9 573	1 094	555	540	8 479	1 144	2 412	1 968	1 183	855	917
1991	9 725	1 072	546	526	8 652	1 168	2 417	2 060	1 211	864	933
1992	9 896	1 056	544	512	8 840	1 194	2 409	2 150	1 268	868	951
1993	10 083	1 075	559	516	9 008	1 181	2 425	2 228	1 330	874	969
1994	10 258	1 087	586	501	9 171	1 207	2 399	2 300	1 392	889	985
1995	10 411	1 131	601	530	9 280	1 161	2 388	2 362	1 462	901	1 006
1996	10 575	1 161	623	538	9 414	1 154	2 373	2 413	1 534	914	1 025
1997	10 763	1 188	634	553	9 575	1 153	2 363	2 471	1 607	936	1 045
1998	10 927	1 201	623	578	9 727	1 166	2 335	2 520	1 682	956	1 068
1999	11 143	1 218	628	589	9 926	1 197	2 321	2 566	1 765	986	1 091
2000	11 129	1 178	605	572	9 952	1 195	2 277	2 471	1 889	1 067	1 053
2001	11 172	1 179	606	573	9 993	1 224	2 212	2 440	1 960	1 096	1 060
2002	11 391	1 195	615	580	10 196	1 281	2 223	2 437	2 042	1 137	1 075
2003	11 454	1 176	661	515	10 278	1 291	2 210	2 401	2 094	1 189	1 093
2004	11 656	1 195	680	516	10 461	1 326	2 242	2 382	2 150	1 250	1 111
2005	11 882	1 223	682	541	10 659	1 341	2 277	2 372	2 202	1 319	1 148
2006	12 130	1 266	713	552	10 864	1 355	2 318	2 369	2 261	1 390	1 170
2007	12 361	1 305	742	563	11 057	1 380	2 366	2 352	2 318	1 454	1 186
2008	12 516	1 322	718	604	11 194	1 384	2 398	2 313	2 335	1 519	1 245
2009	12 705	1 326	736	590	11 379	1 410	2 454	2 271	2 392	1 592	1 260
2010	12 939	1 313	715	598	11 626	1 474	2 540	2 234	2 406	1 673	1 299
2011	13 164	1 282	642	640	11 882	1 510	2 612	2 222	2 435	1 759	1 344
2012	13 508	1 319	707	612	12 189	1 586	2 461	2 286	2 484	1 923	1 449
2013	13 747	1 276	685	591	12 471	1 647	2 536	2 299	2 474	1 992	1 522
2014	13 997	1 246	688	558	12 751	1 675	2 634	2 319	2 448	2 062	1 613
2015	14 268	1 237	697	540	13 031	1 662	2 740	2 353	2 454	2 130	1 692
2016	14 525	1 247	666	580	13 278	1 621	2 861	2 378	2 447	2 189	1 782
2017	14 712	1 249	673	576	13 464	1 571	2 963	2 401	2 430	2 234	1 864
2018	14 964	1 241	633	608	13 723	1 535	3 077	2 454	2 400	2 282	1 974
2019	15 102	1 222	656	566	13 881	1 499	3 160	2 493	2 365	2 311	2 053

Table 1-6. Civilian Noninstitutional Population, by Age, Race, Sex, and Hispanic Origin, 1948–2019
—Continued

(Thousands of people.)

Race, Hispanic origin, sex, and year	16 years and over	16 to 19 years			20 years and over						
		Total	16 to 17 years	18 to 19 years	Total	20 to 24 years	25 to 34 years	35 to 44 years	45 to 54 years	55 to 64 years	65 years and over
BLACK											
Women											
1985	10 873	1 101	540	560	9 773	1 447	2 693	1 828	1 312	1 136	1 357
1986	11 033	1 088	542	545	9 945	1 430	2 762	1 893	1 341	1 145	1 374
1987	11 224	1 098	557	541	10 126	1 405	2 819	1 976	1 368	1 153	1 405
1988	11 402	1 105	561	544	10 298	1 376	2 867	2 060	1 403	1 159	1 432
1989	11 582	1 100	541	559	10 482	1 351	2 905	2 159	1 441	1 162	1 464
1990	11 904	1 144	546	598	10 760	1 410	2 995	2 360	1 435	1 114	1 446
1991	12 074	1 115	539	576	10 959	1 417	3 003	2 478	1 471	1 121	1 470
1992	12 251	1 099	542	557	11 152	1 421	2 995	2 573	1 542	1 127	1 495
1993	12 438	1 106	554	552	11 332	1 419	2 983	2 659	1 611	1 142	1 518
1994	12 621	1 125	582	543	11 496	1 410	2 963	2 738	1 692	1 156	1 538
1995	12 835	1 153	597	556	11 682	1 392	2 948	2 816	1 782	1 178	1 565
1996	13 029	1 195	615	580	11 833	1 364	2 938	2 877	1 874	1 196	1 584
1997	13 241	1 225	620	604	12 016	1 362	2 916	2 939	1 964	1 228	1 608
1998	13 446	1 243	618	624	12 203	1 380	2 886	2 991	2 053	1 268	1 626
1999	13 711	1 261	621	640	12 451	1 418	2 876	3 043	2 153	1 310	1 650
2000	13 772	1 211	600	611	12 561	1 416	2 812	3 017	2 279	1 340	1 697
2001	13 966	1 209	606	603	12 758	1 462	2 790	3 026	2 383	1 382	1 714
2002	14 187	1 221	620	601	12 966	1 498	2 792	3 023	2 471	1 434	1 747
2003	14 232	1 206	648	558	13 026	1 482	2 768	2 986	2 534	1 504	1 753
2004	14 409	1 227	670	557	13 182	1 495	2 778	2 954	2 590	1 577	1 789
2005	14 635	1 258	659	598	13 377	1 494	2 797	2 939	2 666	1 661	1 819
2006	14 877	1 299	694	605	13 578	1 495	2 815	2 933	2 731	1 747	1 857
2007	15 124	1 336	755	581	13 788	1 511	2 844	2 918	2 792	1 830	1 893
2008	15 328	1 354	741	613	13 974	1 530	2 864	2 885	2 848	1 910	1 937
2009	15 536	1 357	726	631	14 178	1 563	2 895	2 839	2 898	2 004	1 979
2010	15 769	1 344	723	621	14 425	1 623	2 951	2 796	2 916	2 101	2 038
2011	15 950	1 312	712	600	14 638	1 657	2 994	2 773	2 922	2 196	2 096
2012	16 400	1 324	674	650	15 076	1 740	2 994	2 821	2 963	2 358	2 201
2013	16 629	1 289	659	630	15 340	1 778	3 048	2 832	2 955	2 437	2 289
2014	16 846	1 262	656	605	15 584	1 785	3 108	2 849	2 929	2 511	2 402
2015	17 118	1 254	646	609	15 863	1 764	3 190	2 879	2 929	2 588	2 515
2016	17 365	1 263	711	552	16 102	1 717	3 278	2 895	2 933	2 652	2 627
2017	17 535	1 263	679	584	16 272	1 667	3 344	2 909	2 905	2 700	2 747
2018	17 797	1 257	648	610	16 539	1 636	3 425	2 954	2 895	2 755	2 875
2019	17 934	1 241	653	589	16 693	1 605	3 477	2 981	2 842	2 783	3 005
HISPANIC											
Both Sexes											
1985	11 915	1 298	638	661	10 617	1 864	3 401	2 117	1 377	1 015	843
1986	12 344	1 302	658	644	11 042	1 899	3 510	2 239	1 496	1 023	875
1987	12 867	1 332	651	681	11 536	1 910	3 714	2 464	1 492	1 061	895
1988	13 325	1 354	662	692	11 970	1 948	3 807	2 565	1 571	1 159	920
1989	13 791	1 399	672	727	12 392	1 950	3 953	2 658	1 649	1 182	1 001
1990	15 904	1 737	821	915	14 167	2 428	4 589	3 001	1 817	1 247	1 084
1991	16 425	1 732	819	913	14 693	2 481	4 674	3 243	1 879	1 283	1 134
1992	16 961	1 737	836	901	15 224	2 444	4 806	3 458	1 980	1 321	1 216
1993	17 532	1 756	855	901	15 776	2 487	4 887	3 632	2 094	1 324	1 353
1994	18 117	1 818	902	916	16 300	2 518	5 000	3 756	2 223	1 401	1 401
1995	18 629	1 872	903	969	16 757	2 528	5 050	3 965	2 294	1 483	1 437
1996	19 213	1 948	962	986	17 265	2 524	5 181	4 227	2 275	1 546	1 512
1997	20 321	2 121	1 088	1 033	18 200	2 623	5 405	4 453	2 581	1 580	1 558
1998	21 070	2 204	1 070	1 135	18 865	2 731	5 447	4 636	2 775	1 615	1 662
1999	21 650	2 307	1 113	1 194	19 344	2 700	5 512	4 833	2 868	1 713	1 718
2000	23 938	2 523	1 214	1 309	21 415	3 255	6 466	5 189	3 061	1 736	1 708
2001	24 942	2 508	1 173	1 334	22 435	3 417	6 726	5 346	3 339	1 816	1 792
2002	25 963	2 507	1 216	1 291	23 456	3 508	7 010	5 606	3 494	1 953	1 885
2003	27 551	2 543	1 346	1 197	25 008	3 533	7 506	6 003	3 845	2 093	2 027
2004	28 109	2 608	1 337	1 270	25 502	3 666	7 470	6 055	3 987	2 208	2 115
2005	29 133	2 689	1 415	1 274	26 444	3 647	7 684	6 293	4 217	2 361	2 242
2006	30 103	2 796	1 518	1 277	27 307	3 603	7 856	6 519	4 466	2 516	2 347
2007	31 383	2 944	1 559	1 385	28 440	3 648	8 129	6 785	4 720	2 685	2 473
2008	32 141	3 042	1 620	1 422	29 098	3 620	8 147	6 946	4 937	2 840	2 609
2009	32 891	3 123	1 602	1 522	29 768	3 623	8 099	7 078	5 192	3 017	2 759
2010	33 713	3 243	1 673	1 570	30 469	3 880	8 084	7 123	5 351	3 167	2 864
2011	34 438	3 407	1 808	1 598	31 031	4 193	8 107	7 103	5 414	3 311	2 903
2012	36 759	3 656	1 906	1 750	33 103	4 502	8 512	7 551	5 831	3 613	3 094
2013	37 517	3 651	1 911	1 740	33 867	4 572	8 564	7 663	6 010	3 791	3 267
2014	38 400	3 662	1 949	1 713	34 738	4 642	8 656	7 792	6 192	3 989	3 467
2015	39 617	3 705	1 970	1 736	35 912	4 697	8 762	8 026	6 474	4 255	3 698
2016	40 697	3 777	2 011	1 766	36 919	4 711	8 914	8 194	6 672	4 483	3 946
2017	41 371	3 844	2 045	1 799	37 528	4 686	8 988	8 263	6 800	4 662	4 129
2018	42 734	3 938	2 086	1 852	38 795	4 744	9 263	8 499	6 983	4 892	4 414
2019	43 507	3 989	2 119	1 871	39 517	4 760	9 366	8 585	7 111	5 081	4 615

Table 1-6. Civilian Noninstitutional Population, by Age, Race, Sex, and Hispanic Origin, 1948–2019
—Continued

(Thousands of people.)

Race, Hispanic origin, sex, and year	16 years and over	16 to 19 years			20 years and over						
		Total	16 to 17 years	18 to 19 years	Total	20 to 24 years	25 to 34 years	35 to 44 years	45 to 54 years	55 to 64 years	65 years and over
HISPANIC											
Men											
1985	5 885	...	...	...	5 232	...	...	...	...	...	...
1986	6 106	...	...	...	5 451	...	...	...	...	...	...
1987	6 371	...	...	...	5 700	...	...	...	...	...	...
1988	6 604	...	...	...	5 921	...	...	...	...	...	...
1989	6 825	...	...	...	6 114	...	...	...	...	...	...
1990	8 041	...	...	...	7 126	...	...	...	...	...	...
1991	8 296	...	...	...	7 392	...	...	...	...	...	...
1992	8 553	...	...	...	7 655	...	...	...	...	...	...
1993	8 824	...	...	...	7 930	...	...	...	...	...	...
1994	9 104	926	472	454	8 178	1 346	2 627	1 871	1 076	644	614
1995	9 329	954	481	473	8 375	1 337	2 657	1 966	1 127	668	619
1996	9 604	992	485	507	8 611	1 321	2 692	2 144	1 111	712	630
1997	10 368	1 119	585	534	9 250	1 439	2 872	2 275	1 266	747	651
1998	10 734	1 161	586	575	9 573	1 462	2 907	2 377	1 342	771	714
1999	10 713	1 190	571	619	9 523	1 398	2 805	2 407	1 397	767	749
2000	12 174	1 333	640	693	10 841	1 784	3 380	2 626	1 527	799	725
2001	12 695	1 310	619	690	11 386	1 846	3 529	2 765	1 650	848	749
2002	13 221	1 293	615	678	11 928	1 890	3 727	2 875	1 716	902	817
2003	14 098	1 301	674	627	12 797	1 905	4 033	3 098	1 910	989	862
2004	14 417	1 336	664	672	13 082	1 981	4 024	3 147	1 990	1 046	894
2005	14 962	1 376	730	646	13 586	1 956	4 155	3 284	2 114	1 123	953
2006	15 473	1 428	763	664	14 046	1 916	4 266	3 414	2 251	1 204	996
2007	16 154	1 505	790	714	14 649	1 928	4 430	3 563	2 384	1 287	1 058
2008	16 524	1 553	838	716	14 971	1 890	4 438	3 655	2 502	1 365	1 121
2009	16 897	1 593	818	774	15 305	1 875	4 405	3 735	2 647	1 459	1 184
2010	17 359	1 666	847	819	15 693	2 016	4 381	3 783	2 741	1 538	1 234
2011	17 753	1 812	951	861	15 941	2 278	4 379	3 702	2 717	1 604	1 260
2012	18 434	1 879	970	909	16 555	2 341	4 424	3 822	2 911	1 729	1 329
2013	18 798	1 870	988	882	16 928	2 364	4 453	3 880	3 012	1 818	1 402
2014	19 244	1 873	1 006	867	17 371	2 389	4 509	3 951	3 104	1 920	1 499
2015	19 745	1 886	1 014	872	17 860	2 396	4 516	4 053	3 241	2 050	1 604
2016	20 266	1 920	1 041	879	18 346	2 396	4 588	4 142	3 347	2 166	1 708
2017	20 578	1 951	1 042	908	18 627	2 374	4 617	4 183	3 404	2 256	1 794
2018	21 287	1 998	1 067	931	19 289	2 402	4 777	4 321	3 498	2 374	1 917
2019	21 660	2 020	1 080	940	19 640	2 401	4 821	4 376	3 552	2 470	2 020
HISPANIC											
Women											
1985	6 029	...	...	...	5 385	...	...	...	...	...	...
1986	6 238	...	...	...	5 591	...	...	...	...	...	...
1987	6 496	...	...	...	5 835	...	...	...	...	...	...
1988	6 721	...	...	...	6 050	...	...	...	...	...	...
1989	6 965	...	...	...	6 278	...	...	...	...	...	...
1990	7 863	...	...	...	7 041	...	...	...	...	...	...
1991	8 130	...	...	...	7 301	...	...	...	...	...	...
1992	8 408	...	...	...	7 569	...	...	...	...	...	...
1993	8 708	...	...	...	7 846	...	...	...	...	...	...
1994	9 014	892	430	462	8 122	1 173	2 373	1 885	1 147	757	787
1995	9 300	918	422	496	8 382	1 191	2 393	1 999	1 167	815	818
1996	9 610	956	477	479	8 654	1 203	2 489	2 082	1 164	834	882
1997	9 953	1 003	503	500	8 950	1 184	2 533	2 178	1 315	833	907
1998	10 335	1 044	483	560	9 292	1 269	2 539	2 259	1 433	844	948
1999	10 937	1 116	542	575	9 821	1 302	2 707	2 425	1 470	947	969
2000	11 764	1 190	574	616	10 574	1 471	3 086	2 564	1 534	937	982
2001	12 247	1 198	554	644	11 049	1 571	3 198	2 581	1 689	968	1 043
2002	12 742	1 214	601	613	11 528	1 617	3 283	2 732	1 777	1 051	1 068
2003	13 452	1 242	672	570	12 211	1 628	3 473	2 905	1 935	1 105	1 166
2004	13 692	1 272	674	598	12 420	1 685	3 447	2 908	1 997	1 162	1 221
2005	14 172	1 313	685	628	12 858	1 692	3 529	3 009	2 103	1 237	1 289
2006	14 630	1 368	755	613	13 262	1 688	3 590	3 105	2 215	1 313	1 351
2007	15 229	1 439	769	670	13 791	1 720	3 698	3 222	2 336	1 398	1 416
2008	15 616	1 489	782	706	14 127	1 730	3 710	3 291	2 435	1 475	1 488
2009	15 993	1 531	783	748	14 463	1 748	3 694	3 343	2 545	1 558	1 576
2010	16 354	1 578	826	752	14 776	1 864	3 703	3 340	2 610	1 628	1 630
2011	16 685	1 595	857	738	15 090	1 915	3 727	3 401	2 696	1 707	1 643
2012	18 324	1 776	936	841	16 548	2 161	4 088	3 729	2 920	1 884	1 765
2013	18 719	1 781	923	858	16 938	2 208	4 110	3 783	2 998	1 973	1 866
2014	19 156	1 790	944	846	17 367	2 253	4 147	3 841	3 088	2 070	1 968
2015	19 872	1 820	956	864	18 052	2 301	4 247	3 973	3 233	2 205	2 094
2016	20 430	1 857	971	887	18 573	2 315	4 326	4 052	3 325	2 317	2 238
2017	20 794	1 893	1 002	891	18 900	2 312	4 371	4 079	3 397	2 406	2 335
2018	21 447	1 940	1 020	921	19 507	2 342	4 486	4 178	3 485	2 518	2 497
2019	21 846	1 969	1 038	931	19 877	2 358	4 545	4 209	3 559	2 612	2 595

. . . = Not available.

Table 1-7. Civilian Labor Force, by Age, Sex, and Race, 1948–2019

(Thousands of people.)

Race, Hispanic origin, sex, and year	16 years and over	16 to 19 years			20 years and over						
		Total	16 to 17 years	18 to 19 years	Total	20 to 24 years	25 to 34 years	35 to 44 years	45 to 54 years	55 to 64 years	65 years and over
ALL RACES											
Both Sexes											
1948	60 621	4 435	1 780	2 654	56 187	7 392	14 258	13 397	10 914	7 329	2 897
1949	61 286	4 288	1 704	2 583	57 000	7 340	14 415	13 711	11 107	7 426	3 010
1950	62 208	4 216	1 659	2 557	57 994	7 307	14 619	13 954	11 444	7 633	3 036
1951	62 017	4 103	1 743	2 360	57 914	6 594	14 668	14 100	11 739	7 796	3 020
1952	62 138	4 064	1 806	2 257	58 075	5 840	14 904	14 383	11 961	7 980	3 005
1953	63 015	4 027	1 727	2 299	58 989	5 481	14 898	15 099	12 249	8 024	3 236
1954	63 643	3 976	1 643	2 300	59 666	5 475	14 983	15 221	12 524	8 269	3 192
1955	65 023	4 092	1 711	2 382	60 931	5 666	15 058	15 400	12 992	8 513	3 305
1956	66 552	4 296	1 878	2 418	62 257	5 940	14 961	15 694	13 407	8 830	3 423
1957	66 929	4 275	1 843	2 433	62 653	6 071	14 826	15 847	13 768	8 853	3 290
1958	67 639	4 260	1 818	2 442	63 377	6 272	14 668	16 028	14 179	9 031	3 199
1959	68 369	4 492	1 971	2 522	63 876	6 413	14 435	16 127	14 518	9 227	3 158
1960	69 628	4 841	2 095	2 747	64 788	6 702	14 382	16 269	14 852	9 385	3 195
1961	70 459	4 936	1 984	2 951	65 524	6 950	14 319	16 402	15 071	9 636	3 146
1962	70 614	4 916	1 919	2 997	65 699	7 082	14 023	16 589	15 096	9 757	3 154
1963	71 833	5 139	2 171	2 966	66 695	7 473	14 050	16 788	15 338	10 006	3 041
1964	73 091	5 388	2 449	2 940	67 702	7 963	14 056	16 771	15 637	10 182	3 090
1965	74 455	5 910	2 486	3 425	68 543	8 259	14 233	16 840	15 756	10 350	3 108
1966	75 770	6 558	2 664	3 893	69 219	8 410	14 458	16 738	15 984	10 575	3 053
1967	77 347	6 521	2 734	3 786	70 825	9 010	15 055	16 703	16 172	10 792	3 097
1968	78 737	6 619	2 817	3 803	72 118	9 305	15 708	16 591	16 397	10 964	3 153
1969	80 734	6 970	3 009	3 959	73 763	9 879	16 336	16 458	16 730	11 135	3 227
1970	82 771	7 249	3 135	4 115	75 521	10 597	17 036	16 437	16 949	11 283	3 222
1971	84 382	7 470	3 192	4 278	76 913	11 331	17 714	16 305	17 024	11 390	3 149
1972	87 034	8 054	3 420	4 636	78 980	12 130	18 960	16 398	16 967	11 412	3 114
1973	89 429	8 507	3 665	4 839	80 924	12 846	20 376	16 492	16 983	11 256	2 974
1974	91 949	8 871	3 810	5 059	83 080	13 314	21 654	16 763	17 131	11 284	2 934
1975	93 775	8 870	3 740	5 131	84 904	13 750	22 864	16 903	17 084	11 346	2 956
1976	96 158	9 056	3 767	5 288	87 103	14 284	24 203	17 317	16 982	11 422	2 895
1977	99 009	9 351	3 919	5 431	89 658	14 825	25 500	17 943	16 878	11 577	2 934
1978	102 251	9 652	4 127	5 526	92 598	15 370	26 703	18 821	16 891	11 744	3 070
1979	104 962	9 638	4 079	5 559	95 325	15 769	27 938	19 685	16 897	11 931	3 104
1980	106 940	9 378	3 883	5 496	97 561	15 922	29 227	20 463	16 910	11 985	3 054
1981	108 670	8 988	3 647	5 340	99 682	16 099	30 392	21 211	16 970	11 969	3 042
1982	110 204	8 526	3 336	5 189	101 679	16 082	31 186	22 431	16 889	12 062	3 030
1983	111 550	8 171	3 073	5 098	103 379	16 052	31 834	23 611	16 851	11 992	3 040
1984	113 544	7 943	3 050	4 894	105 601	16 046	32 723	24 933	17 006	11 961	2 933
1985	115 461	7 901	3 154	4 747	107 560	15 718	33 550	26 073	17 322	11 991	2 907
1986	117 834	7 926	3 287	4 639	109 908	15 441	34 591	27 232	17 739	11 894	3 010
1987	119 865	7 988	3 384	4 604	111 878	14 977	35 233	28 460	18 210	11 877	3 119
1988	121 669	8 031	3 286	4 745	113 638	14 505	35 503	29 435	19 104	11 808	3 284
1989	123 869	7 954	3 125	4 828	115 916	14 180	35 896	30 601	19 916	11 877	3 446
1990	125 840	7 792	2 937	4 856	118 047	14 700	35 929	32 145	20 248	11 575	3 451
1991	126 346	7 265	2 789	4 476	119 082	14 548	35 507	33 312	20 828	11 473	3 413
1992	128 105	7 096	2 769	4 327	121 009	14 521	35 369	33 899	22 160	11 587	3 473
1993	129 200	7 170	2 831	4 338	122 030	14 354	34 780	34 562	23 296	11 599	3 439
1994	131 056	7 481	3 134	4 347	123 576	14 131	34 353	35 226	24 318	11 713	3 834
1995	132 304	7 765	3 225	4 540	124 539	13 688	34 198	35 751	25 223	11 860	3 819
1996	133 943	7 806	3 263	4 543	126 137	13 377	33 833	36 556	26 397	12 146	3 828
1997	136 297	7 932	3 237	4 695	128 365	13 532	33 380	37 326	27 574	12 665	3 887
1998	137 673	8 256	3 335	4 921	129 417	13 638	32 813	37 556	28 368	13 215	3 847
1999	139 368	8 333	3 337	4 996	131 034	13 933	32 143	37 882	29 388	13 682	4 005
2000	142 583	8 271	3 261	5 010	134 312	14 250	32 755	37 567	31 071	14 356	4 312
2001	143 734	7 902	3 088	4 814	135 832	14 557	32 361	37 404	32 025	15 104	4 382
2002	144 863	7 585	2 870	4 715	137 278	14 781	32 196	36 926	32 597	16 309	4 469
2003	146 510	7 170	2 857	4 313	139 340	14 928	32 343	36 695	33 270	17 312	4 792
2004	147 401	7 114	2 747	4 367	140 287	15 154	32 207	36 158	33 758	18 013	4 998
2005	149 320	7 164	2 825	4 339	142 157	15 127	32 341	36 030	34 402	18 979	5 278
2006	151 428	7 281	2 952	4 329	144 147	15 113	32 573	35 848	35 146	19 984	5 484
2007	153 124	7 012	2 771	4 242	146 112	15 205	33 130	35 527	35 697	20 750	5 804
2008	154 287	6 858	2 552	4 306	147 429	15 174	33 332	35 061	36 003	21 615	6 243
2009	154 142	6 390	2 227	4 163	147 752	14 971	33 298	34 239	36 205	22 505	6 534
2010	153 889	5 906	2 000	3 905	147 983	15 028	33 614	33 366	35 960	23 297	6 718
2011	153 617	5 727	1 873	3 853	147 890	15 270	33 724	32 660	35 360	23 765	7 112
2012	154 975	5 823	1 952	3 870	149 152	15 462	33 465	32 734	35 054	24 710	7 727
2013	155 389	5 785	2 023	3 762	149 604	15 595	33 746	32 563	34 467	25 116	8 116
2014	155 922	5 654	1 971	3 683	150 268	15 641	34 199	32 506	34 062	25 502	8 358
2015	157 130	5 700	1 987	3 713	151 430	15 523	34 647	32 603	33 902	25 954	8 801
2016	159 187	5 889	2 127	3 763	153 298	15 313	35 519	32 820	33 909	26 465	9 272
2017	160 320	5 901	2 237	3 664	154 418	15 259	36 086	33 034	33 563	26 899	9 577
2018	162 075	5 885	2 133	3 753	156 190	15 099	36 774	33 619	33 311	27 354	10 032
2019	163 539	5 896	2 081	3 816	157 642	15 196	37 191	34 057	32 932	27 603	10 663

Table 1-7. Civilian Labor Force, by Age, Sex, and Race, 1948–2019—*Continued*

(Thousands of people.)

Race, Hispanic origin, sex, and year	16 years and over	16 to 19 years			20 years and over						
		Total	16 to 17 years	18 to 19 years	Total	20 to 24 years	25 to 34 years	35 to 44 years	45 to 54 years	55 to 64 years	65 years and over
ALL RACES											
Men											
1948	43 286	2 600	1 109	1 490	40 687	4 673	10 327	9 596	7 943	5 764	2 384
1949	43 498	2 477	1 056	1 420	41 022	4 682	10 418	9 722	8 008	5 748	2 454
1950	43 819	2 504	1 048	1 456	41 316	4 632	10 527	9 793	8 117	5 794	2 453
1951	43 001	2 347	1 081	1 266	40 655	3 935	10 375	9 799	8 205	5 873	2 469
1952	42 869	2 312	1 101	1 210	40 558	3 338	10 585	9 945	8 326	5 949	2 416
1953	43 633	2 320	1 070	1 249	41 315	3 053	10 736	10 437	8 570	5 975	2 543
1954	43 965	2 295	1 023	1 272	41 669	3 051	10 771	10 513	8 702	6 105	2 526
1955	44 475	2 369	1 070	1 299	42 106	3 221	10 806	10 595	8 838	6 122	2 526
1956	45 091	2 433	1 142	1 291	42 658	3 485	10 685	10 663	9 002	6 220	2 602
1957	45 197	2 415	1 127	1 289	42 780	3 629	10 571	10 731	9 153	6 222	2 477
1958	45 521	2 428	1 133	1 295	43 092	3 771	10 475	10 843	9 320	6 304	2 378
1959	45 886	2 596	1 206	1 390	43 289	3 940	10 346	10 899	9 438	6 345	2 322
1960	46 388	2 787	1 290	1 496	43 603	4 123	10 251	10 967	9 574	6 399	2 287
1961	46 653	2 794	1 210	1 583	43 860	4 253	10 176	11 012	9 668	6 530	2 220
1962	46 600	2 770	1 178	1 592	43 831	4 279	9 920	11 115	9 715	6 560	2 241
1963	47 129	2 907	1 321	1 586	44 222	4 514	9 876	11 187	9 836	6 675	2 135
1964	47 679	3 074	1 499	1 575	44 604	4 754	9 876	11 156	9 956	6 741	2 124
1965	48 255	3 397	1 532	1 866	44 857	4 894	9 903	11 120	10 045	6 763	2 132
1966	48 471	3 685	1 609	2 075	44 788	4 820	9 948	10 983	10 100	6 847	2 089
1967	48 987	3 634	1 658	1 976	45 354	5 043	10 207	10 859	10 189	6 937	2 118
1968	49 533	3 681	1 687	1 995	45 852	5 070	10 610	10 725	10 267	7 025	2 154
1969	50 221	3 870	1 770	2 100	46 351	5 282	10 941	10 556	10 344	7 058	2 170
1970	51 228	4 008	1 810	2 199	47 220	5 717	11 327	10 469	10 417	7 126	2 165
1971	52 180	4 172	1 856	2 315	48 009	6 233	11 731	10 347	10 451	7 155	2 090
1972	53 555	4 476	1 955	2 522	49 079	6 766	12 350	10 372	10 412	7 155	2 026
1973	54 624	4 693	2 073	2 618	49 932	7 183	13 056	10 338	10 416	7 028	1 913
1974	55 739	4 861	2 138	2 721	50 879	7 387	13 665	10 401	10 431	7 063	1 932
1975	56 299	4 805	2 065	2 740	51 494	7 565	14 192	10 398	10 401	7 023	1 914
1976	57 174	4 886	2 069	2 817	52 288	7 866	14 784	10 500	10 293	7 020	1 826
1977	58 396	5 048	2 155	2 893	53 348	8 109	15 353	10 771	10 158	7 100	1 857
1978	59 620	5 149	2 227	2 923	54 471	8 327	15 814	11 159	10 083	7 151	1 936
1979	60 726	5 111	2 192	2 919	55 615	8 535	16 387	11 531	10 008	7 212	1 943
1980	61 453	4 999	2 102	2 897	56 455	8 607	16 971	11 836	9 905	7 242	1 893
1981	61 974	4 777	1 957	2 820	57 197	8 648	17 479	12 166	9 868	7 170	1 866
1982	62 450	4 470	1 776	2 694	57 980	8 604	17 793	12 781	9 784	7 174	1 845
1983	63 047	4 303	1 621	2 682	58 744	8 601	18 038	13 398	9 746	7 119	1 842
1984	63 835	4 134	1 591	2 542	59 701	8 594	18 488	14 037	9 776	7 050	1 755
1985	64 411	4 134	1 663	2 471	60 277	8 283	18 808	14 506	9 870	7 060	1 750
1986	65 422	4 102	1 707	2 395	61 320	8 148	19 383	15 029	9 994	6 954	1 811
1987	66 207	4 112	1 745	2 367	62 095	7 837	19 656	15 587	10 176	6 940	1 899
1988	66 927	4 159	1 714	2 445	62 768	7 594	19 742	16 074	10 566	6 831	1 960
1989	67 840	4 136	1 630	2 505	63 704	7 458	19 905	16 622	10 919	6 783	2 017
1990	69 011	4 094	1 537	2 557	64 916	7 866	19 872	17 481	11 103	6 627	1 967
1991	69 168	3 795	1 452	2 343	65 374	7 820	19 641	18 077	11 362	6 550	1 924
1992	69 964	3 751	1 453	2 297	66 213	7 770	19 495	18 347	12 040	6 551	2 010
1993	70 404	3 762	1 497	2 265	66 642	7 671	19 214	18 713	12 562	6 502	1 980
1994	70 817	3 896	1 630	2 266	66 921	7 540	18 854	18 966	12 962	6 423	2 176
1995	71 360	4 036	1 668	2 368	67 324	7 338	18 670	19 189	13 421	6 504	2 201
1996	72 087	4 043	1 665	2 378	68 044	7 104	18 430	19 602	13 967	6 693	2 247
1997	73 261	4 095	1 676	2 419	69 166	7 184	18 110	20 058	14 564	6 952	2 298
1998	73 959	4 244	1 728	2 516	69 715	7 221	17 796	20 242	14 963	7 253	2 240
1999	74 512	4 318	1 732	2 587	70 194	7 291	17 318	20 382	15 394	7 477	2 333
2000	76 280	4 269	1 676	2 594	72 010	7 521	17 844	20 093	16 269	7 795	2 488
2001	76 886	4 070	1 568	2 501	72 816	7 640	17 671	20 018	16 804	8 171	2 511
2002	77 500	3 870	1 431	2 439	73 630	7 769	17 596	19 828	17 143	8 751	2 542
2003	78 238	3 614	1 405	2 209	74 623	7 906	17 767	19 762	17 352	9 144	2 692
2004	78 980	3 616	1 329	2 288	75 364	8 057	17 798	19 539	17 635	9 547	2 787
2005	80 033	3 590	1 368	2 222	76 443	8 054	17 837	19 495	18 053	10 045	2 959
2006	81 255	3 693	1 453	2 240	77 562	8 116	17 944	19 407	18 489	10 509	3 096
2007	82 136	3 541	1 354	2 187	78 596	8 095	18 308	19 299	18 801	10 904	3 188
2008	82 520	3 472	1 238	2 235	79 047	8 065	18 302	18 972	18 928	11 345	3 436
2009	82 123	3 226	1 103	2 123	78 897	7 839	18 211	18 518	19 001	11 730	3 598
2010	81 985	2 991	990	2 002	78 994	7 864	18 352	18 119	18 856	12 103	3 701
2011	81 975	2 895	917	1 978	79 080	8 101	18 469	17 686	18 483	12 350	3 990
2012	82 327	2 940	950	1 990	79 387	8 110	18 083	17 607	18 363	12 879	4 345
2013	82 667	2 923	987	1 936	79 744	8 156	18 287	17 605	18 071	13 117	4 507
2014	82 882	2 827	959	1 868	80 056	8 182	18 478	17 547	17 900	13 361	4 587
2015	83 620	2 885	997	1 888	80 735	8 038	18 776	17 556	17 893	13 627	4 845
2016	84 755	2 995	1 028	1 967	81 759	7 954	19 151	17 686	17 890	13 938	5 141
2017	85 145	2 939	1 057	1 882	82 206	7 948	19 374	17 777	17 662	14 156	5 289
2018	86 096	2 909	1 003	1 906	83 188	7 786	19 789	18 123	17 528	14 436	5 525
2019	86 687	2 950	1 027	1 923	83 737	7 789	19 948	18 296	17 287	14 547	5 869

Table 1-7. Civilian Labor Force, by Age, Sex, and Race, 1948–2019—*Continued*

(Thousands of people.)

Race, Hispanic origin, sex, and year	16 years and over	16 to 19 years			20 years and over						
		Total	16 to 17 years	18 to 19 years	Total	20 to 24 years	25 to 34 years	35 to 44 years	45 to 54 years	55 to 64 years	65 years and over
ALL RACES											
Women											
1948	17 335	1 835	671	1 164	15 500	2 719	3 931	3 801	2 971	1 565	513
1949	17 788	1 811	648	1 163	15 978	2 658	3 997	3 989	3 099	1 678	556
1950	18 389	1 712	611	1 101	16 678	2 675	4 092	4 161	3 327	1 839	583
1951	19 016	1 756	662	1 094	17 259	2 659	4 293	4 301	3 534	1 923	551
1952	19 269	1 752	705	1 047	17 517	2 502	4 319	4 438	3 635	2 031	589
1953	19 382	1 707	657	1 050	17 674	2 428	4 162	4 662	3 679	2 049	693
1954	19 678	1 681	620	1 028	17 997	2 424	4 212	4 708	3 822	2 164	666
1955	20 548	1 723	641	1 083	18 825	2 445	4 252	4 805	4 154	2 391	779
1956	21 461	1 863	736	1 127	19 599	2 455	4 276	5 031	4 405	2 610	821
1957	21 732	1 860	716	1 144	19 873	2 442	4 255	5 116	4 615	2 631	813
1958	22 118	1 832	685	1 147	20 285	2 501	4 193	5 185	4 859	2 727	821
1959	22 483	1 896	765	1 132	20 587	2 473	4 089	5 228	5 080	2 882	836
1960	23 240	2 054	805	1 251	21 185	2 579	4 131	5 302	5 278	2 986	908
1961	23 806	2 142	774	1 368	21 664	2 697	4 143	5 390	5 403	3 106	926
1962	24 014	2 146	741	1 405	21 868	2 803	4 103	5 474	5 381	3 197	913
1963	24 704	2 232	850	1 380	22 473	2 959	4 174	5 601	5 502	3 331	906
1964	25 412	2 314	950	1 365	23 098	3 209	4 180	5 615	5 681	3 441	966
1965	26 200	2 513	954	1 559	23 686	3 365	4 330	5 720	5 711	3 587	976
1966	27 299	2 873	1 055	1 818	24 431	3 590	4 510	5 755	5 884	3 728	964
1967	28 360	2 887	1 076	1 810	25 475	3 966	4 848	5 844	5 983	3 855	979
1968	29 204	2 938	1 130	1 808	26 266	4 235	5 098	5 866	6 130	3 939	999
1969	30 513	3 100	1 239	1 859	27 413	4 597	5 395	5 902	6 386	4 077	1 057
1970	31 543	3 241	1 325	1 916	28 301	4 880	5 708	5 968	6 532	4 157	1 056
1971	32 202	3 298	1 336	1 963	28 904	5 098	5 983	5 957	6 573	4 234	1 059
1972	33 479	3 578	1 464	2 114	29 901	5 364	6 610	6 027	6 555	4 257	1 089
1973	34 804	3 814	1 592	2 221	30 991	5 663	7 320	6 154	6 567	4 228	1 061
1974	36 211	4 010	1 672	2 338	32 201	5 926	7 989	6 362	6 699	4 221	1 002
1975	37 475	4 065	1 674	2 391	33 410	6 185	8 673	6 505	6 683	4 323	1 042
1976	38 983	4 170	1 698	2 470	34 814	6 418	9 419	6 817	6 689	4 402	1 069
1977	40 613	4 303	1 765	2 538	36 310	6 717	10 149	7 171	6 720	4 477	1 078
1978	42 631	4 503	1 900	2 603	38 128	7 043	10 888	7 662	6 807	4 593	1 134
1979	44 235	4 527	1 887	2 639	39 708	7 234	11 551	8 154	6 889	4 719	1 161
1980	45 487	4 381	1 781	2 599	41 106	7 315	12 257	8 627	7 004	4 742	1 161
1981	46 696	4 211	1 691	2 520	42 485	7 451	12 912	9 045	7 101	4 799	1 176
1982	47 755	4 056	1 561	2 495	43 699	7 477	13 393	9 651	7 105	4 888	1 185
1983	48 503	3 868	1 452	2 416	44 636	7 451	13 796	10 213	7 105	4 873	1 198
1984	49 709	3 810	1 458	2 351	45 900	7 451	14 234	10 896	7 230	4 911	1 177
1985	51 050	3 767	1 491	2 276	47 283	7 434	14 742	11 567	7 452	4 932	1 156
1986	52 413	3 824	1 580	2 244	48 589	7 293	15 208	12 204	7 746	4 940	1 199
1987	53 658	3 875	1 638	2 237	49 783	7 140	15 577	12 873	8 034	4 937	1 221
1988	54 742	3 872	1 572	2 300	50 870	6 910	15 761	13 361	8 537	4 977	1 324
1989	56 030	3 818	1 495	2 323	52 212	6 721	15 990	13 980	8 997	5 095	1 429
1990	56 829	3 698	1 400	2 298	53 131	6 834	16 058	14 663	9 145	4 948	1 483
1991	57 178	3 470	1 337	2 133	53 708	6 728	15 867	15 235	9 465	4 924	1 489
1992	58 141	3 345	1 316	2 030	54 796	6 750	15 875	15 552	10 120	5 035	1 464
1993	58 795	3 408	1 335	2 073	55 388	6 683	15 566	15 849	10 733	5 097	1 459
1994	60 239	3 585	1 504	2 081	56 655	6 592	15 499	16 259	11 357	5 289	1 658
1995	60 944	3 729	1 557	2 172	57 215	6 349	15 528	16 562	11 801	5 356	1 618
1996	61 857	3 763	1 599	2 164	58 094	6 273	15 403	16 954	12 430	5 452	1 581
1997	63 036	3 837	1 561	2 277	59 198	6 348	15 271	17 268	13 010	5 713	1 590
1998	63 714	4 012	1 607	2 405	59 702	6 418	15 017	17 294	13 405	5 962	1 607
1999	64 855	4 015	1 606	2 410	60 840	6 643	14 826	17 501	13 994	6 204	1 673
2000	66 303	4 002	1 585	2 416	62 301	6 730	14 912	17 473	14 802	6 561	1 823
2001	66 848	3 832	1 520	2 313	63 016	6 917	14 690	17 386	15 221	6 932	1 870
2002	67 363	3 715	1 439	2 277	63 648	7 012	14 600	17 098	15 454	7 559	1 926
2003	68 272	3 556	1 452	2 104	64 716	7 021	14 576	16 933	15 919	8 168	2 099
2004	68 421	3 498	1 418	2 080	64 923	7 097	14 409	16 619	16 123	8 466	2 211
2005	69 288	3 574	1 457	2 117	65 714	7 073	14 503	16 535	16 349	8 934	2 319
2006	70 173	3 588	1 499	2 089	66 585	6 997	14 628	16 441	16 656	9 475	2 388
2007	70 988	3 471	1 417	2 055	67 516	7 110	14 822	16 227	16 896	9 846	2 615
2008	71 767	3 385	1 314	2 071	68 382	7 109	15 030	16 089	17 075	10 270	2 808
2009	72 019	3 163	1 124	2 039	68 856	7 132	15 087	15 720	17 204	10 776	2 937
2010	71 904	2 914	1 011	1 904	68 990	7 164	15 263	15 247	17 104	11 194	3 017
2011	71 642	2 832	957	1 875	68 810	7 169	15 255	14 973	16 876	11 414	3 121
2012	72 648	2 883	1 003	1 880	69 765	7 352	15 382	15 127	16 692	11 830	3 383
2013	72 722	2 862	1 036	1 826	69 860	7 440	15 459	14 957	16 396	12 000	3 609
2014	73 039	2 827	1 012	1 815	70 212	7 459	15 721	14 958	16 163	12 141	3 771
2015	73 510	2 815	991	1 824	70 695	7 485	15 871	15 047	16 009	12 326	3 957
2016	74 432	2 894	1 099	1 795	71 538	7 359	16 369	15 134	16 019	12 527	4 130
2017	75 175	2 962	1 180	1 782	72 213	7 311	16 712	15 257	15 901	12 743	4 288
2018	75 978	2 977	1 130	1 847	73 002	7 312	16 985	15 497	15 783	12 918	4 508
2019	76 852	2 946	1 054	1 892	73 906	7 406	17 243	15 761	15 644	13 056	4 795

Table 1-7. Civilian Labor Force, by Age, Sex, and Race, 1948–2019—*Continued*

(Thousands of people.)

Race, Hispanic origin, sex, and year	16 years and over	16 to 19 years			20 years and over						
		Total	16 to 17 years	18 to 19 years	Total	20 to 24 years	25 to 34 years	35 to 44 years	45 to 54 years	55 to 64 years	65 years and over
WHITE											
Both Sexes											
1954	56 816	3 501	1 448	2 054	53 315	4 752	13 226	13 540	11 258	7 591	2 946
1955	58 085	3 598	1 511	2 087	54 487	4 941	13 267	13 729	11 680	7 810	3 062
1956	59 428	3 771	1 656	2 113	55 657	5 194	13 154	14 000	12 061	8 080	3 166
1957	59 754	3 775	1 637	2 135	55 979	5 283	13 044	14 117	12 382	8 091	3 049
1958	60 293	3 757	1 615	2 144	56 536	5 449	12 884	14 257	12 727	8 254	2 964
1959	60 952	4 000	1 775	2 225	56 952	5 544	12 670	14 355	13 048	8 411	2 925
1960	61 915	4 275	1 871	2 405	57 640	5 787	12 594	14 450	13 322	8 522	2 964
1961	62 656	4 362	1 767	2 594	58 294	6 026	12 503	14 557	13 517	8 773	2 917
1962	62 750	4 354	1 709	2 645	58 396	6 164	12 218	14 695	13 551	8 856	2 912
1963	63 830	4 559	1 950	2 608	59 271	6 537	12 229	14 859	13 789	9 067	2 790
1964	64 921	4 784	2 211	2 572	60 137	6 952	12 235	14 852	14 043	9 239	2 817
1965	66 137	5 267	2 221	3 044	60 870	7 189	12 391	14 900	14 162	9 392	2 839
1966	67 276	5 827	2 367	3 460	61 449	7 324	12 591	14 785	14 370	9 583	2 793
1967	68 699	5 749	2 432	3 318	62 950	7 886	13 123	14 765	14 545	9 817	2 821
1968	69 976	5 839	2 519	3 320	64 137	8 109	13 740	14 683	14 756	9 968	2 884
1969	71 778	6 168	2 698	3 470	65 611	8 614	14 289	14 564	15 057	10 132	2 954
1970	73 556	6 442	2 824	3 617	67 113	9 238	14 896	14 525	15 269	10 255	2 930
1971	74 963	6 681	2 894	3 787	68 282	9 889	15 445	14 374	15 343	10 351	2 880
1972	77 275	7 193	3 096	4 098	70 082	10 605	16 584	14 399	15 283	10 402	2 809
1973	79 151	7 579	3 320	4 260	71 572	11 182	17 764	14 440	15 256	10 240	2 687
1974	81 281	7 899	3 441	4 459	73 381	11 600	18 862	14 644	15 375	10 241	2 656
1975	82 831	7 899	3 375	4 525	74 932	12 019	19 897	14 753	15 308	10 287	2 668
1976	84 767	8 088	3 410	4 679	76 678	12 444	20 990	15 088	15 187	10 371	2 599
1977	87 141	8 352	3 562	4 790	78 789	12 892	22 099	15 604	15 053	10 495	2 647
1978	89 634	8 555	3 715	4 839	81 079	13 309	23 067	16 353	15 004	10 602	2 745
1979	91 923	8 548	3 668	4 881	83 375	13 632	24 101	17 123	14 965	10 767	2 787
1980	93 600	8 312	3 485	4 827	85 286	13 769	25 181	17 811	14 956	10 812	2 759
1981	95 052	7 962	3 274	4 688	87 089	13 926	26 208	18 445	14 993	10 764	2 753
1982	96 143	7 518	3 001	4 518	88 625	13 866	26 814	19 491	14 879	10 832	2 742
1983	97 021	7 186	2 765	4 421	89 835	13 816	27 237	20 488	14 798	10 732	2 766
1984	98 492	6 952	2 720	4 232	91 540	13 733	27 958	21 588	14 899	10 701	2 660
1985	99 926	6 841	2 777	4 065	93 085	13 469	28 640	22 591	15 101	10 679	2 605
1986	101 801	6 862	2 895	3 967	94 939	13 176	29 497	23 571	15 379	10 583	2 732
1987	103 290	6 893	2 963	3 931	96 396	12 764	29 956	24 581	15 792	10 497	2 806
1988	104 756	6 940	2 861	4 079	97 815	12 311	30 167	25 358	16 573	10 462	2 943
1989	106 355	6 809	2 685	4 124	99 546	11 940	30 388	26 312	17 278	10 533	3 094
1990	107 447	6 683	2 543	4 140	100 764	12 397	30 174	27 265	17 515	10 290	3 123
1991	107 743	6 245	2 432	3 813	101 498	12 248	29 794	28 213	18 028	10 129	3 086
1992	108 837	6 022	2 388	3 633	102 815	12 187	29 518	28 580	19 200	10 196	3 135
1993	109 700	6 105	2 458	3 647	103 595	11 987	29 027	29 056	20 181	10 215	3 129
1994	111 082	6 357	2 681	3 677	104 725	11 688	28 580	29 626	21 026	10 319	3 486
1995	111 950	6 545	2 749	3 796	105 404	11 266	28 325	30 112	21 804	10 432	3 466
1996	113 108	6 607	2 780	3 826	106 502	11 003	27 901	30 683	22 781	10 648	3 485
1997	114 693	6 720	2 779	3 941	107 973	11 127	27 362	31 171	23 709	11 086	3 517
1998	115 415	6 965	2 860	4 105	108 450	11 244	26 707	31 221	24 282	11 548	3 448
1999	116 509	7 048	2 849	4 199	109 461	11 436	25 978	31 391	25 102	11 960	3 595
2000	118 545	6 955	2 768	4 186	111 590	11 626	26 336	30 968	26 353	12 463	3 846
2001	119 399	6 661	2 626	4 035	112 737	11 883	26 010	30 778	27 062	13 121	3 883
2002	120 150	6 366	2 445	3 921	113 784	12 073	25 908	30 286	27 405	14 148	3 965
2003	120 546	5 973	2 414	3 560	114 572	12 064	25 752	29 788	27 786	14 944	4 238
2004	121 086	5 929	2 309	3 620	115 156	12 192	25 548	29 305	28 181	15 522	4 408
2005	122 299	5 950	2 390	3 560	116 349	12 109	25 548	29 107	28 685	16 275	4 624
2006	123 834	6 009	2 473	3 536	117 825	12 128	25 681	28 849	29 231	17 132	4 805
2007	124 935	5 795	2 326	3 470	119 139	12 176	26 076	28 394	29 627	17 782	5 085
2008	125 635	5 644	2 126	3 518	119 990	12 142	26 210	27 932	29 780	18 464	5 463
2009	125 644	5 295	1 883	3 413	120 349	11 995	26 277	27 263	29 903	19 199	5 711
2010	125 084	4 861	1 693	3 168	120 223	11 948	26 455	26 510	29 632	19 808	5 869
2011	124 579	4 714	1 581	3 134	119 865	12 120	26 511	25 834	29 036	20 188	6 175
2012	123 684	4 669	1 605	3 065	119 015	11 914	25 806	25 445	28 384	20 752	6 714
2013	123 412	4 608	1 669	2 939	118 804	11 962	25 898	25 167	27 776	20 945	7 056
2014	123 327	4 476	1 591	2 885	118 851	11 927	26 172	25 029	27 336	21 181	7 207
2015	123 607	4 487	1 579	2 908	119 120	11 755	26 305	24 929	27 066	21 534	7 531
2016	124 658	4 618	1 692	2 926	120 040	11 553	26 725	24 996	26 929	21 889	7 948
2017	124 941	4 542	1 766	2 776	120 399	11 481	27 040	25 056	26 474	22 209	8 139
2018	125 815	4 576	1 692	2 884	121 238	11 383	27 332	25 442	26 113	22 464	8 504
2019	126 600	4 594	1 644	2 950	122 006	11 395	27 534	25 806	25 687	22 599	8 986

Table 1-7. Civilian Labor Force, by Age, Sex, and Race, 1948–2019—*Continued*

(Thousands of people.)

Race, Hispanic origin, sex, and year	16 years and over	16 to 19 years			20 years and over						
		Total	16 to 17 years	18 to 19 years	Total	20 to 24 years	25 to 34 years	35 to 44 years	45 to 54 years	55 to 64 years	65 years and over
WHITE											
Men											
1954	39 759	1 989	896	1 095	37 770	2 654	9 695	9 516	7 913	5 653	2 339
1955	40 197	2 056	935	1 121	38 141	2 803	9 721	9 597	8 025	5 654	2 343
1956	40 734	2 114	1 002	1 110	38 620	3 036	9 595	9 661	8 175	5 736	2 417
1957	40 826	2 108	992	1 114	38 718	3 152	9 483	9 719	8 317	5 735	2 307
1958	41 080	2 116	1 001	1 116	38 964	3 278	9 386	9 822	8 465	5 800	2 213
1959	41 397	2 279	1 077	1 202	39 118	3 409	9 261	9 876	8 581	5 833	2 158
1960	41 743	2 433	1 140	1 293	39 310	3 559	9 153	9 919	8 689	5 861	2 129
1961	41 986	2 439	1 067	1 372	39 547	3 681	9 072	9 961	8 776	5 988	2 068
1962	41 931	2 432	1 041	1 391	39 499	3 726	8 846	10 029	8 820	5 995	2 082
1963	42 404	2 563	1 183	1 380	39 841	3 955	8 805	10 079	8 944	6 090	1 967
1964	42 894	2 716	1 345	1 371	40 178	4 166	8 800	10 055	9 053	6 161	1 942
1965	43 400	2 999	1 359	1 639	40 401	4 279	8 824	10 023	9 130	6 188	1 959
1966	43 572	3 253	1 423	1 830	40 319	4 200	8 859	9 892	9 189	6 250	1 928
1967	44 041	3 191	1 464	1 727	40 851	4 416	9 102	9 785	9 260	6 348	1 944
1968	44 553	3 236	1 504	1 732	41 318	4 432	9 477	9 662	9 340	6 427	1 981
1969	45 185	3 413	1 583	1 830	41 772	4 615	9 773	9 509	9 413	6 467	1 996
1970	46 035	3 551	1 629	1 922	42 483	4 988	10 099	9 414	9 487	6 517	1 978
1971	46 904	3 719	1 681	2 039	43 185	5 448	10 444	9 294	9 528	6 550	1 922
1972	48 118	3 980	1 758	2 223	44 138	5 937	11 039	9 278	9 473	6 562	1 846
1973	48 920	4 174	1 875	2 300	44 747	6 274	11 621	9 212	9 445	6 452	1 740
1974	49 843	4 312	1 922	2 391	45 532	6 470	12 135	9 246	9 455	6 464	1 759
1975	50 324	4 290	1 871	2 418	46 034	6 642	12 579	9 231	9 415	6 425	1 742
1976	51 033	4 357	1 869	2 489	46 675	6 890	13 092	9 289	9 310	6 437	1 657
1977	52 033	4 496	1 949	2 548	47 537	7 097	13 575	9 509	9 175	6 492	1 688
1978	52 955	4 565	2 002	2 563	48 390	7 274	13 939	9 858	9 068	6 508	1 744
1979	53 856	4 537	1 974	2 563	49 320	7 421	14 415	10 183	8 968	6 571	1 761
1980	54 473	4 424	1 881	2 543	50 049	7 479	14 893	10 455	8 877	6 618	1 727
1981	54 895	4 224	1 751	2 473	50 671	7 521	15 340	10 740	8 836	6 530	1 704
1982	55 133	3 933	1 602	2 331	51 200	7 438	15 549	11 289	8 727	6 520	1 677
1983	55 480	3 764	1 452	2 312	51 716	7 406	15 707	11 817	8 649	6 446	1 691
1984	56 062	3 609	1 420	2 189	52 453	7 370	16 037	12 348	8 683	6 410	1 606
1985	56 472	3 576	1 467	2 109	52 895	7 122	16 306	12 767	8 730	6 376	1 595
1986	57 217	3 542	1 502	2 040	53 675	6 986	16 769	13 207	8 791	6 260	1 663
1987	57 779	3 547	1 524	2 023	54 232	6 717	16 963	13 674	8 945	6 200	1 733
1988	58 317	3 583	1 487	2 095	54 734	6 468	17 018	14 068	9 285	6 108	1 787
1989	58 988	3 546	1 401	2 146	55 441	6 316	17 077	14 516	9 615	6 082	1 835
1990	59 638	3 522	1 333	2 189	56 116	6 688	16 920	15 026	9 713	5 957	1 811
1991	59 656	3 269	1 266	2 003	56 387	6 619	16 709	15 523	9 926	5 847	1 763
1992	60 168	3 192	1 260	1 932	56 976	6 542	16 512	15 701	10 570	5 821	1 830
1993	60 484	3 200	1 292	1 908	57 284	6 449	16 244	15 971	11 010	5 784	1 825
1994	60 727	3 315	1 403	1 912	57 411	6 294	15 879	16 188	11 327	5 726	1 998
1995	61 146	3 427	1 429	1 998	57 719	6 096	15 669	16 414	11 730	5 809	2 000
1996	61 783	3 444	1 421	2 023	58 340	5 922	15 475	16 728	12 217	5 943	2 054
1997	62 639	3 513	1 440	2 073	59 126	6 029	15 120	17 019	12 710	6 154	2 094
1998	63 034	3 614	1 487	2 127	59 421	6 063	14 770	17 157	13 003	6 415	2 013
1999	63 413	3 666	1 478	2 188	59 747	6 151	14 292	17 201	13 368	6 618	2 117
2000	64 466	3 615	1 422	2 193	60 850	6 244	14 666	16 880	13 977	6 840	2 243
2001	64 966	3 446	1 334	2 112	61 519	6 363	14 536	16 809	14 400	7 169	2 241
2002	65 308	3 241	1 215	2 026	62 067	6 444	14 499	16 583	14 615	7 665	2 261
2003	65 509	3 036	1 193	1 843	62 473	6 479	14 529	16 398	14 708	7 973	2 386
2004	65 994	3 050	1 127	1 923	62 944	6 586	14 429	16 192	14 934	8 326	2 478
2005	66 694	2 988	1 162	1 826	63 705	6 562	14 426	16 080	15 273	8 734	2 631
2006	67 613	3 074	1 222	1 852	64 540	6 597	14 469	15 962	15 606	9 152	2 753
2007	68 158	2 944	1 147	1 798	65 214	6 567	14 715	15 765	15 846	9 500	2 821
2008	68 351	2 868	1 040	1 829	65 483	6 526	14 715	15 436	15 905	9 855	3 046
2009	68 051	2 679	933	1 746	65 372	6 348	14 669	15 066	15 943	10 160	3 186
2010	67 728	2 463	844	1 619	65 265	6 342	14 734	14 713	15 791	10 422	3 263
2011	67 551	2 386	780	1 606	65 165	6 539	14 785	14 317	15 400	10 629	3 494
2012	66 921	2 382	785	1 596	64 540	6 339	14 256	14 018	15 121	10 970	3 835
2013	66 842	2 337	821	1 516	64 505	6 353	14 325	13 909	14 804	11 125	3 990
2014	66 680	2 250	764	1 486	64 430	6 309	14 401	13 827	14 617	11 266	4 011
2015	67 018	2 308	798	1 511	64 710	6 165	14 533	13 757	14 539	11 489	4 227
2016	67 564	2 395	855	1 539	65 169	6 082	14 675	13 803	14 451	11 694	4 464
2017	67 592	2 296	855	1 441	65 296	6 062	14 765	13 818	14 210	11 863	4 579
2018	68 082	2 270	805	1 465	65 812	5 951	14 958	14 055	14 020	12 031	4 796
2019	68 367	2 330	828	1 501	66 037	5 930	15 002	14 189	13 729	12 130	5 057

Table 1-7. Civilian Labor Force, by Age, Sex, and Race, 1948–2019—*Continued*

(Thousands of people.)

Race, Hispanic origin, sex, and year	16 years and over	16 to 19 years			20 years and over						
		Total	16 to 17 years	18 to 19 years	Total	20 to 24 years	25 to 34 years	35 to 44 years	45 to 54 years	55 to 64 years	65 years and over
WHITE											
Women											
1954	17 057	1 512	552	959	15 545	2 098	3 531	4 024	3 345	1 938	607
1955	17 888	1 542	576	966	16 346	2 138	3 546	4 132	3 655	2 156	719
1956	18 694	1 657	654	1 003	17 037	2 158	3 559	4 339	3 886	2 344	749
1957	18 928	1 667	645	1 021	17 261	2 131	3 561	4 398	4 065	2 356	742
1958	19 213	1 641	614	1 028	17 572	2 171	3 498	4 435	4 262	2 454	751
1959	19 555	1 721	698	1 023	17 834	2 135	3 409	4 479	4 467	2 578	767
1960	20 172	1 842	731	1 112	18 330	2 228	3 441	4 531	4 633	2 661	835
1961	20 670	1 923	700	1 222	18 747	2 345	3 431	4 596	4 741	2 785	849
1962	20 819	1 922	668	1 254	18 897	2 438	3 372	4 666	4 731	2 861	830
1963	21 426	1 996	767	1 228	19 430	2 582	3 424	4 780	4 845	2 977	823
1964	22 027	2 068	866	1 201	19 959	2 786	3 435	4 797	4 990	3 078	875
1965	22 737	2 268	862	1 405	20 469	2 910	3 567	4 877	5 032	3 204	880
1966	23 704	2 574	944	1 630	21 130	3 124	3 732	4 893	5 181	3 333	865
1967	24 658	2 558	968	1 591	22 100	3 471	4 021	4 980	5 285	3 469	877
1968	25 423	2 603	1 015	1 588	22 821	3 677	4 263	5 021	5 416	3 541	903
1969	26 593	2 755	1 115	1 640	23 839	3 999	4 516	5 055	5 644	3 665	958
1970	27 521	2 891	1 195	1 695	24 630	4 250	4 797	5 111	5 781	3 738	952
1971	28 060	2 962	1 213	1 748	25 097	4 441	5 001	5 080	5 816	3 801	958
1972	29 157	3 213	1 338	1 875	25 945	4 668	5 544	5 121	5 810	3 839	963
1973	30 231	3 405	1 445	1 960	26 825	4 908	6 143	5 228	5 811	3 788	947
1974	31 437	3 588	1 520	2 068	27 850	5 131	6 727	5 399	5 920	3 777	897
1975	32 508	3 610	1 504	2 107	28 898	5 378	7 318	5 522	5 892	3 862	926
1976	33 735	3 731	1 541	2 189	30 004	5 554	7 898	5 799	5 877	3 935	940
1977	35 108	3 856	1 614	2 243	31 253	5 795	8 523	6 095	5 877	4 003	959
1978	36 679	3 990	1 713	2 276	32 689	6 035	9 128	6 495	5 936	4 094	1 001
1979	38 067	4 011	1 694	2 318	34 056	6 211	9 687	6 940	5 997	4 196	1 024
1980	39 127	3 888	1 605	2 284	35 239	6 290	10 289	7 356	6 079	4 194	1 032
1981	40 157	3 739	1 523	2 216	36 418	6 406	10 868	7 704	6 157	4 235	1 049
1982	41 010	3 585	1 399	2 186	37 425	6 428	11 264	8 202	6 152	4 313	1 065
1983	41 541	3 422	1 314	2 109	38 119	6 410	11 530	8 670	6 149	4 285	1 074
1984	42 431	3 343	1 300	2 043	39 087	6 363	11 922	9 240	6 217	4 292	1 054
1985	43 455	3 265	1 310	1 955	40 190	6 348	12 334	9 824	6 371	4 303	1 010
1986	44 584	3 320	1 393	1 927	41 264	6 191	12 729	10 364	6 588	4 323	1 069
1987	45 510	3 347	1 439	1 908	42 164	6 047	12 993	10 907	6 847	4 297	1 073
1988	46 439	3 358	1 374	1 984	43 081	5 844	13 149	11 291	7 288	4 354	1 156
1989	47 367	3 262	1 284	1 978	44 105	5 625	13 311	11 796	7 663	4 451	1 259
1990	47 809	3 161	1 210	1 951	44 648	5 709	13 254	12 239	7 802	4 333	1 312
1991	48 087	2 976	1 166	1 810	45 111	5 629	13 085	12 689	8 101	4 282	1 324
1992	48 669	2 830	1 128	1 702	45 839	5 645	13 006	12 879	8 630	4 375	1 305
1993	49 216	2 905	1 167	1 739	46 311	5 539	12 783	13 085	9 171	4 430	1 304
1994	50 356	3 042	1 278	1 764	47 314	5 394	12 702	13 439	9 699	4 593	1 487
1995	50 804	3 118	1 320	1 798	47 686	5 170	12 656	13 697	10 074	4 622	1 466
1996	51 325	3 163	1 360	1 803	48 162	5 081	12 426	13 955	10 563	4 706	1 431
1997	52 054	3 207	1 339	1 867	48 847	5 099	12 242	14 153	10 999	4 932	1 422
1998	52 380	3 351	1 373	1 977	49 029	5 180	11 937	14 064	11 279	5 133	1 435
1999	53 096	3 382	1 371	2 010	49 714	5 285	11 685	14 190	11 734	5 342	1 478
2000	54 079	3 339	1 346	1 993	50 740	5 381	11 669	14 088	12 376	5 623	1 602
2001	54 433	3 215	1 292	1 923	51 218	5 519	11 474	13 969	12 662	5 952	1 642
2002	54 842	3 125	1 229	1 895	51 717	5 628	11 409	13 703	12 790	6 482	1 704
2003	55 037	2 937	1 221	1 716	52 099	5 584	11 223	13 390	13 078	6 970	1 852
2004	55 092	2 879	1 182	1 697	52 212	5 606	11 119	13 114	13 247	7 197	1 930
2005	55 605	2 962	1 228	1 733	52 643	5 546	11 123	13 027	13 413	7 542	1 993
2006	56 221	2 935	1 251	1 684	53 286	5 530	11 212	12 886	13 625	7 980	2 052
2007	56 777	2 851	1 179	1 672	53 925	5 609	11 360	12 629	13 781	8 282	2 264
2008	57 284	2 776	1 086	1 690	54 508	5 616	11 495	12 495	13 875	8 609	2 417
2009	57 593	2 616	950	1 667	54 976	5 647	11 608	12 197	13 960	9 039	2 525
2010	57 356	2 398	849	1 549	54 957	5 607	11 721	11 796	13 841	9 386	2 607
2011	57 028	2 328	800	1 528	54 700	5 581	11 726	11 517	13 636	9 559	2 681
2012	56 763	2 288	819	1 469	54 475	5 575	11 550	11 428	13 263	9 782	2 879
2013	56 571	2 271	848	1 423	54 299	5 609	11 573	11 258	12 973	9 820	3 066
2014	56 648	2 226	827	1 399	54 421	5 618	11 771	11 202	12 719	9 915	3 196
2015	56 589	2 178	782	1 397	54 410	5 589	11 772	11 172	12 527	10 045	3 304
2016	57 095	2 224	837	1 387	54 871	5 471	12 050	11 193	12 478	10 195	3 484
2017	57 349	2 247	911	1 335	55 103	5 419	12 275	11 238	12 264	10 346	3 560
2018	57 732	2 307	887	1 420	55 426	5 432	12 374	11 387	12 093	10 434	3 707
2019	58 233	2 265	816	1 449	55 968	5 465	12 532	11 617	11 958	10 469	3 928

Table 1-7. Civilian Labor Force, by Age, Sex, and Race, 1948–2019—*Continued*

(Thousands of people.)

Race, Hispanic origin, sex, and year	16 years and over	16 to 19 years			20 years and over						
		Total	16 to 17 years	18 to 19 years	Total	20 to 24 years	25 to 34 years	35 to 44 years	45 to 54 years	55 to 64 years	65 years and over
BLACK											
Both Sexes											
2000	16 397	941	356	585	15 456	1 873	4 281	4 515	3 203	1 264	320
2001	16 421	898	332	565	15 524	1 878	4 180	4 483	3 298	1 335	350
2002	16 565	870	297	574	15 695	1 908	4 134	4 458	3 435	1 407	353
2003	16 526	771	289	482	15 755	1 892	4 060	4 465	3 506	1 466	366
2004	16 638	762	272	489	15 876	1 926	4 076	4 380	3 578	1 538	380
2005	17 013	803	279	525	16 209	1 957	4 145	4 370	3 686	1 647	403
2006	17 314	871	318	553	16 443	1 960	4 197	4 348	3 785	1 739	414
2007	17 496	801	300	501	16 695	1 974	4 254	4 357	3 866	1 811	432
2008	17 740	787	270	517	16 953	1 981	4 328	4 316	3 945	1 908	476
2009	17 632	729	231	499	16 902	1 961	4 300	4 175	3 976	1 995	495
2010	17 862	677	203	473	17 186	2 072	4 418	4 095	3 991	2 104	506
2011	17 881	647	188	459	17 234	2 105	4 434	4 029	3 957	2 155	555
2012	18 400	711	213	498	17 689	2 210	4 333	4 120	4 057	2 369	599
2013	18 580	717	218	499	17 863	2 236	4 383	4 144	4 021	2 462	617
2014	18 873	681	227	454	18 192	2 305	4 541	4 159	4 013	2 528	648
2015	19 318	701	233	469	18 616	2 337	4 707	4 226	4 051	2 584	711
2016	19 637	729	240	489	18 908	2 259	4 926	4 283	4 039	2 669	732
2017	20 088	754	250	504	19 334	2 241	5 094	4 368	4 068	2 741	822
2018	20 414	763	232	530	19 651	2 173	5 260	4 441	4 075	2 846	856
2019	20 632	741	234	507	19 891	2 186	5 344	4 431	4 086	2 905	939
Men											
2000	7 702	462	181	281	7 240	875	1 999	2 105	1 497	612	151
2001	7 647	447	166	281	7 200	853	1 915	2 073	1 537	645	177
2002	7 794	446	149	297	7 347	906	1 909	2 064	1 623	664	181
2003	7 711	365	138	228	7 346	918	1 872	2 058	1 627	685	186
2004	7 773	359	128	231	7 414	927	1 931	2 000	1 654	714	188
2005	7 998	399	139	260	7 600	940	1 948	2 028	1 732	756	196
2006	8 128	409	152	256	7 720	971	1 986	1 999	1 792	777	195
2007	8 252	384	137	247	7 867	981	2 037	2 030	1 822	791	206
2008	8 347	385	124	261	7 962	984	2 047	2 008	1 846	852	225
2009	8 265	350	111	239	7 914	954	2 041	1 932	1 852	904	231
2010	8 415	339	96	244	8 076	986	2 118	1 924	1 862	950	236
2011	8 454	329	89	241	8 125	1 012	2 159	1 860	1 854	983	257
2012	8 594	338	99	239	8 256	1 054	2 030	1 908	1 884	1 099	281
2013	8 733	347	105	242	8 386	1 091	2 081	1 934	1 867	1 132	281
2014	8 909	323	115	208	8 586	1 138	2 174	1 931	1 870	1 176	297
2015	9 099	326	112	213	8 773	1 145	2 250	1 956	1 899	1 204	320
2016	9 315	350	92	259	8 965	1 091	2 365	2 003	1 887	1 270	349
2017	9 508	345	103	242	9 163	1 091	2 460	2 041	1 887	1 304	380
2018	9 694	367	98	269	9 327	1 046	2 573	2 087	1 900	1 343	379
2019	9 790	336	98	237	9 454	1 062	2 631	2 079	1 925	1 336	421
BLACK											
Women											
2000	8 695	479	175	305	8 215	998	2 282	2 409	1 706	652	168
2001	8 774	451	166	284	8 323	1 025	2 265	2 410	1 762	690	173
2002	8 772	424	148	276	8 348	1 002	2 225	2 394	1 812	743	171
2003	8 815	406	151	255	8 409	973	2 188	2 407	1 879	781	180
2004	8 865	403	144	259	8 462	999	2 144	2 380	1 924	824	192
2005	9 014	405	140	265	8 610	1 017	2 197	2 342	1 954	891	207
2006	9 186	462	166	297	8 723	989	2 211	2 349	1 993	963	218
2007	9 244	417	163	254	8 828	993	2 218	2 328	2 044	1 019	227
2008	9 393	402	146	256	8 991	997	2 281	2 308	2 099	1 056	251
2009	9 367	379	119	260	8 988	1 008	2 258	2 243	2 124	1 091	264
2010	9 447	337	108	230	9 110	1 086	2 299	2 171	2 129	1 153	270
2011	9 427	318	99	219	9 110	1 093	2 275	2 168	2 104	1 172	298
2012	9 805	373	114	258	9 433	1 157	2 303	2 212	2 173	1 271	317
2013	9 846	370	113	257	9 476	1 145	2 303	2 210	2 153	1 330	336
2014	9 964	358	112	246	9 606	1 167	2 367	2 227	2 142	1 352	351
2015	10 218	376	120	255	9 843	1 192	2 457	2 270	2 152	1 381	391
2016	10 321	379	148	231	9 943	1 168	2 561	2 280	2 152	1 399	383
2017	10 580	409	146	262	10 171	1 151	2 634	2 327	2 181	1 437	441
2018	10 720	395	134	261	10 324	1 128	2 687	2 354	2 175	1 503	478
2019	10 842	405	135	270	10 437	1 124	2 714	2 352	2 161	1 569	518

Table 1-8. Civilian Labor Force Participation Rates, by Age, Sex, Race, and Hispanic Origin, 1948–2019

(Percent.)

Race, Hispanic origin, sex, and year	16 years and over	16 to 19 years	20 years and over Total	20 to 24 years	25 to 34 years	35 to 44 years	45 to 54 years	55 to 64 years	65 years and over
ALL RACES									
Both Sexes									
1948	58.8	52.5	59.4	64.1	63.1	66.7	65.1	56.9	27.0
1949	58.9	52.2	59.5	64.9	63.2	67.2	65.3	56.2	27.3
1950	59.2	51.8	59.9	65.9	63.5	67.5	66.4	56.7	26.7
1951	59.2	52.2	59.8	64.8	64.2	67.6	67.2	56.9	25.8
1952	59.0	51.3	59.7	62.2	64.7	68.0	67.5	57.5	24.8
1953	58.9	50.2	59.6	61.2	64.0	68.9	68.1	58.0	24.8
1954	58.8	48.3	59.6	61.6	64.3	68.8	68.4	58.7	23.9
1955	59.3	48.9	60.1	62.7	64.8	68.9	69.7	59.5	24.1
1956	60.0	50.9	60.7	64.1	64.8	69.5	70.5	60.8	24.3
1957	59.6	49.6	60.4	64.0	64.9	69.5	70.9	60.1	22.9
1958	59.5	47.4	60.5	64.4	65.0	69.6	71.5	60.5	21.8
1959	59.3	46.7	60.4	64.3	65.0	69.5	71.9	61.0	21.1
1960	59.4	47.5	60.5	65.2	65.4	69.4	72.2	60.9	20.8
1961	59.3	46.9	60.5	65.7	65.6	69.5	72.1	61.5	20.1
1962	58.8	46.1	60.0	65.3	65.2	69.7	72.2	61.5	19.1
1963	58.7	45.2	60.1	65.1	65.6	70.1	72.5	62.0	17.9
1964	58.7	44.5	60.2	66.3	65.8	70.0	72.9	61.9	18.0
1965	58.9	45.7	60.3	66.4	66.4	70.7	72.5	61.9	17.8
1966	59.2	48.2	60.5	66.5	67.1	71.0	72.7	62.2	17.2
1967	59.6	48.4	60.9	67.1	68.2	71.6	72.7	62.3	17.2
1968	59.6	48.3	60.9	67.0	68.6	72.0	72.8	62.2	17.2
1969	60.1	49.4	61.3	68.2	69.1	72.5	73.4	62.1	17.3
1970	60.4	49.9	61.6	69.2	69.7	73.1	73.5	61.8	17.0
1971	60.2	49.7	61.4	69.3	69.9	73.2	73.2	61.3	16.2
1972	60.4	51.9	61.4	70.8	70.9	73.3	72.7	60.0	15.6
1973	60.8	53.7	61.7	72.6	72.3	74.0	72.5	58.4	14.6
1974	61.3	54.8	62.0	74.0	73.6	74.6	72.7	57.8	14.0
1975	61.2	54.0	62.1	73.9	74.4	75.0	72.6	57.2	13.7
1976	61.6	54.5	62.4	74.7	75.7	76.0	72.5	56.6	13.1
1977	62.3	56.0	63.0	75.7	77.0	77.0	72.8	56.3	13.0
1978	63.2	57.8	63.8	76.8	78.3	78.1	73.5	56.3	13.3
1979	63.7	57.9	64.3	77.5	79.2	79.2	74.3	56.2	13.1
1980	63.8	56.7	64.5	77.2	79.9	80.0	74.9	55.7	12.5
1981	63.9	55.4	64.8	77.3	80.5	80.7	75.7	55.0	12.2
1982	64.0	54.1	65.0	77.1	81.0	81.2	75.9	55.1	11.9
1983	64.0	53.5	65.0	77.2	81.3	81.6	76.0	54.5	11.7
1984	64.4	53.9	65.3	77.6	81.8	82.4	76.5	54.2	11.1
1985	64.8	54.5	65.7	78.2	82.5	83.1	77.3	54.2	10.8
1986	65.3	54.7	66.2	78.9	82.9	83.7	78.0	54.0	10.9
1987	65.6	54.7	66.5	78.9	83.3	84.3	78.6	54.4	11.1
1988	65.9	55.3	66.8	78.7	83.3	84.6	79.6	54.6	11.5
1989	66.5	55.9	67.3	78.7	83.8	85.1	80.5	55.5	11.8
1990	66.5	53.7	67.6	77.8	83.6	85.2	80.7	55.9	11.8
1991	66.2	51.6	67.3	76.7	83.2	85.2	81.0	55.5	11.5
1992	66.4	51.3	67.6	77.0	83.7	85.1	81.5	56.2	11.5
1993	66.3	51.5	67.5	77.0	83.3	84.9	81.6	56.4	11.2
1994	66.6	52.7	67.7	77.0	83.2	84.8	81.7	56.8	12.4
1995	66.6	53.5	67.7	76.6	83.8	84.6	81.4	57.2	12.1
1996	66.8	52.3	67.9	76.8	84.1	84.8	82.1	57.9	12.1
1997	67.1	51.6	68.4	77.6	84.4	85.1	82.6	58.9	12.2
1998	67.1	52.8	68.3	77.5	84.6	84.7	82.5	59.3	11.9
1999	67.1	52.0	68.3	77.5	84.6	84.9	82.6	59.3	12.3
2000	67.1	52.0	68.3	77.8	84.6	84.8	82.5	59.2	12.9
2001	66.8	49.6	68.2	77.1	84.0	84.6	82.3	60.4	13.0
2002	66.6	47.4	68.1	76.4	83.7	84.1	82.1	61.9	13.2
2003	66.2	44.5	67.9	75.4	82.9	83.9	82.1	62.4	14.0
2004	66.0	43.9	67.7	75.0	82.7	83.6	81.8	62.3	14.4
2005	66.0	43.7	67.8	74.6	82.8	83.8	81.7	62.9	15.1
2006	66.2	43.7	67.9	74.6	83.0	83.8	81.9	63.7	15.4
2007	66.0	41.3	68.0	74.4	83.3	83.8	82.0	63.8	16.0
2008	66.0	40.2	68.0	74.4	83.3	84.1	81.9	64.5	16.8
2009	65.4	37.5	67.5	72.9	82.7	83.7	81.6	64.9	17.2
2010	64.7	34.9	67.0	71.4	82.2	83.2	81.2	64.9	17.4
2011	64.1	34.1	66.4	71.3	81.5	82.7	80.7	64.3	17.9
2012	63.7	34.3	65.9	70.9	81.7	82.6	80.2	64.5	18.5
2013	63.2	34.5	65.4	70.7	81.2	82.2	79.7	64.4	18.7
2014	62.9	34.0	65.0	70.8	81.2	82.2	79.6	64.1	18.6
2015	62.7	34.3	64.7	70.7	81.0	82.1	79.5	63.9	18.9
2016	62.8	35.2	64.7	70.5	81.6	82.4	80.0	64.1	19.3
2017	62.9	35.2	64.8	71.3	82.1	82.7	80.3	64.5	19.3
2018	62.9	35.1	64.8	71.1	82.5	82.9	80.8	65.0	19.6
2019	63.1	35.3	65.0	72.2	82.9	83.1	81.4	65.3	20.2

Table 1-8. Civilian Labor Force Participation Rates, by Age, Sex, Race, and Hispanic Origin, 1948–2019
—Continued
(Percent.)

Race, Hispanic origin, sex, and year	16 years and over	16 to 19 years	20 years and over Total	20 to 24 years	25 to 34 years	35 to 44 years	45 to 54 years	55 to 64 years	65 years and over
ALL RACES									
Men									
1948	86.6	63.7	88.6	84.6	95.9	97.9	95.8	89.5	46.8
1949	86.4	62.8	88.5	86.6	95.8	97.9	95.6	87.5	47.0
1950	86.4	63.2	88.4	87.9	96.0	97.6	95.8	86.9	45.8
1951	86.3	63.0	88.2	88.4	96.9	97.5	95.9	87.2	44.9
1952	86.3	61.3	88.3	88.1	97.5	97.8	96.2	87.5	42.6
1953	86.0	60.7	88.0	87.7	97.4	98.2	96.5	87.9	41.6
1954	85.5	58.0	87.8	86.9	97.3	98.1	96.5	88.7	40.5
1955	85.4	58.9	87.6	86.9	97.6	98.1	96.4	87.9	39.6
1956	85.5	60.5	87.6	87.8	97.3	97.9	96.6	88.5	40.0
1957	84.8	59.1	86.9	87.1	97.1	97.9	96.3	87.5	37.5
1958	84.2	56.6	86.6	86.9	97.1	97.9	96.3	87.8	35.6
1959	83.7	55.8	86.3	87.8	97.4	97.8	96.0	87.4	34.2
1960	83.3	56.1	86.0	88.1	97.5	97.7	95.7	86.8	33.1
1961	82.9	54.6	85.7	87.8	97.5	97.6	95.6	87.3	31.7
1962	82.0	53.8	84.8	86.9	97.2	97.6	95.6	86.2	30.3
1963	81.4	52.9	84.4	86.1	97.1	97.5	95.7	86.2	28.4
1964	81.0	52.4	84.2	86.1	97.3	97.3	95.7	85.6	28.0
1965	80.7	53.8	83.9	85.8	97.2	97.3	95.6	84.6	27.9
1966	80.4	55.3	83.6	85.1	97.3	97.2	95.3	84.5	27.1
1967	80.4	55.6	83.4	84.4	97.2	97.3	95.2	84.4	27.1
1968	80.1	55.1	83.1	82.8	96.9	97.1	94.9	84.3	27.3
1969	79.8	55.9	82.8	82.8	96.7	96.9	94.6	83.4	27.2
1970	79.7	56.1	82.6	83.3	96.4	96.9	94.3	83.0	26.8
1971	79.1	56.1	82.1	83.0	95.9	96.5	93.9	82.1	25.5
1972	78.9	58.1	81.6	83.9	95.7	96.4	93.2	80.4	24.3
1973	78.8	59.7	81.3	85.2	95.7	96.2	93.0	78.2	22.7
1974	78.7	60.7	81.0	85.9	95.8	96.0	92.2	77.3	22.4
1975	77.9	59.1	80.3	84.5	95.2	95.6	92.1	75.6	21.6
1976	77.5	59.3	79.8	85.2	95.2	95.4	91.6	74.3	20.2
1977	77.7	60.9	79.7	85.6	95.3	95.7	91.1	73.8	20.0
1978	77.9	62.0	79.8	85.9	95.3	95.7	91.3	73.3	20.4
1979	77.8	61.5	79.8	86.4	95.3	95.7	91.4	72.8	19.9
1980	77.4	60.5	79.4	85.9	95.2	95.5	91.2	72.1	19.0
1981	77.0	59.0	79.0	85.5	94.9	95.4	91.4	70.6	18.4
1982	76.6	56.7	78.7	84.9	94.7	95.3	91.2	70.2	17.8
1983	76.4	56.2	78.5	84.8	94.2	95.2	91.2	69.4	17.4
1984	76.4	56.0	78.3	85.0	94.4	95.4	91.2	68.5	16.3
1985	76.3	56.8	78.1	85.0	94.7	95.0	91.0	67.9	15.8
1986	76.3	56.4	78.1	85.8	94.6	94.8	91.0	67.3	16.0
1987	76.2	56.1	78.0	85.2	94.6	94.6	90.7	67.6	16.3
1988	76.2	56.9	77.9	85.0	94.3	94.5	90.9	67.0	16.5
1989	76.4	57.9	78.1	85.3	94.4	94.5	91.1	67.2	16.6
1990	76.4	55.7	78.2	84.4	94.1	94.3	90.7	67.8	16.3
1991	75.8	53.2	77.7	83.5	93.6	94.1	90.5	67.0	15.7
1992	75.8	53.4	77.7	83.3	93.8	93.7	90.7	67.0	16.1
1993	75.4	53.2	77.3	83.2	93.4	93.4	90.1	66.5	15.6
1994	75.1	54.1	76.8	83.1	92.6	92.8	89.1	65.5	16.8
1995	75.0	54.8	76.7	83.1	93.0	92.3	88.8	66.0	16.8
1996	74.9	53.2	76.8	82.5	93.2	92.4	89.1	67.0	16.9
1997	75.0	52.3	77.0	82.5	93.0	92.6	89.5	67.6	17.1
1998	74.9	53.3	76.8	82.0	93.2	92.6	89.2	68.1	16.5
1999	74.7	52.9	76.7	81.9	93.3	92.8	88.8	67.9	16.9
2000	74.8	52.8	76.7	82.6	93.4	92.7	88.6	67.3	17.7
2001	74.4	50.2	76.5	81.6	92.7	92.5	88.5	68.3	17.7
2002	74.1	47.5	76.3	80.7	92.4	92.1	88.5	69.2	17.9
2003	73.5	44.3	75.9	80.0	91.8	92.1	87.7	68.7	18.6
2004	73.3	43.9	75.8	79.6	91.9	91.9	87.5	68.7	19.0
2005	73.3	43.2	75.8	79.1	91.7	92.1	87.7	69.3	19.8
2006	73.5	43.7	75.9	79.6	91.7	92.1	88.1	69.6	20.3
2007	73.2	41.1	75.9	78.7	92.2	92.3	88.2	69.6	20.5
2008	73.0	40.1	75.7	78.7	91.5	92.2	88.0	70.4	21.5
2009	72.0	37.3	74.8	76.2	90.3	91.7	87.4	70.2	21.9
2010	71.2	34.9	74.1	74.5	89.7	91.5	86.8	70.0	22.1
2011	70.5	33.7	73.4	74.7	89.2	90.9	86.2	69.3	22.8
2012	70.2	34.0	73.0	74.5	89.5	90.7	86.1	69.9	23.6
2013	69.7	34.2	72.5	73.9	89.2	90.7	85.5	70.0	23.5
2014	69.2	33.5	71.9	73.9	88.7	90.5	85.6	69.9	23.0
2015	69.1	34.2	71.7	73.0	90.3	88.8	85.9	69.8	23.4
2016	69.2	35.3	71.7	73.0	88.8	90.6	86.3	70.2	24.0
2017	69.1	34.6	71.6	74.1	88.8	90.7	86.4	70.6	23.9
2018	69.1	34.2	71.6	73.2	89.1	90.9	87.0	71.2	24.0
2019	69.2	34.9	71.6	74.0	89.1	90.8	87.4	71.5	24.7

Table 1-8. Civilian Labor Force Participation Rates, by Age, Sex, Race, and Hispanic Origin, 1948–2019
—*Continued*

(Percent.)

Race, Hispanic origin, sex, and year	16 years and over	16 to 19 years	20 years and over						
			Total	20 to 24 years	25 to 34 years	35 to 44 years	45 to 54 years	55 to 64 years	65 years and over
ALL RACES									
Women									
1948	32.7	42.0	31.8	45.3	33.2	36.9	35.0	24.3	9.1
1949	33.1	42.4	32.3	45.0	33.4	38.1	35.9	25.3	9.6
1950	33.9	41.0	33.3	46.0	34.0	39.1	37.9	27.0	9.7
1951	34.6	42.4	34.0	46.5	35.4	39.8	39.7	27.6	8.9
1952	34.7	42.2	34.1	44.7	35.4	40.4	40.1	28.7	9.1
1953	34.4	40.7	33.9	44.3	34.0	41.3	40.4	29.1	10.0
1954	34.6	39.4	34.2	45.1	34.4	41.2	41.2	30.0	9.3
1955	35.7	39.7	35.4	45.9	34.9	41.6	43.8	32.5	10.6
1956	36.9	42.2	36.4	46.3	35.4	43.1	45.5	34.9	10.8
1957	36.9	41.1	36.5	45.9	35.6	43.3	46.5	34.5	10.5
1958	37.1	39.0	36.9	46.3	35.6	43.4	47.8	35.2	10.3
1959	37.1	38.2	37.1	45.1	35.3	43.4	49.0	36.6	10.2
1960	37.7	39.3	37.6	46.1	36.0	43.4	49.9	37.2	10.8
1961	38.1	39.7	38.0	47.0	36.4	43.8	50.1	37.9	10.7
1962	37.9	39.0	37.8	47.3	36.3	44.1	50.0	38.7	10.0
1963	38.3	38.0	38.3	47.5	37.2	44.9	50.6	39.7	9.6
1964	38.7	37.0	38.9	49.4	37.2	45.0	51.4	40.2	10.1
1965	39.3	38.0	39.4	49.9	38.5	46.1	50.9	41.1	10.0
1966	40.3	41.4	40.1	51.5	39.8	46.8	51.7	41.8	9.6
1967	41.1	41.6	41.1	53.3	41.9	48.1	51.8	42.4	9.6
1968	41.6	41.9	41.6	54.5	42.6	48.9	52.3	42.4	9.6
1969	42.7	43.2	42.7	56.7	43.7	49.9	53.8	43.1	9.9
1970	43.3	44.0	43.3	57.7	45.0	51.1	54.4	43.0	9.7
1971	43.4	43.4	43.3	57.7	45.6	51.6	54.3	42.9	9.5
1972	43.9	45.8	43.7	59.1	47.8	52.0	53.9	42.1	9.3
1973	44.7	47.8	44.4	61.1	50.4	53.3	53.7	41.1	8.9
1974	45.7	49.1	45.3	63.1	52.6	54.7	54.6	40.7	8.1
1975	46.3	49.1	46.0	64.1	54.9	55.8	54.6	40.9	8.2
1976	47.3	49.8	47.0	65.0	57.3	57.8	55.0	41.0	8.2
1977	48.4	51.2	48.1	66.5	59.7	59.6	55.8	40.9	8.1
1978	50.0	53.7	49.6	68.3	62.2	61.6	57.1	41.3	8.3
1979	50.9	54.2	50.6	69.0	63.9	63.6	58.3	41.7	8.3
1980	51.5	52.9	51.3	68.9	65.5	65.5	59.9	41.3	8.1
1981	52.1	51.8	52.1	69.6	66.7	66.8	61.1	41.4	8.0
1982	52.6	51.4	52.7	69.8	68.0	68.0	61.6	41.8	7.9
1983	52.9	50.8	53.1	69.9	69.0	68.7	61.9	41.5	7.8
1984	53.6	51.8	53.7	70.4	69.8	70.1	62.9	41.7	7.5
1985	54.5	52.1	54.7	71.8	70.9	71.8	64.4	42.0	7.3
1986	55.3	53.0	55.5	72.4	71.6	73.1	65.9	42.3	7.4
1987	56.0	53.3	56.2	73.0	72.4	74.5	67.1	42.7	7.4
1988	56.6	53.6	56.8	72.7	72.7	75.2	69.0	43.5	7.9
1989	57.4	53.9	57.7	72.4	73.5	76.0	70.5	45.0	8.4
1990	57.5	51.6	58.0	71.3	73.5	76.4	71.2	45.2	8.6
1991	57.4	50.0	57.9	70.1	73.1	76.5	72.0	45.2	8.5
1992	57.8	49.1	58.5	70.9	73.9	76.7	72.6	46.5	8.3
1993	57.9	49.7	58.5	70.9	73.4	76.6	73.5	47.2	8.1
1994	58.8	51.3	59.3	71.0	74.0	77.1	74.6	48.9	9.2
1995	58.9	52.2	59.4	70.3	74.9	77.2	74.4	49.2	8.8
1996	59.3	51.3	59.9	71.3	75.2	77.5	75.4	49.6	8.6
1997	59.8	51.0	60.5	72.7	76.0	77.7	76.0	50.9	8.6
1998	59.8	52.3	60.4	73.0	76.3	77.1	76.2	51.2	8.6
1999	60.0	51.0	60.7	73.2	76.4	77.2	76.7	51.5	8.9
2000	59.9	51.2	60.6	73.1	76.1	77.2	76.8	51.9	9.4
2001	59.8	49.0	60.6	72.7	75.5	77.1	76.4	53.2	9.6
2002	59.6	47.3	60.5	72.1	75.1	76.4	76.0	55.2	9.8
2003	59.5	44.8	60.6	70.8	74.1	76.0	76.8	56.6	10.6
2004	59.2	43.8	60.3	70.5	73.6	75.6	76.5	56.3	11.1
2005	59.3	44.2	60.4	70.1	73.9	75.8	76.0	57.0	11.5
2006	59.4	43.7	60.5	69.5	74.4	75.9	76.0	58.2	11.7
2007	59.3	41.5	60.6	70.1	74.5	75.5	76.0	58.3	12.6
2008	59.5	40.2	60.9	70.0	75.2	76.1	76.1	59.1	13.3
2009	59.2	37.7	60.8	69.6	75.0	75.9	76.0	60.0	13.6
2010	58.6	35.0	60.3	68.3	74.7	75.2	75.7	60.2	13.8
2011	58.1	34.6	59.8	67.8	73.9	74.7	75.4	59.5	14.0
2012	57.7	34.6	59.3	67.4	74.1	74.8	74.7	59.4	14.4
2013	57.2	34.7	58.8	67.5	73.5	74.0	74.1	59.2	14.9
2014	57.0	34.5	58.5	67.7	73.8	74.1	73.8	58.8	15.1
2015	56.7	34.4	58.2	68.3	73.4	74.3	73.4	58.5	15.3
2016	56.8	35.1	58.3	68.0	74.5	74.5	73.9	58.4	15.5
2017	57.0	35.9	58.5	68.5	75.5	75.0	74.5	58.9	15.7
2018	57.1	36.0	58.5	69.0	75.9	75.1	74.9	59.1	15.9
2019	57.4	35.7	58.9	70.4	76.7	75.7	75.7	59.6	16.4

Table 1-8. Civilian Labor Force Participation Rates, by Age, Sex, Race, and Hispanic Origin, 1948–2019
    —Continued

(Percent.)

Race, Hispanic origin, sex, and year	16 years and over	16 to 19 years	20 years and over						
			Total	20 to 24 years	25 to 34 years	35 to 44 years	45 to 54 years	55 to 64 years	65 years and over
WHITE									
Both Sexes									
1954	58.2	48.8	58.9	61.0	63.5	68.0	67.9	58.4	23.7
1955	58.7	49.3	59.5	62.4	64.0	68.3	69.2	59.3	23.9
1956	59.4	51.3	60.1	64.1	64.0	68.9	70.1	60.6	24.2
1957	59.1	50.3	59.8	63.7	64.1	68.8	70.5	59.9	22.8
1958	58.9	47.9	59.8	64.1	64.2	68.8	71.0	60.3	21.7
1959	58.7	47.4	59.7	63.7	64.3	68.7	71.5	60.7	21.0
1960	58.8	47.9	59.8	64.8	64.7	68.6	71.7	60.6	20.8
1961	58.8	47.4	59.9	65.5	64.8	68.8	71.7	61.3	20.0
1962	58.3	46.6	59.4	65.0	64.4	69.0	71.8	61.3	19.0
1963	58.2	45.7	59.4	64.9	64.8	69.4	72.3	61.8	17.9
1964	58.2	45.1	59.6	65.8	64.9	69.5	72.5	61.8	17.8
1965	58.4	46.5	59.7	65.7	65.6	70.1	72.2	61.7	17.7
1966	58.7	49.1	59.8	66.0	66.3	70.4	72.5	61.9	17.1
1967	59.2	49.2	60.3	66.8	67.4	71.2	72.5	62.3	17.0
1968	59.3	49.3	60.4	66.6	67.9	71.7	72.7	62.2	17.1
1969	59.9	50.6	60.9	67.9	68.4	72.3	73.3	62.1	17.2
1970	60.2	51.4	61.2	69.2	69.1	72.9	73.5	61.8	16.8
1971	60.1	51.6	61.1	69.6	69.3	73.0	73.4	61.3	16.1
1972	60.4	54.1	61.2	71.2	70.4	73.2	72.9	60.3	15.4
1973	60.8	56.0	61.4	73.3	72.0	73.9	72.7	58.6	14.4
1974	61.4	57.3	61.9	74.8	73.4	74.6	73.0	58.0	13.9
1975	61.5	56.7	62.0	75.2	74.4	75.1	73.0	57.4	13.6
1976	61.8	57.5	62.3	76.0	75.6	76.1	73.0	56.9	13.0
1977	62.5	59.3	62.9	77.1	77.0	77.1	73.2	56.6	12.9
1978	63.3	60.8	63.6	78.1	78.3	78.1	73.8	56.4	13.1
1979	63.9	61.1	64.2	78.9	79.4	79.3	74.6	56.5	12.9
1980	64.1	60.0	64.5	78.7	80.2	80.3	75.4	56.0	12.5
1981	64.3	58.9	64.8	79.1	81.0	81.0	76.2	55.2	12.2
1982	64.3	57.5	65.0	78.9	81.6	81.5	76.4	55.3	12.0
1983	64.3	56.9	65.0	79.0	81.8	81.9	76.5	54.7	11.8
1984	64.6	57.2	65.3	79.4	82.5	82.6	77.0	54.5	11.1
1985	65.0	57.5	65.7	79.9	83.1	83.4	77.8	54.4	10.7
1986	65.5	57.8	66.1	80.6	83.6	84.0	78.5	54.3	11.0
1987	65.8	57.7	66.5	80.7	84.0	84.7	79.1	54.6	11.1
1988	66.2	58.6	66.8	80.6	84.1	85.0	80.3	55.1	11.4
1989	66.7	59.1	67.3	80.2	84.5	85.5	81.2	56.2	11.8
1990	66.9	57.5	67.6	79.8	84.6	85.9	81.3	56.5	11.9
1991	66.6	55.8	67.4	78.9	84.3	85.9	81.8	56.0	11.6
1992	66.8	54.7	67.7	79.4	84.6	85.8	82.2	56.8	11.6
1993	66.8	55.1	67.6	79.5	84.5	85.7	82.5	57.1	11.4
1994	67.1	56.4	67.9	79.5	84.4	85.7	82.7	57.6	12.5
1995	67.1	57.1	67.8	78.7	84.9	85.5	82.5	58.0	12.3
1996	67.2	55.9	68.1	79.1	84.9	85.7	83.1	58.7	12.3
1997	67.5	55.2	68.4	79.6	85.3	85.8	83.5	59.9	12.3
1998	67.3	56.0	68.2	79.5	85.4	85.3	83.4	60.1	12.0
1999	67.3	55.5	68.2	79.5	85.1	85.4	83.5	60.2	12.5
2000	67.3	55.5	68.2	79.9	85.1	85.4	83.5	60.0	13.0
2001	67.0	53.1	68.1	79.2	84.5	85.2	83.3	61.2	13.0
2002	66.8	50.5	68.1	78.6	84.5	84.7	83.0	62.8	13.3
2003	66.5	47.7	67.9	77.7	83.6	84.3	83.0	63.3	14.1
2004	66.3	47.1	67.7	77.1	83.5	84.1	82.9	63.2	14.6
2005	66.3	46.9	67.7	76.3	83.5	84.2	82.8	63.7	15.1
2006	66.5	46.7	67.9	76.5	83.8	84.3	83.0	64.7	15.5
2007	66.4	44.4	68.0	76.4	84.1	84.1	83.1	64.9	16.2
2008	66.3	43.1	68.0	76.3	83.9	84.4	82.9	65.7	17.0
2009	65.8	40.6	67.7	75.1	83.5	84.2	82.7	66.2	17.4
2010	65.1	37.7	67.1	73.4	83.2	83.8	82.2	66.1	17.6
2011	64.5	36.8	66.5	73.2	82.5	83.3	81.7	65.5	18.1
2012	64.0	36.9	65.9	73.1	82.6	83.2	81.2	65.9	18.7
2013	63.5	36.9	65.3	73.1	82.2	82.7	80.7	65.5	19.0
2014	63.1	36.2	64.9	73.0	82.3	82.7	80.5	65.3	18.8
2015	62.8	36.4	64.5	72.7	82.1	82.6	80.5	65.2	19.1
2016	62.9	37.4	64.6	72.4	82.5	82.9	81.0	65.4	19.5
2017	62.8	36.8	64.5	73.1	83.1	83.0	81.0	65.9	19.5
2018	62.8	37.2	64.5	73.2	83.4	83.3	81.5	66.3	19.7
2019	63.0	37.5	64.7	73.9	83.9	83.9	82.0	66.6	20.3

Table 1-8. Civilian Labor Force Participation Rates, by Age, Sex, Race, and Hispanic Origin, 1948–2019
—*Continued*

(Percent.)

Race, Hispanic origin, sex, and year	16 years and over	16 to 19 years	20 years and over						
			Total	20 to 24 years	25 to 34 years	35 to 44 years	45 to 54 years	55 to 64 years	65 years and over
WHITE									
Men									
1954	85.6	57.6	87.8	86.3	97.5	98.2	96.8	89.1	40.4
1955	85.4	58.6	87.5	86.5	97.8	98.2	96.7	88.4	39.6
1956	85.6	60.4	87.6	87.6	97.4	98.1	96.8	88.9	40.0
1957	84.8	59.2	86.9	86.6	97.2	98.0	96.7	88.0	37.7
1958	84.3	56.5	86.6	86.7	97.2	98.0	96.6	88.2	35.7
1959	83.8	55.9	86.3	87.3	97.5	98.0	96.3	87.9	34.3
1960	83.4	55.9	86.0	87.8	97.7	97.9	96.1	87.2	33.3
1961	83.0	54.5	85.7	87.6	97.7	97.9	95.9	87.8	31.9
1962	82.1	53.8	84.9	86.5	97.4	97.9	96.0	86.7	30.6
1963	81.5	53.1	84.4	85.8	97.4	97.8	96.2	86.6	28.4
1964	81.1	52.7	84.2	85.7	97.5	97.6	96.1	86.1	27.9
1965	80.8	54.1	83.9	85.3	97.4	97.7	95.9	85.2	27.9
1966	80.6	55.9	83.6	84.4	97.5	97.6	95.8	84.9	27.2
1967	80.6	56.3	83.5	84.0	97.5	97.7	95.6	84.9	27.1
1968	80.4	55.9	83.2	82.4	97.2	97.6	95.4	84.7	27.4
1969	80.2	56.8	83.0	82.6	97.0	97.4	95.1	83.9	27.3
1970	80.0	57.5	82.8	83.3	96.7	97.3	94.9	83.3	26.7
1971	79.6	57.9	82.3	83.2	96.3	97.0	94.7	82.6	25.6
1972	79.6	60.1	82.0	84.3	96.0	97.0	94.0	81.1	24.4
1973	79.4	62.0	81.6	85.8	96.2	96.8	93.5	78.9	22.7
1974	79.4	62.9	81.4	86.6	96.3	96.7	93.0	78.0	22.4
1975	78.7	61.9	80.7	85.5	95.8	96.4	92.9	76.4	21.7
1976	78.4	62.3	80.3	86.3	95.9	96.0	92.5	75.2	20.2
1977	78.5	64.0	80.2	86.8	96.0	96.2	92.1	74.6	20.0
1978	78.6	65.0	80.1	87.3	95.9	96.3	92.1	73.7	20.3
1979	78.6	64.8	80.1	87.6	96.0	96.4	92.2	73.4	20.0
1980	78.2	63.7	79.8	87.2	95.9	96.2	92.1	73.1	19.1
1981	77.9	62.4	79.5	87.0	95.8	96.1	92.4	71.5	18.5
1982	77.4	60.0	79.2	86.3	95.6	96.0	92.2	71.0	17.9
1983	77.1	59.4	78.9	86.1	95.2	96.0	91.9	70.0	17.7
1984	77.1	59.0	78.7	86.5	95.4	96.1	92.0	69.5	16.4
1985	77.0	59.7	78.5	86.4	95.7	95.7	92.0	68.8	15.9
1986	76.9	59.3	78.5	87.3	95.5	95.4	91.8	68.0	16.3
1987	76.8	59.0	78.4	86.9	95.5	95.4	91.6	68.1	16.5
1988	76.9	60.0	78.3	86.6	95.2	95.4	91.8	67.9	16.7
1989	77.1	61.0	78.5	86.8	95.4	95.3	92.2	68.3	16.8
1990	77.1	59.6	78.5	86.2	95.2	95.3	91.7	68.6	16.6
1991	76.5	57.3	78.0	85.4	94.9	95.0	91.4	67.7	15.9
1992	76.5	56.9	78.0	85.2	94.9	94.7	91.8	67.7	16.2
1993	76.2	56.6	77.7	85.5	94.7	94.5	91.3	67.3	15.9
1994	75.9	57.7	77.3	85.5	93.9	93.9	90.3	66.4	17.2
1995	75.7	58.5	77.1	85.1	94.1	93.4	90.0	67.1	16.9
1996	75.8	57.1	77.3	85.0	94.4	93.6	90.4	68.0	17.2
1997	75.9	56.1	77.5	85.1	94.2	93.7	90.6	68.9	17.4
1998	75.6	56.6	77.2	84.6	94.4	93.7	90.3	69.1	16.6
1999	75.6	56.4	77.2	84.9	94.3	93.8	90.1	69.1	17.2
2000	75.5	56.5	77.1	85.2	94.5	93.8	89.7	68.2	17.9
2001	75.1	53.7	76.9	84.1	93.9	93.6	89.7	69.1	17.8
2002	74.8	50.3	76.7	83.2	93.7	93.2	89.6	70.2	17.8
2003	74.2	47.5	76.3	82.5	93.3	93.1	88.8	69.7	18.6
2004	74.1	47.4	76.2	82.1	93.2	93.0	88.7	69.8	19.1
2005	74.1	46.2	76.2	81.4	93.0	93.0	89.0	70.4	20.0
2006	74.3	46.9	76.4	81.9	92.9	93.1	89.3	71.0	20.6
2007	74.0	44.3	76.3	80.9	93.4	93.1	89.6	71.2	20.8
2008	73.7	43.0	76.1	80.8	92.6	93.0	89.2	71.9	21.8
2009	72.8	40.3	75.3	78.6	91.6	92.7	88.8	71.8	22.2
2010	72.0	37.4	74.6	77.0	91.1	92.4	88.1	71.2	22.3
2011	71.3	36.1	73.9	77.1	90.5	92.1	87.5	70.8	23.0
2012	71.0	36.7	73.5	77.2	90.9	91.8	87.5	71.6	24.0
2013	70.5	36.6	72.9	76.9	90.5	91.6	86.9	71.6	24.0
2014	69.8	35.6	72.2	76.5	90.0	91.5	86.9	71.3	23.3
2015	69.7	36.7	72.0	75.5	90.3	91.3	87.2	71.5	23.7
2016	69.8	38.1	72.0	75.5	90.1	91.7	87.5	71.7	24.3
2017	69.5	36.5	71.8	76.5	90.2	91.6	87.6	72.3	24.2
2018	69.5	36.2	71.8	75.8	90.5	91.9	88.1	72.8	24.5
2019	69.6	37.4	71.8	76.3	90.6	92.1	88.2	73.4	25.1

Table 1-8. Civilian Labor Force Participation Rates, by Age, Sex, Race, and Hispanic Origin, 1948–2019
   —*Continued*

(Percent.)

Race, Hispanic origin, sex, and year	16 years and over	16 to 19 years	20 years and over						
			Total	20 to 24 years	25 to 34 years	35 to 44 years	45 to 54 years	55 to 64 years	65 years and over
WHITE									
Women									
1954	33.3	40.6	32.7	44.4	32.5	39.3	39.8	29.1	9.1
1955	34.5	40.7	34.0	45.8	32.8	40.0	42.7	31.8	10.5
1956	35.7	43.1	35.1	46.5	33.2	41.5	44.4	34.0	10.6
1957	35.7	42.2	35.2	45.8	33.6	41.5	45.4	33.7	10.2
1958	35.8	40.1	35.5	46.0	33.6	41.4	46.5	34.5	10.1
1959	36.0	39.6	35.6	44.5	33.4	41.4	47.8	35.7	10.0
1960	36.5	40.3	36.2	45.7	34.1	41.5	48.6	36.2	10.6
1961	36.9	40.6	36.6	46.9	34.3	41.8	48.9	37.2	10.5
1962	36.7	39.8	36.5	47.1	34.1	42.2	48.9	38.0	9.8
1963	37.2	38.7	37.0	47.3	34.8	43.1	49.5	38.9	9.4
1964	37.5	37.8	37.5	48.8	35.0	43.3	50.2	39.4	9.9
1965	38.1	39.2	38.0	49.2	36.3	44.4	49.9	40.3	9.7
1966	39.2	42.6	38.8	51.0	37.7	45.0	50.6	41.1	9.4
1967	40.1	42.5	39.8	53.1	39.7	46.4	50.9	41.9	9.3
1968	40.7	43.0	40.4	54.0	40.6	47.5	51.5	42.0	9.4
1969	41.8	44.6	41.5	56.4	41.7	48.6	53.0	42.6	9.7
1970	42.6	45.6	42.2	57.7	43.2	49.9	53.7	42.6	9.5
1971	42.6	45.4	42.3	58.0	43.7	50.2	53.6	42.5	9.3
1972	43.2	48.1	42.7	59.4	46.0	50.7	53.4	41.9	9.0
1973	44.1	50.1	43.5	61.7	48.7	52.2	53.4	40.7	8.7
1974	45.2	51.7	44.4	63.9	51.3	53.6	54.3	40.4	8.0
1975	45.9	51.5	45.3	65.5	53.8	54.9	54.3	40.6	8.0
1976	46.9	52.8	46.2	66.3	56.0	57.1	54.7	40.7	7.9
1977	48.0	54.5	47.3	67.8	58.5	58.9	55.3	40.7	7.9
1978	49.4	56.7	48.7	69.3	61.2	60.7	56.7	41.1	8.1
1979	50.5	57.4	49.8	70.5	63.1	63.0	58.1	41.5	8.1
1980	51.2	56.2	50.6	70.6	64.8	65.0	59.6	40.9	7.9
1981	51.9	55.4	51.5	71.5	66.4	66.4	60.9	40.9	7.9
1982	52.4	55.0	52.2	71.8	67.8	67.5	61.4	41.5	7.8
1983	52.7	54.5	52.5	72.1	68.7	68.2	61.9	41.1	7.8
1984	53.3	55.4	53.1	72.5	69.8	69.6	62.7	41.2	7.5
1985	54.1	55.2	54.0	73.8	70.9	71.4	64.2	41.5	7.0
1986	55.0	56.3	54.9	74.1	71.8	72.9	65.8	42.1	7.3
1987	55.7	56.5	55.6	74.8	72.5	74.2	67.2	42.4	7.2
1988	56.4	57.2	56.3	74.9	73.0	74.9	69.2	43.6	7.7
1989	57.2	57.1	57.2	74.0	73.8	75.9	70.6	45.2	8.2
1990	57.4	55.3	57.6	73.4	74.1	76.6	71.3	45.5	8.5
1991	57.4	54.1	57.6	72.5	73.8	76.8	72.4	45.4	8.5
1992	57.7	52.5	58.1	73.5	74.4	77.0	72.8	46.8	8.2
1993	58.0	53.5	58.3	73.4	74.3	76.9	74.0	47.6	8.1
1994	58.9	55.1	59.2	73.4	74.9	77.5	75.2	49.4	9.2
1995	59.0	55.5	59.2	72.3	75.8	77.6	75.2	49.5	9.0
1996	59.1	54.7	59.4	73.3	75.5	77.8	76.1	50.1	8.7
1997	59.5	54.1	59.9	73.9	76.3	77.9	76.6	51.5	8.6
1998	59.4	55.4	59.7	74.3	76.3	76.9	76.6	51.6	8.7
1999	59.6	54.5	59.9	73.9	76.0	77.1	77.1	52.0	8.9
2000	59.5	54.5	59.9	74.5	75.7	77.2	77.5	52.4	9.4
2001	59.4	52.4	59.9	74.2	75.1	77.0	77.1	53.8	9.6
2002	59.3	50.8	60.0	74.0	75.0	76.3	76.6	55.8	9.9
2003	59.2	47.9	59.9	72.7	73.7	75.5	77.3	57.4	10.8
2004	58.9	46.7	59.7	71.9	73.6	75.2	77.1	57.0	11.2
2005	58.9	47.6	59.7	71.0	73.7	75.4	76.7	57.5	11.4
2006	59.0	46.6	59.9	70.9	74.3	75.5	76.7	58.7	11.6
2007	59.0	44.6	60.1	71.6	74.5	75.0	76.6	58.9	12.7
2008	59.2	43.3	60.3	71.6	74.9	75.8	76.6	59.7	13.3
2009	59.1	40.9	60.4	71.6	75.1	75.7	76.7	60.8	13.6
2010	58.5	38.0	59.9	69.7	74.9	75.0	76.3	61.1	13.9
2011	58.0	37.5	59.4	69.1	74.2	74.4	76.1	60.6	14.1
2012	57.4	37.1	58.7	69.0	74.3	74.5	75.2	60.5	14.4
2013	56.9	37.2	58.2	69.2	73.9	73.9	74.7	59.9	14.9
2014	56.7	36.8	57.9	69.5	74.5	74.0	74.3	57.2	14.5
2015	56.2	36.1	57.5	69.8	73.8	73.9	73.9	59.3	15.2
2016	56.3	36.7	57.6	69.3	74.8	74.2	74.5	59.3	15.6
2017	56.4	37.1	57.6	69.7	75.9	74.5	74.6	59.8	15.6
2018	56.4	38.1	57.6	70.5	76.2	74.7	75.0	60.0	15.7
2019	56.8	37.6	57.9	71.4	77.1	75.6	75.9	60.2	16.2

Table 1-8. Civilian Labor Force Participation Rates, by Age, Sex, Race, and Hispanic Origin, 1948–2019
—*Continued*

(Percent.)

Race, Hispanic origin, sex, and year	16 years and over	16 to 19 years	20 years and over						
			Total	20 to 24 years	25 to 34 years	35 to 44 years	45 to 54 years	55 to 64 years	65 years and over
BLACK									
Both Sexes									
1985	62.9	41.2	65.6	70.0	79.8	81.5	73.4	51.4	11.2
1986	63.3	41.3	65.9	71.7	80.1	81.9	74.3	50.6	9.7
1987	63.8	41.6	66.5	70.5	80.7	82.6	74.7	52.4	10.7
1988	63.8	40.8	66.5	70.5	80.8	82.6	75.0	50.6	11.5
1989	64.2	42.5	66.7	72.2	80.9	82.7	75.5	48.3	11.6
1990	64.0	38.7	66.9	68.8	79.7	82.4	76.5	49.6	11.1
1991	63.3	35.4	66.4	67.7	78.5	82.0	76.2	50.4	10.7
1992	63.9	37.9	66.8	67.4	79.7	81.4	76.2	51.6	10.6
1993	63.2	37.0	66.0	67.8	78.3	81.0	75.2	50.2	9.5
1994	63.4	38.5	66.0	68.8	78.3	80.8	74.8	49.3	10.6
1995	63.7	39.9	66.3	68.7	80.0	80.4	74.1	50.3	10.5
1996	64.1	39.2	66.9	69.0	81.1	81.0	74.9	50.9	9.8
1997	64.7	38.7	67.6	70.9	82.0	81.4	76.3	50.5	10.0
1998	65.6	41.6	68.2	70.6	83.0	82.2	76.7	52.3	10.3
1999	65.8	38.7	68.9	71.4	85.2	83.0	76.4	51.4	10.4
2000	65.8	39.4	68.7	71.8	84.1	82.3	76.9	52.5	11.6
2001	65.3	37.6	68.2	69.9	83.6	82.0	75.9	53.9	12.6
2002	64.8	36.0	67.8	68.6	82.4	81.6	76.1	54.7	12.5
2003	64.3	32.4	67.6	68.2	81.6	82.9	75.8	54.4	12.9
2004	63.8	31.4	67.2	68.3	81.2	82.1	75.5	54.4	13.1
2005	64.2	32.4	67.4	69.0	81.7	82.3	75.7	55.3	13.6
2006	64.1	34.0	67.3	68.8	81.8	82.0	75.8	55.4	13.7
2007	63.7	30.3	67.2	68.3	81.7	82.7	75.7	55.1	14.0
2008	63.7	29.4	67.4	68.0	82.2	83.0	76.1	55.6	15.0
2009	62.4	27.2	66.1	66.0	80.4	81.7	75.2	55.5	15.3
2010	62.2	25.5	66.0	66.9	80.5	81.4	75.0	55.7	15.2
2011	61.4	24.9	65.0	66.5	79.1	80.6	73.9	54.5	16.1
2012	61.5	26.9	64.9	66.5	79.4	80.7	74.5	55.3	16.4
2013	61.2	28.0	64.2	65.3	78.5	80.7	74.1	55.6	16.2
2014	61.2	27.2	64.2	66.6	79.1	80.5	74.6	55.3	16.1
2015	61.5	28.1	64.4	68.2	79.4	80.8	75.3	54.8	16.9
2016	61.6	29.0	64.4	67.7	80.3	81.2	75.1	55.1	16.6
2017	62.3	30.0	65.0	69.2	80.8	82.3	76.2	55.6	17.8
2018	62.3	30.5	64.9	68.5	80.9	82.1	77.0	56.5	17.7
2019	62.5	30.1	65.1	70.4	80.5	80.9	78.5	57.0	18.6
Men									
1985	70.8	44.6	74.4	79.0	88.8	89.8	83.0	58.9	13.9
1986	71.2	43.7	74.8	80.1	89.6	89.6	84.1	59.1	12.6
1987	71.1	43.6	74.7	77.8	89.4	88.6	83.7	62.1	13.7
1988	71.0	43.8	74.6	79.3	89.3	88.2	83.5	59.4	14.3
1989	71.0	44.6	74.4	80.2	89.7	88.7	82.5	55.5	14.3
1990	71.0	40.7	75.0	76.8	88.8	88.1	83.5	58.0	13.0
1991	70.4	37.3	74.6	76.7	87.3	87.7	83.4	58.7	13.0
1992	70.7	40.6	74.3	75.4	88.0	86.5	81.8	60.0	13.7
1993	69.6	39.5	73.2	74.1	87.3	86.1	80.0	57.9	11.6
1994	69.1	40.8	72.5	73.9	86.2	85.9	79.1	54.5	12.7
1995	69.0	40.1	72.5	74.6	87.5	84.1	78.5	54.4	14.9
1996	68.7	39.5	72.3	73.4	87.5	84.4	78.5	55.6	12.9
1997	68.3	37.4	72.2	72.1	86.8	84.8	80.1	54.3	12.9
1998	69.0	40.7	72.5	71.8	87.1	85.0	79.9	57.3	14.0
1999	68.7	38.6	72.4	69.8	89.2	86.0	78.5	55.5	12.7
2000	69.2	39.2	72.8	73.3	87.8	85.2	79.2	57.4	14.4
2001	68.4	37.9	72.1	69.7	86.6	84.9	78.4	58.9	16.7
2002	68.4	37.3	72.1	70.7	85.9	84.7	79.5	58.4	16.9
2003	67.3	31.1	71.5	71.1	84.7	85.7	77.7	57.6	17.0
2004	66.7	30.0	70.9	69.9	86.1	84.0	76.9	57.1	17.0
2005	67.3	32.6	71.3	70.1	85.5	85.5	78.6	57.3	17.1
2006	67.0	32.3	71.1	71.6	85.7	84.4	79.2	55.9	16.7
2007	66.8	29.4	71.2	71.1	86.1	86.3	78.6	54.4	17.3
2008	66.7	29.1	71.1	71.1	85.3	86.8	79.1	56.1	18.1
2009	65.0	26.4	69.6	67.6	83.2	85.1	77.4	56.8	18.3
2010	65.0	25.8	69.5	66.9	83.4	86.1	77.4	56.8	18.1
2011	64.2	25.7	68.4	67.0	82.6	83.7	76.1	55.9	19.1
2012	63.6	25.6	67.7	66.4	82.5	83.5	75.9	57.1	19.4
2013	63.5	27.2	67.2	66.2	82.0	84.1	75.5	56.8	18.5
2014	63.6	25.9	67.3	67.9	82.5	83.3	76.4	57.0	18.4
2015	63.8	26.3	67.3	68.9	82.1	83.1	77.4	56.5	18.9
2016	64.1	28.1	67.5	67.3	82.7	84.2	77.1	58.0	19.6
2017	64.6	27.6	68.1	69.4	83.0	85.0	77.6	58.4	20.4
2018	64.8	29.6	68.0	68.1	83.6	85.0	79.2	58.9	19.2
2019	64.8	27.5	68.1	70.9	83.3	83.4	81.4	57.8	20.5

Table 1-8. Civilian Labor Force Participation Rates, by Age, Sex, Race, and Hispanic Origin, 1948–2019
—Continued

(Percent.)

Race, Hispanic origin, sex, and year	16 years and over	16 to 19 years	20 years and over						
			Total	20 to 24 years	25 to 34 years	35 to 44 years	45 to 54 years	55 to 64 years	65 years and over
BLACK									
Women									
1985	56.5	37.9	58.6	62.5	72.4	74.8	65.7	45.3	9.4
1986	56.9	39.1	58.9	64.6	72.4	75.8	66.5	43.6	7.8
1987	58.0	39.6	60.0	64.4	73.5	77.8	67.5	44.4	8.6
1988	58.0	37.9	60.1	63.2	73.7	78.1	68.3	43.4	9.6
1989	58.7	40.4	60.6	65.5	73.6	78.0	70.0	42.4	9.8
1990	58.3	36.8	60.6	62.4	72.3	77.7	70.7	43.2	9.9
1991	57.5	33.5	60.0	60.3	71.4	77.2	70.2	44.1	9.2
1992	58.5	35.2	60.8	60.8	73.1	77.1	71.7	45.1	8.6
1993	57.9	34.6	60.2	62.6	70.9	76.8	71.2	44.4	8.3
1994	58.7	36.3	60.9	64.5	71.9	76.4	71.3	45.3	9.2
1995	59.5	39.8	61.4	63.7	73.9	77.3	70.5	47.2	7.7
1996	60.4	38.9	62.6	65.2	75.9	78.2	72.0	47.2	7.7
1997	61.7	39.9	64.0	69.9	78.1	78.4	73.2	47.6	8.2
1998	62.8	42.5	64.8	69.6	79.6	79.9	74.0	48.5	7.9
1999	63.5	38.8	66.1	72.7	82.1	80.4	74.6	48.4	8.9
2000	63.1	39.6	65.4	70.5	81.1	79.9	74.9	48.6	9.9
2001	62.8	37.3	65.2	70.1	81.2	79.6	73.9	49.9	10.1
2002	61.8	34.7	64.4	66.9	79.7	79.2	73.3	51.8	9.8
2003	61.9	33.7	64.6	65.7	79.1	80.6	74.2	51.9	10.3
2004	61.5	32.8	64.2	66.8	77.2	80.6	74.3	52.3	10.7
2005	61.6	32.2	64.4	68.1	78.5	79.7	73.3	53.7	11.4
2006	61.7	35.6	64.2	66.2	78.6	80.1	73.0	55.1	11.8
2007	61.1	31.2	64.0	65.7	78.0	79.8	73.2	55.7	12.0
2008	61.3	29.7	64.3	65.2	79.6	80.0	73.7	55.3	13.0
2009	60.3	27.9	63.4	64.5	78.0	79.0	73.3	54.4	13.3
2010	59.9	25.1	63.2	66.9	77.9	77.7	73.0	54.9	13.3
2011	59.1	24.2	62.2	65.9	76.0	78.2	72.0	53.4	14.2
2012	59.8	28.2	62.6	66.5	76.9	78.4	73.3	53.9	14.4
2013	59.2	28.7	61.8	64.4	75.5	78.0	72.9	54.6	14.7
2014	59.2	28.4	61.6	65.4	76.2	78.2	73.2	53.8	14.6
2015	59.7	29.9	62.0	67.6	77.0	78.9	73.5	53.4	15.6
2016	59.4	30.0	61.8	68.0	78.1	78.7	73.4	52.7	14.6
2017	60.3	32.4	62.5	69.0	78.8	80.0	75.1	53.2	16.1
2018	60.2	31.4	62.4	68.9	78.5	79.7	75.1	54.5	16.6
2019	60.5	32.7	62.5	70.0	78.1	78.9	76.0	56.4	17.2
HISPANIC									
Both Sexes									
1985	64.6	44.6	69.0	. . .	. . .	. . .	. . .	. . .	. . .
1986	65.4	43.9	67.1	. . .	. . .	. . .	. . .	. . .	. . .
1987	66.4	45.8	69.0	. . .	. . .	. . .	. . .	. . .	. . .
1988	67.4	49.6	73.6	. . .	. . .	. . .	. . .	. . .	. . .
1989	67.6	48.6	71.9	. . .	. . .	. . .	. . .	. . .	. . .
1990	67.4	47.8	70.9	. . .	. . .	. . .	. . .	. . .	. . .
1991	66.5	45.1	67.8	. . .	. . .	. . .	. . .	. . .	. . .
1992	66.8	45.8	68.6	. . .	. . .	. . .	. . .	. . .	. . .
1993	66.2	43.9	66.3	. . .	. . .	. . .	. . .	. . .	. . .
1994	66.1	44.4	67.2	74.0	77.3	78.9	73.1	49.8	10.7
1995	65.8	45.4	69.0	71.9	78.1	78.5	72.8	48.6	10.5
1996	66.5	43.4	65.3	73.1	78.2	79.5	74.6	52.2	11.0
1997	67.9	43.0	63.3	76.4	79.5	80.9	75.4	53.8	11.9
1998	67.9	45.7	67.3	76.1	80.3	80.0	75.3	55.4	10.1
1999	67.7	45.5	67.2	76.0	78.6	81.3	75.9	54.1	11.6
2000	69.7	46.3	66.4	78.2	80.4	81.7	78.0	54.2	12.3
2001	69.5	46.9	67.5	76.6	80.0	81.9	77.4	55.1	10.9
2002	69.1	44.0	63.7	76.3	80.5	81.1	76.1	55.8	11.9
2003	68.3	37.7	55.2	75.6	79.4	81.1	75.3	57.4	12.8
2004	68.6	38.2	55.7	74.5	79.4	81.4	77.6	58.1	14.5
2005	68.0	38.6	56.8	72.7	79.1	81.2	77.2	58.4	13.9
2006	68.7	38.3	55.7	74.4	80.1	81.9	77.3	59.2	15.7
2007	68.8	37.1	53.9	74.8	80.7	81.8	78.6	58.5	16.0
2008	68.5	36.9	53.9	73.7	80.5	82.0	78.2	59.9	16.0
2009	68.0	34.0	50.0	73.1	79.5	81.3	79.3	61.9	17.1
2010	67.5	30.9	45.8	71.1	80.6	81.2	79.2	61.1	17.9
2011	66.5	28.3	42.6	72.0	79.1	80.3	78.9	60.8	17.6
2012	66.4	30.9	46.5	71.2	79.1	80.2	78.4	60.5	16.5
2013	66.0	31.0	47.0	71.7	78.3	79.5	78.1	61.0	17.0
2014	66.1	30.3	69.8	71.4	78.8	79.9	78.3	61.7	17.0
2015	65.9	30.9	69.6	71.6	78.3	79.5	78.3	62.7	17.2
2016	65.8	31.2	69.4	71.8	78.9	79.6	78.0	61.7	18.1
2017	66.1	31.9	69.6	71.0	79.3	80.5	77.9	63.0	18.8
2018	66.3	32.5	69.7	71.6	80.0	80.4	78.4	63.6	18.6
2019	66.8	32.2	70.3	73.0	80.3	80.5	79.3	65.4	19.5

. . . = Not available.

Table 1-8. Civilian Labor Force Participation Rates, by Age, Sex, Race, and Hispanic Origin, 1948–2019
    —*Continued*

(Percent.)

Race, Hispanic origin, sex, and year	16 years and over	16 to 19 years	20 years and over						
			Total	20 to 24 years	25 to 34 years	35 to 44 years	45 to 54 years	55 to 64 years	65 years and over
HISPANIC									
Men									
1985	80.3	...	84.0	...	...	...	...	...	...
1986	81.0	...	84.6	...	...	...	...	...	...
1987	81.0	...	84.5	...	...	...	...	...	...
1988	81.9	...	85.0	...	...	...	...	...	...
1989	82.0	...	85.0	...	...	...	...	...	...
1990	81.4	...	84.7	...	...	...	...	...	...
1991	80.3	...	83.8	...	...	...	...	...	...
1992	80.7	...	84.0	...	...	...	...	...	...
1993	80.2	...	83.5	...	...	...	...	...	...
1994	79.2	50.0	82.5	88.0	92.5	91.5	85.7	63.6	14.4
1995	79.1	50.2	82.4	86.2	92.9	91.3	85.6	62.4	15.8
1996	79.6	50.0	83.0	85.7	93.2	91.7	87.0	65.9	16.7
1997	80.1	47.4	84.1	88.1	93.5	91.9	87.8	68.4	17.3
1998	79.8	48.7	83.6	88.1	94.0	91.4	86.7	70.2	14.9
1999	79.8	50.1	83.5	88.1	93.9	92.2	86.2	68.6	18.2
2000	81.5	50.7	85.3	89.1	94.1	93.3	87.6	69.4	18.5
2001	81.0	52.2	84.3	86.8	93.4	92.7	86.7	68.6	16.8
2002	80.2	48.8	83.6	86.1	93.5	92.1	86.1	67.3	16.3
2003	80.1	40.9	84.1	86.2	93.6	92.9	85.4	68.8	17.4
2004	80.4	42.4	84.2	84.4	93.6	93.2	87.2	69.6	20.8
2005	80.1	41.9	84.0	84.1	93.3	93.1	87.7	69.3	20.1
2006	80.7	42.0	84.6	85.9	94.1	93.8	87.1	69.6	22.9
2007	80.5	40.0	84.7	85.3	94.1	93.9	88.3	70.3	22.0
2008	80.2	40.3	84.4	84.3	94.0	93.7	88.6	71.7	21.7
2009	78.8	36.4	83.2	82.3	91.9	93.0	88.8	71.7	23.0
2010	77.8	33.2	82.6	80.0	92.7	92.9	87.8	69.0	24.5
2011	76.5	30.1	81.7	79.5	91.6	92.4	87.3	69.9	23.3
2012	76.1	33.0	81.0	78.5	91.6	91.1	87.3	70.3	21.1
2013	76.3	32.8	81.1	78.6	91.0	91.9	87.8	70.7	23.1
2014	76.1	31.2	81.0	77.9	90.5	92.9	87.8	72.9	21.9
2015	76.2	32.4	80.9	77.3	90.9	92.6	88.3	73.9	22.2
2016	76.0	32.3	80.5	77.1	90.5	92.5	88.6	72.4	23.8
2017	75.8	31.6	80.5	77.0	90.1	92.7	88.6	73.5	24.9
2018	75.7	32.5	80.2	76.6	89.6	92.8	88.2	74.8	24.6
2019	75.9	33.7	80.2	77.1	89.4	92.6	88.9	75.9	25.4
HISPANIC									
Women									
1985	49.3	50.6	50.6	...	...	...	...	...	...
1986	50.1	51.7	51.7	...	...	...	...	...	...
1987	52.0	53.3	53.3	...	...	...	...	...	...
1988	53.2	54.2	54.2	...	...	...	...	...	...
1989	53.5	54.9	54.9	...	...	...	...	...	...
1990	53.1	54.8	54.8	...	...	...	...	...	...
1991	52.4	54.0	54.0	...	...	...	...	...	...
1992	52.8	54.3	54.3	...	...	...	...	...	...
1993	52.1	53.8	53.8	...	...	...	...	...	...
1994	52.9	54.4	54.4	57.9	60.5	66.4	61.4	38.1	7.9
1995	52.6	53.9	53.9	55.9	61.6	65.9	60.5	37.2	6.6
1996	53.4	55.2	55.2	59.2	62.0	67.0	62.7	40.5	6.9
1997	55.1	57.0	57.0	62.3	63.7	69.3	63.3	40.6	8.1
1998	55.6	57.1	57.1	62.2	64.5	67.9	64.7	41.9	6.6
1999	55.9	57.7	57.7	63.0	62.7	70.5	66.2	42.4	6.5
2000	57.5	59.3	59.3	65.0	65.3	69.9	68.5	41.2	7.7
2001	57.6	59.3	59.3	64.6	65.2	70.3	68.3	43.2	6.7
2002	57.6	59.5	59.5	65.0	65.8	69.5	66.3	46.1	8.5
2003	55.9	58.1	58.1	63.3	62.9	68.5	65.3	47.1	9.4
2004	56.1	58.4	58.4	62.9	62.9	68.7	67.9	47.8	9.8
2005	55.3	57.4	57.4	59.4	62.4	68.2	66.6	48.4	9.3
2006	56.1	58.3	58.3	61.3	63.5	68.7	67.4	49.7	10.4
2007	56.5	58.8	58.8	62.9	64.6	68.4	68.7	47.6	11.4
2008	56.2	58.6	58.6	62.1	64.3	69.1	67.6	48.9	11.7
2009	56.5	59.2	59.2	63.2	64.7	68.2	69.4	52.6	12.7
2010	56.5	59.5	59.5	61.6	66.3	67.9	70.2	53.7	13.0
2011	55.9	59.0	59.0	63.0	64.5	67.1	70.4	52.3	13.2
2012	56.6	59.5	59.5	63.3	65.6	69.0	69.4	51.4	13.2
2013	55.7	58.5	58.5	64.3	64.5	66.9	68.4	52.0	12.5
2014	56.0	29.3	58.7	64.5	66.1	66.4	68.8	51.3	13.3
2015	55.7	29.3	58.4	65.8	64.9	66.2	68.3	52.2	13.4
2016	55.8	30.0	58.4	66.4	66.5	66.3	67.3	51.6	13.8
2017	56.4	32.1	58.9	64.7	67.9	67.9	67.1	53.2	14.2
2018	57.0	32.5	59.4	66.5	69.8	67.6	68.6	53.1	13.9
2019	57.7	30.6	60.4	68.8	70.7	68.0	69.7	55.4	14.9

. . . = Not available.

Table 1-9. Employed and Unemployed Full- and Part-Time Workers, by Age, Sex, and Race, 2005–2019

(Thousands of people.)

Race, sex, age, and year	Employed[1]								Unemployed	
	Full-time workers				Part-time workers					
		At work				At work[2]				
	Total	35 hours or more	1 to 34 hours for economic or noneconomic reasons	Not at work	Total	For economic reasons	For noneconomic reasons	Not at work	Looking for full-time work	Looking for part-time work
ALL RACES										
Both Sexes, 16 Years and Over										
2005	117 016	103 044	9 983	3 990	24 714	2 963	20 229	1 522	6 175	1 415
2006	119 688	105 328	10 223	4 137	24 739	2 774	20 356	1 609	5 675	1 326
2007	121 091	106 990	9 976	4 125	24 956	2 851	20 511	1 594	5 789	1 289
2008	120 030	105 575	10 426	4 030	25 332	3 814	20 009	1 509	7 446	1 478
2009	112 634	95 911	12 853	3 870	27 244	6 353	19 327	1 563	12 523	1 741
2010	111 714	97 946	10 217	3 551	27 350	6 965	18 876	1 509	12 970	1 854
2011	112 556	98 976	10 047	3 534	27 313	6 872	18 984	1 525	11 914	1 833
2012	114 809	101 877	9 324	3 607	27 661	6 626	19 509	1 525	10 699	1 807
2013	116 314	104 069	8 756	3 489	27 615	6 479	19 621	1 514	9 726	1 733
2014	118 718	105 416	9 772	3 531	27 587	5 904	20 185	1 498	8 055	1 561
2015	121 492	106 611	11 263	3 618	27 341	5 143	20 750	1 448	6 888	1 409
2016	123 761	110 540	9 507	3 713	27 675	4 684	21 421	1 571	6 345	1 406
2017	125 967	111 686	10 295	3 987	27 370	4 104	21 646	1 620	5 649	1 334
2018	128 572	115 402	9 357	3 814	27 189	3 564	22 072	1 553	6 314	1 262
2019	130 597	117 625	9 233	3 738	26 941	3 207	22 175	1 560	4 843	1 157
Both Sexes, 20 Years and Over										
2005	115 206	101 534	9 729	3 942	20 546	2 698	16 489	1 359	5 619	786
2006	117 844	103 779	9 974	4 090	20 421	2 510	16 478	1 433	5 117	765
2007	119 317	105 499	9 738	4 080	20 819	2 587	16 819	1 413	5 234	742
2008	118 404	104 212	10 204	3 989	21 385	3 492	16 543	1 350	6 790	849
2009	111 414	94 928	12 647	3 839	23 626	5 934	16 286	1 406	11 651	1 061
2010	110 622	97 037	10 057	3 528	24 064	6 552	16 138	1 373	12 155	1 142
2011	111 500	98 103	9 888	3 508	24 043	6 457	16 259	1 327	11 180	1 167
2012	113 667	100 919	9 167	3 582	24 376	6 240	16 750	1 385	9 968	1 141
2013	115 106	103 041	8 601	3 464	24 365	6 103	16 877	1 386	9 043	1 090
2014	117 514	104 403	9 604	3 506	24 244	5 551	17 334	1 358	7 503	1 008
2015	120 199	105 523	11 088	3 588	23 901	4 822	17 771	1 308	6 378	953
2016	122 363	109 351	9 332	3 681	24 108	4 399	18 279	1 430	5 881	945
2017	124 525	110 459	10 112	3 953	23 739	3 842	18 439	1 459	5 261	894
2018	127 095	114 129	9 184	3 781	23 540	3 320	18 822	1 398	4 697	858
2019	129 072	116 305	9 059	3 708	23 316	2 966	18 947	1 404	4 487	768
Men, 16 Years and Over										
2005	67 858	60 825	5 096	1 937	8 115	1 316	6 370	429	3 444	616
2006	69 307	62 087	5 237	1 984	8 194	1 232	6 510	452	3 192	561
2007	70 035	62 965	5 095	1 975	8 220	1 319	6 424	477	3 326	556
2008	68 853	61 436	5 443	1 974	8 634	1 842	6 349	442	4 396	637
2009	63 951	55 317	6 772	1 862	9 719	3 035	6 170	514	7 696	757
2010	63 501	56 425	5 352	1 723	9 858	3 316	6 066	476	7 827	799
2011	64 333	57 413	5 189	1 731	9 957	3 262	6 216	479	6 903	781
2012	65 477	58 956	4 803	1 719	10 078	3 089	6 491	498	5 988	784
2013	66 335	60 112	4 531	1 692	10 017	2 985	6 526	507	5 563	752
2014	67 829	61 128	5 004	1 697	9 863	2 712	6 663	487	4 516	674
2015	69 351	61 892	5 737	1 722	9 780	2 368	6 927	485	3 888	602
2016	70 567	63 943	4 841	1 782	10 002	2 194	7 305	502	3 607	580
2017	71 571	64 472	5 189	1 910	9 831	1 914	7 392	525	3 174	569
2018	72 935	66 314	4 774	1 847	9 764	1 650	7 587	527	2 877	521
2019	73 824	67 313	4 694	1 816	9 637	1 514	7 622	501	2 730	496
Men, 20 Years and Over										
2005	66 803	59 934	4 955	1 914	6 247	1 182	4 705	360	3 118	274
2006	68 193	61 140	5 095	1 958	6 238	1 100	4 762	376	2 861	270
2007	68 968	62 057	4 959	1 952	6 369	1 190	4 782	397	2 990	268
2008	67 895	60 625	5 315	1 955	6 855	1 675	4 802	378	3 994	303
2009	63 242	54 738	6 659	1 845	8 099	2 827	4 828	445	7 151	404
2010	62 854	55 887	5 258	1 710	8 376	3 102	4 857	417	7 336	427
2011	63 690	56 870	5 104	1 715	8 492	3 059	5 010	423	6 461	437
2012	64 810	58 386	4 719	1 705	8 593	2 883	5 271	439	5 547	437
2013	65 631	59 504	4 448	1 679	8 545	2 797	5 301	447	5 144	424
2014	67 093	60 498	4 911	1 684	8 378	2 532	5 422	424	4 192	393
2015	68 588	61 240	5 642	1 706	8 189	2 200	5 570	419	3 594	365
2016	69 747	63 242	4 740	1 765	8 337	2 039	5 857	441	3 329	346
2017	70 729	63 750	5 087	1 892	8 190	1 779	5 962	449	2 941	346
2018	72 061	65 556	4 678	1 828	8 150	1 525	6 162	463	2 658	318
2019	72 936	66 537	4 600	1 799	7 982	1 381	6 173	428	2 522	297

[1]Employed persons are classified as full- or part-time workers based on their usual weekly hours at all jobs, regardless of the number of hours they were at work during the reference week. Persons absent from work are also classified according to their usual status.
[2]Includes some persons at work 35 hours or more classified by their reason for working part time.

Table 1-9. Employed and Unemployed Full- and Part-Time Workers, by Age, Sex, and Race, 2005–2019
—*Continued*

(Thousands of people.)

Race, sex, age, and year	Employed[1]								Unemployed	
	Full-time workers				Part-time workers					
		At work				At work[2]				
	Total	35 hours or more	1 to 34 hours for economic or noneconomic reasons	Not at work	Total	For economic reasons	For noneconomic reasons	Not at work	Looking for full-time work	Looking for part-time work

ALL RACES—*Continued*

Women, 16 Years and Over

2005	49 158	42 219	4 887	2 052	16 598	1 647	13 859	1 092	2 732	799
2006	50 380	43 241	4 986	2 153	16 545	1 542	13 846	1 157	2 483	764
2007	51 056	44 025	4 881	2 150	16 736	1 532	14 087	1 117	2 463	732
2008	51 178	44 139	4 983	2 056	16 698	1 972	13 660	1 067	3 050	841
2009	48 683	40 594	6 080	2 009	17 525	3 318	13 157	1 050	4 827	984
2010	48 214	41 521	4 865	1 828	17 491	3 648	12 810	1 033	5 144	1 055
2011	48 224	41 563	4 858	1 802	17 355	3 610	12 767	977	5 011	1 052
2012	49 331	42 921	4 521	1 888	17 583	3 538	13 018	1 026	4 711	1 023
2013	49 979	43 957	4 225	1 797	17 598	3 495	13 095	1 008	4 164	982
2014	50 889	44 287	4 768	1 834	17 724	3 192	13 521	1 011	3 539	887
2015	52 142	44 719	5 527	1 896	17 561	2 775	13 823	963	3 000	807
2016	53 194	46 597	4 666	1 931	17 674	2 490	14 115	1 069	2 739	826
2017	54 396	47 214	5 105	2 077	17 539	2 190	14 254	1 095	2 474	765
2018	55 638	49 088	4 583	1 966	17 425	1 914	14 485	1 026	2 175	741
2019	56 773	50 313	4 539	1 922	17 304	1 693	14 553	1 059	2 113	661

Women, 20 Years and Over

2005	48 403	41 600	4 774	2 028	14 299	1 516	11 784	999	2 501	512
2006	49 651	42 639	4 880	2 132	14 183	1 410	11 716	1 057	2 256	495
2007	50 349	43 442	4 779	2 128	14 450	1 397	12 037	1 016	2 244	474
2008	50 509	43 587	4 888	2 034	14 530	1 817	11 740	973	2 796	546
2009	48 171	40 190	5 988	1 994	15 527	3 107	11 459	961	4 500	657
2010	47 767	41 150	4 799	1 818	15 688	3 450	11 282	956	4 819	715
2011	47 810	41 233	4 784	1 792	15 551	3 398	11 249	904	4 719	730
2012	48 857	42 533	4 448	1 877	15 783	3 358	11 480	946	4 420	704
2013	49 475	43 537	4 153	1 785	15 820	3 306	11 575	939	3 900	665
2014	50 421	43 905	4 693	1 823	15 865	3 019	11 912	934	3 311	615
2015	51 611	44 284	5 446	1 881	15 712	2 622	12 201	889	2 784	588
2016	52 616	46 109	4 591	555	15 770	2 360	12 422	989	2 553	599
2017	53 796	46 709	5 025	2 061	15 549	2 062	12 477	1 010	2 320	548
2018	55 033	48 574	4 506	1 953	15 390	1 795	12 660	935	2 039	540
2019	56 136	49 768	4 458	1 909	15 335	1 585	12 774	976	1 965	470

WHITE[3]

Men, 16 Years and Over

2005	56 955	50 965	4 334	1 656	6 808	1 014	5 424	370	2 459	471
2006	58 063	51 894	4 484	1 685	6 820	947	5 481	393	2 299	432
2007	58 494	52 460	4 359	1 676	6 795	1 022	5 368	406	2 444	425
2008	57 432	51 104	4 653	1 675	7 192	1 433	5 379	379	3 235	492
2009	53 506	46 153	5 770	1 583	8 124	2 438	5 240	446	5 819	602
2010	53 086	47 055	4 554	1 477	8 166	2 662	5 102	402	5 832	644
2011	53 727	47 865	4 397	1 465	8 193	2 560	5 227	405	5 020	611
2012	53 857	48 409	4 009	1 439	8 133	2 383	5 334	416	4 330	600
2013	54 263	49 091	3 775	1 397	8 059	2 281	5 357	421	3 941	579
2014	55 281	49 766	4 107	1 408	7 827	2 027	5 402	399	3 086	486
2015	56 176	50 088	4 673	1 415	7 716	1 752	5 567	397	2 678	448
2016	56 735	51 333	3 941	1 460	7 877	1 598	5 873	407	2 526	426
2017	57 296	51 552	4 202	1 543	7 704	1 386	5 890	427	2 176	416
2018	58 015	52 678	3 849	1 487	7 687	1 183	6 083	421	1 998	383
2019	58 541	53 319	3 773	1 449	7 560	1 079	6 074	407	1 882	384

Men, 20 Years and Over

2005	56 050	50 203	4 213	1 634	5 205	905	3 990	310	2 242	209
2006	57 108	51 081	4 365	1 662	5 150	840	3 987	324	2 074	208
2007	57 591	51 691	4 243	1 656	5 216	915	3 967	334	2 204	204
2008	56 623	50 421	4 542	1 660	5 681	1 302	4 055	324	2 944	235
2009	52 899	45 654	5 676	1 569	6 728	2 269	4 075	384	5 421	325
2010	52 530	46 592	4 472	1 466	6 907	2 484	4 071	352	5 481	347
2011	53 186	47 406	4 328	1 451	6 933	2 392	4 184	357	4 702	344
2012	53 302	47 934	3 941	1 427	6 891	2 218	4 306	367	4 014	333
2013	53 660	48 569	3 706	1 386	6 850	2 132	4 349	370	3 657	337
2014	54 671	49 249	4 026	1 395	6 619	1 889	4 382	348	2 855	286
2015	55 533	49 536	4 593	1 403	6 426	1 622	4 460	345	2 480	271
2016	56 071	50 764	3 861	1 447	6 504	1 480	4 668	356	2 344	250
2017	56 620	50 967	4 123	1 530	6 388	1 293	4 730	365	2 028	259
2018	57 312	52 068	3 775	1 470	6 406	1 093	4 944	369	1 858	235
2019	57 838	52 704	3 700	1 434	6 231	980	4 903	348	1 739	228

[1]Employed persons are classified as full- or part-time workers based on their usual weekly hours at all jobs, regardless of the number of hours they were at work during the reference week. Persons absent from work are also classified according to their usual status.
[2]Includes some persons at work 35 hours or more classified by their reason for working part time.
[3]Beginning in 2003, persons who selected this race group only; persons who selected more than one race group are not included. Prior to 2003, persons who reported more than one race group were included in the group they identified as their main race.

Table 1-9. Employed and Unemployed Full- and Part-Time Workers, by Age, Sex, and Race, 2005–2019
—Continued

(Thousands of people.)

Race, sex, age, and year	Employed[1]								Unemployed	
	Full-time workers				Part-time workers					
		At work				At work[2]				
	Total	35 hours or more	1 to 34 hours for economic or noneconomic reasons	Not at work	Total	For economic reasons	For noneconomic reasons	Not at work	Looking for full-time work	Looking for part-time work

WHITE[3]—Continued

Women, 16 Years and Over
2005	38 973	33 325	3 976	1 672	14 213	1 207	12 043	963	1 807	612
2006	39 813	33 980	4 082	1 751	14 137	1 157	11 967	1 013	1 670	601
2007	40 238	34 486	4 014	1 738	14 265	1 143	12 148	973	1 694	579
2008	40 292	34 569	4 076	1 647	14 209	1 518	11 761	931	2 119	664
2009	38 456	31 885	4 946	1 626	14 910	2 579	11 418	913	3 442	785
2010	38 158	32 710	3 958	1 490	14 758	2 846	11 029	883	3 612	828
2011	38 152	32 731	3 944	1 477	14 618	2 775	10 994	850	3 450	807
2012	38 362	33 244	3 614	1 504	14 416	2 674	10 875	867	3 191	794
2013	38 629	33 870	3 329	1 430	14 428	2 605	10 986	837	2 756	757
2014	39 241	22 994	3 770	1 477	14 439	2 345	11 242	852	2 304	664
2015	39 823	34 038	4 311	1 474	14 228	2 035	11 395	798	1 945	592
2016	40 477	35 331	3 640	1 506	14 225	1 784	11 560	881	1 781	613
2017	41 145	35 554	3 961	1 630	14 031	1 554	11 571	905	1 593	580
2018	41 825	36 781	3 541	1 504	13 934	1 363	11 740	831	1 414	560
2019	42 523	37 525	3 514	1 484	13 817	1 192	11 752	873	1 391	502

Women, 20 Years and Over
2005	38 354	32 820	3 882	1 652	12 235	1 108	10 248	879	1 653	401
2006	39 232	33 500	3 998	1 733	12 128	1 050	10 151	927	1 524	402
2007	39 670	34 015	3 932	1 722	12 326	1 037	10 402	887	1 547	383
2008	39 765	34 128	4 005	1 632	12 359	1 392	10 116	851	1 949	435
2009	38 033	31 547	4 872	1 614	13 198	2 411	9 952	835	3 216	529
2010	37 789	32 404	3 904	1 481	13 208	2 684	9 705	818	3 389	571
2011	37 816	32 466	3 882	1 468	13 065	2 597	9 683	785	3 255	563
2012	38 362	32 936	3 556	1 497	12 923	2 533	9 591	799	3 009	555
2013	38 233	33 544	3 269	1 420	12 964	2 462	9 719	783	2 586	516
2014	39 241	33 994	3 770	1 477	14 439	2 345	11 242	852	2 304	664
2015	39 418	33 707	4 249	1 462	12 743	1 915	10 091	736	1 812	437
2016	40 037	34 955	3 587	1 495	12 733	1 689	10 226	819	1 652	448
2017	40 696	35 177	3 899	1 619	12 484	1 460	10 185	838	1 496	427
2018	41 369	36 395	3 480	1 494	12 313	1 271	10 286	756	1 329	415
2019	42 055	37 128	3 454	1 473	12 249	1 106	10 339	805	1 298	366

BLACK[3]

Men, 16 Years and Over
2005	6 381	5 745	463	174	773	207	533	33	742	102
2006	6 529	5 907	446	176	825	201	590	34	681	93
2007	6 673	6 068	429	176	826	195	589	42	660	92
2008	6 548	5 935	440	173	850	276	542	32	849	100
2009	5 871	5 166	556	150	946	379	530	36	1 348	100
2010	5 856	5 279	446	130	1 009	419	550	41	1 448	102
2011	5 892	5 293	445	154	1 060	452	566	43	1 393	108
2012	6 185	5 579	453	153	1 117	442	629	46	1 169	123
2013	6 331	5 752	423	156	1 166	471	651	44	1 124	112
2014	6 678	6 032	488	158	1 140	442	651	47	973	118
2015	6 974	6 258	553	164	1 190	400	740	50	839	96
2016	7 279	6 616	490	173	1 192	375	764	53	751	94
2017	7 533	6 791	534	209	1 208	336	818	54	673	93
2018	7 899	7 239	463	197	1 119	299	759	61	591	85
2019	8 023	7 353	484	186	1 122	288	783	51	576	69

Men, 20 Years and Over
2005	6 287	5 662	452	174	614	189	397	28	655	44
2006	6 424	5 816	433	175	655	185	441	30	596	44
2007	6 574	5 983	417	174	671	181	452	37	580	43
2008	6 461	5 860	430	171	690	252	409	29	764	46
2009	5 811	5 119	544	148	817	355	428	34	1 238	49
2010	5 803	5 235	439	129	877	392	447	37	1 344	52
2011	5 830	5 242	435	153	935	428	470	38	1 299	61
2012	6 117	5 522	443	152	987	421	526	40	1 081	71
2013	6 279	5 707	416	156	1 025	450	534	41	1 026	56
2014	6 614	5 975	482	158	998	418	539	41	909	64
2015	6 974	6 258	553	164	1 190	400	740	50	839	96
2016	7 192	6 545	476	171	1 036	348	642	47	675	62
2017	7 452	6 724	522	206	1 049	312	688	49	609	53
2018	7 797	7 150	450	197	948	274	619	55	531	51
2019	7 924	7 268	472	184	959	263	654	43	529	41

[1]Employed persons are classified as full- or part-time workers based on their usual weekly hours at all jobs, regardless of the number of hours they were at work during the reference week. Persons absent from work are also classified according to their usual status.
[2]Includes some persons at work 35 hours or more classified by their reason for working part time.
[3]Beginning in 2003, persons who selected this race group only; persons who selected more than one race group are not included. Prior to 2003, persons who reported more than one race group were included in the group they identified as their main race.

Table 1-9. Employed and Unemployed Full- and Part-Time Workers, by Age, Sex, and Race, 2005–2019
—Continued

(Thousands of people.)

Race, sex, age, and year	Employed[1]								Unemployed	
	Full-time workers				Part-time workers				Looking for full-time work	Looking for part-time work
	Total	At work		Not at work	Total	At work[2]		Not at work		
		35 hours or more	1 to 34 hours for economic or noneconomic reasons			For economic reasons	For noneconomic reasons			
BLACK[3]—Continued										
Women, 16 Years and Over										
2005	6 750	5 871	619	260	1 407	320	1 018	70	723	133
2006	7 001	6 131	605	265	1 410	274	1 054	82	655	120
2007	7 119	6 272	584	263	1 432	273	1 085	75	589	104
2008	7 105	6 238	596	272	1 449	302	1 070	77	717	122
2009	6 666	5 696	718	252	1 542	480	984	78	1 027	132
2010	6 525	5 727	582	215	1 621	528	1 010	82	1 142	160
2011	6 450	5 651	592	207	1 648	573	1 004	72	1 165	164
2012	6 750	5 956	557	236	1 803	559	1 157	88	1 099	153
2013	6 868	6 097	553	218	1 786	572	1 128	86	1 043	150
2014	7 063	6 213	626	224	1 852	538	1 229	85	899	151
2015	7 424	6 457	715	252	1 884	504	1 298	82	777	134
2016	7 591	6 722	622	247	1 920	474	1 342	104	674	136
2017	7 901	6 949	684	267	1 945	435	1 413	97	621	113
2018	8 154	7 261	617	275	1 920	365	1 454	101	534	112
2019	8 425	7 575	596	253	1 811	307	1 415	89	505	102
Women, 20 Years and Over										
2005	6 653	5 789	606	258	1 222	298	861	63	660	74
2006	6 893	6 042	588	263	1 175	255	848	72	588	67
2007	7 024	6 194	570	260	1 216	254	897	65	527	61
2008	7 006	6 160	580	267	1 254	283	902	68	654	78
2009	6 600	5 644	705	250	1 356	449	837	71	951	82
2010	6 471	5 681	575	215	1 473	504	894	75	1 063	103
2011	6 402	5 610	586	207	1 504	549	888	67	1 095	108
2012	6 682	5 901	547	235	1 631	531	1 021	79	1 021	98
2013	6 802	6 039	546	216	1 606	541	986	79	969	100
2014	7 063	6 213	626	224	1 852	538	1 229	85	899	151
2015	7 345	6 389	705	250	1 687	482	1 130	74	714	97
2016	7 506	6 651	609	245	1 713	452	1 166	95	630	94
2017	7 803	6 863	675	265	1 711	411	1 210	90	580	77
2018	8 058	7 179	607	272	1 693	350	1 250	93	495	79
2019	8 310	7 476	582	252	1 599	294	1 220	85	464	63

[1]Employed persons are classified as full- or part-time workers based on their usual weekly hours at all jobs, regardless of the number of hours they were at work during the reference week. Persons absent from work are also classified according to their usual status.
[2]Includes some persons at work 35 hours or more classified by their reason for working part time.
[3]Beginning in 2003, persons who selected this race group only; persons who selected more than one race group are not included. Prior to 2003, persons who reported more than one race group were included in the group they identified as their main race.

Table 1-10. Persons Not in the Labor Force, by Age, Sex, and Desire and Availability for Work, 2016–2019

(Thousands of people.)

Category	Total		Age						Sex			
			16 to 24 years		25 to 54 years		55 years and over		Men		Women	
	2016	2017	2016	2017	2016	2017	2016	2017	2016	2017	2016	2017
TOTAL, NOT IN THE LABOR FORCE	94 351	94 759	17 232	16 989	23 513	23 014	53 606	54 756	37 743	38 130	56 608	56 629
Do Not Want a Job Now[1]	88 502	89 242	15 452	15 335	21 032	20 732	52 018	53 175	35 009	35 591	53 492	53 650
Want a Job[1]	5 849	5 518	1 780	1 655	2 481	2 282	1 587	1 581	2 733	2 539	3 116	2 979
Did not search for work in the previous year	3 415	3 320	994	953	1 353	1 281	1 069	1 086	1 522	1 450	1 894	1 870
Searched for work in the previous year[2]	2 434	2 198	787	702	1 128	1 001	519	495	1 211	1 089	1 222	1 109
Not available to work now	630	610	257	263	287	258	86	90	251	254	379	357
Available to work now	1 804	1 587	530	439	841	743	433	405	960	835	843	752
Reason not currently looking:												
Discouragement over job prospects[3]	553	476	130	115	267	223	156	138	345	299	208	177
Reasons other than discouragement	1 250	1 112	400	324	573	519	277	268	615	536	635	575
Family responsibilities	199	188	26	23	127	121	46	44	61	53	138	135
In school or training	224	187	171	141	47	41	7	6	120	103	105	84
Ill health or disability	144	139	16	13	67	54	62	71	77	68	67	71
Other[4]	682	598	187	147	333	304	162	147	356	312	326	286

Category	Total		Age						Sex			
			16 to 24 years		25 to 54 years		55 years and over		Men		Women	
	2018	2019	2018	2019	2018	2019	2018	2019	2018	2019	2018	2019
TOTAL, NOT IN THE LABOR FORCE	95 716	95 636	17 020	16 656	22 685	22 102	56 010	56 879	38 582	38 667	57 134	56 970
Do Not Want a Job Now[1]	90 467	90 593	15 430	15 153	20 513	20 023	54 524	55 417	36 133	36 252	54 334	54 341
Want a Job[1]	5 249	5 043	1 590	1 503	2 172	2 078	1 487	1 462	2 448	2 415	2 800	2 629
Did not search for work in the previous year	3 161	3 084	925	883	1 195	1 157	1 040	1 045	1 399	1 430	1 762	1 654
Searched for work in the previous year[2]	2 088	1 959	665	620	977	921	447	418	1 049	984	1 039	975
Not available to work now	571	556	232	229	267	252	72	75	232	242	338	314
Available to work now	1 517	1 403	433	391	709	669	375	343	817	742	700	661
Reason not currently looking:												
Discouragement over job prospects[3]	423	382	93	86	211	193	120	103	266	239	158	143
Reasons other than discouragement	1 094	1 021	340	306	499	476	255	240	551	503	542	519
Family responsibilities	173	156	25	21	114	103	35	32	50	44	123	112
In school or training	184	146	144	116	36	27	4	4	99	76	85	70
Ill health or disability	152	135	16	14	64	63	72	58	85	73	67	63
Other[4]	584	584	156	155	285	283	143	147	317	310	267	274

[1]Includes some persons who were not asked if they wanted a job.
[2]Persons who had a job during the prior 12 months must have searched since the end of that job.
[3]Includes believes no work available, could not find work, lacks necessary schooling or training, employer thinks too young or old, and other types of discrimination.
[4]Includes those who did not actively look for work in the prior four weeks for reasons such as childcare and transportation problems, as well as a small number for whom reason for nonparticipation was not ascertained.

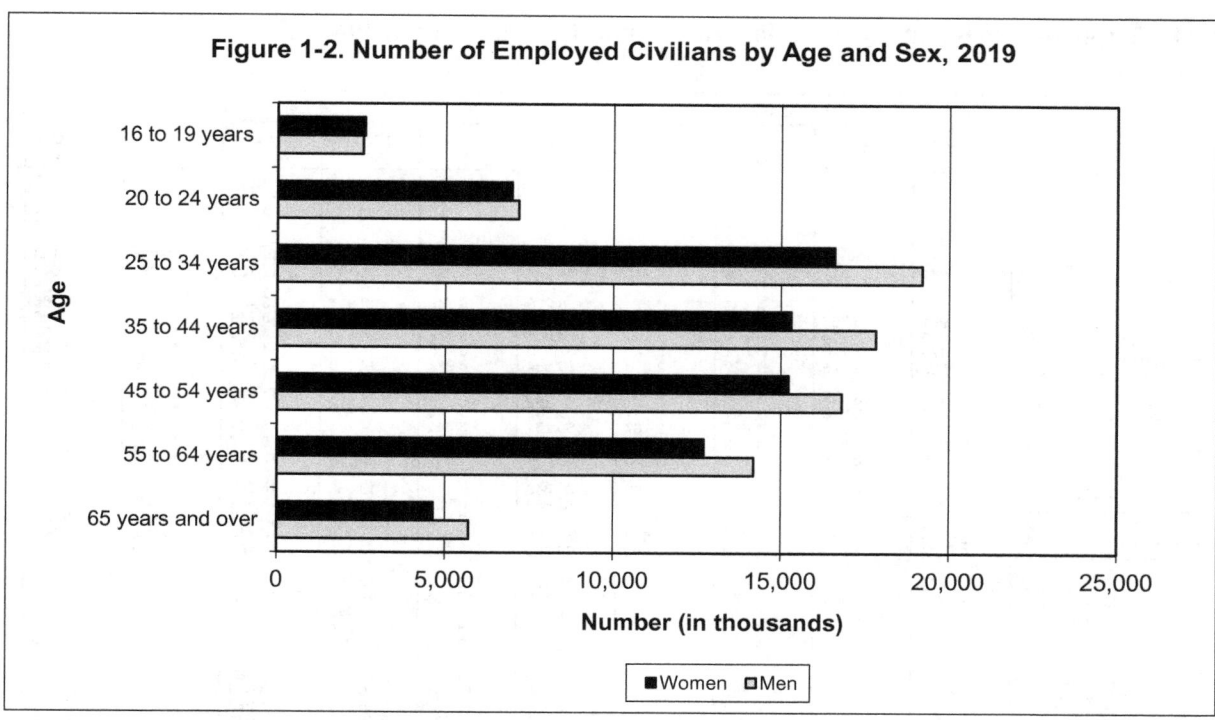

Figure 1-2. Number of Employed Civilians by Age and Sex, 2019

There were over 157 million employed civilians in the labor force in 2019—the highest amount ever. This represented an increase of 1.1 percent from 2018. From 2007 to 2011, the number of employed civilians declined 4.2 percent. (See Table 1-11.)

OTHER HIGHLIGHTS

- While men made up 53.0 percent of employed civilians in 2019, they only made up 13.1 percent of employees in healthcare support occupations; 26.4 percent of employees in education, training, and library occupations; and 29.1 percent of employees in office and administrative support occupations. (See Table 1-13.)

- In 2019, employment increased for all groups except for those with less than a high school degree or those with some college but no degree. It increased 1.3 percent for those with an associate's degree, 0.8 percent for high school graduates and 3.0 percent for those that are college graduates or higher. (See Table 1-16.)

- The multiple jobholding rate decreased significantly in May 2020 as employment declined after the global pandemic impacted the United States. It remained higher for women 4.4 percent) than for men (3.7 percent). (See Table 1-17.)

- In 2019, more than 4.0 million families had an unemployed member—a decline from 4.3 million in 2018, 4.7 million in 2017, and 5.3 million in 2016. (See Table 1-20.)

Table 1-11. Employed Civilians, by Age, Sex, Race, and Hispanic Origin, 1948–2019

(Thousands of people.)

Race, Hispanic origin, sex, and year	16 years and over	16 to 19 years			20 years and over						
		Total	16 to 17 years	18 to 19 years	Total	20 to 24 years	25 to 34 years	35 to 44 years	45 to 54 years	55 to 64 years	65 years and over
ALL RACES											
Both Sexes											
1948	58 343	4 026	1 600	2 426	54 318	6 937	13 801	13 050	10 624	7 103	2 804
1949	57 651	3 712	1 466	2 246	53 940	6 660	13 639	13 108	10 636	7 042	2 864
1950	58 918	3 703	1 433	2 270	55 218	6 746	13 917	13 424	10 966	7 265	2 899
1951	59 961	3 767	1 575	2 192	56 196	6 321	14 233	13 746	11 421	7 558	2 917
1952	60 250	3 719	1 626	2 092	56 536	5 572	14 515	14 058	11 687	7 785	2 919
1953	61 179	3 720	1 577	2 142	57 460	5 225	14 519	14 774	11 969	7 806	3 166
1954	60 109	3 475	1 422	2 053	56 634	4 971	14 190	14 541	11 976	7 895	3 060
1955	62 170	3 642	1 500	2 143	58 528	5 270	14 481	14 879	12 556	8 158	3 185
1956	63 799	3 818	1 647	2 171	59 983	5 545	14 407	15 218	12 978	8 519	3 314
1957	64 071	3 778	1 613	2 167	60 291	5 641	14 253	15 348	13 320	8 553	3 179
1958	63 036	3 582	1 519	2 063	59 454	5 571	13 675	15 157	13 448	8 559	3 045
1959	64 630	3 838	1 670	2 168	60 791	5 870	13 709	15 454	13 915	8 822	3 023
1960	65 778	4 129	1 770	2 360	61 648	6 119	13 630	15 598	14 238	8 989	3 073
1961	65 746	4 108	1 621	2 486	61 638	6 227	13 429	15 552	14 320	9 120	2 987
1962	66 702	4 195	1 607	2 588	62 508	6 446	13 311	15 901	14 491	9 346	3 013
1963	67 762	4 255	1 751	2 504	63 508	6 815	13 318	16 114	14 749	9 596	2 915
1964	69 305	4 516	2 013	2 503	64 789	7 303	13 449	16 166	15 094	9 804	2 973
1965	71 088	5 036	2 075	2 962	66 052	7 702	13 704	16 294	15 320	10 028	3 005
1966	72 895	5 721	2 269	3 452	67 178	7 964	14 017	16 312	15 615	10 310	2 961
1967	74 372	5 682	2 334	3 348	68 690	8 499	14 575	16 281	15 789	10 536	3 011
1968	75 920	5 781	2 403	3 377	70 141	8 762	15 265	16 220	16 083	10 745	3 065
1969	77 902	6 117	2 573	3 543	71 785	9 319	15 883	16 100	16 410	10 919	3 155
1970	78 678	6 144	2 598	3 546	72 534	9 731	16 318	15 922	16 473	10 974	3 118
1971	79 367	6 208	2 596	3 613	73 158	10 201	16 781	15 675	16 451	11 009	3 040
1972	82 153	6 746	2 787	3 959	75 407	10 999	18 082	15 822	16 457	11 044	3 003
1973	85 064	7 271	3 032	4 239	77 793	11 839	19 509	16 041	16 553	10 966	2 886
1974	86 794	7 448	3 111	4 338	79 347	12 101	20 610	16 203	16 633	10 964	2 835
1975	85 846	7 104	2 941	4 162	78 744	11 885	21 087	15 953	16 190	10 827	2 801
1976	88 752	7 336	2 972	4 363	81 416	12 570	22 493	16 468	16 224	10 912	2 747
1977	92 017	7 688	3 138	4 550	84 329	13 196	23 850	17 157	16 212	11 126	2 787
1978	96 048	8 070	3 330	4 739	87 979	13 887	25 281	18 128	16 338	11 400	2 946
1979	98 824	8 083	3 340	4 743	90 741	14 327	26 492	18 981	16 357	11 585	2 999
1980	99 303	7 710	3 106	4 605	91 593	14 087	27 204	19 523	16 234	11 586	2 960
1981	100 397	7 225	2 866	4 359	93 172	14 122	28 180	20 145	16 255	11 525	2 945
1982	99 526	6 549	2 505	4 044	92 978	13 690	28 149	20 879	15 923	11 414	2 923
1983	100 834	6 342	2 320	4 022	94 491	13 722	28 756	21 960	15 812	11 315	2 927
1984	105 005	6 444	2 404	4 040	98 562	14 207	30 348	23 598	16 178	11 395	2 835
1985	107 150	6 434	2 492	3 941	100 716	13 980	31 208	24 732	16 509	11 474	2 813
1986	109 597	6 472	2 622	3 850	103 125	13 790	32 201	25 861	16 949	11 405	2 919
1987	112 440	6 640	2 736	3 905	105 800	13 524	33 105	27 179	17 487	11 465	3 041
1988	114 968	6 805	2 713	4 092	108 164	13 244	33 574	28 269	18 447	11 433	3 197
1989	117 342	6 759	2 588	4 172	110 582	12 962	34 045	29 443	19 279	11 499	3 355
1990	118 793	6 581	2 410	4 171	112 213	13 401	33 935	30 817	19 525	11 189	3 346
1991	117 718	5 906	2 202	3 704	111 812	12 975	33 061	31 593	19 882	11 001	3 300
1992	118 492	5 669	2 128	3 540	112 824	12 872	32 667	31 923	21 022	10 998	3 341
1993	120 259	5 805	2 226	3 579	114 455	12 840	32 385	32 666	22 175	11 058	3 331
1994	123 060	6 161	2 510	3 651	116 899	12 758	32 286	33 599	23 348	11 228	3 681
1995	124 900	6 419	2 573	3 846	118 481	12 443	32 356	34 202	24 378	11 435	3 666
1996	126 708	6 500	2 646	3 853	120 208	12 138	32 077	35 051	25 514	11 739	3 690
1997	129 558	6 661	2 648	4 012	122 897	12 380	31 809	35 908	26 744	12 296	3 761
1998	131 463	7 051	2 762	4 289	124 413	12 557	31 394	36 278	27 587	12 872	3 725
1999	133 488	7 172	2 793	4 379	126 316	12 891	30 865	36 728	28 635	13 315	3 882
2000	136 891	7 189	2 759	4 431	129 701	13 229	31 549	36 433	30 310	14 002	4 179
2001	136 933	6 740	2 558	4 182	130 194	13 348	30 863	36 049	31 036	14 645	4 253
2002	136 485	6 332	2 330	4 002	130 154	13 351	30 306	35 235	31 281	15 674	4 306
2003	137 736	5 919	2 312	3 607	131 817	13 433	30 383	34 881	31 914	16 598	4 608
2004	139 252	5 907	2 193	3 714	133 345	13 723	30 423	34 580	32 469	17 331	4 819
2005	141 730	5 978	2 284	3 694	135 752	13 792	30 680	34 630	33 207	18 349	5 094
2006	144 427	6 162	2 444	3 719	138 265	13 878	31 051	34 569	34 052	19 389	5 325
2007	146 047	5 911	2 286	3 625	140 136	13 964	31 586	34 302	34 563	20 108	5 614
2008	145 362	5 573	1 989	3 584	139 790	13 629	31 383	33 457	34 529	20 812	5 979
2009	139 877	4 837	1 651	3 187	135 040	12 764	30 014	31 517	33 613	21 019	6 114
2010	139 064	4 378	1 418	2 960	134 686	12 699	30 229	30 663	33 191	21 636	6 268
2011	139 869	4 327	1 355	2 972	135 542	13 036	30 537	30 270	32 867	22 186	6 647
2012	142 469	4 426	1 419	3 007	138 043	13 408	30 701	30 576	32 874	23 239	7 245
2013	143 929	4 458	1 487	2 971	139 471	13 599	31 242	30 650	32 523	23 776	7 681
2014	146 305	4 548	1 545	3 003	141 757	13 894	31 975	30 966	32 556	24 395	7 971
2015	148 834	4 734	1 624	3 110	144 099	14 022	32 742	31 252	32 643	24 975	8 465
2016	151 436	4 965	1 747	3 218	146 471	14 027	33 722	31 562	32 720	25 524	8 916
2017	153 337	5 074	1 890	3 184	148 263	14 132	34 439	31 892	32 503	26 064	9 234
2018	155 761	5 126	1 838	3 289	150 635	14 051	35 324	32 616	32 373	26 565	9 705
2019	157 538	5 150	1 789	3 361	152 388	14 172	35 807	33 127	32 042	26 893	10 347

Table 1-11. Employed Civilians, by Age, Sex, Race, and Hispanic Origin, 1948–2019—*Continued*

(Thousands of people.)

Race, Hispanic origin, sex, and year	16 years and over	16 to 19 years			20 years and over						
		Total	16 to 17 years	18 to 19 years	Total	20 to 24 years	25 to 34 years	35 to 44 years	45 to 54 years	55 to 64 years	65 years and over
ALL RACES											
Men											
1948	41 725	2 344	996	1 348	39 382	4 349	10 038	9 363	7 742	5 587	2 303
1949	40 925	2 124	911	1 213	38 803	4 197	9 879	9 308	7 661	5 438	2 329
1950	41 578	2 186	909	1 277	39 394	4 255	10 060	9 445	7 790	5 508	2 336
1951	41 780	2 156	979	1 177	39 626	3 780	10 134	9 607	8 012	5 711	2 382
1952	41 682	2 107	985	1 121	39 578	3 183	10 352	9 753	8 144	5 804	2 343
1953	42 430	2 136	976	1 159	40 296	2 901	10 500	10 229	8 374	5 808	2 483
1954	41 619	1 985	881	1 104	39 634	2 724	10 254	10 082	8 330	5 830	2 414
1955	42 621	2 095	936	1 159	40 526	2 973	10 453	10 267	8 553	5 857	2 424
1956	43 379	2 164	1 008	1 156	41 216	3 245	10 337	10 385	8 732	6 004	2 512
1957	43 357	2 115	987	1 130	41 239	3 346	10 222	10 427	8 851	6 002	2 394
1958	42 423	2 012	948	1 064	40 411	3 293	9 790	10 291	8 828	5 955	2 254
1959	43 466	2 198	1 015	1 183	41 267	3 597	9 862	10 492	9 048	6 058	2 210
1960	43 904	2 361	1 090	1 271	41 543	3 754	9 759	10 552	9 182	6 105	2 191
1961	43 656	2 315	989	1 325	41 342	3 795	9 591	10 505	9 195	6 155	2 098
1962	44 177	2 362	990	1 372	41 815	3 898	9 475	10 711	9 333	6 260	2 138
1963	44 657	2 406	1 073	1 334	42 251	4 118	9 431	10 801	9 478	6 385	2 038
1964	45 474	2 587	1 242	1 345	42 886	4 370	9 531	10 832	9 637	6 478	2 039
1965	46 340	2 918	1 285	1 634	43 422	4 583	9 611	10 837	9 792	6 542	2 057
1966	46 919	3 253	1 389	1 863	43 668	4 599	9 709	10 764	9 904	6 668	2 024
1967	47 479	3 186	1 417	1 769	44 294	4 809	9 988	10 674	9 990	6 774	2 058
1968	48 114	3 255	1 453	1 802	44 859	4 812	10 405	10 554	10 102	6 893	2 093
1969	48 818	3 430	1 526	1 904	45 388	5 012	10 736	10 441	10 187	6 931	2 122
1970	48 990	3 409	1 504	1 905	45 581	5 237	10 936	10 216	10 170	6 928	2 094
1971	49 390	3 478	1 510	1 968	45 912	5 593	11 218	10 028	10 139	6 916	2 019
1972	50 896	3 765	1 598	2 167	47 130	6 138	11 884	10 088	10 139	6 929	1 953
1973	52 349	4 039	1 721	2 318	48 310	6 655	12 617	10 126	10 197	6 857	1 856
1974	53 024	4 103	1 744	2 359	48 922	6 739	13 119	10 135	10 181	6 880	1 869
1975	51 857	3 839	1 621	2 219	48 018	6 484	13 205	9 891	9 902	6 722	1 811
1976	53 138	3 947	1 626	2 321	49 190	6 915	13 869	10 069	9 881	6 724	1 732
1977	54 728	4 174	1 733	2 441	50 555	7 232	14 483	10 399	9 832	6 848	1 761
1978	56 479	4 336	1 800	2 535	52 143	7 559	15 124	10 845	9 806	6 954	1 855
1979	57 607	4 300	1 799	2 501	53 308	7 791	15 688	11 202	9 735	7 015	1 876
1980	57 186	4 085	1 672	2 412	53 101	7 532	15 832	11 355	9 548	6 999	1 835
1981	57 397	3 815	1 526	2 289	53 582	7 504	16 266	11 613	9 478	6 909	1 812
1982	56 271	3 379	1 307	2 072	52 891	7 197	16 002	11 902	9 234	6 781	1 776
1983	56 787	3 300	1 213	2 087	53 487	7 232	16 216	12 450	9 133	6 686	1 770
1984	59 091	3 322	1 244	2 078	55 769	7 571	17 166	13 309	9 326	6 694	1 703
1985	59 891	3 328	1 300	2 029	56 562	7 339	17 564	13 800	9 411	6 753	1 695
1986	60 892	3 323	1 352	1 971	57 569	7 250	18 092	14 266	9 554	6 654	1 753
1987	62 107	3 381	1 393	1 988	58 726	7 058	18 487	14 898	9 750	6 682	1 850
1988	63 273	3 492	1 403	2 089	59 781	6 918	18 702	15 457	10 201	6 591	1 911
1989	64 315	3 477	1 327	2 150	60 837	6 799	18 952	16 002	10 569	6 548	1 968
1990	65 104	3 427	1 254	2 173	61 678	7 151	18 779	16 771	10 690	6 378	1 909
1991	64 223	3 044	1 135	1 909	61 178	6 909	18 265	17 086	10 813	6 245	1 860
1992	64 440	2 944	1 096	1 848	61 496	6 819	17 966	17 230	11 365	6 173	1 943
1993	65 349	2 994	1 155	1 839	62 355	6 805	17 877	17 665	11 927	6 166	1 916
1994	66 450	3 156	1 288	1 868	63 294	6 771	17 741	18 111	12 439	6 142	2 089
1995	67 377	3 292	1 316	1 977	64 085	6 665	17 709	18 374	12 958	6 272	2 108
1996	68 207	3 310	1 318	1 992	64 897	6 429	17 527	18 816	13 483	6 470	2 172
1997	69 685	3 401	1 355	2 045	66 284	6 548	17 338	19 327	14 107	6 735	2 229
1998	70 693	3 558	1 398	2 161	67 135	6 638	17 097	19 634	14 544	7 052	2 171
1999	71 446	3 685	1 437	2 249	67 761	6 729	16 694	19 811	14 991	7 274	2 263
2000	73 305	3 671	1 394	2 276	69 634	6 974	17 241	19 537	15 871	7 606	2 406
2001	73 196	3 420	1 268	2 151	69 776	6 952	16 915	19 305	16 268	7 900	2 437
2002	72 903	3 169	1 130	2 040	69 734	6 978	16 573	18 932	16 419	8 378	2 455
2003	73 332	2 917	1 115	1 802	70 415	7 065	16 670	18 774	16 588	8 733	2 585
2004	74 524	2 952	1 037	1 915	71 572	7 246	16 818	18 700	16 951	9 174	2 683
2005	75 973	2 923	1 067	1 855	73 050	7 279	16 993	18 780	17 429	9 714	2 857
2006	77 502	3 071	1 182	1 888	74 431	7 412	17 134	18 765	17 920	10 192	3 008
2007	78 254	2 917	1 091	1 827	75 337	7 374	17 452	18 666	18 210	10 556	3 080
2008	77 486	2 736	926	1 810	74 750	7 145	17 183	18 097	18 124	10 919	3 282
2009	73 670	2 328	786	1 543	71 341	6 510	16 223	16 918	17 443	10 890	3 357
2010	73 359	2 129	675	1 454	71 230	6 466	16 358	16 585	17 242	11 140	3 439
2011	74 290	2 108	650	1 459	72 182	6 826	16 674	16 370	17 113	11 469	3 730
2012	75 555	2 152	659	1 493	73 403	6 948	16 607	16 483	17 221	12 068	4 077
2013	76 353	2 177	700	1 477	74 176	7 013	16 907	16 590	17 033	12 276	4 257
2014	77 692	2 222	729	1 493	75 471	7 187	17 293	16 735	17 118	12 762	4 377
2015	79 131	2 354	799	1 555	76 776	7 173	17 746	16 861	17 245	13 092	4 661
2016	80 568	2 484	825	1 659	78 084	7 212	18 185	17 042	17 287	13 410	4 948
2017	81 402	2 483	882	1 601	78 919	7 281	18 490	17 202	17 125	13 710	5 111
2018	82 698	2 487	847	1 640	80 211	7 190	19 027	17 608	17 038	14 001	5 348
2019	83 460	2 543	879	1 664	80 917	7 187	19 207	17 822	16 816	14 187	5 699

Table 1-11. Employed Civilians, by Age, Sex, Race, and Hispanic Origin, 1948–2019—*Continued*

(Thousands of people.)

Race, Hispanic origin, sex, and year	16 years and over	16 to 19 years			20 years and over						
		Total	16 to 17 years	18 to 19 years	Total	20 to 24 years	25 to 34 years	35 to 44 years	45 to 54 years	55 to 64 years	65 years and over
ALL RACES											
Women											
1948	16 617	1 682	604	1 078	14 936	2 588	3 763	3 687	2 882	1 516	501
1949	16 723	1 588	555	1 033	15 137	2 463	3 760	3 800	2 975	1 604	535
1950	17 340	1 517	524	993	15 824	2 491	3 857	3 979	3 176	1 757	563
1951	18 181	1 611	596	1 015	16 570	2 541	4 099	4 139	3 409	1 847	535
1952	18 568	1 612	641	971	16 958	2 389	4 163	4 305	3 543	1 981	576
1953	18 749	1 584	601	983	17 164	2 324	4 019	4 545	3 595	1 998	683
1954	18 490	1 490	541	949	17 000	2 247	3 936	4 459	3 646	2 065	646
1955	19 551	1 547	564	984	18 002	2 297	4 028	4 612	4 003	2 301	761
1956	20 419	1 654	639	1 015	18 767	2 300	4 070	4 833	4 246	2 515	802
1957	20 714	1 663	626	1 037	19 052	2 295	4 031	4 921	4 469	2 551	785
1958	20 613	1 570	571	999	19 043	2 278	3 885	4 866	4 620	2 604	791
1959	21 164	1 640	655	985	19 524	2 273	3 847	4 962	4 867	2 764	813
1960	21 874	1 768	680	1 089	20 105	2 365	3 871	5 046	5 056	2 884	882
1961	22 090	1 793	632	1 161	20 296	2 432	3 838	5 047	5 125	2 965	889
1962	22 525	1 833	617	1 216	20 693	2 548	3 836	5 190	5 158	3 086	875
1963	23 105	1 849	678	1 170	21 257	2 697	3 887	5 313	5 271	3 211	877
1964	23 831	1 929	771	1 158	21 903	2 933	3 918	5 334	5 457	3 326	934
1965	24 748	2 118	790	1 328	22 630	3 119	4 093	5 457	5 528	3 486	948
1966	25 976	2 468	880	1 589	23 510	3 365	4 308	5 548	5 711	3 642	937
1967	26 893	2 496	917	1 579	24 397	3 690	4 587	5 607	5 799	3 762	953
1968	27 807	2 526	950	1 575	25 281	3 950	4 860	5 666	5 981	3 852	972
1969	29 084	2 687	1 047	1 639	26 397	4 307	5 147	5 699	6 223	3 988	1 033
1970	29 688	2 735	1 094	1 641	26 952	4 494	5 382	5 706	6 303	4 046	1 023
1971	29 976	2 730	1 086	1 645	27 246	4 609	5 563	5 647	6 313	4 093	1 021
1972	31 257	2 980	1 188	1 792	28 276	4 861	6 197	5 734	6 318	4 115	1 051
1973	32 715	3 231	1 310	1 920	29 484	5 184	6 893	5 915	6 356	4 109	1 029
1974	33 769	3 345	1 367	1 978	30 424	5 363	7 492	6 068	6 451	4 084	966
1975	33 989	3 263	1 320	1 943	30 726	5 401	7 882	6 061	6 288	4 105	989
1976	35 615	3 389	1 346	2 043	32 226	5 655	8 624	6 400	6 343	4 188	1 017
1977	37 289	3 514	1 403	2 110	33 775	5 965	9 367	6 758	6 380	4 279	1 027
1978	39 569	3 734	1 530	2 204	35 836	6 328	10 157	7 282	6 532	4 446	1 091
1979	41 217	3 783	1 541	2 242	37 434	6 538	10 802	7 779	6 622	4 569	1 124
1980	42 117	3 625	1 433	2 192	38 492	6 555	11 370	8 168	6 686	4 587	1 125
1981	43 000	3 411	1 340	2 070	39 590	6 618	11 914	8 532	6 777	4 616	1 133
1982	43 256	3 170	1 198	1 972	40 086	6 492	12 147	8 977	6 689	4 634	1 147
1983	44 047	3 043	1 107	1 935	41 004	6 490	12 540	9 510	6 678	4 629	1 157
1984	45 915	3 122	1 161	1 962	42 793	6 636	13 182	10 289	6 852	4 700	1 133
1985	47 259	3 105	1 193	1 913	44 154	6 640	13 644	10 933	7 097	4 721	1 118
1986	48 706	3 149	1 270	1 879	45 556	6 540	14 109	11 595	7 395	4 751	1 165
1987	50 334	3 260	1 343	1 917	47 074	6 466	14 617	12 281	7 737	4 783	1 191
1988	51 696	3 313	1 310	2 003	48 383	6 326	14 872	12 811	8 246	4 841	1 286
1989	53 027	3 282	1 261	2 021	49 745	6 163	15 093	13 440	8 711	4 950	1 388
1990	53 689	3 154	1 156	1 998	50 535	6 250	15 155	14 046	8 835	4 811	1 437
1991	53 496	2 862	1 067	1 794	50 634	6 066	14 796	14 507	9 069	4 756	1 440
1992	54 052	2 724	1 032	1 692	51 328	6 053	14 701	14 693	9 657	4 825	1 398
1993	54 910	2 811	1 071	1 740	52 099	6 035	14 508	15 002	10 248	4 892	1 414
1994	56 610	3 005	1 222	1 783	53 606	5 987	14 545	15 488	10 908	5 085	1 592
1995	57 523	3 127	1 258	1 869	54 396	5 779	14 647	15 828	11 421	5 163	1 558
1996	58 501	3 190	1 328	1 862	55 311	5 709	14 549	16 235	12 031	5 269	1 518
1997	59 873	3 260	1 293	1 967	56 613	5 831	14 471	16 581	12 637	5 561	1 532
1998	60 771	3 493	1 364	2 128	57 278	5 919	14 298	16 644	13 043	5 820	1 554
1999	62 042	3 487	1 357	2 130	58 555	6 163	14 171	16 917	13 644	6 041	1 619
2000	63 586	3 519	1 364	2 154	60 067	6 255	14 308	16 897	14 438	6 396	1 773
2001	63 737	3 320	1 289	2 031	60 417	6 396	13 948	16 744	14 768	6 745	1 815
2002	63 582	3 162	1 200	1 962	60 420	6 374	13 733	16 303	14 863	7 296	1 851
2003	64 404	3 002	1 197	1 805	61 402	6 367	13 714	16 106	15 326	7 866	2 023
2004	64 728	2 955	1 156	1 799	61 773	6 477	13 605	15 880	15 518	8 157	2 135
2005	65 757	3 055	1 217	1 838	62 702	6 513	13 687	15 850	15 779	8 635	2 238
2006	66 925	3 091	1 261	1 830	63 834	6 467	13 917	15 804	16 132	9 198	2 316
2007	67 792	2 994	1 195	1 798	64 799	6 590	14 133	15 636	16 353	9 553	2 534
2008	67 876	2 837	1 063	1 774	65 039	6 484	14 200	15 360	16 406	9 893	2 697
2009	66 208	2 509	865	1 644	63 699	6 254	13 791	14 599	16 170	10 128	2 757
2010	65 705	2 249	743	1 506	63 456	6 233	13 870	14 078	15 949	10 496	2 830
2011	65 579	2 219	705	1 514	63 360	6 209	13 863	13 900	15 753	10 717	2 917
2012	66 914	2 274	760	1 514	64 640	6 460	14 094	14 093	15 653	11 171	3 168
2013	67 577	2 281	787	1 494	65 295	6 586	14 336	14 060	15 490	11 400	3 424
2014	68 613	2 326	817	1 510	66 287	6 707	14 682	14 232	15 438	11 634	3 594
2015	69 703	2 380	825	1 555	67 323	6 849	14 996	14 391	15 399	11 884	3 804
2016	70 868	2 481	922	1 559	68 387	6 815	15 537	14 520	15 433	12 114	3 968
2017	71 936	2 591	1 008	1 583	69 344	6 851	15 949	14 690	15 377	12 354	4 124
2018	73 063	2 639	991	1 648	70 424	6 861	16 298	15 008	15 335	12 564	4 358
2019	74 078	2 607	911	1 696	71 470	6 985	16 600	15 306	15 225	12 706	4 648

Table 1-11. Employed Civilians, by Age, Sex, Race, and Hispanic Origin, 1948–2019—*Continued*

(Thousands of people.)

Race, Hispanic origin, sex, and year	16 years and over	16 to 19 years			20 years and over						
		Total	16 to 17 years	18 to 19 years	Total	20 to 24 years	25 to 34 years	35 to 44 years	45 to 54 years	55 to 64 years	65 years and over
WHITE											
Both Sexes											
1954	53 957	3 078	1 257	1 822	50 879	4 358	12 616	13 000	10 811	7 262	2 831
1955	55 833	3 225	1 330	1 896	52 608	4 637	12 855	13 327	11 322	7 510	2 957
1956	57 269	3 389	1 465	1 922	53 880	4 897	12 748	13 637	11 706	7 822	3 068
1957	57 465	3 374	1 442	1 931	54 091	4 952	12 619	13 716	12 009	7 829	2 951
1958	56 613	3 216	1 370	1 847	53 397	4 908	12 128	13 571	12 113	7 849	2 828
1959	58 006	3 475	1 520	1 955	54 531	5 138	12 144	13 830	12 552	8 063	2 805
1960	58 850	3 700	1 598	2 103	55 150	5 331	12 021	13 930	12 820	8 192	2 855
1961	58 913	3 693	1 472	2 220	55 220	5 460	11 835	13 905	12 906	8 335	2 778
1962	59 698	3 774	1 447	2 327	55 924	5 676	11 703	14 173	13 066	8 511	2 795
1963	60 622	3 851	1 600	2 250	56 771	6 036	11 689	14 341	13 304	8 718	2 683
1964	61 922	4 076	1 846	2 230	57 846	6 444	11 794	14 380	13 596	8 916	2 717
1965	63 446	4 562	1 892	2 670	58 884	6 752	11 992	14 473	13 804	9 116	2 748
1966	65 021	5 176	2 052	3 124	59 845	6 986	12 268	14 449	14 072	9 356	2 713
1967	66 361	5 114	2 121	2 993	61 247	7 493	12 763	14 429	14 224	9 596	2 746
1968	67 750	5 195	2 193	3 002	62 555	7 687	13 410	14 386	14 487	9 781	2 804
1969	69 518	5 508	2 347	3 161	64 010	8 182	13 935	14 270	14 788	9 947	2 888
1970	70 217	5 571	2 386	3 185	64 645	8 559	14 326	14 092	14 854	9 979	2 835
1971	70 878	5 670	2 404	3 266	65 208	9 000	14 713	13 858	14 843	10 014	2 780
1972	73 370	6 173	2 581	3 592	67 197	9 718	15 904	13 940	14 845	10 077	2 714
1973	75 708	6 623	2 806	3 816	69 086	10 424	17 099	14 083	14 886	9 983	2 610
1974	77 184	6 796	2 881	3 916	70 388	10 676	18 040	14 196	14 948	9 958	2 568
1975	76 411	6 487	2 721	3 770	69 924	10 546	18 485	13 979	14 555	9 827	2 533
1976	78 853	6 724	2 762	3 962	72 129	11 119	19 662	14 407	14 549	9 923	2 470
1977	81 700	7 068	2 926	4 142	74 632	11 696	20 844	14 984	14 483	10 107	2 518
1978	84 936	7 367	3 085	4 282	77 569	12 251	22 008	15 809	14 550	10 311	2 642
1979	87 259	7 356	3 079	4 278	79 904	12 594	23 033	16 578	14 522	10 477	2 699
1980	87 715	7 021	2 861	4 161	80 694	12 405	23 653	17 071	14 405	10 475	2 684
1981	88 709	6 588	2 645	3 943	82 121	12 477	24 551	17 617	14 414	10 386	2 676
1982	87 903	5 984	2 317	3 667	81 918	12 097	24 531	18 268	14 083	10 283	2 656
1983	88 893	5 799	2 156	3 643	83 094	12 138	24 955	19 194	13 961	10 169	2 678
1984	92 120	5 836	2 209	3 627	86 284	12 451	26 235	20 552	14 239	10 227	2 580
1985	93 736	5 768	2 270	3 498	87 968	12 235	26 945	21 552	14 459	10 247	2 530
1986	95 660	5 792	2 386	3 406	89 869	12 027	27 746	22 515	14 750	10 176	2 654
1987	97 789	5 898	2 468	3 431	91 890	11 748	28 429	23 596	15 216	10 164	2 738
1988	99 812	6 030	2 424	3 606	93 782	11 438	28 796	24 468	16 054	10 153	2 874
1989	101 584	5 946	2 278	3 668	95 638	11 084	29 091	25 442	16 775	10 223	3 024
1990	102 261	5 779	2 141	3 638	96 481	11 498	28 773	26 282	16 933	9 960	3 035
1991	101 182	5 216	1 971	3 246	95 966	11 116	27 989	26 883	17 269	9 719	2 990
1992	101 669	4 985	1 904	3 081	96 684	11 031	27 552	27 097	18 285	9 701	3 019
1993	103 045	5 113	1 990	3 123	97 932	10 931	27 274	27 645	19 273	9 772	3 037
1994	105 190	5 398	2 210	3 188	99 792	10 736	27 101	28 442	20 247	9 912	3 354
1995	106 490	5 593	2 273	3 320	100 897	10 400	27 014	28 951	21 127	10 070	3 335
1996	107 808	5 667	2 325	3 343	102 141	10 149	26 678	29 566	22 071	10 313	3 364
1997	109 856	5 807	2 341	3 466	104 049	10 362	26 294	30 137	23 061	10 785	3 411
1998	110 931	6 089	2 436	3 653	104 842	10 512	25 729	30 320	23 662	11 272	3 347
1999	112 235	6 204	2 435	3 769	106 032	10 716	25 113	30 548	24 507	11 657	3 491
2000	114 424	6 160	2 383	3 777	108 264	10 944	25 500	30 151	25 762	12 169	3 738
2001	114 430	5 817	2 224	3 593	108 613	11 054	24 948	29 793	26 301	12 743	3 774
2002	114 013	5 441	2 037	3 404	108 572	11 096	24 568	29 049	26 401	13 630	3 828
2003	114 235	5 064	1 999	3 065	109 171	11 052	24 399	28 501	26 762	14 375	4 083
2004	115 239	5 039	1 895	3 145	110 199	11 233	24 337	28 176	27 228	14 965	4 260
2005	116 949	5 105	1 999	3 106	111 844	11 231	24 443	28 102	27 801	15 788	4 480
2006	118 833	5 215	2 099	3 117	113 618	11 296	24 652	27 929	28 419	16 652	4 670
2007	119 792	4 990	1 965	3 026	114 802	11 325	25 024	27 492	28 779	17 262	4 921
2008	119 126	4 697	1 703	2 994	114 428	11 055	24 875	26 736	28 686	17 829	5 247
2009	114 996	4 138	1 443	2 696	110 858	10 438	23 957	25 237	27 891	17 978	5 357
2010	114 168	3 733	1 248	2 485	110 435	10 334	24 097	24 540	27 502	18 464	5 496
2011	114 690	3 691	1 189	2 501	111 000	10 574	24 376	24 156	27 176	18 937	5 780
2012	114 769	3 665	1 207	2 458	111 104	10 561	23 925	23 931	26 769	19 608	6 309
2013	115 379	3 671	1 274	2 397	111 708	10 662	24 247	23 833	26 363	19 913	6 690
2014	116 788	3 701	1 289	2 412	113 087	10 842	24 771	23 970	26 251	20 351	6 902
2015	117 944	3 824	1 319	2 505	114 120	10 784	25 111	24 012	26 154	20 783	7 276
2016	119 313	3 967	1 419	2 549	115 346	10 722	25 568	24 159	26 070	21 169	7 658
2017	120 176	3 989	1 520	2 469	116 188	10 738	26 001	24 289	25 716	21 581	7 863
2018	121 461	4 060	1 485	2 575	117 401	10 697	26 400	24 771	25 437	21 855	8 241
2019	122 441	4 067	1 429	2 638	118 374	10 739	26 641	25 174	25 042	22 046	8 733

Table 1-11. Employed Civilians, by Age, Sex, Race, and Hispanic Origin, 1948–2019—*Continued*

(Thousands of people.)

Race, Hispanic origin, sex, and year	16 years and over	16 to 19 years			20 years and over						
		Total	16 to 17 years	18 to 19 years	Total	20 to 24 years	25 to 34 years	35 to 44 years	45 to 54 years	55 to 64 years	65 years and over
WHITE											
Men											
1954	37 846	1 723	771	953	36 123	2 394	9 287	9 175	7 614	5 412	2 241
1955	38 719	1 824	821	1 004	36 895	2 607	9 461	9 351	7 792	5 431	2 254
1956	39 368	1 893	890	1 002	37 475	2 850	9 330	9 449	7 950	5 559	2 336
1957	39 349	1 865	874	990	37 484	2 930	9 226	9 480	8 067	5 542	2 234
1958	38 591	1 783	852	932	36 808	2 896	8 861	9 386	8 061	5 501	2 103
1959	39 494	1 961	915	1 046	37 533	3 153	8 911	9 560	8 261	5 588	2 060
1960	39 755	2 092	973	1 119	37 663	3 264	8 777	9 589	8 372	5 618	2 043
1961	39 588	2 055	891	1 164	37 533	3 311	8 630	9 566	8 394	5 670	1 961
1962	40 016	2 098	883	1 215	37 918	3 426	8 514	9 718	8 512	5 749	1 998
1963	40 428	2 156	972	1 184	38 272	3 646	8 463	9 782	8 650	5 844	1 887
1964	41 115	2 316	1 128	1 188	38 799	3 856	8 538	9 800	8 787	5 945	1 872
1965	41 844	2 612	1 159	1 453	39 232	4 025	8 598	9 795	8 924	5 998	1 892
1966	42 331	2 913	1 245	1 668	39 418	4 028	8 674	9 719	9 029	6 096	1 871
1967	42 833	2 849	1 278	1 571	39 985	4 231	8 931	9 632	9 093	6 208	1 892
1968	43 411	2 908	1 319	1 589	40 503	4 226	9 315	9 522	9 198	6 316	1 926
1969	44 048	3 070	1 385	1 685	40 978	4 401	9 608	9 379	9 279	6 359	1 953
1970	44 178	3 066	1 374	1 692	41 112	4 601	9 784	9 202	9 271	6 340	1 914
1971	44 595	3 157	1 393	1 764	41 438	4 935	10 026	9 026	9 256	6 339	1 856
1972	45 944	3 416	1 470	1 947	42 528	5 431	10 664	9 047	9 236	6 363	1 786
1973	47 085	3 660	1 590	2 071	43 424	5 863	11 268	9 046	9 257	6 299	1 689
1974	47 674	3 728	1 611	2 117	43 946	5 965	11 701	9 027	9 242	6 304	1 706
1975	46 697	3 505	1 502	2 002	43 192	5 770	11 783	8 818	9 005	6 160	1 656
1976	47 775	3 604	1 501	2 103	44 171	6 140	12 362	8 944	8 968	6 176	1 579
1977	49 150	3 824	1 607	2 217	45 326	6 437	12 893	9 212	8 898	6 279	1 605
1978	50 544	3 950	1 664	2 286	46 594	6 717	13 413	9 608	8 840	6 339	1 677
1979	51 452	3 904	1 654	2 250	47 546	6 868	13 888	9 930	8 748	6 406	1 707
1980	51 127	3 708	1 534	2 174	47 419	6 652	14 009	10 077	8 586	6 412	1 684
1981	51 315	3 469	1 402	2 066	47 846	6 652	14 398	10 307	8 518	6 309	1 662
1982	50 287	3 079	1 214	1 865	47 209	6 372	14 164	10 593	8 267	6 188	1 624
1983	50 621	3 003	1 124	1 879	47 618	6 386	14 297	11 062	8 152	6 084	1 637
1984	52 462	3 001	1 140	1 861	49 461	6 647	15 045	11 776	8 320	6 108	1 564
1985	53 046	2 985	1 185	1 800	50 061	6 428	15 374	12 214	8 374	6 118	1 552
1986	53 785	2 966	1 225	1 741	50 818	6 340	15 790	12 620	8 442	6 012	1 612
1987	54 647	2 999	1 252	1 747	51 649	6 150	16 084	13 138	8 596	5 991	1 690
1988	55 550	3 084	1 248	1 836	52 466	5 987	16 241	13 590	8 992	5 909	1 748
1989	56 352	3 060	1 171	1 889	53 292	5 839	16 383	14 046	9 335	5 891	1 797
1990	56 703	3 018	1 119	1 899	53 685	6 179	16 124	14 496	9 383	5 744	1 760
1991	55 797	2 694	1 017	1 677	53 103	5 942	15 644	14 743	9 488	5 578	1 707
1992	55 959	2 602	990	1 612	53 357	5 855	15 357	14 842	10 027	5 503	1 772
1993	56 656	2 634	1 031	1 603	54 021	5 830	15 230	15 178	10 497	5 514	1 772
1994	57 452	2 776	1 144	1 632	54 676	5 738	15 052	15 562	10 910	5 490	1 925
1995	58 146	2 892	1 169	1 723	55 254	5 613	14 958	15 793	11 359	5 609	1 921
1996	58 888	2 911	1 161	1 750	55 977	5 444	14 820	16 136	11 834	5 755	1 987
1997	59 998	3 011	1 206	1 806	56 986	5 590	14 567	16 470	12 352	5 972	2 037
1998	60 604	3 103	1 233	1 870	57 500	5 659	14 259	16 715	12 661	6 251	1 955
1999	61 139	3 205	1 254	1 951	57 934	5 753	13 851	16 781	13 046	6 447	2 056
2000	62 289	3 169	1 205	1 965	59 119	5 876	14 238	16 477	13 675	6 678	2 175
2001	62 212	2 967	1 102	1 865	59 245	5 870	13 989	16 280	13 987	6 941	2 178
2002	61 849	2 725	987	1 738	59 124	5 882	13 727	15 910	14 060	7 360	2 184
2003	61 866	2 518	972	1 546	59 348	5 890	13 731	15 675	14 117	7 640	2 295
2004	62 712	2 553	903	1 650	60 159	6 026	13 735	15 572	14 418	8 018	2 390
2005	63 763	2 508	942	1 566	61 255	6 041	13 840	15 544	14 810	8 471	2 550
2006	64 883	2 625	1 020	1 605	62 259	6 114	13 903	15 480	15 189	8 893	2 680
2007	65 289	2 483	951	1 531	62 806	6 066	14 112	15 287	15 399	9 215	2 727
2008	64 624	2 320	808	1 512	62 304	5 858	13 931	14 775	15 300	9 518	2 922
2009	61 630	2 004	692	1 312	59 626	5 379	13 230	13 858	14 710	9 465	2 984
2010	61 252	1 815	598	1 217	59 438	5 347	13 282	13 583	14 542	9 637	3 047
2011	61 920	1 802	573	1 229	60 118	5 630	13 548	13 366	14 370	9 932	3 271
2012	61 990	1 797	563	1 234	60 193	5 547	13 212	13 224	14 264	10 334	3 611
2013	62 322	1 811	608	1 203	60 511	5 597	13 381	13 182	14 035	10 541	3 775
2014	63 108	1 819	599	1 219	61 289	5 681	13 627	13 258	14 060	10 817	3 847
2015	63 892	1 934	653	1 280	61 959	5 585	13 866	13 273	14 059	11 088	4 088
2016	64 612	2 037	708	1 328	62 575	5 598	14 022	13 358	14 005	11 284	4 308
2017	65 000	1 991	727	1 264	63 009	5 613	14 190	13 422	13 819	11 531	4 434
2018	65 702	1 983	696	1 287	63 719	5 561	14 450	13 711	13 658	11 692	4 647
2019	66 100	2 030	711	1 320	64 070	5 543	14 517	13 865	13 385	11 840	4 921

Table 1-11. Employed Civilians, by Age, Sex, Race, and Hispanic Origin, 1948–2019—*Continued*

(Thousands of people.)

Race, Hispanic origin, sex, and year	16 years and over	16 to 19 years			20 years and over						
		Total	16 to 17 years	18 to 19 years	Total	20 to 24 years	25 to 34 years	35 to 44 years	45 to 54 years	55 to 64 years	65 years and over
WHITE											
Women											
1954	16 111	1 355	486	869	14 756	1 964	3 329	3 825	3 197	1 850	590
1955	17 114	1 401	509	892	15 713	2 030	3 394	3 976	3 530	2 079	703
1956	17 901	1 496	575	920	16 405	2 047	3 418	4 188	3 756	2 263	732
1957	18 116	1 509	568	941	16 607	2 022	3 393	4 236	3 942	2 287	717
1958	18 022	1 433	518	915	16 589	2 012	3 267	4 185	4 052	2 348	725
1959	18 512	1 514	605	909	16 998	1 985	3 233	4 270	4 291	2 475	745
1960	19 095	1 608	625	984	17 487	2 067	3 244	4 341	4 448	2 574	812
1961	19 325	1 638	581	1 056	17 687	2 149	3 205	4 339	4 512	2 665	817
1962	19 682	1 676	564	1 112	18 006	2 250	3 189	4 455	4 554	2 762	797
1963	20 194	1 695	628	1 066	18 499	2 390	3 226	4 559	4 654	2 874	796
1964	20 807	1 760	718	1 042	19 047	2 588	3 256	4 580	4 809	2 971	845
1965	21 602	1 950	733	1 217	19 652	2 727	3 394	4 678	4 880	3 118	856
1966	22 690	2 263	807	1 456	20 427	2 958	3 594	4 730	5 043	3 260	842
1967	23 528	2 265	843	1 422	21 263	3 262	3 832	4 797	5 131	3 388	854
1968	24 339	2 287	874	1 413	22 052	3 461	4 095	4 864	5 289	3 465	878
1969	25 470	2 438	962	1 476	23 032	3 781	4 327	4 891	5 509	3 588	935
1970	26 039	2 505	1 012	1 493	23 534	3 959	4 542	4 890	5 582	3 640	921
1971	26 283	2 513	1 011	1 502	23 770	4 065	4 687	4 831	5 588	3 675	924
1972	27 426	2 755	1 111	1 645	24 669	4 286	5 240	4 893	5 608	3 714	928
1973	28 623	2 962	1 217	1 746	25 661	4 562	5 831	5 036	5 628	3 684	920
1974	29 511	3 069	1 269	1 799	26 442	4 711	6 340	5 169	5 706	3 654	862
1975	29 714	2 983	1 215	1 767	26 731	4 775	6 701	5 161	5 550	3 667	877
1976	31 078	3 120	1 260	1 860	27 958	4 978	7 300	5 462	5 580	3 746	891
1977	32 550	3 244	1 319	1 923	29 306	5 259	7 950	5 772	5 585	3 829	912
1978	34 392	3 416	1 420	1 996	30 975	5 535	8 595	6 201	5 710	3 972	964
1979	35 807	3 451	1 423	2 027	32 357	5 726	9 145	6 648	5 773	4 071	993
1980	36 587	3 314	1 327	1 986	33 275	5 753	9 644	6 994	5 818	4 064	1 001
1981	37 394	3 119	1 242	1 877	34 275	5 826	10 153	7 311	5 896	4 077	1 013
1982	37 615	2 905	1 103	1 802	34 710	5 724	10 367	7 675	5 816	4 095	1 032
1983	38 272	2 796	1 032	1 764	35 476	5 751	10 659	8 132	5 809	4 084	1 041
1984	39 659	2 835	1 069	1 766	36 823	5 804	11 190	8 776	5 920	4 118	1 015
1985	40 690	2 783	1 085	1 698	37 907	5 807	11 571	9 338	6 084	4 128	978
1986	41 876	2 825	1 160	1 665	39 050	5 687	11 956	9 895	6 307	4 164	1 042
1987	43 142	2 900	1 216	1 684	40 242	5 598	12 345	10 459	6 620	4 172	1 047
1988	44 262	2 946	1 176	1 770	41 316	5 450	12 555	10 878	7 062	4 244	1 126
1989	45 232	2 886	1 107	1 779	42 346	5 245	12 708	11 395	7 440	4 332	1 227
1990	45 558	2 762	1 023	1 739	42 796	5 319	12 649	11 785	7 551	4 217	1 275
1991	45 385	2 523	954	1 569	42 862	5 174	12 344	12 139	7 781	4 141	1 283
1992	45 710	2 383	915	1 468	43 327	5 176	12 195	12 254	8 258	4 198	1 246
1993	46 390	2 479	959	1 520	43 910	5 101	12 044	12 467	8 776	4 258	1 265
1994	47 738	2 622	1 066	1 556	45 116	4 997	12 049	12 880	9 338	4 423	1 429
1995	48 344	2 701	1 104	1 597	45 643	4 787	12 056	13 157	9 768	4 461	1 415
1996	48 920	2 756	1 164	1 592	46 164	4 705	11 858	13 430	10 237	4 558	1 376
1997	49 859	2 796	1 136	1 660	47 063	4 773	11 727	13 667	10 709	4 813	1 374
1998	50 327	2 986	1 203	1 783	47 342	4 853	11 470	13 604	11 001	5 021	1 392
1999	51 096	2 999	1 181	1 817	48 098	4 963	11 262	13 767	11 461	5 211	1 435
2000	52 136	2 991	1 178	1 813	49 145	5 068	11 262	13 674	12 087	5 490	1 564
2001	52 218	2 850	1 122	1 727	49 369	5 184	10 959	13 513	12 314	5 802	1 597
2002	52 164	2 716	1 050	1 665	49 448	5 214	10 842	13 138	12 341	6 269	1 644
2003	52 369	2 546	1 027	1 519	49 823	5 161	10 668	12 826	12 645	6 735	1 788
2004	52 527	2 486	991	1 495	50 040	5 207	10 602	12 604	12 810	6 947	1 870
2005	53 186	2 597	1 057	1 540	50 589	5 190	10 603	12 558	12 991	7 317	1 930
2006	53 950	2 590	1 079	1 512	51 359	5 182	10 750	12 449	13 230	7 758	1 991
2007	54 503	2 507	1 013	1 494	51 996	5 259	10 912	12 205	13 380	8 047	2 193
2008	54 501	2 377	895	1 482	52 124	5 197	10 943	11 961	13 386	8 312	2 325
2009	53 366	2 134	751	1 383	51 231	5 060	10 727	11 379	13 181	8 513	2 373
2010	52 916	1 918	650	1 268	50 997	4 988	10 815	10 958	12 960	8 827	2 450
2011	52 770	1 889	617	1 272	50 881	4 943	10 828	10 789	12 806	9 005	2 509
2012	52 779	1 868	644	1 224	50 911	5 014	10 713	10 708	12 505	9 274	2 698
2013	53 057	1 860	665	1 195	51 198	5 066	10 866	10 651	12 328	9 371	2 915
2014	53 680	1 882	690	1 192	51 798	5 161	11 143	10 712	12 192	9 535	3 055
2015	54 052	1 891	666	1 225	52 161	5 200	11 245	10 739	12 094	9 695	3 188
2016	54 701	1 931	711	1 220	52 771	5 124	11 546	10 800	12 065	9 885	3 350
2017	55 176	1 997	792	1 205	53 179	5 126	11 811	10 867	11 897	10 050	3 428
2018	55 759	2 077	788	1 288	53 682	5 137	11 950	11 060	11 779	10 163	3 594
2019	56 341	2 036	718	1 318	54 304	5 196	12 124	11 309	11 657	10 206	3 812

Table 1-11. Employed Civilians, by Age, Sex, Race, and Hispanic Origin, 1948–2019—*Continued*

(Thousands of people.)

Race, Hispanic origin, sex, and year	16 years and over	16 to 19 years			20 years and over						
		Total	16 to 17 years	18 to 19 years	Total	20 to 24 years	25 to 34 years	35 to 44 years	45 to 54 years	55 to 64 years	65 years and over
BLACK											
Both Sexes											
1985	10 501	532	175	356	9 969	1 399	3 325	2 427	1 598	985	235
1986	10 814	536	183	353	10 278	1 429	3 464	2 524	1 666	982	214
1987	11 309	587	203	385	10 722	1 421	3 614	2 695	1 714	1 036	241
1988	11 658	601	223	378	11 057	1 433	3 725	2 839	1 783	1 018	261
1989	11 953	625	237	388	11 328	1 467	3 801	2 981	1 844	970	265
1990	12 175	598	194	404	11 577	1 409	3 803	3 287	1 897	933	248
1991	12 074	494	161	334	11 580	1 373	3 714	3 401	1 892	957	243
1992	12 151	492	157	335	11 659	1 343	3 699	3 441	1 964	965	246
1993	12 382	494	171	323	11 888	1 377	3 700	3 584	2 059	941	226
1994	12 835	552	224	328	12 284	1 449	3 732	3 722	2 178	953	251
1995	13 279	586	223	363	12 693	1 443	3 844	3 861	2 288	1 004	253
1996	13 542	613	233	380	12 929	1 411	3 851	3 974	2 426	1 025	241
1997	13 969	631	229	401	13 339	1 456	3 903	4 094	2 588	1 048	249
1998	14 556	736	246	490	13 820	1 496	3 967	4 238	2 739	1 118	262
1999	15 056	691	243	448	14 365	1 594	4 091	4 404	2 872	1 134	271
2000	15 156	711	260	451	14 444	1 593	3 993	4 261	3 073	1 226	300
2001	15 006	637	230	408	14 368	1 571	3 840	4 200	3 139	1 283	335
2002	14 872	611	193	417	14 262	1 543	3 726	4 109	3 220	1 332	332
2003	14 739	516	196	320	14 222	1 516	3 618	4 080	3 289	1 373	346
2004	14 909	520	169	351	14 389	1 572	3 635	4 039	3 332	1 452	359
2005	15 313	536	164	372	14 776	1 599	3 722	4 060	3 464	1 555	375
2006	15 765	618	215	402	15 147	1 643	3 809	4 072	3 570	1 659	394
2007	16 051	566	202	364	15 485	1 674	3 888	4 120	3 658	1 732	413
2008	15 953	541	172	369	15 411	1 625	3 870	4 015	3 670	1 791	440
2009	15 025	442	131	310	14 584	1 474	3 582	3 686	3 562	1 827	453
2010	15 010	386	106	280	14 624	1 532	3 641	3 561	3 531	1 899	460
2011	15 051	380	99	281	14 671	1 574	3 632	3 499	3 513	1 943	508
2012	15 856	438	119	319	15 417	1 700	3 693	3 662	3 660	2 161	540
2013	16 151	439	117	322	15 712	1 727	3 780	3 730	3 644	2 263	567
2014	16 732	456	142	315	16 276	1 839	3 936	3 834	3 728	2 342	596
2015	17 472	502	164	338	16 970	1 953	4 190	3 928	3 806	2 433	660
2016	17 982	535	167	368	17 447	1 930	4 492	3 997	3 814	2 526	689
2017	18 587	573	189	384	18 015	1 984	4 667	4 115	3 858	2 606	786
2018	19 091	596	176	420	18 496	1 940	4 910	4 208	3 898	2 728	812
2019	19 381	588	180	408	18 793	1 935	5 014	4 230	3 920	2 799	895
Men											
1985	5 270	278	92	186	4 992	726	1 669	1 187	795	501	114
1986	5 428	278	96	182	5 150	732	1 756	1 211	831	507	112
1987	5 661	304	109	195	5 357	728	1 821	1 283	853	547	124
1988	5 824	316	122	193	5 509	736	1 881	1 348	878	536	131
1989	5 928	327	124	202	5 602	742	1 931	1 415	886	498	131
1990	5 995	303	99	204	5 692	702	1 895	1 586	926	469	114
1991	5 961	255	85	170	5 706	695	1 859	1 634	923	481	114
1992	5 930	249	78	170	5 681	679	1 819	1 650	930	478	124
1993	6 047	254	88	166	5 793	674	1 858	1 717	978	461	106
1994	6 241	276	107	169	5 964	718	1 850	1 795	1 030	455	115
1995	6 422	285	111	174	6 137	714	1 895	1 836	1 085	468	138
1996	6 456	289	109	180	6 167	685	1 867	1 878	1 129	482	126
1997	6 607	282	108	174	6 325	668	1 874	1 955	1 215	487	127
1998	6 871	341	120	221	6 530	686	1 886	2 008	1 284	524	142
1999	7 027	325	120	205	6 702	700	1 926	2 092	1 327	525	131
2000	7 082	341	129	211	6 741	730	1 865	1 984	1 425	596	142
2001	6 938	311	115	196	6 627	703	1 757	1 931	1 452	614	170
2002	6 959	306	95	212	6 652	725	1 729	1 899	1 503	624	172
2003	6 820	234	89	145	6 586	726	1 660	1 868	1 518	638	176
2004	6 912	231	76	155	6 681	739	1 720	1 840	1 534	668	180
2005	7 155	254	76	178	6 901	748	1 759	1 886	1 616	711	182
2006	7 354	275	99	175	7 079	804	1 797	1 882	1 680	734	184
2007	7 500	254	82	172	7 245	816	1 851	1 916	1 717	750	195
2008	7 398	247	70	177	7 151	794	1 805	1 854	1 703	792	204
2009	6 817	189	56	133	6 628	689	1 635	1 662	1 622	813	206
2010	6 865	185	48	137	6 680	692	1 710	1 638	1 594	834	211
2011	6 953	187	49	138	6 765	734	1 733	1 583	1 621	858	236
2012	7 302	198	52	146	7 104	784	1 723	1 667	1 693	988	249
2013	7 497	192	51	141	7 304	818	1 782	1 738	1 675	1 036	256
2014	7 818	205	70	134	7 613	887	1 879	1 772	1 721	1 081	272
2015	8 164	226	75	150	7 938	936	1 995	1 816	1 780	1 115	297
2016	8 471	242	57	185	8 228	906	2 156	1 865	1 779	1 195	327
2017	8 742	241	74	168	8 500	946	2 249	1 920	1 789	1 231	365
2018	9 018	273	69	204	8 745	913	2 408	1 973	1 810	1 281	361
2019	9 145	262	78	183	8 883	916	2 462	1 976	1 838	1 291	400

Table 1-11. Employed Civilians, by Age, Sex, Race, and Hispanic Origin, 1948–2019—*Continued*

(Thousands of people.)

Race, Hispanic origin, sex, and year	16 years and over	16 to 19 years			20 years and over						
		Total	16 to 17 years	18 to 19 years	Total	20 to 24 years	25 to 34 years	35 to 44 years	45 to 54 years	55 to 64 years	65 years and over
BLACK											
Women											
1985	5 231	254	83	171	4 977	673	1 656	1 240	804	484	121
1986	5 386	259	87	171	5 128	696	1 708	1 313	835	475	102
1987	5 648	283	93	190	5 365	693	1 793	1 412	860	489	117
1988	5 834	285	101	184	5 548	697	1 844	1 491	905	482	129
1989	6 025	298	113	185	5 727	725	1 870	1 566	959	472	134
1990	6 180	296	96	200	5 884	707	1 907	1 701	971	464	135
1991	6 113	239	76	164	5 874	677	1 855	1 768	969	476	129
1992	6 221	243	79	164	5 978	664	1 880	1 791	1 034	487	123
1993	6 334	239	82	157	6 095	703	1 842	1 867	1 081	480	121
1994	6 595	275	117	158	6 320	731	1 882	1 926	1 147	497	136
1995	6 857	301	112	189	6 556	729	1 949	2 025	1 202	536	114
1996	7 086	324	124	200	6 762	726	1 984	2 096	1 297	543	115
1997	7 362	349	122	227	7 013	789	2 029	2 139	1 373	561	122
1998	7 685	395	126	268	7 290	810	2 081	2 230	1 455	594	120
1999	8 029	366	123	243	7 663	893	2 165	2 312	1 545	609	139
2000	8 073	370	131	240	7 703	862	2 128	2 277	1 647	630	158
2001	8 068	327	115	212	7 741	868	2 084	2 269	1 686	668	165
2002	7 914	304	99	205	7 610	819	1 997	2 209	1 717	708	160
2003	7 919	283	107	175	7 636	790	1 959	2 211	1 770	735	171
2004	7 997	289	93	196	7 707	833	1 914	2 199	1 798	784	179
2005	8 158	282	88	194	7 876	852	1 964	2 175	1 848	844	193
2006	8 410	343	116	227	8 068	839	2 012	2 191	1 890	925	210
2007	8 551	311	120	191	8 240	858	2 037	2 205	1 941	982	218
2008	8 554	294	102	192	8 260	831	2 065	2 161	1 967	1 000	236
2009	8 208	252	75	178	7 956	784	1 947	2 024	1 939	1 014	246
2010	8 145	201	58	143	7 944	841	1 931	1 923	1 936	1 065	248
2011	8 098	193	50	142	7 906	840	1 899	1 916	1 892	1 086	272
2012	8 553	240	67	173	8 313	916	1 970	1 995	1 968	1 173	291
2013	8 654	246	66	180	8 408	909	1 998	1 992	1 970	1 228	311
2014	8 915	252	71	180	8 663	952	2 057	2 061	2 007	1 261	325
2015	9 308	276	89	188	9 032	1 017	2 195	2 112	2 026	1 319	363
2016	9 511	292	110	183	9 219	1 025	2 335	2 132	2 035	1 330	362
2017	9 845	331	115	216	9 514	1 038	2 418	2 194	2 069	1 375	421
2018	10 073	322	107	215	9 751	1 027	2 502	2 235	2 088	1 448	451
2019	10 236	326	101	225	9 910	1 019	2 552	2 254	2 081	1 508	495
HISPANIC											
Both Sexes											
1985	6 888	438	144	294	6 449	1 187	2 316	1 473	913	486	75
1986	7 219	430	146	284	6 789	1 231	2 427	1 570	1 011	474	76
1987	7 790	474	149	325	7 316	1 273	2 668	1 775	1 010	512	76
1988	8 250	523	171	353	7 727	1 341	2 749	1 876	1 078	585	97
1989	8 573	548	165	383	8 025	1 325	2 900	1 968	1 129	589	114
1990	9 845	668	208	460	9 177	1 672	3 327	2 229	1 235	611	103
1991	9 828	602	169	433	9 225	1 622	3 264	2 333	1 266	637	103
1992	10 027	577	169	408	9 450	1 575	3 350	2 468	1 316	628	112
1993	10 361	570	160	410	9 792	1 574	3 446	2 605	1 402	630	135
1994	10 788	609	195	415	10 178	1 643	3 517	2 737	1 495	647	139
1995	11 127	645	194	450	10 483	1 609	3 618	2 889	1 565	666	135
1996	11 642	646	199	447	10 996	1 628	3 758	3 115	1 595	748	152
1997	12 726	714	228	487	12 012	1 798	4 029	3 371	1 846	794	173
1998	13 291	793	230	563	12 498	1 883	4 113	3 504	1 994	846	158
1999	13 720	854	254	600	12 866	1 881	4 097	3 738	2 074	886	190
2000	15 735	973	285	688	14 762	2 356	4 950	4 052	2 308	898	197
2001	16 190	969	268	701	15 221	2 404	5 065	4 149	2 472	944	187
2002	16 590	882	254	628	15 708	2 413	5 272	4 273	2 511	1 029	209
2003	17 372	768	242	525	16 604	2 399	5 541	4 573	2 711	1 132	249
2004	17 930	792	211	581	17 138	2 477	5 560	4 671	2 932	1 210	288
2005	18 632	847	253	595	17 785	2 423	5 756	4 879	3 114	1 317	296
2006	19 613	900	287	614	18 712	2 487	6 001	5 106	3 324	1 441	354
2007	20 382	894	269	625	19 488	2 516	6 237	5 314	3 547	1 499	376
2008	20 346	870	248	622	19 476	2 361	6 119	5 371	3 620	1 619	385
2009	19 647	742	192	550	18 905	2 218	5 704	5 168	3 700	1 680	435
2010	19 906	680	165	515	19 226	2 281	5 781	5 185	3 779	1 737	464
2011	20 269	665	155	510	19 604	2 544	5 747	5 179	3 848	1 820	465
2012	21 878	808	204	604	21 070	2 761	6 119	5 552	4 188	1 983	467
2013	22 514	821	217	604	21 693	2 857	6 157	5 652	4 374	2 140	514
2014	23 492	859	225	634	22 633	2 947	6 354	5 869	4 593	2 313	557
2015	24 400	922	253	669	23 477	3 027	6 432	6 063	4 831	2 523	601
2016	25 249	977	284	693	24 272	3 086	6 652	6 251	4 975	2 627	681
2017	25 938	1 041	311	730	24 898	3 073	6 767	6 395	5 098	2 825	533
2018	27 012	1 094	307	787	25 918	3 160	7 093	6 600	5 305	2 982	778
2019	27 805	1 085	313	772	26 720	3 242	7 218	6 711	5 468	3 217	862

Table 1-11. Employed Civilians, by Age, Sex, Race, and Hispanic Origin, 1948–2019—*Continued*

(Thousands of people.)

Race, Hispanic origin, sex, and year	16 years and over	16 to 19 years			20 years and over						
		Total	16 to 17 years	18 to 19 years	Total	20 to 24 years	25 to 34 years	35 to 44 years	45 to 54 years	55 to 64 years	65 years and over
HISPANIC											
Men											
1985	4 245	251	82	169	3 994	727	1 473	888	550	308	. . .
1986	4 428	254	82	172	4 174	773	1 510	929	614	297	. . .
1987	4 713	268	81	188	4 444	777	1 664	1 044	606	303	. . .
1988	4 972	292	87	205	4 680	815	1 706	1 120	645	331	. . .
1989	5 172	319	94	225	4 853	821	1 787	1 152	676	350	. . .
1990	6 021	412	126	286	5 609	1 083	2 076	1 312	722	355	. . .
1991	5 979	356	94	263	5 623	1 063	2 050	1 360	719	369	. . .
1992	6 093	336	97	238	5 757	985	2 127	1 437	768	372	. . .
1993	6 328	337	95	242	5 992	1 003	2 200	1 527	822	360	. . .
1994	6 530	341	109	233	6 189	1 056	2 227	1 600	847	379	79
1995	6 725	358	110	248	6 367	1 030	2 284	1 675	908	384	85
1996	7 039	384	107	277	6 655	1 015	2 345	1 842	918	438	96
1997	7 728	420	130	290	7 307	1 142	2 547	1 978	1 059	477	105
1998	8 018	449	133	315	7 570	1 173	2 592	2 077	1 115	512	101
1999	8 067	491	139	352	7 576	1 135	2 524	2 135	1 151	502	130
2000	9 428	570	159	411	8 859	1 486	3 063	2 358	1 295	532	126
2001	9 668	568	149	419	9 100	1 473	3 142	2 446	1 375	545	119
2002	9 845	504	141	363	9 341	1 476	3 271	2 503	1 396	569	125
2003	10 479	415	121	294	10 063	1 485	3 537	2 724	1 533	639	144
2004	10 832	446	108	338	10 385	1 514	3 557	2 801	1 654	687	174
2005	11 337	465	137	328	10 872	1 511	3 711	2 939	1 781	748	183
2006	11 887	496	146	350	11 391	1 535	3 845	3 088	1 894	809	220
2007	12 310	483	145	338	11 827	1 524	3 982	3 220	2 012	869	220
2008	12 248	479	140	340	11 769	1 406	3 897	3 233	2 080	929	224
2009	11 640	383	94	289	11 256	1 287	3 576	3 108	2 104	930	251
2010	11 800	361	78	283	11 438	1 319	3 591	3 169	2 137	949	273
2011	12 049	364	76	287	11 685	1 535	3 615	3 124	2 141	1 006	266
2012	12 643	431	97	334	12 212	1 584	3 714	3 229	2 334	1 097	256
2013	13 078	440	111	329	12 638	1 609	3 748	3 332	2 471	1 181	296
2014	13 655	453	108	344	13 202	1 655	3 830	1 949	2 600	1 317	307
2015	14 111	487	127	359	13 624	1 655	3 873	3 604	2 730	1 432	331
2016	14 563	508	147	361	14 055	1 677	3 952	3 693	2 859	1 490	384
2017	14 874	519	146	373	14 355	1 692	3 972	3 746	2 921	1 601	423
2018	15 418	545	149	396	14 873	1 705	4 125	3 892	3 002	1 704	446
2019	15 782	578	182	396	15 204	1 717	4 158	3 954	3 067	1 816	492
HISPANIC											
Women											
1985	2 642	187	62	125	2 456	460	843	585	362	178	. . .
1986	2 791	176	64	112	2 615	458	917	641	397	177	. . .
1987	3 077	206	69	137	2 872	496	1 004	732	405	209	. . .
1988	3 278	231	84	147	3 047	526	1 042	756	434	254	. . .
1989	3 401	229	71	158	3 172	504	1 114	816	453	239	. . .
1990	3 823	256	82	174	3 567	588	1 251	917	513	256	. . .
1991	3 848	246	76	170	3 603	559	1 214	972	548	268	. . .
1992	3 934	242	72	170	3 693	591	1 223	1 031	548	256	. . .
1993	4 033	233	65	168	3 800	571	1 246	1 077	581	269	. . .
1994	4 258	268	86	182	3 989	587	1 290	1 137	648	268	59
1995	4 403	287	85	202	4 116	579	1 334	1 213	657	282	50
1996	4 602	261	92	169	4 341	612	1 412	1 273	677	310	56
1997	4 999	294	98	196	4 705	656	1 482	1 393	787	318	69
1998	5 273	345	97	247	4 928	710	1 521	1 428	879	334	57
1999	5 653	363	115	248	5 290	746	1 574	1 603	923	384	60
2000	6 307	404	127	277	5 903	870	1 887	1 695	1 013	366	72
2001	6 522	401	119	282	6 121	931	1 923	1 703	1 097	398	67
2002	6 744	378	113	265	6 367	937	2 001	1 770	1 114	460	84
2003	6 894	353	121	231	6 541	914	2 004	1 849	1 178	493	105
2004	7 098	346	103	243	6 752	964	2 003	1 870	1 279	523	114
2005	7 295	382	116	266	6 913	912	2 045	1 940	1 333	569	113
2006	7 725	404	140	264	7 321	951	2 155	2 018	1 430	632	135
2007	8 072	410	124	287	7 662	991	2 255	2 094	1 535	631	155
2008	8 098	391	108	282	7 707	955	2 222	2 138	1 541	690	161
2009	8 007	358	98	261	7 649	931	2 128	2 060	1 596	751	183
2010	8 106	318	87	231	7 788	962	2 189	2 016	1 642	788	191
2011	8 220	301	79	223	7 918	1 010	2 132	2 055	1 707	814	200
2012	9 235	377	107	269	8 858	1 178	2 405	2 323	1 854	887	212
2013	9 437	381	107	274	9 056	1 249	2 409	2 320	1 902	959	217
2014	9 838	407	117	290	9 431	1 291	2 524	2 376	1 993	997	250
2015	10 289	436	126	310	9 853	1 372	2 560	2 460	2 101	1 091	270
2016	10 686	470	138	332	10 217	1 409	2 700	2 557	2 116	1 137	297
2017	11 064	522	165	357	10 543	1 381	2 795	2 649	2 176	1 224	317
2018	11 594	549	158	391	11 045	1 456	2 968	2 708	2 303	1 278	331
2019	12 023	508	131	376	11 516	1 525	3 060	2 757	2 402	1 401	370

. . . = Not available.

Table 1-12. Civilian Employment-Population Ratios, by Sex, Age, Race, and Hispanic Origin, 1948–2019

(Percent.)

Race, Hispanic origin, and year	Both sexes			Men			Women		
	16 years and over	16 to 19 years	20 years and over	16 years and over	16 to 19 years	20 years and over	16 years and over	16 to 19 years	20 years and over
ALL RACES									
1948	56.6	47.7	57.4	83.5	57.5	85.8	31.3	38.5	30.7
1949	55.4	45.2	56.3	81.3	53.8	83.7	31.2	37.2	30.6
1950	56.1	45.5	57.0	82.0	55.2	84.2	32.0	36.3	31.6
1951	57.3	47.9	58.1	84.0	57.9	86.1	33.1	38.9	32.6
1952	57.3	46.9	58.1	83.9	55.9	86.2	33.4	38.8	33.0
1953	57.1	46.4	58.0	83.6	55.9	85.9	33.3	37.8	32.9
1954	55.5	42.3	56.6	81.0	50.2	83.5	32.5	34.9	32.3
1955	56.7	43.5	57.8	81.8	52.1	84.3	34.0	35.6	33.8
1956	57.5	45.3	58.5	82.3	53.8	84.6	35.1	37.5	34.9
1957	57.1	43.9	58.2	81.3	51.8	83.8	35.1	36.7	35.0
1958	55.4	39.9	56.8	78.5	46.9	81.2	34.5	33.5	34.6
1959	56.0	39.9	57.5	79.3	47.2	82.3	35.0	33.0	35.1
1960	56.1	40.5	57.6	78.9	47.6	81.9	35.5	33.8	35.7
1961	55.4	39.1	56.9	77.6	45.3	80.8	35.4	33.2	35.6
1962	55.5	39.4	57.1	77.7	45.9	80.9	35.6	33.3	35.8
1963	55.4	37.4	57.2	77.1	43.8	80.6	35.8	31.5	36.3
1964	55.7	37.3	57.7	77.3	44.1	80.9	36.3	30.9	36.9
1965	56.2	38.9	58.2	77.5	46.2	81.2	37.1	32.0	37.6
1966	56.9	42.1	58.7	77.9	48.9	81.5	38.3	35.6	38.6
1967	57.3	42.2	59.0	78.0	48.7	81.5	39.0	35.9	39.3
1968	57.5	42.2	59.3	77.8	48.7	81.3	39.6	36.0	40.0
1969	58.0	43.4	59.7	77.6	49.5	81.1	40.7	37.5	41.1
1970	57.4	42.3	59.2	76.2	47.7	79.7	40.8	37.1	41.2
1971	56.6	41.3	58.4	74.9	46.8	78.5	40.4	36.0	40.9
1972	57.0	43.5	58.6	75.0	48.9	78.4	41.0	38.2	41.3
1973	57.8	45.9	59.3	75.5	51.4	78.6	42.0	40.5	42.2
1974	57.8	46.0	59.2	74.9	51.2	77.9	42.6	41.0	42.8
1975	56.1	43.3	57.6	71.7	47.2	74.8	42.0	39.4	42.3
1976	56.8	44.2	58.3	72.0	47.9	75.1	43.2	40.5	43.5
1977	57.9	46.1	59.2	72.8	50.4	75.6	44.5	41.8	44.8
1978	59.3	48.3	60.6	73.8	52.2	76.4	46.4	44.5	46.6
1979	59.9	48.5	61.2	73.8	51.7	76.5	47.5	45.3	47.7
1980	59.2	46.6	60.6	72.0	49.5	74.6	47.7	43.8	48.1
1981	59.0	44.6	60.5	71.3	47.1	74.0	48.0	42.0	48.6
1982	57.8	41.5	59.4	69.0	42.9	71.8	47.7	40.2	48.4
1983	57.9	41.5	59.5	68.8	43.1	71.4	48.0	40.0	48.8
1984	59.5	43.7	61.0	70.7	45.0	73.2	49.5	42.5	50.1
1985	60.1	44.4	61.5	70.9	45.7	73.3	50.4	42.9	51.0
1986	60.7	44.6	62.1	71.0	45.7	73.3	51.4	43.6	52.0
1987	61.5	45.5	62.9	71.5	46.1	73.8	52.5	44.8	53.1
1988	62.3	46.8	63.6	72.0	47.8	74.2	53.4	45.9	54.0
1989	63.0	47.5	64.2	72.5	48.7	74.5	54.3	46.4	54.9
1990	62.8	45.3	64.3	72.0	46.6	74.3	54.3	44.0	55.2
1991	61.7	42.0	63.2	70.4	42.7	72.7	53.7	41.2	54.6
1992	61.5	41.0	63.0	69.8	41.9	72.1	53.8	40.0	54.8
1993	61.7	41.7	63.3	70.0	42.3	72.3	54.1	41.0	55.0
1994	62.5	43.4	64.0	70.4	43.8	72.6	55.3	43.0	56.2
1995	62.9	44.2	64.4	70.8	44.7	73.0	55.6	43.8	56.5
1996	63.2	43.5	64.7	70.9	43.6	73.2	56.0	43.5	57.0
1997	63.8	43.4	65.5	71.3	43.4	73.7	56.8	43.3	57.8
1998	64.1	45.1	65.6	71.6	44.7	73.9	57.1	45.5	58.0
1999	64.3	44.7	65.9	71.6	45.1	74.0	57.4	44.3	58.5
2000	64.4	45.2	66.0	71.9	45.4	74.2	57.5	45.0	58.4
2001	63.7	42.3	65.4	70.9	42.2	73.3	57.0	42.4	58.1
2002	62.7	39.6	64.6	69.7	38.9	72.3	56.3	40.3	57.5
2003	62.3	36.8	64.3	68.9	35.7	71.7	56.1	37.8	57.5
2004	62.3	36.4	64.4	69.2	35.9	71.9	56.0	37.0	57.4
2005	62.7	36.5	64.7	69.6	35.1	72.4	56.2	37.8	57.6
2006	63.1	36.9	65.2	70.1	36.3	72.9	56.6	37.6	58.0
2007	63.0	34.8	65.2	69.8	33.8	72.8	56.6	35.8	58.2
2008	62.2	32.6	64.5	68.5	31.6	71.6	56.2	33.7	57.9
2009	59.3	28.4	61.7	64.5	26.9	67.6	54.4	29.9	56.2
2010	58.5	25.9	61.0	63.7	24.8	66.8	53.6	27.0	55.5
2011	58.4	25.8	60.8	63.9	24.6	67.0	53.2	27.1	55.0
2012	58.6	26.1	61.0	64.4	24.9	67.5	53.1	27.3	55.0
2013	58.6	26.6	60.9	64.4	25.5	67.4	53.2	27.7	54.9
2014	59.0	27.3	61.3	64.9	26.3	67.8	53.5	28.4	55.2
2015	59.3	28.5	61.5	65.3	27.9	68.1	53.7	29.1	55.4
2016	59.7	29.7	61.8	65.8	29.3	68.5	54.1	30.1	55.7
2017	60.1	30.3	62.2	66.0	29.2	68.8	54.6	31.4	56.1
2018	60.4	30.6	62.5	66.3	29.3	69.0	54.9	31.9	56.4
2019	60.8	30.9	62.8	66.6	30.1	69.2	55.4	31.6	56.9

Table 1-12. Civilian Employment-Population Ratios, by Sex, Age, Race, and Hispanic Origin, 1948–2019 —*Continued*

(Percent.)

Race, Hispanic origin, and year	Both sexes			Men			Women		
	16 years and over	16 to 19 years	20 years and over	16 years and over	16 to 19 years	20 years and over	16 years and over	16 to 19 years	20 years and over
WHITE									
1954	55.2	42.9	56.2	81.5	49.9	84.0	31.4	36.4	31.1
1955	56.5	44.2	57.4	82.2	52.0	84.7	33.0	37.0	32.7
1956	57.3	46.1	58.2	82.7	54.1	85.0	34.2	38.9	33.8
1957	56.8	45.0	57.8	81.8	52.4	84.1	34.2	38.2	33.9
1958	55.3	41.0	56.5	79.2	47.6	81.8	33.6	35.0	33.5
1959	55.9	41.2	57.2	79.9	48.1	82.8	34.0	34.8	34.0
1960	55.9	41.5	57.2	79.4	48.1	82.4	34.6	35.1	34.5
1961	55.3	40.1	56.7	78.2	45.9	81.4	34.5	34.6	34.5
1962	55.4	40.4	56.9	78.4	46.4	81.5	34.7	34.8	34.7
1963	55.3	38.6	56.9	77.7	44.7	81.1	35.0	32.9	35.2
1964	55.5	38.4	57.3	77.8	45.0	81.3	35.5	32.2	35.8
1965	56.0	40.3	57.8	77.9	47.1	81.5	36.2	33.7	36.5
1966	56.8	43.6	58.3	78.3	50.1	81.7	37.5	37.5	37.5
1967	57.2	43.8	58.7	78.4	50.2	81.7	38.3	37.7	38.3
1968	57.4	43.9	59.0	78.3	50.3	81.6	38.9	37.8	39.1
1969	58.0	45.2	59.4	78.2	51.1	81.4	40.1	39.5	40.1
1970	57.5	44.5	59.0	76.8	49.6	80.1	40.3	39.5	40.4
1971	56.8	43.8	58.3	75.7	49.2	79.0	39.9	38.6	40.1
1972	57.4	46.4	58.6	76.0	51.5	79.0	40.7	41.3	40.6
1973	58.2	48.9	59.3	76.5	54.3	79.2	41.8	43.6	41.6
1974	58.3	49.3	59.3	75.9	54.4	78.6	42.4	44.3	42.2
1975	56.7	46.5	57.9	73.0	50.6	75.7	42.0	42.5	41.9
1976	57.5	47.8	58.6	73.4	51.5	76.0	43.2	44.2	43.1
1977	58.6	50.1	59.6	74.1	54.4	76.5	44.5	45.9	44.4
1978	60.0	52.4	60.8	75.0	56.3	77.2	46.3	48.5	46.1
1979	60.6	52.6	61.5	75.1	55.7	77.3	47.5	49.4	47.3
1980	60.0	50.7	61.0	73.4	53.4	75.6	47.8	47.9	47.8
1981	60.0	48.7	61.1	72.8	51.3	75.1	48.3	46.2	48.5
1982	58.8	45.8	60.1	70.6	47.0	73.0	48.1	44.6	48.4
1983	58.9	45.9	60.1	70.4	47.4	72.6	48.5	44.5	48.9
1984	60.5	48.0	61.5	72.1	49.1	74.3	49.8	47.0	50.0
1985	61.0	48.5	62.0	72.3	49.9	74.3	50.7	47.1	51.0
1986	61.5	48.8	62.6	72.3	49.6	74.3	51.7	47.9	52.0
1987	62.3	49.4	63.4	72.7	49.9	74.7	52.8	49.0	53.1
1988	63.1	50.9	64.1	73.2	51.7	75.1	53.8	50.2	54.0
1989	63.8	51.6	64.7	73.7	52.6	75.4	54.6	50.5	54.9
1990	63.7	49.7	64.8	73.3	51.0	75.1	54.7	48.3	55.2
1991	62.6	46.6	63.7	71.6	47.2	73.5	54.2	45.9	54.8
1992	62.4	45.3	63.6	71.1	46.4	73.1	54.2	44.2	54.9
1993	62.7	46.2	63.9	71.4	46.6	73.3	54.6	45.7	55.2
1994	63.5	47.9	64.7	71.8	48.3	73.6	55.8	47.5	56.4
1995	63.8	48.8	64.9	72.0	49.4	73.8	56.1	48.1	56.7
1996	64.1	47.9	65.3	72.3	48.2	74.2	56.3	47.6	57.0
1997	64.6	47.7	65.9	72.7	48.1	74.7	57.0	47.2	57.8
1998	64.7	49.0	65.9	72.7	48.6	74.7	57.1	49.3	57.7
1999	64.8	48.9	66.1	72.8	49.3	74.8	57.3	48.4	58.0
2000	64.9	49.1	66.1	73.0	49.5	74.9	57.4	48.8	58.0
2001	64.2	46.3	65.6	72.0	46.2	74.0	57.0	46.5	57.7
2002	63.4	43.2	64.9	70.8	42.3	73.1	56.4	44.1	57.3
2003	63.0	40.4	64.7	70.1	39.4	72.5	56.3	41.5	57.3
2004	63.1	40.0	64.8	70.4	39.7	72.8	56.1	40.3	57.2
2005	63.4	40.2	65.1	70.8	38.8	73.3	56.3	41.8	57.4
2006	63.8	40.6	65.5	71.3	40.0	73.7	56.6	41.1	57.7
2007	63.6	38.3	65.5	70.9	37.3	73.5	56.7	39.2	57.9
2008	62.9	35.9	64.8	69.7	34.8	72.4	56.3	37.1	57.7
2009	60.2	31.7	62.3	66.0	30.2	68.7	54.8	33.4	56.2
2010	59.4	29.0	61.6	65.1	27.6	67.9	54.0	30.4	55.6
2011	59.4	28.8	61.6	65.3	27.3	68.2	53.7	30.4	55.3
2012	59.4	29.0	61.5	65.8	27.7	68.6	53.3	30.3	54.9
2013	59.4	29.4	61.4	65.7	28.3	68.4	53.3	30.5	54.8
2014	59.7	29.9	61.8	66.1	28.8	68.7	56.7	36.8	57.9
2015	59.9	31.0	61.8	66.5	30.8	68.9	53.7	31.3	55.1
2016	60.2	32.1	62.1	66.7	32.4	69.1	54.0	31.9	55.4
2017	60.4	32.3	62.3	66.9	31.7	69.3	54.2	33.0	55.6
2018	60.7	33.0	62.5	67.1	31.6	69.5	54.5	34.3	55.8
2019	61.0	33.2	62.8	67.3	44.5	69.6	54.9	33.8	56.2

Table 1-12. Civilian Employment-Population Ratios, by Sex, Age, Race, and Hispanic Origin, 1948–2019
  —*Continued*

(Percent.)

Race, Hispanic origin, and year	Both sexes			Men			Women		
	16 years and over	16 to 19 years	20 years and over	16 years and over	16 to 19 years	20 years and over	16 years and over	16 to 19 years	20 years and over
BLACK									
1985	53.4	24.6	57.0	60.0	26.3	64.6	48.1	23.1	50.9
1986	54.1	25.1	57.6	60.6	26.5	65.1	48.8	23.8	51.6
1987	55.6	27.1	58.9	62.0	28.5	66.4	50.3	25.8	53.0
1988	56.3	27.6	59.7	62.7	29.4	67.1	51.2	25.8	53.9
1989	56.9	28.7	60.1	62.8	30.4	67.0	52.0	27.1	54.6
1990	56.7	26.7	60.2	62.6	27.7	67.1	51.9	25.9	54.7
1991	55.4	22.6	59.0	61.3	23.8	66.0	50.6	21.4	53.6
1992	54.9	22.8	58.3	59.9	23.6	64.3	50.8	22.1	53.6
1993	55.0	22.7	58.4	60.0	23.6	64.3	50.9	21.6	53.8
1994	56.1	25.0	59.4	60.8	25.4	65.0	52.3	24.4	55.0
1995	57.1	25.7	60.6	61.7	25.2	66.1	53.4	26.1	56.1
1996	57.4	26.0	60.8	61.0	24.9	65.5	54.4	27.1	57.1
1997	58.2	26.2	61.8	61.4	23.7	66.1	55.6	28.5	58.4
1998	59.7	30.1	63.0	62.9	28.4	67.1	57.2	31.8	59.7
1999	60.6	27.9	64.2	63.1	26.7	67.5	58.6	29.0	61.5
2000	60.9	29.8	64.2	63.6	28.9	67.7	58.6	30.6	61.3
2001	59.7	26.7	63.2	62.1	26.4	66.3	57.8	27.0	60.7
2002	58.1	25.3	61.6	61.1	25.6	65.2	55.8	24.9	58.7
2003	57.4	21.7	61.0	59.5	19.9	64.1	55.6	23.5	58.6
2004	57.2	21.5	60.9	59.3	19.3	63.9	55.5	23.6	58.5
2005	57.7	21.6	61.5	60.2	20.8	64.7	55.7	22.4	58.9
2006	58.4	24.1	62.0	60.6	21.7	65.2	56.5	26.4	59.4
2007	58.4	21.4	62.3	60.7	19.5	65.5	56.5	23.3	59.8
2008	57.3	20.2	61.2	59.1	18.7	63.9	55.8	21.7	59.1
2009	53.2	16.5	57.1	53.7	14.3	58.2	52.8	18.6	56.1
2010	52.3	14.5	56.1	53.1	14.1	57.5	51.7	15.0	55.1
2011	51.7	14.6	55.3	52.8	14.6	56.9	50.8	14.7	54.0
2012	53.0	16.6	56.5	54.1	15.0	58.3	52.2	18.1	55.1
2013	53.2	17.1	56.5	54.5	15.0	58.6	52.0	19.1	54.8
2014	54.3	18.2	57.4	55.9	16.4	59.7	52.9	19.9	55.6
2015	55.7	20.1	58.7	57.2	18.2	60.9	54.4	22.0	56.9
2016	56.4	21.3	59.4	58.3	19.4	62.0	54.8	23.1	57.3
2017	57.6	22.8	60.6	59.4	19.3	63.1	56.1	26.2	58.5
2018	58.3	23.8	61.1	60.3	22.0	63.7	56.6	25.6	59.0
2019	58.7	23.9	61.5	60.6	21.4	64.0	57.1	26.3	59.4
HISPANIC									
1985	57.8	33.7	60.7	. . .	. . .	. . .	. . .	. . .	. . .
1986	58.5	33.0	61.5	. . .	. . .	. . .	. . .	. . .	. . .
1987	60.5	35.6	63.4	. . .	. . .	. . .	. . .	. . .	. . .
1988	61.9	38.6	64.6	. . .	. . .	. . .	. . .	. . .	. . .
1989	62.2	39.2	64.8	. . .	. . .	. . .	. . .	. . .	. . .
1990	61.9	38.5	64.8	. . .	. . .	. . .	. . .	. . .	. . .
1991	59.8	34.8	62.8	. . .	. . .	. . .	. . .	. . .	. . .
1992	59.1	33.2	62.1	. . .	. . .	. . .	. . .	. . .	. . .
1993	59.1	32.5	62.1	. . .	. . .	. . .	. . .	. . .	. . .
1994	59.5	33.5	62.4	71.7	36.8	. . .	47.2	30.1	. . .
1995	59.7	34.5	62.6	72.1	37.5	. . .	47.3	31.3	. . .
1996	60.6	33.2	63.7	73.3	38.8	. . .	47.9	27.3	. . .
1997	62.6	33.7	66.0	74.5	37.6	. . .	50.2	29.3	. . .
1998	63.1	36.0	66.2	74.7	38.6	. . .	51.0	33.0	. . .
1999	63.4	37.0	66.5	75.3	41.2	. . .	51.7	32.5	. . .
2000	65.7	38.6	68.9	77.4	42.8	81.7	53.6	33.9	55.8
2001	64.9	38.6	67.8	76.2	43.3	79.9	53.3	33.5	55.4
2002	63.9	35.2	67.0	74.5	39.0	78.3	52.9	31.1	55.2
2003	63.1	30.2	66.4	74.3	31.9	78.6	51.2	28.4	53.6
2004	63.8	30.4	67.2	75.1	33.4	79.4	51.8	27.2	54.4
2005	64.0	31.5	67.3	75.8	33.8	80.0	51.5	29.1	53.8
2006	65.2	32.2	68.5	76.8	34.8	81.1	52.8	29.5	55.2
2007	64.9	30.4	68.5	76.2	32.1	80.7	53.0	28.5	55.6
2008	63.3	28.6	66.9	74.1	30.9	78.6	51.9	26.2	54.6
2009	59.7	23.8	63.5	68.9	24.1	73.5	50.1	23.4	52.9
2010	59.0	21.0	63.1	68.0	21.7	72.9	49.6	20.2	52.7
2011	58.9	19.5	63.2	67.9	20.1	73.3	49.3	18.9	52.5
2012	59.5	22.1	63.6	68.6	22.9	73.8	50.4	21.2	53.5
2013	60.0	22.5	64.1	69.6	23.5	74.7	50.4	21.4	53.5
2014	61.2	23.5	65.2	71.0	24.2	76.0	51.4	22.7	54.3
2015	61.6	24.9	65.4	71.5	25.8	76.3	51.8	23.9	54.6
2016	62.0	25.9	65.7	71.9	26.4	76.6	52.3	25.3	55.0
2017	62.7	27.1	66.3	72.3	26.6	77.1	53.2	27.6	55.8
2018	63.2	27.8	66.8	72.4	27.3	77.1	54.1	28.3	56.6
2019	63.9	27.2	67.6	72.9	28.6	77.4	55.0	25.8	57.9

. . . = Not available.

Table 1-13. Employed Civilians, by Sex, Race, Hispanic Origin, and Occupation, 2017–2019

(Thousands of people.)

Year and occupation	Total	Men	Women	White	Black	Hispanic[1]
2017						
All Occupations	153 337	81 402	71 936	120 176	18 587	25 938
Management, professional, and related occupations	60 901	29 488	31 413	48 748	5 719	5 826
Management, business, and financial operations occupations	25 379	14 207	11 171	21 065	2 075	2 532
Computer and mathematical occupations	4 804	3 578	1 226	3 258	416	352
Architecture and engineering occupations	3 224	2 702	521	2 556	182	281
Life, physical and social science occupations	1 431	753	678	1 093	81	129
Community and social service occupations	2 635	893	1 742	1 925	524	326
Legal occupations	1 827	862	965	1 582	126	157
Education, training, and library occupations	9 215	2 486	6 729	7 553	987	967
Arts, design, entertainment, sports, and media occupations	3 246	1 723	1 523	2 722	237	332
Healthcare practitioner and technical occupations	9 141	2 285	6 857	6 994	1 091	751
Healthcare support occupations	3 506	451	3 055	2 301	879	661
Protective service occupations	3 113	2 418	694	2 261	638	399
Food preparation and serving related occupations	8 305	3 840	4 465	6 179	1 155	2 117
Building and grounds cleaning and maintenance occupations	5 888	3 491	2 397	4 560	875	2 235
Personal care and service occupations	5 939	1 421	4 518	4 127	955	1 016
Sales and related occupations	15 815	8 045	7 770	12 640	1 756	2 515
Office and administrative support occupations	17 751	4 929	12 823	13 717	2 593	2 824
Farming, fishing, and forestry occupations	1 184	907	278	1 058	58	524
Construction and extraction occupations	8 031	7 788	243	7 050	554	2 890
Installation, maintenance, and repair occupations	4 977	4 778	200	4 232	149	946
Production occupations	8 482	6 031	2 450	6 514	1 132	1 935
Transportation and material moving occupations	9 445	7 815	1 630	6 790	1 844	2 051
2018						
All Occupations	155 761	82 698	73 063	121 461	19 091	27 012
Management, professional, and related occupations	62 436	30 287	32 149	49 555	5 982	6 048
Management, business, and financial operations occupations	25 850	14 464	11 387	21 309	2 127	2 535
Computer and mathematical occupations	5 126	3 814	1 313	3 436	431	382
Architecture and engineering occupations	3 263	2 745	518	2 588	211	290
Life, physical and social science occupations	1 529	815	714	1 194	108	133
Community and social service occupations	2 680	898	1 783	1 925	546	325
Legal occupations	1 891	915	976	1 620	139	187
Education, training, and library occupations	9 313	2 495	6 819	7 588	987	995
Arts, design, entertainment, sports, and media occupations	3 362	1 790	1 572	2 812	247	397
Healthcare practitioner and technical occupations	9 420	2 352	7 068	7 083	1 183	803
Healthcare support occupations	3 629	469	3 161	2 333	952	665
Protective service occupations	3 203	2 483	720	2 353	645	441
Food preparation and serving related occupations	8 220	3 655	4 565	6 014	1 214	2 126
Building and grounds cleaning and maintenance occupations	5 854	3 434	2 421	4 526	869	2 273
Personal care and service occupations	5 947	1 375	4 572	4 118	972	1 059
Sales and related occupations	15 806	7 999	7 807	12 677	1 738	2 582
Office and administrative support occupations	17 655	5 010	12 646	13 614	2 543	2 976
Farming, fishing, and forestry occupations	1 121	848	273	1 007	42	516
Construction and extraction occupations	8 338	8 053	285	7 294	590	3 088
Installation, maintenance, and repair occupations	5 012	4 825	187	4 180	473	1 006
Production occupations	8 621	6 140	2 480	6 604	1 167	8 621
Transportation and material moving occupations	9 918	8 121	1 797	7 186	1 903	2 213
2019						
All Occupations	157 538	83 460	74 078	122 441	19 381	27 805
Management, professional, and related occupations	64 218	30 950	33 267	50 706	6 186	6 490
Management, business, and financial operations occupations	26 981	15 072	11 909	22 140	2 269	2 800
Computer and mathematical occupations	5 352	3 973	1 379	3 517	465	420
Architecture and engineering occupations	3 305	2 785	520	2 563	224	302
Life, physical and social science occupations	1 485	752	733	1 142	93	141
Community and social service occupations	2 717	884	1 833	1 981	547	354
Legal occupations	1 955	925	1 030	1 622	162	186
Education, training, and library occupations	9 455	2 500	6 955	7 729	963	1 037
Arts, design, entertainment, sports, and media occupations	3 285	1 676	1 609	2 719	253	3 285
Healthcare practitioner and technical occupations	9 684	2 384	7 300	7 295	1 209	870
Healthcare support occupations	3 758	491	3 267	2 411	1 002	717
Protective service occupations	3 128	2 437	692	2 311	634	479
Food preparation and serving related occupations	8 378	3 808	4 569	6 172	1 167	2 264
Building and grounds cleaning and maintenance occupations	5 746	3 332	2 413	4 444	856	2 193
Personal care and service occupations	5 968	1 376	4 592	4 144	962	1 086
Sales and related occupations	33 370	13 148	20 222	26 059	4 324	2 606
Office and administrative support occupations	17 789	5 169	12 620	13 623	2 580	3 115
Farming, fishing, and forestry occupations	1 156	865	291	1 032	51	550
Construction and extraction occupations	8 325	8 033	292	7 251	604	3 032
Installation, maintenance, and repair occupations	4 862	4 671	191	4 084	445	4 862
Production occupations	18 628	14 348	4 281	13 827	3 149	8 565
Transportation and material moving occupations	10 063	8 233	1 831	7 268	1 272	2 306

[1]May be of any race.

Table 1-14. Employed Civilians, by Selected Occupation and Industry, 2017–2019

(Thousands of people.)

Year and occupation	Total employed	Agriculture, forestry, fishing, and hunting	Mining	Construction	Manufacturing Total	Durable goods	Nondurable goods	Wholesale trade
2017								
All Occupations	153 337	2 454	748	10 692	15 408	9 698	5 710	3 594
Management, professional, and related occupations	60 901	1 108	257	2 249	4 899	3 316	1 583	686
Management, business, and financial operations occupations	25 379	1 056	146	1 984	2 645	1 692	952	513
Computer and mathematical occupations	4 804	4	19	27	475	369	106	64
Architecture and engineering occupations	3 224	4	60	178	1 182	989	193	31
Life, physical and social science occupations	1 431	31	21	5	260	53	207	9
Community and social service occupations	2 635	1	...	0	3	2	0	2
Legal occupations	1 827	3	6	6	35	22	13	10
Education, training, and library occupations	9 215	1	1	4	31	20	11	11
Arts, design, entertainment, sports, and media occupations	3 246	5	2	41	230	150	80	23
Healthcare practitioner and technical occupations	9 141	3	2	4	39	19	20	23
Healthcare support occupations	3 506	1	0	1	10	7	3	2
Protective service occupations	3 113	14	4	15	36	25	12	3
Food preparation and serving related occupations	8 305	3	2	5	58	8	50	9
Building and grounds cleaning and maintenance occupations	5 888	41	3	40	133	69	64	21
Personal care and service occupations	5 939	32	0	2	15	6	9	2
Sales and related occupations	15 815	18	11	111	608	296	312	1 304
Office and administrative support occupations	17 751	80	52	492	1 292	823	469	542
Farming, fishing, and forestry occupations	1 184	1 001	1	5	61	5	56	52
Construction and extraction occupations	8 031	11	235	6 769	304	234	71	22
Installation, maintenance, and repair occupations	4 977	30	55	612	675	434	241	126
Production occupations	8 482	24	47	161	6 078	3 823	2 255	122
Transportation and material moving occupations	9 445	90	81	232	1 239	654	585	701
2018								
All Occupations	155 761	2 425	784	11 181	15 560	9 831	5 729	3 671
Management, professional, and related occupations	62 436	1 072	253	2 451	4 927	3 311	1 616	695
Management, business, and financial operations occupations	25 850	1 032	144	2 149	2 630	1 661	969	516
Computer and mathematical occupations	5 126	5 126	3	13	473	375	98	75
Architecture and engineering occupations	3 263	6	55	201	1 229	1 028	200	37
Life, physical and social science occupations	1 529	24	30	10	253	46	207	12
Community and social service occupations	2 680	3	...	0	4	1	3	0
Legal occupations	1 891	1	5	7	26	15	10	8
Education, training, and library occupations	9 313	2	3	5	23	12	11	7
Arts, design, entertainment, sports, and media occupations	3 362	1	1	42	223	137	86	25
Healthcare practitioner and technical occupations	9 420	1	1	6	67	35	32	14
Healthcare support occupations	3 629	0	0	1	11	9	2	5
Protective service occupations	3 203	14	4	18	26	12	14	6
Food preparation and serving related occupations	8 220	9	1	4	70	14	57	13
Building and grounds cleaning and maintenance occupations	5 854	31	8	38	141	64	76	30
Personal care and service occupations	5 947	44	0	6	16	6	10	2
Sales and related occupations	15 806	15	11	124	602	313	289	1 297
Office and administrative support occupations	17 655	83	51	543	1 243	783	460	557
Farming, fishing, and forestry occupations	1 121	966	0	3	56	4	52	33
Construction and extraction occupations	8 338	15	246	6 992	313	246	67	27
Installation, maintenance, and repair occupations	5 012	36	55	585	710	441	269	126
Production occupations	8 621	41	51	185	6 103	3 872	2 231	133
Transportation and material moving occupations	9 918	15	...	18	1 344	757	587	747
2019								
All Occupations	157 538	2 425	750	11 373	15 741	9 970	5 771	3 525
Management, professional, and related occupations	64 218	1 051	282	2 601	5 156	3 422	1 734	688
Management, business, and financial operations occupations	26 981	1 008	155	2 311	2 851	1 757	1 094	518
Computer and mathematical occupations	5 352	5	21	35	480	372	109	61
Architecture and engineering occupations	3 305	7	62	189	1 255	1 059	197	32
Life, physical and social science occupations	1 485	20	33	6	236	51	184	15
Community and social service occupations	2 717	3	...	0	7	2	5	1
Legal occupations	1 955	...	4	6	24	12	12	4
Education, training, and library occupations	9 455	2	1	5	38	20	18	13
Arts, design, entertainment, sports, and media occupations	3 285	2	3	40	212	129	83	31
Healthcare practitioner and technical occupations	9 684	3	3	7	54	21	33	13
Healthcare support occupations	3 758	0	1	1	14	7	7	8
Protective service occupations	3 128	15	2	24	30	17	12	7
Food preparation and serving related occupations	8 378	4	0	5	65	8	57	9
Building and grounds cleaning and maintenance occupations	5 746	35	4	29	146	87	59	28
Personal care and service occupations	5 968	59	...	2	7	5	3	2
Sales and related occupations	15 582	17	11	118	608	341	267	1 309
Office and administrative support occupations	17 789	81	63	529	1 275	765	510	525
Farming, fishing, and forestry occupations	1 156	993	0	4	50	4	46	40
Construction and extraction occupations	8 325	12	212	7 044	300	241	59	23
Installation, maintenance, and repair occupations	4 862	26	53	589	706	443	263	128
Production occupations	8 565	38	40	160	6 150	3 955	2 196	113
Transportation and material moving occupations	10 063	93	81	267	1 235	676	559	646

... = Not available.

Table 1-14. Employed Civilians, by Selected Occupation and Industry, 2017–2019—*Continued*

(Thousands of people.)

Year and occupation	Retail trade	Transportation and warehousing	Utilities	Information	Finance and insurance	Real estate and rental and leasing	Professional and technical services
2017							
All Occupations	16 720	6 810	1 349	2 903	7 288	3 194	11 764
Management, professional, and related occupations	2 020	762	493	1 698	4 182	1 124	9 548
Management, business, and financial operations occupations	984	610	265	564	3 363	1 036	3 774
Computer and mathematical occupations	200	69	57	301	537	23	2 004
Architecture and engineering occupations	26	40	112	95	21	12	1 109
Life, physical and social science occupations	4	1	31	4	14	3	369
Community and social service occupations	1	1	1	2	30	6	20
Legal occupations	13	8	6	13	82	20	1 206
Education, training, and library occupations	29	11	9	124	18	1	39
Arts, design, entertainment, sports, and media occupations	215	18	9	590	36	16	761
Healthcare practitioner and technical occupations	548	3	3	6	80	8	265
Healthcare support occupations	42	2	0	0	7	3	69
Protective service occupations	66	20	14	6	43	19	25
Food preparation and serving related occupations	392	22	1	27	6	20	10
Building and grounds cleaning and maintenance occupations	143	60	16	15	19	227	28
Personal care and service occupations	59	50	0	30	7	37	40
Sales and related occupations	8 824	100	23	330	1 168	1 116	366
Office and administrative support occupations	2 776	1 464	189	428	1 790	323	1 322
Farming, fishing, and forestry occupations	10	2	2	0	...	0	4
Construction and extraction occupations	73	66	110	13	8	42	56
Installation, maintenance, and repair occupations	582	352	191	279	23	163	78
Production occupations	456	114	259	40	25	16	145
Transportation and material moving occupations	1 276	3 797	50	37	10	105	74
2018							
All Occupations	16 599	7 207	1 345	2 919	7 376	3 273	12 105
Management, professional, and related occupations	1 971	809	520	1 770	4 321	1 144	9 913
Management, business, and financial operations occupations	940	629	282	611	3 456	1 042	3 780
Computer and mathematical occupations	209	81	72	319	548	33	2 237
Architecture and engineering occupations	27	42	111	90	21	17	1 070
Life, physical and social science occupations	8	4	29	7	14	...	378
Community and social service occupations	1	2	...	4	26	5	17
Legal occupations	13	12	5	13	104	27	1 252
Education, training, and library occupations	30	18	1	113	27	3	50
Arts, design, entertainment, sports, and media occupations	203	16	16	607	49	12	833
Healthcare practitioner and technical occupations	541	6	4	5	77	5	296
Healthcare support occupations	36	4	...	0	7	4	59
Protective service occupations	55	20	10	6	36	17	24
Food preparation and serving related occupations	366	24	1	28	6	22	4
Building and grounds cleaning and maintenance occupations	162	70	12	10	20	213	31
Personal care and service occupations	57	54	0	29	7	29	43
Sales and related occupations	8 766	99	31	319	1 185	1 196	396
Office and administrative support occupations	2 678	1 547	182	379	1 731	329	1 245
Farming, fishing, and forestry occupations	13	0	1	...	...	...	2
Construction and extraction occupations	74	76	109	14	6	56	76
Installation, maintenance, and repair occupations	577	366	194	291	18	143	89
Production occupations	472	135	242	33	29	14	141
Transportation and material moving occupations	1 372	4 003	41	39	9	106	82
2019							
All Occupations	16 217	7 614	1 377	2 766	7 464	3 301	12 808
Management, professional, and related occupations	1 923	831	512	1 690	4 453	1 235	10 466
Management, business, and financial operations occupations	937	662	271	566	3 524	1 122	4 202
Computer and mathematical occupations	196	63	58	315	611	37	2 338
Architecture and engineering occupations	33	56	129	102	24	12	1 050
Life, physical and social science occupations	6	4	28	9	6	2	340
Community and social service occupations	1	...	...	2	34	5	25
Legal occupations	19	10	4	8	89	27	1 326
Education, training, and library occupations	23	21	2	113	29	5	65
Arts, design, entertainment, sports, and media occupations	196	12	13	569	45	22	833
Healthcare practitioner and technical occupations	512	3	7	5	91	2	286
Healthcare support occupations	51	2	0	0	11	7	62
Protective service occupations	50	27	15	9	41	16	30
Food preparation and serving related occupations	347	13	3	31	7	13	7
Building and grounds cleaning and maintenance occupations	159	58	15	18	14	185	41
Personal care and service occupations	55	49	1	27	11	30	52
Sales and related occupations	8 450	109	27	267	1 126	1 192	429
Office and administrative support occupations	2 572	1 730	158	375	1 747	300	1 342
Farming, fishing, and forestry occupations	19	5	2	0	0	...	1
Construction and extraction occupations	74	63	115	16	6	51	64
Installation, maintenance, and repair occupations	590	305	212	254	19	168	86
Production occupations	452	144	262	31	21	17	146
Transportation and material moving occupations	1 475	4 277	55	46	8	87	84

... = Not available.

Table 1-14. Employed Civilians, by Selected Occupation and Industry, 2017–2019—*Continued*

(Thousands of people.)

Year and occupation	Management, administrative, and waste services	Educational services	Health care and social assistance	Arts, entertainment, and recreation	Accommodation and food services	Other services (except public administration)	Public administration
2017							
All Occupations	7 072	13 763	20 720	3 399	10 891	7 485	7 083
Management, professional, and related occupations	1 422	10 849	11 754	1 252	1 763	1 671	3 163
Management, business, and financial operations occupations	1 067	1 453	1 856	358	1 660	695	1 351
Computer and mathematical occupations	111	276	225	27	14	51	319
Architecture and engineering occupations	38	55	34	11	5	19	193
Life, physical and social science occupations	13	221	223	13	1	20	189
Community and social service occupations	14	366	1 155	9	5	638	381
Legal occupations	32	12	25	8	2	16	321
Education, training, and library occupations	28	7 883	726	108	42	64	84
Arts, design, entertainment, sports, and media occupations	40	272	56	708	22	133	69
Healthcare practitioner and technical occupations	80	311	7 454	10	12	36	255
Healthcare support occupations	52	39	3 060	19	7	151	41
Protective service occupations	532	121	60	160	41	27	1 905
Food preparation and serving related occupations	28	369	387	256	6 634	48	29
Building and grounds cleaning and maintenance occupations	2 780	558	474	255	506	440	127
Personal care and service occupations	32	263	2 023	888	99	2 232	127
Sales and related occupations	278	39	61	159	882	385	31
Office and administrative support occupations	957	1 041	2 497	239	469	603	1 195
Farming, fishing, and forestry occupations	14	1	3	4	1	2	21
Construction and extraction occupations	75	52	30	20	16	24	105
Installation, maintenance, and repair occupations	225	114	87	64	46	1 110	165
Production occupations	166	34	134	19	120	442	80
Transportation and material moving occupations	511	283	149	62	305	349	94
2018							
All Occupations	6 845	13 910	21 133	3 362	10 905	7 742	7 419
Management, professional, and related occupations	1 374	11 047	12 041	1 217	1 862	1 709	3 339
Management, business, and financial operations occupations	997	1 483	1 898	348	1 747	713	1 451
Computer and mathematical occupations	112	238	261	29	23	50	318
Architecture and engineering occupations	46	44	33	13	6	12	204
Life, physical and social science occupations	22	257	231	10	5	17	219
Community and social service occupations	17	382	1 173	7	5	652	383
Legal occupations	19	11	21	5	3	13	349
Education, training, and library occupations	28	8 032	692	89	42	56	92
Arts, design, entertainment, sports, and media occupations	52	280	53	705	20	159	65
Healthcare practitioner and technical occupations	82	319	7 678	11	12	38	257
Healthcare support occupations	53	31	3 207	23	4	137	48
Protective service occupations	597	116	67	171	34	29	1 954
Food preparation and serving related occupations	31	382	384	269	6 522	50	34
Building and grounds cleaning and maintenance occupations	2 664	534	460	234	500	559	138
Personal care and service occupations	24	255	1 985	879	98	2 254	163
Sales and related occupations	252	43	67	149	858	363	35
Office and administrative support occupations	905	1 009	2 516	244	539	638	1 238
Farming, fishing, and forestry occupations	11	2	1	5	1	3	23
Construction and extraction occupations	85	46	31	30	15	16	111
Installation, maintenance, and repair occupations	193	119	97	61	46	1 153	153
Production occupations	162	38	143	17	111	490	79
Transportation and material moving occupations	493	288	134	64	316	343	105
2019							
All Occupations	6 799	14 193	21 701	3 444	11 200	7 617	7 225
Management, professional, and related occupations	1 397	11 294	12 541	1 266	1 871	1 716	3 246
Management, business, and financial operations occupations	1 022	1 514	2 058	367	1 755	739	1 397
Computer and mathematical occupations	120	267	277	31	24	61	352
Architecture and engineering occupations	34	52	35	8	8	16	200
Life, physical and social science occupations	18	268	265	11	2	16	200
Community and social service occupations	10	394	1 207	9	5	631	383
Legal occupations	37	15	21	3	2	19	335
Education, training, and library occupations	28	8 191	641	86	44	63	82
Arts, design, entertainment, sports, and media occupations	42	257	69	727	19	129	65
Healthcare practitioner and technical occupations	86	335	7 968	23	13	41	233
Healthcare support occupations	39	33	3 294	17	9	154	56
Protective service occupations	576	100	65	172	34	14	1 902
Food preparation and serving related occupations	15	390	381	267	6 745	51	27
Building and grounds cleaning and maintenance occupations	2 614	523	440	240	532	534	131
Personal care and service occupations	38	292	1 983	834	103	2 262	162
Sales and related occupations	253	39	72	178	946	396	37
Office and administrative support occupations	930	1 039	2 509	268	502	650	1 194
Farming, fishing, and forestry occupations	11	4	1	6	0	4	16
Construction and extraction occupations	88	51	36	28	15	18	109
Installation, maintenance, and repair occupations	183	114	99	72	41	1 061	156
Production occupations	156	38	134	22	108	459	73
Transportation and material moving occupations	499	276	147	76	293	298	118

Table 1-15. Employed Civilians in Agriculture and Nonagricultural Industries, by Class of Worker and Sex, 1995–2019

(Thousands of people.)

| Sex and year | Total employed | Agriculture | | | | Nonagricultural industries | | | | | | |
| | | Total | Wage and salary workers | Self-employed workers | Unpaid family workers | Total employed | Wage and salary workers | | | | Self-employed workers | Unpaid family workers |
							Total	Government	Private household	Other industries except private households		
Both Sexes												
1995	124 900	3 440	1 814	1 580	45	121 460	112 448	18 362	963	93 123	8 902	110
1996	126 707	3 443	1 869	1 518	56	123 264	114 171	18 217	928	95 026	8 971	122
1997	129 558	3 399	1 890	1 457	51	126 159	116 983	18 131	915	97 937	9 056	120
1998	131 463	3 378	2 000	1 341	38	128 085	119 019	18 383	962	99 674	8 962	103
1999	133 488	3 281	1 944	1 297	40	130 207	121 323	18 903	933	101 487	8 790	95
2000	136 891	2 464	1 421	1 010	33	134 427	125 114	19 248	718	105 148	9 205	108
2001	136 933	2 299	1 283	988	28	134 635	125 407	19 335	694	105 378	9 121	107
2002	136 485	2 311	1 282	1 003	26	134 174	125 156	19 636	757	104 764	8 923	95
2003	137 736	2 275	1 299	951	25	135 461	126 015	19 634	764	105 616	9 344	101
2004	139 252	2 232	1 242	964	27	137 020	127 463	19 983	779	106 701	9 467	90
2005	141 730	2 197	1 212	955	30	139 532	129 931	20 357	812	108 761	9 509	93
2006	144 427	2 206	1 287	901	18	142 221	132 449	20 337	803	111 309	9 685	87
2007	146 047	2 095	1 220	856	19	143 952	134 283	21 003	813	112 467	9 557	112
2008	145 362	2 168	1 279	860	28	143 194	133 882	21 258	805	111 819	9 219	93
2009	139 877	2 103	1 242	836	25	137 775	128 713	21 178	783	106 752	836	25
2010	139 064	2 206	1 353	821	33	136 858	127 914	21 003	667	106 244	8 860	84
2011	139 869	2 254	1 380	846	28	137 615	128 934	20 536	722	107 676	8 603	78
2012	142 469	2 186	1 377	780	29	140 283	131 452	20 360	738	110 355	8 749	81
2013	143 929	2 130	1 310	789	31	141 799	133 111	20 247	723	112 141	8 619	70
2014	146 305	2 237	1 459	756	22	144 068	135 402	20 135	820	114 446	8 602	64
2015	148 834	2 422	1 547	844	32	146 411	137 678	20 601	798	116 279	8 665	68
2016	151 436	2 460	1 583	853	23	148 976	140 161	20 630	724	118 807	8 751	65
2017	153 337	2 454	1 640	790	24	150 883	142 096	20 835	657	120 603	8 736	52
2018	155 761	2 425	1 632	766	27	153 336	144 326	20 942	777	122 607	8 941	69
2019	157 538	2 425	1 658	741	26	155 113	146 262	20 976	821	124 465	8 799	53
Men												
1995	67 377	2 559	1 395	1 138	26	64 818	59 332	8 267	96	50 969	5 461	25
1996	68 207	2 573	1 418	1 124	31	65 634	60 133	8 110	99	51 924	5 465	36
1997	69 685	2 552	1 439	1 084	29	67 133	61 595	8 015	81	53 499	5 506	31
1998	70 693	2 553	1 526	1 005	23	68 140	62 630	8 178	86	54 366	5 480	29
1999	71 446	2 432	1 450	962	20	69 014	63 624	8 278	74	55 272	5 366	25
2000	73 305	1 861	1 116	725	20	71 444	65 838	8 309	71	57 458	5 573	33
2001	73 196	1 708	990	703	15	71 488	65 930	8 342	63	57 524	5 527	31
2002	72 903	1 724	979	731	14	71 179	65 726	8 437	76	57 212	5 425	29
2003	73 332	1 695	991	694	11	71 636	65 871	8 368	59	57 444	5 736	30
2004	74 525	1 687	970	702	15	72 838	66 951	8 616	60	58 275	5 860	27
2005	75 973	1 654	949	688	17	74 319	68 345	8 760	67	59 518	5 944	30
2006	77 502	1 663	989	664	10	75 838	69 811	8 696	60	61 055	6 004	23
2007	78 254	1 604	973	623	8	76 650	70 697	9 022	76	61 599	5 920	32
2008	77 486	1 650	997	637	16	75 836	70 072	9 089	70	60 912	5 736	29
2009	73 670	1 607	977	613	17	72 062	66 517	9 013	74	57 430	5 527	19
2010	73 359	1 665	1 051	598	17	71 694	66 189	9 059	60	57 070	5 472	33
2011	74 290	1 698	1 050	632	16	72 592	67 306	8 922	78	58 307	5 262	24
2012	75 555	1 626	1 048	562	16	73 930	68 629	8 760	82	59 786	5 266	34
2013	76 353	1 611	1 020	571	20	74 742	69 606	8 799	62	60 744	5 111	25
2014	77 692	1 685	1 119	554	12	76 007	70 828	8 633	64	62 131	5 158	22
2015	79 131	1 826	1 194	615	17	77 305	72 016	8 870	58	63 088	5 269	21
2016	80 568	1 839	1 211	614	14	78 729	73 342	8 890	60	64 392	5 366	22
2017	81 402	1 843	1 263	568	13	79 559	74 352	9 043	55	65 255	5 191	15
2018	82 698	1 797	1 236	542	19	80 902	75 456	9 016	53	66 387	5 423	22
2019	83 460	1 790	1 233	541	16	81 670	76 389	8 903	74	67 412	5 266	15
Women												
1995	57 523	881	419	442	20	56 642	53 115	10 095	867	42 153	3 440	86
1996	58 501	871	452	394	25	57 630	54 037	10 107	830	43 100	3 506	87
1997	59 873	847	451	373	23	59 026	55 388	10 116	834	44 438	3 550	89
1998	60 770	825	474	336	15	59 945	56 389	10 205	876	45 308	3 482	74
1999	62 042	849	494	335	20	61 193	57 699	10 625	859	46 215	3 424	70
2000	63 586	602	305	285	12	62 983	59 277	10 939	647	47 690	3 631	76
2001	63 737	591	293	284	13	63 147	59 477	10 993	630	47 853	3 594	75
2002	63 582	587	303	272	12	62 995	59 431	11 199	680	47 552	3 499	66
2003	64 404	580	309	257	14	63 824	60 144	11 267	705	48 172	3 609	72
2004	64 728	546	271	262	12	64 182	60 512	11 367	719	48 426	3 607	63
2005	65 757	544	263	267	13	65 213	61 586	11 598	745	49 243	3 565	63
2006	66 925	543	298	237	8	66 382	62 638	11 641	742	50 254	3 681	64
2007	67 792	490	247	233	11	67 302	63 586	11 981	737	50 868	3 637	80
2008	67 876	518	282	224	12	67 358	63 810	12 169	735	50 907	3 483	65
2009	66 208	496	265	223	8	65 712	62 197	12 165	709	49 322	3 468	47
2010	65 705	541	302	223	16	65 164	61 725	11 944	607	49 174	3 388	51
2011	65 579	556	330	214	12	65 023	61 628	11 614	644	49 370	3 341	54
2012	66 914	560	329	218	13	66 353	62 824	11 600	656	50 568	3 483	47
2013	67 577	519	290	218	11	67 058	63 505	11 447	661	51 396	3 508	45
2014	68 613	552	340	202	10	68 061	64 574	11 502	757	52 316	3 444	43
2015	69 703	597	353	229	14	69 106	65 663	11 731	741	53 191	3 396	48
2016	70 868	621	372	239	10	70 247	66 819	11 740	664	54 415	3 385	43
2017	71 936	611	378	222	11	71 324	67 743	11 793	602	55 349	3 544	37
2018	73 063	628	396	224	9	72 435	68 870	11 926	725	56 220	3 518	47
2019	74 078	635	424	200	10	73 443	69 873	12 073	747	57 052	3 532	38

Table 1-16. Number of Employed Persons Age 25 Years and Over, by Educational Attainment, Sex, Race, and Hispanic Origin, 2008–2019

(Thousands of people.)

Race, Hispanic origin, sex, and year	Total	Less than a high school diploma	High school graduate, no college	Some college, no degree	Associate's degree	College graduate or higher	
						Total	Bachelor's degree only
Both Sexes							
2008	126 161	11 073	36 097	22 092	12 948	43 951	28 460
2009	122 277	10 371	34 487	21 016	12 872	43 531	27 964
2010	121 987	10 115	34 293	20 838	12 910	43 832	27 977
2011	122 507	9 967	33 823	20 712	13 182	44 822	28 333
2012	124 635	9 923	33 718	20 936	13 770	46 288	29 371
2013	125 872	9 798	33 619	20 914	14 011	47 531	30 140
2014	127 863	9 852	33 865	21 159	14 139	48 848	30 789
2015	130 077	10 098	33 402	21 573	14 213	50 792	31 772
2016	132 444	9 884	33 801	21 668	14 718	52 374	32 475
2017	134 132	9 668	34 210	21 440	14 842	53 971	33 620
2018	136 584	9 701	34 550	21 128	15 209	55 995	35 026
2019	138 216	9 441	34 837	20 882	15 400	57 655	35 850
Men							
2008	67 605	7 108	20 093	11 356	6 021	23 027	14 845
2009	64 831	6 569	19 085	10 772	5 864	22 541	14 368
2010	64 765	6 434	19 159	10 737	5 829	22 606	14 359
2011	65 356	6 388	19 059	10 741	6 029	23 138	14 637
2012	66 455	6 309	19 192	10 862	6 364	23 729	15 024
2013	67 163	6 335	19 103	10 946	6 446	24 333	15 487
2014	68 284	6 410	19 403	11 151	6 531	24 791	15 706
2015	69 604	6 573	19 302	11 293	6 660	25 776	16 323
2016	70 872	6 354	19 691	11 311	6 928	26 588	16 670
2017	71 638	6 129	20 013	11 355	6 969	27 172	17 137
2018	73 021	6 201	20 294	11 279	7 182	28 066	17 803
2019	73 731	6 047	20 512	11 161	7 406	28 605	18 151
Women							
2008	58 555	3 965	16 004	10 737	6 926	20 924	13 614
2009	57 445	3 802	15 402	10 244	7 008	20 990	13 597
2010	57 222	3 681	15 134	10 101	7 080	21 226	13 618
2011	57 151	3 579	14 764	9 971	7 153	21 684	13 697
2012	58 180	3 614	14 527	10 074	7 405	22 559	14 347
2013	58 710	3 463	14 516	9 968	7 565	23 198	14 653
2014	59 579	3 442	14 462	10 009	7 609	24 057	15 083
2015	60 474	3 525	14 100	10 280	7 553	25 016	15 449
2016	61 572	3 530	14 110	10 357	7 790	25 786	15 805
2017	62 494	3 540	14 197	10 085	7 873	26 799	16 483
2018	63 563	3 501	14 256	9 850	8 028	27 929	17 223
2019	64 485	3 394	14 325	9 722	7 994	29 051	17 699
White[1]							
2008	103 373	9 036	29 495	17 873	10 742	36 228	23 511
2009	100 419	8 497	28 372	16 983	10 714	35 854	23 109
2010	100 100	8 290	28 128	16 800	10 707	36 176	23 179
2011	100 426	8 248	27 568	16 713	10 922	36 975	23 533
2012	100 543	8 100	27 112	16 594	11 260	37 476	23 942
2013	101 046	7 885	27 049	16 425	11 460	38 228	24 419
2014	102 245	7 895	27 132	16 556	11 556	39 106	24 879
2015	103 336	8 128	26 508	16 820	11 501	40 380	25 395
2016	104 624	7 879	26 623	16 786	11 881	41 454	25 967
2017	105 449	7 690	26 710	16 515	11 872	42 662	26 986
2018	106 704	7 713	26 870	16 281	12 067	43 772	27 708
2019	107 636	7 519	27 183	15 992	12 190	44 752	28 139
Black[1]							
2008	13 786	1 234	4 719	2 972	1 439	3 423	2 354
2009	13 110	1 096	4 375	2 855	1 422	3 363	2 253
2010	13 092	1 103	4 234	2 864	1 482	3 409	2 260
2011	13 097	1 013	4 298	2 792	1 519	3 474	2 257
2012	13 717	1 016	4 397	2 919	1 584	3 801	2 479
2013	13 985	1 064	4 343	3 034	1 583	3 961	2 582
2014	14 437	1 084	4 442	3 119	1 674	4 117	2 623
2015	15 017	1 033	4 549	3 242	1 775	4 418	2 850
2016	15 517	1 069	4 737	4 737	1 817	4 612	2 942
2017	16 031	1 038	4 889	3 335	1 894	4 874	3 050
2018	16 556	1 009	4 986	3 276	1 994	5 291	3 395
2019	16 858	1 029	5 007	3 275	2 041	5 506	3 488
Hispanic[2]							
2008	17 115	5 426	5 232	2 484	1 236	2 736	1 930
2009	18 642	6 064	5 658	2 670	1 357	2 894	2 063
2010	16 946	5 183	5 175	2 474	1 252	2 862	2 025
2011	17 059	5 156	5 216	2 513	1 317	2 857	1 982
2012	18 309	5 269	5 613	2 734	1 482	3 210	2 221
2013	18 836	5 297	5 754	2 781	1 543	3 460	2 428
2014	19 686	5 365	5 954	2 990	1 636	3 741	2 648
2015	20 450	5 592	6 064	3 119	1 739	3 936	2 694
2016	21 186	5 472	6 398	3 227	1 826	4 263	2 884
2017	21 825	5 462	6 642	3 258	1 937	4 525	3 139
2018	22 758	5 488	7 145	3 341	2 012	4 770	3 312
2019	23 477	5 411	7 394	3 411	2 097	5 164	3 543

[1]Beginning in 2003, persons who selected this race group only; persons who selected more than one race group are not included. Prior to 2003, persons who reported more than one race group were included in the group they identified as their main race.
[2]May be of any race.

Table 1-16. Number of Employed Persons Age 25 Years and Over, by Educational Attainment, Sex, Race, and Hispanic Origin, 2008–2019—*Continued*

(Thousands of people.)

Race, Hispanic origin, sex, and year	Total	Less than a high school diploma	High school graduate, no college	Some college, no degree	Associate's degree	College graduate or higher	
						Total	Bachelor's degree only
White Men[1]							
2008	56 446	6 066	16 741	9 397	5 070	19 171	12 482
2009	54 248	5 583	15 966	8 937	4 948	18 813	12 112
2010	54 091	5 461	15 952	8 846	4 922	18 910	12 128
2011	54 488	5 450	15 776	8 878	5 082	19 303	12 344
2012	54 646	5 339	15 711	8 809	5 273	19 513	12 495
2013	54 914	5 286	15 672	9 356	5 611	20 542	13 287
2014	55 608	5 299	15 830	8 942	5 424	20 113	12 957
2015	56 374	5 484	15 617	9 037	5 533	20 702	13 265
2016	56 977	5 258	15 844	8 970	5 705	21 199	13 488
2017	57 396	5 074	16 029	8 954	5 670	21 670	13 966
2018	58 158	5 138	16 122	8 930	5 814	22 153	14 286
2019	58 527	4 988	16 389	8 749	5 993	22 407	14 424
White Women[1]							
2008	46 928	2 970	12 753	8 477	5 672	17 056	11 029
2009	46 172	2 913	12 406	8 046	5 766	17 040	10 997
2010	46 010	2 829	12 176	7 953	5 785	17 266	11 051
2011	45 938	2 798	11 792	7 835	5 840	17 672	11 189
2012	45 897	2 761	11 402	7 784	5 987	17 963	11 447
2013	46 132	2 598	11 377	7 649	6 111	18 396	11 637
2014	46 637	2 596	11 302	7 614	6 132	18 993	11 923
2015	46 962	2 643	10 891	7 782	5 968	19 677	12 131
2016	47 647	2 621	10 779	7 816	6 176	20 255	12 479
2017	48 053	2 616	10 681	7 562	6 203	20 992	13 020
2018	48 546	2 575	10 748	7 351	6 253	21 619	13 422
2019	49 109	2 531	10 794	7 243	6 197	22 345	13 714
Black Men[1]							
2008	6 357	616	2 358	1 296	579	1 508	1 036
2009	5 939	551	2 199	1 225	544	1 419	958
2010	5 988	561	2 164	1 270	567	1 426	960
2011	6 031	532	2 225	1 235	591	1 449	968
2012	6 320	530	2 281	1 328	639	1 541	1 024
2013	6 487	569	2 222	1 400	623	1 673	1 134
2014	6 726	592	2 319	1 433	662	1 720	1 136
2015	7 003	545	2 407	1 477	679	1 895	1 283
2016	7 323	562	2 504	1 482	751	2 023	1 342
2017	7 554	535	2 564	1 535	821	2 098	1 361
2018	7 832	505	2 661	1 543	840	2 283	1 549
2019	7 968	553	2 646	1 560	845	2 364	1 626
Black Women[1]							
2007	7 429	617	2 361	1 676	859	1 915	1 318
2009	7 171	544	2 176	1 631	877	1 943	1 295
2010	7 104	542	2 070	1 594	915	1 983	1 300
2011	7 066	481	2 073	1 558	928	2 026	1 289
2012	7 397	487	2 115	1 591	945	2 260	1 455
2013	7 498	495	2 121	1 634	961	2 288	1 448
2014	7 711	492	2 123	1 686	1 012	2 398	1 487
2015	8 014	488	2 142	1 765	1 096	2 523	1 567
2016	8 194	507	2 233	1 799	1 066	2 589	1 600
2017	8 477	503	2 325	1 800	1 073	2 775	1 689
2018	8 724	504	2 325	1 733	1 155	3 007	1 846
2019	8 891	476	2 361	1 715	1 196	3 143	1 862
Hispanic Men[2]							
2008	10 363	3 714	3 231	1 371	607	1 439	1 008
2009	9 969	3 508	3 114	1 321	595	1 431	992
2010	10 120	3 517	3 176	1 341	595	1 491	1 045
2011	10 151	3 487	3 158	1 377	636	1 492	1 044
2012	10 629	3 512	3 391	1 420	693	1 612	1 115
2013	11 029	3 599	3 475	1 486	718	1 751	1 236
2014	11 546	3 651	3 584	1 637	791	1 883	1 362
2015	11 969	3 787	3 664	1 642	875	2 001	1 402
2016	12 378	3 669	3 960	1 697	896	2 156	1 488
2017	12 663	3 662	4 067	1 771	915	2 248	1 598
2018	13 168	3 679	4 369	1 822	951	2 346	1 654
2019	13 487	3 590	4 522	1 844	1 024	2 507	1 760
Hispanic Women[2]							
2007	6 752	1 712	2 001	1 113	629	1 297	922
2009	6 718	1 724	1 955	1 093	647	1 298	941
2010	6 826	1 666	1 999	1 133	656	1 371	979
2011	6 908	1 669	2 058	1 136	681	1 365	938
2012	7 680	1 757	2 222	1 315	788	1 598	1 106
2013	7 807	1 698	2 280	1 295	826	1 709	1 192
2014	8 140	1 713	2 370	1 353	845	1 859	1 287
2015	8 481	1 805	2 401	1 477	864	1 935	1 292
2016	8 807	1 803	2 438	1 530	930	2 107	1 396
2017	9 162	1 799	2 575	1 488	1 023	2 277	1 542
2018	9 589	1 809	2 776	1 519	1 061	2 424	1 658
2019	9 991	1 821	2 872	1 567	1 074	2 657	1 783

[1]Beginning in 2003, persons who selected this race group only; persons who selected more than one race group are not included. Prior to 2003, persons who reported more than one race group were included in the group they identified as their main race.
[2]May be of any race.

Table 1-17. Multiple Jobholders and Multiple Jobholding Rates, by Selected Characteristics, May of Selected Years, 1970–2020

(Thousands of people, percent, not seasonally adjusted.)

| Year | Total employed | Multiple jobholders | | | | Multiple jobholding rate[1] | | | | | | |
| | | Total | Men | Women | | Total | Men | Women | White | Black[2] | Asian | Hispanic[3] |
				Number	Percent of all multiple jobholders							
1970	78 358	4 048	3 412	636	15.7	5.2	7.0	2.2	5.3	4.4	. . .	. . .
1971	78 708	4 035	3 270	765	19.0	5.1	6.7	2.6	5.3	3.8	. . .	. . .
1972	81 224	3 770	3 035	735	19.5	4.6	6.0	2.4	4.8	3.7	. . .	. . .
1973	83 758	4 262	3 393	869	20.4	5.1	6.6	2.7	5.1	4.7	. . .	. . .
1974	85 786	3 889	3 022	867	22.3	4.5	5.8	2.6	4.6	3.8	. . .	. . .
1975	84 146	3 918	2 962	956	24.4	4.7	5.8	2.9	4.8	3.7	. . .	. . .
1976	87 278	3 948	3 037	911	23.1	4.5	5.8	2.6	4.7	2.8	. . .	. . .
1977	90 482	4 558	3 317	1 241	27.2	5.0	6.2	3.4	5.3	2.6	. . .	. . .
1978	93 904	4 493	3 212	1 281	28.5	4.8	5.8	3.3	5.0	3.1	. . .	. . .
1979	96 327	4 724	3 317	1 407	29.8	4.9	5.9	3.5	5.1	3.0	. . .	. . .
1980	96 809	4 759	3 210	1 549	32.5	4.9	5.8	3.8	5.1	3.2	. . .	. . .
1985	106 878	5 730	3 537	2 192	38.3	5.4	5.9	4.7	5.7	3.2	. . .	. . .
1989	117 084	7 225	4 115	3 109	43.0	6.2	6.4	5.9	6.5	4.3	. . .	. . .
1991	116 626	7 183	4 054	3 129	43.6	6.2	6.4	5.9	6.4	4.9	. . .	. . .
1994	122 946	7 316	3 973	3 343	45.7	6.0	6.0	5.9	6.1	4.9	. . .	3.8
1995	124 554	7 952	4 225	3 727	46.9	6.4	6.3	6.5	6.6	5.2	. . .	3.6
1996	126 391	7 846	4 352	3 494	44.5	6.2	6.4	6.0	6.4	5.1	. . .	4.0
1997	129 565	8 197	4 398	3 800	46.4	6.3	6.3	6.4	6.5	5.7	. . .	4.1
1998	131 476	8 126	4 438	3 688	45.4	6.2	6.3	6.1	6.3	5.5	. . .	4.4
1999	133 411	7 895	4 117	3 778	47.9	5.9	5.8	6.1	6.0	5.5	. . .	3.6
2000	136 685	7 751	4 084	3 667	47.3	5.7	5.6	5.8	5.9	4.9	3.4	3.2
2001	137 121	7 540	3 914	3 626	48.1	5.5	5.3	5.7	5.6	5.3	3.7	3.4
2002	136 559	7 247	3 736	3 511	48.4	5.3	5.1	5.5	5.5	4.7	4.0	3.8
2003	137 567	7 338	3 841	3 498	47.7	5.3	5.3	5.4	5.5	4.3	4.2	3.4
2004	138 867	7 258	3 653	3 605	49.7	5.2	4.9	5.6	5.3	5.1	3.7	3.4
2005	141 591	7 348	3 741	3 607	49.1	5.2	4.9	5.5	5.4	4.4	3.5	2.8
2006	144 041	7 641	3 863	3 778	49.4	5.3	5.0	5.7	5.3	5.4	3.7	3.1
2007	145 864	7 693	3 835	3 858	50.1	5.3	4.9	5.7	5.5	4.4	3.7	3.0
2008	145 927	7 653	3 842	3 812	49.8	5.2	4.9	5.6	5.4	4.9	3.8	2.9
2009	140 363	7 265	3 540	3 725	51.3	5.2	4.8	5.6	5.3	4.8	3.9	3.0
2010	139 497	7 261	3 559	3 702	51.0	5.2	4.8	5.6	5.4	4.6	3.1	3.1
2011	140 028	7 084	3 491	3 593	50.7	5.1	4.7	5.5	5.3	4.5	3.1	3.3
2012	142 727	7 174	3 605	3 569	49.7	5.0	4.8	5.3	5.2	4.9	3.3	3.1
2013	144 432	7 123	3 570	3 553	49.9	4.9	4.7	5.2	5.1	4.4	3.7	3.7
2014	146 398	7 305	3 647	3 658	50.1	5.0	4.7	5.3	5.0	4.9	4.0	3.7
2015	149 349	7 081	3 441	3 641	51.4	4.7	4.3	5.2	4.8	5.1	2.9	3.1
2016	151 594	7 472	3 677	3 796	50.8	4.9	4.6	5.4	5.0	5.4	3.0	2.7
2017	153 407	7 584	3 831	3 752	49.5	4.9	4.7	5.2	5.0	5.0	3.8	3.2
2018	156 009	7 411	3 687	3 724	50.2	4.8	4.4	5.1	4.8	4.7	2.9	3.7
2019	157 152	7 857	3 774	4 083	52.0	5.0	4.5	5.5	5.0	5.3	3.4	3.4
2020	137 461	5 509	2 703	2 807	51.0	4.0	3.7	4.4	4.0	4.7	2.8	2.5

Note: Data prior to 1985 reflect 1970 census–based population controls; years 1985–1991 reflect 1980 census–based controls; years 1994–1999 reflect 1990 census–based controls adjusted for the estimated undercount; and data for years 2000–2002 have been revised to incorporate population controls from the 2000 census. Prior to 1994, data on multiple jobholders were collected only through special periodic supplements to the Current Population Survey (CPS) in May of various years; these supplemental surveys were not conducted in 1981–1984, 1986–1988, 1990, or 1992–1993. Beginning in 1994, data reflect the introduction of a major redesign of the CPS, including the collection of monthly data on multiple jobholders.

[1] Multiple jobholders as a percent of all employed persons in specified group.
[2] Data for years prior to 1977 refer to the Black-and-Other population group.
[3] May be of any race.
. . . = Not available.

Table 1-18. Multiple Jobholders, by Sex, Age, Marital Status, Race, Hispanic Origin, and Job Status, 2016–2019

(Thousands of people, percent.)

Characteristic	Both sexes				Men				Women			
	Number		Rate[1]		Number		Rate[1]		Number		Rate[1]	
	2016	2017	2016	2017	2016	2017	2016	2017	2016	2017	2016	2017
Age												
Total, 16 years and over[2]	7 531	7 545	5.0	4.9	3 645	3 748	4.5	4.6	3 887	3 798	5.5	5.3
16 to 19 years	205	189	4.1	3.7	81	81	3.3	3.3	124	109	5.0	4.2
20 to 24 years	848	828	6.0	5.9	335	359	4.6	4.9	514	469	7.5	6.8
25 to 34 years	1 727	1 724	5.1	5.0	858	846	4.7	4.6	869	878	5.6	5.5
35 to 44 years	1 548	1 578	4.9	4.9	783	801	4.6	4.7	765	776	5.3	5.3
45 to 54 years	1 687	1 687	5.2	5.2	819	825	4.7	4.8	868	862	5.6	5.6
55 to 64 years	1 161	1 183	4.5	4.5	571	621	4.3	4.5	589	563	4.9	4.6
65 years and over	356	356	4.0	3.9	198	215	4.0	4.2	158	141	4.0	3.4
Marital Status												
Single	2 463	2 447	5.3	5.1	1 089	1 123	4.3	4.4	1 374	1 324	6.4	5.9
Married, spouse present	3 761	3 769	4.7	4.6	2 114	2 161	4.7	4.7	1 647	1 608	4.7	4.5
Widowed, divorced, or separated	1 307	1 329	5.4	5.6	442	463	4.4	4.4	865	866	6.2	6.3
Race and Hispanic Origin												
White	5 999	5 988	5.0	5.0	2 926	2 995	4.5	5.0	3 072	2 993	5.6	5.4
Black	958	979	5.3	5.3	449	469	5.3	5.3	510	510	5.4	5.2
Hispanic[3]	820	880	3.2	3.4	433	464	3.0	3.3	387	388	3.6	3.5
Full- or Part-Time Status												
Primary job full time, secondary job part time	4 084	4 499	...	...	2 235	2 268	...	...	1 849	1 883	...	...
Primary and secondary jobs, both part time	2 075	2 062	...	...	703	694	...	...	1 372	1 298	...	...
Primary and secondary jobs, both full time	278	307	...	...	167	192	...	...	112	106	...	...
Hours vary on primary or secondary job	1 038	1 127	...	...	512	571	...	...	526	481	...	...

Characteristic	Both sexes				Men				Women			
	Number		Rate[1]		Number		Rate[1]		Number		Rate[1]	
	2018	2019	2018	2019	2018	2019	2018	2019	2018	2019	2018	2019
Age												
Total, 16 years and over[2]	7 769	8 050	5.0	5.1	3 835	3 908	5.0	4.7	3 934	4 141	5.4	5.6
16 to 19 years	183	201	3.6	3.9	61	82	3.6	3.2	122	119	4.6	4.5
20 to 24 years	780	769	5.6	5.4	328	297	5.6	4.1	452	472	6.6	6.8
25 to 34 years	1 867	1 876	5.3	5.2	915	907	5.3	4.7	952	969	5.8	5.8
35 to 44 years	1 646	1 737	5.0	5.2	834	888	5.0	5.0	811	849	5.4	5.5
45 to 54 years	1 684	1 752	5.2	5.5	847	839	5.2	5.0	837	913	5.5	6.0
55 to 64 years	1 220	1 275	4.6	4.7	629	646	4.6	4.6	591	628	4.7	4.9
65 years and over	390	440	4.0	4.2	221	249	4.0	4.4	169	191	3.9	4.1
Marital Status												
Single	2 579	2 690	5.2	5.3	1 160	1 203	5.2	4.4	1 419	1 487	6.1	6.3
Married, spouse present	3 842	3 971	4.7	4.8	2 191	2 233	4.7	4.9	1 651	1 738	4.6	4.8
Widowed, divorced, or separated	1 348	1 388	5.6	5.7	484	472	5.6	4.6	864	916	6.2	6.5
Race and Hispanic Origin												
White	6 166	6 304	5.1	5.1	3 057	3 086	4.7	4.7	3 110	3 218	5.6	5.7
Black	993	1 074	5.2	5.5	469	488	5.2	5.3	523	586	5.2	5.7
Hispanic[3]	951	1 027	3.5	3.7	538	550	3.5	3.5	413	478	3.6	4.0
Full- or Part-Time Status												
Primary job full time, secondary job part time	4 290	4 499	...	...	2 327	2 381	...	...	1 963	2 118	...	...
Primary and secondary jobs, both part time	2 031	2 062	...	...	717	720	...	...	1 314	1 342	...	...
Primary and secondary jobs, both full time	316	307	...	...	196	203	...	...	120	104	...	...
Hours vary on primary or secondary job	1 080	1 127	...	...	570	580	...	...	510	547	...	...

Note: Estimates for the above race groups (White or Black) do not sum to totals because data are not presented for all races. Beginning in January 2003, data reflect the revised population controls used in the household survey.

[1]Multiple jobholders as a percent of all employed persons in specified group.
[2]Includes a small number of persons who work part time at their primary job and full time at their secondary job(s), not shown separately.
[3]May be of any race.
. . . = Not available.

Table 1-19. Multiple Jobholders, by Sex and Industry of Principal Secondary Job, Annual Averages, 2017–2019

(Thousands of people.)

Year and industry of secondary job	Both sexes	Men	Women
2017			
All Nonagricultural Industries, Wage and Salary Workers	5 472	2 575	2 897
Mining, quarrying, and oil and gas extraction	3	2	1
Construction	125	102	23
Manufacturing	128	75	53
Durable goods	62	48	14
Nondurable goods	66	27	39
Wholesale and retail trade	785	313	473
Wholesale trade	46	26	21
Retail trade	739	287	452
Transportation and utilities	217	149	68
Transportation and warehousing	202	140	62
Utilities	15	9	5
Information	110	61	49
Financial activities	235	140	95
Professional and business services	536	317	219
Education and health services	1 526	559	967
Leisure and hospitality	1 141	535	605
Other services	451	189	262
Other services, except private households	386	182	204
Other services, private households	386	182	204
Public administration	217	134	83
2018			
All Nonagricultural Industries, Wage and Salary Workers	5 608	2 631	2 977
Mining, quarrying, and oil and gas extraction	4	2	2
Construction	129	98	30
Manufacturing	125	75	50
Durable goods	54	43	11
Nondurable goods	71	31	39
Wholesale and retail trade	794	329	464
Wholesale trade	34	15	19
Retail trade	759	314	445
Transportation and utilities	244	179	64
Transportation and warehousing	227	169	57
Utilities	17	10	7
Information	115	71	44
Financial activities	263	167	97
Professional and business services	521	293	229
Education and health services	1 666	602	1 064
Leisure and hospitality	1 057	454	603
Other services	466	202	264
Other services, except private households	392	193	199
Other services, private households	74	9	65
Public administration	225	159	66
2019			
All Nonagricultural Industries, Wage and Salary Workers	5 821	2 660	3 160
Mining, quarrying, and oil and gas extraction	6	4	3
Construction	129	98	31
Manufacturing	143	94	49
Durable goods	59	46	13
Nondurable goods	84	48	36
Wholesale and retail trade	778	323	455
Wholesale trade	59	41	18
Retail trade	719	282	437
Transportation and utilities	265	182	83
Transportation and warehousing	254	175	79
Utilities	11	8	3
Information	107	71	36
Financial activities	287	177	110
Professional and business services	589	324	266
Education and health services	1 688	547	1 141
Leisure and hospitality	1 114	487	627
Other services	476	198	278
Other services, except private households	396	187	210
Other services, private households	80	12	68
Public administration	238	155	83

Table 1-20. Employment and Unemployment in Families, by Race and Hispanic Origin, Annual Averages, 2007–2019

(Thousands of people, percent.)

Characteristic	2007	2008	2009	2010	2011	2012	2013	2014	2015	2016	2017	2018	2019
ALL RACES													
Total Families	77 894	77 943	78 361	78 246	78 362	80 141	80 445	80 889	81 410	82 092	82 015	82 502	82 633
With employed member(s)	64 330	64 058	63 010	62 560	62 529	64 091	64 318	64 832	65 360	66 023	66 027	66 655	67 006
As percent of total families	82.6	82.2	80.4	80.0	79.8	80.0	80.0	80.1	80.3	80.4	80.5	80.8	81.1
Some usually work full time[1]	59 616	59 116	57 037	56 471	56 498	58 007	58 113	58 762	59 520	60 065	60 395	61 159	61 551
With no employed member	13 564	13 884	15 351	15 686	15 833	16 050	16 127	16 057	16 050	16 069	15 988	15 847	15 627
As percent of total families	17.4	17.8	19.6	20.0	20.2	20.0	20.0	19.9	19.7	19.6	19.5	19.2	18.9
With unemployed member(s)	4 914	6 104	9 381	9 695	9 043	8 444	7 685	6 486	5 615	5 301	4 744	4 300	4 076
As percent of total families	6.3	7.8	12.0	12.4	11.5	10.5	9.6	8.0	6.9	6.5	5.8	5.2	4.9
Some member(s) employed	3 497	4 319	6 438	6 566	6 079	5 702	5 192	4 419	3 831	3 656	3 277	3 012	2 902
As percent of families with unemployed member(s)	71.2	70.8	68.6	67.7	67.2	67.5	67.6	68.1	68.2	69.0	69.1	70.0	71.2
Some usually work full time[1]	3 096	3 830	5 460	5 572	5 211	4 902	4 453	3 819	3 302	3 162	2 870	2 636	2 542
As percent of families with unemployed member(s)	63.0	62.7	58.2	57.5	57.6	58.1	58.0	58.9	58.8	59.7	60.5	61.3	62.4
WHITE[2]													
Total Families	63 667	63 490	63 774	63 551	63 635	64 246	64 294	64 476	64 663	65 083	64 910	65 042	65 082
With employed member(s)	52 669	52 273	51 494	51 048	51 030	51 491	51 471	51 661	51 769	52 209	52 016	52 264	52 435
As percent of total families	82.7	82.3	80.7	80.3	80.2	80.1	80.1	80.1	80.1	80.2	80.1	80.4	80.6
Some usually work full time[1]	48 879	48 271	46 629	46 150	46 203	46 710	46 636	46 937	47 225	47 611	47 621	47 973	48 146
With no employed member	10 997	11 217	12 280	12 502	12 605	12 755	12 822	12 815	12 894	12 873	12 894	12 778	12 647
As percent of total families	17.3	17.7	19.3	19.7	19.8	19.9	19.9	19.9	19.9	19.8	19.9	19.6	19.4
With unemployed member(s)	3 587	4 506	7 089	7 202	6 608	6 133	5 471	4 499	3 908	3 711	3 343	3 042	2 903
As percent of total families	5.6	7.1	11.1	11.3	10.4	9.5	8.5	7.0	6.0	5.7	5.2	4.7	4.5
Some member(s) employed	2 653	3 332	5 072	5 069	4 627	4 321	3 845	3 195	2 784	2 684	2 385	2 184	2 139
As percent of families with unemployed member(s)	73.9	74.0	71.5	70.4	70.0	70.5	70.3	71.0	71.2	72.3	71.3	71.8	73.7
Some usually work full time[1]	2 350	2 955	4 294	4 289	3 964	3 719	3 310	2 767	2 408	2 343	2 098	1 917	1 871
As percent of families with unemployed member(s)	65.5	65.6	60.6	59.6	60.0	60.6	60.5	61.5	61.6	63.1	62.8	63.0	64.5
BLACK[2]													
Total Families	9 184	9 297	9 318	9 404	9 370	9 671	9 737	9 793	9 854	9 976	10 017	10 008	9 966
With employed member(s)	7 249	7 290	7 022	7 030	6 954	7 290	7 373	7 481	7 652	7 764	7 886	7 934	7 975
As percent of total families	78.9	78.4	75.4	74.8	74.2	75.4	75.7	76.4	77.7	77.8	78.7	79.3	80.0
Some usually work full time[1]	6 608	6 622	6 265	6 222	6 105	6 419	6 451	6 596	6 792	6 835	7 053	7 149	7 228
With no employed member	1 935	2 006	2 296	2 374	2 416	2 380	2 363	2 312	2 202	2 212	2 131	2 074	1 991
As percent of total families	21.1	21.6	24.6	25.2	25.8	24.6	24.3	23.6	22.3	22.2	21.3	20.7	20.0
With unemployed member(s)	990	1 188	1 624	1 807	1 767	1 629	1 555	1 376	1 184	1 086	951	837	791
As percent of total families	10.8	12.8	17.4	19.2	18.9	16.8	16.0	14.1	12.0	10.9	10.0	8.0	7.9
Some member(s) employed	591	686	886	1 009	985	885	880	780	666	628	553	504	476
As percent of families with unemployed member(s)	59.7	57.8	54.5	55.8	55.7	54.3	56.6	56.7	56.3	57.8	58.1	60.3	60.2
Some usually work full time[1]	519	605	748	862	835	752	733	666	558	524	469	437	416
As percent of families with unemployed member(s)	52.4	50.9	46.0	47.7	47.3	46.1	47.1	48.4	47.2	48.2	49.4	52.3	52.6
HISPANIC[3]													
Total Families	10 332	10 500	10 489	10 561	10 902	11 769	12 023	12 178	12 602	12 900	12 936	13 194	13 281
With employed member(s)	9 048	9 135	8 852	8 897	9 178	9 962	10 231	10 456	10 883	11 182	11 244	11 546	11 721
As percent of total families	87.6	87.0	84.4	84.2	84.2	84.6	85.1	85.9	86.4	86.7	86.9	87.5	88.3
Some usually work full time[1]	8 492	8 466	7 923	7 934	8 201	8 978	9 242	9 429	9 914	10 217	10 383	10 706	10 882
With no employed member	1 285	1 365	1 637	1 664	1 724	1 808	1 792	1 722	1 719	1 718	1 692	1 649	1 559
As percent of total families	12.4	13.0	15.6	15.8	15.8	15.4	14.9	14.1	13.6	13.3	13.1	12.5	11.7
With unemployed member(s)	876	1 159	1 770	1 841	1 781	1 707	1 547	1 311	1 220	1 117	994	918	879
As percent of total families	8.5	11.0	16.9	17.4	16.3	14.5	12.9	10.8	9.7	8.7	7.7	7.0	6.6
Some member(s) employed	619	846	1 228	1 262	1 226	1 197	1 078	933	864	811	715	657	650
As percent of families with unemployed member(s)	70.6	73.0	69.3	68.6	68.8	70.1	69.7	71.1	70.8	72.6	71.9	71.5	73.9
Some usually work full time[1]	554	743	1 021	1 060	1 030	1 020	919	798	740	702	634	584	568
As percent of families with unemployed member(s)	63.2	64.1	57.7	57.6	57.8	59.7	59.4	60.9	60.7	62.9	63.8	63.6	64.6

Note: The race or ethnicity of the family is determined by the race of the householder. Estimates for the above race groups (White or Black) do not sum to totals because data are not presented for all races.

[1]Usually work 35 hours or more a week at all jobs.
[2]Beginning in 2003, families where the householder selected this race group only; families where the householder selected more than one race group are excluded. Prior to 2003, families where the householder selected more than one race group were included in the group that the householder identified as the main race.
[3]May be of any race.

Table 1-21. Families, by Presence and Relationship of Employed Members and Family Type, Annual Averages, 2007–2019

(Thousands of people, percent.)

Characteristic	Number of families												
	2007	2008	2009	2010	2011	2012	2013	2014	2015	2016	2017	2018	2019
MARRIED-COUPLE FAMILIES													
Total	58 145	58 125	58 124	57 524	57 290	58 431	58 529	58 806	59 217	59 747	59 910	60 094	60 300
Member(s) employed, total	48 676	48 541	47 876	47 238	46 910	47 830	47 722	47 852	48 205	48 440	48 525	48 791	48 984
Husband only	11 509	11 351	11 371	11 311	11 426	11 815	11 755	11 713	11 726	11 649	11 425	11 469	11 163
Wife only	3 858	4 036	4 909	4 937	4 764	4 696	4 578	4 422	4 209	4 253	4 265	4 085	4 078
Husband and wife	30 055	29 854	28 211	27 501	27 229	27 708	27 748	28 042	28 434	28 693	28 944	29 317	29 809
Other employment combinations	3 254	3 300	3 384	3 489	3 491	3 612	3 640	3 676	3 837	3 845	3 891	3 921	3 934
No member(s) employed	9 469	9 585	10 248	10 286	10 379	10 601	10 807	10 954	11 012	11 307	11 386	11 302	11 317
FAMILIES MAINTAINED BY WOMEN[1]													
Total	14 423	14 383	14 610	14 913	15 147	15 517	15 507	15 581	15 693	15 669	15 438	15 452	15 317
Member(s) employed, total	11 087	10 929	10 642	10 715	10 867	11 236	11 360	11 585	11 765	12 001	11 861	12 003	12 025
Householder only	6 307	6 250	6 135	6 189	6 248	6 403	6 359	6 368	6 451	6 502	6 333	6 250	6 163
Householder and other member(s)	2 994	2 870	2 642	2 603	2 683	2 896	2 933	3 059	3 181	3 293	3 372	3 484	3 548
Other member(s), not householder	1 785	1 809	1 866	1 923	1 937	1 937	2 069	2 159	2 133	2 205	2 156	2 269	2 315
No member(s) employed	3 336	3 454	3 968	4 198	4 280	4 281	4 147	3 995	3 928	3 668	3 577	3 449	3 292
FAMILIES MAINTAINED BY MEN[1]													
Total	5 327	5 435	5 627	5 809	5 926	6 192	6 410	6 502	6 499	6 676	6 666	6 956	7 016
Member(s) employed, total	4 568	4 589	4 492	4 607	4 752	5 025	5 236	5 394	5 389	5 582	5 641	5 861	5 998
Householder only	2 170	2 178	2 104	2 215	2 399	2 514	2 529	2 568	2 517	2 577	2 564	2 703	2 724
Householder and other member(s)	1 696	1 659	1 557	1 525	1 506	1 622	1 736	1 891	1 932	2 050	2 101	2 173	2 268
Other member(s), not householder	701	752	831	867	847	889	971	935	940	955	976	985	1 006
No member(s) employed	759	845	1 135	1 202	1 174	1 168	1 174	1 108	1 110	1 094	1 025	1 096	1 018

Characteristic	Percent distribution												
	2007	2008	2009	2010	2011	2012	2013	2014	2015	2016	2017	2018	2019
MARRIED-COUPLE FAMILIES													
Total	100.0	100.0	100.0	100.0	100.0	100.0	100.0	100.0	100.0	100.0	100.0	100.0	100.0
Member(s) employed, total	83.7	83.5	82.4	82.1	81.9	81.9	81.5	81.4	81.4	81.1	81.0	81.2	81.2
Husband only	19.8	19.5	19.6	19.7	19.9	20.2	20.1	19.9	19.8	19.5	19.1	19.1	18.5
Wife only	6.6	6.9	8.4	8.6	8.3	8.0	7.8	7.5	7.1	7.1	7.1	6.8	6.8
Husband and wife	51.7	51.4	48.5	47.8	47.5	47.4	47.4	47.7	48.0	48.0	48.3	48.8	49.4
Other employment combinations	5.6	5.7	5.8	6.1	6.1	6.2	6.2	6.3	6.5	6.4	6.5	6.5	6.5
No member(s) employed	16.3	16.5	17.6	17.9	18.1	18.1	18.5	18.6	18.6	18.9	19.0	18.8	18.8
FAMILIES MAINTAINED BY WOMEN[1]													
Total	100.0	100.0	100.0	100.0	100.0	100.0	100.0	100.0	100.0	100.0	100.0	100.0	100.0
Member(s) employed, total	76.9	76.0	72.8	71.9	71.7	72.4	73.3	74.4	75.0	76.6	76.8	77.7	78.5
Householder only	43.7	43.5	42.0	41.5	41.2	41.3	41.0	40.9	41.1	41.5	41.0	40.4	40.2
Householder and other member(s)	20.8	20.0	18.1	17.5	17.7	18.7	18.9	19.6	20.3	21.0	21.8	22.5	23.2
Other member(s), not householder	12.4	12.6	12.8	12.9	12.8	12.5	13.3	13.9	13.6	14.1	14.0	14.7	15.1
No member(s) employed	23.1	24.0	27.2	28.1	28.3	27.6	26.7	25.6	25.0	23.4	23.2	22.3	21.5
FAMILIES MAINTAINED BY MEN[1]													
Total	100.0	100.0	100.0	100.0	100.0	100.0	100.0	100.0	100.0	100.0	100.0	100.0	100.0
Member(s) employed, total	85.7	84.4	79.8	79.3	80.2	81.1	81.7	83.0	82.9	83.6	84.6	84.3	85.5
Householder only	40.7	40.1	37.4	38.1	40.5	40.6	39.5	39.5	38.7	38.6	38.5	38.9	38.8
Householder and other member(s)	31.8	30.5	27.7	26.2	25.4	26.2	27.1	29.1	29.7	30.7	31.5	31.2	32.3
Other member(s), not householder	13.2	13.8	14.8	14.9	14.3	14.4	15.1	14.4	14.5	14.3	14.6	14.2	14.3
No member(s) employed	14.3	15.6	20.2	20.7	19.8	18.9	18.3	17.0	17.1	16.4	15.4	15.7	14.5

Note: Detail may not sum to total due to rounding.

[1]No spouse present.

Table 1-22. Unemployment in Families, by Presence and Relationship of Employed Members and Family Type, Annual Averages, 2007–2019

(Thousands of people, percent.)

Characteristic	Number												
	2007	2008	2009	2010	2011	2012	2013	2014	2015	2016	2017	2018	2019
MARRIED-COUPLE FAMILIES													
With Unemployed Member(s), Total	2 978	3 796	6 056	6 147	5 576	5 140	4 586	3 765	3 292	3 122	2 783	2 528	2 367
No member employed	512	663	1 218	4 884	4 413	4 123	3 639	3 028	2 653	2 511	2 245	2 075	1 942
Some member(s) employed	2 467	3 133	4 838	1 263	1 162	1 017	946	737	639	612	537	452	425
Husband unemployed	1 110	1 439	2 808	2 813	2 387	2 066	1 824	1 398	1 194	1 149	1 009	877	784
Wife employed	725	927	1 799	1 783	1 497	1 307	1 134	872	739	702	632	558	506
Wife unemployed	902	1 114	1 630	1 697	1 610	1 567	1 346	1 121	947	913	850	766	712
Husband employed	783	975	1 397	1 455	1 350	1 328	1 129	943	786	775	700	654	604
Other family member unemployed	966	1 243	1 618	1 637	1 579	1 507	1 416	1 246	1 151	1 060	923	885	871
FAMILIES MAINTAINED BY WOMEN[1]													
With Unemployed Member(s), Total	1 416	1 666	2 309	2 446	2 498	2 372	2 165	1 933	1 666	1 543	1 389	1 233	1 163
No member employed	701	849	1 244	1 094	1 146	1 081	1 026	936	804	774	691	633	624
Some member(s) employed	714	817	1 065	1 351	1 352	1 290	1 139	997	862	770	697	600	538
Householder unemployed	650	796	1 141	1 227	1 268	1 191	1 053	892	770	710	644	559	510
Other member(s) employed	144	181	225	254	275	250	251	216	181	174	165	154	152
Other member(s) unemployed	766	870	1 168	1 218	1 229	1 180	1 112	1 040	896	833	744	673	653
FAMILIES MAINTAINED BY MEN[1]													
With Unemployed Member(s), Total	520	642	1 016	1 102	970	932	934	789	657	635	573	539	547
No member employed	205	274	482	587	520	497	527	455	375	372	340	303	336
Some member(s) employed	316	368	535	515	450	435	408	333	282	264	233	236	211
Householder unemployed	294	385	626	680	575	535	550	446	378	354	312	306	286
Other member(s) employed	137	164	239	259	231	209	238	200	158	153	132	125	137
Other member(s) unemployed	226	257	391	422	394	397	385	343	280	282	260	233	260

Characteristic	Percent distribution												
	2007	2008	2009	2010	2011	2012	2013	2014	2015	2016	2017	2018	2019
MARRIED-COUPLE FAMILIES													
With Unemployed Member(s), Total	100.0	100.0	100.0	100.0	100.0	100.0	100.0	100.0	100.0	100.0	100.0	100.0	100.0
No member employed	17.2	17.5	20.1	79.4	79.2	80.2	79.4	80.4	80.6	80.4	80.7	82.1	82.1
Some member(s) employed	82.8	82.5	79.9	20.6	20.8	19.8	20.6	19.6	19.4	19.6	19.3	17.9	17.9
Husband unemployed	37.3	37.9	46.4	45.8	42.8	40.2	39.8	37.1	36.3	36.8	36.3	34.7	33.1
Wife employed	24.3	24.4	29.7	29.0	26.9	25.4	24.7	23.2	22.5	22.5	22.7	22.1	21.4
Wife unemployed	30.3	29.3	26.9	27.6	28.9	30.5	29.4	29.8	28.8	29.2	30.6	30.3	30.1
Husband employed	26.3	25.7	23.1	23.7	24.2	25.8	24.6	25.1	23.9	24.8	25.1	25.9	25.5
Other family member unemployed	32.4	32.7	26.7	26.6	28.3	29.3	30.9	33.1	35.0	34.0	33.2	35.0	36.8
FAMILIES MAINTAINED BY WOMEN[1]													
With Unemployed Member(s), Total	100.0	100.0	100.0	100.0	100.0	100.0	100.0	100.0	100.0	100.0	100.0	100.0	100.0
No member employed	49.5	50.9	53.9	44.7	45.9	45.6	47.4	48.4	48.2	50.1	49.8	51.4	53.7
Some member(s) employed	50.5	49.1	46.1	55.3	54.1	54.4	52.6	51.6	51.8	49.9	50.2	48.6	46.3
Householder unemployed	45.9	47.8	49.4	50.2	50.8	50.2	48.6	46.2	46.2	46.0	46.4	45.4	43.8
Other member(s) employed	10.2	10.9	9.7	10.4	11.0	10.6	11.6	11.2	10.8	11.3	11.9	12.5	13.1
Other member(s) unemployed	54.1	52.2	50.6	49.8	49.2	49.8	51.4	53.8	53.8	54.0	53.6	54.6	56.2
FAMILIES MAINTAINED BY MEN[1]													
With Unemployed Member(s), Total	100.0	100.0	100.0	100.0	100.0	100.0	100.0	100.0	100.0	100.0	100.0	100.0	100.0
No member employed	39.3	42.7	47.4	53.3	53.6	53.3	56.4	57.7	57.0	58.5	59.4	56.2	61.4
Some member(s) employed	60.7	57.3	52.6	46.7	46.4	46.7	43.6	42.3	43.0	41.5	40.6	43.8	38.6
Householder unemployed	56.6	60.0	61.6	61.7	59.4	57.4	58.8	56.5	57.5	55.6	54.5	56.7	52.4
Other member(s) employed	26.3	25.6	23.5	23.5	23.8	22.5	25.5	25.4	24.1	24.0	23.1	23.2	25.1
Other member(s) unemployed	43.4	40.0	38.4	38.3	40.6	42.6	41.2	43.5	42.5	44.4	45.5	43.3	47.6

Note: Detail may not sum to total due to rounding.

[1] No spouse present.

Table 1-23. Employment Status of the Population, by Sex, Marital Status, and Presence and Age of Own Children Under 18 Years, Annual Averages, 2010–2019

(Thousands of people, percent.)

Characteristic	2010			2011			2012			2013			2014		
	Both sexes	Men	Women	Both sexes	Men	Women	Both sexes	Men	Women	Both sexes	Men	Women	Both sexes	Men	Women
With Own Children Under 18 Years, Total															
Civilian noninstitutional population	64 488	28 463	36 025	63 885	28 143	35 743	65 620	28 943	36 676	65 385	28 947	36 438	65 643	29 040	36 602
Civilian labor force	52 159	26 661	25 499	51 521	26 302	25 219	52 754	26 954	25 800	52 335	26 869	25 466	52 580	26 939	25 641
Participation rate	80.9	93.7	70.8	80.6	93.5	70.6	80.4	93.1	70.3	80.0	92.8	69.9	80.1	92.8	70.1
Employed	47 863	24 653	23 210	47 578	24 619	22 959	49 101	25 460	23 641	49 146	25 540	23 606	49 948	25 899	24 049
Employment-population ratio	74.2	86.6	64.4	74.5	87.5	64.2	74.8	88.0	64.5	75.2	88.2	64.8	76.1	89.2	65.7
Full-time workers[1]	7 581	1 477	6 104	7 303	1 374	5 930	41 698	24 055	17 643	41 844	24 207	17 637	42 727	24 615	18 112
Part-time workers[2]	74	87	64	74	88	64	7 403	1 405	5 999	7 302	1 333	5 969	7 221	1 284	5 937
Unemployed	4 296	2 008	2 289	3 943	1 683	2 260	3 653	1 494	2 159	3 189	1 329	1 860	2 632	1 040	1 592
Unemployment rate	8.2	7.5	9.0	7.7	6.4	9.0	6.9	5.5	8.4	6.1	4.9	7.3	5.0	3.9	6.2
Married, Spouse Present															
Civilian noninstitutional population	50 868	25 820	25 049	49 999	25 392	24 607	49 595	25 013	24 582	49 595	25 035	24 560	49 739	25 098	24 641
Civilian labor force	41 600	24 332	17 268	40 783	23 873	16 911	40 277	23 481	16 796	40 096	23 447	16 650	40 220	23 505	16 715
Participation rate	81.8	94.2	68.9	81.6	94.0	68.7	81.2	93.9	68.3	80.8	93.7	67.8	80.9	93.7	67.8
Employed	38 870	22 689	16 181	38 379	22 480	15 900	38 261	22 374	15 886	38 325	22 478	15 847	38 804	22 762	16 042
Employment-population ratio	76.4	87.9	64.6	76.8	88.5	64.6	77.1	89.5	64.6	77.3	89.8	64.5	78.0	90.7	65.1
Full-time workers[1]	5 728	1 245	4 482	5 440	1 158	4 282	32 961	21 277	11 684	33 196	21 436	11 759	33 773	21 751	12 022
Part-time workers[2]	76	88	65	77	88	65	5 299	1 097	4 202	5 130	1 042	4 088	5 032	1 012	4 020
Unemployed	2 730	1 643	1 087	2 404	1 393	1 011	2 017	1 106	910	1 771	969	802	1 415	742	673
Unemployment rate	6.6	6.8	6.3	5.9	5.8	6.0	5.0	4.7	5.4	4.4	4.1	4.8	3.5	3.2	4.0
Other Marital Status[3]															
Civilian noninstitutional population	13 620	2 643	10 977	13 886	2 751	11 135	16 025	3 930	12 095	15 789	3 912	11 878	15 904	3 943	11 961
Civilian labor force	10 559	2 329	8 230	10 737	2 429	8 308	12 477	3 473	9 004	12 238	3 422	8 817	12 360	3 434	8 926
Participation rate	77.5	88.1	75.0	77.3	88.3	74.6	77.9	88.4	74.4	77.5	87.5	74.2	77.7	87.1	74.6
Employed	8 994	1 964	7 029	9 198	2 139	7 059	10 840	3 085	7 755	10 820	3 062	7 759	11 143	3 137	8 007
Employment-population ratio	66.0	74.3	64.0	66.2	77.8	63.4	67.6	78.5	64.1	68.5	78.3	65.3	70.1	79.6	66.9
Full-time workers[1]	1 853	232	1 621	1 864	216	1 647	8 736	2 777	5 959	8 648	2 771	5 878	8 955	2 864	6 090
Part-time workers[2]	66	74	64	66	78	63	2 104	308	1 796	2 172	291	1 881	2 189	272	1 917
Unemployed	1 566	365	1 201	1 539	290	1 249	1 636	388	1 249	1 418	360	1 058	1 217	298	919
Unemployment rate	14.8	15.7	14.6	14.3	11.9	15.0	13.1	11.2	13.9	11.6	10.5	12.0	9.8	8.7	10.3
With Own Children 6 to 17 Years, None Younger															
Civilian noninstitutional population	35 402	15 639	19 763	35 027	15 431	19 596	35 786	15 777	20 009	36 218	16 007	20 212	36 486	16 114	20 372
Civilian labor force	29 625	14 515	15 110	29 193	14 289	14 904	29 573	14 545	15 028	29 815	14 714	15 101	29 989	14 768	15 221
Participation rate	83.7	92.8	76.5	77.6	87.0	70.2	82.6	92.2	75.1	82.3	91.9	74.7	82.2	91.6	74.7
Employed	27 421	13 482	13 939	27 178	13 422	13 756	27 722	13 791	13 931	28 216	14 047	14 169	28 689	14 244	14 445
Employment-population ratio	77.5	86.2	70.5	77.6	87.0	70.2	77.5	87.4	69.6	77.9	87.8	70.1	78.6	88.4	70.9
Full-time workers[1]	4 182	757	3 425	3 992	686	3 306	23 783	13 074	10 709	24 181	13 361	10 819	24 746	13 594	11 153
Part-time workers[2]	78	86	71	78	87	70	3 939	717	3 222	4 035	686	3 349	3 943	650	3 292
Unemployed	2 204	1 032	1 172	2 015	867	1 148	1 851	754	1 097	1 599	667	933	1 300	524	775
Unemployment rate	7.4	7.1	7.8	6.9	6.1	7.7	6.3	5.2	7.3	5.4	4.5	6.2	4.3	3.6	5.1
With Own Children Under 6 Years															
Civilian noninstitutional population	29 086	12 824	16 262	28 858	12 712	16 146	29 834	13 167	16 667	29 166	12 940	16 226	29 157	12 927	16 230
Civilian labor force	22 534	12 146	10 388	22 328	12 013	10 315	23 181	12 409	10 772	22 519	12 155	10 365	22 591	12 171	10 420
Participation rate	77.5	94.7	63.9	77.4	94.5	63.9	77.7	94.2	64.6	77.2	93.9	63.9	77.5	94.2	64.2
Employed	20 442	11 171	9 271	20 400	11 197	9 203	21 379	11 669	9 710	20 930	11 493	9 437	21 259	11 655	9 604
Employment-population ratio	70.3	87.1	57.0	70.7	88.1	57.0	71.7	88.6	58.3	71.8	88.8	58.2	72.9	90.2	59.2
Full-time workers[1]	3 399	720	2 679	3 311	687	2 624	17 915	10 981	6 934	17 663	10 846	6 817	17 981	11 021	6 959
Part-time workers[2]	70	87	57	71	88	57	3 464	688	2 776	3 267	647	2 620	3 278	634	2 644
Unemployed	2 092	975	1 117	1 928	816	1 112	1 802	740	1 062	1 589	662	928	1 332	516	816
Unemployment rate	9.3	8.0	10.8	8.6	6.8	10.8	7.8	6.0	9.9	7.1	5.4	8.9	5.9	4.2	7.8
With No Own Children Under 18 Years															
Civilian noninstitutional population	173 342	86 711	86 631	175 732	88 175	87 558	177 665	88 400	89 264	180 295	89 609	90 686	182 304	90 707	91 596
Civilian labor force	101 729	55 324	46 405	102 096	55 673	46 423	102 221	55 373	46 848	103 055	55 798	47 256	103 342	55 943	47 399
Participation rate	58.7	63.8	53.6	58.1	63.1	53.0	57.5	62.6	52.5	57.2	62.3	52.1	56.7	61.7	51.7
Employed	91 201	48 706	42 495	92 291	49 671	42 620	93 368	50 096	43 272	94 783	50 813	43 971	96 357	51 793	44 564
Employment-population ratio	52.6	56.2	49.1	52.5	56.3	48.7	52.6	56.7	48.5	52.6	56.7	48.5	52.9	57.1	48.7
Full-time workers[1]	19 769	8 381	11 387	20 010	8 584	11 426	73 111	41 423	31 688	74 470	42 128	32 342	75 991	43 214	32 777
Part-time workers[2]	53	56	49	52	56	49	20 257	8 673	11 584	20 313	8 685	11 629	20 366	8 579	11 787
Unemployed	10 528	6 618	3 910	9 805	6 002	3 803	8 853	5 277	3 575	8 271	4 986	3 285	6 985	4 150	2 835
Unemployment rate	10.3	12.0	8.4	9.6	10.8	8.2	8.7	9.5	7.6	8.0	8.9	7.0	6.8	7.4	6.0

Note: Own children include sons, daughters, stepchildren, and adopted children. Not included are nieces, nephews, grandchildren, and other related and unrelated children. Detail may not sum to total due to rounding.

[1]Usually work 35 hours or more a week at all jobs.
[2]Usually work less than 35 hours a week at all jobs.
[3]Includes never-married, divorced, separated, and widowed persons.

Table 1-23. Employment Status of the Population, by Sex, Marital Status, and Presence and Age of Own Children Under 18 Years, Annual Averages, 2010–2019—*Continued*

(Thousands of people, percent.)

Characteristic	2015 Both sexes	2015 Men	2015 Women	2016 Both sexes	2016 Men	2016 Women	2017 Both sexes	2017 Men	2017 Women	2018 Both sexes	2018 Men	2018 Women	2019 Both sexes	2019 Men	2019 Women
With Own Children Under 18 Years, Total															
Civilian noninstitutional population	65 564	29 095	36 469	65 055	28 992	36 063	64 188	28 740	35 448	64 235	28 913	35 321	63 638	28 658	34 979
Civilian labor force	52 476	26 978	25 498	52 321	26 902	25 419	51 875	26 662	25 213	52 206	26 967	25 239	52 033	26 756	25 277
Participation rate	80.0	92.7	70.0	80.4	92.8	70.5	80.8	92.8	71.1	81.3	93.3	71.5	81.8	93.4	72.3
Employed	50 238	26 079	24 159	50 240	26 039	24 201	50 036	25 920	24 117	50 590	26 316	24 274	50 551	26 162	24 390
Employment-population ratio	76.6	89.6	66.2	77.2	89.8	67.1	78.0	90.2	68.0	78.8	91.0	68.7	79.4	91.3	69.7
Full-time workers[1]	43 250	24 880	18 370	43 352	24 896	18 456	43 433	24 807	18 626	44 177	25 231	18 946	44 303	25 159	19 144
Part-time workers[2]	6 989	1 199	5 790	6 887	1 143	5 744	6 604	1 113	5 491	6 414	1 085	5 328	6 248	1 002	5 246
Unemployed	2 238	899	1 339	2 082	864	1 218	1 838	742	1 096	1 616	651	965	1 482	594	888
Unemployment rate	4.3	3.3	5.3	4.0	3.2	4.8	3.5	2.8	4.3	3.1	2.4	3.8	2.8	2.2	3.5
Married, Spouse Present															
Civilian noninstitutional population	49 822	25 122	24 700	49 472	25 007	24 465	48 974	24 779	24 195	49 007	24 809	24 198	48 746	24 613	24 132
Civilian labor force	40 226	23 532	16 694	40 016	23 409	16 607	39 781	23 172	16 609	40 043	23 341	16 703	40 040	23 175	16 866
Participation rate	80.7	93.7	67.6	80.9	93.6	67.9	81.2	93.5	68.6	81.7	94.1	69.0	82.1	94.2	69.9
Employed	39 026	22 889	16 137	38 866	22 791	16 075	38 775	22 633	16 142	39 183	22 895	16 288	39 242	22 770	16 472
Employment-population ratio	78.3	91.1	65.3	78.6	91.1	65.7	79.2	91.3	66.7	80.0	92.3	67.3	80.5	92.5	68.3
Full-time workers[1]	34 148	21 958	12 190	34 112	21 899	12 214	34 081	21 746	12 334	34 625	22 044	12 581	34 708	21 988	12 720
Part-time workers[2]	4 877	931	3 947	4 754	892	3 861	4 695	887	3 808	4 558	851	3 707	4 534	782	3 752
Unemployed	1 200	643	557	1 150	618	532	1 006	539	467	860	445	415	798	404	394
Unemployment rate	3.0	2.7	3.3	2.9	2.6	3.2	2.5	2.3	2.8	2.1	1.9	2.5	2.0	1.7	2.3
Other Marital Status[3]															
Civilian noninstitutional population	15 742	3 973	11 769	15 583	3 985	11 598	15 213	3 961	11 253	15 228	4 104	11 123	14 892	4 045	10 847
Civilian labor force	12 250	3 446	8 804	12 305	3 494	8 811	12 093	3 490	8 603	12 163	3 627	8 536	11 993	3 581	8 412
Participation rate	77.8	86.7	74.8	79.0	87.7	76.0	79.5	88.1	76.5	79.9	88.4	76.7	80.5	88.5	77.6
Employed	11 213	3 190	8 022	11 374	3 248	8 125	11 261	3 287	7 975	11 407	3 421	7 987	11 309	3 392	7 918
Employment-population ratio	71.2	80.3	68.2	73.0	81.5	70.1	74.0	83.0	70.9	74.9	83.3	71.8	75.9	83.8	73.0
Full-time workers[1]	9 101	2 922	6 179	9 240	2 997	6 243	9 352	3 061	6 291	9 552	3 187	6 365	9 595	3 171	6 424
Part-time workers[2]	2 111	268	1 843	2 134	251	1 883	1 909	226	1 683	1 856	234	1 622	1 714	220	1 493
Unemployed	1 038	256	782	931	246	686	832	203	629	755	206	550	684	189	494
Unemployment rate	8.5	7.4	8.9	7.6	7.0	7.8	6.9	5.8	7.3	6.2	5.7	6.4	5.7	5.3	5.9
With Own Children 6 to 17 Years, None Younger															
Civilian noninstitutional population	36 616	16 171	20 445	36 491	16 152	20 338	36 286	16 153	20 133	35 880	15 995	19 886	35 706	15 987	19 719
Civilian labor force	30 057	14 840	15 218	30 088	14 836	15 252	30 060	14 812	15 248	29 936	14 753	15 183	29 858	14 714	15 144
Participation rate	82.1	91.8	74.4	82.5	91.9	75.0	82.8	91.7	75.7	83.4	92.2	76.4	83.6	92.0	76.8
Employed	28 923	14 392	14 531	28 998	14 393	14 605	29 063	14 428	14 635	29 097	14 429	14 668	29 049	14 385	14 664
Employment-population ratio	79.0	89.0	71.1	79.5	89.1	71.8	80.1	89.3	72.7	81.1	90.2	73.8	81.4	90.0	74.4
Full-time workers[1]	25 073	13 785	11 288	25 166	13 785	11 381	25 391	13 830	11 561	25 604	13 860	11 744	25 608	13 841	11 768
Part-time workers[2]	3 850	607	3 243	3 831	607	3 224	3 672	598	3 074	3 493	569	2 924	3 441	544	2 897
Unemployed	1 134	448	687	1 090	444	646	997	384	612	840	324	515	809	329	480
Unemployment rate	3.8	3.0	4.5	3.6	3.0	4.2	3.3	2.6	4.0	2.8	2.2	3.4	2.7	2.2	3.2
With Own Children Under 6 Years															
Civilian noninstitutional population	28 948	12 924	16 024	28 565	12 840	15 724	27 902	12 587	15 315	28 354	12 919	15 436	27 932	12 672	15 260
Civilian labor force	22 419	12 138	10 281	22 233	12 066	10 167	21 815	11 849	9 965	22 270	12 214	10 056	22 175	12 042	10 133
Participation rate	77.4	93.9	64.0	77.8	94.0	64.7	78.2	94.1	65.1	78.5	94.5	65.0	79.4	95.0	66.4
Employed	21 315	11 687	9 628	21 242	11 646	9 596	20 973	11 492	9 481	21 494	11 888	9 606	21 502	11 777	9 725
Employment-population ratio	73.6	90.4	60.1	74.4	90.7	61.0	75.2	91.3	61.9	75.8	92.0	62.2	77.0	92.9	63.7
Full-time workers[1]	18 177	11 095	7 082	18 186	11 110	7 076	18 041	10 977	7 064	18 573	11 371	7 201	18 695	11 319	7 376
Part-time workers[2]	3 139	592	2 547	3 056	536	2 520	2 932	515	2 417	2 921	516	2 405	2 807	458	2 349
Unemployed	1 104	451	652	992	420	572	841	358	484	776	327	449	673	265	408
Unemployment rate	4.9	3.7	6.3	4.5	3.5	5.6	3.9	3.0	4.9	3.5	2.7	4.5	3.0	2.2	4.0
With No Own Children Under 18 Years															
Civilian noninstitutional population	185 237	92 006	93 231	188 482	93 505	94 978	190 891	94 535	96 356	193 556	95 765	97 791	195 538	96 695	98 842
Civilian labor force	104 654	56 643	48 011	106 866	57 852	49 014	108 445	58 483	49 962	109 869	59 129	50 740	111 506	59 931	51 574
Participation rate	56.5	61.6	51.5	56.7	61.9	51.6	56.8	61.9	51.9	56.8	61.7	51.9	57.0	62.0	52.2
Employed	98 595	53 052	45 544	101 196	54 529	46 667	103 301	55 482	47 819	105 171	56 382	48 789	106 987	57 299	49 688
Employment-population ratio	53.2	57.7	48.9	53.7	58.3	49.1	54.1	58.7	49.6	54.3	58.9	49.9	54.7	59.3	50.3
Full-time workers[1]	78 243	44 471	33 772	80 408	45 671	34 738	82 535	46 764	35 770	84 396	47 704	36 692	86 294	48 664	37 630
Part-time workers[2]	20 353	8 581	11 772	20 788	8 858	11 930	20 766	8 718	12 048	20 775	8 678	12 096	20 693	8 634	12 059
Unemployed	6 058	3 591	2 468	5 670	3 323	2 346	5 144	3 001	2 143	4 698	2 747	1 951	4 519	2 633	1 886
Unemployment rate	5.8	6.3	5.1	5.3	5.7	4.8	4.7	5.1	4.3	4.3	4.6	3.8	4.1	4.4	3.7

Note: Own children include sons, daughters, stepchildren, and adopted children. Not included are nieces, nephews, grandchildren, and other related and unrelated children. Detail may not sum to total due to rounding.

[1]Usually work 35 hours or more a week at all jobs.
[2]Usually work less than 35 hours a week at all jobs.
[3]Includes never-married, divorced, separated, and widowed persons.

Table 1-24. Employment Status of Mothers with Own Children Under 3 Years of Age, by Age of Youngest Child and Marital Status, Annual Averages, 2010–2019

(Thousands of people, percent.)

Year and characteristic	Civilian noninsti-tutional population	Civilian labor force		Employed				Unemployed	
		Total	Percent of population	Total	Percent of population	Full-time workers[1]	Part-time workers[2]	Number	Percent of labor force
2010									
Total Mothers with Own Children Under 3 Years	9 503	5 770	60.7	5 114	53.8	3 570	1 543	656	11.4
2 years	2 968	1 908	64.3	1 708	57.5	1 200	509	199	10.5
1 year	3 351	2 062	61.5	1 815	54.2	1 243	572	246	12.0
Under 1 year	3 184	1 800	56.5	1 590	49.9	1 128	462	210	11.7
Married, Spouse Present with Own Children Under 3 Years	6 642	3 941	59.3	3 670	55.3	2 596	1 074	271	6.9
2 years	2 055	1 275	62.1	1 195	58.2	841	354	80	6.3
1 year	2 344	1 403	59.8	1 301	55.5	896	405	101	7.2
Under 1 year	3 184	1 800	56.5	1 590	49.9	1 128	462	210	11.7
Other Marital Status with Own Children Under 3 Years[3]	2 862	1 828	63.9	1 444	50.5	974	470	385	21.0
2 years	914	633	69.2	514	56.2	359	155	119	18.8
1 year	1 007	659	65.5	514	51.0	346	168	145	22.0
Under 1 year	941	537	57.0	416	44.2	269	147	121	22.5
2011									
Total Mothers with Own Children Under 3 Years	9 259	5 613	60.6	4 977	53.8	3 486	1 492	635	11.3
2 years	2 893	1 848	63.9	1 645	56.9	1 169	476	202	11.0
1 year	3 353	2 083	62.1	1 844	55.0	1 296	548	239	11.5
Under 1 year	3 013	1 682	55.8	1 488	49.4	1 021	467	194	11.5
Married, Spouse Present with Own Children Under 3 Years	6 488	3 854	59.4	3 603	55.5	2 594	1 009	251	6.5
2 years	1 999	1 220	61.0	1 138	56.9	822	316	82	6.7
1 year	2 381	1 434	60.2	1 342	56.4	967	375	92	6.4
Under 1 year	2 109	1 200	56.9	1 123	53.3	805	318	77	6.4
Other Marital Status with Own Children Under 3 Years[3]	2 771	1 759	63.5	1 375	49.6	892	483	384	21.8
2 years	894	628	70.3	508	56.8	347	161	120	19.2
1 year	973	649	66.8	502	51.6	329	173	147	22.6
Under 1 year	905	482	53.2	365	40.3	216	149	117	24.2
2012									
Total Mothers with Own Children Under 3 Years	9 540	5 839	61.2	5 245	55.0	3 690	1 555	594	10.2
2 years	2 922	1 890	64.7	1 708	58.5	1 215	493	181	9.6
1 year	3 393	2 119	62.5	1 909	56.3	1 314	595	210	9.9
Under 1 year	3 224	1 830	56.7	1 628	50.5	1 161	467	202	11.0
Married, Spouse Present with Own Children Under 3 Years	6 334	3 808	60.1	3 600	56.8	2 595	1 005	208	5.5
2 years	1 940	1 198	61.8	1 134	58.5	816	318	64	5.4
1 year	2 288	1 409	61.6	1 332	58.2	928	405	77	5.5
Under 1 year	2 106	1 200	57.0	1 134	53.8	852	282	66	5.5
Other Marital Status with Own Children Under 3 Years[3]	3 206	2 031	63.4	1 645	51.3	1 095	550	386	19.0
2 years	982	691	70.4	574	58.5	399	175	117	17.0
1 year	1 105	710	64.2	577	52.2	386	191	133	18.8
Under 1 year	1 119	630	56.3	494	44.2	309	185	136	21.6
2013									
Total Mothers with Own Children Under 3 Years	9 211	5 626	61.1	5 113	55.5	3 615	1 497	514	9.1
2 years	2 877	1 875	65.2	1 723	59.9	1 240	482	152	8.1
1 year	3 266	1 995	61.1	1 798	55.0	1 251	547	197	9.9
Under 1 year	3 069	1 757	57.3	1 593	51.9	1 124	469	164	9.3
Married, Spouse Present with Own Children Under 3 Years	6 224	3 689	59.3	3 503	56.3	2 541	962	186	5.0
2 years	1 913	1 194	62.4	1 141	59.6	835	305	54	4.5
1 year	2 232	1 299	58.2	1 224	54.9	867	357	75	5.8
Under 1 year	2 080	1 196	57.5	1 138	54.7	839	299	58	4.8
Other Marital Status with Own Children Under 3 Years[3]	2 987	1 937	64.9	1 610	53.9	1 075	535	327	16.9
2 years	964	681	70.6	582	60.3	405	177	99	14.5
1 year	1 034	695	67.3	573	55.5	384	189	122	17.5
Under 1 year	989	561	56.7	455	46.0	285	169	107	19.0
2014									
Total Mothers with Own Children Under 3 Years	9 224	5 624	61.0	5 169	56.0	3 685	1 484	456	8.1
2 years	2 834	1 799	63.5	1 661	58.6	1 185	477	137	7.6
1 year	3 293	2 056	62.4	1 880	57.1	1 325	555	176	8.6
Under 1 year	3 097	1 770	57.1	1 628	52.6	1 175	453	142	8.0
Married, Spouse Present with Own Children Under 3 Years	6 243	3 691	59.1	3 526	56.5	2 602	925	165	4.5
2 years	1 934	1 153	59.6	1 104	57.1	807	296	49	4.3
1 year	2 300	1 376	59.8	1 307	56.8	950	357	68	5.0
Under 1 year	2 009	1 163	57.9	1 116	55.5	844	271	47	4.1
Other Marital Status with Own Children Under 3 Years[3]	2 981	1 933	64.9	1 642	55.1	1 083	559	291	15.0
2 years	900	646	71.8	558	62.0	377	180	88	13.6
1 year	993	681	68.6	573	57.7	375	197	108	15.8
Under 1 year	1 088	607	55.8	512	47.0	330	182	95	15.6

Note: Own children include sons, daughters, stepchildren, and adopted children. Not included are nieces, nephews, grandchildren, and other related and unrelated children. Detail may not sum to total due to rounding. Updated population controls are introduced annually with the release of January data.

[1]Usually work 35 hours or more a week at all jobs.
[2]Usually work less than 35 hours a week at all jobs.
[3]Includes never-married, divorced, separated, and widowed persons.

Table 1-24. Employment Status of Mothers with Own Children Under 3 Years of Age, by Age of Youngest Child and Marital Status, Annual Averages, 2010–2019—Continued

(Thousands of people, percent.)

Year and characteristic	Civilian noninsti-tutional population	Civilian labor force						Unemployed	
		Total	Percent of population	Employed				Number	Percent of labor force
				Total	Percent of population	Full-time workers[1]	Part-time workers[2]		
2015									
Total Mothers with Own Children Under 3 Years	9 308	5 714	61.4	5 336	57.3	3 882	1 455	377	6.6
2 years	2 920	1 869	64.0	1 741	59.6	1 280	462	127	6.8
1 year	3 254	2 024	62.2	1 897	58.3	1 370	526	128	6.3
Under 1 year	3 134	1 821	58.1	1 698	54.2	1 232	466	123	6.7
Married, Spouse Present with Own Children Under 3 Years	6 341	3 772	59.5	3 628	57.2	2 698	931	144	3.8
2 years	1 974	1 198	60.7	1 149	58.2	864	285	49	4.1
1 year	2 252	1 356	60.2	1 300	57.7	961	339	55	4.1
Under 1 year	2 114	1 218	57.6	1 179	55.8	873	306	39	3.2
Other Marital Status with Own Children Under 3 Years[3]	2 967	1 942	65.4	1 708	57.6	1 184	524	234	12.0
2 years	946	670	70.9	592	62.6	415	177	78	11.6
1 year	1 001	669	66.8	596	59.5	409	187	72	10.8
Under 1 year	1 020	603	59.1	519	50.9	359	160	84	13.9
2016									
Total Mothers with Own Children Under 3 Years	9 158	5 662	61.8	5 343	58.3	3 870	1 473	319	5.6
2 years	2 850	1 858	65.2	1 764	61.9	1 312	452	94	5.0
1 year	3 322	2 055	61.9	1 933	58.2	1 392	540	123	6.0
Under 1 year	2 985	1 749	58.6	1 645	55.1	1 165	480	103	5.9
Married, Spouse Present with Own Children Under 3 Years	6 335	3 768	59.5	3 648	57.6	2 691	957	120	3.2
2 years	1 964	1 210	61.6	1 171	59.6	876	294	39	3.3
1 year	2 302	1 367	59.4	1 321	57.4	966	356	46	3.4
Under 1 year	2 069	1 191	57.6	1 156	55.9	849	307	35	3.0
Other Marital Status with Own Children Under 3 Years[3]	2 823	1 894	67.1	1 695	60.0	1 179	516	199	10.5
2 years	886	648	73.1	594	67.0	436	158	54	8.4
1 year	1 020	689	67.5	612	60.0	427	185	77	11.2
Under 1 year	917	557	60.8	489	53.4	316	173	68	12.2
2017									
Total Mothers with Own Children Under 3 Years	8 877	5 528	62.0	5 250	59.1	3 837	1 413	277	5.0
2 years	2 804	1 835	65.4	1 742	62.1	1 315	427	93	5.1
1 year	3 208	2 016	62.8	1 923	59.9	1 385	538	93	4.6
Under 1 year	2 865	1 677	58.5	1 585	55.3	1 138	447	92	5.5
Married, Spouse Present with Own Children Under 3 Years	6 193	3 716	60.0	3 618	58.4	2 660	958	98	2.6
2 years	1 951	1 207	61.9	1 167	59.8	871	296	40	3.3
1 year	2 253	1 354	60.1	1 324	58.8	970	353	30	2.2
Under 1 year	1 989	1 155	58.1	1 128	56.7	819	309	27	2.4
Other Marital Status with Own Children Under 3 Years[3]	2 684	1 812	67.5	1 632	60.8	1 177	455	180	9.9
2 years	853	628	73.6	575	67.4	443	131	53	8.5
1 year	956	662	69.3	600	62.7	415	185	62	9.4
Under 1 year	876	522	59.6	457	52.2	319	138	64	12.3
2018									
Total Mothers with Own Children Under 3 Years	8 825	5 462	61.9	5 210	59.0	3 827	1 383	251	4.6
2 years	2 842	1 858	65.4	1 775	62.5	1 323	452	83	4.5
1 year	3 133	1 956	62.4	1 866	59.6	1 347	519	90	4.6
Under 1 year	2 849	1 648	57.8	1 569	55.1	1 157	412	78	4.8
Married, Spouse Present with Own Children Under 3 Years	6 195	3 694	59.6	3 597	60.8	3 940	1 344	228	4.1
2 years	1 996	1 221	61.2	1 187	63.9	1 271	436	71	4.0
1 year	2 195	1 328	60.5	1 294	61.4	1 463	485	85	4.2
Under 1 year	2 004	1 145	57.1	1 116	57.4	1 206	424	72	4.2
Other Marital Status with Own Children Under 3 Years[3]	2 630	1 768	67.2	1 614	58.1	2 656	940	97	2.6
2 years	846	637	75.2	589	59.4	881	306	35	2.9
1 year	938	628	67.0	572	59.0	945	349	33	2.5
Under 1 year	845	503	59.5	453	55.7	831	285	29	2.5
2019									
Total Mothers with Own Children Under 3 Years	8 685	5 512	63.5	5 284	60.8	2 825	934	90	2.3
2 years	2 673	1 778	66.5	1 707	61.4	869	295	27	2.3
1 year	3 171	2 032	64.1	1 947	61.6	1 064	340	34	2.4
Under 1 year	2 842	1 702	59.9	1 630	59.1	891	299	28	2.3
Married, Spouse Present with Own Children Under 3 Years	6 187	3 849	62.2	3 759	61.4	1 170	443	154	8.7
2 years	1 896	1 192	62.9	1 165	69.5	442	147	48	7.6
1 year	2 278	1 438	63.2	1 404	60.9	402	170	57	9.0
Under 1 year	2 013	1 219	60.5	1 191	53.6	327	127	50	9.8
Other Marital Status with Own Children Under 3 Years[3]	2 499	1 663	66.6	1 525	61.0	1 116	410	138	8.3
2 years	777	586	75.4	542	69.8	402	140	44	7.5
1 year	893	594	66.5	544	60.8	399	145	50	8.5
Under 1 year	828	483	58.3	439	53.0	315	124	44	9.1

Note: Own children include sons, daughters, stepchildren, and adopted children. Not included are nieces, nephews, grandchildren, and other related and unrelated children. Detail may not sum to total due to rounding. Updated population controls are introduced annually with the release of January data.

[1]Usually work 35 hours or more a week at all jobs.
[2]Usually work less than 35 hours a week at all jobs.
[3]Includes never-married, divorced, separated, and widowed persons.

UNEMPLOYMENT

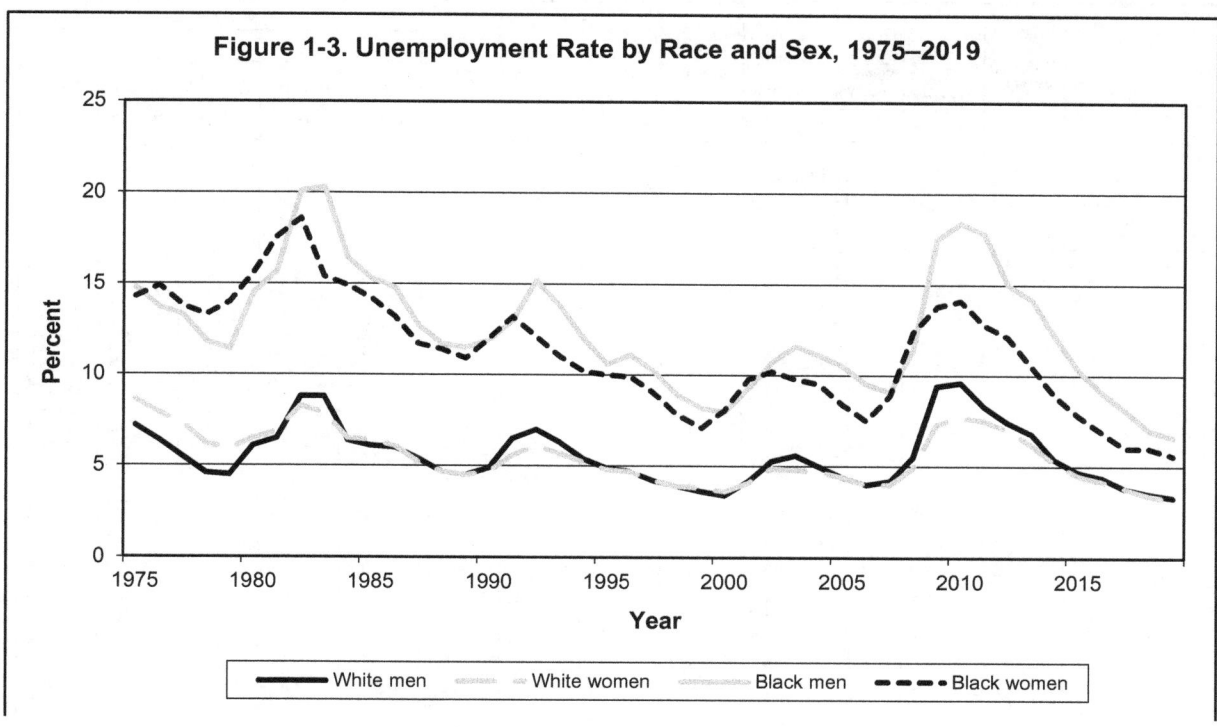

Figure 1-3. Unemployment Rate by Race and Sex, 1975–2019

The unemployment rate declined for the ninth consecutive year in 2019 from 3.9 percent in 2018 to 3.7 percent in 2019. Although the unemployment rate was slightly higher for men (3.7 percent) than for women (3.6 percent), the gap is getting far more narrow. In 2010, men had an unemployment rate of 10.5 percent compared with an unemployment rate of 8.6 percent for women. In 2019, Black men had the highest unemployment rate at 6.6 percent followed by Black women with an unemployment rate of 5.6 percent. From 2018 to 2019, the unemployment rate decreased by 0.4 percent for both Blacks and 0.2 percent for Whites. (See Table 1-27.)

OTHER HIGHLIGHTS

• While the unemployment rate decreased or remained steady for most age groups in 2019, the disparity in unemployment rates among age groups continued to be substantial as younger workers typically experience much higher levels of unemployment. In 2019, the unemployment rate for those age 16 to 19 years was 12.7 percent, while it was only 2.6 percent for those age 55 to 64 years. (See Table 1-27.)

• Among the major industries, agriculture and private wage salary workers continued to have the highest unemployment rate at 7.4 percent, followed by and leisure and hospitality workers at 5.2 percent. Financial activities had the lowest unemployment rate at 2.1 percent. (See Table 1-29.)

• The number of persons unemployed 27 weeks and over declined again in 2018 to 1.26 million. This was the ninth consecutive year that this number has declined since 2011 and was only slightly higher than the number of people unemployed 27 weeks or over in 2006. (See Table 1-31.)

• In 2019, the unemployment rate declined in 35 states and the District of Columbia, remained stable in five states (New Hampshire, Michigan, Delaware, North Carolina, and Kentucky), and increased in ten states (Pennsylvania, Minnesota, Missouri, South Dakota, Mississippi, Idaho, Iowa, Nebraska, and Wisconsin and Hawaii). (See Table 1-5.)

Table 1-25. Unemployment Rate, by Selected Characteristics, 1948–2019

(Unemployment as a percent of civilian labor force.)

Year	All civilian workers	Both sexes, 16 to 19 years	Men, 20 years and over	Women, 20 years and over	White[1]	Black[1]	Asian[1]	Hispanic[2]	Men Single, never married	Men Married, spouse present	Men Widowed, divorced, or separated	Women Single, never married	Women Married, spouse present	Women Widowed, divorced, or separated
1948	3.8	9.2	3.2	3.6	...	...	...	...	...	...	...	...	...	...
1949	5.9	13.4	5.4	5.3	...	...	...	...	...	...	...	...	...	...
1950	5.3	12.2	4.7	5.1	...	...	...	...	...	...	...	...	...	...
1951	3.3	8.2	2.5	4.0	...	...	...	...	...	...	...	...	...	...
1952	3.0	8.5	2.4	3.2	...	...	...	...	...	...	...	...	...	...
1953	2.9	7.6	2.5	2.9	...	...	...	...	...	...	...	...	...	...
1954	5.5	12.6	4.9	5.5	5.0	...	...	...	...	...	...	...	...	...
1955	4.4	11.0	3.8	4.4	3.9	...	...	...	8.6	2.6	7.1	5.0	3.7	5.0
1956	4.1	11.1	3.4	4.2	3.6	...	...	...	7.7	2.3	6.2	5.3	3.6	5.0
1957	4.3	11.6	3.6	4.1	3.8	...	...	...	9.2	2.8	6.8	5.6	4.3	4.7
1958	6.8	15.9	6.2	6.1	6.1	...	...	...	13.3	5.1	11.2	7.4	6.5	6.7
1959	5.5	14.6	4.7	5.2	4.8	...	...	...	11.6	3.6	8.6	7.1	5.2	6.2
1960	5.5	14.7	4.7	5.1	5.0	...	...	...	11.7	3.7	8.4	7.5	5.2	5.9
1961	6.7	16.8	5.7	6.3	6.0	...	...	...	13.1	4.6	10.3	8.7	6.4	7.4
1962	5.5	14.7	4.6	5.4	4.9	...	...	...	11.2	3.6	9.9	7.9	5.4	6.4
1963	5.7	17.2	4.5	5.4	5.0	...	...	...	12.4	3.4	9.6	8.9	5.4	6.7
1964	5.2	16.2	3.9	5.2	4.6	...	...	...	11.5	2.8	8.9	8.7	5.1	6.4
1965	4.5	14.8	3.2	4.5	4.1	...	...	...	10.1	2.4	7.2	8.2	4.5	5.4
1966	3.8	12.8	2.5	3.8	3.4	...	...	...	8.6	1.9	5.5	7.9	3.7	4.7
1967	3.8	12.9	2.3	4.2	3.4	...	...	...	8.3	1.8	4.9	7.5	4.5	4.6
1968	3.6	12.7	2.2	3.8	3.2	...	...	...	8.0	1.6	4.2	7.6	3.9	4.2
1969	3.5	12.2	2.1	3.7	3.1	...	...	...	8.0	1.5	4.0	7.3	3.9	4.0
1970	4.9	15.3	3.5	4.8	4.5	...	...	...	11.2	2.6	6.4	9.0	4.9	5.2
1971	5.9	16.9	4.4	5.7	5.4	...	...	...	13.2	3.2	7.4	10.5	5.7	6.3
1972	5.6	16.2	4.0	5.4	5.1	10.4	...	...	12.4	2.8	7.0	10.1	5.4	6.1
1973	4.9	14.5	3.3	4.9	4.3	9.4	...	7.5	10.4	2.3	5.4	9.4	4.7	5.8
1974	5.6	16.0	3.8	5.5	5.0	10.5	...	8.1	11.8	2.7	6.2	10.5	5.3	6.3
1975	8.5	19.9	6.8	8.0	7.8	14.8	...	12.2	16.1	5.1	11.0	13.0	7.9	8.9
1976	7.7	19.0	5.9	7.4	7.0	14.0	...	11.5	14.9	4.2	9.8	12.1	7.1	8.7
1977	7.1	17.8	5.2	7.0	6.2	14.0	...	10.1	13.5	3.6	8.2	12.1	6.5	7.9
1978	6.1	16.4	4.3	6.0	5.2	12.8	...	9.1	11.7	2.8	6.6	10.9	5.5	6.9
1979	5.8	16.1	4.2	5.7	5.1	12.3	...	8.3	11.1	2.8	6.5	10.4	5.1	6.7
1980	7.1	17.8	5.9	6.4	6.3	14.3	...	10.1	13.6	4.2	8.6	10.9	5.8	7.2
1981	7.6	19.6	6.3	6.8	6.7	15.6	...	10.4	14.6	4.3	9.1	11.9	6.0	8.1
1982	9.7	23.2	8.8	8.3	8.6	18.9	...	13.8	17.7	6.5	12.4	13.6	7.4	9.5
1983	9.6	22.4	8.9	8.1	8.4	19.5	...	13.7	17.3	6.5	13.0	13.1	7.0	9.9
1984	7.5	18.9	6.6	6.8	6.5	15.9	...	10.7	13.5	4.6	9.4	11.1	5.7	8.4
1985	7.2	18.6	6.2	6.6	6.2	15.1	...	10.5	12.7	4.3	9.2	10.7	5.6	8.3
1986	7.0	18.3	6.1	6.2	6.0	14.5	...	10.6	12.2	4.4	8.8	10.7	5.2	7.7
1987	6.2	16.9	5.4	5.4	5.3	13.0	...	8.8	11.1	3.9	7.6	9.5	4.3	7.0
1988	5.5	15.3	4.8	4.9	4.7	11.7	...	8.2	9.9	3.3	7.0	8.6	3.9	6.3
1989	5.3	15.0	4.5	4.7	4.5	11.4	...	8.0	9.6	3.0	6.3	8.4	3.7	5.9
1990	5.6	15.5	5.0	4.9	4.8	11.4	...	8.2	10.1	3.4	6.9	8.7	3.8	6.0
1991	6.8	18.7	6.4	5.7	6.1	12.5	...	10.0	12.4	4.4	9.0	10.1	4.5	6.9
1992	7.5	20.1	7.1	6.3	6.6	14.2	...	11.6	13.2	5.1	9.8	10.8	5.0	7.6
1993	6.9	19.0	6.4	5.9	6.1	13.0	...	10.8	12.4	4.4	9.0	10.3	4.6	7.3
1994	6.1	17.6	5.4	5.4	5.3	11.5	...	9.9	11.0	3.7	7.4	9.7	4.1	6.6
1995	5.6	17.3	4.8	4.9	4.9	10.4	...	9.3	10.1	3.3	6.9	9.1	3.9	5.9
1996	5.4	16.7	4.6	4.8	4.7	10.5	...	8.9	10.0	3.0	6.5	9.1	3.6	5.7
1997	4.9	16.0	4.2	4.4	4.2	10.0	...	7.7	9.2	2.7	5.8	8.8	3.1	5.2
1998	4.5	14.6	3.7	4.1	3.9	8.9	...	7.2	8.5	2.4	4.8	7.8	2.9	4.9
1999	4.2	13.9	3.5	3.8	3.7	8.0	...	6.4	7.8	2.2	4.6	7.4	2.7	4.5
2000	4.0	13.1	3.3	3.6	3.5	7.6	3.6	5.7	7.6	2.0	4.3	6.8	2.7	4.2
2001	4.7	14.7	4.2	4.1	4.2	8.6	4.5	6.6	8.9	2.7	5.1	7.7	3.1	4.7
2002	5.8	16.5	5.3	5.1	5.1	10.2	5.9	7.5	10.3	3.6	6.8	8.9	3.7	6.1
2003	6.0	17.5	5.6	5.1	5.2	10.8	6.0	7.7	11.0	3.8	7.3	9.1	3.7	6.1
2004	5.5	17.0	5.0	4.9	4.8	10.4	4.4	7.0	10.5	3.1	6.3	8.7	3.5	5.9
2005	5.1	16.6	4.4	4.6	4.4	10.0	4.0	6.0	9.5	2.8	5.6	8.3	3.3	5.4
2006	4.6	15.4	4.0	4.1	4.0	8.9	3.0	5.2	8.6	2.4	5.2	7.7	2.9	4.9
2007	4.6	15.7	4.1	4.0	4.1	8.3	3.2	5.6	8.8	2.5	5.3	7.2	2.8	5.0
2008	5.8	18.7	5.4	4.9	5.2	10.1	4.0	7.6	11.0	3.4	7.1	8.5	3.6	5.9
2009	9.3	24.3	9.6	7.5	8.5	14.8	7.3	12.1	16.3	6.6	12.8	12.0	5.5	9.2
2010	9.6	25.9	9.8	8.0	8.7	16.0	7.5	12.5	16.5	6.8	12.8	12.8	5.9	9.6
2011	8.9	24.4	8.7	7.9	7.9	15.8	7.0	11.5	15.1	5.8	11.1	12.5	5.6	9.7
2012	8.1	24.0	7.5	7.3	7.2	13.8	5.9	10.3	13.7	4.9	9.4	11.8	5.3	8.7
2013	7.4	22.9	7.0	6.5	6.5	13.1	5.2	9.1	13.0	4.3	8.7	10.8	4.6	7.7
2014	6.2	19.6	5.7	5.6	5.3	11.3	5.0	7.4	11.0	3.4	6.9	9.4	3.8	6.6
2015	5.3	16.9	4.9	4.8	4.6	9.6	3.8	6.6	9.5	2.8	6.1	8.2	3.1	5.5
2016	4.9	15.7	4.5	4.4	4.3	8.4	3.6	5.8	8.5	2.7	5.6	7.4	3.0	5.1
2017	4.4	14.0	4.0	4.0	3.8	7.5	3.4	5.1	7.7	2.4	4.6	6.5	2.7	4.8
2018	3.9	12.9	3.6	3.5	3.5	6.5	3.0	4.7	6.9	2.0	4.5	5.8	2.4	4.0
2019	3.7	12.7	3.4	3.3	3.3	6.1	2.7	4.3	6.7	1.8	4.0	5.5	2.2	3.8

Note: See notes and definitions for information on historical comparability.

[1]Beginning in 2003, persons who selected this race group only; persons who selected more than one race group are not included. Prior to 2003, persons who reported more than one race group were included in the group they identified as their main race.
[2]May be of any race.
. . . = Not available.

Table 1-26. Unemployed Persons, by Age, Sex, Race, and Hispanic Origin, 1948–2019

(Thousands of people.)

Race, Hispanic origin, sex, and year	16 years and over	16 to 19 years			20 years and over						
		Total	16 to 17 years	18 to 19 years	Total	20 to 24 years	25 to 34 years	35 to 44 years	45 to 54 years	55 to 64 years	65 years and over
ALL RACES											
Both Sexes											
1948	2 276	409	180	228	1 869	455	457	347	290	226	93
1949	3 637	576	238	337	3 060	680	776	603	471	384	146
1950	3 288	513	226	287	2 776	561	702	530	478	368	137
1951	2 055	336	168	168	1 718	273	435	354	318	238	103
1952	1 883	345	180	165	1 539	268	389	325	274	195	86
1953	1 834	307	150	157	1 529	256	379	325	280	218	70
1954	3 532	501	221	247	3 032	504	793	680	548	374	132
1955	2 852	450	211	239	2 403	396	577	521	436	355	120
1956	2 750	478	231	247	2 274	395	554	476	429	311	109
1957	2 859	497	230	266	2 362	430	573	499	448	300	111
1958	4 602	678	299	379	3 923	701	993	871	731	472	154
1959	3 740	654	301	354	3 085	543	726	673	603	405	135
1960	3 852	712	325	387	3 140	583	752	671	614	396	122
1961	4 714	828	363	465	3 886	723	890	850	751	516	159
1962	3 911	721	312	409	3 191	636	712	688	605	411	141
1963	4 070	884	420	462	3 187	658	732	674	589	410	126
1964	3 786	872	436	437	2 913	660	607	605	543	378	117
1965	3 366	874	411	463	2 491	557	529	546	436	322	103
1966	2 875	837	395	441	2 041	446	441	426	369	265	92
1967	2 975	839	400	438	2 140	511	480	422	383	256	86
1968	2 817	838	414	426	1 978	543	443	371	314	219	88
1969	2 832	853	436	416	1 978	560	453	358	320	216	72
1970	4 093	1 106	537	569	2 987	866	718	515	476	309	104
1971	5 016	1 262	596	665	3 755	1 130	933	630	573	381	109
1972	4 882	1 308	633	676	3 573	1 132	878	576	510	368	111
1973	4 365	1 235	634	600	3 130	1 008	866	451	430	290	88
1974	5 156	1 422	699	722	3 733	1 212	1 044	559	498	321	99
1975	7 929	1 767	799	968	6 161	1 865	1 776	951	893	520	155
1976	7 406	1 719	796	924	5 687	1 714	1 710	849	758	510	147
1977	6 991	1 663	781	881	5 330	1 629	1 650	785	666	450	147
1978	6 202	1 583	796	787	4 620	1 483	1 422	694	552	345	123
1979	6 137	1 555	739	816	4 583	1 442	1 446	705	540	346	104
1980	7 637	1 669	778	890	5 969	1 835	2 024	940	676	399	94
1981	8 273	1 763	781	981	6 510	1 976	2 211	1 065	715	444	98
1982	10 678	1 977	831	1 145	8 701	2 392	3 037	1 552	966	647	107
1983	10 717	1 829	753	1 076	8 888	2 330	3 078	1 650	1 039	677	114
1984	8 539	1 499	646	854	7 039	1 838	2 374	1 335	828	566	97
1985	8 312	1 468	662	806	6 844	1 738	2 341	1 340	813	518	93
1986	8 237	1 454	665	789	6 783	1 651	2 390	1 371	790	489	91
1987	7 425	1 347	648	700	6 077	1 453	2 129	1 281	723	412	78
1988	6 701	1 226	573	653	5 475	1 261	1 929	1 166	657	375	87
1989	6 528	1 194	537	657	5 333	1 218	1 851	1 159	637	379	91
1990	7 047	1 212	527	685	5 835	1 299	1 995	1 328	723	386	105
1991	8 628	1 359	587	772	7 269	1 573	2 447	1 719	946	473	113
1992	9 613	1 427	641	787	8 186	1 649	2 702	1 976	1 138	589	132
1993	8 940	1 365	606	759	7 575	1 514	2 395	1 896	1 121	541	108
1994	7 996	1 320	624	696	6 676	1 373	2 067	1 627	971	485	153
1995	7 404	1 346	652	695	6 058	1 244	1 841	1 549	844	425	153
1996	7 236	1 306	617	689	5 929	1 239	1 757	1 505	883	406	139
1997	6 739	1 271	589	683	5 467	1 152	1 571	1 418	830	369	127
1998	6 210	1 205	573	632	5 005	1 081	1 419	1 258	782	343	122
1999	5 880	1 162	544	618	4 718	1 042	1 278	1 154	753	367	124
2000	5 692	1 081	502	579	4 611	1 022	1 207	1 133	762	355	132
2001	6 801	1 162	531	632	5 638	1 209	1 498	1 355	989	458	129
2002	8 378	1 253	540	714	7 124	1 430	1 890	1 691	1 315	635	163
2003	8 774	1 251	545	706	7 523	1 495	1 960	1 815	1 356	713	183
2004	8 149	1 208	554	653	6 942	1 431	1 784	1 578	1 288	682	179
2005	7 591	1 186	541	645	6 405	1 335	1 661	1 400	1 195	630	184
2006	7 001	1 119	509	610	5 882	1 234	1 521	1 279	1 094	595	159
2007	7 078	1 101	485	616	5 976	1 241	1 544	1 225	1 135	642	190
2008	8 924	1 285	563	722	7 639	1 545	1 949	1 604	1 473	803	264
2009	14 265	1 552	576	976	12 712	2 207	3 284	2 722	2 592	1 487	421
2010	14 825	1 528	582	945	13 297	2 329	3 386	2 703	2 769	1 660	449
2011	13 747	1 400	519	881	12 348	2 234	3 187	2 389	2 493	1 579	465
2012	12 506	1 397	533	863	11 109	2 054	2 764	2 158	2 181	1 470	482
2013	11 460	1 327	536	791	10 133	1 997	2 504	1 913	1 945	1 340	435
2014	9 617	680	426	1 106	8 511	1 747	2 224	1 539	1 507	1 107	387
2015	8 296	966	363	603	7 330	1 501	1 905	1 351	1 259	978	337
2016	7 751	925	380	545	6 826	1 286	1 797	1 258	1 189	941	355
2017	6 982	827	347	480	6 155	1 127	1 647	1 143	1 060	835	343
2018	6 314	759	295	464	5 555	1 048	1 450	1 003	938	789	327
2019	6 001	746	291	455	5 254	1 024	1 384	930	890	710	317

Table 1-26. Unemployed Persons, by Age, Sex, Race, and Hispanic Origin, 1948–2019—*Continued*

(Thousands of people.)

Race, Hispanic origin, sex, and year	16 years and over	16 to 19 years			20 years and over						
		Total	16 to 17 years	18 to 19 years	Total	20 to 24 years	25 to 34 years	35 to 44 years	45 to 54 years	55 to 64 years	65 years and over
ALL RACES											
Men											
1948	1 559	256	113	142	1 305	324	289	233	201	177	81
1949	2 572	353	145	207	2 219	485	539	414	347	310	125
1950	2 239	318	139	179	1 922	377	467	348	327	286	117
1951	1 221	191	102	89	1 029	155	241	192	193	162	87
1952	1 185	205	116	89	980	155	233	192	182	145	73
1953	1 202	184	94	90	1 019	152	236	208	196	167	60
1954	2 344	310	142	168	2 035	327	517	431	372	275	112
1955	1 854	274	134	140	1 580	248	353	328	285	265	102
1956	1 711	269	134	135	1 442	240	348	278	270	216	90
1957	1 841	300	140	159	1 541	283	349	304	302	220	83
1958	3 098	416	185	231	2 681	478	685	552	492	349	124
1959	2 420	398	191	207	2 022	343	484	407	390	287	112
1960	2 486	426	200	225	2 060	369	492	415	392	294	96
1961	2 997	479	221	258	2 518	458	585	507	473	375	122
1962	2 423	408	188	220	2 016	381	445	404	382	300	103
1963	2 472	501	248	252	1 971	396	445	386	358	290	97
1964	2 205	487	257	230	1 718	384	345	324	319	263	85
1965	1 914	479	247	232	1 435	311	292	283	253	221	75
1966	1 551	432	220	212	1 120	221	239	219	196	179	65
1967	1 508	448	241	207	1 060	235	219	185	199	163	60
1968	1 419	426	234	193	993	258	205	171	165	132	61
1969	1 403	440	244	196	963	270	205	155	157	127	48
1970	2 238	599	306	294	1 638	479	391	253	247	198	71
1971	2 789	693	346	347	2 097	640	513	320	313	239	71
1972	2 659	711	357	355	1 948	628	466	284	272	227	73
1973	2 275	653	352	300	1 624	528	439	211	219	171	57
1974	2 714	757	394	362	1 957	649	546	266	250	183	63
1975	4 442	966	445	521	3 476	1 081	986	507	499	302	103
1976	4 036	939	443	496	3 098	951	914	431	411	296	94
1977	3 667	874	421	453	2 794	877	869	373	326	252	97
1978	3 142	813	426	388	2 328	768	691	314	277	198	81
1979	3 120	811	393	418	2 308	744	699	329	272	196	67
1980	4 267	913	429	485	3 353	1 076	1 137	482	357	243	58
1981	4 577	962	431	531	3 615	1 144	1 213	552	390	261	55
1982	6 179	1 090	469	621	5 089	1 407	1 791	879	550	393	69
1983	6 260	1 003	408	595	5 257	1 369	1 822	947	613	433	73
1984	4 744	812	348	464	3 932	1 023	1 322	728	450	356	53
1985	4 521	806	363	443	3 715	944	1 244	706	459	307	55
1986	4 530	779	355	424	3 751	899	1 291	763	440	301	58
1987	4 101	732	353	379	3 369	779	1 169	689	426	258	49
1988	3 655	667	311	356	2 987	676	1 040	617	366	240	49
1989	3 525	658	303	355	2 867	660	953	619	351	234	49
1990	3 906	667	283	384	3 239	715	1 092	711	413	249	59
1991	4 946	751	317	433	4 195	911	1 375	990	550	305	64
1992	5 523	806	357	449	4 717	951	1 529	1 118	675	378	67
1993	5 055	768	342	426	4 287	865	1 338	1 049	636	336	64
1994	4 367	740	342	398	3 627	768	1 113	855	522	281	88
1995	3 983	744	352	391	3 239	673	961	815	464	233	94
1996	3 880	733	347	387	3 146	675	903	786	484	223	76
1997	3 577	694	321	373	2 882	636	772	732	457	217	69
1998	3 266	686	330	355	2 580	583	699	609	420	201	69
1999	3 066	633	295	338	2 433	562	624	571	403	203	70
2000	2 975	599	281	317	2 376	547	602	557	398	189	83
2001	3 690	650	300	350	3 040	688	756	714	536	272	74
2002	4 597	700	301	399	3 896	792	1 023	897	725	373	87
2003	4 906	697	291	407	4 209	841	1 097	988	764	412	107
2004	4 456	664	292	372	3 791	811	980	839	684	373	104
2005	4 059	667	300	367	3 392	775	844	715	624	331	102
2006	3 753	622	271	352	3 131	705	810	642	569	318	88
2007	3 882	623	263	360	3 259	721	856	634	591	349	108
2008	5 033	736	312	425	4 297	920	1 119	875	804	425	153
2009	8 453	898	317	581	7 555	1 329	1 988	1 600	1 558	840	241
2010	8 626	863	315	548	7 763	1 398	1 993	1 534	1 614	962	262
2011	7 684	786	267	520	6 898	1 275	1 795	1 316	1 370	882	261
2012	6 771	787	291	497	5 984	1 163	1 476	1 124	1 142	811	268
2013	6 314	746	287	459	5 568	1 143	1 381	1 015	1 039	741	250
2014	5 190	605	230	375	4 585	996	1 185	813	782	600	210
2015	4 490	531	197	333	3 959	865	1 030	695	649	536	184
2016	4 187	512	203	309	3 675	742	966	644	602	528	193
2017	3 743	457	175	282	3 287	667	884	575	537	445	179
2018	3 398	422	156	266	2 976	596	763	335	229	435	177
2019	3 227	408	149	259	2 819	602	741	475	471	361	170

Table 1-26. Unemployed Persons, by Age, Sex, Race, and Hispanic Origin, 1948–2019—*Continued*

(Thousands of people.)

Race, Hispanic origin, sex, and year	16 years and over	16 to 19 years			20 years and over						
		Total	16 to 17 years	18 to 19 years	Total	20 to 24 years	25 to 34 years	35 to 44 years	45 to 54 years	55 to 64 years	65 years and over
ALL RACES											
Women											
1948	717	153	67	86	564	131	168	114	89	49	12
1949	1 065	223	93	130	841	195	237	189	124	74	21
1950	1 049	195	87	108	854	184	235	182	151	82	20
1951	834	145	66	79	689	118	194	162	125	76	16
1952	698	140	64	76	559	113	156	133	92	50	13
1953	632	123	56	67	510	104	143	117	84	51	10
1954	1 188	191	79	79	997	177	276	249	176	99	20
1955	998	176	77	99	823	148	224	193	151	90	18
1956	1 039	209	97	112	832	155	206	198	159	95	19
1957	1 018	197	90	107	821	147	224	195	146	80	28
1958	1 504	262	114	148	1 242	223	308	319	239	123	30
1959	1 320	256	110	147	1 063	200	242	266	213	118	23
1960	1 366	286	125	162	1 080	214	260	256	222	102	26
1961	1 717	349	142	207	1 368	265	305	343	278	141	37
1962	1 488	313	124	189	1 175	255	267	284	223	111	38
1963	1 598	383	172	210	1 216	262	287	288	231	120	29
1964	1 581	385	179	207	1 195	276	262	281	224	115	32
1965	1 452	395	164	231	1 056	246	237	263	183	101	28
1966	1 324	405	175	229	921	225	202	207	173	86	27
1967	1 468	391	159	231	1 078	277	261	237	184	93	26
1968	1 397	412	180	233	985	285	238	200	149	87	27
1969	1 429	413	192	220	1 015	290	248	203	163	89	24
1970	1 855	506	231	275	1 349	387	327	262	229	111	33
1971	2 227	568	250	318	1 658	489	420	310	260	142	38
1972	2 222	598	276	322	1 625	503	413	293	237	141	38
1973	2 089	583	282	301	1 507	480	427	240	212	119	31
1974	2 441	665	305	360	1 777	564	497	294	248	137	36
1975	3 486	802	355	447	2 684	783	791	444	395	219	52
1976	3 369	780	352	429	2 588	763	795	417	346	214	53
1977	3 324	789	361	428	2 535	752	782	412	340	198	50
1978	3 061	769	370	399	2 292	714	731	381	275	148	43
1979	3 018	743	346	396	2 276	697	748	375	268	150	38
1980	3 370	755	349	407	2 615	760	886	459	318	155	36
1981	3 696	800	350	450	2 895	833	998	513	325	184	43
1982	4 499	886	362	524	3 613	985	1 246	673	416	254	38
1983	4 457	825	344	481	3 632	961	1 255	703	427	244	41
1984	3 794	687	298	390	3 107	815	1 052	607	378	211	45
1985	3 791	661	298	363	3 129	794	1 098	634	355	211	39
1986	3 707	675	310	365	3 032	752	1 099	609	350	189	33
1987	3 324	616	295	321	2 709	674	960	592	298	155	30
1988	3 046	558	262	297	2 487	585	889	550	291	136	38
1989	3 003	536	234	302	2 467	558	897	540	286	144	41
1990	3 140	544	243	301	2 596	584	902	617	310	137	46
1991	3 683	608	270	338	3 074	662	1 071	728	396	168	49
1992	4 090	621	283	338	3 469	698	1 173	858	463	210	66
1993	3 885	597	264	333	3 288	648	1 058	847	485	205	45
1994	3 629	580	282	298	3 049	605	954	772	449	204	66
1995	3 421	602	299	303	2 819	571	880	735	381	193	60
1996	3 356	573	270	303	2 783	564	854	720	399	183	63
1997	3 162	577	268	310	2 585	516	800	686	373	152	58
1998	2 944	519	242	277	2 424	498	720	650	362	141	53
1999	2 814	529	249	280	2 285	480	654	584	350	163	54
2000	2 717	483	221	262	2 235	475	604	577	364	165	50
2001	3 111	512	230	282	2 599	521	742	641	453	187	55
2002	3 781	553	238	315	3 228	638	866	795	591	263	76
2003	3 868	554	255	299	3 314	654	863	827	592	302	76
2004	3 694	543	262	281	3 150	619	804	739	605	309	75
2005	3 531	519	240	278	3 013	560	817	685	571	299	82
2006	3 247	496	238	258	2 751	530	711	637	524	277	71
2007	3 196	478	222	256	2 718	520	688	591	544	293	81
2008	3 891	549	251	297	3 342	625	830	730	669	377	111
2009	5 811	654	259	395	5 157	878	1 296	1 121	1 034	647	180
2010	6 199	665	268	397	5 534	931	1 392	1 169	1 156	698	187
2011	6 063	613	252	362	5 450	960	1 392	1 073	1 123	697	204
2012	5 734	609	242	367	5 125	891	1 288	1 034	1 039	659	214
2013	5 146	581	249	332	4 565	854	1 123	898	906	600	185
2014	4 426	501	196	305	3 926	751	1 039	726	725	507	177
2015	3 807	435	166	269	3 371	636	874	656	610	442	153
2016	3 564	413	177	236	3 151	545	832	614	586	413	162
2017	3 239	371	172	199	2 868	460	763	568	523	389	164
2018	2 916	338	139	198	2 578	452	687	295	448	223	150
2019	2 774	339	143	196	2 435	421	643	455	419	350	147

Table 1-26. Unemployed Persons, by Age, Sex, Race, and Hispanic Origin, 1948–2019—*Continued*

(Thousands of people.)

Race, Hispanic origin, sex, and year	16 years and over	16 to 19 years			20 years and over						
		Total	16 to 17 years	18 to 19 years	Total	20 to 24 years	25 to 34 years	35 to 44 years	45 to 54 years	55 to 64 years	65 years and over
WHITE											
Both Sexes											
1954	2 859	423	191	232	2 436	394	610	540	447	329	115
1955	2 252	373	181	191	1 879	304	412	402	358	300	105
1956	2 159	382	191	191	1 777	297	406	363	355	258	98
1957	2 289	401	195	204	1 888	331	425	401	373	262	98
1958	3 680	541	245	297	3 139	541	756	686	614	405	136
1959	2 946	525	255	270	2 421	406	526	525	496	348	120
1960	3 065	575	273	302	2 490	456	573	520	502	330	109
1961	3 743	669	295	374	3 074	566	668	652	611	438	139
1962	3 052	580	262	318	2 472	488	515	522	485	345	117
1963	3 208	708	350	358	2 500	501	540	518	485	349	107
1964	2 999	708	365	342	2 291	508	441	472	447	323	100
1965	2 691	705	329	374	1 986	437	399	427	358	276	91
1966	2 255	651	315	336	1 604	338	323	336	298	227	80
1967	2 338	635	311	325	1 703	393	360	336	321	221	75
1968	2 226	644	326	318	1 582	422	330	297	269	187	80
1969	2 260	660	351	309	1 601	432	354	294	269	185	66
1970	3 339	871	438	432	2 468	679	570	433	415	275	95
1971	4 085	1 011	491	521	3 074	887	732	517	500	338	100
1972	3 906	1 021	515	506	2 885	887	679	459	439	324	95
1973	3 442	955	513	443	2 486	758	664	358	371	257	77
1974	4 097	1 104	561	544	2 993	925	821	448	427	283	88
1975	6 421	1 413	657	755	5 007	1 474	1 413	774	753	460	136
1976	5 914	1 364	649	715	4 550	1 326	1 329	682	637	448	128
1977	5 441	1 284	636	648	4 157	1 195	1 255	621	569	388	129
1978	4 698	1 189	631	558	3 509	1 059	1 059	543	453	290	104
1979	4 664	1 193	589	603	3 472	1 038	1 068	545	443	290	87
1980	5 884	1 291	625	666	4 593	1 364	1 528	740	550	335	74
1981	6 343	1 374	629	745	4 968	1 449	1 658	827	578	379	77
1982	8 241	1 534	683	851	6 707	1 770	2 283	1 223	796	549	86
1983	8 128	1 387	609	778	6 741	1 678	2 282	1 294	837	563	88
1984	6 372	1 116	510	605	5 256	1 282	1 723	1 036	660	475	81
1985	6 191	1 074	507	567	5 117	1 235	1 695	1 039	642	432	75
1986	6 140	1 070	509	561	5 070	1 149	1 751	1 056	629	407	78
1987	5 501	995	495	500	4 506	1 017	1 527	984	576	333	68
1988	4 944	910	437	473	4 033	874	1 371	890	520	309	69
1989	4 770	863	407	456	3 908	856	1 297	871	503	311	70
1990	5 186	903	401	502	4 283	899	1 401	983	582	330	88
1991	6 560	1 029	461	568	5 532	1 132	1 805	1 330	759	410	96
1992	7 169	1 037	484	553	6 132	1 156	1 967	1 483	915	495	116
1993	6 655	992	468	523	5 663	1 057	1 754	1 411	907	442	92
1994	5 892	960	471	489	4 933	952	1 479	1 184	779	407	132
1995	5 459	952	476	476	4 507	866	1 311	1 161	676	362	131
1996	5 300	939	456	484	4 361	854	1 223	1 117	709	336	122
1997	4 836	912	438	475	3 924	765	1 068	1 035	648	302	106
1998	4 484	876	424	451	3 608	731	978	901	620	276	101
1999	4 273	844	414	430	3 429	720	865	843	595	303	104
2000	4 121	795	386	409	3 326	682	835	817	591	294	107
2001	4 969	845	402	443	4 124	829	1 062	985	761	378	109
2002	6 137	925	407	518	5 212	977	1 340	1 237	1 004	518	137
2003	6 311	909	414	495	5 401	1 012	1 354	1 287	1 025	569	155
2004	5 847	890	414	476	4 957	959	1 211	1 130	953	557	148
2005	5 350	845	391	454	4 505	878	1 106	1 006	884	488	144
2006	5 002	794	375	419	4 208	832	1 029	920	813	480	135
2007	5 143	805	361	444	4 338	851	1 052	902	848	520	164
2008	6 509	947	422	524	5 562	1 087	1 336	1 196	1 094	634	216
2009	10 648	1 157	440	717	9 491	1 556	2 320	2 026	2 012	1 221	355
2010	10 916	1 128	445	683	9 788	1 614	2 358	1 969	2 130	1 344	373
2011	9 889	1 024	391	633	8 865	1 546	2 135	1 678	1 859	1 251	395
2012	8 915	1 004	397	607	7 911	1 353	1 881	1 514	1 614	1 144	405
2013	8 033	937	395	542	7 096	1 299	1 651	1 334	1 414	1 032	366
2014	6 540	775	302	473	5 764	1 084	1 402	1 059	1 085	829	305
2015	5 662	662	260	402	5 000	970	1 194	917	913	751	255
2016	5 345	651	273	378	4 694	831	1 157	837	858	720	290
2017	4 765	554	247	307	4 211	743	1 039	766	759	628	277
2018	4 354	516	207	309	3 837	685	932	671	677	610	262
2019	4 159	528	215	312	3 631	656	893	633	645	553	253

Table 1-26. Unemployed Persons, by Age, Sex, Race, and Hispanic Origin, 1948–2019—*Continued*

(Thousands of people.)

Race, Hispanic origin, sex, and year	16 years and over	16 to 19 years			20 years and over						
		Total	16 to 17 years	18 to 19 years	Total	20 to 24 years	25 to 34 years	35 to 44 years	45 to 54 years	55 to 64 years	65 years and over
WHITE											
Men											
1954	1 913	266	125	142	1 647	260	408	341	299	241	98
1955	1 478	232	114	117	1 246	196	260	246	233	223	89
1956	1 366	221	112	108	1 145	186	265	212	225	177	81
1957	1 477	243	118	124	1 234	222	257	239	250	193	73
1958	2 489	333	149	184	2 156	382	525	436	404	299	110
1959	1 903	318	162	156	1 585	256	350	316	320	245	98
1960	1 988	341	167	174	1 647	295	376	330	317	243	86
1961	2 398	384	176	208	2 014	370	442	395	382	318	107
1962	1 915	334	158	176	1 581	300	332	311	308	246	84
1963	1 976	407	211	196	1 569	309	342	297	294	246	80
1964	1 779	400	217	183	1 379	310	262	255	266	216	70
1965	1 556	387	200	186	1 169	254	226	228	206	190	67
1966	1 241	340	178	162	901	172	185	173	160	154	57
1967	1 208	342	186	156	866	185	171	153	167	140	52
1968	1 142	328	185	143	814	206	162	140	142	111	55
1969	1 137	343	198	145	794	214	165	130	134	108	43
1970	1 857	485	255	230	1 372	388	316	212	216	177	64
1971	2 309	562	288	275	1 747	513	418	268	272	211	66
1972	2 173	564	288	276	1 610	506	375	231	237	199	60
1973	1 836	513	284	229	1 323	411	353	166	188	153	51
1974	2 169	584	311	274	1 585	505	434	218	213	161	53
1975	3 627	785	369	416	2 841	871	796	412	411	265	86
1976	3 258	754	368	385	2 504	750	730	346	341	259	78
1977	2 883	672	342	330	2 211	660	682	297	276	213	82
1978	2 411	615	338	277	1 797	558	525	250	227	169	68
1979	2 405	633	319	313	1 773	553	526	253	220	165	56
1980	3 345	716	347	369	2 629	827	884	378	291	206	44
1981	3 580	755	349	406	2 825	869	943	433	317	221	42
1982	4 846	854	387	467	3 991	1 066	1 385	696	460	331	53
1983	4 859	761	328	433	4 098	1 019	1 410	755	497	362	54
1984	3 600	608	280	328	2 992	722	991	572	363	302	42
1985	3 426	592	282	310	2 834	694	931	553	356	257	43
1986	3 433	576	276	299	2 857	645	978	586	349	248	51
1987	3 132	548	272	276	2 584	568	879	536	350	209	43
1988	2 766	499	239	260	2 268	480	777	477	293	200	40
1989	2 636	487	230	257	2 149	476	694	470	280	191	38
1990	2 935	504	214	290	2 431	510	796	530	330	214	51
1991	3 859	575	249	327	3 284	677	1 064	780	438	269	55
1992	4 209	590	270	319	3 620	686	1 155	858	543	318	58
1993	3 828	565	261	305	3 263	619	1 015	793	512	270	53
1994	3 275	540	259	280	2 735	555	827	626	417	236	74
1995	2 999	535	260	275	2 465	483	711	621	371	200	79
1996	2 896	532	260	273	2 363	478	655	592	383	188	67
1997	2 641	502	234	268	2 140	439	553	549	358	182	58
1998	2 431	510	254	257	1 920	405	512	441	342	164	58
1999	2 274	461	223	237	1 813	398	441	419	322	172	61
2000	2 177	446	217	229	1 731	368	428	403	302	162	68
2001	2 754	479	232	247	2 275	494	547	529	413	229	64
2002	3 459	516	228	288	2 943	562	772	672	554	305	77
2003	3 643	518	221	298	3 125	589	798	723	591	333	91
2004	3 282	497	224	274	2 785	560	694	620	516	307	88
2005	2 931	480	220	260	2 450	522	586	536	463	263	81
2006	2 730	449	202	247	2 281	483	567	482	417	259	73
2007	2 869	461	195	266	2 408	501	604	478	447	285	93
2008	3 727	548	231	317	3 179	668	784	662	604	337	124
2009	6 421	675	241	434	5 746	969	1 439	1 208	1 233	695	202
2010	6 476	648	246	402	5 828	995	1 452	1 131	1 249	785	216
2011	5 631	585	208	377	5 046	909	1 237	951	1 030	697	223
2012	4 931	584	222	362	4 347	792	1 044	794	856	637	224
2013	4 520	526	213	313	3 994	756	944	727	769	583	215
2014	3 572	431	165	266	3 141	628	774	568	558	449	164
2015	3 126	375	144	231	2 751	581	667	484	480	400	139
2016	2 952	358	147	211	2 594	484	653	444	446	410	156
2017	2 592	304	128	177	2 288	449	575	396	391	331	144
2018	2 380	286	109	178	2 094	390	508	344	344	331	144
2019	2 266	299	118	182	1 967	387	486	325	344	290	136

Table 1-26. Unemployed Persons, by Age, Sex, Race, and Hispanic Origin, 1948–2019—*Continued*

(Thousands of people.)

Race, Hispanic origin, sex, and year	16 years and over	16 to 19 years			20 years and over						
		Total	16 to 17 years	18 to 19 years	Total	20 to 24 years	25 to 34 years	35 to 44 years	45 to 54 years	55 to 64 years	65 years and over
WHITE											
Women											
1954	946	157	66	90	789	134	202	199	148	88	17
1955	774	141	67	74	633	108	152	156	125	77	16
1956	793	161	79	83	632	111	141	151	130	81	17
1957	812	158	77	80	654	109	168	162	123	69	25
1958	1 191	208	96	113	983	159	231	250	210	106	26
1959	1 043	207	93	114	836	150	176	209	176	103	22
1960	1 077	234	106	128	843	161	197	190	185	87	23
1961	1 345	285	119	166	1 060	196	226	257	229	120	32
1962	1 137	246	104	142	891	188	183	211	177	99	33
1963	1 232	301	139	162	931	192	198	221	191	103	27
1964	1 220	308	148	159	912	198	179	217	181	107	30
1965	1 135	318	129	188	817	183	173	199	152	86	24
1966	1 014	311	137	174	703	166	138	163	138	73	23
1967	1 130	293	125	169	837	209	189	183	154	81	23
1968	1 084	316	141	175	768	216	168	157	127	76	25
1969	1 123	317	153	164	806	218	189	164	135	77	23
1970	1 482	386	183	202	1 096	291	254	221	199	98	31
1971	1 777	449	203	246	1 328	376	314	249	228	126	34
1972	1 733	457	227	230	1 275	381	304	227	202	125	35
1973	1 606	442	228	214	1 164	347	311	192	183	104	26
1974	1 927	519	250	270	1 408	420	387	230	214	122	35
1975	2 794	628	288	340	2 166	602	617	362	342	195	49
1976	2 656	611	280	330	2 045	577	598	336	296	188	49
1977	2 558	612	294	318	1 946	536	573	323	293	175	47
1978	2 287	574	292	281	1 713	500	533	294	226	122	37
1979	2 260	560	270	290	1 699	485	542	293	223	125	32
1980	2 540	576	278	298	1 964	537	645	362	259	129	31
1981	2 762	620	281	339	2 143	580	715	394	261	158	36
1982	3 395	680	296	384	2 715	704	898	527	337	217	33
1983	3 270	626	282	345	2 643	659	872	539	340	201	33
1984	2 772	508	231	277	2 264	559	731	464	297	173	39
1985	2 765	482	225	257	2 283	541	763	486	286	175	32
1986	2 708	495	233	262	2 213	504	773	470	281	159	27
1987	2 369	447	223	224	1 922	449	648	448	227	124	25
1988	2 177	412	198	214	1 766	393	594	413	227	110	30
1989	2 135	376	177	199	1 758	380	603	401	223	120	32
1990	2 251	399	187	212	1 852	389	605	453	251	116	37
1991	2 701	453	212	241	2 248	455	741	550	320	141	41
1992	2 959	447	214	233	2 512	469	811	625	372	177	58
1993	2 827	426	208	219	2 400	438	739	618	395	172	39
1994	2 617	420	211	208	2 197	397	652	558	361	170	58
1995	2 460	418	216	201	2 042	384	600	540	306	162	52
1996	2 404	407	196	211	1 998	376	568	525	326	148	55
1997	2 195	411	204	207	1 784	326	515	486	290	119	49
1998	2 053	365	171	195	1 688	327	467	460	279	112	43
1999	1 999	383	190	193	1 616	322	423	423	273	131	43
2000	1 944	349	168	180	1 595	314	407	414	289	133	39
2001	2 215	366	170	196	1 849	335	515	456	348	150	45
2002	2 678	409	179	230	2 269	415	567	565	449	213	60
2003	2 668	391	194	197	2 276	423	555	564	434	235	64
2004	2 565	393	191	202	2 172	399	516	510	437	250	60
2005	2 419	365	172	193	2 054	356	520	469	421	225	63
2006	2 271	345	173	172	1 927	349	462	437	395	222	62
2007	2 274	344	166	178	1 930	350	448	425	401	235	71
2008	2 782	399	191	207	2 384	419	552	534	489	298	92
2009	4 227	482	199	283	3 745	587	881	818	780	526	153
2010	4 440	480	199	281	3 960	619	906	839	881	559	157
2011	4 257	439	184	255	3 818	637	899	728	829	554	171
2012	3 985	420	176	245	3 564	561	837	720	758	508	181
2013	3 513	411	183	228	3 102	543	707	607	645	449	151
2014	2 968	344	138	207	2 623	457	628	490	527	380	141
2015	2 537	288	116	172	2 249	390	527	433	433	351	116
2016	2 393	293	126	167	2 100	347	504	393	412	310	134
2017	2 173	249	119	130	1 923	293	464	228	367	297	132
2018	1 973	230	99	131	1 743	295	424	327	153	271	113
2019	1 893	228	98	131	1 664	269	407	308	301	263	116

Table 1-26. Unemployed Persons, by Age, Sex, Race, and Hispanic Origin, 1948–2019—*Continued*

(Thousands of people.)

Race, Hispanic origin, sex, and year	16 years and over	16 to 19 years			20 years and over						
		Total	16 to 17 years	18 to 19 years	Total	20 to 24 years	25 to 34 years	35 to 44 years	45 to 54 years	55 to 64 years	65 years and over
BLACK											
Both Sexes											
1985	1 864	357	135	221	1 507	455	562	254	143	74	18
1986	1 840	347	138	209	1 493	453	564	269	127	69	10
1987	1 684	312	134	178	1 373	397	533	247	124	62	10
1988	1 547	288	121	167	1 259	349	502	230	111	51	10
1989	1 544	300	116	184	1 245	322	494	246	109	53	20
1990	1 565	268	112	156	1 297	349	505	278	106	44	14
1991	1 723	280	105	175	1 443	378	539	318	151	44	13
1992	2 011	324	127	197	1 687	421	610	402	178	64	13
1993	1 844	313	112	201	1 530	387	532	376	153	72	11
1994	1 666	300	127	173	1 366	351	468	346	130	55	16
1995	1 538	325	143	182	1 213	311	423	303	116	42	18
1996	1 592	310	133	177	1 282	327	454	313	127	48	13
1997	1 560	302	123	179	1 258	327	426	307	136	45	16
1998	1 426	281	124	156	1 146	301	366	294	125	45	16
1999	1 309	268	109	159	1 041	273	339	249	121	46	14
2000	1 241	230	96	134	1 011	281	289	254	131	38	20
2001	1 416	260	102	158	1 155	307	340	283	159	52	15
2002	1 693	260	103	156	1 433	365	407	349	215	76	21
2003	1 787	255	93	162	1 532	375	442	385	217	93	20
2004	1 729	241	103	138	1 487	353	441	341	245	86	21
2005	1 700	267	115	152	1 433	358	423	310	222	92	28
2006	1 549	253	102	151	1 296	318	388	276	214	81	19
2007	1 445	235	98	138	1 210	300	367	237	208	79	19
2008	1 788	246	98	148	1 542	355	458	301	275	117	36
2009	2 606	288	99	189	2 319	488	717	489	415	168	42
2010	2 852	291	97	194	2 562	539	776	534	461	204	47
2011	2 831	267	88	179	2 564	531	801	529	444	212	47
2012	2 544	272	94	179	2 272	510	640	457	397	209	59
2013	2 429	278	101	177	2 151	509	603	414	376	199	50
2014	2 141	225	85	139	1 916	466	605	325	284	186	51
2015	1 846	199	69	131	1 646	384	517	298	245	151	51
2016	1 655	194	73	122	1 460	329	435	286	225	143	43
2017	1 501	181	61	120	1 320	258	428	253	210	135	36
2018	1 322	167	56	111	1 155	234	349	234	177	117	44
2019	1 251	153	54	99	1 098	251	330	201	166	106	44
Men											
1985	951	193	69	124	757	224	268	127	85	43	11
1986	946	180	68	112	765	225	273	148	70	44	5
1987	826	160	70	90	666	186	253	122	61	39	6
1988	771	154	64	90	617	177	233	111	58	30	8
1989	773	153	65	88	619	162	226	129	59	33	10
1990	806	142	62	80	664	177	247	146	62	27	6
1991	890	145	54	91	745	201	252	172	87	25	7
1992	1 067	180	71	109	886	221	301	208	107	42	6
1993	971	170	66	104	801	201	260	201	87	46	7
1994	848	167	69	97	682	173	218	180	72	29	10
1995	762	168	73	95	593	153	195	150	63	21	11
1996	808	169	73	96	639	163	210	158	75	26	7
1997	747	162	70	92	585	165	178	141	72	22	7
1998	671	147	61	86	524	151	148	133	60	24	8
1999	626	145	60	85	480	135	143	114	60	22	7
2000	620	121	52	70	499	145	134	121	72	17	9
2001	709	136	51	85	573	150	159	142	84	31	7
2002	835	140	54	85	695	181	180	165	120	40	9
2003	891	132	49	83	760	192	212	189	109	47	10
2004	860	128	52	75	733	188	211	160	120	46	8
2005	844	145	63	82	699	192	189	143	116	45	14
2006	774	134	53	81	640	167	189	118	112	43	11
2007	752	130	55	75	622	166	186	114	106	41	10
2008	949	138	54	84	811	190	242	154	143	61	21
2009	1 448	161	55	106	1 286	264	406	270	230	91	24
2010	1 550	154	47	107	1 396	294	408	286	268	116	24
2011	1 502	142	39	102	1 360	278	426	277	233	125	21
2012	1 292	140	47	93	1 152	269	308	241	191	110	32
2013	1 236	154	54	101	1 082	273	298	196	193	96	26
2014	1 091	118	44	74	973	251	295	159	149	95	25
2015	935	100	37	63	835	209	254	140	119	89	23
2016	845	108	35	73	737	186	208	138	108	75	22
2017	766	104	29	74	663	144	211	121	98	49	15
2018	676	94	29	65	582	133	165	114	52	62	18
2019	645	74	20	54	571	147	169	103	87	45	21

Table 1-26. Unemployed Persons, by Age, Sex, Race, and Hispanic Origin, 1948–2019—*Continued*

(Thousands of people.)

Race, Hispanic origin, sex, and year	16 years and over	16 to 19 years			20 years and over						
		Total	16 to 17 years	18 to 19 years	Total	20 to 24 years	25 to 34 years	35 to 44 years	45 to 54 years	55 to 64 years	65 years and over
BLACK											
Women											
1985	913	164	66	98	750	231	295	913	58	31	7
1986	894	167	70	97	728	228	291	894	57	25	5
1987	858	152	64	88	706	211	280	858	63	23	4
1988	776	134	57	78	642	172	269	776	53	22	7
1989	772	147	51	96	625	160	267	772	50	21	9
1990	758	126	49	76	633	172	258	758	44	17	8
1991	833	135	51	84	698	177	288	833	64	19	6
1992	944	144	56	88	800	200	308	944	71	22	6
1993	872	143	46	97	729	186	272	872	66	26	5
1994	818	133	57	76	685	178	249	818	59	26	6
1995	777	157	. . .	87	620	158	228	777	53	20	7
1996	784	141	60	80	643	164	244	784	52	21	7
1997	813	140	53	87	673	163	248	813	64	24	9
1998	756	134	63	71	622	150	218	756	65	21	8
1999	684	123	49	74	561	138	196	684	61	25	7
2000	621	109	44	65	512	136	154	621	59	22	10
2001	706	124	52	72	582	157	181	706	75	21	8
2002	858	120	49	71	738	183	228	858	95	35	12
2003	895	123	44	79	772	183	230	895	109	46	10
2004	868	114	51	63	755	166	230	868	126	40	13
2005	856	123	52	70	734	166	233	856	106	47	14
2006	775	120	50	70	656	150	199	775	102	38	8
2007	693	106	43	63	588	135	181	693	103	38	9
2008	839	108	44	64	732	166	216	839	132	56	15
2009	1 159	127	44	82	1 032	223	311	1 159	185	77	17
2010	1 302	137	50	87	1 165	245	369	1 302	193	88	22
2011	1 329	125	49	76	1 204	253	376	1 329	211	86	25
2012	1 252	133	47	85	1 119	241	333	1 252	205	98	26
2013	1 192	124	47	77	1 069	235	305	1 192	184	103	24
2014	1 050	106	41	65	943	215	310	166	136	91	26
2015	911	99	32	68	811	174	263	158	126	62	28
2016	810	86	38	48	724	143	226	148	117	68	21
2017	735	77	32	46	657	113	216	133	112	62	21
2018	646	73	27	46	573	101	185	120	87	55	26
2019	607	79	34	45	527	105	162	98	79	61	22
HISPANIC											
Both Sexes											
1985	811	141	55	85	670	171	256	123	73	41	7
1986	857	141	57	84	716	183	258	143	85	38	9
1987	751	136	57	79	615	152	222	128	75	33	5
1988	732	148	63	84	585	145	209	120	69	36	6
1989	750	132	59	73	618	158	218	124	76	36	6
1990	876	161	68	94	714	167	263	156	85	36	7
1991	1 092	179	79	99	913	214	332	206	110	44	8
1992	1 311	219	94	124	1 093	240	390	267	126	59	10
1993	1 248	201	86	115	1 047	237	354	261	132	54	10
1994	1 187	198	90	108	989	220	348	227	132	51	12
1995	1 140	205	96	109	934	209	325	224	106	54	16
1996	1 132	199	85	114	933	217	296	246	101	59	14
1997	1 069	197	87	110	872	206	269	229	99	56	13
1998	1 026	214	89	125	812	194	260	203	96	48	11
1999	945	196	79	117	750	171	233	190	104	42	10
2000	954	194	83	112	759	190	247	189	79	42	12
2001	1 138	208	84	123	931	212	315	228	111	56	9
2002	1 353	221	81	140	1 132	265	373	271	146	62	15
2003	1 441	192	79	113	1 249	273	419	294	183	69	10
2004	1 342	203	86	117	1 139	255	371	261	161	74	18
2005	1 191	191	78	113	1 000	227	324	231	142	61	15
2006	1 081	170	74	97	911	194	294	231	128	49	14
2007	1 220	197	78	119	1 023	213	322	238	161	70	19
2008	1 678	251	105	146	1 427	307	437	328	242	81	32
2009	2 706	321	109	212	2 385	429	731	584	416	186	38
2010	2 843	322	99	223	2 520	479	736	598	459	199	49
2011	2 629	300	96	203	2 329	473	669	524	424	195	45
2012	2 514	324	111	213	2 190	444	618	502	381	201	44
2013	2 257	312	111	201	1 945	418	549	442	321	172	43
2014	1 878	250	89	160	1 628	368	469	355	255	147	33
2015	1 726	221	74	147	1 505	338	430	319	239	143	36
2016	1 548	201	71	130	1 347	298	377	269	230	137	34
2017	1 401	184	73	111	1 217	253	362	254	197	113	38
2018	1 323	186	64	122	1 138	239	320	237	170	131	42
2019	1 248	198	70	128	1 050	230	305	201	172	104	37

. . . = Not available.

Table 1-26. Unemployed Persons, by Age, Sex, Race, and Hispanic Origin, 1948–2019—*Continued*

(Thousands of people.)

Race, Hispanic origin, sex, and year	16 years and over	16 to 19 years			20 years and over						
		Total	16 to 17 years	18 to 19 years	Total	20 to 24 years	25 to 34 years	35 to 44 years	45 to 54 years	55 to 64 years	65 years and over
HISPANIC											
Men											
1985	483	82	34	49	401	108	156	69	40	23	. . .
1986	520	82	33	50	438	115	159	86	46	26	. . .
1987	451	77	32	45	374	88	137	77	46	22	. . .
1988	437	86	36	50	351	83	128	70	42	24	. . .
1989	423	81	36	45	342	88	113	69	43	25	. . .
1990	524	100	40	60	425	99	154	91	53	25	. . .
1991	685	110	47	62	575	139	210	126	62	33	. . .
1992	807	132	56	75	675	156	239	156	75	42	. . .
1993	747	118	50	68	629	144	217	148	79	33	. . .
1994	680	121	54	67	558	128	203	113	75	30	9
1995	651	121	59	63	530	123	185	120	57	33	13
1996	607	112	49	63	495	117	165	124	49	31	9
1997	582	110	47	63	471	125	137	113	54	35	8
1998	552	117	54	62	436	115	142	97	54	29	5
1999	480	106	42	63	374	96	109	83	54	24	7
2000	494	106	46	60	388	105	118	93	42	23	8
2001	611	117	52	65	495	129	152	116	55	36	6
2002	764	127	42	86	636	151	213	144	82	38	8
2003	809	116	42	74	693	157	239	153	98	41	5
2004	755	120	48	72	635	158	207	133	82	41	13
2005	647	112	42	70	536	134	168	119	74	31	9
2006	601	104	43	61	497	110	169	114	66	29	8
2007	695	119	44	74	576	121	189	126	92	35	13
2008	1 007	147	63	84	860	188	275	192	136	50	19
2009	1 670	196	66	131	1 474	255	470	364	246	117	21
2010	1 711	191	54	137	1 519	294	470	346	269	112	28
2011	1 527	182	53	129	1 345	277	395	297	231	116	28
2012	1 383	189	66	123	1 195	254	339	251	208	119	24
2013	1 263	173	58	115	1 090	248	305	232	173	105	28
2014	996	132	48	83	864	207	251	179	124	82	22
2015	943	124	40	84	820	196	232	151	133	83	25
2016	833	113	40	74	720	171	201	139	107	78	23
2017	730	98	30	68	632	137	190	132	93	57	23
2018	695	104	34	70	591	136	155	119	83	73	26
2019	657	104	35	69	553	133	152	98	92	58	21
HISPANIC											
Women											
1985	327	58	22	37	269	63	100	54	32	18	. . .
1986	337	59	25	35	278	68	99	57	39	12	. . .
1987	300	59	25	34	241	64	85	51	29	11	. . .
1988	296	62	27	34	234	63	81	50	27	12	. . .
1989	327	51	23	28	276	70	105	55	33	11	. . .
1990	351	62	28	34	289	68	109	65	32	11	. . .
1991	407	69	32	37	339	74	122	80	48	12	. . .
1992	504	87	38	49	418	84	151	111	51	17	. . .
1993	501	83	36	47	418	93	136	113	53	21	. . .
1994	508	77	36	40	431	92	145	115	57	21	2
1995	488	84	38	46	404	86	140	104	50	21	3
1996	525	88	36	52	438	100	131	122	52	27	5
1997	488	87	40	46	401	81	132	117	46	21	4
1998	473	98	35	63	376	80	118	106	48	19	5
1999	466	90	36	54	376	75	124	107	50	17	3
2000	460	88	37	51	371	86	129	96	38	19	4
2001	527	91	33	58	436	83	163	112	56	20	3
2002	590	94	39	54	496	113	160	127	65	24	7
2003	631	76	37	39	555	116	180	141	86	28	5
2004	587	83	38	45	504	97	164	128	78	32	5
2005	544	80	36	43	464	93	156	112	68	30	6
2006	480	67	31	36	414	84	125	116	62	20	6
2007	525	79	34	45	446	92	134	111	69	35	6
2008	672	104	42	62	567	119	162	136	105	32	13
2009	1 036	125	44	81	911	174	260	220	170	70	17
2010	1 132	131	45	86	1 001	186	267	252	190	87	20
2011	1 102	118	44	74	984	196	274	227	192	78	17
2012	1 130	135	45	90	995	190	278	251	173	83	20
2013	994	139	52	86	855	170	244	210	148	67	15
2014	882	118	41	77	764	162	218	176	131	65	11
2015	783	98	34	63	686	142	198	168	107	60	11
2016	715	88	31	56	627	127	176	130	123	59	12
2017	671	86	43	43	585	116	172	122	103	56	15
2018	628	82	31	51	547	103	165	118	87	58	9
2019	591	94	35	59	497	97	154	103	80	46	17

. . . = Not available.

Table 1-27. Unemployment Rates of Civilian Workers, by Age, Sex, Race, and Hispanic Origin, 1948–2019

(Percent of labor force.)

Race, Hispanic origin, sex, and year	16 years and over	16 to 19 years			20 years and over						
		Total	16 to 17 years	18 to 19 years	Total	20 to 24 years	25 to 34 years	35 to 44 years	45 to 54 years	55 to 64 years	65 years and over
ALL RACES											
Both Sexes											
1948	3.8	9.2	10.1	8.6	3.3	6.2	3.2	2.6	2.7	3.1	3.2
1949	5.9	13.4	14.0	13.0	5.4	9.3	5.4	4.4	4.2	5.2	4.9
1950	5.3	12.2	13.6	11.2	4.8	7.7	4.8	3.8	4.2	4.8	4.5
1951	3.3	8.2	9.6	7.1	3.0	4.1	3.0	2.5	2.7	3.1	3.4
1952	3.0	8.5	10.0	7.3	2.7	4.6	2.6	2.3	2.3	2.4	2.9
1953	2.9	7.6	8.7	6.8	2.6	4.7	2.5	2.2	2.3	2.7	2.2
1954	5.5	12.6	13.5	10.7	5.1	9.2	5.3	4.5	4.4	4.5	4.1
1955	4.4	11.0	12.3	10.0	3.9	7.0	3.8	3.4	3.4	4.2	3.6
1956	4.1	11.1	12.3	10.2	3.7	6.6	3.7	3.0	3.2	3.5	3.2
1957	4.3	11.6	12.5	10.9	3.8	7.1	3.9	3.1	3.3	3.4	3.4
1958	6.8	15.9	16.4	15.5	6.2	11.2	6.8	5.4	5.2	5.2	4.8
1959	5.5	14.6	15.3	14.0	4.8	8.5	5.0	4.2	4.2	4.4	4.3
1960	5.5	14.7	15.5	14.1	4.8	8.7	5.2	4.1	4.1	4.2	3.8
1961	6.7	16.8	18.3	15.8	5.9	10.4	6.2	5.2	5.0	5.4	5.1
1962	5.5	14.7	16.3	13.6	4.9	9.0	5.1	4.1	4.0	4.2	4.5
1963	5.7	17.2	19.3	15.6	4.8	8.8	5.2	4.0	3.8	4.1	4.1
1964	5.2	16.2	17.8	14.9	4.3	8.3	4.3	3.6	3.5	3.7	3.8
1965	4.5	14.8	16.5	13.5	3.6	6.7	3.7	3.2	2.8	3.1	3.3
1966	3.8	12.8	14.8	11.3	2.9	5.3	3.1	2.5	2.3	2.5	3.0
1967	3.8	12.9	14.6	11.6	3.0	5.7	3.2	2.5	2.4	2.4	2.8
1968	3.6	12.7	14.7	11.2	2.7	5.8	2.8	2.2	1.9	2.0	2.8
1969	3.5	12.2	14.5	10.5	2.7	5.7	2.8	2.2	1.9	1.9	2.2
1970	4.9	15.3	17.1	13.8	4.0	8.2	4.2	3.1	2.8	2.7	3.2
1971	5.9	16.9	18.7	15.5	4.9	10.0	5.3	3.9	3.4	3.3	3.5
1972	5.6	16.2	18.5	14.6	4.5	9.3	4.6	3.5	3.0	3.2	3.6
1973	4.9	14.5	17.3	12.4	3.9	7.8	4.2	2.7	2.5	2.6	3.0
1974	5.6	16.0	18.3	14.3	4.5	9.1	4.8	3.3	2.9	2.8	3.4
1975	8.5	19.9	21.4	18.9	7.3	13.6	7.8	5.6	5.2	4.6	5.2
1976	7.7	19.0	21.1	17.5	6.5	12.0	7.1	4.9	4.5	4.5	5.1
1977	7.1	17.8	19.9	16.2	5.9	11.0	6.5	4.4	3.9	3.9	5.0
1978	6.1	16.4	19.3	14.2	5.0	9.6	5.3	3.7	3.3	2.9	4.0
1979	5.8	16.1	18.1	14.7	4.8	9.1	5.2	3.6	3.2	2.9	3.4
1980	7.1	17.8	20.0	16.2	6.1	11.5	6.9	4.6	4.0	3.3	3.1
1981	7.6	19.6	21.4	18.4	6.5	12.3	7.3	5.0	4.2	3.7	3.2
1982	9.7	23.2	24.9	22.1	8.6	14.9	9.7	6.9	5.7	5.4	3.5
1983	9.6	22.4	24.5	21.1	8.6	14.5	9.7	7.0	6.2	5.6	3.7
1984	7.5	18.9	21.2	17.4	6.7	11.5	7.3	5.4	4.9	4.7	3.3
1985	7.2	18.6	21.0	17.0	6.4	11.1	7.0	5.1	4.7	4.3	3.2
1986	7.0	18.3	20.2	17.0	6.2	10.7	6.9	5.0	4.5	4.1	3.0
1987	6.2	16.9	19.1	15.2	5.4	9.7	6.0	4.5	4.0	3.5	2.5
1988	5.5	15.3	17.4	13.8	4.8	8.7	5.4	4.0	3.4	3.2	2.7
1989	5.3	15.0	17.2	13.6	4.6	8.6	5.2	3.8	3.2	3.2	2.6
1990	5.6	15.5	17.9	14.1	4.9	8.8	5.6	4.1	3.6	3.3	3.0
1991	6.8	18.7	21.0	17.2	6.1	10.8	6.9	5.2	4.5	4.1	3.3
1992	7.5	20.1	23.1	18.2	6.8	11.4	7.6	5.8	5.1	5.1	3.8
1993	6.9	19.0	21.4	17.5	6.2	10.5	6.9	5.5	4.8	4.7	3.2
1994	6.1	17.6	19.9	16.0	5.4	9.7	6.0	4.6	4.0	4.1	4.0
1995	5.6	17.3	20.2	15.3	4.9	9.1	5.4	4.3	3.3	3.6	4.0
1996	5.4	16.7	18.9	15.2	4.7	9.3	5.2	4.1	3.3	3.3	3.6
1997	4.9	16.0	18.2	14.5	4.3	8.5	4.7	3.8	3.0	2.9	3.3
1998	4.5	14.6	17.2	12.8	3.9	7.9	4.3	3.4	2.8	2.6	3.2
1999	4.2	13.9	16.3	12.4	3.6	7.5	4.0	3.0	2.6	2.7	3.1
2000	4.0	13.1	15.4	11.6	3.4	7.2	3.7	3.0	2.5	2.5	3.1
2001	4.7	14.7	17.2	13.1	4.2	8.3	4.6	3.6	3.1	3.0	2.9
2002	5.8	16.5	18.8	15.1	5.2	9.7	5.9	4.6	4.0	3.9	3.6
2003	6.0	17.5	19.1	16.4	5.4	10.0	6.1	4.9	4.1	4.1	3.8
2004	5.5	17.0	20.2	15.0	4.9	9.4	5.5	4.4	3.8	3.8	3.6
2005	5.1	16.6	19.1	14.9	4.5	8.8	5.1	3.9	3.5	3.3	3.5
2006	4.6	15.4	17.2	14.1	4.1	8.2	4.7	3.6	3.1	3.0	2.9
2007	4.6	15.7	17.5	14.5	4.1	8.2	4.7	3.4	3.2	3.1	3.3
2008	5.8	18.7	22.1	16.8	5.2	10.2	5.8	4.6	4.1	3.7	4.2
2009	9.3	24.3	25.9	23.4	8.6	14.7	9.9	7.9	7.2	6.6	6.4
2010	9.6	25.9	29.1	24.2	9.0	15.5	10.1	8.1	7.7	7.1	6.7
2011	8.9	24.4	27.7	22.9	8.3	14.6	9.5	7.3	7.1	6.6	6.5
2012	8.1	24.0	27.3	22.3	7.4	13.3	8.3	6.6	6.2	5.9	6.2
2013	7.4	22.9	26.5	21.0	6.8	12.8	7.4	5.9	5.6	5.3	5.4
2014	6.2	19.6	21.6	18.5	5.7	11.2	6.5	4.7	4.4	4.3	4.1
2015	5.3	16.9	18.3	16.2	4.8	9.7	5.5	4.1	3.7	3.8	3.8
2016	4.9	15.7	17.9	14.5	4.5	8.4	5.1	3.8	3.6	3.6	3.8
2017	4.4	14.0	15.5	13.1	4.0	7.4	4.6	3.5	3.2	3.1	3.6
2018	3.9	12.9	13.8	12.4	3.6	6.9	3.9	3.5	2.8	2.8	3.3
2019	3.7	12.7	14.0	11.9	3.3	6.7	3.7	2.7	2.7	2.6	3.0

Table 1-27. Unemployment Rates of Civilian Workers, by Age, Sex, Race, and Hispanic Origin, 1948–2019
—Continued

(Percent of labor force.)

Race, Hispanic origin, sex, and year	16 years and over	16 to 19 years			20 years and over						
		Total	16 to 17 years	18 to 19 years	Total	20 to 24 years	25 to 34 years	35 to 44 years	45 to 54 years	55 to 64 years	65 years and over
ALL RACES											
Men											
1985	7.0	19.5	21.9	17.9	6.2	11.4	6.6	4.9	4.6	4.3	3.1
1986	6.9	19.0	20.8	17.7	6.1	11.0	6.7	5.1	4.4	4.3	3.2
1987	6.2	17.8	20.2	16.0	5.4	9.9	5.9	4.4	4.2	3.7	2.6
1988	5.5	16.0	18.2	14.6	4.8	8.9	5.3	3.8	3.5	3.5	2.5
1989	5.2	15.9	18.6	14.2	4.5	8.8	4.8	3.7	3.2	3.5	2.4
1990	5.7	16.3	18.4	15.0	5.0	9.1	5.5	4.1	3.7	3.8	3.0
1991	7.2	19.8	21.8	18.5	6.4	11.6	7.0	5.5	4.8	4.6	3.3
1992	7.9	21.5	24.6	19.5	7.1	12.2	7.8	6.1	5.6	5.8	3.3
1993	7.2	20.4	22.9	18.8	6.4	11.3	7.0	5.6	5.1	5.2	3.2
1994	6.2	19.0	21.0	17.6	5.4	10.2	5.9	4.5	4.0	4.4	4.0
1995	5.6	18.4	21.1	16.5	4.8	9.2	5.1	4.2	3.5	3.6	4.3
1996	5.4	18.1	20.8	16.3	4.6	9.5	4.9	4.0	3.5	3.3	3.4
1997	4.9	16.9	19.1	15.4	4.2	8.9	4.3	3.6	3.1	3.1	3.0
1998	4.4	16.2	19.1	14.1	3.7	8.1	3.9	3.0	2.8	2.8	3.1
1999	4.1	14.7	17.0	13.1	3.5	7.7	3.6	2.8	2.6	2.7	3.0
2000	3.9	14.0	16.8	12.2	3.3	7.3	3.4	2.8	2.4	2.4	3.3
2001	4.8	16.0	19.1	14.0	4.2	9.0	4.3	3.6	3.2	3.3	3.0
2002	5.9	18.1	21.1	16.4	5.3	10.2	5.8	4.5	4.2	4.3	3.4
2003	6.3	19.3	20.7	18.4	5.6	10.6	6.2	5.0	4.4	4.5	4.0
2004	5.6	18.4	22.0	16.3	5.0	10.1	5.5	4.3	3.9	3.9	3.7
2005	5.1	18.6	22.0	16.5	4.4	9.6	4.7	3.7	3.5	3.3	3.4
2006	4.6	16.9	18.6	15.7	4.0	8.7	4.5	3.3	3.1	3.0	2.8
2007	4.7	17.6	19.4	16.5	4.1	8.9	4.7	3.3	3.1	3.2	3.4
2008	6.1	21.2	25.2	19.0	5.4	11.4	6.1	4.6	4.2	3.8	4.5
2009	10.3	27.8	28.7	27.4	9.6	17.0	10.9	8.6	8.2	7.2	6.7
2010	10.5	28.8	31.8	27.4	9.8	17.8	10.9	8.5	8.6	8.0	7.1
2011	9.4	27.2	29.1	26.3	8.7	15.7	9.7	7.4	7.4	7.1	6.5
2012	8.2	26.8	30.6	25.0	7.5	14.3	8.2	6.4	6.2	6.3	6.2
2013	7.6	25.5	29.1	23.7	7.0	14.0	7.6	5.8	5.7	5.6	5.5
2014	6.3	21.4	24.0	20.1	5.7	12.2	6.4	4.6	4.4	4.5	4.6
2015	5.4	18.4	19.8	17.6	4.9	10.8	5.5	4.0	3.6	3.9	3.8
2016	4.9	17.1	19.7	15.7	4.5	9.3	5.0	3.6	3.4	3.8	3.8
2017	4.4	15.5	16.5	15.0	4.0	8.4	4.6	3.2	3.0	3.1	3.4
2018	3.9	14.5	15.5	13.9	3.6	7.7	3.9	2.8	2.8	3.0	3.2
2019	3.7	13.8	14.5	13.5	3.4	7.7	3.7	2.6	2.7	2.5	2.9
ALL RACES											
Women											
1985	7.4	17.6	20.0	16.0	6.6	10.7	7.4	5.5	4.8	4.3	3.3
1986	7.1	17.6	19.6	16.3	6.2	10.3	7.2	5.0	4.5	3.8	2.8
1987	6.2	15.9	18.0	14.3	5.4	9.4	6.2	4.6	3.7	3.1	2.4
1988	5.6	14.4	16.6	12.9	4.9	8.5	5.6	4.1	3.4	2.7	2.9
1989	5.4	14.0	15.7	13.0	4.7	8.3	5.6	3.9	3.2	2.8	2.9
1990	5.5	14.7	17.4	13.1	4.9	8.5	5.6	4.2	3.4	2.8	3.1
1991	6.4	17.5	20.2	15.9	5.7	9.8	6.8	4.8	4.2	3.4	3.3
1992	7.0	18.6	21.5	16.6	6.3	10.3	7.4	5.5	4.6	4.2	4.5
1993	6.6	17.5	19.8	16.1	5.9	9.7	6.8	5.3	4.5	4.0	3.1
1994	6.0	16.2	18.7	14.3	5.4	9.2	6.2	4.7	4.0	3.9	4.0
1995	5.6	16.1	19.2	14.0	4.9	9.0	5.7	4.4	3.2	3.6	3.7
1996	5.4	15.2	16.9	14.0	4.8	9.0	5.5	4.2	3.2	3.4	4.0
1997	5.0	15.0	17.2	13.6	4.4	8.1	5.2	4.0	2.9	2.7	3.6
1998	4.6	12.9	15.1	11.5	4.1	7.8	4.8	3.8	2.7	2.4	3.3
1999	4.3	13.2	15.5	11.6	3.8	7.2	4.4	3.3	2.5	2.6	3.2
2000	4.1	12.1	13.9	10.8	3.6	7.1	4.1	3.3	2.5	2.5	2.7
2001	4.7	13.4	15.2	12.2	4.1	7.5	5.1	3.7	3.0	2.7	2.9
2002	5.6	14.9	16.6	13.8	5.1	9.1	5.9	4.6	3.8	3.5	3.9
2003	5.7	15.6	17.5	14.2	5.1	9.3	5.9	4.9	3.7	3.7	3.6
2004	5.4	15.5	18.5	13.5	4.9	8.7	5.6	4.4	3.7	3.6	3.4
2005	5.1	14.5	16.5	13.1	4.6	7.9	5.6	4.1	3.5	3.3	3.5
2006	4.6	13.8	15.9	12.4	4.1	7.6	4.9	3.9	3.1	2.9	3.0
2007	4.5	13.8	15.7	12.5	4.0	7.3	4.6	3.6	3.2	3.0	3.1
2008	5.4	16.2	19.1	14.3	4.9	8.8	5.5	4.5	3.9	3.7	3.9
2009	8.1	20.7	23.1	19.4	7.5	12.3	8.6	7.1	6.0	6.0	6.1
2010	8.6	22.8	26.5	20.9	8.0	13.0	9.1	7.7	6.8	6.2	6.2
2011	8.5	21.7	26.3	19.3	7.9	13.4	9.1	7.2	6.7	6.1	6.5
2012	7.9	21.1	24.2	19.5	7.3	12.1	8.4	6.8	6.2	5.6	6.3
2013	7.1	20.3	24.0	18.2	6.5	11.5	7.3	6.0	5.5	5.0	5.1
2014	6.1	17.7	19.3	16.8	5.6	10.1	6.6	4.9	4.5	4.2	4.7
2015	5.2	15.5	16.7	14.8	4.8	8.5	5.5	4.4	3.8	3.6	3.9
2016	4.8	14.3	16.1	13.2	4.4	7.4	5.1	4.1	3.7	3.3	3.9
2017	4.3	12.5	14.6	11.1	4.0	6.3	4.6	3.7	3.3	3.1	3.8
2018	3.8	11.3	12.3	10.7	3.5	6.2	4.0	3.2	2.8	2.7	3.3
2019	3.6	11.5	13.6	10.4	3.3	5.7	3.7	2.9	2.7	2.7	3.1

Table 1-27. Unemployment Rates of Civilian Workers, by Age, Sex, Race, and Hispanic Origin, 1948–2019
—*Continued*

(Percent of labor force.)

Race, Hispanic origin, sex, and year	16 years and over	16 to 19 years			20 years and over						
		Total	16 to 17 years	18 to 19 years	Total	20 to 24 years	25 to 34 years	35 to 44 years	45 to 54 years	55 to 64 years	65 years and over
WHITE											
Both Sexes											
1954	5.0	12.1	13.2	11.3	4.6	8.3	4.6	4.0	4.0	4.3	3.9
1955	3.9	10.4	12.0	9.2	3.4	6.2	3.1	2.9	3.1	3.8	3.4
1956	3.6	10.1	11.5	9.0	3.2	5.7	3.1	2.6	2.9	3.2	3.1
1957	3.8	10.6	11.9	9.6	3.4	6.3	3.3	2.8	3.0	3.2	3.2
1958	6.1	14.4	15.2	13.9	5.6	9.9	5.9	4.8	4.8	4.9	4.6
1959	4.8	13.1	14.4	12.1	4.3	7.3	4.2	3.7	3.8	4.1	4.1
1960	5.0	13.5	14.6	12.6	4.3	7.9	4.5	3.6	3.8	3.9	3.7
1961	6.0	15.3	16.7	14.4	5.3	9.4	5.3	4.5	4.5	5.0	4.8
1962	4.9	13.3	15.3	12.0	4.2	7.9	4.2	3.6	3.6	3.9	4.0
1963	5.0	15.5	17.9	13.7	4.2	7.7	4.4	3.5	3.5	3.8	3.8
1964	4.6	14.8	16.5	13.3	3.8	7.3	3.6	3.2	3.2	3.5	3.5
1965	4.1	13.4	14.8	12.3	3.3	6.1	3.2	2.9	2.5	2.9	3.2
1966	3.4	11.2	13.3	9.7	2.6	4.6	2.6	2.3	2.1	2.4	2.9
1967	3.4	11.0	12.8	9.8	2.7	5.0	2.7	2.3	2.2	2.3	2.7
1968	3.2	11.0	12.9	9.6	2.5	5.2	2.4	2.0	1.8	1.9	2.8
1969	3.1	10.7	13.0	8.9	2.4	5.0	2.5	2.0	1.8	1.8	2.2
1970	4.5	13.5	15.5	11.9	3.7	7.3	3.8	3.0	2.7	2.7	3.2
1971	5.4	15.1	17.0	13.8	4.5	9.0	4.7	3.6	3.3	3.3	3.5
1972	5.1	14.2	16.6	12.3	4.1	8.4	4.1	3.2	2.9	3.1	3.4
1973	4.3	12.6	15.4	10.4	3.5	6.8	3.7	2.5	2.4	2.5	2.9
1974	5.0	14.0	16.3	12.2	4.1	8.0	4.4	3.1	2.8	2.8	3.3
1975	7.8	17.9	19.5	16.7	6.7	12.3	7.1	5.2	4.9	4.5	5.1
1976	7.0	16.9	19.0	15.3	5.9	10.7	6.3	4.5	4.2	4.3	4.9
1977	6.2	15.4	17.9	13.5	5.3	9.3	5.7	4.0	3.8	3.7	4.9
1978	5.2	13.9	17.0	11.5	4.3	8.0	4.6	3.3	3.0	2.7	3.8
1979	5.1	14.0	16.1	12.4	4.2	7.6	4.4	3.2	3.0	2.7	3.1
1980	6.3	15.5	17.9	13.8	5.4	9.9	6.1	4.2	3.7	3.1	2.7
1981	6.7	17.3	19.2	15.9	5.7	10.4	6.3	4.5	3.9	3.5	2.8
1982	8.6	20.4	22.8	18.8	7.6	12.8	8.5	6.3	5.4	5.1	3.1
1983	8.4	19.3	22.0	17.6	7.5	12.1	8.4	6.3	5.7	5.2	3.2
1984	6.5	16.0	18.8	14.3	5.7	9.3	6.2	4.8	4.4	4.4	3.0
1985	6.2	15.7	18.3	13.9	5.5	9.2	5.9	4.6	4.3	4.0	2.9
1986	6.0	15.6	17.6	14.1	5.3	8.7	5.9	4.5	4.1	3.8	2.9
1987	5.3	14.4	16.7	12.7	4.7	8.0	5.1	4.0	3.7	3.2	2.4
1988	4.7	13.1	15.3	11.6	4.1	7.1	4.5	3.5	3.1	3.0	2.4
1989	4.5	12.7	15.2	11.1	3.9	7.2	4.3	3.3	2.9	3.0	2.3
1990	4.8	13.5	15.8	12.1	4.3	7.3	4.6	3.6	3.3	3.2	2.8
1991	6.1	16.5	19.0	14.9	5.5	9.2	6.1	4.7	4.2	4.0	3.1
1992	6.6	17.2	20.3	15.2	6.0	9.5	6.7	5.2	4.8	4.9	3.7
1993	6.1	16.2	19.0	14.4	5.5	8.8	6.0	4.9	4.5	4.3	3.0
1994	5.3	15.1	17.6	13.3	4.7	8.1	5.2	4.0	3.7	3.9	3.8
1995	4.9	14.5	17.3	12.5	4.3	7.7	4.6	3.9	3.1	3.5	3.8
1996	4.7	14.2	16.4	12.6	4.1	7.8	4.4	3.6	3.1	3.2	3.5
1997	4.2	13.6	15.8	12.0	3.6	6.9	3.9	3.3	2.7	2.7	3.0
1998	3.9	12.6	14.8	11.0	3.3	6.5	3.7	2.9	2.6	2.4	2.9
1999	3.7	12.0	14.5	10.2	3.1	6.3	3.3	2.7	2.4	2.5	2.9
2000	3.5	11.4	13.9	9.8	3.0	5.9	3.2	2.6	2.2	2.4	2.8
2001	4.2	12.7	15.3	11.0	3.7	7.0	4.1	3.2	2.8	2.9	2.8
2002	5.1	14.5	16.7	13.2	4.6	8.1	5.2	4.1	3.7	3.7	3.5
2003	5.2	15.2	17.2	13.9	4.7	8.4	5.3	4.3	3.7	3.8	3.7
2004	4.8	15.0	17.9	13.1	4.3	7.9	4.7	3.9	3.4	3.6	3.3
2005	4.4	14.2	16.4	12.7	3.9	7.2	4.3	3.5	3.1	3.0	3.1
2006	4.0	13.2	15.1	11.9	3.6	6.9	4.0	3.2	2.8	2.8	2.8
2007	4.1	13.9	15.5	12.8	3.6	7.0	4.0	3.2	2.9	2.9	3.2
2008	5.2	16.8	19.9	14.9	4.6	9.0	5.1	4.3	3.7	3.4	4.0
2009	8.5	21.8	23.4	21.0	7.9	13.0	8.8	7.4	6.7	6.4	6.2
2010	8.7	23.2	26.3	21.6	8.1	13.5	8.9	7.4	7.2	6.8	6.4
2011	7.9	21.7	24.7	20.2	7.4	12.8	8.1	6.5	6.4	6.2	6.4
2012	7.2	21.5	24.8	19.8	6.6	11.4	7.3	5.9	5.7	5.5	6.0
2013	6.5	20.3	23.7	18.4	6.0	10.9	6.4	5.3	5.1	4.9	5.2
2014	5.3	17.3	19.0	16.4	4.9	9.1	5.4	4.2	4.0	3.9	4.2
2015	4.6	14.8	16.5	13.8	4.2	8.3	4.5	3.7	3.4	3.5	3.4
2016	4.3	14.1	16.1	12.9	3.9	7.2	4.3	3.3	3.2	3.3	3.7
2017	3.8	12.2	14.0	11.1	3.5	6.5	3.8	3.1	2.9	2.8	3.4
2018	3.5	11.3	12.3	10.7	3.2	6.0	3.4	2.6	2.6	2.7	3.1
2019	3.3	11.5	13.1	10.6	3.0	5.8	3.2	2.5	2.5	2.4	2.8

Table 1-27. Unemployment Rates of Civilian Workers, by Age, Sex, Race, and Hispanic Origin, 1948–2019 —Continued

(Percent of labor force.)

Race, Hispanic origin, sex, and year	16 years and over	16 to 19 years			20 years and over						
		Total	16 to 17 years	18 to 19 years	Total	20 to 24 years	25 to 34 years	35 to 44 years	45 to 54 years	55 to 64 years	65 years and over
WHITE											
Men											
1954	4.8	13.4	14.0	13.0	4.4	9.8	4.2	3.6	3.8	4.3	4.2
1955	3.7	11.3	12.2	10.4	3.3	7.0	2.7	2.6	2.9	3.9	3.8
1956	3.4	10.5	11.2	9.7	3.0	6.1	2.8	2.2	2.8	3.1	3.4
1957	3.6	11.5	11.9	11.1	3.2	7.0	2.7	2.5	3.0	3.4	3.2
1958	6.1	15.7	14.9	16.5	5.5	11.7	5.6	4.4	4.8	5.2	5.0
1959	4.6	14.0	15.0	13.0	4.1	7.5	3.8	3.2	3.7	4.2	4.5
1960	4.8	14.0	14.6	13.5	4.2	8.3	4.1	3.3	3.6	4.1	4.0
1961	5.7	15.7	16.5	15.2	5.1	10.1	4.9	4.0	4.4	5.3	5.2
1962	4.6	13.7	15.2	12.7	4.0	8.1	3.8	3.1	3.5	4.1	4.0
1963	4.7	15.9	17.8	14.2	3.9	7.8	3.9	2.9	3.3	4.0	4.1
1964	4.1	14.7	16.1	13.3	3.4	7.4	3.0	2.5	2.9	3.5	3.6
1965	3.6	12.9	14.7	11.3	2.9	5.9	2.6	2.3	2.3	3.1	3.4
1966	2.8	10.5	12.5	8.9	2.2	4.1	2.1	1.7	1.7	2.5	3.0
1967	2.7	10.7	12.7	9.0	2.1	4.2	1.9	1.6	1.8	2.2	2.7
1968	2.6	10.1	12.3	8.3	2.0	4.6	1.7	1.4	1.5	1.7	2.8
1969	2.5	10.0	12.5	7.9	1.9	4.6	1.7	1.4	1.4	1.7	2.2
1970	4.0	13.7	15.7	12.0	3.2	7.8	3.1	2.3	2.3	2.7	3.2
1971	4.9	15.1	17.1	13.5	4.0	9.4	4.0	2.9	2.9	3.2	3.4
1972	4.5	14.2	16.4	12.4	3.6	8.5	3.4	2.5	2.5	3.0	3.3
1973	3.8	12.3	15.2	10.0	3.0	6.6	3.0	1.8	2.0	2.4	2.9
1974	4.4	13.5	16.2	11.5	3.5	7.8	3.6	2.4	2.2	2.5	3.0
1975	7.2	18.3	19.7	17.2	6.2	13.1	6.3	4.5	4.4	4.1	5.0
1976	6.4	17.3	19.7	15.5	5.4	10.9	5.6	3.7	3.7	4.0	4.7
1977	5.5	15.0	17.6	13.0	4.7	9.3	5.0	3.1	3.0	3.3	4.9
1978	4.6	13.5	16.9	10.8	3.7	7.7	3.8	2.5	2.5	2.6	3.9
1979	4.5	13.9	16.1	12.2	3.6	7.5	3.7	2.5	2.5	2.5	3.2
1980	6.1	16.2	18.5	14.5	5.3	11.1	5.9	3.6	3.3	3.1	2.5
1981	6.5	17.9	19.9	16.4	5.6	11.6	6.1	4.0	3.6	3.4	2.4
1982	8.8	21.7	24.2	20.0	7.8	14.3	8.9	6.2	5.3	5.1	3.2
1983	8.8	20.2	22.6	18.7	7.9	13.8	9.0	6.4	5.7	5.6	3.2
1984	6.4	16.8	19.7	15.0	5.7	9.8	6.2	4.6	4.2	4.7	2.6
1985	6.1	16.5	19.2	14.7	5.4	9.7	5.7	4.3	4.1	4.0	2.7
1986	6.0	16.3	18.4	14.7	5.3	9.2	5.8	4.4	4.0	4.0	3.0
1987	5.4	15.5	17.9	13.7	4.8	8.4	5.2	3.9	3.9	3.4	2.5
1988	4.7	13.9	16.1	12.4	4.1	7.4	4.6	3.4	3.2	3.3	2.2
1989	4.5	13.7	16.4	12.0	3.9	7.5	4.1	3.2	2.9	3.1	2.1
1990	4.9	14.3	16.1	13.2	4.3	7.6	4.7	3.5	3.4	3.6	2.8
1991	6.5	17.6	19.7	16.3	5.8	10.2	6.4	5.0	4.4	4.6	3.1
1992	7.0	18.5	21.5	16.5	6.4	10.5	7.0	5.5	5.1	5.5	3.2
1993	6.3	17.7	20.2	16.0	5.7	9.6	6.2	5.0	4.7	4.7	2.9
1994	5.4	16.3	18.5	14.7	4.8	8.8	5.2	3.9	3.7	4.1	3.7
1995	4.9	15.6	18.2	13.8	4.3	7.9	4.5	3.8	3.2	3.4	4.0
1996	4.7	15.5	18.3	13.5	4.1	8.1	4.2	3.5	3.1	3.2	3.2
1997	4.2	14.3	16.3	12.9	3.6	7.3	3.7	3.2	2.8	3.0	2.7
1998	3.9	14.1	17.1	12.1	3.2	6.7	3.5	2.6	2.6	2.6	2.9
1999	3.6	12.6	15.1	10.8	3.0	6.5	3.1	2.4	2.4	2.6	2.9
2000	3.4	12.3	15.3	10.4	2.8	5.9	2.9	2.4	2.2	2.4	3.0
2001	4.2	13.9	17.4	11.7	3.7	7.8	3.8	3.1	2.9	3.2	2.8
2002	5.3	15.9	18.8	14.2	4.7	8.7	5.3	4.1	3.8	4.0	3.4
2003	5.6	17.1	18.5	16.1	5.0	9.1	5.5	4.4	4.0	4.2	3.8
2004	5.0	16.3	19.8	14.2	4.4	8.5	4.8	3.8	3.5	3.7	3.5
2005	4.4	16.1	18.9	14.3	3.8	7.9	4.1	3.3	3.0	3.0	3.1
2006	4.0	14.6	16.5	13.4	3.5	7.3	3.9	3.0	2.7	2.8	2.7
2007	4.2	15.7	17.0	14.8	3.7	7.6	4.1	3.0	2.8	3.0	3.3
2008	5.5	19.1	22.2	17.3	4.9	10.2	5.3	4.3	3.8	3.4	4.1
2009	9.4	25.2	25.9	24.8	8.8	15.3	9.8	8.0	7.7	6.8	6.3
2010	9.6	26.3	29.2	24.8	8.9	15.7	9.9	7.7	7.9	7.5	6.6
2011	8.3	24.5	26.6	23.5	7.7	13.9	8.4	6.6	6.7	6.6	6.4
2012	7.4	24.5	28.3	22.7	6.7	12.5	7.3	5.7	5.7	5.8	5.8
2013	6.8	22.5	25.9	20.7	6.2	11.9	6.6	5.2	5.2	5.2	5.4
2014	5.4	19.2	21.6	17.9	4.9	9.9	5.4	4.1	3.8	4.0	4.1
2015	4.7	16.2	18.1	15.3	4.3	9.4	4.6	3.5	3.3	3.5	3.3
2016	4.4	14.9	17.2	13.7	4.0	8.0	4.5	3.2	3.1	3.5	3.5
2017	3.8	13.3	14.9	12.3	3.5	7.4	3.9	2.9	2.8	2.8	3.2
2018	3.5	12.6	13.5	12.1	3.2	6.6	3.4	2.4	2.6	2.8	3.1
2019	3.3	12.8	14.2	12.1	3.0	6.5	3.2	2.3	2.5	2.4	2.7

Table 1-27. Unemployment Rates of Civilian Workers, by Age, Sex, Race, and Hispanic Origin, 1948–2019
—Continued

(Percent of labor force.)

Race, Hispanic origin, sex, and year	16 years and over	16 to 19 years			20 years and over						
		Total	16 to 17 years	18 to 19 years	Total	20 to 24 years	25 to 34 years	35 to 44 years	45 to 54 years	55 to 64 years	65 years and over
ALL RACES											
Men											
1948	3.6	9.8	10.2	9.5	3.2	6.9	2.8	2.4	2.5	3.1	3.4
1949	5.9	14.3	13.7	14.6	5.4	10.4	5.2	4.3	4.3	5.4	5.1
1950	5.1	12.7	13.3	12.3	4.7	8.1	4.4	3.6	4.0	4.9	4.8
1951	2.8	8.1	9.4	7.0	2.5	3.9	2.3	2.0	2.4	2.8	3.5
1952	2.8	8.9	10.5	7.4	2.4	4.6	2.2	1.9	2.2	2.4	3.0
1953	2.8	7.9	8.8	7.2	2.5	5.0	2.2	2.0	2.3	2.8	2.4
1954	5.3	13.5	13.9	13.2	4.9	10.7	4.8	4.1	4.3	4.5	4.4
1955	4.2	11.6	12.5	10.8	3.8	7.7	3.3	3.1	3.2	4.3	4.0
1956	3.8	11.1	11.7	10.5	3.4	6.9	3.3	2.6	3.0	3.5	3.5
1957	4.1	12.4	12.4	12.3	3.6	7.8	3.3	2.8	3.3	3.5	3.4
1958	6.8	17.1	16.3	17.8	6.2	12.7	6.5	5.1	5.3	5.5	5.2
1959	5.2	15.3	15.8	14.9	4.7	8.7	4.7	3.7	4.1	4.5	4.8
1960	5.4	15.3	15.5	15.0	4.7	8.9	4.8	3.8	4.1	4.6	4.2
1961	6.4	17.1	18.3	16.3	5.7	10.8	5.7	4.6	4.9	5.7	5.5
1962	5.2	14.7	16.0	13.8	4.6	8.9	4.5	3.6	3.9	4.6	4.6
1963	5.2	17.2	18.8	15.9	4.5	8.8	4.5	3.5	3.6	4.3	4.5
1964	4.6	15.8	17.1	14.6	3.9	8.1	3.5	2.9	3.2	3.9	4.0
1965	4.0	14.1	16.1	12.4	3.2	6.4	2.9	2.5	2.5	3.3	3.5
1966	3.2	11.7	13.7	10.2	2.5	4.6	2.4	2.0	1.9	2.6	3.1
1967	3.1	12.3	14.5	10.5	2.3	4.7	2.1	1.7	2.0	2.3	2.8
1968	2.9	11.6	13.9	9.7	2.2	5.1	1.9	1.6	1.6	1.9	2.8
1969	2.8	11.4	13.8	9.3	2.1	5.1	1.9	1.5	1.5	1.8	2.2
1970	4.4	15.0	16.9	13.4	3.5	8.4	3.5	2.4	2.4	2.8	3.3
1971	5.3	16.6	18.7	15.0	4.4	10.3	4.4	3.1	3.0	3.3	3.4
1972	5.0	15.9	18.3	14.1	4.0	9.3	3.8	2.7	2.6	3.2	3.6
1973	4.2	13.9	17.0	11.4	3.3	7.3	3.4	2.0	2.1	2.4	3.0
1974	4.9	15.6	18.4	13.3	3.8	8.8	4.0	2.6	2.4	2.6	3.3
1975	7.9	20.1	21.6	19.0	6.8	14.3	6.9	4.9	4.8	4.3	5.4
1976	7.1	19.2	21.4	17.6	5.9	12.1	6.2	4.1	4.0	4.2	5.1
1977	6.3	17.3	19.5	15.6	5.2	10.8	5.7	3.5	3.2	3.6	5.2
1978	5.3	15.8	19.1	13.3	4.3	9.2	4.4	2.8	2.7	2.8	4.2
1979	5.1	15.9	17.9	14.3	4.2	8.7	4.3	2.9	2.7	2.7	3.4
1980	6.9	18.3	20.4	16.7	5.9	12.5	6.7	4.1	3.6	3.4	3.1
1981	7.4	20.1	22.0	18.8	6.3	13.2	6.9	4.5	4.0	3.6	2.9
1982	9.9	24.4	26.4	23.1	8.8	16.4	10.1	6.9	5.6	5.5	3.7
1983	9.9	23.3	25.2	22.2	8.9	15.9	10.1	7.1	6.3	6.1	3.9
1984	7.4	19.6	21.9	18.3	6.6	11.9	7.2	5.2	4.6	5.0	3.0
1985	7.0	19.5	21.9	17.9	6.2	11.4	6.6	4.9	4.6	4.3	3.1
1986	6.9	19.0	20.8	17.7	6.1	11.0	6.7	5.1	4.4	4.3	3.2
1987	6.2	17.8	20.2	16.0	5.4	9.9	5.9	4.4	4.2	3.7	2.6
1988	5.5	16.0	18.2	14.6	4.8	8.9	5.3	3.8	3.5	3.5	2.5
1989	5.2	15.9	18.6	14.2	4.5	8.8	4.8	3.7	3.2	3.5	2.4
1990	5.7	16.3	18.4	15.0	5.0	9.1	5.5	4.1	3.7	3.8	3.0
1991	7.2	19.8	21.8	18.5	6.4	11.6	7.0	5.5	4.8	4.6	3.3
1992	7.9	21.5	24.6	19.5	7.1	12.2	7.8	6.1	5.6	5.8	3.3
1993	7.2	20.4	22.9	18.8	6.4	11.3	7.0	5.6	5.1	5.2	3.2
1994	6.2	19.0	21.0	17.6	5.4	10.2	5.9	4.5	4.0	4.4	4.0
1995	5.6	18.4	21.1	16.5	4.8	9.2	5.1	4.2	3.5	3.6	4.3
1996	5.4	18.1	20.8	16.3	4.6	9.5	4.9	4.0	3.5	3.3	3.4
1997	4.9	16.9	19.1	15.4	4.2	8.9	4.3	3.6	3.1	3.1	3.0
1998	4.4	16.2	19.1	14.1	3.7	8.1	3.9	3.0	2.8	2.8	3.1
1999	4.1	14.7	17.0	13.1	3.5	7.7	3.6	2.8	2.6	2.7	3.0
2000	3.9	14.0	16.8	12.2	3.3	7.3	3.4	2.8	2.4	2.4	3.3
2001	4.8	16.0	19.1	14.0	4.2	9.0	4.3	3.6	3.2	3.3	3.0
2002	5.9	18.1	21.1	16.4	5.3	10.2	5.8	4.5	4.2	4.3	3.4
2003	6.3	19.3	20.7	18.4	5.6	10.6	6.2	5.0	4.4	4.5	4.0
2004	5.6	18.4	22.0	16.3	5.0	10.1	5.5	4.3	3.9	3.9	3.7
2005	5.1	18.6	22.0	16.5	4.4	9.6	4.7	3.7	3.5	3.3	3.4
2006	4.6	16.9	18.6	15.7	4.0	8.7	4.5	3.3	3.1	3.0	2.8
2007	4.7	17.6	19.4	16.5	4.1	8.9	4.7	3.3	3.1	3.2	3.4
2008	6.1	21.2	25.2	19.0	5.4	11.4	6.1	4.6	4.2	3.8	4.5
2009	10.3	27.8	28.7	27.4	9.6	17.0	10.9	8.6	8.2	7.2	6.7
2010	10.5	28.8	31.8	27.4	9.8	17.8	10.9	8.5	8.6	8.0	7.1
2011	9.4	27.2	29.1	26.3	8.7	15.7	9.7	7.4	7.4	7.1	6.5
2012	8.2	26.8	30.6	25.0	7.5	14.3	8.2	6.4	6.2	6.3	6.2
2013	7.6	25.5	29.1	23.7	7.0	14.0	7.6	5.8	5.7	5.6	5.5
2014	6.3	21.4	24.0	20.1	5.7	12.2	6.4	4.6	4.4	4.5	4.6
2015	5.4	18.4	19.8	17.6	4.9	10.8	5.5	4.0	3.6	3.9	3.8
2016	4.9	17.1	19.7	15.7	4.5	9.3	5.0	3.6	3.4	3.8	3.8
2017	4.4	15.5	16.5	15.0	4.0	8.4	4.6	3.2	3.0	3.1	3.4
2018	3.9	14.5	15.5	13.9	3.6	7.7	3.9	2.8	2.8	3.0	3.2
2019	3.7	13.8	14.5	13.5	3.4	7.7	3.7	2.6	2.7	2.5	2.9

**Table 1-27. Unemployment Rates of Civilian Workers, by Age, Sex, Race, and Hispanic Origin, 1948–2019
—Continued**

(Percent of labor force.)

Race, Hispanic origin, sex, and year	16 years and over	16 to 19 years			20 years and over						
		Total	16 to 17 years	18 to 19 years	Total	20 to 24 years	25 to 34 years	35 to 44 years	45 to 54 years	55 to 64 years	65 years and over
WHITE											
Women											
1954	5.5	10.4	12.0	9.4	5.1	6.4	5.7	4.9	4.4	4.5	2.8
1955	4.3	9.1	11.6	7.7	3.9	5.1	4.3	3.8	3.4	3.6	2.2
1956	4.2	9.7	12.1	8.3	3.7	5.1	4.0	3.5	3.3	3.5	2.3
1957	4.3	9.5	11.9	7.8	3.8	5.1	4.7	3.7	3.0	2.9	3.4
1958	6.2	12.7	15.6	11.0	5.6	7.3	6.6	5.6	4.9	4.3	3.5
1959	5.3	12.0	13.3	11.1	4.7	7.0	5.2	4.7	3.9	4.0	2.9
1960	5.3	12.7	14.5	11.5	4.6	7.2	5.7	4.2	4.0	3.3	2.8
1961	6.5	14.8	17.0	13.6	5.7	8.4	6.6	5.6	4.8	4.3	3.8
1962	5.5	12.8	15.6	11.3	4.7	7.7	5.4	4.5	3.7	3.5	4.0
1963	5.8	15.1	18.1	13.2	4.8	7.4	5.8	4.6	3.9	3.5	3.3
1964	5.5	14.9	17.1	13.2	4.6	7.1	5.2	4.5	3.6	3.5	3.4
1965	5.0	14.0	15.0	13.4	4.0	6.3	4.9	4.1	3.0	2.7	2.7
1966	4.3	12.1	14.5	10.7	3.3	5.3	3.7	3.3	2.7	2.2	2.7
1967	4.6	11.5	12.9	10.6	3.8	6.0	4.7	3.7	2.9	2.3	2.6
1968	4.3	12.1	13.9	11.0	3.4	5.9	3.9	3.1	2.3	2.1	2.8
1969	4.2	11.5	13.7	10.0	3.4	5.5	4.2	3.2	2.4	2.1	2.4
1970	5.4	13.4	15.3	11.9	4.4	6.9	5.3	4.3	3.4	2.6	3.3
1971	6.3	15.1	16.7	14.1	5.3	8.5	6.3	4.9	3.9	3.3	3.6
1972	5.9	14.2	17.0	12.3	4.9	8.2	5.5	4.4	3.5	3.3	3.7
1973	5.3	13.0	15.8	10.9	4.3	7.1	5.1	3.7	3.2	2.7	2.8
1974	6.1	14.5	16.4	13.0	5.1	8.2	5.8	4.3	3.6	3.2	3.9
1975	8.6	17.4	19.2	16.1	7.5	11.2	8.4	6.5	5.8	5.0	5.3
1976	7.9	16.4	18.2	15.1	6.8	10.4	7.6	5.8	5.0	4.8	5.3
1977	7.3	15.9	18.2	14.2	6.2	9.3	6.7	5.3	5.0	4.4	4.9
1978	6.2	14.4	17.1	12.4	5.2	8.3	5.8	4.5	3.8	3.0	3.7
1979	5.9	14.0	15.9	12.5	5.0	7.8	5.6	4.2	3.7	3.0	3.1
1980	6.5	14.8	17.3	13.1	5.6	8.5	6.3	4.9	4.3	3.1	3.0
1981	6.9	16.6	18.4	15.3	5.9	9.1	6.6	5.1	4.2	3.7	3.4
1982	8.3	19.0	21.2	17.6	7.3	10.9	8.0	6.4	5.5	5.0	3.1
1983	7.9	18.3	21.4	16.4	6.9	10.3	7.6	6.2	5.5	4.7	3.1
1984	6.5	15.2	17.8	13.6	5.8	8.8	6.1	5.0	4.8	4.0	3.7
1985	6.4	14.8	17.2	13.1	5.7	8.5	6.2	4.9	4.5	4.1	3.1
1986	6.1	14.9	16.7	13.6	5.4	8.1	6.1	4.5	4.3	3.7	2.6
1987	5.2	13.4	15.5	11.7	4.6	7.4	5.0	4.1	3.3	2.9	2.4
1988	4.7	12.3	14.4	10.8	4.1	6.7	4.5	3.7	3.1	2.5	2.6
1989	4.5	11.5	13.8	10.1	4.0	6.8	4.5	3.4	2.9	2.7	2.5
1990	4.7	12.6	15.5	10.9	4.1	6.8	4.6	3.7	3.2	2.7	2.8
1991	5.6	15.2	18.2	13.3	5.0	8.1	5.7	4.3	4.0	3.3	3.1
1992	6.1	15.8	18.9	13.7	5.5	8.3	6.2	4.9	4.3	4.0	4.5
1993	5.7	14.7	17.8	12.6	5.2	7.9	5.8	4.7	4.3	3.9	3.0
1994	5.2	13.8	16.6	11.8	4.6	7.4	5.1	4.2	3.7	3.7	3.9
1995	4.8	13.4	16.4	11.2	4.3	7.4	4.7	3.9	3.0	3.5	3.5
1996	4.7	12.9	14.4	11.7	4.1	7.4	4.6	3.8	3.1	3.1	3.8
1997	4.2	12.8	15.2	11.1	3.7	6.4	4.2	3.4	2.6	2.4	3.5
1998	3.9	10.9	12.4	9.8	3.4	6.3	3.9	3.3	2.5	2.2	3.4
1999	3.8	11.3	13.9	9.6	3.3	6.1	3.6	3.0	2.3	2.5	2.9
2000	3.6	10.4	12.5	9.0	3.1	5.8	3.5	2.9	2.3	2.4	2.4
2001	4.1	11.4	13.1	10.2	3.6	6.1	4.5	3.3	2.7	2.5	2.7
2002	4.9	13.1	14.6	12.1	4.4	7.4	5.0	4.1	3.5	3.3	3.5
2003	4.8	13.3	15.9	11.5	4.4	7.6	4.9	4.2	3.3	3.4	3.5
2004	4.7	13.6	16.1	11.9	4.2	7.1	4.6	3.9	3.3	3.5	3.1
2005	4.4	12.3	14.0	11.1	3.9	6.4	4.7	3.6	3.1	3.0	3.2
2006	4.0	11.7	13.8	10.2	3.6	6.3	4.1	3.4	2.9	2.8	3.0
2007	4.0	12.1	14.1	10.6	3.6	6.2	3.9	3.4	2.9	2.8	3.1
2008	4.9	14.4	17.6	12.3	4.4	7.5	4.8	4.3	3.5	3.5	3.8
2009	7.3	18.4	20.9	17.0	6.8	10.4	7.6	6.7	5.6	5.8	6.0
2010	7.7	20.0	23.4	18.1	7.2	11.0	7.7	7.1	6.4	6.0	6.0
2011	7.5	18.9	22.9	16.7	7.0	11.4	7.7	6.3	6.1	5.8	6.4
2012	7.0	18.4	21.4	16.7	6.5	10.1	7.2	6.3	5.7	5.2	6.3
2013	6.2	18.1	21.5	16.0	5.7	9.7	6.1	5.4	5.0	4.6	4.9
2014	5.2	15.5	16.6	14.8	4.8	8.1	5.3	4.4	4.1	3.8	4.4
2015	4.5	13.2	14.8	12.3	4.1	7.0	4.5	3.9	3.5	3.5	3.5
2016	4.2	13.2	15.1	12.0	3.8	6.3	4.2	3.5	3.3	3.0	3.9
2017	3.8	11.1	13.1	9.8	3.5	5.4	3.8	3.3	3.0	2.9	3.7
2018	3.4	10.0	11.1	9.3	3.1	5.4	3.4	2.9	2.6	2.6	3.0
2019	3.2	10.1	12.0	9.0	3.0	4.9	3.2	2.6	2.5	2.5	3.0

Table 1-27. Unemployment Rates of Civilian Workers, by Age, Sex, Race, and Hispanic Origin, 1948–2019
 —*Continued*

(Percent of labor force.)

Race, Hispanic origin, sex, and year	16 years and over	16 to 19 years			20 years and over						
		Total	16 to 17 years	18 to 19 years	Total	20 to 24 years	25 to 34 years	35 to 44 years	45 to 54 years	55 to 64 years	65 years and over
BLACK											
Both Sexes											
1985	15.1	40.2	43.6	38.3	13.1	24.5	14.5	9.5	8.2	7.0	7.0
1986	14.5	39.3	43.0	37.2	12.7	24.1	14.0	9.6	7.1	6.6	4.5
1987	13.0	34.7	39.7	31.6	11.3	21.8	12.8	8.4	6.8	5.6	3.9
1988	11.7	32.4	35.1	30.7	10.2	19.6	11.9	7.5	5.9	4.8	5.5
1989	11.4	32.4	32.9	32.2	9.9	18.0	11.5	7.6	5.6	5.2	6.9
1990	11.4	30.9	36.5	27.8	10.1	19.9	11.7	7.8	5.3	4.6	5.3
1991	12.5	36.1	39.5	34.4	11.1	21.6	12.7	8.5	7.4	4.4	5.2
1992	14.2	39.7	44.7	37.1	12.6	23.8	14.2	10.5	8.3	6.2	4.9
1993	13.0	38.8	39.7	38.4	11.4	21.9	12.6	9.5	6.9	7.1	4.7
1994	11.5	35.2	36.1	34.6	10.0	19.5	11.1	8.5	5.6	5.4	6.2
1995	10.4	35.7	39.1	33.4	8.7	17.7	9.9	7.3	4.8	4.0	6.7
1996	10.5	33.6	36.3	31.7	9.0	18.8	10.5	7.3	5.0	4.4	5.3
1997	10.0	32.4	35.0	30.8	8.6	18.3	9.9	7.0	5.0	4.2	6.1
1998	8.9	27.6	33.6	24.2	7.7	16.8	8.4	6.5	4.4	3.9	5.6
1999	8.0	27.9	31.0	26.2	6.8	14.6	7.6	5.3	4.0	3.9	5.0
2000	7.6	24.5	26.9	22.9	6.5	15.0	6.7	5.6	4.1	3.0	6.1
2001	8.6	29.0	30.8	27.9	7.4	16.3	8.1	6.3	4.8	3.9	4.3
2002	10.2	29.8	34.9	27.2	9.1	19.1	9.9	7.8	6.3	5.4	5.9
2003	10.8	33.0	32.2	33.5	9.7	19.8	10.9	8.6	6.2	6.3	5.4
2004	10.4	31.7	37.8	28.3	9.4	18.4	10.8	7.8	6.9	5.6	5.5
2005	10.0	33.3	41.2	29.0	8.8	18.3	10.2	7.1	6.0	5.6	6.9
2006	8.9	29.1	32.2	27.3	7.9	16.2	9.3	6.3	5.7	4.6	4.7
2007	8.3	29.4	32.6	27.4	7.2	15.2	8.6	5.4	5.4	4.3	4.5
2008	10.1	31.2	36.3	28.5	9.1	17.9	10.6	7.0	7.0	6.1	7.5
2009	14.8	39.5	43.1	37.8	13.7	24.9	16.7	11.7	10.4	8.4	8.5
2010	16.0	43.0	47.8	40.9	14.9	26.0	17.6	13.0	11.5	9.7	9.2
2011	15.8	41.3	47.1	38.9	14.9	25.2	18.1	13.1	11.2	9.8	8.4
2012	13.8	38.3	44.0	35.9	12.8	23.1	14.8	11.1	9.8	8.8	9.8
2013	13.1	38.8	46.2	35.5	12.0	22.8	13.8	10.0	9.4	8.1	8.1
2014	11.3	33.0	37.6	30.7	10.5	20.2	13.3	7.8	7.1	7.3	6.7
2015	9.6	28.4	29.6	27.9	8.8	16.4	11.0	7.1	6.1	5.8	7.2
2016	8.4	26.7	30.4	24.9	7.7	14.5	8.8	6.7	5.6	5.4	5.8
2017	7.5	24.0	24.5	23.8	6.8	11.5	8.4	5.8	5.2	4.9	4.4
2018	6.5	21.9	24.3	20.9	5.9	10.8	6.6	5.3	4.3	4.1	5.2
2019	6.1	20.7	23.1	19.6	5.5	11.5	6.2	4.6	4.1	3.6	4.6
Men											
1985	15.3	41.0	42.9	40.0	13.2	23.5	13.8	9.6	9.7	7.9	8.9
1986	14.8	39.3	41.4	38.2	12.9	23.5	13.5	10.9	7.8	8.0	4.3
1987	12.7	34.4	39.0	31.6	11.1	20.3	12.2	8.7	6.7	6.6	4.3
1988	11.7	32.7	34.4	31.7	10.1	19.4	11.0	7.6	6.2	5.2	5.6
1989	11.5	31.9	34.4	30.3	10.0	17.9	10.5	8.4	6.2	6.2	7.4
1990	11.9	31.9	38.8	28.0	10.4	20.1	11.5	8.4	6.3	5.4	4.6
1991	13.0	36.3	39.0	34.8	11.5	22.4	11.9	9.5	8.6	5.0	6.1
1992	15.2	42.0	47.5	39.1	13.5	24.6	14.2	11.2	10.3	8.1	4.9
1993	13.8	40.1	42.7	38.6	12.1	23.0	12.3	10.5	8.1	9.0	5.8
1994	12.0	37.6	39.3	36.5	10.3	19.4	10.6	9.1	6.5	6.0	8.2
1995	10.6	37.1	39.7	35.4	8.8	17.6	9.3	7.6	5.5	4.4	7.6
1996	11.1	36.9	39.9	34.9	9.4	19.2	10.1	7.8	6.3	5.2	5.0
1997	10.2	36.5	39.5	34.4	8.5	19.8	8.7	6.7	5.6	4.2	5.5
1998	8.9	30.1	33.9	27.9	7.4	18.0	7.3	6.2	4.4	4.5	5.2
1999	8.2	30.9	33.3	29.4	6.7	16.2	6.9	5.2	4.3	3.9	5.0
2000	8.0	26.2	28.5	24.7	6.9	16.6	6.7	5.8	4.8	2.7	6.3
2001	9.3	30.4	30.5	30.4	8.0	17.6	8.3	6.9	5.5	4.8	4.0
2002	10.7	31.3	36.6	28.7	9.5	20.0	9.4	8.0	7.4	6.1	5.0
2003	11.6	36.0	35.6	36.3	10.3	20.9	11.3	9.2	6.7	6.8	5.6
2004	11.1	35.6	40.8	32.7	9.9	20.3	10.9	8.0	7.2	6.4	4.2
2005	10.5	36.3	45.1	31.5	9.2	20.5	9.7	7.0	6.7	5.9	7.1
2006	9.5	32.7	34.8	31.5	8.3	17.2	9.5	5.9	6.3	5.5	5.8
2007	9.1	33.8	40.1	30.2	7.9	16.9	9.1	5.6	5.8	5.2	5.0
2008	11.4	35.9	43.9	32.0	10.2	19.3	11.8	7.7	7.7	7.1	9.5
2009	17.5	46.0	49.3	44.5	16.3	27.7	19.9	14.0	12.4	10.1	10.6
2010	18.4	45.4	49.4	43.9	17.3	29.8	19.3	14.9	14.4	12.2	10.4
2011	17.8	43.1	44.5	42.5	16.7	27.4	19.7	14.9	12.5	12.7	8.2
2012	15.0	41.3	47.2	38.9	14.0	25.6	15.2	12.6	10.2	10.1	11.5
2013	14.2	44.5	51.2	41.6	12.9	25.1	14.3	10.1	10.3	8.5	9.1
2014	12.2	36.5	38.5	35.5	11.3	22.1	13.6	8.2	7.9	8.0	8.5
2015	10.3	30.8	33.1	29.5	9.5	18.3	11.3	7.2	6.3	7.4	7.2
2016	9.1	30.9	37.8	28.4	8.2	17.0	8.8	6.9	5.7	5.9	6.2
2017	8.1	30.0	28.5	30.7	7.2	13.2	8.6	5.9	5.2	5.6	4.0
2018	7.0	25.7	30.0	24.1	6.2	12.7	6.4	5.5	4.7	4.6	4.7
2019	6.6	22.0	20.2	22.8	6.0	13.8	6.4	4.9	4.5	3.4	5.0

Table 1-27. Unemployment Rates of Civilian Workers, by Age, Sex, Race, and Hispanic Origin, 1948–2019
—*Continued*

(Percent of labor force.)

Race, Hispanic origin, sex, and year	16 years and over	16 to 19 years			20 years and over						
		Total	16 to 17 years	18 to 19 years	Total	20 to 24 years	25 to 34 years	35 to 44 years	45 to 54 years	55 to 64 years	65 years and over
BLACK											
Women											
1985	14.2	39.2	44.6	36.1	12.4	24.7	14.6	8.5	6.4	5.9	4.9
1986	13.2	34.9	40.5	31.7	11.6	23.3	13.5	8.1	6.9	6.0	3.4
1987	11.7	32.0	35.9	29.6	10.4	19.8	12.7	7.4	5.6	5.0	5.4
1988	11.4	33.0	31.1	34.0	9.8	18.1	12.5	7.0	5.0	4.5	6.4
1989	10.9	29.9	34.1	27.6	9.7	19.6	11.9	7.2	4.3	4.3	5.9
1990	12.0	36.0	40.1	33.9	10.6	20.7	13.4	7.6	6.2	4.2	4.4
1991	13.2	37.2	41.7	34.8	11.8	23.1	14.1	9.8	6.4	3.6	5.0
1992	12.1	37.4	36.1	38.1	10.7	20.9	12.9	8.6	5.8	3.8	3.6
1993	11.0	32.6	32.9	32.5	9.8	19.6	11.7	8.0	4.9	4.2	4.4
1994	10.2	34.3	38.5	31.5	8.6	17.8	10.5	7.0	4.2	5.1	5.6
1995	10.0	30.3	32.8	28.6	8.7	18.4	11.0	6.9	3.8	4.9	6.6
1996	9.9	28.7	30.3	27.8	8.8	17.1	10.9	7.2	4.4	3.6	6.1
1997	9.0	25.3	33.2	20.9	7.9	15.7	9.5	6.7	4.3	3.8	5.0
1998	7.8	25.1	28.5	23.3	6.8	13.4	8.3	5.5	3.8	4.1	6.0
1999	7.1	22.8	25.3	21.3	6.2	13.6	6.8	5.5	3.4	3.4	4.6
2000	8.1	27.5	31.2	25.4	7.0	15.3	8.0	5.8	4.3	3.9	6.9
2001	9.8	28.3	33.2	25.6	8.8	18.3	10.2	7.7	5.3	3.3	5.3
2002	10.2	30.3	29.1	31.1	9.2	18.8	10.5	8.1	5.8	3.1	6.8
2003	9.8	28.2	35.2	24.3	8.9	16.6	10.7	7.6	6.5	4.7	6.6
2004	9.5	30.3	37.3	26.6	8.5	16.3	10.6	7.2	5.4	5.9	3.7
2005	8.4	25.9	29.9	23.6	7.5	15.2	9.0	6.7	5.1	4.8	4.0
2006	7.5	25.3	26.4	24.7	6.7	13.6	8.1	5.3	5.0	5.3	5.8
2007	8.9	26.8	29.9	25.0	8.1	16.6	9.5	6.4	6.3	3.9	6.6
2008	12.4	33.4	37.2	31.7	11.5	22.2	13.8	9.7	8.7	3.7	8.2
2009	13.8	40.5	46.4	37.7	12.8	22.6	16.0	11.4	9.1	5.3	8.5
2010	14.1	39.4	49.5	34.8	13.2	23.1	16.5	11.6	10.0	7.1	8.2
2011	12.8	35.6	41.3	33.1	11.9	20.8	14.4	9.8	9.4	7.6	7.2
2012	12.1	33.4	41.6	29.8	11.3	20.6	13.2	9.8	8.5	7.4	7.2
2013	10.5	29.7	36.7	26.6	9.8	18.4	13.1	7.4	7.9	6.7	7.4
2014	8.9	26.4	26.3	26.5	8.2	14.6	10.7	7.0	5.9	4.5	7.2
2015	7.8	22.8	25.7	20.9	7.3	12.3	8.8	6.5	5.4	4.9	5.4
2016	6.9	18.9	21.7	17.4	6.5	9.8	8.2	5.7	5.1	4.3	4.7
2017	6.0	18.4	20.2	17.6	5.6	8.9	6.9	5.1	4.0	3.7	5.5
2018	6.0	18.4	20.2	17.6	5.6	8.9	6.9	5.1	5.1	3.7	5.5
2019	5.6	19.6	25.2	16.8	5.1	9.3	6.0	4.2	3.7	3.9	4.3
HISPANIC											
Both Sexes											
1985	10.6	24.7	28.1	22.9	9.5	12.9	9.6	8.4	7.8	7.3	10.1
1986	8.8	22.3	27.7	19.5	7.8	10.6	7.7	6.7	6.9	6.0	6.5
1987	8.2	22.0	27.1	19.3	7.0	9.8	7.1	6.0	6.0	5.8	5.6
1988	8.0	19.4	26.4	16.0	7.2	10.7	7.0	5.9	6.3	5.8	5.3
1989	8.2	19.5	24.5	16.9	7.2	9.1	7.3	6.6	6.4	5.6	6.0
1990	10.0	22.9	31.9	18.7	9.0	11.6	9.2	8.1	8.0	6.5	7.0
1991	11.6	27.5	35.7	23.4	10.4	13.2	10.4	9.8	8.8	8.6	8.1
1992	10.8	26.1	35.1	21.8	9.7	13.1	9.3	9.1	8.6	8.0	6.6
1993	9.9	24.5	31.7	20.6	8.9	11.8	9.0	7.7	8.1	7.3	7.9
1994	9.3	24.1	33.1	19.5	8.2	11.5	8.2	7.2	6.4	7.5	10.6
1995	8.9	23.6	30.0	20.3	7.8	11.8	7.3	7.3	6.0	7.3	8.2
1996	7.7	21.6	27.7	18.4	6.8	10.3	6.3	6.4	5.1	6.5	6.8
1997	7.2	21.3	28.0	18.1	6.1	9.4	5.9	5.5	4.6	5.3	6.4
1998	6.4	18.6	23.7	16.3	5.5	8.3	5.4	4.8	4.8	4.5	5.0
1999	5.7	16.6	22.5	13.9	4.9	7.5	4.8	4.5	3.3	4.5	5.7
2000	6.6	17.7	24.0	15.0	5.8	8.1	5.9	5.2	4.3	5.6	4.5
2001	7.5	20.1	24.2	18.2	6.7	9.9	6.6	6.0	5.5	5.7	6.8
2002	7.7	20.0	24.6	17.7	7.0	10.2	7.0	6.0	6.3	5.7	3.9
2003	7.0	20.4	29.0	16.8	6.2	9.3	6.3	5.3	5.2	5.8	6.0
2004	6.0	18.4	23.6	16.0	5.3	8.6	5.3	4.5	4.4	4.4	4.9
2005	5.2	15.9	20.4	13.6	4.6	7.2	4.7	4.3	3.7	3.3	3.9
2006	5.6	18.1	22.5	16.0	5.0	7.8	4.9	4.3	4.3	4.5	4.9
2007	7.6	22.4	29.8	19.0	6.8	11.5	6.7	5.8	6.3	4.8	7.8
2008	12.1	30.2	36.3	27.8	11.2	16.2	11.4	10.2	10.1	10.0	8.0
2009	12.5	32.2	37.6	30.2	11.6	17.4	11.3	10.3	10.8	10.3	9.5
2010	11.5	31.1	38.3	28.5	10.6	15.7	10.4	9.2	9.9	9.7	8.8
2011	10.3	28.6	35.2	26.1	9.4	13.8	9.2	8.3	8.3	9.2	8.7
2012	9.1	27.5	33.7	25.0	8.2	12.8	8.2	7.3	6.8	7.4	7.7
2013	7.4	22.5	28.5	20.2	6.7	11.1	6.9	5.7	5.3	6.0	5.7
2014	6.6	19.3	22.6	18.0	6.0	10.0	6.3	5.0	4.7	5.4	5.8
2015	5.8	17.1	20.0	15.8	5.3	8.8	5.4	4.1	4.4	5.0	4.8
2016	5.1	15.0	19.0	13.2	4.7	7.6	5.1	3.8	3.7	3.9	4.9
2017	4.7	14.5	17.3	13.4	4.2	7.0	4.3	3.5	3.1	4.2	5.1
2018	4.7	14.5	17.3	13.4	4.2	7.0	4.3	3.5	3.5	4.2	5.1
2019	4.3	15.4	18.2	14.3	3.8	6.6	4.1	2.9	3.1	3.1	4.2

Table 1-27. Unemployment Rates of Civilian Workers, by Age, Sex, Race, and Hispanic Origin, 1948–2019
—Continued

(Percent of labor force.)

Race, Hispanic origin, sex, and year	16 years and over	16 to 19 years			20 years and over						
		Total	16 to 17 years	18 to 19 years	Total	20 to 24 years	25 to 34 years	35 to 44 years	45 to 54 years	55 to 64 years	65 years and over
HISPANIC											
Men											
1985	10.5	24.5	28.5	22.4	9.5	13.0	9.5	8.5	7.0	8.0	. . .
1986	8.7	22.2	28.2	19.3	7.8	10.2	7.6	6.9	7.1	6.7	. . .
1987	8.1	22.7	29.5	19.5	7.0	9.2	7.0	5.9	6.1	6.7	. . .
1988	7.6	20.2	27.6	16.8	6.6	9.7	5.9	5.7	6.0	6.6	. . .
1989	8.0	19.5	24.0	17.4	7.0	8.4	6.9	6.5	6.8	6.5	. . .
1990	10.3	23.5	33.6	19.2	9.3	11.6	9.3	8.5	7.9	8.1	. . .
1991	11.7	28.2	36.6	24.0	10.5	13.7	10.1	9.8	8.9	10.2	. . .
1992	10.6	25.9	34.5	21.9	9.5	12.6	9.0	8.8	8.8	8.5	. . .
1993	9.4	26.3	33.3	22.5	8.3	10.8	8.4	6.6	8.1	7.4	10.5
1994	8.8	25.3	34.8	20.2	7.7	10.6	7.5	6.7	5.9	7.9	12.9
1995	7.9	22.5	31.5	18.4	6.9	10.3	6.6	6.3	5.1	6.7	8.3
1996	7.0	20.8	26.5	17.9	6.1	9.8	5.1	5.4	4.8	6.8	7.2
1997	6.4	20.6	29.0	16.4	5.4	8.9	5.2	4.5	4.2	5.3	5.0
1998	5.6	17.8	23.4	15.3	4.7	7.8	4.1	3.8	4.5	4.6	5.0
1999	5.0	15.7	22.3	12.8	4.2	6.6	3.7	3.8	3.1	4.1	6.2
2000	5.9	17.1	25.8	13.4	5.2	8.1	4.6	4.5	3.8	6.3	4.8
2001	7.2	20.2	22.9	19.1	6.4	9.3	6.1	5.4	5.5	6.2	6.3
2002	7.2	21.9	25.9	20.1	6.4	9.6	6.3	5.3	6.0	6.0	3.6
2003	6.5	21.2	30.7	17.6	5.8	9.4	5.5	4.5	4.7	5.7	6.9
2004	5.4	19.3	23.4	17.5	4.7	8.2	4.3	3.9	4.0	4.0	4.8
2005	4.8	17.3	22.6	14.8	4.2	6.7	4.2	3.6	3.4	3.5	3.7
2006	5.3	19.7	23.4	18.0	4.6	7.4	4.5	3.8	4.4	3.9	5.5
2007	7.6	23.4	30.9	19.9	6.8	11.8	6.6	5.6	6.2	5.1	7.8
2008	12.5	33.8	41.1	31.1	11.6	16.6	11.6	10.5	10.5	11.2	7.8
2009	12.7	34.6	41.0	32.6	11.7	18.2	11.6	9.8	11.2	10.6	9.4
2010	11.2	33.3	40.7	31.0	10.3	15.3	9.9	8.7	9.8	10.4	9.5
2011	9.9	30.5	40.6	26.9	8.9	13.8	8.4	7.2	8.2	9.8	8.6
2012	8.8	28.2	34.5	25.8	7.9	13.4	7.5	6.5	6.5	8.2	8.5
2013	6.8	22.5	30.8	19.5	6.1	11.1	6.1	4.9	4.6	5.9	6.6
2014	6.3	20.3	23.8	18.9	5.7	10.6	5.7	4.0	4.6	5.5	5.7
2015	5.4	18.3	21.4	16.9	4.9	9.3	4.8	3.6	3.6	5.0	5.6
2016	4.7	15.9	17.3	15.3	4.2	7.5	4.6	3.4	3.1	3.4	5.1
2017	4.3	16.0	18.5	15.1	3.8	7.4	3.6	3.0	2.7	4.1	5.5
2018	4.3	16.0	18.5	15.1	3.8	7.4	3.6	3.0	2.7	4.1	5.5
2019	4.0	15.3	16.0	14.9	3.5	7.2	3.5	2.4	2.9	3.1	4.1
HISPANIC											
Women											
1985	10.8	25.1	27.6	23.6	9.6	12.9	9.8	8.2	8.9	6.2	. . .
1986	8.9	22.4	27.1	19.9	7.7	11.4	7.8	6.5	6.7	5.0	. . .
1987	8.3	21.0	24.5	18.9	7.1	10.7	7.2	6.2	5.9	4.6	. . .
1988	8.8	18.2	24.7	14.9	8.0	12.2	8.6	6.3	6.7	4.5	. . .
1989	8.4	19.4	25.4	16.2	7.5	10.4	8.0	6.7	6.0	4.3	. . .
1990	9.6	21.9	29.6	17.9	8.6	11.7	9.1	7.6	8.1	4.1	. . .
1991	11.4	26.4	34.5	22.4	10.2	12.4	11.0	9.7	8.5	6.2	. . .
1992	11.0	26.3	36.0	21.7	9.9	14.0	9.9	9.5	8.3	7.2	. . .
1993	10.7	22.2	29.7	18.1	9.8	13.5	10.1	9.2	8.0	7.1	3.6
1994	10.0	22.6	30.7	18.7	8.9	13.0	9.5	7.9	7.0	6.8	6.4
1995	10.2	25.1	28.2	23.3	9.2	14.1	8.5	8.7	7.2	8.1	8.0
1996	8.9	22.7	29.2	19.1	7.9	11.0	8.2	7.7	5.5	6.1	6.0
1997	8.2	22.1	26.4	20.2	7.1	10.1	7.2	6.9	5.1	5.4	8.8
1998	7.6	19.8	24.0	17.7	6.6	9.1	7.3	6.3	5.1	4.3	4.8
1999	6.8	18.0	22.7	15.6	5.9	9.0	6.4	5.4	3.6	5.0	4.8
2000	7.5	18.5	21.6	17.1	6.6	8.2	7.8	6.2	4.8	4.8	4.0
2001	8.0	19.9	25.8	17.0	7.2	10.8	7.4	6.7	5.5	5.0	7.5
2002	8.4	17.7	23.2	14.4	7.8	11.3	8.2	7.1	6.8	5.3	4.4
2003	7.6	19.3	27.0	15.5	7.0	9.1	7.6	6.4	5.8	5.8	4.6
2004	6.9	17.2	23.8	14.0	6.3	9.2	7.1	5.5	4.8	5.0	5.1
2005	5.9	14.1	18.1	11.9	5.3	8.1	5.5	5.5	4.2	3.1	4.2
2006	6.1	16.1	21.3	13.6	5.5	8.5	5.6	5.1	4.3	5.2	4.0
2007	7.7	21.1	28.1	18.0	6.9	11.1	6.8	6.0	6.4	4.4	7.7
2008	11.5	25.8	30.8	23.8	10.6	15.7	10.9	9.7	9.6	8.5	8.3
2009	12.3	29.1	34.2	27.0	11.4	16.2	10.9	11.1	10.4	9.9	9.6
2010	11.8	28.1	35.7	25.0	11.1	16.3	11.4	9.9	10.1	8.8	8.0
2011	10.9	26.4	29.4	25.1	10.1	13.9	10.4	9.7	8.5	8.5	8.8
2012	9.5	26.7	33.0	23.9	8.6	12.0	9.2	8.3	7.2	6.5	6.7
2013	8.2	22.5	26.1	21.0	7.5	11.1	7.9	6.9	6.2	6.1	4.5
2014	7.1	18.3	21.4	16.9	6.5	9.4	7.2	6.4	4.8	5.2	3.9
2015	6.3	15.8	18.6	14.5	5.8	8.3	6.1	4.8	5.5	4.9	3.7
2016	5.7	14.1	20.5	10.8	5.3	7.7	5.8	4.4	4.5	4.4	4.6
2017	5.1	12.9	16.2	11.6	4.7	6.6	5.3	4.2	3.6	4.4	4.5
2018	5.1	12.9	16.2	11.6	4.7	6.6	5.3	4.2	3.6	4.4	4.5
2019	4.7	15.6	21.1	13.5	4.1	6.0	4.8	3.6	3.2	3.2	4.3

. . . = Not available.

Table 1-28. Unemployed Persons and Unemployment Rates, by Selected Occupation, 2010–2019

(Thousands of people, percent of civilian labor force.)

Occupation	2010	2011	2012	2013	2014	2015	2016	2017	2018	2019
Total Unemployed Persons, 16 Years and Over[1]	14 825	13 747	12 506	11 460	9 617	8 296	7 751	6 982	6 314	6 001
Management, professional, and related	2 566	2 458	2 318	2 036	1 777	1 504	1 513	1 383	1 346	1 310
Management, business, and financial operations	1 117	1 067	935	831	704	602	629	558	523	499
Professional and related	1 449	1 392	1 383	1 205	1 073	902	884	825	822	811
Services	2 819	2 727	2 540	2 444	2 048	1 855	1 655	1 530	1 353	1 255
Sales and office	3 315	3 135	2 775	2 575	2 119	1 792	1 623	1 443	1 337	1 274
Sales and related	1 596	1 481	1 318	1 212	1 022	909	799	699	669	614
Office and administrative support	1 719	1 653	1 457	1 363	1 096	883	825	744	668	659
Natural resources, construction, and maintenance	2 504	2 000	1 668	1 423	1 171	1 058	953	903	780	703
Farming, fishing, and forestry	193	181	167	124	134	132	127	113	114	123
Construction and extraction	1 809	1 414	1 181	1 016	813	701	618	611	530	452
Installation, maintenance, and repair	503	406	320	284	224	225	207	179	136	129
Production, transportation, and material moving	2 365	2 099	1 845	1 690	1 385	1 182	1 160	1 014	881	847
Production	1 206	1 025	865	792	632	513	516	435	361	350
Transportation and material moving	1 159	1 073	980	898	754	668	644	579	520	497
Total Unemployment Rate, 16 Years and Over[1]	9.6	8.9	8.1	7.4	6.2	5.3	4.9	4.4	3.9	3.7
Management, professional, and related	4.7	4.5	4.1	3.6	3.1	2.5	2.5	2.2	2.1	2.0
Management, business, and financial operations	5.1	4.7	4.0	3.5	2.9	2.4	2.5	2.2	2.0	1.8
Professional and related	4.5	4.3	4.2	3.6	3.2	2.6	2.5	2.3	2.2	2.1
Services	10.3	9.9	9.1	8.6	7.3	6.7	5.8	5.4	4.8	4.4
Sales and office	9.0	8.7	7.7	7.2	6.0	5.1	4.6	4.1	3.8	3.7
Sales and related	9.4	8.8	7.9	7.3	6.1	5.5	4.8	4.2	4.1	3.8
Office and administrative support	8.7	8.5	7.6	7.1	5.8	4.7	4.5	4.0	3.6	3.6
Natural resources, construction, and maintenance	16.1	13.3	11.5	9.8	8.0	7.2	6.4	6.0	5.1	4.7
Farming, fishing, and forestry	16.3	15.3	14.4	11.4	11.6	10.9	10.4	8.7	9.2	9.6
Construction and extraction	20.1	16.6	14.4	12.5	9.6	8.4	7.2	7.1	6.0	5.2
Installation, maintenance, and repair	9.3	7.7	6.2	5.4	4.4	4.3	4.1	3.5	2.6	2.6
Production, transportation, and material moving	12.8	11.3	9.8	9.1	7.4	6.3	6.1	5.4	4.5	4.3
Production	13.1	11.2	9.3	8.7	7.0	5.7	5.7	4.9	4.0	3.9
Transportation and material moving	12.4	11.4	10.3	9.4	7.7	6.8	6.5	5.8	5.0	4.7

[1]Includes persons with no work experience and persons whose last job was in the armed forces.

Table 1-29. Unemployed Persons and Unemployment Rates, by Class of Worker and Industry, 2010–2019

(Thousands of people, percent.)

Class of worker and industry	2010	2011	2012	2013	2014	2015	2016	2017	2018	2019
Total Unemployed Persons,16 Years and Over	14 825	13 747	12 506	11 460	9 617	8 296	7 751	6 982	6 314	6 001
Nonagricultural private wage and salary workers	11 808	10 655	9 531	8 693	7 267	6 299	5 824	5 323	4 798	4 522
Mining, quarrying, and oil and gas extraction	73	52	59	64	52	84	67	31	27	24
Construction	1 801	1 383	1 129	935	762	624	558	559	494	435
Manufacturing	1 622	1 373	1 122	1 019	754	677	667	563	517	468
Durable goods	1 074	887	693	612	454	410	412	360	295	274
Nondurable goods	548	485	430	407	300	267	255	203	222	194
Wholesale trade and retail trade	1 963	1 834	1 663	1 463	1 260	1 135	1 009	942	881	803
Transportation and utilities	492	484	410	406	357	275	278	271	236	256
Information	303	222	218	175	153	108	123	120	99	89
Financial activities	626	582	466	424	373	247	266	240	215	216
Professional and business services	1 561	1 430	1 358	1 284	1 083	894	842	775	671	647
Education and health services	1 243	1 217	1 232	1 098	935	823	772	714	638	621
Leisure and hospitality	1 592	1 527	1 403	1 379	1 168	1 092	949	856	791	746
Other services	533	551	470	445	368	340	293	251	229	217
Agriculture and related private wage and salary workers ...	211	190	188	141	146	155	139	122	124	129
Government workers	969	1 013	923	851	678	573	582	527	505	496
Self-employed and unpaid family workers	617	605	547	527	440	389	383	319	285	263
Total Unemployment Rate,16 Years and Over[1]	9.6	8.9	8.1	7.4	6.2	5.3	4.9	4.4	3.9	3.7
Nonagricultural private wage and salary workers	9.9	9.0	7.9	7.2	5.9	5.1	4.6	4.2	3.7	3.5
Mining	9.4	6.1	6.0	5.8	4.7	8.6	8.0	4.1	3.4	3.2
Construction	20.6	16.4	13.9	11.3	8.9	7.3	6.3	6.0	5.1	4.5
Manufacturing	10.6	9.0	7.3	6.6	4.9	4.3	4.3	3.6	3.3	3.0
Durable goods	11.2	9.2	7.2	6.3	4.7	4.1	4.2	3.7	3.0	2.7
Nondurable goods	9.6	8.5	7.5	7.1	5.2	4.6	4.4	3.5	3.8	3.3
Wholesale trade and retail trade	9.5	8.9	8.1	7.3	6.1	5.5	5.0	4.6	4.3	4.1
Transportation and utilities	8.4	8.2	6.9	6.6	5.7	4.4	4.2	4.1	3.4	3.5
Information	9.7	7.3	7.6	6.2	5.2	3.9	4.6	4.5	3.7	3.5
Financial activities	6.9	6.4	5.1	4.5	4.0	2.6	2.7	2.4	2.2	2.1
Professional and business services	10.8	9.7	8.9	8.3	6.9	5.6	5.1	4.5	3.9	3.6
Education and health services	5.8	5.6	5.5	4.9	4.2	3.6	3.3	3.0	2.6	2.5
Leisure and hospitality	12.2	11.6	10.4	10.0	8.6	7.9	6.8	6.1	5.7	5.2
Other services	8.5	8.8	7.2	6.9	5.7	5.2	4.4	3.8	3.3	3.2
Agriculture and related private wage and salary workers	13.9	12.5	12.4	10.1	9.4	9.4	8.3	7.2	7.2	7.4
Government workers	4.4	4.7	4.3	4.0	3.2	2.7	2.7	2.5	2.3	2.3
Self-employed and unpaid family workers	5.9	6.0	5.4	5.3	4.4	3.9	3.8	3.2	2.8	2.7

Note: See notes and definitions for information on historical comparability.

[1]Includes persons with no work experience and persons whose last job was in the armed forces.

Table 1-30. Unemployed Persons, by Duration of Unemployment, 1948–2019

(Thousands of people, number of weeks.)

Year	Total unemployed	Less than 5 weeks Number	Percent	5 to 14 weeks Number	Percent	15 weeks and over Number	Percent	15 to 26 weeks Number	Percent	27 weeks and over Number	Percent	Average duration, in weeks	Median duration, in weeks
1948	2 276	1 300	57.1	669	29.4	309	13.6	193	8.5	116	5.1	8.6	...
1949	3 637	1 756	48.3	1 194	32.8	684	18.8	428	11.8	256	7.0	10.0	...
1950	3 288	1 450	44.1	1 055	32.1	782	23.8	425	12.9	357	10.9	12.1	...
1951	2 055	1 177	57.3	574	27.9	303	14.7	166	8.1	137	6.7	9.7	...
1952	1 883	1 135	60.3	516	27.4	232	12.3	148	7.9	84	4.5	8.4	...
1953	1 834	1 142	62.3	482	26.3	210	11.5	132	7.2	78	4.3	8.0	...
1954	3 532	1 605	45.4	1 116	31.6	812	23.0	495	14.0	317	9.0	11.8	...
1955	2 852	1 335	46.8	815	28.6	702	24.6	366	12.8	336	11.8	13.0	...
1956	2 750	1 412	51.3	805	29.3	533	19.4	301	10.9	232	8.4	11.3	...
1957	2 859	1 408	49.2	891	31.2	560	19.6	321	11.2	239	8.4	10.5	...
1958	4 602	1 753	38.1	1 396	30.3	1 452	31.6	785	17.1	667	14.5	13.9	...
1959	3 740	1 585	42.4	1 114	29.8	1 040	27.8	469	12.5	571	15.3	14.4	...
1960	3 852	1 719	44.6	1 176	30.5	957	24.8	503	13.1	454	11.8	12.8	...
1961	4 714	1 806	38.3	1 376	29.2	1 532	32.5	728	15.4	804	17.1	15.6	...
1962	3 911	1 663	42.5	1 134	29.0	1 119	28.6	534	13.7	585	15.0	14.7	...
1963	4 070	1 751	43.0	1 231	30.2	1 088	26.7	535	13.1	553	13.6	14.0	...
1964	3 786	1 697	44.8	1 117	29.5	973	25.7	491	13.0	482	12.7	13.3	...
1965	3 366	1 628	48.4	983	29.2	755	22.4	404	12.0	351	10.4	11.8	...
1966	2 875	1 573	54.7	779	27.1	526	18.3	287	10.0	239	8.3	10.4	...
1967	2 975	1 634	54.9	893	30.0	448	15.1	271	9.1	177	5.9	8.7	2.3
1968	2 817	1 594	56.6	810	28.8	412	14.6	256	9.1	156	5.5	8.4	4.5
1969	2 832	1 629	57.5	827	29.2	375	13.2	242	8.5	133	4.7	7.8	4.4
1970	4 093	2 139	52.3	1 290	31.5	663	16.2	428	10.4	235	5.8	8.6	4.9
1971	5 016	2 245	44.8	1 585	31.6	1 187	23.7	668	13.3	519	10.4	11.3	6.3
1972	4 882	2 242	45.9	1 472	30.2	1 167	23.9	601	12.3	566	11.6	12.0	6.2
1973	4 365	2 224	51.0	1 314	30.1	826	18.9	483	11.1	343	7.9	10.0	5.2
1974	5 156	2 604	50.5	1 597	31.0	955	18.5	574	11.1	381	7.4	9.8	5.2
1975	7 929	2 940	37.1	2 484	31.3	2 505	31.6	1 303	16.4	1 203	15.2	14.2	8.4
1976	7 406	2 844	38.4	2 196	29.6	2 366	32.0	1 018	13.8	1 348	18.2	15.8	8.2
1977	6 991	2 919	41.8	2 132	30.5	1 942	27.8	913	13.1	1 028	14.7	14.3	7.0
1978	6 202	2 865	46.2	1 923	31.0	1 414	22.8	766	12.3	648	10.5	11.9	5.9
1979	6 137	2 950	48.1	1 946	31.7	1 241	20.2	706	11.5	535	8.7	10.8	5.4
1980	7 637	3 295	43.2	2 470	32.3	1 871	24.5	1 052	13.8	820	10.7	11.9	6.5
1981	8 273	3 449	41.7	2 539	30.7	2 285	27.6	1 122	13.6	1 162	14.0	13.7	6.9
1982	10 678	3 883	36.4	3 311	31.0	3 485	32.6	1 708	16.0	1 776	16.6	15.6	8.7
1983	10 717	3 570	33.3	2 937	27.4	4 210	39.3	1 652	15.4	2 559	23.9	20.0	10.1
1984	8 539	3 350	39.2	2 451	28.7	2 737	32.1	1 104	12.9	1 634	19.1	18.2	7.9
1985	8 312	3 498	42.1	2 509	30.2	2 305	27.7	1 025	12.3	1 280	15.4	15.6	6.8
1986	8 237	3 448	41.9	2 557	31.0	2 232	27.1	1 045	12.7	1 187	14.4	15.0	6.9
1987	7 425	3 246	43.7	2 196	29.6	1 983	26.7	943	12.7	1 040	14.0	14.5	6.5
1988	6 701	3 084	46.0	2 007	30.0	1 610	24.0	801	12.0	809	12.1	13.5	5.9
1989	6 528	3 174	48.6	1 978	30.3	1 375	21.1	730	11.2	646	9.9	11.9	4.8
1990	7 047	3 265	46.3	2 257	32.0	1 525	21.6	822	11.7	703	10.0	12.0	5.3
1991	8 628	3 480	40.3	2 791	32.4	2 357	27.3	1 246	14.4	1 111	12.9	13.7	6.8
1992	9 613	3 376	35.1	2 830	29.4	3 408	35.4	1 453	15.1	1 954	20.3	17.7	8.7
1993	8 940	3 262	36.5	2 584	28.9	3 094	34.6	1 297	14.5	1 798	20.1	18.0	8.3
1994	7 996	2 728	34.1	2 408	30.1	2 860	35.8	1 237	15.5	1 623	20.3	18.8	9.2
1995	7 404	2 700	36.5	2 342	31.6	2 363	31.9	1 085	14.6	1 278	17.3	16.6	8.3
1996	7 236	2 633	36.4	2 287	31.6	2 316	32.0	1 053	14.6	1 262	17.4	16.7	8.3
1997	6 739	2 538	37.7	2 138	31.7	2 062	30.6	995	14.8	1 067	15.8	15.8	8.0
1998	6 210	2 622	42.2	1 950	31.4	1 637	26.4	763	12.3	875	14.1	14.5	6.7
1999	5 880	2 568	43.7	1 832	31.2	1 480	25.2	755	12.8	725	12.3	13.4	6.4
2000	5 692	2 558	44.9	1 815	31.9	1 318	23.2	669	11.8	649	11.4	12.6	5.9
2001	6 801	2 853	42.0	2 196	32.3	1 752	25.8	951	14.0	801	11.8	13.1	6.8
2002	8 378	2 893	34.5	2 580	30.8	2 904	34.7	1 369	16.3	1 535	18.3	16.6	9.1
2003	8 774	2 785	31.7	2 612	29.8	3 378	38.5	1 442	16.4	1 936	22.1	19.2	10.1
2004	8 149	2 696	33.1	2 382	29.2	3 072	37.7	1 293	15.9	1 779	21.8	19.6	9.8
2005	7 591	2 667	35.1	2 304	30.4	2 619	34.5	1 130	14.9	1 490	19.6	18.4	8.9
2006	7 001	2 614	37.3	2 121	30.3	2 266	32.4	1 031	14.7	1 235	17.6	16.8	8.3
2007	7 078	2 542	35.9	2 232	31.5	2 303	32.5	1 061	15.0	1 243	17.6	16.8	8.5
2008	8 924	2 932	32.8	2 804	31.4	3 188	35.7	1 427	16.0	1 761	19.7	17.9	9.4
2009	14 265	3 165	22.2	3 828	26.8	7 272	51.0	2 775	19.5	4 496	31.5	24.4	15.1
2010	14 825	2 771	18.7	3 267	22.0	8 786	59.3	2 371	16.0	6 415	43.3	33.0	21.4
2011	13 747	2 677	19.5	2 993	21.8	8 077	58.8	2 061	15.0	6 016	43.8	39.3	21.4
2012	12 506	2 644	21.1	2 866	22.9	6 996	55.9	1 859	14.9	5 136	41.1	39.4	19.3
2013	11 460	2 584	22.5	2 759	24.1	6 117	53.4	1 807	15.8	4 310	37.6	36.5	17.0
2014	9 617	2 471	25.7	2 432	25.3	4 714	49.0	1 497	15.6	3 218	33.5	33.7	14.0
2015	8 296	2 399	28.9	2 302	27.7	3 595	43.3	1 267	15.3	2 328	28.1	29.2	11.6
2016	7 751	2 362	30.5	2 226	28.7	3 163	40.8	1 158	14.9	2 005	25.9	27.5	10.6
2017	6 982	2 270	32.5	2 008	28.8	2 704	38.7	1 017	14.6	1 687	24.2	25.0	10.0
2018	6 314	2 170	34.4	1 876	29.7	2 268	35.9	917	14.5	1 350	21.4	22.7	9.3
2019	6 001	2 086	34.8	1 789	29.8	2 126	35.4	860	14.3	1 266	21.1	21.6	9.1

. . . = Not available.

Table 1-31. Long-Term Unemployment, by Industry and Selected Occupation, 2005–2019

(Thousands of people.)

Characteristic	2005	2006	2007	2008	2009	2010	2011	2012	2013	2014	2015	2016	2017	2018	2019
UNEMPLOYED 15 WEEKS AND OVER															
Total	2 619	2 266	2 303	3 188	7 272	8 786	8 077	6 996	6 117	4 714	3 595	3 163	2 704	2 268	2 126
Wage and Salary Workers, by Industry															
Agriculture and related	29	30	28	42	96	100	99	92	71	71	62	53	37	47	45
Mining [1]	8	5	6	7	44	46	31	25	27	23	28	28	17	12	7
Construction	216	177	215	339	907	1 083	822	643	476	340	264	195	206	178	131
Manufacturing	326	257	259	385	1 059	1 122	922	702	611	410	311	304	229	199	171
Durable goods	199	140	162	246	702	773	611	443	367	246	189	180	148	112	99
Nondurable goods	127	116	97	139	357	350	311	259	244	165	122	124	81	87	73
Wholesale and retail trade	415	337	334	440	962	1 215	1 118	971	834	635	522	432	383	344	299
Transportation and utilities	91	87	95	142	290	343	343	262	249	212	135	133	117	99	108
Information	76	55	49	66	170	204	146	142	109	84	53	63	56	46	40
Financial activities	91	103	100	168	357	446	411	312	261	220	130	139	115	89	93
Professional and business services	299	266	247	346	810	985	878	793	739	541	429	356	315	249	260
Education and health services	271	263	253	320	691	898	910	907	772	588	443	388	351	305	259
Leisure and hospitality	277	259	274	356	755	898	830	740	682	562	441	358	309	248	248
Other services	117	97	80	132	245	310	336	261	236	179	295	122	109	80	86
Public administration	62	34	51	55	107	164	185	144	141	101	74	67	68	54	62
Experienced Workers, by Occupation															
Management, professional, and related	436	373	368	569	1 331	1 600	1 482	1 362	1 116	884	662	634	566	509	487
Services	511	464	482	595	1 243	1 557	1 500	1 356	1 261	984	788	649	582	447	487
Sales and office	641	561	560	741	1 675	2 048	1 949	1 622	1 446	1 099	809	679	591	505	476
Natural resources, construction, and maintenance	341	294	299	463	1 224	1 445	1 150	914	715	534	436	356	325	277	221
Production, transportation, and material moving	461	380	384	570	1 302	1 498	1 290	1 041	944	683	508	485	373	310	292
UNEMPLOYED 27 WEEKS AND OVER															
Total	1 490	1 235	1 243	1 761	4 496	6 415	6 016	5 136	4 310	3 218	2 328	2 005	1 687	1 350	1 266
Wage and Salary Workers, by Industry															
Agriculture and related	16	13	14	17	51	57	58	55	39	40	33	27	17	23	22
Mining [1]	4	3	3	4	23	37	22	17	15	13	15	18	11	5	4
Construction	108	92	107	168	530	773	617	464	324	218	161	117	109	94	76
Manufacturing	195	140	152	230	657	888	725	533	439	291	202	196	139	121	99
Durable goods	124	75	93	150	428	619	486	341	273	172	123	114	86	69	60
Nondurable goods	71	64	58	80	229	269	239	192	166	118	79	82	54	52	38
Wholesale and retail trade	230	183	171	237	607	904	833	731	604	427	336	278	240	200	178
Transportation and utilities	50	42	58	77	180	263	265	198	180	141	90	88	78	64	69
Information	41	30	29	38	115	159	116	107	77	60	40	47	36	32	25
Financial activities	56	56	50	97	232	332	315	245	185	156	130	86	77	54	58
Professional and business services	172	144	130	184	510	722	641	580	518	369	429	221	204	153	153
Education and health services	156	144	132	182	432	644	671	668	561	417	443	234	216	182	152
Leisure and hospitality	148	135	142	196	445	624	596	519	472	379	441	212	178	145	152
Other services	74	51	43	73	161	223	249	192	161	126	156	79	77	48	53
Public administration	38	21	29	29	66	121	140	112	101	74	74	45	43	33	36
Experienced Workers, by Occupation															
Management, professional, and related	269	206	207	569	840	6 415	1 121	1 022	801	625	442	414	370	312	306
Services	284	249	251	595	750	1 094	1 086	971	896	673	513	398	360	257	245
Sales and office	354	299	285	741	1 067	1 513	1 486	1 211	1 042	760	521	429	375	315	283
Natural resources, construction, and maintenance	186	158	157	463	724	1 042	855	676	487	346	265	218	194	151	121
Production, transportation, and material moving	261	206	219	570	814	1 142	973	773	656	461	331	306	221	185	171

[1] Starting in 2009, mining includes quarrying, and oil and gas extraction.

Table 1-32. Unemployed Persons and Unemployment Rates, by Reason for Unemployment, Sex, and Age, 1985–2019

(Thousands of people, percent.)

Sex, age, and year	Number of unemployed					Unemployed as a percent of the total civilian labor force			
	Total	Job losers and persons who completed temporary jobs	Job leavers	Entrants		Job losers and persons who completed temporary jobs	Job leavers	Entrants	
				Reentrants	New entrants			Reentrants	New entrants
Both Sexes, 16 Years and Over									
1985	8 312	4 139	877	2 256	1 039	3.6	0.8	2.0	0.9
1986	8 237	4 033	1 015	2 160	1 029	3.4	0.9	1.8	0.9
1987	7 425	3 566	965	1 974	920	3.0	0.8	1.6	0.8
1988	6 701	3 092	983	1 809	816	2.5	0.8	1.5	0.7
1989	6 528	2 983	1 024	1 843	677	2.4	0.8	1.5	0.5
1990	7 047	3 387	1 041	1 930	688	2.7	0.8	1.5	0.5
1991	8 628	4 694	1 004	2 139	792	3.7	0.8	1.7	0.6
1992	9 613	5 389	1 002	2 285	937	4.2	0.8	1.8	0.7
1993	8 940	4 848	976	2 198	919	3.8	0.8	1.7	0.7
1994	7 996	3 815	791	2 786	604	2.9	0.6	2.1	0.5
1995	7 404	3 476	824	2 525	579	2.6	0.6	1.9	0.4
1996	7 236	3 370	774	2 512	580	2.5	0.6	1.9	0.4
1997	6 739	3 037	795	2 338	569	2.2	0.6	1.7	0.4
1998	6 210	2 822	734	2 132	520	2.1	0.5	1.5	0.4
1999	5 880	2 622	783	2 005	469	1.9	0.6	1.4	0.3
2000	5 692	2 517	780	1 961	434	1.8	0.5	1.4	0.3
2001	6 801	3 476	835	2 031	459	2.4	0.6	1.4	0.3
2002	8 378	4 607	866	2 368	536	3.2	0.6	1.6	0.4
2003	8 774	4 838	818	2 477	641	3.3	0.6	1.7	0.4
2004	8 149	4 197	858	2 408	686	2.8	0.6	1.6	0.5
2005	7 591	3 667	872	2 386	666	2.5	0.6	1.6	0.4
2006	7 001	3 321	827	2 237	616	2.2	0.5	1.5	0.4
2007	7 078	3 515	793	2 142	627	2.3	0.5	1.4	0.4
2008	8 924	4 789	896	2 472	766	3.1	0.6	1.6	0.5
2009	14 265	9 160	882	3 187	1 035	5.9	0.6	2.1	0.7
2010	14 825	9 250	889	3 466	1 220	6.0	0.6	2.3	0.8
2011	13 747	8 106	956	3 401	1 284	5.3	0.6	2.2	0.8
2012	12 506	6 877	967	3 345	1 316	4.4	0.6	2.2	0.8
2013	11 460	6 073	932	3 207	1 247	3.9	0.6	2.1	0.8
2014	9 617	4 878	824	2 829	1 086	3.1	0.5	1.8	0.7
2015	8 296	4 063	819	2 535	879	2.6	0.5	1.6	0.6
2016	7 751	3 740	858	2 330	823	2.3	0.5	1.5	0.5
2017	6 982	3 434	778	2 079	690	2.1	0.5	1.3	0.4
2018	6 314	2 990	794	1 928	602	1.8	0.5	1.2	0.4
2019	6 001	2 786	814	1 810	591	1.7	0.5	1.1	0.4
Both Sexes, 16 to 19 Years									
1985	1 468	275	113	390	689	3.5	1.4	4.9	8.7
1986	1 454	240	145	374	695	3.0	1.8	4.7	8.8
1987	1 347	210	146	375	617	2.7	1.8	4.7	7.7
1988	1 226	207	159	310	550	2.6	2.0	3.9	6.8
1989	1 194	198	200	345	452	2.5	2.5	4.3	5.7
1990	1 212	233	181	338	460	3.0	2.3	4.3	5.9
1991	1 359	289	180	365	524	4.0	2.5	5.0	7.2
1992	1 427	259	149	377	643	3.6	2.1	5.3	9.1
1993	1 365	233	151	353	628	3.3	2.1	4.9	8.8
1994	1 320	185	84	634	416	2.5	1.1	8.5	5.6
1995	1 346	214	102	615	415	2.8	1.3	7.9	5.3
1996	1 306	182	91	625	409	2.3	1.2	8.0	5.2
1997	1 271	174	104	606	388	2.2	1.3	7.6	4.9
1998	1 205	181	86	577	361	2.2	1.0	7.0	4.4
1999	1 162	173	114	547	328	2.1	1.4	6.6	3.9
2000	1 081	157	109	516	299	1.9	1.3	6.2	3.6
2001	1 162	185	98	568	311	2.3	1.2	7.2	3.9
2002	1 253	197	91	597	368	2.6	1.2	7.9	4.9
2003	1 251	188	85	554	424	2.6	1.2	7.7	5.9
2004	1 208	165	76	510	456	2.3	1.1	7.2	6.4
2005	1 186	155	76	489	466	2.2	1.1	6.8	6.5
2006	1 119	145	78	461	435	2.0	1.1	6.3	6.0
2007	1 101	176	71	435	419	2.5	1.0	6.2	6.0
2008	1 285	203	80	490	511	3.0	1.2	7.1	7.5
2009	1 552	271	56	548	677	4.2	0.9	8.6	10.6
2010	1 528	220	42	487	778	3.7	0.7	8.2	13.2
2011	1 400	181	52	429	739	3.2	0.9	7.5	12.9
2012	1 397	176	43	419	758	3.0	0.7	7.2	13.0
2013	1 327	170	53	386	718	2.9	0.9	6.7	12.4
2014	1 106	140	44	327	595	2.5	0.8	5.8	10.5
2015	966	132	51	301	481	2.6	0.5	1.6	0.6
2016	925	113	53	307	453	1.9	0.9	5.2	7.7
2017	827	116	44	267	399	2.0	0.7	4.5	6.8
2018	759	111	52	256	340	1.9	0.9	4.3	5.8
2019	746	106	52	265	323	1.8	0.9	4.5	5.5

Note: See notes and definitions for information on historical comparability.

Table 1-32. Unemployed Persons and Unemployment Rates, by Reason for Unemployment, Sex, and Age, 1985–2019—*Continued*

(Thousands of people, percent.)

| Sex, age, and year | Number of unemployed | | | | | Unemployed as a percent of the total civilian labor force | | | |
| | Total | Job losers and persons who completed temporary jobs | Job leavers | Entrants | | Job losers and persons who completed temporary jobs | Job leavers | Entrants | |
				Reentrants	New entrants			Reentrants	New entrants
Men, 20 Years and Over									
1985	3 715	2 568	352	671	124	4.3	0.6	1.1	0.2
1986	3 751	2 568	444	611	128	4.1	0.7	1.0	0.2
1987	3 369	2 289	413	558	108	3.7	0.7	0.9	0.2
1988	2 987	1 939	416	534	98	3.1	0.7	0.9	0.2
1989	2 867	1 843	394	541	88	2.9	0.6	0.8	0.1
1990	3 239	2 100	431	626	82	3.2	0.7	1.0	0.1
1991	4 195	2 982	411	698	105	4.6	0.6	1.1	0.2
1992	4 717	3 420	421	765	111	5.2	0.6	1.2	0.2
1993	4 287	2 996	429	747	114	4.5	0.6	1.1	0.2
1994	3 627	2 296	367	898	65	3.4	0.5	1.3	0.1
1995	3 239	2 051	356	775	57	3.0	0.5	1.2	0.1
1996	3 146	2 043	322	731	51	3.0	0.5	1.1	0.1
1997	2 882	1 795	358	675	55	2.6	0.5	1.0	0.1
1998	2 580	1 588	318	611	63	2.3	0.5	0.9	0.1
1999	2 433	1 459	336	592	46	2.1	0.5	0.8	0.1
2000	2 376	1 416	328	577	55	2.0	0.5	0.8	0.1
2001	3 040	1 999	372	612	56	2.7	0.5	0.8	0.1
2002	3 896	2 702	386	743	65	3.7	0.5	1.0	0.1
2003	4 209	2 899	376	846	88	3.9	0.5	1.1	0.1
2004	3 791	2 503	398	791	99	3.3	0.5	1.0	0.1
2005	4 059	2 188	445	1 067	359	2.7	0.5	1.0	0.1
2006	3 131	1 927	368	757	78	2.5	0.5	1.0	0.1
2007	3 259	2 064	371	723	101	2.6	0.5	0.9	0.1
2008	4 297	2 918	410	969	856	3.7	0.5	1.1	0.1
2009	7 555	5 796	407	1 190	162	7.3	0.5	1.5	0.2
2010	7 763	5 773	433	1 346	211	7.3	0.5	1.7	0.3
2011	6 898	4 856	464	1 312	267	6.1	0.6	1.7	0.3
2012	5 984	3 996	464	1 250	274	5.0	0.6	1.6	0.3
2013	5 568	3 582	440	1 285	261	4.5	0.6	1.6	0.3
2014	4 585	2 839	392	1 109	245	3.5	0.5	1.4	0.3
2015	3 959	2 361	379	1 014	206	4.9	0.5	1.3	0.3
2016	3 675	2 165	388	936	185	2.6	0.5	1.1	0.2
2017	3 287	1 970	359	815	142	2.4	0.4	1.0	0.2
2018	2 976	1 706	381	759	130	2.1	0.5	0.9	0.2
2019	2 819	1 548	418	708	144	1.8	0.5	0.8	0.2
Women, 20 Years and Over									
1985	3 129	1 296	412	1 195	227	2.7	0.9	2.5	0.5
1986	3 032	1 225	426	1 175	206	2.5	0.9	2.4	0.4
1987	2 709	1 067	406	1 041	194	2.2	0.8	2.1	0.4
1988	2 487	946	408	965	168	1.9	0.8	1.9	0.3
1989	2 467	942	430	958	137	1.8	0.8	1.8	0.3
1990	2 596	1 054	429	966	146	2.0	0.8	1.8	0.3
1991	3 074	1 423	413	1 075	163	2.6	0.8	2.0	0.3
1992	3 469	1 710	433	1 142	183	3.1	0.8	2.1	0.3
1993	3 288	1 619	395	1 098	176	2.9	0.7	2.0	0.3
1994	3 049	1 334	339	1 253	122	2.4	0.6	2.2	0.2
1995	2 819	1 211	366	1 135	107	2.1	0.6	2.0	0.2
1996	2 783	1 145	361	1 156	120	2.0	0.6	2.0	0.2
1997	2 585	1 069	333	1 057	126	1.8	0.6	1.8	0.2
1998	2 424	1 053	330	944	97	1.8	0.6	1.6	0.2
1999	2 285	990	333	866	96	1.6	0.5	1.4	0.2
2000	2 235	943	343	868	80	1.5	0.6	1.4	0.1
2001	2 599	1 291	365	850	92	2.0	0.6	1.3	0.1
2002	3 228	1 708	389	1 028	102	2.7	0.6	1.6	0.2
2003	3 314	1 751	357	1 076	130	2.7	0.6	1.7	0.2
2004	3 150	1 529	384	1 107	131	2.4	0.6	1.7	0.2
2005	3 013	1 417	391	1 103	101	2.2	0.6	1.7	0.2
2006	2 751	1 249	380	1 019	103	1.9	0.6	1.5	0.2
2007	2 718	1 276	351	984	107	1.9	0.5	1.7	0.4
2008	3 342	1 668	406	1 126	143	2.4	0.6	1.6	0.2
2009	5 157	3 093	419	1 449	196	4.5	0.6	2.1	0.3
2010	5 534	3 257	413	1 633	231	4.7	0.6	2.4	0.3
2011	5 450	3 070	441	1 661	279	4.5	0.6	2.4	0.4
2012	5 125	2 705	460	1 676	284	3.9	0.7	2.4	0.4
2013	4 565	2 322	439	1 536	269	3.3	0.6	2.2	0.4
2014	3 926	1 899	388	1 393	245	2.7	0.6	2.0	0.3
2015	3 371	1 570	389	1 220	192	2.2	0.6	1.7	0.3
2016	3 151	1 461	417	1 087	186	2.0	0.6	1.5	0.3
2017	2 868	1 348	375	996	149	1.9	0.5	1.5	0.4
2018	2 578	1 173	361	912	132	1.6	0.5	1.2	0.2
2019	2 435	1 132	344	836	123	1.5	0.5	1.1	0.2

Note: See notes and definitions for information on historical comparability.

Table 1-33. Percent of the Population with Work Experience During the Year, by Age and Sex, 1995–2019

(Percent.)

Sex and year	Total	16 to 17 years	18 to 19 years	20 to 24 years	25 to 34 years	35 to 44 years	45 to 54 years	55 to 59 years	60 to 64 years	65 to 69 years	70 years and over
Both Sexes											
1995	69.6	44.4	71.2	82.0	85.6	85.9	83.4	72.2	53.3	28.0	10.2
1996	69.9	43.3	70.5	83.1	86.1	85.7	84.3	73.3	54.3	27.8	10.4
1997	70.1	43.6	70.5	83.0	87.1	85.9	84.4	73.8	53.8	28.5	10.0
1998	70.1	42.1	69.9	82.9	86.7	86.3	84.2	73.7	54.5	29.2	10.6
1999	70.7	43.7	71.2	82.7	87.3	86.9	85.0	72.3	55.8	30.5	11.6
2000	70.5	42.2	69.6	82.6	87.1	87.0	84.6	72.9	55.1	30.8	11.4
2001	69.4	37.7	66.7	80.8	86.1	85.8	83.7	73.5	56.7	30.6	10.5
2002	68.5	34.5	62.8	78.5	84.4	85.0	83.7	74.7	56.8	33.1	10.4
2003	67.8	32.0	61.7	77.5	83.7	84.0	82.9	73.9	56.5	33.2	11.4
2004	67.7	32.6	59.8	76.9	83.3	84.2	82.6	73.9	57.0	32.7	12.2
2005	67.8	31.1	60.1	77.3	83.7	84.1	82.8	74.4	58.2	32.0	12.1
2006	67.9	30.9	58.3	76.9	84.4	84.3	82.8	74.5	58.2	33.6	12.6
2007	67.8	28.5	57.3	76.6	84.2	84.4	82.4	75.6	59.7	35.2	13.0
2008	67.1	24.6	55.3	76.0	84.1	83.9	81.8	74.6	60.3	34.9	13.5
2009	65.0	21.9	48.7	71.0	81.6	82.0	80.5	73.8	59.3	35.3	12.8
2010	63.8	17.8	43.9	69.1	80.2	81.3	79.2	73.8	58.4	37.1	13.0
2011	63.4	17.0	44.8	69.8	79.7	81.3	79.0	72.0	59.5	36.5	13.3
2012	63.9	19.9	47.1	70.1	80.6	81.3	79.4	74.5	59.2	37.5	14.0
2013	63.6	19.9	46.3	71.0	80.2	81.0	79.9	72.4	59.3	36.8	14.7
2014	63.7	20.4	46.7	70.0	80.5	82.0	79.5	73.0	60.4	37.7	14.7
2015	64.3	22.4	48.6	71.3	81.7	82.3	80.1	74.6	60.5	38.2	14.9
2016	64.4	23.6	49.0	72.7	82.8	82.6	80.3	73.4	60.9	38.0	15.6
2017	64.3	23.5	49.1	73.1	82.5	83.0	80.8	73.4	62.2	38.0	15.5
2018	64.5	22.4	49.4	73.2	83.3	82.9	81.8	74.2	61.9	39.2	15.9
2019	65.0	25.4	49.9	73.1	84.0	84.2	83.6	75.5	63.1	39.4	15.6
Men											
1995	77.0	43.7	73.6	86.4	92.6	92.2	89.7	81.5	62.1	34.5	14.9
1996	77.2	44.1	71.8	86.7	93.4	92.1	90.4	81.8	62.5	33.6	15.2
1997	77.1	43.4	70.3	86.6	94.1	92.3	90.7	81.4	62.9	33.8	13.9
1998	76.9	40.4	71.6	86.4	93.5	92.7	90.1	81.7	63.5	35.5	14.7
1999	77.3	44.7	72.3	85.5	93.9	93.2	89.9	79.2	65.1	37.4	16.5
2000	77.1	42.1	70.2	85.1	93.4	93.6	89.8	80.6	64.4	38.4	16.0
2001	76.3	37.4	67.7	84.8	93.2	92.2	89.1	80.4	64.3	37.8	14.5
2002	75.2	34.7	62.8	82.1	91.6	91.8	88.9	80.7	64.3	39.3	14.6
2003	74.3	32.8	61.7	80.2	90.8	90.9	87.7	80.9	63.1	37.3	15.8
2004	74.2	32.1	58.9	80.2	91.0	91.1	87.9	80.1	64.5	37.1	16.7
2005	74.6	31.1	60.7	80.8	91.3	91.6	88.2	80.1	64.3	37.6	17.0
2006	74.5	30.9	57.9	80.1	91.9	91.8	88.0	80.6	64.1	38.3	17.3
2007	74.3	28.5	59.0	80.5	90.5	91.5	88.2	80.3	66.2	39.3	17.9
2008	73.2	24.4	55.1	78.7	90.7	91.1	86.4	79.3	66.0	40.3	17.9
2009	70.8	22.2	48.0	73.3	87.7	89.1	85.0	78.3	64.8	39.8	17.2
2010	69.4	16.9	43.2	71.3	86.0	88.0	84.1	78.9	62.8	43.4	17.5
2011	69.0	16.1	43.2	71.6	86.2	88.1	84.3	76.7	64.0	42.6	18.2
2012	69.7	19.1	45.9	72.2	86.9	88.9	84.8	79.9	64.2	43.2	18.5
2013	69.3	18.4	46.6	72.5	86.5	88.0	85.8	77.0	64.6	42.0	19.4
2014	69.4	20.5	44.9	70.4	87.2	89.0	85.1	78.1	66.5	42.2	19.4
2015	70.2	22.2	48.2	72.9	87.8	89.4	86.2	79.4	66.1	43.5	19.8
2016	70.1	22.2	48.1	74.1	88.2	90.0	86.1	78.1	67.5	44.2	20.0
2017	70.2	23.2	47.8	75.3	88.3	90.4	86.1	79.5	67.8	43.6	20.5
2018	69.9	21.8	46.3	73.6	88.8	90.1	87.3	80.1	68.2	43.2	20.0
2019	70.2	24.2	51.3	73.7	88.3	90.7	89.1	81.1	68.1	45.9	19.7
Women											
1995	62.8	45.2	68.7	77.7	78.8	79.8	77.6	63.2	45.6	22.4	7.1
1996	63.2	42.5	69.2	79.5	78.9	79.5	78.4	65.4	46.9	23.0	7.1
1997	63.6	43.9	70.7	79.5	80.1	79.6	78.4	66.7	45.6	24.0	7.3
1998	63.7	44.1	68.2	79.4	80.1	80.0	78.6	66.3	46.2	23.8	7.8
1999	64.5	42.6	70.1	79.9	80.9	80.7	80.3	66.2	47.3	24.4	8.2
2000	64.3	42.3	69.0	80.2	80.9	80.5	79.5	65.7	47.0	23.9	8.2
2001	63.1	38.1	65.7	76.9	79.2	79.5	78.6	67.1	49.8	24.2	7.9
2002	62.3	34.3	62.8	74.9	77.2	78.4	78.7	69.1	50.0	27.8	7.4
2003	61.7	31.2	61.6	74.6	76.6	77.2	78.4	67.3	50.7	29.6	8.3
2004	61.5	33.1	60.7	73.7	75.6	77.4	77.5	68.2	50.3	28.7	9.0
2005	61.4	31.2	59.6	73.7	76.1	76.8	77.6	68.9	52.7	27.1	8.7
2006	61.6	30.9	58.7	73.7	76.9	76.9	77.9	68.8	53.0	29.5	9.3
2007	61.6	28.5	55.6	72.6	77.8	77.4	76.9	71.2	53.7	31.5	9.5
2008	61.3	24.8	55.4	73.2	77.3	76.7	77.3	70.1	55.0	30.1	10.3
2009	59.6	21.6	49.5	68.6	75.4	75.0	76.1	69.5	54.4	31.1	9.7
2010	58.5	18.7	44.5	66.9	74.3	74.7	74.4	69.1	54.2	31.6	9.6
2011	58.1	18.0	46.5	68.0	73.4	74.7	73.8	67.7	55.4	31.0	9.6
2012	58.4	20.7	48.3	68.1	74.3	73.8	74.3	69.4	54.8	32.2	10.6
2013	58.2	21.4	46.1	69.5	74.0	74.2	74.3	68.0	54.4	32.1	11.2
2014	58.3	20.2	48.5	69.6	73.8	75.1	74.1	68.3	54.7	33.7	11.2
2015	58.8	22.6	49.1	69.7	75.7	75.4	74.3	70.1	55.4	33.5	11.3
2016	59.0	25.0	50.0	71.3	77.4	75.5	74.8	69.0	55.0	32.4	12.1
2017	58.8	23.9	50.5	71.0	76.6	75.7	75.7	67.5	57.2	33.0	11.6
2018	59.4	22.9	52.4	72.7	77.6	75.9	76.5	68.9	56.2	35.6	12.6
2019	60.1	26.6	48.5	72.5	79.7	77.8	78.3	70.3	58.5	33.6	12.3

Note: See notes and definitions for information on historical comparability.

Table 1-34. Persons with Work Experience During the Year, by Industry and Class of Worker of Job Held the Longest, 2010–2019

(Thousands of people.)

Industry and class of worker	2010	2011	2012	2013	2014	2015	2016	2017	2018	2019
TOTAL	153 141	154 330	157 050	157 878	159 881	163 169	164 435	166 045	167 261	169 522
Agriculture	2 383	2 470	2 176	2 497	2 748	2 890	2 591	2 715	2 344	2 688
Wage and salary workers	1 578	1 679	1 504	1 769	1 918	2 041	1 823	1 933	1 760	2 063
Self-employed workers	788	750	649	706	794	831	735	750	573	593
Unpaid family workers	17	42	22	22	36	19	33	32	11	32
Nonagricultural Industries	150 759	151 859	154 874	155 381	157 133	160 279	161 844	163 330	164 917	166 834
Wage and salary workers	141 686	142 962	145 787	146 688	148 247	151 029	152 914	154 158	156 139	157 853
Mining	771	890	1 146	1 173	1 114	1 000	814	777	817	876
Construction	8 633	8 607	8 445	8 589	9 015	9 173	9 467	9 844	9 921	10 225
Manufacturing	14 865	15 139	15 139	15 688	15 445	15 748	15 828	16 257	16 114	15 901
Durable goods	9 288	9 586	9 585	9 916	9 981	9 897	9 945	10 064	10 038	10 052
Nondurable goods	5 577	5 552	5 554	5 773	5 465	5 851	5 883	6 193	6 077	5 849
Wholesale and retail trade	20 854	20 685	20 485	21 353	21 352	21 339	21 557	20 896	20 683	20 219
Wholesale trade	3 921	3 601	3 606	3 738	3 840	3 761	3 566	3 810	3 429	3 489
Retail trade	16 933	17 084	16 879	17 615	17 512	17 578	17 991	17 086	17 254	16 729
Transportation and utilities	6 993	7 173	7 573	7 493	7 504	8 128	8 086	8 289	8 726	8 974
Transportation and warehousing	5 701	5 944	6 336	6 318	6 215	6 737	6 638	6 782	7 350	7 542
Utilities	1 292	1 229	1 237	1 175	1 290	1 392	1 448	1 507	1 377	1 432
Information	3 380	3 137	3 144	3 384	3 010	3 005	2 977	2 946	2 849	2 910
Financial activities	9 239	9 443	9 889	9 987	9 835	9 993	10 160	10 330	10 239	10 602
Finance and insurance	6 726	6 909	7 293	7 231	7 073	7 101	7 351	7 490	7 231	7 716
Real estate and rental and leasing	2 512	2 534	2 595	2 756	2 762	2 892	2 809	2 840	3 007	2 886
Professional and business services	15 094	15 339	15 924	15 923	16 375	16 949	17 346	17 309	18 482	18 509
Professional, scientific, and technical services	8 841	9 054	9 370	9 401	10 077	10 485	10 802	11 076	11 727	12 257
Management, administration, and waste management services	6 253	6 285	6 553	6 522	6 297	6 464	6 544	6 233	6 755	6 252
Education and health services	33 596	33 424	34 156	33 943	34 724	35 682	35 960	36 321	37 126	37 641
Education services	14 157	13 917	14 256	14 394	14 770	14 899	14 836	15 633	15 499	15 743
Health care and social assistance services	19 439	19 507	19 900	19 549	19 953	20 783	21 124	20 688	21 627	21 898
Leisure and hospitality	13 718	14 293	15 103	14 688	14 998	15 291	15 573	15 402	15 673	16 076
Arts, entertainment, and recreation	2 993	3 116	3 332	3 232	3 022	3 120	3 232	3 471	3 581	3 775
Accommodation and food services	10 725	11 177	11 771	11 457	11 976	12 171	12 340	11 931	12 092	12 302
Other services and private household	6 111	6 717	6 643	6 571	6 818	6 558	6 931	7 284	7 026	7 170
Private households	816	773	833	942	929	769	857	819	884	937
Public administration	7 597	7 270	7 333	7 094	7 245	7 398	7 565	7 723	7 781	7 937
Self-employed workers	8 962	8 778	8 955	8 605	8 786	9 122	8 836	9 079	8 680	8 869
Unpaid family workers	111	120	132	87	101	129	94	92	98	112

Note: See notes and definitions for information on historical comparability.

Table 1-35. Number of Persons with Work Experience During the Year, by Extent of Employment and Sex, 1995–2019

(Thousands of people.)

Sex and year	Total	Full-time workers				Part-time workers			
		Total	50 to 52 weeks	27 to 49 weeks	1 to 26 weeks	Total	50 to 52 weeks	27 to 49 weeks	1 to 26 weeks
Both Sexes									
1995	139 724	110 063	88 173	12 970	8 920	29 661	12 725	6 831	10 105
1996	142 201	112 313	90 252	12 997	9 064	29 888	13 382	6 643	9 863
1997	143 968	113 879	92 631	12 508	8 740	30 089	13 810	6 565	9 714
1998	145 566	116 412	95 772	12 156	8 484	29 155	13 538	6 480	9 714
1999	148 295	119 096	97 941	12 294	8 861	29 199	13 680	6 317	9 202
2000	149 361	120 591	100 349	12 071	8 171	28 770	13 865	6 161	8 744
2001	151 042	121 921	100 357	13 172	8 392	29 121	14 038	6 139	8 944
2002	151 546	121 726	100 659	12 544	8 523	29 819	14 635	6 184	9 000
2003	151 553	121 158	100 700	11 972	8 486	30 395	15 333	6 027	9 035
2004	153 024	122 404	102 427	11 862	8 115	30 621	15 552	6 077	8 992
2005	155 127	124 683	104 876	11 816	7 991	30 444	15 374	6 161	8 909
2006	157 352	127 340	107 734	11 736	7 870	30 012	15 131	6 223	8 657
2007	158 468	128 332	108 617	11 901	7 814	30 136	15 477	6 194	8 466
2008	158 317	125 937	104 023	13 421	8 493	32 380	16 562	6 630	9 188
2009	154 772	121 355	99 306	12 350	9 698	33 418	17 417	6 674	9 327
2010	153 141	119 940	99 250	11 705	8 985	33 201	17 122	6 582	9 497
2011	154 330	121 400	101 700	11 040	8 661	32 929	17 261	6 288	9 380
2012	157 050	123 229	103 078	11 708	8 442	33 821	17 494	6 681	9 646
2013	157 878	124 875	105 839	10 945	8 090	33 003	17 151	6 733	9 119
2014	159 881	127 353	108 687	11 297	7 369	32 528	17 144	6 539	8 845
2015	163 169	130 053	111 079	11 586	7 388	33 116	17 305	6 472	9 339
2016	164 435	131 340	113 306	10 842	7 192	33 095	17 447	6 611	9 037
2017	166 045	133 632	115 671	11 038	6 923	32 413	17 472	6 247	8 694
2018	167 261	135 277	117 957	10 743	6 578	31 984	17 381	6 383	8 220
2019	169 522	137 088	119 145	10 856	7 087	32 434	17 252	6 395	8 786
Men									
1995	74 381	64 145	52 671	6 973	4 501	10 236	4 034	2 257	3 945
1996	75 760	65 356	53 795	6 891	4 670	10 404	4 321	2 136	3 947
1997	76 408	66 089	54 918	6 638	4 533	10 319	4 246	2 274	3 799
1998	76 918	67 250	56 953	6 208	4 089	9 669	4 197	2 090	3 382
1999	78 145	68 347	57 520	6 401	4 426	9 797	4 297	2 062	3 438
2000	78 804	68 925	58 756	6 094	4 075	9 879	4 485	1 957	3 437
2001	79 971	70 074	58 715	7 087	4 272	9 897	4 306	1 989	3 602
2002	80 282	70 132	58 765	6 804	4 563	10 151	4 519	2 042	3 590
2003	80 317	69 766	58 778	6 479	4 509	10 551	5 042	1 872	3 637
2004	81 261	70 780	60 096	6 428	4 256	10 482	4 987	1 992	3 503
2005	82 735	72 056	61 510	6 299	4 247	10 679	5 153	2 074	3 452
2006	83 767	73 578	63 058	6 373	4 147	10 189	4 747	2 046	3 396
2007	84 292	73 734	62 994	6 583	4 157	10 558	4 933	2 165	3 460
2008	83 889	72 204	59 869	7 645	4 690	11 685	5 425	2 457	3 803
2009	81 835	69 178	56 058	7 339	5 780	12 658	5 911	2 526	4 221
2010	81 076	68 402	56 416	6 760	5 225	12 674	5 883	2 523	4 267
2011	81 272	69 029	58 004	6 183	4 842	12 243	5 797	2 408	4 037
2012	82 910	70 181	59 022	6 547	4 611	12 729	6 199	2 481	4 049
2013	83 420	71 388	60 769	6 024	4 595	12 032	5 863	2 306	3 863
2014	84 358	72 398	62 445	6 016	3 937	11 960	6 018	2 313	3 628
2015	86 270	73 900	63 869	6 027	4 003	12 371	6 050	2 414	3 907
2016	86 768	74 574	64 970	5 723	3 882	12 194	6 129	2 339	3 726
2017	87 939	76 236	66 373	6 051	3 813	11 703	5 854	2 178	3 671
2018	87 956	76 305	67 185	5 627	3 493	11 651	6 018	2 275	3 358
2019	88 856	76 646	67 104	5 886	3 656	12 210	6 176	2 424	3 609
Women									
1995	65 342	45 917	35 502	5 997	4 418	19 425	8 691	4 574	6 160
1996	66 439	46 955	36 457	6 105	4 393	19 484	9 061	4 507	5 916
1997	67 559	47 790	37 713	5 870	4 207	19 769	9 564	4 291	5 914
1998	68 648	49 162	38 819	5 948	4 395	19 486	9 341	4 390	5 755
1999	70 150	50 748	40 421	5 892	4 435	19 402	9 383	4 255	5 764
2000	70 556	51 665	41 593	5 977	4 095	18 891	9 380	4 204	5 307
2001	71 071	51 848	41 642	6 085	4 120	19 223	9 731	4 150	5 342
2002	71 263	51 593	41 893	5 741	3 959	19 671	10 117	4 143	5 411
2003	71 236	51 391	41 921	5 493	3 977	19 844	10 291	4 155	5 398
2004	71 763	51 624	42 331	5 434	3 859	20 139	10 565	4 085	5 489
2005	72 392	52 627	43 366	5 517	3 744	19 765	10 222	4 087	5 456
2006	73 585	53 762	44 676	5 364	3 723	19 823	10 384	4 178	5 261
2007	74 176	54 598	45 622	5 318	3 657	19 579	10 543	4 029	5 006
2008	74 428	53 733	44 154	5 776	3 803	20 695	11 137	4 172	5 385
2009	72 937	52 177	43 248	5 012	3 918	20 760	11 506	4 147	5 107
2010	72 066	51 538	42 834	4 944	3 760	20 528	11 239	4 058	5 230
2011	73 058	52 371	43 696	4 857	3 818	20 687	11 464	3 880	5 343
2012	74 140	53 048	44 055	5 161	3 831	21 092	11 295	4 200	5 597
2013	74 458	53 486	45 070	4 922	3 495	20 972	11 288	4 427	5 256
2014	75 523	54 955	46 241	5 281	3 432	20 568	11 125	4 226	5 217
2015	76 899	56 153	47 210	5 558	3 385	20 745	11 254	4 058	5 433
2016	77 667	56 766	48 337	5 119	3 310	20 901	11 318	4 272	5 311
2017	78 106	57 396	49 299	4 987	3 110	20 710	11 618	4 068	5 023
2018	79 305	58 972	50 771	5 116	3 084	20 333	11 364	4 107	4 862
2019	80 666	60 442	52 041	4 970	3 431	20 224	11 076	3 971	5 177

Note: See notes and definitions for information on historical comparability.

Table 1-36. Percent Distribution of the Population with Work Experience During the Year, by Extent of Employment and Sex, 1995–2019

(Percent of total people with work experience.)

Sex and year	Total	Full-time workers				Part-time workers			
		Total	50 to 52 weeks	27 to 49 weeks	1 to 26 weeks	Total	50 to 52 weeks	27 to 49 weeks	1 to 26 weeks
Both Sexes									
1995	100.0	78.8	63.1	9.3	6.4	21.2	9.1	4.9	7.2
1996	100.0	79.0	63.5	9.1	6.4	21.0	9.4	4.7	6.9
1997	100.0	79.1	64.3	8.7	6.1	20.9	9.6	4.6	6.7
1998	100.0	80.0	65.8	8.4	5.8	20.1	9.3	4.5	6.3
1999	100.0	80.3	66.0	8.3	6.0	19.7	9.2	4.3	6.2
2000	100.0	80.8	67.2	8.1	5.5	19.3	9.3	4.1	5.9
2001	100.0	80.7	66.4	8.7	5.6	19.3	9.3	4.1	5.9
2002	100.0	80.3	66.4	8.3	5.6	19.7	9.7	4.1	5.9
2003	100.0	79.9	66.4	7.9	5.6	20.1	10.1	4.0	6.0
2004	100.0	80.0	66.9	7.8	5.3	20.1	10.2	4.0	5.9
2005	100.0	80.4	67.6	7.6	5.2	19.6	9.9	4.0	5.7
2006	100.0	80.9	68.5	7.5	5.0	19.1	9.6	4.0	5.5
2007	100.0	81.0	68.5	7.5	4.9	19.0	9.8	3.9	5.3
2008	100.0	79.5	65.7	8.5	5.4	20.5	10.5	4.2	5.8
2009	100.0	78.4	64.2	8.0	6.3	21.6	11.3	4.3	6.0
2010	100.0	78.3	64.8	7.6	5.9	21.7	11.2	4.3	6.2
2011	100.0	78.7	65.9	7.2	5.6	21.3	11.2	4.1	6.1
2012	100.0	78.5	65.6	7.5	5.4	21.5	11.1	4.3	6.1
2013	100.0	79.1	67.0	6.9	5.1	20.9	10.9	4.3	5.8
2014	100.0	79.7	68.0	7.1	4.6	20.3	10.7	4.1	5.5
2015	100.0	79.7	68.1	7.1	4.5	20.3	10.6	4.0	5.7
2016	100.0	79.9	68.9	6.6	4.4	20.1	10.6	4.0	5.5
2017	100.0	80.5	69.7	6.6	4.2	19.5	10.5	3.8	5.2
2018	100.0	80.9	70.5	6.4	3.9	19.1	10.4	3.8	4.9
2019	100.0	80.9	70.3	6.4	4.2	19.1	10.2	3.8	5.2
Men									
1995	100.0	86.3	70.8	9.4	6.1	13.7	5.4	3.0	5.3
1996	100.0	86.3	71.0	9.1	6.2	13.7	5.7	2.8	5.2
1997	100.0	86.5	71.9	8.7	5.9	13.6	5.6	3.0	5.0
1998	100.0	87.4	74.0	8.1	5.3	12.6	5.5	2.7	4.4
1999	100.0	87.5	73.6	8.2	5.7	12.5	5.5	2.6	4.4
2000	100.0	87.5	74.6	7.7	5.2	12.6	5.7	2.5	4.4
2001	100.0	87.6	73.4	8.9	5.3	12.4	5.4	2.5	4.5
2002	100.0	87.4	73.2	8.5	5.7	12.6	5.6	2.5	4.5
2003	100.0	86.9	73.2	8.1	5.6	13.1	6.3	2.3	4.5
2004	100.0	87.1	74.0	7.9	5.2	12.9	6.1	2.5	4.3
2005	100.0	87.0	74.3	7.6	5.1	12.9	6.2	2.5	4.2
2006	100.0	87.8	75.3	7.6	5.0	12.2	5.7	2.4	4.1
2007	100.0	87.5	74.7	7.8	4.9	12.5	5.9	2.6	4.1
2008	100.0	86.1	71.4	9.1	5.6	13.9	6.5	2.9	4.5
2009	100.0	84.5	68.5	9.0	7.1	15.5	7.2	3.1	5.2
2010	100.0	84.4	69.6	8.3	6.4	15.6	7.3	3.1	5.3
2011	100.0	84.9	71.4	7.6	6.0	15.1	7.1	3.0	5.0
2012	100.0	84.6	71.2	7.9	5.6	15.4	7.5	3.0	4.9
2013	100.0	85.6	72.8	7.2	5.5	14.4	7.0	2.8	4.6
2014	100.0	85.8	74.0	7.1	4.7	14.2	7.1	2.7	4.3
2015	100.0	85.7	74.0	7.0	4.6	14.3	7.0	2.8	4.5
2016	100.0	85.9	74.9	6.6	4.5	14.1	7.1	2.7	4.3
2017	100.0	86.7	75.5	6.9	4.3	13.3	6.7	2.5	4.2
2018	100.0	86.8	76.4	6.4	4.0	13.2	6.8	2.6	3.8
2019	100.0	86.3	75.5	6.6	4.1	13.7	7.0	2.7	4.1
Women									
1995	100.0	70.3	54.3	9.2	6.8	29.7	13.3	7.0	9.4
1996	100.0	70.7	54.9	9.2	6.6	29.3	13.6	6.8	8.9
1997	100.0	70.7	55.8	8.7	6.2	29.4	14.2	6.4	8.8
1998	100.0	71.6	56.5	8.7	6.4	28.4	13.6	6.4	8.4
1999	100.0	72.3	57.6	8.4	6.3	27.7	13.4	6.1	8.2
2000	100.0	73.2	58.9	8.5	5.8	26.8	13.3	6.0	7.5
2001	100.0	73.0	58.6	8.6	5.8	27.0	13.7	5.8	7.5
2002	100.0	72.5	58.8	8.1	5.6	27.6	14.2	5.8	7.6
2003	100.0	72.1	58.8	7.7	5.6	27.8	14.4	5.8	7.6
2004	100.0	72.0	59.0	7.6	5.4	28.0	14.7	5.7	7.6
2005	100.0	72.7	59.9	7.6	5.2	27.2	14.1	5.6	7.5
2006	100.0	73.1	60.7	7.3	5.1	26.9	14.1	5.7	7.1
2007	100.0	73.6	61.5	7.2	4.9	26.4	14.2	5.4	6.7
2008	100.0	72.2	59.3	7.8	5.1	27.8	15.0	5.6	7.2
2009	100.0	71.5	59.3	6.9	5.4	28.5	15.8	5.7	7.0
2010	100.0	71.5	59.4	6.9	5.2	28.5	15.6	5.6	7.3
2011	100.0	71.7	59.8	6.6	5.2	28.3	15.7	5.3	7.3
2012	100.0	71.6	59.4	7.0	5.2	28.4	15.2	5.7	7.5
2013	100.0	71.8	60.5	6.6	4.7	28.2	15.2	5.9	7.1
2014	100.0	72.8	61.2	7.0	4.5	27.2	14.7	5.6	6.9
2015	100.0	73.0	61.4	7.2	4.4	27.0	14.6	5.3	7.1
2016	100.0	73.1	62.2	6.6	4.3	26.9	14.6	5.5	6.8
2017	100.0	73.5	63.1	6.4	4.0	26.5	14.9	5.2	6.4
2018	100.0	74.4	64.0	6.5	3.9	25.6	14.3	5.2	6.1
2019	100.0	74.9	64.5	6.2	4.3	25.1	13.7	4.9	6.4

Note: See notes and definitions for information on historical comparability.

Table 1-37. Extent of Unemployment During the Year, by Sex, 1995–2005

(Thousands of people, percent.)

Sex and extent of unemployment	1995	1996	1997	1998	1999	2000	2001	2002	2003	2004	2005
BOTH SEXES											
Total Who Worked or Looked for Work	142 413	144 528	146 096	147 295	149 798	150 786	153 056	154 205	154 315	155 576	157 549
Percent with unemployment	12.7	11.6	10.7	9.5	8.7	8.1	10.4	10.9	10.7	9.7	9.2
Total with Unemployment	18 067	16 789	15 637	14 044	13 068	12 269	15 843	16 824	16 462	15 074	14 558
Did not work but looked for work	2 690	2 329	2 129	1 729	1 503	1 425	2 014	2 660	2 762	2 551	2 422
Worked during the year	15 377	14 460	13 508	12 316	11 566	10 845	13 829	14 164	13 699	12 522	12 136
Year-round workers with 1 or 2 weeks of unemployment	715	589	611	630	562	573	602	584	534	465	431
Part-year workers with unemployment	14 662	13 871	12 897	11 686	11 004	10 272	13 227	13 580	13 165	12 057	11 705
1 to 4 weeks	2 812	2 550	2 582	2 323	2 361	2 233	2 368	2 002	1 839	1 985	1 941
5 to 10 weeks	2 725	2 671	2 601	2 495	2 218	2 014	2 557	2 373	2 264	2 100	2 170
11 to 14 weeks	2 147	2 020	1 822	1 701	1 594	1 505	2 038	1 970	1 749	1 773	1 698
15 to 26 weeks	4 013	3 662	3 378	3 019	2 803	2 641	3 683	3 848	3 778	3 448	3 349
27 weeks or more	2 965	2 968	2 514	2 148	2 028	1 879	2 582	3 387	3 535	2 751	2 547
With 2 or more spells of unemployment	4 468	4 237	4 044	3 628	3 225	3 079	3 421	3 226	3 093	2 896	3 095
2 spells	1 963	1 982	1 853	1 650	1 449	1 397	1 643	1 556	1 585	1 344	1 477
3 or more spells	2 505	2 255	2 191	1 978	1 776	1 682	1 779	1 670	1 508	1 552	1 618
MEN											
Total Who Worked or Looked for Work	75 698	76 786	77 385	77 704	78 905	79 546	80 975	81 651	81 804	82 478	83 951
Percent with unemployment	13.2	11.9	11.1	9.4	9.0	8.6	11.0	11.8	11.4	10.0	9.7
Total with Unemployment	9 996	9 157	8 604	7 284	7 091	6 806	8 928	9 621	9 339	8 256	8 116
Did not work but looked for work	1 317	1 026	978	787	760	742	1 004	1 369	1 487	1 217	1 216
Worked during the year	8 679	8 130	7 626	6 497	6 332	6 064	7 924	8 252	7 854	7 039	6 899
Year-round workers with 1 or 2 weeks of unemployment	462	395	382	386	373	379	421	365	359	289	296
Part-year workers with unemployment	8 217	7 735	7 244	6 111	5 959	5 685	7 502	7 887	7 495	6 750	6 603
1 to 4 weeks	1 398	1 272	1 275	1 085	1 166	1 070	1 247	1 075	958	1 028	1 052
5 to 10 weeks	1 434	1 478	1 474	1 363	1 168	1 135	1 446	1 342	1 314	1 170	1 209
11 to 14 weeks	1 253	1 258	1 068	980	937	880	1 207	1 186	1 039	1 021	1 024
15 to 26 weeks	2 439	2 076	1 949	1 585	1 655	1 595	2 191	2 282	2 178	2 065	1 923
27 weeks or more	1 693	1 651	1 478	1 098	1 033	1 005	1 412	2 002	2 006	1 466	1 395
With 2 or more spells of unemployment	2 793	2 554	2 437	2 014	1 845	1 809	2 100	1 920	1 882	1 828	1 975
2 spells	1 110	1 109	1 078	880	787	804	1 002	914	946	808	940
3 or more spells	1 683	1 445	1 359	1 134	1 058	1 005	1 099	1 006	936	1 020	1 035
WOMEN											
Total Who Worked or Looked for Work	66 716	67 742	68 710	69 591	70 893	71 240	72 081	72 554	72 511	73 097	73 598
Percent with unemployment	12.1	11.3	10.2	9.7	8.4	7.7	9.6	9.9	9.8	9.3	8.8
Total with Unemployment	8 070	7 632	7 033	6 760	5 976	5 463	6 915	7 203	7 123	6 818	6 442
Did not work but looked for work	1 373	1 303	1 151	942	743	683	1 010	1 291	1 275	1 334	1 206
Worked during the year	6 696	6 330	5 882	5 816	5 234	4 779	5 905	5 913	5 848	5 484	5 236
Year-round workers with 1 or 2 weeks of unemployment	253	194	229	243	189	193	180	220	176	177	136
Part-year workers with unemployment	6 443	6 136	5 653	5 573	5 045	4 586	5 725	5 693	5 672	5 307	5 100
1 to 4 weeks	1 413	1 279	1 307	1 237	1 194	1 164	1 121	927	882	957	888
5 to 10 weeks	1 291	1 192	1 127	1 131	1 050	878	1 111	1 031	950	929	961
11 to 14 weeks	893	762	754	721	657	625	831	784	710	752	674
15 to 26 weeks	1 574	1 586	1 429	1 434	1 148	1 045	1 492	1 566	1 600	1 384	1 426
27 weeks or more	1 272	1 317	1 036	1 050	996	874	1 170	1 385	1 530	1 285	1 151
With 2 or more spells of unemployment	1 675	1 682	1 607	1 614	1 379	1 270	1 321	1 306	1 211	1 069	1 120
2 spells	853	872	775	770	662	593	641	642	639	537	537
3 or more spells	822	810	832	844	717	677	680	664	572	532	583

Table 1-38. Percent Distribution of Persons with Unemployment During the Year, by Sex and Extent of Unemployment, 1990–2019

(Percent.)

Sex and extent of unemployment	1990	1991	1992	1993	1994	1995	1996	1997	1998	1999	2000	2001	2002	2003	2004
BOTH SEXES															
Total with Unemployment Who Worked During the Year	100.0	100.0	100.0	100.0	100.0	100.0	100.0	100.0	100.0	100.0	100.0	100.0	100.0	100.0	100.0
Year-round workers with 1 or 2 weeks of unemployment	5.9	5.1	4.7	4.0	4.6	4.6	4.1	4.5	5.1	4.9	5.3	4.4	4.1	3.9	3.7
Part-year workers with unemployment	94.1	94.8	95.4	96.1	95.4	95.4	96.0	95.5	95.0	95.1	94.8	95.6	95.9	96.1	96.3
1 to 4 weeks	20.3	17.1	15.7	15.4	17.3	18.3	17.6	19.1	18.9	20.4	20.6	17.1	14.1	13.4	15.9
5 to 10 weeks	20.5	19.4	18.7	17.0	18.5	17.7	18.5	19.3	20.3	19.2	18.6	18.5	16.8	16.5	16.8
11 to 14 weeks	13.9	13.7	13.8	13.5	14.1	14.0	14.0	13.5	13.8	13.9	14.7	13.9	12.8	14.2
15 to 26 weeks	24.1	26.1	26.1	26.6	25.8	26.1	25.3	25.0	24.5	24.2	24.4	26.6	27.2	27.6	27.5
27 weeks or more	15.3	18.5	21.1	23.6	19.7	19.3	20.6	18.6	17.5	17.5	17.3	18.7	23.9	25.8	22.0
With 2 or more spells of unemployment	32.4	31.1	30.6	31.2	29.7	29.1	29.3	29.9	29.5	27.9	28.4	24.8	22.8	22.6	23.1
2 spells	15.9	14.5	14.4	15.0	13.7	12.8	13.7	13.7	13.4	12.5	12.9	11.9	11.0	11.6	10.7
3 or more spells	16.5	16.6	16.2	16.2	16.0	16.3	15.6	16.2	16.1	15.4	15.5	12.9	11.8	11.0	12.4
MEN															
Total with Unemployment Who Worked During the Year	100.0	100.0	100.0	100.0	100.0	100.0	100.0	100.0	100.0	100.0	100.0	100.0	100.0	100.0	100.0
Year-round workers with 1 or 2 weeks of unemployment	6.8	5.4	4.9	4.4	5.7	5.3	4.9	5.0	5.9	5.9	6.3	5.3	4.4	4.6	4.1
Part-year workers with unemployment	93.2	94.6	95.0	95.5	94.3	94.7	95.1	95.1	94.1	94.0	93.6	94.7	95.6	95.4	95.9
1 to 4 weeks	17.5	13.9	13.6	13.3	14.7	16.1	15.6	16.7	16.7	18.4	17.6	15.7	13.0	12.2	14.6
5 to 10 weeks	19.6	18.5	17.8	16.3	17.9	16.5	18.2	19.3	21.0	18.4	18.7	18.2	16.3	16.7	16.6
11 to 14 weeks	14.0	14.5	14.1	13.4	14.7	14.4	15.5	14.0	15.1	14.8	14.5	15.2	14.4	13.2	14.5
15 to 26 weeks	25.4	28.0	27.6	28.4	26.4	28.1	25.5	25.6	24.4	26.1	26.3	27.6	27.7	27.7	29.3
27 weeks or more	16.7	19.7	21.9	24.1	20.6	19.5	20.3	19.4	16.9	16.3	16.5	17.8	24.3	25.5	20.8
With 2 or more spells of unemployment	35.4	34.0	33.9	34.3	31.6	32.2	31.4	31.9	31.0	29.1	29.9	26.5	23.3	24.0	26.0
2 spells	16.1	15.2	15.5	15.7	13.6	12.8	13.6	14.1	13.5	12.4	13.3	12.6	11.1	12.1	11.5
3 or more spells	19.3	18.8	18.4	18.6	18.0	19.4	17.8	17.8	17.5	16.7	16.6	13.9	12.2	11.9	14.5
WOMEN															
Total With Unemployment Who Worked During the Year	100.0	100.0	100.0	100.0	100.0	100.0	100.0	100.0	100.0	100.0	100.0	100.0	100.0	100.0	100.0
Year-round workers with 1 or 2 weeks of unemployment	4.6	4.8	4.2	3.4	3.2	3.8	3.1	3.9	4.2	3.6	4.0	3.1	3.7	3.0	3.2
Part-year workers with unemployment	95.3	95.3	95.7	96.6	96.7	96.2	96.9	96.1	95.8	96.4	96.0	96.9	96.3	97.0	96.8
1 to 4 weeks	24.3	22.0	19.0	18.3	20.9	21.1	20.2	22.2	21.3	22.8	24.3	19.0	15.7	15.1	17.4
5 to 10 weeks	21.6	20.8	20.1	17.8	19.3	19.3	18.8	19.2	19.4	20.1	18.4	18.8	17.4	16.2	16.9
11 to 14 weeks	13.8	12.5	13.2	13.5	13.1	13.3	12.0	12.8	12.4	12.6	13.1	14.1	13.3	12.1	13.7
15 to 26 weeks	22.2	23.2	23.6	24.1	25.1	23.5	25.1	24.3	24.7	21.9	21.9	25.3	26.5	27.4	25.2
27 weeks or more	13.4	16.8	19.8	22.9	18.3	19.0	20.8	17.6	18.0	19.0	18.3	19.8	23.4	26.2	23.5
With 2 or more spells of unemployment	28.2	26.6	25.4	26.9	27.0	25.0	26.6	27.3	27.7	26.3	26.6	22.4	22.1	20.7	19.5
2 spells	15.7	13.4	12.6	14.1	13.8	12.7	13.8	13.2	13.2	12.6	12.4	10.9	10.9	10.9	9.8
3 or more spells	12.5	13.2	12.8	12.8	13.2	12.3	12.8	14.1	14.5	13.7	14.2	11.5	11.2	9.8	9.7

Table 1-38. Percent Distribution of Persons with Unemployment During the Year, by Sex and Extent of Unemployment, 1990–2019—*Continued*

(Percent.)

Sex and extent of unemployment	2005	2006	2007	2008	2009	2010	2011	2012	2013	2014	2015	2016	2017	2018	2019
BOTH SEXES															
Total with Unemployment Who Worked During the Year	100.0	100.0	100.0	100.0	100.0	100.0	100.0	100.0	100.0	100.0	100.0	100.0	100.0	100.0	100.0
Year-round workers with 1 or 2 weeks of unemployment	3.6	3.6	3.8	4.2	3.4	3.2	2.4	2.7	2.9	2.8	2.8	3.7	3.5	4.2	3.7
Part-year workers with unemployment	96.4	96.4	96.1	95.8	96.5	96.8	97.6	97.3	97.1	97.2	97.2	96.3	96.5	95.8	96.3
1 to 4 weeks	16.0	20.7	19.9	15.5	12.5	12.1	12.6	13.3	14.9	16.9	19.0	19.7	22.9	21.5	20.6
5 to 10 weeks	17.9	16.8	16.0	16.3	12.6	12.8	13.0	13.9	13.5	14.3	15.3	16.0	15.7	15.1	16.0
11 to 14 weeks	14.0	12.9	14.5	13.5	11.9	12.3	11.8	12.8	12.6	13.5	13.9	12.0	13.1	13.0	13.6
15 to 26 weeks	27.6	25.3	25.9	26.9	28.1	27.4	28.2	27.8	27.9	27.5	25.9	25.3	23.6	25.5	24.4
27 weeks or more	20.9	20.7	19.8	23.5	31.5	32.2	32.0	29.4	28.2	25.0	22.9	23.3	21.2	20.8	21.7
With 2 or more spells of unemployment	25.5	24.5	23.8	22.1	20.5	20.7	20.1	22.2	20.7	20.5	21.6	22.1	20.2	21.7	20.9
2 spells	12.2	12.5	10.9	11.0	9.4	9.6	10.0	10.2	10.0	10.5	10.0	11.1	9.3	10.2	10.3
3 or more spells	13.3	12.1	12.9	11.1	11.0	11.2	10.2	12.0	10.7	10.0	11.6	11.0	10.9	11.5	10.7
MEN															
Total with Unemployment Who Worked During the Year	100.0	100.0	100.0	100.0	100.0	100.0	100.0	100.0	100.0	100.0	100.0	100.0	100.0	100.0	100.0
Year-round workers with 1 or 2 weeks of unemployment	4.3	4.1	4.8	4.5	3.7	3.4	2.7	3.3	2.8	3.6	3.3	4.0	3.9	4.8	4.1
Part-year workers with unemployment	95.7	95.9	95.2	95.5	96.4	96.6	97.3	96.7	97.2	96.4	96.7	96.0	96.1	95.2	95.9
1 to 4 weeks	15.3	18.0	17.9	14.3	11.7	10.5	11.6	12.5	13.6	15.7	18.4	18.0	21.0	18.3	18.0
5 to 10 weeks	17.5	17.7	15.9	16.0	12.7	12.7	12.3	14.3	13.6	14.9	15.6	15.3	16.0	14.8	15.9
11 to 14 weeks	14.8	13.4	15.3	13.8	12.4	12.8	12.7	13.1	12.4	14.0	13.3	12.1	13.5	13.0	13.9
15 to 26 weeks	27.9	26.1	27.0	28.5	28.4	28.8	29.2	28.6	28.6	27.2	26.9	27.0	23.4	27.0	25.9
27 weeks or more	20.2	20.6	19.1	22.9	31.2	31.8	31.4	28.3	29.0	24.6	22.5	23.5	22.2	22.2	22.2
With 2 or more spells of unemployment	28.6	27.1	26.1	24.6	22.8	23.3	24.4	24.5	22.7	22.8	23.7	23.4	22.1	23.6	22.3
2 spells	13.6	13.2	11.1	11.6	10.3	10.1	11.1	10.5	10.5	11.9	10.3	11.3	9.3	10.4	11.4
3 or more spells	15.0	13.9	15.0	13.0	12.5	13.3	13.2	13.9	12.3	10.9	13.4	12.1	12.8	13.3	10.9
WOMEN															
Total With Unemployment Who Worked During the Year	100.0	100.0	100.0	100.0	100.0	100.0	100.0	100.0	100.0	100.0	100.0	100.0	100.0	100.0	100.0
Year-round workers with 1 or 2 weeks of unemployment	2.6	2.9	2.5	3.8	3.0	2.8	2.0	2.1	2.9	1.7	2.3	3.3	3.0	3.3	3.3
Part-year workers with unemployment	97.4	97.1	97.4	96.2	96.9	97.2	98.0	97.9	97.1	98.3	97.7	96.7	97.0	96.7	96.7
1 to 4 weeks	17.0	24.4	22.6	17.2	13.7	14.5	13.9	14.3	16.6	18.4	19.8	21.6	25.2	25.4	23.6
5 to 10 weeks	18.4	15.6	16.2	16.8	12.5	13.1	13.9	13.3	13.4	13.4	14.9	16.9	15.5	15.4	16.1
11 to 14 weeks	12.9	12.1	13.4	13.1	11.1	11.5	10.5	12.6	13.0	12.8	14.6	11.9	12.7	13.1	13.3
15 to 26 weeks	27.2	24.2	24.3	24.7	27.5	25.2	26.8	26.9	27.0	28.0	24.8	23.3	23.8	23.7	22.5
27 weeks or more	22.0	20.8	20.9	24.4	32.1	32.8	32.9	30.8	27.1	25.6	23.6	23.0	19.9	19.1	21.2
With 2 or more spells of unemployment	21.4	21.1	20.6	18.5	16.6	16.8	14.4	19.3	18.0	17.5	19.1	20.7	17.8	19.4	19.3
2 spells	10.3	11.5	10.7	10.2	8.0	8.8	8.3	9.8	9.4	8.7	9.6	10.9	9.3	10.1	8.9
3 or more spells	11.1	9.7	9.9	8.3	8.6	8.0	6.1	9.5	8.5	8.8	9.5	9.7	8.5	9.3	10.4

Table 1-39. Number and Median Annual Earnings of Year-Round, Full-Time Wage and Salary Workers, by Age, Sex, and Race, 1995–2019

(Thousands of people, dollars.)

Sex, age, and race	1995	1996	1997	1998	1999	2000	2001	2002	2003	2004	2005	2006
NUMBER												
Both Sexes, 16 Years and Over	83 407	85 611	86 905	89 748	91 722	94 359	94 531	94 526	94 731	96 098	98 632	101 353
16 to 24 years	6 892	6 809	7 063	7 618	7 631	8 384	7 989	7 903	7 631	7 702	7 956	8 113
25 to 44 years	48 695	49 225	49 513	50 264	50 532	51 159	49 939	49 120	48 343	48 421	49 149	50 056
25 to 34 years	23 310	23 071	23 186	23 048	22 952	23 044	22 744	22 657	22 512	22 405	22 808	23 613
35 to 44 years	25 385	26 154	26 327	27 216	27 580	28 115	27 195	26 463	25 831	26 016	26 341	26 443
45 to 54 years	18 436	19 714	20 109	21 274	22 375	23 307	23 855	23 999	24 507	25 074	25 661	26 338
55 to 64 years	8 122	8 455	8 901	9 273	9 594	9 870	10 948	11 584	12 207	12 812	13 605	14 340
65 years and over	1 263	1 408	1 318	1 318	1 590	1 639	1 800	1 921	2 042	2 090	2 262	2 507
Men, 16 Years and Over	49 334	50 407	50 772	52 509	53 132	54 477	54 630	54 420	54 575	55 610	57 020	58 533
16 to 24 years	4 094	3 942	4 021	4 479	4 347	4 602	4 605	4 570	4 421	4 493	4 663	4 812
25 to 44 years	28 940	29 282	29 453	29 763	29 738	30 080	29 271	28 855	28 499	28 763	29 151	29 589
25 to 34 years	13 844	13 817	13 735	13 612	13 471	13 497	13 386	13 400	13 288	13 430	13 629	13 933
35 to 44 years	15 096	15 465	15 718	16 151	16 267	16 583	15 885	15 455	15 211	15 333	15 522	15 655
45 to 54 years	10 589	11 372	11 388	12 030	12 546	13 045	13 363	13 330	13 616	13 975	14 382	14 758
55 to 64 years	4 884	4 908	5 133	5 438	5 498	5 693	6 253	6 502	6 872	7 165	7 489	7 905
65 years and over	827	903	775	801	1 003	1 057	1 138	1 163	1 165	1 213	1 334	1 469
Women, 16 Years and Over	34 073	35 203	36 133	37 239	38 591	39 887	39 901	40 106	40 156	40 488	41 613	42 820
16 to 24 years	2 798	2 867	3 041	3 140	3 285	3 782	3 384	3 333	3 210	3 209	3 293	3 301
25 to 44 years	19 755	19 942	20 060	20 503	20 794	21 081	20 668	20 264	19 844	19 656	19 997	20 467
25 to 34 years	9 467	9 254	9 451	9 437	9 481	9 548	9 358	9 257	9 224	8 974	9 179	9 679
35 to 44 years	10 288	10 688	10 609	11 066	11 313	11 533	11 310	11 007	10 620	10 682	10 818	10 788
45 to 54 years	7 847	8 343	8 721	9 244	9 829	10 263	10 493	10 669	10 891	11 099	11 279	11 580
55 to 64 years	3 238	3 547	3 767	3 836	4 096	4 178	4 695	5 082	5 335	5 647	6 116	6 434
65 years and over	436	505	543	517	586	583	662	758	877	877	927	1 038
White, 16 Years and Over	70 430	72 068	72 650	75 046	76 203	77 790	78 306	77 632	77 545	78 236	80 546	82 411
Men	42 608	43 554	43 429	44 901	45 211	46 105	46 373	45 823	45 816	46 317	47 790	48 897
Women	27 822	28 514	29 221	30 145	30 992	31 685	31 933	31 809	31 729	31 919	32 756	33 513
Black, 16 Years and Over	9 446	9 706	10 248	10 532	11 145	11 899	11 001	10 966	10 979	11 301	11 417	11 988
Men	4 686	4 682	5 026	5 202	5 411	5 636	5 281	5 150	5 196	5 470	5 402	5 679
Women	4 759	5 024	5 222	5 329	5 734	6 264	5 720	5 816	5 783	5 832	6 015	6 309
MEDIAN ANNUAL EARNINGS												
Both Sexes, 16 Years and Over	27 000	28 000	30 000	30 000	31 000	32 000	34 000	35 000	35 000	35 672	36 400	38 000
16 to 24 years	15 500	15 600	16 000	18 000	18 000	19 000	20 000	20 000	20 000	20 000	20 000	21 000
25 to 34 years	25 000	25 300	27 000	28 500	30 000	30 000	31 000	31 800	32 000	33 000	33 000	35 000
35 to 44 years	30 000	31 000	32 000	33 000	34 992	35 000	36 000	37 000	39 000	40 000	40 000	41 000
45 to 54 years	32 000	33 000	35 000	35 000	36 000	38 000	39 500	40 000	40 000	40 000	42 000	44 000
55 to 64 years	30 000	30 000	32 000	34 000	35 000	35 000	36 400	39 145	40 000	40 000	41 000	43 000
65 years and over	29 600	26 496	28 200	26 000	30 000	32 000	32 000	33 000	32 000	35 000	35 000	35 001
Men, 16 Years and Over	31 000	32 000	34 000	35 000	36 000	37 600	38 500	40 000	40 000	40 000	40 051	42 000
16 to 24 years	16 000	17 000	17 000	18 720	19 000	20 000	20 000	20 000	20 800	20 800	20 800	22 000
25 to 34 years	27 000	28 000	29 852	30 000	32 000	33 500	34 000	34 740	35 000	35 000	35 000	36 000
35 to 44 years	35 000	36 000	37 000	38 000	40 000	40 000	42 000	43 000	43 900	45 000	45 000	48 000
45 to 54 years	40 000	40 000	41 000	42 000	44 616	45 000	45 000	47 000	48 000	48 000	50 000	50 000
55 to 64 years	36 000	36 000	39 000	40 000	40 853	44 000	45 000	47 000	50 000	50 000	50 000	50 000
65 years and over	36 000	33 000	36 400	35 000	36 000	35 999	35 000	37 861	42 000	40 000	41 000	44 000
Women, 16 Years and Over	23 000	24 000	25 000	25 000	26 000	27 500	29 000	30 000	30 000	30 001	32 000	33 000
16 to 24 years	15 000	15 000	15 000	17 000	17 000	18 000	19 000	19 000	20 000	20 000	20 000	20 000
25 to 34 years	22 000	23 000	24 000	25 000	26 000	27 000	28 080	29 500	30 000	30 000	30 000	31 000
35 to 44 years	25 000	25 000	26 000	27 200	28 000	29 000	30 000	30 400	32 000	32 800	35 000	35 000
45 to 54 years	25 000	26 000	27 040	28 132	30 000	30 000	32 000	32 000	33 466	34 771	35 000	36 000
55 to 64 years	22 500	24 000	24 800	25 775	27 000	28 000	30 000	31 410	32 000	33 000	33 000	35 000
65 years and over	23 290	20 800	24 000	22 000	20 800	24 000	25 000	28 000	26 000	27 000	28 768	27 878
White, 16 Years and Over	28 000	29 000	30 000	31 000	32 000	34 000	35 000	35 000	36 000	37 000	38 000	40 000
Men	32 000	33 000	35 000	36 000	37 200	39 000	40 000	40 000	40 000	42 000	42 000	44 707
Women	23 000	24 000	25 000	26 000	27 000	28 000	30 000	30 000	31 000	31 800	32 000	34 000
Black, 16 Years and Over	22 000	23 784	24 000	25 000	25 760	26 000	28 500	29 000	30 000	30 000	30 000	31 000
Men	24 500	26 000	26 000	27 000	30 000	30 000	30 000	30 000	32 000	30 000	33 000	34 000
Women	20 000	21 000	22 000	23 000	24 000	25 000	26 000	26 000	27 000	28 000	29 141	30 000

Table 1-39. Number and Median Annual Earnings of Year-Round, Full-Time Wage and Salary Workers, by Age, Sex, and Race, 1995–2019—*Continued*

(Thousands of people, dollars.)

Sex, age, and race	2007	2008	2009	2010	2011	2012	2013	2014	2015	2016	2017	2018	2019
NUMBER													
Both Sexes, 16 Years and Over	102 441	98 493	94 012	94 110	96 562	97 879	100 711	103 308	105 520	107 999	110 095	112 659	113 617
16 to 24 years	8 064	7 242	6 302	6 073	6 411	6 424	6 969	7 135	7 241	7 504	7 848	8 285	7 753
25 to 44 years	49 725	47 364	44 579	44 441	45 166	45 812	46 478	48 188	49 130	50 826	52 287	53 415	54 216
25 to 34 years	23 646	22 786	21 572	21 894	21 989	22 690	23 141	24 099	25 008	26 209	26 666	27 530	27 843
35 to 44 years	26 080	24 578	23 007	22 546	23 177	23 122	23 337	24 090	24 123	24 616	25 621	25 886	26 373
45 to 54 years	26 566	25 722	24 877	24 388	24 782	24 593	25 245	25 018	25 334	25 397	25 300	25 411	25 255
55 to 64 years	15 248	15 286	15 274	16 073	16 622	17 255	17 721	18 416	19 152	19 433	19 543	20 078	20 680
65 years and over	2 837	2 879	2 980	3 135	3 582	3 795	4 299	4 551	4 663	4 839	5 117	5 469	5 713
Men, 16 Years and Over	58 673	55 973	52 362	52 793	54 542	55 489	57 263	58 719	60 012	61 295	62 437	63 486	63 389
16 to 24 years	4 719	4 112	3 494	3 462	3 649	3 730	3 952	3 914	4 107	4 186	4 482	4 498	4 224
25 to 44 years	29 004	27 546	25 324	25 449	25 959	26 476	26 924	27 941	28 399	29 193	30 010	30 645	30 510
25 to 34 years	13 706	13 208	12 085	12 475	12 616	13 043	13 370	14 123	14 406	14 885	15 167	15 759	15 420
35 to 44 years	15 298	14 337	13 239	12 974	13 343	13 433	13 555	13 818	13 993	14 308	14 844	14 886	15 090
45 to 54 years	14 810	14 199	13 521	13 373	13 723	13 690	14 094	14 026	14 278	14 235	14 134	14 059	13 781
55 to 64 years	8 449	8 397	8 289	8 727	9 066	9 315	9 747	10 199	10 461	10 775	10 752	11 140	11 427
65 years and over	1 692	1 720	1 733	1 782	2 146	2 278	2 546	2 640	2 767	2 906	3 058	3 144	3 449
Women, 16 Years and Over	43 768	42 520	41 650	41 318	42 020	42 390	43 448	44 589	45 508	46 704	47 658	49 172	50 228
16 to 24 years	3 345	3 130	2 808	2 611	2 762	2 694	3 016	3 222	3 134	3 318	3 366	3 788	3 530
25 to 44 years	20 721	19 819	19 255	18 992	19 207	19 336	19 554	20 248	20 731	21 632	22 276	22 770	23 706
25 to 34 years	9 940	9 578	9 487	9 420	9 373	9 647	9 771	9 976	10 602	11 324	11 499	11 770	12 423
35 to 44 years	10 782	10 240	9 768	9 572	9 834	9 689	9 782	10 272	10 130	10 308	10 777	11 000	11 283
45 to 54 years	11 757	11 524	11 356	11 016	11 059	10 903	11 151	10 992	11 056	11 162	11 166	11 352	11 474
55 to 64 years	6 799	6 889	6 984	7 346	7 556	7 940	7 974	8 217	8 691	8 659	8 791	8 938	9 253
65 years and over	1 146	1 158	1 247	1 354	1 436	1 518	1 753	1 911	1 896	1 933	2 059	2 324	2 265
White, 16 Years and Over	83 139	79 980	76 470	76 557	77 669	78 266	80 188	81 557	82 879	84 303	85 613	87 180	87 737
Men	48 825	46 608	43 622	44 018	45 037	45 460	46 764	47 591	48 333	49 079	49 758	50 493	50 232
Women	34 314	33 372	32 848	32 540	32 632	32 806	33 424	33 966	34 546	35 224	35 855	36 687	37 504
Black, 16 Years and Over	11 987	11 424	10 716	10 676	11 009	11 193	11 865	12 370	12 754	13 419	13 832	14 384	14 301
Men	5 689	5 377	4 952	4 957	5 111	5 323	5 617	5 910	6 178	6 471	6 702	6 889	6 751
Women	6 299	6 046	5 764	5 719	5 898	5 870	6 248	6 460	6 577	6 948	7 129	7 495	7 550
MEDIAN ANNUAL EARNINGS													
Both Sexes, 16 Years and Over	40 000	40 000	41 000	42 000	42 000	44 000	44 000	45 000	45 000	47 500	48 000	50 000	52 000
16 to 24 years	22 421	24 000	23 532	23 000	22 650	23 000	24 570	25 000	25 000	26 000	27 000	29 000	30 000
25 to 34 years	35 000	36 500	38 000	37 815	38 000	39 000	40 000	40 000	40 000	40 023	42 000	44 847	47 000
35 to 44 years	43 000	45 000	45 000	45 000	45 000	48 000	48 000	48 000	50 000	52 000	52 002	55 000	58 000
45 to 54 years	45 000	45 000	46 000	48 000	48 000	50 000	49 920	50 000	50 000	52 000	54 000	56 000	60 000
55 to 64 years	45 000	46 000	48 000	49 000	50 000	50 000	50 000	50 000	51 000	52 000	52 000	55 000	59 000
65 years and over	40 000	42 000	42 000	45 000	44 200	48 000	48 000	50 000	50 000	54 167	54 000	54 000	56 000
Men, 16 Years and Over	45 000	46 000	48 000	48 000	48 000	50 000	50 000	50 000	50 000	51 000	52 000	55 000	58 000
16 to 24 years	23 000	25 000	25 000	24 000	24 000	24 480	25 000	26 000	25 000	28 000	28 000	30 000	32 000
25 to 34 years	38 000	40 000	40 000	40 000	40 000	40 000	40 000	42 000	43 000	45 000	45 000	48 000	50 000
35 to 44 years	50 000	50 000	50 000	50 000	51 000	52 000	52 000	52 000	55 132	58 000	60 000	60 000	62 000
45 to 54 years	50 000	52 000	53 004	55 000	55 000	57 000	56 000	60 000	60 000	60 000	60 000	63 000	68 000
55 to 64 years	52 000	54 000	55 000	55 000	57 000	55 000	57 998	58 000	60 000	60 000	60 000	63 000	68 000
65 years and over	44 000	50 000	49 000	50 002	50 000	53 700	55 000	60 000	60 000	65 000	60 000	60 000	65 000
Women, 16 Years and Over	35 000	35 000	36 000	37 000	37 000	38 000	39 000	40 000	40 000	41 000	42 000	45 000	47 201
16 to 24 years	22 000	22 000	22 000	20 816	22 000	22 000	23 000	22 880	24 000	25 000	25 000	26 400	30 000
25 to 34 years	33 000	34 000	35 000	35 000	35 000	35 002	37 000	36 000	38 000	38 000	40 000	40 000	44 000
35 to 44 years	36 000	38 000	38 000	40 000	40 000	40 000	40 000	40 000	45 000	46 000	46 000	50 000	50 000
45 to 54 years	37 163	38 000	40 000	40 000	40 000	40 000	40 000	42 000	43 000	45 000	46 000	50 000	50 000
55 to 64 years	37 100	39 000	40 000	40 000	40 000	41 000	41 161	41 000	44 000	45 000	45 000	48 000	50 000
65 years and over	31 000	34 193	36 000	40 000	37 000	38 000	40 000	40 000	42 500	42 000	48 000	47 000	50 000
White, 16 Years and Over	40 000	41 600	42 000	43 502	44 000	45 000	45 000	45 000	48 000	49 000	50 000	50 000	54 000
Men	45 000	48 000	49 000	50 000	50 000	50 000	50 000	50 000	52 000	53 000	54 200	56 000	60 000
Women	35 000	35 500	36 002	38 000	38 000	39 520	40 000	40 000	40 000	42 000	44 000	45 000	48 800
Black, 16 Years and Over	33 000	34 000	35 000	35 000	35 000	35 000	36 000	36 000	38 000	38 000	40 000	40 000	42 000
Men	35 000	37 500	38 000	36 000	39 000	38 000	40 000	40 000	40 000	40 000	42 000	44 000	45 000
Women	30 000	30 002	32 000	32 000	34 000	34 000	34 000	33 000	35 000	35 000	36 000	38 000	40 000

Table 1-40. Number and Median Annual Earnings of Year-Round, Full-Time Wage and Salary Workers, by Sex and Occupation of Job Held the Longest, 2010–2019

(Thousands of people, dollars.)

Sex and occupation	2010	2011	2012	2013	2014	2015	2016	2017	2018	2019
Both Sexes, Number of Workers										
Management, business, and financial operations	16 889	17 396	17 799	18 241	19 020	19 937	20 642	20 609	21 556	22 803
Management	11 804	12 140	12 548	12 646	13 240	13 928	14 370	14 215	14 958	15 403
Business and financial operations	5 085	5 256	5 251	5 595	5 780	6 009	6 272	6 395	6 597	7 400
Professional and related	21 966	22 165	22 751	23 251	24 109	24 721	25 883	26 797	27 234	28 727
Computer and mathematical	2 993	3 171	3 524	3 439	3 690	4 044	4 190	4 395	4 510	5 074
Architecture and engineering	2 409	2 451	2 398	2 302	2 362	2 602	2 776	2 868	3 045	2 884
Life, physical, and social sciences	993	991	1 050	1 075	1 090	1 085	1 172	1 245	1 184	1 374
Community and social services	1 905	1 784	1 846	1 982	1 947	2 002	1 974	2 157	2 148	2 139
Legal	1 255	1 226	1 350	1 350	1 360	1 271	1 319	1 408	1 327	1 492
Education, training, and library	5 510	5 390	5 285	5 588	5 683	5 546	5 956	6 188	6 181	6 245
Arts, design, entertainment, sports, and media	1 380	1 449	1 445	1 582	1 658	1 660	1 767	1 883	1 815	1 953
Health care practitioner and technical	5 521	5 703	5 852	5 932	6 319	6 512	6 731	6 653	7 024	7 567
Services	12 855	13 676	13 456	13 650	13 795	14 426	14 771	15 003	15 451	14 855
Health care support	2 008	2 236	2 037	2 307	2 144	2 261	2 309	2 511	2 425	3 087
Protective services	2 589	2 571	2 535	2 582	2 498	2 482	2 503	2 539	2 607	2 662
Food preparation and serving related	3 408	3 797	3 631	3 508	3 641	4 130	4 140	4 060	4 285	4 061
Building and grounds cleaning and maintenance	2 942	3 098	3 056	3 190	3 243	3 205	3 344	3 306	3 479	3 256
Personal care and services	1 908	1 974	2 196	2 062	2 269	2 348	2 474	2 588	2 654	1 789
Sales and office	21 859	21 949	22 121	22 841	22 843	22 520	22 571	22 598	23 056	21 691
Sales and related	9 187	9 191	9 312	10 010	9 937	9 757	9 929	10 026	10 172	9 562
Office and administrative support	12 671	12 758	12 810	12 831	12 906	12 763	12 642	12 571	12 883	12 130
Natural resources, construction, and maintenance	8 298	8 584	8 897	9 317	9 715	9 846	10 212	10 561	10 429	10 329
Farming, fishing, and forestry	532	562	539	621	631	768	737	730	708	723
Construction and extraction	4 029	4 283	4 329	4 604	5 077	5 081	5 303	5 664	5 795	5 525
Installation, maintenance, and repair	3 737	3 739	4 029	4 093	4 006	3 997	4 172	4 167	3 926	4 081
Production, transportation, and material moving	11 518	12 041	12 166	12 724	13 129	13 388	13 327	13 817	14 309	14 472
Production	6 226	6 574	6 410	6 723	6 904	7 080	6 946	6 966	7 291	6 677
Transportation and material moving	5 292	5 467	5 756	6 001	6 225	6 308	6 381	6 851	7 018	7 794
Armed forces	727	749	689	687	697	681	593	710	625	739
Both Sexes, Median Annual Earnings										
Management, business, and financial operations	64 000	65 000	65 000	65 000	65 000	70 000	70 000	72 000	75 000	76 000
Management	68 000	70 000	70 000	70 000	70 000	75 000	75 000	76 000	80 000	80 000
Business and financial operations	56 000	57 000	57 000	60 000	60 000	60 000	60 000	65 000	66 000	71 000
Professional and related	55 000	56 000	58 705	58 000	59 000	60 000	61 000	64 000	65 000	67 500
Computer and mathematical	70 000	73 000	75 000	75 000	80 000	80 000	80 000	87 000	86 000	88 000
Architecture and engineering	75 000	75 000	75 000	80 000	76 000	80 000	80 000	85 000	82 000	85 000
Life, physical, and social sciences	60 000	61 599	67 000	70 000	65 000	70 000	75 500	65 000	70 000	70 000
Community and social services	40 000	40 000	41 000	42 000	44 000	45 000	46 000	45 000	47 000	49 000
Legal	75 000	85 000	80 000	86 000	90 000	88 000	94 209	92 000	100 000	109 000
Education, training, and library	45 000	46 200	47 000	45 000	47 907	49 000	50 000	50 000	50 000	52 000
Arts, design, entertainment, sports, and media	48 000	50 000	50 000	50 000	52 000	52 000	54 000	60 000	58 908	60 000
Health care practitioner and technical	57 638	58 000	60 000	60 000	58 000	60 000	60 998	62 000	65 000	65 000
Services	26 000	26 000	27 000	26 255	27 040	29 044	30 000	30 000	30 000	32 000
Health care support	26 270	26 000	26 000	28 000	26 922	28 000	29 100	30 000	30 000	30 500
Protective services	48 000	50 000	50 000	50 000	50 000	50 000	50 000	52 000	55 000	58 000
Food preparation and serving related	20 800	21 000	21 840	22 000	22 607	25 000	25 000	24 960	25 000	26 000
Building and grounds cleaning and maintenance	25 000	24 002	25 000	24 000	25 301	28 000	27 560	30 000	30 000	30 000
Personal care and services	25 000	25 000	25 000	24 000	25 500	30 000	30 000	30 000	29 799	31 000
Sales and office	35 000	35 002	36 000	37 440	37 000	39 000	40 000	40 000	42 000	45 000
Sales and related	40 000	40 000	40 000	40 000	40 000	43 000	44 000	45 000	48 000	50 000
Office and administrative support	34 000	35 000	35 000	35 000	35 000	36 000	37 010	38 000	40 000	42 000
Natural resources, construction, and maintenance	40 000	40 000	40 000	40 000	40 000	41 000	43 000	42 000	45 000	48 000
Farming, fishing, and forestry	23 000	24 000	24 000	25 600	27 300	26 443	30 400	30 000	32 000	32 000
Construction and extraction	40 000	39 500	38 000	40 000	40 000	40 000	41 700	40 555	43 000	48 000
Installation, maintenance, and repair	43 981	44 018	44 000	45 000	45 000	46 000	46 000	45 002	50 000	51 000
Production, transportation, and material moving	34 000	35 000	36 000	35 761	36 000	37 000	38 000	40 000	40 000	40 000
Production	34 000	35 000	36 000	36 000	36 000	36 000	38 000	40 000	40 000	41 600
Transportation and material moving	33 000	35 000	36 000	35 000	35 000	38 000	38 000	40 000	40 000	40 000
Armed forces	47 000	45 000	45 000	47 000	48 000	50 000	50 156	50 000	52 000	52 000

Table 1-40. Number and Median Annual Earnings of Year-Round, Full-Time Wage and Salary Workers, by Sex and Occupation of Job Held the Longest, 2010–2019—*Continued*

(Thousands of people, dollars.)

Sex and occupation	2010	2011	2012	2013	2014	2015	2016	2017	2018	2019
Men, Number of Workers										
Management, business, and financial operations	9 569	9 886	9 917	10 137	10 773	11 084	11 513	11 388	11 885	12 307
Management	7 249	7 497	7 666	7 742	8 103	8 344	8 593	8 381	8 875	8 953
Business and financial operations	2 320	2 389	2 252	2 395	2 670	2 739	2 919	3 007	3 010	3 354
Professional and related	10 126	10 228	10 731	10 858	11 194	11 520	11 977	12 548	12 516	13 371
Computer and mathematical	2 244	2 329	2 564	2 636	2 821	3 100	3 125	3 372	3 383	3 838
Architecture and engineering	2 110	2 144	2 073	2 004	2 044	2 231	2 322	2 402	2 635	2 482
Life, physical, and social sciences	562	605	615	589	622	656	667	680	611	684
Community and social services	701	679	742	792	740	704	740	791	727	753
Legal	605	616	686	615	666	611	620	697	640	688
Education, training, and library	1 601	1 522	1 504	1 586	1 653	1 577	1 690	1 790	1 702	1 719
Arts, design, entertainment, sports, and media	839	860	824	989	937	940	1 013	1 083	979	1 103
Health care practitioner and technical	1 464	1 473	1 724	1 645	1 711	1 701	1 799	1 732	1 839	2 104
Services	6 426	6 923	7 040	6 931	6 922	7 323	7 417	7 471	7 465	7 153
Health care support	242	268	269	277	284	280	329	352	307	457
Protective services	2 070	2 108	2 041	2 087	2 054	1 998	2 008	2 065	2 077	2 099
Food preparation and serving related	1 743	2 050	2 068	1 880	1 896	2 309	2 286	2 116	2 255	2 126
Building and grounds cleaning and maintenance	1 862	1 974	2 055	2 069	2 057	2 050	2 171	2 220	2 104	2 036
Personal care and services	508	523	606	618	629	685	624	718	722	435
Sales and office	8 872	8 971	8 874	9 386	9 395	9 234	9 333	9 452	9 718	8 716
Sales and related	5 363	5 425	5 436	5 867	5 680	5 631	5 614	5 719	5 849	5 351
Office and administrative support	3 509	3 545	3 439	3 519	3 715	3 603	3 719	3 733	3 870	3 365
Natural resources, construction, and maintenance	7 936	8 274	8 550	8 996	9 330	9 456	9 820	10 117	9 949	9 794
Farming, fishing, and forestry	430	474	445	501	521	617	589	580	545	596
Construction and extraction	3 909	4 192	4 245	4 534	4 948	4 959	5 182	5 513	5 600	5 276
Installation, maintenance, and repair	3 597	3 608	3 860	3 961	3 861	3 880	4 049	4 024	3 805	3 922
Production, transportation, and material moving	9 214	9 583	9 754	10 331	10 490	10 775	10 710	10 818	11 357	11 391
Production	4 612	4 813	4 814	5 090	5 098	5 281	5 142	5 011	5 398	4 962
Transportation and material moving	4 602	4 770	4 940	5 241	5 392	5 495	5 568	5 806	5 959	6 429
Armed forces	649	677	622	625	616	620	525	644	596	657
Men, Median Annual Earnings										
Management, business, and financial operations	75 000	75 000	75 000	75 000	75 000	80 000	80 000	82 000	85 000	90 000
Management	78 000	80 000	75 056	77 975	78 000	82 000	83 000	85 000	90 000	90 000
Business and financial operations	67 000	65 000	67 500	70 000	68 000	70 000	72 000	75 000	75 000	84 000
Professional and related	67 000	70 000	70 000	71 000	70 000	75 000	75 000	78 000	80 000	80 000
Computer and mathematical	75 000	79 000	80 000	78 000	81 000	85 000	84 000	90 002	90 000	90 000
Architecture and engineering	77 000	75 000	79 002	80 000	78 000	80 000	80 000	90 000	85 000	90 000
Life, physical, and social sciences	64 000	65 000	72 000	76 000	70 000	75 000	84 152	68 797	76 000	72 000
Community and social services	42 002	42 000	42 000	42 640	45 000	50 000	50 000	45 000	50 000	50 000
Legal	120 000	120 000	100 000	125 000	127 000	120 000	133 125	135 000	140 000	152 000
Education, training, and library	53 000	55 000	55 000	56 000	55 000	56 000	60 000	60 000	60 000	60 000
Arts, design, entertainment, sports, and media	50 000	55 000	55 000	55 000	58 000	51 000	56 800	60 000	60 000	62 000
Health care practitioner and technical	75 000	75 000	75 000	78 000	75 000	85 000	80 000	78 893	88 000	90 000
Services	30 002	30 000	30 000	31 000	32 000	32 000	34 320	35 000	35 000	37 000
Health care support	34 000	29 904	30 000	35 000	30 000	30 000	32 170	35 000	39 700	35 000
Protective services	50 000	50 000	54 000	51 000	54 000	52 002	54 522	55 000	57 000	60 000
Food preparation and serving related	23 000	23 400	24 000	22 709	24 000	25 000	26 000	26 000	28 000	27 118
Building and grounds cleaning and maintenance	28 600	27 000	28 000	28 000	29 000	30 000	30 000	32 000	32 400	35 000
Personal care and services	30 000	32 000	32 000	30 000	32 000	35 000	35 000	40 000	33 000	36 137
Sales and office	42 000	43 000	45 000	44 400	45 000	48 000	49 000	48 000	50 000	51 186
Sales and related	48 000	50 000	49 000	50 000	50 000	51 000	52 000	52 000	57 000	59 000
Office and administrative support	37 000	37 000	40 000	40 000	40 000	40 000	40 000	40 000	42 000	46 000
Natural resources, construction, and maintenance	40 000	40 000	40 000	40 000	40 000	42 000	44 000	42 500	45 000	49 000
Farming, fishing, and forestry	23 400	25 000	25 000	28 705	29 900	28 000	32 000	32 517	35 000	34 000
Construction and extraction	40 000	40 000	39 000	40 000	40 000	40 000	42 000	40 560	44 000	48 000
Installation, maintenance, and repair	44 000	45 000	44 000	45 000	45 000	47 000	47 000	45 000	50 000	51 909
Production, transportation, and material moving	36 000	38 500	40 000	39 000	40 000	40 000	40 000	42 000	43 000	45 000
Production	36 944	40 000	40 000	40 000	40 000	40 000	42 000	44 120	45 000	48 000
Transportation and material moving	35 000	37 440	38 638	37 000	38 000	40 000	40 000	40 000	42 000	43 000
Armed forces	47 000	45 000	45 000	49 999	48 000	50 000	51 600	50 000	52 000	54 000

Table 1-40. Number and Median Annual Earnings of Year-Round, Full-Time Wage and Salary Workers, by Sex and Occupation of Job Held the Longest, 2010–2019—*Continued*

(Thousands of people, dollars.)

Sex and occupation	2010	2011	2012	2013	2014	2015	2016	2017	2018	2019
Women, Number of Workers										
Management, business, and financial operations	7 320	7 511	7 881	8 104	8 248	8 853	9 129	9 221	9 670	10 496
Management	4 555	4 643	4 882	4 904	5 137	5 584	5 776	5 834	6 083	6 450
Business and financial operations	2 765	2 867	2 999	3 200	3 110	3 269	3 353	3 388	3 587	4 046
Professional and related	11 840	11 937	12 020	12 394	12 915	13 202	13 906	14 249	14 718	15 356
Computer and mathematical	748	842	960	803	869	944	1 064	1 023	1 127	1 236
Architecture and engineering	299	307	325	298	318	371	454	466	410	402
Life, physical, and social sciences	431	386	435	486	468	429	505	565	574	690
Community and social services	1 204	1 105	1 104	1 190	1 208	1 298	1 233	1 366	1 421	1 386
Legal	650	610	664	735	694	660	699	711	688	804
Education, training, and library	3 909	3 868	3 781	4 001	4 030	3 969	4 266	4 398	4 479	4 526
Arts, design, entertainment, sports, and media	541	589	622	593	721	720	753	800	836	850
Health care practitioner and technical	4 057	4 230	4 129	4 287	4 608	4 811	4 932	4 920	5 184	5 462
Services	6 429	6 753	6 416	6 718	6 874	7 103	7 353	7 532	7 986	7 702
Health care support	1 766	1 969	1 768	2 030	1 860	1 980	1 980	2 159	2 118	2 630
Protective services	519	463	494	495	443	484	496	474	531	564
Food preparation and serving related	1 665	1 747	1 562	1 628	1 745	1 821	1 854	1 943	2 030	1 935
Building and grounds cleaning and maintenance	1 079	1 125	1 001	1 121	1 186	1 155	1 172	1 086	1 376	1 220
Personal care and services	1 400	1 451	1 590	1 444	1 640	1 663	1 851	1 870	1 932	1 354
Sales and office	12 986	12 979	13 247	13 455	13 448	13 285	13 238	13 146	13 338	12 975
Sales and related	3 824	3 766	3 876	4 143	4 256	4 126	4 315	4 307	4 324	4 211
Office and administrative support	9 162	9 213	9 371	9 313	9 191	9 159	8 923	8 839	9 014	8 764
Natural resources, construction, and maintenance	361	310	347	321	385	390	392	444	480	535
Farming, fishing, and forestry	102	87	94	120	110	151	148	150	163	127
Construction and extraction	120	91	85	70	130	122	121	151	195	249
Installation, maintenance, and repair	140	131	169	132	145	117	122	143	121	159
Production, transportation, and material moving	2 304	2 458	2 412	2 393	2 639	2 613	2 617	3 000	2 951	3 081
Production	1 614	1 761	1 596	1 633	1 806	1 800	1 804	1 955	1 893	1 715
Transportation and material moving	690	697	816	760	833	813	813	1 045	1 058	1 366
Armed forces	78	72	67	62	81	61	68	66	29	83
Women, Median Annual Earnings										
Management, business, and financial operations	52 779	52 000	54 000	55 000	56 000	59 000	60 000	60 000	63 000	65 000
Management	55 000	55 000	58 000	57 000	60 000	60 000	62 000	65 000	65 000	67 000
Business and financial operations	50 000	50 000	50 000	52 000	52 000	52 000	54 574	57 000	60 000	63 000
Professional and related	49 000	50 000	50 000	50 000	50 000	51 500	54 000	55 000	55 000	59 000
Computer and mathematical	65 000	65 000	66 002	71 000	73 000	70 000	70 000	80 000	75 000	82 500
Architecture and engineering	60 000	62 400	65 000	64 000	65 000	65 000	75 000	72 000	75 000	70 000
Life, physical, and social sciences	56 000	55 000	61 008	63 000	56 627	65 465	70 000	63 000	60 000	70 000
Community and social services	39 000	40 000	40 000	40 000	42 720	43 000	45 000	45 600	45 000	48 000
Legal	57 257	51 875	55 000	57 075	60 000	66 000	72 000	70 000	70 000	80 000
Education, training, and library	42 000	45 000	44 000	43 000	45 000	45 040	47 849	47 000	48 000	50 000
Arts, design, entertainment, sports, and media	42 000	43 000	45 000	48 000	49 000	53 000	50 000	55 000	55 000	60 000
Health care practitioner and technical	53 000	53 000	55 000	55 000	55 000	56 000	59 000	60 000	60 000	60 000
Services	23 000	23 000	24 000	24 000	24 000	25 000	26 000	26 000	28 000	29 000
Health care support	25 000	26 000	26 000	27 000	26 000	27 040	28 500	29 000	30 000	30 000
Protective services	38 500	42 000	42 000	43 419	38 000	39 800	39 915	45 000	47 454	46 000
Food preparation and serving related	19 000	20 000	20 000	22 000	20 000	24 000	23 000	22 000	25 000	25 000
Building and grounds cleaning and maintenance	20 000	20 020	20 000	20 000	21 000	22 000	22 000	23 000	25 000	24 002
Personal care and services	23 000	23 000	25 000	22 000	25 000	26 000	27 262	26 000	27 000	30 000
Sales and office	32 000	33 000	33 000	35 000	34 000	35 000	35 000	36 400	38 000	40 000
Sales and related	30 000	30 000	30 000	30 000	30 000	32 000	32 000	35 000	35 000	40 000
Office and administrative support	33 000	34 000	35 000	35 000	35 000	35 000	36 000	37 000	39 000	40 000
Natural resources, construction, and maintenance	30 000	30 000	32 000	30 000	30 000	30 000	30 000	38 000	33 218	37 613
Farming, fishing, and forestry	20 000	20 000	20 498	22 093	23 000	25 000	28 013	24 000	28 392	25 000
Construction and extraction	33 670	28 323	30 645	31 200	29 052	38 801	34 965	41 002	36 296	40 000
Installation, maintenance, and repair	41 888	35 000	43 889	43 000	37 000	38 639	37 000	48 000	38 000	48 000
Production, transportation, and material moving	25 000	25 000	27 560	28 000	27 000	29 000	30 000	30 000	30 000	30 368
Production	25 000	25 000	27 000	27 901	27 000	29 000	29 000	31 200	30 090	32 000
Transportation and material moving	25 000	26 000	28 000	28 000	27 000	29 000	30 000	28 000	30 000	30 000
Armed forces	50 000	52 000	48 000	39 000	45 000	50 121	47 860	48 000	55 648	46 487

Table 1-41. Distribution of Employed Wage and Salary Workers by Tenure with Current Employer, Age, Sex, Race, and Hispanic Origin, January 2020

(Thousands of people, percent.)

Characteristic	Number employed/ (in thousands)	Percent distribution by tenure with current employer								
		Total	12 months or less	13 to 23 months	2 years	3 to 4 years	5 to 9 years	10 to 14 years	15 to 19 years	20 years or more
Both Sexes										
16 years and over	141 374	100.0	22.2	7.0	5.7	17.8	19.3	10.6	6.6	10.8
16 to 19 years	4 792	100.0	74.9	11.3	7.7	5.8	0.3	-	-	-
20 years and over	136 581	100.0	20.4	6.8	5.6	18.3	19.9	11.0	6.8	11.2
20 to 24 years	13 514	100.0	50.8	13.5	10.8	20.2	4.6	-	-	-
25 to 34 years	34 141	100.0	27.6	9.5	7.9	26.4	23.0	5.0	0.7	-
35 to 44 years	30 001	100.0	16.9	5.9	4.9	18.6	24.7	16.2	8.8	4.0
45 to 54 years	27 932	100.0	12.7	4.6	3.5	13.6	20.7	14.8	11.4	18.6
55 to 64 years	23 027	100.0	9.7	4.0	3.3	12.7	18.1	13.5	10.6	28.2
65 years and over	7 966	100.0	9.0	3.5	3.6	11.2	17.4	14.8	10.6	30.0
Men										
16 years and over	72 676	100.0	21.2	6.6	5.6	18.0	19.7	10.6	6.7	11.7
16 to 19 years	2 310	100.0	73.8	11.2	7.6	7.3	-	-	-	-
20 years and over	70 366	100.0	19.5	6.4	5.6	18.3	20.3	11.0	6.9	12.1
20 to 24 years	6 870	100.0	48.5	13.6	11.3	21.8	4.8	0.1	-	-
25 to 34 years	17 795	100.0	25.9	9.0	7.8	27.0	23.9	5.5	0.8	-
35 to 44 years	15 649	100.0	15.9	5.3	5.0	17.7	25.4	16.6	9.3	4.8
45 to 54 years	14 321	100.0	12.0	4.3	3.5	13.1	20.3	14.6	11.3	20.8
55 to 64 years	11 646	100.0	9.8	3.9	2.9	12.4	18.1	12.4	10.4	30.2
65 years and over	4 085	100.0	9.7	3.0	3.1	11.9	17.6	14.2	10.1	30.4
Women										
16 years and over	68 697	100.0	23.3	7.4	5.7	17.7	18.8	10.6	6.6	9.9
16 to 19 years	2 482	100.0	76.0	11.5	7.7	4.3	0.5	-	-	-
20 years and over	66 215	100.0	21.4	7.2	5.6	18.2	19.5	11.0	6.8	10.3
20 to 24 years	6 644	100.0	53.2	13.5	10.3	18.6	4.4	-	-	-
25 to 34 years	16 346	100.0	29.4	10.1	8.0	25.7	21.9	4.4	0.5	-
35 to 44 years	14 352	100.0	17.9	6.7	4.7	19.5	24.0	15.7	8.4	3.1
45 to 54 years	13 612	100.0	13.5	4.9	3.5	14.1	21.2	15.0	11.5	16.4
55 to 64 years	11 381	100.0	9.5	4.1	3.7	13.0	18.2	14.7	10.7	26.1
65 years and over	3 881	100.0	8.2	4.0	4.1	10.4	17.2	15.4	11.2	29.6
White										
16 years and over	109 188	100.0	21.5	7.0	5.4	17.3	19.5	10.7	6.8	11.7
Men	56 942	100.0	20.6	6.5	5.4	17.3	19.9	10.6	7.0	12.8
Women	52 247	100.0	22.6	7.5	5.4	17.4	19.1	10.8	6.7	10.5
Black										
16 years and over	17 353	100.0	25.8	6.4	6.4	20.1	17.9	9.2	5.6	8.5
Men	8 039	100.0	25.3	6.5	6.4	21.5	17.3	9.3	5.3	8.4
Women	9 315	100.0	26.3	6.4	6.4	18.9	18.4	9.1	5.9	8.6
Asian										
16 years and over	9 321	100.0	19.5	7.4	6.8	19.4	20.8	12.1	7.0	7.0
Men	4 886	100.0	18.5	7.6	5.8	19.9	22.1	12.3	7.0	6.9
Women	4 435	100.0	20.7	7.2	8.0	18.7	19.5	12.0	7.0	7.0
Hispanic[1]										
16 years and over	25 806	100.0	25.5	6.2	6.8	20.0	19.3	9.8	5.4	7.0
Men	14 242	100.0	24.6	5.1	6.7	19.6	20.6	10.4	5.6	7.4
Women	11 564	100.0	26.6	7.4	7.0	20.5	17.8	9.2	5.0	6.5

[1]May be of any race.
- = Data represents or rounds to zero.

Table 1-42. Median Years of Tenure with Current Employer for Employed Wage and Salary Workers, 25 Years and Over, by Educational Attainment, Sex, and Age, January 2020

(Number of years.)

Year, sex, and age	Total employed	25 to 34 years	35 to 44 years	45 to 54 years	55 to 64 years	65 years and over
Both Sexes	4.9	2.8	4.9	7.5	9.9	10.3
Less than a high school diploma	4.6	2.7	4.3	5.3	7.4	9.6
High school graduates, no college	5.0	2.8	4.7	6.7	10.2	10.3
Some college, no degree	4.7	2.7	4.8	6.9	9.8	10.1
Associate degree	5.0	2.9	4.7	7.4	10.4	10.2
College graduates	5.0	2.8	5.2	8.7	9.7	10.8
Bachelor's degree	4.8	2.9	5.2	8.0	9.4	10.1
Master's degree	5.4	3.0	5.2	9.1	10.2	10.9
Doctoral or professional degree	5.5	2.0	5.1	10.7	10.3	14.7
Men	5.1	2.9	5.1	8.2	10.0	10.3
Less than a high school diploma	4.8	2.8	4.7	5.5	9.5	9.1
High school graduates, no college	5.1	3.0	4.9	7.0	10.5	9.6
Some college, no degree	4.9	2.8	5.1	8.7	9.9	10.0
Associate degree	5.1	3.1	5.2	8.3	11.2	9.6
College graduates	5.2	2.9	5.4	9.6	9.5	11.6
Bachelor's degree	5.0	2.9	5.6	9.0	9.2	11.0
Master's degree	5.6	3.1	5.1	9.9	9.6	11.3
Doctoral or professional degree	6.2	2.2	5.3	11.1	10.2	14.7
Women	4.8	2.7	4.6	6.8	9.8	10.4
Less than a high school diploma	4.1	2.6	3.4	5.0	5.4	10.0
High school graduates, no college	4.9	2.4	4.4	6.2	9.9	11.6
Some college, no degree	4.4	2.6	4.5	5.2	9.6	10.2
Associate degree	4.9	2.7	4.2	6.6	10.2	11.1
College graduates	4.9	2.8	5.0	7.9	9.9	10.2
Bachelor's degree	4.6	2.9	4.8	7.2	9.5	9.5
Master's degree	5.3	2.8	5.2	8.4	10.8	10.5
Doctoral or professional degree	5.1	1.9	5.0	10.4	10.3	14.8

Table 1-43. Median Years of Tenure with Current Employer for Employed Wage and Salary Workers, by Age and Sex, Selected Years, February 1998–January 2020

(Number of years.)

Sex and age	February 1998	February 2000	January 2002	January 2004	January 2006	January 2008	January 2010	January 2012	January 2014	January 2016	January 2018	January 2020
Both Sexes												
16 years and over	3.6	3.5	3.7	4.0	4.0	4.1	4.4	4.6	4.6	4.2	4.2	4.1
16 to 17 years	0.6	0.6	0.7	0.7	0.6	0.7	0.7	0.7	0.7	0.6	0.6	0.7
18 to 19 years	0.7	0.7	0.8	0.8	0.7	0.8	1.0	0.8	0.8	0.8	0.8	0.8
20 to 24 years	1.1	1.1	1.2	1.3	1.3	1.3	1.5	1.3	1.3	1.3	1.2	1.3
25 years and over	4.7	4.7	4.7	4.9	4.9	5.1	5.2	5.4	5.5	5.1	5.0	4.9
25 to 34 years	2.7	2.6	2.7	2.9	2.9	2.7	3.1	3.2	3.0	2.8	2.8	2.8
35 to 44 years	5.0	4.8	4.6	4.9	4.9	4.9	5.1	5.3	5.2	4.9	4.9	4.9
45 to 54 years	8.1	8.2	7.6	7.7	7.3	7.6	7.8	7.8	7.9	7.9	7.6	7.5
55 to 64 years	10.1	10.0	9.9	9.6	9.3	9.9	10.0	10.3	10.4	10.1	10.1	9.9
65 years and over	7.8	9.4	8.6	9.0	8.8	10.2	9.9	10.3	10.3	10.3	10.2	10.3
Men												
16 years and over	3.8	3.8	3.9	4.1	4.1	4.2	4.6	4.7	4.7	4.3	4.3	4.3
16 to 17 years	0.6	0.6	0.8	0.7	0.7	0.7	0.7	0.6	0.7	0.6	0.5	0.7
18 to 19 years	0.7	0.7	0.8	0.8	0.7	0.8	1.0	0.8	0.9	0.8	0.8	0.8
20 to 24 years	1.2	1.2	1.4	1.3	1.4	1.4	1.6	1.4	1.4	1.3	1.3	1.4
25 years and over	4.9	4.9	4.9	5.1	5.0	5.2	5.3	5.5	5.5	5.2	5.1	5.1
25 to 34 years	2.8	2.7	2.8	3.0	2.9	2.8	3.2	3.2	3.1	2.9	2.9	2.9
35 to 44 years	5.5	5.3	5.0	5.2	5.1	5.2	5.3	5.4	5.4	5.0	5.0	5.1
45 to 54 years	9.4	9.5	9.1	9.6	8.1	8.2	8.5	8.5	8.2	8.4	8.1	8.2
55 to 64 years	11.2	10.2	10.2	9.8	9.5	10.1	10.4	10.7	10.7	10.2	10.2	10.0
65 years and over	7.1	9.0	8.1	8.2	8.3	10.4	9.7	10.2	10.0	10.2	10.2	10.3
Women												
16 years and over	3.4	3.3	3.4	3.8	3.9	3.9	4.2	4.6	4.5	4.0	4.0	3.9
16 to 17 years	0.6	0.6	0.7	0.6	0.6	0.6	0.7	0.7	0.7	0.6	0.7	0.7
18 to 19 years	0.7	0.7	0.8	0.8	0.7	0.8	1.0	0.8	0.8	0.8	0.8	0.8
20 to 24 years	1.1	1.0	1.1	1.3	1.2	1.3	1.5	1.3	1.3	1.2	1.2	1.2
25 years and over	4.4	4.4	4.4	4.7	4.8	4.9	5.1	5.4	5.4	5.0	4.9	4.8
25 to 34 years	2.5	2.5	2.5	2.8	2.8	2.6	3.0	3.1	2.9	2.6	2.7	2.7
35 to 44 years	4.5	4.3	4.2	4.5	4.6	4.7	4.9	5.2	5.1	4.8	4.7	4.6
45 to 54 years	7.2	7.3	6.5	6.4	6.7	7.0	7.1	7.3	7.6	7.5	7.1	6.8
55 to 64 years	9.6	9.9	9.6	9.2	9.2	9.8	9.7	10.0	10.2	10.0	10.1	9.8
65 years and over	8.7	9.7	9.4	9.6	9.5	9.9	10.1	10.5	10.5	10.4	10.1	10.4

Table 1-44. Median Years of Tenure with Current Employer for Employed Wage and Salary Workers, by Industry, Selected Years, February 2000–January 2020

(Number of years.)

Industry	February 2000	January 2002	January 2004	January 2006	January 2008	January 2010	January 2012	January 2014	January 2016	January 2018	January 2020
TOTAL, 16 YEARS AND OVER	3.5	3.7	4.0	4.0	4.1	4.4	4.6	4.6	4.2	4.2	4.1
Private Sector	3.2	3.3	3.5	3.6	3.6	4.0	4.2	4.1	3.7	3.8	3.7
Agriculture and related industries	3.7	4.2	3.7	3.8	4.3	4.8	4.1	3.6	4.5	4.6	3.5
Nonagricultural industries	3.2	3.3	3.5	3.6	3.6	4.0	4.2	4.1	3.7	3.8	3.7
Mining	4.8	4.5	5.2	3.8	4.1	4.8	3.5	4.0	4.6	5.1	4.6
Construction	2.7	3.0	3.0	3.0	3.5	4.2	4.3	3.9	4.0	4.1	4.0
Manufacturing	4.9	5.4	5.8	5.5	5.9	6.1	6.0	5.9	5.3	5.0	5.1
Durable goods manufacturing	4.8	5.5	6.0	5.6	6.1	6.6	6.1	6.0	5.4	5.3	5.3
Nonmetallic mineral product	5.5	5.3	4.8	5.0	4.8	7.7	7.0	7.6	5.1	5.2	5.2
Primary metals and fabricated metal product	5.0	6.3	6.4	6.2	5.2	7.2	5.6	6.1	6.0	6.0	5.4
Machinery manufacturing	5.3	6.8	6.4	6.6	6.0	8.3	5.4	6.2	5.5	5.7	5.3
Computers and electronic product	3.9	4.7	5.2	5.9	6.7	5.9	7.7	5.1	5.3	5.8	6.1
Electrical equipment and appliances	5.0	5.5	9.8	6.2	6.2	5.0	5.9	5.8	4.7	4.5	4.5
Transportation equipment	6.4	7.0	7.7	7.2	7.8	8.3	7.1	7.1	6.1	5.7	5.5
Wood product	3.7	4.3	5.0	4.7	6.2	4.7	5.3	4.6	4.7	3.5	3.9
Furniture and fixtures	4.4	4.7	4.7	4.2	5.2	5.0	6.5	5.9	4.8	4.8	5.5
Miscellaneous manufacturing	3.7	4.5	4.6	3.9	4.7	5.4	4.8	5.1	5.0	4.8	4.7
Nondurable goods manufacturing	5.0	5.3	5.5	5.4	5.4	5.5	5.8	5.9	5.1	4.7	4.8
Food manufacturing	4.6	5.0	4.9	5.2	4.3	4.7	4.9	4.7	4.5	3.9	4.2
Beverage and tobacco product	5.5	4.6	8.0	5.4	6.9	8.1	6.4	4.8	4.3	4.1	3.9
Textiles, apparel, and leather	4.7	5.0	5.0	4.4	4.6	4.7	4.3	5.3	5.6	5.0	5.0
Paper and printing	5.1	6.2	6.9	6.3	5.5	6.8	9.7	9.7	5.3	5.4	5.9
Petroleum and coal product	9.5	9.8	11.4	5.0	4.3	5.1	6.4	6.1	6.6	5.0	5.7
Chemicals	6.0	5.7	5.3	6.1	7.6	7.3	6.1	7.1	5.3	4.7	5.2
Plastics and rubber product	4.6	5.3	5.7	5.0	5.3	7.4	6.1	6.5	5.3	5.0	4.5
Wholesale and retail trade	2.7	2.8	3.1	3.1	3.2	3.6	3.7	3.6	3.3	3.2	3.3
Wholesale trade	3.9	3.9	4.3	4.6	5.0	5.2	5.5	5.8	5.2	5.1	5.0
Retail trade	2.5	2.6	2.8	2.8	2.9	3.3	3.3	3.3	3.0	3.0	3.1
Transportation and utilities	4.7	4.9	5.3	4.9	5.1	5.3	5.6	5.1	4.6	4.8	4.3
Transportation and warehousing	4.0	4.3	4.7	4.3	4.6	5.0	5.3	4.7	4.4	4.2	3.9
Utilities	11.5	13.4	13.3	10.4	10.1	9.1	9.5	9.2	7.4	9.5	7.7
Information[1]	3.4	3.3	4.3	4.8	4.7	5.0	5.4	4.8	4.3	4.4	4.2
Publishing, except Internet	4.2	4.8	4.7	5.3	4.7	5.6	6.6	5.3	5.7	4.1	5.4
Motion picture and sound recording industries	1.6	2.3	2.2	1.9	1.9	3.8	2.6	2.4	2.4	2.9	2.7
Broadcasting, except Internet	3.6	3.1	4.0	4.6	3.4	4.3	4.9	4.1	3.6	5.0	5.3
Telecommunications	4.3	3.4	4.6	5.3	6.9	6.6	7.4	7.8	6.0	5.2	6.6
Financial activities	3.5	3.6	3.9	4.0	4.5	4.6	4.9	5.0	4.8	4.7	4.8
Finance and insurance	3.6	3.9	4.1	4.1	4.7	4.8	5.0	5.3	5.0	5.0	4.9
Finance	3.3	3.6	4.0	3.9	4.4	4.5	4.7	5.0	5.0	4.8	4.8
Insurance	4.4	4.5	4.4	4.7	5.2	5.5	5.7	6.0	5.2	5.4	5.0
Real estate and rental and leasing	3.1	3.0	3.3	3.4	3.7	3.9	4.5	4.4	3.8	3.6	4.6
Real estate	3.1	3.2	3.5	3.5	3.9	4.1	4.5	4.6	3.9	3.7	4.7
Rental and leasing services	3.0	2.2	2.9	3.1	3.0	3.3	4.2	3.5	3.4	3.4	3.8
Professional and business services	2.4	2.7	3.2	3.2	3.1	3.4	3.8	3.6	3.4	3.6	3.5
Professional and technical services	2.6	3.1	3.6	3.8	3.3	4.0	4.4	4.2	3.9	3.9	3.9
Management, administrative, and waste services[1]	2.0	2.1	2.6	2.5	2.5	2.9	3.1	3.1	2.8	3.3	2.9
Administrative and support services	1.8	1.9	2.4	2.4	2.4	2.8	3.0	3.0	2.6	3.1	2.8
Waste management and remediation services	3.6	4.3	3.4	4.1	4.1	2.9	4.4	4.7	4.6	5.8	5.3
Education and health services	3.4	3.5	3.6	4.0	4.1	4.1	4.4	4.5	3.9	3.9	3.8
Education services	3.2	3.6	3.8	4.0	4.3	4.4	4.3	4.8	4.0	4.2	3.9
Health care and social assistance	3.5	3.5	3.6	4.1	4.1	4.1	4.4	4.4	3.9	3.9	3.8
Hospitals	5.1	4.9	4.7	5.2	5.4	5.3	6.0	5.7	5.6	4.9	5.0
Health services, except hospitals	3.2	3.1	3.3	3.6	3.6	3.6	3.8	3.9	3.4	3.5	3.4
Social assistance	2.4	2.5	2.8	3.1	3.0	3.1	3.1	3.2	2.6	3.0	2.9
Leisure and hospitality	1.7	1.8	2.0	1.9	2.1	2.5	2.4	2.3	2.2	2.2	2.3
Arts, entertainment, and recreation	2.6	2.3	2.8	3.1	2.8	3.3	3.1	3.0	3.2	3.0	3.3
Accommodation and food services	1.5	1.6	1.9	1.6	1.9	2.3	2.3	2.1	2.0	2.1	2.1
Accommodation	2.8	2.7	3.1	2.5	3.1	3.3	3.8	3.5	3.0	3.1	3.2
Food services and drinking places	1.4	1.4	1.6	1.4	1.6	2.2	2.1	2.0	1.8	2.0	2.0
Other services	3.1	3.3	3.3	3.2	3.3	4.0	3.8	4.0	3.9	4.0	4.1
Other services, except private households	3.2	3.3	3.5	3.3	3.4	4.1	3.8	4.2	4.1	3.9	4.1
Repair and maintenance	3.0	3.0	3.2	2.9	3.0	4.0	3.7	4.0	3.5	3.3	3.3
Personal and laundry services	2.7	2.8	3.4	2.8	3.2	3.5	3.5	3.7	3.8	3.6	3.8
Membership associations and organizations	4.0	4.1	3.9	4.2	4.4	4.5	4.3	4.9	4.9	4.5	4.8
Other services, private households	3.0	2.7	2.3	2.8	2.8	3.4	3.3	3.0	3.3	4.5	4.0
Public Sector	7.1	6.7	6.9	6.9	7.2	7.2	7.8	7.8	7.7	6.8	6.5
Federal government	11.5	11.3	10.4	9.9	9.9	7.9	9.5	8.5	8.8	8.3	8.2
State government	5.5	5.4	6.4	6.3	6.5	6.4	6.4	7.4	5.8	5.9	5.6
Local government	6.7	6.2	6.4	6.6	7.1	7.5	8.1	7.9	8.3	6.9	6.6

[1]Includes other industries not shown separately.

Table 1-45. Employment Status of the Population, by Sex and Marital Status, March 1996–March 2020

(Thousands of people, percent.)

Marital status and year	Men						Women					
	Population	Labor force					Population	Labor force				
		Total		Employed	Unemployed			Total		Employed	Unemployed	
		Number	Percent of population		Number	Percent of labor force		Number	Percent of population		Number	Percent of labor force
Single												
1996	28 695	20 561	71.7	18 097	2 464	12.0	23 632	15 417	65.2	14 084	1 333	8.6
1997	29 294	20 942	71.5	18 683	2 259	10.8	24 215	16 178	66.8	14 747	1 431	8.8
1998	29 558	21 255	71.9	19 124	2 131	10.0	24 808	16 885	68.1	15 626	1 259	7.5
1999	29 883	21 329	71.4	19 465	1 864	8.7	25 674	17 486	68.1	16 185	1 301	7.4
2000	30 232	21 641	71.6	19 823	1 818	8.4	25 863	17 749	68.6	16 446	1 303	7.3
2001	30 968	22 232	71.8	20 239	1 993	9.0	26 180	17 900	68.4	16 631	1 269	7.1
2002	32 220	22 761	70.6	20 066	2 695	11.8	26 942	18 079	67.1	16 499	1 580	8.7
2003	32 852	22 821	69.5	20 194	2 627	11.5	27 527	17 901	65.0	16 219	1 682	9.4
2004	33 786	23 212	68.7	20 434	2 778	12.0	28 033	18 089	64.5	16 506	1 583	8.8
2005	34 069	23 335	68.5	20 831	2 504	10.7	28 508	18 554	65.1	16 902	1 652	8.9
2006	34 906	24 369	69.8	21 961	2 408	9.9	29 357	18 989	64.7	17 444	1 545	8.1
2007	35 359	24 506	69.3	22 224	2 281	9.3	29 695	19 218	64.7	17 935	1 284	6.7
2008	36 522	25 229	69.1	22 695	2 534	10.0	30 772	19 889	64.6	18 369	1 520	7.6
2009	36 907	24 930	67.5	20 645	4 284	17.2	31 038	19 785	63.7	17 714	2 071	10.5
2010	38 110	25 663	67.3	21 038	4 626	18.0	32 085	19 973	62.3	17 517	2 457	12.3
2011	38 766	25 646	66.2	21 389	4 256	16.6	33 041	20 581	62.3	18 117	2 463	12.0
2012	38 933	25 615	65.8	21 838	3 778	14.7	34 241	21 417	62.5	18 895	2 523	11.8
2013	39 482	25 881	65.6	22 306	3 575	13.8	34 889	21 739	62.3	19 319	2 419	11.1
2014	40 338	26 602	65.9	23 220	3 382	12.7	35 288	22 174	62.8	19 974	2 200	9.9
2015	40 893	26 949	65.9	24 094	2 855	10.6	36 036	22 385	62.1	20 530	1 855	8.3
2016	41 933	27 894	66.5	25 275	2 619	9.4	37 035	23 216	62.7	21 359	1 856	8.0
2017	41 801	27 652	66.2	25 397	2 255	8.2	37 174	23 748	63.9	22 262	1 486	6.3
2018	42 654	28 755	67.4	26 516	2 239	7.8	37 786	24 390	64.5	23 031	1 359	5.6
2019	43 173	29 170	67.6	27 001	2 169	7.4	38 062	24 576	64.6	23 261	1 315	5.3
2020	43 825	29 066	66.3	26 490	2 576	8.9	38 888	24 752	63.7	22 955	1 797	7.3
Married, Spouse Present												
1996	53 996	41 837	77.5	40 356	1 481	3.5	54 640	33 382	61.1	32 258	1 124	3.4
1997	53 981	41 967	77.7	40 628	1 339	3.2	54 611	33 907	62.1	32 836	1 071	3.2
1998	54 685	42 288	77.3	41 039	1 249	3.0	55 241	34 136	61.8	33 028	1 108	3.2
1999	55 256	42 557	77.0	41 476	1 081	2.5	55 801	34 349	61.6	33 403	946	2.8
2000	55 897	43 254	77.4	42 261	993	2.3	56 432	34 959	61.9	33 998	961	2.7
2001	56 152	43 463	77.4	42 245	1 218	2.8	56 740	35 234	62.1	34 273	961	2.7
2002	57 325	44 271	77.2	42 508	1 763	4.0	57 883	35 624	61.5	34 295	1 329	3.7
2003	57 940	44 700	77.1	42 797	1 903	4.3	58 545	36 185	61.8	34 806	1 379	3.8
2004	58 395	44 860	76.8	43 247	1 613	3.6	59 008	35 918	60.9	34 582	1 336	3.7
2005	58 854	45 263	76.9	43 763	1 500	3.3	59 449	35 809	60.2	34 738	1 071	3.0
2006	58 850	45 082	76.6	43 877	1 205	2.7	59 476	36 192	60.9	35 185	1 007	2.8
2007	60 126	46 129	76.7	44 813	1 317	2.9	60 656	37 335	61.6	36 370	965	2.6
2008	59 455	45 451	76.4	43 958	1 493	3.3	60 108	37 074	61.7	35 919	1 155	3.1
2009	60 132	45 741	76.1	42 667	3 074	6.7	60 818	37 536	61.7	35 540	1 996	5.3
2010	59 694	45 110	75.6	41 762	3 348	7.4	60 339	37 201	61.7	34 964	2 237	6.0
2011	59 477	44 553	74.9	41 667	2 886	6.5	60 095	36 383	60.5	34 340	2 043	5.6
2012	60 346	44 915	74.4	42 387	2 528	5.6	61 011	36 363	59.6	34 423	1 940	5.3
2013	60 630	44 904	74.1	42 760	2 145	4.8	61 269	36 292	59.2	34 601	1 691	4.7
2014	61 224	44 874	73.3	43 091	1 784	4.0	61 917	36 257	58.6	34 759	1 499	4.1
2015	61 568	45 185	73.4	43 783	1 403	3.1	62 171	36 388	58.5	35 314	1 074	3.0
2016	61 973	45 348	73.2	44 021	1 327	2.9	62 577	36 858	58.9	35 731	1 127	3.1
2017	62 699	45 820	73.1	44 536	1 284	2.8	63 295	37 414	59.1	36 383	1 031	2.8
2018	63 026	45 855	72.8	44 759	1 096	2.4	63 683	37 136	58.3	36 176	960	2.6
2019	63 648	46 038	72.3	45 104	935	2.0	64 505	38 204	59.2	37 375	829	2.2
2020	64 075	45 927	71.7	44 440	1 487	3.2	64 851	37 863	58.4	36 545	1 318	3.5
Widowed, Divorced, or Separated												
1996	13 176	8 697	66.0	7 976	721	8.3	25 786	12 430	48.2	11 742	688	5.5
1997	14 113	9 420	66.7	8 715	705	7.5	26 301	12 814	48.7	12 071	743	5.8
1998	14 166	9 482	66.9	8 954	528	5.6	26 092	12 880	49.4	12 235	645	5.0
1999	14 225	9 449	66.4	8 971	478	5.1	26 199	12 951	49.4	12 307	644	5.0
2000	14 289	9 623	67.3	9 152	471	4.9	26 354	13 228	50.2	12 657	571	4.3
2001	14 392	9 421	65.5	8 927	494	5.2	26 747	13 454	50.3	12 887	567	4.2
2002	14 617	9 650	66.0	8 931	719	7.5	27 802	13 716	49.3	12 855	861	6.3
2003	15 180	9 855	64.9	9 020	835	8.5	28 240	14 154	50.1	13 240	914	6.5
2004	15 059	9 789	65.0	9 059	730	7.5	28 228	14 194	50.3	13 324	870	6.1
2005	15 779	10 256	65.0	9 569	687	6.7	28 576	14 233	49.8	13 472	761	5.3
2006	16 405	10 815	65.9	10 141	674	6.2	28 981	14 220	49.1	13 539	681	4.8
2007	16 247	10 799	66.5	10 150	650	6.0	28 950	14 320	49.5	13 620	700	4.9
2008	16 718	10 896	65.2	10 083	812	7.5	29 419	14 553	49.5	13 765	787	5.4
2009	16 719	10 687	63.9	9 224	1 463	13.7	29 471	14 449	49.0	13 169	1 281	8.9
2010	17 016	10 863	63.8	9 188	1 675	15.4	29 915	14 707	49.2	13 285	1 422	9.7
2011	17 744	11 095	62.5	9 676	1 420	12.8	29 876	14 610	48.9	13 221	1 389	9.5
2012	17 704	11 076	62.6	9 884	1 192	10.8	30 367	14 825	48.8	13 543	1 283	8.7
2013	18 090	11 045	61.1	9 968	1 077	10.8	30 633	14 688	47.9	13 494	1 193	8.1
2014	17 833	10 681	59.9	9 842	839	7.9	30 657	14 853	48.4	13 789	1 064	7.2
2015	18 277	10 973	60.0	10 110	864	7.9	31 135	14 607	46.9	13 792	815	5.6
2016	18 205	10 901	59.9	10 210	691	6.3	31 044	14 659	47.2	13 966	693	4.7
2017	18 445	10 883	59.0	10 333	549	5.0	31 000	14 375	46.4	13 643	731	5.1
2018	18 652	10 987	58.9	10 445	542	4.9	31 296	14 503	46.3	13 889	615	4.2
2019	18 206	10 540	57.9	10 029	511	4.8	30 932	14 181	45.8	13 647	534	3.8
2020	17 738	10 256	57.8	9 651	605	5.9	30 380	13 923	45.8	13 227	696	5.0

Note: See notes and definitions for information on historical comparability.

Table 1-45. Employment Status of the Population, by Sex and Marital Status, March 1996–March 2020 —Continued

(Thousands of people, percent.)

Marital status and year	Men						Women					
	Population	Labor force					Population	Labor force				
		Total		Employed	Unemployed			Total		Employed	Unemployed	
		Number	Percent of population		Number	Percent of labor force		Number	Percent of population		Number	Percent of labor force
Widowed												
1996	2 476	487	19.7	466	21	4.3	11 070	1 916	17.3	1 820	96	5.0
1997	2 686	559	20.8	529	30	5.4	11 058	2 018	18.2	1 926	92	4.6
1998	2 567	563	21.9	551	12	2.1	11 027	2 157	19.6	2 071	86	4.0
1999	2 540	562	22.1	532	30	5.3	10 943	2 039	18.6	1 942	97	4.8
2000	2 601	583	22.4	547	36	6.2	11 061	2 011	18.2	1 911	100	5.0
2001	2 638	568	21.5	546	22	3.9	11 182	2 137	19.1	2 045	92	4.3
2002	2 635	629	23.9	581	48	7.6	11 411	2 001	17.5	1 887	114	5.7
2003	2 694	628	23.3	588	40	6.4	11 295	2 087	18.5	1 991	96	4.6
2004	2 651	581	21.9	558	23	4.0	11 159	2 157	19.3	2 048	109	5.1
2005	2 729	618	22.6	590	28	4.5	11 125	2 111	19.0	2 005	106	5.0
2006	2 626	610	23.2	563	47	7.7	11 305	2 164	19.1	2 094	70	3.2
2007	2 697	631	23.4	588	43	6.8	11 220	2 058	18.3	1 971	87	4.2
2008	2 911	656	22.5	611	44	6.8	11 399	2 218	19.5	2 101	117	5.3
2009	2 813	632	22.5	543	90	14.2	11 446	2 174	19.0	2 032	143	6.6
2010	2 969	776	26.1	684	92	11.8	11 379	2 214	19.5	2 036	178	8.0
2011	2 931	698	23.8	648	50	7.1	11 310	2 291	20.3	2 118	173	7.6
2012	2 864	639	22.3	595	43	6.8	11 197	2 179	19.5	2 044	135	6.2
2013	3 122	686	22.0	631	55	8.1	11 234	2 132	19.0	1 987	145	6.8
2014	3 068	722	23.5	668	54	7.5	11 132	2 079	18.7	1 922	157	7.6
2015	3 271	782	23.9	746	36	4.6	11 333	2 153	19.0	2 035	119	5.5
2016	3 471	904	26.1	862	42	4.7	11 423	2 224	19.5	2 139	85	3.8
2017	3 280	810	24.7	758	52	6.5	11 684	2 369	20.3	2 244	125	5.3
2018	3 410	841	24.7	784	57	6.8	11 704	2 331	19.9	2 231	101	4.3
2019	3 471	828	23.8	801	26	3.2	11 433	2 123	18.6	2 041	81	3.8
2020	3 487	842	24.2	776	66	7.9	11 280	2 062	18.3	1 967	96	4.6
Divorced												
1996	7 734	5 954	77.0	5 468	486	8.2	10 508	7 829	74.5	7 468	361	4.6
1997	8 191	6 298	76.9	5 851	447	7.1	11 102	8 092	72.9	7 666	426	5.3
1998	8 307	6 378	76.8	6 045	333	5.2	11 065	8 038	72.6	7 687	351	4.4
1999	8 529	6 481	76.0	6 151	330	5.1	11 130	8 171	73.4	7 841	330	4.0
2000	8 532	6 583	77.2	6 279	304	4.6	11 061	8 505	76.9	8 217	288	3.4
2001	8 580	6 403	74.6	6 074	329	5.1	11 719	8 662	73.9	8 335	327	3.8
2002	8 643	6 519	75.4	6 053	466	7.1	12 227	8 902	72.8	8 416	486	5.5
2003	8 938	6 621	74.1	6 052	569	8.6	12 653	9 191	72.6	8 673	518	5.6
2004	8 942	6 622	74.1	6 104	518	7.8	12 817	9 246	72.1	8 706	540	5.8
2005	9 196	6 754	73.4	6 281	473	7.0	12 950	9 253	71.5	8 836	417	4.5
2006	9 646	7 065	73.2	6 631	434	6.1	13 107	9 188	70.1	8 799	389	4.2
2007	9 608	7 110	74.0	6 679	431	6.1	13 214	9 334	70.6	8 896	439	4.7
2008	9 767	7 106	72.8	6 607	499	7.0	13 551	9 387	69.3	8 938	449	4.8
2009	9 938	7 052	71.0	6 064	988	14.0	13 301	9 176	69.0	8 402	774	8.4
2010	9 944	7 018	70.6	5 888	1 131	16.1	13 758	9 394	68.3	8 510	885	9.4
2011	10 635	7 394	69.5	6 430	965	13.0	13 757	9 230	67.1	8 407	823	8.9
2012	10 662	7 394	69.3	6 572	822	11.1	14 210	9 416	66.3	8 620	797	8.5
2013	10 923	7 420	67.9	6 718	702	9.5	14 428	9 416	65.3	8 704	713	7.6
2014	10 630	7 044	66.3	6 456	588	8.3	14 633	9 615	65.7	9 020	596	6.2
2015	10 928	7 197	65.9	6 598	600	8.3	14 855	9 365	63.0	8 901	464	5.0
2016	10 689	7 117	66.6	6 671	446	6.3	14 835	9 358	63.1	8 923	435	4.7
2017	10 873	7 084	65.1	6 754	330	4.7	14 606	9 048	61.9	8 658	390	4.3
2018	11 031	7 188	65.2	6 845	343	4.8	14 830	9 143	61.6	8 822	321	3.5
2019	10 618	6 845	64.5	6 504	341	5.0	14 803	9 077	61.3	8 780	298	3.3
2020	10 666	6 875	64.5	6 476	400	5.8	14 677	9 010	61.4	8 609	402	2.7
Separated												
1996	2 966	2 255	76.0	2 041	214	9.5	4 209	2 684	63.8	2 453	231	8.6
1997	3 236	2 563	79.2	2 335	228	8.9	4 141	2 705	65.3	2 480	225	8.3
1998	3 293	2 542	77.2	2 358	184	7.2	4 000	2 683	67.1	2 476	207	7.7
1999	3 156	2 405	76.2	2 287	118	4.9	4 126	2 740	66.4	2 523	217	7.9
2000	3 157	2 456	77.8	2 326	130	5.3	4 012	2 711	67.6	2 528	183	6.8
2001	3 174	2 450	77.2	2 307	143	5.8	3 846	2 654	69.0	2 507	147	5.5
2002	3 339	2 502	74.9	2 297	205	8.2	4 164	2 812	67.5	2 551	261	9.3
2003	3 548	2 606	73.4	2 380	226	8.7	4 293	2 877	67.0	2 576	301	10.5
2004	3 466	2 586	74.6	2 397	189	7.3	4 251	2 791	65.7	2 569	222	8.0
2005	3 855	2 884	74.8	2 698	186	6.4	4 501	2 870	63.8	2 632	238	8.3
2006	4 132	3 141	76.0	2 947	194	6.2	4 569	2 869	62.8	2 647	222	7.7
2007	3 943	3 058	77.6	2 883	176	5.7	4 516	2 927	64.8	2 753	174	6.0
2008	4 040	3 134	77.6	2 865	269	8.6	4 469	2 947	65.9	2 726	221	7.5
2009	3 968	3 002	75.7	2 617	386	12.8	4 725	3 099	65.6	2 734	364	11.8
2010	4 103	3 069	74.8	2 616	452	14.7	4 778	3 099	64.8	2 739	359	11.6
2011	4 178	3 004	71.9	2 598	406	13.5	4 809	3 089	64.2	2 696	393	12.7
2012	4 177	3 044	72.9	2 717	327	10.7	4 960	3 230	65.1	2 879	351	10.9
2013	4 045	2 939	72.7	2 619	320	10.9	4 970	3 139	63.2	2 803	336	10.7
2014	4 134	2 915	70.5	2 718	197	6.8	4 892	3 159	64.6	2 848	311	9.9
2015	4 078	2 994	73.4	2 766	228	7.6	4 946	3 089	62.5	2 856	233	7.5
2016	4 045	2 879	71.2	2 677	202	7.0	4 786	3 077	64.3	2 905	172	5.6
2017	4 291	2 989	69.6	2 822	167	5.6	4 710	2 958	62.8	2 742	216	7.3
2018	4 211	2 958	70.2	2 816	142	4.8	4 762	3 029	63.6	2 836	193	6.4
2019	4 117	2 868	69.7	2 724	144	5.0	4 696	2 981	63.5	2 826	155	5.2
2020	3 585	2 538	70.8	2 400	139	5.5	4 423	2 851	64.4	2 652	199	7.0

Note: See notes and definitions for information on historical comparability.

Table 1-46. Employment Status of All Women and Single Women, by Presence and Age of Children, March 1996–March 2020

(Thousands of women, percent.)

Presence and age of children and year	All women							Single women						
	Civilian labor force	Civilian labor force as percent of population	Employed			Unemployed		Civilian labor force	Civilian labor force as percent of population	Employed			Unemployed	
			Number	Percent full time	Percent part time	Number	Percent of labor force			Number	Percent full time	Percent part time	Number	Percent of labor force
Women with No Children Under 18 Years														
1996	36 509	53.0	34 698	73.3	26.7	1 811	5.0	13 172	66.1	12 255	64.6	35.4	918	7.0
1997	37 295	53.6	35 572	73.7	26.3	1 723	4.6	13 405	66.5	12 442	64.0	36.0	964	7.2
1998	38 253	54.1	36 680	74.1	25.9	1 573	4.1	13 888	67.2	13 082	64.8	35.2	806	5.8
1999	39 316	54.3	37 589	74.6	25.4	1 727	4.4	14 435	67.1	13 491	65.6	34.4	944	6.5
2000	40 142	54.8	38 408	75.4	24.6	1 733	4.3	14 677	67.6	13 713	66.6	33.4	964	6.6
2001	40 836	54.9	39 219	75.7	24.3	1 617	4.0	14 877	67.4	13 993	67.3	32.7	884	5.9
2002	41 278	54.0	39 038	75.1	24.9	2 241	5.4	14 855	65.6	13 682	65.9	34.1	1 173	7.9
2003	42 039	54.1	39 667	74.8	25.2	2 372	5.6	14 678	63.5	13 430	65.1	34.9	1 249	8.5
2004	42 289	53.8	40 000	74.6	25.4	2 289	5.4	14 828	63.0	13 670	65.5	34.5	1 157	7.8
2005	42 039	54.1	39 667	74.8	25.2	2 372	5.6	14 678	63.5	13 430	65.1	34.9	1 249	8.5
2006	43 392	53.6	41 440	75.3	24.7	1 952	4.5	15 673	63.4	14 547	66.5	33.5	1 125	7.2
2007	44 039	53.9	42 279	75.3	24.7	1 760	4.0	15 704	63.4	14 801	66.4	33.6	903	5.7
2008	45 585	54.3	43 417	75.7	24.3	2 168	4.8	16 378	63.4	15 261	67.4	32.6	1 116	6.8
2009	45 649	53.8	42 343	73.3	26.7	3 306	7.2	16 112	62.1	14 607	64.9	35.1	1 506	9.3
2010	46 098	53.5	42 256	73.5	26.5	3 842	8.3	16 331	60.7	14 533	65.6	34.4	1 798	11.0
2011	46 198	53.0	42 569	73.3	26.7	3 629	7.9	16 758	60.8	15 016	65.2	34.8	1 743	10.4
2012	47 222	52.6	43 494	74.0	26.0	3 728	7.9	17 310	60.7	15 473	66.3	33.7	1 837	10.6
2013	47 607	52.3	44 294	73.6	26.4	3 313	7.0	17 650	60.5	15 915	65.5	34.5	1 735	9.8
2014	48 076	52.1	44 980	73.3	26.7	3 096	6.4	18 168	61.2	16 552	65.1	34.9	1 616	8.9
2015	48 273	51.7	45 794	74.4	25.6	2 479	5.1	18 199	60.2	16 873	67.9	32.1	1 326	7.3
2016	49 663	52.1	47 180	74.5	25.5	2 484	5.0	19 130	60.9	17 699	68.0	32.0	1 430	7.5
2017	50 675	52.5	48 541	74.7	25.3	2 134	4.2	19 711	62.2	18 603	68.6	31.4	1 108	5.6
2018	51 227	52.3	49 247	74.7	25.3	1 980	3.9	20 359	62.8	19 323	68.6	31.4	1 035	5.1
2019	52 068	52.5	50 244	75.4	24.6	1 824	3.5	20 692	62.9	19 682	70.3	29.7	1 010	4.9
2020	51 915	51.8	49 336	76.8	23.2	2 579	5.0	20 979	62.0	19 514	71.9	28.1	1 465	7.0
Women with Children Under 18 Years														
1996	24 720	70.2	23 386	72.6	27.4	1 334	5.4	2 245	60.5	1 829	73.5	26.5	416	18.5
1997	25 604	72.1	24 082	74.1	25.9	1 522	5.9	2 772	68.1	2 305	76.6	23.4	467	16.8
1998	25 647	72.3	24 209	74.0	26.0	1 438	5.6	2 997	72.5	2 544	75.6	24.4	453	15.1
1999	25 469	72.1	24 305	74.1	25.9	1 165	4.6	3 051	73.4	2 694	75.8	24.2	357	11.7
2000	25 795	72.9	24 693	74.6	25.4	1 102	4.3	3 073	73.9	2 734	79.7	20.3	339	11.0
2001	25 751	73.1	24 572	75.6	24.4	1 179	4.6	3 022	73.8	2 638	81.8	18.2	385	12.7
2002	26 140	72.2	24 612	74.8	25.2	1 529	5.8	3 224	75.3	2 818	79.1	20.9	406	12.6
2003	26 202	71.7	24 598	74.3	25.7	1 603	6.1	3 222	73.1	2 789	79.5	20.5	433	13.4
2004	25 913	70.7	24 413	74.2	25.8	1 501	5.8	3 262	72.6	2 836	76.8	23.2	426	13.1
2005	26 202	71.7	24 598	74.3	25.7	1 603	6.1	3 222	73.1	2 789	79.5	20.5	433	13.4
2006	26 009	70.6	24 728	75.6	24.4	1 281	4.9	3 317	71.5	2 896	77.8	22.2	420	12.7
2007	26 834	71.3	25 646	75.2	24.8	1 188	4.4	3 514	71.4	3 133	76.4	23.6	381	10.8
2008	25 930	71.2	24 637	75.7	24.3	1 294	5.0	3 511	71.0	3 108	78.0	22.0	403	11.5
2009	26 122	71.6	24 079	74.6	25.4	2 043	7.8	3 673	72.0	3 108	75.8	24.2	566	18.2
2010	25 783	71.3	23 510	73.7	26.3	2 273	8.8	3 642	70.1	2 984	71.9	28.1	659	18.1
2011	25 376	70.9	23 109	74.2	25.8	2 266	8.9	3 822	70.0	3 102	71.9	28.1	721	18.9
2012	25 384	70.9	23 366	75.4	24.6	2 018	7.9	4 108	71.5	3 422	73.2	26.8	686	16.7
2013	25 112	70.3	23 121	74.8	25.2	1 991	7.9	4 088	71.3	3 404	71.9	28.1	684	16.7
2014	25 209	70.8	23 542	75.6	24.4	1 667	6.6	4 007	71.4	3 423	74.8	25.2	584	14.6
2015	25 107	69.9	23 841	76.3	23.7	1 265	5.0	4 186	72.2	3 657	74.5	25.5	529	12.6
2016	25 070	70.8	23 877	76.4	23.6	1 193	4.8	4 086	72.8	3 660	73.3	26.7	426	10.4
2017	24 863	71.3	23 748	77.2	22.8	1 114	4.5	4 038	73.4	3 659	77.0	23.0	378	9.4
2018	24 802	71.4	23 849	77.9	22.1	953	3.8	4 031	75.0	3 708	77.8	22.2	324	8.0
2019	24 892	72.4	24 038	78.8	21.2	854	3.4	3 884	74.9	3 579	78.4	21.6	305	7.8
2020	24 623	72.5	23 391	79.2	20.8	1 232	5.0	3 773	74.8	3 441	79.8	20.2	332	8.8
Women with Children Under 6 Years														
1996	10 293	62.3	9 592	68.4	31.6	701	6.8	1 378	55.1	1 099	67.3	32.7	279	20.2
1997	10 610	65.0	9 800	70.5	29.5	810	7.6	1 755	65.1	1 424	71.6	28.4	330	18.8
1998	10 619	65.2	9 839	69.8	30.2	780	7.3	1 755	67.3	1 448	71.7	28.3	307	17.5
1999	10 322	64.4	9 674	69.0	31.0	648	6.3	1 811	68.1	1 565	71.0	29.0	246	13.6
2000	10 316	65.3	9 763	70.5	29.5	553	5.4	1 835	70.5	1 603	75.3	24.7	232	12.6
2001	10 200	64.9	9 618	71.2	28.8	582	5.7	1 783	69.7	1 542	79.1	20.9	242	13.6
2002	10 193	64.1	9 441	70.4	29.6	752	7.4	1 819	71.0	1 568	74.5	25.5	251	13.8
2003	10 209	62.9	9 433	70.0	30.0	776	7.6	1 893	70.2	1 614	75.2	24.8	279	14.7
2004	10 131	62.2	9 407	69.4	30.6	724	7.1	1 885	68.4	1 605	70.1	29.9	279	14.8
2005	10 209	62.9	9 433	70.0	30.0	776	7.6	1 893	70.2	1 614	75.2	24.8	279	14.7
2006	10 430	63.0	9 779	72.0	28.0	651	6.2	1 934	68.6	1 659	72.8	27.2	276	14.3
2007	10 894	63.5	10 305	71.9	28.1	589	5.4	2 066	67.4	1 827	72.7	27.3	239	11.6
2008	10 452	63.6	9 794	72.1	27.9	657	6.3	1 982	66.0	1 705	72.2	27.8	277	14.0
2009	10 497	63.6	9 517	71.8	28.2	980	9.3	2 137	67.8	1 754	70.3	29.7	383	17.9
2010	10 536	64.2	9 452	70.9	29.1	1 085	10.3	2 076	65.6	1 643	67.0	33.0	433	20.9
2011	10 403	64.2	9 268	71.3	28.7	1 135	10.9	2 177	65.8	1 678	65.5	34.5	499	22.9
2012	10 462	64.7	9 458	72.6	27.4	1 004	9.6	2 408	68.1	1 958	69.0	31.0	450	18.7
2013	10 171	64.7	9 212	72.8	27.2	958	9.4	2 305	68.2	1 864	66.7	33.3	441	19.1
2014	9 982	64.3	9 153	73.5	26.5	829	8.3	2 221	67.6	1 836	71.7	28.3	385	17.3
2015	10 048	63.9	9 405	73.4	26.6	643	6.4	2 333	68.5	1 993	68.9	31.1	340	14.6
2016	9 934	65.3	9 358	73.9	26.1	576	5.8	2 161	68.6	1 903	69.4	30.6	258	11.9
2017	9 783	65.1	9 268	74.5	25.5	515	5.3	2 088	68.9	1 852	72.4	27.6	236	11.3
2018	9 749	64.7	9 304	74.5	25.5	445	4.6	2 078	71.3	1 884	73.1	26.9	194	9.3
2019	9 920	66.4	9 513	75.9	24.1	407	4.1	2 003	70.9	1 816	75.0	25.0	187	9.3
2020	10 048	67.4	9 492	76.0	24.0	556	5.5	1 913	71.3	1 724	75.9	24.1	189	9.9

Note: See notes and definitions for information on historical comparability.

Table 1-47. Employment Status of Ever-Married Women and Married Women, Spouse Present, by Presence and Age of Children, March 1996–March 2020

(Thousands of women, percent.)

Presence and age of children and year	Ever-married women[1] Civilian labor force	Civilian labor force as percent of population	Employed Number	Percent full time	Percent part time	Unemployed Number	Percent of labor force	Married women, spouse present Civilian labor force	Civilian labor force as percent of population	Employed Number	Percent full time	Percent part time	Unemployed Number	Percent of labor force
Women with No Children Under 18 Years														
1996	23 337	47.7	22 444	78.1	21.9	893	3.8	15 628	53.4	15 123	76.8	23.2	506	3.2
1997	23 890	48.3	23 130	78.9	21.1	760	3.2	15 750	54.2	15 315	77.7	22.3	435	2.8
1998	24 366	48.7	23 598	79.3	20.7	767	3.1	16 007	54.1	15 581	78.3	21.7	426	2.7
1999	24 881	48.9	24 098	79.7	20.3	783	3.1	16 484	54.4	16 061	78.2	21.8	423	2.6
2000	25 465	49.4	24 695	80.3	19.7	769	3.0	16 786	54.7	16 357	79.1	20.9	429	2.6
2001	25 959	49.6	25 226	80.4	19.6	733	2.8	16 909	54.8	16 528	78.7	21.3	381	2.3
2002	26 423	49.1	25 356	80.0	20.0	1 068	4.0	17 353	54.8	16 780	78.4	21.6	573	3.3
2003	27 361	50.1	26 238	79.7	20.3	1 123	4.1	17 901	55.7	17 273	78.6	21.4	628	3.5
2004	27 461	49.8	26 329	79.3	20.7	1 131	4.1	17 965	55.0	17 367	78.6	21.4	598	3.3
2005	27 361	50.1	26 238	79.7	20.3	1 123	4.1	17 901	55.7	17 273	78.6	21.4	628	3.5
2006	27 719	49.3	26 893	80.1	19.9	827	3.0	18 124	54.8	17 691	79.3	20.7	434	2.4
2007	28 335	49.8	27 477	80.1	19.9	858	3.0	18 766	55.4	18 326	79.6	20.4	441	2.3
2008	29 207	50.3	28 156	80.2	19.8	1 052	3.6	19 188	55.9	18 650	79.8	20.2	539	2.8
2009	29 536	50.2	27 737	77.8	22.2	1 800	6.1	19 541	55.8	18 521	77.3	22.7	1 019	5.2
2010	29 767	50.2	27 723	77.7	22.3	2 044	6.9	19 579	55.8	18 454	77.3	22.7	1 125	5.7
2011	29 440	49.4	27 553	77.7	22.3	1 886	6.4	19 316	54.6	18 285	77.4	22.6	1 031	5.3
2012	29 912	48.8	28 021	78.2	21.8	1 891	6.3	19 617	53.6	18 536	77.8	22.2	1 081	5.5
2013	29 956	48.4	28 379	78.1	21.9	1 578	5.3	19 507	53.3	18 706	77.5	22.5	801	4.1
2014	29 908	47.8	28 428	78.0	22.0	1 480	4.9	19 350	52.0	18 582	77.5	22.5	768	4.1
2015	30 074	47.6	28 921	78.2	21.8	1 153	3.8	19 609	52.5	19 009	77.6	22.4	600	3.1
2016	30 534	47.8	29 481	78.3	21.7	1 053	3.4	19 977	52.6	19 392	78.2	21.8	584	2.9
2017	30 964	47.7	29 938	78.4	21.6	1 026	3.3	20 483	52.7	19 978	77.9	22.1	505	2.5
2018	30 868	47.0	29 924	78.6	21.4	945	3.1	20 227	51.6	19 698	78.5	21.5	529	2.6
2019	31 376	47.4	30 563	78.7	21.3	814	2.6	21 006	52.6	20 568	78.6	21.4	438	2.1
2020	30 936	46.7	29 822	80.0	20.0	1 114	3.6	20 621	51.1	19 990	79.8	20.2	631	3.1
Women with Children Under 18 Years														
1996	22 475	71.4	21 556	72.5	27.5	919	4.1	17 754	70.0	17 136	69.6	30.4	618	3.5
1997	22 831	72.6	21 777	73.9	26.1	1 054	4.6	18 157	71.1	17 521	71.6	28.4	636	3.5
1998	22 650	72.3	21 665	73.8	26.2	985	4.3	18 129	70.6	17 447	71.5	28.5	682	3.8
1999	22 419	71.9	21 611	73.9	26.1	808	3.6	17 865	70.1	17 342	71.5	28.5	523	2.9
2000	22 722	72.7	21 960	74.0	26.0	763	3.4	18 174	70.6	17 641	71.7	28.3	533	2.9
2001	22 729	73.0	21 934	74.9	25.1	795	3.5	18 325	70.8	17 745	72.6	27.4	580	3.2
2002	22 917	71.8	21 794	74.3	25.7	1 122	4.9	18 271	69.6	17 515	71.7	28.3	756	4.1
2003	22 979	71.5	21 809	73.7	26.3	1 170	5.1	18 284	69.2	17 533	71.0	29.0	751	4.1
2004	22 651	70.5	21 576	73.8	26.2	1 075	4.7	17 953	68.2	17 215	71.3	28.7	738	4.1
2005	22 979	71.5	21 809	73.7	26.3	1 170	5.1	18 284	69.2	17 533	71.0	29.0	751	4.1
2006	22 692	70.5	21 831	75.3	24.7	861	3.8	18 067	68.4	17 494	73.0	27.0	574	3.2
2007	23 320	71.3	22 513	75.0	25.0	807	3.5	18 569	69.3	18 045	72.6	27.4	524	2.8
2008	22 419	71.2	21 529	75.4	24.6	890	4.0	17 886	69.4	17 269	73.6	26.4	616	3.4
2009	22 449	71.5	20 972	74.5	25.5	1 477	6.6	17 995	69.8	17 018	73.1	26.9	977	5.4
2010	22 141	71.5	20 526	74.0	26.0	1 615	7.3	17 622	69.7	16 510	72.6	27.4	1 112	6.3
2011	21 553	71.1	20 008	74.6	25.4	1 546	7.2	17 067	69.1	16 055	73.1	26.9	1 012	5.9
2012	21 276	70.7	19 944	75.8	24.2	1 332	6.3	16 746	68.5	15 887	74.1	25.9	859	5.1
2013	21 024	70.1	19 717	75.3	24.7	1 306	6.2	16 786	68.1	15 896	74.1	25.9	890	5.3
2014	21 202	70.6	20 120	75.8	24.2	1 083	5.1	16 907	68.4	16 176	74.7	25.3	730	4.3
2015	20 921	69.5	20 185	76.7	23.3	736	3.5	16 779	67.6	16 305	75.3	24.7	474	2.8
2016	20 984	70.5	20 217	77.0	23.0	767	3.7	16 882	68.6	16 339	76.3	23.7	543	3.2
2017	20 825	70.9	20 089	77.2	22.8	736	3.5	16 931	69.3	16 406	76.2	23.8	525	3.1
2018	20 771	70.7	20 141	77.9	22.1	630	3.0	16 908	69.0	16 478	77.0	23.0	431	2.5
2019	21 008	71.9	20 459	78.9	21.1	549	2.6	17 197	70.1	16 807	77.9	22.1	390	2.3
2020	20 850	72.1	19 950	79.1	20.9	900	4.3	17 241	70.4	16 555	77.9	22.1	687	4.0
Women with Children Under 6 Years														
1996	8 915	63.6	8 493	68.6	31.4	422	4.7	7 590	62.7	7 297	66.5	33.5	293	3.9
1997	8 856	64.9	8 376	70.3	29.7	480	5.4	7 582	63.6	7 252	69.1	30.9	330	4.4
1998	8 864	64.8	8 391	69.5	30.5	473	5.3	7 655	63.7	7 309	68.1	31.9	346	4.5
1999	8 511	63.7	8 109	68.6	31.4	402	4.7	7 246	61.8	6 979	67.1	32.9	267	3.7
2000	8 481	64.3	8 159	69.5	30.5	321	3.8	7 341	62.8	7 087	68.1	31.9	254	3.5
2001	8 417	64.0	8 077	69.7	30.3	340	4.0	7 319	62.5	7 062	68.5	31.5	257	3.5
2002	8 373	62.8	7 873	69.6	30.4	501	6.0	7 166	60.8	6 804	67.7	32.3	363	5.1
2003	8 315	61.4	7 818	68.9	31.1	497	6.0	7 175	59.8	6 826	67.1	32.9	349	4.9
2004	8 246	61.0	7 801	69.3	30.7	445	5.4	7 107	59.3	6 774	68.1	31.9	332	4.7
2005	8 315	61.4	7 818	68.9	31.1	497	6.0	7 175	59.8	6 826	67.1	32.9	349	4.9
2006	8 496	61.9	8 121	71.8	28.2	375	4.4	7 366	60.3	7 092	70.6	29.4	274	3.7
2007	8 829	62.7	8 479	71.7	28.3	350	4.0	7 664	61.5	7 407	70.8	29.2	257	3.4
2008	8 470	63.0	8 089	72.1	27.9	381	4.5	7 285	61.6	6 999	70.9	29.1	285	3.9
2009	8 360	62.6	7 763	72.1	27.9	597	7.1	7 231	61.6	6 805	71.4	28.6	426	5.9
2010	8 460	63.8	7 809	71.7	28.3	651	7.7	7 227	62.5	6 741	71.5	28.5	486	6.7
2011	8 226	63.7	7 590	72.5	27.5	636	7.7	7 061	62.3	6 608	71.9	28.1	453	6.4
2012	8 054	63.7	7 501	73.5	26.5	554	6.9	6 878	62.3	6 491	72.7	27.3	387	5.6
2013	7 866	63.7	7 349	74.3	25.7	517	6.6	6 737	62.0	6 384	74.1	25.9	352	5.2
2014	7 761	63.4	7 317	73.9	26.1	444	5.7	6 663	61.5	6 326	73.7	26.3	336	5.0
2015	7 714	62.7	7 411	74.6	25.4	303	3.9	6 653	61.3	6 454	74.4	25.6	198	3.0
2016	7 773	64.4	7 455	75.0	25.0	318	4.1	6 715	62.9	6 483	74.6	25.4	232	3.4
2017	7 695	64.1	7 416	75.1	24.9	279	3.6	6 732	62.9	6 523	74.6	25.4	209	3.1
2018	7 671	63.1	7 420	74.8	25.2	251	3.3	6 789	61.8	6 596	74.2	25.8	193	2.8
2019	7 917	65.4	7 697	76.1	23.9	221	2.8	7 034	64.2	6 867	75.8	24.2	167	2.4
2020	8 135	66.6	7 769	76.0	24.0	367	4.5	7 225	65.4	6 925	75.5	24.5	300	4.1

[1]Ever-married women are women who are, or have ever been, married.

Table 1-48. Employment Status of Women Who Maintain Families, by Marital Status and Presence and Age of Children, March 2005–March 2020

(Thousands of women, percent.)

Marital status, age of children, and year	Civilian noninstitutional population	Civilian labor force					Not in the labor force
		Number	Percent of the population	Employed	Unemployed		
					Number	Percent of the labor force	
Total, Women Who Maintain Families							
2005	14 391	9 941	69.1	9 140	801	8.1	4 450
2006	14 485	9 966	68.8	9 227	739	7.4	4 520
2007	14 833	10 172	68.6	9 510	661	6.5	4 662
2008	14 820	10 166	68.6	9 447	719	7.1	4 654
2009	14 813	10 140	68.5	9 034	1 106	10.9	4 673
2010	15 214	10 206	67.1	9 027	1 179	11.6	5 008
2011	15 461	10 462	67.7	9 141	1 321	12.6	5 000
2012	16 122	11 009	68.3	9 807	1 202	10.9	5 113
2013	15 914	10 793	67.8	9 589	1 204	11.2	5 121
2014	15 612	10 505	67.3	9 511	994	9.5	5 107
2015	16 017	10 691	66.7	9 848	843	7.9	5 326
2016	16 003	10 695	66.8	9 988	707	6.6	5 308
2017	15 882	10 663	67.1	10 040	623	5.8	5 219
2018	15 700	10 460	66.6	9 875	585	5.6	5 241
2019	15 345	10 350	67.5	9 827	523	5.1	4 995
2020	15 092	10 163	67.3	9 538	625	6.2	4 930
Women with No Children Under 18 Years							
2005	5 692	3 095	54.4	2 961	134	4.3	2 597
2006	5 693	3 088	54.2	2 945	143	4.6	2 604
2007	5 823	3 124	53.7	2 990	134	4.3	2 699
2008	6 022	3 352	55.7	3 167	185	5.5	2 670
2009	6 068	3 332	54.9	3 075	258	7.7	2 735
2010	6 414	3 417	53.3	3 131	286	8.4	2 997
2011	6 403	3 455	54.0	3 131	324	9.4	2 948
2012	6 773	3 779	55.8	3 464	316	8.4	2 994
2013	6 822	3 790	55.5	3 466	324	8.5	3 032
2014	6 715	3 566	53.1	3 301	265	7.4	3 149
2015	6 977	3 732	53.5	3 521	211	5.7	3 246
2016	7 084	3 798	53.6	3 593	205	5.4	3 286
2017	7 317	4 034	55.1	3 860	173	4.3	3 284
2018	7 259	3 808	52.5	3 632	176	4.6	3 451
2019	7 335	3 952	53.9	3 798	154	3.9	3 383
2020	7 347	3 993	54.3	3 797	196	4.9	3 354
Women with Children Under 18 Years							
2005	8 699	6 846	78.7	6 179	667	9.7	1 853
2006	8 793	6 878	78.2	6 282	596	8.7	1 915
2007	9 010	7 047	78.2	6 520	527	7.5	1 963
2008	8 798	6 814	77.4	6 280	535	7.8	1 984
2009	8 745	6 807	77.8	5 959	848	12.5	1 938
2010	8 800	6 789	77.1	5 896	893	13.2	2 011
2011	9 059	7 007	77.4	6 009	998	14.2	2 052
2012	9 349	7 230	77.3	6 343	887	12.3	2 119
2013	9 092	7 003	77.0	6 123	880	12.6	2 089
2014	8 896	6 939	78.0	6 210	729	10.5	1 957
2015	9 040	6 959	77.0	6 327	632	9.1	2 081
2016	8 920	6 897	77.3	6 396	502	7.3	2 022
2017	8 565	6 630	77.4	6 180	450	6.8	1 935
2018	8 441	6 652	78.8	6 243	409	6.2	1 790
2019	8 010	6 398	79.9	6 029	369	5.8	1 612
2020	7 745	6 170	79.7	5 741	429	7.0	1 575
Single Women with No Children Under 18 Years							
2005	1 388	926	66.7	855	71	7.7	463
2006	1 370	933	68.1	861	72	7.7	437
2007	1 413	986	69.8	930	57	5.7	427
2008	1 515	1 057	69.8	989	68	6.5	458
2009	1 531	1 069	69.8	967	102	9.6	462
2010	1 718	1 166	67.9	1 041	125	10.7	552
2011	1 729	1 178	68.2	1 047	132	11.2	551
2012	1 836	1 241	67.6	1 099	143	11.5	595
2013	1 933	1 322	68.4	1 178	144	10.9	611
2014	1 840	1 224	66.5	1 105	119	9.7	616
2015	2 008	1 288	64.1	1 203	85	6.6	720
2016	2 097	1 412	67.3	1 320	92	6.5	685
2017	2 301	1 579	68.6	1 493	87	5.5	722
2018	2 247	1 452	64.6	1 369	83	5.7	796
2019	2 323	1 622	69.8	1 551	71	4.4	701
2020	2 353	1 599	67.9	1 499	99	6.2	754

Note: See notes and definitions for information on historical comparability.

Table 1-48. Employment Status of Women Who Maintain Families, by Marital Status and Presence and Age of Children, March 2005–March 2020—*Continued*

(Thousands of women, percent.)

Marital status, age of children, and year	Civilian noninstitutional population	Civilian labor force					Not in the labor force
		Number	Percent of the population	Employed	Unemployed		
					Number	Percent of the labor force	
Single Women with Children Under 18 Years							
2005	3 591	2 708	75.4	2 325	383	14.1	882
2006	3 671	2 710	73.8	2 370	340	12.5	961
2007	3 748	2 782	74.2	2 491	291	10.4	966
2008	3 721	2 743	73.7	2 448	295	10.8	978
2009	3 872	2 877	74.3	2 448	429	14.9	995
2010	3 948	2 868	72.6	2 379	488	17.0	1 081
2011	4 193	3 072	73.3	2 522	550	17.9	1 120
2012	4 442	3 263	73.5	2 746	517	15.8	1 179
2013	4 403	3 220	73.1	2 698	522	16.2	1 183
2014	4 297	3 137	73.0	2 698	439	14.0	1 161
2015	4 438	3 296	74.3	2 889	407	12.4	1 142
2016	4 362	3 252	74.5	2 941	310	9.5	1 110
2017	4 278	3 201	74.8	2 928	273	8.5	1 078
2018	4 187	3 222	77.0	2 988	234	7.3	965
2019	4 002	3 074	76.8	2 830	244	7.9	928
2020	3 906	3 013	77.1	2 756	257	8.5	893
Widowed, Divorced, or Separated Women with No Children Under 18 Years							
2005	4 304	2 170	50.4	2 106	64	2.9	2 135
2006	4 323	2 156	49.9	2 084	72	3.3	2 168
2007	4 410	2 138	48.5	2 061	77	3.6	2 272
2008	4 507	2 295	50.9	2 178	117	5.1	2 213
2009	4 536	2 263	49.9	2 108	155	6.9	2 273
2010	4 696	2 251	47.9	2 090	161	7.1	2 445
2011	4 674	2 276	48.7	2 084	192	8.4	2 397
2012	4 937	2 538	51.4	2 365	173	6.8	2 399
2013	4 889	2 468	50.5	2 288	180	7.3	2 421
2014	4 875	2 342	48.0	2 196	146	6.2	2 533
2015	4 969	2 444	49.2	2 317	126	5.2	2 526
2016	4 987	2 386	47.8	2 273	113	4.7	2 601
2017	5 016	2 454	48.9	2 368	87	3.5	2 562
2018	5 012	2 356	47.0	2 263	93	4.0	2 655
2019	5 012	2 330	46.5	2 247	83	3.6	2 682
2020	4 994	2 394	47.9	2 298	97	4.0	2 600
Widowed, Divorced, or Separated Women with Children Under 18 Years							
2005	5 108	4 137	81.0	3 854	283	6.8	971
2006	5 121	4 167	81.4	3 912	255	6.1	955
2007	5 262	4 266	81.1	4 029	237	5.5	997
2008	5 077	4 071	80.2	3 832	239	5.9	1 006
2009	4 873	3 930	80.7	3 511	420	10.7	943
2010	4 852	3 922	80.8	3 517	405	10.3	931
2011	4 866	3 935	80.9	3 487	448	11.4	931
2012	4 907	3 966	80.8	3 597	370	9.3	940
2013	4 689	3 783	80.7	3 425	358	9.5	906
2014	4 599	3 802	82.7	3 512	290	7.6	797
2015	4 602	3 663	79.6	3 438	225	6.1	939
2016	4 558	3 646	80.0	3 455	191	5.2	912
2017	4 286	3 429	80.0	3 252	176	5.1	858
2018	4 255	3 430	80.6	3 255	175	5.1	825
2019	4 008	3 324	82.9	3 199	125	3.8	684
2020	3 839	3 157	82.2	2 985	172	5.5	683

Note: See notes and definitions for information on historical comparability.

Table 1-49. Number and Age of Children in Families, by Type of Family and Labor Force Status of Mother, March 2005–March 2020

(Thousands of children.)

Age of children and year	Total children	Mother in labor force	Mother not in labor force	Married-couple families			Families maintained by women			Families maintained by men
				Total	Mother in labor force	Mother not in labor force	Total	Mother in labor force	Mother not in labor force	
Children Under 18 Years										
2005	66 526	43 239	20 179	48 688	31 886	16 802	14 729	11 352	3 377	3 108
2006	66 883	43 278	20 440	48 853	31 946	16 908	14 865	11 332	3 532	3 165
2007	67 228	44 116	20 073	48 927	32 496	16 431	15 263	11 620	3 643	3 038
2008	67 153	43 798	19 966	48 303	32 110	16 193	15 461	11 688	3 773	3 388
2009	66 913	43 509	20 074	48 384	32 065	16 315	15 204	11 444	3 759	3 326
2010	66 811	43 335	19 913	47 730	31 686	16 044	15 518	11 649	3 869	3 563
2011	66 804	42 882	20 260	47 051	30 902	16 149	16 091	11 980	4 111	3 662
2012	66 472	42 643	19 885	45 989	30 228	15 761	16 539	12 414	4 125	3 944
2013	66 661	42 454	20 012	46 254	30 294	15 960	16 211	12 159	4 052	4 195
2014	66 137	42 447	19 718	46 428	30 471	15 958	15 737	11 977	3 760	3 972
2015	65 916	41 721	20 356	46 256	29 949	16 307	15 820	11 772	4 048	3 839
2016	66 124	42 427	19 675	46 198	30 450	15 748	15 903	11 976	3 927	4 022
2017	65 798	42 531	19 280	46 344	30 919	15 425	15 467	11 612	3 855	3 987
2018	65 979	42 506	19 275	46 563	30 666	15 897	15 218	11 840	3 378	4 198
2019	65 911	42 973	18 612	46 994	31 557	15 406	14 622	11 416	3 207	4 295
2020	65 068	42 640	18 421	46 930	31 707	15 184	14 169	10 933	3 236	3 969
Children 6 to 17 Years										
2005	45 027	30 930	11 995	32 412	22 565	9 847	10 514	8 366	2 148	2 102
2006	45 039	30 591	12 250	32 311	22 315	9 996	10 530	8 276	2 254	2 198
2007	45 155	31 252	11 855	32 417	22 788	9 629	10 690	8 464	2 226	2 048
2008	44 909	30 853	11 874	31 990	22 413	9 577	10 737	8 440	2 297	2 182
2009	44 595	30 600	11 811	31 966	22 425	9 537	10 449	8 175	2 274	2 180
2010	44 456	30 209	11 922	31 468	21 957	9 510	10 663	8 251	2 412	2 325
2011	44 471	29 904	12 244	31 072	21 365	9 707	11 076	8 539	2 537	2 323
2012	45 049	30 143	12 315	30 923	21 163	9 760	11 535	8 980	2 556	2 591
2013	45 492	30 091	12 694	31 411	21 352	10 058	11 375	8 738	2 636	2 707
2014	45 059	30 205	12 233	31 471	21 540	9 931	10 968	8 665	2 302	2 621
2015	44 817	29 490	12 830	31 359	21 090	10 269	10 961	8 400	2 560	2 498
2016	45 131	29 929	12 553	31 251	21 243	10 008	11 230	8 685	2 545	2 649
2017	44 756	30 136	12 002	31 118	21 617	9 500	11 021	8 519	2 502	2 618
2018	44 784	30 121	11 898	31 144	21 449	9 695	10 875	8 672	2 204	2 765
2019	44 815	30 341	11 554	31 460	21 939	9 504	10 451	8 401	2 050	2 903
2020	44 354	29 778	11 766	31 367	21 754	9 588	10 202	8 024	2 178	2 785
Children Under 6 Years										
2005	21 498	12 308	8 184	16 276	9 321	6 955	4 216	2 987	1 229	1 006
2006	21 844	12 687	8 190	16 542	9 631	6 911	4 335	3 057	1 278	968
2007	22 073	12 864	8 218	16 509	9 708	6 802	4 572	3 156	1 416	991
2008	22 244	12 946	8 092	16 313	9 697	6 616	4 724	3 248	1 476	1 207
2009	22 318	12 909	8 263	16 418	9 640	6 778	4 755	3 270	1 485	1 146
2010	22 355	13 127	7 991	16 262	9 729	6 533	4 855	3 398	1 457	1 237
2011	22 333	12 978	8 015	15 979	9 537	6 442	5 015	3 441	1 573	1 340
2012	21 423	12 500	7 570	15 066	9 065	6 001	5 004	3 435	1 569	1 353
2013	21 169	12 363	7 317	14 844	8 942	5 902	4 837	3 421	1 416	1 489
2014	21 078	12 242	7 484	14 958	8 931	6 027	4 769	3 312	1 457	1 351
2015	21 099	12 231	7 526	14 898	8 859	6 038	4 860	3 372	1 488	1 341
2016	20 993	12 498	7 121	14 947	9 207	5 739	4 673	3 291	1 382	1 373
2017	21 041	12 395	7 278	15 227	9 302	5 925	4 446	3 093	1 353	1 368
2018	21 195	12 385	7 377	15 419	9 217	6 202	4 343	3 168	1 174	1 434
2019	21 096	12 632	7 059	15 533	9 618	5 902	4 171	3 014	1 157	1 392
2020	20 713	12 862	6 654	15 562	9 953	5 596	3 967	2 909	1 058	1 184

Note: See notes and definitions for information on historical comparability.

Table 1-50. Number of Families and Median Family Income, by Type of Family and Earner Status of Members, 1995–2019

(Thousands of families, dollars.)

Number and type of families and median family income	1995	1996	1997	1998	1999	2000	2001	2002	2003	2004	2005	2006
NUMBER OF FAMILIES												
Married-Couple Families, Total	53 621	53 654	54 362	54 829	55 352	55 650	56 798	57 362	57 767	58 180	58 225	59 050
No earners	7 276	7 145	7 286	7 257	7 160	7 297	7 662	7 803	8 043	7 998	8 017	8 091
One earner	11 708	11 493	11 700	12 246	12 290	12 450	12 852	13 503	14 061	14 385	14 301	14 562
Husband	8 792	8 611	8 770	9 173	9 062	9 319	9 573	10 121	10 478	10 853	10 611	10 706
Wife	2 251	2 207	2 298	2 411	2 585	2 545	2 689	2 821	3 027	2 993	3 097	3 264
Other family member	666	674	632	662	643	586	590	560	557	539	593	591
Two earners	27 180	27 260	27 712	27 593	28 010	28 329	28 779	28 891	28 693	28 806	28 802	29 216
Husband and wife	25 274	25 274	25 731	25 696	26 134	26 447	26 829	26 966	26 860	26 758	26 833	27 241
Husband and other family member	1 393	1 483	1 406	1 306	1 325	1 277	1 424	1 391	1 322	1 462	1 376	1 358
Husband not an earner	513	502	575	590	552	605	526	534	511	586	594	616
Three earners or more	7 456	7 756	7 664	7 733	7 892	7 575	7 504	7 165	6 970	6 991	7 104	7 181
Husband and wife	6 770	7 126	7 023	7 102	7 220	6 917	6 859	6 565	6 349	6 459	6 535	6 620
Husband, not wife	531	479	478	456	528	537	530	455	467	381	445	397
Husband not an earner	155	150	163	176	144	120	115	145	154	152	124	165
Families Maintained by Women, Total	13 007	13 277	13 115	13 206	13 164	12 950	13 517	14 033	14 196	14 404	14 505	14 852
No earners	2 664	2 574	2 332	2 143	1 883	1 786	2 076	2 228	2 451	2 610	2 616	2 627
One earner	6 815	7 027	7 091	7 351	7 441	7 462	7 693	8 153	8 012	8 074	8 052	8 303
Householder	5 590	5 817	5 841	6 167	6 127	6 132	6 436	6 832	6 725	6 788	6 724	6 904
Other family member	1 225	1 211	1 251	1 183	1 314	1 331	1 257	1 321	1 286	1 285	1 329	1 398
Two earners or more	3 527	3 675	3 692	3 712	3 840	3 702	3 748	3 652	3 733	3 720	3 836	3 923
Householder and other family member(s)	3 225	3 431	3 398	3 399	3 508	3 376	3 442	3 290	3 364	3 399	3 468	3 547
Householder not an earner	302	245	294	313	332	325	306	362	369	321	368	376
Families Maintained by Men, Total	3 557	3 924	3 982	4 041	4 086	4 316	4 499	4 747	4 778	4 953	5 193	5 119
No earners	357	359	344	381	376	380	461	466	530	492	537	555
One earner	1 800	1 972	2 104	2 027	2 044	2 223	2 319	2 434	2 466	2 573	2 661	2 584
Householder	1 548	1 667	1 791	1 725	1 721	1 879	1 911	2 026	2 053	2 152	2 196	2 155
Other family member	253	305	313	302	323	344	408	408	413	421	464	429
Two earners or more	1 400	1 593	1 534	1 634	1 666	1 713	1 719	1 847	1 782	1 888	1 995	1 979
Householder and other family member(s)	1 302	1 469	1 427	1 532	1 522	1 585	1 629	1 709	1 625	1 736	1 848	1 828
Householder not an earner	98	124	107	102	143	128	90	138	157	152	147	152
MEDIAN FAMILY INCOME												
Married-Couple Families, Total	47 000	49 614	51 475	54 043	56 792	59 200	60 100	61 000	62 388	63 627	65 586	69 300
No earners	21 888	22 622	23 782	24 525	25 262	25 356	25 900	25 954	26 312	26 798	28 376	30 000
One earner	35 100	36 468	39 140	40 519	41 261	44 424	44 400	45 000	46 546	47 749	50 000	50 400
Husband	36 052	38 150	40 300	42 000	44 200	47 010	47 500	48 004	48 948	50 000	50 000	53 360
Wife	32 098	30 301	34 050	35 625	35 546	36 458	36 140	39 072	41 180	41 000	43 505	45 000
Other family member	37 784	39 644	40 317	42 414	41 120	45 492	44 270	40 927	45 936	46 324	50 263	49 352
Two earners	53 500	56 000	58 020	61 300	64 007	67 500	69 543	71 282	73 309	75 100	76 960	81 500
Husband and wife	53 626	56 392	58 564	61 900	64 950	68 132	70 000	72 150	74 500	76 000	77 539	82 762
Husband and other family member	52 530	49 610	53 854	57 680	53 541	56 503	65 240	62 848	60 100	66 120	67 350	68 828
Husband not an earner	47 121	46 990	47 979	50 955	52 466	53 430	58 725	54 840	58 000	63 050	65 622	63 657
Three earners or more	68 996	70 400	75 593	78 973	81 940	83 990	86 090	88 632	93 000	94 212	98 000	103 803
Husband and wife	69 371	71 148	76 105	79 907	83 000	84 634	87 000	89 962	94 353	95 524	99 800	104 045
Husband, not wife	60 360	61 824	68 890	71 001	69 561	79 050	76 230	82 180	77 316	87 000	79 417	91 965
Husband not an earner	61 196	55 495	62 684	63 205	69 275	68 050	80 661	68 400	91 771	73 137	84 638	97 510
Families Maintained by Women, Total	19 306	19 416	20 470	21 875	23 100	25 000	25 064	26 000	26 000	26 400	27 000	28 218
No earners	7 440	7 092	7 476	7 737	8 010	8 988	8 160	8 808	8 344	8 400	8 228	8 657
One earner	18 824	18 500	19 000	20 000	20 092	22 306	23 008	24 597	24 752	25 040	25 308	26 393
Householder	17 890	18 000	18 000	18 800	19 000	21 400	22 001	23 760	23 832	24 801	24 505	25 381
Other family member	23 166	21 000	22 870	25 981	26 800	27 524	28 476	29 524	28 857	29 700	31 700	31 462
Two earners or more	35 000	36 400	39 275	40 000	41 144	43 035	45 244	46 580	47 576	48 549	50 000	52 400
Householder and other family member(s)	34 674	36 400	39 000	39 713	40 855	43 000	44 842	46 000	46 701	47 974	48 989	51 479
Householder not an earner	39 444	38 249	47 471	43 725	48 004	45 600	51 000	51 248	57 267	56 799	64 805	61 699
Families Maintained by Men, Total	30 000	31 500	32 984	35 000	37 000	37 040	36 000	37 440	37 914	40 000	40 293	41 130
No earners	12 240	12 030	14 252	15 468	13 752	14 946	12 840	15 200	15 408	14 167	13 950	15 462
One earner	25 337	26 100	26 897	29 125	31 038	30 160	30 800	30 139	32 097	35 000	35 001	35 100
Householder	25 069	25 874	27 000	29 125	30 483	30 816	30 500	30 014	31 355	35 000	35 075	35 011
Other family member	27 291	28 584	25 486	28 241	34 756	29 118	31 052	32 000	35 525	35 438	35 000	37 840
Two earners or more	43 100	44 275	49 900	51 288	51 040	55 010	55 024	55 000	57 840	57 600	60 024	61 000
Householder and other family member(s)	43 000	43 065	50 000	50 954	50 960	55 400	54 850	55 220	57 400	57 058	60 000	61 000
Householder not an earner	55 133	47 001	44 786	68 257	57 407	51 945	61 824	49 852	64 658	65 400	70 879	62 000

Note: See notes and definitions for information on historical comparability.

Table 1-50. Number of Families and Median Family Income, by Type of Family and Earner Status of Members, 1995–2019—*Continued*

(Thousands of families, dollars.)

Number and type of families and median family income	2007	2008	2009	2010	2011	2012	2013	2014	2015	2016	2017	2018	2019
NUMBER OF FAMILIES													
Married-Couple Families, Total	58 490	59 181	58 521	58 135	59 071	59 327	59 795	60 091	60 338	60 912	61 348	61 692	61 840
No earners	7 914	8 083	8 467	8 626	9 152	9 101	9 556	9 437	9 380	9 814	9 944	10 039	10 351
One earner	14 272	14 625	15 046	15 421	15 981	15 841	15 828	15 642	15 653	15 496	15 895	15 600	15 045
Husband	10 396	10 567	10 570	10 895	11 308	11 276	11 370	11 246	11 185	11 057	11 394	10 925	10 475
Wife	3 267	3 437	3 854	3 935	4 016	3 894	3 788	3 776	3 739	3 744	3 841	3 976	3 741
Other family member	608	620	621	591	658	671	669	620	729	695	660	699	829
Two earners	29 256	29 466	28 371	27 821	27 661	27 902	27 978	28 255	28 505	28 754	28 469	29 159	29 135
Husband and wife	27 264	27 531	26 298	25 801	25 581	25 718	25 846	25 978	26 251	26 502	26 181	26 597	26 904
Husband and other family member	1 393	1 308	1 363	1 317	1 370	1 447	1 457	1 561	1 520	1 553	1 540	1 454	1 470
Husband not an earner	599	627	710	703	710	738	675	716	735	699	748	790	761
Three earners or more	7 048	7 008	6 638	6 267	6 277	6 482	6 434	6 756	6 800	6 848	7 040	6 894	7 309
Husband and wife	6 452	6 393	6 024	5 609	5 621	5 865	5 839	6 002	6 061	6 139	6 239	6 065	6 476
Husband, not wife	452	432	425	466	462	435	389	521	514	501	552	547	620
Husband not an earner	144	182	189	192	193	182	206	233	224	208	249	249	212
Families Maintained by Women, Total	14 846	14 842	15 236	15 491	16 154	15 949	15 632	16 055	16 038	15 913	15 716	15 360	15 117
No earners	2 502	2 678	3 076	3 297	3 373	3 300	3 143	3 173	3 022	2 821	2 921	2 703	2 485
One earner	8 418	8 381	8 475	8 638	8 790	8 621	8 537	8 702	8 672	8 618	8 388	8 103	8 044
Householder	7 020	6 978	6 941	7 158	7 303	7 170	6 998	7 158	7 076	6 924	6 785	6 445	6 442
Other family member	1 398	1 404	1 533	1 480	1 487	1 451	1 538	1 544	1 596	1 695	1 604	1 658	1 601
Two earners or more	3 925	3 783	3 685	3 555	3 991	4 028	3 953	4 180	4 344	4 473	4 407	4 554	4 588
Householder and other family member(s)	3 572	3 467	3 281	3 149	3 552	3 623	3 438	3 700	3 880	3 971	3 897	4 045	4 087
Householder not an earner	353	316	405	406	439	405	515	480	465	502	509	509	501
Families Maintained by Men, Total	5 181	5 301	5 630	5 649	5 975	6 308	6 384	6 236	6 386	6 526	6 485	6 567	6 555
No earners	532	611	539	775	838	883	824	817	802	765	781	755	723
One earner	2 703	2 636	2 801	2 911	3 106	3 242	3 311	3 230	3 236	3 262	3 291	3 265	3 206
Householder	2 297	2 199	2 261	2 389	2 535	2 698	2 715	2 664	2 634	2 622	2 732	2 650	2 590
Other family member	406	437	539	521	571	544	595	566	601	640	558	615	615
Two earners or more	1 947	2 054	2 030	1 963	2 031	2 183	2 249	2 190	2 348	2 500	2 413	2 548	2 627
Householder and other family member(s)	1 812	1 889	1 822	1 751	1 811	1 951	2 029	1 981	2 156	2 271	2 213	2 343	2 398
Householder not an earner	134	165	208	212	220	232	220	208	193	228	200	204	228
MEDIAN FAMILY INCOME													
Married-Couple Families, Total	72 802	72 805	71 464	72 224	73 678	75 002	76 000	80 234	84 076	86 508	90 000	93 041	101 742
No earners	30 134	31 164	32 093	32 350	33 756	33 584	35 948	36 748	37 678	39 378	41 656	44 737	50 399
One earner	52 686	53 865	53 087	55 000	56 609	58 415	57 000	60 009	63 015	65 333	68 000	70 000	75 002
Husband	55 350	56 000	55 333	56 533	59 842	60 002	59 748	60 381	64 490	69 174	70 008	72 000	75 511
Wife	47 000	47 015	47 550	50 150	52 007	52 517	52 000	57 189	59 914	58 595	61 139	65 030	70 470
Other family member	48 922	55 114	55 166	57 264	56 914	53 195	56 949	59 818	62 842	60 000	70 942	66 516	80 324
Two earners	85 012	85 500	86 361	88 500	90 001	91 651	94 100	98 023	102 256	104 247	109 302	112 235	122 782
Husband and wife	86 000	86 842	87 939	90 000	90 976	93 125	95 200	100 000	104 113	106 200	111 106	113 825	124 778
Husband and other family member	71 573	68 755	73 720	74 973	77 888	76 408	75 099	78 161	82 000	84 354	88 673	93 233	102 576
Husband not an earner	68 032	66 445	70 017	72 317	72 644	73 906	74 198	80 716	81 897	78 750	87 119	93 492	102 043
Three earners or more	106 747	105 618	107 000	107 542	111 000	114 201	118 408	123 850	127 000	130 249	136 207	144 064	151 153
Husband and wife	107 630	106 493	108 703	108 714	112 943	115 800	119 184	126 250	128 423	131 598	138 113	144 303	154 500
Husband, not wife	101 771	99 731	85 574	93 000	96 756	90 956	105 360	109 076	108 423	116 014	109 803	139 001	125 940
Husband not an earner	92 428	93 961	95 251	100 105	97 491	96 968	120 913	110 120	121 350	121 150	128 859	141 459	125 070
Families Maintained by Women, Total	30 000	29 698	29 025	28 774	29 848	30 000	30 500	30 816	33 405	36 003	36 800	39 714	42 840
No earners	8 873	9 404	10 037	9 600	9 600	10 299	10 224	10 205	10 736	10 200	11 904	11 382	13 916
One earner	27 795	28 060	29 000	29 009	27 488	29 558	30 000	29 740	30 205	33 259	33 895	35 987	38 068
Householder	26 644	27 000	27 928	27 924	27 488	28 077	28 000	28 000	29 402	31 308	32 002	34 036	36 138
Other family member	31 950	34 814	34 421	33 957	35 161	35 000	38 003	38 446	37 334	40 000	40 468	44 680	45 033
Two earners or more	55 749	54 369	54 500	55 047	56 000	58 694	58 535	59 008	63 651	67 001	69 086	71 898	74 304
Householder and other family member(s)	55 010	54 306	54 448	54 000	55 500	57 561	58 004	58 016	62 405	66 090	67 226	70 255	73 508
Householder not an earner	64 094	54 978	56 203	61 781	60 015	71 367	63 773	62 676	75 555	77 805	78 451	78 721	81 846
Families Maintained by Men, Total	44 001	43 050	41 000	42 500	43 000	42 000	44 394	47 159	49 000	50 936	52 407	53 628	61 216
No earners	12 921	15 557	15 653	16 176	17 945	18 006	16 440	15 828	17 107	18 810	17 865	16 920	17 520
One earner	37 716	36 806	35 116	37 707	38 000	38 500	38 300	40 754	40 989	45 000	45 000	46 111	51 472
Householder	37 720	37 569	35 117	37 990	38 069	36 000	39 185	40 530	42 000	45 039	45 000	47 005	52 000
Other family member	37 522	34 404	35 086	37 041	36 983	34 892	35 600	41 426	39 457	42 948	43 000	44 015	49 189
Two earners or more	63 600	64 077	64 747	66 000	67 301	65 017	69 505	71 997	77 729	77 000	80 000	79 610	87 206
Householder and other family member(s)	64 000	63 416	64 743	65 200	66 708	65 024	68 029	72 000	78 088	77 000	79 331	78 985	86 866
Householder not an earner	60 498	69 794	65 618	71 962	73 242	64 799	79 466	70 000	73 516	76 863	92 318	82 778	92 101

Note: See notes and definitions for information on historical comparability.

Table 1-51. Employment Status of the Foreign-Born and Native-Born Populations, by Selected Characteristics, 2018–2019

(Thousands of people, percent.)

Year and characteristic	Civilian noninstitutional population	Civilian labor force				
		Total	Participation rate	Employed	Unemployed	
					Number	Rate
2018						
TOTAL						
Both sexes, 16 years and over	257 791	162 075	62.9	155 761	6 314	3.9
Men	124 678	86 096	69.1	82 698	3 398	3.9
Women	133 112	75 978	57.1	73 063	2 916	3.8
FOREIGN BORN						
Both sexes, 16 years and over	42 898	28 202	65.7	27 217	986	3.5
Men	20 803	16 203	77.9	15 714	488	3.0
Women	22 095	12 000	54.3	11 502	497	4.1
Age						
16 to 24 years	3 443	1 761	51.2	1 638	124	7.0
25 to 34 years	7 946	6 092	76.7	5 877	215	3.5
35 to 44 years	9 499	7 520	79.2	7 302	219	2.9
45 to 54 years	8 715	7 044	80.8	6 844	200	2.8
55 to 64 years	6 542	4 425	67.6	4 255	170	3.8
65 years and over	6 754	1 360	20.1	1 301	58	4.3
Race and Hispanic Origin						
White, non-Hispanic	7 837	4 676	59.7	4 517	160	3.4
Black, non-Hispanic	3 786	2 682	70.8	2 560	122	4.6
Asian, non-Hispanic	11 118	7 082	63.7	6 895	187	2.6
Hispanic[1]	19 683	13 457	68.4	12 950	507	3.8
Educational Attainment						
Total, 25 years and over	39 455	26 441	67.0	25 579	862	3.3
Less than a high school diploma	9 616	5 607	58.3	5 378	229	4.1
High school graduate, no college[2]	10 127	6 629	65.5	6 415	214	3.2
Some college or associate's degree	6 366	4 448	69.9	4 301	147	3.3
Bachelor's degree or higher[3]	13 347	9 758	73.1	9 485	273	2.8
NATIVE BORN						
Both sexes, 16 years and over	214 892	133 872	62.3	128 544	5 328	4.0
Men	103 875	69 894	67.3	66 984	2 910	4.2
Women	111 018	63 979	57.6	61 560	2 418	3.8
Age						
16 to 24 years	34 561	19 223	55.6	17 539	1 684	8.8
25 to 34 years	36 635	30 682	83.8	29 447	1 235	4.0
35 to 44 years	31 071	26 099	84.0	25 315	784	3.0
45 to 54 years	32 525	26 267	80.8	25 529	738	2.8
55 to 64 years	35 572	22 929	64.5	22 310	619	2.7
65 years and over	44 529	8 673	19.5	8 404	269	3.1
Race and Hispanic Origin						
White, non-Hispanic or Latino	154 396	95 991	62.2	92 952	3 038	3.2
Black, non-Hispanic or Latino	27 076	16 484	60.9	15 355	1 129	6.8
Asian, non-Hispanic or Latino	4 408	2 761	62.6	2 657	104	3.8
Hispanic[1]	23 051	14 879	64.5	14 063	816	5.5
Educational Attainment						
Total, 25 years and over	180 332	114 650	63.6	111 005	3 644	3.2
Less than a high school diploma	12 635	4 671	37.0	4 323	347	7.4
High school graduates, no college[2]	52 465	29 382	56.0	28 135	1 247	4.2
Some college or associate's degree	51 038	33 138	64.9	32 036	1 101	3.3
Bachelor's degree or higher[3]	64 193	47 459	73.9	46 511	949	2.0

Note: Updated population controls are introduced annually with the release of January data.

[1]May be of any race.
[2]Includes persons with a high school diploma or equivalent.
[3]Includes persons with bachelor's, master's, professional, and doctoral degrees.

Table 1-51. Employment Status of the Foreign-Born and Native-Born Populations, by Selected Characteristics, 2018–2019—*Continued*

(Thousands of people, percent.)

Year and characteristic	Civilian noninstitutional population	Civilian labor force				
		Total	Participation rate	Employed	Unemployed	
					Number	Rate
2019						
TOTAL						
Both sexes, 16 years and over	259 175	163 539	63.1	157 538	6 001	3.7
Men	125 353	86 687	69.2	83 460	3 227	3.7
Women	133 822	76 852	57.4	74 078	2 774	3.6
FOREIGN BORN						
Both sexes, 16 years and over	42 990	28 390	66.0	27 502	888	3.1
Men	20 814	16 234	78.0	15 791	443	2.7
Women	22 176	12 156	54.8	11 711	446	3.7
Age						
16 to 24 years	3 330	1 735	52.1	1 619	116	6.7
25 to 34 years	7 665	5 917	77.2	5 726	191	3.2
35 to 44 years	9 361	7 459	79.7	7 273	187	2.5
45 to 54 years	8 878	7 219	81.3	7 018	201	2.8
55 to 64 years	6 699	4 585	68.5	4 450	135	3.0
65 years and over	7 057	1 475	20.9	1 416	59	4.0
Race and Hispanic Origin						
White, non-Hispanic	7 710	4 651	60.3	4 515	136	2.9
Black, non-Hispanic	3 837	2 716	70.8	2 606	110	4.1
Asian, non-Hispanic	11 180	7 187	64.3	7 013	174	2.4
Hispanic[1]	19 753	13 506	68.4	13 046	460	3.4
Educational Attainment						
Total, 25 years and over	39 660	26 655	67.2	25 883	773	2.9
Less than a high school diploma	9 494	5 432	57.2	5 217	214	3.9
High school graduates, no college[2]	9 983	6 632	66.4	6 454	178	2.7
Some college or associate degree	6 233	4 312	69.2	4 196	116	2.7
Bachelor's degree and higher[3]	13 950	10 280	73.7	10 015	264	2.6
NATIVE BORN						
Both sexes, 16 years and over	216 185	135 148	62.5	130 036	5 112	3.8
Men	104 540	70 453	67.4	67 669	2 784	4.0
Women	111 645	64 696	57.9	62 367	2 328	3.6
Age						
16 to 24 years	34 418	19 358	56.2	17 703	1 654	8.5
25 to 34 years	37 211	31 274	84.0	30 081	1 193	3.8
35 to 44 years	31 599	26 598	84.2	25 854	743	2.8
45 to 54 years	31 566	25 713	81.5	25 024	689	2.7
55 to 64 years	35 542	23 018	64.8	22 443	575	2.5
65 years and over	45 848	9 188	20.0	8 931	257	2.8
Race and Hispanic Origin						
White, non-Hispanic	154 457	96 132	62.2	93 210	2 922	3.0
Black, non-Hispanic	27 105	16 566	61.1	15 497	1 069	6.5
Asian, non-Hispanic	4 720	2 973	63.0	2 874	99	3.3
Hispanic[1]	23 754	15 547	65.4	14 759	788	5.1
Educational Attainment						
Total, 25 years and over	181 767	115 791	63.7	112 333	3 458	3.0
Less than a high school diploma	12 132	4 544	37.5	4 224	320	7.0
High school graduates, no college[2]	52 476	29 530	56.3	28 383	1 146	3.9
Some college or associate degree	51 280	33 108	64.6	32 086	1 022	3.1
Bachelor's degree or higher[3]	65 878	48 609	73.8	47 640	969	2.0

Note: Updated population controls are introduced annually with the release of January data.

[1]May be of any race.
[2]Includes persons with a high school diploma or equivalent.
[3]Includes persons with bachelor's, master's, professional, and doctoral degrees.

Table 1-52. Employment Status of the Foreign-Born and Native-Born Populations Age 16 Years and Over, by Sex and Presence and Age of Youngest Child, Annual Averages, 2018–2019

(Thousands of people, percent.)

Characteristic	2018			2019		
	Both sexes	Men	Women	Both sexes	Men	Women
FOREIGN BORN						
With Own Children Under 18 Years						
Civilian noninstitutional population	15 770	7 446	8 324	15 499	7 341	8 159
Civilian labor force	12 062	6 984	5 078	11 926	6 891	5 035
Participation rate	76.5	93.8	61.0	76.9	93.9	61.7
Employed	11 675	6 815	4 860	11 574	6 735	4 840
Employment-population ratio	74.0	91.5	58.4	74.7	91.7	59.3
Unemployed	387	168	219	352	156	195
Unemployment rate	3.2	2.4	4.3	3.0	2.3	3.9
With Own Children 6 to 17 Years, None Younger						
Civilian noninstitutional population	8 948	4 120	4 827	8 938	4 127	4 810
Civilian labor force	7 127	3 824	3 303	7 093	3 820	3 273
Participation rate	79.7	92.8	68.4	79.4	92.5	68.0
Employed	6 904	3 733	3 171	6 880	3 724	3 157
Employment-population ratio	77.2	90.6	65.7	77.0	90.2	65.6
Unemployed	223	91	132	212	96	116
Unemployment rate	3.1	2.4	4.0	3.0	2.5	3.6
With Own Children Under 6 Years						
Civilian noninstitutional population	6 823	3 326	3 497	6 562	3 213	3 348
Civilian labor force	4 935	3 160	1 775	4 834	3 071	1 762
Participation rate	72.3	95.0	50.8	73.7	95.6	52.6
Employed	4 771	3 082	1 689	4 694	3 011	1 683
Employment-population ratio	69.9	92.7	48.3	71.5	93.7	50.3
Unemployed	164	77	87	139	60	79
Unemployment rate	3.3	2.4	4.9	2.9	2.0	4.5
With Own Children Under 3 Years						
Civilian noninstitutional population	3 720	1 828	1 892	3 566	1 774	1 792
Civilian labor force	2 589	1 732	857	2 566	1 695	871
Participation rate	69.6	94.8	45.3	72.0	95.5	48.6
Employed	2 504	1 695	809	2 495	1 664	831
Employment-population ratio	67.3	92.7	42.8	70.0	93.8	46.4
Unemployed	85	37	48	71	31	40
Unemployment rate	3.3	2.2	5.6	2.8	1.8	4.6
With No Own Children Under 18 Years						
Civilian noninstitutional population	27 128	13 357	13 771	27 491	13 473	14 018
Civilian labor force	16 140	9 219	6 921	16 464	9 343	7 121
Participation rate	59.5	69.0	50.3	59.9	69.3	50.8
Employed	15 542	8 899	6 643	15 927	9 056	6 871
Employment-population ratio	57.3	66.6	48.2	57.9	67.2	49.0
Unemployed	599	320	279	537	287	250
Unemployment rate	3.7	3.5	4.0	3.3	3.1	3.5

Note: Updated population controls are introduced annually with the release of January data.

Table 1-52. Employment Status of the Foreign-Born and Native-Born Populations Age 16 Years and Over, by Sex and Presence and Age of Youngest Child, Annual Averages, 2018–2019—*Continued*

(Thousands of people, percent.)

Characteristic	2018			2019		
	Both sexes	Men	Women	Both sexes	Men	Women
NATIVE BORN						
With Own Children Under 18 Years						
Civilian noninstitutional population	48 464	21 467	26 998	48 138	21 318	26 820
Civilian labor force	40 144	19 984	20 161	40 107	19 865	20 242
Participation rate	82.8	93.1	74.7	83.3	93.2	75.5
Employed	38 915	19 501	19 414	38 977	19 427	19 550
Employment-population ratio	80.3	90.8	71.9	81.0	91.0	73.0
Unemployed	1 229	483	746	1 130	438	692
Unemployment rate	3.1	2.4	3.7	2.8	2.2	3.4
With Own Children 6 to 17 Years, None Younger						
Civilian noninstitutional population	26 933	11 874	15 059	26 768	11 859	14 909
Civilian labor force	22 810	10 929	11 880	22 765	10 894	11 871
Participation rate	84.7	92.0	78.9	85.0	91.9	79.6
Employed	22 193	10 696	11 497	22 169	10 661	11 508
Employment-population ratio	82.4	90.1	76.3	82.8	89.9	77.2
Unemployed	617	233	384	596	233	363
Unemployment rate	2.7	2.1	3.2	2.6	2.1	3.1
With Own Children Under 6 Years						
Civilian noninstitutional population	21 532	9 593	11 939	21 370	9 458	11 912
Civilian labor force	17 335	9 055	8 280	17 342	8 971	8 371
Participation rate	80.5	94.4	69.4	81.1	94.8	70.3
Employed	16 723	8 805	7 918	16 808	8 766	8 042
Employment-population ratio	77.7	91.8	66.3	78.7	92.7	67.5
Unemployed	612	249	363	534	204	329
Unemployment rate	3.5	2.8	4.4	3.1	2.3	3.9
With Own Children Under 3 Years						
Civilian noninstitutional population	12 556	5 623	6 933	12 464	5 571	6 894
Civilian labor force	9 932	5 328	4 605	9 941	5 300	4 641
Participation rate	79.1	94.8	66.4	79.8	95.1	67.3
Employed	9 576	5 174	4 401	9 626	5 173	4 453
Employment-population ratio	76.3	92.0	63.5	77.2	92.9	64.6
Unemployed	357	153	204	315	127	188
Unemployment rate	3.6	2.9	4.4	3.2	2.4	4.1
With No Own Children Under 18 Years						
Civilian noninstitutional population	166 428	82 408	84 020	168 047	83 222	84 825
Civilian labor force	93 728	49 910	43 818	95 042	50 588	44 453
Participation rate	56.3	60.6	52.2	56.6	60.8	52.4
Employed	89 629	47 483	42 146	91 060	48 242	42 817
Employment-population ratio	53.9	57.6	50.2	54.2	58.0	50.5
Unemployed	4 099	2 427	1 672	3 982	2 346	1 636
Unemployment rate	4.4	4.9	3.8	4.2	4.6	3.7

Note: Updated population controls are introduced annually with the release of January data.

Table 1-53. Employment Status of the Foreign-Born and Native-Born Populations Age 25 Years and Over, by Educational Attainment, Race, and Hispanic Origin, Annual Averages, 2018–2019

(Thousands of people, percent.)

Characteristic	2018				2019			
	Less than a high school diploma	High school graduate, no college[1]	Some college or associate's degree	Bachelor's degree or higher[2]	Less than a high school diploma	High school graduate, no college[1]	Some college or associate's degree	Bachelor's degree or higher[2]
FOREIGN BORN								
White, Non-Hispanic								
Civilian noninstitutional population	644	1 708	1 361	3 617	563	1 686	1 369	3 610
Civilian labor force	250	849	817	2 515	186	897	794	2 523
Participation rate	38.9	49.7	60.0	69.5	33.0	53.2	58.0	69.9
Employed	238	823	791	2 440	179	871	771	2 456
Employment-population ratio	36.9	48.2	58.1	67.5	31.9	51.7	56.3	68.0
Unemployed	12	26	27	75	6	25	22	67
Unemployment rate	4.9	3.1	3.3	3.0	3.4	2.8	2.8	2.7
Black, Non-Hispanic								
Civilian noninstitutional population	391	946	908	1 156	374	967	838	1 240
Civilian labor force	196	666	684	950	199	663	638	1 011
Participation rate	50.0	70.0	75.3	82.1	53.2	68.5	76.2	81.5
Employed	187	637	653	911	187	637	614	976
Employment-population ratio	47.8	67.4	71.9	78.8	49.9	65.9	73.3	78.7
Unemployed	10	28	31	38	12	26	24	36
Unemployment rate	4.9	4.2	4.5	4.0	6.1	3.9	3.8	3.5
Asian, Non-Hispanic								
Civilian noninstitutional population	1 015	1 955	1 402	5 844	1 079	1 829	1 318	6 096
Civilian labor force	403	1 145	934	4 257	410	1 062	878	4 478
Participation rate	39.7	58.6	66.7	73.0	38.0	58.1	66.6	73.5
Employed	393	1 121	910	4 152	399	1 044	857	4 378
Employment-population ratio	38.7	57.3	64.9	71.0	37.0	57.1	65.0	71.8
Unemployed	10	24	24	106	11	17	21	100
Unemployment rate	2.5	2.1	2.6	2.5	2.6	1.6	2.4	2.2
Hispanic[3]								
Civilian noninstitutional population	7 514	5 410	2 577	2 585	7 436	5 392	2 572	2 834
Civilian labor force	4 730	3 908	1 930	1 923	4 618	3 941	1 910	2 142
Participation rate	62.9	72.0	74.9	74.4	62.1	73.1	74.2	75.6
Employed	4 534	3 777	1 867	1 870	4 433	3 835	1 863	2 082
Employment-population ratio	60.3	69.8	72.4	72.4	59.6	71.1	72.4	73.5
Unemployed	196	131	63	53	184	106	47	59
Unemployment rate	4.1	3.4	3.2	2.7	4.0	2.7	2.5	2.8
NATIVE BORN								
White, Non-Hispanic								
Civilian noninstitutional population	7 423	37 857	37 328	52 012	7 075	37 579	37 225	53 021
Civilian labor force	2 641	20 379	23 507	37 817	2 550	20 377	23 175	38 437
Participation rate	35.6	53.8	63.0	72.7	36.0	54.2	62.3	72.5
Employed	2 479	19 670	22 855	37 117	2 399	19 725	22 570	37 726
Employment-population ratio	33.4	52.0	61.2	71.4	33.9	52.5	60.6	71.2
Unemployed	162	708	652	700	151	652	606	711
Unemployment rate	6.1	3.5	2.8	1.9	5.9	3.2	2.6	1.8
Black, Non-Hispanic								
Civilian noninstitutional population	2 427	7 487	6 713	5 555	2 315	7 571	6 820	5 708
Civilian labor force	782	4 340	4 571	4 259	759	4 326	4 632	4 373
Participation rate	32.2	58.0	68.1	76.7	32.8	57.1	67.9	76.6
Employed	684	4 029	4 324	4 146	668	4 035	4 427	4 256
Employment-population ratio	28.2	53.8	64.4	74.6	28.9	53.3	64.9	74.6
Unemployed	98	311	247	112	91	291	205	118
Unemployment rate	12.6	7.2	5.4	2.6	12.0	6.7	4.4	2.7
Asian, Non-Hispanic								
Civilian noninstitutional population	164	516	602	1 854	145	509	685	2 035
Civilian labor force	69	309	414	1 468	55	294	471	1 637
Participation rate	41.8	60.0	68.7	79.2	38.1	57.8	68.7	80.4
Employed	65	299	400	1 440	53	285	455	1 598
Employment-population ratio	39.7	58.0	66.4	77.7	36.3	56.0	66.5	78.5
Unemployed	4	10	14	28	3	9	15	39
Unemployment rate	5.1	3.4	3.3	1.9	4.9	3.2	3.3	2.4
Hispanic[3]								
Civilian noninstitutional population	2 223	5 227	4 903	3 613	2 215	5 446	5 004	3 858
Civilian labor force	1 023	3 531	3 624	2 989	1 042	3 698	3 790	3 157
Participation rate	46.0	67.6	73.9	82.7	47.0	67.9	75.7	81.8
Employed	954	3 369	3 487	2 900	978	3 559	3 646	3 081
Employment-population ratio	42.9	64.5	71.1	80.3	44.2	65.4	72.9	79.9
Unemployed	69	162	137	88	64	139	144	76
Unemployment rate	6.8	4.6	3.8	3.0	6.1	3.8	3.8	2.4

Note: Updated population controls are introduced annually with the release of January data.

[1]Includes persons with a high school diploma or equivalent.
[2]Includes persons with bachelor's, master's, professional, and doctoral degrees.
[3]May be of any race.

Table 1-54. Employed Foreign-Born and Native-Born Persons Age 16 Years and Over, by Occupation and Sex, Annual Averages, 2018–2019

(Thousands of people, percent.)

| Occupation | 2018 | | | | | |
| | Foreign born | | | Native born | | |
	Both sexes	Male	Female	Both sexes	Male	Female
TOTAL EMPLOYED	26 254	15 171	11 083	127 083	66 231	60 852
Percent Employed	100.0	100.0	100.0	100.0	100.0	100.0
Management, professional, and related	32.3	30.7	34.3	41.3	37.5	45.4
Management, business, and financial operations	12.3	12.6	11.9	17.4	18.6	16.2
Management	8.6	9.6	7.4	12.2	14.0	10.3
Business and financial operations	3.7	3.0	4.6	5.2	4.6	5.9
Professional and related	20.0	18.2	22.4	23.8	18.9	29.2
Computer and mathematical	4.8	6.4	2.5	2.8	3.9	1.6
Architecture and engineering	2.3	3.2	1.0	2.1	3.3	0.7
Life, physical, and social sciences	1.3	1.2	1.4	0.9	0.9	0.9
Community and social services	0.9	0.6	1.2	1.9	1.2	2.6
Legal	0.5	0.4	0.8	1.3	1.2	1.4
Education, training, and library	3.7	2.2	5.7	6.5	3.3	10.0
Arts, design, entertainment, sports, and media	1.4	1.3	1.5	2.3	2.3	2.2
Health care practitioner and technical	5.2	2.9	8.4	6.1	2.8	9.7
Services	23.9	17.2	33.1	16.1	13.6	18.8
Health care support	2.8	0.6	5.8	2.2	0.5	4.0
Protective services	0.8	1.1	0.4	2.3	3.4	1.1
Food preparation and serving related	7.1	6.6	7.8	5.1	4.3	5.9
Building and grounds cleaning and maintenance	8.4	7.0	10.3	2.9	3.7	2.1
Personal care and services	4.8	1.8	8.8	3.7	1.7	5.8
Sales and office	15.0	11.1	20.4	23.3	17.0	30.1
Sales and related	7.5	6.7	8.7	10.9	10.6	11.2
Office and administrative support	7.5	4.4	11.8	12.4	6.4	18.9
Natural resources, construction, and maintenance	13.9	22.6	2.0	8.3	15.2	0.8
Farming, fishing, and forestry	1.7	2.1	1.2	0.6	0.9	0.2
Construction and extraction	9.3	15.6	0.5	4.4	8.2	0.3
Installation, maintenance, and repair	2.9	4.8	0.2	3.3	6.1	0.3
Production, transportation, and material moving	14.9	18.4	10.1	11.0	16.7	4.9
Production	7.5	7.9	7.0	5.1	7.3	2.7
Transportation and material moving	7.4	10.5	3.1	5.9	9.4	2.1

| Occupation | 2019 | | | | | |
| | Foreign born | | | Native born | | |
	Both sexes	Male	Female	Both sexes	Male	Female
TOTAL EMPLOYED	27 502	15 791	11 711	130 036	67 669	62 367
Percent Employed	100.0	100.0	100.0	100.0	100.0	100.0
Management, professional, and related	33.9	32.0	36.4	42.2	38.3	46.5
Management, business, and financial operations	13.1	13.5	12.6	18.0	19.1	16.7
Management	9.2	10.4	7.6	12.6	14.4	10.7
Business and financial operations	3.9	3.1	5.0	5.3	4.7	6.0
Professional and related	20.8	18.5	23.8	24.2	19.2	29.8
Computer and mathematical	5.2	6.6	3.2	3.0	4.3	1.6
Architecture and engineering	2.3	3.3	1.1	2.0	3.4	0.6
Life, physical, and social sciences	1.2	1.1	1.2	0.9	0.8	0.9
Community and social services	1.0	0.7	1.4	1.9	1.1	2.7
Legal	0.6	0.4	0.8	1.4	1.3	1.5
Education, training, and library	3.8	2.1	6.0	6.5	3.2	10.0
Arts, design, entertainment, sports, and media	1.5	1.4	1.6	2.2	2.1	2.3
Health care practitioner and technical	5.2	2.8	8.5	6.3	2.9	10.1
Services	22.5	15.9	31.4	16.0	13.2	19.0
Health care support	2.6	0.6	5.2	2.3	0.6	4.3
Protective services	0.9	1.3	0.4	2.2	3.3	1.0
Food preparation and serving related	6.7	6.0	7.7	5.0	4.2	5.9
Building and grounds cleaning and maintenance	7.6	6.3	9.4	2.8	3.5	2.1
Personal care and services	4.8	1.7	8.8	3.6	1.6	5.7
Sales and office	15.5	12.0	20.2	22.4	16.6	28.6
Sales and related	7.7	7.3	8.3	10.3	10.1	10.6
Office and administrative support	7.8	4.7	11.9	12.0	6.5	18.0
Natural resources, construction, and maintenance	13.4	21.8	2.0	8.2	15.0	0.9
Farming, fishing, and forestry	1.7	2.0	1.2	0.5	0.8	0.2
Construction and extraction	9.1	15.3	0.7	4.5	8.3	0.3
Installation, maintenance, and repair	2.6	4.4	0.2	3.2	5.9	0.3
Production, transportation, and material moving	14.7	18.2	10.0	11.2	16.9	5.0
Production	7.2	7.6	6.6	5.1	7.3	2.7
Transportation and material moving	7.5	10.6	3.4	6.1	9.7	2.3

Note: Updated population controls are introduced annually with the release of January data.

Table 1-55. Median Usual Weekly Earnings of Full-Time Wage and Salary Workers for the Foreign-Born and Native-Born Populations, by Selected Characteristics, Annual Averages, 2018–2019

(Thousands of people, dollars, percent.)

Year and characteristic	Foreign born		Native born		Earnings of foreign born as a percent of earnings of native born[1]
	Number	Median weekly earnings	Number	Median weekly earnings	
2018					
Both Sexes, 16 Years and Over	20 627	758	94 939	910	83.3
Men	12 469	815	51 673	1 007	80.9
Women	8 158	678	43 266	810	83.7
Age					
16 to 24 years	993	522	9 436	551	94.7
25 to 34 years	4 668	752	24 207	819	91.8
35 to 44 years	5 803	802	20 648	1 035	77.5
45 to 54 years	5 215	779	20 351	1 059	73.6
55 to 64 years	3 154	774	16 430	1 035	74.8
65 years and over	795	733	3 867	977	75.0
Race and Hispanic Origin					
White, non-Hispanic	3 135	1 083	67 771	986	109.8
Black, non-Hispanic	2 023	699	12 109	697	100.3
Asian, non-Hispanic	5 387	1 129	2 041	1 065	106.0
Hispanic[2]	9 852	621	10 445	741	83.8
Educational Attainment					
Total, 25 years and over	19 635	775	85 503	965	80.3
Less than a high school diploma	4 097	535	2 902	578	92.6
High school graduate, no college[3]	4 879	632	21 358	754	83.8
Some college	3 125	755	24 350	837	90.2
Bachelor's degree or higher[4]	7 534	1 362	36 893	1 309	104.0
2019					
Both Sexes, 16 Years and Over	21 007	800	96 576	941	85.0
Men	12 584	863	52 423	1 042	82.8
Women	8 423	719	44 154	841	85.5
Age					
16 to 24 years	987	564	9 778	583	96.7
25 to 34 years	4 682	797	24 894	854	93.3
35 to 44 years	5 704	864	21 078	1 083	79.8
45 to 54 years	5 491	815	19 899	1 102	74.0
55 to 64 years	3 293	815	16 773	1 065	76.5
65 years and over	850	749	4 155	964	77.7
Race and Hispanic Origin					
White, non-Hispanic	3 203	1 141	68 143	1 016	112.3
Black, non-Hispanic	2 089	749	12 353	735	101.9
Asian, non-Hispanic	5 466	1 198	2 218	1 168	102.6
Hispanic[2]	10 008	658	11 219	759	86.7
Educational Attainment					
Total, 25 years and over	20 020	819	86 798	999	82.0
Less than a high school diploma	4 038	577	2 972	617	93.5
High school graduates, no college[3]	4 950	675	21 806	766	88.1
Some college	3 093	779	24 185	868	89.7
Bachelor's degree and higher[4]	7 939	1 418	37 834	1 360	104.3

Note: Updated population controls are introduced annually with the release of January data.

[1]These figures are computed using unrounded medians and may differ slightly from percentages computed using the rounded medians displayed in this table.
[2]May be of any race.
[3]Includes persons with a high school diploma or equivalent.
[4]Includes persons with bachelor's, master's, professional, and doctoral degrees.

Table 1-56. Percent Distribution of the Civilian Labor Force Age 25 to 64 Years, by Educational Attainment, Sex, and Race, March 2000–March 2020

(Thousands of people, percent.)

Sex, race, and year	Civilian labor force	Percent distribution				
		Total	Less than a high school diploma	4 years of high school only	1 to 3 years of college	4 or more years of college
Both Sexes						
2000	114 052	99.9	9.8	31.8	27.9	30.4
2001	115 073	100.0	9.8	31.4	28.1	30.7
2002	117 738	100.0	10.1	30.6	27.7	31.6
2003	119 261	99.9	10.1	30.1	27.8	31.9
2004	119 392	100.0	9.7	30.1	27.8	32.4
2005	120 461	100.0	9.8	30.1	27.8	32.3
2006	122 541	100.0	9.8	29.6	28.0	32.6
2007	124 581	100.0	9.8	29.3	27.3	33.6
2008	125 493	100.0	9.0	28.8	27.9	34.4
2009	125 655	100.0	9.0	28.7	27.9	34.3
2010	126 363	100.0	8.8	29.1	27.5	34.5
2011	125 385	100.0	8.5	28.2	28.0	35.4
2012	125 726	100.0	8.6	27.5	27.9	36.0
2013	125 744	100.0	8.2	27.0	28.1	36.7
2014	125 847	100.0	8.4	26.9	27.8	37.0
2015	126 863	100.0	8.2	26.3	27.7	37.7
2016	128 660	100.0	7.9	25.8	27.6	38.8
2017	129 313	100.0	7.3	25.9	27.6	39.1
2018	130 447	100.0	7.2	25.5	26.8	40.5
2019	131 173	100.0	7.1	25.3	26.3	41.3
2020	130 965	100.0	6.4	24.6	26.0	43.0
Men						
2000	60 510	99.9	11.1	31.8	26.1	30.9
2001	61 091	100.0	11.0	31.6	26.3	31.1
2002	62 794	100.0	11.8	30.6	25.9	31.7
2003	63 466	100.0	12.0	30.1	25.8	32.1
2004	63 699	100.0	11.5	30.5	25.8	32.2
2005	64 562	100.0	11.6	31.4	25.4	31.6
2006	65 708	100.0	11.8	30.7	25.7	31.8
2007	66 742	100.0	11.7	30.6	25.1	32.7
2008	66 957	100.0	11.0	30.3	25.8	33.0
2009	66 843	100.0	10.8	30.4	26.0	32.8
2010	67 261	100.0	10.6	31.2	25.3	32.9
2011	66 801	100.0	10.2	30.4	25.5	33.9
2012	66 539	100.0	10.1	29.7	25.9	34.3
2013	66 594	100.0	9.9	29.1	26.2	34.8
2014	66 625	100.0	10.2	29.4	25.8	34.7
2015	67 578	100.0	10.0	29.1	25.8	35.1
2016	68 329	100.0	9.5	28.5	25.8	36.1
2017	68 312	100.0	8.8	28.9	25.9	36.3
2018	69 208	100.0	8.7	28.6	25.2	37.5
2019	69 463	100.0	8.7	28.3	25.0	38.0
2020	68 970	100.0	7.8	27.8	24.8	39.6
Women						
2000	53 541	100.0	8.4	31.8	30.0	29.8
2001	53 982	99.9	8.5	31.1	30.1	30.2
2002	54 944	100.0	8.2	30.6	29.7	31.5
2003	55 795	100.0	8.0	30.1	30.1	31.8
2004	55 693	100.0	7.7	29.6	30.2	32.5
2005	55 899	100.0	7.8	28.6	30.5	33.1
2006	56 833	100.0	7.6	28.2	30.6	33.6
2007	57 839	100.0	7.5	27.9	29.9	34.6
2008	58 536	100.0	6.7	27.0	30.4	35.9
2009	58 811	100.0	7.0	26.9	30.2	35.9
2010	59 102	100.0	6.8	26.8	30.1	36.3
2011	58 584	100.0	6.5	25.7	30.7	37.1
2012	59 187	100.0	6.8	25.1	30.2	37.9
2013	59 150	100.0	6.3	24.6	30.2	38.9
2014	59 222	100.0	6.4	24.1	30.0	39.6
2015	59 285	100.0	6.2	23.2	29.9	40.7
2016	60 331	100.0	6.1	22.6	29.6	41.7
2017	61 002	100.0	5.7	22.6	29.4	42.3
2018	61 239	100.0	5.5	22.1	28.5	43.9
2019	61 710	100.0	5.3	21.9	27.7	45.1
2020	61 996	100.0	4.8	21.1	27.3	46.8

Table 1-56. Percent Distribution of the Civilian Labor Force Age 25 to 64 Years, by Educational Attainment, Sex, and Race, March 2000–March 2020—*Continued*

(Thousands of people, percent.)

Sex, race, and year	Civilian labor force	Percent distribution				
		Total	Less than a high school diploma	4 years of high school only	1 to 3 years of college	4 or more years of college
White[1]						
2000	95 073	100.0	9.5	31.8	27.7	31.0
2001	95 562	99.9	9.5	31.0	28.0	31.4
2002	97 699	100.0	9.8	30.6	27.6	32.0
2003	98 241	100.0	9.9	30.0	27.7	32.4
2004	98 030	100.0	9.5	29.8	27.8	32.9
2005	98 581	100.0	9.7	29.8	27.8	32.7
2006	100 205	100.0	9.7	29.3	28.1	32.9
2007	101 548	100.0	9.7	29.1	27.3	33.9
2008	102 077	100.0	8.9	28.7	27.8	34.6
2009	102 261	100.0	9.1	28.6	27.7	34.6
2010	102 634	100.0	8.8	29.0	27.4	34.8
2011	101 707	100.0	8.4	27.8	27.9	35.8
2012	100 382	100.0	8.6	27.4	27.7	36.4
2013	99 964	100.0	8.2	27.0	27.9	36.9
2014	99 664	100.0	8.3	26.8	27.8	37.2
2015	99 813	100.0	8.4	26.3	27.5	37.9
2016	100 886	100.0	8.0	25.7	27.4	38.9
2017	100 794	100.0	7.4	25.9	27.5	39.2
2018	101 234	100.0	7.3	25.5	26.6	40.6
2019	101 321	100.0	7.2	25.4	26.1	41.3
2020	101 216	100.0	6.6	24.6	26.2	42.6
Black[1]						
2000	13 383	100.1	11.8	36.1	31.5	20.7
2001	13 617	100.0	12.0	37.1	31.1	19.8
2002	13 319	99.9	12.4	34.5	32.0	21.0
2003	13 315	100.0	11.3	35.6	31.5	21.6
2004	13 372	100.0	11.0	36.6	30.5	21.9
2005	13 635	100.0	11.2	37.3	29.9	21.6
2006	13 855	99.9	10.9	35.6	30.4	23.0
2007	14 186	100.0	10.1	35.4	31.4	23.1
2008	14 356	100.0	9.5	34.3	32.1	24.1
2009	14 325	100.0	8.5	35.1	33.0	23.5
2010	14 483	100.0	8.9	34.5	32.4	24.2
2011	14 377	100.0	8.5	33.8	33.1	24.6
2012	14 721	100.0	8.5	32.0	33.4	26.0
2013	14 869	100.0	8.5	31.4	33.4	26.7
2014	15 121	100.0	8.9	31.3	32.2	27.6
2015	15 415	100.0	7.1	31.2	34.1	27.5
2016	15 666	100.0	7.5	30.7	33.1	28.7
2017	16 108	100.0	6.9	30.3	33.5	29.3
2018	16 420	100.0	6.5	30.4	32.3	30.9
2019	16 687	100.0	6.7	29.5	31.8	32.0
2020	16 433	100.0	5.8	30.2	30.3	33.7

[1]Beginning in 2003, persons who selected this race group only; persons who selected more than one race group are not included. Prior to 2003, persons who reported more than one race group were included in the group they identified as their main race.

Table 1-57. Labor Force Participation Rates of Persons Age 25 to 64 Years, by Educational Attainment, Sex, and Race, March 2000–March 2020

(Civilian labor force as a percent of the civilian noninstitutional population.)

Sex, race, and year	Participation rates				
	Total	Less than a high school diploma	4 years of high school only	1 to 3 years of college	4 or more years of college
Both Sexes					
2000	80.3	62.7	78.4	83.2	87.8
2001	80.2	63.5	78.4	83.0	87.0
2002	79.7	63.5	77.7	82.1	86.7
2003	79.4	64.1	76.9	81.9	86.2
2004	78.8	63.2	76.1	81.2	85.9
2005	78.5	62.9	75.7	81.1	85.7
2006	78.7	63.2	75.9	81.0	85.9
2007	79.0	63.7	76.3	81.1	85.9
2008	79.0	62.5	76.0	80.9	86.1
2009	78.6	62.3	75.7	80.3	85.9
2010	78.7	62.7	76.2	79.7	85.7
2011	77.6	61.0	74.3	78.6	85.3
2012	77.4	61.7	73.2	78.5	85.5
2013	77.2	60.9	73.0	78.1	85.1
2014	76.7	61.3	72.3	77.3	84.9
2015	76.7	60.2	71.8	77.9	84.8
2016	77.2	61.6	71.9	77.3	85.6
2017	77.5	60.6	72.2	78.3	85.5
2018	77.7	60.8	72.4	77.8	85.7
2019	78.1	60.0	72.8	78.8	85.9
2020	78.1	60.1	72.1	78.3	86.0
Men					
2000	87.5	74.9	86.2	88.9	93.3
2001	87.4	75.4	85.8	89.1	92.9
2002	87.0	75.5	85.3	88.8	92.4
2003	86.4	76.1	84.3	87.5	92.2
2004	85.9	75.2	83.8	87.0	91.9
2005	86.0	75.7	83.7	87.5	91.7
2006	86.0	76.3	83.4	87.8	91.7
2007	86.2	75.7	83.9	87.2	92.4
2008	85.8	74.8	83.6	86.5	91.9
2009	85.1	73.7	82.3	86.0	91.9
2010	85.3	74.5	83.2	85.3	91.5
2011	84.0	73.3	81.8	83.2	91.1
2012	84.1	72.9	80.7	84.3	91.4
2013	84.0	72.7	80.5	83.8	91.4
2014	83.2	73.1	79.8	82.4	90.8
2015	83.6	73.4	80.0	83.7	90.6
2016	83.8	74.0	79.7	83.0	91.4
2017	83.8	72.3	79.7	83.6	91.2
2018	84.3	73.2	80.7	83.7	91.0
2019	84.6	72.6	80.5	85.0	91.2
2020	84.2	72.2	79.0	84.2	91.3
Women					
2000	73.5	50.4	71.2	78.3	82.0
2001	73.4	51.7	71.3	77.7	80.9
2002	72.7	50.4	70.4	76.4	81.0
2003	72.6	50.5	69.8	77.1	80.1
2004	72.0	49.7	68.6	76.2	80.0
2005	71.4	48.7	67.4	75.8	79.8
2006	71.7	48.3	68.2	75.3	80.4
2007	72.1	49.6	68.4	76.0	79.7
2008	72.5	47.9	68.2	76.1	80.9
2009	72.4	49.0	68.7	75.4	80.5
2010	72.3	48.9	68.6	75.0	80.4
2011	71.3	46.8	66.1	74.7	80.0
2012	71.1	49.2	65.2	73.5	80.3
2013	70.8	47.3	65.1	73.3	79.6
2014	70.6	47.6	64.1	72.9	79.8
2015	70.1	45.3	62.6	72.9	79.9
2016	70.8	47.6	63.2	72.4	80.5
2017	71.4	47.2	63.6	73.6	80.6
2018	71.3	46.8	63.0	72.7	81.1
2019	71.9	45.4	63.9	73.3	81.4
2020	72.4	46.1	63.9	73.1	81.6

Table 1-57. Labor Force Participation Rates of Persons Age 25 to 64 Years, by Educational Attainment, Sex, and Race, March 2000–March 2020—*Continued*

(Civilian labor force as a percent of the civilian noninstitutional population.)

Sex, race, and year	Participation rates				
	Total	Less than a high school diploma	4 years of high school only	1 to 3 years of college	4 or more years of college
White[1]					
2000	80.8	64.2	78.7	83.1	87.9
2001	80.7	64.5	78.7	83.1	87.2
2002	80.3	65.0	78.2	82.4	87.0
2003	80.1	65.7	77.5	82.3	86.5
2004	79.5	64.6	76.7	81.6	86.2
2005	79.2	63.8	76.4	81.5	86.1
2006	79.5	65.1	76.5	81.4	86.2
2007	79.6	65.1	77.2	81.4	86.1
2008	79.6	63.8	76.8	81.2	86.3
2009	79.4	64.7	76.4	80.7	86.2
2010	79.5	64.5	77.1	80.4	86.0
2011	78.5	62.9	75.3	79.3	85.5
2012	78.3	63.8	74.2	78.8	86.0
2013	78.0	63.0	73.9	78.5	85.6
2014	77.6	62.9	73.4	77.8	85.4
2015	77.5	62.4	72.8	78.1	85.4
2016	78.0	63.6	73.1	77.7	86.2
2017	78.2	62.6	73.1	78.5	86.0
2018	78.4	63.3	73.2	78.1	86.3
2019	78.8	61.7	73.8	78.9	86.5
2020	79.1	62.1	73.5	79.0	86.7
Black[1]					
2000	77.9	55.5	77.0	84.2	90.3
2001	78.1	58.7	76.8	83.0	90.5
2002	76.4	56.6	75.0	81.7	88.9
2003	75.8	55.4	73.9	81.2	88.2
2004	75.0	55.2	73.4	79.0	87.9
2005	75.2	58.2	72.6	79.5	87.2
2006	75.0	54.0	73.3	79.6	87.7
2007	75.6	55.3	72.5	80.7	88.0
2008	75.6	54.3	72.8	80.0	87.5
2009	74.4	50.0	72.6	78.7	86.2
2010	74.2	52.2	71.7	77.5	87.0
2011	72.4	49.0	69.6	76.3	85.5
2012	72.9	50.8	68.6	77.2	85.7
2013	73.0	50.2	69.2	77.7	84.2
2014	72.8	54.4	67.9	75.4	86.0
2015	72.8	49.0	66.6	78.1	85.4
2016	72.7	50.9	66.9	76.2	85.8
2017	73.9	50.9	67.7	78.1	86.0
2018	74.3	48.7	69.6	76.6	86.8
2019	74.9	50.0	68.8	78.8	86.7
2020	73.1	49.6	66.3	76.2	84.7

[1]Beginning in 2003, persons who selected this race group only; persons who selected more than one race group are not included. Prior to 2003, persons who reported more than one race group were included in the group they identified as their main race.

Table 1-58. Unemployment Rates of Persons Age 25 to 64 Years, by Educational Attainment and Sex, March 2000–March 2020

(Unemployment as a percent of the civilian labor force.)

Sex, race, and year	Unemployment rates				
	Total	Less than a high school diploma	4 years of high school only	1 to 3 years of college	4 or more years of college
Both Sexes					
2000	3.3	7.9	3.8	3.0	1.5
2001	3.5	8.1	4.2	2.9	2.0
2002	5.0	10.2	6.1	4.5	2.8
2003	5.3	9.9	6.4	5.2	3.0
2004	5.1	10.5	5.9	4.9	2.9
2005	4.4	9.0	5.5	4.1	2.3
2006	4.1	8.3	4.7	3.9	2.3
2007	3.9	8.5	4.7	3.7	1.8
2008	4.4	10.1	5.8	4.2	2.1
2009	8.1	15.8	10.4	8.0	4.3
2010	9.1	16.8	12.1	8.8	4.7
2011	8.3	16.2	10.9	8.1	4.4
2012	7.4	14.3	9.2	7.9	4.1
2013	6.6	12.7	8.7	6.5	3.8
2014	5.8	10.6	7.4	6.1	3.4
2015	4.7	9.2	6.2	4.9	2.4
2016	4.4	8.1	6.1	4.5	2.4
2017	3.9	8.3	5.2	3.8	2.3
2018	3.5	6.6	4.7	3.7	2.2
2019	3.2	6.5	4.0	3.5	1.9
2020	4.5	8.3	6.0	4.7	2.9
Men					
2000	3.3	7.1	3.9	3.1	1.6
2001	3.7	7.5	4.6	3.2	1.9
2002	5.5	9.9	6.7	4.9	3.0
2003	5.8	9.5	6.9	6.0	3.2
2004	5.4	9.4	6.6	5.4	3.0
2005	4.7	7.9	6.0	4.3	2.5
2006	4.3	7.6	5.0	4.2	2.4
2007	4.3	8.4	5.5	3.9	1.9
2008	4.9	10.9	6.3	4.2	2.0
2009	9.5	16.5	12.4	9.3	4.7
2010	10.5	17.8	13.8	10.2	5.1
2011	9.2	16.7	12.2	8.7	4.6
2012	8.0	13.6	10.1	8.2	4.3
2013	6.9	11.9	9.2	6.5	3.7
2014	5.9	9.4	7.8	5.9	3.4
2015	5.0	8.4	6.7	4.9	2.8
2016	4.5	7.5	6.3	4.7	2.3
2017	4.1	8.0	5.2	4.1	2.4
2018	3.7	6.0	5.0	3.8	2.2
2019	3.4	6.1	4.2	3.7	2.0
2020	4.6	8.0	6.0	4.8	2.8
Women					
2000	3.2	9.1	3.6	2.9	1.4
2001	3.3	8.9	3.8	2.6	2.0
2002	4.6	10.6	5.4	4.1	2.6
2003	4.8	10.6	5.9	4.4	2.8
2004	4.7	12.2	5.2	4.3	2.9
2005	4.2	10.9	4.8	4.0	2.2
2006	3.8	9.4	4.4	3.7	2.1
2007	3.4	8.5	3.8	3.6	1.8
2008	4.0	8.5	5.1	4.2	2.1
2009	6.6	14.5	7.9	6.7	4.0
2010	7.5	15.0	9.8	7.5	4.3
2011	7.2	15.2	9.1	7.5	4.3
2012	6.8	15.4	8.1	7.7	3.8
2013	6.3	14.1	8.1	6.4	3.8
2014	5.7	12.7	6.8	6.3	3.4
2015	4.3	10.6	5.6	5.0	2.1
2016	4.2	9.2	5.8	4.3	2.6
2017	3.7	8.7	5.3	3.5	2.3
2018	3.3	7.8	4.3	3.6	2.1
2019	2.9	7.2	3.7	3.3	1.8
2020	4.3	8.8	5.9	4.5	2.9

Table 1-58. Unemployment Rates of Persons Age 25 to 64 Years, by Educational Attainment and Sex, March 2000–March 2020—*Continued*

(Unemployment as a percent of the civilian labor force.)

Sex, race, and year	Unemployment rates				
	Total	Less than a high school diploma	4 years of high school only	1 to 3 years of college	4 or more years of college
White[1]					
2000	3.0	7.5	3.3	2.7	1.4
2001	3.1	7.2	3.6	2.7	1.8
2002	4.6	9.1	5.5	4.1	2.6
2003	4.7	9.0	5.7	4.5	2.7
2004	4.6	9.6	5.4	4.4	2.8
2005	3.9	7.7	4.9	3.6	2.2
2006	3.5	7.1	4.0	3.5	2.1
2007	3.5	7.8	4.2	3.3	1.7
2008	4.0	9.2	5.1	3.7	1.9
2009	7.6	15.2	9.9	7.4	4.0
2010	8.4	16.3	11.3	8.1	4.3
2011	7.5	15.1	9.9	7.2	4.0
2012	6.7	13.5	8.3	6.9	3.7
2013	5.9	11.2	7.7	5.7	3.5
2014	5.1	9.2	6.3	5.4	3.1
2015	4.1	8.2	5.3	4.2	2.3
2016	3.8	6.7	5.2	3.8	2.3
2017	3.5	7.3	4.6	3.3	2.1
2018	3.2	5.9	4.2	3.3	2.0
2019	2.8	5.4	3.5	3.1	1.8
2020	3.9	7.5	4.9	4.2	2.6
Black[1]					
2000	5.4	10.4	6.3	4.3	2.5
2001	6.5	14.0	7.7	4.3	3.3
2002	8.1	15.4	9.7	6.0	4.1
2003	9.0	14.7	9.9	8.9	4.7
2004	8.4	15.8	9.3	7.9	3.7
2005	8.3	17.9	8.6	7.5	3.6
2006	7.8	16.4	9.0	6.5	3.6
2007	6.5	14.0	7.7	5.7	2.5
2008	7.6	16.7	9.3	6.5	3.3
2009	12.1	22.0	14.0	11.2	7.2
2010	14.1	22.4	17.5	12.9	7.9
2011	13.9	25.0	16.6	12.7	7.7
2012	12.3	21.4	14.2	12.7	6.3
2013	11.4	22.8	14.2	10.0	6.1
2014	10.7	19.7	13.8	10.0	5.0
2015	8.8	17.6	10.8	8.6	4.3
2016	7.9	17.3	10.5	7.4	3.3
2017	6.7	16.4	8.5	5.9	3.4
2018	5.6	11.6	7.3	5.2	2.9
2019	5.4	15.0	6.6	5.3	2.5
2020	7.0	11.4	10.6	6.8	3.3

[1]Beginning in 2003, persons who selected this race group only; persons who selected more than one race group are not included. Prior to 2003, persons who reported more than one race group were included in the group they identified as their main race.

Table 1-59. Workers Age 25 to 64 Years, by Educational Attainment, Occupation of Longest Job Held, and Sex, 2018–2019

(Thousands of people with work experience during the year.)

Year, sex, and occupation	Total	Less than a high school diploma	4 years of high school only	1 to 3 years of college	4 or more years of college
2018					
Both Sexes	133 412	9 326	33 677	35 394	55 015
Management, business, and financial operations	23 946	457	3 189	5 292	15 008
Management	16 673	405	2 548	3 809	9 911
Business and financial operations	7 272	52	640	1 483	5 097
Professional and related	32 863	129	2 137	6 015	24 582
Computer and mathematical	4 732	15	309	776	3 632
Architecture and engineering	3 037	9	241	544	2 243
Life, physical, and social sciences	1 353	. . .	68	105	1 181
Community and social services	2 379	22	185	351	1 822
Legal	1 492	. . .	87	194	1 211
Education, training, and library	8 610	47	509	1 040	7 014
Arts, design, entertainment, sports, and media	2 772	20	277	587	1 889
Health care practitioner and technical	8 488	16	462	2 419	5 591
Services	20 739	2 985	7 591	6 617	3 546
Health care support	3 012	164	952	1 416	480
Protective services	2 669	50	596	1 125	898
Food preparation and serving related	5 429	931	2 274	1 517	706
Building and grounds cleaning and maintenance	5 053	1 405	2 266	924	458
Personal care and services	4 577	435	1 504	1 634	1 004
Sales and office	26 658	1 062	7 738	9 232	8 626
Sales and related	12 115	597	3 371	3 668	4 479
Office and administrative support	14 542	464	4 367	5 564	4 147
Natural resources, construction, and maintenance	12 554	2 427	5 399	3 574	1 153
Farming, fishing, and forestry	982	449	315	148	70
Construction and extraction	7 481	1 616	3 358	1 804	703
Installation, maintenance, and repair	4 091	362	1 726	1 623	379
Production, transportation, and material moving	16 109	2 265	7 523	4 446	1 875
Production	7 657	1 126	3 511	2 227	794
Transportation and material moving	8 452	1 139	4 012	2 220	1 081
Armed forces	544	1	99	218	226
Men	70 580	5 967	19 978	17 858	26 777
Management, business, and financial operations	13 068	317	1 892	2 816	8 043
Management	9 802	289	1 639	2 296	5 578
Business and financial operations	3 266	28	253	520	2 465
Professional and related	13 725	49	886	2 167	10 623
Computer and mathematical	3 519	12	210	596	2 702
Architecture and engineering	2 586	9	191	492	1 894
Life, physical, and social sciences	644	. . .	44	49	551
Community and social services	741	10	80	109	541
Legal	676	. . .	13	15	648
Education, training, and library	2 164	13	92	186	1 872
Arts, design, entertainment, sports, and media	1 397	6	173	330	889
Health care practitioner and technical	1 999	. . .	83	389	1 526
Services	8 703	1 277	3 136	2 628	1 661
Health care support	364	9	117	136	102
Protective services	2 074	38	452	920	664
Food preparation and serving related	2 508	483	1 004	690	331
Building and grounds cleaning and maintenance	2 756	661	1 269	528	298
Personal care and services	1 001	86	293	355	267
Sales and office	10 343	474	2 910	3 169	3 790
Sales and related	6 333	249	1 663	1 817	2 604
Office and administrative support	4 010	225	1 247	1 352	1 186
Natural resources, construction, and maintenance	11 862	2 222	5 169	3 409	1 062
Farming, fishing, and forestry	707	323	227	111	47
Construction and extraction	7 220	1 558	3 274	1 733	655
Installation, maintenance, and repair	3 935	341	1 668	1 565	360
Production, transportation, and material moving	12 372	1 629	5 889	3 459	1 395
Production	5 435	694	2 541	1 670	530
Transportation and material moving	6 937	934	3 349	1 789	865
Armed forces	507	. . .	96	208	203
Women	62 832	3 358	13 699	17 537	28 238
Management, business, and financial operations	10 877	140	1 297	2 476	6 965
Management	6 871	117	909	1 512	4 333
Business and financial operations	4 006	24	387	963	2 632
Professional and related	19 138	79	1 251	3 848	13 959
Computer and mathematical	1 213	3	100	180	931
Architecture and engineering	451	. . .	50	52	350
Life, physical, and social sciences	709	. . .	24	55	630
Community and social services	1 639	12	104	241	1 281
Legal	816	. . .	74	179	563
Education, training, and library	6 446	34	417	854	5 141
Arts, design, entertainment, sports, and media	1 375	14	104	257	1 000
Health care practitioner and technical	6 489	16	379	2 030	4 064
Services	12 036	1 708	4 456	3 988	1 884
Health care support	2 649	155	835	1 280	379
Protective services	594	12	143	206	234
Food preparation and serving related	2 921	448	1 270	827	375
Building and grounds cleaning and maintenance	2 296	745	996	396	159
Personal care and services	3 576	349	1 211	1 279	737
Sales and office	16 315	588	4 828	6 063	4 836
Sales and related	5 782	348	1 708	1 851	1 875
Office and administrative support	10 532	239	3 120	4 212	2 961
Natural resources, construction, and maintenance	692	206	230	166	91
Farming, fishing, and forestry	275	126	89	37	23
Construction and extraction	261	58	84	71	49
Installation, maintenance, and repair	156	22	58	57	19
Production, transportation, and material moving	3 737	636	1 634	987	480
Production	2 222	432	970	557	264
Transportation and material moving	1 515	204	664	431	216
Armed forces	36	1	3	9	23

. . . = Not available.

Table 1-59. Workers Age 25 to 64 Years, by Educational Attainment, Occupation of Longest Job Held, and Sex, 2018–2019—*Continued*

(Thousands of people with work experience during the year.)

Year, sex, and occupation	Total	Less than a high school diploma	4 years of high school only	1 to 3 years of college	4 or more years of college
2019					
Both Sexes	135 207	8 656	33 410	35 454	57 687
Management, business, and financial operations	25 204	453	3 489	5 377	15 885
Management	17 082	404	2 713	3 911	10 054
Business and financial operations	8 123	50	776	1 466	5 831
Professional and related	34 324	208	2 095	6 145	25 876
Computer and mathematical	5 415	14	290	920	4 191
Architecture and engineering	2 913	29	202	482	2 200
Life, physical, and social sciences	1 503	7	58	105	1 333
Community and social services	2 363	39	142	312	1 870
Legal	1 637	5	76	167	1 388
Education, training, and library	8 549	49	499	967	7 034
Arts, design, entertainment, sports, and media	2 945	29	280	723	1 913
Health care practitioner and technical	9 000	35	547	2 469	5 949
Services	20 395	2 590	7 428	6 492	3 885
Health care support	4 224	312	1 408	1 669	835
Protective services	2 754	42	593	1 175	944
Food preparation and serving related	5 352	798	2 287	1 482	786
Building and grounds cleaning and maintenance	4 864	1 224	2 072	1 021	546
Personal care and services	3 201	215	1 067	1 145	774
Sales and office	25 200	757	7 177	8 841	8 425
Sales and related	11 267	408	3 155	3 422	4 282
Office and administrative support	13 933	350	4 022	5 419	4 142
Natural resources, construction, and maintenance	12 660	2 270	5 472	3 747	1 171
Farming, fishing, and forestry	1 044	415	340	174	114
Construction and extraction	7 404	1 538	3 309	1 933	625
Installation, maintenance, and repair	4 212	317	1 824	1 640	431
Production, transportation, and material moving	16 760	2 372	7 633	4 630	2 125
Production	7 090	1 003	3 321	1 998	768
Transportation and material moving	9 670	1 369	4 312	2 632	1 357
Armed forces	665	5	116	223	321
Men	70 853	5 505	19 734	17 801	27 813
Management, business, and financial operations	13 306	310	2 048	2 701	8 246
Management	9 772	286	1 753	2 223	5 511
Business and financial operations	3 534	25	295	479	2 736
Professional and related	14 642	94	835	2 388	11 325
Computer and mathematical	4 010	10	226	742	3 032
Architecture and engineering	2 494	23	173	442	1 855
Life, physical, and social sciences	723	3	32	61	628
Community and social services	766	16	65	76	609
Legal	723	. . .	8	32	683
Education, training, and library	2 116	8	50	176	1 882
Arts, design, entertainment, sports, and media	1 647	21	170	439	1 016
Health care practitioner and technical	2 164	12	112	419	1 620
Services	8 511	1 024	3 085	2 654	1 748
Health care support	532	13	179	158	182
Protective services	2 119	27	476	930	687
Food preparation and serving related	2 527	393	1 068	697	370
Building and grounds cleaning and maintenance	2 668	562	1 133	641	332
Personal care and services	664	28	229	229	178
Sales and office	9 273	293	2 506	2 825	3 649
Sales and related	5 689	161	1 505	1 609	2 414
Office and administrative support	3 584	132	1 001	1 216	1 235
Natural resources, construction, and maintenance	11 864	2 067	5 210	3 559	1 029
Farming, fishing, and forestry	762	293	263	138	69
Construction and extraction	7 065	1 465	3 178	1 850	572
Installation, maintenance, and repair	4 037	309	1 770	1 571	387
Production, transportation, and material moving	12 673	1 714	5 938	3 480	1 540
Production	5 034	619	2 463	1 474	477
Transportation and material moving	7 639	1 094	3 475	2 007	1 063
Armed forces	585	5	111	193	276
Women	64 355	3 151	13 675	17 654	29 875
Management, business, and financial operations	11 898	143	1 441	2 676	7 638
Management	7 310	118	961	1 689	4 543
Business and financial operations	4 589	25	480	987	3 095
Professional and related	19 682	114	1 260	3 757	14 552
Computer and mathematical	1 405	4	64	178	1 159
Architecture and engineering	420	6	29	40	344
Life, physical, and social sciences	780	4	26	45	705
Community and social services	1 597	23	77	236	1 260
Legal	913	5	68	135	705
Education, training, and library	6 432	41	449	791	5 152
Arts, design, entertainment, sports, and media	1 299	8	110	283	897
Health care practitioner and technical	6 836	22	435	2 049	4 329
Services	11 884	1 567	4 343	3 837	2 137
Health care support	3 692	299	1 229	1 511	653
Protective services	635	15	117	245	257
Food preparation and serving related	2 825	404	1 219	785	417
Building and grounds cleaning and maintenance	2 195	661	940	380	214
Personal care and services	2 537	188	838	916	596
Sales and office	15 927	465	4 670	6 016	4 776
Sales and related	5 578	247	1 649	1 813	1 869
Office and administrative support	10 349	218	3 021	4 203	2 907
Natural resources, construction, and maintenance	795	203	262	188	142
Farming, fishing, and forestry	281	123	77	37	45
Construction and extraction	340	73	131	83	53
Installation, maintenance, and repair	175	8	54	69	44
Production, transportation, and material moving	4 088	659	1 695	1 149	585
Production	2 057	384	858	524	291
Transportation and material moving	2 031	274	837	625	294
Armed forces	80	. . .	5	29	46

. . . = Not available.

Table 1-60. Percent Distribution of Workers Age 25 to 64 Years, by Educational Attainment, Occupation of Longest Job Held, and Sex, 2018–2019

(Percent of total workers in occupation.)

Year, sex, and occupation	Total	Less than a high school diploma	4 years of high school only	1 to 3 years of college	4 or more years of college
2018					
Both Sexes	100.0	7.0	25.2	26.5	41.2
Management, business, and financial operations	100.0	1.9	13.3	22.1	62.7
Management	100.0	2.4	15.3	22.8	59.4
Business and financial operations	100.0	0.7	8.8	20.4	70.1
Professional and related	100.0	0.4	6.5	18.3	74.8
Computer and mathematical	100.0	0.3	6.5	16.4	76.8
Architecture and engineering	100.0	0.3	7.9	17.9	73.9
Life, physical, and social sciences	100.0	. . .	5.0	7.7	87.3
Community and social services	100.0	0.9	7.8	14.7	76.6
Legal	100.0	. . .	5.8	13.0	81.2
Education, training, and library	100.0	0.6	5.9	12.1	81.5
Arts, design, entertainment, sports, and media	100.0	0.7	10.0	21.2	68.1
Health care practitioner and technical	100.0	0.2	5.4	28.5	65.9
Services	100.0	14.4	36.6	31.9	17.1
Health care support	100.0	5.4	31.6	47.0	15.9
Protective services	100.0	1.9	22.3	42.2	33.6
Food preparation and serving related	100.0	17.2	41.9	27.9	13.0
Building and grounds cleaning and maintenance	100.0	27.8	44.8	18.3	9.1
Personal care and services	100.0	9.5	32.9	35.7	21.9
Sales and office	100.0	4.0	29.0	34.6	32.4
Sales and related	100.0	4.9	27.8	30.3	37.0
Office and administrative support	100.0	3.2	30.0	38.3	28.5
Natural resources, construction, and maintenance	100.0	19.3	43.0	28.5	9.2
Farming, fishing, and forestry	100.0	45.7	32.1	15.1	7.2
Construction and extraction	100.0	21.6	44.9	24.1	9.4
Installation, maintenance, and repair	100.0	8.9	42.2	39.7	9.3
Production, transportation, and material moving	100.0	14.1	46.7	27.6	11.6
Production	100.0	14.7	45.9	29.1	10.4
Transportation and material moving	100.0	13.5	47.5	26.3	12.8
Armed forces	100.0	0.2	18.2	40.1	41.5
Men	100.0	8.5	28.3	25.3	37.9
Management, business, and financial operations	100.0	2.4	14.5	21.6	61.5
Management	100.0	2.9	16.7	23.4	56.9
Business and financial operations	100.0	0.9	7.7	15.9	75.5
Professional and related	100.0	0.4	6.5	15.8	77.4
Computer and mathematical	100.0	0.3	6.0	16.9	76.8
Architecture and engineering	100.0	0.3	7.4	19.0	73.2
Life, physical, and social sciences	100.0	. . .	6.8	7.7	85.5
Community and social services	100.0	1.3	10.8	14.8	73.1
Legal	100.0	. . .	1.9	2.3	95.8
Education, training, and library	100.0	0.6	4.3	8.6	86.5
Arts, design, entertainment, sports, and media	100.0	0.4	12.4	23.6	63.6
Health care practitioner and technical	100.0	. . .	4.1	19.5	76.4
Services	100.0	14.7	36.0	30.2	19.1
Health care support	100.0	2.4	32.2	37.5	27.9
Protective services	100.0	1.8	21.8	44.3	32.0
Food preparation and serving related	100.0	19.3	40.0	27.5	13.2
Building and grounds cleaning and maintenance	100.0	24.0	46.1	19.2	10.8
Personal care and services	100.0	8.6	29.3	35.4	26.7
Sales and office	100.0	4.6	28.1	30.6	36.6
Sales and related	100.0	3.9	26.3	28.7	41.1
Office and administrative support	100.0	5.6	31.1	33.7	29.6
Natural resources, construction, and maintenance	100.0	18.7	43.6	28.7	9.0
Farming, fishing, and forestry	100.0	45.6	32.0	15.6	6.7
Construction and extraction	100.0	21.6	45.3	24.0	9.1
Installation, maintenance, and repair	100.0	8.7	42.4	39.8	9.2
Production, transportation, and material moving	100.0	13.2	47.6	28.0	11.3
Production	100.0	12.8	46.7	30.7	9.7
Transportation and material moving	100.0	13.5	48.3	25.8	12.5
Armed forces	100.0	. . .	18.9	41.1	40.0
Women	100.0	5.3	21.8	27.9	44.9
Management, business, and financial operations	100.0	1.3	11.9	22.8	64.0
Management	100.0	1.7	13.2	22.0	63.1
Business and financial operations	100.0	0.6	9.7	24.0	65.7
Professional and related	100.0	0.4	6.5	20.1	72.9
Computer and mathematical	100.0	0.2	8.2	14.8	76.7
Architecture and engineering	100.0	. . .	11.0	11.4	77.5
Life, physical, and social sciences	100.0	. . .	3.4	7.8	88.8
Community and social services	100.0	0.7	6.4	14.7	78.2
Legal	100.0	. . .	9.1	21.9	69.0
Education, training, and library	100.0	0.5	6.5	13.2	79.8
Arts, design, entertainment, sports, and media	100.0	1.0	7.6	18.7	72.7
Health care practitioner and technical	100.0	0.3	5.8	31.3	62.6
Services	100.0	14.2	37.0	33.1	15.7
Health care support	100.0	5.9	31.5	48.3	14.3
Protective services	100.0	2.0	24.1	34.6	39.4
Food preparation and serving related	100.0	15.3	43.5	28.3	12.8
Building and grounds cleaning and maintenance	100.0	32.4	43.4	17.3	6.9
Personal care and services	100.0	9.8	33.9	35.8	20.6
Sales and office	100.0	3.6	29.6	37.2	29.6
Sales and related	100.0	6.0	29.5	32.0	32.4
Office and administrative support	100.0	2.3	29.6	40.0	28.1
Natural resources, construction, and maintenance	100.0	29.7	33.3	23.9	13.1
Farming, fishing, and forestry	100.0	45.9	32.2	13.6	8.3
Construction and extraction	100.0	22.2	32.1	27.2	18.6
Installation, maintenance, and repair	100.0	13.8	37.1	36.8	12.3
Production, transportation, and material moving	100.0	17.0	43.7	26.4	12.8
Production	100.0	19.4	43.7	25.0	11.9
Transportation and material moving	100.0	13.5	43.8	28.4	14.3
Armed forces	100.0	2.6	9.1	25.7	62.6

. . . = Not available.

Table 1-60. Percent Distribution of Workers Age 25 to 64 Years, by Educational Attainment, Occupation of Longest Job Held, and Sex, 2018–2019—*Continued*

(Percent of total workers in occupation.)

Year, sex, and occupation	Total	Less than a high school diploma	4 years of high school only	1 to 3 years of college	4 or more years of college
2019					
Both Sexes					
Management, business, and financial operations	100.0	6.4	24.7	26.2	42.7
Management	100.0	1.8	13.8	21.3	63.0
Business and financial operations	100.0	2.4	15.9	22.9	58.9
Professional and related	100.0	0.6	9.6	18.0	71.8
Computer and mathematical	100.0	0.6	6.1	17.9	75.4
Architecture and engineering	100.0	0.3	5.4	17.0	77.4
Life, physical, and social sciences	100.0	1.0	6.9	16.6	75.5
Community and social services	100.0	1.6	6.0	13.2	79.1
Legal	100.0	0.3	4.6	10.2	84.8
Education, training, and library	100.0	0.6	5.8	11.3	82.3
Arts, design, entertainment, sports, and media	100.0	1.0	9.5	24.5	64.9
Health care practitioner and technical	100.0	0.4	6.1	27.4	66.1
Services	100.0	12.7	36.4	31.8	19.0
Health care support	100.0	7.4	33.3	39.5	19.8
Protective services	100.0	1.5	21.5	42.7	34.3
Food preparation and serving related	100.0	14.9	42.7	27.7	14.7
Building and grounds cleaning and maintenance	100.0	25.2	42.6	21.0	11.2
Personal care and services	100.0	6.7	33.3	35.8	24.2
Sales and office	100.0	3.0	28.5	35.1	33.4
Sales and related	100.0	3.6	28.0	30.4	38.0
Office and administrative support	100.0	2.5	28.9	38.9	29.7
Natural resources, construction, and maintenance	100.0	17.9	43.2	29.6	9.2
Farming, fishing, and forestry	100.0	39.8	32.6	16.7	10.9
Construction and extraction	100.0	20.8	44.7	26.1	8.4
Installation, maintenance, and repair	100.0	7.5	43.3	38.9	10.2
Production, transportation, and material moving	100.0	14.2	45.5	27.6	12.7
Production	100.0	14.2	46.8	28.2	10.8
Transportation and material moving	100.0	14.2	44.6	27.2	14.0
Armed forces	100.0	0.7	17.4	33.5	48.3
Men					
Management, business, and financial operations	100.0	7.8	27.9	25.1	39.3
Management	100.0	2.3	15.4	20.3	62.0
Business and financial operations	100.0	2.9	17.9	22.7	56.4
Professional and related	100.0	0.7	8.4	13.5	77.4
Computer and mathematical	100.0	0.6	5.7	16.3	77.3
Architecture and engineering	100.0	0.3	5.6	18.5	75.6
Life, physical, and social sciences	100.0	0.9	6.9	17.7	74.4
Community and social services	100.0	2.1	8.5	9.9	79.5
Legal	100.0	. . .	1.1	4.5	94.5
Education, training, and library	100.0	0.4	2.3	8.3	88.9
Arts, design, entertainment, sports, and media	100.0	1.3	10.3	26.7	61.7
Health care practitioner and technical	100.0	0.6	5.2	19.4	74.9
Services	100.0	12.0	36.2	31.2	20.5
Health care support	100.0	2.5	33.6	29.7	34.2
Protective services	100.0	1.3	22.4	43.9	32.4
Food preparation and serving related	100.0	15.6	42.3	27.6	14.6
Building and grounds cleaning and maintenance	100.0	21.1	42.5	24.0	12.4
Personal care and services	100.0	4.2	34.5	34.5	26.8
Sales and office	100.0	3.2	27.0	30.5	39.4
Sales and related	100.0	2.8	26.5	28.3	42.4
Office and administrative support	100.0	3.7	27.9	33.9	34.5
Natural resources, construction, and maintenance	100.0	17.4	43.9	30.0	8.7
Farming, fishing, and forestry	100.0	38.4	34.5	18.0	9.1
Construction and extraction	100.0	20.7	45.0	26.2	8.1
Installation, maintenance, and repair	100.0	7.7	43.8	38.9	9.6
Production, transportation, and material moving	100.0	13.5	46.9	27.5	12.2
Production	100.0	12.3	48.9	29.3	9.5
Transportation and material moving	100.0	14.3	45.5	26.3	13.9
Armed forces	100.0	0.8	19.0	33.0	47.1
Women					
Management, business, and financial operations	100.0	4.9	21.3	27.4	46.4
Management	100.0	1.2	12.1	22.5	64.2
Business and financial operations	100.0	1.6	13.1	23.1	62.1
Professional and related	100.0	0.6	10.5	21.5	67.5
Computer and mathematical	100.0	0.6	6.4	19.1	73.9
Architecture and engineering	100.0	0.3	4.6	12.6	82.5
Life, physical, and social sciences	100.0	1.5	6.9	9.6	82.1
Community and social services	100.0	1.4	4.8	14.8	78.9
Legal	100.0	0.6	7.5	14.8	77.2
Education, training, and library	100.0	0.6	7.0	12.3	80.1
Arts, design, entertainment, sports, and media	100.0	0.6	8.5	21.8	69.0
Health care practitioner and technical	100.0	0.3	6.4	30.0	63.3
Services	100.0	13.2	36.5	32.3	18.0
Health care support	100.0	8.1	33.3	40.9	17.7
Protective services	100.0	2.4	18.5	38.7	40.5
Food preparation and serving related	100.0	14.3	43.2	27.8	14.7
Building and grounds cleaning and maintenance	100.0	30.1	42.8	17.3	9.8
Personal care and services	100.0	7.4	33.0	36.1	23.5
Sales and office	100.0	2.9	29.3	37.8	30.0
Sales and related	100.0	4.4	29.6	32.5	33.5
Office and administrative support	100.0	2.1	29.2	40.6	28.1
Natural resources, construction, and maintenance	100.0	25.6	32.9	23.7	17.8
Farming, fishing, and forestry	100.0	43.6	27.4	13.0	16.0
Construction and extraction	100.0	21.5	38.5	24.4	15.6
Installation, maintenance, and repair	100.0	4.4	30.9	39.5	25.1
Production, transportation, and material moving	100.0	16.1	41.5	28.1	14.3
Production	100.0	18.7	41.7	25.5	14.1
Transportation and material moving	100.0	13.5	41.2	30.8	14.5
Armed forces	100.0	. . .	5.8	37.0	57.2

. . . = Not available.

Table 1-61. Median Annual Earnings of Year-Round, Full-Time Wage and Salary Workers Age 25 to 64 Years, by Educational Attainment and Sex, 2006–2019

(Thousands of workers, dollars.)

Year and sex	Total	Less than a high school diploma	4 years of high school only	1 to 3 years of college	4 or more years of college
2006					
Both Sexes					
Number of workers	90 733	7 951	26 233	24 737	31 812
Median annual earnings	40 000	23 000	32 000	39 482	57 588
Men					
Number of workers	52 252	5 485	15 525	13 204	18 038
Median annual earnings	45 000	25 000	36 665	45 000	68 000
Women					
Number of workers	38 481	2 466	10 708	11 533	13 774
Median annual earnings	35 000	19 000	26 800	33 000	49 000
2007					
Both Sexes					
Number of workers	91 540	7 123	25 925	25 574	32 918
Median annual earnings	41 000	24 000	33 000	40 000	60 000
Men					
Number of workers	52 262	4 902	15 390	13 655	18 316
Median annual earnings	47 000	25 000	38 000	45 188	70 000
Women					
Number of workers	39 277	2 221	10 535	11 919	14 603
Median annual earnings	35 000	19 200	27 120	35 000	50 000
2008					
Both Sexes					
Number of workers	88 373	6 600	24 531	24 887	32 355
Median annual earnings	42 000	24 000	34 000	40 000	60 000
Men					
Number of workers	50 141	4 503	14 480	13 283	17 876
Median annual earnings	49 564	27 000	39 040	47 000	72 000
Women					
Number of workers	38 231	2 097	10 051	11 604	14 479
Median annual earnings	36 000	19 567	28 000	35 000	50 000
2009					
Both Sexes					
Number of workers	84 730	5 847	23 277	23 515	32 091
Median annual earnings	43 000	24 000	34 320	40 000	60 000
Men					
Number of workers	47 135	3 809	13 620	12 283	17 424
Median annual earnings	50 000	26 000	40 000	49 000	71 000
Women					
Number of workers	37 595	2 037	9 657	11 233	14 667
Median annual earnings	38 000	20 000	29 000	35 000	52 000
2010					
Both Sexes					
Number of workers	84 902	5 548	22 768	23 725	32 861
Median annual earnings	44 217	24 000	35 000	40 000	60 000
Men					
Number of workers	47 549	3 653	13 526	12 405	17 965
Median annual earnings	50 000	26 500	40 000	48 000	72 000
Women					
Number of workers	37 353	1 895	9 241	11 321	14 896
Median annual earnings	38 000	20 000	30 000	35 000	51 000
2011					
Both Sexes					
Number of workers	86 570	5 858	22 921	23 947	33 843
Median annual earnings	45 000	25 000	35 000	41 000	62 000
Men					
Number of workers	48 748	3 971	13 750	12 705	18 322
Median annual earnings	50 000	27 819	40 000	50 000	75 000
Women					
Number of workers	37 822	1 887	9 171	11 243	15 521
Median annual earnings	39 000	20 000	30 000	35 000	52 000
2012					
Both Sexes					
Number of workers	87 660	5 671	22 628	24 217	35 144
Median annual earnings	45 000	24 750	35 000	41 500	63 000
Men					
Number of workers	49 481	3 874	13 629	13 051	18 927
Median annual earnings	50 000	26 000	40 000	49 000	75 000
Women					
Number of workers	38 179	1 797	8 999	11 165	16 217
Median annual earnings	40 000	20 000	30 000	35 395	54 000

Table 1-61. Median Annual Earnings of Year-Round, Full-Time Wage and Salary Workers Age 25 to 64 Years, by Educational Attainment and Sex, 2006–2019—*Continued*

(Thousands of workers, dollars.)

Year and sex	Total	Less than a high school diploma	4 years of high school only	1 to 3 years of college	4 or more years of college
2013					
Both Sexes					
Number of workers	89 443	6 100	23 427	24 477	35 440
Median annual earnings	45 000	25 000	35 000	42 000	65 000
Men					
Number of workers	50 765	4 260	14 338	13 201	18 965
Median annual earnings	50 000	28 000	40 000	49 999	75 000
Women					
Number of workers	38 678	1 840	9 089	11 275	16 475
Median annual earnings	40 000	20 800	30 000	35 340	55 000
2014					
Both Sexes					
Number of workers	91 622	6 280	23 537	24 967	36 837
Median annual earnings	46 000	25 000	35 000	41 600	65 000
Men					
Number of workers	52 165	4 377	14 649	13 402	19 736
Median annual earnings	50 000	29 000	40 000	49 000	75 000
Women					
Number of workers	39 456	1 903	8 888	11 565	17 101
Median annual earnings	40 000	20 800	30 000	35 000	55 000
2015					
Both Sexes					
Number of workers	93 616	6 208	23 376	25 747	38 284
Median annual earnings	48 000	27 000	36 000	43 000	68 000
Men					
Number of workers	53 137	4 313	14 495	13 830	20 499
Median annual earnings	53 000	30 000	40 000	50 000	80 000
Women					
Number of workers	40 478	1 895	8 881	11 917	17 785
Median annual earnings	41 600	20 800	30 000	37 000	57 747
2016					
Both Sexes					
Number of workers	95 656	5 916	23 927	26 180	39 632
Median annual earnings	50 000	30 000	37 010	45 000	69 507
Men					
Number of workers	54 203	4 067	15 038	14 138	20 960
Median annual earnings	54 000	32 000	42 000	50 000	80 000
Women					
Number of workers	41 453	1 849	8 889	12 042	18 672
Median annual earnings	44 000	24 000	31 000	38 000	60 000
2017					
Both Sexes					
Number of workers	97 130	5 920	24 030	25 853	41 327
Median annual earnings	50 000	30 000	39 000	45 000	70 000
Men					
Number of workers	54 897	4 067	15 157	13 997	21 676
Median annual earnings	55 000	32 000	42 500	51 000	80 000
Women					
Number of workers	42 233	1 853	8 873	11 856	19 651
Median annual earnings	45 000	24 002	32 000	38 000	60 000
2018					
Both Sexes					
Number of workers	98 904	5 920	24 601	25 630	42 753
Median annual earnings	51 000	30 000	40 000	47 466	71 000
Men					
Number of workers	55 844	4 075	15 548	13 991	22 230
Median annual earnings	58 000	34 000	45 000	54 000	84 000
Women					
Number of workers	43 060	1 845	9 053	11 639	20 523
Median annual earnings	45 760	24 000	32 000	40 000	60 000
2019					
Both Sexes					
Number of workers	100 151	5 521	24 020	25 606	45 003
Median annual earnings	55 000	31 000	40 000	50 000	75 000
Men					
Number of workers	55 717	3 724	14 994	13 775	23 224
Median annual earnings	60 000	35 000	46 000	55 000	87 000
Women					
Number of workers	44 434	1 797	9 026	11 832	21 779
Median annual earnings	50 000	25 002	35 000	40 425	63 000

Table 1-62. Employment Status of the Civilian Noninstitutional Population by Disability Status and Selected Characteristics, 2019 Annual Averages

(Thousands of people, percent.)

Characteristic	Civilian noninstitutional population	Civilian labor force						Not in labor force
		Total	Participation rate	Employed		Unemployed		
				Total	Percent	Total	Rate	
TOTAL								
Total, 16 Years and Over	259 175	163 539	63.1	157 538	60.8	6 001	3.7	95 636
Men	125 353	86 687	69.2	83 460	66.6	3 227	3.7	38 667
Women	133 822	76 852	57.4	74 078	55.4	2 774	3.6	56 970
PERSONS WITH A DISABILITY	30 392	6 321	20.8	5 858	19.3	463	7.3	24 070
Sex								
Men	14 184	3 442	24.3	3 189	22.5	254	7.4	10 741
Women	16 208	2 879	17.8	2 669	16.5	210	7.3	13 329
Age								
16 to 64 years	15 231	5 117	33.6	4 706	30.9	411	8.0	10 113
16 to 19 years	667	157	23.5	123	18.4	34	21.7	510
20 to 24 years	909	412	45.4	365	40.2	47	11.4	497
25 to 34 years	1 992	973	48.8	866	43.5	107	11.0	1 019
35 to 44 years	2 168	899	41.5	836	38.5	63	7.0	1 269
45 to 54 years	3 393	1 154	34.0	1 069	31.5	86	7.4	2 238
55 to 64 years	6 103	1 522	24.9	1 448	23.7	74	4.9	4 580
65 years and over	15 161	1 204	7.9	1 152	7.6	52	4.3	13 957
Race and Hispanic Origin								
White	24 189	5 092	21.0	4 755	19.7	337	6.6	19 097
Black or African American	4 192	742	17.7	654	15.6	88	11.8	3 450
Asian	873	177	20.3	165	18.9	12	6.7	696
Hispanic[1]	3 481	781	22.4	714	20.5	67	8.6	2 699
Educational Attainment								
Total, 25 years and over	28 816	5 752	20.0	5 370	18.6	382	6.6	23 064
Less than a high school diploma	5 090	510	10.0	462	9.1	48	9.3	4 580
High school graduates, no college[2]	10 262	1 718	16.7	1 594	15.5	124	7.2	8 544
Some college or associate degree	7 900	1 879	23.8	1 743	22.1	135	7.2	6 022
Bachelor's degree and higher[3]	5 563	1 645	29.6	1 570	28.2	75	4.5	3 918

[1]May be of any race.
[2]Includes persons with a high school diploma or equivalent.
[3]Includes persons with bachelor's, master's, professional, and doctoral degrees.

Table 1-63. Employed Full- and Part-Time Workers by Disability Status and Age, 2019 Annual Averages

(Thousands of people.)

Disability status and age	Employed			At work part-time for economic reasons[1]
	Total	Usually work full-time	Usually work part-time	
TOTAL				
Total, 16 Years and Over	157 538	130 597	26 941	4 407
16 to 64 years	147 191	124 175	23 016	4 187
65 years and over	10 347	6 422	3 925	219
Persons With a Disability				
16 years and over	5 858	3 985	1 873	248
16 to 64 years	4 706	3 401	1 305	220
65 years and over	1 152	584	568	28
Persons Without a Disability				
16 years and over	151 680	126 612	25 068	4 159
16 to 64 years	142 485	120 774	21 711	3 967
65 years and over	9 195	5 838	3 357	191

Note: Full time refers to persons who usually work 35 hours or more per week; part time refers to persons who usually work less than 35 hours per week.

[1]Refers to persons who, whether they usually work full or part time, worked 1 to 34 hours during the reference week for an economic reason such as slack work or unfavorable business conditions, inability to find full-time work, or seasonal declines in demand.

Table 1-64. Employed Persons by Disability Status, Occupation, and Sex, 2019 Annual Averages

(Number in thousands, percent.)

Occupation	Persons with a disability			Persons with no disability		
	Total	Men	Women	Total	Men	Women
TOTAL EMPLOYED	5 858	3 189	2 669	151 680	80 272	71 409
Occupation as a Percent of Total Employed						
Total	100.0	100.0	100.0	100.0	100.0	100.0
Management, professional, and related	34.1	32.4	36.1	41.0	37.3	45.2
Management, business, and financial operations	15.6	17.6	13.2	17.2	18.1	16.2
Management	11.4	13.9	8.4	12.1	13.6	10.3
Business and financial operations	4.2	3.7	4.8	5.1	4.4	5.9
Professional and related	18.5	14.8	22.9	23.8	19.2	29.1
Computer and mathematical	2.2	3.0	1.2	3.4	4.8	1.9
Architecture and engineering	1.2	1.8	0.6	2.1	3.4	0.7
Life, physical, and social science	0.8	0.7	0.8	0.9	0.9	1.0
Community and social services	1.9	1.2	2.7	1.7	1.1	2.5
Legal	1.1	1.4	0.8	1.2	1.1	1.4
Education, training, and library	4.8	2.8	7.3	6.0	3.0	9.5
Arts, design, entertainment, sports, and media	2.1	2.0	2.3	2.1	2.0	2.2
Healthcare practitioner and technical	4.3	1.9	7.2	6.2	2.9	10.0
Service	20.7	16.5	25.8	17.0	13.6	20.8
Healthcare support	2.5	0.6	4.8	2.4	0.6	4.4
Protective service	2.2	3.1	1.1	2.0	2.9	0.9
Food preparation and serving related	5.7	4.8	6.8	5.3	4.6	6.1
Building and grounds cleaning and maintenance	5.6	6.0	5.1	3.6	3.9	3.2
Personal care and service	4.7	2.0	8.0	3.8	1.6	6.1
Sales and office	22.3	17.0	28.6	21.1	15.7	27.3
Sales and related	9.7	8.8	10.8	9.9	9.6	10.2
Office and administrative support	12.6	8.2	17.8	11.2	6.1	17.0
Natural resources, construction, and maintenance	8.4	14.5	1.0	9.1	16.3	1.0
Farming, fishing, and forestry	0.7	1.0	0.3	0.7	1.0	0.4
Construction and extraction	4.4	7.8	0.3	5.3	9.7	0.4
Installation, maintenance, and repair	3.3	5.7	0.4	3.1	5.6	0.3
Production, transportation, and material moving	14.5	19.5	8.5	11.7	17.1	5.7
Production	6.4	7.8	4.7	5.4	7.3	3.3
Transportation and material moving	8.1	11.8	3.8	6.3	9.8	2.4

Table 1-65. Persons Not in the Labor Force by Disability Status, Age, and Sex, 2019 Annual Averages

(Thousands of people, percent distribution.)

Category	Total, 16 years and over	16 to 64 years			Total, 65 years and over
		Total	Men	Women	
Persons With a Disability					
Total not in the labor force	24 070	10 113	4 788	5 325	13 957
Persons who currently want a job	650	430	219	212	220
Marginally attached to the labor force[1]	155	122	66	57	33
Discouraged workers[2]	33	22	12	10	11
Other persons marginally attached to the labor force[3]	122	100	53	47	21
Persons Without a Disability					
Total not in the labor force	71 566	43 282	16 007	27 274	28 284
Persons who currently want a job	4 393	3 815	1 818	1 997	578
Marginally attached to the labor force[1]	1 248	1 134	609	525	114
Discouraged workers[2]	348	315	206	109	34
Other persons marginally attached to the labor force[3]	900	820	404	416	80

[1]Data refer to persons who want a job, have searched for work during the prior 12 months, and were available to take a job during the reference week, but had not looked for work in the past 4 weeks.
[2]Includes those who did not actively look for work in the prior 4 weeks for reasons such as thinks no work available, could not find work, lacks schooling or training, employer thinks too young or old, and other types of discrimination.
[3]Includes those who did not actively look for work in the prior 4 weeks for such reasons as school or family responsibilities, ill health, and transportation problems, as well as a number for whom reason for nonparticipation was not determined.

Table 1-66. Employment Status of Persons 18 Years and Over by Veteran Status, Period of Service, Sex, Race, and Hispanic or Latino Ethnicity, 2019

(Thousands of people, percent.)

Characteristic	Civilian noninstitutional population	Civilian labor force						Not in labor force
		Total	Percent of population	Employed		Unemployed		
				Total	Percent of population	Total	Percent of labor force	
TOTAL								
Total, 18 Years and Over	250 377	161 458	64.5	155 749	62.2	5 709	3.5	88 919
Veterans	18 822	9 270	49.2	8 986	47.7	284	3.1	9 552
Gulf War era, total	7 399	5 808	78.5	5 624	76.0	183	3.2	1 591
Gulf War era II	4 328	3 468	80.1	3 345	77.3	123	3.5	860
Gulf War era I	3 070	2 339	76.2	2 279	74.2	60	2.6	731
WW II, Korean War, and Vietnam era	7 213	1 479	20.5	1 437	19.9	42	2.8	5 735
Other service periods	4 210	1 983	47.1	1 925	45.7	59	3.0	2 227
Nonveterans	231 555	152 188	65.7	146 763	63.4	5 425	3.6	79 367
MEN								
Total, 18 Years and Over	120 898	85 660	70.9	82 582	68.3	3 078	3.6	35 238
Veterans	16 938	8 169	48.2	7 926	46.8	243	3.0	8 769
Gulf War era, total	6 170	4 968	80.5	4 815	78.0	153	3.1	1 202
Gulf War era II	3 602	2 974	82.6	2 874	79.8	100	3.4	628
Gulf War era I	2 568	1 994	77.6	1 941	75.6	53	2.7	574
WW II, Korean War, and Vietnam era	6 964	1 425	20.5	1 386	19.9	39	2.7	5 539
Other service periods	3 803	1 776	46.7	1 726	45.4	51	2.8	2 027
Nonveterans	103 960	77 491	74.5	74 655	71.8	2 835	3.7	26 469
WOMEN								
Total, 18 Years and Over	129 479	75 798	58.5	73 167	56.5	2 631	3.5	53 681
Veterans	1 884	1 101	58.4	1 060	56.2	41	3.7	784
Gulf War era, total	1 228	840	68.4	810	65.9	30	3.6	389
Gulf War era II	726	495	68.1	471	64.9	23	4.7	232
Gulf War era I	502	345	68.7	338	67.4	7	2.0	157
WW II, Korean War, and Vietnam era	249	54	21.6	51	20.4	3	5.4	195
Other service periods	407	207	50.9	199	49.0	8	3.9	200
Nonveterans	127 595	74 697	58.5	72 107	56.5	2 590	3.5	52 898
WHITE								
Total, 18 Years and Over	194 408	124 956	64.3	121 012	62.2	3 944	3.2	69 453
Veterans	15 580	7 466	47.9	7 260	46.6	206	2.8	8 114
Gulf War era, total	5 710	4 533	79.4	4 406	77.2	127	2.8	1 177
Gulf War era II	3 313	2 692	81.3	2 612	78.8	81	3.0	621
Gulf War era I	2 397	1 841	76.8	1 794	74.9	46	2.5	557
WW II, Korean War, and Vietnam era	6 379	1 308	20.5	1 274	20.0	35	2.6	5 071
Other service periods	3 491	1 624	46.5	1 580	45.3	44	2.7	1 867
Nonveterans	178 828	117 490	65.7	113 752	63.6	3 738	3.2	61 338
BLACK								
Total, 18 Years and Over	31 764	20 431	64.3	19 232	60.5	1 199	5.9	11 333
Veterans	2 322	1 272	54.8	1 210	52.1	62	4.9	1 049
Gulf War era, total	1 173	882	75.2	837	71.3	45	5.1	291
Gulf War era II	677	512	75.7	477	70.5	35	6.8	165
Gulf War era I	495	369	74.6	359	72.5	10	2.8	126
WW II, Korean War, and Vietnam era	586	103	17.6	97	16.6	6	5.7	483
Other service periods	563	287	51.0	276	49.0	11	3.9	276
Nonveterans	29 442	19 159	65.1	18 022	61.2	1 137	5.9	10 283
ASIAN								
Total, 18 Years and Over	15 788	10 334	65.5	10 062	63.7	272	2.6	5 454
Veterans	333	193	57.8	186	55.8	7	3.6	140
Gulf War era, total	179	133	74.6	128	71.3	6	4.4	45
Gulf War era II	108	87	80.1	83	77.0	3	3.9	21
Gulf War era I	71	47	66.2	44	62.6	3	5.4	24
WW II, Korean War, and Vietnam era	110	40	36.2	40	36.0	0	0.6	70
Other service periods	44	19	43.8	19	42.1	1	. . .	25
Nonveterans	15 455	10 142	65.6	9 876	63.9	266	2.6	5 313
HISPANIC[1]								
Total, 18 Years and Over	41 326	28 600	69.2	27 425	66.4	1 176	4.1	12 726
Veterans	1 358	856	63.0	835	61.5	21	2.4	502
Gulf War era, total	812	655	80.6	636	78.3	19	2.9	158
Gulf War era II	540	440	81.4	426	78.8	14	3.2	100
Gulf War era I	272	215	79.0	210	77.3	5	2.2	57
WW II, Korean War, and Vietnam era	311	79	25.4	78	25.1	1	1.2	232
Other service periods	235	122	52.0	121	51.6	1	0.8	113
Nonveterans	39 968	27 744	69.4	26 589	66.5	1 155	4.2	12 224

Note: Veterans are men and women who served in the U.S. Armed Forces during World War II, the Korean War, the Vietnam era, the Gulf War era, and all other service periods. Nonveterans are men and women who never served in the U.S. Armed Forces. Other service periods include the periods between World War II and the Korean War, between the Korean War and the Vietnam era, and between the Vietnam era and the Gulf War era. Estimates for the above race groups (White, Black, and Asian) do not sum to totals because data are not presented for all races.

[1]May be of any race.
. . . = Not available.

Table 1-67. Employment Status of Persons 18 Years and Over by Veteran Status, Age, Period of Service, and Sex, 2019 Annual Averages

(Thousands of people, percent.)

Veteran status, age, period of service, and sex	Civilian noninstitutional population	Civilian labor force		Employed		Unemployed		Not in labor force
		Total	Percent of population	Total	Percent of population	Total	Percent of labor force	
TOTAL VETERANS								
Total, 18 years and over	18 822	9 270	49.2	8 986	47.7	284	3.1	9 552
18 to 24 years	261	193	73.9	179	68.4	14	7.4	68
25 to 34 years	1 585	1 302	82.2	1 260	79.5	43	3.3	283
35 to 44 years	2 013	1 699	84.4	1 641	81.6	57	3.4	314
45 to 54 years	2 622	2 199	83.9	2 140	81.6	59	2.7	422
55 to 64 years	3 519	2 234	63.5	2 169	61.6	65	2.9	1 285
65 years and over	8 823	1 642	18.6	1 597	18.1	45	2.8	7 181
Gulf War Era, Total								
Total, 18 years and over	7 399	5 808	78.5	5 624	76.0	183	3.2	1 591
18 to 24 years	261	193	73.9	179	68.4	14	7.4	68
25 to 34 years	1 585	1 302	82.2	1 260	79.5	43	3.3	283
35 to 44 years	2 013	1 699	84.4	1 641	81.6	57	3.4	314
45 to 54 years	2 092	1 763	84.3	1 717	82.1	46	2.6	329
55 to 64 years	1 058	749	70.8	728	68.9	21	2.8	309
65 years and over	391	102	26.1	100	25.5	2	2.1	289
Gulf War Era II								
Total, 18 years and over	4 328	3 468	80.1	3 345	77.3	123	3.5	860
18 to 24 years	261	193	73.9	179	68.4	14	7.4	68
25 to 34 years	1 585	1 302	82.2	1 260	79.5	43	3.3	283
35 to 44 years	1 349	1 125	83.4	1 082	80.2	43	3.8	224
45 to 54 years	660	538	81.5	523	79.2	15	2.8	122
55 to 64 years	378	282	74.6	274	72.7	7	2.5	96
65 years and over	96	29	30.3	28	29.6	1	. . .	67
Gulf War Era I								
Total, 25 years and over	3 070	2 339	76.2	2 279	74.2	60	2.6	731
35 to 44 years	664	574	86.5	560	84.3	14	2.5	90
45 to 54 years	1 432	1 225	85.5	1 194	83.4	31	2.5	207
55 to 64 years	680	467	68.7	454	66.7	14	2.9	213
65 years and over	295	73	24.7	71	24.2	2	2.2	222
World War II, Korean War, Vietnam War								
Total, 55 years and over	7 213	1 479	20.5	1 437	19.9	42	2.8	5 735
55 to 64 years	431	185	42.9	180	41.8	5	2.6	246
65 years and over	6 782	1 294	19.1	1 257	18.5	37	2.9	5 488
Other Service Periods								
Total, 45 years and over	4 210	1 983	47.1	1 925	45.7	59	3.0	2 227
45 to 54 years	530	437	82.5	424	80.0	13	3.0	93
55 to 64 years	2 031	1 300	64.0	1 261	62.1	39	3.0	730
65 years and over	1 650	246	14.9	240	14.6	6	2.5	1 404
TOTAL NONVETERANS								
Total, 18 years and over	231 555	152 188	65.7	146 763	63.4	5 425	3.6	79 367
18 to 24 years	28 689	18 818	65.6	17 354	60.5	1 464	7.8	9 870
25 to 34 years	43 292	35 889	82.9	34 548	79.8	1 341	3.7	7 403
35 to 44 years	38 947	32 358	83.1	31 486	80.8	873	2.7	6 589
45 to 54 years	37 823	30 732	81.3	29 901	79.1	831	2.7	7 091
55 to 64 years	38 725	25 372	65.5	24 724	63.8	648	2.6	13 353
65 years and over	44 079	9 018	20.5	8 750	19.9	268	3.0	35 061

Note: Veterans are men and women who served in the U.S. Armed Forces during World War II, the Korean War, the Vietnam era, the Gulf War era, and all other service periods. Nonveterans are men and women who never served in the U.S. Armed Forces. Other service periods include the periods between World War II and the Korean War, between the Korean War and the Vietnam era, and between the Vietnam era and the Gulf War era.

. . . = Not available.

Table 1-67. Employment Status of Persons 18 Years and Over by Veteran Status, Age, Period of Service, and Sex, 2019 Annual Averages—*Continued*

(Thousands of people, percent.)

Veteran status, age, period of service, and sex	Civilian noninstitutional population	Civilian labor force						Not in labor force
		Total	Percent of population	Employed		Unemployed		
				Total	Percent of population	Total	Percent of labor force	
VETERANS, MEN								
Total, 18 years and over	16 938	8 169	48.2	7 926	46.8	243	3.0	8 769
18 to 24 years	203	161	79.3	150	73.7	11	7.1	42
25 to 34 years	1 281	1 098	85.7	1 064	83.1	34	3.1	183
35 to 44 years	1 636	1 418	86.7	1 372	83.9	47	3.3	217
45 to 54 years	2 253	1 925	85.5	1 873	83.1	52	2.7	328
55 to 64 years	3 088	1 987	64.3	1 930	62.5	57	2.9	1 102
65 years and over	8 477	1 580	18.6	1 538	18.1	42	2.7	6 897
Gulf War Era, Total								
Total, 18 years and over	6 170	4 968	80.5	4 815	78.0	153	3.1	1 202
18 to 24 years	203	161	79.3	150	73.7	11	7.1	42
25 to 34 years	1 281	1 098	85.7	1 064	83.1	34	3.1	183
35 to 44 years	1 636	1 418	86.7	1 372	83.9	47	3.3	217
45 to 54 years	1 798	1 541	85.7	1 501	83.5	41	2.6	257
55 to 64 years	902	656	72.6	637	70.5	19	2.9	247
65 years and over	350	94	26.9	92	26.3	2	2.3	256
Gulf War Era II								
Total, 18 years and over	3 602	2 974	82.6	2 874	79.8	100	3.4	628
18 to 24 years	203	161	79.3	150	73.7	11	7.1	42
25 to 34 years	1 281	1 098	85.7	1 064	83.1	34	3.1	183
35 to 44 years	1 108	950	85.7	916	82.6	34	3.6	158
45 to 54 years	584	482	82.5	468	80.0	14	3.0	102
55 to 64 years	340	257	75.6	251	74.0	5	2.1	83
65 years and over	85	26	29.9	25	29.2	1	. . .	60
Gulf War Era I								
Total, 25 years and over	2 568	1 994	77.6	1 941	75.6	53	2.7	574
35 to 44 years	527	468	88.8	456	86.4	12	2.6	59
45 to 54 years	1 214	1 059	87.2	1 033	85.1	26	2.5	155
55 to 64 years	563	399	70.9	385	68.5	14	3.4	164
65 years and over	265	69	25.9	67	25.3	2	2.3	196
World War II, Korean War, and Vietnam War								
Total, 55 years and over	6 964	1 425	20.5	1 386	19.9	39	2.7	5 539
55 to 64 years	397	169	42.5	165	41.7	3	2.0	228
65 years and over	6 568	1 256	19.1	1 221	18.6	35	2.8	5 311
Other Service Periods								
Total, 45 years and over	3 803	1 776	46.7	1 726	45.4	51	2.8	2 027
45 to 54 years	455	384	84.4	373	81.9	11	3.0	71
55 to 64 years	1 789	1 163	65.0	1 128	63.0	35	3.0	627
65 years and over	1 559	229	14.7	225	14.4	4	1.9	1 330
NONVETERANS, MEN								
Total, 18 years and over	103 960	77 491	74.5	74 655	71.8	2 835	3.7	26 469
18 to 24 years	14 317	9 552	66.7	8 702	60.8	850	8.9	4 765
25 to 34 years	21 105	18 850	89.3	18 143	86.0	707	3.8	2 255
35 to 44 years	18 508	16 878	91.2	16 450	88.9	428	2.5	1 630
45 to 54 years	17 521	15 362	87.7	14 943	85.3	419	2.7	2 159
55 to 64 years	17 249	12 563	72.8	12 257	71.1	306	2.4	4 686
65 years and over	15 260	4 286	28.1	4 161	27.3	125	2.9	10 974

Note: Veterans are men and women who served in the U.S. Armed Forces during World War II, the Korean War, the Vietnam era, the Gulf War era, and all other service periods. Nonveterans are men and women who never served in the U.S. Armed Forces. Other service periods include the periods between World War II and the Korean War, between the Korean War and the Vietnam era, and between the Vietnam era and the Gulf War era.

. . . = Not available.

Table 1-67.   Employment Status of Persons 18 Years and Over by Veteran Status, Age, Period of Service, and Sex, 2019 Annual Averages—*Continued*

(Thousands of people, percent.)

Veteran status, age, period of service, and sex	Civilian noninstitutional population	Civilian labor force						Not in labor force
		Total	Percent of population	Employed		Unemployed		
				Total	Percent of population	Total	Percent of labor force	
VETERANS, WOMEN								
Total, 18 years and over	1 884	1 101	58.4	1 060	56.2	41	3.7	784
18 to 24 years	58	32	55.0	29	50.0	3	. . .	26
25 to 34 years	303	204	67.3	195	64.3	9	4.4	99
35 to 44 years	377	281	74.4	270	71.5	11	3.9	97
45 to 54 years	369	274	74.4	267	72.5	7	2.6	94
55 to 64 years	431	247	57.4	239	55.5	8	3.2	184
65 years and over	346	63	18.1	59	17.1	3	5.3	284
Gulf War Era, Total								
Total, 18 years and over	1 228	840	68.4	810	65.9	30	3.6	389
18 to 24 years	58	32	55.0	29	50.0	3	. . .	26
25 to 34 years	303	204	67.3	195	64.3	9	4.4	99
35 to 44 years	377	281	74.4	270	71.5	11	3.9	97
45 to 54 years	294	222	75.4	216	73.5	5	2.4	72
55 to 64 years	155	93	60.2	92	59.0	2	2.0	62
65 years and over	41	8	. . .	8	. . .	0	. . .	33
Gulf War Era II								
Total, 18 years and over	726	495	68.1	471	64.9	23	4.7	232
18 to 24 years	58	32	55.0	29	50.0	3	. . .	26
25 to 34 years	303	204	67.3	195	64.3	9	4.4	99
35 to 44 years	240	174	72.5	165	68.9	9	5.0	66
45 to 54 years	76	56	73.5	55	72.4	1	1.4	20
55 to 64 years	38	25	65.6	23	60.9	2	. . .	13
65 years and over	11	4	. . .	4	. . .	0	. . .	7
Gulf War Era I								
Total, 25 Years and over	502	345	68.7	338	67.4	7	2.0	157
35 to 44 years	137	106	77.7	104	76.1	2	2.0	31
45 to 54 years	218	166	76.1	161	73.9	5	2.8	52
55 to 64 years	117	69	58.5	69	58.4	0	0.2	49
65 years and over	30	4	. . .	4	. . .	0	. . .	26
World War II, Korean War, and Vietnam Era								
Total, 55 years and over	249	54	21.6	51	20.4	3	5.4	195
55 to 64 years	34	16	. . .	14	. . .	1	. . .	18
65 years and over	215	38	17.6	36	16.9	1	3.9	177
Other Service Periods								
Total, 45 years and over	407	207	50.9	199	49.0	8	3.9	200
45 to 54 years	75	53	70.5	51	68.3	2	3.1	22
55 to 64 years	241	138	57.0	133	55.1	5	3.3	104
65 years and over	91	17	18.7	15	16.7	2	. . .	74
NONVETERANS, WOMEN								
Total, 18 years and over	127 595	74 697	58.5	72 107	56.5	2 590	3.5	52 898
18 to 24 years	14 372	9 267	64.5	8 652	60.2	614	6.6	5 105
25 to 34 years	22 187	17 039	76.8	16 405	73.9	634	3.7	5 148
35 to 44 years	20 439	15 480	75.7	15 036	73.6	445	2.9	4 959
45 to 54 years	20 302	15 370	75.7	14 958	73.7	412	2.7	4 932
55 to 64 years	21 476	12 809	59.6	12 467	58.1	342	2.7	8 667
65 years and over	28 819	4 732	16.4	4 589	15.9	143	3.0	24 087

Note: Veterans are men and women who served in the U.S. Armed Forces during World War II, the Korean War, the Vietnam era, the Gulf War era, and all other service periods. Nonveterans are men and women who never served in the U.S. Armed Forces. Other service periods include the periods between World War II and the Korean War, between the Korean War and the Vietnam era, and between the Vietnam era and the Gulf War era.

. . . = Not available.

Table 1-68. Employment Status of Gulf War Era Veterans by Reserve or National Guard Status, August 2019, Not Seasonally Adjusted

(Thousands of people, percent.)

Reserve or National Guard status	Civilian noninstitutional population	Civilian labor force							Not in labor force
		Total	Percent of population	Employed		Unemployed			
				Total	Percent of population	Total	Percent of labor force		
GULF WAR ERA									
Total	7 419	5 832	78.6	5 596	75.4	236	4.1		1 587
Current or past member of Reserve or National Guard	2 476	2 029	81.9	1 934	78.1	95	4.7		447
Never a member of Reserve or National Guard	4 731	3 623	76.6	3 481	73.6	141	3.9		1 108
Reserve or National Guard membership not reported	212	181	85.2	181	85.2	0	0.0		32
GULF WAR ERA II									
Total	4 411	3 520	79.8	3 356	76.1	164	4.7		891
Current or past member of Reserve or National Guard	1 451	1 232	84.9	1 162	80.0	71	5.7		219
Never a member of Reserve or National Guard	2 821	2 172	77.0	2 079	73.7	93	4.3		649
Reserve or National Guard membership not reported	138	115	83.3	115	83.3	0	0.0		23
GULF WAR ERA I									
Total	3 008	2 313	76.9	2 240	74.5	72	3.1		695
Current or past member of Reserve or National Guard	1 024	796	77.8	772	75.4	24	3.1		228
Never a member of Reserve or National Guard	1 910	1 451	76.0	1 403	73.4	48	3.3		459
Reserve or National Guard membership not reported	74	66	-	66	-	0	-		8

Note: Veterans are men and women who served in the U.S. Armed Forces during World War II, the Korean War, the Vietnam era, the Gulf War era, and all other service periods. The Gulf War era began in August 1990 and continues to the present day. It is divided into two periods of service: Gulf War era II (September 2001–present) and Gulf War era I (August 1990– August 2001).

Table 1-69. Employed Persons 18 Years and Over by Occupation, Sex, Veteran Status, and Period of Service, 2019 Annual Averages

(Number in thousands, percent distribution.)

Occupation	Total veterans	Gulf War era			WWII, Korean War, and Vietnam War	Other services periods	Non-veteran
		Total	Gulf War era II	Gulf War era I			
TOTAL							
Total, 18 Years and Over	8 986	5 624	3 345	2 279	1 437	1 925	146 763
Percent	100.0	100.0	100.0	100.0	100.0	100.0	100.0
Management, professional, and related occupations	40.4	40.5	38.1	43.9	43.7	37.7	41.2
Management, business, and financial operations occupations	19.5	18.4	17.5	19.7	25.3	18.4	17.2
Professional and related occupations	20.9	22.1	20.6	24.3	18.5	19.2	24.0
Service occupations	13.9	14.7	16.5	12.1	12.0	12.8	16.9
Sales and office occupations	15.6	15.6	16.0	15.0	16.4	15.2	21.4
Sales and related occupations	7.8	7.1	6.9	7.5	10.5	7.9	9.8
Office and administrative support occupations	7.8	8.4	9.1	7.5	5.9	7.3	11.5
Natural resources, construction, and maintenance occupations	13.1	13.3	13.4	13.2	11.0	13.8	8.9
Farming, fishing, and forestry occupations	0.5	0.5	0.5	0.4	0.7	0.5	0.7
Construction and extraction occupations	5.9	5.5	5.4	5.6	6.0	7.3	5.3
Installation, maintenance, and repair occupations	6.6	7.4	7.5	7.1	4.3	6.0	2.9
Production, transportation, and material moving occupations	17.1	15.9	16.0	15.9	16.9	20.5	11.6
Production occupations	6.7	6.9	6.9	6.8	4.1	8.3	5.4
Transportation and material moving occupations	10.3	9.0	9.0	9.1	12.8	12.2	6.2
MEN							
Total, 18 Years and Over	7 926	4 815	2 874	1 941	1 386	1 726	74 655
Percent	100.0	100.0	100.0	100.0	100.0	100.0	100.0
Management, professional, and related occupations	38.9	38.5	36.1	42.1	43.3	36.5	37.3
Management, business, and financial operations occupations	19.6	18.3	17.5	19.5	25.4	18.4	18.1
Professional and related occupations	19.3	20.2	18.6	22.6	17.9	18.1	19.2
Service occupations	13.7	14.6	16.6	11.7	11.6	12.7	13.3
Sales and office occupations	14.3	14.1	14.6	13.3	16.5	13.3	15.8
Sales and related occupations	7.8	7.1	6.9	7.3	10.8	7.5	9.6
Office and administrative support occupations	6.5	7.0	7.7	6.1	5.6	5.9	6.1
Natural resources, construction, and maintenance occupations	14.6	15.2	15.3	15.2	11.4	15.3	16.5
Farming, fishing, and forestry occupations	0.5	0.5	0.5	0.5	0.7	0.5	1.1
Construction and extraction occupations	6.7	6.3	6.2	6.5	6.2	8.0	10.0
Installation, maintenance, and repair occupations	7.4	8.4	8.6	8.2	4.5	6.7	5.5
Production, transportation, and material moving occupations	18.5	17.6	17.4	17.8	17.2	22.1	17.1
Production occupations	7.3	7.6	7.7	7.5	4.1	8.8	7.4
Transportation and material moving occupations	11.2	9.9	9.7	10.3	13.0	13.3	9.7
WOMEN							
Total, 18 Years and Over	1 060	810	471	338	51	199	72 107
Percent	100.0	100.0	100.0	100.0	100.0	100.0	100.0
Management, professional, and related occupations	51.2	52.0	50.1	54.7	54.3	47.5	45.3
Management, business, and financial operations occupations	18.9	18.9	17.5	20.9	21.4	18.4	16.2
Professional and related occupations	32.3	33.1	32.6	33.8	33.0	29.0	29.1
Service occupations	15.4	15.6	16.4	14.4	20.9	13.4	20.7
Sales and office occupations	25.3	24.4	24.4	24.3	14.7	31.5	27.2
Sales and related occupations	8.1	7.6	6.9	8.7	1.9	11.4	10.1
Office and administrative support occupations	17.2	16.8	17.6	15.7	12.7	20.1	17.1
Natural resources, construction, and maintenance occupations	1.7	1.9	2.0	1.8	1.1	1.3	1.0
Farming, fishing, and forestry occupations	0.2	0.2	0.2	0.0	0.7	0.2	0.4
Construction and extraction occupations	0.7	0.6	0.5	0.7	0.5	1.2	0.4
Installation, maintenance, and repair occupations	0.9	1.2	1.3	1.0	0.0	0.0	0.3
Production, transportation, and material moving occupations	6.3	6.2	7.1	4.8	8.9	6.3	5.8
Production occupations	2.7	2.4	2.3	2.7	2.7	3.7	3.3
Transportation and material moving occupations	3.7	3.7	4.9	2.2	6.2	2.7	2.5

Note: Veterans are men and women who served in the U.S. Armed Forces during World War II, the Korean War, the Vietnam era, the Gulf War era, and all other service periods. Nonveterans are men and women who never served in the U.S. Armed Forces. Other service periods include the periods between World War II and the Korean War, between the Korean War and the Vietnam era, and between the Vietnam era and the Gulf War era.

Table 1-70. Employed Persons 18 Years and Over by Industry, Class of Worker, Sex, Veteran Status, and Period of Service, 2019 Annual Averages

(Number in thousands, percent distribution.)

Industry and class of worker	Total veterans	Gulf War era			WWII, Korean War, and Vietnam War	Other services periods	Non-veteran
		Total	Gulf War era II	Gulf War era I			
TOTAL							
Total, 18 Years and Over	8 986	5 624	3 345	2 279	1 437	1 925	146 763
Percent	100.0	100.0	100.0	100.0	100.0	100.0	100.0
Agriculture and related industries	1.8	0.9	0.9	0.8	5.3	1.6	1.5
Wage and salary workers	0.9	0.7	0.8	0.5	1.9	0.8	1.0
Self-employed workers	0.9	0.2	0.1	0.3	3.4	0.9	0.4
Nonagricultural industries	98.2	99.1	99.1	99.2	94.7	98.4	98.5
Wage and salary workers	92.6	95.8	96.0	95.4	82.7	90.8	92.9
Private industries	71.1	70.9	70.6	71.3	69.9	72.8	79.8
Mining	0.7	0.8	0.6	0.9	0.5	0.6	0.5
Construction	6.6	6.3	6.5	6.1	6.4	7.4	5.9
Manufacturing	12.0	12.3	12.3	12.3	8.9	13.5	9.7
Wholesale trade	2.4	2.5	2.3	2.7	2.3	2.1	2.2
Retail trade	7.9	7.2	7.2	7.5	10.4	8.2	9.8
Transportation and utilities	7.5	7.4	7.4	7.3	6.7	8.5	4.4
Information	1.6	1.8	1.5	2.3	1.6	1.0	1.6
Financial activities	4.9	4.6	4.3	5.0	6.2	5.0	6.4
Professional and business services	11.8	12.5	12.7	12.2	11.6	9.9	10.9
Education and health services	8.5	8.7	8.4	9.0	6.6	9.3	15.9
Leisure and hospitality	4.1	4.1	4.9	3.1	4.6	3.8	8.3
Other services	3.1	2.8	2.8	2.8	4.0	3.4	4.2
Government	21.5	24.9	25.4	24.1	12.9	18.1	13.0
Federal	10.8	13.7	14.8	12.1	3.4	7.6	2.0
State	4.4	4.7	4.5	5.1	3.4	4.1	4.4
Local	6.3	6.4	6.1	6.9	6.1	6.3	6.6
Self-employed workers	5.6	3.3	3.0	3.8	11.8	7.5	5.6
MEN							
Total, 18 Years and Over	7 926	4 815	2 874	1 941	1 386	1 726	74 655
Percent	100.0	100.0	100.0	100.0	100.0	100.0	100.0
Agriculture and related industries	1.9	0.9	1.0	0.8	5.5	1.8	2.1
Wage and salary workers	1.0	0.7	0.9	0.6	2.0	0.8	1.5
Self-employed workers	0.9	0.2	0.2	0.3	3.5	1.0	0.6
Nonagricultural industries	98.1	99.1	99.0	99.2	94.5	98.2	97.9
Wage and salary workers	92.3	95.6	95.9	95.3	82.5	90.8	91.5
Private industries	72.0	71.9	71.4	72.6	70.1	73.7	81.6
Mining	0.8	0.9	0.7	1.1	0.5	0.6	0.7
Construction	7.2	7.1	7.2	6.8	6.6	8.1	10.2
Manufacturing	12.9	13.5	13.4	13.5	9.0	14.4	13.1
Wholesale trade	2.5	2.7	2.5	3.1	2.4	2.2	3.0
Retail trade	7.9	7.0	6.9	7.3	10.5	8.2	9.8
Transportation and utilities	8.2	8.2	8.2	8.3	6.9	9.3	6.4
Information	1.7	1.9	1.6	2.4	1.6	1.0	1.8
Financial activities	4.6	4.1	4.1	4.2	6.2	4.8	5.7
Professional and business services	12.1	12.9	13.2	12.2	11.7	10.1	12.2
Education and health services	6.8	6.7	6.1	7.6	6.1	7.8	7.0
Leisure and hospitality	4.1	4.0	4.7	3.0	4.6	3.8	7.8
Other services	3.2	2.8	2.8	2.7	4.1	3.4	3.7
Government	20.3	23.8	24.5	22.7	12.3	17.1	9.9
Federal	10.1	13.2	14.3	11.7	3.3	7.0	1.8
State	4.1	4.4	4.4	4.3	3.2	4.0	3.2
Local	6.1	6.1	5.8	6.6	5.8	6.1	4.8
Self-employed workers	5.8	3.4	3.1	3.9	11.9	7.5	6.4
WOMEN							
Total, 18 Years and Over	1 060	810	471	338	51	199	72 107
Percent	100.0	100.0	100.0	100.0	100.0	100.0	100.0
Agriculture and related industries	0.5	0.5	0.5	0.6	0.7	0.5	0.9
Wage and salary workers	0.3	0.4	0.5	0.2	0.0	0.3	0.6
Self-employed workers	0.2	0.2	0.0	0.4	0.7	0.2	0.3
Nonagricultural industries	99.5	99.5	99.5	99.4	99.3	99.5	99.1
Wage and salary workers	95.3	96.6	97.0	96.0	89.4	91.6	94.3
Private industries	64.9	65.1	66.1	63.8	62.4	64.8	78.0
Mining	0.1	0.1	0.2	0.0	0.0	0.0	0.2
Construction	1.8	2.0	2.0	2.0	0.0	1.7	1.4
Manufacturing	5.6	5.3	5.3	5.4	7.1	6.3	6.1
Wholesale trade	1.0	1.2	1.4	0.8	0.0	0.7	1.3
Retail trade	8.0	8.1	7.4	9.1	7.0	7.7	9.9
Transportation and utilities	2.1	2.2	2.6	1.5	1.8	2.1	2.3
Information	1.3	1.4	1.2	1.6	2.4	0.7	1.3
Financial activities	7.0	7.1	5.2	9.7	4.0	7.2	7.1
Professional and business services	9.5	9.8	9.9	9.6	9.0	8.3	9.6
Education and health services	21.1	20.6	22.9	17.3	22.6	22.9	25.1
Leisure and hospitality	4.7	4.8	5.7	3.5	5.6	4.3	8.9
Other services	2.7	2.7	2.3	3.2	3.0	2.9	4.7
Government	30.4	31.4	30.9	32.2	27.0	26.8	16.3
Federal	15.4	16.7	18.2	14.6	6.1	12.6	2.1
State	6.6	6.8	4.8	9.5	7.2	5.6	5.7
Local	8.3	7.9	7.9	8.0	13.7	8.6	8.4
Self-employed workers	4.2	2.9	2.5	3.4	10.0	7.9	4.8

Note: Veterans are men and women who served in the U.S. Armed Forces during World War II, the Korean War, the Vietnam era, the Gulf War era, and all other service periods. Nonveterans are men and women who never served in the U.S. Armed Forces. Other service periods include the periods between World War II and the Korean War, between the Korean War and the Vietnam era, and between the Vietnam era and the Gulf War era.

Table 1-71. Employed Persons 18 Years and Over by Veteran Status, Presence of Service-Connected Disability, Period of Service, and Class of Worker, August 2019, Not Seasonally Adjusted

(Numbers in thousands, percent distribution.)

Veteran status, presence of disability, and period of service	Total employed (number)	Total employed (percent)	Agriculture and related industries	Nonagricultural industries					Self-employed, unincorporated, and unpaid family workers
				Wage and salary workers					
				Total	Private sector	Government			
						Total	Federal	State and local	
Veterans, Total[1]	8 664	100.0	1.6	98.4	71.1	21.1	11.2	9.8	6.3
With service-connected disability	2 144	100.0	1.2	98.8	63.5	30.8	20.4	10.4	4.5
Without service-connected disability	6 260	100.0	1.7	98.3	74.1	17.2	7.7	9.5	7.0
Gulf War Era, Total[1]	5 596	100.0	0.9	99.1	70.6	24.3	15.0	9.4	4.2
With service-connected disability	1 698	100.0	1.1	98.9	62.8	32.8	22.8	9.9	3.4
Without service-connected disability	3 688	100.0	0.8	99.2	74.9	19.8	10.8	9.0	4.6
Gulf War Era II[1]	3 356	100.0	0.8	99.2	71.9	23.3	14.2	9.1	4.0
With service-connected disability	1 230	100.0	1.1	98.9	65.7	29.4	21.5	7.9	3.7
Without service-connected disability	1 998	100.0	0.6	99.4	77.0	18.4	8.6	9.8	4.0
Gulf War Era I[1]	2 240	100.0	1.0	99.0	68.7	25.8	16.1	9.7	4.4
With service-connected disability	468	100.0	1.0	99.0	55.0	41.7	26.4	15.3	2.4
Without service-connected disability	1 690	100.0	0.9	99.1	72.5	21.4	13.4	8.0	5.2
WW II, Korean War, and Vietnam Era[1]	1 225	100.0	4.3	95.7	70.8	12.0	2.0	10.0	12.9
With service-connected disability	213	100.0	1.8	98.2	74.1	12.9	2.7	10.2	11.3
Without service-connected disability	1 006	100.0	4.8	95.2	69.9	11.9	1.9	10.0	13.3
Other Service Periods[1]	1 843	100.0	1.9	98.1	72.7	17.2	6.0	11.2	8.2
With service-connected disability	232	100.0	1.3	98.7	59.4	32.7	18.6	14.1	6.7
Without service-connected disability	1 566	100.0	2.0	98.0	74.8	14.5	4.0	10.5	8.7
Nonveterans	146 901	100.0	1.5	98.5	80.1	12.7	2.0	10.7	5.6

Note: Veterans are men and women who served in the U.S. Armed Forces during World War II, the Korean War, the Vietnam era, the Gulf War era, and all other service periods. Nonveterans are men and women who never served in the U.S. Armed Forces. Other service periods include the periods between World War II and the Korean War, between the Korean War and the Vietnam era, and between the Vietnam era and the Gulf War era.

[1]Includes veterans who did not report presence of disability.

Table 1-72. Long-Tenured Displaced Workers[1] by Age, Sex, Race, and Hispanic Origin, January 2020

(Numbers in thousands, percent.)

Characteristic	Total	Percent distribution by employment status			
		Total	Employed	Unemployed	Not in the labor force
TOTAL					
Total, 20 years and over	2 672	100.0	70.1	12.4	17.5
20 to 24 years	63	100.0	(2)	(2)	(2)
25 to 54 years	1 676	100.0	75.1	13.9	11.0
55 to 64 years	702	100.0	66.5	10.7	22.8
65 years and over	232	100.0	44.1	7.4	48.5
Men					
Total, 20 years and over	1 466	100.0	71.9	12.3	15.7
20 to 24 years	20	100.0	(2)	(2)	(2)
25 to 54 years	947	100.0	74.5	14.6	10.9
55 to 64 years	382	100.0	71.7	8.3	20.0
65 years and over	117	100.0	52.6	9.3	38.2
Women					
Total, 20 years and over	1 206	100.0	67.8	12.5	19.7
20 to 24 years	42	100.0	(2)	(2)	(2)
25 to 54 years	729	100.0	75.9	12.9	11.2
55 to 64 years	321	100.0	60.3	13.4	26.3
65 years and over	115	100.0	35.4	5.6	59.1
White					
Total, 20 years and over	2 162	100.0	70.9	10.5	18.6
Men	1 211	100.0	73.5	11.0	15.5
Women	951	100.0	67.7	9.7	22.6
Black					
Total, 20 years and over	335	100.0	61.8	22.2	16.0
Men	152	100.0	58.5	21.8	19.7
Women	183	100.0	64.6	22.6	12.9
Asian					
Total, 20 years and over	110	100.0	73.5	25.6	0.9
Men	62	100.0	-	-	-
Women	48	100.0	(2)	(2)	(2)
Hispanic[3]					
Total, 20 years and over	461	100.0	67.6	8.5	23.9
Men	262	100.0	72.6	7.0	20.5
Women	199	100.0	61.2	10.5	28.3

[1]Data refer to persons who had three or more years of tenure on a job that they had lost between January 2017 and December 209 because of plant or company closings or moves, insufficient work, or the abolishment of their positions or skills.
[2]Data not shown where the base is less than 75,000.
[3]Persons of Hispanic origin may be of any race.

Table 1-73. Long-Tenured Displaced Workers[1] by Age, Sex, Race, and Hispanic Origin and Reason for Job Loss, January 2020

(Numbers in thousands, percent.)

Characteristic	Total	Percent distribution by reasons for job loss			
		Total	Plant or company closed down or moving	Insufficient work	Position or shift abolished
TOTAL					
Total, 20 years and over	2 672	100.0	40.6	23.2	36.2
20 to 24 years	63	100.0	([2])	([2])	([2])
25 to 54 years	1 676	100.0	42.6	23.2	34.2
55 to 64 years	702	100.0	33.2	24.7	42.1
65 years and over	232	100.0	43.8	19.5	36.7
Men					
Total, 20 years and over	1 466	100.0	40.2	25.7	34.2
20 to 24 years	20	100.0	([2])	([2])	([2])
25 to 54 years	947	100.0	40.0	27.5	32.5
55 to 64 years	382	100.0	36.6	22.1	41.3
65 years and over	117	100.0	48.8	21.2	30.0
Women					
Total, 20 years and over	1 206	100.0	41.0	20.3	38.7
20 to 24 years	42	100.0	([2])	([2])	([2])
25 to 54 years	729	100.0	46.0	17.7	36.3
55 to 64 years	321	100.0	29.1	27.7	43.1
65 years and over	115	100.0	38.7	17.7	43.6
White					
Total, 20 years and over	2 162	100.0	40.7	23.0	36.3
Men	1 211	100.0	40.8	25.1	34.1
Women	951	100.0	40.6	20.3	39.1
Black					
Total, 20 years and over	335	100.0	47.3	21.4	31.3
Men	152	100.0	46.1	26.0	27.9
Women	183	100.0	48.3	17.6	34.1
Asian					
Total, 20 years and over	110	100.0	13.8	24.4	61.8
Men	62	100.0	([2])	([2])	([2])
Women	48	100.0	([2])	([2])	([2])
Hispanic[3]					
Total, 20 years and over	461	100.0	50.6	27.5	22.0
Men	262	100.0	50.2	29.6	20.2
Women	199	100.0	51.0	24.7	24.3

[1]Data refer to persons who had three or more years of tenure on a job that they had lost between January 2017 and December 2019 because of plant or company closings or moves, insufficient work, or the abolishment of their positions or skills.
[2]Data not shown where the base is less than 75,000.
[3]Persons of Hispanic origin may be of any race.

Table 1-74. Long-Tenured Displaced Workers[1] by Whether they Received Written Advance Notice, Reason for Job Loss, and Employment Status, January 2020

(Numbers in thousands, percent.)

Characteristic	Total	Percent distribution by employment status			
		Total	Employed	Unemployed	Not in the labor force
TOTAL					
Total, 20 years and over[2]	2 672	100.0	70.1	12.4	17.5
Received written advance notice	1 254	100.0	67.8	13.1	19.1
Did not receive written advance notice	1 377	100.0	72.9	11.8	15.3
Plant or Company Closed Down or Moved					
Total, 20 years and over[2]	1 084	100.0	69.9	11.7	18.4
Received written advance notice	646	100.0	69.4	13.5	17.1
Did not receive written advance notice	415	100.0	73.1	8.3	18.5
Insufficient Work					
Total, 20 years and over[2]	621	100.0	73.7	8.4	17.9
Received written advance notice	183	100.0	68.1	5.0	26.9
Did not receive written advance notice	431	100.0	76.4	10.0	13.7
Position or Shift Abolished					
Total, 20 years and over[2]	967	100.0	67.9	15.7	16.4
Received written advance notice	425	100.0	65.4	15.9	18.7
Did not receive written advance notice	532	100.0	69.9	16.0	14.2

[1] Data refer to persons who had three or more years of tenure on a job that they had lost between January 2017 and December 2019 because of plant or company closings or moves, insufficient work, or the abolishment of their positions or skills.
[2] Includes a small number who did not report information on advance notice.

Table 1-75. Long-Tenured Displaced Workers[1] by Industry and Class of Worker of Lost Job and Employment Status, January 2020

(Numbers in thousands, percent.)

Industry of class of worker of lost job	Total	Percent distribution by employment status			
		Total	Employed	Unemployed	Not in the labor force
TOTAL, 20 YEARS AND OVER[2]	2 672	100.0	70.1	12.4	17.5
Agriculture and related industries wage and salary workers	26	100.0	([3])	([3])	([3])
Nonagricultural industries wage and salary workers	2 621	100.0	70.4	12.2	17.4
Private nonagricultural wage and salary workers	2 481	100.0	70.3	12.4	17.3
Mining, quarrying, and oil and gas extraction	31	100.0	([3])	([3])	-
Construction	189	100.0	63.6	20.0	16.5
Manufacturing	461	100.0	64.4	13.1	22.4
Durable goods manufacturing	279	100.0	62.1	15.3	22.6
Primary metals and fabricated metal products	57	100.0	([3])	([3])	([3])
Machinery manufacturing	49	100.0	([3])	([3])	([3])
Computers and electronic products	55	100.0	([3])	([3])	([3])
Electrical equipment and appliances	19	100.0	([3])	([3])	([3])
Transportation equipment	25	100.0	([3])	([3])	([3])
Miscellaneous manufacturing	27	100.0	([3])	([3])	([3])
Other durable goods industries	47	100.0	([3])	([3])	([3])
Nondurable goods manufacturing	182	100.0	68.0	9.7	22.3
Food manufacturing	48	100.0	([3])	([3])	([3])
Textiles, apparel, and leather	30	100.0	([3])	([3])	([3])
Paper and printing	41	100.0	([3])	([3])	([3])
Other nondurable goods industries	64	100.0	([3])	([3])	([3])
Wholesale and retail trade	435	100.0	76.5	7.0	16.5
Wholesale trade	96	100.0	70.1	4.5	25.4
Retail trade	340	100.0	78.3	7.7	14.0
Transportation and utilities	85	100.0	72.5	14.1	13.4
Transportation and warehousing	78	100.0	([3])	([3])	([3])
Information	126	100.0	80.2	2.9	16.9
Telecommunications	48	100.0	([3])	([3])	([3])
Financial activities	256	100.0	67.0	18.2	14.8
Finance and insurance	221	100.0	70.3	14.2	15.5
Finance	116	100.0	([3])	([3])	9.3
Insurance	105	100.0	64.8	12.8	22.4
Real estate and rental and leasing	35	100.0	([3])	([3])	([3])
Professional and business services	393	100.0	71.4	13.2	15.5
Professional and technical services	232	100.0	72.9	16.5	10.6
Management, administrative, and waste services	161	100.0	69.1	8.4	22.4
Education and health services	278	100.0	68.2	13.9	17.8
Educational services	60	100.0	([3])	([3])	([3])
Health care and social assistance	218	100.0	67.0	12.1	20.9
Hospitals	53	100.0	([3])	([3])	([3])
Health services, except hospitals	118	100.0	75.0	6.3	18.7
Leisure and hospitality	140	100.0	78.3	5.2	16.5
Accommodation and food services	117	100.0	74.2	6.2	19.6
Food services and drinking places	94	100.0	71.8	7.7	20.5
Other services	86	100.0	72.6	21.9	5.5
Government wage and salary workers	140	100.0	71.9	8.1	20.0

[1]Data refer to persons who had three or more years of tenure on a job that they had lost between January 2017 and December 2019 because of plant or company closings or moves, insufficient work, or the abolishment of their positions or skills.
[2]Total includes a small number of unpaid family workers and persons who did not report industry or class of worker, not shown separately.
[3]Data not shown where base is less than 75,000.

Table 1-76. Long-Tenured Displaced Workers[1] by Occupation of Lost Job and Employment Status, January 2020

(Numbers in thousands, percent.)

Occupation of lost job	Total	Percent distribution by employment status			
		Total	Employed	Unemployed	Not in the labor force
TOTAL, 20 YEARS AND OVER[2]	2 672	100.0	70.1	12.4	17.5
Management, professional, and related occupations	1 195	100.0	73.5	13.7	12.8
Management, business, and financial operations occupations	715	100.0	71.7	16.2	12.1
Professional and related occupations	481	100.0	76.1	10.0	14.0
Service occupations	252	100.0	69.6	8.9	21.5
Sales and office occupations	603	100.0	71.1	9.8	19.0
Sales and related occupations	283	100.0	76.9	10.3	12.8
Office and administrative support occupations	321	100.0	66.1	9.4	24.5
Natural resources, construction, and maintenance occupations	237	100.0	59.1	14.9	26.0
Farming, fishing, and forestry occupations	8	100.0	(3)	(3)	(3)
Construction and extraction occupations	124	100.0	57.2	14.1	28.8
Installation, maintenance, and repair occupations	106	100.0	65.7	10.1	24.2
Production, transportation, and material moving occupations	364	100.0	66.3	10.6	23.2
Production occupations	201	100.0	64.5	13.8	21.7
Transportation and material moving occupations	163	100.0	68.4	6.6	25.0

[1]Data refer to persons who had three or more years of tenure on a job that they had lost between January 2017 and December 2019 because of plant or company closings or moves, insufficient work, or the abolishment of their positions or skills.
[2]Includes a small number who did not report occupation.
[3]Data not shown where base is 75,000.

Table 1-77. Long-Tenured Displaced Workers[1] by Selected Characteristics and Area of Residence, January 2020

(Numbers in thousands.)

Characteristic	Total	New England	Middle Atlantic	East North Central	West North Central
Workers who Lost Jobs					
Total, 20 years and over	2 672	147	326	408	177
Men	1 466	78	189	215	109
Women	1 206	69	137	193	68
Reason for Loss					
Plant or company closed down or moved	1 084	48	114	184	66
Insufficient work	621	45	82	84	41
Position or shift abolished	967	54	130	140	70
Industry and Class of Worker who Lost Job[2]					
Agriculture and related industries wage and salary workers	26	-	-	10	-
Nonagricultural industries wage and salary workers	2 621	143	326	398	172
Private nonagricultural wage and salary	2 481	134	316	376	161
Mining, quarrying, and oil and gas extraction	31	-	-	-	-
Construction	189	12	25	13	4
Manufacturing	461	24	54	92	44
Durable goods	279	21	29	59	20
Nondurable goods	182	3	25	32	23
Wholesale and retail trade	435	18	51	65	24
Transportation and utilities	85	4	11	23	5
Information	126	9	19	21	13
Financial activities	256	9	40	55	15
Professional and business services	393	25	52	34	29
Education and health services	278	22	36	46	14
Leisure and hospitality	140	6	19	9	9
Other services	86	5	10	18	3
Government wage and salary workers	140	8	10	21	11
Employment Status in January 2014					
Employed	1 872	103	206	300	137
Unemployed	331	19	41	47	17
Not in the labor force	469	25	79	61	23

Characteristic	South Atlantic	East South Central	West South Central	Mountain	Pacific
Workers who Lost Jobs					
Total, 20 years and over	445	108	404	215	442
Men	236	59	199	127	255
Women	210	49	206	88	187
Reason for Loss					
Plant or company closed down or moved	185	52	152	85	198
Insufficient work	112	28	91	45	93
Position or shift abolished	148	27	162	84	151
Industry and Class of Worker who Lost Job[2]					
Agriculture and related industries wage and salary workers	-	-	-	3	13
Nonagricultural industries wage and salary workers	440	108	395	211	429
Private nonagricultural wage and salary	409	103	379	201	401
Mining, quarrying, and oil and gas extraction	-	1	25	1	4
Construction	53	15	15	27	27
Manufacturing	70	18	41	25	94
Durable goods	45	12	21	21	51
Nondurable goods	25	6	19	4	43
Wholesale and retail trade	79	17	87	34	60
Transportation and utilities	4	2	19	6	12
Information	6	12	22	3	20
Financial activities	30	14	56	4	33
Professional and business services	74	16	58	38	67
Education and health services	51	4	30	38	36
Leisure and hospitality	34	5	15	17	27
Other services	9	-	12	7	21
Government wage and salary workers	31	4	16	10	28
Employment Status in January 2014					
Employed	301	56	292	176	301
Unemployed	68	13	35	15	75
Not in the labor force	77	38	77	24	65

[1]Data refer to persons who had three or more years of tenure on a job that they had lost between January 2017 and December 2019 because of plant or company closings or moves, insufficient work, or the abolishment of their positions or skills.
[2]Total includes a small number of unpaid family workers and persons who did not report industry or class of worker, not shown separately.
- = Represents or rounds to zero.

Table 1-78. Long-Tenured Displaced Workers Who Lost Full-Time Wage and Salary Jobs and Were Reemployed in January 2020 by Industry of Lost Job and Characteristic of New Job

(Numbers in thousands.)

Industry and class of worker of lost job[1]	Reemployed in January 2016							Self-employed and unpaid family workers
	Total	Wage and salary workers						
		Part-time	Full-time					
			Total[2]	Earnings relative to those of lost job				
				20 percent or more below	Below, but within 20 percent	Equal or above, but within 20 percent	20 percent or more above	
TOTAL WHO LOST FULL-TIME WAGE AND SALARY JOBS[3]	1 672	186	1 335	172	181	383	269	151
Agriculture and related industries wage and salary workers	11	4	7	-	-	5	1	-
Nonagricultural industries wage and salary workers	1 645	181	1 314	172	180	373	267	150
Private nonagricultural wage and salary workers	1 569	168	1 250	156	175	362	244	150
Mining, quarrying, and oil and gas extraction	18	-	14	2	6	0	5	4
Construction	116	9	84	15	14	15	10	24
Manufacturing	285	18	244	28	26	86	47	23
Durable goods	169	10	141	23	17	48	24	18
Nondurable goods	116	8	103	5	9	38	23	5
Wholesale and retail trade	286	46	237	51	14	61	38	3
Transportation and utilities	62	-	53	9	13	19	7	9
Information	100	0	77	17	16	21	6	22
Financial activities	172	11	150	15	20	51	22	11
Professional and business services	260	12	214	2	38	63	68	34
Education and health services	144	30	109	16	16	32	17	6
Leisure and hospitality	67	15	43	1	12	4	12	9
Other services	59	27	27	1	1	10	12	5
Government wage and salary workers	77	13	64	16	5	11	23	-

Note: Dash represents or rounds to zero.

[1]Data refer to persons who had three or more years of tenure on a job that they had lost between January 2017 and December 2019 because of plant or company closings or moves, insufficient work, or the abolishment of their positions or skills.
[2]Includes about 330,000 persons who did not report earnings on lost job.
[3]Includes a small number who did not report industry.

Table 1-79. Total Displaced Workers by Selected Characteristics and Employment Status in January 2020

(Numbers in thousands, percent.)

Characteristic[1]	Total	Percent Distribution by Employment Status			
		Total	Employed	Unemployed	Not in the labor force
WORKERS WHO LOST JOBS					
Sex and Age					
Total, 20 years and over	6 334	100.0	70.9	15.0	14.1
20 to 24 years	670	100.0	75.1	11.8	13.1
25 to 54 years	4 177	100.0	74.4	16.2	9.4
55 to 64 years	1 142	100.0	64.8	13.3	21.9
65 years and over	344	100.0	40.1	13.0	47.0
Men, 20 years and over	3 412	100.0	71.4	15.8	12.8
20 to 24 years	328	100.0	69.6	15.6	14.8
25 to 54 years	2 276	100.0	75.0	16.3	8.7
55 to 64 years	622	100.0	67.6	13.5	18.9
65 years and over	186	100.0	43.0	17.7	39.3
Women, 20 years and over	2 922	100.0	70.3	14.1	15.6
20 to 24 years	341	100.0	80.3	8.2	11.5
25 to 54 years	1 902	100.0	73.8	16.0	10.2
55 to 64 years	520	100.0	61.4	13.0	25.5
65 years and over	158	100.0	36.6	7.4	55.9
Race and Hispanic Origin					
White	4 813	100.0	72.0	12.6	15.3
Black or African American	954	100.0	62.7	25.9	11.4
Asian	304	100.0	71.6	22.4	6.0
Hispanic[2]	1 235	100.0	70.7	14.3	15.0
Reason for Job Loss					
Plant or company closed down or moved	2 275	100.0	70.5	13.4	16.1
Insufficient work	2 260	100.0	71.3	16.1	12.5
Position or shift abolished	1 798	100.0	70.8	15.7	13.5
Occupation of Lost Job[3]					
Management, professional, and related occupations	2 266	100.0	74.2	14.9	10.9
Management, business, and financial operations occupations	1 252	100.0	72.4	18.2	9.4
Professional and related occupations	1 014	100.0	76.4	10.8	12.8
Service occupations	890	100.0	73.9	14.5	11.7
Sales and office occupations	1 414	100.0	71.2	11.9	16.8
Sales and related occupations	698	100.0	69.7	15.1	15.2
Office and administrative support occupations	716	100.0	72.8	8.8	18.4
Natural resources, construction, and maintenance occupations	620	100.0	68.2	14.4	17.4
Farming, fishing, and forestry occupations	14	100.0	-	-	-
Construction and extraction occupations	420	100.0	72.6	13.3	14.1
Installation, maintenance, and repair occupations	186	100.0	63.2	14.3	22.5
Production, transportation, and material moving occupations	948	100.0	63.5	18.9	17.6
Production occupations	508	100.0	59.8	19.1	21.1
Transportation and material moving occupations	441	100.0	67.8	18.7	13.6
Agriculture and related industries wage and salary workers	36	100.0	-	-	-
Nonagricultural industries wage and salary workers	6 094	100.0	71.3	14.8	13.9
Private nonagricultural wage and salary workers	5 842	100.0	70.9	15.2	13.9
Mining, quarrying, and oil and gas extraction	54	100.0	-	-	-
Construction	544	100.0	68.3	19.2	12.5
Manufacturing	908	100.0	63.6	18.2	18.2
Durable goods	576	100.0	62.0	21.0	17.0
Nondurable goods	332	100.0	66.3	13.3	20.3
Wholesale and retail trade	1 045	100.0	70.5	12.5	17.0
Transportation and utilities	194	100.0	78.3	14.5	7.2
Information	202	100.0	80.1	7.9	12.0
Financial activities	402	100.0	65.6	19.1	15.3
Professional and business services	975	100.0	71.2	17.7	11.2
Education and health services	632	100.0	76.5	10.7	12.8
Leisure and hospitality	598	100.0	76.7	12.1	11.2
Other services	268	100.0	70.3	20.4	9.4
Government wage and salary workers	252	100.0	79.8	4.5	15.7

Note: Dash represents or rounds to zero.

[1]Data refer to all persons (regardless of years of tenure on lost job) who had lost or left a job between January 2017 and December 2019 because of plant or company closings or moves, insufficient work, or the abolishment of their positions or shifts.
[2]Persons of Hispanic origin may be of any race.
[3]Total includes a small number of unpaid family workers and persons who did not report occupation, industry, or class of worker, not shown separately.

CHAPTER 2: EMPLOYMENT, HOURS, AND EARNINGS

HIGHLIGHTS

The employment, hours, and earnings data in this section are presented by industry and state and are derived from the Current Employment Statistics (CES) survey, which covers approximately 697,000 individual worksites and 144,000 business and government agencies. The employment numbers differ from those presented in from the household survey in Chapter 1 because of dissimilarities in methodology, concepts, definitions, and coverage. As the CES survey data are obtained from payroll records, they are consistent for industry classifications.

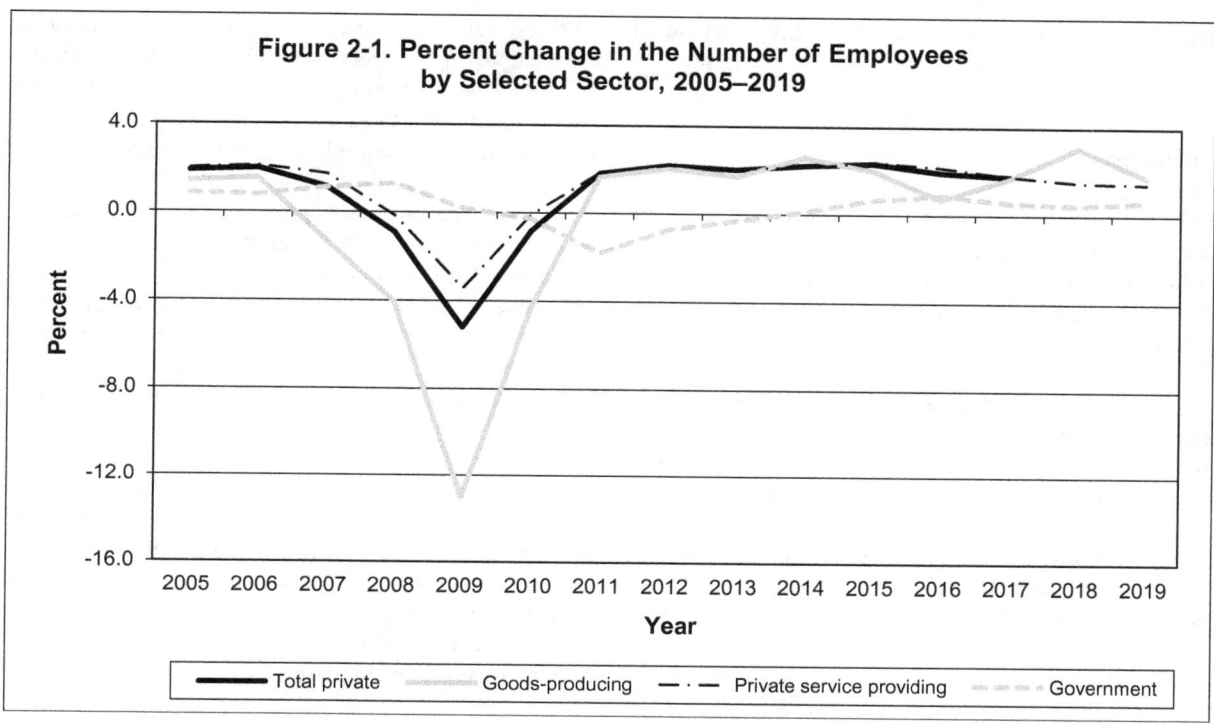

Figure 2-1. Percent Change in the Number of Employees by Selected Sector, 2005–2019

In 2019, total nonfarm employment increased for the ninth consecutive year after declining each year from 2008 to 2010. Private employment increased 1.5 percent while goods-producing employment increased 1.8 percent and 1.4 percent in private-service providing industries. (See Table 2-1.)

OTHER HIGHLIGHTS:

- Employment increased in all major sectors in 2019 except in retail trade and utilities which both experienced a small decrease. Within retail trade, clothing and clothing accessory stores experienced the largest decline in employment at 4.4 percent followed sporting goods, hobby, and music stores at 4.0 percent and electronic and appliance stores at -2.9 percent. Gasoline stations, food and beverage stores, and motor vehicle parts and dealers were the only industries within retail trade that did not experience a decline in unemployment between 2018 and 2019. (See Table 2-1.)

- From 2005 to 2019, the number of women employees on nonfarm payrolls increased 15.9 percent. Millions of women left the labor force in 2020, as they were often the ones that had to handle childcare after COVID-19 forced schools to close all over the country. (See Table 2-2.)

- Average weekly hours of all employees on private nonfarm payrolls decreased slightly to 34.4 hours in 2019. Employees in mining and logging worked the longest week (46.2 hours) followed by workers in utilities (42.2 hours) and manufacturing (40.6 hours). Workers in leisure and hospitality worked the lowest number of hours (25.9 hours). (See Table 2-6.)

NOTES AND DEFINITIONS

EMPLOYMENT, HOURS, AND EARNINGS

Collection and Coverage

The Bureau of Labor Statistics (BLS) conducts the Current Employment Statistics (CES), or establishment, survey. This survey collects monthly data on employment, hours, and earnings from a sample of nonfarm establishments (including government).

The CES sample includes about 144,000 businesses and government agencies and covers approximately 697,000 individual worksites. The reference period for the CES survey is the pay period which includes the 12th of the month.

The BLS publishes:

- Approximately 2,000 not seasonally adjusted employment series for all employees, production and nonsupervisory employees, and women employees are published monthly. The series for all employees include over 900 industries at various levels of aggregation.

- About 8,200 not seasonally adjusted special derivative series such as average weekly earnings, indexes, and constant dollar series for all employees and production and nonsupervisory employees are also published for over 600 industries.

- Approximately 4,500 seasonally adjusted employment, hours, and earnings series for all employees, production and nonsupervisory employees, and women employees are published.

- About 2,400 all employees and production and nonsupervisory employees series for average hourly earnings, average weekly hours, and, in manufacturing, average weekly overtime hours are published monthly on a not seasonally adjusted basis and cover over 600 industries.

Industry Classification

The CES survey completed a conversion from its original quota sample design to a probability-based sample survey design, and switched from the Standard Industrial Classification (SIC) system to the North American Industry Classification System (NAICS) in 2003. The industry-coding update included reconstruction of historical estimates in order to preserve time series for data users. The foundation of industrial classification with NAICS has changed how establishments are classified into industries and how businesses, as they exist today, are recognized. With the release of January 2008 data on February 1, 2008, the CES National Nonfarm Payroll series was updated to the 2007 North American Industry Classification System (NAICS) from the 2002 NAICS basis. In February 2012, the CES National Nonfarm Payroll series was updated again from the 2007 version to the 2012 version of NAICS with the release of January data. CES data are classified according to the 2017 North American Industry Classification System (NAICS).

Industry Employment

Employment data refer to persons on establishment payrolls who received pay for any part of the pay period containing the 12th day of the month. The data exclude proprietors, the self-employed, unpaid volunteer or family workers, farm workers, and domestic workers. Salaried officers of corporations are included. Government employment covers only civilian employees; military personnel are excluded. Employees of the Central Intelligence Agency, the National Security Agency, the National Imagery and Mapping Agency, and the Defense Intelligence Agency are also excluded.

Persons on establishment payrolls who were on paid sick leave (for cases in which pay is received directly from the firm), paid holiday, or vacation leave, or who work during part of the pay period despite being unemployed or on strike during the rest of the period were counted as employed. Not counted as employed were persons on layoff, on leave without pay, on strike for the entire period, or who had been hired but had not yet reported during to their new jobs.

Beginning with the June 2003 publication of May 2003 data, the CES national federal government employment series has been estimated from a sample of federal establishments and benchmarked annually to counts from unemployment insurance tax records. It reflects employee counts as of the pay period containing the 12th day of the month, which is consistent with other CES industry series. Previously, the national series was an end-of-month count produced by the Office of Personnel Management.

The exclusion of farm employment, self-employment, and domestic service employment accounts from the payroll survey accounts for the differences in employment figures between the household and payroll surveys. The payroll survey also excludes workers on leave without pay. (These workers are counted as employed in the household survey.) Persons who worked in more than one establishment during the reporting period are counted each time their names appear on payrolls; these persons are only counted once in the household survey.

Concepts and Definitions

Production and related workers. This category includes working supervisors and all nonsupervisory workers (including group leaders and trainees) engaged in fabricating, processing, assembling, inspecting, receiving, storing, handling, packing, warehousing, shipping, trucking, hauling, maintenance, repair, janitorial, guard services, product development, auxiliary production for plant's own use (such as a power plant), record-keeping, and other services closely associated with production operations.

Construction workers. This group includes the following employees in the construction division: working supervisors, qualified craft workers, mechanics, apprentices, helpers, and laborers engaged in new work, alterations, demolition, repair, maintenance, and the like, whether working at the site of construction or at jobs in shops or yards at jobs (such as precutting and pre-assembling) ordinarily performed by members of the construction trades.

Nonsupervisory workers. This category consists of employees such as office and clerical workers, repairers, salespersons, operators, drivers, physicians, lawyers, accountants, nurses, social workers, research aides, teachers, drafters, photographers, beauticians, musicians, restaurant workers, custodial workers, attendants, line installers and repairers, laborers, janitors, guards, and other employees at similar occupational levels whose services are closely associated with those of the employees listed. It excludes persons in executive, managerial, and supervisory positions.

Payroll. This refers to payments made to full- and part-time production, construction, or nonsupervisory workers who received pay for any part of the pay period containing the 12th day of the month. The payroll is reported before deductions of any kind, such as those for old age and unemployment insurance, group insurance, withholding tax, bonds, or union dues. Also included is pay for overtime, holidays, and vacation, as well as for sick leave paid directly by the firm. Bonuses (unless earned and paid regularly each pay period), other pay not earned in the pay period reported (such as retroactive pay), tips, and the value of free rent, fuel, meals, or other payment-in-kind are excluded. Employee benefits (such as health and other types of insurance and contributions to retirement, as paid by the employer) are also excluded.

Total hours. During the pay period, total hours include all hours worked (including overtime hours), hours paid for standby or reporting time, and equivalent hours for which employees received pay directly from the employer for sick leave, holidays, vacations, and other leave. Overtime and other premium pay hours are not converted to straight-time equivalent hours. The concept of total hours differs from those of scheduled hours and hours worked. The average weekly hours derived from paid total hours reflect the effects of such factors as unpaid absenteeism, labor turnover, part-time work, and work stoppages, as well as fluctuations in work schedules.

Average weekly hours. The workweek information relates to the average hours for which pay was received and is different from standard or scheduled hours. Such factors as unpaid absenteeism, labor turnover, part-time work, and work stoppages cause average weekly hours to be lower than scheduled hours of work for an establishment. Group averages further reflect changes in the workweeks of component industries.

Overtime hours. These are hours worked by production or related workers for which overtime premiums were paid because the hours were in excess of the number of hours of either the straight-time workday or the total workweek. Weekend and holiday hours are included only if overtime premiums were paid. Hours for which only shift differential, hazard, incentive, or other similar types of premiums were paid are excluded.

Average overtime hours. Overtime hours represent the portion of average weekly hours that exceeded regular hours and for which overtime premiums were paid. If an employee worked during a paid holiday at regular rates, receiving as total compensation his or her holiday pay plus straight-time pay for hours worked that day, no overtime hours would be reported.

Since overtime hours are premium hours by definition, weekly hours and overtime hours do not necessarily move in the same direction from month to month. Factors such as work stoppages, absenteeism, and labor turnover may not have the same influence on overtime hours as on average hours. Diverse trends at the industry group level may also be caused by a marked change in hours for a component industry in which little or no overtime was worked in both the previous and current months.

Industry hours and earnings. Average hours and earnings data are derived from reports of payrolls and hours for production and related workers in manufacturing and natural resources and mining, construction workers in construction, and nonsupervisory employees in private service-providing industries.

Average hourly earnings. Average hourly earnings are on a "gross" basis. They reflect not only changes in basic hourly and incentive wage rates, but also such variable factors as premium pay for overtime and late-shift work and changes in output of workers paid on an incentive plan. They also reflect shifts in the number of employees between relatively high-paid and low-paid work and changes in workers' earnings in individual establishments. Averages for groups and divisions further reflect changes in average hourly earnings for individual industries.

Averages of hourly earnings differ from wage rates. Earnings are the actual return to the worker for a stated period; rates are the amount stipulated for a given unit of work or time. The earnings series do not measure the level of total labor costs on the part of the employer because the following items are excluded: irregular bonuses, retroactive items, payroll taxes paid by employers, and earnings for those employees not covered under the definitions of production workers, construction workers, or nonsupervisory employees.

Average hourly earnings, excluding overtime-premium pay, are computed by dividing the total production worker payroll for the industry group by the sum of total production worker hours and one-half of total overtime hours. No adjustments are made for other premium payment provisions, such as holiday pay, late-shift premiums, and overtime rates other than time and one-half.

Average weekly earnings. These estimates are derived by multiplying average weekly hours estimates by average hourly earnings estimates. Therefore, weekly earnings are affected not only by changes in average hourly earnings but also by changes in the length of the workweek. Monthly variations in factors, such as the proportion of part-time workers, work stoppages, labor turnover during the survey period, and absenteeism for which employees are not paid may cause the average workweek to fluctuate.

Long-term trends of average weekly earnings can be affected by structural changes in the makeup of the workforce. For example, persistent long-term increases in the proportion of part-time workers in retail trade and many of the services industries have reduced average workweeks in these industries and have affected the average weekly earnings series.

These earnings are in constant dollars and are calculated from the earnings averages for the current month using a deflator derived from the Consumer Price Index for Urban Wage Earnings and Clerical Workers (CPI-W). The reference year for these series is 1982.

Seasonally adjustment removes the change in employment that is due to normal seasonal hiring or layoffs, thus leaving an over-the-month change that reflects only employment changes due to trend and irregular movements. Seasonally adjusted estimates of employment and other series are generated using the X-12 ARIMA program developed by the United States Census Bureau.

Data Revisions

CES revises published estimates to improve its data series by incorporating additional information that was not available at the time of the initial publication of the estimates. Each year, the CES incorporates a benchmark revision that re-anchors estimates to nearly complete employment counts available from Quarterly Census of Employment and Wages (QCEW) data, County Business Pattern data, and other state collected data. The benchmark helps to control for sampling error in the estimates. See more about the QCEW later in this chapter.

It can be nearly two years before not seasonally adjusted CES estimates are considered final. The first preliminary CES estimates of employment, hours, and earnings are published each month approximately three weeks after the reference period. Estimates are then revised twice before being held constant until the annual benchmark release. Second preliminary estimates for a given month are published the month following the initial release, and final sample-based estimates are published two months after the initial release. The annual benchmark revisions affect nearly two years of data, so most months are subject to revisions during two separate benchmark periods.

Sources of Additional Information

For further information on sampling, estimation methods, and data revisions for national data visit the Employment, Hours, and Earnings homepage on the BLS Web site at <https://www.bls.gov/ces>. For more information on state and area data, please visit the BLS Web site at <https://www.bls.gov/sae>.

Table 2-1. Employees on Nonfarm Payrolls, by Super Sector and Selected Component Groups, NAICS Basis, 2005–2019

(Thousands of people.)

Industry	2005	2006	2007	2008	2009	2010	2011	2012	2013	2014	2015	2016	2017	2018	2019
TOTAL	134 034	136 435	137 981	137 224	131 296	130 345	131 914	134 157	136 364	138 940	141 825	144 336	146 608	148 908	150 939
Total Private	112 230	114 462	115 763	114 714	108 741	107 855	109 828	112 237	114 511	117 058	119 796	122 112	124 258	126 454	128 346
Goods-Producing	22 190	22 530	22 233	21 335	18 558	17 751	18 047	18 420	18 738	19 226	19 610	19 750	20 084	20 704	21 067
Mining and Logging	628	684	724	767	694	705	788	848	863	891	813	668	676	727	735
Mining	562	620	664	710	643	655	739	797	811	839	760	617	626	677	685
Logging	65	64	60	57	50	50	49	51	52	52	52	51	50	50	51
Construction	7 336	7 691	7 630	7 162	6 016	5 518	5 533	5 646	5 856	6 151	6 461	6 728	6 969	7 288	7 492
Construction of buildings	1 712	1 805	1 774	1 642	1 357	1 230	1 222	1 240	1 286	1 358	1 424	1 493	1 545	1 625	1 660
Heavy and civil engineering	951	985	1 005	965	851	825	837	868	885	912	938	952	996	1 051	1 078
Specialty trade contractors	4 673	4 901	4 850	4 556	3 808	3 463	3 474	3 537	3 684	3 881	4 100	4 283	4 427	4 613	4 755
Manufacturing	14 227	14 155	13 879	13 406	11 847	11 528	11 726	11 927	12 020	12 185	12 336	12 354	12 439	12 688	12 840
Durable goods	8 956	8 981	8 808	8 463	7 284	7 064	7 273	7 470	7 548	7 674	7 765	7 714	7 741	7 946	8 059
Wood product	561	561	517	458	360	342	337	339	353	372	383	393	397	406	409
Nonmetallic mineral product	505	510	501	465	394	371	367	365	373	384	398	406	410	417	422
Primary metals	466	464	456	442	362	362	388	402	395	399	394	375	371	380	385
Fabricated metal product	1 522	1 553	1 563	1 528	1 312	1 282	1 347	1 410	1 432	1 454	1 458	1 422	1 425	1 470	1 492
Machinery	1 166	1 183	1 187	1 188	1 029	996	1 056	1 099	1 105	1 127	1 121	1 077	1 079	1 117	1 126
Computer and electronic product	1 316	1 308	1 273	1 244	1 137	1 095	1 104	1 089	1 066	1 049	1 053	1 048	1 039	1 054	1 081
Electrical equipment and appliances	434	433	429	424	374	360	366	373	374	378	384	383	386	400	405
Transportation equipment	1 772	1 769	1 712	1 608	1 348	1 333	1 382	1 461	1 509	1 559	1 605	1 630	1 643	1 702	1 734
Furniture and related product	566	558	529	478	384	357	353	351	360	370	381	390	395	393	388
Miscellaneous manufacturing	647	644	642	629	584	567	574	580	581	582	590	591	595	608	618
Nondurable goods	5 271	5 174	5 071	4 943	4 564	4 464	4 453	4 457	4 472	4 512	4 571	4 640	4 699	4 742	4 781
Food manufacturing	1 478	1 479	1 484	1 481	1 456	1 451	1 459	1 469	1 474	1 484	1 512	1 557	1 598	1 621	1 643
Textile mills	218	195	170	151	124	119	120	119	117	117	117	115	113	112	109
Textile product mills	176	167	158	147	126	119	118	116	114	115	116	116	116	116	113
Apparel	251	232	215	199	168	157	152	148	145	140	137	131	119	114	110
Paper and paper product	484	471	458	445	407	395	387	380	378	373	373	371	366	366	365
Printing and related support activities	646	634	622	594	522	488	472	462	452	454	450	448	440	432	425
Petroleum and coal product	112	113	115	117	115	114	112	112	110	112	113	113	115	115	115
Chemicals	872	866	861	847	804	787	784	783	793	803	807	812	824	835	850
Plastics and rubber product	802	786	757	729	625	625	635	645	659	674	689	702	717	730	737
Private Service-Providing	90 039	91 931	93 530	93 380	90 184	90 104	91 781	93 817	95 773	97 832	100 186	102 362	104 174	105 750	107 279
Trade, Transportation, and Utilities	25 892	26 206	26 556	26 219	24 834	24 565	24 990	25 399	25 783	26 303	26 806	27 179	27 393	27 607	27 715
Wholesale Trade	5 706	5 842	5 948	5 875	5 521	5 387	5 475	5 595	5 660	5 740	5 780	5 787	5 814	5 841	5 903
Durable goods	3 119	3 203	3 257	3 191	2 944	2 848	2 905	2 978	3 013	3 056	3 080	3 083	3 108	3 149	3 203
Nondurable goods	2 109	2 134	2 161	2 148	2 063	2 026	2 041	2 071	2 092	2 121	2 137	2 145	2 153	2 151	2 169
Electronic markets, agents, and brokers	478	505	530	536	514	513	529	547	556	563	564	559	553	541	531
Retail Trade	15 285	15 359	15 526	15 289	14 528	14 446	14 674	14 847	15 085	15 363	15 611	15 832	15 846	15 786	15 644
Motor vehicle and parts dealers	1 919	1 910	1 908	1 831	1 638	1 629	1 691	1 737	1 793	1 862	1 929	1 980	2 005	2 015	2 035
Furniture and home furnishing stores	576	587	575	531	449	438	439	439	446	456	467	471	476	477	473
Electronic and appliance stores	586	581	583	570	516	523	528	508	497	498	523	522	503	491	477
Building material and garden supply stores	1 277	1 325	1 310	1 249	1 156	1 133	1 147	1 175	1 209	1 229	1 235	1 268	1 277	1 303	1 296
Food and beverage stores	2 818	2 821	2 844	2 862	2 830	2 808	2 823	2 861	2 930	3 004	3 062	3 090	3 086	3 073	3 078
Health and personal care stores	954	961	993	1 003	986	981	981	998	1 016	1 023	1 034	1 053	1 067	1 063	1 052
Gasoline stations	871	864	862	842	826	819	831	844	866	881	905	923	930	932	945
Clothing and clothing accessories stores	1 415	1 451	1 500	1 468	1 364	1 353	1 361	1 391	1 391	1 370	1 354	1 359	1 374	1 359	1 299
Sporting goods, hobby, and music stores	598	606	623	622	589	579	578	582	603	619	623	620	606	573	550
General merchandise stores	2 934	2 935	3 021	3 026	2 966	2 998	3 085	3 065	3 060	3 102	3 131	3 169	3 126	3 098	3 043
Miscellaneous store retailers	900	881	865	843	782	762	772	794	803	818	828	832	828	835	834
Nonstore retailers	438	437	442	442	425	425	438	452	472	501	519	543	567	569	563
Transportation and Warehousing	4 348	4 457	4 528	4 496	4 225	4 179	4 289	4 404	4 486	4 649	4 859	5 004	5 178	5 426	5 618
Air transportation	501	487	492	491	463	458	457	459	444	444	459	478	492	497	503
Rail transportation	193	192	198	195	185	183	193	195	196	200	204	184	182	182	175
Water transportation	61	63	66	67	63	62	61	64	65	67	66	66	65	65	66
Truck transportation	1 398	1 436	1 440	1 389	1 269	1 251	1 301	1 350	1 383	1 418	1 453	1 448	1 457	1 496	1 531
Transit and ground passenger transportation	396	407	419	430	428	436	447	448	456	474	485	490	495	495	499
Pipeline transportation	38	39	40	42	43	42	43	44	45	47	50	50	49	50	51
Scenic and sightseeing transportation	29	28	29	28	28	27	28	28	29	31	33	35	35	35	36
Support activities for transportation	563	581	595	603	559	553	573	591	609	637	663	678	701	729	754
Couriers and messengers	571	582	581	573	546	528	529	534	544	577	613	645	676	740	816
Warehousing and storage	599	643	670	677	642	638	658	692	716	755	834	932	1 027	1 139	1 188

Table 2-1. Employees on Nonfarm Payrolls, by Super Sector and Selected Component Groups, NAICS Basis, 2005–2019—*Continued*

(Thousands of people.)

Industry	2005	2006	2007	2008	2009	2010	2011	2012	2013	2014	2015	2016	2017	2018	2019
Utilities	554	549	553	559	560	553	553	553	552	552	556	556	555	553	549
Information	3 061	3 038	3 032	2 984	2 804	2 707	2 674	2 676	2 706	2 726	2 750	2 794	2 814	2 839	2 860
Publishing industries, except Internet	904	902	901	880	796	759	749	740	733	727	727	730	729	739	760
Motion picture and sound recording industry	378	376	381	371	358	370	362	362	371	379	398	426	433	441	444
Broadcasting, except Internet	328	328	325	319	301	290	283	285	284	283	277	271	268	270	267
Internet publishing and broadcasting and web search portals	67	69	73	81	83	92	110	125	142	163	184	204	224	245	272
Telecommunications	1 071	1 048	1 031	1 019	966	903	874	857	853	839	811	801	781	750	713
Other information services	118	121	126	134	135	142	160	177	196	219	241	262	286	309	338
Financial Activities	8 197	8 367	8 348	8 206	7 838	7 695	7 697	7 784	7 886	7 977	8 123	8 287	8 451	8 590	8 746
Finance and insurance	6 063	6 194	6 179	6 076	5 844	5 761	5 769	5 828	5 886	5 931	6 035	6 148	6 262	6 337	6 425
Monetary authorities, central bank	21	21	22	22	21	20	18	18	18	18	18	19	19	20	20
Credit intermediation	2 869	2 925	2 866	2 733	2 590	2 550	2 554	2 583	2 614	2 564	2 571	2 610	2 645	2 651	2 652
Securities, commodity contracts, investments, and funds and trusts	834	869	900	916	862	850	860	859	865	883	908	927	938	954	964
Insurance carriers and related activities	2 339	2 379	2 392	2 405	2 371	2 341	2 336	2 368	2 389	2 466	2 538	2 593	2 660	2 713	2 790
Real estate and rental and leasing	2 134	2 173	2 169	2 130	1 994	1 934	1 927	1 955	2 000	2 046	2 088	2 139	2 189	2 253	2 321
Real estate	1 461	1 499	1 500	1 485	1 420	1 396	1 401	1 420	1 459	1 487	1 517	1 557	1 606	1 663	1 718
Rental and leasing services	646	646	640	617	547	514	502	511	518	535	548	558	560	567	579
Lessors of nonfinancial intangible assets	27	28	28	28	27	25	24	24	24	24	24	24	24	23	23
Professional and Business Services	17 003	17 619	17 998	17 792	16 634	16 783	17 389	17 992	18 575	19 124	19 695	20 114	20 508	20 950	21 313
Professional and technical services	7 065	7 399	7 705	7 845	7 553	7 486	7 713	7 941	8 170	8 386	8 658	8 881	9 058	9 282	9 543
Management and technical consulting services	853	917	985	1 035	1 027	1 031	1 098	1 152	1 215	1 268	1 318	1 394	1 433	1 482	1 531
Administrative and management consulting services	308	331	357	374	369	376	399	416	444	475	507	565	588	620	653
Waste management and remediation services	338	348	355	357	352	357	365	372	378	386	397	404	415	436	454
Education and Health Services	17 676	18 154	18 676	19 228	19 630	19 975	20 318	20 769	21 086	21 439	22 029	22 639	23 188	23 638	24 177
Education services	2 836	2 901	2 941	3 040	3 090	3 155	3 250	3 341	3 354	3 417	3 472	3 570	3 668	3 715	3 765
Health care and social assistance	14 840	15 253	15 735	16 188	16 540	16 820	17 069	17 428	17 731	18 022	18 557	19 069	19 520	19 923	20 413
Ambulatory health care services	5 114	5 286	5 474	5 647	5 793	5 975	6 136	6 307	6 477	6 632	6 856	7 080	7 297	7 477	7 697
Hospitals	4 345	4 423	4 515	4 627	4 667	4 679	4 722	4 779	4 786	4 787	4 896	5 015	5 072	5 130	5 199
Nursing and residential health facilities	2 855	2 893	2 958	3 016	3 082	3 124	3 168	3 196	3 229	3 258	3 291	3 318	3 348	3 357	3 379
Social assistance	2 527	2 651	2 788	2 898	2 997	3 043	3 043	3 147	3 240	3 346	3 515	3 655	3 803	3 958	4 137
Leisure and Hospitality	12 816	13 110	13 427	13 436	13 077	13 049	13 353	13 768	14 254	14 696	15 160	15 660	16 051	16 295	16 576
Arts, entertainment, and recreation	1 892	1 929	1 969	1 970	1 916	1 913	1 919	1 969	2 030	2 103	2 166	2 252	2 333	2 383	2 433
Performing arts and spectator sports	376	399	405	406	397	406	394	402	419	443	450	464	494	506	516
Museums, historical sites	121	124	130	132	129	128	133	136	140	147	153	160	166	170	173
Amusements, gambling, and recreation	1 395	1 406	1 434	1 433	1 389	1 379	1 392	1 430	1 470	1 513	1 563	1 628	1 674	1 707	1 744
Accommodation and food services	10 923	11 181	11 457	11 466	11 162	11 135	11 434	11 800	12 224	12 593	12 994	13 408	13 718	13 913	14 143
Accommodation	1 819	1 832	1 867	1 869	1 763	1 760	1 801	1 825	1 865	1 895	1 923	1 960	2 003	2 035	2 078
Food services and drinking places	9 104	9 349	9 590	9 598	9 399	9 376	9 633	9 975	10 359	10 698	11 071	11 448	11 715	11 878	12 065
Other Services	5 395	5 438	5 494	5 515	5 367	5 331	5 360	5 430	5 483	5 567	5 622	5 691	5 770	5 831	5 893
Repair and maintenance	1 236	1 249	1 253	1 227	1 150	1 139	1 169	1 194	1 217	1 242	1 277	1 293	1 311	1 327	1 352
Personal and laundry services	1 277	1 288	1 310	1 323	1 281	1 265	1 289	1 314	1 342	1 371	1 405	1 444	1 478	1 507	1 525
Membership associations and organizations	2 882	2 901	2 931	2 966	2 936	2 926	2 903	2 922	2 925	2 954	2 940	2 953	2 981	2 998	3 016
Government	21 804	21 974	22 218	22 509	22 555	22 490	22 086	21 920	21 853	21 882	22 029	22 224	22 350	22 455	22 594
Federal	2 732	2 732	2 734	2 762	2 832	2 977	2 859	2 820	2 769	2 733	2 757	2 795	2 805	2 800	2 834
Federal, excluding U.S. Postal Service	1 957	1 963	1 965	2 014	2 129	2 318	2 228	2 209	2 175	2 140	2 160	2 186	2 189	2 192	2 227
State	5 032	5 075	5 122	5 177	5 169	5 137	5 078	5 055	5 046	5 050	5 077	5 110	5 165	5 173	5 177
State, excluding education	2 772	2 782	2 804	2 823	2 809	2 764	2 704	2 666	2 653	2 661	2 676	2 681	2 686	2 686	2 692
Local	14 041	14 167	14 362	14 571	14 554	14 376	14 150	14 045	14 037	14 098	14 195	14 319	14 379	14 481	14 583
Local, excluding education	6 185	6 254	6 376	6 487	6 475	6 363	6 278	6 267	6 260	6 283	6 324	6 414	6 458	6 518	6 574

Table 2-2. Women Employees on Nonfarm Payrolls, by Super Sector and Selected Component Groups, NAICS Basis, 2005–2019

(Thousands of people.)

Industry	2005	2006	2007	2008	2009	2010	2011	2012	2013	2014	2015	2016	2017	2018	2019
TOTAL NONFARM	64 996	65 823	67 137	67 455	65 620	65 089	65 447	66 377	67 431	68 573	69 983	71 520	72 625	73 941	75 309
Total Private	52 607	53 605	54 558	54 546	52 720	52 260	52 835	53 884	54 963	56 078	57 378	58 779	59 807	61 014	62 264
Goods-Producing	5 104	5 083	5 041	4 866	4 289	4 088	4 057	4 093	4 125	4 211	4 286	4 322	4 403	4 576	4 712
Mining and logging	79	82	93	101	98	98	105	113	116	119	114	98	91	92	96
Construction	890	944	947	916	801	723	711	724	746	780	813	841	881	934	971
Manufacturing	4 135	4 057	4 001	3 848	3 390	3 268	3 241	3 256	3 263	3 312	3 360	3 384	3 431	3 550	3 645
Private Service-Providing	47 504	48 523	49 517	49 681	48 431	48 172	48 779	49 792	50 838	51 867	53 092	54 457	55 404	56 439	57 552
Trade, transportation, and utilities	10 518	10 611	10 833	10 766	10 218	9 992	10 074	10 236	10 449	10 664	10 860	11 060	11 029	11 076	11 096
Wholesale trade	1 719	1 775	1 809	1 798	1 684	1 619	1 644	1 676	1 676	1 691	1 700	1 708	1 712	1 740	1 776
Retail trade	7 525	7 589	7 760	7 714	7 363	7 228	7 282	7 392	7 575	7 733	7 863	7 992	7 913	7 856	7 758
Transportation and warehousing	1 130	1 102	1 114	1 102	1 029	1 006	1 013	1 031	1 062	1 106	1 163	1 229	1 276	1 351	1 430
Utilities	143	146	150	151	143	139	135	137	136	134	133	131	128	129	132
Information	1 333	1 306	1 285	1 260	1 170	1 104	1 084	1 076	1 079	1 094	1 102	1 116	1 117	1 119	1 136
Financial activities	4 923	5 055	4 988	4 851	4 648	4 530	4 490	4 519	4 547	4 572	4 635	4 715	4 782	4 862	4 954
Professional and business services	7 590	7 797	8 026	7 964	7 490	7 472	7 706	7 954	8 267	8 522	8 755	9 006	9 220	9 484	9 718
Education and health services	13 661	14 037	14 478	14 904	15 218	15 435	15 637	15 964	16 202	16 469	16 948	17 444	17 861	18 232	18 694
Leisure and hospitality	6 708	6 903	7 054	7 056	6 861	6 819	6 964	7 190	7 421	7 636	7 858	8 133	8 349	8 568	8 809
Other services	2 772	2 814	2 854	2 880	2 824	2 820	2 823	2 852	2 874	2 912	2 935	2 984	3 046	3 098	3 146
Government	12 389	12 218	12 578	12 908	12 900	12 829	12 611	12 493	12 468	12 495	12 605	12 741	12 819	12 927	13 045
Federal	1 177	1 194	1 202	1 224	1 259	1 326	1 269	1 249	1 230	1 209	1 220	1 236	1 244	1 249	1 274
State	2 575	2 630	2 651	2 684	2 628	2 639	2 643	2 648	2 649	2 651	2 702	2 740	2 779	2 797	2 805
Local	8 637	8 395	8 725	9 000	9 014	8 864	8 700	8 596	8 589	8 635	8 683	8 766	8 796	8 880	8 966

Table 2-3. Production Workers on Private Nonfarm Payrolls, by Super Sector, NAICS Basis, 2005–2019

(Thousands of people.)

Industry	2005	2006	2007	2008	2009	2010	2011	2012	2013	2014	2015	2016	2017	2018	2019
TOTAL PRIVATE	91 426	93 759	95 243	94 660	89 616	88 940	90 605	92 766	94 573	96 688	98 769	100 555	102 411	104 169	105 612
Goods-Producing	16 145	16 559	16 405	15 724	13 399	12 774	13 005	13 287	13 481	13 858	14 141	14 215	14 450	14 876	15 094
Mining and logging	473	519	547	574	510	525	594	641	636	652	592	471	490	541	541
Construction	5 611	5 903	5 883	5 521	4 567	4 172	4 184	4 246	4 423	4 640	4 866	5 074	5 230	5 437	5 579
Manufacturing	10 060	10 137	9 975	9 629	8 322	8 077	8 228	8 400	8 422	8 565	8 683	8 670	8 730	8 898	8 975
Private Service-Providing	75 282	77 200	78 838	78 936	76 217	76 166	77 600	79 479	81 093	82 830	84 628	86 340	87 961	89 293	90 518
Trade, transportation, and utilities	21 776	22 109	22 486	22 277	21 059	20 816	21 174	21 554	21 811	22 217	22 566	22 842	23 094	23 348	23 443
Wholesale trade	4 538	4 676	4 799	4 768	4 453	4 324	4 388	4 505	4 563	4 638	4 644	4 634	4 661	4 688	4 739
Retail trade	13 033	13 114	13 322	13 139	12 476	12 430	12 652	12 798	12 928	13 112	13 269	13 433	13 486	13 488	13 354
Transportation and warehousing	3 761	3 876	3 922	3 920	3 678	3 618	3 693	3 810	3 875	4 022	4 207	4 328	4 500	4 728	4 910
Utilities	443	443	444	450	451	444	441	441	445	446	447	447	447	444	440
Information	2 386	2 399	2 403	2 388	2 240	2 170	2 148	2 164	2 194	2 209	2 226	2 252	2 268	2 286	2 301
Financial activities	6 127	6 312	6 365	6 320	6 066	5 942	5 900	5 986	6 068	6 155	6 278	6 430	6 571	6 654	6 767
Professional and business services	13 892	14 487	14 828	14 631	13 565	13 744	14 298	14 851	15 352	15 818	16 183	16 455	16 751	17 079	17 333
Education and health services	15 401	15 832	16 318	16 842	17 240	17 531	17 818	18 230	18 505	18 827	19 337	19 859	20 365	20 763	21 234
Leisure and hospitality	11 263	11 568	11 861	11 873	11 560	11 507	11 772	12 154	12 590	12 968	13 360	13 782	14 139	14 334	14 563
Other services	4 438	4 494	4 578	4 606	4 488	4 458	4 491	4 541	4 573	4 637	4 678	4 720	4 775	4 828	4 876

Table 2-4. Production Workers on Manufacturing Payrolls, by Industry, NAICS Basis, 2005–2019

(Thousands of people.)

Industry	2005	2006	2007	2008	2009	2010	2011	2012	2013	2014	2015	2016	2017	2018	2019
Total Manufacturing	10 060	10 137	9 975	9 629	8 322	8 077	8 228	8 400	8 422	8 565	8 683	8 670	8 730	8 898	8 975
Durable Goods	6 220	6 355	6 250	5 975	4 990	4 829	4 986	5 152	5 185	5 282	5 350	5 303	5 315	5 464	5 546
Wood products	454	451	407	358	278	269	269	272	283	298	306	309	311	319	321
Nometallic mineral products	387	391	384	363	303	284	278	273	275	280	297	306	305	311	314
Primary metals	363	363	358	348	273	275	301	317	306	310	307	293	292	295	300
Fabricated metal products	1 129	1 162	1 171	1 143	961	935	994	1 050	1 063	1 071	1 069	1 036	1 045	1 087	1 111
Machinery	749	770	774	772	641	616	662	700	699	716	711	686	691	716	709
Computer and electronic products	700	756	744	730	654	629	630	628	610	589	594	596	598	612	641
Electrical equipment and appliances	300	303	305	305	266	251	248	249	245	248	258	259	253	261	264
Transportation equipment	1 277	1 304	1 275	1 177	948	937	972	1 024	1 053	1 103	1 139	1 151	1 149	1 189	1 203
Furniture and related products	436	433	409	364	284	263	260	259	266	276	284	287	290	290	289
Miscellaneous manufacturing	424	423	425	416	382	370	373	380	386	390	384	382	381	384	394
Nondurable Goods	3 841	3 782	3 725	3 653	3 332	3 248	3 241	3 248	3 237	3 283	3 333	3 367	3 415	3 434	3 429
Food manufacturing	1 170	1 172	1 184	1 184	1 161	1 152	1 158	1 169	1 169	1 176	1 189	1 212	1 251	1 272	1 289
Textile mills	174	158	137	122	99	96	98	96	93	91	90	90	88	87	85
Textile products mills	143	135	123	115	98	92	89	85	83	86	88	89	89	85	78
Apparel	193	182	173	163	132	120	112	109	106	103	104	99	88	82	74
Paper and paper products	365	357	351	344	313	302	295	288	279	277	277	275	278	275	272
Printing and related support	447	447	443	425	369	342	327	316	310	312	310	312	305	296	284
Petroleum and coal products	75	72	73	77	70	70	70	72	70	72	74	76	80	77	77
Chemicals	510	508	504	513	479	474	480	491	490	497	507	516	525	546	558
Plastics and rubber products	620	608	592	572	477	472	482	487	497	518	532	536	543	548	552

Table 2-5. Total Employees on Manufacturing Payrolls, by Industry, NAICS Basis, 2005–2019

(Thousands of people.)

Industry	2005	2006	2007	2008	2009	2010	2011	2012	2013	2014	2015	2016	2017	2018	2019
Total Manufacturing	14 227	14 155	13 879	13 406	11 847	11 528	11 726	11 927	12 020	12 185	12 336	12 354	12 439	12 688	12 840
Durable Goods	8 956	8 981	8 808	8 463	7 284	7 064	7 273	7 470	7 548	7 674	7 765	7 714	7 741	7 946	8 059
Wood products	561	561	517	458	360	342	337	339	353	372	383	393	397	406	409
Nometallic mineral products	505	510	501	465	394	371	367	365	373	384	398	406	410	416	422
Primary metals	466	464	456	442	362	362	388	402	395	399	394	375	371	380	385
Fabricated metal products	1 522	1 553	1 563	1 528	1 312	1 282	1 347	1 410	1 432	1 454	1 458	1 422	1 425	1 470	1 492
Machinery	1 166	1 183	1 187	1 188	1 029	996	1 056	1 099	1 105	1 127	1 121	1 077	1 079	1 117	1 126
Computer and electronic products	1 316	1 308	1 273	1 244	1 137	1 095	1 104	1 089	1 066	1 049	1 053	1 048	1 039	1 054	1 081
Electrical equipment and appliances	434	433	429	424	374	360	366	373	374	378	384	383	386	400	405
Transportation equipment	1 772	1 769	1 712	1 608	1 348	1 333	1 382	1 461	1 509	1 559	1 605	1 630	1 643	1 702	1 734
Furniture and related products	566	558	529	478	384	357	353	351	360	370	381	390	395	393	388
Miscellaneous manufacturing	647	644	642	629	584	567	574	580	581	582	590	591	595	608	618
Nondurable Goods	5 271	5 174	5 071	4 943	4 564	4 464	4 453	4 457	4 472	4 512	4 571	4 640	4 699	4 742	4 781
Food manufacturing	1 478	1 479	1 484	1 481	1 456	1 451	1 459	1 469	1 474	1 484	1 512	1 557	1 598	1 621	1 643
Textile mills	218	195	170	151	124	119	120	119	117	117	117	115	113	112	109
Textile products mills	176	167	158	147	126	119	118	116	114	115	116	116	116	116	113
Apparel	251	232	215	199	168	157	152	148	145	140	137	131	119	114	110
Paper and paper products	484	471	458	445	407	395	387	380	378	373	373	371	366	366	365
Printing and related support	646	634	622	594	522	488	472	462	452	454	450	448	440	432	425
Petroleum and coal products	112	113	115	117	115	114	112	112	110	112	113	113	115	115	114

Table 2-6. Average Weekly Hours of All Employees on Private Nonfarm Payrolls by NAICS Super Sector, 2010–2019

(Hours per week, seasonally adjusted.)

| Year and month | Total private | Mining and logging | Construc-tion | Manufac-turing | Trade, transportation, and utilities | | | | Informa-tion | Financial activities | Profes-sional and business services | Education and health services | Leisure and hospitality | Other services |
					Total	Wholesale trade	Retail trade	Utilities						
2010	34.1	43.4	37.8	40.2	34.2	38.1	31.4	41.1	36.5	36.9	35.4	32.7	25.7	31.6
2011	34.3	44.5	38.3	40.5	34.5	38.7	31.6	41.8	36.6	37.3	35.7	32.7	25.9	31.7
2012	34.5	44.0	38.7	40.7	34.6	38.7	31.7	41.8	36.6	37.4	36.0	32.8	26.1	31.6
2013	34.4	44.0	39.0	40.8	34.5	38.7	31.4	42.2	36.6	37.1	36.1	32.7	26.0	31.7
2014	34.5	44.8	39.0	41.0	34.5	38.9	31.3	42.4	36.8	37.3	36.3	32.7	26.2	31.8
2015	34.5	44.0	39.1	40.8	34.6	38.9	31.4	42.5	36.3	37.6	36.2	32.8	26.3	31.9
2016	34.4	43.3	39.1	40.7	34.3	38.8	31.0	42.3	35.9	37.4	36.0	32.8	26.1	31.9
2017	34.4	45.2	39.2	40.8	34.4	39.1	31.0	42.2	36.2	37.5	36.1	32.9	26.1	31.8
2018	34.5	46.0	39.3	40.9	34.5	39.1	31.0	42.1	36.1	37.6	36.2	32.9	26.1	31.8
2019	34.4	46.2	39.3	40.6	34.2	38.9	30.6	42.2	36.3	37.6	36.2	33.0	25.9	31.9
2015														
January	34.5	45.1	39.0	40.9	34.5	38.9	31.3	42.3	36.5	37.4	36.2	32.8	26.3	31.9
February	34.6	44.3	39.5	41.0	34.6	38.9	31.4	42.7	36.4	37.4	36.2	32.8	26.3	31.9
March	34.5	43.9	39.2	40.8	34.6	38.8	31.4	42.8	36.3	37.5	36.1	32.8	26.2	31.8
April	34.5	43.7	39.0	40.8	34.6	38.8	31.4	42.6	36.3	37.6	36.1	32.8	26.2	31.8
May	34.5	43.6	38.9	40.7	34.7	38.9	31.5	42.4	36.3	37.6	36.2	32.8	26.2	31.8
June	34.5	43.7	39.2	40.6	34.5	38.8	31.3	42.2	36.3	37.6	36.2	32.8	26.3	31.8
July	34.5	43.9	39.1	40.8	34.5	38.9	31.3	42.5	36.3	37.6	36.2	32.8	26.2	31.8
August	34.5	43.7	39.3	40.9	34.6	38.8	31.4	42.8	36.2	37.7	36.2	32.8	26.2	31.8
September	34.5	44.1	38.8	40.6	34.9	38.9	31.8	42.5	36.0	37.7	36.1	32.8	26.3	31.8
October	34.6	44.0	39.4	40.7	34.6	38.9	31.4	42.6	36.1	37.6	36.3	32.8	26.3	31.9
November	34.5	44.1	39.1	40.7	34.6	38.9	31.4	42.6	36.1	37.6	36.1	32.8	26.2	31.9
December	34.5	44.3	39.6	40.7	34.5	39.0	31.2	42.4	36.0	37.7	36.2	32.8	26.3	31.9
2016														
January	34.6	44.0	39.3	40.8	34.6	39.0	31.3	42.6	36.3	37.7	36.3	32.9	26.2	32.0
February	34.5	43.2	39.3	40.8	34.5	38.9	31.3	41.7	36.0	37.6	36.1	32.8	26.2	31.9
March	34.4	42.8	38.9	40.7	34.4	38.8	31.1	41.7	36.0	37.6	36.1	32.8	26.1	31.9
April	34.4	42.9	39.1	40.8	34.4	38.9	31.1	42.4	36.0	37.7	36.2	32.8	26.1	31.9
May	34.4	43.0	39.0	40.8	34.3	38.8	31.0	42.4	36.0	37.5	36.1	32.8	26.1	31.9
June	34.4	43.0	39.0	40.7	34.3	38.8	31.0	42.4	35.9	37.4	36.0	32.9	26.1	31.9
July	34.4	43.2	39.1	40.7	34.3	38.9	31.0	42.5	36.1	37.7	36.2	32.9	26.1	31.9
August	34.3	43.6	38.9	40.6	34.2	38.8	30.9	42.4	36.0	37.5	36.0	32.9	26.0	32.0
September	34.4	43.7	39.1	40.7	34.3	39.0	30.9	42.2	35.8	37.5	36.1	32.9	26.2	32.0
October	34.4	43.8	39.3	40.8	34.3	39.0	30.9	43.0	35.9	37.4	36.1	32.9	26.0	32.0
November	34.3	43.8	39.1	40.6	34.2	38.9	30.8	41.8	36.0	37.4	36.0	32.9	26.1	31.9
December	34.3	43.7	38.9	40.7	34.4	38.9	31.1	42.5	36.0	37.4	36.0	32.9	25.9	31.9
2017														
January	34.4	44.0	39.0	40.8	34.3	38.9	30.9	42.5	36.6	37.2	36.1	32.9	26.0	31.8
February	34.3	44.5	39.0	40.6	34.2	38.9	30.8	42.1	36.3	37.4	36.1	32.9	25.9	31.8
March	34.3	45.0	38.9	40.6	34.2	38.9	30.9	42.3	36.3	37.4	36.0	32.9	26.0	31.8
April	34.4	45.2	39.1	40.7	34.5	39.0	31.2	42.0	36.3	37.4	36.1	32.9	26.2	31.8
May	34.4	45.4	39.2	40.8	34.4	39.0	31.0	42.1	36.3	37.4	36.0	32.8	26.0	31.8
June	34.4	45.0	39.1	40.8	34.4	39.0	31.0	42.3	36.2	37.6	36.1	32.9	26.1	31.8
July	34.4	45.5	39.1	40.9	34.4	39.1	31.0	42.4	36.3	37.5	36.1	32.9	26.1	31.7
August	34.4	45.0	39.0	40.8	34.4	39.1	30.9	41.8	36.1	37.5	36.0	32.9	26.0	31.7
September	34.4	45.3	39.0	40.8	34.4	39.1	30.9	42.4	36.0	37.5	36.1	32.8	26.0	31.7
October	34.4	45.4	39.2	40.9	34.4	39.0	31.0	42.2	36.1	37.5	36.0	32.9	26.1	31.7
November	34.5	45.6	39.3	41.0	34.6	39.2	31.3	42.0	36.0	37.6	36.2	32.9	26.1	31.7
December	34.5	45.6	39.2	40.8	34.5	39.3	31.1	42.0	36.1	37.6	36.0	33.0	26.2	31.8
2018														
January	34.4	45.4	38.9	40.7	34.5	39.0	31.1	41.9	35.9	37.5	35.9	32.9	26.0	31.6
February	34.5	46.0	39.3	41.0	34.5	39.0	31.1	41.8	36.0	37.6	36.2	33.0	26.1	31.7
March	34.5	45.8	39.3	40.9	34.5	39.0	31.2	42.1	36.1	37.5	36.2	32.9	26.1	31.7
April	34.5	46.0	39.5	41.1	34.5	39.0	31.0	42.3	36.1	37.6	36.2	33.0	26.1	31.8
May	34.5	46.2	39.5	40.9	34.5	39.1	31.1	42.0	35.9	37.6	36.1	32.9	26.2	31.7
June	34.6	46.4	39.2	40.9	34.6	39.1	31.1	42.0	35.7	37.7	36.2	33.0	26.2	31.8
July	34.5	46.0	39.5	41.0	34.6	39.0	31.1	41.9	36.1	37.5	36.2	32.9	26.1	31.8
August	34.5	46.1	39.2	40.9	34.5	39.1	30.9	41.9	36.1	37.6	36.1	33.0	26.1	31.8
September	34.5	45.9	39.0	40.9	34.5	39.0	30.9	42.2	36.2	37.6	36.1	32.9	26.0	31.9
October	34.5	46.0	38.9	40.8	34.4	39.0	30.8	42.1	36.2	37.8	36.2	32.9	26.0	31.9
November	34.4	45.9	38.7	40.8	34.5	39.0	30.9	42.4	36.2	37.6	36.1	32.9	25.9	31.9
December	34.5	46.2	39.3	40.9	34.3	39.0	30.6	42.3	36.3	37.6	36.1	33.0	26.0	31.9
2019														
January	34.5	46.4	39.9	40.8	34.3	39.0	30.7	42.3	36.2	37.7	36.3	33.0	26.1	31.9
February	34.4	46.3	38.8	40.7	34.2	39.0	30.6	42.4	36.2	37.7	36.2	33.0	26.0	31.8
March	34.5	46.6	39.4	40.7	34.3	39.0	30.7	42.2	36.3	37.7	36.3	33.0	26.1	32.0
April	34.4	46.8	39.2	40.6	34.3	39.0	30.7	41.8	36.2	37.7	36.2	33.0	25.9	31.9
May	34.4	46.3	39.1	40.6	34.3	38.9	30.7	42.1	36.4	37.6	36.2	33.0	25.9	31.9
June	34.4	46.3	39.3	40.6	34.2	38.9	30.7	42.5	36.4	37.5	36.2	33.0	25.9	31.9
July	34.3	46.2	39.1	40.4	34.1	38.8	30.6	42.0	36.2	37.5	36.1	33.0	25.8	31.9
August	34.4	46.2	39.4	40.5	34.2	38.9	30.6	42.4	36.5	37.7	36.2	33.0	25.8	31.8
September	34.4	46.2	39.7	40.5	34.2	38.9	30.7	42.1	36.5	37.6	36.1	33.0	25.9	31.8
October	34.4	46.1	39.3	40.3	34.2	39.0	30.6	42.2	36.4	37.7	36.1	33.0	25.8	31.9
November	34.3	45.7	39.1	40.4	34.0	39.0	30.3	42.5	36.3	37.7	36.1	33.1	25.8	31.9
December	34.3	45.8	39.0	40.4	34.1	38.8	30.6	42.4	36.3	37.5	36.1	33.0	25.8	31.8

Table 2-7. Average Weekly Hours of Production Workers on Private Nonfarm Payrolls, by Super Sector, NAICS Basis, 2005–2019

(Hours.)

Industry	2005	2006	2007	2008	2009	2010	2011	2012	2013	2014	2015	2016	2017	2018	2019
TOTAL PRIVATE	33.8	33.9	33.8	33.6	33.1	33.4	33.6	33.7	33.7	33.7	33.7	33.6	33.7	33.8	33.6
Goods-Producing	40.1	40.5	40.6	40.2	39.2	40.4	40.9	41.1	41.3	41.5	41.2	41.2	41.3	41.5	41.1
Mining and logging	45.6	45.6	45.9	45.1	43.2	44.6	46.7	46.6	45.9	47.3	45.8	45.3	46.1	46.8	46.8
Construction	38.6	39.0	39.0	38.5	37.6	38.4	39.0	39.3	39.6	39.6	39.6	39.7	39.7	40.0	39.8
Manufacturing	40.7	41.1	41.2	40.8	39.8	41.1	41.4	41.7	41.8	42.0	41.8	41.9	41.9	42.2	41.6
Private Service-Providing	32.4	32.4	32.4	32.3	32.1	32.2	32.4	32.5	32.4	32.4	32.4	32.3	32.4	32.5	32.4
Trade, transportation, and utilities	33.4	33.4	33.3	33.1	32.8	33.3	33.7	33.8	33.7	33.6	33.7	33.5	33.8	33.9	33.8
Wholesale trade	37.7	38.0	38.2	38.3	37.7	37.9	38.5	38.7	38.7	38.6	38.6	38.6	39.0	38.9	38.7
Retail trade	30.6	30.5	30.2	30.0	29.9	30.2	30.5	30.6	30.2	30.0	30.1	29.7	30.2	30.4	30.3
Transportation and warehousing	37.0	36.8	36.9	36.4	36.0	37.1	37.8	38.0	38.5	38.4	38.7	38.8	38.4	38.4	37.9
Utilities	41.1	41.4	42.4	42.7	42.0	42.0	42.1	41.1	41.7	42.3	42.4	42.5	42.5	42.7	42.4
Information	36.5	36.6	36.5	36.7	36.6	36.3	36.2	36.0	35.9	35.9	35.7	35.5	35.8	35.6	35.3
Financial activities	36.0	35.8	35.9	35.9	36.1	36.2	36.4	36.8	36.7	36.7	37.1	36.9	37.0	37.0	36.9
Professional and business services	34.3	34.6	34.8	34.8	34.7	35.1	35.2	35.3	35.4	35.6	35.5	35.4	35.4	35.4	35.4
Education and health services	32.6	32.5	32.5	32.4	32.2	32.0	32.2	32.3	32.1	32.0	32.1	32.2	32.2	32.2	32.2
Leisure and hospitality	25.7	25.7	25.5	25.2	24.8	24.8	24.8	25.0	25.0	25.1	25.1	24.9	24.9	24.9	24.7
Other services	30.9	30.9	30.9	30.8	30.5	30.7	30.8	30.7	30.8	30.7	30.7	30.8	30.7	30.8	30.8

Table 2-8. Employees on Total Nonfarm Payrolls, by State and Selected Territory, 1975–2019

(Thousands of people.)

State	1975	1976	1977	1978	1979	1980	1981	1982	1983	1984	1985	1986	1987	1988	1989	1990
UNITED STATES	77 069	79 502	82 593	86 826	89 933	90 533	91 297	89 689	90 295	94 548	97 532	99 500	102 116	105 378	108 051	109 526
Alabama	1 155	1 207	1 269	1 337	1 362	1 356	1 348	1 313	1 329	1 388	1 427	1 463	1 508	1 559	1 601	1 645
Alaska	162	172	163	164	167	169	186	200	214	226	231	221	210	214	227	238
Arizona	729	759	809	895	980	1 014	1 041	1 030	1 078	1 182	1 279	1 338	1 386	1 419	1 455	1 483
Arkansas	624	660	696	733	750	742	740	720	741	780	797	814	837	865	893	923
California	7 847	8 154	8 600	9 200	9 666	9 853	9 993	9 822	9 933	10 408	10 792	11 111	11 501	11 944	12 274	12 540
Colorado	964	1 003	1 058	1 150	1 218	1 251	1 295	1 317	1 327	1 402	1 419	1 408	1 413	1 436	1 482	1 521
Connecticut	1 223	1 240	1 282	1 346	1 398	1 427	1 438	1 429	1 444	1 517	1 558	1 598	1 638	1 667	1 666	1 625
Delaware	230	237	239	248	257	259	259	259	266	280	293	303	321	334	345	347
District of Columbia	577	576	579	596	613	616	611	598	597	614	629	640	656	674	681	687
Florida	2 746	2 784	2 933	3 181	3 381	3 576	3 736	3 762	3 905	4 204	4 410	4 599	4 848	5 067	5 261	5 363
Georgia	1 756	1 839	1 927	2 050	2 128	2 159	2 199	2 202	2 280	2 449	2 570	2 672	2 782	2 876	2 941	3 027
Hawaii	343	349	359	377	394	404	405	399	406	413	426	439	460	478	506	528
Idaho	273	291	307	331	338	330	328	312	318	331	336	328	333	349	366	385
Illinois	4 419	4 565	4 656	4 789	4 880	4 850	4 732	4 593	4 531	4 672	4 755	4 791	4 928	5 098	5 214	5 288
Indiana	1 942	2 024	2 114	2 206	2 236	2 130	2 115	2 028	2 030	2 122	2 169	2 222	2 305	2 396	2 479	2 522
Iowa	999	1 037	1 079	1 119	1 132	1 110	1 089	1 042	1 040	1 075	1 074	1 074	1 109	1 156	1 200	1 226
Kansas	801	835	871	913	947	945	950	921	922	961	968	985	1 005	1 035	1 064	1 092
Kentucky	1 058	1 103	1 148	1 210	1 245	1 210	1 196	1 161	1 152	1 214	1 250	1 274	1 328	1 382	1 433	1 460
Louisiana	1 250	1 314	1 365	1 464	1 517	1 579	1 631	1 607	1 565	1 602	1 591	1 519	1 484	1 512	1 539	1 590
Maine	357	375	388	406	416	418	419	416	425	446	458	477	501	527	542	535
Maryland	1 479	1 498	1 546	1 626	1 691	1 712	1 716	1 676	1 724	1 814	1 888	1 952	2 028	2 102	2 155	2 178
Massachusetts	2 273	2 324	2 416	2 526	2 604	2 654	2 672	2 642	2 697	2 856	2 931	2 992	3 071	3 138	3 118	2 988
Michigan	3 137	3 283	3 442	3 609	3 637	3 443	3 364	3 193	3 223	3 381	3 562	3 657	3 736	3 819	3 922	3 944
Minnesota	1 474	1 521	1 597	1 689	1 767	1 770	1 761	1 707	1 718	1 820	1 866	1 893	1 963	2 028	2 087	2 136
Mississippi	692	728	766	814	838	829	819	791	793	821	839	848	864	896	919	938
Missouri	1 741	1 798	1 862	1 953	2 011	1 970	1 957	1 923	1 937	2 033	2 095	2 143	2 198	2 259	2 315	2 345
Montana	238	251	265	280	284	280	282	274	276	281	279	275	274	283	291	297
Nebraska	558	572	594	610	631	628	623	610	611	635	651	653	667	688	708	731
Nevada	263	280	308	350	384	400	411	401	403	426	446	468	500	538	581	621
New Hampshire	293	313	337	360	379	385	395	394	410	442	466	490	513	529	529	507
New Jersey	2 700	2 754	2 837	2 962	3 027	3 060	3 099	3 093	3 165	3 329	3 414	3 488	3 576	3 651	3 690	3 635
New Mexico	370	390	415	444	461	465	476	474	480	503	520	526	529	548	562	580
New York	6 830	6 790	6 858	7 045	7 179	7 207	7 287	7 255	7 313	7 570	7 751	7 908	8 059	8 187	8 247	8 204
North Carolina	1 980	2 083	2 171	2 278	2 373	2 380	2 392	2 347	2 419	2 565	2 651	2 744	2 863	2 987	3 074	3 121
North Dakota	204	215	221	234	244	245	249	250	251	253	252	250	252	257	260	266
Ohio	4 016	4 095	4 230	4 395	4 485	4 367	4 318	4 124	4 093	4 260	4 373	4 472	4 583	4 701	4 818	4 882
Oklahoma	900	931	972	1 036	1 088	1 138	1 201	1 217	1 171	1 180	1 165	1 124	1 109	1 132	1 164	1 210
Oregon	837	879	937	1 009	1 056	1 045	1 019	961	967	1 007	1 030	1 059	1 100	1 153	1 206	1 256
Pennsylvania	4 436	4 513	4 565	4 716	4 806	4 753	4 729	4 580	4 524	4 655	4 730	4 791	4 915	5 042	5 139	5 173
Rhode Island	349	367	382	396	400	398	401	391	396	416	429	443	452	459	462	457
South Carolina	983	1 038	1 082	1 138	1 176	1 189	1 197	1 162	1 189	1 263	1 296	1 338	1 392	1 449	1 500	1 528
South Dakota	209	219	227	237	241	238	236	230	235	247	249	252	257	266	276	289
Tennessee	1 506	1 575	1 648	1 737	1 777	1 747	1 755	1 703	1 719	1 832	1 868	1 938	2 012	2 092	2 167	2 196
Texas	4 463	4 684	4 907	5 272	5 602	5 851	6 180	6 263	6 194	6 492	6 663	6 564	6 517	6 678	6 840	7 126
Utah	440	463	489	525	548	551	558	561	567	601	624	634	640	660	691	726
Vermont	162	168	178	191	198	200	204	203	206	215	225	234	246	256	262	258
Virginia	1 779	1 848	1 930	2 034	2 115	2 157	2 161	2 146	2 207	2 333	2 455	2 558	2 680	2 773	2 862	2 896
Washington	1 226	1 283	1 367	1 485	1 581	1 608	1 612	1 569	1 586	1 660	1 710	1 770	1 852	1 942	2 048	2 148
West Virginia	575	596	612	633	659	646	629	608	582	597	597	598	599	610	615	613
Wisconsin	1 677	1 726	1 799	1 887	1 960	1 938	1 923	1 867	1 867	1 949	1 983	2 024	2 090	2 169	2 236	2 292
Wyoming	146	157	171	187	201	210	224	218	203	204	207	196	183	189	193	199
Puerto Rico	. . .	. . .	. . .	. . .	. . .	693	680	642	646	684	693	728	764	818	837	846
Virgin Islands	33	31	32	34	36	37	38	37	36	37	37	38	40	42	42	43

. . . = Not available.

Table 2-8. Employees on Total Nonfarm Payrolls, by State and Selected Territory, 1975–2019—*Continued*

(Thousands of people.)

State	1991	1992	1993	1994	1995	1996	1997	1998	1999	2000	2001	2002	2003	2004
UNITED STATES	108 425	108 799	110 931	114 393	117 400	119 828	122 941	126 146	129 228	132 011	132 073	130 634	130 331	131 769
Alabama	1 651	1 684	1 727	1 770	1 815	1 841	1 879	1 912	1 934	1 947	1 924	1 898	1 891	1 917
Alaska	243	247	253	259	262	264	269	275	279	284	289	295	299	304
Arizona	1 491	1 517	1 585	1 692	1 793	1 892	1 985	2 075	2 163	2 243	2 266	2 268	2 299	2 385
Arkansas	935	962	993	1 033	1 069	1 087	1 104	1 122	1 141	1 158	1 153	1 146	1 144	1 157
California	12 407	12 208	12 096	12 213	12 478	12 806	13 202	13 689	14 094	14 587	14 720	14 601	14 576	14 749
Colorado	1 545	1 597	1 670	1 756	1 834	1 900	1 980	2 057	2 132	2 213	2 226	2 183	2 152	2 179
Connecticut	1 563	1 533	1 536	1 549	1 567	1 587	1 612	1 648	1 674	1 698	1 686	1 669	1 649	1 656
Delaware	342	341	349	356	366	376	388	400	413	420	420	415	415	425
District of Columbia	678	674	671	659	643	623	619	614	628	650	654	664	666	674
Florida	5 274	5 337	5 549	5 777	5 973	6 159	6 395	6 611	6 801	7 054	7 145	7 154	7 235	7 483
Georgia	2 976	3 029	3 144	3 300	3 435	3 560	3 646	3 771	3 885	3 979	3 971	3 897	3 870	3 923
Hawaii	539	543	539	536	533	531	532	532	535	552	556	557	568	584
Idaho	398	415	434	459	476	489	506	522	539	560	568	569	572	588
Illinois	5 233	5 235	5 330	5 462	5 591	5 681	5 766	5 894	5 956	6 042	5 993	5 883	5 810	5 816
Indiana	2 508	2 556	2 629	2 715	2 789	2 818	2 862	2 921	2 974	3 005	2 939	2 909	2 904	2 936
Iowa	1 238	1 253	1 279	1 320	1 358	1 383	1 407	1 443	1 469	1 479	1 466	1 447	1 441	1 457
Kansas	1 097	1 117	1 135	1 168	1 200	1 229	1 270	1 315	1 329	1 347	1 349	1 337	1 314	1 326
Kentucky	1 464	1 498	1 537	1 587	1 632	1 661	1 701	1 742	1 785	1 817	1 795	1 779	1 773	1 789
Louisiana	1 613	1 627	1 659	1 722	1 772	1 810	1 850	1 890	1 896	1 920	1 918	1 898	1 908	1 920
Maine	514	512	520	532	538	543	554	570	587	604	608	607	607	612
Maryland	2 108	2 088	2 109	2 153	2 191	2 221	2 276	2 332	2 394	2 457	2 473	2 482	2 489	2 517
Massachusetts	2 825	2 799	2 844	2 908	2 982	3 042	3 116	3 187	3 250	3 338	3 350	3 272	3 214	3 213
Michigan	3 883	3 917	3 997	4 139	4 267	4 351	4 438	4 513	4 584	4 676	4 564	4 487	4 416	4 399
Minnesota	2 146	2 194	2 252	2 320	2 387	2 442	2 499	2 564	2 621	2 683	2 688	2 663	2 658	2 679
Mississippi	939	962	1 004	1 057	1 076	1 090	1 109	1 135	1 155	1 155	1 131	1 125	1 116	1 126
Missouri	2 310	2 334	2 395	2 472	2 522	2 569	2 642	2 687	2 730	2 752	2 734	2 703	2 686	2 700
Montana	304	317	326	340	352	362	367	376	384	391	391	396	400	411
Nebraska	741	752	770	799	820	839	858	880	896	913	919	911	914	921
Nevada	628	639	671	738	786	843	891	926	983	1 027	1 051	1 052	1 088	1 153
New Hampshire	481	486	501	522	538	552	569	588	604	620	625	616	616	625
New Jersey	3 498	3 456	3 490	3 548	3 595	3 632	3 717	3 798	3 897	3 990	3 999	3 983	3 976	3 996
New Mexico	585	602	626	657	682	695	709	720	730	745	757	766	776	790
New York	7 879	7 722	7 750	7 819	7 879	7 923	8 056	8 223	8 445	8 619	8 576	8 448	8 399	8 453
North Carolina	3 074	3 138	3 239	3 348	3 447	3 531	3 647	3 752	3 842	3 907	3 885	3 829	3 781	3 827
North Dakota	271	277	285	295	302	309	314	320	324	328	330	330	333	338
Ohio	4 819	4 848	4 918	5 076	5 221	5 296	5 392	5 482	5 564	5 625	5 543	5 445	5 397	5 408
Oklahoma	1 225	1 236	1 261	1 294	1 330	1 367	1 407	1 454	1 475	1 502	1 520	1 499	1 471	1 487
Oregon	1 253	1 277	1 318	1 373	1 428	1 485	1 537	1 562	1 586	1 618	1 605	1 585	1 574	1 606
Pennsylvania	5 086	5 078	5 125	5 195	5 256	5 309	5 409	5 498	5 588	5 693	5 684	5 642	5 613	5 645
Rhode Island	427	427	433	437	441	443	452	460	468	479	481	482	487	492
South Carolina	1 497	1 512	1 553	1 592	1 636	1 670	1 719	1 780	1 826	1 854	1 815	1 795	1 799	1 827
South Dakota	296	308	318	331	342	347	353	360	370	378	379	378	378	384
Tennessee	2 186	2 248	2 331	2 426	2 503	2 537	2 588	2 642	2 689	2 733	2 688	2 664	2 663	2 706
Texas	7 204	7 301	7 515	7 786	8 059	8 292	8 643	8 974	9 190	9 462	9 545	9 447	9 401	9 529
Utah	748	771	812	862	910	956	994	1 023	1 049	1 076	1 081	1 074	1 074	1 104
Vermont	249	251	258	264	270	275	280	285	292	299	302	300	299	303
Virginia	2 830	2 849	2 920	3 004	3 072	3 138	3 235	3 321	3 414	3 520	3 523	3 500	3 502	3 587
Washington	2 182	2 228	2 267	2 317	2 361	2 431	2 536	2 622	2 679	2 746	2 735	2 694	2 702	2 740
West Virginia	611	621	634	655	667	676	682	692	697	705	704	702	696	706
Wisconsin	2 302	2 358	2 412	2 490	2 558	2 600	2 655	2 717	2 783	2 832	2 812	2 780	2 772	2 802
Wyoming	203	206	210	217	219	221	225	228	233	239	245	248	250	255
Puerto Rico	838	858	872	898	930	973	989	997	1 011	1 025	1 009	1 005	1 024	1 050
Virgin Islands	44	45	49	45	42	41	42	42	41	42	44	43	42	43

Table 2-8. Employees on Total Nonfarm Payrolls, by State and Selected Territory, 1975–2019—*Continued*

(Thousands of people.)

State	2005	2006	2007	2008	2009	2010	2011	2012	2013	2014	2015	2016	2017	2018	2019
UNITED STATES	134 034	136 435	137 981	137 224	131 296	130 345	131 914	134 157	136 364	138 940	141 825	144 336	146 608	148 908	150 939
Alabama	1 961	1 996	2 023	2 010	1 905	1 890	1 890	1 906	1 924	1 944	1 971	1 997	2 019	2 045	2 073
Alaska	310	315	318	322	321	325	330	335	337	338	339	334	329	328	329
Arizona	2 513	2 639	2 679	2 622	2 433	2 386	2 411	2 462	2 520	2 570	2 636	2 709	2 777	2 858	2 937
Arkansas	1 177	1 198	1 204	1 203	1 165	1 163	1 170	1 177	1 178	1 190	1 213	1 233	1 249	1 266	1 276
California	15 046	15 326	15 462	15 300	14 439	14 283	14 435	14 762	15 151	15 576	16 052	16 481	16 827	17 173	17 425
Colorado	2 225	2 278	2 330	2 349	2 244	2 221	2 257	2 312	2 381	2 464	2 541	2 602	2 660	2 727	2 786
Connecticut	1 668	1 690	1 701	1 704	1 631	1 612	1 628	1 642	1 655	1 666	1 679	1 684	1 687	1 690	1 687
Delaware	433	438	439	436	416	414	417	419	428	438	448	453	456	461	466
District of Columbia	682	688	694	704	702	712	726	733	743	748	764	777	785	793	798
Florida	7 783	7 985	8 001	7 717	7 235	7 175	7 255	7 400	7 586	7 828	8 111	8 388	8 572	8 783	8 953
Georgia	4 024	4 111	4 166	4 122	3 900	3 860	3 900	3 954	4 032	4 145	4 261	4 371	4 453	4 536	4 620
Hawaii	602	618	626	620	593	588	595	608	620	629	639	648	655	658	656
Idaho	611	638	655	649	609	603	610	622	637	654	672	694	715	739	759
Illinois	5 862	5 931	5 977	5 946	5 655	5 610	5 678	5 751	5 803	5 879	5 966	6 013	6 055	6 102	6 118
Indiana	2 963	2 982	2 994	2 965	2 794	2 802	2 848	2 905	2 941	2 983	3 038	3 078	3 113	3 147	3 166
Iowa	1 481	1 504	1 519	1 524	1 479	1 469	1 486	1 509	1 528	1 547	1 561	1 571	1 573	1 584	1 586
Kansas	1 335	1 355	1 382	1 393	1 345	1 331	1 340	1 358	1 373	1 392	1 401	1 405	1 404	1 416	1 423
Kentucky	1 814	1 837	1 857	1 842	1 760	1 760	1 784	1 811	1 831	1 858	1 886	1 908	1 920	1 930	1 939
Louisiana	1 894	1 856	1 918	1 940	1 904	1 888	1 906	1 930	1 957	1 987	1 996	1 975	1 974	1 989	1 989
Maine	612	615	618	618	597	593	595	599	602	606	611	619	624	630	636
Maryland	2 557	2 591	2 611	2 603	2 526	2 522	2 548	2 578	2 603	2 625	2 665	2 697	2 726	2 752	2 769
Massachusetts	3 231	3 267	3 305	3 318	3 211	3 223	3 259	3 310	3 365	3 432	3 499	3 565	3 612	3 653	3 690
Michigan	4 390	4 327	4 268	4 162	3 871	3 864	3 952	4 034	4 110	4 182	4 243	4 320	4 369	4 418	4 433
Minnesota	2 721	2 756	2 769	2 760	2 652	2 638	2 683	2 726	2 774	2 813	2 859	2 899	2 938	2 963	2 978
Mississippi	1 132	1 143	1 154	1 149	1 098	1 093	1 093	1 102	1 111	1 121	1 134	1 146	1 152	1 154	1 158
Missouri	2 742	2 781	2 803	2 798	2 695	2 664	2 673	2 692	2 718	2 746	2 804	2 846	2 872	2 885	2 902
Montana	420	434	444	445	429	428	431	440	449	453	462	468	473	478	484
Nebraska	934	946	962	969	950	945	953	969	980	993	1 007	1 015	1 019	1 024	1 027
Nevada	1 223	1 279	1 292	1 264	1 148	1 118	1 126	1 145	1 174	1 216	1 259	1 299	1 340	1 384	1 418
New Hampshire	634	640	645	647	625	622	625	631	636	643	654	666	673	678	684
New Jersey	4 036	4 067	4 074	4 045	3 890	3 844	3 842	3 885	3 929	3 961	4 005	4 065	4 122	4 159	4 195
New Mexico	809	832	844	847	812	803	802	805	812	821	827	828	832	844	857
New York	8 523	8 604	8 719	8 778	8 540	8 545	8 692	8 820	8 957	9 123	9 292	9 436	9 561	9 685	9 786
North Carolina	3 904	4 030	4 134	4 124	3 897	3 863	3 910	3 981	4 052	4 135	4 236	4 335	4 407	4 488	4 574
North Dakota	345	352	359	368	367	377	397	430	445	462	454	435	432	435	439
Ohio	5 427	5 435	5 427	5 362	5 072	5 036	5 108	5 202	5 267	5 344	5 424	5 481	5 526	5 563	5 587
Oklahoma	1 525	1 566	1 595	1 618	1 568	1 556	1 578	1 614	1 635	1 656	1 668	1 654	1 663	1 689	1 703
Oregon	1 654	1 703	1 731	1 718	1 612	1 602	1 620	1 640	1 674	1 722	1 781	1 834	1 875	1 913	1 941
Pennsylvania	5 703	5 757	5 799	5 800	5 617	5 622	5 686	5 726	5 741	5 789	5 835	5 883	5 941	6 010	6 064
Rhode Island	494	496	495	484	463	462	464	469	475	482	489	494	497	501	504
South Carolina	1 863	1 906	1 945	1 926	1 814	1 811	1 833	1 864	1 901	1 951	2 007	2 055	2 096	2 155	2 189
South Dakota	390	399	407	411	404	403	408	414	418	424	429	432	434	438	441
Tennessee	2 743	2 783	2 797	2 775	2 620	2 615	2 661	2 715	2 760	2 822	2 894	2 965	3 012	3 063	3 122
Texas	9 773	10 099	10 429	10 643	10 342	10 376	10 606	10 915	11 241	11 594	11 866	12 014	12 228	12 519	12 801
Utah	1 148	1 204	1 253	1 252	1 189	1 183	1 208	1 250	1 290	1 327	1 378	1 426	1 468	1 516	1 561
Vermont	306	308	309	307	297	298	301	305	307	310	312	313	315	316	316
Virginia	3 667	3 732	3 771	3 772	3 652	3 646	3 693	3 736	3 762	3 783	3 859	3 915	3 959	4 011	4 059
Washington	2 813	2 894	2 968	2 994	2 863	2 836	2 873	2 920	2 984	3 057	3 145	3 243	3 321	3 401	3 469
West Virginia	715	726	726	731	715	717	725	734	732	729	726	717	716	726	720
Wisconsin	2 836	2 859	2 876	2 868	2 741	2 725	2 752	2 781	2 810	2 853	2 892	2 927	2 948	2 975	2 981
Wyoming	264	278	290	299	287	284	289	293	294	298	297	286	284	286	290
Puerto Rico	1 051	1 045	1 032	1 014	965	932	924	940	926	910	901	894	871	864	880
Virgin Islands	44	46	46	46	44	44	44	40	39	38	38	38	37	34	37

Table 2-9. Employees on Total Private Payrolls, by State and Selected Territory, 2005–2019

(Thousands of people.)

State	2005	2006	2007	2008	2009	2010	2011	2012	2013	2014	2015	2016	2017	2018	2019
UNITED STATES	112 230	114 462	115 763	114 714	108 741	107 855	109 828	112 237	114 511	117 058	119 796	122 112	124 258	126 454	128 346
Alabama	1 595	1 623	1 643	1 622	1 518	1 499	1 504	1 524	1 543	1 563	1 590	1 615	1 634	1 658	1 681
Alaska	229	234	237	240	237	240	245	251	254	256	257	252	248	247	250
Arizona	2 110	2 231	2 258	2 190	2 010	1 970	2 004	2 054	2 111	2 160	2 227	2 298	2 364	2 442	2 515
Arkansas	974	991	994	989	948	945	953	961	963	977	1 001	1 021	1 038	1 054	1 065
California	12 626	12 874	12 967	12 781	11 959	11 835	12 030	12 386	12 777	13 162	13 589	13 965	14 273	14 591	14 817
Colorado	1 863	1 911	1 956	1 966	1 854	1 828	1 865	1 917	1 977	2 056	2 125	2 174	2 224	2 282	2 330
Connecticut	1 416	1 432	1 447	1 444	1 376	1 362	1 381	1 397	1 410	1 421	1 435	1 443	1 449	1 454	1 450
Delaware	373	377	377	374	353	350	353	356	364	373	383	387	390	395	399
District of Columbia	448	454	462	469	461	465	479	489	503	513	526	536	544	554	560
Florida	6 700	6 884	6 876	6 588	6 118	6 061	6 159	6 317	6 506	6 751	7 026	7 291	7 466	7 668	7 829
Georgia	3 357	3 431	3 474	3 411	3 192	3 162	3 214	3 270	3 353	3 469	3 585	3 692	3 768	3 846	3 924
Hawaii	483	497	504	495	467	463	470	482	495	502	513	522	529	533	529
Idaho	496	522	538	529	490	485	493	505	520	536	552	573	592	613	632
Illinois	5 016	5 085	5 130	5 092	4 799	4 757	4 839	4 919	4 975	5 053	5 140	5 191	5 236	5 282	5 293
Indiana	2 537	2 555	2 563	2 525	2 356	2 365	2 418	2 477	2 517	2 558	2 611	2 652	2 685	2 717	2 737
Iowa	1 235	1 257	1 269	1 271	1 224	1 216	1 233	1 255	1 274	1 292	1 306	1 313	1 313	1 323	1 325
Kansas	1 084	1 101	1 124	1 133	1 084	1 068	1 081	1 100	1 116	1 135	1 144	1 149	1 148	1 157	1 163
Kentucky	1 513	1 532	1 547	1 532	1 448	1 443	1 463	1 488	1 507	1 535	1 567	1 592	1 605	1 617	1 627
Louisiana	1 518	1 505	1 560	1 573	1 533	1 519	1 546	1 578	1 615	1 655	1 667	1 646	1 645	1 659	1 658
Maine	507	511	514	513	493	489	493	497	502	506	511	518	524	530	534
Maryland	2 091	2 120	2 132	2 114	2 032	2 020	2 043	2 075	2 100	2 123	2 161	2 194	2 222	2 246	2 262
Massachusetts	2 806	2 838	2 873	2 881	2 773	2 783	2 825	2 873	2 922	2 981	3 048	3 111	3 159	3 199	3 233
Michigan	3 716	3 662	3 612	3 512	3 224	3 228	3 335	3 425	3 511	3 586	3 649	3 720	3 765	3 809	3 819
Minnesota	2 306	2 340	2 354	2 342	2 235	2 221	2 273	2 314	2 361	2 395	2 440	2 479	2 515	2 538	2 551
Mississippi	891	903	910	901	848	844	847	856	866	876	890	902	909	913	917
Missouri	2 312	2 347	2 363	2 352	2 243	2 216	2 234	2 254	2 282	2 314	2 370	2 412	2 437	2 450	2 465
Montana	334	346	357	357	339	336	341	351	359	363	372	377	382	388	393
Nebraska	773	783	799	806	781	775	785	800	812	823	836	842	846	851	854
Nevada	1 080	1 130	1 136	1 102	991	964	976	995	1 023	1 064	1 104	1 141	1 180	1 222	1 253
New Hampshire	543	548	552	551	529	526	533	540	546	553	564	576	583	588	594
New Jersey	3 396	3 421	3 428	3 398	3 241	3 207	3 227	3 273	3 319	3 350	3 399	3 461	3 517	3 555	3 589
New Mexico	608	635	649	649	613	604	608	612	620	629	637	639	644	657	668
New York	7 034	7 119	7 218	7 262	7 017	7 033	7 187	7 336	7 487	7 659	7 824	7 958	8 077	8 198	8 297
North Carolina	3 238	3 347	3 436	3 408	3 178	3 147	3 202	3 273	3 341	3 425	3 521	3 614	3 682	3 760	3 842
North Dakota	270	277	283	291	289	297	318	350	365	382	373	352	349	352	356
Ohio	4 627	4 635	4 629	4 563	4 280	4 250	4 332	4 427	4 499	4 576	4 650	4 704	4 743	4 777	4 801
Oklahoma	1 204	1 236	1 261	1 281	1 219	1 208	1 234	1 267	1 287	1 308	1 317	1 301	1 313	1 341	1 350
Oregon	1 369	1 417	1 441	1 420	1 313	1 302	1 325	1 349	1 385	1 428	1 480	1 527	1 566	1 618	1 642
Pennsylvania	4 949	5 002	5 044	5 041	4 849	4 852	4 935	4 994	5 020	5 077	5 131	5 180	5 238	5 307	5 357
Rhode Island	426	428	427	417	397	396	400	405	411	418	425	429	433	436	438
South Carolina	1 527	1 566	1 599	1 571	1 459	1 456	1 484	1 513	1 548	1 595	1 647	1 692	1 730	1 787	1 817
South Dakota	315	323	331	335	326	325	330	337	341	346	351	354	355	359	361
Tennessee	2 333	2 369	2 379	2 350	2 194	2 185	2 236	2 293	2 337	2 398	2 469	2 537	2 582	2 628	2 685
Texas	8 061	8 364	8 666	8 835	8 491	8 485	8 751	9 088	9 399	9 733	9 981	10 093	10 288	10 567	10 830
Utah	946	999	1 046	1 041	974	965	988	1 027	1 065	1 097	1 144	1 186	1 224	1 268	1 307
Vermont	253	254	255	253	243	243	246	250	251	254	257	257	259	260	259
Virginia	3 005	3 057	3 086	3 077	2 949	2 940	2 980	3 022	3 050	3 073	3 148	3 201	3 242	3 288	3 328
Washington	2 286	2 364	2 435	2 448	2 313	2 286	2 329	2 378	2 441	2 507	2 583	2 667	2 735	2 814	2 882
West Virginia	572	580	582	584	565	563	573	580	578	577	573	561	562	573	568
Wisconsin	2 421	2 444	2 460	2 446	2 320	2 305	2 337	2 370	2 401	2 441	2 483	2 515	2 541	2 567	2 576
Wyoming	199	212	222	230	217	213	217	221	222	227	226	215	214	217	221
Puerto Rico	747	744	734	714	676	664	665	681	681	675	670	667	654	656	677
Virgin Islands	32	33	33	33	31	31	31	29	28	27	27	28	26	23	27

Table 2-10. Employees on Manufacturing Payrolls, by State and Selected Territory, NAICS Basis, 2005–2019

(Thousands of people.)

State	2005	2006	2007	2008	2009	2010	2011	2012	2013	2014	2015	2016	2017	2018	2019
UNITED STATES	14 227	14 155	13 879	13 406	11 847	11 528	11 726	11 927	12 020	12 185	12 336	12 354	12 439	12 688	12 840
Alabama	299	303	296	284	247	236	238	244	249	253	258	261	264	267	269
Alaska	13	13	13	13	13	13	14	14	14	15	14	14	13	13	13
Arizona	183	186	182	174	155	149	151	156	156	158	160	162	165	171	177
Arkansas	202	200	191	184	164	160	159	155	153	154	155	155	157	161	162
California	1 505	1 491	1 466	1 429	1 286	1 247	1 254	1 260	1 262	1 280	1 302	1 309	1 312	1 323	1 323
Colorado	148	147	145	142	128	124	128	131	133	137	141	143	144	148	150
Connecticut	193	191	188	185	168	163	163	162	160	157	157	157	159	161	162
Delaware	33	34	33	32	28	26	26	26	25	25	26	26	26	27	27
District of Columbia	2	2	2	2	1	1	1	1	1	1	1	1	1	1	1
Florida	416	417	399	371	324	309	313	318	323	332	344	356	363	373	385
Georgia	448	445	429	407	356	344	349	353	356	366	378	388	396	405	406
Hawaii	15	16	16	15	14	13	14	14	14	14	14	15	15	15	14
Idaho	64	66	66	63	55	53	55	57	60	61	62	64	66	68	69
Illinois	689	684	676	658	577	561	574	583	580	581	582	575	576	587	586
Indiana	570	565	550	521	441	447	463	481	491	507	518	523	532	542	542
Iowa	229	231	230	228	203	201	206	211	215	217	216	214	216	223	226
Kansas	178	181	184	184	164	157	158	159	160	161	160	159	160	164	167
Kentucky	262	261	256	245	213	209	213	223	229	235	241	248	251	252	252
Louisiana	152	153	157	153	142	138	140	142	145	148	144	136	135	136	138
Maine	61	60	59	59	52	51	51	51	50	50	51	51	51	52	53
Maryland	141	137	134	130	121	117	115	112	108	106	106	106	108	110	113
Massachusetts	303	298	293	284	257	250	250	249	247	246	246	243	242	242	244
Michigan	668	638	608	563	455	466	502	531	549	575	592	606	616	629	627
Minnesota	347	346	342	336	300	293	301	306	307	312	318	318	318	322	324
Mississippi	178	176	170	160	141	136	135	137	137	140	142	143	144	145	147
Missouri	312	310	304	293	257	246	250	252	253	257	262	264	267	273	277
Montana	20	20	21	20	17	17	17	18	18	19	19	20	20	21	21
Nebraska	101	102	101	101	93	92	93	95	97	98	97	97	98	100	100
Nevada	48	50	50	48	40	38	38	39	41	42	42	44	48	56	59
New Hampshire	80	78	78	76	68	66	67	66	66	66	67	68	69	71	72
New Jersey	329	323	310	297	263	254	249	243	241	241	241	244	247	250	252
New Mexico	36	38	37	35	30	29	30	30	29	28	28	27	26	27	29
New York	580	567	552	532	476	457	459	459	456	454	455	451	445	443	439
North Carolina	565	553	539	516	448	432	434	440	443	449	462	465	468	475	478
North Dakota	26	26	26	26	24	23	24	25	25	26	26	25	25	26	26
Ohio	813	797	772	740	630	621	639	657	664	676	688	686	687	699	701
Oklahoma	152	156	158	157	136	130	137	142	142	145	143	134	134	139	141
Oregon	204	207	204	195	167	164	168	172	175	180	186	188	190	195	198
Pennsylvania	680	671	660	644	575	561	566	568	566	569	569	561	563	571	575
Rhode Island	55	53	51	48	42	40	40	40	40	40	41	41	40	40	40
South Carolina	260	252	249	241	213	207	215	219	223	228	234	236	241	250	258
South Dakota	40	42	42	43	38	37	39	41	42	42	43	42	43	44	45
Tennessee	406	397	378	359	307	297	302	311	316	323	331	342	346	351	355
Texas	901	928	939	929	843	817	842	870	876	888	879	847	853	882	907
Utah	119	124	128	126	113	111	114	117	119	121	124	126	129	133	137
Vermont	37	36	36	35	31	31	31	32	32	31	31	30	30	30	30
Virginia	296	288	278	265	240	231	231	232	231	232	234	233	235	241	243
Washington	273	286	294	292	266	259	269	281	287	289	292	290	284	288	294
West Virginia	62	61	59	57	51	49	50	49	48	48	48	47	47	47	47
Wisconsin	507	508	504	495	439	433	447	458	460	467	470	468	471	480	484
Wyoming	10	10	10	10	9	9	9	9	10	10	10	9	9	10	10
Puerto Rico	115	110	107	101	92	87	84	82	77	75	74	74	71	72	75
Virgin Islands	2	2	2	2	2	2	2	1	1	1	1	1	1	1	1

Table 2-11. Employees on Government Payrolls, by State and Selected Territory, NAICS Basis, 2005–2019

(Thousands of people.)

State	2005	2006	2007	2008	2009	2010	2011	2012	2013	2014	2015	2016	2017	2018	2019
UNITED STATES	21 804	21 974	22 218	22 509	22 555	22 490	22 086	21 920	21 853	21 882	22 029	22 224	22 350	22 455	22 594
Alabama	366	374	380	387	388	391	386	381	381	382	381	382	385	387	392
Alaska	81	81	81	82	84	85	85	84	83	82	82	82	81	80	80
Arizona	403	409	421	432	423	416	407	409	409	410	410	411	413	416	423
Arkansas	203	207	211	214	217	218	216	216	215	213	212	212	211	212	211
California	2 420	2 452	2 495	2 519	2 480	2 448	2 405	2 376	2 374	2 414	2 463	2 516	2 554	2 582	2 608
Colorado	362	367	374	384	390	393	392	394	403	408	417	428	437	446	455
Connecticut	252	257	254	260	255	251	247	246	245	245	244	241	239	236	236
Delaware	60	61	62	63	63	64	64	64	64	65	65	66	66	66	67
District of Columbia	234	233	232	235	241	247	248	244	241	236	238	241	241	238	239
Florida	1 084	1 102	1 125	1 130	1 117	1 115	1 096	1 082	1 079	1 077	1 085	1 098	1 106	1 115	1 123
Georgia	667	680	692	710	708	698	686	684	679	676	677	680	684	690	690
Hawaii	120	121	122	125	126	125	125	126	125	126	126	126	126	126	126
Idaho	115	116	117	119	120	119	117	117	117	118	119	121	123	125	127
Illinois	846	846	848	854	856	852	839	832	828	826	827	822	819	820	825
Indiana	426	426	431	441	438	437	430	428	425	425	427	426	428	430	429
Iowa	245	247	250	253	255	253	253	254	255	255	256	258	260	261	261
Kansas	251	255	258	260	261	262	260	259	257	257	257	256	256	259	260
Kentucky	301	305	310	310	311	317	321	324	324	323	318	316	316	313	311
Louisiana	376	350	358	367	372	369	360	352	341	332	330	329	330	330	331
Maine	105	104	104	104	104	104	102	102	101	100	100	100	100	100	101
Maryland	466	471	480	489	495	502	504	503	503	502	503	503	504	506	507
Massachusetts	425	429	433	437	438	439	435	437	443	452	451	454	453	454	457
Michigan	674	665	656	650	647	636	617	609	599	596	594	599	604	609	613
Minnesota	415	416	415	419	417	417	410	412	413	419	419	419	424	426	427
Mississippi	241	239	244	248	250	249	246	246	245	244	243	244	243	241	242
Missouri	429	434	440	446	452	448	439	438	435	432	434	434	435	435	436
Montana	86	88	87	88	90	92	90	90	90	90	90	91	91	90	91
Nebraska	161	162	162	164	169	170	168	168	169	170	171	173	173	173	174
Nevada	143	149	156	161	157	154	150	149	151	153	155	158	161	162	165
New Hampshire	91	92	93	95	97	96	92	92	90	91	90	91	90	90	90
New Jersey	641	646	646	647	649	637	615	612	610	612	606	604	605	604	606
New Mexico	201	198	195	198	199	200	195	193	192	192	190	189	187	187	189
New York	1 489	1 485	1 501	1 516	1 524	1 511	1 505	1 483	1 470	1 464	1 468	1 477	1 484	1 487	1 489
North Carolina	666	683	698	716	719	716	708	708	711	710	715	721	725	729	733
North Dakota	75	76	76	76	78	80	79	79	80	80	81	83	83	83	83
Ohio	800	800	798	799	792	786	776	775	768	768	773	778	783	786	786
Oklahoma	321	330	334	337	348	349	344	347	349	348	351	352	349	349	353
Oregon	285	286	290	298	300	300	295	291	289	294	301	307	310	295	299
Pennsylvania	754	755	755	760	768	771	751	732	721	711	705	703	703	703	707
Rhode Island	68	68	68	67	66	65	64	64	64	64	64	64	65	65	65
South Carolina	336	340	346	356	355	355	348	352	353	356	360	363	366	368	372
South Dakota	75	75	76	76	78	79	78	78	77	78	78	78	79	80	80
Tennessee	410	414	419	425	426	431	426	422	423	424	425	428	430	436	437
Texas	1 712	1 735	1 764	1 809	1 852	1 891	1 854	1 827	1 842	1 861	1 885	1 921	1 940	1 952	1 972
Utah	202	205	207	212	215	218	220	223	225	230	234	239	244	248	254
Vermont	53	54	54	54	55	55	55	55	55	56	56	56	56	56	57
Virginia	661	675	685	695	703	707	713	714	713	711	711	714	717	723	731
Washington	527	530	534	546	550	550	544	541	543	551	562	576	586	587	588
West Virginia	143	146	144	148	150	154	152	154	154	153	153	156	154	153	152
Wisconsin	415	415	416	422	421	420	415	411	409	412	409	412	407	408	406
Wyoming	65	65	67	69	70	71	72	72	72	71	71	71	70	69	69
Puerto Rico	305	300	297	299	289	268	259	259	245	235	231	228	217	208	203
Virgin Islands	12	13	13	13	13	13	13	12	11	11	11	11	11	11	11

EARNINGS

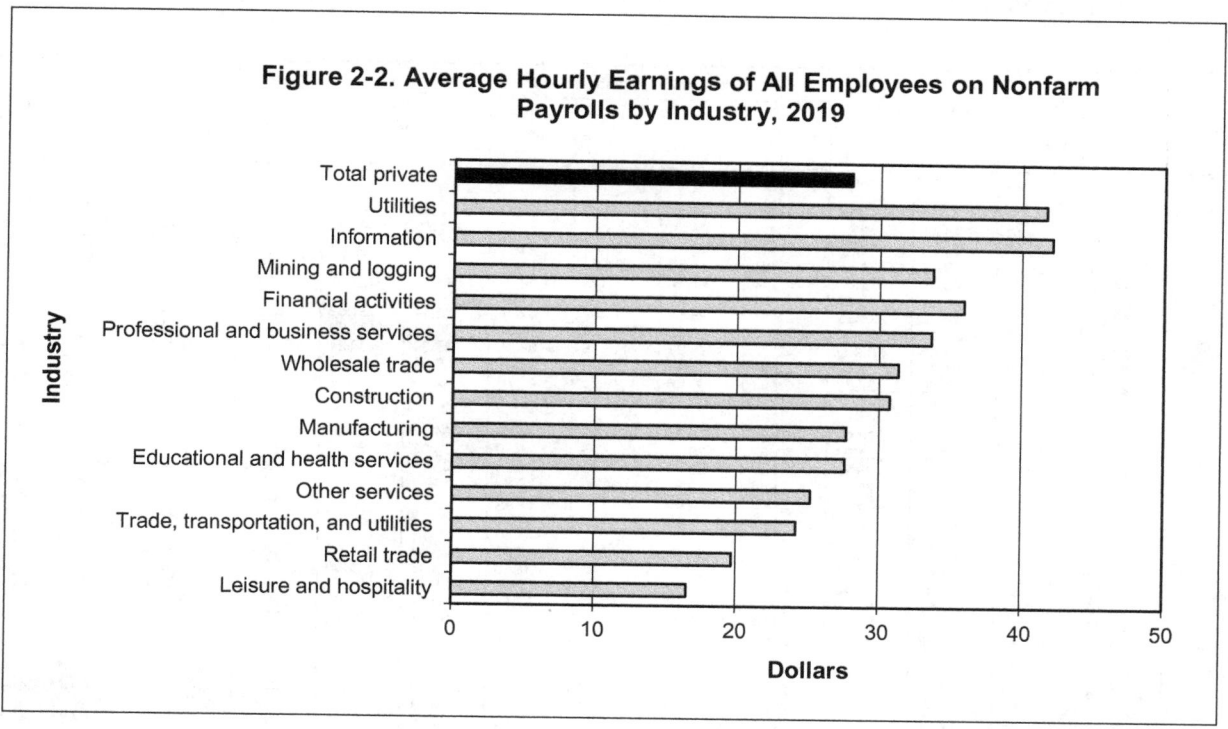

Figure 2-2. Average Hourly Earnings of All Employees on Nonfarm Payrolls by Industry, 2019

Average hourly earnings increased in all super sectors in 2019. Total private average hourly earnings were $28.00 in all super sectors in 2019, workers in information had the highest average hourly earnings at $42.15 followed by those in utilities ($41.73), financial activities ($35.94), and mining and logging at ($33.77). (See Table 2-12.)

OTHER HIGHLIGHTS

- Average hourly earnings for all employees also varied significantly by state and region in 2019. Earnings were highest in the District of Columbia ($45.44) followed by Washington ($33.99) and Massachusetts ($33.93). Mississippi had the lowest average hourly earnings ($21.57) followed by Arkansas ($22.21) and Kentucky ($22.83). (See Table 2-13.)

- In 2019, average weekly earnings increased 2.9 percent for all employees on nonfarm payrolls. When adjusted for inflation, average weekly earnings increased 1.0 percent. Average weekly earnings of all employees on nonfarm payrolls ranged from $428.87 in leisure and hospitality to $1,761.89 in utilities. (See Table 2-15.)

- From 2018 to 2019, average weekly earnings increased in each state in the United States. Mississippi experienced the highest increase in average weekly earnings at 6.8 percent followed by the District of Columbia and Nevada at 6.3 percent. Conversely, Rhode Island experienced the smallest increase in average weekly earnings at 0.1 percent followed by Maryland at 0.3 percent. (See Table 2-17.)

Table 2-12. Average Hourly Earnings of All Employees on Total Private Payrolls by NAICS Super Sector, 2010–2019

(Dollars, seasonally adjusted.)

Year and month	Total private	Mining and logging	Construc-tion	Manufact-uring	Trade, transportation, and utilities				Informa-tion	Financial activities	Profes-sional and business services	Education and health services	Leisure and hospitality	Other services
					Total	Whole-sale trade	Retail trade	Utilities						
2010	22.56	27.39	25.19	23.31	19.60	26.04	15.57	32.55	30.53	27.21	27.26	22.76	13.08	20.16
2011	23.03	28.10	25.41	23.69	19.99	26.28	15.87	33.62	31.59	27.91	27.79	23.42	13.23	20.50
2012	23.49	28.76	25.73	23.92	20.45	26.79	16.31	34.25	31.83	29.26	28.16	24.01	13.37	20.85
2013	23.95	29.72	26.12	24.35	20.91	27.54	16.64	35.17	32.91	30.15	28.58	24.42	13.50	21.40
2014	24.46	30.79	26.69	24.81	21.32	27.97	17.01	35.60	34.07	30.76	29.32	24.72	13.91	21.97
2015	25.01	31.15	27.37	25.25	21.77	28.53	17.52	37.14	35.14	31.52	30.11	25.24	14.32	22.48
2016	25.64	31.91	28.12	26.00	22.26	29.36	17.88	38.32	36.67	32.29	30.82	25.74	14.87	23.05
2017	26.32	32.05	28.90	26.60	22.72	29.92	18.18	39.25	38.30	33.24	31.67	26.32	15.47	23.85
2018	27.11	32.49	29.90	27.05	23.33	30.45	18.79	40.61	40.08	34.79	32.59	27.00	15.98	24.56
2019	28.00	33.77	30.75	27.70	24.22	31.36	19.70	41.73	42.15	35.94	33.67	27.63	16.55	25.23
2015														
January	24.73	30.51	27.07	24.99	21.54	28.21	17.32	36.00	34.51	31.07	29.74	24.99	14.15	22.18
February	24.78	30.67	27.12	25.04	21.62	28.32	17.35	36.59	34.66	31.17	29.77	25.02	14.17	22.25
March	24.84	30.83	27.24	25.10	21.60	28.27	17.32	36.84	34.74	31.22	29.88	25.12	14.22	22.35
April	24.89	30.70	27.28	25.11	21.65	28.35	17.39	36.86	34.74	31.36	29.98	25.11	14.26	22.32
May	24.96	31.16	27.32	25.14	21.72	28.59	17.43	36.99	34.89	31.54	30.04	25.22	14.30	22.42
June	24.98	31.03	27.34	25.14	21.70	28.52	17.47	36.95	34.93	31.60	30.07	25.24	14.30	22.54
July	25.00	31.18	27.36	25.23	21.77	28.55	17.52	37.21	35.04	31.50	30.10	25.21	14.31	22.48
August	25.10	31.41	27.44	25.36	21.86	28.71	17.61	37.63	35.38	31.59	30.18	25.29	14.34	22.56
September	25.11	31.52	27.35	25.40	21.83	28.62	17.68	37.31	35.43	31.70	30.28	25.33	14.38	22.60
October	25.19	31.43	27.52	25.42	21.94	28.74	17.72	37.51	35.58	31.70	30.33	25.41	14.43	22.64
November	25.24	31.68	27.67	25.52	21.95	28.72	17.72	38.00	35.72	31.72	30.39	25.44	14.46	22.66
December	25.27	31.47	27.62	25.53	21.98	28.73	17.76	37.72	35.87	31.82	30.35	25.49	14.52	22.72
2016														
January	25.36	31.79	27.66	25.63	22.01	28.90	17.72	37.84	36.02	32.03	30.53	25.54	14.58	22.77
February	25.38	31.77	27.76	25.66	22.02	28.89	17.78	37.70	36.21	32.00	30.57	25.58	14.63	22.80
March	25.45	31.95	27.88	25.76	22.13	29.20	17.84	37.90	36.16	32.19	30.56	25.60	14.67	22.86
April	25.53	31.98	27.98	25.86	22.19	29.31	17.84	38.16	36.26	32.15	30.70	25.68	14.75	22.90
May	25.58	32.13	28.08	25.97	22.20	29.32	17.87	38.32	36.48	32.19	30.80	25.64	14.80	22.96
June	25.63	32.12	28.13	25.98	22.29	29.35	17.96	38.49	36.51	32.22	30.88	25.68	14.86	23.02
July	25.70	32.01	28.20	26.01	22.32	29.57	17.89	38.42	36.65	32.41	30.92	25.72	14.93	23.11
August	25.72	31.65	28.20	26.12	22.33	29.50	17.91	38.36	36.81	32.49	30.93	25.71	14.98	23.15
September	25.77	31.87	28.23	26.12	22.37	29.53	17.93	38.38	37.04	32.58	30.97	25.83	15.02	23.17
October	25.88	31.98	28.40	26.28	22.49	29.70	18.00	38.92	37.40	32.44	31.11	25.89	15.08	23.32
November	25.91	31.90	28.35	26.26	22.51	29.60	18.10	38.42	37.46	32.64	31.15	25.94	15.12	23.33
December	25.94	32.08	28.42	26.33	22.43	29.70	17.94	38.80	37.53	32.69	31.22	25.97	15.16	23.38
2017														
January	26.00	32.20	28.53	26.36	22.52	29.78	18.01	39.27	37.50	32.63	31.28	25.98	15.23	23.51
February	26.08	32.14	28.52	26.41	22.54	29.80	18.02	38.77	37.56	32.83	31.37	26.09	15.29	23.64
March	26.11	32.03	28.61	26.41	22.56	29.77	18.05	38.77	37.65	32.78	31.51	26.09	15.35	23.61
April	26.17	31.81	28.60	26.55	22.59	29.87	18.07	39.32	38.00	32.90	31.59	26.21	15.37	23.66
May	26.21	31.84	28.72	26.53	22.65	29.84	18.14	38.92	38.20	32.88	31.52	26.26	15.50	23.69
June	26.27	31.91	28.90	26.56	22.71	29.89	18.18	39.12	38.49	33.08	31.55	26.26	15.45	23.75
July	26.36	32.21	28.95	26.67	22.77	29.96	18.22	39.30	38.60	33.25	31.63	26.39	15.48	23.86
August	26.38	32.04	29.00	26.60	22.76	29.88	18.25	38.85	38.64	33.36	31.68	26.41	15.54	23.93
September	26.51	31.98	29.18	26.69	22.85	30.00	18.27	39.52	38.60	33.50	31.86	26.53	15.62	24.06
October	26.48	32.02	29.11	26.74	22.81	29.87	18.27	39.74	38.51	33.69	31.83	26.44	15.59	24.10
November	26.55	32.12	29.22	26.73	22.87	30.05	18.30	39.55	38.71	33.71	31.92	26.55	15.64	24.18
December	26.64	32.20	29.29	26.78	22.94	30.11	18.33	39.48	38.82	34.03	32.03	26.62	15.70	24.21
2018														
January	26.71	32.31	29.39	26.87	22.97	30.09	18.40	39.75	38.98	34.23	32.13	26.66	15.74	24.23
February	26.75	32.22	29.55	26.85	23.00	30.11	18.45	39.94	39.11	34.23	32.12	26.69	15.74	24.26
March	26.84	32.45	29.49	26.90	23.04	30.13	18.48	40.14	39.29	34.42	32.24	26.82	15.82	24.41
April	26.91	32.36	29.66	26.94	23.12	30.14	18.60	40.24	39.46	34.45	32.30	26.85	15.86	24.46
May	26.98	32.28	29.70	26.97	23.21	30.28	18.72	40.19	39.60	34.65	32.40	26.96	15.89	24.50
June	27.04	32.51	29.78	27.03	23.24	30.45	18.68	40.33	39.78	34.68	32.50	27.01	15.94	24.52
July	27.11	32.44	29.94	27.01	23.30	30.41	18.78	40.85	39.73	34.82	32.62	27.05	16.01	24.56
August	27.22	32.60	30.02	27.09	23.41	30.50	18.87	40.82	40.08	34.91	32.80	27.12	16.06	24.60
September	27.31	32.88	30.18	27.12	23.49	30.69	18.93	41.02	40.76	35.10	32.83	27.15	16.10	24.69
October	27.36	32.61	30.24	27.14	23.58	30.69	19.04	41.06	40.98	34.99	32.86	27.19	16.16	24.75
November	27.44	32.74	30.30	27.24	23.60	30.73	19.08	41.16	41.15	35.30	32.96	27.24	16.22	24.80
December	27.54	32.68	30.44	27.32	23.79	30.92	19.24	41.62	41.45	35.36	33.04	27.28	16.27	24.88
2019														
January	27.58	32.74	30.32	27.27	23.80	30.83	19.34	41.37	41.78	35.39	33.07	27.42	16.28	24.97
February	27.69	32.95	30.45	27.43	23.93	30.99	19.42	41.59	41.77	35.51	33.23	27.46	16.38	25.00
March	27.76	32.96	30.50	27.46	24.02	31.26	19.44	41.83	41.96	35.54	33.33	27.52	16.40	25.05
April	27.81	33.33	30.63	27.48	24.01	31.12	19.48	41.55	41.97	35.73	33.43	27.49	16.45	25.09
May	27.87	33.47	30.70	27.57	24.13	31.30	19.55	41.81	42.00	35.82	33.52	27.43	16.51	25.16
June	27.96	33.65	30.74	27.68	24.20	31.38	19.65	41.71	41.84	35.91	33.63	27.54	16.55	25.18
July	28.05	34.11	30.75	27.75	24.28	31.39	19.73	41.54	42.26	35.93	33.75	27.64	16.59	25.21
August	28.16	34.15	30.87	27.81	24.38	31.62	19.79	41.92	42.80	36.19	33.86	27.71	16.62	25.30
September	28.16	34.44	30.87	27.88	24.38	31.56	19.84	41.75	42.28	36.03	33.94	27.74	16.67	25.32
October	28.24	34.72	30.98	27.91	24.44	31.66	19.89	41.63	42.30	36.14	34.04	27.85	16.70	25.39
November	28.34	34.57	31.09	28.02	24.52	31.74	20.00	41.89	42.58	36.40	34.17	27.87	16.76	25.48
December	28.37	34.57	31.15	28.14	24.50	31.61	20.04	42.14	42.57	36.53	34.23	27.86	16.77	25.55

Table 2-13. Average Hourly Earnings of All Employees on Total Private Payrolls, by State, NAICS Basis, 2007–2019

(Dollars.)

State	2007	2008	2009	2010	2011	2012	2013	2014	2015	2016	2017	2018	2019
UNITED STATES	20.92	21.56	22.17	22.56	23.03	23.49	23.95	24.46	25.01	25.64	26.32	27.11	28.00
Alabama	19.37	19.56	19.67	19.85	20.14	20.21	20.27	20.86	21.36	22.07	22.67	23.47	24.21
Alaska	24.70	25.01	24.80	23.90	24.49	25.58	26.74	27.15	27.89	28.22	28.28	28.78	29.02
Arizona	19.84	20.69	22.03	22.16	22.56	22.61	22.88	22.81	23.17	23.93	25.21	25.57	26.43
Arkansas	16.27	17.21	17.97	18.08	18.36	18.57	19.26	19.53	19.51	20.11	20.59	21.05	22.21
California	24.69	24.72	25.48	26.36	26.91	26.90	27.01	27.49	28.13	28.97	30.05	30.97	32.44
Colorado	23.13	23.79	23.78	23.79	23.95	24.61	25.64	26.29	26.85	27.07	27.60	28.92	30.37
Connecticut	26.59	27.71	27.81	28.08	28.23	28.14	27.96	28.16	29.14	30.43	31.16	32.05	33.02
Delaware	21.98	22.73	22.30	22.71	22.32	22.01	22.12	21.70	22.63	24.40	26.22	26.20	26.94
District of Columbia	33.54	32.37	31.37	34.18	35.44	36.84	38.31	38.95	38.33	38.42	40.67	43.10	45.44
Florida	20.57	21.00	21.61	21.44	21.46	21.62	21.95	22.19	22.63	23.31	24.04	24.81	25.66
Georgia	20.44	20.77	21.08	21.57	21.83	21.75	22.47	23.34	23.76	24.22	25.35	26.37	26.62
Hawaii	20.69	20.81	21.13	21.67	22.18	22.73	23.75	24.35	24.65	25.44	26.19	27.77	28.81
Idaho	16.52	17.53	19.26	21.04	20.79	21.00	20.89	21.34	21.94	22.28	22.33	22.74	23.20
Illinois	22.94	22.67	23.06	23.15	23.58	24.34	24.89	25.50	26.01	26.56	26.79	27.68	28.81
Indiana	19.93	20.30	20.55	20.57	20.64	21.38	22.08	22.60	22.85	23.52	24.45	24.91	25.58
Iowa	18.01	18.35	20.01	20.38	20.22	20.86	21.48	21.78	22.55	23.14	23.22	23.92	24.74
Kansas	19.63	20.12	20.17	20.07	20.50	21.03	21.48	22.09	22.56	22.77	23.20	24.10	25.43
Kentucky	17.73	18.07	18.82	19.40	19.80	20.06	20.15	20.53	21.08	21.26	21.82	22.11	22.83
Louisiana	18.74	19.22	19.46	19.55	20.63	21.37	21.98	22.12	22.20	22.65	22.99	23.49	24.20
Maine	18.74	18.96	19.16	19.45	19.95	20.96	21.01	21.33	21.85	22.25	23.22	23.86	24.92
Maryland	24.04	24.56	25.41	26.17	25.80	25.94	26.95	27.53	27.41	27.82	28.56	30.02	30.38
Massachusetts	26.08	26.39	26.86	27.15	27.65	28.14	28.72	29.49	30.38	31.03	31.79	32.84	33.93
Michigan	21.55	21.61	21.89	22.26	22.35	22.46	22.94	23.60	23.98	24.00	24.52	25.48	26.55
Minnesota	23.13	23.23	23.41	23.85	24.54	24.95	25.64	25.79	26.06	27.11	28.42	29.06	30.31
Mississippi	16.46	16.89	17.87	18.05	18.13	18.83	19.42	19.31	19.56	20.11	20.55	20.26	21.57
Missouri	19.79	20.57	20.94	21.20	20.79	21.47	21.73	21.86	21.97	22.41	23.83	24.65	25.38
Montana	17.80	18.44	19.86	20.19	20.67	20.66	20.62	21.20	21.67	21.96	22.83	23.70	24.36
Nebraska	19.92	19.79	20.19	20.89	20.84	20.94	20.91	21.35	22.16	22.99	24.09	24.72	25.71
Nevada	19.64	19.75	19.56	19.13	19.35	19.83	20.21	20.95	21.95	22.15	22.52	23.34	24.52
New Hampshire	22.06	22.66	22.70	22.99	23.01	23.72	24.31	24.33	24.91	25.72	26.30	26.59	27.00
New Jersey	24.84	25.32	25.92	25.95	25.63	26.45	26.76	26.87	27.78	28.11	29.22	29.85	30.36
New Mexico	18.57	18.73	18.92	19.57	19.70	19.83	20.15	20.44	20.43	20.60	21.39	22.10	22.97
New York	25.27	25.49	25.71	26.07	26.48	27.18	27.81	28.23	28.85	29.27	30.06	31.14	32.21
North Carolina	19.25	19.92	20.60	20.62	20.91	21.71	21.67	21.87	22.30	23.43	24.04	25.00	25.45
North Dakota	18.34	18.75	19.21	20.19	21.45	22.73	23.61	24.58	25.22	25.59	26.19	26.74	27.46
Ohio	20.22	20.11	19.95	20.22	21.07	22.01	22.21	22.29	22.75	23.41	24.03	24.81	25.33
Oklahoma	17.35	17.44	18.09	19.21	20.36	20.91	21.23	21.54	21.82	22.03	22.87	23.69	24.44
Oregon	20.61	20.93	21.33	21.56	21.75	22.23	22.52	22.91	23.53	24.72	25.66	26.22	27.17
Pennsylvania	20.08	20.44	20.75	21.22	21.86	22.63	23.29	23.73	24.22	24.68	25.10	25.75	26.16
Rhode Island	22.17	22.50	22.52	22.67	23.73	25.00	25.42	25.10	24.94	25.99	26.97	27.68	27.97
South Carolina	18.76	18.80	19.18	19.89	20.58	20.09	20.52	21.05	21.42	22.11	22.89	23.97	24.72
South Dakota	16.47	16.53	17.94	18.55	19.05	19.42	19.62	20.17	20.98	21.37	21.95	22.62	23.24
Tennessee	19.01	19.41	19.53	19.94	20.20	20.14	20.29	20.76	20.87	21.63	22.53	23.36	24.19
Texas	21.07	21.30	21.40	21.36	21.97	22.20	22.86	23.80	24.39	24.59	25.42	25.91	26.22
Utah	21.41	21.10	22.48	24.31	23.11	22.24	23.02	23.70	24.34	24.57	25.18	25.62	26.97
Vermont	20.43	21.35	22.41	23.01	23.03	22.79	22.77	23.17	24.06	24.34	24.43	25.39	25.92
Virginia	22.46	22.31	22.58	23.54	24.66	24.98	25.23	25.34	26.14	26.96	27.56	28.39	29.30
Washington	24.18	25.21	26.31	26.94	27.25	27.32	27.70	28.44	29.60	30.31	31.36	32.73	33.99
West Virginia	17.12	17.78	18.17	18.71	19.00	19.62	20.43	20.60	20.80	20.98	21.76	23.00	23.69
Wisconsin	20.46	20.68	21.13	21.36	21.85	22.38	23.11	23.24	23.46	24.03	24.74	25.93	26.42
Wyoming	20.04	20.82	21.05	21.43	22.15	22.52	22.91	23.17	23.11	23.22	23.86	25.39	26.28

. . . = Not available.

Table 2-14. Average Hourly Earnings of Production Workers on Private Nonfarm Payrolls, by Super Sector, NAICS Basis, 2005–2019

(Dollars.)

Industry	2005	2006	2007	2008	2009	2010	2011	2012	2013	2014	2015	2016	2017	2018	2019
TOTAL PRIVATE	16.12	16.74	17.41	18.06	18.60	19.04	19.43	19.73	20.13	20.60	21.03	21.53	22.05	22.71	23.51
Goods-Producing	17.60	18.02	18.67	19.33	19.90	20.28	20.67	20.94	21.24	21.59	21.96	22.58	23.18	24.00	24.74
Mining and logging	18.72	19.90	20.97	22.50	23.29	23.82	24.50	25.79	26.80	26.84	26.48	26.97	27.44	28.27	29.95
Construction	19.46	20.02	20.95	21.87	22.66	23.22	23.65	23.97	24.22	24.67	25.20	25.97	26.74	27.75	28.51
Manufacturing	16.56	16.81	17.26	17.75	18.24	18.61	18.93	19.08	19.30	19.56	19.91	20.44	20.90	21.54	22.15
Private Service-Providing	15.72	16.40	17.09	17.75	18.33	18.78	19.17	19.48	19.90	20.39	20.83	21.31	21.82	22.44	23.25
Trade, transportation, and utilities	14.90	15.36	15.74	16.13	16.44	16.78	17.10	17.38	17.69	18.21	18.61	18.93	19.29	19.88	20.64
Wholesale trade	18.13	18.87	19.54	20.08	20.78	21.46	21.88	22.13	22.52	23.14	23.52	24.07	24.58	25.17	26.06
Retail trade	12.36	12.58	12.76	12.87	13.02	13.25	13.52	13.82	14.03	14.40	14.83	15.05	15.33	15.91	16.62
Transportation and warehousing	16.65	17.21	17.67	18.36	18.74	19.10	19.42	19.47	19.73	20.43	20.66	20.83	21.22	21.75	22.40
Utilities	26.68	27.40	27.88	28.83	29.48	30.04	30.82	31.61	32.27	32.86	34.02	35.33	36.22	36.76	36.91
Information	22.06	23.23	23.96	24.78	25.45	25.87	26.62	27.04	27.98	28.70	29.05	30.05	30.74	31.97	33.89
Financial activities	17.98	18.83	19.67	20.32	20.90	21.55	21.93	22.82	23.87	24.71	25.34	26.12	26.57	26.93	27.67
Professional and business services	18.09	19.14	20.16	21.19	22.36	22.80	23.14	23.31	23.74	24.31	24.81	25.43	26.05	26.82	27.78
Education and health services	16.62	17.28	17.99	18.73	19.34	19.95	20.60	20.91	21.29	21.64	22.09	22.52	23.03	23.64	24.35
Leisure and hospitality	9.38	9.75	10.41	10.84	11.12	11.31	11.45	11.62	11.78	12.09	12.41	12.85	13.38	13.87	14.49
Other services	14.34	14.77	15.42	16.09	16.59	17.06	17.32	17.59	18.00	18.51	19.01	19.36	20.10	20.78	21.41

Table 2-15. Average Weekly Earnings of All Employees on Nonfarm Payrolls, by Industry, in Current and 1982–1984 Dollars, NAICS Basis, 2010–2019

(Dollars.)

Industry	2010	2011	2012	2013	2014	2015	2016	2017	2018	2019
TOTAL PRIVATE										
Current dollars	769.57	790.74	809.46	824.91	844.80	864.07	881.09	906.19	936.37	963.09
1982–1984 dollars	352.92	351.54	352.56	354.10	356.85	364.56	367.11	369.69	372.90	376.71
Goods-Producing										
Current dollars	952.07	976.19	994.41	1 016.09	1 041.52	1 057.13	1 083.97	1 113.61	1 145.02	1 169.92
1982–1984 dollars	436.62	433.98	433.12	436.17	439.95	446.01	451.64	454.31	455.99	457.61
Mining and logging										
Current dollars	1 189.32	1 250.91	1 263.98	1 306.16	1 380.77	1 371.13	1 383.16	1 448.75	1 494.46	1 559.64
1982–1984 dollars	545.42	556.11	550.53	560.69	583.25	578.49	576.30	591.04	595.15	610.05
Construction										
Current dollars	952.78	973.85	997.01	1 018.01	1 040.85	1 070.93	1 100.94	1 131.76	1 174.87	1 208.94
1982–1984 dollars	436.94	432.94	434.25	436.99	439.67	451.84	458.71	461.72	467.88	472.88
Manufacturing										
Current dollars	937.34	958.84	973.96	994.30	1 016.42	1 029.68	1 057.77	1 084.86	1 107.27	1 124.08
1982–1984 dollars	429.86	426.27	424.21	426.82	429.35	434.43	440.72	442.58	440.96	439.68
Private Service-Providing										
Current dollars	733.07	754.34	773.67	787.71	805.82	826.44	841.85	866.05	895.13	922.91
1982–1984 dollars	336.18	335.35	336.97	338.14	340.39	348.68	350.76	353.32	356.47	361.00
Trade, transportation, and utilities										
Current dollars	670.87	690.43	707.20	721.19	735.94	753.57	764.27	781.98	804.94	828.06
1982–1984 dollars	307.66	306.94	308.02	309.58	310.87	317.94	318.44	319.02	320.56	323.89
Wholesale trade										
Current dollars	991.59	1 015.85	1 038.30	1 066.81	1 088.33	1 109.79	1 140.05	1 169.15	1 189.45	1 220.83
1982–1984 dollars	454.74	451.61	452.23	457.94	459.72	468.23	475.01	476.97	473.68	477.53
Retail trade										
Current dollars	488.08	501.04	516.10	522.57	532.88	550.74	554.27	563.80	582.14	602.54
1982–1984 dollars	223.83	222.74	224.79	224.32	225.09	232.36	230.94	230.01	231.83	235.68
Transportation and warehousing										
Current dollars	801.27	831.80	841.76	861.63	879.66	886.60	897.87	922.04	946.11	952.22
1982–1984 dollars	367.46	369.79	366.63	369.87	371.58	374.07	374.10	376.16	376.78	372.46
Utilities										
Current dollars	1 338.50	1 404.36	1 432.93	1 484.54	1 508.94	1 580.30	1 620.24	1 655.22	1 708.84	1 761.89
1982–1984 dollars	613.83	624.33	624.11	637.26	637.39	666.75	675.08	675.27	680.52	689.16
Information										
Current dollars	1 114.65	1 156.56	1 166.45	1 206.05	1 252.44	1 274.99	1 315.74	1 388.30	1 447.26	1 529.95
1982–1984 dollars	511.18	514.17	508.05	517.71	529.05	537.93	548.21	566.38	576.35	598.44
Financial activities										
Current dollars	1 003.94	1 039.70	1 093.00	1 119.71	1 146.22	1 185.77	1 208.20	1 246.39	1 309.49	1 351.25
1982–1984 dollars	460.40	462.21	476.06	480.65	484.18	500.29	503.40	508.48	521.49	528.54
Professional and business services										
Current dollars	964.60	992.94	1 014.67	1 031.57	1 063.71	1 089.87	1 110.34	1 142.52	1 178.94	1 217.95
1982–1984 dollars	442.36	441.43	441.94	442.82	449.32	459.83	462.63	466.11	469.50	476.40
Education and health services										
Current dollars	743.41	766.88	787.43	798.73	809.11	828.36	844.80	865.65	889.44	911.45
1982–1984 dollars	340.93	340.93	342.97	342.87	341.78	349.49	351.99	353.15	354.21	356.51
Leisure and hospitality										
Current dollars	336.83	342.67	349.12	350.95	364.07	376.20	387.80	403.77	416.89	428.87
1982–1984 dollars	154.47	152.34	152.06	150.65	153.79	158.72	161.58	164.72	166.02	167.75
Other services										
Current dollars	637.65	649.87	659.49	679.43	698.41	716.17	734.90	757.95	781.48	803.75
1982–1984 dollars	292.42	288.91	287.24	291.65	295.02	302.16	306.20	309.22	311.21	314.39

Table 2-16. Average Weekly Earnings of Production Workers on Nonfarm Payrolls, by Industry, in Current and 1982–1984 Dollars, NAICS Basis, 2005–2019

(Dollars.)

Industry	2005	2006	2007	2008	2009	2010	2011	2012	2013	2014	2015	2016	2017	2018	2019
TOTAL PRIVATE															
Current dollars	543.94	566.94	589.09	607.10	615.82	636.02	652.72	665.54	677.62	694.74	708.70	723.20	742.48	766.99	790.67
1982–1984 dollars	284.79	287.64	290.53	287.65	293.77	297.25	294.58	294.19	295.49	298.47	305.72	308.96	310.59	312.87	317.26
Goods-Producing															
Current dollars	705.28	730.16	757.53	776.63	779.68	818.96	844.85	861.39	877.09	895.09	905.43	930.34	956.83	996.67	1 017.62
1982–1984 dollars	369.26	370.45	373.60	367.98	371.93	382.75	381.29	380.76	382.47	384.54	390.59	397.45	400.26	406.56	408.32
Mining and logging															
Current dollars	853.87	907.95	962.63	1 014.69	1 006.67	1 063.11	1 144.64	1 201.69	1 229.70	1 270.91	1 211.91	1 221.69	1 265.92	1 322.45	1 402.86
1982–1984 dollars	447.05	460.65	474.75	480.77	480.21	496.86	516.59	531.18	536.23	545.99	522.80	521.92	529.56	539.45	562.90
Construction															
Current dollars	750.37	781.59	816.23	842.61	851.76	891.83	921.84	942.14	958.72	977.11	998.02	1 031.88	1 061.98	1 108.59	1 135.17
1982–1984 dollars	392.86	396.54	402.55	399.24	406.32	416.81	416.04	416.45	418.06	419.77	430.53	440.83	444.25	452.22	455.49
Manufacturing															
Current dollars	673.30	690.88	711.53	724.46	726.12	765.18	784.29	794.67	807.37	822.03	832.25	855.77	876.10	908.01	921.66
1982–1984 dollars	352.51	350.52	350.91	343.26	346.38	357.62	353.96	351.27	352.07	353.15	359.02	365.59	366.49	370.40	369.81
Private Service-Providing															
Current dollars	509.00	532.11	554.05	573.23	587.37	604.91	620.78	632.87	644.65	661.42	675.83	689.13	707.04	728.42	752.65
1982–1984 dollars	266.49	269.97	273.24	271.60	280.19	282.71	280.17	279.75	281.11	284.15	291.54	294.40	295.77	297.14	302.00
Trade, transportation, and utilities															
Current dollars	497.07	512.82	524.57	534.44	540.19	558.05	575.88	587.09	595.36	611.77	626.54	633.77	652.11	674.74	697.53
1982–1984 dollars	260.25	260.18	258.71	253.23	257.69	260.81	259.90	259.51	259.62	262.82	270.28	270.75	272.79	275.24	279.88
Wholesale trade															
Current dollars	683.99	717.42	747.08	768.14	782.62	814.04	842.06	857.06	871.89	894.06	907.72	929.09	957.95	979.82	1 007.57
1982–1984 dollars	358.11	363.99	368.44	363.96	373.33	380.45	380.03	378.85	380.20	384.09	391.58	396.92	400.73	399.69	404.29
Retail trade															
Current dollars	377.58	383.25	385.18	386.44	388.74	400.38	412.29	422.35	423.44	431.97	446.01	447.69	463.10	483.03	503.07
1982–1984 dollars	197.69	194.44	189.96	183.10	185.44	187.12	186.07	186.69	184.65	185.58	192.40	191.26	193.72	197.04	201.86
Transportation and warehousing															
Current dollars	615.26	633.23	651.78	667.57	674.19	707.93	734.06	739.12	758.79	785.50	800.14	807.25	813.69	835.39	849.29
1982–1984 dollars	322.13	321.27	321.44	316.30	321.61	330.86	331.29	326.71	330.88	337.46	345.17	344.87	340.38	340.77	340.78
Utilities															
Current dollars	1 095.91	1 135.57	1 182.65	1 230.65	1 239.34	1 262.89	1 296.92	1 298.23	1 344.70	1 388.91	1 444.03	1 502.09	1 540.27	1 569.38	1 566.66
1982–1984 dollars	573.77	576.14	583.26	583.10	591.20	590.23	585.32	573.86	586.38	596.69	622.94	641.71	644.33	640.18	628.62
Information															
Current dollars	805.11	850.64	874.45	908.78	931.08	939.85	964.85	973.52	1 003.65	1 030.17	1 038.10	1 068.23	1 100.03	1 139.52	1 196.36
1982–1984 dollars	421.52	431.58	431.26	430.59	444.15	439.25	435.45	430.33	437.66	442.57	447.82	456.36	460.17	464.83	480.04
Financial activities															
Current dollars	646.51	673.66	706.52	729.64	754.90	780.25	798.68	839.84	875.04	908.15	939.46	962.95	982.09	997.26	1 020.28
1982–1984 dollars	338.49	341.79	348.44	345.71	360.11	364.66	360.46	371.23	381.57	390.15	405.27	411.38	410.83	406.80	409.39
Professional and business services															
Current dollars	619.65	662.80	701.42	738.31	776.30	799.43	814.74	823.37	839.86	865.25	879.63	899.79	922.51	949.18	984.07
1982–1984 dollars	324.42	336.28	345.92	349.82	370.32	373.62	367.70	363.95	366.23	371.72	379.46	384.40	385.91	387.19	394.86
Education and health services															
Current dollars	541.40	561.02	585.44	607.82	622.30	639.37	663.04	674.48	683.24	692.56	709.25	723.91	741.55	761.86	784.18
1982–1984 dollars	283.46	284.64	288.73	287.99	296.86	298.82	299.24	298.14	297.94	297.53	305.96	309.26	310.21	310.78	314.65
Leisure and hospitality															
Current dollars	241.36	250.34	265.54	273.39	275.95	280.87	283.82	290.54	294.31	303.81	311.32	319.67	332.54	345.21	358.10
1982–1984 dollars	126.37	127.01	130.96	129.54	131.64	131.27	128.09	128.43	128.34	130.52	134.30	136.57	139.11	140.82	143.69
Other services															
Current dollars	443.40	456.50	477.06	495.57	506.26	523.70	532.63	539.46	553.77	568.92	583.54	595.68	617.91	640.70	660.02
1982–1984 dollars	232.15	231.61	235.27	234.81	241.50	244.76	240.38	238.46	241.48	244.41	251.73	254.48	258.48	261.35	264.83

Table 2-17. Average Weekly Earnings of All Employees on Total Private Payrolls, by State, NAICS Basis, 2007–2019

(Dollars.)

State	2007	2008	2009	2010	2011	2012	2013	2014	2015	2016	2017	2018	2019
UNITED STATES	719.74	738.96	749.74	769.57	790.74	809.46	824.91	844.80	864.07	881.09	906.19	936.37	963.09
Alabama	708.94	704.16	684.52	696.74	708.93	727.56	731.75	740.53	758.28	785.69	800.25	828.49	852.19
Alaska	876.85	882.85	868.00	843.67	884.09	905.53	943.92	939.39	967.78	970.77	992.63	1 010.18	1 021.50
Arizona	698.37	720.01	766.64	780.03	789.60	791.35	793.94	786.95	806.32	825.59	879.83	894.95	919.76
Arkansas	571.08	605.79	621.76	630.99	642.60	648.09	672.17	681.60	673.10	691.78	718.59	738.86	777.35
California	851.81	845.42	861.22	896.24	925.70	925.36	929.14	945.66	973.30	996.57	1 036.73	1 071.56	1 115.94
Colorado	807.24	827.89	815.65	816.00	826.28	861.35	892.27	907.01	912.90	906.85	924.60	974.60	1 011.32
Connecticut	912.04	939.37	917.73	935.06	957.00	956.76	939.46	946.18	976.19	1 022.45	1 050.09	1 086.50	1 116.08
Delaware	753.91	768.27	729.21	735.80	738.79	726.33	718.90	713.93	751.32	810.08	862.64	864.60	889.02
District of Columbia	1 217.50	1 158.85	1 135.59	1 203.14	1 258.12	1 318.87	1 379.16	1 409.99	1 364.55	1 367.75	1 443.79	1 517.12	1 613.12
Florida	728.18	739.20	756.35	761.12	746.81	741.57	755.08	763.34	776.21	792.54	824.57	863.39	880.14
Georgia	727.66	733.18	729.37	748.48	757.50	761.25	790.94	821.57	833.98	842.86	879.65	920.31	926.38
Hawaii	674.49	678.41	686.73	710.78	740.81	770.55	788.50	818.16	820.85	831.89	866.89	913.63	942.09
Idaho	566.64	594.27	647.14	704.84	704.78	705.60	691.46	710.62	732.80	733.01	754.75	775.43	781.84
Illinois	789.14	777.58	793.26	796.36	815.87	847.03	858.71	879.75	897.35	905.70	913.54	949.42	979.54
Indiana	707.52	710.50	711.03	722.01	722.40	741.89	763.97	788.74	797.47	816.14	858.20	874.34	897.86
Iowa	615.94	620.23	666.33	694.96	687.48	715.50	741.06	764.48	782.49	798.33	798.77	822.85	848.58
Kansas	681.16	698.16	687.80	684.39	705.20	733.95	743.21	762.11	771.55	767.35	791.12	824.22	874.79
Kentucky	652.46	654.13	666.23	684.82	693.00	696.08	699.21	716.50	744.12	746.23	765.88	773.85	801.33
Louisiana	670.89	701.53	702.51	713.58	748.87	773.59	786.88	802.96	796.98	795.02	816.15	847.99	876.04
Maine	640.91	650.33	638.03	657.41	678.30	714.74	714.34	725.22	749.46	754.28	789.48	816.01	842.30
Maryland	836.59	852.23	876.65	892.40	887.52	881.96	910.91	938.77	937.42	948.66	979.61	1 035.69	1 039.00
Massachusetts	873.68	886.70	899.81	912.24	915.22	928.62	956.38	982.02	1 017.73	1 039.51	1 064.97	1 096.86	1 126.48
Michigan	752.10	739.06	728.94	750.16	764.37	768.13	784.55	811.84	827.31	825.60	845.94	884.16	910.67
Minnesota	781.79	778.21	763.17	787.05	817.18	838.32	864.07	876.86	886.04	921.74	969.12	988.04	1 021.45
Mississippi	587.62	601.28	632.60	648.00	652.68	670.35	689.41	689.37	684.60	699.83	717.20	703.02	750.64
Missouri	680.78	709.67	709.87	718.68	721.41	742.86	747.51	747.61	744.78	748.49	798.31	830.71	852.77
Montana	633.68	595.61	619.63	658.19	680.04	683.85	680.46	695.36	708.61	720.29	753.39	791.58	813.62
Nebraska	667.32	666.92	680.40	712.35	710.64	711.96	715.12	728.04	755.66	777.06	823.88	835.54	863.86
Nevada	732.57	730.75	700.25	659.99	665.64	674.22	677.04	699.73	737.52	750.89	767.93	795.89	845.94
New Hampshire	734.60	743.25	742.29	760.97	763.93	785.13	814.39	812.62	836.98	869.34	891.57	888.11	901.80
New Jersey	844.56	850.75	870.91	877.11	868.86	888.72	899.14	902.83	938.96	955.74	990.56	1 020.87	1 038.31
New Mexico	642.52	663.04	664.09	684.95	691.47	690.08	699.21	705.18	694.62	688.04	718.70	746.98	780.98
New York	861.71	869.21	866.43	883.77	902.97	924.12	939.98	951.35	975.13	980.55	1 004.00	1 036.96	1 062.93
North Carolina	669.90	683.26	696.28	703.14	717.21	749.00	747.62	758.89	771.58	805.99	829.38	862.50	875.48
North Dakota	605.22	607.50	614.72	658.19	731.45	795.55	840.52	877.51	885.22	880.30	911.41	941.25	972.08
Ohio	687.48	681.73	658.35	677.37	710.06	750.54	757.36	760.09	780.33	802.96	824.23	850.98	863.75
Oklahoma	608.99	619.12	634.96	683.88	722.78	742.31	745.17	758.21	759.34	771.05	811.89	843.36	872.51
Oregon	704.86	707.43	708.16	724.42	735.15	751.37	758.92	776.65	800.02	842.95	875.01	894.10	923.78
Pennsylvania	678.70	690.87	684.75	706.63	732.31	751.32	780.22	799.70	823.48	834.18	848.38	880.65	894.67
Rhode Island	742.70	767.25	763.43	768.51	783.09	827.50	836.32	828.30	825.51	849.87	887.31	921.74	923.01
South Carolina	675.36	669.28	665.55	692.17	716.18	705.16	716.15	726.23	743.27	762.80	791.99	829.36	852.84
South Dakota	543.51	543.84	597.40	626.99	645.80	673.87	676.89	693.85	713.32	726.58	739.72	762.29	787.84
Tennessee	669.15	683.23	687.46	703.88	711.04	712.96	716.24	732.83	734.62	767.87	797.56	826.94	851.49
Texas	769.06	773.19	753.28	766.82	808.50	808.08	832.10	871.08	880.48	880.32	912.58	937.94	946.54
Utah	747.21	730.06	804.78	863.01	808.85	782.85	805.70	834.24	847.03	852.58	883.82	894.14	935.86
Vermont	696.66	734.44	764.18	786.94	776.11	768.02	769.63	773.88	801.20	812.96	818.41	848.03	870.91
Virginia	790.59	780.85	781.27	833.32	872.96	874.30	870.44	881.83	917.51	940.90	959.09	985.13	1 004.99
Washington	851.14	872.27	902.43	918.65	940.13	942.54	950.11	972.65	1 018.24	1 048.73	1 091.33	1 139.00	1 172.66
West Virginia	604.34	627.63	626.87	654.85	657.40	676.89	706.88	718.94	723.84	736.40	772.48	816.50	843.36
Wisconsin	673.13	682.44	680.39	700.61	725.42	749.73	774.19	785.51	790.60	805.01	836.21	871.25	874.50
Wyoming	725.45	764.09	747.28	769.34	799.62	817.48	822.47	824.85	811.16	770.90	816.01	886.11	935.57

NOTES AND DEFINITIONS

QUARTERLY CENSUS OF EMPLOYMENT AND WAGES

The Quarterly Census of Employment and Wages (QCEW), often referred to as the ES-202 program, is a cooperative endeavor of the Bureau of Labor Statistics (BLS) and the State Employment Security Agencies (SESAs). Using quarterly data submitted by the agencies, BLS summarizes the employment and wage data for workers covered by state unemployment insurance laws and civilian workers covered by the Unemployment Compensation for Federal Employees (UCFE) program.

Since the introduction of 2001 data, the QCEW data have been coded according to the North American Classification System, either NAICS 2002, which was used for the data up through 2006; NAICS 2007, which was used for data from 2007 through 2010; or NAICS 2012 which was introduced with the release of first quarter data in 2011. As a result of the revision, approximately 8 percent of establishments, 11 percent of employment, and 6 percent of total wages were reclassified into different industries within private industry.

NAICS is the statistical classification standard underlying all establishment-based federal economic statistics classified by industry. Before 2001, QCEW data were coded according to the Standard Industrial Classification (SIC) system. Due to the differences in the classification systems, data coded according to NAICS are often not directly comparable to SIC coded data.

The QCEW data series is the most complete universe of employment and wage information by industry, county, and state. It includes 98 percent of all wage and salary civilian employment. These data serve as the basic source of benchmark information for employment by industry in the Current Employment Statistics (CES) survey, which is described in the first section of notes in this chapter. Therefore, the entire employment series is not presented here. The wage series is presented because the CES only provides earnings only for production and nonsupervisory employees. The QCEW is more comprehensive. BLS aggregates the data by industry and ownership; these aggregations are available at the national, state, county, and metropolitan statistical area (MSA) levels.

Collection and Coverage

Employment data under the QCEW program represent the number of covered workers who worked during, or received pay for, the pay period including the 12th of the month. Excluded are members of the armed forces, the self-employed, proprietors, domestic workers, unpaid family workers, and railroad workers covered by the railroad unemployment insurance system. Wages represent total compensation paid during the calendar quarter, regardless of when services were performed. Included in wages are pay for vacation and other paid leave, bonuses, stock options, tips, the cash value of meals and lodging, and in some states, contributions to deferred compensation plans (such as 401(k) plans). The QCEW program does provide partial information on agricultural industries and employees in private households.

Data from the QCEW program serve as an important input to many BLS programs. The QCEW data are used as the benchmark source for employment by the Current Employment Statistics program and the Occupational employment statistics program. The UI administrative records collected under the QCEW program serve as a sampling frame for BLS establishment surveys.

In addition, data from the QCEW program serve as an input to other federal and state programs. The Bureau of Economic Analysis (BEA) of the Department of Commerce uses QCEW data as the base for developing the wage and salary component of personal income. The Employment and Training Administration (ETA) of the Department of Labor and the SESAs use QCEW data to administer the employment security program. The QCEW data accurately reflect the extent of coverage of the state UI laws and are used to measure UI revenues; national, state and local area employment; and total and UI taxable wage trends.

Sources of Additional Information

Additional information is available on the BLS Web site at <http://www.bls.gov/cew>.

Table 2-18. Employment and Average Annual Pay for Covered Workers,[1] by Industry, NAICS Basis, 2014–2019

(Number, dollars.)

Industry	2014		2015		2016	
	Employment	Average annual pay	Employment	Average annual pay	Employment	Average annual pay
Total Private	115 568 686	51 296	118 307 717	52 876	120 504 622	53 515
Natural resources and mining	2 073 041	59 660	2 001 103	58 461	1 872 879	56 115
Agriculture, forestry, fishing, and hunting	1 231 162	30 614	1 249 192	31 977	1 259 490	33 287
Construction	6 108 673	55 037	6 423 866	57 009	6 686 142	58 647
Manufacturing	12 156 537	62 976	12 291 676	64 305	12 296 697	64 870
Wholesale trade	5 815 992	71 043	5 874 282	73 363	5 859 605	73 710
Retail trade	15 343 711	28 742	15 642 116	29 742	15 824 396	30 299
Transportation and warehousing	4 391 274	48 708	4 600 012	49 931	4 765 869	50 459
Utilities	548 993	98 123	553 685	101 445	553 007	102 868
Information	2 732 191	90 823	2 754 109	95 098	2 796 947	98 458
Financial activities	7 674 037	85 267	7 828 679	87 915	7 953 761	88 841
Professional and business services	19 074 275	66 668	19 607 372	69 270	20 024 917	69 992
Education and health services	20 573 137	45 950	21 080 792	47 383	21 654 265	48 058
Leisure and hospitality	14 626 556	20 995	15 100 935	21 807	15 556 625	22 445
Other services	4 235 390	33 936	4 308 880	35 116	4 387 613	35 921
Total Government	21 044 923	51 733	21 183 982	53 309	21 365 445	54 221
Federal	2 729 603	75 797	2 756 434	77 900	2 792 987	78 379
State	4 545 441	54 179	4 566 622	55 878	4 569 606	57 168
Local	13 769 879	46 155	13 860 926	47 573	14 002 852	48 440

Industry	2017		2018		2019	
	Employment	Average annual pay	Employment	Average annual pay	Employment	Average annual pay
Total Private	122 386 565	55 338	124 551 838	57 198	126 358 743	59 202
Natural resources and mining	1 885 246	56 859	1 937 219	59 628	1 938 254	61 862
Agriculture, forestry, fishing, and hunting	1 261 312	34 464	1 263 676	35 841	1 263 160	37 212
Construction	6 919 107	60 735	7 225 870	62 727	7 451 476	64 826
Manufacturing	12 406 757	66 840	12 647 900	68 525	12 776 157	69 920
Wholesale trade	5 898 637	75 904	5 855 477	77 870	5 883 948	80 193
Retail trade	15 854 454	31 217	15 791 102	32 362	15 602 881	33 611
Transportation and warehousing	4 947 369	51 726	5 208 134	53 197	5 491 748	54 365
Utilities	551 935	107 194	551 920	109 957	548 712	113 354
Information	2 793 429	105 722	2 815 363	113 781	2 849 185	119 605
Financial activities	8 088 405	92 923	8 187 308	95 561	8 319 844	98 516
Professional and business services	20 339 284	72 525	20 872 036	75 169	21 233 982	78 385
Education and health services	22 146 912	49 201	22 632 823	50 444	23 121 291	51 902
Leisure and hospitality	15 900 633	23 188	16 196 857	24 087	16 457 253	25 081
Other services	4 434 678	37 320	4 501 913	38 464	4 553 161	39 922
Total Government	21 473 291	55 686	21 579 916	57 658	21 746 349	59 249
Federal	2 802 583	80 432	2 795 195	83 657	2 824 154	84 310
State	4 628 557	58 802	4 624 977	60 751	4 666 127	62 830
Local	14 042 151	49 720	14 159 744	51 515	14 256 068	53 112

[1]Includes workers covered by unemployment insurance (UI) and Unemployment Compensation for Federal Employees (UCFE) programs.

Table 2-19. Employment and Average Annual Pay for Covered Workers,[1] by State and Selected Territory, 2010–2019

(Number, dollars.)

State	2010 Employment	2010 Average annual pay	2011 Employment	2011 Average annual pay	2012 Employment	2012 Average annual pay	2013 Employment	2013 Average annual pay	2014 Employment	2014 Average annual pay
UNITED STATES	127 820 442	46 751	129 411 095	48 043	131 696 378	49 289	133 968 434	49 808	136 613 609	51 364
Alabama	1 813 155	40 289	1 813 497	41 186	1 828 248	41 990	1 845 086	42 276	1 863 561	43 287
Alaska	316 691	48 230	322 084	49 383	327 378	50 614	328 716	51 566	330 105	53 418
Arizona	2 356 789	43 299	2 378 248	44 581	2 431 788	45 593	2 488 009	45 921	2 539 253	46 919
Arkansas	1 134 071	36 254	1 139 682	37 280	1 146 811	38 226	1 146 274	38 941	1 157 630	39 975
California	14 414 461	53 285	14 567 128	55 013	14 959 808	56 784	15 378 962	57 111	15 809 082	59 042
Colorado	2 176 986	47 868	2 213 059	49 082	2 266 503	50 563	2 335 803	50 873	2 417 735	52 724
Connecticut	1 595 713	59 465	1 612 292	61 145	1 627 748	62 085	1 640 333	62 357	1 653 573	63 919
Delaware	399 078	48 669	402 959	50 499	405 646	51 734	413 825	52 040	423 598	53 212
District of Columbia	693 274	80 200	707 359	81 529	714 930	82 783	724 270	83 054	729 349	85 877
Florida	7 109 630	41 581	7 195 232	42 313	7 341 002	43 211	7 518 448	43 649	7 755 371	44 803
Georgia	3 753 934	43 899	3 792 209	45 090	3 841 767	46 267	3 918 085	46 760	4 032 488	48 138
Hawaii	586 772	41 709	593 668	42 473	605 240	43 385	618 195	43 845	626 146	45 210
Idaho	605 571	34 900	607 504	35 626	614 463	36 152	630 328	36 836	646 305	37 982
Illinois	5 502 322	49 497	5 566 648	50 840	5 636 918	52 194	5 687 541	52 590	5 762 156	54 106
Indiana	2 709 831	39 256	2 755 826	40 248	2 812 347	41 240	2 849 311	41 660	2 890 758	42 553
Iowa	1 436 340	38 146	1 452 769	39 204	1 475 884	40 343	1 496 426	41 107	1 515 822	42 538
Kansas	1 297 779	38 936	1 303 799	39 989	1 320 285	41 118	1 336 948	41 548	1 357 090	42 716
Kentucky	1 712 178	38 720	1 734 503	39 646	1 761 043	40 451	1 779 777	40 793	1 807 068	41 941
Louisiana	1 832 357	41 461	1 848 399	42 375	1 871 037	43 300	1 893 823	44 008	1 923 745	45 336
Maine	577 790	37 338	579 838	38 020	583 196	38 606	586 525	39 279	590 377	40 442
Maryland	2 453 197	51 739	2 478 505	53 008	2 511 669	54 035	2 531 656	54 052	2 552 623	55 389
Massachusetts	3 149 169	57 770	3 189 753	59 671	3 242 273	60 898	3 295 647	61 790	3 360 035	64 103
Michigan	3 770 225	44 439	3 854 837	45 828	3 935 694	46 720	4 018 602	47 131	4 090 009	48 487
Minnesota	2 558 310	46 787	2 602 988	47 858	2 644 408	49 349	2 691 832	50 116	2 730 301	51 602
Mississippi	1 074 617	34 343	1 076 488	34 976	1 085 748	35 875	1 093 581	36 455	1 102 603	37 111
Missouri	2 573 703	40 679	2 585 009	41 461	2 607 420	42 695	2 637 273	43 066	2 667 996	44 258
Montana	419 231	34 595	422 726	35 791	430 315	37 096	436 867	37 575	440 198	38 878
Nebraska	896 936	37 324	901 584	38 269	920 295	39 268	932 768	39 965	946 110	41 185
Nevada	1 108 238	42 512	1 115 062	43 102	1 132 140	43 667	1 160 115	44 119	1 202 475	44 727
New Hampshire	600 697	45 957	605 853	47 281	612 419	48 272	618 781	48 963	626 566	51 165
New Jersey	3 735 703	56 382	3 734 660	57 546	3 768 935	58 644	3 812 940	59 467	3 841 854	60 597
New Mexico	781 694	39 264	781 226	40 032	785 455	40 698	791 804	40 809	798 912	41 925
New York	8 340 732	60 291	8 444 791	61 792	8 563 125	62 669	8 685 758	63 089	8 846 774	65 880
North Carolina	3 788 581	41 119	3 838 300	42 121	3 907 085	43 110	3 974 937	43 795	4 057 439	44 973
North Dakota	358 635	38 128	379 432	41 778	411 709	45 909	427 108	47 779	444 652	50 855
Ohio	4 908 571	41 788	4 968 724	42 972	5 048 166	44 244	5 110 011	44 671	5 183 462	46 000
Oklahoma	1 485 400	38 237	1 507 558	40 108	1 540 292	41 633	1 560 799	42 457	1 582 712	43 773
Oregon	1 598 173	41 675	1 616 634	43 090	1 642 434	44 258	1 678 726	45 019	1 725 906	46 529
Pennsylvania	5 472 171	45 733	5 535 283	47 035	5 578 414	48 397	5 596 841	49 077	5 644 443	50 567
Rhode Island	447 408	44 645	448 570	45 705	450 711	46 716	456 112	47 732	463 303	49 297
South Carolina	1 758 204	37 553	1 780 690	38 427	1 810 150	39 286	1 846 621	39 792	1 895 420	40 797
South Dakota	389 198	34 331	393 744	35 413	400 475	36 534	404 652	37 225	410 929	38 690
Tennessee	2 558 438	41 572	2 602 604	42 454	2 653 392	43 961	2 694 288	44 091	2 750 032	45 202
Texas	10 182 150	46 952	10 422 295	48 735	10 727 642	50 579	11 031 907	51 201	11 379 184	53 218
Utah	1 150 737	39 389	1 176 530	40 279	1 215 983	41 301	1 254 582	41 792	1 291 859	42 942
Vermont	293 058	39 434	295 512	40 293	299 519	40 967	301 586	42 043	304 472	43 025
Virginia	3 536 676	49 651	3 578 848	50 657	3 619 176	51 646	3 640 209	51 918	3 654 831	52 929
Washington	2 808 698	48 516	2 844 622	50 256	2 894 703	51 962	2 960 123	53 050	3 043 562	55 016
West Virginia	692 448	37 675	701 905	39 092	710 590	39 727	703 916	40 201	700 846	41 201
Wisconsin	2 633 572	39 966	2 664 920	41 003	2 695 404	41 966	2 721 960	42 777	2 758 496	43 829
Wyoming	271 151	41 963	274 743	43 394	278 595	44 580	279 748	44 972	284 394	46 492

[1]Includes workers covered by the unemployment insurance (UI) and Unemployment Compensation for Federal Employees (UCFE) programs.

Table 2-19. Employment and Average Annual Pay for Covered Workers,[1] by State and Selected Territory, 2010–2019—*Continued*

(Number, dollars.)

State	2015 Employment	2015 Average annual pay	2016 Employment	2016 Average annual pay	2017 Employment	2017 Average annual pay	2018 Employment	2018 Average annual pay	2019 Employment	2019 Average annual pay
UNITED STATES	139 491 699	52 942	141 870 066	53 621	143 859 855	55 390	146 131 754	57 266	148 105 092	59 209
Alabama	1 890 340	44 273	1 915 306	44 832	1 936 819	45 997	1 961 625	47 414	1 989 555	48 839
Alaska	331 681	54 755	326 295	53 605	322 136	53 714	321 078	55 668	323 695	57 518
Arizona	2 609 770	47 933	2 680 065	48 523	2 747 638	50 146	2 826 095	51 865	2 908 826	53 807
Arkansas	1 177 884	40 895	1 191 763	41 571	1 200 542	42 959	1 211 021	43 950	1 218 106	45 448
California	16 295 204	61 698	16 718 647	62 964	17 019 702	65 857	17 355 855	68 478	17 631 489	71 351
Colorado	2 494 450	54 182	2 552 503	54 664	2 609 770	56 914	2 674 030	58 941	2 736 105	61 820
Connecticut	1 662 825	65 530	1 666 554	65 870	1 669 616	66 636	1 673 925	67 742	1 670 704	69 771
Delaware	433 748	53 991	438 238	53 765	441 873	55 828	447 075	56 814	452 776	58 479
District of Columbia	743 596	88 159	756 646	89 481	763 847	92 544	771 750	95 909	776 041	98 051
Florida	8 039 635	46 260	8 309 351	47 035	8 494 623	48 455	8 700 654	50 094	8 884 066	51 741
Georgia	4 151 011	49 551	4 262 937	50 676	4 346 453	52 189	4 430 136	53 496	4 513 028	55 263
Hawaii	637 854	46 919	647 545	48 178	654 185	49 671	658 341	50 977	659 045	52 686
Idaho	664 792	38 857	687 919	39 637	706 820	41 345	730 716	42 882	752 351	44 264
Illinois	5 848 451	55 989	5 895 633	56 447	5 934 549	57 971	5 973 316	59 941	5 995 905	61 572
Indiana	2 941 991	43 903	2 987 091	44 590	3 018 177	46 192	3 051 879	47 590	3 077 767	48 793
Iowa	1 530 234	44 095	1 539 752	44 910	1 540 435	46 074	1 549 958	47 511	1 553 350	48 672
Kansas	1 367 329	43 878	1 370 665	44 142	1 371 633	45 116	1 383 119	46 607	1 393 184	48 060
Kentucky	1 835 550	43 365	1 861 063	44 099	1 874 455	45 166	1 884 653	46 302	1 897 896	47 723
Louisiana	1 930 688	45 928	1 908 397	45 622	1 907 721	46 500	1 921 498	48 116	1 923 825	49 286
Maine	595 889	41 791	603 785	42 596	609 271	43 911	615 271	45 370	621 691	47 188
Maryland	2 591 189	57 176	2 627 172	58 106	2 653 569	59 603	2 679 064	61 151	2 698 113	62 976
Massachusetts	3 428 020	66 692	3 494 553	67 432	3 543 383	69 929	3 586 034	72 606	3 636 617	75 404
Michigan	4 161 641	50 063	4 242 537	50 943	4 294 711	52 487	4 340 045	53 803	4 358 167	54 972
Minnesota	2 776 684	53 527	2 815 248	54 297	2 856 105	56 140	2 882 944	58 007	2 902 225	59 630
Mississippi	1 114 379	37 642	1 124 854	38 144	1 128 498	38 788	1 130 786	39 762	1 135 598	40 687
Missouri	2 715 579	45 565	2 755 477	46 122	2 781 242	47 364	2 794 483	49 053	2 812 888	50 536
Montana	448 688	40 056	454 819	40 716	459 431	42 045	464 818	43 407	470 525	44 883
Nebraska	959 176	42 854	968 601	43 597	972 764	44 851	978 066	46 262	982 504	47 854
Nevada	1 244 635	45 739	1 283 642	47 114	1 326 151	48 126	1 371 030	50 041	1 408 753	51 422
New Hampshire	636 806	52 553	647 347	53 563	653 487	55 138	658 836	56 782	665 320	58 671
New Jersey	3 889 975	62 365	3 953 972	62 777	4 006 799	64 042	4 043 517	65 727	4 083 014	67 364
New Mexico	806 762	42 555	807 387	42 599	810 516	43 535	822 351	45 167	836 674	47 043
New York	9 014 385	67 521	9 154 025	67 940	9 276 868	70 682	9 432 830	72 900	9 542 899	75 365
North Carolina	4 161 654	46 530	4 259 276	47 269	4 330 606	48 920	4 410 791	50 756	4 498 572	52 379
North Dakota	437 072	50 696	417 119	48 873	414 038	50 313	417 578	52 356	422 837	54 102
Ohio	5 257 971	47 146	5 319 679	47 700	5 364 626	49 153	5 405 891	50 573	5 439 352	52 125
Oklahoma	1 594 011	44 306	1 575 978	43 906	1 581 198	45 121	1 605 887	46 727	1 622 058	48 023
Oregon	1 787 398	48 328	1 840 874	49 474	1 883 407	51 118	1 920 804	53 053	1 953 467	55 023
Pennsylvania	5 691 613	52 187	5 737 759	52 460	5 799 123	54 000	5 867 783	55 628	5 925 588	57 497
Rhode Island	469 981	50 651	473 406	51 453	477 362	52 840	481 569	53 736	485 638	54 918
South Carolina	1 949 881	42 002	1 996 297	42 881	2 035 341	44 177	2 091 683	44 729	2 129 271	46 383
South Dakota	416 020	40 181	420 460	41 178	422 489	42 432	426 927	43 694	430 117	45 150
Tennessee	2 820 198	46 742	2 887 754	47 403	2 930 932	48 820	2 976 889	50 450	3 032 893	51 702
Texas	11 655 919	54 281	11 805 698	54 333	12 014 802	55 795	12 302 358	57 747	12 590 406	59 794
Utah	1 340 591	44 318	1 388 878	45 255	1 430 588	46 575	1 478 493	48 513	1 520 688	50 766
Vermont	307 058	44 234	308 044	45 030	309 442	46 186	310 334	47 640	310 611	49 337
Virginia	3 735 713	54 276	3 789 744	54 836	3 838 368	56 503	3 893 254	58 239	3 938 841	60 200
Washington	3 122 749	56 661	3 215 014	59 024	3 290 209	62 041	3 372 533	66 119	3 439 158	69 593
West Virginia	696 195	41 727	684 322	41 665	683 807	43 419	693 478	46 120	688 761	46 618
Wisconsin	2 794 170	45 365	2 828 166	46 008	2 850 145	47 238	2 876 534	48 872	2 887 018	50 413
Wyoming	282 667	46 306	271 813	44 974	269 586	46 270	272 171	48 059	277 114	49 880

[1]Includes workers covered by the unemployment insurance (UI) and Unemployment Compensation for Federal Employees (UCFE) programs.

BUSINESS EMPLOYMENT DYNAMICS

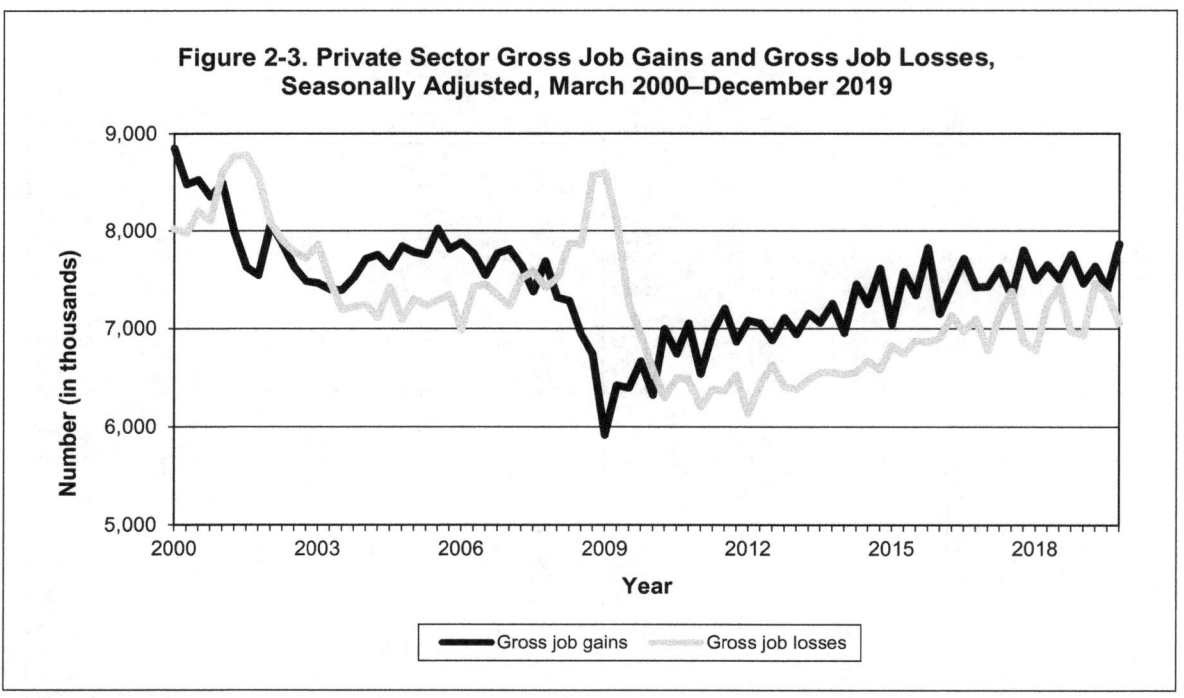

Figure 2-3. Private Sector Gross Job Gains and Gross Job Losses, Seasonally Adjusted, March 2000–December 2019

The change in the number of jobs is the net result of the gross increase in the number of jobs from expanding and opening establishments and the gross decrease in jobs from contracting and closing establishments. The net gain of over 800,000 jobs in the fourth quarter of 2019 resulted from 7.864 million gross job gains and 7.051 million gross job losses. There was a net gain of jobs in 29 consecutive quarters from June 2010 to June 2017. In September 2017, there was a net loss of 55,000 jobs. There has been a net gain in the following nine quarters between December 2017 and December 2019. (See Table 2-20.)

OTHER HIGHLIGHTS

• Of the nearly 7.0 million jobs that were lost in the fourth quarter of 2019, 81.2 percent resulted from contracting establishments while 18.8 percent were the result of establishments closing. (See Table 2-20.)

• In 2020, most sectors experienced a decrease in employment due to the global pandemic. The service-providing industry experienced a net employment change of -764,000 jobs while the goods-producing industries experienced a net loss of 9,000 jobs. The leisure and hospitality industry was particularly impacted and experienced a net decline of 544,000 jobs. (See Table 2-22.)

• Construction, information, retail trade, and utilities were the only sectors which experienced a net increase in employment in the first quarter of 2020. Gross job gains were highest in construction (57,000) followed by retail trade (32,000), information (13,000) and utilities (1,000). (See Table 2-22.)

• Job losses exceeded job gains in 46 states and the District of Columbia by the end of the first quarter 2020 as much of the nation was under stay-at-home orders due to COVID-19. California experienced the highest net loss in jobs at nearly 94,000 followed by New York at 72,000 and Illinois at nearly at 56,000. Only Washington, Utah, North Carolina, and Idaho experienced a net increase in job gains by the end of March 2020. (See Table 2-23.)

NOTES AND DEFINITIONS

BUSINESS EMPLOYMENT DYNAMICS (BED)

The Business Employment Dynamics (BED) data are a set of statistics generated from the federal-state cooperative program known as the Quarterly Census of Employment and Wages (QCEW), or the ES-202 program. These quarterly data series consist of gross job gains and gross job losses statistics from 1992 forward.

The Bureau of Labor Statistics (BLS) compiles the BED data from existing quarterly state unemployment insurance (UI) records. Most employers in the United States are required to file quarterly reports on the employment and wages of workers covered by UI laws and to pay quarterly UI taxes. The quarterly UI reports are sent by the State Workforce Agencies (SWAs) to BLS. These reports form the basis of the BLS establishment universe-sampling frame.

In the BED program, the quarterly UI records are linked across quarters to provide a longitudinal history for each establishment. The linkage process allows the tracking of net employment changes at the establishment level, which in turn allows estimations of jobs gained at opening and expanding establishments and of jobs lost at closing and contracting establishments. BLS publishes three different establishment-based employment measures for every given quarter. Each of these measures—the Current Employment Statistics (CES) survey, the QCEW program, and the BED data each make use of the quarterly UI employment reports. However, each measure has somewhat different types of universal coverage, estimation procedures, and publication products. (See the notes and corresponding tables for CES and QCEW in earlier sections of this chapter.)

Concepts and Definitions

The BED data measure the net change in employment at the establishment level. These changes can come about in four different ways. A net increase in employment can come from either opening establishments or expanding establishments. A net decrease in employment can come from either closing establishments or contracting establishments.

Gross job gains include the sum of all jobs added at either opening or expanding establishments.

Gross job losses include the sum of all jobs lost in either closing or contracting establishments. The net change in employment is the difference between gross job gains and gross job losses.

Openings consist of establishments with positive third-month employment for the first time in the current quarter, with no links to the prior quarter, or with positive third-month employment in the current quarter, following zero employment in the previous quarter.

Expansions include establishments with positive employment in the third month in both the previous and current quarters, with a net increase in employment over this period.

Closings consist of establishments with positive third-month employment in the previous quarter, with no employment or zero employment reported in the current quarter.

Contractions include establishments with positive employment in the third month in both the previous and current quarters, with a net decrease in employment over this period.

Sources of Additional Information

For additional information, see BLS news release 20-1996 "Business Employment Dynamics: First Quarter 2020."

Table 2-20. Private Sector Gross Job Gains and Job Losses, Seasonally Adjusted, March 2007–December 2019

(Thousands of jobs.)

Year and month	Net change[1]	Gross job gains			Gross job losses		
		Total	Expanding establishments	Opening establishments	Total	Contracting establishments	Closing establishments
2007							
March	584	7 815	6 331	1 484	7 231	5 894	1 337
June	132	7 647	6 205	1 442	7 515	6 084	1 431
September	-209	7 376	5 870	1 506	7 585	6 190	1 395
December	268	7 687	6 181	1 506	7 419	6 040	1 379
2008							
March	-199	7 320	5 860	1 460	7 519	6 111	1 408
June	-593	7 281	5 833	1 448	7 874	6 363	1 511
September	-913	6 944	5 535	1 409	7 857	6 436	1 421
December	-1 838	6 738	5 345	1 393	8 576	7 056	1 520
2009							
March	-2 680	5 918	4 675	1 243	8 598	7 142	1 456
June	-1 667	6 425	5 080	1 345	8 092	6 674	1 418
September	-849	6 399	5 139	1 260	7 248	5 854	1 394
December	-264	6 665	5 308	1 357	6 929	5 605	1 324
2010							
March	-247	6 325	5 108	1 217	6 572	5 324	1 248
June	698	6 995	5 674	1 321	6 297	5 090	1 207
September	237	6 741	5 438	1 303	6 504	5 231	1 273
December	566	7 052	5 639	1 413	6 486	5 219	1 267
2011							
March	334	6 540	5 322	1 218	6 206	5 025	1 181
June	582	6 966	5 625	1 341	6 384	5 115	1 269
September	841	7 205	5 810	1 395	6 364	5 172	1 192
December	335	6 865	5 503	1 362	6 530	5 273	1 257
2012							
March	948	7 080	5 746	1 334	6 132	5 005	1 127
June	616	7 051	5 724	1 327	6 435	5 266	1 169
September	252	6 881	5 571	1 310	6 629	5 430	1 199
December	695	7 110	5 753	1 357	6 415	5 225	1 190
2013							
March	558	6 941	5 705	1 236	6 383	5 201	1 182
June	674	7 152	5 830	1 322	6 478	5 271	1 207
September	507	7 058	5 719	1 339	6 551	5 408	1 143
December	700	7 255	5 926	1 329	6 555	5 353	1 202
2014							
March	419	6 953	5 687	1 266	6 534	5 380	1 154
June	895	7 454	6 114	1 340	6 559	5 342	1 217
September	577	7 247	5 918	1 329	6 670	5 487	1 183
December	1 038	7 617	6 248	1 369	6 579	5 346	1 233
2015							
March	216	7 040	5 727	1 313	6 824	5 622	1 202
June	838	7 580	6 236	1 344	6 742	5 550	1 192
September	466	7 340	5 977	1 363	6 874	5 665	1 209
December	968	7 827	6 367	1 460	6 859	5 594	1 265
2016							
March	243	7 149	5 864	1 285	6 906	5 702	1 204
June	310	7 446	6 074	1 372	7 136	5 829	1 307
September	750	7 717	6 253	1 464	6 967	5 722	1 245
December	329	7 423	6 012	1 411	7 094	5 795	1 299
2017							
March	654	7 428	6 091	1 337	6 774	5 591	1 183
June	480	7 621	6 252	1 369	7 141	5 873	1 268
September	-55	7 324	5 970	1 354	7 379	6 080	1 299
December	933	7 801	6 366	1 435	6 868	5 571	1 297
2018							
March	717	7 494	6 141	1 353	6 777	5 587	1 190
June	407	7 652	6 254	1 398	7 245	5 960	1 285
September	79	7 506	6 126	1 380	7 427	6 104	1 323
December	790	7 756	6 309	1 447	6 966	5 634	1 332
2019							
March	533	7 460	6 102	1 358	6 927	5 682	1 245
June	171	7 637	6 253	1 384	7 466	6 105	1 361
September	53	7 404	6 022	1 382	7 351	6 077	1 274
December	813	7 864	6 364	1 500	7 051	5 725	1 326

[1]Net change is the difference between total gross job gains and total gross job losses.

Table 2-21. Private Sector Gross Job Gains and Job Losses, as a Percent of Employment,[1] Seasonally Adjusted, March 2007–December 2019

(Percent.)

Year and month	Net change[2]	Gross job gains			Gross job losses		
		Total	Expanding establishments	Opening establishments	Total	Contracting establishments	Closing establishments
2007							
March	0.5	6.9	5.6	1.3	6.4	5.2	1.2
June	0.1	6.7	5.4	1.3	6.6	5.3	1.3
September	-0.2	6.4	5.1	1.3	6.6	5.4	1.2
December	0.2	6.7	5.4	1.3	6.5	5.3	1.2
2008							
March	-0.1	6.4	5.1	1.3	6.5	5.3	1.2
June	-0.5	6.4	5.1	1.3	6.9	5.6	1.3
September	-0.9	6.1	4.9	1.2	7.0	5.7	1.3
December	-1.7	6.0	4.8	1.2	7.7	6.3	1.4
2009							
March	-2.4	5.4	4.3	1.1	7.8	6.5	1.3
June	-1.5	6.0	4.7	1.3	7.5	6.2	1.3
September	-0.8	6.0	4.8	1.2	6.8	5.5	1.3
December	-0.3	6.3	5.0	1.3	6.6	5.3	1.3
2010							
March	-0.2	6.0	4.8	1.2	6.2	5.0	1.2
June	0.7	6.6	5.4	1.2	5.9	4.8	1.1
September	0.2	6.3	5.1	1.2	6.1	4.9	1.2
December	0.5	6.6	5.3	1.3	6.1	4.9	1.2
2011							
March	0.3	6.1	5.0	1.1	5.8	4.7	1.1
June	0.5	6.4	5.2	1.2	5.9	4.7	1.2
September	0.8	6.7	5.4	1.3	5.9	4.8	1.1
December	0.4	6.4	5.1	1.3	6.0	4.8	1.2
2012							
March	0.8	6.4	5.2	1.2	5.6	4.6	1.0
June	0.5	6.4	5.2	1.2	5.9	4.8	1.1
September	0.2	6.2	5.0	1.2	6.0	4.9	1.1
December	0.6	6.4	5.2	1.2	5.8	4.7	1.1
2013							
March	0.5	6.2	5.1	1.1	5.7	4.6	1.1
June	0.6	6.4	5.2	1.2	5.8	4.7	1.1
September	0.5	6.3	5.1	1.2	5.8	4.8	1.0
December	0.6	6.4	5.2	1.2	5.8	4.7	1.1
2014							
March	0.4	6.1	5.0	1.1	5.7	4.7	1.0
June	0.8	6.5	5.3	1.2	5.7	4.6	1.1
September	0.5	6.2	5.1	1.1	5.7	4.7	1.0
December	0.9	6.6	5.4	1.2	5.7	4.6	1.1
2015							
March	0.2	6.0	4.9	1.1	5.8	4.8	1.0
June	0.7	6.4	5.3	1.1	5.7	4.7	1.0
September	0.5	6.3	5.1	1.2	5.8	4.8	1.0
December	0.7	6.5	5.3	1.2	5.8	4.7	1.1
2016							
March	0.2	6.0	4.9	1.1	5.8	4.8	1.0
June	0.2	6.2	5.1	1.1	6.0	4.9	1.1
September	0.6	6.4	5.2	1.2	5.8	4.8	1.0
December	0.3	6.2	5.0	1.2	5.9	4.8	1.1
2017							
March	0.5	6.1	5.0	1.1	5.6	4.6	1.0
June	0.4	6.2	5.1	1.1	5.8	4.8	1.0
September	-0.1	6.0	4.9	1.1	6.1	5.0	1.1
December	0.8	6.4	5.2	1.2	5.6	4.5	1.1
2018							
March	0.6	6.1	5.0	1.1	5.5	4.5	1.0
June	0.3	6.1	5.0	1.1	5.8	4.8	1.0
September	0.0	6.0	4.9	1.1	6.0	4.9	1.1
December	0.7	6.3	5.1	1.2	5.6	4.5	1.1
2019							
March	0.5	6.0	4.9	1.1	5.5	4.5	1.0
June	0.2	6.1	5.0	1.1	5.9	4.8	1.1
September	0.1	5.9	4.8	1.1	5.8	4.8	1.0
December	0.7	6.2	5.0	1.2	5.5	4.5	1.0

[1] The rates measure gross job gains and job losses as a percentage of the average of the previous and current employment.
[2] Net change is the difference between total gross job gains and total gross job losses.

Table 2-22. Three-Month Private Sector Job Gains and Losses, by Industry, Seasonally Adjusted, March 2019–March 2020

(Thousands of jobs.)

Industry	Gross job gains and job losses (3 months ended)					Gross job gains and losses as a percent of employment (3 months ended)				
	March 2019	June 2019	September 2019	December 2019	March 2020	March 2019	June 2019	September 2019	December 2019	March 2020
TOTAL PRIVATE[1]										
Gross job gains	7 460	7 637	7 404	7 864	6 963	6.0	6.1	5.9	6.2	5.5
Gross job losses	6 927	7 466	7 351	7 051	7 736	5.5	5.9	5.8	5.5	6.1
Net employment change	533	171	53	813	-773	0.5	0.2	0.1	0.7	-0.6
Goods-Producing										
Gross job gains	1 359	1 372	1 254	1 319	1 286	6.1	6.2	5.7	5.9	5.7
Gross job losses	1 255	1 351	1 331	1 329	1 295	5.7	6.1	6.1	6.0	5.8
Net employment change	104	21	-77	-10	-9	0.4	0.1	-0.4	-0.1	-0.1
Natural Resources and Mining										
Gross job gains	244	266	228	234	239	12.5	13.7	11.9	12.2	12.4
Gross job losses	250	250	243	273	251	12.7	12.9	12.7	14.2	13.1
Net employment change	-6	16	-15	-39	-12	-0.2	0.8	-0.8	-2.0	-0.7
Construction										
Gross job gains	711	690	649	676	683	9.5	9.2	8.8	9.1	9.0
Gross job losses	623	673	647	649	626	8.4	9.0	8.7	8.7	8.3
Net employment change	88	17	2	27	57	1.1	0.2	0.1	0.4	0.7
Manufacturing										
Gross job gains	404	416	377	409	364	3.2	3.2	3.0	3.2	2.9
Gross job losses	382	428	441	407	418	3.0	3.3	3.4	3.2	3.3
Net employment change	22	-12	-64	2	-54	0.2	-0.1	-0.4	0.0	-0.4
Service-Providing[1]										
Gross job gains	6 101	6 265	6 150	6 545	5 677	5.9	6.0	5.9	6.2	5.5
Gross job losses	5 672	6 115	6 020	5 722	6 441	5.5	5.9	5.8	5.5	6.2
Net employment change	429	150	130	823	-764	0.4	0.1	0.1	0.7	-0.7
Wholesale Trade										
Gross job gains	264	270	256	267	250	4.5	4.6	4.3	4.6	4.3
Gross job losses	246	264	266	249	258	4.2	4.5	4.5	4.2	4.4
Net employment change	18	6	-10	18	-8	0.3	0.1	-0.2	0.4	-0.1
Retail Trade										
Gross job gains	914	876	858	891	906	5.8	5.6	5.5	5.7	5.8
Gross job losses	872	976	943	887	874	5.5	6.2	6.1	5.8	5.6
Net employment change	42	-100	-85	4	32	0.3	-0.6	-0.6	-0.1	0.2
Transportation and Warehousing										
Gross job gains	290	312	343	508	278	5.4	5.8	6.3	8.9	4.9
Gross job losses	348	269	255	254	416	6.4	5.0	4.7	4.4	7.2
Net employment change	-58	43	88	254	-138	-1.0	0.8	1.6	4.5	-2.3
Utilities										
Gross job gains	14	14	14	13	10	2.6	2.6	2.6	2.4	1.8
Gross job losses	13	14	14	12	9	2.4	2.6	2.6	2.2	1.7
Net employment change	1	0	0	1	1	0.2	0.0	0.0	0.2	0.1
Information										
Gross job gains	162	164	162	155	152	5.7	5.8	5.7	5.4	5.3
Gross job losses	133	163	154	161	139	4.8	5.7	5.4	5.6	4.9
Net employment change	29	1	8	-6	13	0.9	0.1	0.3	-0.2	0.4
Financial Activities										
Gross job gains	373	410	386	406	356	4.5	4.9	4.6	4.9	4.2
Gross job losses	351	364	364	362	363	4.2	4.4	4.4	4.3	4.3
Net employment change	22	46	22	44	-7	0.3	0.5	0.2	0.6	-0.1
Professional and Business Services										
Gross job gains	1 347	1 490	1 408	1 506	1 270	6.4	7.0	6.6	7.0	5.9
Gross job losses	1 333	1 370	1 375	1 378	1 377	6.3	6.4	6.4	6.5	6.5
Net employment change	14	120	33	128	-107	0.1	0.6	0.2	0.5	-0.6
Education and Health Services										
Gross job gains	1 036	1 020	1 052	1 034	976	4.5	4.4	4.6	4.4	4.2
Gross job losses	863	977	921	904	983	3.8	4.2	4.0	3.8	4.2
Net employment change	173	43	131	130	-7	0.7	0.2	0.6	0.6	0.0
Leisure and Hospitality										
Gross job gains	1 354	1 353	1 337	1 407	1 116	8.2	8.2	8.2	8.5	6.8
Gross job losses	1 215	1 407	1 409	1 218	1 660	7.4	8.6	8.6	7.4	10.1
Net employment change	139	-54	-72	189	-544	0.8	-0.4	-0.4	1.1	-3.3
Other Services										
Gross job gains	305	314	299	307	283	7.2	7.4	7.0	7.1	6.6
Gross job losses	279	293	300	279	336	6.5	6.9	7.0	6.5	7.9
Net employment change	26	21	-1	28	-53	0.7	0.5	0.0	0.6	-1.3

[1]Includes unclassified sector, not shown separately.

Table 2-23. Private Sector Gross Job Gains and Losses, by State and Selected Territory, Seasonally Adjusted, March 2019–March 2020

(Number.)

State	Gross job gains (3 months ended)					Gross job losses (3 months ended)				
	March 2019	June 2019	September 2019	December 2019	March 2020	March 2019	June 2019	September 2019	December 2019	March 2020
UNITED STATES	7 460 000	7 637 000	7 404 000	7 864 000	6 963 000	6 927 000	7 466 000	7 351 000	7 051 000	7 736 000
Alabama	98 440	94 193	94 423	101 210	88 038	89 875	96 296	94 743	89 724	96 125
Alaska	25 046	26 837	24 031	25 708	22 994	22 341	25 164	25 082	25 494	23 781
Arizona	142 509	140 914	158 912	161 684	142 660	136 506	138 413	122 446	131 921	151 494
Arkansas	54 288	51 536	56 712	66 058	52 888	52 811	58 717	59 055	49 413	56 439
California	964 053	991 200	957 511	1 033 526	922 323	913 878	972 002	910 802	902 580	1 016 052
Colorado	151 438	161 505	151 336	154 775	146 864	142 316	142 271	148 249	143 528	161 908
Connecticut	75 200	82 854	79 268	78 282	74 079	82 197	82 692	82 472	79 999	84 157
Delaware	25 137	23 284	24 058	25 783	23 973	21 563	25 651	24 066	24 376	25 771
District of Columbia	29 568	29 197	29 652	28 907	28 449	26 336	29 577	28 702	25 084	28 599
Florida	476 216	500 015	510 367	518 476	427 989	434 028	485 529	446 393	463 711	482 375
Georgia	258 363	238 049	240 087	253 759	217 790	217 934	247 803	231 298	214 268	230 425
Hawaii	29 548	25 534	29 731	30 150	27 999	31 937	31 198	27 699	27 912	31 192
Idaho	46 915	45 245	43 568	49 082	49 081	38 324	42 034	42 672	39 995	39 897
Illinois	273 223	291 180	258 724	288 093	254 939	270 604	276 155	290 410	268 919	310 548
Indiana	156 429	138 368	144 096	160 186	133 045	131 461	157 118	150 279	135 961	160 208
Iowa	67 469	76 335	68 869	76 115	68 219	73 171	74 873	73 909	71 270	77 348
Kansas	64 164	65 865	64 305	72 463	62 633	64 879	66 180	64 958	65 013	68 682
Kentucky	93 600	92 471	94 832	100 449	85 377	89 014	95 700	91 725	89 006	97 894
Louisiana	97 072	100 827	95 554	94 925	84 883	99 012	105 384	98 111	92 085	100 952
Maine	38 883	38 753	34 024	38 413	33 604	35 107	38 846	38 081	36 140	36 819
Maryland	142 136	140 100	135 677	141 093	124 904	125 430	142 571	139 786	128 868	148 152
Massachusetts	193 777	192 844	168 415	187 728	165 169	166 994	177 352	187 880	177 913	193 240
Michigan	195 103	210 494	192 884	218 726	189 764	177 223	217 822	221 284	199 952	215 440
Minnesota	131 255	147 507	134 330	146 583	125 105	129 687	136 492	143 662	139 721	141 062
Mississippi	51 412	52 644	50 622	56 241	49 812	56 110	54 610	52 011	50 181	56 733
Missouri	130 095	135 649	139 066	149 173	123 536	125 923	140 017	138 282	126 959	138 015
Montana	29 543	30 891	28 367	33 231	29 990	31 111	29 789	29 594	27 933	30 358
Nebraska	46 577	47 077	46 815	51 291	47 643	46 116	46 496	45 346	46 946	49 831
Nevada	75 792	74 040	75 765	85 282	67 736	66 925	77 042	69 258	63 901	79 198
New Hampshire	37 051	37 172	33 686	38 739	35 160	33 256	36 948	38 396	34 427	37 525
New Jersey	201 917	215 885	211 609	229 606	202 323	201 756	207 181	218 949	204 729	222 150
New Mexico	43 176	41 097	44 494	45 847	40 322	38 087	42 452	39 997	41 643	42 675
New York	487 174	489 954	469 675	480 529	442 737	435 506	476 870	482 643	465 753	515 065
North Carolina	238 204	229 161	218 043	235 197	223 550	192 337	224 574	224 248	203 674	218 100
North Dakota	24 889	23 563	23 085	23 552	24 097	22 444	23 630	24 976	23 417	24 502
Ohio	262 791	268 764	253 121	269 713	239 254	245 625	268 195	275 676	249 121	264 866
Oklahoma	76 446	77 538	82 603	83 429	69 577	75 769	81 043	80 343	80 887	85 430
Oregon	106 313	104 398	103 032	111 629	104 027	96 277	100 951	102 740	96 963	108 302
Pennsylvania	270 548	277 104	275 857	283 898	261 356	250 120	279 063	272 037	255 290	296 782
Rhode Island	24 981	26 967	25 104	27 573	25 545	24 396	27 606	26 536	25 146	27 474
South Carolina	115 324	113 102	106 943	115 720	97 016	114 382	109 288	103 035	104 081	116 474
South Dakota	20 457	22 101	20 692	22 892	21 343	22 278	21 022	21 235	20 534	23 763
Tennessee	140 108	142 942	143 410	147 817	128 960	125 770	134 010	134 154	132 149	140 158
Texas	593 214	616 107	621 816	646 101	544 673	553 074	570 355	569 866	548 150	598 020
Utah	93 282	88 988	87 882	87 902	85 420	79 848	84 678	80 452	81 579	83 326
Vermont	17 709	18 167	16 048	17 695	14 932	16 213	18 440	19 565	16 345	19 399
Virginia	204 719	195 103	177 767	211 840	181 461	175 869	187 642	200 915	177 757	196 921
Washington	182 351	190 598	174 815	190 519	216 627	171 257	167 681	175 064	167 332	215 647
West Virginia	33 843	34 489	32 234	34 064	32 860	37 599	36 536	37 364	39 055	37 162
Wisconsin	128 771	139 554	120 219	136 067	126 388	122 544	135 059	146 059	124 896	132 770
Wyoming	19 105	18 039	17 931	19 831	18 182	16 664	20 291	18 641	18 365	19 707
Puerto Rico	48 574	44 047	40 432	36 994	34 391	34 864	39 887	37 460	33 546	35 428
Virgin Islands	3 279	2 357	3 268	2 927	2 087	1 932	1 827	1 754	2 086	2 389

Table 2-24. Private Sector Gross Job Gains and Losses as a Percent of Total Employment, by State and Selected Territory, Seasonally Adjusted, March 2019–March 2020

(Percent.)

State	Gross job gains (3 months ended)					Gross job losses (3 months ended)				
	March 2019	June 2019	September 2019	December 2019	March 2020	March 2019	June 2019	September 2019	December 2019	March 2020
UNITED STATES	6.0	6.1	5.9	6.2	5.5	5.5	5.9	5.8	5.5	6.1
Alabama	6.1	5.9	5.8	6.2	5.5	5.6	5.9	5.9	5.5	5.9
Alaska	10.1	10.7	9.6	10.3	9.2	9.0	10.1	10.1	10.2	9.5
Arizona	5.7	5.7	6.3	6.4	5.6	5.5	5.6	4.9	5.2	5.9
Arkansas	5.3	5.0	5.6	6.5	5.1	5.1	5.7	5.8	4.9	5.5
California	6.4	6.6	6.3	6.8	6.1	6.1	6.4	6.0	6.0	6.7
Colorado	6.6	7.0	6.6	6.7	6.3	6.3	6.2	6.4	6.2	7.0
Connecticut	5.3	5.8	5.5	5.5	5.2	5.7	5.8	5.8	5.6	5.9
Delaware	6.5	6.0	6.2	6.7	6.2	5.6	6.6	6.3	6.2	6.6
District of Columbia	5.5	5.4	5.5	5.4	5.2	5.0	5.5	5.3	4.7	5.3
Florida	6.2	6.5	6.6	6.6	5.4	5.6	6.3	5.8	5.9	6.2
Georgia	6.7	6.1	6.2	6.5	5.6	5.7	6.5	6.0	5.5	5.9
Hawaii	5.5	4.8	5.6	5.7	5.2	5.9	5.8	5.2	5.2	5.8
Idaho	7.5	7.1	7.0	7.7	7.6	6.1	6.7	6.8	6.3	6.1
Illinois	5.2	5.6	5.0	5.6	5.0	5.2	5.3	5.6	5.2	6.0
Indiana	5.8	5.1	5.4	6.0	4.9	4.8	5.9	5.6	5.1	6.0
Iowa	5.1	5.8	5.3	5.8	5.2	5.6	5.8	5.7	5.5	5.9
Kansas	5.6	5.7	5.6	6.3	5.4	5.7	5.8	5.7	5.7	6.0
Kentucky	5.8	5.8	5.9	6.2	5.3	5.5	6.0	5.7	5.6	6.1
Louisiana	6.1	6.2	5.9	5.9	5.3	6.1	6.5	6.1	5.7	6.3
Maine	7.5	7.4	6.5	7.3	6.4	6.7	7.4	7.3	6.9	7.0
Maryland	6.4	6.4	6.2	6.4	5.7	5.7	6.5	6.3	5.9	6.7
Massachusetts	6.1	6.0	5.3	5.8	5.2	5.2	5.6	5.9	5.6	6.0
Michigan	5.2	5.5	5.1	5.8	5.0	4.6	5.7	5.9	5.3	5.7
Minnesota	5.2	5.8	5.4	5.8	5.0	5.2	5.5	5.8	5.6	5.6
Mississippi	5.7	5.8	5.7	6.2	5.6	6.2	6.1	5.7	5.6	6.2
Missouri	5.4	5.7	5.8	6.2	5.2	5.3	5.8	5.8	5.3	5.7
Montana	7.6	8.1	7.4	8.6	7.7	8.1	7.7	7.7	7.2	7.7
Nebraska	5.7	5.7	5.7	6.2	5.8	5.7	5.7	5.5	5.8	6.1
Nevada	6.1	6.0	6.1	6.8	5.4	5.4	6.2	5.5	5.0	6.3
New Hampshire	6.4	6.4	5.8	6.6	6.0	5.7	6.3	6.6	6.0	6.4
New Jersey	5.7	6.2	6.0	6.5	5.7	5.7	5.9	6.2	5.8	6.3
New Mexico	6.7	6.3	6.8	7.0	6.1	5.8	6.5	6.1	6.3	6.5
New York	6.0	6.1	5.8	6.0	5.5	5.4	5.9	5.9	5.7	6.4
North Carolina	6.4	6.0	5.8	6.3	5.8	5.1	5.9	6.0	5.4	5.7
North Dakota	7.1	6.7	6.5	6.7	6.8	6.4	6.7	7.1	6.6	7.0
Ohio	5.6	5.7	5.3	5.7	5.1	5.2	5.7	5.9	5.3	5.6
Oklahoma	5.9	6.0	6.4	6.5	5.4	5.9	6.3	6.2	6.2	6.7
Oregon	6.4	6.3	6.2	6.7	6.2	5.8	6.1	6.2	5.8	6.5
Pennsylvania	5.2	5.3	5.2	5.4	4.9	4.8	5.4	5.1	4.9	5.6
Rhode Island	5.9	6.3	6.0	6.5	6.1	5.7	6.5	6.2	5.9	6.5
South Carolina	6.6	6.4	6.0	6.5	5.5	6.5	6.2	5.9	5.9	6.6
South Dakota	5.7	6.2	5.9	6.4	6.0	6.2	5.9	6.0	5.8	6.6
Tennessee	5.4	5.5	5.5	5.7	4.9	4.9	5.2	5.1	5.0	5.3
Texas	5.6	5.8	5.9	6.0	5.0	5.3	5.3	5.3	5.1	5.5
Utah	7.3	7.0	6.8	6.8	6.6	6.2	6.6	6.3	6.3	6.4
Vermont	6.9	7.1	6.3	6.9	5.8	6.3	7.1	7.6	6.4	7.6
Virginia	6.4	6.1	5.5	6.5	5.6	5.5	5.8	6.3	5.5	6.1
Washington	6.4	6.6	6.1	6.6	7.4	6.1	5.8	6.1	5.8	7.4
West Virginia	6.1	6.2	5.9	6.2	6.0	6.7	6.6	6.7	7.1	6.8
Wisconsin	5.2	5.5	4.8	5.4	5.0	4.9	5.3	5.9	5.0	5.3
Wyoming	9.0	8.5	8.6	9.4	8.6	7.8	9.5	8.9	8.7	9.3
Puerto Rico	7.2	6.4	5.9	5.4	5.0	5.2	5.8	5.5	4.9	5.2
Virgin Islands	12.9	8.9	12.0	10.3	7.2	7.6	6.9	6.4	7.3	8.3

CHAPTER 3: OCCUPATIONAL EMPLOYMENT AND WAGES

HIGHLIGHTS

This chapter presents employment and wage statistics from the Bureau of Labor Statistics Occupational Employment Statistics (OES) program.

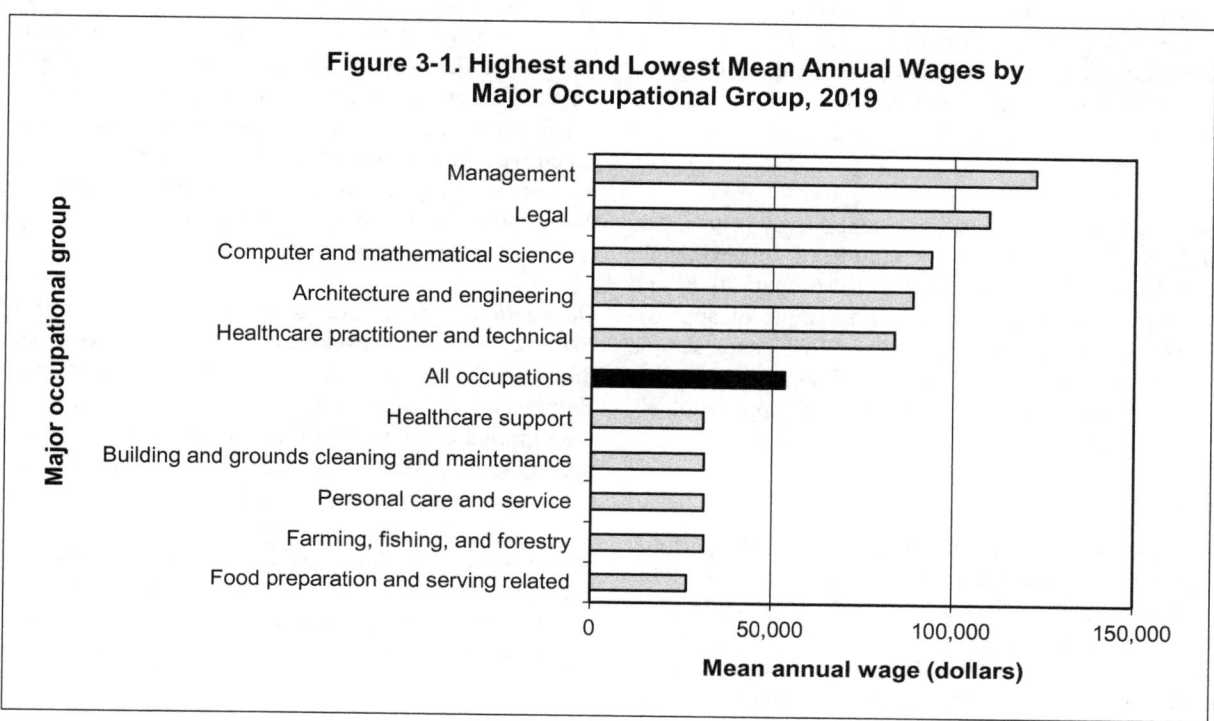

Figure 3-1. Highest and Lowest Mean Annual Wages by Major Occupational Group, 2019

Workers in management continued to have the highest mean annual wage ($122,480) followed by those in legal occupations ($109,630), and computer and mathematical science occupations ($93,760) in 2019. Meanwhile, workers in food preparation and serving related workers ($26,670) and farming, fishing, and forestry ($31,340) had the lowest mean annual wages. (See Table 3-1.)

OTHER HIGHLIGHTS

- Most of the largest occupations were relatively low paying. Food preparation and serving related occupations, which employed over 13 million people, had a mean annual wage of $26,670 in 2019. Likewise, office and administrative support occupations employed 19.5 million people and had a mean annual wage of $41,040 in 2019. Of the ten largest occupations, registered nurses ($77,460) and general operations managers ($123,030) were the only occupations with above-average wages. (See Table 3-1.)

- The highest paying occupations typically requiring less than a bachelor's degree for entry included air traffic controllers ($120,140), which typically require an associate's degree for entry, and transportation, storage, and distribution managers ($103,320) which typically require a high school diploma or the equivalent. (See Table 3-2.)

- There were over 9.3 million jobs representing 6.4 percent of total U.S. employment. STEM occupations had annual mean wage of $95,350 compared with $50,600 for non-STEM occupations. (Table 3-2.)

NOTES AND DEFINITIONS

Collection and Coverage

The Occupational Employment Statistics (OES) survey is a federal-state cooperative program conducted by the Bureau of Labor Statistics (BLS) and the State Workforce Agencies (SWAs). The OES program collects data on wage and salary workers in nonfarm establishments in order to produce employment and wage estimates for over 810 occupations. The survey does not include the self-employed, owners and partners in unincorporated firms, household workers, or unpaid family workers. BLS funds the survey and provides procedural and technical support, while the SWAs collect the necessary data.

The OES sample has been reduced in recent survey panels. The May 2019 OES survey panel had a sample of approximately 183,000 establishments. The November 2017, May 2018, and November 2018 survey panels each had a sample of approximately 186,000 establishments. The May 2017 panel sample consisted of approximately 195,000 establishments, and the November 2016 panel sample consisted of approximately 202,000 establishments.

Scope of the Survey

Prior to 1996, the OES program collected only occupational employment data for selected industries in each year of the three-year survey cycle, and produced only industry-specific estimates of occupational employment. The 1996 survey round was the first year that the OES program began collecting occupational employment and wage data in every State. In addition, the program's three-year survey cycle was modified to collect data from all covered industries each year. In 1997, the OES program began producing estimates of cross-industry as well as industry-specific occupational employment and wages.

In 1999, the OES survey began using the Standard Occupational Classification (SOC) system. The SOC system is the first occupational classification system for federal agencies required by the Office of Management and Budget (OMB). The May 2012 estimates were the first estimates based on the 2010 Standard Occupational Classification (SOC) system. The OES program began implementing the 2018 Standard Occupational Classification (SOC) system with the May 2019 estimates.

In 2002, the OES survey switched from the Standard Industrial Classification System (SIC) to the North American Industry Classification System (NAICS). In 2008, the OES survey switched to the 2007 NAICS from the 2002 NAICS. The most significant revisions were in the information sector, particularly within the telecommunications area. The May 2018 OES estimates use the 2017 North American Industry Classification System (NAICS).

More information about NAICS can be found on the BLS Web site at <https://www.bls.gov/bls/naics.htm >.

Concepts and Definitions

Employment is the estimate of total wage and salary employment in an occupation across the industries in which it was reported. The OES survey defines employment as the number of workers who can be classified as full-time or part-time employees, including workers on paid vacations or other types of leave; workers on unpaid short-term absences; employees who are salaried officers, executives, or staff members of incorporated firms; employees temporarily assigned to other units; and employees for whom the reporting unit is their permanent duty station regardless of whether that unit prepares their paycheck.

Occupations are classified based on work performed and required skills. Employees are assigned to an occupation based on the work they perform and not on their education or training. Employees who perform the duties of two or more occupations are reported as being in either the occupation that requires the highest level of skill or the occupation in which the most time is spent (if there is no measurable difference in skill requirements).

Wages are money that is paid or received for work or services performed in a specified period. Base rate, cost-of-living allowances, guaranteed pay, hazardous-duty pay, incentive pay (including commissions and production bonuses), tips, and on-call pay are included.

Mean wage refers to an average wage; an occupational mean wage estimate is calculated by summing the wages of all the employees in a given occupation and then dividing the total wages by the number of employees.

An *establishment* is defined as an economic unit that processes goods or provides services, such as a factory, store, or mine. The establishment is generally at a single physical location and is primarily engaged in one type of economic activity.

An *industry* is a group of establishments that produce similar products or provide similar services. A given industry, or even a particular establishment in that industry, might have employees in dozens of occupations. The North American Industry Classification System (NAICS) groups similar establishments into industries.

Additional Information

For additional data including area data, see BLS news release USDL 20-0520 "Occupational Employment and Wages, May 2019," and special reports on the BLS Web site at < https://www.bls.gov/OES/>.

Table 3-1. Employment and Wages, by Major Occupational Group, May 2016–May 2019

(Number, percent, dollars.)

Occupation	May 2016				May 2017			
	Employment		Mean hourly wage	Mean annual wage[1]	Employment		Mean hourly wage	Mean annual wage[1]
	Number	Percent			Number	Percent		
All Occupations	140 400 040	100.0	23.86	49 630	142 549 250	100.0	24.34	50 620
Management	7 090 790	5.1	56.74	118 020	7 280 330	5.1	57.65	119 910
Business and financial operations	7 281 190	5.2	36.09	75 070	7 472 750	5.2	36.70	76 330
Computer and mathematical sciences	4 165 140	3.0	42.25	87 880	4 261 460	3.0	43.18	89 810
Architecture and engineering	2 499 050	1.8	40.53	84 300	2 516 780	1.8	41.44	86 190
Life, physical, and social sciences	1 152 840	0.8	35.06	72 930	1 148 300	0.8	35.76	74 370
Community and social services	2 019 250	1.4	22.69	47 200	2 096 740	1.5	23.10	48 050
Legal	1 075 520	0.8	50.95	105 980	1 095 770	0.8	51.62	107 370
Education, training, and library	8 636 430	6.2	26.21	54 520	8 727 710	6.1	26.67	55 470
Arts, design, entertainment, sports, and media	1 902 970	1.4	28.07	58 390	1 925 140	1.4	28.34	58 950
Health care practitioner and technical	8 318 500	5.9	38.06	79 160	8 506 740	6.0	38.83	80 760
Health care support	4 043 480	2.9	14.65	30 470	4 113 410	2.9	15.05	31 310
Protective services	3 386 360	2.4	22.03	45 810	3 408 680	2.4	22.69	47 190
Food preparation and serving related	12 981 720	9.2	11.47	23 850	13 193 090	9.3	11.88	24 710
Building and grounds cleaning and maintenance	4 426 090	3.2	13.47	28 010	4 424 440	3.1	13.91	28 930
Personal care and services	4 514 960	3.2	12.74	26 510	5 159 100	3.6	13.11	27 270
Sales and related	14 536 530	10.4	19.50	40 560	14 522 580	10.2	19.56	40 680
Office and administrative support	22 026 080	15.7	17.91	37 260	21 965 480	15.4	18.24	37 950
Farming, fishing, and forestry	463 640	0.3	13.37	27 810	470 920	0.3	13.87	28 840
Construction and extraction	5 585 420	4.0	23.51	48 900	5 728 460	4.0	24.01	49 930
Installation, maintenance, and repair	5 456 640	3.9	22.45	46 690	5 528 390	3.9	17.82	47 870
Production	9 105 650	6.5	17.88	37 190	9 024 560	6.3	18.30	38 070
Transportation and material moving	9 731 790	6.9	17.34	36 070	9 978 390	7.0	17.82	37 070

Occupation	May 2018				May 2019			
	Employment		Mean hourly wage	Mean annual wage[1]	Employment		Mean hourly wage	Mean annual wage[1]
	Number	Percent			Number	Percent		
All Occupations	144 733 270	100.0	24.98	51 960	146 875 480	100.0	25.72	53 490
Management	7 616 650	5.3	58.44	121 560	8 054 120	5.5	58.88	122 480
Business and financial operations	7 721 300	5.3	36.98	76 910	8 183 750	5.6	37.56	78 130
Computer and mathematical sciences	4 384 300	3.0	44.01	91 530	4 552 880	3.1	45.08	93 760
Architecture and engineering	2 556 220	1.8	42.01	87 370	2 592 680	1.8	42.69	88 800
Life, physical, and social sciences	1 171 910	0.8	36.62	76 160	1 288 920	0.9	37.28	77 540
Community and social services	2 171 820	1.5	23.69	49 280	2 244 310	1.5	24.27	50 480
Legal	1 127 900	0.8	52.25	108 690	1 150 780	0.8	52.71	109 630
Education, training, and library	8 779 780	6.1	27.22	56 620	8 886 600	6.1	27.75	57 710
Arts, design, entertainment, sports, and media	1 951 170	1.3	28.74	59 780	2 017 810	1.4	29.79	61 960
Health care practitioner and technical	8 646 730	6.0	39.42	82 000	8 673 140	5.9	40.21	83 640
Health care support	4 117 450	2.8	15.57	32 380	6 521 790	4.4	14.91	31 010
Protective services	3 437 410	2.4	23.36	48 580	3 498 800	2.4	23.98	49 880
Food preparation and serving related	13 374 620	9.2	12.30	25 580	13 494 590	9.2	12.82	26 670
Building and grounds cleaning and maintenance	4 421 980	3.1	14.43	30 020	4 429 100	3.0	15.03	31 250
Personal care and services	5 451 330	3.8	13.51	28 090	3 303 200	2.2	15.03	31 260
Sales and related	14 542 290	10.0	20.09	41 790	14 371 410	9.8	20.70	43 060
Office and administrative support	21 828 990	15.1	18.75	38 990	19 528 250	13.3	19.73	41 040
Farming, fishing, and forestry	480 130	0.3	14.49	30 140	484 750	0.3	15.07	31 340
Construction and extraction	5 962 640	4.1	24.62	51 220	6 194 140	4.2	25.28	52 580
Installation, maintenance, and repair	5 628 880	3.9	23.54	48 960	5 713 450	3.9	24.10	50 130
Production	9 115 530	6.3	18.84	39 190	9 158 980	6.2	19.30	40 140
Transportation and material moving	10 244 260	7.1	18.41	38 290	12 532 030	8.5	18.23	37 920

[1]The annual wage has been calculated by multiplying the hourly mean wage by a "year-round, full-time" hours figure of 2,080 hours; for occupations with no published hourly mean wage, the annual wage has been directly calculated from the reported survey data.

Table 3-2. Employment and Wages, by Occupation, May 2019

(Number of people, dollars.)

Occupation	May 2019			
	Employment	Mean hourly wage	Mean annual wage[1]	Median hourly wage
All Occupations	146 875 480	25.72	53 490	19.14
Management Occupations	8 054 120	58.88	122 480	50.80
Top Executives	2 658 440	61.09	127 070	49.63
Chief Executives	205 890	93.20	193 850	88.68
General and Operations Managers	2 400 280	59.15	123 030	48.45
Legislators	52 280	([2])	49 440	([2])
Advertising, Marketing, Promotions, Public Relations, and Sales Managers	770 540	68.91	143 330	61.96
Advertising and Promotions Managers	25 100	68.22	141 890	60.34
Marketing Managers	263 680	71.73	149 200	65.79
Sales Managers	402 600	68.12	141 690	60.89
Public Relations and Fundraising Managers	79 160	63.77	132 630	55.86
Operations Specialties Managers	1 996 160	64.69	134 550	58.15
Administrative Services and Facilities Managers	307 280	51.23	106 550	46.61
Computer and Information Systems Managers	433 960	75.19	156 390	70.37
Financial Managers	654 790	70.93	147 530	62.45
Industrial Production Managers	185 790	55.34	115 110	50.71
Purchasing Managers	72 100	61.73	128 400	58.23
Transportation, Storage, and Distribution Managers	132 040	49.67	103 320	45.46
Compensation and Benefits Managers	16 900	64.52	134 210	58.78
Human Resources Managers	154 800	62.29	129 570	56.11
Training and Development Managers	38 510	59.36	123 470	54.50
Other Management Occupations	2 628 970	49.31	102 560	43.90
Farmers, Ranchers, and Other Agricultural Managers	5 060	38.63	80 360	34.21
Construction Managers	293 380	50.48	105 000	45.80
Education and Childcare Administrators, Preschool and Daycare	52 360	25.81	53 690	23.18
Education Administrators, Kindergarten through Secondary	271 020	([2])	100 340	([2])
Education Administrators, Postsecondary	144 880	54.04	112 400	45.87
Education Administrators, All Other	44 550	44.30	92 150	41.08
Architectural and Engineering Managers	194 250	73.52	152 930	69.63
Food Service Managers	235 470	28.76	59 820	26.60
Gambling Managers	4 450	40.72	84 700	36.04
Lodging Managers	38 340	30.56	63 570	26.17
Medical and Health Services Managers	394 910	55.37	115 160	48.55
Natural Sciences Managers	67 720	69.93	145 450	62.07
Postmasters and Mail Superintendents	13 850	37.60	78 220	36.97
Property, Real Estate, and Community Association Managers	220 750	34.48	71 720	28.25
Social and Community Service Managers	156 460	35.05	72 900	32.28
Emergency Management Directors	10 060	39.68	82 530	35.86
Funeral Home Managers	9 400	45.78	95 220	36.71
Personal Service Managers, All Other; Entertainment and Recreation Managers, Except Gambling; and Managers, All Other	472 060	57.07	118 710	53.19
Business and Financial Operations Occupations	8 183 750	37.56	78 130	33.57
Business Operations Specialists	5 427 140	36.31	75 530	33.04
Agents and Business Managers of Artists, Performers, and Athletes	17 060	46.72	97 170	35.45
Buyers and Purchasing Agents	421 280	33.50	69 680	30.95
Claims Adjusters, Examiners, and Investigators	287 960	33.15	68 940	32.11
Insurance Appraisers, Auto Damage	13 750	31.85	66 240	30.42
Compliance Officers	317 600	35.03	72 850	33.20
Cost Estimators	210 000	34.31	71 350	31.37
Human Resources Specialists	633 040	32.58	67 760	29.77
Farm Labor Contractors	160	29.84	62 060	29.77
Labor Relations Specialists	75 580	34.55	71 870	33.18
Logisticians	182 050	37.83	78 680	35.94
Management Analysts	709 750	45.94	95 560	40.99
Meeting, Convention, and Event Planners	117 610	26.39	54 880	24.33
Fundraisers	81 660	30.21	62 830	27.87
Compensation, Benefits, and Job Analysis Specialists	89 300	33.58	69 840	31.04
Training and Development Specialists	312 450	31.56	65 640	29.43
Market Research Analysts and Marketing Specialists	678 500	34.41	71 570	30.67
Project Management Specialists and Business Operations Specialists, All Other	1 279 390	38.57	80 220	35.37
Financial Specialists	2 756 610	40.03	83 260	34.59
Accountants and Auditors	1 280 700	38.23	79 520	34.40
Property Appraisers and Assessors	56 320	30.58	63 610	27.41
Budget Analysts	51 460	38.61	80 300	36.80
Credit Analysts	73 930	40.83	84 930	35.41
Personal Financial Advisors	210 190	57.35	119 290	42.24
Insurance Underwriters	100 050	37.33	77 640	33.67
Financial Examiners	64 550	44.39	92 330	38.99
Credit Counselors	32 110	24.15	50 230	22.09
Loan Officers	308 370	36.64	76 200	30.42
Tax Examiners and Collectors, and Revenue Agents	53 760	29.31	60 960	26.39
Tax Preparers	66 670	23.82	49 550	20.71
Financial and Investment Analysts, Financial Risk Specialists, and Financial Specialists, All Other	458 510	45.27	94 160	39.22

[1]Annual wages have been calculated by multiplying the hourly mean wage by a "year-round, full-time" hours figure of 2,080 hours; for occupations with no published hourly mean wage, the annual wage has been directly calculated from the reported survey data.
[2]Wages for some occupations that do not generally entail year-round, full-time employment are reported as either hourly wages or annual salaries (depending on how employees are typically paid).

Table 3-2. Employment and Wages, by Occupation, May 2019—*Continued*

(Number of people, dollars.)

Occupation	May 2019			
	Employment	Mean hourly wage	Mean annual wage[1]	Median hourly wage
Computer and Mathematical Occupations	4 552 880	45.08	93 760	42.47
Computer Occupations	4 358 410	45.01	93 620	42.43
Computer Systems Analysts	589 060	46.23	96 160	43.71
Information Security Analysts	125 570	50.10	104 210	47.95
Computer and Information Research Scientists	30 780	61.28	127 460	59.06
Computer Network Support Specialists	185 430	33.10	68 860	30.51
Computer User Support Specialists	647 330	27.19	56 550	25.13
Computer Network Architects	152 420	55.34	115 110	54.18
Network and Computer Systems Administrators	354 450	42.51	88 410	40.15
Database Administrators and Architects	125 460	46.21	96 110	45.07
Computer Programmers	199 540	44.53	92 610	41.61
Software Developers and Software Quality Assurance Analysts and Testers	1 406 870	53.66	111 620	51.69
Web Developers and Digital Interface Designers	148 340	39.60	82 370	35.46
Computer Occupations, All Other	393 160	44.43	92 410	42.57
Mathematical Science Occupations	194 460	46.59	96 900	43.47
Actuaries	22 260	58.16	120 970	52.09
Mathematicians	2 630	51.57	107 280	50.50
Operations Research Analysts	99 680	43.56	90 600	40.78
Statisticians	39 090	46.00	95 680	43.83
Data Scientists and Mathematical Science Occupations, All Other	30 810	48.35	100 560	45.33
Architecture and Engineering Occupations	2 592 680	42.69	88 800	39.15
Architects, Surveyors, and Cartographers	182 650	39.06	81 250	35.83
Architects, Except Landscape and Naval	105 850	43.06	89 560	38.82
Landscape Architects	20 280	35.56	73 970	33.35
Cartographers and Photogrammetrists	11 300	33.55	69 790	31.47
Surveyors	45 220	32.66	67 920	30.49
Engineers	1 730 720	48.45	100 770	45.43
Aerospace Engineers	63 200	57.32	119 220	56.01
Agricultural Engineers	1 550	47.26	98 290	38.81
Bioengineers and Biomedical Engineers	19 780	46.68	97 090	43.95
Chemical Engineers	30 120	56.29	117 090	52.30
Civil Engineers	310 850	45.36	94 360	41.86
Computer Hardware Engineers	67 880	59.15	123 030	56.36
Electrical Engineers	185 570	49.75	103 480	47.37
Electronics Engineers, Except Computer	128 800	52.99	110 210	50.76
Environmental Engineers	53 150	45.30	94 220	42.72
Health and Safety Engineers, Except Mining Safety Engineers and Inspectors	25 860	45.58	94 810	43.95
Industrial Engineers	291 710	44.55	92 660	42.32
Marine Engineers and Naval Architects	11 360	47.47	98 730	44.42
Materials Engineers	26 820	47.06	97 890	44.88
Mechanical Engineers	306 990	44.97	93 540	42.51
Mining and Geological Engineers, Including Mining Safety Engineers	6 280	46.63	96 990	43.83
Nuclear Engineers	15 850	58.03	120 700	54.55
Petroleum Engineers	32 620	75.37	156 780	66.21
Engineers, All Other	152 340	49.26	102 460	47.62
Drafters, Engineering Technicians, and Mapping Technicians	679 310	29.00	60 320	27.73
Architectural and Civil Drafters	98 800	27.92	58 080	27.09
Electrical and Electronics Drafters	24 140	31.60	65 720	29.58
Mechanical Drafters	55 210	29.09	60 500	27.43
Drafters, All Other	14 600	26.37	54 840	25.40
Aerospace Engineering and Operations Technologists and Technicians	11 540	32.86	68 340	31.74
Civil Engineering Technologists and Technicians	68 870	26.67	55 480	25.68
Electrical and Electronic Engineering Technologists and Technicians	122 550	31.84	66 240	31.38
Electro-Mechanical and Mechatronics Technologists and Technicians	14 290	29.53	61 420	28.05
Environmental Engineering Technologists and Technicians	18 010	26.32	54 740	24.34
Industrial Engineering Technologists and Technicians	67 110	28.56	59 400	27.19
Mechanical Engineering Technologists and Technicians	42 820	28.44	59 160	27.40
Surveying and Mapping Technicians	53 030	23.32	48 500	21.64
Calibration Technologists and Technicians and Engineering Technologists and Technicians, Except Drafters, All Other	88 330	31.70	65 940	30.28
Life, Physical, and Social Science Occupations	1 288 920	37.28	77 540	32.77
Life Scientists	311 910	42.68	88 770	37.54
Animal Scientists	2 690	32.96	68 570	28.99
Food Scientists and Technologists	13 460	36.63	76 190	33.16
Soil and Plant Scientists	14 150	33.58	69 860	30.39
Biochemists and Biophysicists	31 360	52.01	108 180	45.43
Microbiologists	18 270	39.79	82 760	36.37
Zoologists and Wildlife Biologists	19 250	32.31	67 200	30.42
Biological Scientists, All Other	40 100	42.11	87 590	39.53
Conservation Scientists	22 070	32.23	67 040	30.12
Foresters	9 510	30.42	63 270	29.71
Epidemiologists	7 410	37.64	78 290	34.13
Medical Scientists, Except Epidemiologists	127 180	47.49	98 770	42.69
Life Scientists, All Other	6 450	41.29	85 890	36.49
Physical Scientists	255 790	43.80	91 110	39.07

[1]Annual wages have been calculated by multiplying the hourly mean wage by a "year-round, full-time" hours figure of 2,080 hours; for occupations with no published hourly mean wage, the annual wage has been directly calculated from the reported survey data.

Table 3-2. Employment and Wages, by Occupation, May 2019—*Continued*

(Number of people, dollars.)

Occupation	May 2019			
	Employment	Mean hourly wage	Mean annual wage[1]	Median hourly wage
Life, Physical, and Social Science Occupations—*Continued*				
Astronomers	2 070	58.79	122 270	55.09
Physicists	16 730	63.02	131 080	59.06
Atmospheric and Space Scientists	9 290	46.71	97 160	45.86
Chemists	83 530	40.46	84 150	37.32
Materials Scientists	6 710	48.28	100 430	46.54
Environmental Scientists and Specialists, Including Health	84 290	37.47	77 940	34.31
Geoscientists, Except Hydrologists and Geographers	29 200	52.09	108 350	44.25
Hydrologists	6 440	41.50	86 330	39.07
Physical Scientists, All Other	17 550	53.88	112 070	52.84
Social Scientists and Related Workers	249 120	42.32	88 030	38.57
Economists	19 000	56.07	116 630	50.49
Survey Researchers	9 930	31.61	65 760	28.45
Clinical, Counseling, and School Psychologists	113 270	42.04	87 450	37.59
Industrial-Organizational Psychologists	630	53.44	111 150	44.66
Psychologists, All Other	14 220	47.23	98 230	48.94
Sociologists	2 630	43.55	90 590	40.10
Urban and Regional Planners	38 560	37.38	77 750	35.75
Anthropologists and Archeologists	6 720	32.12	66 810	30.61
Geographers	1 400	39.41	81 970	39.20
Historians	3 040	33.02	68 690	30.62
Political Scientists	6 010	57.82	120 260	58.76
Social Scientists and Related Workers, All Other	33 690	42.16	87 690	40.06
Life, Physical, and Social Science Technicians	358 740	25.17	52 340	23.19
Agricultural and Food Science Technicians	21 870	21.37	44 440	19.82
Biological Technicians	79 530	23.61	49 110	22.05
Chemical Technicians	65 760	25.44	52 910	23.68
Environmental Science and Protection Technicians, Including Health	32 620	24.41	50 760	22.38
Geological and Hydrologic Technicians	17 110	29.23	60 800	24.58
Nuclear Technicians	6 420	39.77	82 710	39.46
Social Science Research Assistants	35 580	24.68	51 340	22.84
Forest and Conservation Technicians	19 060	22.05	45 860	21.87
Forensic Science Technicians	16 520	30.37	63 170	28.44
Life, Physical, and Social Science Technicians, All Other	64 260	25.80	53 670	24.30
Occupational Health and Safety Specialists and Technicians	113 360	34.95	72 690	33.88
Occupational Health and Safety Specialists	92 780	36.68	76 290	35.63
Occupational Health and Safety Technicians	20 580	27.15	56 470	24.79
Community and Social Service Occupations	2 244 310	24.27	50 480	22.16
Counselors, Social Workers, and Other Community and Social Service Specialists	2 159 870	24.23	50 410	22.15
Educational, Guidance, and Career Counselors and Advisors	296 460	29.33	61 000	27.42
Marriage and Family Therapists	59 050	26.25	54 590	23.85
Rehabilitation Counselors	109 040	19.31	40 160	17.28
Substance Abuse, Behavioral Disorder, and Mental Health Counselors	283 540	24.01	49 950	22.23
Counselors, All Other	25 420	23.46	48 800	20.64
Child, Family, and School Social Workers	327 710	24.53	51 030	22.78
Healthcare Social Workers	174 890	28.51	59 300	27.29
Mental Health and Substance Abuse Social Workers	117 770	24.84	51 670	22.43
Social Workers, All Other	58 410	29.69	61 750	29.44
Health Education Specialists	58 590	29.09	60 500	26.55
Probation Officers and Correctional Treatment Specialists	88 120	28.80	59 910	26.10
Social and Human Service Assistants	404 450	17.81	37 050	16.85
Community Health Workers	58 950	21.34	44 390	19.41
Community and Social Service Specialists, All Other	97 480	22.55	46 900	21.05
Religious Workers	84 440	25.12	52 260	22.54
Clergy	53 180	26.53	55 190	24.23
Directors, Religious Activities and Education	21 820	24.28	50 490	21.09
Religious Workers, All Other	9 450	19.15	39 830	15.21
Legal Occupations	1 150 780	52.71	109 630	39.34
Lawyers, Judges, and Related Workers	722 940	67.87	141 180	57.68
Lawyers	657 170	69.86	145 300	59.11
Judicial Law Clerks	16 630	28.79	59 890	25.97
Administrative Law Judges, Adjudicators, and Hearing Officers	14 380	48.19	100 230	47.05
Arbitrators, Mediators, and Conciliators	6 090	35.44	73 720	30.74
Judges, Magistrate Judges, and Magistrates	28 670	61.80	128 550	65.82
Legal Support Workers	427 840	27.08	56 320	24.96
Paralegals and Legal Assistants	329 870	26.45	55 020	24.87
Title Examiners, Abstractors, and Searchers	52 890	25.02	52 050	23.17
Legal Support Workers, All Other	45 080	34.06	70 840	28.08
Educational Instruction and Library Occupations	8 886 600	27.75	57 710	24.42
Postsecondary Teachers	1 407 110	(2)	90 830	(2)
Business Teachers, Postsecondary	83 920	(2)	105 440	(2)
Computer Science Teachers, Postsecondary	31 800	(2)	98 430	(2)
Mathematical Science Teachers, Postsecondary	51 150	(2)	86 330	(2)
Architecture Teachers, Postsecondary	6 780	(2)	98 980	(2)
Engineering Teachers, Postsecondary	36 080	(2)	112 110	(2)
Agricultural Sciences Teachers, Postsecondary	9 470	(2)	89 320	(2)
Biological Science Teachers, Postsecondary	53 090	(2)	98 700	(2)
Forestry and Conservation Science Teachers, Postsecondary	1 770	(2)	90 940	(2)

[1]Annual wages have been calculated by multiplying the hourly mean wage by a "year-round, full-time" hours figure of 2,080 hours; for occupations with no published hourly mean wage, the annual wage has been directly calculated from the reported survey data.
[2]Wages for some occupations that do not generally entail year-round, full-time employment are reported as either hourly wages or annual salaries (depending on how employees are typically paid).

Table 3-2. Employment and Wages, by Occupation, May 2019—*Continued*

(Number of people, dollars.)

Occupation	May 2019			
	Employment	Mean hourly wage	Mean annual wage[1]	Median hourly wage
Educational Instruction and Library Occupations—*Continued*				
Atmospheric, Earth, Marine, and Space Sciences Teachers, Postsecondary	11 020	(2)	102 690	(2)
Chemistry Teachers, Postsecondary	21 380	(2)	92 650	(2)
Environmental Science Teachers, Postsecondary	6 060	(2)	93 450	(2)
Physics Teachers, Postsecondary	13 780	(2)	101 110	(2)
Anthropology and Archeology Teachers, Postsecondary	5 850	(2)	95 140	(2)
Area, Ethnic, and Cultural Studies Teachers, Postsecondary	10 600	(2)	88 410	(2)
Economics Teachers, Postsecondary	13 270	(2)	119 160	(2)
Geography Teachers, Postsecondary	3 970	(2)	86 540	(2)
Political Science Teachers, Postsecondary	15 750	(2)	102 290	(2)
Psychology Teachers, Postsecondary	37 480	(2)	87 530	(2)
Sociology Teachers, Postsecondary	13 850	(2)	85 240	(2)
Social Sciences Teachers, Postsecondary, All Other	16 830	(2)	85 390	(2)
Health Specialties Teachers, Postsecondary	201 920	(2)	121 620	(2)
Nursing Instructors and Teachers, Postsecondary	59 680	(2)	83 160	(2)
Education Teachers, Postsecondary	61 300	(2)	74 560	(2)
Library Science Teachers, Postsecondary	4 390	(2)	77 170	(2)
Criminal Justice and Law Enforcement Teachers, Postsecondary	14 070	(2)	72 980	(2)
Law Teachers, Postsecondary	16 180	(2)	129 950	(2)
Social Work Teachers, Postsecondary	13 640	(2)	77 910	(2)
Art, Drama, and Music Teachers, Postsecondary	94 060	(2)	83 220	(2)
Communications Teachers, Postsecondary	29 120	(2)	79 830	(2)
English Language and Literature Teachers, Postsecondary	67 930	(2)	80 180	(2)
Foreign Language and Literature Teachers, Postsecondary	24 860	(2)	80 170	(2)
History Teachers, Postsecondary	21 030	(2)	84 210	(2)
Philosophy and Religion Teachers, Postsecondary	23 490	(2)	88 970	(2)
Family and Consumer Sciences Teachers, Postsecondary	2 150	(2)	85 270	(2)
Recreation and Fitness Studies Teachers, Postsecondary	15 880	(2)	73 720	(2)
Career/Technical Education Teachers, Postsecondary	112 210	29.05	60 420	26.26
Postsecondary Teachers, All Other	201 320	(2)	80 720	(2)
Preschool, Elementary, Middle, Secondary, and Special Education Teachers	4 211 470	(2)	61 420	(2)
Preschool Teachers, Except Special Education	431 350	16.66	34 650	14.67
Kindergarten Teachers, Except Special Education	124 290	(2)	60 210	(2)
Elementary School Teachers, Except Special Education	1 430 480	(2)	63 930	(2)
Middle School Teachers, Except Special and Career/Technical Education	622 330	(2)	63 550	(2)
Career/Technical Education Teachers, Middle School	11 860	(2)	64 900	(2)
Secondary School Teachers, Except Special and Career/Technical Education	1 035 850	(2)	65 930	(2)
Career/Technical Education Teachers, Secondary School	74 520	(2)	64 800	(2)
Special Education Teachers, Preschool	22 340	(2)	67 060	(2)
Special Education Teachers, Kindergarten and Elementary School	193 830	(2)	64 420	(2)
Special Education Teachers, Middle School	85 840	(2)	65 740	(2)
Special Education Teachers, Secondary School	143 170	(2)	65 710	(2)
Special Education Teachers, All Other	35 600	(2)	65 350	(2)
Other Teachers and Instructors	1 212 090	19.58	40 730	15.93
Adult Basic Education, Adult Secondary Education, and English as a Second Language Instructors	51 950	28.36	58 980	26.13
Self-Enrichment Teachers	252 780	22.17	46 120	18.84
Substitute Teachers, Short-Term	587 120	15.61	32 460	13.84
Tutors and Teachers and Instructors, All Other	320 250	(2)	48 700	(2)
Librarians, Curators, and Archivists	257 060	25.16	52 330	23.57
Archivists	6 560	27.65	57 500	25.94
Curators	12 890	28.43	59 130	26.24
Museum Technicians and Conservators	13 190	23.09	48 030	21.36
Librarians and Media Collections Specialists	135 690	29.77	61 920	28.61
Library Technicians	88 720	17.76	36 950	16.78
Other Educational Instruction and Library Occupations	1 798 860	(2)	35 330	(2)
Farm and Home Management Educators	8 720	25.34	52 720	23.90
Instructional Coordinators	176 690	33.26	69 180	31.87
Teaching Assistants, Postsecondary	137 500	(2)	36 460	(2)
Teaching Assistants, Except Postsecondary	1 346 910	(2)	29 640	(2)
Educational Instruction and Library Workers, All Other	129 040	22.10	45 970	19.38
Arts, Design, Entertainment, Sports, and Media Occupations	2 017 810	29.79	61 960	24.59
Art and Design Workers	633 420	27.54	57 290	23.14
Art Directors	42 890	52.69	109 600	45.30
Craft Artists	4 640	18.63	38 740	16.69
Fine Artists, Including Painters, Sculptors, and Illustrators	12 350	30.30	63 030	24.30
Special Effects Artists and Animators	29 340	40.76	84 780	36.19
Artists and Related Workers, All Other	7 550	32.57	67 750	31.01
Commercial and Industrial Designers	32 770	35.49	73 820	33.12
Fashion Designers	22 030	41.40	86 110	35.48
Floral Designers	41 770	14.31	29 760	13.48
Graphic Designers	215 930	27.17	56 510	25.05
Interior Designers	60 650	29.32	60 990	26.94
Merchandise Displayers and Window Trimmers	140 850	15.84	32 940	14.16
Set and Exhibit Designers	12 040	30.04	62 480	26.25
Designers, All Other	10 610	35.34	73 510	31.07

[1]Annual wages have been calculated by multiplying the hourly mean wage by a "year-round, full-time" hours figure of 2,080 hours; for occupations with no published hourly mean wage, the annual wage has been directly calculated from the reported survey data.
[2]Wages for some occupations that do not generally entail year-round, full-time employment are reported as either hourly wages or annual salaries (depending on how employees are typically paid).

Table 3-2. Employment and Wages, by Occupation, May 2019—*Continued*

(Number of people, dollars.)

Occupation	May 2019			
	Employment	Mean hourly wage	Mean annual wage[1]	Median hourly wage
Arts, Design, Entertainment, Sports, and Media Occupations—*Continued*				
Entertainers and Performers, Sports and Related Workers	536 540	30.10	62 600	21.76
Actors	52 620	29.14	([2])	20.43
Producers and Directors	129 210	45.16	93 940	35.78
Athletes and Sports Competitors	11 330	([2])	93 140	([2])
Coaches and Scouts	241 390	([2])	44 910	([2])
Umpires, Referees, and Other Sports Officials	20 120	([2])	38 810	([3])
Dancers	9 690	22.91	([2])	17.49
Choreographers	4 630	25.77	53 590	22.27
Music Directors and Composers	10 580	31.09	64 670	24.84
Musicians and Singers	41 130	39.96	([2])	30.39
Miscellaneous Entertainers and Performers, Sports and Related Workers	15 840	23.40	([2])	15.86
Media and Communication Workers	609 210	32.61	67 830	28.48
Broadcast Announcers and Radio Disc Jockeys	29 230	25.76	53 580	16.65
News Analysts, Reporters, and Journalists	44 100	30.00	62 400	22.25
Public Relations Specialists	244 730	33.75	70 190	29.40
Editors	95 970	34.57	71 910	29.50
Technical Writers	50 760	36.95	76 860	35.03
Writers and Authors	45 860	35.51	73 860	30.39
Interpreters and Translators	58 870	27.40	57 000	24.92
Court Reporters and Simultaneous Captioners	14 530	31.25	64 990	28.91
Media and Communication Workers, All Other	25 160	25.51	53 060	22.88
Media and Communication Equipment Workers	238 630	27.86	57 950	23.21
Audio and Video Technicians	73 960	24.65	51 260	22.07
Broadcast Technicians	28 650	22.50	46 800	19.51
Sound Engineering Technicians	12 890	32.25	67 090	26.32
Photographers	50 620	21.85	45 440	17.44
Camera Operators, Television, Video, and Film	21 500	31.23	64 960	26.52
Film and Video Editors	27 570	41.97	87 300	30.66
Lighting Technicians and Media and Communication Equipment Workers, All Other	23 440	35.43	73 700	35.32
Healthcare Practitioners and Technical Occupations	8 673 140	40.21	83 640	32.78
Healthcare Diagnosing or Treating Practitioners	5 685 500	49.26	102 470	39.61
Chiropractors	35 010	40.87	85 010	33.82
Dentists, General	110 730	85.70	178 260	74.81
Oral and Maxillofacial Surgeons	4 650	114.21	237 570	([3])
Orthodontists	5 990	110.98	230 830	([3])
Prosthodontists	490	106.17	220 840	([3])
Dentists, All Other Specialists	5 330	85.59	178 040	70.78
Dietitians and Nutritionists	67 670	29.97	62 330	29.46
Optometrists	39 420	59.12	122 980	55.41
Pharmacists	311 200	60.34	125 510	61.58
Physician Assistants	120 090	54.04	112 410	53.97
Podiatrists	9 770	68.60	142 680	60.69
Occupational Therapists	133 570	41.45	86 210	40.84
Physical Therapists	233 350	43.35	90 170	43.00
Radiation Therapists	17 860	44.05	91 620	41.14
Recreational Therapists	19 070	24.58	51 130	23.18
Respiratory Therapists	132 090	30.75	63 950	29.48
Speech-Language Pathologists	154 360	39.43	82 000	38.04
Exercise Physiologists	7 280	26.32	54 750	23.64
Therapists, All Other	12 170	28.17	58 600	25.31
Veterinarians	74 540	50.39	104 820	45.90
Registered Nurses	2 982 280	37.24	77 460	35.24
Nurse Anesthetists	43 570	87.04	181 040	84.03
Nurse Midwives	6 930	52.31	108 810	50.50
Nurse Practitioners	200 600	53.77	111 840	52.80
Audiologists	13 590	40.34	83 900	37.31
Anesthesiologists	31 010	125.83	261 730	([3])
Family Medicine Physicians	109 370	102.53	213 270	98.84
General Internal Medicine Physicians	44 610	96.85	201 440	96.92
Obstetricians and Gynecologists	18 620	112.31	233 610	([3])
Pediatricians, General	29 740	88.66	184 410	84.28
Psychiatrists	25 530	105.98	220 430	([3])
Physicians, All Other; and Ophthalmologists, Except Pediatric	390 680	97.81	203 450	99.28
Surgeons, Except Ophthalmologists	36 270	121.17	252 040	([3])
Dental Hygienists	221 560	37.13	77 230	36.65
Acupuncturists and Healthcare Diagnosing or Treating Practitioners, All Other	36 500	42.82	89 060	36.37
Health Technologists and Technicians	2 902 300	22.86	47 540	21.34
Clinical Laboratory Technologists and Technicians	326 020	26.34	54 780	25.54
Cardiovascular Technologists and Technicians	56 110	28.66	59 600	27.75
Diagnostic Medical Sonographers	72 790	36.44	75 780	35.73
Nuclear Medicine Technologists	18 110	38.58	80 240	37.48
Radiologic Technologists and Technicians	207 360	30.34	63 120	29.09
Magnetic Resonance Imaging Technologists	37 900	35.70	74 270	35.30
Emergency Medical Technicians and Paramedics	260 600	18.67	38 830	17.02

[1] Annual wages have been calculated by multiplying the hourly mean wage by a "year-round, full-time" hours figure of 2,080 hours; for occupations with no published hourly mean wage, the annual wage has been directly calculated from the reported survey data.
[2] Wages for some occupations that do not generally entail year-round, full-time employment are reported as either hourly wages or annual salaries (depending on how employees are typically paid).
[3] Median hourly wage is equal to or greater than $100.00 per hour.

Table 3-2. Employment and Wages, by Occupation, May 2019—*Continued*

(Number of people, dollars.)

Occupation	May 2019			
	Employment	Mean hourly wage	Mean annual wage[1]	Median hourly wage
Healthcare Practitioners and Technical Occupations—*Continued*				
Dietetic Technicians	29 230	14.99	31 180	13.66
Pharmacy Technicians	417 780	16.95	35 250	16.32
Psychiatric Technicians	78 470	18.05	37 550	16.24
Surgical Technologists	109 000	24.09	50 110	23.22
Veterinary Technologists and Technicians	110 650	17.63	36 670	16.98
Ophthalmic Medical Technicians	58 600	18.64	38 760	17.76
Licensed Practical and Licensed Vocational Nurses	697 510	23.32	48 500	22.83
Opticians, Dispensing	72 330	19.58	40 730	18.19
Orthotists and Prosthetists	9 830	35.01	72 810	32.89
Hearing Aid Specialists	8 210	26.62	55 360	25.68
Medical Dosimetrists, Medical Records Specialists, and Health Technologists and Technicians, All Other	331 790	22.40	46 590	20.50
Other Healthcare Practitioners and Technical Occupations	85 340	27.22	56 620	23.93
Athletic Trainers	28 600	(2)	50 540	(2)
Genetic Counselors	2 390	40.54	84 310	39.36
Health Information Technologists, Medical Registrars, Surgical Assistants, and Healthcare Practitioners and Technical Workers, All Other	54 350	28.17	58 600	23.97
Healthcare Support Occupations				
Home Health and Personal Care Aides; and Nursing Assistants, Orderlies, and Psychiatric Aides	6 521 790	14.91	31 010	13.69
Home Health and Personal Care Aides	4 683 430	13.39	27 860	12.68
Nursing Assistants	3 161 500	12.71	26 440	12.15
Orderlies	1 419 920	14.77	30 720	14.26
Psychiatric Aides	46 990	14.76	30 710	13.93
Occupational Therapy and Physical Therapist Assistants and Aides	55 020	15.67	32 590	14.96
Occupational Therapy Assistants	198 660	24.56	51 080	25.44
Occupational Therapy Aides	44 990	29.75	61 880	29.57
Physical Therapist Assistants	7 560	16.50	34 310	14.05
Physical Therapist Aides	96 840	28.14	58 520	28.26
Other Healthcare Support Occupations	49 270	14.03	29 180	12.98
Massage Therapists	1 639 700	18.07	37 580	17.24
Dental Assistants	107 240	22.68	47 180	20.59
Medical Assistants	351 470	19.79	41 170	19.27
Medical Equipment Preparers	712 430	17.17	35 720	16.73
Medical Transcriptionists	56 900	19.01	39 530	18.00
Pharmacy Aides	55 780	16.93	35 210	16.05
Veterinary Assistants and Laboratory Animal Caretakers	37 280	14.66	30 490	13.39
Phlebotomists	97 030	14.28	29 690	13.75
	128 290	17.54	36 480	17.07
Healthcare Support Workers, All Other	93 270	19.24	40 010	18.49
Protective Service Occupations				
Supervisors of Protective Service Workers	3 498 800	23.98	49 880	19.99
First-Line Supervisors of Correctional Officers	319 960	37.31	77 600	34.35
First-Line Supervisors of Police and Detectives	46 430	33.18	69 000	30.64
	121 340	45.65	94 950	43.79
First-Line Supervisors of Firefighting and Prevention Workers	69 590	39.43	82 010	37.40
Miscellaneous First-Line Supervisors, Protective Service Workers	82 590	25.58	53 210	24.27
Firefighting and Prevention Workers	340 490	26.46	55 040	24.68
Firefighters	324 620	26.27	54 650	24.45
Fire Inspectors and Investigators	13 710	31.12	64 730	29.65
Forest Fire Inspectors and Prevention Specialists	2 160	25.65	53 350	21.77
Law Enforcement Workers	1 232 740	30.17	62 740	27.42
Bailiffs	19 650	24.92	51 840	22.99
Correctional Officers and Jailers	423 050	24.10	50 130	21.72
Detectives and Criminal Investigators	105 620	41.36	86 030	39.99
Fish and Game Wardens	6 800	27.73	57 690	27.64
Parking Enforcement Workers	7 650	20.88	43 420	19.67
Police and Sheriff's Patrol Officers	665 280	32.50	67 600	30.36
Transit and Railroad Police	4 690	34.19	71 120	34.53
Other Protective Service Workers	1 605 610	16.05	33 380	14.31
Animal Control Workers	11 980	19.09	39 710	18.07
Private Detectives and Investigators	35 000	27.40	57 000	24.28
Gambling Surveillance Officers and Gambling Investigators	10 280	18.28	38 030	16.44
Security Guards	1 126 370	15.88	33 030	14.27
Crossing Guards and Flaggers	84 920	15.83	32 920	14.31
Lifeguards, Ski Patrol, and Other Recreational Protective Service Workers	143 940	12.20	25 380	11.26
Transportation Security Screeners	46 730	20.34	42 310	20.08
School Bus Monitors and Protective Service Workers, All Other	146 390	16.77	34 880	14.90
Food Preparation and Serving Related Occupations				
Supervisors of Food Preparation and Serving Workers	13 494 590	12.82	26 670	11.65
Chefs and Head Cooks	1 139 290	18.82	39 140	16.74
First-Line Supervisors of Food Preparation and Serving Workers	128 190	27.07	56 310	24.78
Cooks and Food Preparation Workers	1 011 100	17.77	36 960	16.06
	3 367 740	13.03	27 100	12.45
Cooks, Fast Food	527 220	11.31	23 530	11.30
Cooks, Institution and Cafeteria	402 480	13.96	29 030	13.34
Cooks, Private Household	390	21.92	45 600	18.21
Cooks, Restaurant	1 401 890	13.80	28 700	13.36
Cooks, Short Order	152 670	12.62	26 240	12.09

[1]Annual wages have been calculated by multiplying the hourly mean wage by a "year-round, full-time" hours figure of 2,080 hours; for occupations with no published hourly mean wage, the annual wage has been directly calculated from the reported survey data.

[2]Wages for some occupations that do not generally entail year-round, full-time employment are reported as either hourly wages or annual salaries (depending on how employees are typically paid).

Table 3-2. Employment and Wages, by Occupation, May 2019—*Continued*

(Number of people, dollars.)

Occupation	May 2019			
	Employment	Mean hourly wage	Mean annual wage[1]	Median hourly wage
Food Preparation and Serving Related Occupations—*Continued*				
Cooks, All Other	19 340	15.50	32 240	14.79
Food Preparation Workers	863 740	12.41	25 820	11.92
Food and Beverage Serving Workers	7 500 280	12.01	24 990	11.02
Bartenders	646 850	13.46	28 000	11.39
Fast Food and Counter Workers	3 996 820	11.18	23 250	10.93
Waiters and Waitresses	2 579 020	12.88	26 800	11.00
Food Servers, Nonrestaurant	277 580	12.54	26 080	11.74
Other Food Preparation and Serving Related Workers	1 487 290	11.82	24 590	11.37
Dining Room and Cafeteria Attendants and Bartender Helpers	477 270	12.03	25 020	11.28
Dishwashers	514 330	11.74	24 410	11.53
Hosts and Hostesses, Restaurant, Lounge, and Coffee Shop	423 380	11.54	24 010	11.10
Food Preparation and Serving Related Workers, All Other	72 300	12.74	26 510	12.01
Building and Grounds Cleaning and Maintenance Occupations	4 429 100	15.03	31 250	13.62
Supervisors of Building and Grounds Cleaning and Maintenance Workers	259 140	22.80	47 430	21.39
First-Line Supervisors of Housekeeping and Janitorial Workers	155 550	21.23	44 160	19.61
First-Line Supervisors of Landscaping, Lawn Service, and Groundskeeping Workers	103 580	25.16	52 340	23.73
Building Cleaning and Pest Control Workers	3 170 010	14.11	29 350	12.78
Janitors and Cleaners, Except Maids and Housekeeping Cleaners	2 145 450	14.43	30 010	13.19
Maids and Housekeeping Cleaners	926 960	12.89	26 810	11.95
Building Cleaning Workers, All Other	18 150	16.96	35 270	15.01
Pest Control Workers	79 450	19.19	39 910	17.95
Grounds Maintenance Workers	999 960	15.91	33 100	14.85
Landscaping and Groundskeeping Workers	912 660	15.56	32 360	14.63
Pesticide Handlers, Sprayers, and Applicators, Vegetation	25 780	18.86	39 230	17.23
Tree Trimmers and Pruners	47 210	20.44	42 510	19.22
Grounds Maintenance Workers, All Other	14 310	18.21	37 870	15.43
Personal Care and Service Occupations	3 303 200	15.03	31 260	12.61
Supervisors of Personal Care and Service Workers	247 100	21.35	44 400	19.68
First-Line Supervisors of Gambling Services Workers	29 420	24.93	51 850	24.38
First-Line Supervisors of Personal Service and Entertainment and Recreation Workers, Except Gambling Services	217 680	20.86	43 400	19.14
Animal Care and Service Workers	228 980	13.33	27 720	12.02
Animal Trainers	16 530	17.43	36 240	14.63
Animal Caretakers	212 450	13.01	27 060	11.91
Entertainment Attendants and Related Workers	628 090	12.05	25 060	11.18
Gambling Dealers	98 890	11.53	23 980	10.22
Gambling and Sports Book Writers and Runners	9 970	13.38	27 830	11.90
Gambling Service Workers, All Other	10 470	15.38	32 000	13.61
Motion Picture Projectionists	4 540	14.37	29 890	12.09
Ushers, Lobby Attendants, and Ticket Takers	138 160	11.96	24 870	11.30
Amusement and Recreation Attendants	338 110	11.70	24 330	11.23
Costume Attendants	7 460	23.55	48 970	19.91
Locker Room, Coatroom, and Dressing Room Attendants	15 990	13.57	28 230	12.07
Entertainment Attendants and Related Workers, All Other	4 500	15.28	31 790	12.72
Embalmers	3 890	24.09	50 100	22.96
Funeral Attendants	34 370	14.34	29 830	13.43
Morticians, Undertakers, and Funeral Arrangers	25 440	28.06	58 360	26.04
Personal Appearance Workers	589 960	15.24	31 700	12.71
Barbers	20 030	16.92	35 190	14.50
Hairdressers, Hairstylists, and Cosmetologists	385 960	15.16	31 530	12.54
Makeup Artists, Theatrical and Performance	3 400	39.23	81 600	36.41
Manicurists and Pedicurists	111 780	13.17	27 390	12.39
Shampooers	12 120	11.02	22 910	10.84
Skincare Specialists	56 660	18.74	38 970	16.39
Baggage Porters, Bellhops, and Concierges	81 460	15.06	31 330	13.73
Baggage Porters and Bellhops	39 790	13.57	28 230	12.30
Concierges	41 670	16.48	34 290	15.09
Tour and Travel Guides	48 710	14.74	30 670	13.27
Childcare Workers	561 520	12.27	25 510	11.65
Exercise Trainers and Group Fitness Instructors	325 500	21.69	45 110	19.42
Recreation Workers	358 750	14.10	29 330	12.67
Residential Advisors	107 930	15.20	31 610	14.16
Crematory Operators and Personal Care and Service Workers, All Other	61 510	14.03	29 190	13.04
Sales and Related Occupations	14 371 410	20.70	43 060	14.24
Supervisors of Sales Workers	1 420 990	25.43	52 900	21.27
First-Line Supervisors of Retail Sales Workers	1 171 900	22.03	45 830	19.40
First-Line Supervisors of Non-Retail Sales Workers	249 090	41.43	86 180	35.94
Retail Sales Workers	8 603 590	13.27	27 600	11.84
Cashiers	3 596 630	11.72	24 370	11.37
Gambling Change Persons and Booth Cashiers	21 290	13.46	28 010	12.35
Counter and Rental Clerks	411 560	15.67	32 600	13.86
Parts Salespersons	256 170	16.93	35 220	15.24
Retail Salespersons	4 317 950	14.12	29 360	12.14
Sales Representatives, Services	2 084 000	34.45	71 660	26.62

[1]Annual wages have been calculated by multiplying the hourly mean wage by a "year-round, full-time" hours figure of 2,080 hours; for occupations with no published hourly mean wage, the annual wage has been directly calculated from the reported survey data.

Table 3-2. Employment and Wages, by Occupation, May 2019—*Continued*

(Number of people, dollars.)

Occupation	May 2019			
	Employment	Mean hourly wage	Mean annual wage[1]	Median hourly wage
Sales and Related Occupations—*Continued*				
Advertising Sales Agents	129 740	31.09	64 660	25.63
Insurance Sales Agents	410 050	32.59	67 780	24.49
Securities, Commodities, and Financial Services Sales Agents	437 880	44.75	93 090	29.94
Travel Agents	66 670	21.49	44 690	19.55
Sales Representatives of Services, Except Advertising, Insurance, Financial Services, and Travel	1 039 670	32.10	66 760	26.99
Sales Representatives, Wholesale and Manufacturing	1 651 500	36.14	75 180	30.29
Sales Representatives, Wholesale and Manufacturing, Technical and Scientific Products	306 980	44.70	92 980	38.95
Sales Representatives, Wholesale and Manufacturing, Except Technical and Scientific Products	1 344 530	34.19	71 110	28.81
Other Sales and Related Workers	611 330	25.72	53 500	17.89
Demonstrators and Product Promoters	77 760	16.98	35 320	14.87
Models	2 320	17.52	36 430	13.63
Real Estate Brokers	42 730	39.16	81 450	28.71
Real Estate Sales Agents	162 330	29.83	62 060	23.53
Sales Engineers	63 550	54.22	112 780	49.95
Telemarketers	134 800	14.31	29 770	12.64
Door-to-Door Sales Workers, News and Street Vendors, and Related Workers	8 930	16.90	35 150	13.19
Sales and Related Workers, All Other	118 910	19.53	40 620	15.30
Office and Administrative Support Occupations	19 528 250	19.73	41 040	18.07
Supervisors of Office and Administrative Support Workers	1 487 870	28.91	60 130	27.22
First-Line Supervisors of Office and Administrative Support Workers	1 487 870	28.91	60 130	27.22
Communications Equipment Operators	76 030	16.29	33 890	14.94
Switchboard Operators, Including Answering Service	68 050	15.88	33 030	14.72
Telephone Operators	4 740	18.24	37 940	17.19
Communications Equipment Operators, All Other	3 240	22.14	46 050	20.57
Financial Clerks	2 910 660	19.60	40 770	18.52
Bill and Account Collectors	235 870	18.90	39 300	17.79
Billing and Posting Clerks	466 450	19.53	40 620	18.63
Bookkeeping, Accounting, and Auditing Clerks	1 512 660	20.65	42 960	19.82
Gambling Cage Workers	14 330	14.23	29 600	13.48
Payroll and Timekeeping Clerks	142 700	22.79	47 390	22.20
Procurement Clerks	66 030	21.14	43 980	20.82
Tellers	442 120	15.22	31 660	15.02
Financial Clerks, All Other	30 500	21.51	44 740	20.40
Information and Record Clerks	5 780 040	17.59	36 580	16.37
Brokerage Clerks	47 990	26.53	55 190	25.36
Correspondence Clerks	6 250	19.03	39 570	18.34
Court, Municipal, and License Clerks	154 020	20.21	42 030	18.93
Credit Authorizers, Checkers, and Clerks	26 700	20.13	41 880	19.28
Customer Service Representatives	2 919 230	17.94	37 320	16.69
Eligibility Interviewers, Government Programs	139 780	22.65	47 110	22.40
File Clerks	102 300	16.64	34 610	15.73
Hotel, Motel, and Resort Desk Clerks	267 940	12.47	25 950	11.76
Interviewers, Except Eligibility and Loan	188 570	17.49	36 390	16.81
Library Assistants, Clerical	85 910	14.34	29 820	13.22
Loan Interviewers and Clerks	208 530	20.17	41 960	19.54
New Accounts Clerks	43 420	18.50	38 490	17.57
Order Clerks	137 180	17.60	36 600	16.46
Human Resources Assistants, Except Payroll and Timekeeping	117 340	20.49	42 620	19.92
Receptionists and Information Clerks	1 057 370	15.02	31 250	14.45
Reservation and Transportation Ticket Agents and Travel Clerks	123 660	21.34	44 390	18.45
Information and Record Clerks, All Other	153 850	20.39	42 410	19.89
Material Recording, Scheduling, Dispatching, and Distributing Workers	2 155 080	21.13	43 950	19.39
Cargo and Freight Agents	95 810	22.48	46 770	21.03
Couriers and Messengers	74 720	15.21	31 640	14.28
Public Safety Telecommunicators	95 320	21.31	44 310	20.15
Dispatchers, Except Police, Fire, and Ambulance	199 360	21.20	44 100	19.32
Meter Readers, Utilities	30 450	22.23	46 250	20.33
Postal Service Clerks	81 170	24.33	50 610	23.23
Postal Service Mail Carriers	339 650	25.09	52 180	24.67
Postal Service Mail Sorters, Processors, and Processing Machine Operators	102 390	24.61	51 190	28.91
Production, Planning, and Expediting Clerks	370 380	24.35	50 640	23.20
Shipping, Receiving, and Inventory Clerks	704 910	17.32	36 030	16.44
Weighers, Measurers, Checkers, and Samplers, Recordkeeping	60 920	17.62	36 650	16.85
Secretaries and Administrative Assistants	3 353 950	20.87	43 410	19.16
Executive Secretaries and Executive Administrative Assistants	542 690	30.25	62 920	29.27
Legal Secretaries and Administrative Assistants	168 140	24.47	50 900	22.74
Medical Secretaries and Administrative Assistants	604 780	18.31	38 090	17.59
Secretaries and Administrative Assistants, Except Legal, Medical, and Executive	2 038 340	18.84	39 180	18.12
Other Office and Administrative Support Workers	3 764 620	17.75	36 920	16.67
Data Entry Keyers	159 930	16.74	34 820	16.10
Word Processors and Typists	47 460	20.13	41 880	19.39
Desktop Publishers	8 740	23.43	48 740	21.82
Insurance Claims and Policy Processing Clerks	257 000	20.81	43 280	19.59
Mail Clerks and Mail Machine Operators, Except Postal Service	83 580	15.68	32 620	14.89
Office Clerks, General	2 956 060	17.48	36 360	16.37
Office Machine Operators, Except Computer	45 960	16.90	35 150	16.08
Proofreaders and Copy Markers	7 730	20.77	43 200	19.54
Statistical Assistants	9 810	24.83	51 640	23.97
Office and Administrative Support Workers, All Other	188 360	18.41	38 290	17.05

[1]Annual wages have been calculated by multiplying the hourly mean wage by a "year-round, full-time" hours figure of 2,080 hours; for occupations with no published hourly mean wage, the annual wage has been directly calculated from the reported survey data.

Table 3-2. Employment and Wages, by Occupation, May 2019—Continued

(Number of people, dollars.)

Occupation	May 2019			
	Employment	Mean hourly wage	Mean annual wage[1]	Median hourly wage
Farming, Fishing, and Forestry Occupations	484 750	15.07	31 340	13.07
Supervisors of Farming, Fishing, and Forestry Workers	22 560	25.25	52 520	23.21
First-Line Supervisors of Farming, Fishing, and Forestry Workers	22 560	25.25	52 520	23.21
Agricultural Workers	415 390	14.00	29 120	12.52
Agricultural Inspectors	13 760	22.67	47 160	21.87
Animal Breeders	1 610	22.32	46 420	20.64
Graders and Sorters, Agricultural Products	34 340	13.25	27 570	12.34
Agricultural Equipment Operators	26 990	16.01	33 300	15.36
Farmworkers and Laborers, Crop, Nursery, and Greenhouse	295 520	13.36	27 780	12.23
Farmworkers, Farm, Ranch, and Aquacultural Animals	36 630	14.37	29 880	13.38
Agricultural Workers, All Other	6 540	16.31	33 930	14.23
Forest, Conservation, and Logging Workers	44 720	19.78	41 130	18.79
Forest and Conservation Workers	6 760	15.76	32 790	15.27
Fallers	4 890	23.88	49 670	21.46
Logging Equipment Operators	26 030	20.22	42 060	19.92
Log Graders and Scalers	3 300	18.80	39 110	17.92
Logging Workers, All Other	3 750	19.42	40 390	19.12
Construction and Extraction Occupations	6 194 140	25.28	52 580	22.80
Supervisors of Construction and Extraction Workers	626 180	34.35	71 440	31.83
First-Line Supervisors of Construction Trades and Extraction Workers	626 180	34.35	71 440	31.83
Construction Trades Workers	4 617 440	24.68	51 330	22.28
Boilermakers	15 820	31.27	65 040	30.34
Brickmasons and Blockmasons	60 650	27.15	56 470	25.53
Stonemasons	12 390	23.11	48 070	20.81
Carpenters	734 170	25.41	52 850	23.24
Carpet Installers	26 010	21.79	45 320	19.27
Floor Layers, Except Carpet, Wood, and Hard Tiles	16 290	23.37	48 610	21.27
Floor Sanders and Finishers	4 940	20.34	42 300	19.04
Tile and Stone Setters	40 470	22.74	47 300	20.70
Cement Masons and Concrete Finishers	196 120	23.24	48 330	21.54
Terrazzo Workers and Finishers	2 970	27.09	56 340	25.09
Construction Laborers	1 020 350	20.06	41 730	17.72
Paving, Surfacing, and Tamping Equipment Operators	45 770	21.46	44 630	19.29
Pile Driver Operators	3 540	33.76	70 230	30.10
Operating Engineers and Other Construction Equipment Operators	405 750	26.06	54 210	23.55
Drywall and Ceiling Tile Installers	102 850	24.31	50 560	21.97
Tapers	17 970	29.59	61 550	28.40
Electricians	688 620	29.02	60 370	27.01
Glaziers	52 400	23.95	49 810	21.46
Insulation Workers, Floor, Ceiling, and Wall	33 550	21.68	45 100	19.41
Insulation Workers, Mechanical	26 670	26.02	54 120	23.41
Painters, Construction and Maintenance	232 760	21.46	44 640	19.37
Paperhangers	3 380	21.38	44 470	19.48
Pipelayers	36 270	20.96	43 600	18.66
Plumbers, Pipefitters, and Steamfitters	442 870	28.75	59 800	26.52
Plasterers and Stucco Masons	27 360	23.90	49 710	21.85
Reinforcing Iron and Rebar Workers	18 870	26.27	54 650	23.60
Roofers	129 690	22.03	45 820	20.24
Sheet Metal Workers	131 300	26.19	54 480	24.23
Structural Iron and Steel Workers	76 570	28.45	59 170	26.46
Solar Photovoltaic Installers	11 080	22.52	46 850	21.58
Helpers, Construction Trades	242 400	16.49	34 300	15.73
Helpers--Brickmasons, Blockmasons, Stonemasons, and Tile and Marble Setters	23 480	18.48	38 440	17.02
Helpers--Carpenters	32 920	16.26	33 830	15.89
Helpers--Electricians	79 260	16.49	34 300	15.78
Helpers--Painters, Paperhangers, Plasterers, and Stucco Masons	10 850	15.83	32 930	15.07
Helpers--Pipelayers, Plumbers, Pipefitters, and Steamfitters	58 400	16.23	33 750	15.43
Helpers--Roofers	8 960	16.04	33 350	15.44
Helpers, Construction Trades, All Other	28 530	16.06	33 400	15.34
Other Construction and Related Workers	437 730	24.81	51 600	22.36
Construction and Building Inspectors	110 420	30.96	64 390	29.19
Elevator and Escalator Installers and Repairers	28 350	40.02	83 250	40.86
Fence Erectors	25 900	18.56	38 600	17.21
Hazardous Materials Removal Workers	44 240	22.95	47 740	21.11
Highway Maintenance Workers	150 860	20.39	42 410	19.58
Rail-Track Laying and Maintenance Equipment Operators	16 180	27.48	57 160	26.97
Septic Tank Servicers and Sewer Pipe Cleaners	29 750	20.56	42 760	19.17
Miscellaneous Construction and Related Workers	32 040	21.17	44 030	19.10
Extraction Workers	270 390	23.16	48 180	21.61
Derrick Operators, Oil and Gas	12 110	23.09	48 030	22.59
Rotary Drill Operators, Oil and Gas	21 010	27.44	57 070	26.43
Service Unit Operators, Oil and Gas	51 760	24.71	51 390	22.47
Excavating and Loading Machine and Dragline Operators, Surface Mining	44 090	23.36	48 580	21.54
Continuous Mining Machine Operators	14 630	27.18	56 530	26.58
Roof Bolters, Mining	3 140	28.63	59 560	28.41
Loading and Moving Machine Operators, Underground Mining	4 200	25.83	53 730	26.06
Rock Splitters, Quarry	5 080	17.97	37 390	17.34
Roustabouts, Oil and Gas	58 930	19.85	41 280	18.71
Helpers--Extraction Workers	16 700	18.46	38 390	17.85

[1]Annual wages have been calculated by multiplying the hourly mean wage by a "year-round, full-time" hours figure of 2,080 hours; for occupations with no published hourly mean wage, the annual wage has been directly calculated from the reported survey data.

Table 3-2. Employment and Wages, by Occupation, May 2019—_Continued_

(Number of people, dollars.)

Occupation	May 2019			
	Employment	Mean hourly wage	Mean annual wage[1]	Median hourly wage
Construction and Extraction Occupations—_Continued_				
Earth Drillers, Except Oil and Gas; and Explosives Workers, Ordnance Handling Experts, and Blasters	24 940	23.50	48 890	22.24
Underground Mining Machine Operators and Extraction Workers, All Other	13 790	25.13	52 280	24.11
Installation, Maintenance, and Repair Occupations	5 713 450	24.10	50 130	22.42
Supervisors of Installation, Maintenance, and Repair Workers	485 700	33.92	70 550	32.44
First-Line Supervisors of Mechanics, Installers, and Repairers	485 700	33.92	70 550	32.44
Electrical and Electronic Equipment Mechanics, Installers, and Repairers	557 620	26.27	54 630	25.28
Computer, Automated Teller, and Office Machine Repairers	98 260	20.23	42 070	19.01
Radio, Cellular, and Tower Equipment Installers and Repairers	14 370	27.80	57 820	26.62
Telecommunications Equipment Installers and Repairers, Except Line Installers	208 480	28.15	58 560	27.84
Avionics Technicians	21 750	32.20	66 970	31.59
Electric Motor, Power Tool, and Related Repairers	15 890	22.41	46 620	21.19
Electrical and Electronics Installers and Repairers, Transportation Equipment	9 790	30.61	63 670	30.06
Electrical and Electronics Repairers, Commercial and Industrial Equipment	58 930	29.02	60 360	28.51
Electrical and Electronics Repairers, Powerhouse, Substation, and Relay	22 650	39.08	81 280	39.80
Electronic Equipment Installers and Repairers, Motor Vehicles	10 310	18.71	38 910	17.97
Audiovisual Equipment Installers and Repairers	25 590	20.25	42 130	18.99
Security and Fire Alarm Systems Installers	71 600	24.14	50 210	23.54
Vehicle and Mobile Equipment Mechanics, Installers, and Repairers	1 638 920	22.81	47 440	21.44
Aircraft Mechanics and Service Technicians	133 310	32.27	67 110	30.81
Automotive Body and Related Repairers	144 180	22.79	47 390	20.95
Automotive Glass Installers and Repairers	19 410	18.00	37 440	17.20
Automotive Service Technicians and Mechanics	655 330	21.58	44 890	20.24
Bus and Truck Mechanics and Diesel Engine Specialists	266 330	24.21	50 360	23.32
Farm Equipment Mechanics and Service Technicians	36 290	20.97	43 630	20.29
Mobile Heavy Equipment Mechanics, Except Engines	147 800	26.36	54 840	25.66
Rail Car Repairers	25 930	27.31	56 810	27.11
Motorboat Mechanics and Service Technicians	22 940	20.89	43 440	19.87
Motorcycle Mechanics	15 590	19.22	39 970	18.08
Outdoor Power Equipment and Other Small Engine Mechanics	32 160	18.11	37 670	17.36
Bicycle Repairers	13 190	15.07	31 360	14.58
Recreational Vehicle Service Technicians	15 580	20.03	41 660	18.54
Tire Repairers and Changers	110 880	14.59	30 350	13.77
Other Installation, Maintenance, and Repair Occupations	3 031 220	22.83	47 480	21.20
Mechanical Door Repairers	23 050	21.03	43 740	19.99
Control and Valve Installers and Repairers, Except Mechanical Door	52 270	28.81	59 920	27.93
Heating, Air Conditioning, and Refrigeration Mechanics and Installers	342 040	24.72	51 420	23.43
Home Appliance Repairers	31 100	20.38	42 400	19.36
Industrial Machinery Mechanics	387 630	26.60	55 320	25.77
Maintenance Workers, Machinery	72 890	23.77	49 450	22.85
Millwrights	47 320	27.43	57 050	26.71
Refractory Materials Repairers, Except Brickmasons	820	26.80	55 750	25.95
Electrical Power-Line Installers and Repairers	111 660	34.60	71 960	34.86
Telecommunications Line Installers and Repairers	120 900	28.69	59 670	27.29
Camera and Photographic Equipment Repairers	3 620	19.58	40 720	18.69
Medical Equipment Repairers	46 370	25.54	53 130	23.69
Musical Instrument Repairers and Tuners	8 020	19.11	39 750	17.62
Watch and Clock Repairers	2 780	21.77	45 280	20.44
Precision Instrument and Equipment Repairers, All Other	10 570	28.82	59 940	28.23
Maintenance and Repair Workers, General	1 418 990	20.17	41 960	18.79
Wind Turbine Service Technicians	5 960	27.26	56 700	25.44
Coin, Vending, and Amusement Machine Servicers and Repairers	31 370	17.97	37 380	17.03
Commercial Divers	3 420	32.26	67 100	24.03
Locksmiths and Safe Repairers	17 010	21.38	44 460	20.16
Manufactured Building and Mobile Home Installers	2 810	16.49	34 300	16.29
Riggers	23 000	25.20	52 420	24.45
Signal and Track Switch Repairers	6 860	34.95	72 690	35.52
Helpers--Installation, Maintenance, and Repair Workers	99 460	15.66	32 570	14.68
Installation, Maintenance, and Repair Workers, All Other	161 290	21.06	43 800	19.15
Production Occupations	9 158 980	19.30	40 140	17.31
Supervisors of Production Workers	631 100	31.35	65 220	29.48
First-Line Supervisors of Production and Operating Workers	631 100	31.35	65 220	29.48
Assemblers and Fabricators	1 856 870	17.46	36 310	16.21
Aircraft Structure, Surfaces, Rigging, and Systems Assemblers	42 940	27.15	56 460	26.06
Coil Winders, Tapers, and Finishers	12 690	18.63	38 760	17.56
Electrical, Electronic, and Electromechanical Assemblers, Except Coil Winders, Tapers, and Finishers	285 190	17.75	36 930	16.74
Engine and Other Machine Assemblers	45 980	22.39	46 570	21.95
Structural Metal Fabricators and Fitters	76 890	20.67	43 000	19.42
Fiberglass Laminators and Fabricators	20 010	17.78	36 970	17.06
Timing Device Assemblers and Adjusters	1 260	18.32	38 110	16.87
Miscellaneous Assemblers and Fabricators	1 371 920	16.73	34 800	15.55
Food Processing Workers	802 290	14.94	31 080	14.09
Bakers	184 990	14.25	29 630	13.32
Butchers and Meat Cutters	136 770	16.35	34 010	15.62
Meat, Poultry, and Fish Cutters and Trimmers	153 990	13.85	28 810	13.51
Slaughterers and Meat Packers	73 390	14.23	29 600	14.05
Food and Tobacco Roasting, Baking, and Drying Machine Operators and Tenders	20 830	16.29	33 880	15.19
Food Batchmakers	159 390	15.92	33 120	14.80
Food Cooking Machine Operators and Tenders	30 030	15.54	32 320	14.96

[1]Annual wages have been calculated by multiplying the hourly mean wage by a "year-round, full-time" hours figure of 2,080 hours; for occupations with no published hourly mean wage, the annual wage has been directly calculated from the reported survey data.

Table 3-2. Employment and Wages, by Occupation, May 2019—*Continued*

(Number of people, dollars.)

Occupation	May 2019			
	Employment	Mean hourly wage	Mean annual wage[1]	Median hourly wage
Production Occupations—*Continued*				
Food Processing Workers, All Other	42 890	13.85	28 820	13.24
Metal Workers and Plastic Workers	1 825 170	20.22	42 050	18.96
Extruding and Drawing Machine Setters, Operators, and Tenders, Metal and Plastic	76 940	18.16	37 770	17.46
Forging Machine Setters, Operators, and Tenders, Metal and Plastic	16 320	19.81	41 200	19.07
Rolling Machine Setters, Operators, and Tenders, Metal and Plastic	32 470	20.15	41 920	19.47
Cutting, Punching, and Press Machine Setters, Operators, and Tenders, Metal and Plastic	195 040	17.94	37 310	17.12
Drilling and Boring Machine Tool Setters, Operators, and Tenders, Metal and Plastic	10 870	20.49	42 630	18.71
Grinding, Lapping, Polishing, and Buffing Machine Tool Setters, Operators, and Tenders, Metal and Plastic	76 810	18.20	37 860	17.36
Lathe and Turning Machine Tool Setters, Operators, and Tenders, Metal and Plastic	28 070	20.19	41 990	19.28
Milling and Planing Machine Setters, Operators, and Tenders, Metal and Plastic	18 730	21.55	44 820	20.77
Machinists	383 470	22.17	46 120	21.36
Metal-Refining Furnace Operators and Tenders	17 150	20.81	43 280	20.31
Pourers and Casters, Metal	8 010	19.64	40 850	18.57
Model Makers, Metal and Plastic	4 300	27.61	57 420	27.41
Patternmakers, Metal and Plastic	3 010	23.10	48 050	22.55
Foundry Mold and Coremakers	17 590	17.75	36 920	17.11
Molding, Coremaking, and Casting Machine Setters, Operators, and Tenders, Metal and Plastic	172 520	16.67	34 670	15.45
Multiple Machine Tool Setters, Operators, and Tenders, Metal and Plastic	146 950	18.47	38 410	17.47
Tool and Die Makers	70 770	26.43	54 980	25.92
Welders, Cutters, Solderers, and Brazers	410 750	21.73	45 190	20.43
Welding, Soldering, and Brazing Machine Setters, Operators, and Tenders	35 110	19.35	40 240	18.42
Heat Treating Equipment Setters, Operators, and Tenders, Metal and Plastic	19 560	19.16	39 840	18.39
Layout Workers, Metal and Plastic	8 150	23.51	48 900	24.01
Plating Machine Setters, Operators, and Tenders, Metal and Plastic	41 810	17.14	35 640	16.10
Tool Grinders, Filers, and Sharpeners	6 440	20.18	41 970	18.91
Metal Workers and Plastic Workers, All Other	24 340	18.17	37 790	16.75
Printing Workers	249 300	18.65	38 790	17.60
Prepress Technicians and Workers	30 270	20.45	42 540	19.48
Printing Press Operators	173 430	18.80	39 100	17.74
Print Binding and Finishing Workers	45 600	16.89	35 130	15.89
Textile, Apparel, and Furnishings Workers	569 260	13.78	28 660	12.68
Laundry and Dry-Cleaning Workers	209 330	12.22	25 420	11.64
Pressers, Textile, Garment, and Related Materials	38 070	11.93	24 820	11.63
Sewing Machine Operators	133 410	13.46	28 000	12.70
Shoe and Leather Workers and Repairers	8 760	14.70	30 580	14.21
Shoe Machine Operators and Tenders	5 020	14.68	30 540	14.70
Sewers, Hand	4 770	14.92	31 020	14.40
Tailors, Dressmakers, and Custom Sewers	24 110	16.60	34 530	15.15
Textile Bleaching and Dyeing Machine Operators and Tenders	8 690	14.81	30 810	14.16
Textile Cutting Machine Setters, Operators, and Tenders	13 210	14.26	29 660	13.81
Textile Knitting and Weaving Machine Setters, Operators, and Tenders	21 130	15.05	31 300	14.41
Textile Winding, Twisting, and Drawing Out Machine Setters, Operators, and Tenders	31 190	14.78	30 740	14.32
Extruding and Forming Machine Setters, Operators, and Tenders, Synthetic and Glass Fibers	18 230	18.16	37 760	17.36
Fabric and Apparel Patternmakers	5 870	25.35	52 740	21.67
Upholsterers	29 420	17.62	36 640	16.89
Textile, Apparel, and Furnishings Workers, All Other	18 060	14.76	30 710	13.45
Woodworkers	253 080	16.66	34 660	15.75
Cabinetmakers and Bench Carpenters	99 400	18.09	37 620	17.21
Furniture Finishers	16 220	16.51	34 350	15.62
Model Makers, Wood	810	27.56	57 320	28.49
Patternmakers, Wood	370	30.53	63 490	31.19
Sawing Machine Setters, Operators, and Tenders, Wood	50 730	15.46	32 150	14.62
Woodworking Machine Setters, Operators, and Tenders, Except Sawing	78 850	15.47	32 180	14.90
Woodworkers, All Other	6 700	16.96	35 270	15.92
Plant and System Operators	302 270	30.40	63 230	29.01
Nuclear Power Reactor Operators	5 050	48.55	100 990	48.33
Power Distributors and Dispatchers	10 770	42.74	88 910	43.61
Power Plant Operators	33 620	38.16	79 370	39.42
Stationary Engineers and Boiler Operators	32 520	31.71	65 970	29.88
Water and Wastewater Treatment Plant and System Operators	123 730	24.28	50 490	22.96
Chemical Plant and System Operators	28 840	30.15	62 710	30.07
Gas Plant Operators	14 410	34.16	71 050	34.00
Petroleum Pump System Operators, Refinery Operators, and Gaugers	40 370	35.49	73 830	35.66
Plant and System Operators, All Other	12 950	28.61	59 500	28.07
Other Production Occupations	2 669 650	18.64	38 770	17.11
Chemical Equipment Operators and Tenders	87 120	24.78	51 540	23.62
Separating, Filtering, Clarifying, Precipitating, and Still Machine Setters, Operators, and Tenders	51 160	21.81	45 370	19.87
Crushing, Grinding, and Polishing Machine Setters, Operators, and Tenders	33 360	18.88	39 270	18.06
Grinding and Polishing Workers, Hand	29 170	15.90	33 060	14.71
Mixing and Blending Machine Setters, Operators, and Tenders	125 340	19.19	39 920	18.17
Cutters and Trimmers, Hand	9 670	15.55	32 340	14.52
Cutting and Slicing Machine Setters, Operators, and Tenders	57 960	17.67	36 750	17.11
Extruding, Forming, Pressing, and Compacting Machine Setters, Operators, and Tenders	71 850	17.90	37 240	17.06
Furnace, Kiln, Oven, Drier, and Kettle Operators and Tenders	18 970	19.88	41 350	19.27
Inspectors, Testers, Sorters, Samplers, and Weighers	576 950	20.67	43 000	18.82
Jewelers and Precious Stone and Metal Workers	23 590	22.09	45 950	19.65
Dental Laboratory Technicians	34 460	21.31	44 330	19.87

[1]Annual wages have been calculated by multiplying the hourly mean wage by a "year-round, full-time" hours figure of 2,080 hours; for occupations with no published hourly mean wage, the annual wage has been directly calculated from the reported survey data.

Table 3-2. Employment and Wages, by Occupation, May 2019—*Continued*

(Number of people, dollars.)

Occupation	May 2019			
	Employment	Mean hourly wage	Mean annual wage[1]	Median hourly wage
Production Occupations—*Continued*				
Medical Appliance Technicians	14 130	21.25	44 200	19.56
Ophthalmic Laboratory Technicians	29 150	16.73	34 800	15.68
Packaging and Filling Machine Operators and Tenders	390 540	16.15	33 590	14.90
Painting, Coating, and Decorating Workers	12 430	17.11	35 600	15.84
Coating, Painting, and Spraying Machine Setters, Operators, and Tenders	146 350	19.84	41 260	18.34
Semiconductor Processing Technicians	27 680	20.17	41 950	18.30
Photographic Process Workers and Processing Machine Operators	11 940	17.74	36 890	15.52
Computer Numerically Controlled Tool Operators	151 700	20.75	43 170	19.81
Computer Numerically Controlled Tool Programmers	25 570	28.72	59 730	27.14
Adhesive Bonding Machine Operators and Tenders	13 890	17.31	36 010	16.51
Cleaning, Washing, and Metal Pickling Equipment Operators and Tenders	16 410	16.46	34 230	15.31
Cooling and Freezing Equipment Operators and Tenders	8 740	17.80	37 010	16.97
Etchers and Engravers	10 310	16.24	33 770	14.72
Molders, Shapers, and Casters, Except Metal and Plastic	44 890	17.31	36 000	16.36
Paper Goods Machine Setters, Operators, and Tenders	100 290	19.70	40 980	18.85
Tire Builders	20 790	21.64	45 010	22.12
Helpers--Production Workers	303 030	14.68	30 540	13.99
Production Workers, All Other	222 230	16.26	33 830	14.33
Transportation and Material Moving Occupations	12 532 030	18.23	37 920	15.60
Supervisors of Transportation and Material Moving Workers	464 890	27.81	57 850	26.46
Aircraft Cargo Handling Supervisors	9 500	27.87	57 960	25.89
First-Line Supervisors of Transportation and Material Moving Workers, Except Aircraft Cargo Handling Supervisors	455 390	27.81	57 840	26.47
Air Transportation Workers	275 960	(2)	104 130	(2)
Airline Pilots, Copilots, and Flight Engineers	84 520	(2)	174 870	(2)
Commercial Pilots	37 830	(2)	102 870	(2)
Air Traffic Controllers	22 090	57.76	120 140	59.13
Airfield Operations Specialists	10 680	27.70	57 620	25.31
Flight Attendants	120 840	(2)	56 230	(2)
Motor Vehicle Operators	4 174 700	19.57	40 710	18.53
Ambulance Drivers and Attendants, Except Emergency Medical Technicians	14 740	14.23	29 600	12.45
Driver/Sales Workers	444 660	14.53	30 230	12.43
Heavy and Tractor-Trailer Truck Drivers	1 856 130	22.52	46 850	21.76
Light Truck Drivers	923 050	18.52	38 520	16.70
Bus Drivers, Transit and Intercity	179 510	22.03	45 830	20.69
Passenger Vehicle Drivers, Except Bus Drivers, Transit and Intercity	700 030	15.97	33 210	15.07
Motor Vehicle Operators, All Other	56 590	17.93	37 300	15.82
Rail Transportation Workers	111 090	32.33	67 240	31.20
Locomotive Engineers	35 520	34.41	71 570	32.26
Rail Yard Engineers, Dinkey Operators, and Hostlers	5 400	25.33	52 690	23.72
Railroad Brake, Signal, and Switch Operators and Locomotive Firers	11 080	29.99	62 380	28.97
Railroad Conductors and Yardmasters	45 710	32.86	68 350	31.73
Subway and Streetcar Operators	10 730	30.66	63 770	32.63
Rail Transportation Workers, All Other	2 650	26.04	54 170	24.81
Water Transportation Workers	75 180	34.25	71 240	27.56
Sailors and Marine Oilers	31 290	25.60	53 250	20.90
Captains, Mates, and Pilots of Water Vessels	33 370	42.03	87 420	34.78
Motorboat Operators	2 120	23.57	49 030	23.20
Ship Engineers	8 410	38.24	79 540	35.87
Other Transportation Workers	368 840	15.98	33 240	12.87
Bridge and Lock Tenders	3 150	23.02	47 880	24.09
Parking Attendants	147 390	12.72	26 450	12.09
Automotive and Watercraft Service Attendants	117 670	12.91	26 860	12.11
Traffic Technicians	7 470	25.28	52 590	22.83
Transportation Inspectors	30 020	37.27	77 530	36.45
Passenger Attendants	28 200	14.15	29 420	12.78
Aircraft Service Attendants and Transportation Workers, All Other	34 940	20.65	42 940	17.79
Material Moving Workers	7 061 370	15.28	31 790	13.97
Conveyor Operators and Tenders	24 050	17.38	36 150	16.66
Crane and Tower Operators	45 480	29.10	60 530	27.26
Dredge Operators	1 550	24.68	51 340	22.62
Hoist and Winch Operators	4 800	30.14	62 690	28.71
Industrial Truck and Tractor Operators	629 270	18.24	37 930	17.40
Cleaners of Vehicles and Equipment	382 670	13.43	27 940	12.40
Laborers and Freight, Stock, and Material Movers, Hand	2 953 170	15.45	32 130	14.19
Machine Feeders and Offbearers	63 280	15.87	33 010	14.99
Packers and Packagers, Hand	633 640	13.31	27 680	12.46
Stockers and Order Fillers	2 135 850	14.26	29 660	13.16
Gas Compressor and Gas Pumping Station Operators	3 440	30.15	62 710	31.81
Pump Operators, Except Wellhead Pumpers	10 000	23.61	49 120	21.65
Wellhead Pumpers	12 970	26.48	55 080	26.46
Refuse and Recyclable Material Collectors	121 330	19.90	41 400	18.19
Tank Car, Truck, and Ship Loaders	11 620	22.88	47 580	20.36
Material Moving Workers, All Other	28 240	17.56	36 530	15.28

[1]Annual wages have been calculated by multiplying the hourly mean wage by a "year-round, full-time" hours figure of 2,080 hours; for occupations with no published hourly mean wage, the annual wage has been directly calculated from the reported survey data.

[2]Wages for some occupations that do not generally entail year-round, full-time employment are reported as either hourly wages or annual salaries (depending on how employees are typically paid).

CHAPTER 4: LABOR FORCE AND EMPLOYMENT PROJECTIONS BY INDUSTRY AND OCCUPATION

HIGHLIGHTS

Every two years, the Bureau of Labor Statistics (BLS) develops decade-long projections for industry output, employment, and occupations. This chapter presents the employment outlook for the 2019–2029 period. The projections are based on a set of explicit assumptions and an application of a model of economic relationships.

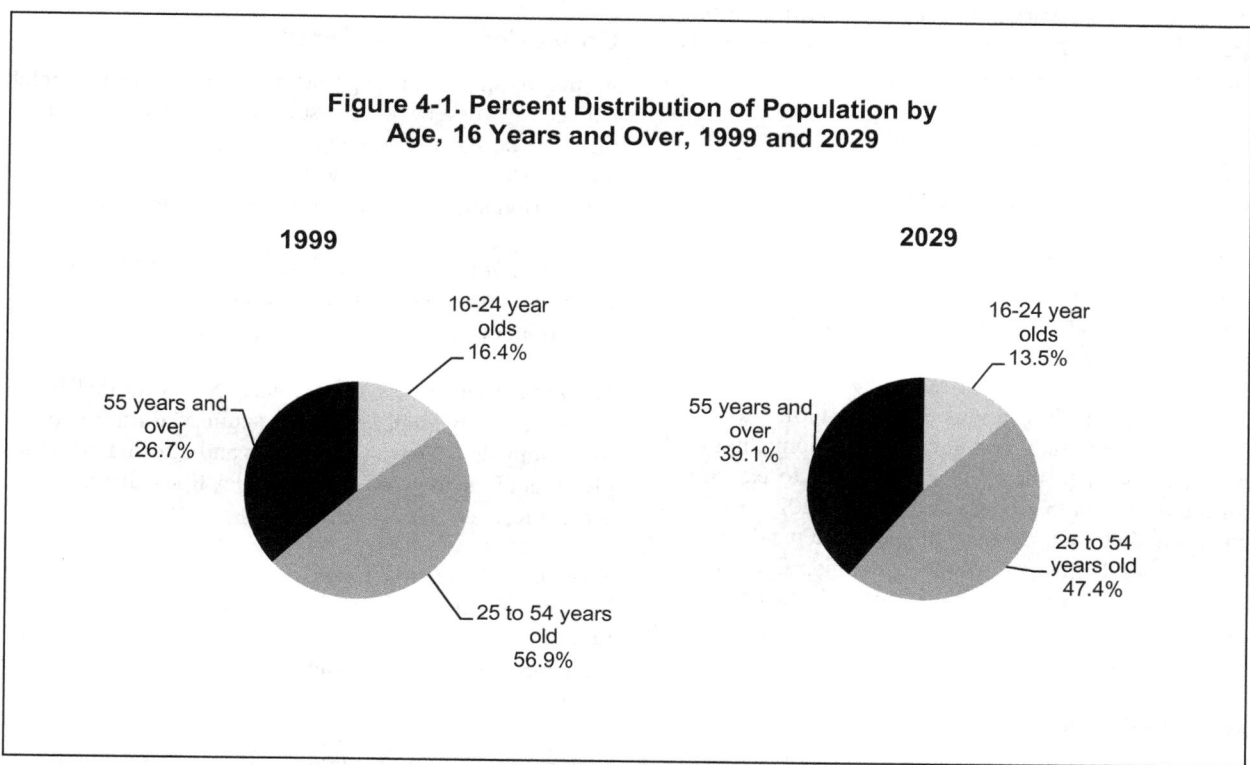

Figure 4-1. Percent Distribution of Population by Age, 16 Years and Over, 1999 and 2029

From 2019 to 2029, the civilian non-institutional population is projected to grow at an annual rate of 0.8 percent. The number of Hispanics is expected to grow at a much faster rate than the general population, increasing at a rate of 2.4 percent per year. In contrast, the number of White people is expected to increase at a rate of 0.5 percent. (See Table 4-1.)

OTHER HIGHLIGHTS

- It is projected that there will also be significant variation in growth rates by age group. While the number of persons 75 years and over is expected to increase by 4.1 percent, the number of those aged 55 to 64 is expected to decline 0.8 percent and the 16 to 19 age population is expected to decline 0.1 percent. (See Table 4-1.)

- The healthcare and social assistance sector is the fastest growing major sector in the economy. Healthcare occupations will account for 13 of the 30 fastest growing occupations from 2019 to 2029. Increased demand for healthcare services from an aging population and people with chronic conditions will drive much of the expected employment growth. (See Table 4-8)

- Meanwhile, employment is expected to decline for several occupations such as mail carriers, administrative assistants, and data entry workers due to advances in technology and automation. (See Table 4-4)

- The labor force continues to age. The median age of the labor force was 39.0 in 1999, 41.5 in 2009, 41.9 in 2019, and is projected to be 42.6 in 2029. (See Table 4-7.)

NOTES AND DEFINITIONS

The Bureau of Labor Statistics (BLS) develops long-term projections of likely employment patterns in the U.S. economy. Since the early 1970s, projections have been prepared on a 2-year cycle. The last projections were released in September 2020. The projections cover the future size and composition of the labor force, aggregate economic growth, detailed estimates of industry production, and industry and occupational employment. The resulting data serve a variety of users who need information about expected patterns of economic growth and the effects these patterns are expected to have on employment.

The 2019–2029 projections do not include impacts of the COVID-19 pandemic and response efforts. The BLS Employment Projections are developed using models based on historical data, which in this set of projections cover the time period through 2019; all input data therefore precede the pandemic. In addition, the 2019–2029 projections were finalized in the spring of 2020 when there was still significant uncertainty about the duration and impacts of the pandemic.

The BLS Employment Projections are long-term projections intended to capture structural change in the economy, not cyclical fluctuations. As such, they are not intended to capture the impacts of the recession that began in February 2020. However, besides the immediate recessionary impacts, the pandemic may cause new structural changes to the economy. BLS releases new employment projections annually, and subsequent projections will incorporate new information on economic structural changes as it becomes available.

Concepts and Definitions

Economic dependency ratio. This ratio is measured *by* measured by estimating the number of persons in the total population (including all Armed Forces personnel overseas and children) who are *not* in the labor force per hundred of those who are.

Employment. In the employment projections survey, employment is defined as a count of jobs, not a count of individual workers.

Employment change. The numerical change in employment measures the projected number of job gains or losses.

Employment change, percent. The percent change in employment measures the projected rate of change of employment in an occupation. A rapidly growing occupation usually indicates favorable prospects for employment. However, even modest employment growth in a large occupation can result in many more job openings due to growth than can rapid employment growth in a small occupation.

Job openings due to growth and replacement needs. Estimates of the projected number of net entrants into an occupation. For occupations that require training, the data may be used to assess the minimum number of workers who will need to be trained.

On-the-Job Training Terms:

Apprenticeship. An apprenticeship is a formal relationship between a worker and sponsor that combines technical instruction and on-the-job training. The typical programs provides at least 2,000 hours of on-the-job training per year over a 3-to-5 year period and 144 hours of technical instruction.

Internship/residency. An internship or residency typically involves supervised training in a professional setting such as a classroom or hospital.

Moderate-term on-the-job training. Skills needed for a worker to become fully qualified can be acquired during 1 to 12 months of combined on-the-job experience and informal training. Examples include heavy and tractor-trailer truck drivers and medical secretaries.

Short-term on-the-job training. Skills needed for a worker to become fully qualified can be acquired during a short demonstration of job duties or during 1 month or less of on-the-job experience or instruction. Examples include retail salespersons and waiters and waitresses.

Long-term on-the-job training. More than 12 months of on-the-job training or, alternatively, combined work experience and formal classroom instruction are needed for workers to develop the skills to become fully qualified. This category includes formal or informal apprenticeships that may last up to 5 years. Long-term on-the-job training also includes intensive occupation-specific, employer-sponsored programs that workers must complete.

Sources of Additional Information

A complete presentation of the projections, including analysis of results and additional tables and a comprehensive description of the methodology, can be found in the September 2020 edition of the Monthly Labor Review which is available on the BLS Web site at https://www.bls.gov/mlr/. In addition, more information on employment projections can be found on the BLS Web site at <https://www.bls.gov/emp/home.htm />.

Table 4-1. Civilian Noninstitutional Population, by Age, Sex, Race, and Hispanic Origin, 1999, 2009, 2019, and Projected 2029

(Numbers in thousands, percent.)

Age, sex, race, and Hispanic origin	Level				Change		
	1999	2009	2019	2029	1999–2009	2009–2019	2019–2029
Both Sexes, 16 Years and Over	207 752	235 800	259 174	280 407	28 048	23 374	21 233
16 to 24 years	34 007	37 567	37 747	37 952	3 560	180	205
16 to 19 years	16 039	17 043	17 692	16 578	1 004	-351	-114
20 to 24 years	17 968	20 524	21 055	21 374	2 556	531	319
25 to 54 years	118 197	125 565	126 280	132 955	7 368	715	6 675
25 to 34 years	37 976	40 281	44 876	44 997	2 305	4 595	121
35 to 44 years	44 634	40 918	40 960	46 879	-3 716	42	5 919
45 to 54 years	35 587	44 366	40 444	41 079	8 779	-3 922	635
55 years and over	55 548	72 668	95 147	109 500	17 120	22 479	14 353
55 to 64 years	23 064	34 670	42 241	38 996	11 606	7 571	-3 245
65 to 74 years	17 821	20 532	31 279	38 231	2 711	10 747	6 952
75 years and over	14 663	17 466	21 627	32 273	2 803	4 161	10 646
Men, 16 Years and Over	99 722	114 135	125 354	135 992	14 413	11 219	10 638
16 to 24 years	17 066	18 927	18 975	19 064	1 861	48	89
16 to 19 years	8 167	8 643	8 445	8 400	476	-198	-45
20 to 24 years	8 899	10 284	10 530	10 664	1 385	246	134
25 to 54 years	57 869	62 097	62 304	66 125	4 228	207	3 821
25 to 34 years	18 565	20 167	22 386	22 484	1 602	2 219	98
35 to 44 years	21 968	20 198	20 144	23 460	-1 770	-54	3 316
45 to 54 years	17 336	21 732	19 774	20 181	4 396	-1 958	407
55 years and over	24 787	33 111	44 075	50 803	8 324	10 964	6 728
55 to 64 years	11 008	16 697	20 335	18 888	5 689	3 638	-1 447
65 to 74 years	8 055	9 470	14 577	17 932	1 415	5 107	3 355
75 years and over	5 724	6 944	9 163	13 983	1 220	2 219	4 820
Women, 16 Years and Over	108 030	121 665	133 820	144 415	13 635	12 155	10 595
16 to 24 years	16 941	18 640	18 772	18 888	1 699	132	116
16 to 19 years	7 872	8 400	8 247	8 177	528	-153	-70
20 to 24 years	9 069	10 240	10 525	10 710	1 171	285	185
25 to 54 years	60 328	63 468	63 976	66 830	3 140	508	2 854
25 to 34 years	19 411	20 114	22 490	22 513	703	2 376	23
35 to 44 years	22 666	20 720	20 816	23 419	-1 946	96	2 603
45 to 54 years	18 251	22 634	20 670	20 898	4 383	-1 964	228
55 years and over	30 761	39 557	51 072	58 698	8 796	11 515	7 626
55 to 64 years	12 056	17 973	21 906	20 108	5 917	3 933	-1 798
65 to 74 years	9 766	11 062	16 702	20 300	1 296	5 640	3 598
75 years and over	8 939	10 522	12 464	18 290	1 583	1 942	5 826
White, 16 Years and Over	173 085	190 902	200 827	211 644	17 817	9 925	10 817
Men	83 930	93 433	98 221	103 765	9 503	4 788	5 544
Women	89 156	97 469	102 606	107 878	8 313	5 137	5 272
Black, 16 Years and Over	24 855	28 241	33 038	36 900	3 386	4 797	3 862
Men	11 144	12 705	15 103	17 036	1 562	2 398	1 933
Women	13 711	15 536	17 935	19 864	1 825	2 399	1 929
All Other Groups,[1] 16 Years and Over	9 812	16 657	25 309	31 864	6 845	8 652	6 555
Men	4 649	7 997	12 030	15 190	3 348	4 033	3 160
Women	5 163	8 660	13 279	16 673	3 497	4 619	3 394
Hispanic,[2] 16 Years and Over	21 650	32 890	43 506	54 974	11 240	10 616	11 468
Men	10 713	16 897	21 660	27 493	6 184	4 763	5 833
Women	10 937	15 993	21 846	27 481	5 056	5 853	5 635
Other than Hispanic origin	186 102	202 910	215 668	225 433	16 808	12 758	9 765
Men	89 009	97 238	103 694	108 499	8 229	6 456	4 805
Women	97 093	105 672	111 974	116 934	8 579	6 302	4 960

[1] The "All other groups" category includes respondents who reported the racial categories of "American Indian and Alaska Native" or "Native Hawaiian and Other Pacific Islander," as well as those who reported two or more races. This category was not defined prior to 2003.
[2] May be of any race.
. . . = Not available.

Table 4-1. Civilian Noninstitutional Population, by Age, Sex, Race, and Hispanic Origin, 1999, 2009, 2019, and Projected 2029—*Continued*

(Numbers in thousands, percent.)

Age, sex, race, and Hispanic origin	Percent distribution				Annual growth rate (percent)		
	1999	2009	2019	2029	1999–2009	2009–2019	2019–2029
Both Sexes, 16 Years and Over	100.0	100.0	100.0	100.0	1.3	0.9	0.8
16 to 24 years	16.4	15.9	14.6	13.5	1.0	0.0	0.1
16 to 19 years	7.7	7.2	6.4	5.9	0.6	-0.2	-0.1
20 to 24 years	8.6	8.7	8.1	7.6	1.3	0.3	0.2
25 to 54 years	56.9	53.3	48.7	47.4	0.6	0.1	0.5
25 to 34 years	18.3	17.1	17.3	16.0	0.6	1.1	0.0
35 to 44 years	21.5	17.4	15.8	16.7	-0.9	0.0	1.4
45 to 54 years	17.1	18.8	15.6	14.6	2.2	-0.9	0.2
55 years and over	26.7	30.8	36.7	39.1	2.7	2.7	1.4
55 to 64 years	11.1	14.7	16.3	13.9	4.2	2.0	-0.8
65 to 74 years	8.6	8.7	12.1	13.6	1.4	4.3	2.0
75 years and over	7.1	7.4	8.3	11.5	1.8	2.2	4.1
Men, 16 Years and Over	48.0	48.4	48.4	48.5	1.4	0.9	0.8
16 to 24 years	8.2	8.0	7.3	6.8	1.0	0.0	0.0
16 to 19 years	3.9	3.7	3.3	3.0	0.6	-0.2	-0.1
20 to 24 years	4.3	4.4	4.1	3.8	1.5	0.2	0.1
25 to 54 years	27.9	26.3	24.0	23.6	0.7	0.0	0.6
25 to 34 years	8.9	8.6	8.6	8.0	0.8	1.0	0.0
35 to 44 years	10.6	8.6	7.8	8.4	-0.8	0.0	1.5
45 to 54 years	8.3	9.2	7.6	7.2	2.3	-0.9	0.2
55 years and over	11.9	14.0	17.0	18.1	2.9	2.9	1.4
55 to 64 years	5.3	7.1	7.8	6.7	4.3	2.0	-0.7
65 to 74 years	3.9	4.0	5.6	6.4	1.6	4.4	2.1
75 years and over	2.8	2.9	3.5	5.0	2.0	2.8	4.3
Women, 16 Years and Over	52.0	51.6	51.6	51.5	1.2	1.0	0.8
16 to 24 years	8.2	7.9	7.2	6.7	1.0	0.1	0.1
16 to 19 years	3.8	3.6	3.2	2.9	0.7	-0.2	-0.1
20 to 24 years	4.4	4.3	4.1	3.8	1.2	0.3	0.2
25 to 54 years	29.0	26.9	24.7	23.8	0.5	0.1	0.4
25 to 34 years	9.3	8.5	8.7	8.0	0.4	1.1	0.0
35 to 44 years	10.9	8.8	8.0	8.4	-0.9	0.0	1.2
45 to 54 years	8.8	9.6	8.0	7.5	2.2	-0.9	0.1
55 years and over	14.8	16.8	19.7	20.9	2.5	2.6	1.4
55 to 64 years	5.8	7.6	8.5	7.2	4.1	2.0	-0.9
65 to 74 years	4.7	4.7	6.4	7.2	1.3	4.2	2.0
75 years and over	4.3	4.5	4.8	6.5	1.6	1.7	3.9
White, 16 Years and Over	83.3	81.0	77.5	75.5	1.0	0.5	0.5
Men	40.4	39.6	37.9	37.0	1.1	0.5	0.6
Women	42.9	41.3	39.6	38.5	0.9	0.5	0.5
Black, 16 Years and Over	12.0	12.0	12.7	13.2	1.3	1.6	1.1
Men	5.4	5.4	5.8	6.1	1.3	1.7	1.2
Women	6.6	6.6	6.9	7.1	1.3	1.4	1.0
All Other Groups,[1] 16 Years and Over	4.7	7.1	9.8	11.4	5.4	4.3	2.3
Men	2.2	3.4	4.6	5.4	5.6	4.2	2.4
Women	2.5	3.7	5.1	5.9	5.3	4.4	2.3
Hispanic,[2] 16 Years and Over	10.4	13.9	16.8	19.6	4.3	2.8	2.4
Men	5.2	7.2	8.4	9.8	4.7	2.5	2.4
Women	5.3	6.8	8.4	9.8	3.9	3.2	2.3
Other than Hispanic origin	89.6	86.1	83.2	80.4	0.9	0.6	0.4
Men	42.8	41.2	40.0	38.7	0.9	0.6	0.5
Women	46.7	44.8	43.2	41.7	0.9	0.6	0.4

[1]The "All other groups" category includes respondents who reported the racial categories of "American Indian and Alaska Native" or "Native Hawaiian and Other Pacific Islander," as well as those who reported two or more races. This category was not defined prior to 2003.
[2]May be of any race.
. . . = Not available.

Table 4-2. Fastest-Growing Occupations, 2019 and Projected 2029

(Numbers in thousands, percent.)

Occupation	Employment		Change, 2019–2029		Mean annual wage, 2019
	2019	2029	Number	Percent	
Total, All Occupations	162 795.6	168 834.7	6 039.2	3.7	39 810
Wind turbine service technicians	7.0	11.3	4.3	60.7	52 910
Nurse practitioners	211.3	322.0	110.7	52.4	109 820
Solar photovoltaic installers	12.0	18.1	6.1	50.5	44 890
Occupational therapy assistants	47.1	63.5	16.3	34.6	61 510
Statisticians	42.7	57.5	14.8	34.6	91 160
Home health and personal care aides	3 439.7	4 599.2	1 159.5	33.7	25 280
Physical therapist assistants	98.7	130.9	32.2	32.6	58 790
Medical and health services managers	422.3	555.5	133.2	31.5	100 980
Physician assistants	125.5	164.8	39.3	31.3	112 260
Information security analysts	131.0	171.9	40.9	31.2	99 730
Data scientists and mathematical science occupations, all other	33.2	43.4	10.3	30.9	94 280
Derrick operators, oil and gas	12.0	15.7	3.7	30.5	46 990
Rotary drill operators, oil and gas	20.9	26.6	5.6	26.9	54 980
Roustabouts, oil and gas	58.5	73.1	14.7	25.1	38 910
Speech-language pathologists	162.6	203.1	40.5	24.9	79 120
Operations research analysts	105.1	131.3	26.1	24.8	84 810
Substance abuse, behavioral disorder, and mental health counselors	319.4	398.4	79.0	24.7	46 240
Forest fire inspectors and prevention specialists	2.3	2.8	0.5	24.3	45 270
Cooks, restaurant	1 417.3	1 744.6	327.3	23.1	27 790
Animal caretakers	300.7	369.5	68.8	22.9	24 780
Service unit operators, oil and gas	51.7	63.6	11.8	22.9	46 740
Marriage and family therapists	66.2	80.9	14.8	22.3	49 610
Computer numerically controlled tool programmers	25.7	31.3	5.6	21.9	56 450
Film and video editors	38.3	46.5	8.3	21.6	63 780
Software developers and software quality assurance analysts and testers	1 469.2	1 785.2	316.0	21.5	107 510
Genetic counselors	2.6	3.2	0.6	21.5	81 880
Physical therapist aides	50.6	61.3	10.8	21.3	27 000
Massage therapists	166.7	201.1	34.4	20.6	42 820
Health specialties teachers, postsecondary	254.0	306.1	52.1	20.5	97 320
Helpers--extraction workers	16.9	20.3	3.4	20.2	37 120

Table 4-3. Occupations with the Largest Job Growth, 2019–2029

(Numbers in thousands, percent.)

Occupation	Employment		Change, 2019–2029		Mean annual wage, 2019
	2019	2029	Number	Percent	
Total, All Occupations	162 795.6	168 834.7	6 039.2	3.7	39 810
Home health and personal care aides	3 439.7	4 599.2	1 159.5	33.7	25 280
Fast food and counter workers	4 047.7	4 508.6	460.9	11.4	22 740
Cooks, restaurant	1 417.3	1 744.6	327.3	23.1	27 790
Software developers and software quality assurance analysts and testers	1 469.2	1 785.2	316.0	21.5	107 510
Registered nurses	3 096.7	3 318.7	221.9	7.2	73 300
General and operations managers	2 486.4	2 630.2	143.8	5.8	100 780
Medical assistants	725.2	864.4	139.2	19.2	34 800
Medical and health services managers	422.3	555.5	133.2	31.5	100 980
Market research analysts and marketing specialists	738.1	868.4	130.3	17.7	63 790
Laborers and freight, stock, and material movers, hand	2 986.0	3 111.7	125.7	4.2	29 510
Landscaping and groundskeeping workers	1 188.0	1 307.9	119.9	10.1	30 440
Nursing assistants	1 528.5	1 645.5	116.9	7.6	29 660
Nurse practitioners	211.3	322.0	110.7	52.4	109 820
Financial managers	697.9	806.0	108.1	15.5	129 890
Janitors and cleaners, except maids and housekeeping cleaners	2 374.2	2 479.8	105.6	4.4	27 430
Waiters and waitresses	2 613.8	2 711.4	97.6	3.7	22 890
Passenger vehicle drivers, except bus drivers, transit and intercity	853.3	947.8	94.4	11.1	31 340
Management analysts	876.3	970.2	93.8	10.7	85 260
Project management specialists and business operations specialists, all other	1 361.8	1 441.6	79.8	5.9	73 570
Substance abuse, behavioral disorder, and mental health counselors	319.4	398.4	79.0	24.7	46 240
Construction laborers	1 398.0	1 473.4	75.4	5.4	36 860
Social and human service assistants	425.6	497.1	71.5	16.8	35 060
Animal caretakers	300.7	369.5	68.8	22.9	24 780
Licensed practical and licensed vocational nurses	721.7	787.4	65.7	9.1	47 480
Sales representatives of services, except advertising, insurance, financial services, and travel	1 070.5	1 134.7	64.2	6.0	56 130
Maintenance and repair workers, general	1 516.4	1 579.4	63.0	4.2	39 080
Industrial machinery mechanics	399.4	461.7	62.3	15.6	53 590
Electricians	739.2	801.4	62.2	8.4	56 180
Accountants and auditors	1 436.1	1 497.9	61.7	4.3	71 550
First-line supervisors of food preparation and serving workers	1 039.3	1 100.2	60.9	5.9	33 400

Table 4-4. Fastest Declining Occupations, 2019 and Projected 2029

(Numbers in thousands, percent, dollars.)

Occupation	2019	2029	Number	Percent	Median annual wage, 2019
Total, All Occupations	162 795.6	168 834.7	6 039.2	3.7	39 810
Word processors and typists	52.7	33.5	-19.2	-36.4	40 340
Parking enforcement workers	8.1	5.2	-2.9	-36.2	40 920
Nuclear power reactor operators	5.3	3.4	-1.9	-35.7	100 530
Watch and clock repairers	3.2	2.1	-1.0	-32.3	42 520
Cutters and trimmers, hand	9.8	6.9	-2.9	-29.9	30 200
Telephone operators	5.0	3.6	-1.4	-27.9	35 750
Travel agents	82.0	60.8	-21.3	-25.9	40 660
Data entry keyers	172.4	130.0	-42.4	-24.6	33 490
Electronic equipment installers and repairers, motor vehicles	10.4	8.0	-2.4	-23.2	37 380
Switchboard operators, including answering service	69.9	54.1	-15.7	-22.5	30 610
Manufactured building and mobile home installers	2.9	2.2	-0.6	-22.3	33 890
Timing device assemblers and adjusters	1.3	1.0	-0.3	-22.3	35 080
Legal secretaries and administrative assistants	171.8	133.8	-38.0	-22.1	47 300
Postmasters and mail superintendents	13.4	10.5	-2.9	-21.9	76 900
Forging machine setters, operators, and tenders, metal and plastic	16.4	13.0	-3.5	-21.1	39 670
Prepress technicians and workers	30.2	24.0	-6.3	-20.7	40 510
Executive secretaries and executive administrative assistants	593.4	472.4	-121.1	-20.4	60 890
Floral designers	51.8	41.4	-10.4	-20.1	28 040
Door-to-door sales workers, news and street vendors, and related workers	72.9	58.3	-14.6	-20.0	27 420
Grinding and polishing workers, hand	29.0	23.4	-5.6	-19.5	30 600
Photographic process workers and processing machine operators	12.3	9.9	-2.4	-19.4	32 280
Refractory materials repairers, except brickmasons	0.8	0.7	-0.2	-19.3	53 990
Desktop publishers	10.4	8.4	-2.0	-19.0	45 390
Drilling and boring machine tool setters, operators, and tenders, metal and plastic	11.2	9.1	-2.1	-19.0	38 910
Nuclear technicians	6.7	5.4	-1.3	-18.9	82 080
Pressers, textile, garment, and related materials	38.3	31.1	-7.2	-18.9	24 190
Coil winders, tapers, and finishers	13.0	10.5	-2.4	-18.7	36 520
Milling and planing machine setters, operators, and tenders, metal and plastic	19.2	15.6	-3.6	-18.6	43 210
Postal service mail sorters, processors, and processing machine operators	98.5	80.9	-17.6	-17.8	60 140
Aircraft structure, surfaces, rigging, and systems assemblers	43.9	36.3	-7.6	-17.4	54 210

Table 4-5. Economic Dependency Ratio, 1999, 2009, 2019, and Projected 2029

(Number.)

Group	1999	2009	2019	2029
TOTAL POPULATION	93.6	97.2	100.2	104.1
Under age 16	44.2	42.1	39.7	38.8
Ages 16 to 64	28.8	34.7	35.0	34.2
Ages 65 and older	21.7	21.3	26.4	32.0

Table 4-6. Industries with the Largest Wage and Salary Employment Growth and Declines, 2019–2029

(Number in thousands, percent.)

Industry	Sector	Employment		Change, 2019–2029	Annual rate of change, 2019–2029
		2019	2029		
Largest Growth					
Individual and family services	Health care and social assistance	2 611.3	3 663.9	1 052.6	3.4
Food services and drinking places	Leisure and hospitality	12 064.7	12 941.5	876.8	0.7
Computer systems design and related services	Professional and business services	2 202.2	2 776.7	574.5	2.3
Home health care services	Health care and social assistance	1 527.4	1 983.4	456.0	2.6
Nursing and residential care facilities	Health care and social assistance	3 379.3	3 734.4	355.1	1.0
Management, scientific, and technical consulting services	Professional and business services	1 531.1	1 865.3	334.2	2.0
Offices of physicians	Health care and social assistance	2 672.0	2 978.9	306.9	1.1
Construction	Construction	7 492.2	7 792.4	300.2	0.4
Outpatient care centers	Health care and social assistance	963.0	1 239.6	276.6	2.6
Hospitals	Health care and social assistance	5 198.7	5 454.3	255.6	0.5
Largest Declines					
All other retail	Retail trade	7 488.5	7 278.0	-210.5	-0.3
General Merchandise stores	Retail trade	3 043.3	2 927.4	-115.9	-0.4
Wholesale trade	Wholesale trade	5 903.4	5 801.3	-102.1	-0.2
Wired telecommunications carriers	Information	519.5	419.3	-100.2	-2.1
Newspaper, periodical, book, and directory publishers	Information	298.5	199.3	-99.2	-4.0
Postal Service	Federal government	607.3	519.1	-88.2	-1.6
Printing and related support activities	Manufacturing	424.6	342.3	-82.3	-2.1
Federal non-defense government compensation	Federal government	1 598.0	1 517.3	-80.8	-0.5
Travel arrangement and reservation services	Professional and business services	219.5	153.5	-66.0	-3.5
Food and beverage stores	Retail trade	3 077.6	3 012.2	-65.4	-0.2

Table 4-7. Median Age of the Labor Force, by Sex, Race, and Ethnicity, 1999, 2009, 2019, and Projected 2029

(Number.)

	1999	2009	2019	2029
TOTAL	39.0	41.5	41.9	42.6
Sex				
Men	39.1	41.4	41.9	42.5
Women	39.0	41.8	41.9	42.8
Race				
White	39.4	42.1	42.7	43.4
Black	37.0	39.4	39.6	40.9
Asian	34.7	36.8	38.3	39.8

[1] May be of any race.

Table 4-8. Employment and Output, by Industry, 2009, 2019, and Projected 2029

(Number, percent, dollars.)

Industry	Employment							Output				
	Number of jobs (thousands)			Change		Compound annual rate of change (percent)		Billions of chained (2005) dollars			Compound annual rate of change (percent)	
	2009	2019	2029	2009–2019	2019–2029	2009–2019	2019–2029	2009	2019	2029	2009–2019	2019–2029
Total[1,2]	143 036	162 795	168 834	19 759	6 039	1.3	0.4	27 293	34 049	40 867	2.2	1.8
Nonagriculture Wage and Salary	132 029	151 710	158 116	19 680	6 406	1.4	0.4	26 836	33 487	40 193	2.2	1.8
Mining	643	685	778	41	93	0.6	1.3	486	635	836	2.7	2.8
Oil and gas extraction	160	150	130	-10	-20	-0.6	-1.4	278	474	660	5.5	3.4
Mining, except oil and gas	208	191	194	-17	2	-0.8	0.1	125	108	114	-1.4	0.6
Coal mining	82	52	44	-30	-8.3	-4.4	-1.7	51	45	44	-1.3	-0.2
Metal ore mining	35	42	49	7	6.8	1.8	1.5	41	36	38	-1.2	0.5
Nonmetallic mineral mining and quarrying	92	98	102	6	4	0.6	0.4	33	27	32	-2.0	1.6
Support activities for mining	275	343	454	67.9	111	2.2	2.8	84	82	109	-0.1	2.9
Utilities	560	549	507	-11	-42	-0.2	-0.8	444	459	534	0.3	1.5
Electric power generation, transmission and distribution	404	386	352	-19	-34	-0.5	-0.9	340	357	422	0.5	1.7
Natural gas distribution	109	110	99	2	-11	0.1	-1.1	89	91	99	0.2	0.8
Water, sewage and other systems	47.3	53.2	55.6	5.9	2.4	1.2	0.4	13.0	11.4	12.8	-1.3	1.1
Construction	6 016	7 492	7 792	1 476	300	2.2	0.4	1 162	1 419	1 616	2.0	1.3
Manufacturing	11 848	12 840	12 395	992	-445	0.8	-0.4	5 262	6 384	7 434	2.0	1.5
Food manufacturing	1 456	1 643	1 650	187	6	1.2	0.0	736	825	972	1.1	1.7
Animal food manufacturing	52	64	75	12	10.8	2.1	1.6	53	66	81	2.2	2.1
Grain and oilseed milling	60	61	56	1	-4	0.1	-0.8	95	143	178	4.2	2.3
Sugar and confectionery product manufacturing	71	79	67	8	-12	1.1	-1.6	34	37	39	1.0	0.4
Fruit and vegetable preserving and specialty food manufacturing	172	173	159	1	-15	0.1	-0.9	65	67	72	0.3	0.9
Dairy product manufacturing	131	156	159	25	3	1.8	0.2	117	123	149	0.5	2.0
Animal slaughtering and processing	497	531	545	34	14	0.7	0.3	213	220	258	0.3	1.6
Seafood product preparation and packaging	38	35	29	-3	-6	-0.8	-1.8	12	11	13	-0.6	1.8
Bakeries and tortilla manufacturing	273	316	303	43	-13	1.5	-0.4	61	66	75	0.9	1.2
Other food manufacturing	163	228	257	66	28	3.5	1.2	88	97	115	0.9	1.7
Beverage and tobacco product	187	286	296	98	10	4.3	0.4	167	168	181	0.1	0.8
Beverage manufacturing	169	275	289	106	14	5.0	0.5	104	122	148	1.6	2.0
Tobacco manufacturing	19	11	7	-7	-5	-4.9	-5.2	64	47	38	-2.9	-2.1
Textile mills and textile product mills	250	222	198	-28	-24	-1.2	-1.1	51	53	50	0.3	-0.5
Apparel, leather and allied product manufacturing	196	138	94	-59	-44	-3.5	-3.7	26	19	20	-2.8	0.5
Wood product manufacturing	360	409	382	49	-26	1.3	-0.7	74	94	108	2.4	1.4
Sawmills and wood preservation	83	92	85	9	-7	1.0	-0.8	21	26	30	2.0	1.6
Veneer, plywood, and engineered wood product manufacturing	68	82	87	14	4.9	1.9	0.6	18	20	24	1.5	1.6
Other wood product manufacturing, including wood tv, radio and sewing machine cabinet manufacturing	209	234	210	26	-24	1.2	-1.1	35	48	54	3.1	1.3
Paper manufacturing	407	365	340	-42	-25	-1.1	-0.7	173	177	183	0.2	0.4
Pulp, paper, and paperboard mills	117	96	92	-20	-4	-1.9	-0.4	79	81	84	0.2	0.4
Converted paper product manufacturing	290	269	248	-21	-21	-0.8	-0.8	93	96	99	0.2	0.3
Printing and related support activities	522	425	342	-97	-82	-2.0	-2.1	86	84	90	-0.3	0.7
Petroleum and coal products manufacturing	115	114	109	-1	-5	-0.1	-0.5	841	900	1 132	0.7	2.3
Chemical manufacturing	804	850	877	46	27	0.6	0.3	744	864	1 034	1.5	1.8
Basic chemical manufacturing	145	153	160	7.7	7	0.5	0.4	256	332	409	2.6	2.1
Resin, synthetic rubber, and artificial synthetic fibers and filaments manufacturing	92	95	94	3	-1	0.4	-0.1	103	116	139	1.2	1.8
Pesticide, fertilizer, and other agricultural chemical manufacturing	36	37	35	>0	-2	0.0	-0.5	34	54	60	4.8	1.2
Pharmaceutical and medicine manufacturing	284	306	322	22	16	0.7	0.5	201	194	232	-0.4	1.8
Paint, coating, and adhesive manufacturing	57	65	69	8	4	1.3	0.6	34	38	40	1.2	0.6
Soap, cleaning compound, and toilet preparation manufacturing	103	110	117	8	7	0.7	0.6	75	88	111	1.6	2.3
Other chemical product and preparation manufacturing	86	83	79	-2	-4	-0.3	-0.5	42	47	50	1.2	0.5
Plastics and rubber products manufacturing	625	737	683	112	-54	1.7	-0.8	189	226	259	1.8	1.4
Plastics product manufacturing	502	599	549	97	-50	1.8	-0.9	150	177	203	1.7	1.4
Rubber product manufacturing	123	138	134	15	-4	1.2	-0.3	38	48	56	2.4	1.4
Nonmetallic mineral product manufacturing	394	422	348	27	-74	0.7	-1.9	94	121	141	2.5	1.5
Clay product and refractory manufacturing	44	39	29	-5	-9	-1.2	-2.8	8	10	10	2.6	0.3
Glass and glass product manufacturing	84	86	79	2	-7	0.3	-0.8	19	28	34	4.3	1.8
Cement and concrete product manufacturing	185	199	142	14	-57	0.7	-3.3	42	49	57	1.4	1.6
Lime, gypsum and other nonmetallic mineral product manufacturing	82	98	98	16	<0	1.8	0.0	25	34	40	3.0	1.6
Primary metal manufacturing	362	385	369	23	-16	0.6	-0.4	203	249	269	2.0	0.8
Iron and steel mills and ferroalloy manufacturing	85	86	79	1	-7	0.1	-0.8	86	102	108	1.8	0.6

[1] Employment data for wage and salary workers are from the BLS Current Employment Statistics (CES) Survey, which counts jobs, whereas data for self-employed, unpaid family workers, and agriculture, forestry, fishing, and hunting workers are from the Current Population Survey (CPS, or household, survey), which counts workers.
[2] Output subcategories do not necessarily add to higher categories as a by-product of chain weighting.
<0 Negative value too near zero to display.
>0 Value too small to display.

Table 4-8. Employment and Output, by Industry, 2009, 2019, and Projected 2029—*Continued*

(Number, percent, dollars.)

Industry	Employment							Output				
	Number of jobs (thousands)			Change		Compound annual rate of change (percent)		Billions of chained (2005) dollars			Compound annual rate of change (percent)	
	2009	2019	2029	2009–2019	2019–2029	2009–2019	2019–2029	2009	2019	2029	2009–2019	2019–2029
Manufacturing—*Continued*												
Steel product manufacturing from purchased steel	50	58	58	8	>0	1.5	0.0	18	22	25	2.2	1.3
Alumina and aluminum production and processing	56	60	53	4	-7	0.7	-1.2	29	32	29	0.8	-0.9
Nonferrous metal (except aluminum) production and processing	58	62	60	4	-2	0.6	-0.4	48	62	74	2.6	1.8
Foundries	113	119	119	6	<0	0.5	0.0	23	31	32	3.3	0.4
Fabricated metal product manufacturing	1 312	1 492	1 446	180	-45	1.3	-0.3	297	386	431	2.7	1.1
Forging and stamping	89	101	96	12	-5	1.3	-0.5	28	42	46	3.9	1.1
Cutlery and handtool manufacturing	42	36	34	-6	-2	-1.4	-0.5	9	11	11	1.9	0.1
Architectural and structural metals manufacturing	345	400	404	56	3	1.5	0.1	74	84	96	1.3	1.4
Boiler, tank, and shipping container manufacturing	89	96	95	8	-1	0.8	-0.1	27	39	44	3.9	1.1
Hardware manufacturing	24	26	24	1	-2	0.5	-0.7	8	8	8	0.2	0.5
Spring and wire product manufacturing	43	44	41	1	-2	0.2	-0.6	7	10	10	2.9	0.5
Machine shops; turned product; and screw, nut, and bolt manufacturing	309	365	378	55.7	13	1.7	0.3	54	78	87	3.8	1.1
Coating, engraving, heat treating, and allied activities	121	142	137	21	-5.2	1.6	-0.4	23	31	32	2.8	0.4
Other fabricated metal product manufacturing	250	282	237	31	-44	1.2	-1.7	66	83	95	2.3	1.3
Machinery manufacturing	1 029	1 126	1 112	97	-14	0.9	-0.1	300	385	446	2.5	1.5
Agriculture, construction, and mining machinery manufacturing	214	221	219	7	-2	0.3	-0.1	77	110	130	3.7	1.7
Industrial machinery manufacturing	102	118	109	16	-9	1.5	-0.8	30	32	38	0.8	1.6
Commercial and service industry machinery manufacturing, including digital camera manufacturing	96	94	94	-2	<0	-0.2	0.0	22	26	30	1.6	1.6
Ventilation, heating, air-conditioning, and commercial refrigeration equipment manufacturing	128	138	134	9	-4	0.7	-0.3	35	45	50	2.6	1.2
Metalworking machinery manufacturing	158	180	178	22	-2	1.3	-0.1	24	29	31	2.1	0.7
Engine, turbine, and power transmission equipment manufacturing	95	100	100	5	1	0.5	0.1	37	54	62	3.9	1.5
Other general purpose machinery manufacturing	237	276	278	39	2	1.5	0.1	76	90	104	1.6	1.5
Computer and electronic product manufacturing	1 137	1 080	1 062	-56	-18	-0.5	-0.2	336	404	474	1.9	1.6
Computer and peripheral equipment manufacturing, excluding digital camera manufacturing	166	163	169	-3	6	-0.2	0.3	44	56	73	2.3	2.7
Communications equipment manufacturing	120	84	58	-37	-26	-3.6	-3.6	58	65	82	1.2	2.3
Audio and video equipment manufacturing	23	20	18	-3	-2	-1.2	-1.1	8	3	4	-8.0	1.4
Semiconductor and other electronic component manufacturing	378	377	374	-1	-3	0.0	-0.1	91	127	129	3.4	0.1
Navigational, measuring, electromedical, and control instruments manufacturing	422	424	431	2	7	0.1	0.2	131	152	188	1.5	2.2
Manufacturing and reproducing magnetic and optical media	28	13	12	-15	<0	-7.4	-0.4	4	4	5	-0.2	2.1
Electrical equipment, appliance, and component manufacturing	374	405	392	32	-13	0.8	-0.3	114	143	158	2.3	1.0
Electric lighting equipment manufacturing	48	46	31	-2	-15	-0.5	-3.9	12	18	18	4.0	0.2
Household appliance manufacturing	60	62	60	2	-2	0.4	-0.3	21	23	29	0.9	2.3
Electrical equipment manufacturing	145	147	142	2	-5	0.2	-0.4	36	43	49	1.9	1.3
Other electrical equipment and component manufacturing	121	150	159	29	9	2.2	0.6	46	60	63	2.7	0.5
Transportation equipment manufacturing	1 348	1 734	1 715	386	-19	2.6	-0.1	625	1 043	1 250	5.3	1.8
Motor vehicle manufacturing	146	237	249	91	12	4.9	0.5	179	355	452	7.1	2.5
Motor vehicle body and trailer manufacturing	104	166	155	62	-10	4.8	-0.6	24	45	51	6.4	1.3
Motor vehicle parts manufacturing	414	596	610	182	14	3.7	0.2	153	324	360	7.8	1.0
Aerospace product and parts manufacturing	492	534	530	42	-4	0.8	-0.1	200	244	300	2.0	2.1
Railroad rolling stock manufacturing	23	24	20	1	-4.3	0.5	-1.9	13	20	21	4.0	0.6
Ship and boat building	131	142	121	12	-21	0.8	-1.6	32	33	38	0.4	1.4
Other transportation equipment manufacturing	38	35	30	-3	-6	-0.8	-1.7	25	24	30	-0.2	2.2
Furniture and related product manufacturing	384	388	359	4	-29	0.1	-0.8	62	74	84	1.8	1.2
Household and institutional furniture and kitchen cabinet manufacturing, excluding wood tv, radio and sewing maching cabinet manufacturing	243	243	242	>0	-1	0.0	-0.1	34	38	43	1.0	1.3
Office furniture (including fixtures) manufacturing	103	111	86	8	-24.7	0.7	-2.5	20	26	28	2.4	0.6
Other furniture related product manufacturing	38	34	31	-4	-3.2	-1.1	-1.0	8	11	13	3.6	1.9
Miscellaneous manufacturing	584	618	620	33	2	0.6	0.0	168	170	198	0.1	1.5
Medical equipment and supplies manufacturing	307	324	327	18	3	0.6	0.1	92	102	118	1.0	1.5
Other miscellaneous manufacturing	278	293	292	16	-1	0.5	0.0	76	68	80	-1.0	1.6
Wholesale Trade	5 521	5 903	5 801	382	-102	0.7	-0.2	1 224	1 886	2 441	4.4	2.6
Retail Trade	14 528	15 644	15 276	1 117	-368	0.7	-0.2	1 271	1 842	2 339	3.8	2.4
Motor vehicle and parts dealers	1 637	2 035	2 058	397	23	2.2	0.1	156	379	491	9.3	2.6
Food and beverage stores	2 830	3 078	3 012	248	-65	0.8	-0.2	204	212	240	0.4	1.2
General Merchandise stores	2 966	3 043	2 927	77	-116	0.3	-0.4	236	257	292	0.9	1.3
All other retail	7 094	7 488	7 278	394	-210	0.5	-0.3	677	1 003	1 332	4.0	2.9

<0 Negative value too near zero to display.
>0 Value too small to display.

Table 4-8. Employment and Output, by Industry, 2009, 2019, and Projected 2029—*Continued*

(Number, percent, dollars.)

Industry	Employment							Output				
	Number of jobs (thousands)			Change		Compound annual rate of change (percent)		Billions of chained (2005) dollars			Compound annual rate of change (percent)	
	2009	2019	2029	2009–2019	2019–2029	2009–2019	2019–2029	2009	2019	2029	2009–2019	2019–2029
Transportation and Warehousing	4 225	5 618	5 944	1 393	326	2.9	0.6	940	1 128	1 328	1.8	1.6
Air transportation	463	503	532	40	29.5	0.8	0.6	178	244	293	3.2	1.9
Rail transportation	185	174	167	-10	-8	-0.6	-0.5	65	75	85	1.4	1.3
Water transportation	63	66	67	2	2	0.4	0.2	51	52	54	0.1	0.5
Truck transportation	1 269	1 531	1 557	262	26	1.9	0.2	258	338	417	2.7	2.1
Transit and ground passenger transportation	428	499	526	71	26	1.5	0.5	48	76	92	4.8	2.0
Pipeline transportation	43	51	53	9	2	1.9	0.3	38	44	46	1.5	0.6
Scenic and sightseeing transportation and support activities for transportation	586	790	808	204	18	3.0	0.2	94	130	160	3.3	2.1
Postal Service	703	607	519	-96	-88	-1.5	-1.6	74	54	49	-3.1	-0.8
Couriers and messengers	546	816	942	270	126	4.1	1.4	86	82	93	-0.4	1.3
Warehousing and storage	642	1 188	1 292	545.9	104	6.3	0.8	127	94	98	-3.0	0.5
Information	2 804	2 859	2 853	56	-6	0.2	0.0	1 227	1 914	2 490	4.6	2.7
Publishing industries	796	760	755	-37	-5	-0.5	-0.1	293	357	495	2.0	3.3
Newspaper, periodical, book, and directory publishers	539	298	199	-240	-99	-5.7	-4.0	139	121	123	-1.4	0.1
Software publishers	258	461	555	203	94	6.0	1.9	154	236	378	4.4	4.8
Motion picture, video, and sound recording industries	358	444	493	86	49	2.2	1.0	129	128	140	-0.1	0.9
Broadcasting (except Internet)	301	266	247	-34	-20	-1.2	-0.8	131	198	247	4.2	2.3
Radio and television broadcasting	215	214	215	-2	1	-0.1	0.1	65	98	124	4.2	2.4
Cable and other subscription programming	85	53	32	-32	-21	-4.6	-4.8	66	99	123	4.2	2.1
Telecommunications	966	713	0	-253	0	-3.0	0.0	531	763	934	3.7	2.0
Wired telecommunications carriers	635	520	419	-116	-100	-2.0	-2.1	327	335	391	0.3	1.6
Wireless telecommunications carriers (except satellite)	187	106	104	-81	-2	-5.5	-0.2	173	398	514	8.7	2.6
Satellite, telecommunications resellers, and all other telecommunications	144	88	78	-56	-9.8	-4.8	-1.2	34	50	64	3.9	2.6
Data processing, hosting, and related services	248	339	377	90	38	3.1	1.1	90	236	322	10.2	3.2
Other information services	135	338	380	203	43	9.6	1.2	54	242	365	16.2	4.2
Finance and Insurance	5 844	6 425	6 491	581	66	1.0	0.1	2 111	2 344	2 700	1.1	1.4
Monetary authorities, credit intermediation, and related activities	2 611	2 671	2 665	60	-6	0.2	0.0	803	637	695	-2.3	0.9
Securities, commodity contracts, funds, trusts and other financial investments and related activities	862	964	990	102	26	1.1	0.3	628	600	657	-0.5	0.9
Insurance carriers and related activities	2 371	2 790	2 836	419	46	1.6	0.2	684	1 142	1 407	5.3	2.1
Insurance carriers	1 463	1 598	1 587	135	-12	0.9	-0.1	496	719	887	3.8	2.1
Agencies, brokerages, and other insurance related activities	908	1 192	1 250	284	58	2.8	0.5	189	424	520	8.4	2.1
Real estate, rental, and leasing	1 994	2 321	2 308	327	-12	1.5	-0.1	1 506	1 887	2 266	2.3	1.8
Real estate	1 420	1 718	1 726	298	8	1.9	0.0	1 245	1 569	1 888	2.3	1.9
Rental and leasing services and lessors of intangible assets	574	603	582	29	-21	0.5	-0.3	261	314	372	1.9	1.7
Automotive equipment rental and leasing	168	227	231	59	4	3.0	0.2	44	62	78	3.5	2.3
Consumer goods rental and general rental centers	264	177	132	-87	-45	-3.9	-2.9	28	32	36	1.6	1.1
Commercial and industrial machinery and equipment rental and leasing	116	176	200	60	24	4.3	1.3	55	66	82	1.9	2.1
Lessors of nonfinancial intangible assets (except copyrighted works)	26	23	20	-3	-4	-1.3	-1.7	135	154	176	1.3	1.4
Professional, Scientific, and Technical Services	7 553	9 543	10 577	1 990	1 034	2.4	1.0	1 639	2 249	2 826	3.2	2.3
Legal services	1 125	1 150	1 140	25	-10	0.2	-0.1	305	315	368	0.3	1.6
Accounting, tax preparation, bookkeeping, and payroll services	915	1 026	1 044	111	18	1.2	0.2	153	188	230	2.1	2.1
Architectural, engineering, and related services	1 326	1 513	1 519	187	6	1.3	0.0	287	348	427	2.0	2.1
Specialized design services	124	144	138	21	-6	1.6	-0.4	27	35	42	2.4	2.0
Computer systems design and related services	1 429	2 202	2 777	773	574	4.4	2.3	269	518	712	6.8	3.2
Management, scientific, and technical consulting services	1 026	1 531	1 865	505	334	4.1	2.0	198	338	433	5.5	2.5
Scientific research and development services	619	729	759	110	30	1.6	0.4	171	226	279	2.8	2.1
Advertising and related services	424	493	486	69	-7	1.5	-0.1	120	139	178	1.4	2.5
Other professional, scientific, and technical services	566	755	849	189	94	2.9	1.2	112	156	190	3.4	2.0
Management of companies and enterprises	1 872	2 427	2 558	555	131	2.6	0.5	459	492	619	0.7	2.3
Administrative and support and waste management and remediation services	7 208	9 343	9 696	2 134	353	2.6	0.4	654	1 034	1 288	4.7	2.2
Administrative and support services	6 857	8 888	9 210	2 032	321	2.6	0.4	575	941	1 178	5.0	2.3
Office administrative services	401	526	625	125	99	2.8	1.7	43	71	90	5.1	2.4
Facilities support services	133	164	165	31	1	2.1	0.0	27	39	49	3.9	2.2
Employment services	2 482	3 637	3 620	1 156	-18	3.9	0.0	190	365	465	6.7	2.5
Business support services	822	878	1 006	56	128	0.7	1.4	65	97	121	4.1	2.3
Travel arrangement and reservation services	194	220	154	26	-66	1.3	-3.5	38	59	72	4.5	2.0
Investigation and security services	790	956	1 018	166	62	1.9	0.6	43	69	86	4.9	2.2
Services to buildings and dwellings	1 753	2 168	2 274	415	106	2.1	0.5	132	189	231	3.7	2.0
Other support services	282	339	349	57	10	1.9	0.3	38	54	67	3.5	2.3

Table 4-8. Employment and Output, by Industry, 2009, 2019, and Projected 2029—*Continued*

(Number, percent, dollars.)

Industry	Employment							Output				
	Number of jobs (thousands)			Change		Compound annual rate of change (percent)		Billions of chained (2005) dollars			Compound annual rate of change (percent)	
	2009	2019	2029	2009–2019	2019–2029	2009–2019	2019–2029	2009	2019	2029	2009–2019	2019–2029
Professional, Scientific, and Technical Services—*Continued*												
Waste management and remediation services	352	454	486	103	32	2.6	0.7	79	94	111	1.8	1.7
Education services	3 090	3 764	4 230	674	466	2.0	1.2	314	313	371	0.0	1.7
Elementary and secondary schools	856	1 106	1 255	251	148	2.6	1.3	40	36	42	-1.1	1.5
Junior colleges, colleges, universities, and professional schools	1 643	1 841	1 983	198	142	1.1	0.7	206	208	245	0.1	1.7
Other educational services	591	817	992	226	175	3.3	2.0	68	70	85	0.2	2.0
Health care and social assistance	16 540	20 413	23 492	3 873	3 079	2.1	1.4	1 830	2 402	3 201	2.8	2.9
Ambulatory health care services	5 793	7 697	9 124	1 904.0	1 427	2.9	1.7	811	1 087	1 458	3.0	3.0
Offices of physicians	2 231	2 672	2 979	441	307	1.8	1.1	400	541	739	3.1	3.2
Offices of dentists	818	969	1 022	152	53	1.7	0.5	110	119	142	0.8	1.8
Offices of other health practitioners	647	969	1 208	322	239	4.1	2.2	77	111	151	3.7	3.1
Outpatient care centers	606	963	1 240	357	277	4.7	2.6	88	122	168	3.4	3.2
Medical and diagnostic laboratories	219	283	326	64	42	2.6	1.4	43	71	96	5.0	3.1
Home health care services	1 027	1 527	1 983	500	456	4.0	2.6	60	85	114	3.7	3.0
Other ambulatory health care services	246	314	367	68	53	2.5	1.6	35	39	53	1.2	3.1
Hospitals	4 667	5 199	5 454	531	256	1.1	0.5	658	894	1 192	3.1	2.9
Nursing and residential care facilities	3 082	3 379	3 734	297	355	0.9	1.0	196	227	302	1.5	2.9
Social assistance	2 997	4 137	5 179	1 140	1 042	3.3	2.3	164	196	253	1.8	2.6
Individual and family services	1 603	2 611	3 664	1 008	1 053	5.0	3.4	76	100	133	2.8	2.9
Community, and vocational rehabilitation services	541	508	501	-34	-7	-0.6	-0.1	42	48	62	1.4	2.7
Child day care services	853	1 018	1 014	166	-4	1.8	0.0	47	48	58	0.3	1.8
Arts, entertainment, and recreation	1 916	2 433	2 668	518	234	2.4	0.9	257	325	404	2.4	2.2
Performing arts, spectator sports, and related industries	397	516	544	119	28	2.7	0.5	127	160	197	2.4	2.1
Performing arts companies	114	132	112	18	-20	1.5	-1.6	21	26	32	2.3	2.0
Spectator sports	130	150	164	21	14	1.5	0.9	38	43	54	1.3	2.2
Promoters of events, and agents and managers	109	181	203	72	22	5.2	1.2	33	45	55	3.2	2.0
Independent artists, writers, and performers	45	53	64	8	11	1.7	1.9	35	45	56	2.7	2.1
Museums, historical sites, and similar institutions	129	173	203	44	30	2.9	1.6	13	17	22	2.9	2.7
Amusement, gambling, and recreation industries	1 389	1 744	1 921	355	177	2.3	1.0	117	148	185	2.3	2.3
Amusement parks and arcades	152	225	247	73	22	4.0	0.9	19	17	22	-0.9	2.1
Gambling industries (except casino hotels)	132	115	103	-17	-12	-1.4	-1.1	30	39	50	2.5	2.6
Other amusement and recreation industries	1 105	1 404	1 571	299	167	2.4	1.1	68	92	114	3.0	2.2
Accomodation and food services	11 162	14 143	15 024	2 981	881	2.4	0.6	757	1 022	1 259	3.1	2.1
Accomodation	1 763	2 078	2 082	315	5	1.7	0.0	191	255	328	2.9	2.5
Food services and drinking places	9 399	12 065	12 942	2 666	877	2.5	0.7	565	767	931	3.1	2.0
Other services	6 150	6 714	6 995	564	281	0.9	0.4	564	652	774	1.5	1.7
Repair and mantenance	1 150	1 352	1 420	202	68	1.6	0.5	184	216	253	1.6	1.6
Automotive repair and maintenance	806	949	982	143	33	1.6	0.3	111	132	148	1.7	1.1
Electronic and precision equipment repair and maintenance ...	98	105	119	7	14	0.7	1.2	19	26	32	3.3	2.2
Commercial and industrial machinery and equipment (except automotive and electronic) repair and maintenance	176	220	253	43.5	33	2.2	1.4	32	39	49	1.9	2.2
Personal and household goods repair and maintenance	70	79	66	8	-12	1.1	-1.7	22	20	25	-0.9	2.3
Personal and laundry services	1 281	1 525	1 640	245	115	1.8	0.7	162	193	232	1.7	1.9
Personal care services	604	738	778	133	41	2.0	0.5	64	80	100	2.3	2.2
Death care services	133	137	130	3	-7	0.2	-0.5	19	23	24	1.8	0.5
Drycleaning and laundry services	311	294	278	-18	-16	-0.6	-0.6	26	29	32	0.8	1.0
Other personal services	232	357	454	126	97	4.4	2.4	53	62	76	1.5	2.2
Religious, grantmaking, civic, professional, and similar organizatons	2 936	3 016	3 142	80	126	0.3	0.4	200	224	267	1.1	1.8
Religious organizations	1 690	1 728	1 731	38	3	0.2	0.0	86	90	102	0.5	1.3
Grantmaking and giving services and social advocacy organizations	363	419	518	56	99	1.4	2.2	44	49	60	1.1	2.1
Civic, social, professional, and similar organizations	882	868	892	-14	24	-0.2	0.3	71	86	104	1.9	2.0
Private households	783	821	792	38	-28.3	0.5	-0.4	17	19	22	0.8	1.7
Federal Government	2 832	2 834	2 650	2	-184	0.0	-0.7	1 126	1 119	1 112	-0.1	-0.1
Postal Service	703	607	519	-96	-88	-1.5	-1.6	74	54	49	-3.1	-0.8
Federal electric utilities	23	15	10	-8	-5	-4.2	-3.8	12	16	19	2.9	1.7
Federal enterprises except the Postal Service and electric utilities	86	71	73	-15	3	-1.9	0.4	19	21	25	1.0	1.9
Federal defense government compensation	519	543	530	24	-12	0.5	-0.2	243	234	227	-0.4	-0.3
Federal defense government consumption of fixed capital	0	0	0	0	0	0.0	0.0	151	152	148	0.1	-0.3
Federal defense government except compensation and consumption of fixed capital	0	0	0	0	0	0.0	0.0	273	247	246	-1.0	-0.1
Federal non-defense government compensation - except enterprises	1 501	1 598	1 517	97	-81	0.6	-0.5	155	159	158	0.2	-0.1
Federal non-defense government consumption of fixed capital	0	0	0	0	0	0.0	0.0	88	108	108	2.2	-0.1
Federal non-defense government except compensation and consumption of fixed capital	0	0	0	0	0	0.0	0.0	111	128	134	1.4	0.4
Federal government except enterprises	2 020	2 141	2 048	121	-93	0.6	-0.4	1 021	1 029	1 019	0.1	-0.1

Table 4-8. Employment and Output, by Industry, 2009, 2019, and Projected 2029—*Continued*

(Number, percent, dollars.)

Industry	Employment							Output				
	Number of jobs (thousands)			Change		Compound annual rate of change (percent)		Billions of chained (2005) dollars			Compound annual rate of change (percent)	
	2009	2019	2029	2009–2019	2019–2029	2009–2019	2019–2029	2009	2019	2029	2009–2019	2019–2029
State and Local Government	19 723	19 759	20 080	37	321	0.0	0.2	2 334	2 475	2 754	0.6	1.1
Local government passenger transit	269	289	307	19	19	0.7	0.6	15	16	19	0.4	2.0
Local government enterprises except passenger transit	1 346	1 347	1 368	1	22	0.0	0.2	177	198	234	1.1	1.7
Local government hospitals - compensation	661	684	714	23	30.4	0.3	0.4	64	66	70	0.3	0.6
Local government educational services - compensation	8 079	8 010	8 033	-69	23	-0.1	0.0	437	420	447	-0.4	0.6
Local government excluding enterprises, educational services, and hospitals - compensation	4 199	4 254	4 463	56	208	0.1	0.5	344	347	370	0.1	0.6
State government enterprises	531	481	464	-50	-16	-1.0	-0.3	87	96	114	1.0	1.7
State government hospitals - compensation	359	386	407	28	20	0.7	0.5	44	39	42	-1.2	0.6
State government educational services - compensation	2 360	2 484	2 529	123.8	45	0.5	0.2	128	143	153	1.1	0.6
State government, other compensation	1 919	1 825	1 795	-94	-29.8	-0.5	-0.2	182	173	184	-0.5	0.6
State and local government capital services	0	0	0	0	0	0.0	0.0	171	196	209	1.4	0.6
General state and local government except compensation and capital services	0	0	0	0	0	0.0	0.0	684	790	929	1.5	1.6
Owner-Occupied Dwellings	0	0	0	0	0	0.0	0.0	1 274	1 506	1 671	1.7	1.0
Agriculture, Forestry, Fishing, and Hunting[3]	2 012	2 304	2 265	292	-39	1.4	-0.2	460	572	684	2.2	1.8
Crop production	904	1 240	1 307	336	66	3.2	0.5	213	309	377	3.8	2.0
Animal production	847	750	646	-97	-103	-1.2	-1.5	200	216	254	0.8	1.6
Forestry	16	16	20	<0	4	-0.1	2.0	5	4	4	-2.7	0.9
Logging	72	73	58	1	-15	0.2	-2.2	14	15	17	0.7	1.2
Fishing, hunting and trapping	41	56	52	15	-5	3.2	-0.9	8	10	11	2.6	1.3
Support activities for agriculture and forestry	132	168	182	36	15	2.5	0.8	20	24	30	1.9	2.3
Nonagriculture Self-Employed[4]	8 995	8 782	8 454	-213.0	-328	-0.2	-0.4	. . .	. . .	. . .	0.0	0.0

[3]Includes agriculture, forestry, fishing, and hunting wage and salary, and self-employed data from the Current Population Survey, except logging, which is from Current Employment Statistics survey.
[4]Comparable estimate of output growth is not available.
. . . = Not available.
<0 Negative value too near zero to display.

Table 4-9. Employment and Wages by Typical Entry Level Education, Projected 2019–2029

(Numbers in thousands, percent, dollars.)

Education, work experience, and on-the-job training	2019 Employment		Employment changes, 2019–2029 (percent)	Median annual wage, 2019
	Number	Percent distribution		
TOTAL, ALL OCCUPATIONS	162 796	100.0	3.7	39 810
Doctoral or professional degree	4 413	2.7	5.9	107 660
Master's degree	2 634	1.6	15.0	76 180
Bachelor's degree	36 864	22.6	6.4	75 440
Associate's degree	3 602	2.2	6.2	54 940
Postsecondary nondegree award	10 093	6.2	5.6	39 940
Some college, no degree	4 085	2.5	-0.1	36 790
High school diploma or equivalent	62 410	38.3	1.5	37 930
No formal educational credential	38 695	23.8	3.3	25 700

Table 4-10. Employment in STEM Occupations 2019 and Projected 2029

(Numbers, percent, dollars.)

Education, work experience, and on-the-job training	Employment		Change 2019–2029		Median annual wage, 2019[1]
	2018	2028	Number	Percent	
TOTAL, ALL OCCUPATIONS	162 796	168 835	6 039	3.7	39 810
STEM Occupations[2]	9 955	10 753	798	8.0	86 980
Non-STEM occupations	152 840	158 082	5 241	3.4	38 160

[1]Science, technology, engineering, and math (STEM) occupations include computer and mathematical, architecture and engineering, and life and physical science occupations, as well as managerial and postsecondary teaching occupations related to these functional areas and sales occupations requiring scientific or technical knowledge at the postsecondary level.
[2]Wage data cover non-farm wage and salary workers and do not cover the self-employed, owners and partners in unincorporated firms, or household workers.

CHAPTER 5: PRODUCTIVITY AND COSTS

HIGHLIGHTS

This chapter covers two kinds of productivity measures produced by the Bureau of Labor Statistics (BLS): output per hour (or labor productivity) and multifactor productivity. Multifactor productivity is designed to combine the joint influence of technological change, efficiency improvements, returns to scale, and other factors on economic growth.

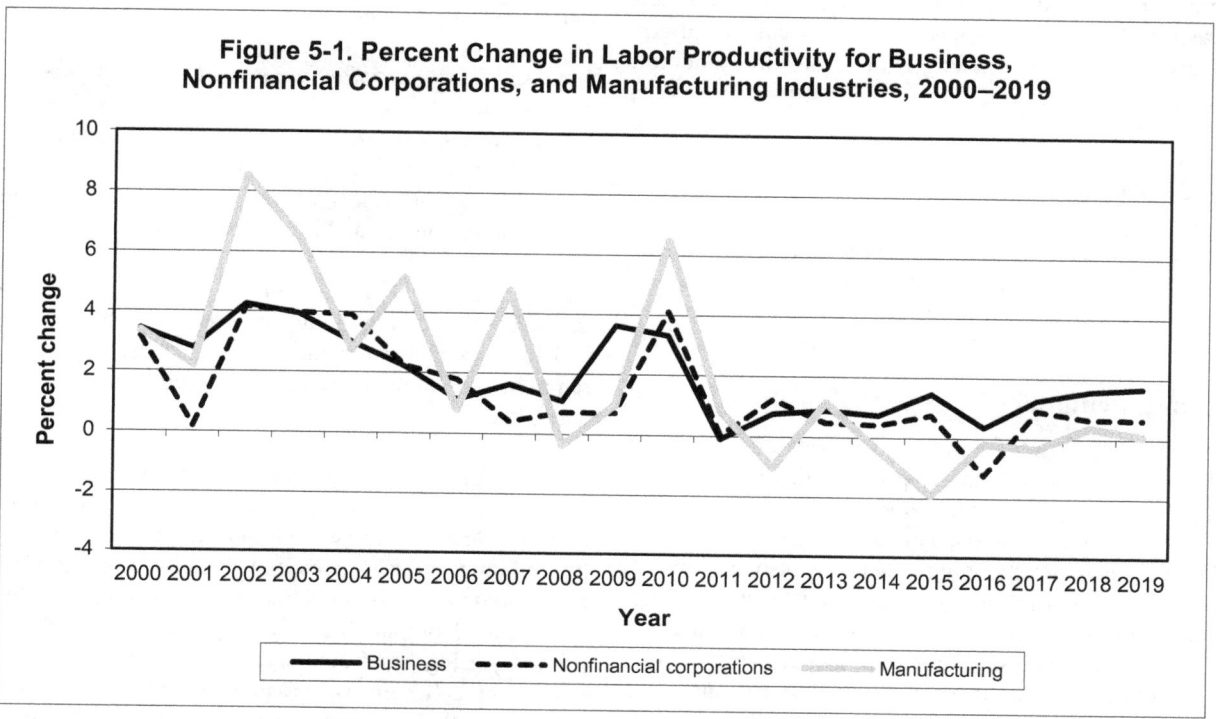

Figure 5-1. Percent Change in Labor Productivity for Business, Nonfinancial Corporations, and Manufacturing Industries, 2000–2019

In 2019, labor productivity increased in all major sectors. It increased 1.7 percent in business and nonfarm business, 0.6 percent in nonfinancial corporations, and 0.1 percent in manufacturing. (See Table 5-1.)

OTHER HIGHLIGHTS:

- Over the entire 1987–2019 period, labor productivity rose in 83 of the 91 manufacturing and mining industries. Output rose in 58 industries, while hours worked increased in 17. In the 17 industries where hours worked increased, they rose at slow pace, 0.7 percent per year on average. (See Table 5-2.)

- During the more recent 2007–2019 period, which included the Great Recession of 2007-09, productivity increased in 45 industries. These increases are predominantly the result of a decline in hours worked rather than an increase in output, as hours worked fell in 35 of these industries while output increased in only 18. (See Table 5-2.)

- During the 1987–2019 period, unit labor costs increased in 76 of the 86 NAICS 4-digit manufacturing industries. All five mining industries saw an increase in unit labor costs. (See Table 5-2.)

- Multifactor productivity increased again in 2019 in both private business and private nonfarm business after last declining in 2016. (See Table 5-4.)

NOTES AND DEFINITIONS

PRODUCTIVITY AND COSTS

The Bureau of Labor Statistics (BLS) produces labor productivity and costs (LPC) measures for sectors of the U.S. economy. Productivity is a measure of economic efficiency that shows how effectively economic inputs are converted into output. The Major Sector Productivity program develops quarterly labor productivity measures for the major U.S. economic sectors including the business sector, the nonfarm business sector, nonfinancial corporations, and manufacturing, along with subsectors of durable and nondurable goods manufacturing. The Industry Productivity program develops annual labor productivity and unit labor cost measures for U.S. industries. In addition, the BLS produces multifactor productivity measures.

Quarterly labor productivity measures are available for business and nonfarm business sectors, nonfinancial corporations and Manufacturing sector. Annual labor productivity measures are available for selected 2-, 3-, 4-, 5-, and 6-digit NAICS industries.

Concepts and Definitions

Business sector output is an annual-weighted index constructed after excluding from gross domestic product (GDP) the following outputs: General government, nonprofit institutions, paid employees of private households, and the rental value of owner-occupied dwellings. Corresponding exclusions also are made in labor inputs. The nonfarm business sector output also excludes the farm sector. Gross domestic product data are prepared by the Bureau of Economic Analysis of the U.S. Department of Commerce as part of the National Income and Product Accounts.

Hourly compensation costs are defined as the sum of wage and salary accruals and supplements to wages and salaries. Wage and salary accruals consist of the monetary remuneration of employees, including the compensation of corporate officers; commissions, tips, and bonuses; voluntary employee contributions to certain deferred compensation plans, such as 401(k) plans; employee gains from exercising nonqualified stock options; and receipts in kind that represent income. Supplements to wages and salaries consist of employer contributions for social insurance and employer payments (including payments in kind) to private pension and profit-sharing plans, group health and life insurance plans, privately administered workers' compensation plans. For employees (wage and salary workers), hourly compensation is measured relative to hours at work and includes payments made by employers for time not at work, such as vacation, holiday, and sick pay. Because compensation costs for the business and nonfarm business sectors would otherwise be severely understated, an estimate of the hourly compensation of proprietors of unincorporated businesses is made by assuming that their hourly compensation is equal to that of employees in the same sector.

Hours at work include paid time working, traveling between job sites, coffee breaks, and machine downtime. Hours at work, however, exclude hours for which employees are paid but not at work.

The *Nonfarm business sector* is a subset of the domestic economy and excludes the economic activities of the following: general government, private households, nonprofit organizations serving individuals, and farms.

Nonfinancial corporations are a subset of the domestic economy and excludes the economic activities of the following: general government, private households, nonprofit organizations serving individuals, and those corporations classified as offices of bank holding companies, offices of other holding companies, or offices in the finance and insurance sector.

Nonlabor payments include profits, consumption of fixed capital, taxes on production and imports less subsidies, net interest and miscellaneous payments, business current transfer payments, rental income of persons, and the current surplus of government enterprises.

Output is measured as an annual-weighted index of the changes in the various products or services (in real terms) provided for sale outside the industry. Real industry output is usually derived by deflating nominal sales or values of production using BLS price indexes, but for some industries it is measured by physical quantities of output. Industry output measures are constructed primarily using data from the economic censuses and annual surveys of the U.S. Census Bureau, U.S. Department of Commerce, together with information on price changes primarily from BLS. Output measures for some mining and utilities industries are based on physical quantity data from the Energy Information Administration, U.S. Department of Energy, while output measures for some transportation industries are based on physical quantity data from the Bureau of Transportation Statistics, U.S. Department of Transportation. Other data sources for some industries include the U.S. Geological Survey, U.S. Department of the Interior; the U.S. Postal Service; the Federal Deposit Insurance Corporation; and the Postal Rate Commission.

Productivity measures describe the relationship between industry output and the labor time involved in its production. They show the changes from period to period in the amount of goods and services produced per hour. Although the labor productivity measures relate output to hours of employees or all persons in an industry, they do not measure the specific contribution of labor or any other factor of production. Rather, they reflect the joint effects of many influences, including changes in technology; capital investment; utilization of capacity, energy, and materials; the use of purchased services inputs, including contract employment services; the organization of production; managerial skill; and the characteristics and effort of the workforce.

Unit labor costs show the growth in compensation relative to that of real output. These costs are calculated by dividing total labor compensation by real output. Changes in unit labor costs can be approximated by subtracting the change in productivity from the change in hourly compensation.

Multifactor Productivity Concepts and Definitions

For the private business and private nonfarm business sectors, the growth rate of multifactor productivity is measured as the growth rate of output less the growth rate of combined inputs of labor and capital. Labor is measured by a weighted average of the number of hours worked classified by education, work experience, and gender. Capital services measure the flow of services from the stocks of equipment and software, structures, land, and inventories. For the manufacturing sector, multifactor productivity is the growth rate of output less the combined inputs of labor, capital, and intermediate purchases. Labor is measured by the number of hours worked. Capital services measure the flow of services from the stocks of equipment and software, structures, land, and inventories. Intermediate purchases are composed of materials, fuels, electricity, and purchased services.

Sectoral output is defined as gross output excluding intra-industry transactions. This measure defines output as deliveries to consumers outside the sector, in an effort to avoid the problem of double-counting that occurs when one establishment provides materials used by other establishments in the same industry.

Value-added output is defined as gross output (sales or receipts and other income, plus inventory change) minus intermediate inputs (goods and service inputs purchased from other domestic industries and foreign sources).

Sources of Additional Information

Productivity concepts and methodology are described in the *BLS Handbook of Methods*. More information on productivity can be found in BLS news releases on the BLS Web site at <https://www.bls.gov/lpc/>. More information can also be found in BLS new releases USDL 20-1276 "Productivity and Costs by Industry: Manufacturing and Mining Industries, 2019"; USDL 20-1465 "Wholesale and Retail Trade Industries, 2019" as well as BLS news release 20-1103 "Productivity and Costs by Industry: Selected Service-Providing Industries, 2019."

Table 5-1. Indexes of Productivity and Related Data, 1947–2019

(2012 = 100.)

Year	Business											
	Output per hour	Output	Hours	Hourly compen-sation	Real hourly compen-sation	Unit labor costs	Unit nonlabor payments	Implicit price deflator	Employment	Output per job	Compen-sation in current dollars	Nonlabor payments in current dollars
1947	20.4	11.2	54.8	3.6	33.9	17.7	11.8	15.1	47.2	23.7	2.0	1.3
1948	21.3	11.7	55.2	3.9	34.0	18.4	13.0	16.0	47.7	24.6	2.2	1.5
1949	21.8	11.6	53.4	4.0	34.9	18.2	12.9	15.9	46.6	24.9	2.1	1.5
1950	23.5	12.7	54.1	4.2	36.9	18.0	13.5	16.1	47.1	27.1	2.3	1.7
1951	24.3	13.6	55.9	4.6	37.5	19.2	14.9	17.3	48.3	28.0	2.6	2.0
1952	25.0	14.0	56.0	4.9	39.0	19.7	14.6	17.5	48.6	28.8	2.8	2.0
1953	25.9	14.7	56.7	5.2	41.2	20.2	14.3	17.6	49.3	29.8	3.0	2.1
1954	26.5	14.5	54.8	5.4	42.2	20.4	14.2	17.7	48.0	30.2	3.0	2.1
1955	27.6	15.7	56.8	5.6	43.4	20.1	15.2	18.0	49.4	31.7	3.2	2.4
1956	27.7	16.0	57.7	5.9	45.6	21.4	14.9	18.5	50.5	31.7	3.4	2.4
1957	28.6	16.3	56.9	6.3	47.0	22.1	15.4	19.1	50.3	32.3	3.6	2.5
1958	29.4	16.0	54.3	6.6	47.8	22.4	15.7	19.5	48.4	33.0	3.6	2.5
1959	30.4	17.2	56.6	6.9	49.3	22.5	16.1	19.7	49.9	34.5	3.9	2.8
1960	31.0	17.6	56.7	7.1	50.5	23.0	15.9	19.9	50.2	35.0	4.0	2.8
1961	32.1	17.9	55.8	7.4	52.0	23.1	16.2	20.1	49.7	36.1	4.1	2.9
1962	33.6	19.1	56.8	7.7	53.7	23.0	16.7	20.2	50.3	38.0	4.4	3.2
1963	34.9	20.0	57.2	8.0	54.9	23.0	17.0	20.4	50.6	39.5	4.6	3.4
1964	36.0	21.2	58.9	8.3	56.2	23.1	17.4	20.6	51.5	41.2	4.9	3.7
1965	37.3	22.7	60.9	8.6	57.4	23.1	18.1	20.9	53.0	42.9	5.3	4.1
1966	38.9	24.3	62.5	9.2	59.5	23.7	18.6	21.4	54.6	44.5	5.8	4.5
1967	39.8	24.8	62.3	9.7	61.0	24.5	18.9	22.0	55.3	44.8	6.1	4.7
1968	41.2	26.0	63.3	10.5	63.2	25.5	19.5	22.9	56.4	46.2	6.6	5.1
1969	41.4	26.8	64.9	11.2	64.1	27.1	19.8	23.9	58.2	46.1	7.3	5.3
1970	42.2	26.8	63.6	12.1	65.2	28.6	20.3	24.9	58.0	46.3	7.7	5.4
1971	43.9	27.9	63.4	12.8	66.2	29.1	22.0	26.0	58.1	47.9	8.1	6.1
1972	45.4	29.7	65.4	13.6	68.2	30.0	22.9	26.9	59.8	49.6	8.9	6.8
1973	46.8	31.7	67.9	14.7	69.3	31.4	24.3	28.3	62.4	50.8	10.0	7.7
1974	46.0	31.2	68.0	16.0	68.2	34.9	26.1	31.1	63.4	49.3	10.9	8.2
1975	47.6	31.0	65.0	17.8	69.2	37.3	29.9	34.1	61.5	50.4	11.6	9.2
1976	49.2	33.0	67.2	19.2	70.7	39.0	31.8	35.8	63.4	52.1	12.9	10.5
1977	50.1	34.9	69.8	20.7	71.7	41.4	33.6	38.0	66.1	52.8	14.5	11.7
1978	50.7	37.2	73.3	22.5	72.6	44.3	35.8	40.6	69.8	53.3	16.5	13.3
1979	50.7	38.5	75.9	24.6	72.7	48.6	38.1	44.0	72.5	53.1	18.7	14.7
1980	50.7	38.1	75.2	27.3	72.4	53.8	40.3	47.9	72.6	52.5	20.5	15.4
1981	51.8	39.2	75.7	29.8	72.4	57.6	45.5	52.3	73.4	53.5	22.6	17.9
1982	51.5	38.1	73.9	32.1	73.4	62.2	46.4	55.3	72.2	52.8	23.7	17.7
1983	53.3	40.1	75.3	33.5	73.5	62.8	50.1	57.3	72.8	55.1	25.2	20.1
1984	54.8	43.7	79.7	35.0	73.7	63.8	52.6	58.9	76.5	57.1	27.9	23.0
1985	56.1	45.7	81.5	36.8	74.9	65.5	53.9	60.4	78.4	58.3	30.0	24.6
1986	57.7	47.4	82.2	38.8	77.8	67.3	53.4	61.3	79.7	59.5	31.9	25.3
1987	58.0	49.1	84.7	40.3	78.0	69.5	53.3	62.4	81.8	60.0	34.1	26.2
1988	58.9	51.2	87.0	42.4	79.3	72.1	54.5	64.4	84.3	60.7	36.9	27.9
1989	59.6	53.2	89.3	43.7	78.2	73.4	58.2	66.8	86.2	61.7	39.0	31.0
1990	60.7	54.0	88.9	46.5	79.2	76.5	59.3	69.0	86.7	62.3	41.3	32.1
1991	61.7	53.7	87.0	48.6	80.0	78.8	61.0	71.0	85.4	62.9	42.3	32.7
1992	64.6	56.0	86.6	51.6	82.9	79.9	62.1	72.1	84.9	65.9	44.7	34.8
1993	64.7	57.6	89.0	52.4	82.0	81.0	64.5	73.8	86.7	66.4	46.6	37.1
1994	65.0	60.3	92.8	52.8	80.9	81.1	67.4	75.1	89.7	67.3	48.9	40.7
1995	65.5	62.2	94.9	54.0	80.9	82.5	68.7	76.5	92.2	67.4	51.3	42.7
1996	67.1	65.1	97.0	56.0	81.7	83.4	70.3	77.7	94.2	69.0	54.3	45.7
1997	68.6	68.5	99.9	58.2	83.2	84.9	71.0	78.8	96.8	70.8	58.2	48.6
1998	70.7	72.0	101.9	61.7	86.9	87.2	69.0	79.3	98.8	72.9	62.8	49.7
1999	73.5	76.1	103.5	64.7	89.2	87.9	69.3	79.8	100.4	75.8	66.9	52.7
2000	76.1	79.8	104.9	69.1	92.3	90.9	68.2	81.0	102.1	78.1	72.5	54.4
2001	78.2	80.4	102.8	72.3	93.8	92.5	69.2	82.3	101.4	79.3	74.3	55.6
2002	81.5	81.8	100.3	73.9	94.4	90.7	72.9	82.9	99.2	82.5	74.2	59.6
2003	84.7	84.5	99.7	76.7	95.8	90.5	75.5	83.9	99.0	85.3	76.5	63.8
2004	87.3	88.1	100.9	80.3	97.7	92.0	78.5	86.1	100.3	87.8	81.0	69.1
2005	89.2	91.5	102.6	83.2	97.9	93.2	82.9	88.7	102.2	89.6	85.3	75.9
2006	90.3	94.6	104.8	86.4	98.4	95.7	85.2	91.1	104.1	90.9	90.6	80.6
2007	91.7	96.8	105.5	90.3	100.0	98.4	86.6	93.2	105.0	92.2	95.2	83.8
2008	92.7	95.8	103.3	92.8	99.0	100.0	87.8	94.7	103.5	92.6	95.8	84.1
2009	96.1	92.3	96.0	93.6	100.2	97.4	91.7	94.9	97.7	94.5	89.8	84.6
2010	99.3	95.2	95.9	95.3	100.4	95.9	96.1	96.0	96.5	98.6	91.3	91.5
2011	99.2	97.1	97.8	97.3	99.4	98.1	98.3	98.2	98.1	99.0	95.2	95.4
2012	100.0	100.0	100.0	100.0	100.0	100.0	100.0	100.0	100.0	100.0	100.0	100.0
2013	100.9	102.4	101.5	101.5	100.0	100.6	102.6	102.6	101.5	101.7	100.8	105.1
2014	101.6	105.6	103.9	104.1	100.9	102.5	104.0	103.1	103.8	101.8	108.2	109.9
2015	103.1	109.6	106.3	107.2	103.7	104.0	103.1	103.6	106.3	103.2	113.9	113.0
2016	103.5	111.6	107.9	108.3	103.5	104.7	104.1	104.4	108.2	103.2	116.9	116.2
2017	104.8	114.7	109.4	112.2	104.9	107.1	105.2	106.3	109.8	104.5	122.8	120.7
2018	106.4	118.7	111.5	116.0	105.9	109.0	108.0	108.6	111.8	106.2	129.4	128.2
2019	108.2	121.6	112.3	120.2	107.8	111.1	109.0	110.2	113.2	107.4	135.0	132.6

Table 5-1. Indexes of Productivity and Related Data, 1947–2019—*Continued*

(2012 = 100.)

Year	Nonfarm business											
	Output per hour	Output	Hours	Hourly compen-sation	Real hourly compen-sation	Unit labor costs	Unit nonlabor payments	Implicit price deflator	Employment	Output per job	Compen-sation in current dollars	Nonlabor payments in current dollars
1947	23.5	10.9	46.5	3.9	36.2	16.4	11.3	14.2	39.6	27.6	1.8	1.2
1948	24.1	11.4	47.2	4.2	36.4	17.4	12.2	15.1	40.4	28.2	2.0	1.4
1949	24.9	11.3	45.4	4.3	38.0	17.3	12.5	15.2	39.3	28.8	2.0	1.4
1950	26.5	12.4	46.9	4.6	39.7	17.2	13.1	15.4	40.2	30.9	2.1	1.6
1951	27.2	13.4	49.1	5.0	40.0	18.2	14.1	16.4	42.0	31.8	2.4	1.9
1952	27.7	13.8	49.6	5.2	41.4	18.9	14.0	16.8	42.6	32.3	2.6	1.9
1953	28.4	14.5	50.9	5.5	43.4	19.5	14.0	17.1	43.8	33.0	2.8	2.0
1954	29.0	14.2	49.1	5.7	44.5	19.7	14.0	17.2	42.6	33.4	2.8	2.0
1955	30.2	15.4	51.1	5.9	46.3	19.6	14.9	17.5	43.9	35.2	3.0	2.3
1956	30.0	15.7	52.4	6.3	48.4	20.9	14.6	18.2	45.2	34.8	3.3	2.3
1957	30.8	16.1	52.1	6.6	49.5	21.5	15.1	18.7	45.4	35.3	3.5	2.4
1958	31.5	15.7	49.9	6.9	50.1	21.9	15.3	19.0	43.8	35.9	3.4	2.4
1959	32.6	17.0	52.2	7.2	51.6	22.0	15.9	19.3	45.4	37.5	3.7	2.7
1960	33.0	17.3	52.5	7.5	53.0	22.6	15.5	19.5	45.9	37.8	3.9	2.7
1961	34.1	17.7	52.0	7.7	54.2	22.6	15.8	19.7	45.5	38.9	4.0	2.8
1962	35.7	18.9	53.1	8.0	55.8	22.5	16.4	19.9	46.4	40.8	4.3	3.1
1963	36.9	19.8	53.7	8.3	56.9	22.5	16.8	20.0	46.9	42.2	4.5	3.3
1964	37.9	21.1	55.7	8.6	57.9	22.6	17.3	20.3	48.1	44.0	4.8	3.7
1965	39.1	22.6	57.9	8.8	58.9	22.6	17.9	20.5	49.8	45.5	5.1	4.0
1966	40.5	24.3	59.9	9.4	60.6	23.1	18.3	21.0	51.7	46.9	5.6	4.4
1967	41.3	24.7	59.9	9.9	62.2	24.0	18.6	21.7	52.6	47.0	5.9	4.6
1968	42.8	26.0	60.9	10.7	64.2	24.9	19.3	22.5	53.8	48.4	6.5	5.0
1969	42.8	26.8	62.7	11.4	65.1	26.6	19.5	23.5	55.7	48.2	7.1	5.2
1970	43.5	26.8	61.7	12.2	65.9	28.0	20.0	24.5	55.8	48.1	7.5	5.4
1971	45.2	27.8	61.5	12.9	67.0	28.6	21.7	25.6	56.0	49.7	8.0	6.0
1972	46.8	29.7	63.5	13.8	69.1	29.5	22.4	26.4	57.6	51.5	8.7	6.6
1973	48.2	31.8	66.1	14.8	70.0	30.8	22.8	27.3	60.2	52.9	9.8	7.3
1974	47.4	31.4	66.2	16.2	69.0	34.2	24.8	30.2	61.2	51.3	10.7	7.8
1975	48.7	30.9	63.3	17.9	69.9	36.8	28.9	33.4	59.4	51.9	11.4	8.9
1976	50.4	33.1	65.6	19.3	71.2	38.4	31.0	35.2	61.4	53.8	12.7	10.3
1977	51.3	35.0	68.2	20.9	72.4	40.8	32.9	37.4	64.2	54.4	14.3	11.5
1978	52.0	37.3	71.7	22.7	73.4	43.7	34.8	39.8	67.8	55.0	16.3	13.0
1979	51.9	38.6	74.3	24.9	73.4	47.9	36.9	43.1	70.7	54.5	18.5	14.2
1980	51.9	38.2	73.7	27.6	73.2	53.1	39.6	47.2	70.9	53.9	20.3	15.1
1981	52.6	39.1	74.3	30.2	73.3	57.4	44.5	51.8	71.7	54.5	22.4	17.4
1982	52.2	37.9	72.6	32.4	74.2	62.1	45.7	55.0	70.6	53.7	23.5	17.3
1983	54.4	40.3	74.0	33.9	74.3	62.3	49.8	56.9	71.3	56.5	25.1	20.1
1984	55.6	43.7	78.6	35.3	74.4	63.6	51.8	58.5	75.1	58.1	27.7	22.6
1985	56.6	45.6	80.6	37.1	75.5	65.5	53.4	60.2	77.3	59.0	29.9	24.3
1986	58.2	47.3	81.2	39.2	78.4	67.3	53.0	61.1	78.6	60.2	31.8	25.1
1987	58.6	49.0	83.7	40.7	78.7	69.4	52.9	62.2	80.8	60.7	34.0	25.9
1988	59.5	51.3	86.1	42.8	79.9	71.8	54.1	64.1	83.4	61.5	36.8	27.7
1989	60.1	53.1	88.4	44.0	78.7	73.2	57.7	66.5	85.3	62.3	38.9	30.6
1990	61.1	53.9	88.3	46.7	79.6	76.3	58.9	68.7	85.9	62.8	41.2	31.7
1991	62.1	53.6	86.3	48.9	80.4	78.7	60.7	70.9	84.5	63.5	42.2	32.6
1992	64.9	55.8	85.9	51.9	83.4	80.0	61.8	72.1	84.0	66.4	44.6	34.5
1993	65.0	57.5	88.5	52.6	82.3	80.9	64.5	73.8	86.0	66.8	46.5	37.1
1994	65.4	60.1	91.9	53.1	81.4	81.1	67.3	75.1	88.8	67.7	48.8	40.5
1995	66.1	62.2	94.1	54.4	81.5	82.2	68.9	76.5	91.4	68.1	51.2	42.9
1996	67.5	65.0	96.3	56.3	82.1	83.3	70.0	77.5	93.5	69.5	54.2	45.5
1997	68.8	68.4	99.3	58.5	83.5	84.9	71.0	78.9	96.2	71.1	58.0	48.5
1998	71.0	72.0	101.4	61.9	87.2	87.2	69.3	79.4	98.3	73.2	62.7	49.9
1999	73.7	76.1	103.3	64.7	89.3	87.9	69.8	80.0	100.1	76.0	66.8	53.1
2000	76.1	79.7	104.7	69.3	92.4	91.0	68.7	81.3	101.9	78.2	72.5	54.7
2001	78.2	80.3	102.7	72.3	93.8	92.4	69.7	82.6	101.3	79.3	74.2	56.0
2002	81.6	81.7	100.1	74.0	94.5	90.7	73.7	83.3	99.0	82.5	74.1	60.2
2003	84.7	84.3	99.6	76.7	95.8	90.6	75.9	84.2	98.9	85.2	76.4	64.0
2004	87.1	87.9	100.9	80.2	97.6	92.1	78.5	86.2	100.3	87.6	80.9	69.0
2005	89.0	91.3	102.6	83.2	97.8	93.4	83.4	89.1	102.2	89.4	85.3	76.2
2006	90.0	94.4	104.9	86.3	98.4	95.9	85.9	91.6	104.2	90.7	90.6	81.1
2007	91.6	96.7	105.6	90.1	99.8	98.4	86.9	93.4	105.1	92.0	95.2	84.1
2008	92.6	95.7	103.4	92.7	98.9	100.1	88.1	94.9	103.6	92.4	95.8	84.3
2009	95.9	92.0	96.0	93.5	100.2	97.5	92.5	95.4	97.7	94.2	89.8	85.2
2010	99.2	95.0	95.9	95.3	100.4	96.1	96.6	96.3	96.5	98.5	91.4	91.8
2011	99.2	96.9	97.8	97.4	99.5	98.2	98.1	98.2	98.0	98.9	95.2	95.1
2012	100.0	100.0	100.0	100.0	100.0	100.0	100.0	100.0	100.0	100.0	100.0	100.0
2013	100.5	102.2	101.7	101.3	99.8	100.8	102.3	101.5	101.8	100.4	103.0	104.6
2014	101.4	105.4	104.0	104.1	100.9	102.7	104.0	103.3	103.9	101.5	108.3	109.7
2015	103.0	109.4	106.2	107.4	103.9	104.3	103.6	104.0	106.2	103.0	114.1	113.3
2016	103.3	111.3	107.8	108.6	103.7	105.1	105.0	105.0	108.1	103.0	117.0	116.9
2017	104.6	114.4	109.4	112.4	105.1	107.5	105.9	106.8	109.8	104.2	123.0	121.2
2018	106.1	118.4	111.6	116.2	106.0	109.5	108.8	109.2	111.9	105.9	129.6	128.9
2019	107.9	121.3	112.4	120.4	107.9	111.5	110.0	110.8	113.3	107.1	135.3	133.4

Table 5-1. Indexes of Productivity and Related Data, 1947–2019—*Continued*

(2012 = 100.)

Year	Output per hour	Output	Hours	Hourly compensation	Real hourly compensation	Unit labor costs	Unit nonlabor costs	Unit profits	Implicit price deflator	Employment	Output per job	Compensation in current dollars	Nonlabor payments in current dollars
1947	22.5	8.8	38.9	4.4	41.3	19.5	10.9	21.3	17.3	33.6	26.0	1.7	1.3
1948	24.0	9.4	39.3	4.8	42.0	20.1	11.5	25.4	18.4	34.2	27.6	1.9	1.5
1949	25.3	9.3	37.0	5.0	43.9	19.7	12.4	23.1	18.1	32.6	28.7	1.8	1.5
1950	27.2	10.6	38.9	5.3	45.8	19.4	11.8	26.1	18.2	33.8	31.2	2.0	1.8
1951	26.9	11.1	41.4	5.8	46.4	21.4	12.4	28.0	19.8	36.0	31.0	2.4	2.0
1952	27.5	11.6	42.0	6.1	48.1	22.1	13.0	25.3	19.9	36.5	31.7	2.6	2.0
1953	28.7	12.4	43.3	6.4	50.4	22.4	12.9	23.7	19.9	37.8	32.9	2.8	2.1
1954	29.9	12.3	41.1	6.6	51.8	22.2	13.3	23.1	19.8	36.3	33.9	2.7	2.0
1955	31.7	13.8	43.5	6.9	53.8	21.7	12.9	26.9	19.9	37.9	36.4	3.0	2.4
1956	31.9	14.3	44.7	7.3	56.4	23.0	13.7	25.2	20.7	39.2	36.3	3.3	2.5
1957	32.6	14.4	44.3	7.8	57.8	23.8	14.8	24.2	21.3	39.3	36.7	3.4	2.6
1958	33.2	13.9	41.8	8.1	58.4	24.2	16.2	22.0	21.6	37.4	37.2	3.4	2.5
1959	34.9	15.5	44.3	8.4	60.2	24.0	15.6	25.5	21.8	39.1	39.5	3.7	2.9
1960	35.5	16.0	45.0	8.7	61.6	24.5	16.0	23.5	21.9	40.0	40.0	3.9	3.0
1961	36.7	16.4	44.6	9.0	62.9	24.5	16.3	23.6	22.0	39.7	41.2	4.0	3.1
1962	38.3	17.8	46.4	9.3	64.7	24.4	16.1	25.3	22.1	41.0	43.3	4.3	3.4
1963	39.7	18.8	47.5	9.6	65.8	24.2	16.0	26.8	22.2	41.9	45.0	4.6	3.7
1964	40.3	20.2	50.0	9.8	66.2	24.3	16.0	27.8	22.4	43.4	46.5	4.9	4.0
1965	41.4	21.9	52.9	10.1	67.0	24.4	15.9	29.9	22.7	45.7	47.9	5.3	4.5
1966	42.2	23.5	55.7	10.6	68.8	25.2	16.0	30.0	23.3	48.3	48.7	5.9	4.8
1967	42.9	24.2	56.2	11.2	70.5	26.2	16.9	28.1	23.8	49.6	48.7	6.3	5.0
1968	44.5	25.7	57.8	12.0	72.6	27.1	18.0	28.1	24.7	51.4	50.1	7.0	5.5
1969	44.6	26.7	60.0	12.9	73.5	28.9	19.6	25.4	25.7	53.7	49.8	7.7	5.8
1970	44.8	26.5	59.1	13.7	74.3	30.6	22.1	20.9	26.8	53.8	49.3	8.1	5.7
1971	46.7	27.6	59.1	14.6	75.4	31.2	23.2	23.7	27.8	54.0	51.1	8.6	6.4
1972	47.6	29.6	62.2	15.3	76.9	32.2	23.1	25.9	28.7	56.7	52.3	9.5	7.1
1973	48.1	31.5	65.4	16.4	77.6	34.2	24.4	26.8	30.3	59.8	52.6	10.7	7.9
1974	47.2	31.0	65.7	17.9	76.3	38.0	28.0	24.5	33.2	61.0	50.8	11.8	8.3
1975	49.0	30.5	62.3	19.8	77.2	40.4	32.0	29.6	36.5	58.7	52.1	12.3	9.5
1976	50.7	33.1	65.2	21.3	78.5	42.0	31.8	34.9	38.1	61.3	53.9	13.9	10.9
1977	52.0	35.5	68.2	23.0	79.6	44.2	33.0	37.9	40.1	64.4	55.1	15.7	12.3
1978	52.7	37.8	71.7	25.1	81.1	47.6	34.4	40.4	42.8	68.0	55.6	18.0	13.7
1979	52.3	39.0	74.6	27.4	80.9	52.4	37.2	38.7	46.1	71.2	54.8	20.5	14.7
1980	52.2	38.6	74.1	30.2	80.2	57.9	43.7	35.0	50.6	71.5	54.1	22.4	15.8
1981	53.5	40.2	75.2	32.9	79.8	61.5	49.6	41.0	55.2	72.7	55.3	24.7	18.8
1982	53.8	39.3	73.1	35.1	80.4	65.3	55.1	38.2	58.5	71.1	55.4	25.7	19.5
1983	55.6	41.3	74.2	36.5	80.2	65.8	55.4	44.3	59.7	71.4	57.8	27.1	21.3
1984	56.9	44.9	79.0	38.1	80.3	67.0	55.1	51.9	61.5	75.6	59.5	30.1	24.3
1985	58.2	47.0	80.8	40.0	81.5	68.8	56.3	50.1	62.5	77.7	60.5	32.3	25.5
1986	59.5	48.2	81.0	42.3	84.6	71.0	59.2	41.4	63.4	78.8	61.2	34.2	25.7
1987	60.8	50.8	83.6	43.8	84.7	72.0	59.7	44.3	64.6	81.0	62.7	36.6	27.7
1988	62.5	53.9	86.2	45.9	85.8	73.5	60.9	47.3	66.2	83.7	64.4	39.6	30.4
1989	61.8	54.9	88.9	47.3	84.6	76.4	64.2	43.3	68.2	85.8	64.0	42.0	31.4
1990	62.3	55.7	89.4	49.5	84.3	79.4	67.2	40.9	70.4	87.3	63.8	44.2	32.5
1991	63.7	55.4	87.0	51.7	85.0	81.1	70.0	42.0	72.3	85.4	64.9	44.9	33.6
1992	65.5	57.1	87.2	54.5	87.5	83.2	68.6	43.6	73.3	85.5	66.8	47.5	34.4
1993	65.5	58.5	89.4	55.2	86.4	84.2	68.5	50.7	74.9	87.2	67.2	49.3	36.6
1994	66.6	62.1	93.3	55.8	85.6	83.8	68.9	60.5	76.2	90.3	68.8	52.1	41.1
1995	67.7	65.1	96.2	56.9	85.3	84.1	69.1	64.1	77.0	93.6	69.6	54.8	43.9
1996	70.0	68.9	98.5	58.8	85.7	84.0	68.3	68.7	77.3	95.9	71.9	57.9	47.2
1997	72.1	73.6	102.0	60.9	87.0	84.4	67.9	70.4	77.7	99.0	74.3	62.1	50.6
1998	74.4	77.6	104.2	64.4	90.8	86.6	68.3	62.9	78.0	101.4	76.5	67.1	51.6
1999	76.8	81.5	106.1	67.7	93.4	88.1	69.8	58.6	78.7	103.5	78.7	71.8	53.9
2000	79.3	85.4	107.8	72.4	96.7	91.4	72.8	49.2	80.1	105.6	80.9	78.1	55.5
2001	79.4	83.3	104.9	74.1	96.2	93.3	78.2	40.2	81.4	104.3	79.9	77.7	54.6
2002	82.7	84.2	101.7	75.5	96.5	91.3	78.7	49.2	81.7	101.3	83.1	76.8	57.9
2003	86.0	86.0	99.9	78.0	97.5	90.7	77.9	59.5	82.6	100.0	86.0	78.0	61.7
2004	89.4	90.2	100.9	80.9	98.4	90.4	77.4	72.6	84.2	100.8	89.5	81.6	68.4
2005	91.4	93.5	102.3	83.4	98.1	91.2	81.0	82.5	87.0	102.4	91.3	85.3	76.2
2006	93.1	97.1	104.3	85.9	97.8	92.2	82.8	91.8	89.5	104.1	93.3	89.6	83.3
2007	93.5	98.0	104.8	89.2	98.8	95.4	88.1	82.3	91.4	104.7	93.6	93.5	84.4
2008	94.2	96.9	102.9	92.0	98.2	97.7	94.2	73.8	93.3	103.3	93.8	94.7	84.7
2009	94.8	90.0	94.9	93.6	100.2	98.7	99.7	68.1	94.6	96.7	93.1	88.9	80.3
2010	98.7	93.9	95.1	95.1	100.2	96.3	97.9	89.1	95.7	95.7	98.1	90.4	89.2
2011	98.8	96.5	97.7	97.2	99.2	98.4	99.3	93.6	98.0	97.7	98.7	94.9	94.0
2012	100.0	100.0	100.0	100.0	100.0	100.0	100.0	100.0	100.0	100.0	100.0	100.0	100.0
2013	100.5	102.5	102.0	101.4	99.9	100.9	101.2	103.3	101.4	102.1	100.4	103.5	104.5
2014	100.9	105.8	104.8	104.0	100.8	103.1	102.5	104.2	103.1	104.7	101.0	109.1	109.0
2015	101.7	108.9	107.1	107.2	103.7	105.5	103.0	100.2	104.0	107.2	101.6	114.8	111.2
2016	100.4	109.1	108.7	108.4	103.5	107.9	104.1	93.8	104.8	109.1	100.0	117.8	109.9
2017	101.3	112.0	110.5	112.0	104.7	110.5	106.1	93.0	106.8	111.0	100.9	123.8	113.9
2018	102.0	114.9	112.7	115.9	105.8	113.7	105.1	98.7	109.1	113.0	101.7	130.6	118.3
2019	102.6	116.7	113.7	120.2	107.8	117.2	107.1	95.4	111.2	114.6	101.8	136.7	120.5

Table 5-1. Indexes of Productivity and Related Data, 1947–2019—*Continued*

(2012 = 100.)

Year	Manufacturing											
	Output per hour	Output	Hours	Hourly compensation	Real hourly compensation	Unit labor costs	Unit nonlabor payments	Implicit price deflator	Employment	Output per job	Compensation in current dollars	Nonlabor payments in current dollars
1947	...	...	...	...	...	...	...	...	...	...	...	...
1948	...	...	...	...	...	...	...	...	...	...	...	...
1949	...	...	...	...	...	...	...	...	...	...	...	...
1950	...	...	...	...	...	...	...	...	...	...	...	...
1951	...	...	...	...	...	...	...	...	...	...	...	...
1952	...	...	...	...	...	...	...	...	...	...	...	...
1953	...	...	...	...	...	...	...	...	...	...	...	...
1954	...	...	...	...	...	...	...	...	...	...	...	...
1955	...	...	...	...	...	...	...	...	...	...	...	...
1956	...	...	...	...	...	...	...	...	...	...	...	...
1957	...	...	...	...	...	...	...	...	...	...	...	...
1958	...	...	...	...	...	...	...	...	...	...	...	...
1959	...	...	...	...	...	...	...	...	...	...	...	...
1960	...	...	...	...	...	...	...	...	...	...	...	...
1961	...	...	...	...	...	...	...	...	...	...	...	...
1962	...	...	...	...	...	...	...	...	...	...	...	...
1963	...	...	...	...	...	...	...	...	...	...	...	...
1964	...	...	...	...	...	...	...	...	...	...	...	...
1965	...	...	...	...	...	...	...	...	...	...	...	...
1966	...	...	...	...	...	...	...	...	...	...	...	...
1967	...	...	...	...	...	...	...	...	...	...	...	...
1968	...	...	...	...	...	...	...	...	...	...	...	...
1969	...	...	...	...	...	...	...	...	...	...	...	...
1970	...	...	...	...	...	...	...	...	...	...	...	...
1971	...	...	...	...	...	...	...	...	...	...	...	...
1972	...	...	...	...	...	...	...	...	...	...	...	...
1973	...	...	...	...	...	...	...	...	...	...	...	...
1974	...	...	...	...	...	...	...	...	...	...	...	...
1975	...	...	...	...	...	...	...	...	...	...	...	...
1976	...	...	...	...	...	...	...	...	...	...	...	...
1977	...	...	...	...	...	...	...	...	...	...	...	...
1978	...	...	...	...	...	...	...	...	...	...	...	...
1979	...	...	...	...	...	...	...	...	...	...	...	...
1980	...	...	...	...	...	...	...	...	...	...	...	...
1981	...	...	...	...	...	...	...	...	...	...	...	...
1982	...	...	...	...	...	...	...	...	...	...	...	...
1983	...	...	...	...	...	...	...	...	...	...	...	...
1984	...	...	...	...	...	...	...	...	...	...	...	...
1985	...	...	...	...	...	...	...	...	...	...	...	...
1986	...	...	...	...	...	...	...	...	...	...	...	...
1987	45.2	64.6	142.8	42.6	82.4	94.1	52.7	62.3	146.8	45.2	60.8	34.0
1988	45.7	67.3	147.1	44.3	82.7	96.8	55.1	64.8	149.4	45.7	65.1	37.1
1989	46.0	68.1	148.0	45.8	81.9	99.4	57.9	67.6	150.2	46.0	67.7	39.5
1990	47.5	68.2	143.4	48.2	82.3	101.5	59.5	69.3	148.0	47.5	69.2	40.5
1991	48.5	66.9	138.0	50.6	83.2	104.3	58.9	69.5	142.8	48.5	69.8	39.4
1992	50.9	69.6	136.8	53.4	85.7	104.9	59.1	69.7	140.4	50.9	73.0	41.1
1993	52.2	72.2	138.4	54.1	84.7	103.7	59.9	70.1	140.5	52.2	74.9	43.3
1994	53.7	76.3	142.0	54.9	84.2	102.2	61.5	71.0	142.3	53.7	78.0	46.9
1995	55.7	79.6	142.9	56.3	84.4	101.1	64.3	72.9	144.3	55.7	80.5	51.2
1996	57.9	82.7	142.8	57.9	84.4	99.9	64.6	72.9	144.2	57.9	82.6	53.4
1997	60.7	88.4	145.7	58.9	84.1	97.1	64.7	72.2	145.4	60.7	85.8	57.2
1998	63.4	92.6	146.2	62.1	87.5	98.0	61.7	70.1	146.7	63.4	90.7	57.2
1999	67.1	96.5	143.8	65.6	90.6	97.9	61.5	70.0	144.4	67.1	94.4	59.3
2000	69.3	98.9	142.7	69.9	93.3	100.8	62.3	71.3	144.0	69.3	99.7	61.6
2001	70.8	94.5	133.5	72.0	93.4	101.6	61.3	70.7	137.3	70.8	96.0	58.0
2002	76.9	95.3	124.0	74.3	94.9	96.6	62.0	70.0	127.4	76.9	92.1	59.1
2003	81.9	96.5	117.9	78.3	97.8	95.6	63.9	71.3	121.4	81.9	92.3	61.7
2004	84.1	98.6	117.2	81.2	98.8	96.5	68.5	75.0	119.7	84.1	95.2	67.6
2005	88.5	102.6	115.9	84.3	99.1	95.2	75.2	79.9	119.1	88.5	97.6	77.1
2006	89.2	104.2	116.8	86.2	98.3	96.7	79.0	83.1	118.4	89.2	100.7	82.3
2007	93.5	107.4	114.8	89.7	99.4	95.9	83.3	86.3	116.4	93.5	103.0	89.5
2008	93.2	102.5	110.0	92.3	98.5	99.1	90.4	92.4	112.3	93.2	101.5	92.6
2009	94.1	90.2	95.9	95.3	102.1	101.4	82.0	86.5	99.6	94.1	91.4	74.0
2010	100.2	96.0	95.8	96.6	101.7	96.4	89.1	90.8	96.8	100.2	92.5	85.5
2011	101.0	98.7	97.7	98.3	100.4	97.3	98.7	98.4	98.1	101.0	96.1	97.4
2012	100.0	100.0	100.0	100.0	100.0	100.0	100.0	100.0	100.0	100.0	100.0	100.0
2013	101.2	101.9	100.8	100.6	99.1	99.4	100.4	100.2	100.6	101.2	101.3	102.4
2014	100.7	103.1	102.4	103.3	100.1	102.6	99.2	100.0	102.0	100.7	105.8	102.3
2015	98.8	102.2	103.4	105.9	102.5	107.2	90.1	94.1	103.2	98.8	109.5	92.0
2016	98.6	102.0	103.4	106.5	101.7	107.9	87.5	92.3	103.3	98.6	110.1	89.3
2017	98.3	102.7	104.5	109.9	102.8	111.8	91.1	95.9	104.2	98.3	114.8	93.5
2018	98.7	105.0	106.4	112.2	102.4	113.8	96.2	100.3	105.9	98.7	119.5	...
2019	98.8	105.1	106.4	115.5	103.5	117.0	...	...	107.2	98.8	122.9	...

. . . = Not available.

Table 5-2. Average Annual Percent Change in Output Per Hour and Related Series, Selected Industries, 1987–2018

(Number, percent.)

Industry	2017 NAICS code	2018 employment (thousands)	Average annual percent change, 1987–2018				
			Labor productivity	Unit labor costs	Output	Hours worked	Labor compensation
Utilities							
Utilities	221	553	2.2	1.4	1.5	-0.7	2.9
Power generation and supply	2211	391	2.9	0.7	2.1	-0.9	2.7
Natural gas distribution	2212	110	1.2	3.1	0.1	-1.1	3.2
Water, sewage and other systems	2213	52	-1.7	4.6	0.8	2.5	5.4
Transportation and Warehousing							
Air transportation	481	482	3.1	0.9	2.8	-0.3	3.7
Line-haul railroads	482111	166	3.5	-0.4	1.8	-1.6	1.4
Truck transportation	484	1 708	0.6	1.1	2.0	1.1	3.2
General freight trucking	4841	1 229	1.1	1.2	2.4	0.9	3.6
General freight trucking, local	48411	327	2.5	0.3	3.7	0.8	4.0
General freight trucking, long-distance	48412	902	1.3	0.6	2.3	1.0	2.9
Specialized freight trucking	4842	480	0.7	2.1	1.9	1.5	4.1
Used household and office goods moving	48421	101	-0.6	2.6	-0.1	0.5	2.5
Other specialized trucking, local	48422	238	0.3	2.6	1.8	1.6	4.4
Other specialized trucking, long distance	48423	141	1.2	1.7	3.1	2.0	4.9
Postal service	491	608	0.4	2.9	-0.6	-1.0	2.3
Couriers and messengers	492	771	-2.0	3.3	0.7	2.7	4.0
Warehousing and storage	493	1 143	1.0	0.6	5.4	3.8	6.1
General warehousing and storage	49311	1 017	2.0	-0.1	6.7	4.0	6.6
Refrigerated warehousing and storage	49312	64	-0.3	1.7	2.8	2.9	4.6
Information							
Publishing	511	768	3.8	1.7	3.5	-0.4	5.2
Newspaper, book, and directory publishers	5111	350	0.2	4.0	-2.6	-2.8	1.2
Newspaper publishers	51111	152	-0.5	3.8	-4.2	-3.8	-0.6
Periodical publishers	51112	95	-0.3	4.8	-1.7	-1.5	3.0
Book publishers	51113	64	-0.2	4.7	-1.1	-0.9	3.6
Software publishers	5112	418	10.4	-5.0	17.1	6.0	11.2
Motion picture and video exhibition	51213	152	1.2	2.3	1.7	0.5	4.0
Broadcasting, except Internet	515	276	3.0	1.5	2.9	-0.1	4.4
Radio and television broadcasting	5151	221	2.2	1.5	1.9	-0.4	3.4
Radio broadcasting	51511	85	3.7	1.2	2.4	-1.2	3.7
Cable and other subscription programming	5152	54	5.0	2.6	6.3	1.2	9.0
Wired and wireless telecommunications carriers ..	5173	666	6.6	-3.0	5.8	-0.7	2.7
Wired telecommunications carriers	517311	552	3.6	-0.5	2.4	-1.2	1.9
Wireless telecommunications carriers	517312	115	12.1	-7.0	18.2	5.5	9.9
Finance and Insurance							
Commercial banking	52211	1 381	3.0	2.0	2.9	-0.1	5.0
Real Estate and Rental and Leasing							
Passenger car rental	532111	124	2.2	1.6	3.1	0.9	4.7
Truck, trailer, and RV rental and leasing	53212	85	2.2	1.1	3.0	0.8	4.1
Video tape and disc rental	532282	10	5.1	-0.8	-2.7	-7.5	-3.5
Professional and Technical Services							
Accounting and bookkeeping services	5412	1 162	2.4	1.4	3.0	1.0	4.4
Offices of certified public accountants	541211	493	2.0	2.0	3.1	1.4	5.2
Tax preparation services	541213	135	0.7	2.3	2.0	1.3	4.3
Other accounting services	541219	361	4.4	-1.4	4.4	0.5	3.0
Architectural services	54131	212	1.6	1.7	2.7	1.1	4.4
Engineering services	54133	1 015	1.1	2.8	2.7	1.6	5.6
Advertising agencies	54181	229	2.2	1.6	2.9	0.7	4.6
Photography studios, portrait	541921	54	0.7	1.3	1.3	0.6	2.6
Veterinary services	54194	407	-0.9	4.2	1.8	2.7	6.1
Administrative and Waste Services							
Employment placement and executive search ...	56131	303	. . .	. . .	. . .	. . .	. . .
Travel arrangement and reservation services ...	5615	246	6.3	-1.3	4.3	-0.3	2.9
Travel agencies	56151	108	6.0	-1.1	4.9	-1.1	3.7
Janitorial services	56172	1 409	2.0	1.4	3.7	1.6	5.1
Health Care and Social Assistance							
Medical and diagnostic laboratories	6215	288	1.9	0.6	4.9	3.2	5.5
Medical laboratories	621511	206	1.9	0.5	4.9	3.3	5.4

. . . = Not available.

Table 5-2. Average Annual Percent Change in Output Per Hour and Related Series, Selected Industries, 1987–2018—*Continued*

(Number, percent.)

Industry	2017 NAICS code	2018 employment (thousands)	Average annual percent change, 1987–2018				
			Labor productivity	Unit labor costs	Output	Hours worked	Labor compensation
Diagnostic imaging centers	621512	82	2.0	1.1	4.7	3.0	5.8
Hospitals, except psychiatric and substance abuse hospitals	6221	4 886	0.5	3.2	2.0	1.5	5.3
Arts, Entertainment, and Recreation							
Amusement parks and arcades	7131	215	0.4	5.0	-0.1	1.8	4.9
Amusement and theme parks	71311	185	0.1	4.0	1.9	1.7	5.9
Gambling industries	7132	126	3.0	1.3	2.7	4.6	4.0
Golf courses and country clubs	71391	391	-1.0	4.1	0.0	2.9	4.1
Fitness and recreational sports centers	71394	674	3.3	-0.3	4.1	2.6	3.8
Bowling centers	71395	71	0.8	2.6	-0.9	-1.6	1.7
Accommodation and Food Services							
Accommodation and food services	72	14 176	0.8	2.7	2.4	1.6	5.1
Accommodation	721	2 061	1.9	1.8	2.7	0.8	4.6
Traveler accommodation	7211	1 969	1.9	1.8	2.7	0.8	4.6
Hotels and motels, except casino hotels	72111	1 655	1.4	2.5	2.2	0.8	4.7
Food services and drinking places	722	12 115	0.5	3.0	2.2	1.7	5.3
Special food services	7223	870	0.9	1.7	2.3	1.4	4.0
Drinking places, alcoholic beverages	7224	408	-0.3	3.0	0.0	0.3	3.0
Restaurants and other eating places	72251	10 838	0.5	3.2	2.4	1.9	5.6
Full-service restaurants	722511	5 534	0.6	3.6	2.3	1.7	5.9
Limited-service eating places	722513	5 303	0.4	2.8	2.4	2.0	5.2
Other Services							
Automotive repair and maintenance	8111	1 173	1.0	2.3	1.5	0.5	3.8
Reupholstery and furniture repair	81142	20	-0.8	3.6	-2.8	-2.0	0.8
Personal care services	8121	1 302	2.2	1.7	3.5	1.3	5.3
Hair, nail, and skin care services	81211	1 062	2.0	1.8	3.1	1.1	4.9
Funeral homes and funeral services	81221	111	-0.4	4.0	-0.4	0.1	3.6
Drycleaning and laundry services	8123	310	2.2	1.4	1.2	-1.0	2.6
Coin-operated laundries and drycleaners	81231	43	2.9	1.9	0.5	-2.3	2.4
Drycleaning and laundry services	81232	135	0.8	2.2	-1.2	-2.0	0.9
Linen and uniform supply	81233	133	2.5	0.8	3.3	0.8	4.1
Photofinishing	81292	10	3.0	1.7	-3.9	-6.7	-2.3

Table 5-3. Average Annual Percent Change in Output Per Hour and Related Series, Wholesale Trade, and Retail Trade, 1987–2019

(Number, percent.)

Industry	NAICS code	2019 employment (thousands)	Average annual percent change, 1987–2019					
			Labor productivity	Unit labor costs	Output	Hours worked	Labor compensation	Hourly compensation
Wholesale Trade								
Wholesale trade	42	6 028	2.7	1.0	3.0	0.3	4.0	3.7
Durable goods	423	3 262	4.1	-0.3	4.4	0.2	4.0	3.8
Motor vehicles and parts	4231	364	3.2	0.4	3.2	0.0	3.6	3.7
Furniture and furnishings	4232	120	1.7	2.1	1.8	0.1	3.9	3.9
Lumber and construction supplies	4233	254	1.0	1.6	1.8	0.8	3.4	2.7
Commercial equipment	4234	693	11.3	-6.5	11.5	0.2	4.3	4.1
Metals and minerals	4235	139	-0.4	3.8	-0.1	0.3	3.7	3.4
Appliance and electric goods	4236	365	6.9	-2.5	6.7	-0.2	4.0	4.2
Hardware and plumbing	4237	286	1.4	2.1	2.4	1.0	4.5	3.5
Machinery and supplies	4238	722	1.6	2.2	1.7	0.1	4.0	3.9
Miscellaneous durable goods	4239	319	1.1	2.6	1.5	0.5	4.1	3.7
Nondurable goods	424	2 230	1.1	2.7	1.3	0.2	4.1	3.8
Paper and paper products	4241	132	0.6	2.6	0.0	-0.6	2.7	3.3
Druggists' goods	4242	244	2.2	3.5	3.5	1.2	7.1	5.9
Apparel and piece goods	4243	156	1.8	1.5	1.4	-0.4	3.0	3.3
Grocery and related products	4244	812	1.0	2.2	1.7	0.7	4.0	3.3
Farm product raw materials	4245	72	1.1	3.6	-0.5	-1.6	3.0	4.7
Chemicals	4246	153	0.0	3.4	0.7	0.6	4.1	3.4
Petroleum	4247	106	2.5	2.2	1.2	-1.3	3.4	4.7
Alcoholic beverages	4248	208	0.3	2.8	2.1	1.8	4.9	3.1
Miscellaneous nondurable goods	4249	346	0.0	3.3	-0.4	-0.4	2.9	3.3
Electronic markets and agents and brokers	425	536	1.5	0.8	3.0	1.5	3.8	2.3
Retail Trade								
Retail trade	44-45	16 410	2.9	0.0	3.3	0.4	3.3	2.9
Motor vehicle and parts dealers	441	2 093	2.2	0.6	3.0	0.8	3.6	2.8
Automobile dealers	4411	1 331	2.3	0.6	3.1	0.8	3.7	2.9
Other motor vehicle dealers	4412	178	2.5	0.8	3.9	1.4	4.7	3.3
Auto parts, accessories, and tire stores	4413	585	1.0	1.4	1.7	0.7	3.2	2.4
Furniture and home furnishings stores	442	499	3.8	-1.0	3.6	-0.2	2.6	2.8
Furniture stores	4421	232	3.2	-0.6	3.0	-0.2	2.4	2.6
Home furnishings stores	4422	267	4.6	-1.5	4.4	-0.2	2.9	3.0
Electronics and appliance stores	443	490	10.7	-7.2	10.9	0.2	2.9	2.7
Building material and garden supply stores	444	1 329	2.5	0.0	3.2	0.7	3.2	2.5
Building material and supplies dealers	4441	1 163	2.4	0.1	3.2	0.9	3.3	2.4
Lawn and garden equipment and supplies stores	4442	166	3.2	-0.5	3.0	-0.3	2.4	2.7
Food and beverage stores	445	3 147	0.7	2.1	0.7	0.0	2.8	2.8
Grocery stores	4451	2 723	0.5	2.4	0.6	0.1	3.0	2.9
Specialty food stores	4452	243	0.5	1.8	-0.3	-0.8	1.5	2.3
Beer, wine and liquor stores	4453	181	2.0	0.7	1.5	-0.5	2.2	2.7
Health and personal care stores	446	1 103	1.8	1.4	2.8	1.0	4.2	3.2
Gasoline stations	447	950	1.4	1.6	1.1	-0.2	2.8	3.0
Clothing and clothing accessories stores	448	1 398	4.0	-1.0	3.6	-0.4	2.5	2.9
Clothing stores	4481	1 029	4.3	-1.2	4.0	-0.3	2.7	3.0
Shoe stores	4482	204	2.9	-0.7	2.6	-0.3	1.9	2.2
Jewelry, luggage, and leather goods stores	4483	165	3.3	-0.1	2.6	-0.7	2.5	3.2
Sports, hobby, book, and music stores	451	603	3.6	-0.6	3.6	0.0	3.0	3.0
Sporting goods and musical instrument stores	4511	517	4.1	-1.1	4.4	0.3	3.3	3.0
Book stores and news dealers	4512	86	1.8	1.2	0.2	-1.6	1.3	3.0
General merchandise stores	452	3 055	3.0	-0.7	4.1	1.1	3.4	2.3
Department stores	4522	1 083	0.7	0.9	0.3	-0.4	1.3	1.7
Other general merchandise stores	4523	1 972	4.9	-1.7	7.2	2.1	5.3	3.1
Miscellaneous store retailers.	453	982	3.3	-0.8	3.1	-0.2	2.3	2.5
Florists	4531	74	3.1	0.0	0.0	-3.1	0.0	3.1
Office supplies, staionary, and gift stores	4532	257	5.6	-2.4	3.7	-1.8	1.2	3.1
Used merchandise stores	4533	225	4.4	-1.8	5.7	1.2	3.8	2.5
Other miscellaneous store retailers	4539	425	1.0	0.6	2.5	1.5	3.1	1.6
Nonstore retailers	454	762	8.4	-3.8	9.2	0.8	5.1	4.3
Electronic shopping and mail-order houses	4541	483	10.1	-4.7	14.2	3.7	8.9	4.9
Vending machine operators	4542	50	0.3	3.1	-1.8	-2.1	1.3	3.5
Direct selling establishments	4543	229	2.7	-0.1	1.3	-1.4	1.2	2.6

Table 5-4. Indexes of Multifactor Productivity and Related Measures, 1995–2019

(2012 =100 for private business and private nonfarm business, 2009 =100 for manufacturing.)

Sector	1995	1996	1997	1998	1999	2000	2001	2002	2003	2004	2005	2006	2007
PRIVATE BUSINESS													
Productivity													
Labor productivity	65.1	66.7	68.1	70.2	73.0	75.5	77.8	81.2	84.4	87.0	88.9	90.0	91.5
Output per unit of capital services	111.8	111.8	111.8	111.1	110.5	108.9	104.8	103.3	103.8	105.4	105.9	105.6	104.7
Multifactor productivity	82.2	83.3	84.2	85.5	87.5	88.9	89.3	91.1	93.4	95.6	97.0	97.4	97.9
Real value-added output	61.7	64.6	67.9	71.5	75.6	79.2	79.9	81.3	84.0	87.6	91.1	94.3	96.5
Inputs													
Labor input	88.2	90.5	93.6	95.9	97.8	99.4	97.7	95.8	95.6	97.1	98.9	101.4	102.6
Capital services	55.2	57.7	60.8	64.4	68.4	72.8	76.2	78.7	80.9	83.1	86.0	89.3	92.2
Combined input quantity	75.1	77.6	80.7	83.6	86.4	89.2	89.4	89.2	89.9	91.7	93.9	96.7	98.6
PRIVATE NONFARM BUSINESS													
Productivity													
Labor productivity	65.7	67.1	68.4	70.5	73.2	75.6	77.8	81.3	84.4	86.8	88.7	89.7	91.4
Output per unit of capital services	113.6	113.3	113.0	112.2	111.4	109.5	105.3	103.6	104.0	105.5	106.0	105.8	104.9
Multifactor productivity	83.0	83.8	84.6	85.9	87.7	89.0	89.4	91.3	93.4	95.4	96.9	97.3	97.8
Real value-added output	61.7	64.5	67.8	71.5	75.5	79.1	79.8	81.2	83.9	87.4	90.9	94.1	96.4
Inputs													
Labor input	87.3	89.8	93.0	95.4	97.5	99.1	97.5	95.5	95.5	97.0	98.8	101.4	102.6
Capital services	54.3	56.9	60.0	63.7	67.8	72.2	75.8	78.4	80.7	82.9	85.7	88.9	91.9
Combined input quantity	74.3	76.9	80.1	83.2	86.1	88.9	89.2	89.0	89.8	91.6	93.8	96.7	98.6
MANUFACTURING													
Productivity													
Labor productivity	55.5	57.6	60.5	63.2	66.8	69.3	70.9	76.8	81.8	84.0	88.4	89.3	93.4
Output per unit of capital services	118.2	117.7	120.1	119.9	120.0	118.9	111.0	110.2	110.6	112.5	115.6	115.7	116.6
Sector output	79.6	82.7	88.4	92.6	96.5	98.9	94.5	95.3	96.5	98.6	102.6	104.2	107.4
Combined inputs	96.4	99.2	104.2	108.2	110.2	109.5	106.3	104.6	101.0	100.5	103.7	104.2	107.4
Energy	106.0	102.8	104.8	105.2	152.2	177.6	206.3	136.8	113.2	113.6	134.2	103.0	105.5
Materials	87.8	93.2	99.5	105.6	106.6	101.5	93.5	102.4	94.7	100.1	105.3	108.6	120.1
Capital services	67.3	70.2	73.6	77.3	80.4	83.2	85.2	86.5	87.3	87.7	88.7	90.1	92.1
Purchased services	108.7	109.5	117.6	123.3	124.5	121.5	123.5	117.1	118.9	102.4	109.9	115.5	118.2

Sector	2008	2009	2010	2011	2012	2013	2014	2015	2016	2017	2018	2019
PRIVATE BUSINESS												
Productivity												
Labor productivity	92.6	96.2	99.4	99.3	100.0	100.9	101.6	103.1	103.5	104.8	106.4	108.3
Output per unit of capital services	100.9	96.5	98.9	99.0	100.0	100.0	100.4	101.3	100.2	100.2	100.9	100.4
Multifactor productivity	96.8	97.1	99.6	99.4	100.0	100.4	100.9	102.0	101.7	102.2	103.2	103.9
Real value-added output	95.5	92.2	95.2	97.0	100.0	102.5	105.7	109.8	111.8	114.9	118.9	121.9
Inputs												
Labor input	101.2	94.6	95.1	97.4	100.0	101.9	104.5	107.1	109.0	111.0	113.6	114.8
Capital services	94.6	95.5	96.3	98.0	100.0	102.5	105.3	108.4	111.6	114.6	117.8	121.3
Combined input quantity	98.7	95.0	95.5	97.6	100.0	102.1	104.8	107.6	110.0	112.4	115.2	117.2
PRIVATE NONFARM BUSINESS												
Productivity												
Labor productivity	92.4	96.0	99.2	99.2	100.0	100.5	101.3	103.0	103.3	104.6	106.1	108.0
Output per unit of capital services	100.9	96.1	98.6	98.8	100.0	99.8	100.1	100.8	99.6	99.7	100.3	99.8
Multifactor productivity	96.7	96.8	99.4	99.3	100.0	100.1	100.6	101.7	101.3	101.9	102.8	103.5
Real value-added output	95.4	92.0	95.0	96.9	100.0	102.3	105.5	109.5	111.5	114.6	118.6	121.6
Inputs												
Labor input	101.2	94.5	95.0	97.4	100.0	102.0	104.6	107.1	108.9	111.0	113.7	114.8
Capital services	94.6	95.7	96.4	98.1	100.0	102.5	105.4	108.6	111.9	115.0	118.3	121.9
Combined input quantity	98.7	95.0	95.6	97.6	100.0	102.2	104.9	107.7	110.1	112.5	115.4	117.5
MANUFACTURING												
Productivity												
Labor productivity	93.0	94.1	100.0	100.9	100.0	101.1	100.6	98.8	98.4	98.3	98.5	97.5
Output per unit of capital services	107.8	93.6	98.7	100.2	100.0	99.9	98.8	96.0	94.0	93.1	93.8	91.2
Sector output	102.5	90.2	96.0	98.7	100.0	101.9	103.1	102.2	102.0	102.7	105.0	103.9
Combined inputs	100.6	91.9	94.0	97.1	100.0	102.0	102.1	101.9	104.1	104.0	105.6	106.1
Energy	126.3	92.7	89.8	98.8	100.0	103.6	95.2	84.2	81.6	78.8	68.5	62.6
Materials	98.4	85.7	89.6	96.4	100.0	103.1	101.5	101.7	105.4	97.6	99.1	99.2
Capital services	95.1	96.4	97.3	98.5	100.0	102.1	104.3	106.4	108.6	110.3	112.0	113.9
Purchased services	98.3	96.0	99.6	95.8	100.0	100.2	99.5	93.6	96.4	109.1	111.8	112.9

. . . = Not available.

CHAPTER 6: COMPENSATION OF EMPLOYEES

HIGHLIGHTS

This chapter discusses the Employment Cost Index (ECI), which covers changes in wages and salaries and benefits; the Employer Costs for Employee Compensation (ECEC); and employee participation in various benefit plans.

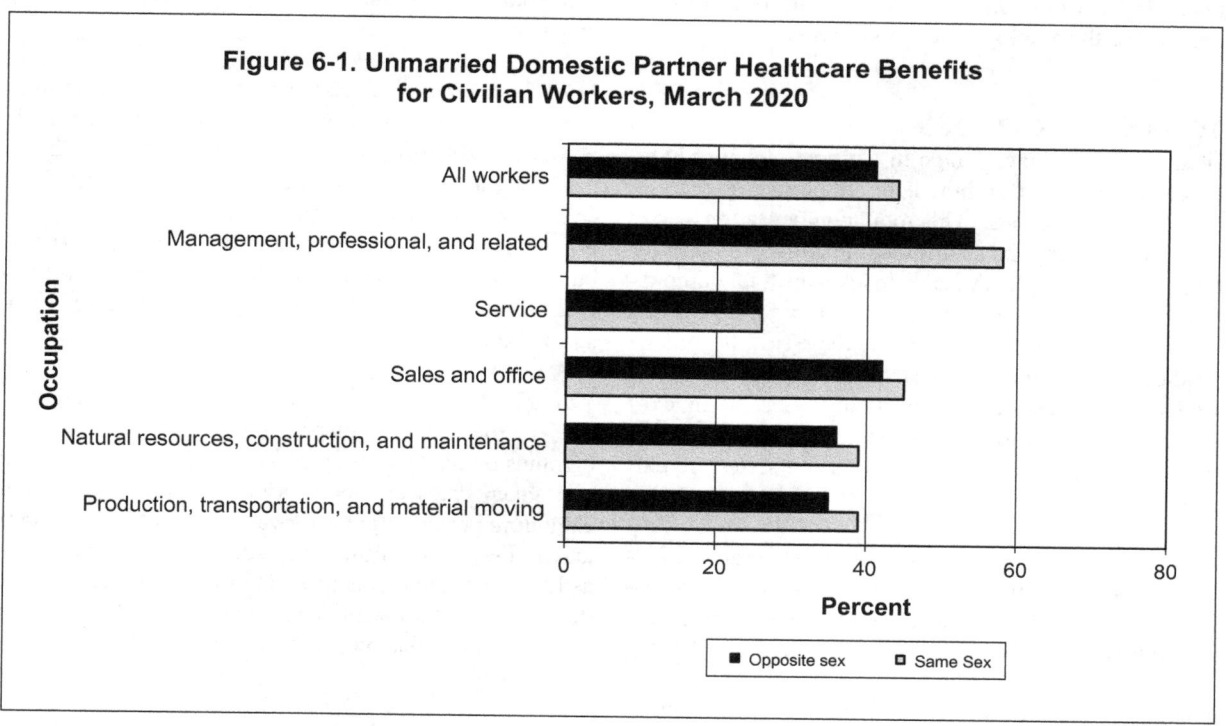

Figure 6-1. Unmarried Domestic Partner Healthcare Benefits for Civilian Workers, March 2020

In March 2020, state and local government workers were far more likely to have access to benefits than those in the private sector. Eighty-nine percent of state and local government workers had access to medical benefits compared while just 69 percent of private industry workers. Similarly, 60 percent of state and government workers had access to retirement benefits while only 25 percent of those in the private industry did. (See Tables 6-9 and 6-10.)

OTHER HIGHLIGHTS

- State and local government workers were also far more likely to have access to life insurance benefits than those in the private industry. In March 2020, 82 percent of state and local government workers had access to life insurance benefits compared with only 56 percent of workers in private industry did. (See Table 6-13.)

- Belonging to a union also increased the chances that an individual would have access to benefits. In March 2020, 94 percent of civilian worked who belonged to a union had access to retirement benefits compared with only 67 percent of nonunion civilian workers. Similarly, 95 percent of civilian union members had access to medical benefits compared with only 68 percent of non-union civilian workers. (See Tables 6-9 and 6-10.)

- The Employment Cost Index (ECI) for total compensation for private industry workers increased 3.0 percent from December 2018 to December 2019 after increasing 3.1 percent the previous year. (See Table 6-1.)

- Many companies now offer nontraditional benefits in order to entice workers. In March 2020, 54 percent had access to employee assistance programs, 44 percent of civilian workers had access to wellness programs, and 11 percent had access to childcare. (Table 6-16.)

NOTES AND DEFINITIONS

NATIONAL COMPENSATION SURVEY

The National Compensation Survey (NCS) is an establishment survey conducted by the Office of Compensation Levels and Trends (OCLT) at the Bureau of Labor Statistics (BLS). It provides data for the Employment Cost Index (ECI), the Employer Costs for Employee Compensation (ECEC), the occupational earnings series, and the employee benefits survey.

EMPLOYMENT COST INDEX

The ECI is a measure of the change in the cost of labor, independent of the influence of employment shifts among occupations and industry categories. The total compensation series includes changes in wages and salaries and in employer costs for employee benefits. The ECI calculates indexes of total compensation, wages and salaries, and benefits separately for all civilian workers in the United States (as defined by the NCS), for private industry workers, and for workers in state and local government. For all of these categories, the ECI calculates the same indexes by occupational group, worker attribute, industry group, and establishment characteristic. Seasonally adjusted series are calculated as well.

It was developed in the mid 1970s in response to the rapid acceleration of both wages and prices at that time. Monetary and fiscal policymakers needed a more accurate measure of the actual changes in employers' labor costs.

Beginning with estimates for March 2006, the following changes were introduced to the ECI:

• The Standard Industrial Classification (SIC) System was replaced by the North American Industry Classification System for classifying establishments by industry.

• The Occupational Classification System (OCS) Manual was replaced by the Standard Occupational Classification Manual for classifying occupations.

• Estimates were weighted to 2002 fixed employment counts until December 2013. For March 1995 through December 2005, ECI estimates were weighted on 1990 fixed employment counts.

• The ECI base was changed to December 2005=100. Prior to this, the base was

June 1989=100, which was used from March 1990 through December 2005.

Concepts and Definitions

Compensation is a term used to encompass the entire range of wages and benefits, both current and deferred, that employees receive in return for their work. In the Employment Cost Index (ECI), compensation includes the employer's cost of wages and salaries, plus the employer's cost of providing employee benefits.

Lump-sum payments are payments made to employees in lieu of a general wage rate increase. The payment may be a fixed amount as set forth in a labor agreement or an amount determined by a formula—for example, 2.5 percent of an employee's earnings during the prior year. Lump-sum payments are not incorporated into an employee's base pay rate or salary, but are considered as nonproduction bonuses in the Employment Cost Index and Employer Costs for Employee Compensation series.

Wages and salaries are defined as the hourly straight-time wage rate or, for workers not paid on an hourly basis, straight-time earnings divided by the corresponding hours. Straight-time wage and salary rates are total earnings before payroll deductions, excluding premium pay for overtime and for work on weekends and holidays, shift differentials, and nonproduction bonuses such as lump-sum payments provided in lieu of wage increases. Production bonuses, incentive earnings, commission payments, and cost-of-living adjustments are included in straight-time wage and salary rates.

Benefits covered by the ECI are: paid leave—vacations, holidays, sick leave, and personal leave; supplemental pay-premium pay for work in addition to the regular work schedule (such as overtime, weekends, and holidays), shift differentials, and nonproduction bonuses (such as referral bonuses and attendance bonuses); insurance benefits—life, health, short-term disability, and long-term disability; retirement and savings benefits—defined benefit and defined contribution plans; and legally required benefits—Social Security, Medicare, federal and state unemployment insurance, and workers' compensation.

Sources of Additional Information

Additional information on ECI methodology and more tables are available in the *BLS Handbook of Methods* and BLS new releases. The BLS publication *Compensation and Working Conditions* contains articles on all aspects of the NCS. All of these resources are on the BLS Web site at <https://www.bls.gov/ncs/ect/>.

Table 6-1. Employment Cost Index, Private Industry Workers, Total Compensation[1] and Wages and Salaries, by Selected Industry and Occupation, 2001–2020

(December 2005 = 100.)

Characteristic and year	Total compensation					Wages and salaries				
	Indexes				Percent change for 12 months (ended December)	Indexes				Percent change for 12 months (ended December)
	March	June	September	December		March	June	September	December	
WORKERS BY INDUSTRY										
Total Private										
2001	85.0	85.8	86.7	87.3	4.1	87.6	88.4	89.2	89.9	3.8
2002	88.2	89.2	89.7	90.0	3.1	90.7	91.6	92.0	92.2	2.6
2003	91.4	92.3	93.2	93.6	4.0	93.3	94.0	94.8	95.1	3.1
2004	94.9	95.9	96.7	97.2	3.8	95.7	96.5	97.3	97.6	2.6
2005	98.2	98.9	99.5	100.0	2.9	98.3	98.9	99.5	100.0	2.5
2006	100.8	101.7	102.5	103.2	3.2	100.7	101.7	102.5	103.2	3.2
2007	104.0	104.9	105.7	106.3	3.0	104.3	105.1	106.0	106.6	3.3
2008	107.3	108.0	108.7	108.9	2.4	107.6	108.4	109.1	109.4	2.6
2009	109.3	109.6	110.0	110.2	1.2	109.8	110.1	110.6	110.8	1.3
2010	111.1	111.7	112.2	112.5	2.1	111.4	111.9	112.4	112.8	1.8
2011	113.3	114.3	114.6	115.0	2.2	113.2	113.8	114.3	114.6	1.6
2012	115.7	116.4	116.8	117.1	1.8	115.3	115.9	116.4	116.6	1.7
2013	117.9	118.6	119.0	119.4	2.0	117.3	118.1	118.5	119.0	2.1
2014	119.9	121.0	121.7	122.2	2.3	119.3	120.3	121.2	121.6	2.2
2015	123.2	123.3	124.0	124.5	1.9	122.6	122.9	123.7	124.2	2.1
2016	125.4	126.2	126.8	127.2	2.2	125.1	126.1	126.7	127.1	2.3
2017	128.3	129.2	130.0	130.5	2.6	128.3	129.1	130.0	130.6	2.8
2018	131.9	132.9	133.8	134.4	3.0	132.0	132.9	134.0	134.7	3.1
2019	135.6	136.4	137.4	138.0	2.7	135.9	136.9	138.0	138.7	3.0
2020	139.4	140.1	140.7	. . .	. . .	140.4	140.9	141.7	. . .	. . .
Goods-Producing[2]										
2001	83.9	84.7	85.3	86.0	3.6	87.9	88.8	89.3	90.0	3.6
2002	87.0	87.7	88.2	89.0	3.5	90.7	91.4	91.9	92.6	2.9
2003	90.5	91.5	92.1	92.6	4.0	93.3	94.1	94.6	94.9	2.5
2004	94.5	95.4	96.5	96.9	4.6	95.6	96.2	97.2	97.2	2.4
2005	98.0	99.0	99.8	100.0	3.2	97.9	98.7	99.5	100.0	2.9
2006	100.3	101.3	102.0	102.5	2.5	100.7	101.8	102.3	102.9	2.9
2007	102.9	103.9	104.4	105.0	2.4	103.9	104.7	105.4	106.0	3.0
2008	106.1	106.8	107.2	107.5	2.4	107.1	108.0	108.6	109.0	2.8
2009	107.9	108.2	108.4	108.6	1.0	109.2	109.5	109.8	110.0	0.9
2010	109.7	110.3	111.0	111.1	2.3	110.5	110.9	111.5	111.6	1.5
2011	112.0	113.2	113.4	113.8	2.4	112.2	112.7	113.2	113.5	1.7
2012	114.1	114.7	115.3	115.6	1.6	114.0	114.5	115.1	115.4	1.7
2013	116.4	117.0	117.5	117.7	1.8	116.1	116.8	117.4	117.6	1.9
2014	118.5	119.1	119.9	120.3	2.2	118.2	119.0	119.6	120.1	2.1
2015	121.0	121.9	122.5	123.2	2.4	120.8	121.8	122.5	123.2	2.6
2016	123.8	124.7	125.2	125.8	2.1	123.9	124.9	125.5	126.2	2.4
2017	126.5	127.3	128.4	128.9	2.5	127.1	127.9	128.8	129.3	2.5
2018	129.9	130.9	131.2	131.9	2.3	130.4	131.4	132.2	133.0	2.9
2019	133.1	134.1	135.1	135.8	3.0	134.2	135.3	136.5	137.5	3.4
2020	136.7	137.7	138.2	. . .	. . .	138.5	139.6	140.2	. . .	. . .
Service-Providing[3]										
2001	85.4	86.2	87.1	87.8	4.4	87.4	88.3	89.2	89.8	3.8
2002	88.7	89.7	90.2	90.4	3.0	90.7	91.7	92.0	92.1	2.6
2003	91.7	92.5	93.6	94.0	4.0	93.3	93.9	94.9	95.2	3.4
2004	95.1	96.1	96.8	97.3	3.5	95.8	96.6	97.3	97.7	2.6
2005	98.3	98.9	99.5	100.0	2.8	98.4	99.0	99.5	100.0	2.4
2006	101.0	101.8	102.7	103.4	3.4	100.8	101.7	102.6	103.3	3.3
2007	104.3	105.2	106.1	106.7	3.2	104.4	105.3	106.1	106.8	3.4
2008	107.7	108.5	109.1	109.4	2.5	107.7	108.6	109.3	109.6	2.6
2009	109.8	110.1	110.5	110.8	1.3	110.0	110.3	110.8	111.1	1.4
2010	111.6	112.1	112.6	113.0	2.0	111.7	112.3	112.7	113.1	1.8
2011	113.8	114.6	115.0	115.3	2.0	113.5	114.1	114.6	114.9	1.6
2012	116.3	117.0	117.3	117.6	2.0	115.6	116.3	116.7	117.0	1.8
2013	118.4	119.1	119.6	120.0	2.0	117.7	118.4	118.9	119.4	2.1
2014	120.4	121.6	122.3	122.8	2.3	119.7	120.7	121.6	122.1	2.3
2015	123.8	123.8	124.5	124.9	1.7	123.1	123.3	124.1	124.5	2.0
2016	125.9	126.7	127.3	127.7	2.2	125.5	126.5	127.1	127.4	2.3
2017	128.9	129.8	130.6	131.0	2.6	128.6	129.5	130.4	131.0	2.8
2018	132.6	133.5	134.6	135.2	3.2	132.5	133.3	134.5	135.2	3.2
2019	136.3	137.1	138.1	138.7	2.6	136.4	137.3	138.4	139.1	2.9
2020	140.2	140.8	141.5	. . .	. . .	140.9	141.3	142.1	. . .	. . .

[1]Includes wages, salaries, and employer costs for employee benefits.
[2]Includes mining, construction, and manufacturing.
[3]Includes the following industries: wholesale trade; retail trade; transportation and warehousing; utilities; information; finance and insurance; real estate and rental and leasing; professional, scientific, and technical services; management of companies and enterprises; administrative and support and waste management and remediation services; education services; health care and social assistance; arts, entertainment, and recreation; accommodation and food services; and other services, except public administration.
. . . = Not available.

Table 6-1. Employment Cost Index, Private Industry Workers, Total Compensation[1] and Wages and Salaries, by Selected Industry and Occupation, 2001–2020—*Continued*

(December 2005 = 100.)

Characteristic and year	Total compensation					Wages and salaries				
	Indexes				Percent change for 12 months (ended December)	Indexes				Percent change for 12 months (ended December)
	March	June	September	December		March	June	September	December	
WORKERS BY OCCUPATION										
Management, Professional, and Related										
2001	85.2	86.1	87.1	87.7	4.8	86.7	87.7	88.7	89.3	4.3
2002	88.6	89.5	89.8	90.1	2.7	90.2	91.1	91.4	91.5	2.5
2003	91.9	92.6	93.6	94.2	4.6	93.2	93.8	94.8	95.3	4.2
2004	95.2	96.0	96.8	97.4	3.4	96.0	96.5	97.4	97.9	2.7
2005	98.6	99.1	99.5	100.0	2.7	98.7	99.2	99.6	100.0	2.1
2006	101.3	102.2	103.2	103.8	3.8	101.1	102.0	103.1	103.7	3.7
2007	105.0	105.9	106.8	107.3	3.4	105.0	105.9	106.8	107.4	3.6
2008	108.5	109.3	110.2	110.6	3.1	108.6	109.4	110.3	110.8	3.2
2009	111.1	111.2	111.4	111.6	0.9	111.4	111.5	111.7	111.9	1.0
2010	112.5	112.9	113.4	113.7	1.9	112.8	113.2	113.7	114.1	2.0
2011	114.8	115.4	115.7	116.0	2.0	114.8	115.2	115.6	115.8	1.5
2012	117.0	117.7	118.0	118.3	2.0	116.6	117.3	117.5	118.0	1.9
2013	119.0	120.0	120.5	120.9	2.2	118.6	119.6	120.1	120.5	2.1
2014	121.3	122.6	123.3	123.7	2.3	120.9	122.0	122.9	123.2	2.2
2015	124.5	124.7	125.5	125.9	1.8	123.7	124.5	125.4	125.9	2.2
2016	126.6	127.0	127.7	128.0	1.7	126.7	127.1	127.9	128.3	1.9
2017	129.1	130.2	130.7	131.1	2.4	129.2	130.3	130.9	131.4	2.4
2018	132.4	133.2	134.1	134.6	2.7	132.6	133.3	134.4	134.9	2.7
2019	135.4	136.3	137.1	137.5	2.2	135.6	136.6	137.5	137.9	2.2
2020	138.6	139.0	139.8	...	...	139.3	139.5	140.2	...	...
Management, Business, and Financial										
2001	86.1	87.1	87.8	88.5	4.4	87.3	88.3	89.1	89.8	4.1
2002	89.5	90.7	90.7	90.6	2.4	90.8	92.2	92.4	92.1	2.6
2003	93.3	93.9	94.9	95.4	5.3	94.8	95.5	96.4	96.7	5.0
2004	95.9	96.8	97.3	97.9	2.6	96.8	97.5	98.1	98.5	1.9
2005	99.1	99.6	99.7	100.0	2.1	99.2	99.7	99.5	100.0	1.5
2006	101.3	102.0	102.7	103.1	3.1	101.3	102.2	102.8	103.1	3.1
2007	104.3	105.1	106.0	106.3	3.1	104.7	105.5	106.3	106.6	3.4
2008	108.0	108.7	109.3	109.5	3.0	108.2	109.0	109.7	110.0	3.2
2009	109.6	109.7	109.7	109.9	0.4	110.3	110.3	110.4	110.8	0.7
2010	111.3	111.7	112.0	112.3	2.2	112.0	112.6	112.8	113.2	2.2
2011	113.6	114.5	114.8	115.0	2.4	113.9	114.4	114.9	115.0	1.6
2012	116.0	116.9	116.9	117.1	1.8	115.7	116.7	116.7	116.9	1.7
2013	118.0	119.3	119.6	119.9	2.4	117.9	119.3	119.4	119.8	2.5
2014	120.3	122.1	123.0	123.0	2.6	120.2	121.7	122.8	122.7	2.4
2015	123.9	124.2	125.4	125.7	2.2	123.4	124.2	125.7	126.2	2.9
2016	126.5	126.8	127.7	128.4	2.1	127.1	127.3	128.4	129.2	2.4
2017	129.5	130.6	131.3	131.7	2.6	129.9	131.0	131.8	132.3	2.4
2018	133.2	133.9	134.7	135.2	2.7	133.7	134.2	135.3	135.8	2.6
2019	136.2	137.3	138.1	138.4	2.4	136.8	137.9	138.9	139.2	2.5
2020	139.5	140.2	140.7	...	...	140.4	141.1	141.4	...	...
Professional and Related										
2001	84.1	85.0	86.0	86.5	4.7	86.9	87.8	88.7	89.3	4.1
2002	87.3	87.9	88.5	89.1	3.0	90.1	90.5	91.0	91.4	2.4
2003	90.3	91.0	92.0	92.6	3.9	92.1	92.7	93.6	94.2	3.1
2004	94.1	94.8	95.8	96.5	4.2	95.3	95.7	96.7	97.2	3.2
2005	98.0	98.8	99.5	100.0	3.6	98.2	98.8	99.6	100.0	2.9
2006	101.0	101.8	103.1	103.9	3.9	100.9	101.8	103.1	104.0	4.0
2007	104.9	105.9	106.7	107.3	3.3	105.1	106.0	107.0	107.6	3.5
2008	108.3	109.0	109.9	110.3	2.8	108.7	109.5	110.4	110.9	3.1
2009	111.0	111.1	111.4	111.4	1.0	111.6	111.8	112.1	112.1	1.1
2010	112.2	112.6	113.3	113.5	1.9	112.8	113.2	113.9	114.1	1.8
2011	114.6	115.1	115.4	115.7	1.9	114.8	115.2	115.6	115.9	1.6
2012	116.8	117.3	117.7	118.2	2.2	116.7	117.2	117.7	118.2	2.0
2013	118.9	119.5	120.2	120.5	1.9	118.8	119.5	120.2	120.5	1.9
2014	121.0	121.9	122.5	122.9	2.0	120.9	121.7	122.3	122.8	1.9
2015	123.7	124.1	124.5	124.9	1.6	123.4	124.2	124.7	125.2	2.0
2016	125.7	126.2	126.7	126.7	1.4	126.0	126.6	127.2	127.2	1.6
2017	127.8	128.7	129.1	129.6	2.3	128.2	129.3	129.6	130.2	2.4
2018	130.8	131.6	132.3	132.8	2.5	131.3	132.1	133.2	133.7	2.7
2019	133.7	134.4	135.1	135.6	2.1	134.4	135.2	136.0	136.6	2.2
2020	136.8	137.0	137.8	...	...	138.1	138.0	138.9	...	...

[1] Includes wages, salaries, and employer costs for employee benefits.
[2] Includes mining, construction, and manufacturing.
[3] Includes the following industries: wholesale trade; retail trade; transportation and warehousing; utilities; information; finance and insurance; real estate and rental and leasing; professional, scientific, and technical services; management of companies and enterprises; administrative and support and waste management and remediation services; education services; health care and social assistance; arts, entertainment, and recreation; accommodation and food services; and other services, except public administration.
... = Not available.

Table 6-1. Employment Cost Index, Private Industry Workers, Total Compensation[1] and Wages and Salaries, by Selected Industry and Occupation, 2001–2020—*Continued*

(December 2005 = 100.)

	Total compensation					Wages and salaries				
	Indexes				Percent change for 12 months (ended December)	Indexes				Percent change for 12 months (ended December)
Characteristic and year	March	June	September	December		March	June	September	December	
Office and Administrative Support										
2001	84.2	84.9	85.9	86.6	4.6	87.0	87.7	88.8	89.4	4.2
2002	87.9	88.6	89.3	89.9	3.8	90.7	91.3	91.8	92.4	3.4
2003	91.0	92.0	92.8	93.3	3.8	93.1	93.9	94.4	94.7	2.5
2004	94.7	95.8	96.5	97.2	4.2	95.6	96.4	97.1	97.6	3.1
2005	98.1	98.9	99.5	100.0	2.9	98.2	99.0	99.4	100.0	2.5
2006	100.9	101.9	102.7	103.4	3.4	100.9	101.9	102.6	103.3	3.3
2007	104.5	105.4	106.0	106.7	3.2	104.5	105.4	106.0	106.7	3.3
2008	107.8	108.5	109.2	109.6	2.7	107.7	108.5	109.2	109.7	2.8
2009	110.5	110.9	111.3	111.6	1.8	110.6	111.1	111.4	111.8	1.9
2010	112.6	113.1	113.7	114.0	2.2	112.2	112.6	113.3	113.6	1.6
2011	115.1	115.8	116.2	116.5	2.2	114.4	114.8	115.4	115.7	1.8
2012	117.5	118.1	118.4	118.7	1.9	116.4	117.0	117.4	117.7	1.7
2013	119.7	120.4	120.7	121.1	2.0	118.6	119.3	119.7	120.1	2.0
2014	121.8	122.9	123.3	123.8	2.2	120.8	121.5	122.0	122.5	2.0
2015	124.6	125.4	125.9	126.6	2.3	123.3	124.2	124.8	125.6	2.5
2016	128.1	129.0	129.6	130.2	2.8	127.1	128.0	128.7	129.5	3.1
2017	131.4	132.1	132.8	133.3	2.4	130.7	131.4	132.2	132.9	2.6
2018	135.0	136.5	137.3	138.0	3.5	134.5	135.9	136.8	137.6	3.5
2019	139.5	140.5	141.4	141.9	2.8	139.2	140.2	141.4	141.9	3.1
2020	143.3	144.1	144.8	. . .	. . .	143.6	144.2	145.0	. . .	. . .
Natural Resources, Construction, and Maintenance										
2001	84.3	85.0	86.4	86.6	4.0	87.6	88.4	89.9	90.0	3.8
2002	87.4	88.5	89.3	89.7	3.6	90.5	91.7	92.3	92.6	2.9
2003	90.8	92.0	92.8	93.3	4.0	93.2	94.1	94.8	95.2	2.8
2004	94.8	96.1	96.5	97.1	4.1	95.8	96.7	97.1	97.5	2.4
2005	97.9	98.9	99.5	100.0	3.0	97.8	98.7	99.4	100.0	2.6
2006	100.8	102.1	103.0	103.6	3.6	100.7	101.8	102.8	103.4	3.4
2007	104.0	105.0	105.9	106.7	3.0	104.2	105.1	106.2	107.1	3.6
2008	107.6	108.3	109.0	109.6	2.7	108.1	109.0	109.8	110.5	3.2
2009	109.9	110.3	110.8	111.2	1.5	110.6	111.0	111.6	112.0	1.4
2010	112.2	112.7	113.1	113.3	1.9	112.5	112.8	113.1	113.3	1.2
2011	113.8	114.9	115.5	115.8	2.2	113.7	114.4	115.2	115.4	1.9
2012	116.3	117.0	117.7	117.8	1.7	115.6	116.0	116.6	116.7	1.1
2013	118.6	119.1	119.9	120.1	2.0	117.2	117.6	118.5	118.8	1.8
2014	120.8	122.0	122.8	123.2	2.6	119.3	120.0	120.9	121.4	2.2
2015	123.6	124.1	124.6	124.9	1.4	121.7	122.7	123.2	123.5	1.7
2016	125.7	126.6	127.1	127.7	2.2	124.3	125.5	126.0	126.7	2.6
2017	128.5	129.7	130.6	131.2	2.7	127.5	128.8	129.8	130.4	2.9
2018	131.8	133.4	133.9	134.5	2.5	130.9	132.0	132.6	133.4	2.3
2019	135.3	136.2	137.3	137.9	2.5	134.1	135.4	136.6	137.4	3.0
2020	139.3	139.9	140.6	. . .	. . .	139.0	139.5	140.3	. . .	. . .
Construction, Extraction, Farming, Fishing, and Forestry										
2001	84.2	85.1	86.2	86.4	3.8	87.8	88.9	89.8	90.0	3.6
2002	87.3	88.1	88.8	89.5	3.6	90.6	91.3	91.9	92.4	2.7
2003	90.3	91.6	92.5	93.1	4.0	92.7	93.7	94.6	94.9	2.7
2004	94.7	95.8	96.4	97.2	4.4	95.8	96.6	96.9	97.5	2.7
2005	97.7	98.7	99.5	100.0	2.9	97.8	98.5	99.3	100.0	2.6
2006	100.7	102.2	103.1	103.7	3.7	100.7	102.0	103.0	103.7	3.7
2007	104.4	105.7	106.5	107.4	3.6	104.7	105.8	106.7	107.8	4.0
2008	108.6	109.7	110.3	110.8	3.2	109.2	110.1	110.8	111.5	3.4
2009	110.9	111.5	112.0	112.4	1.4	111.4	111.7	112.3	112.7	1.1
2010	113.1	113.6	114.3	114.4	1.8	112.9	113.3	113.9	114.0	1.2
2011	114.8	115.5	116.0	116.5	1.8	114.5	114.9	115.4	115.7	1.5
2012	116.6	117.1	117.8	117.9	1.2	115.7	116.0	116.8	116.7	0.9
2013	118.6	118.9	119.9	120.3	2.0	117.1	117.3	118.2	118.5	1.5
2014	120.7	121.4	122.1	122.9	2.2	118.7	119.6	120.3	121.1	2.2
2015	123.1	124.0	124.6	125.1	1.8	121.2	122.0	122.6	123.1	1.7
2016	125.8	127.1	127.3	128.4	2.6	124.0	125.5	125.6	126.9	3.1
2017	129.2	130.2	131.1	131.6	2.5	127.9	128.8	129.9	130.4	2.8
2018	132.2	133.4	133.8	134.4	2.1	131.1	132.3	132.9	133.6	2.5
2019	135.5	136.7	137.9	138.6	3.1	134.6	136.0	137.1	138.0	3.3
2020	140.2	139.9	140.4	. . .	. . .	140.1	139.4	140.1	. . .	. . .

[1]Includes wages, salaries, and employer costs for employee benefits.
[2]Includes mining, construction, and manufacturing.
[3]Includes the following industries: wholesale trade; retail trade; transportation and warehousing; utilities; information; finance and insurance; real estate and rental and leasing; professional, scientific, and technical services; management of companies and enterprises; administrative and support and waste management and remediation services; education services; health care and social assistance; arts, entertainment, and recreation; accommodation and food services; and other services, except public administration.
. . . = Not available.

Table 6-1. Employment Cost Index, Private Industry Workers, Total Compensation[1] and Wages and Salaries, by Selected Industry and Occupation, 2001–2020—*Continued*

(December 2005 = 100.)

Characteristic and year	Total compensation					Wages and salaries				
	Indexes				Percent change for 12 months (ended December)	Indexes				Percent change for 12 months (ended December)
	March	June	September	December		March	June	September	December	
Installation, Maintenance, and Repair										
2001	84.4	84.9	86.8	86.8	4.1	87.4	87.9	90.1	90.1	4.3
2002	87.4	89.1	90.0	90.1	3.8	90.4	92.2	92.9	92.9	3.1
2003	91.4	92.5	93.1	93.6	3.9	93.8	94.6	95.1	95.5	2.8
2004	95.0	96.3	96.7	97.0	3.6	95.9	96.8	97.3	97.4	2.0
2005	98.1	99.3	99.6	100.0	3.1	97.8	99.1	99.5	100.0	2.7
2006	100.9	102.1	103.0	103.4	3.4	100.7	101.6	102.6	103.0	3.0
2007	103.5	104.1	105.2	105.8	2.3	103.7	104.2	105.6	106.1	3.0
2008	106.3	106.6	107.4	108.1	2.2	106.8	107.6	108.5	109.3	3.0
2009	108.6	108.9	109.4	109.8	1.6	109.7	110.2	110.7	111.2	1.7
2010	111.1	111.5	111.6	111.9	1.9	112.1	112.1	112.1	112.5	1.2
2011	112.6	114.2	114.9	115.0	2.8	112.7	113.9	115.0	115.0	2.2
2012	116.1	116.8	117.5	117.8	2.4	115.5	115.9	116.4	116.7	1.5
2013	118.6	119.3	119.9	119.9	1.8	117.5	118.0	119.0	119.2	2.1
2014	121.0	122.6	123.5	123.5	3.0	120.1	120.6	121.6	121.7	2.1
2015	124.1	124.2	124.6	124.8	1.1	122.3	123.4	123.9	124.1	2.0
2016	125.6	126.1	126.9	127.1	1.8	124.8	125.5	126.4	126.6	2.0
2017	127.7	129.2	130.2	130.9	3.0	127.2	128.8	129.7	130.5	3.1
2018	131.3	133.4	133.9	134.6	2.8	130.8	131.8	132.4	133.1	2.0
2019	135.1	135.6	136.7	138.6	3.1	133.5	134.9	136.3	136.9	2.9
2020	138.2	139.9	140.8	...	...	137.9	139.6	140.7	...	...
Production, Transportation, and Material Moving										
2001	85.3	85.8	86.7	87.4	3.6	88.7	89.4	90.2	91.0	3.9
2002	88.4	89.1	89.7	90.3	3.3	91.9	92.4	92.8	93.3	2.5
2003	91.5	92.4	93.2	93.6	3.7	94.0	94.6	95.1	95.4	2.3
2004	95.5	96.5	97.4	97.8	4.5	96.0	96.7	97.6	97.8	2.5
2005	98.5	99.0	99.7	100.0	2.2	98.3	98.9	99.6	100.0	2.2
2006	100.4	101.1	101.7	102.3	2.3	100.6	101.2	101.8	102.4	2.4
2007	102.5	103.3	103.9	104.5	2.2	103.1	103.8	104.5	105.0	2.5
2008	105.5	106.0	106.6	106.9	2.3	106.0	106.8	107.5	107.8	2.7
2009	107.7	108.1	108.6	108.9	1.9	108.3	108.8	109.4	109.6	1.7
2010	109.9	110.5	111.3	111.5	2.4	109.8	110.3	111.1	111.3	1.6
2011	112.2	113.5	113.8	114.2	2.4	111.6	112.0	112.5	112.8	1.3
2012	114.5	115.1	115.7	116.0	1.6	113.7	114.0	114.7	115.1	2.0
2013	116.7	117.2	117.5	118.0	1.7	115.8	116.2	116.7	117.2	1.8
2014	118.9	119.5	120.3	120.6	2.2	118.0	118.7	119.6	119.9	2.3
2015	121.7	122.5	123.1	123.7	2.6	120.8	121.5	122.2	122.8	2.4
2016	124.7	125.6	126.4	127.0	2.7	123.9	124.9	125.9	126.6	3.1
2017	128.3	129.0	130.4	131.0	3.1	128.0	128.8	130.1	130.7	3.2
2018	132.5	133.2	134.1	134.7	2.8	132.3	133.2	134.4	135.1	3.4
2019	136.4	137.2	138.1	139.2	3.3	137.1	137.9	139.1	140.5	4.0
2020	140.6	141.7	142.7	...	...	142.1	143.0	144.2	...	...
Production										
2001	84.9	85.2	86.0	86.7	3.2	88.4	89.1	89.7	90.5	3.7
2002	87.7	88.3	88.8	89.4	3.1	91.3	91.8	92.3	92.8	2.5
2003	91.0	91.7	92.5	93.0	4.0	93.6	94.1	94.8	95.1	2.5
2004	95.3	96.4	97.4	97.7	5.1	95.6	96.5	97.4	97.5	2.5
2005	98.6	99.1	99.6	100.0	2.4	98.3	98.9	99.5	100.0	2.6
2006	100.4	101.0	101.6	102.0	2.0	100.7	101.2	101.7	102.2	2.2
2007	102.1	102.8	103.2	104.0	2.0	103.1	103.6	104.2	104.6	2.3
2008	104.8	105.2	105.8	106.1	2.0	105.6	106.4	107.2	107.4	2.7
2009	107.1	107.6	108.0	108.2	2.0	108.1	108.5	109.0	109.3	1.8
2010	109.5	110.0	110.7	110.8	2.4	109.6	110.0	110.5	110.5	1.1
2011	111.7	113.2	113.4	113.8	2.7	111.1	111.5	112.0	112.3	1.6
2012	113.8	114.4	114.8	115.0	1.1	113.2	113.5	113.9	114.2	1.7
2013	115.7	116.1	116.3	116.7	1.5	115.0	115.5	116.0	116.4	1.9
2014	117.8	118.1	118.8	119.4	2.3	117.4	117.8	118.6	119.1	2.3
2015	120.4	121.0	121.7	122.5	2.6	119.9	120.5	121.2	122.0	2.4
2016	123.4	124.2	125.0	125.5	2.4	123.0	123.9	124.8	125.4	2.8
2017	126.5	127.2	128.6	129.2	2.9	126.5	127.4	128.6	129.3	3.1
2018	130.2	131.1	131.5	132.3	2.4	130.4	131.4	132.2	133.1	2.9
2019	133.5	134.4	135.1	136.0	2.8	134.4	135.4	136.2	137.4	3.2
2020	137.2	138.5	139.3	...	...	138.7	139.9	140.8	...	...

[1]Includes wages, salaries, and employer costs for employee benefits.
[2]Includes mining, construction, and manufacturing.
[3]Includes the following industries: wholesale trade; retail trade; transportation and warehousing; utilities; information; finance and insurance; real estate and rental and leasing; professional, scientific, and technical services; management of companies and enterprises; administrative and support and waste management and remediation services; education services; health care and social assistance; arts, entertainment, and recreation; accommodation and food services; and other services, except public administration.
... = Not available.

Table 6-1. Employment Cost Index, Private Industry Workers, Total Compensation[1] and Wages and Salaries, by Selected Industry and Occupation, 2001–2020—*Continued*

(December 2005 = 100.)

Characteristic and year	Total compensation					Wages and salaries				
	Indexes				Percent change for 12 months (ended December)	Indexes				Percent change for 12 months (ended December)
	March	June	September	December		March	June	September	December	
Transportation and Material Moving										
2001	85.8	86.7	87.7	88.5	4.2	89.0	89.9	90.8	91.6	4.1
2002	89.5	90.2	90.9	91.4	3.3	92.6	93.1	93.6	94.0	2.6
2003	92.4	93.4	94.0	94.4	3.3	94.7	95.3	95.6	95.8	1.9
2004	95.7	96.7	97.5	97.9	3.7	96.4	97.1	97.9	98.2	2.5
2005	98.3	99.0	99.8	100.0	2.1	98.5	98.9	99.7	100.0	1.8
2006	100.4	101.2	102.0	102.6	2.6	100.4	101.2	102.0	102.6	2.6
2007	103.1	104.1	104.9	105.3	2.6	103.2	104.1	105.0	105.4	2.7
2008	106.4	107.2	107.7	107.9	2.5	106.5	107.4	108.0	108.3	2.8
2009	108.4	108.9	109.6	109.7	1.7	108.5	109.2	109.9	110.1	1.7
2010	110.4	111.2	112.2	112.5	2.6	110.2	110.8	111.8	112.2	1.9
2011	113.0	114.0	114.4	114.9	2.1	112.2	112.8	113.2	113.6	1.2
2012	115.5	116.0	117.0	117.6	2.3	114.4	114.8	115.7	116.3	2.4
2013	118.2	118.6	119.2	119.7	1.8	116.9	117.0	117.7	118.2	1.6
2014	120.4	121.4	122.3	122.4	2.3	118.9	119.9	121.0	120.9	2.3
2015	123.5	124.4	125.1	125.3	2.4	121.9	122.8	123.4	123.8	2.4
2016	126.6	127.5	128.4	129.1	3.0	125.1	126.3	127.2	128.1	3.5
2017	130.6	131.4	133.0	133.4	3.3	129.7	130.4	132.1	132.6	3.5
2018	135.4	136.0	137.4	137.8	3.3	134.7	135.3	137.0	137.5	3.7
2019	140.1	140.7	142.0	143.2	3.9	140.3	140.8	142.6	144.0	4.7
2020	144.8	145.7	146.9	. . .	. . .	146.0	146.8	148.2	. . .	. . .
Service										
2001	87.1	87.7	88.2	89.4	3.8	89.7	90.2	90.6	91.7	3.4
2002	90.2	90.6	91.5	92.0	2.9	92.5	92.8	93.4	93.9	2.4
2003	93.0	93.4	94.4	95.0	3.3	94.5	94.8	95.6	96.1	2.3
2004	95.9	96.7	97.2	97.7	2.8	96.4	96.9	97.4	97.9	1.9
2005	98.5	99.0	99.5	100.0	2.4	98.6	99.0	99.6	100.0	2.1
2006	100.8	101.5	102.3	103.1	3.1	100.6	101.3	102.0	102.9	2.9
2007	104.5	105.2	106.4	107.0	3.8	104.6	105.3	106.5	107.1	4.1
2008	107.8	108.7	109.4	109.8	2.6	107.9	108.8	109.7	110.1	2.8
2009	110.7	110.9	111.7	111.8	1.8	111.0	111.2	112.1	112.3	2.0
2010	112.4	112.7	113.3	113.5	1.5	112.6	112.7	113.3	113.5	1.1
2011	114.5	114.7	115.0	115.4	1.7	114.2	114.2	114.6	115.1	1.4
2012	116.0	116.4	116.8	117.4	1.7	115.4	115.8	116.2	116.8	1.5
2013	117.9	118.3	118.4	119.0	1.4	117.2	117.6	117.6	118.3	1.3
2014	119.2	119.6	120.5	121.1	1.8	118.5	119.0	120.1	120.7	2.0
2015	122.0	122.1	122.6	123.2	1.7	121.6	121.6	122.2	122.8	1.7
2016	124.4	125.5	126.5	127.2	3.2	124.0	125.2	126.4	127.1	3.5
2017	128.6	129.2	130.0	130.9	2.9	128.6	129.3	130.2	131.3	3.3
2018	132.7	133.5	134.5	135.6	3.6	133.0	134.0	135.2	136.4	3.9
2019	137.2	138.5	139.2	140.6	3.7	138.3	139.7	140.5	142.2	4.3
2020	142.2	143.2	144.3	. . .	. . .	143.9	144.9	146.2	. . .	. . .

[1]Includes wages, salaries, and employer costs for employee benefits.
[2]Includes mining, construction, and manufacturing.
[3]Includes the following industries: wholesale trade; retail trade; transportation and warehousing; utilities; information; finance and insurance; real estate and rental and leasing; professional, scientific, and technical services; management of companies and enterprises; administrative and support and waste management and remediation services; education services; health care and social assistance; arts, entertainment, and recreation; accommodation and food services; and other services, except public administration.
. . . = Not available.

Table 6-2. Employment Cost Index, Private Industry Workers, Total Compensation[1] and Wages and Salaries, by Bargaining Status and Selected Industry, 2001–2020

(December 2005 = 100.)

Characteristic and year	Total compensation					Wages and salaries				
	Indexes				Percent change for 12 months (ended December)	Indexes				Percent change for 12 months (ended December)
	March	June	September	December		March	June	September	December	
WORKERS BY BARGAINING STATUS AND INDUSTRY										
Union Workers										
2001	82.0	82.9	83.7	84.8	4.2	86.5	87.4	88.3	89.6	4.3
2002	85.7	86.5	87.5	88.2	4.0	90.2	91.1	91.9	92.6	3.3
2003	89.5	90.7	91.6	92.3	4.6	93.0	93.8	94.4	94.9	2.5
2004	94.5	95.9	96.7	97.3	5.4	95.6	96.4	97.1	97.6	2.8
2005	97.9	98.8	99.6	100.0	2.8	97.9	98.7	99.5	100.0	2.5
2006	100.5	101.8	102.4	103.0	3.0	100.3	101.2	101.7	102.3	2.3
2007	102.7	103.9	104.4	105.1	2.0	102.8	103.7	104.4	104.7	2.3
2008	105.9	106.7	107.4	108.0	2.8	105.5	106.7	107.4	108.1	3.2
2009	109.1	109.8	110.5	111.1	2.9	108.8	109.6	110.2	110.9	2.6
2010	112.8	113.7	114.6	114.8	3.3	111.5	112.1	112.7	112.9	1.8
2011	115.6	117.1	117.4	117.9	2.7	113.6	114.0	114.6	114.9	1.8
2012	118.3	119.3	120.2	120.5	2.2	115.6	116.2	116.9	117.4	2.2
2013	121.5	122.1	122.5	122.6	1.7	118.4	119.0	119.6	119.8	2.0
2014	123.5	125.0	125.8	126.7	3.3	120.5	121.2	122.1	123.1	2.8
2015	127.4	127.5	128.0	128.7	1.6	123.7	124.5	124.8	125.5	1.9
2016	129.6	130.0	130.4	130.6	1.5	126.4	126.8	127.2	127.3	1.4
2017	131.9	132.7	133.7	134.5	3.0	128.6	129.2	129.9	130.9	2.8
2018	135.4	137.4	137.8	138.8	3.2	131.6	132.7	133.5	134.6	2.8
2019	140.0	140.8	141.4	142.3	2.5	135.7	137.0	138.1	139.2	3.4
2020	143.1	144.7	145.6	. . .	. . .	140.2	141.2	142.2	. . .	. . .
Union Workers, Goods-Producing[2]										
2001	81.9	82.7	83.4	84.0	2.9	87.2	88.2	88.9	89.5	3.5
2002	84.8	85.5	86.4	87.1	3.7	90.0	90.9	91.7	92.4	3.2
2003	88.9	90.2	90.9	91.7	5.3	92.9	94.0	94.5	95.0	2.8
2004	94.6	95.9	96.7	97.2	6.0	95.4	96.3	96.9	97.1	2.2
2005	97.7	98.8	99.6	100.0	2.9	97.5	98.5	99.2	100.0	3.0
2006	99.9	101.2	101.8	102.2	2.2	100.5	101.6	101.9	102.3	2.3
2007	101.5	102.8	103.1	104.0	1.8	102.7	103.6	104.3	104.3	2.0
2008	104.6	105.6	106.2	106.9	2.8	105.2	106.4	107.1	107.7	3.3
2009	108.0	108.9	109.5	110.0	2.9	108.2	108.8	109.5	109.8	1.9
2010	111.9	112.6	113.8	113.9	3.5	110.2	110.7	111.1	111.2	1.3
2011	114.3	116.4	116.3	116.9	2.6	111.7	112.1	112.8	112.9	1.5
2012	115.8	116.6	117.7	118.0	0.9	113.5	113.8	114.4	115.0	1.9
2013	118.6	118.8	119.2	119.6	1.4	115.7	115.9	116.8	117.0	1.7
2014	120.6	120.9	121.9	122.4	2.3	117.7	118.2	119.0	119.5	2.1
2015	123.0	123.9	124.5	125.4	2.5	119.9	120.7	121.2	121.9	2.0
2016	125.9	126.8	127.1	128.0	2.1	122.3	123.3	123.7	124.7	2.3
2017	128.4	129.4	131.2	131.8	3.0	125.2	126.1	126.8	127.6	2.3
2018	132.3	133.3	132.7	133.2	1.1	127.9	129.1	129.6	130.2	2.0
2019	134.1	135.4	136.3	137.0	2.9	130.9	132.3	133.1	134.1	3.0
2020	137.6	139.1	140.1	. . .	. . .	134.8	135.8	136.9	. . .	. . .
Union Workers, Manufacturing										
2001	81.1	81.4	82.0	83.0	2.7	87.3	88.1	88.8	89.7	3.7
2002	84.1	84.7	85.4	86.5	4.2	90.3	90.8	91.6	92.5	3.1
2003	88.6	89.5	90.1	91.0	5.2	93.3	94.2	94.5	95.0	2.7
2004	95.6	96.7	97.5	97.8	7.5	95.5	96.2	97.0	97.1	2.2
2005	98.3	99.1	99.7	100.0	2.2	97.6	98.3	99.0	100.0	3.0
2006	99.3	100.1	100.5	100.8	0.8	100.6	101.2	101.4	101.7	1.7
2007	99.2	100.0	100.0	101.0	0.2	102.0	102.5	102.9	102.6	0.9
2008	101.4	101.7	102.1	102.8	1.8	103.4	104.4	104.9	105.5	2.8
2009	104.4	104.8	105.3	105.8	2.9	106.0	106.4	107.0	107.3	1.7
2010	108.6	109.1	110.5	110.5	4.4	107.8	108.2	108.6	108.7	1.3
2011	110.9	113.8	113.2	113.8	3.0	109.4	109.8	110.6	110.7	1.8
2012	112.1	112.8	113.6	113.7	-0.1	111.5	111.8	112.1	112.5	1.6
2013	113.9	114.1	113.8	114.2	0.4	113.5	113.9	114.4	114.8	2.0
2014	115.4	115.9	116.8	117.4	2.8	115.6	116.2	116.7	116.9	1.8
2015	118.1	118.6	119.3	120.4	2.6	117.8	118.5	118.8	119.6	2.3
2016	121.1	121.7	121.9	122.8	2.0	120.2	120.8	121.4	122.3	2.3
2017	122.9	123.9	126.8	127.2	3.6	122.7	123.6	124.5	125.2	2.4
2018	127.8	128.2	126.5	126.9	-0.2	125.7	126.3	126.9	127.5	1.8
2019	127.7	128.3	129.1	129.8	2.3	128.0	128.6	129.6	130.9	2.7
2020	130.5	132.7	133.5	. . .	. . .	131.9	133.5	134.7	. . .	. . .

[1]Includes wages, salaries, and employer costs for employee benefits.
[2]Includes mining, construction, and manufacturing.
[3]Includes the following industries: wholesale trade; retail trade; transportation and warehousing; utilities; information; finance and insurance; real estate and rental and leasing; professional, scientific, and technical services; management of companies and enterprises; administrative and support and waste management and remediation services; education services; health care and social assistance; arts, entertainment, and recreation; accommodation and food services; and other services, except public administration.
. . . = Not available.

Table 6-2. Employment Cost Index, Private Industry Workers, Total Compensation[1] and Wages and Salaries, by Bargaining Status and Selected Industry, 2001–2020—*Continued*

(December 2005 = 100.)

Characteristic and year	Total compensation					Wages and salaries				
	Indexes				Percent change for 12 months (ended December)	Indexes				Percent change for 12 months (ended December)
	March	June	September	December		March	June	September	December	
Union Workers, Service-Providing[3]										
2001	82.0	83.0	84.0	85.5	5.2	85.9	86.8	87.8	89.6	4.9
2002	86.4	87.3	88.4	89.1	4.2	90.3	91.2	92.0	92.7	3.5
2003	90.1	91.1	92.3	92.8	4.2	93.1	93.6	94.4	94.8	2.3
2004	94.4	95.8	96.6	97.3	4.8	95.7	96.5	97.3	98.0	3.4
2005	98.1	98.8	99.6	100.0	2.8	98.2	99.0	99.7	100.0	2.0
2006	101.0	102.2	102.9	103.6	3.6	100.1	100.9	101.6	102.2	2.2
2007	103.7	104.7	105.4	106.0	2.3	102.9	103.8	104.6	104.9	2.6
2008	107.0	107.5	108.3	108.8	2.6	105.8	106.9	107.7	108.3	3.2
2009	109.9	110.6	111.3	111.9	2.8	109.2	110.1	110.8	111.6	3.0
2010	113.4	114.5	115.2	115.5	3.2	112.4	113.1	113.8	114.2	2.3
2011	116.8	117.7	118.3	118.8	2.9	115.0	115.3	115.8	116.3	1.8
2012	120.4	121.5	122.2	122.6	3.2	117.0	117.9	118.7	119.1	2.4
2013	123.9	124.9	125.2	125.2	2.1	120.4	121.3	121.7	121.8	2.3
2014	126.0	128.3	129.0	130.0	3.8	122.6	123.4	124.4	125.6	3.1
2015	130.8	130.4	130.8	131.4	1.1	126.3	127.2	127.3	128.0	1.9
2016	132.7	132.7	133.2	133.1	1.3	129.1	129.2	129.8	129.4	1.1
2017	134.8	135.5	136.1	137.1	3.0	131.0	131.5	132.2	133.3	3.0
2018	138.2	140.7	141.6	142.8	4.2	134.2	135.3	136.2	137.5	3.2
2019	144.1	144.7	145.2	146.2	2.4	138.9	140.1	141.4	142.5	3.6
2020	147.2	148.8	149.6	. . .	. . .	143.7	144.7	145.6	. . .	. . .
Nonunion Workers										
2001	85.5	86.3	87.2	87.8	4.2	87.7	88.6	89.3	89.9	3.7
2002	88.7	89.6	90.0	90.3	2.8	90.8	91.7	92.0	92.2	2.6
2003	91.8	92.5	93.5	93.9	4.0	93.3	94.0	94.9	95.1	3.1
2004	95.0	95.9	96.7	97.2	3.5	95.8	96.5	97.3	97.6	2.6
2005	98.3	98.9	99.5	100.0	2.9	98.3	98.9	99.5	100.0	2.5
2006	100.9	101.7	102.6	103.2	3.2	100.8	101.8	102.7	103.3	3.3
2007	104.2	105.1	105.9	106.5	3.2	104.5	105.3	106.2	106.9	3.5
2008	107.5	108.3	108.9	109.1	2.4	107.9	108.7	109.4	109.6	2.5
2009	109.4	109.6	109.9	110.1	0.9	110.0	110.2	110.6	110.9	1.2
2010	110.9	111.4	111.8	112.1	1.8	111.4	111.9	112.4	112.7	1.6
2011	113.0	113.8	114.2	114.5	2.1	113.2	113.8	114.3	114.6	1.7
2012	115.3	116.0	116.3	116.6	1.8	115.2	115.9	116.3	116.5	1.7
2013	117.3	118.0	118.5	119.0	2.1	117.2	117.9	118.4	118.9	2.1
2014	119.4	120.4	121.1	121.5	2.1	119.2	120.2	121.0	121.5	2.2
2015	122.5	122.7	123.4	123.8	1.9	122.4	122.7	123.6	124.0	2.1
2016	124.7	125.7	126.3	126.6	2.3	125.0	126.0	126.6	127.1	2.5
2017	127.8	128.6	129.5	129.9	2.6	128.2	129.1	130.0	130.6	2.8
2018	131.4	132.2	133.2	133.7	2.9	132.1	132.9	134.1	134.7	3.1
2019	134.9	135.8	136.8	137.3	2.7	136.0	136.9	138.0	138.7	3.0
2020	138.8	139.4	140.1	. . .	. . .	140.4	140.9	141.6	. . .	. . .
Nonunion, Goods-Producing[2]										
2001	84.7	85.5	86.0	86.7	3.8	88.1	89.0	89.5	90.1	3.6
2002	87.8	88.5	88.8	89.7	3.5	91.0	91.6	91.9	92.7	2.9
2003	91.1	91.9	92.6	92.9	3.6	93.4	94.1	94.6	94.9	2.4
2004	94.5	95.2	96.4	96.8	4.2	95.6	96.2	97.3	97.3	2.5
2005	98.1	99.0	99.9	100.0	3.3	98.0	98.7	99.6	100.0	2.8
2006	100.5	101.4	102.0	102.5	2.5	100.7	101.9	102.4	103.0	3.0
2007	103.3	104.2	104.8	105.4	2.8	104.2	105.0	105.8	106.4	3.3
2008	106.5	107.1	107.6	107.7	2.2	107.7	108.4	109.0	109.3	2.7
2009	107.9	108.0	108.0	108.2	0.5	109.5	109.7	109.9	110.1	0.7
2010	109.1	109.5	110.1	110.2	1.8	110.6	111.0	111.6	111.7	1.5
2011	111.3	112.2	112.5	112.9	2.5	112.3	112.9	113.3	113.7	1.8
2012	113.5	114.1	114.6	114.9	1.8	114.2	114.7	115.3	115.5	1.6
2013	115.7	116.4	116.9	117.2	2.0	116.2	117.0	117.5	117.8	2.0
2014	117.9	118.6	119.2	119.7	2.1	118.3	119.2	119.8	120.3	2.1
2015	120.4	121.3	121.8	122.5	2.3	121.1	122.1	122.8	123.5	2.7
2016	123.2	124.1	124.6	125.1	2.1	124.3	125.3	125.9	126.6	2.5
2017	125.9	126.6	127.6	128.1	2.4	127.5	128.3	129.3	129.8	2.5
2018	129.2	130.2	130.7	131.4	2.6	131.0	132.0	132.8	133.6	2.9
2019	132.6	133.6	134.7	135.4	3.0	134.9	136.0	137.3	138.2	3.4
2020	136.3	137.2	137.6	. . .	. . .	139.3	140.5	140.9	. . .	. . .

[1]Includes wages, salaries, and employer costs for employee benefits.
[2]Includes mining, construction, and manufacturing.
[3]Includes the following industries: wholesale trade; retail trade; transportation and warehousing; utilities; information; finance and insurance; real estate and rental and leasing; professional, scientific, and technical services; management of companies and enterprises; administrative and support and waste management and remediation services; education services; health care and social assistance; arts, entertainment, and recreation; accommodation and food services; and other services, except public administration.
. . . = Not available.

Table 6-2. Employment Cost Index, Private Industry Workers, Total Compensation[1] and Wages and Salaries, by Bargaining Status and Selected Industry, 2001–2020—*Continued*

(December 2005 = 100.)

Characteristic and year	Total compensation					Wages and salaries				
	Indexes				Percent change for 12 months (ended December)	Indexes				Percent change for 12 months (ended December)
	March	June	September	December		March	June	September	December	
Nonunion Workers, Manufacturing										
2001	84.5	85.3	85.8	86.3	3.6	88.5	89.4	89.8	90.3	3.4
2002	87.6	88.4	88.7	89.4	3.6	91.4	92.0	92.4	92.9	2.9
2003	91.2	91.9	92.6	92.8	3.8	93.9	94.5	94.9	95.2	2.5
2004	94.4	95.3	96.4	96.6	4.1	95.8	96.5	97.5	97.5	2.4
2005	98.2	99.1	99.8	100.0	3.5	98.4	99.0	99.8	100.0	2.6
2006	100.3	101.3	101.7	102.1	2.1	100.7	101.8	102.0	102.5	2.5
2007	102.8	103.7	104.1	104.6	2.4	103.6	104.2	104.9	105.5	2.9
2008	105.6	106.2	106.6	106.8	2.1	106.6	107.3	108.0	108.2	2.6
2009	107.1	107.3	107.3	107.5	0.7	108.6	108.9	109.1	109.3	1.0
2010	108.5	109.2	109.9	110.0	2.3	109.8	110.5	111.1	111.2	1.7
2011	111.6	112.5	112.8	113.0	2.7	112.1	112.6	113.0	113.3	1.9
2012	113.9	114.4	115.0	115.3	2.0	114.1	114.6	115.2	115.4	1.9
2013	116.3	117.0	117.5	117.8	2.2	116.2	117.1	117.5	117.8	2.1
2014	118.8	119.5	120.1	120.6	2.4	118.7	119.6	120.0	120.5	2.3
2015	121.6	122.5	122.9	123.5	2.4	121.5	122.5	123.2	123.8	2.7
2016	124.4	125.3	126.0	126.3	2.3	124.8	125.9	126.6	127.1	2.7
2017	127.3	128.0	129.0	129.5	2.5	128.1	128.9	129.7	130.3	2.5
2018	130.7	131.5	132.0	132.7	2.5	131.4	132.4	133.1	134.0	2.8
2019	134.2	135.1	135.8	136.6	2.9	135.5	136.5	137.4	138.4	3.3
2020	137.6	138.4	138.7	. . .	. . .	139.7	140.5	140.9	. . .	. . .
Nonunion, Service-Providing[3]										
2001	85.7	86.5	87.5	88.0	4.1	87.6	88.5	89.3	89.9	3.8
2002	88.9	89.9	90.4	90.5	2.8	90.8	91.7	92.0	92.1	2.4
2003	91.9	92.7	93.7	94.1	4.0	93.3	94.0	94.9	95.2	3.4
2004	95.2	96.1	96.9	97.3	3.4	95.8	96.6	97.3	97.7	2.6
2005	98.3	98.9	99.4	100.0	2.8	98.4	99.0	99.5	100.0	2.4
2006	101.0	101.8	102.7	103.4	3.4	100.8	101.7	102.7	103.4	3.4
2007	104.4	105.3	106.2	106.8	3.3	104.6	105.4	106.3	107.0	3.5
2008	107.7	108.6	109.2	109.4	2.4	107.9	108.8	109.4	109.7	2.5
2009	109.8	110.0	110.4	110.6	1.1	110.1	110.3	110.8	111.0	1.2
2010	111.3	111.9	112.3	112.7	1.9	111.6	112.2	112.6	113.0	1.8
2011	113.5	114.3	114.7	115.0	2.0	113.4	114.0	114.5	114.8	1.6
2012	115.8	116.5	116.8	117.1	1.8	115.5	116.2	116.5	116.8	1.7
2013	117.8	118.5	119.0	119.4	2.0	117.4	118.2	118.6	119.2	2.1
2014	119.8	120.9	121.6	122.0	2.2	119.4	120.5	121.3	121.7	2.1
2015	123.1	123.1	123.9	124.2	1.8	122.8	122.9	123.8	124.2	2.1
2016	125.2	126.1	126.7	127.1	2.3	125.1	126.2	126.8	127.3	2.5
2017	128.2	129.2	130.0	130.4	2.6	128.4	129.3	130.3	130.8	2.7
2018	132.0	132.8	133.8	134.4	3.1	132.4	133.1	134.4	135.0	3.2
2019	135.5	136.4	137.3	137.9	2.6	136.2	137.1	138.2	138.8	2.8
2020	139.5	140.0	140.7	. . .	. . .	140.7	141.0	141.8	. . .	. . .

[1] Includes wages, salaries, and employer costs for employee benefits.
[2] Includes mining, construction, and manufacturing.
[3] Includes the following industries: wholesale trade; retail trade; transportation and warehousing; utilities; information; finance and insurance; real estate and rental and leasing; professional, scientific, and technical services; management of companies and enterprises; administrative and support and waste management and remediation services; education services; health care and social assistance; arts, entertainment, and recreation; accommodation and food services; and other services, except public administration.
. . . = Not available.

Table 6-3. Employment Cost Index, Private Industry Workers, Total Compensation[1] and Wages and Salaries, by Region, and Metropolitan Area Status, 2001–2020

(December 2005 = 100.)

Geography type and year	Total compensation					Wages and salaries				
	Indexes				Percent change for 12 months (ended December)	Indexes				Percent change for 12 months (ended December)
	March	June	September	December		March	June	September	December	
CENSUS REGIONS AND DIVISIONS										
Northeast										
2001	84.3	85.3	86.2	86.7	3.8	86.8	87.8	88.6	89.2	3.8
2002	87.7	88.6	88.9	89.3	3.0	90.2	91.0	91.1	91.5	2.6
2003	90.6	91.4	92.4	92.9	4.0	92.4	93.2	94.1	94.5	3.3
2004	94.2	95.5	96.3	96.6	4.0	95.3	96.3	97.1	97.2	2.9
2005	97.6	98.5	99.2	100.0	3.5	97.8	98.6	99.2	100.0	2.9
2006	100.9	101.8	102.5	103.3	3.3	100.8	101.7	102.5	103.1	3.1
2007	104.0	105.1	106.2	106.8	3.4	104.0	105.0	106.1	106.6	3.4
2008	107.4	108.1	108.7	109.5	2.5	107.5	108.2	108.7	109.6	2.8
2009	109.8	110.2	110.7	111.0	1.4	109.9	110.3	110.8	111.1	1.4
2010	111.8	112.7	113.1	113.6	2.3	111.7	112.6	112.9	113.4	2.1
2011	114.4	115.3	115.7	116.1	2.2	113.7	114.6	114.9	115.3	1.7
2012	116.5	117.1	117.6	117.8	1.5	115.8	116.4	116.7	117.0	1.5
2013	118.7	119.4	119.7	120.1	2.0	117.6	118.4	118.7	119.1	1.8
2014	120.5	121.8	122.7	123.2	2.6	119.4	120.6	121.7	122.2	2.6
2015	125.3	124.3	125.1	125.6	1.9	124.7	123.2	124.2	124.7	2.0
2016	127.3	127.7	128.2	128.7	2.5	126.9	127.2	127.7	128.3	2.9
2017	130.2	131.2	131.8	132.0	2.6	129.7	130.7	131.5	131.7	2.7
2018	133.7	134.7	135.9	136.5	3.4	133.4	133.9	135.3	136.0	3.3
2019	138.1	139.0	140.0	140.7	3.1	137.6	138.8	139.8	140.7	3.5
2020	141.7	142.6	143.1	. . .	. . .	141.9	142.7	143.1	. . .	. . .
New England										
2006	100.7	101.4	102.1	103.1	3.1	100.7	101.5	102.3	103.1	3.1
2007	103.6	104.8	105.4	106.1	2.9	103.6	104.8	105.7	106.3	3.1
2008	106.7	107.1	107.8	109.5	3.2	107.1	107.6	108.3	110.3	3.8
2009	109.9	110.2	111.2	111.5	1.8	110.5	110.6	111.7	112.1	1.6
2010	112.3	113.1	113.4	114.1	2.3	112.6	113.4	113.5	114.3	2.0
2011	114.8	116.0	116.2	116.3	1.9	114.5	115.9	116.0	116.0	1.5
2012	116.9	117.4	118.0	118.5	1.9	116.6	117.2	117.8	118.2	1.9
2013	118.9	120.0	120.5	121.6	2.6	118.6	119.8	120.5	121.8	3.0
2014	121.5	123.4	125.2	124.8	2.6	121.4	123.5	126.0	125.3	2.9
2015	130.6	125.3	127.6	127.7	2.3	133.1	125.5	128.5	128.4	2.5
2016	131.2	131.3	130.2	131.1	2.7	132.9	132.8	131.1	132.1	2.9
2017	132.7	133.8	134.9	135.3	3.2	134.1	135.2	136.4	136.8	3.6
2018	136.5	136.6	139.7	139.9	3.4	138.0	137.4	141.3	141.5	3.4
2019	141.1	142.0	143.4	144.0	2.9	142.8	143.7	145.4	146.1	3.3
2020	144.9	145.7	146.5	. . .	. . .	147.1	147.8	148.7	. . .	. . .
Middle Atlantic										
2006	100.9	101.9	102.6	103.3	3.3	100.8	101.7	102.5	103.1	3.1
2007	104.2	105.3	106.5	107.1	3.7	104.2	105.1	106.4	106.7	3.5
2008	107.8	108.6	109.1	109.5	2.2	107.6	108.4	109.0	109.4	2.5
2009	109.8	110.2	110.6	110.8	1.2	109.7	110.1	110.4	110.7	1.2
2010	111.6	112.5	113.0	113.4	2.3	111.3	112.3	112.7	113.1	2.2
2011	114.3	115.1	115.5	116.0	2.3	113.4	114.0	114.5	115.0	1.7
2012	116.4	117.0	117.4	117.6	1.4	115.4	116.1	116.4	116.5	1.3
2013	118.6	119.2	119.5	119.6	1.7	117.3	117.9	118.0	118.1	1.4
2014	120.1	121.2	121.8	122.6	2.5	118.6	119.4	120.1	120.9	2.4
2015	123.4	123.9	124.2	124.8	1.8	121.6	122.3	122.6	123.3	2.0
2016	125.9	126.3	127.4	127.8	2.4	124.6	125.2	126.3	126.9	2.9
2017	129.3	130.2	130.7	130.9	2.4	128.0	129.1	129.6	129.8	2.3
2018	132.7	134.0	134.5	135.4	3.4	131.7	132.5	133.1	134.0	3.2
2019	137.1	138.0	138.8	139.5	3.0	135.7	136.9	137.8	138.7	3.5
2020	140.6	141.5	141.9	. . .	. . .	140.0	140.8	141.1	. . .	. . .
South										
2001	86.4	87.2	88.1	88.7	4.2	88.9	89.7	90.5	91.0	3.6
2002	89.5	90.5	91.2	91.2	2.8	91.8	92.7	93.3	93.2	2.4
2003	92.0	92.7	93.6	93.9	3.0	93.5	94.1	94.9	95.0	1.9
2004	95.2	96.2	97.1	97.7	4.0	95.8	96.7	97.5	98.0	3.2
2005	98.9	99.3	99.7	100.0	2.4	98.9	99.3	99.7	100.0	2.0
2006	101.0	101.6	102.8	103.5	3.5	101.0	101.6	102.9	103.6	3.6
2007	104.3	105.3	106.1	106.7	3.1	104.6	105.6	106.5	107.0	3.3
2008	107.8	108.5	109.1	109.3	2.4	108.1	109.1	109.8	110.0	2.8
2009	109.8	110.1	110.6	110.7	1.3	110.4	110.7	111.3	111.5	1.4
2010	111.5	112.0	112.5	112.8	1.9	111.9	112.4	112.9	113.4	1.7
2011	113.4	114.3	114.7	115.0	2.0	113.7	114.4	115.0	115.2	1.6
2012	116.0	116.8	117.2	117.7	2.3	116.0	116.7	117.3	117.8	2.3
2013	118.6	119.3	119.7	120.1	2.0	118.7	119.3	119.7	120.2	2.0
2014	120.6	121.7	122.3	122.7	2.2	120.7	121.7	122.4	122.8	2.2
2015	123.2	123.9	124.3	124.6	1.5	123.3	124.2	124.7	125.0	1.8
2016	125.1	125.9	126.2	126.2	1.3	125.4	126.5	126.8	126.7	1.4
2017	127.1	127.9	128.7	129.2	2.4	127.7	128.6	129.5	130.1	2.7
2018	130.4	131.4	132.0	132.5	2.6	131.3	132.3	133.0	133.6	2.7
2019	133.3	134.2	135.3	135.8	2.5	134.4	135.5	136.7	137.3	2.8
2020	136.7	138.0	138.4	. . .	. . .	138.4	139.7	140.1	. . .	. . .

[1]Includes wages, salaries, and employer costs for employee benefits.
. . . = Not available.

Table 6-3. Employment Cost Index, Private Industry Workers, Total Compensation[1] and Wages and Salaries, by Region, and Metropolitan Area Status, 2001–2020—*Continued*

(December 2005 = 100.)

Geography type and year	Total compensation					Wages and salaries				
	Indexes				Percent change for 12 months (ended December)	Indexes				Percent change for 12 months (ended December)
	March	June	September	December		March	June	September	December	
South Atlantic										
2006	101.2	101.9	103.1	103.8	3.8	101.3	101.9	103.2	103.9	3.9
2007	104.9	106.0	106.8	107.3	3.4	105.0	106.1	106.9	107.5	3.5
2008	108.5	109.1	109.7	109.8	2.3	108.6	109.5	110.2	110.3	2.6
2009	110.3	110.7	111.3	111.5	1.5	110.8	111.3	111.9	112.2	1.7
2010	112.2	112.6	113.0	113.3	1.6	112.5	112.9	113.3	113.7	1.3
2011	113.8	114.6	115.1	115.4	1.9	114.0	114.6	115.4	115.6	1.7
2012	116.4	117.3	117.8	118.3	2.5	116.4	117.3	118.0	118.5	2.5
2013	119.1	119.8	120.2	120.6	1.9	119.2	120.0	120.2	120.7	1.9
2014	121.3	122.4	122.9	123.4	2.3	121.3	122.3	122.9	123.4	2.2
2015	124.2	124.6	125.3	125.6	1.8	124.1	124.7	125.6	126.0	2.1
2016	126.0	127.4	127.4	127.8	1.8	126.4	128.0	127.9	128.3	1.8
2017	128.7	129.7	130.4	131.1	2.6	129.2	130.3	131.1	132.0	2.9
2018	132.3	133.5	134.0	134.8	2.8	133.3	134.5	135.1	135.9	3.0
2019	135.6	136.5	137.5	138.0	2.4	136.7	137.9	139.1	139.7	2.8
2020	138.7	140.3	140.7	. . .	. . .	140.4	142.2	142.7	. . .	. . .
East South Central										
2006	100.7	100.9	101.5	102.3	2.3	100.7	101.5	102.1	103.1	3.1
2007	103.3	103.8	104.8	105.4	3.0	104.2	104.5	105.6	106.3	3.1
2008	106.5	107.2	108.0	108.0	2.5	107.2	107.9	109.0	109.0	2.5
2009	108.5	108.7	109.2	109.3	1.2	109.2	109.5	110.1	110.2	1.1
2010	110.0	110.8	111.0	110.9	1.5	110.8	111.4	111.6	111.5	1.2
2011	112.1	112.7	113.0	113.2	2.1	112.6	112.9	113.4	113.5	1.8
2012	114.0	115.1	115.3	115.8	2.3	114.1	114.8	114.9	115.4	1.7
2013	116.8	116.9	117.5	117.8	1.7	116.3	116.4	116.8	117.3	1.6
2014	118.4	119.1	119.3	119.8	1.7	117.8	118.5	118.8	119.4	1.8
2015	120.7	121.3	121.7	122.4	2.2	120.2	121.2	121.7	122.5	2.6
2016	123.1	124.7	125.1	125.5	2.5	123.0	124.7	125.2	125.5	2.4
2017	126.5	127.0	128.8	128.4	2.3	126.7	127.2	129.1	128.6	2.5
2018	130.0	130.2	131.1	131.3	2.3	130.3	130.6	131.5	131.7	2.4
2019	132.1	132.9	134.9	135.5	3.2	132.4	133.4	135.6	136.3	3.5
2020	136.2	136.9	137.1	. . .	. . .	137.1	137.8	138.0	. . .	. . .
West South Central										
2006	100.7	101.4	102.7	103.4	3.4	100.6	101.2	102.7	103.4	3.4
2007	103.7	104.8	105.6	106.1	2.6	104.1	105.3	106.1	106.6	3.1
2008	107.3	108.2	108.7	109.0	2.7	107.8	108.8	109.4	109.8	3.0
2009	109.4	109.5	109.9	109.9	0.8	110.1	110.2	110.8	110.9	1.0
2010	110.8	111.4	112.2	112.7	2.5	111.3	111.9	112.8	113.5	2.3
2011	113.2	114.4	114.7	115.0	2.0	113.7	114.5	115.0	115.2	1.5
2012	116.2	116.8	117.0	117.6	2.3	116.1	116.6	117.1	117.7	2.2
2013	118.5	119.3	119.8	120.2	2.2	118.7	119.5	120.0	120.6	2.5
2014	120.3	121.7	122.4	122.6	2.0	120.8	121.9	122.9	123.1	2.1
2015	122.6	123.7	123.6	123.6	0.8	123.2	124.5	124.4	124.3	1.0
2016	124.1	123.9	124.6	123.8	0.2	124.8	124.5	125.5	124.5	0.2
2017	124.4	125.3	125.9	126.4	2.1	125.4	126.3	127.1	127.5	2.4
2018	127.4	128.3	129.0	129.2	2.2	128.5	129.4	130.2	130.4	2.3
2019	130.0	130.9	131.8	132.3	2.4	131.3	132.2	133.2	133.7	2.5
2020	133.7	134.7	135.1	. . .	. . .	135.4	136.2	136.5	. . .	. . .
Midwest										
2001	84.8	85.4	86.1	86.7	3.5	86.8	87.6	88.3	88.9	3.3
2002	88.0	88.7	89.0	89.5	3.2	90.3	91.0	91.3	91.7	3.1
2003	92.1	92.8	93.6	94.0	5.0	94.2	94.7	95.2	95.5	4.1
2004	95.0	95.9	96.6	96.9	3.1	95.6	96.1	96.9	97.1	1.7
2005	97.8	98.4	99.5	100.0	3.2	97.8	98.2	99.4	100.0	3.0
2006	100.7	101.7	102.3	102.8	2.8	100.4	101.4	102.0	102.6	2.6
2007	103.3	104.2	104.6	105.3	2.4	103.6	104.4	105.0	105.6	2.9
2008	106.0	107.0	107.4	107.6	2.2	106.3	107.5	107.9	108.0	2.3
2009	107.9	108.1	108.4	108.6	0.9	108.4	108.6	108.9	109.2	1.1
2010	109.9	110.4	111.0	111.3	2.5	109.9	110.4	110.9	111.2	1.8
2011	112.2	113.3	113.6	113.9	2.3	111.8	112.2	112.7	112.9	1.5
2012	114.7	115.3	115.6	115.9	1.8	113.8	114.3	114.7	115.0	1.9
2013	116.4	117.0	117.4	117.8	1.6	115.5	116.0	116.6	117.1	1.8
2014	118.4	119.5	120.0	120.3	2.1	117.4	118.3	118.9	119.1	1.7
2015	121.2	121.4	122.1	122.5	1.8	119.8	120.6	121.4	121.8	2.3
2016	123.4	124.5	125.3	125.7	2.6	122.5	123.9	124.8	125.3	2.9
2017	126.8	127.4	128.0	128.5	2.2	126.4	126.9	127.5	128.1	2.2
2018	129.8	130.6	131.6	132.3	3.0	129.4	130.1	131.4	132.3	3.3
2019	133.5	134.1	135.0	135.7	2.6	133.5	134.0	135.0	136.0	2.8
2020	137.5	137.6	138.2	. . .	. . .	138.2	137.9	138.7	. . .	. . .
East North Central										
2006	100.7	101.7	102.3	102.8	2.8	100.3	101.4	101.9	102.5	2.5
2007	103.2	104.1	104.4	105.0	2.1	103.6	104.4	104.7	105.3	2.7
2008	105.5	106.5	106.9	107.0	1.9	105.8	107.0	107.3	107.4	2.0
2009	107.0	107.3	107.5	107.8	0.7	107.5	107.7	108.0	108.3	0.8
2010	109.2	109.8	110.3	110.5	2.5	109.1	109.7	110.1	110.3	1.8
2011	111.6	112.7	113.1	113.2	2.4	110.9	111.3	111.8	111.9	1.5
2012	113.9	114.5	114.6	114.8	1.4	112.7	113.1	113.4	113.5	1.4
2013	115.4	116.0	116.4	116.7	1.7	114.1	114.7	115.3	115.7	1.9
2014	117.3	118.4	118.8	119.1	2.1	116.0	116.8	117.2	117.5	1.6

[1]Includes wages, salaries, and employer costs for employee benefits.
. . . = Not available.

Table 6-3. Employment Cost Index, Private Industry Workers, Total Compensation[1] and Wages and Salaries, by Region, and Metropolitan Area Status, 2001–2020—*Continued*

(December 2005 = 100.)

Geography type and year	Total compensation					Wages and salaries				
	Indexes				Percent change for 12 months (ended December)	Indexes				Percent change for 12 months (ended December)
	March	June	September	December		March	June	September	December	
East North Central—*Continued*										
2015	120.2	120.4	120.8	121.1	1.7	118.4	119.4	119.8	120.1	2.2
2016	121.9	123.0	123.6	124.1	2.5	120.8	122.1	122.8	123.4	2.7
2017	125.2	126.0	126.5	127.0	2.3	124.5	125.3	125.9	126.5	2.5
2018	128.4	129.0	130.2	130.9	3.1	127.9	128.3	129.7	130.7	3.3
2019	132.3	132.7	133.5	134.1	2.4	132.1	132.4	133.4	134.3	2.8
2020	136.4	136.1	136.7	...	...	137.2	136.3	137.0	...	...
West North Central										
2006	100.6	101.5	102.4	102.7	2.7	100.6	101.5	102.4	102.7	2.7
2007	103.5	104.3	105.3	105.9	3.1	103.8	104.5	105.6	106.3	3.5
2008	107.3	108.4	108.8	109.0	2.9	107.9	108.9	109.5	109.7	3.2
2009	109.9	110.2	110.6	110.7	1.6	110.7	110.8	111.2	111.4	1.5
2010	111.6	112.0	112.8	113.2	2.3	111.9	112.4	113.1	113.5	1.9
2011	113.9	114.8	115.0	115.6	2.1	114.0	114.5	114.9	115.4	1.7
2012	116.9	117.5	118.2	118.7	2.7	116.5	117.1	118.0	118.5	2.7
2013	119.1	119.4	119.9	120.6	1.6	119.0	119.2	119.8	120.7	1.9
2014	121.0	122.3	123.0	123.3	2.2	120.7	122.0	122.8	123.1	2.0
2015	123.7	123.8	125.3	125.8	2.0	123.1	123.5	125.3	125.8	2.2
2016	126.9	128.4	129.5	129.8	3.2	126.5	128.2	129.4	129.8	3.2
2017	130.8	130.9	131.7	132.1	1.8	131.0	130.7	131.6	132.1	1.8
2018	133.3	134.4	135.2	135.8	2.8	133.2	134.4	135.4	136.1	3.0
2019	136.6	137.6	138.7	139.4	2.7	136.9	137.9	139.1	140.0	2.9
2020	140.1	141.3	142.0	...	...	140.8	142.0	142.8	...	...
West										
2001	84.1	85.0	85.9	86.9	5.2	87.4	88.3	89.2	90.2	4.8
2002	87.4	88.5	89.1	89.8	3.3	90.4	91.5	92.0	92.4	2.4
2003	90.9	92.0	93.2	93.8	4.5	93.0	93.9	95.1	95.5	3.4
2004	95.3	96.2	96.9	97.4	3.8	96.4	97.0	97.7	98.0	2.6
2005	98.4	99.3	99.7	100.0	2.7	98.4	99.3	99.6	100.0	2.0
2006	100.6	101.8	102.5	103.0	3.0	100.7	102.1	102.7	103.2	3.2
2007	104.2	104.9	105.7	106.5	3.4	104.8	105.4	106.2	107.0	3.7
2008	107.8	108.4	109.3	109.4	2.7	108.3	108.9	109.9	110.1	2.9
2009	109.9	110.0	110.3	110.6	1.1	110.5	110.8	111.2	111.6	1.4
2010	111.3	111.7	112.3	112.5	1.7	112.0	112.4	112.9	113.0	1.3
2011	113.5	114.3	114.6	115.1	2.3	113.6	114.1	114.5	114.9	1.7
2012	115.7	116.3	116.8	116.8	1.5	115.4	116.1	116.5	116.4	1.3
2013	117.6	118.5	119.2	119.6	2.4	117.1	118.1	118.8	119.2	2.4
2014	120.1	120.9	121.9	122.5	2.4	119.5	120.4	121.5	122.2	2.5
2015	123.1	123.8	124.6	125.3	2.3	122.6	123.4	124.4	125.2	2.5
2016	126.2	127.2	127.9	128.6	2.6	125.8	127.0	127.9	128.7	2.8
2017	129.9	131.0	132.3	132.9	3.3	129.8	130.9	132.2	132.9	3.3
2018	134.6	135.7	136.6	137.2	3.2	134.6	135.8	137.1	137.8	3.7
2019	138.5	139.5	140.4	140.9	2.7	139.3	140.2	141.4	141.9	3.0
2020	142.9	143.1	144.4	...	...	144.3	144.3	145.8	...	...
Mountain										
2006	101.0	101.8	102.7	103.1	3.1	100.6	101.7	102.8	103.2	3.2
2007	105.2	105.2	106.6	107.5	4.3	105.3	105.5	106.7	107.8	4.5
2008	108.4	109.4	110.3	110.4	2.7	108.9	109.9	110.8	111.0	3.0
2009	110.5	110.6	110.9	111.0	0.5	111.1	111.4	111.9	111.9	0.8
2010	111.3	112.3	113.0	112.8	1.6	112.3	113.2	114.1	113.7	1.6
2011	113.4	113.9	114.8	115.3	2.2	113.7	114.1	115.0	115.2	1.3
2012	115.4	116.0	116.5	115.7	0.3	115.2	115.7	116.3	115.2	0.0
2013	116.6	118.1	118.7	119.2	3.0	116.0	117.8	118.3	118.8	3.1
2014	119.5	119.8	120.1	120.6	1.2	119.0	120.5	120.8	121.5	2.3
2015	121.9	122.5	123.4	124.0	2.8	122.5	123.0	124.1	124.9	2.8
2016	124.1	125.4	125.8	126.4	1.9	124.4	125.9	126.4	127.0	1.7
2017	127.5	128.7	129.4	130.0	2.8	128.0	129.3	130.0	130.8	3.0
2018	131.7	132.5	133.2	134.1	3.2	132.5	133.4	134.2	135.2	3.4
2019	135.3	136.6	137.8	138.0	2.9	136.3	137.5	139.0	139.1	2.9
2020	139.5	140.5	141.4	...	...	140.8	141.8	142.8	...	...
Pacific										
2006	100.5	101.8	102.5	103.0	3.0	100.8	102.2	102.7	103.3	3.3
2007	103.9	104.8	105.4	106.1	3.0	104.6	105.3	106.0	106.8	3.4
2008	107.6	108.1	108.9	109.1	2.8	108.1	108.6	109.6	109.8	2.8
2009	109.7	109.9	110.1	110.5	1.3	110.3	110.6	110.9	111.5	1.5
2010	111.4	111.5	112.0	112.4	1.7	112.0	112.1	112.4	112.8	1.2
2011	113.6	114.5	114.6	115.1	2.4	113.6	114.1	114.4	114.9	1.9
2012	115.9	116.5	117.0	117.4	2.0	115.5	116.3	116.7	117.0	1.8
2013	118.1	118.7	119.5	119.9	2.1	117.6	118.3	119.1	119.5	2.1
2014	120.5	121.4	122.7	123.3	2.8	119.8	120.5	121.8	122.5	2.5
2015	123.7	124.4	125.2	125.9	2.1	122.7	123.7	124.6	125.4	2.4
2016	127.1	128.0	128.8	129.6	2.9	126.5	127.5	128.6	129.5	3.3
2017	130.9	132.0	133.6	134.2	3.5	130.7	131.7	133.2	133.8	3.3
2018	135.9	137.1	138.0	138.5	3.2	135.5	136.8	138.4	138.9	3.8
2019	139.9	140.7	141.6	142.2	2.7	140.7	141.4	142.5	143.2	3.1
2020	144.3	144.3	145.7	...	...	145.8	145.5	147.1	...	...

[1]Includes wages, salaries, and employer costs for employee benefits.
. . . = Not available.

Table 6-4. Employment Cost Index, Benefits, by Industry and Occupation, 2005–2020

(December 2005 = 100.)

Characteristic and year	Indexes				Percent change for 3 months (ended December)
	March	June	September	December	
Civilian Workers[1]					
2005	97.5	98.4	99.4	100.2	0.8
2006	100.8	101.7	102.7	103.7	1.0
2007	104.0	105.2	106.0	107.0	0.9
2008	107.5	108.1	108.8	109.3	0.5
2009	109.6	109.9	110.4	110.9	0.5
2010	112.0	112.7	113.5	114.1	0.5
2011	115.4	116.8	117.1	117.7	0.5
2012	118.5	119.3	119.9	120.5	0.5
2013	121.3	121.9	122.6	123.2	0.5
2014	123.8	125.1	125.7	126.4	0.6
2015	127.1	127.2	127.8	128.7	0.7
2016	129.3	129.9	130.7	131.3	0.5
2017	132.2	133.0	134.0	134.7	0.5
2018	135.7	136.9	137.5	138.4	0.7
2019	139.3	140.0	140.8	141.6	0.6
2020	142.1	143.2	144.0	. . .	. . .
Total Private					
2005	98.0	98.8	99.7	100.3	0.6
2006	100.8	101.6	102.5	103.4	0.9
2007	103.1	104.2	105.0	105.9	0.9
2008	106.4	106.9	107.5	107.9	0.4
2009	108.1	108.2	108.6	109.1	0.5
2010	110.3	110.9	111.6	112.1	0.4
2011	113.6	115.2	115.4	116.1	0.6
2012	116.8	117.5	117.9	118.5	0.5
2013	119.1	119.6	120.3	120.8	0.4
2014	121.3	122.5	123.2	123.8	0.5
2015	124.5	124.2	124.8	125.3	0.4
2016	125.9	126.3	127.0	127.5	0.4
2017	128.3	129.1	130.0	130.5	0.4
2018	131.5	132.7	133.2	133.9	0.5
2019	134.6	135.1	135.8	136.5	0.5
2020	136.8	137.8	138.5	. . .	. . .
State and Local Government Workers					
2005	95.6	96.8	98.4	99.9	1.5
2006	100.8	102.0	103.5	105.1	1.5
2007	107.1	108.7	109.7	110.9	1.1
2008	111.4	112.4	113.3	114.1	0.7
2009	115.3	116.2	116.8	117.7	0.8
2010	118.1	119.1	120.2	121.2	0.8
2011	122.0	122.5	123.2	123.7	0.4
2012	124.7	125.8	127.1	127.9	0.6
2013	129.1	129.9	130.9	132.1	0.9
2014	133.0	134.2	134.8	135.8	0.7
2015	136.7	137.8	138.9	140.5	1.2
2016	141.5	142.4	144.0	144.8	0.6
2017	146.0	147.0	148.2	149.6	0.9
2018	150.3	151.7	152.8	154.2	0.9
2019	155.8	157.2	158.1	159.4	0.8
2020	160.8	162.0	163.3	. . .	. . .
WORKERS BY OCCUPATION					
Management, Professional, and Related					
2005	97.9	98.8	99.8	100.4	0.6
2006	101.0	101.7	102.8	103.8	1.0
2007	103.5	104.8	105.5	106.4	0.9
2008	107.1	107.8	108.5	109.0	0.5
2009	108.5	108.7	108.9	109.2	0.3
2010	110.0	110.3	110.9	111.7	0.7
2011	113.2	114.6	114.7	115.6	0.8
2012	116.6	117.1	117.7	118.3	0.5
2013	118.5	119.3	120.2	120.7	0.4
2014	120.9	122.4	123.1	123.8	0.6
2015	124.6	123.9	124.3	124.9	0.5
2016	124.9	125.2	125.8	126.4	0.5
2017	127.2	128.0	129.0	129.6	0.5
2018	130.4	131.4	131.7	132.6	0.7
2019	133.0	133.6	134.5	135.2	0.6
2020	135.2	136.1	136.8	. . .	. . .

[1] Includes workers in the private nonfarm economy, except those in private households, and workers in the public sector, except those in the federal government.
. . . = Not available.

Table 6-4. Employment Cost Index, Benefits, by Industry and Occupation, 2005–2020—*Continued*

(December 2005 = 100.)

Characteristic and year	Indexes				Percent change for 3 months (ended December)
	March	June	September	December	
Sales and Office					
2005	97.5	98.4	99.3	100.2	0.9
2006	100.7	101.5	102.1	103.0	0.9
2007	103.3	104.2	105.2	106.1	0.9
2008	106.5	106.9	107.6	108.0	0.4
2009	108.0	108.0	108.6	108.9	0.3
2010	110.1	110.9	111.6	112.1	0.4
2011	113.3	114.9	115.3	115.8	0.4
2012	116.6	117.4	117.4	117.9	0.4
2013	118.9	119.3	120.1	120.9	0.7
2014	121.2	122.5	123.0	123.8	0.7
2015	123.7	123.9	124.6	125.5	0.7
2016	126.7	127.4	128.2	128.8	0.5
2017	129.2	129.9	130.7	131.3	0.5
2018	132.3	133.8	134.7	135.8	0.8
2019	136.2	136.9	137.4	138.2	0.5
2020	138.5	139.5	140.0	. . .	. . .
Natural Resources, Construction, and Maintenance					
2005	98.0	98.9	99.7	100.4	0.7
2006	101.1	102.4	103.4	104.4	1.0
2007	103.5	104.5	105.2	106.3	1.0
2008	106.6	106.7	107.4	108.0	0.6
2009	108.3	108.5	109.1	109.8	0.6
2010	111.6	112.1	112.8	113.5	0.6
2011	114.2	115.6	116.1	117.1	0.9
2012	117.9	118.8	119.9	120.6	0.6
2013	121.6	122.0	122.6	123.2	0.5
2014	124.0	126.0	126.7	127.4	0.6
2015	127.7	126.9	127.5	128.2	0.5
2016	128.6	128.9	129.4	130.1	0.5
2017	130.6	131.5	132.3	133.1	0.6
2018	133.6	136.0	136.4	137.1	0.5
2019	138.0	137.5	138.5	139.2	0.5
2020	139.8	140.5	141.1	. . .	. . .
Production, Transportation, and Material Moving					
2005	98.7	99.2	99.9	100.1	0.2
2006	100.0	100.8	101.6	102.3	0.7
2007	101.1	102.3	102.7	103.9	1.2
2008	104.4	104.4	104.8	105.3	0.5
2009	106.4	106.7	107.1	107.5	0.4
2010	109.9	110.7	111.7	112.2	0.4
2011	113.5	116.4	116.3	117.1	0.7
2012	116.1	117.0	117.6	118.1	0.4
2013	118.7	119.0	119.1	119.7	0.5
2014	120.5	120.9	121.6	122.3	0.6
2015	123.5	124.2	124.9	125.5	0.5
2016	126.3	126.7	127.4	128.0	0.5
2017	128.7	129.5	131.0	131.6	0.5
2018	132.6	133.3	133.4	134.0	0.4
2019	134.9	135.7	136.1	136.8	0.5
2020	137.5	138.9	139.5	. . .	. . .
Service					
2005	98.0	98.8	99.5	100.3	0.8
2006	101.3	102.1	103.0	103.9	0.9
2007	104.0	105.0	106.0	107.0	0.9
2008	107.4	108.3	108.7	109.2	0.5
2009	109.5	109.8	110.4	110.9	0.5
2010	111.5	112.3	113.3	113.8	0.4
2011	115.2	115.9	116.0	116.7	0.6
2012	117.8	118.2	118.8	119.4	0.5
2013	119.7	120.3	120.8	121.2	0.3
2014	120.9	121.1	121.7	122.4	0.6
2015	122.9	123.3	123.9	124.5	0.5
2016	125.2	126.0	126.7	127.3	0.5
2017	128.0	128.6	129.3	129.9	0.5
2018	131.0	131.5	132.4	133.0	0.5
2019	133.3	134.5	134.9	135.7	0.6
2020	136.0	137.4	138.1	135.7	0.6

. . . = Not available.

Table 6-4. Employment Cost Index, Benefits, by Industry and Occupation, 2005–2020—*Continued*

(December 2005 = 100.)

Characteristic and year	Indexes				Percent change for 3 months (ended December)
	March	June	September	December	
WORKERS BY INDUSTRY					
Goods-Producing Industries[2]					
2005	98.3	99.5	100.3	100.2	-0.1
2006	99.4	100.3	101.3	102.0	0.7
2007	100.9	102.1	102.4	103.4	1.0
2008	104.0	104.3	104.6	105.0	0.4
2009	105.4	105.5	105.6	106.2	0.6
2010	108.4	108.9	110.0	110.2	0.2
2011	111.7	114.1	113.8	114.5	0.6
2012	114.2	114.8	115.7	116.1	0.3
2013	117.0	117.3	117.6	118.1	0.4
2014	119.2	119.4	120.3	120.8	0.4
2015	121.4	122.1	122.3	123.2	0.7
2016	123.6	124.2	124.5	124.9	0.3
2017	125.4	126.0	127.5	128.0	0.4
2018	129.0	129.7	129.2	129.6	0.3
2019	130.8	131.6	132.2	132.6	0.3
2020	133.0	133.8	134.1	. . .	. . .
Manufacturing					
2005	98.2	99.4	100.1	100.1	0.0
2006	98.6	99.6	100.7	101.1	0.4
2007	99.4	100.8	100.9	101.9	1.0
2008	102.2	102.0	102.4	102.8	0.4
2009	103.4	103.4	103.4	104.0	0.6
2010	106.6	107.4	108.7	108.9	0.2
2011	111.0	113.9	113.4	114.0	0.5
2012	113.2	113.9	114.7	115.1	0.3
2013	115.7	116.1	116.4	116.7	0.3
2014	118.1	118.2	119.3	119.9	0.5
2015	120.8	121.5	121.6	122.5	0.7
2016	123.1	123.7	124.0	124.4	0.3
2017	125.0	125.6	127.6	128.1	0.4
2018	129.1	129.7	128.8	129.2	0.3
2019	130.4	131.1	131.6	132.0	0.3
2020	132.2	133.3	133.5	. . .	. . .
Service-Providing[3]					
2005	97.9	98.6	99.4	100.3	0.9
2006	101.3	102.2	103.0	104.0	1.0
2007	104.0	105.1	106.0	106.9	0.8
2008	107.4	108.0	108.7	109.1	0.4
2009	109.2	109.3	109.9	110.2	0.3
2010	111.1	111.7	112.3	112.9	0.5
2011	114.4	115.7	116.0	116.7	0.6
2012	117.8	118.5	118.8	119.4	0.5
2013	120.0	120.6	121.4	121.9	0.4
2014	122.2	123.8	124.3	125.0	0.6
2015	125.7	125.1	125.8	126.3	0.4
2016	126.9	127.3	128.0	128.6	0.5
2017	129.5	130.3	131.0	131.6	0.5
2018	132.6	133.9	134.7	135.5	0.6
2019	136.0	136.5	137.2	137.9	0.5
2020	138.3	139.2	140.1	. . .	. . .

[2]Includes mining, construction, and manufacturing.
[3]Includes the following industries: wholesale trade; retail trade; transportation and warehousing; utilities; information; finance and insurance; real estate and rental and leasing; professional, scientific, and technical services; management of companies and enterprises; administrative and support and waste management and remediation services; education services; health care and social assistance; arts, entertainment, and recreation; accommodation and food services; and other services, except public administration.
. . . = Not available.

NOTES AND DEFINITIONS

EMPLOYER COSTS FOR EMPLOYEE COMPENSATION (ECEC)

The ECEC series measures the average cost to employers for wages and salaries, and for benefits, per employee hour worked. The series provides quarterly data on employer costs per hour worked for total compensation, wages and salaries, total benefits, and the following benefits: paid leave—vacations, holidays, sick leave, and personal leave; supplemental pay—premium pay for work in addition to the regular work schedule (such as overtime, weekend, and holiday work) and for shift differentials, and non-production bonuses (such as yearend, referral, and attendance bonuses); insurance benefits—life, health, short-term disability, and long-term disability insurance; retirement and savings benefits—defined benefit and defined contribution plans; and legally required benefits—Social Security, Medicare, federal and state unemployment insurance, and workers' compensation. Cost data are presented both in dollar amounts and as percentages of total compensation. The ECEC uses current employment weights to reflect the composition of today's labor force.

Differences in the estimates for the state and local government and private industry sectors stem from factors such as variation in work activities and in occupational structures. Manufacturing and sales, for example, make up a large part of private industry work activities but are rare in state and local government. In contrast, professional and administrative support occupations (including teachers) account for two-thirds of the state and local government workforce but less than one-half of private industry

Data for the September 2019 reference period were collected from a probability sample of approximately 26,300 occupational observations selected from a sample of about 6,400 private industry establishments and approximately 7,900 occupational observations selected from a sample of about 1,400 state and local government establishments that provided data at the initial interview.

ECEC includes the civilian economy, which includes data from both private industry and state and local government. Excluded from private industry are the self-employed and farm and private household workers. Federal government workers are excluded from the public sector. The private industry series and the state and local government series provide data for the two sectors separately.

Sources of Additional Information

Additional information may be obtained from BLS news release 20-2266 "Employer Costs for Employee Compensation—September 2020," and Chapter 8 of *the Handbook of Methods*.

Table 6-5. Employer Costs for Employee Compensation by Ownership, September 2020

(Dollars, percent of total cost.)

Compensation component	Civilian workers[1]		Private industry workers		State and local governmnet workers	
	Cost	Percent	Cost	Percent	Cost	Percent
TOTAL COMPENSATION[2]	38.26	100.0	35.95	100.0	52.94	100.0
Wages and Salaries	26.25	68.6	25.23	70.2	32.74	61.8
Total Benefits	12.01	31.4	10.72	29.8	20.20	38.2
Paid leave	2.81	7.4	2.63	7.3	3.99	7.5
Vacation	1.38	3.6	1.35	3.8	1.51	2.8
Holiday	0.83	2.2	0.78	2.2	1.12	2.1
Sick	0.45	1.2	0.36	1.0	1.01	1.9
Personal	0.16	0.4	0.13	0.4	0.34	0.6
Supplemental pay	1.13	3.0	1.23	3.4	0.54	1.0
Overtime and premium pay[3]	0.31	0.8	0.33	0.9	0.24	0.4
Shift differentials	0.08	0.2	0.08	0.2	0.05	0.1
Nonproduction bonuses	0.74	1.9	0.82	2.3	0.25	0.5
Insurance	3.31	8.7	2.86	8.0	6.21	11.7
Life insurance	0.05	0.1	0.04	0.1	0.07	0.1
Health insurance	3.15	8.2	2.70	7.5	6.06	11.4
Short-term disability	0.07	0.2	0.08	0.2	0.03	0.1
Long-term disability	0.05	0.1	0.04	0.1	0.05	0.1
Retirement and savings	1.99	5.2	1.27	3.5	6.56	12.4
Defined benefit plans	1.22	3.2	0.45	1.2	6.11	11.6
Defined contribution plans	0.77	2.0	0.82	2.3	0.44	0.8
Legally required benefits	2.76	7.2	2.73	7.6	2.91	5.5
Social Security and Medicare	2.14	5.6	2.12	5.9	2.27	4.3
Social Security[4]	1.70	4.5	1.70	4.7	1.73	3.3
Medicare	0.44	1.1	0.42	1.2	0.54	1.0
Federal unemployment insurance	0.02	0.1	0.02	0.1	(5)	(6)
State unemployment insurance	0.12	0.3	0.13	0.4	0.06	0.1
Workers' compensation	0.47	1.2	0.45	1.3	0.58	1.1

[1]Includes workers in the private nonfarm economy except those in private households, and workers in the public sector, except the federal government.
[2]Includes costs for wages and salaries and benefits.
[3]Includes premium pay for work (such as overtime, weekends, and holidays) in addition to the regular work schedule.
[4]Social Security refers to the Old-Age, Survivors, and Disability Insurance (OASDI) program.
[5]Cost per hour worked is $0.01 or less.
[6]Less than .05 percent.

Table 6-6. Employer Costs for Employee Compensation for Civilian Workers by Occupational and Industry Group, September 2020

(Dollars, percent of total costs.)

Compensation component	Total compensation[1]		Wages and salaries		Total benefits		Paid leave	
	Cost	Percent	Cost	Percent	Cost	Percent	Cost	Percent
Civilian Workers[2]	38.26	100.0	26.25	68.6	12.01	31.4	2.81	7.4
Occupational Group								
Management, professional, and related	62.45	100.0	42.63	68.3	19.82	31.7	5.38	8.6
Management, business, and financial	71.35	100.0	48.82	68.4	22.53	31.6	6.80	9.5
Professional and related	58.41	100.0	39.82	68.2	18.59	31.8	4.73	8.1
Teachers[3]	66.01	100.0	44.76	67.8	21.25	32.2	3.42	5.2
Prmary, secondary, and special education school teachers	65.76	100.0	43.62	66.3	22.14	33.7	3.01	4.6
Registered nurses	59.92	100.0	38.82	64.8	21.10	35.2	5.87	9.8
Sales and office	27.91	100.0	19.61	70.3	8.30	29.7	1.89	6.8
Sales and related	26.13	100.0	19.89	76.1	6.25	23.9	1.46	5.6
Office and administrative support	28.99	100.0	19.44	67.1	9.55	32.9	2.15	7.4
Service	20.74	100.0	14.73	71.0	6.01	29.0	1.12	5.4
Natural resources, construction, and maintenance	37.89	100.0	25.47	67.2	12.42	32.8	2.07	5.5
Construction, extraction, farming, fishing, and forestry	38.48	100.0	25.50	66.3	12.98	33.7	1.66	4.3
Installation, maintenance, and repair	37.23	100.0	25.44	68.3	11.79	31.7	2.51	6.8
Production, transportation, and material moving	30.18	100.0	19.97	66.2	10.22	33.8	1.85	6.1
Production	28.80	100.0	19.10	66.3	9.71	33.7	1.80	6.2
Transportation and material moving	31.44	100.0	20.76	66.0	10.68	34.0	1.90	6.0
Industry Group								
Education and health services	43.39	100.0	29.36	67.7	14.03	32.3	3.31	7.6
Educational services	54.62	100.0	36.05	66.0	18.57	34.0	3.50	6.4
Elementary and secondaty schools	53.82	100.0	35.21	65.4	18.61	34.6	2.85	5.3
Junior colleges, colleges, and universities	60.61	100.0	40.08	66.1	20.53	33.9	5.27	8.7
Health care and social assistance	37.12	100.0	25.62	69.0	11.50	31.0	3.20	8.6
Hospitals	51.24	100.0	32.83	64.1	18.41	35.9	4.95	9.7

Compensation component	Supplemental pay		Insurance		Retirement and savings		Legally required benefits	
	Cost	Percent	Cost	Percent	Cost	Percent	Cost	Percent
Civilian Workers[2]	1.13	3.0	3.31	8.7	1.99	5.2	2.76	7.2
Occupational Group								
Management, professional, and related	1.81	2.9	5.01	8.0	3.76	6.0	3.86	6.2
Management, business, and financial	2.96	4.2	4.87	6.8	3.47	4.9	4.42	6.2
Professional and related	1.29	2.2	5.07	8.7	3.90	6.7	3.60	6.2
Teachers[3]	0.25	0.4	6.53	9.9	7.67	11.6	3.37	5.1
Prmary, secondary, and special education school teachers	0.22	0.3	7.17	10.9	8.63	13.1	3.12	4.7
Registered nurses	2.31	3.8	5.79	9.7	3.19	5.3	3.94	6.6
Sales and office	0.72	2.6	2.66	9.5	1.00	3.6	2.03	7.3
Sales and related	0.69	2.6	1.52	5.8	0.58	2.2	2.00	7.6
Office and administrative support	0.73	2.5	3.36	11.6	1.26	4.4	2.05	7.1
Service	0.45	2.2	1.73	8.3	0.97	4.7	1.74	8.4
Natural resources, construction, and maintenance	1.34	3.5	3.35	8.8	2.12	5.6	3.54	9.3
Construction, extraction, farming, fishing, and forestry	1.40	3.6	3.42	8.9	2.64	6.9	3.85	10.0
Installation, maintenance, and repair	1.27	3.4	3.28	8.8	1.54	4.1	3.19	8.6
Production, transportation, and material moving	1.28	4.2	3.13	10.4	1.29	4.3	2.67	8.8
Production	1.42	4.9	3.17	11.0	0.87	3.0	2.45	8.5
Transportation and material moving	1.14	3.6	3.09	9.8	1.68	5.3	2.87	9.1
Industry Group								
Education and health services	0.67	1.5	4.32	9.9	3.06	7.0	2.69	6.2
Educational services	0.26	0.5	5.92	10.8	5.99	11.0	2.91	5.3
Elementary and secondaty schools	0.21	0.4	6.17	11.5	6.66	12.4	2.71	5.0
Junior colleges, colleges, and universities	0.37	0.6	6.02	9.9	5.42	8.9	3.44	5.7
Health care and social assistance	0.89	2.4	3.43	9.2	1.42	3.8	2.56	6.9
Hospitals	1.92	3.7	5.54	10.8	2.75	5.4	3.25	6.3

[1]Includes costs for wages and salaries and benefits.
[2]Includes workers in the private nonfarm economy except those in private households, and workers in the public sector, except the federal government.
[3]Includes postsecondary teachers; primary, secondary, and special education teachers; and other teachers and instructors.

Table 6-7. Employer Compensation Costs Per Hour Worked for Employee Compensation and Costs as a Percent of Total Compensation: State and Local Government, by Major Occupational and Industry Group, September 2020

(Dollars, percent of total compensation.)

Characteristic	Total compensation	Wages and salaries	Benefit costs					
			Total	Paid leave	Supplemental pay	Insurance	Retirement and savings	Legally required benefits
COSTS PER HOUR WORKED								
State and Local Government Workers	52.94	32.74	20.20	3.99	0.54	6.21	6.56	2.91
Occupational Group								
Management, professional, and related	63.49	40.68	22.80	4.49	0.42	6.77	7.85	3.28
Professional and related	61.67	39.83	21.84	3.99	0.39	6.73	7.56	3.16
Teachers[1]	69.85	46.44	23.40	3.44	0.25	7.27	9.10	3.34
Primary, secondary, and special education school teachers	69.80	45.81	23.99	3.12	0.23	7.77	9.68	3.18
Sales and office	36.90	21.12	15.79	3.23	0.34	5.87	4.15	2.19
Office and administrative support	37.05	21.15	15.90	3.24	0.34	5.95	4.18	2.19
Service	39.30	22.37	16.93	3.33	0.86	4.96	5.38	2.40
Industry Group								
Education and health services	55.27	35.51	19.76	3.61	0.36	6.35	6.60	2.84
Education services	56.80	36.75	20.05	3.43	0.26	6.47	7.05	2.84
Elementary and secondary schools	55.36	35.86	19.50	2.85	0.22	6.52	7.19	2.71
Junior colleges, colleges, and universities	61.16	39.45	21.71	5.25	0.34	6.29	6.59	3.24
Health care and social assistance	46.88	28.74	18.13	4.57	0.93	5.66	4.13	2.84
Hospitals	49.53	30.91	18.61	4.84	1.07	5.66	4.06	2.98
Public administration	51.31	29.40	21.91	4.82	0.81	6.22	6.98	3.08
PERCENT OF TOTAL COMPENSATION								
State and Local Government Workers	100.0	61.8	38.2	7.5	1.0	11.7	12.4	5.5
Occupational Group								
Management, professional, and related	100.0	64.1	35.9	7.1	0.7	10.7	12.4	5.2
Professional and related	100.0	64.6	35.4	6.5	0.6	10.9	12.3	5.1
Teachers[1]	100.0	66.5	33.5	4.9	0.4	10.4	13.0	4.8
Primary, secondary, and special education school teachers	100.0	65.6	34.4	4.5	0.3	11.1	13.9	4.6
Sales and office	100.0	57.2	42.8	8.8	0.9	15.9	11.3	5.9
Office and administrative support	100.0	57.1	42.9	8.7	0.9	16.0	11.3	5.9
Service	100.0	56.9	43.1	8.5	2.2	12.6	13.7	6.1
Industry Group								
Education and health services	100.0	64.3	35.7	6.5	0.7	11.5	11.9	5.1
Education services	100.0	64.7	35.3	6.0	0.5	11.4	12.4	5.0
Elementary and secondary schools	100.0	64.8	35.2	5.2	0.4	11.8	13.0	4.9
Junior colleges, colleges, and universities	100.0	64.5	35.5	8.6	0.6	10.3	10.8	5.3
Health care and social assistance	100.0	61.3	38.7	9.7	2.0	12.1	8.8	6.1
Hospitals	100.0	62.4	37.6	9.8	2.2	11.4	8.2	6.0
Public administration	100.0	57.3	42.7	9.4	1.6	12.1	13.6	6.0

Note: Individual items may not sum to totals due to rounding.

[1] Includes postsecondary teachers; primary, secondary, and special education teachers; and other teachers and instructors.

Table 6-8. Employer Costs Per Hour Worked for Employee Compensation and Costs as a Percent of Total Compensation: Private Industry Workers, by Occupational Group and Industry, September 2020

(Dollars, percent.)

Compensation component	Total compensation		Wages and salaries		Total benefits		Paid leave	
	Cost	Percent	Cost	Percent	Cost	Percent	Cost	Percent
Private Industry Workers	35.95	100.0	25.23	70.2	10.72	29.8	2.63	7.3
Occupational Group								
Management, professional, and related	62.12	100.0	43.27	69.7	18.85	30.3	5.67	9.1
Management, business, and financial	71.01	100.0	49.25	69.4	21.77	30.6	6.73	9.5
Professional and related	56.98	100.0	39.82	69.9	17.17	30.1	5.06	8.9
Sales and office	27.12	100.0	19.48	71.8	7.65	28.2	1.77	6.5
Sales and related	26.10	100.0	19.89	76.2	6.21	23.8	1.45	5.6
Office and adminsitrative support	27.84	100.0	19.20	69.0	8.64	31.0	1.99	7.1
Service	17.93	100.0	13.57	75.7	4.36	24.3	0.78	4.4
Natural resources, construction, and maintenance	37.30	100.0	25.38	68.0	11.92	32.0	1.91	5.1
Construction, extraction, farming, fishing, and forestry	37.98	100.0	25.45	67.0	12.53	33.0	1.48	3.9
Installation, maintenance, and repair	36.55	100.0	25.30	69.2	11.25	30.8	2.39	6.5
Production, transportation, and material moving	29.73	100.0	19.81	66.6	9.92	33.4	1.81	6.1
Production	28.52	100.0	18.97	66.5	9.55	33.5	1.76	6.2
Transportation and material moving	30.89	100.0	20.62	66.8	10.27	33.2	1.85	6.0
Industry Group								
Goods-producing	40.49	100.0	27.27	67.4	13.21	32.6	2.60	6.4
Construction	40.49	100.0	27.98	69.1	12.52	30.9	1.79	4.4
Manufacturing	39.89	100.0	26.51	66.5	13.37	33.5	3.02	7.6
Aircraft manufacturing	72.71	100.0	44.99	61.9	27.71	38.1	6.79	9.3
Service-providing	35.00	100.0	24.80	70.9	10.20	29.1	2.64	7.5
Trade, transportation, and utlities	29.71	100.0	20.96	70.5	8.75	29.5	1.90	6.4
Wholesale trade	38.34	100.0	27.05	70.5	11.29	29.5	2.81	7.3
Retail trade[4]	21.05	100.0	15.95	75.8	5.10	24.2	1.02	4.9
Transportation and warehousing	41.11	100.0	26.70	64.9	14.41	35.1	2.98	7.2
Utilities	66.97	100.0	41.17	61.5	25.80	38.5	5.94	8.9
Information	57.13	100.0	38.35	67.1	18.78	32.9	5.18	9.1
Financial activities	50.68	100.0	33.97	67.0	16.72	33.0	4.45	8.8
Financial and insurance	55.96	100.0	36.96	66.1	19.00	33.9	5.05	9.0
Credit intermediation and related activities	48.85	100.0	32.56	66.6	16.29	33.4	4.49	9.2
Insurance carriers and related activities[4]	52.36	100.0	34.21	65.3	18.15	34.7	4.63	8.9
Real estate and rental and leasing	34.95	100.0	25.04	71.6	9.91	28.4	2.66	7.6

Compensation component	Supplemental pay		Insurance		retirement and savings		Legally required benfits	
	Cost	Percent	Cost	Percent	Cost	Percent	Cost	Percent
Private Industry Workers	1.23	3.4	2.86	8.0	1.27	3.5	2.73	7.6
Occupational Group								
Management, professional, and related	2.27	3.7	4.44	7.1	2.43	3.9	4.04	6.5
Management, business, and financial	3.28	4.6	4.60	6.5	2.68	3.8	4.48	6.3
Professional and related	1.69	3.0	4.34	7.6	2.29	4.0	3.80	6.7
Sales and office	0.75	2.8	2.38	8.8	0.73	2.7	2.01	7.4
Sales and related	0.69	2.6	1.51	5.8	0.56	2.2	2.00	7.7
Office and adminsitrative support	0.79	2.8	2.99	10.7	0.84	3.0	2.03	7.3
Service	0.39	2.2	1.24	6.9	0.30	1.7	1.64	9.2
Natural resources, construction, and maintenance	1.38	3.7	3.13	8.4	1.91	5.1	3.58	9.6
Construction, extraction, farming, fishing, and forestry	1.46	3.8	3.20	8.4	2.46	6.5	3.92	10.3
Installation, maintenance, and repair	1.29	3.5	3.06	8.4	1.30	3.6	3.20	8.8
Production, transportation, and material moving	1.29	4.4	3.01	10.1	1.15	3.9	2.66	8.9
Production	1.43	5.0	3.12	10.9	0.79	2.8	2.45	8.6
Transportation and material moving	1.17	3.8	2.90	9.4	1.49	4.8	2.86	9.3
Industry Group								
Goods-producing	1.71	4.2	3.72	9.2	1.80	4.4	3.38	8.3
Construction	1.39	3.4	3.29	8.1	2.16	5.3	3.90	9.6
Manufacturing	1.88	4.7	3.94	9.9	1.49	3.7	3.05	7.6
Aircraft manufacturing	3.86	5.3	7.21	9.9	5.17	7.1	4.69	6.4
Service-providing	1.13	3.2	2.68	7.6	1.16	3.3	2.60	7.4
Trade, transportation, and utlities	0.88	3.0	2.39	8.0	1.17	3.9	2.42	8.1
Wholesale trade	1.27	3.3	2.95	7.7	1.33	3.5	2.92	7.6
Retail trade[4]	0.48	2.3	1.37	6.5	0.44	2.1	1.79	8.5
Transportation and warehousing	1.44	3.5	4.17	10.1	2.41	5.9	3.41	8.3
Utilities	2.19	3.3	6.36	9.5	6.55	9.8	4.75	7.1
Information	2.65	4.6	5.01	8.8	2.21	3.9	3.73	6.5
Financial activities	2.94	5.8	4.38	8.6	1.75	3.4	3.20	6.3
Financial and insurance	3.61	6.5	4.87	8.7	2.09	3.7	3.38	6.0
Credit intermediation and related activities	2.52	5.2	4.54	9.3	1.71	3.5	3.03	6.2
Insurance carriers and related activities[4]	3.20	6.1	4.84	9.2	2.19	4.2	3.29	6.3
Real estate and rental and leasing	0.93	2.7	2.90	8.3	0.72	2.1	2.70	7.7

[4]Comprises the Old-Age, Survivors, and Disability Insurance (OASDI) program.

Table 6-8. Employer Costs Per Hour Worked for Employee Compensation and Costs as a Percent of Total Compensation: Private Industry Workers, by Occupational Group and Industry, September 2020—*Continued*

(Dollars, percent.)

Compensation component	Total compensation		Wages and salaries		Total benefits		Paid leave	
	Cost	Percent	Cost	Percent	Cost	Percent	Cost	Percent
Industry Group—*Continued*								
Professional and business services	43.75	100.0	31.37	71.7	12.37	28.3	3.55	8.1
Profesional and technical services	57.29	100.0	41.08	71.7	16.21	28.3	5.12	8.9
Administrative and waste services	24.36	100.0	18.38	75.5	5.98	24.5	1.21	5.0
Education and health services	37.56	100.0	26.34	70.1	11.22	29.9	3.16	8.4
Educational services	47.03	100.0	33.60	71.4	13.43	28.6	3.73	7.9
Junior colleges, colleges, universities and professional schools	59.56	100.0	41.27	69.3	18.28	30.7	5.30	8.9
Health care and social assistance	36.28	100.0	25.36	69.9	10.93	30.1	3.08	8.5
Leisure and hospitality	16.25	100.0	12.88	79.3	3.37	20.7	0.52	3.2
Accomodation and food services	15.65	100.0	12.42	79.4	3.23	20.6	0.47	3.0
Other services	28.38	100.0	21.41	75.4	6.98	24.6	1.74	6.1

Compensation component	Supplemental pay		Insurance		retirement and savings		Legally required benfits	
	Cost	Percent	Cost	Percent	Cost	Percent	Cost	Percent
Industry Group—*Continued*								
Professional and business services	1.58	3.6	2.79	6.4	1.31	3.0	3.14	7.2
Profesional and technical services	1.94	3.4	3.58	6.2	1.72	3.0	3.85	6.7
Administrative and waste services	0.71	2.9	1.52	6.3	0.36	1.5	2.18	8.9
Education and health services	0.81	2.2	3.32	8.8	1.32	3.5	2.61	6.9
Educational services	0.26	0.6	3.98	8.5	2.30	4.9	3.16	6.7
Junior colleges, colleges, universities and professional schools	0.43	0.7	5.53	9.3	3.22	5.4	3.81	6.4
Health care and social assistance	0.89	2.5	3.23	8.9	1.19	3.3	2.53	7.0
Leisure and hospitality	0.24	1.5	0.80	4.9	0.23	1.4	1.58	9.7
Accomodation and food services	0.25	1.6	0.75	4.8	0.22	1.4	1.54	9.8
Other services	0.45	1.6	1.67	5.9	0.74	2.6	2.37	8.4

NOTES AND DEFINITIONS

EMPLOYEE BENEFITS SURVEY

The Employee Benefits Survey provides data on the incidence and provisions of selected employee benefit plans.

Coverage

Data in this section are from the National Compensation Survey (NCS), conducted by the Bureau of Labor Statistics (BLS). This release contains March 2018 data on employer-provided benefits offered to civilian, private industry, and state and local government workers in the United States. Excluded are federal government workers, the military, agricultural workers, private household workers, and the self-employed.

Definitions

Access to a benefit is determined on an occupational basis within an establishment. An employee is considered to have access to a benefit if it is available for his or her use.

Participation refers to the proportion of employees covered by a benefit. There will be cases where employees with access to a plan will not participate. For example, some employees may decline to participate in a health insurance plan if there is an employee cost involved.

A *private establishment* is an economic unit that produces goods or services, a central administrative office, or an auxiliary unit providing support services to a company. For private industries, the establishment is usually at a single physical location. For state and local governments, an establishment is defined as an agency or entity such as a school district, college, university, hospital, nursing home, administrative body, court, police department, fire department, health or social service operation, highway maintenance operation, urban transit operation, or other governmental unit. It provides services under the authority of a specific state or local government organization within a defined geographic area or jurisdiction.

Take-up rates are the percentage of workers with access to a plan who participate in the plan. They are computed by using the number of workers participating in a plan divided by the number of workers with access to the plan, times 100 and rounded to the nearest one percent. Since the computation of take-up rates is based on the number of workers collected, rather the rounded percentage estimates, the take-up rates in the tables may not equal the ratio of participation to access estimates.

An employee is considered to be a *union worker* when all the following conditions are met: 1.) a labor organization is recognized as the bargaining agent for all workers in the occupation. 2.) wage and salary rates are determined through collective bargaining or negotiations. 3.) settlement terms, which must include earnings provisions and may include benefit provisions, are embodied in a signed, mutually binding collective bargaining agreement.

Sources of Additional Information

For more information, see Bureau of Labor Statistics (BLS) news release 20-1792 "Employee Benefits in the United States in the United States–March 2020" which is available on the BLS Web site at <http://www.bls.gov/ncs/ebs/>.

Table 6-9. Retirement Benefits:[1] Access, Participation, and Take-Up Rates, Civilian Workers[2] March 2020

(Percent.)

Characteristic	Civilian[3]			Private industry			State and local government		
	Access	Participation	Take-up rate	Access	Participation	Take-up rate	Access	Participation	Take-up rate
ALL WORKERS	71	55	78	25	20	81	60	43	71
Worker Characteristics									
Management, professional, and related	86	74	86	39	32	81	71	56	78
Management, business, and financial	89	80	90	33	27	81	82	70	85
Professional and related	85	72	84	42	34	81	67	49	74
Teachers	88	78	89	75	66	88	42	22	52
Primary, secondary, and special education school teachers	97	87	90	90	81	90	36	14	39
Registered nurses	90	78	87	43	29	68	80	66	83
Service	46	32	68	15	13	89	37	21	57
Protective service	81	71	88	57	53	93	46	31	67
Sales and office	75	55	73	20	14	72	68	47	69
Sales and related	70	42	60	9	5	53	68	40	59
Office and administrative support	78	62	80	26	20	76	68	51	75
Natural resources, construction, and maintenance	64	51	80	23	21	94	55	39	72
Construction, extraction, farming, fishing, and forestry	59	48	81	25	24	96	47	34	71
Installation, maintenance, and repair	69	54	78	20	18	90	62	45	73
Production, transportation, and material moving	71	55	77	21	17	81	63	46	73
Production	72	58	80	17	14	80	69	54	78
Transportation and material moving	69	51	75	24	19	81	56	38	68
Full-time workers	80	66	82	30	24	82	68	51	75
Part-time workers	40	22	55	10	7	72	34	16	49
Union workers	94	85	90	79	69	87	49	34	69
Nonunion workers	67	51	76	17	13	77	62	44	72
Average Wage Within the Following Percentiles[4]									
Lowest 25 percent	45	26	57	7	5	73	42	22	52
Lowest 10 percent	32	16	51	3	2	78	30	14	48
Second 25 percent	70	53	76	19	15	80	61	43	70
Third 25 percent	83	69	83	32	26	83	70	54	77
Highest 25 percent	90	81	90	47	38	82	73	59	81
Highest 10 percent	92	83	90	45	36	79	79	66	83
Establishment Characteristics									
Goods-producing industries	76	62	82	20	17	84	72	57	79
Service-providing industries	70	54	78	26	21	81	58	41	70
Education and health services	78	64	82	40	33	83	57	38	67
Educational services	88	78	89	73	64	87	42	23	54
Elementary and secondary schools	91	82	90	86	77	90	31	12	40
Junior colleges, colleges, and universities	91	80	88	60	47	79	69	46	67
Health care and social assistance	72	55	76	20	14	74	66	47	72
Hospitals	93	82	87	47	32	68	83	69	83
Public administration	91	85	94	87	79	91	37	21	57
Number of Workers									
1 to 99 workers	55	40	72	12	10	86	50	33	66
1 to 49 workers	50	36	71	9	7	85	46	31	67
50 to 99 workers	71	52	72	20	18	88	61	39	64
100 workers or more	85	71	83	38	31	80	70	53	75
100 to 499 workers	81	64	78	25	21	83	70	50	72
500 workers or more	89	79	88	53	42	78	71	55	78
Geographic Areas[5]									
Northeast	70	58	83	30	25	84	57	43	75
New England	72	58	81	28	22	80	60	46	78
Middle Atlantic	69	58	84	31	26	85	57	42	73
South	68	51	74	23	19	80	60	40	66
South Atlantic	70	51	74	23	17	75	64	42	65
East South Central	68	49	73	25	21	85	58	38	65
West South Central	66	51	77	23	20	87	53	37	69
Midwest	73	58	79	25	20	80	64	47	74
East North Central	73	58	80	26	21	80	66	48	74
West North Central	73	56	77	22	17	80	62	46	74
West	72	58	80	25	20	81	59	44	75
Mountain	74	59	80	24	19	78	61	46	75
Pacific	71	57	80	25	20	82	58	43	74

[1]Includes defined benefit pension plans and defined contribution retirement plans. Workers are considered as having access or as participating if they have access to or participate in at least one of these plan types.
[2]The take-up rate is an estimate of the percentage of workers with access to a plan who participate in the plan, rounded for presentation.
[3]Includes workers in the private nonfarm economy except those in private households, and workers in the public sector, except the federal government.
[4]The percentile groupings are based on the average wage for each occupation surveyed, which may include workers both above and below the threshold.
[5]The states that comprise the Census divisions are: New England—Connecticut, Maine, Massachusetts, New Hampshire, Rhode Island, and Vermont; Middle Atlantic—New Jersey, New York, and Pennsylvania; South Atlantic—Delaware, District of Columbia, Florida, Georgia, Maryland, North Carolina, South Carolina, Virginia, and West Virginia; East South Central—Alabama, Kentucky, Mississippi, and Tennessee; West South Central—Arkansas, Louisiana, Oklahoma, and Texas; East North Central—Illinois, Indiana, Michigan, Ohio, and Wisconsin; West North Central—Iowa, Kansas, Minnesota, Missouri, Nebraska, North Dakota, and South Dakota; Mountain—Arizona, Colorado, Idaho, Montana, Nevada, New Mexico, Utah, and Wyoming; and Pacific—Alaska, California, Hawaii, Oregon, and Washington.
- = No workers in this area or data does not meet standards of reliability or precision.

Table 6-10. Medical Care Benefits: Access, Participation, and Take-Up Rates,[1] March 2020

(Percent.)

Characteristic	Civilian[2]			Private industry			State and local government		
	Access	Participation	Take-up rate	Access	Participation	Take-up rate	Access	Participation	Take-up rate
ALL WORKERS	72	51	71	69	48	69	89	70	78
Worker Characteristics									
Management, professional, and related	88	65	74	87	64	73	92	71	78
Management, business, and financial	94	70	74	94	69	73	-	-	-
Professional and related	85	63	75	82	60	73	91	70	77
Teachers	87	65	75	-	-	-	92	70	76
Primary, secondary, and special education school teachers	97	72	74	-	-	-	99	75	75
Registered nurses	89	63	71	-	-	-	-	-	-
Service	50	30	61	45	26	57	81	62	77
Protective service	81	58	72	67	43	64	90	69	76
Sales and office	69	47	69	67	45	67	88	73	82
Sales and related	53	35	66	53	35	66	-	-	-
Office and administrative support	78	55	70	76	52	68	90	73	82
Natural resources, construction, and maintenance	75	57	75	74	55	75	95	77	81
Construction, extraction, farming, fishing, and forestry	73	55	76	71	53	75	-	-	-
Installation, maintenance, and repair	78	59	75	77	57	75	-	-	-
Production, transportation, and material moving	77	55	71	77	54	71	84	65	78
Production	81	59	73	81	58	73	-	-	-
Transportation and material moving	73	51	70	73	51	69	-	-	-
Full-time workers	87	63	72	85	60	71	99	78	79
Part-time workers	23	11	50	23	11	48	25	18	71
Union workers	95	75	79	95	77	81	95	73	77
Nonunion workers	68	47	69	67	45	68	84	67	80
Average Wage Within the Following Percentiles[3]									
Lowest 25 percent	41	23	57	38	21	55	72	56	78
Lowest 10 percent	27	13	48	27	12	46	62	47	77
Second 25 percent	74	51	69	71	47	67	93	73	79
Third 25 percent	88	66	75	85	62	73	97	77	80
Highest 25 percent	93	70	76	92	69	75	95	73	77
Highest 10 percent	95	72	76	94	71	75	93	73	78
Establishment Characteristics									
Goods-producing industries	85	63	74	85	63	74	-	-	-
Service-providing industries	70	49	70	66	45	68	89	69	78
Education and health services	78	55	70	72	47	66	90	70	77
Educational services	86	65	75	73	50	68	90	69	77
Elementary and secondary schools	88	66	75	-	-	-	90	68	76
Junior colleges, colleges, and universities	89	68	76	90	63	70	89	71	79
Health care and social assistance	73	49	67	72	47	66	92	74	80
Hospitals	91	65	71	-	-	-	91	74	81
Public administration	90	72	80	-	-	-	90	72	80
Number of Workers									
1 to 99 workers	58	39	67	56	37	66	86	68	80
1 to 49 workers	52	35	67	50	33	66	82	66	81
50 to 99 workers	76	52	68	74	49	66	89	70	79
100 workers or more	86	63	73	85	61	71	90	70	78
100 to 499 workers	82	58	71	81	57	70	86	69	80
500 workers or more	91	68	75	90	66	73	92	71	77
Geographic Areas[4]									
Northeast	71	51	72	69	49	71	87	67	77
New England	74	53	71	72	51	70	88	65	74
Middle Atlantic	70	51	72	68	48	71	87	67	78
South	70	49	69	66	44	67	92	74	80
South Atlantic	70	48	69	67	44	66	90	73	80
East South Central	69	50	72	65	44	68	92	80	87
West South Central	70	49	70	65	45	68	96	74	77
Midwest	73	50	69	71	48	68	86	64	75
East North Central	72	50	69	71	48	68	84	65	77
West North Central	73	49	67	71	47	66	88	63	71
West	75	55	74	73	53	73	88	69	79
Mountain	74	54	73	72	52	72	86	66	77
Pacific	76	56	74	74	54	73	88	71	80

[1]The take-up rate is an estimate of the percentage of workers with access to a plan who participate in the plan, rounded for presentation.
[2]Includes workers in the private nonfarm economy except those in private households, and workers in the public sector, except the federal government.
[3]The percentile groupings are based on the average wage for each occupation surveyed, which may include workers both above and below the threshold.
[4]The states that comprise the Census divisions are: New England—Connecticut, Maine, Massachusetts, New Hampshire, Rhode Island, and Vermont; Middle Atlantic—New Jersey, New York, and Pennsylvania; South Atlantic—Delaware, District of Columbia, Florida, Georgia, Maryland, North Carolina, South Carolina, Virginia, and West Virginia; East South Central—Alabama, Kentucky, Mississippi, and Tennessee; West South Central—Arkansas, Louisiana, Oklahoma, and Texas; East North Central—Illinois, Indiana, Michigan, Ohio, and Wisconsin; West North Central—Iowa, Kansas, Minnesota, Missouri, Nebraska, North Dakota, and South Dakota; Mountain—Arizona, Colorado, Idaho, Montana, Nevada, New Mexico, Utah, and Wyoming; and Pacific—Alaska, California, Hawaii, Oregon, and Washington.
- = No workers in this area or data does not meet standards of reliability or precision.

Table 6-11. Medical Plans: Share of Premiums Paid by Employer and Employee for Single Coverage, March 2020

(Percent.)

Characteristic	Civilian[1]		Private industry		State and local government	
	Employer share of premium	Employee share of premium	Employer share of premium	Employee share of premium	Employer share of premium	Employee share of premium
ALL WORKERS	80	20	78	22	86	14
Worker Characteristics						
Management, professional, and related	81	19	79	21	85	15
Management, business, and financial	78	22	77	23	-	-
Professional and related	82	18	80	20	85	15
Teachers	83	17	-	-	84	16
Primary, secondary, and special education school teachers	84	16	-	-	84	16
Registered nurses	83	17	-	-	-	-
Service	81	19	78	22	87	13
Protective service	85	15	77	23	88	12
Sales and office	79	21	78	22	88	12
Sales and related	76	24	76	24	-	-
Office and administrative support	80	20	79	21	88	12
Natural resources, construction, and maintenance	79	21	78	22	90	10
Construction, extraction, farming, fishing, and forestry	80	20	79	21	-	-
Installation, maintenance, and repair	79	21	78	22	-	-
Production, transportation, and material moving	78	22	78	22	86	14
Production	79	21	79	21	-	-
Transportation and material moving	77	23	77	23	-	-
Full-time workers	80	20	78	22	86	14
Part-time workers	81	19	80	20	85	15
Union workers	85	15	84	16	86	14
Nonunion workers	79	21	78	22	87	13
Average Wage Within the Following Percentiles[2]						
Lowest 25 percent	77	23	76	24	87	13
Lowest 10 percent	78	22	77	23	87	13
Second 25 percent	79	21	78	22	87	13
Third 25 percent	80	20	79	21	86	14
Highest 25 percent	81	19	80	20	85	15
Highest 10 percent	81	19	80	20	85	15
Establishment Characteristics						
Goods-producing industries	79	21	79	21	-	-
Service-providing industries	80	20	78	22	86	14
Education and health services	82	18	80	20	85	15
Educational services	84	16	79	21	85	15
Elementary and secondary schools	84	16	-	-	84	16
Junior colleges, colleges, and universities	84	16	80	20	86	14
Health care and social assistance	81	19	81	19	87	13
Hospitals	83	17	-	-	87	13
Public administration	88	12	-	-	88	12
Number of Workers						
1 to 99 workers	79	21	78	22	86	14
1 to 49 workers	79	21	78	22	88	12
50 to 99 workers	78	22	77	23	84	16
100 workers or more	81	19	79	21	86	14
100 to 499 workers	79	21	78	22	87	13
500 workers or more	82	18	80	20	86	14
Geographic Areas[3]						
Northeast	80	20	80	20	85	15
New England	77	23	77	23	77	23
Middle Atlantic	82	18	80	20	87	13
South	79	21	78	22	86	14
South Atlantic	79	21	77	23	86	14
East South Central	81	19	78	22	88	12
West South Central	80	20	78	22	86	14
Midwest	79	21	77	23	87	13
East North Central	79	21	78	22	85	15
West North Central	79	21	76	24	91	9
West	81	19	80	20	86	14
Mountain	80	20	78	22	87	13
Pacific	81	19	81	19	86	14

[1] Includes workers in the private nonfarm economy except those in private households, and workers in the public sector, except the federal government.
[2] The percentile groupings are based on the average wage for each occupation surveyed, which may include workers both above and below the threshold.
[3] The states that comprise the Census divisions are: New England—Connecticut, Maine, Massachusetts, New Hampshire, Rhode Island, and Vermont; Middle Atlantic—New Jersey, New York, and Pennsylvania; South Atlantic—Delaware, District of Columbia, Florida, Georgia, Maryland, North Carolina, South Carolina, Virginia, and West Virginia; East South Central—Alabama, Kentucky, Mississippi, and Tennessee; West South Central—Arkansas, Louisiana, Oklahoma, and Texas; East North Central—Illinois, Indiana, Michigan, Ohio, and Wisconsin; West North Central—Iowa, Kansas, Minnesota, Missouri, Nebraska, North Dakota, and South Dakota; Mountain—Arizona, Colorado, Idaho, Montana, Nevada, New Mexico, Utah, and Wyoming; and Pacific—Alaska, California, Hawaii, Oregon, and Washington.
- = No workers in this area or data does not meet standards of reliability or precision.

Table 6-12. Medical Plans: Share of Premiums Paid by Employer and Employee for Family Coverage, March 2020

(Percent.)

Characteristic	Civilian[1]		Private industry		State and local government	
	Employer share of premium	Employee share of premium	Employer share of premium	Employee share of premium	Employer share of premium	Employee share of premium
ALL WORKERS	67	33	66	34	71	29
Worker Characteristics						
Management, professional, and related	69	31	68	32	70	30
Management, business, and financial	68	32	67	33	-	-
Professional and related	69	31	68	32	69	31
Teachers	66	34	-	-	66	34
Primary, secondary, and special education school teachers	64	36	-	-	65	35
Registered nurses	71	29	-	-	65	35
Service	63	37	60	40	72	28
Protective service	73	27	65	35	77	23
Sales and office	66	34	65	35	73	27
Sales and related	62	38	62	38	-	-
Office and administrative support	68	32	67	33	74	26
Natural resources, construction, and maintenance	68	32	67	33	77	23
Construction, extraction, farming, fishing, and forestry	69	31	68	32	-	-
Installation, maintenance, and repair	67	33	66	34	-	-
Production, transportation, and material moving	69	31	69	31	71	29
Production	72	28	72	28	-	-
Transportation and material moving	67	33	67	33	-	-
Full-time workers	67	33	66	34	71	29
Part-time workers	67	33	66	34	70	30
Union workers	79	21	82	18	76	24
Nonunion workers	64	36	64	36	67	33
Average Wage Within the Following Percentiles[2]						
Lowest 25 percent	59	41	59	41	66	34
Lowest 10 percent	58	42	59	41	61	39
Second 25 percent	65	35	64	36	74	26
Third 25 percent	69	31	67	33	69	31
Highest 25 percent	71	29	71	29	75	25
Highest 10 percent	73	27	72	28	76	24
Establishment Characteristics						
Goods-producing industries	71	29	71	29	-	-
Service-providing industries	67	33	65	35	71	29
Education and health services	66	34	64	36	68	32
Educational services	66	34	64	36	66	34
Elementary and secondary schools	64	36	-	-	65	35
Junior colleges, colleges, and universities	71	29	70	30	72	28
Health care and social assistance	65	35	64	36	74	26
Hospitals	74	26	-	-	74	26
Public administration	77	23	-	-	77	23
Number of Workers						
1 to 99 workers	62	38	61	39	74	26
1 to 49 workers	62	38	61	39	74	26
50 to 99 workers	62	38	60	40	73	27
100 workers or more	70	30	70	30	70	30
100 to 499 workers	67	33	66	34	71	29
500 workers or more	73	27	75	25	70	30
Geographic Areas[3]						
Northeast	73	27	71	29	83	17
New England	71	29	70	30	76	24
Middle Atlantic	74	26	71	29	85	15
South	62	38	62	38	63	37
South Atlantic	63	37	61	39	67	33
East South Central	65	35	66	34	63	37
West South Central	61	39	62	38	57	43
Midwest	69	31	68	32	74	26
East North Central	71	29	70	30	76	24
West North Central	66	34	66	34	70	30
West	68	32	66	34	74	26
Mountain	67	33	67	33	71	29
Pacific	68	32	66	34	75	25

[1] Includes workers in the private nonfarm economy except those in private households, and workers in the public sector, except the federal government.
[2] The percentile groupings are based on the average wage for each occupation surveyed, which may include workers both above and below the threshold.
[3] The states that comprise the Census divisions are: New England—Connecticut, Maine, Massachusetts, New Hampshire, Rhode Island, and Vermont; Middle Atlantic—New Jersey, New York, and Pennsylvania; South Atlantic—Delaware, District of Columbia, Florida, Georgia, Maryland, North Carolina, South Carolina, Virginia, and West Virginia; East South Central—Alabama, Kentucky, Mississippi, and Tennessee; West South Central—Arkansas, Louisiana, Oklahoma, and Texas; East North Central—Illinois, Indiana, Michigan, Ohio, and Wisconsin; West North Central—Iowa, Kansas, Minnesota, Missouri, Nebraska, North Dakota, and South Dakota; Mountain—Arizona, Colorado, Idaho, Montana, Nevada, New Mexico, Utah, and Wyoming; and Pacific—Alaska, California, Hawaii, Oregon, and Washington.
- = No workers in this area or data does not meet standards of reliability or precision.

Table 6-13. Life Insurance Benefits: Access, Participation, and Take-Up Rates, National Compensation Survey, March 2020

(Percent.)

Characteristic	Civilian[1]			Private industry			State and local government		
	Access	Participation	Take-up rates[2]	Access	Participation	Take-up rates[2]	Access	Participation	Take-up rates[2]
ALL WORKERS	60	59	98	56	55	98	82	80	98
Worker Characteristics									
Management, professional, and related	79	78	99	78	77	99	83	81	98
Management, business, and financial	84	82	99	83	82	99	-	-	-
Professional and related	77	76	99	75	74	99	83	80	97
Teachers	77	76	98	-	-	-	82	80	98
Primary, secondary, and special education school teachers	85	83	98	-	-	-	87	86	98
Registered nurses	84	83	99	-	-	-	-	-	-
Service	34	33	95	28	27	94	76	74	97
Protective service	64	61	95	32	27	84	86	84	98
Sales and office	57	56	98	55	54	98	82	81	98
Sales and related	40	39	97	40	39	97	-	-	-
Office and administrative support	67	66	98	65	64	98	83	81	98
Natural resources, construction, and maintenance	56	55	99	53	53	99	90	89	99
Construction, extraction, farming, fishing, and forestry	48	48	99	45	44	99	-	-	-
Installation, maintenance, and repair	65	64	98	62	61	98	-	-	-
Production, transportation, and material moving	64	63	98	64	62	98	80	78	99
Production	69	68	99	69	68	99	-	-	-
Transportation and material moving	60	58	97	59	57	97	-	-	-
Full-time workers	74	73	99	70	70	99	91	89	98
Part-time workers	14	13	89	13	12	88	24	22	94
Union workers	85	83	97	82	80	97	89	87	98
Nonunion workers	56	55	98	54	53	98	76	74	97
Average Wage Within the Following Percentiles[3]									
Lowest 25 percent	28	26	95	25	23	94	66	63	97
Lowest 10 percent	15	13	90	13	12	88	54	53	97
Second 25 percent	58	57	98	55	54	98	87	85	98
Third 25 percent	76	75	99	70	70	99	88	86	98
Highest 25 percent	85	84	99	83	83	99	88	86	98
Highest 10 percent	88	87	99	88	88	99	85	82	97
Establishment Characteristics									
Goods-producing industries	70	69	99	69	69	99	-	-	-
Service-providing industries	58	57	98	53	52	98	82	80	98
Education and health services	68	67	98	61	60	99	82	80	97
Educational services	78	76	98	64	64	100	81	79	98
Elementary and secondary schools	78	76	98	-	-	-	80	78	98
Junior colleges, colleges, and universities	86	84	98	86	85	99	86	83	97
Health care and social assistance	62	61	98	60	59	98	88	84	96
Hospitals	89	87	98	-	-	-	88	83	95
Public administration	84	82	98	-	-	-	84	82	98
Number of Workers									
1 to 99 workers	42	41	98	40	39	98	75	74	98
1 to 49 workers	36	36	99	35	35	99	70	70	99
50 to 99 workers	60	58	97	57	55	97	80	79	98
100 workers or more	77	75	98	75	73	98	84	82	97
100 to 499 workers	70	69	98	69	68	98	78	76	97
500 workers or more	84	81	97	82	80	97	87	84	98
Geographic Areas[4]									
Northeast	58	57	98	54	54	99	82	80	97
New England	65	63	97	62	62	99	83	75	90
Middle Atlantic	56	55	99	51	51	99	82	81	99
South	58	57	98	54	53	98	83	80	97
South Atlantic	58	56	97	54	52	97	85	82	96
East South Central	58	58	99	55	55	99	75	73	97
West South Central	59	57	98	54	52	98	84	82	98
Midwest	63	61	97	60	58	97	81	79	97
East North Central	64	62	98	61	60	98	81	78	96
West North Central	60	58	97	56	55	97	82	81	99
West	61	60	99	57	57	99	80	80	100
Mountain	64	63	99	61	60	99	83	82	100
Pacific	59	59	99	56	55	99	79	79	99

[1]Includes workers in the private nonfarm economy except those in private households, and workers in the public sector, except the federal government.
[2]The take-up rate is an estimate of the percentage of workers with access to a plan who participate in the plan, rounded for presentation.
[3]The percentile groupings are based on the average wage for each occupation surveyed, which may include workers both above and below the threshold.
[4]The states that comprise the Census divisions are: New England—Connecticut, Maine, Massachusetts, New Hampshire, Rhode Island, and Vermont; Middle Atlantic—New Jersey, New York, and Pennsylvania; South Atlantic—Delaware, District of Columbia, Florida, Georgia, Maryland, North Carolina, South Carolina, Virginia, and West Virginia; East South Central—Alabama, Kentucky, Mississippi, and Tennessee; West South Central—Arkansas, Louisiana, Oklahoma, and Texas; East North Central—Illinois, Indiana, Michigan, Ohio, and Wisconsin; West North Central—Iowa, Kansas, Minnesota, Missouri, Nebraska, North Dakota, and South Dakota; Mountain—Arizona, Colorado, Idaho, Montana, Nevada, New Mexico, Utah, and Wyoming; and Pacific—Alaska, California, Hawaii, Oregon, and Washington.
- = No workers in this area or data does not meet standards of reliability or precision.

Table 6-14. Life Insurance Plans: Employee Contribution Requirement, Civilian Workers,[1] March 2020

(Percent.)

Characteristic	Employee contribution required	Employee contribution not required
ALL WORKERS	5	95
Worker Characteristics		
Management, professional, and related	5	95
Management, business, and financial	4	96
Professional and related	5	95
Teachers	10	90
Primary, secondary, and special education school teachers	9	91
Registered nurses	2	98
Service	5	95
Sales and office	8	92
Sales and related	5	95
Office and administrative support	7	93
Natural resources, construction, and maintenance	5	95
Construction, extraction, farming, fishing, and forestry	5	95
Installation, maintenance, and repair	5	95
Production, transportation, and material moving	4	96
Production	5	95
Transportation and material moving	4	96
Full-time workers	5	95
Part-time workers	5	95
Union workers	4	96
Nonunion workers	6	94
Average Wage Within the Following Percentiles[2]		
Lowest 25 percent	5	95
Lowest 10 percent	5	95
Second 25 percent	6	94
Third 25 percent	4	96
Highest 25 percent	5	95
Highest 10 percent	5	95
Establishment Characteristics		
Service-providing industries	5	95
Education and health services	5	95
Educational services	10	90
Elementary and secondary schools	9	91
Junior colleges, colleges, and universities	11	89
Health care and social assistance	2	98
Hospitals	3	97
Public administration	7	93
Number of Workers		
1 to 99 workers	4	96
1 to 49 workers	4	96
50 to 99 workers	4	96
100 workers or more	5	95
100 to 499 workers	5	95
500 workers or more	6	94
Geographic Areas[3]		
Northeast	6	94
New England	10	90
Middle Atlantic	4	96
South	6	94
South Atlantic	4	96
East South Central	7	93
West South Central	7	93
Midwest	4	96
East North Central	4	96
West North Central	4	96
West	4	96
Mountain	5	95
Pacific	3	97

[1]Includes workers in the private nonfarm economy except those in private households, and workers in the public sector, except the federal government.
[2]The percentile groupings are based on the average wage for each occupation surveyed, which may include workers both above and below the threshold.
[3]The states that comprise the Census divisions are: New England—Connecticut, Maine, Massachusetts, New Hampshire, Rhode Island, and Vermont; Middle Atlantic—New Jersey, New York, and Pennsylvania; South Atlantic—Delaware, District of Columbia, Florida, Georgia, Maryland, North Carolina, South Carolina, Virginia, and West Virginia; East South Central—Alabama, Kentucky, Mississippi, and Tennessee; West South Central—Arkansas, Louisiana, Oklahoma, and Texas; East North Central—Illinois, Indiana, Michigan, Ohio, and Wisconsin; West North Central—Iowa, Kansas, Minnesota, Missouri, Nebraska, North Dakota, and South Dakota; Mountain—Arizona, Colorado, Idaho, Montana, Nevada, New Mexico, Utah, and Wyoming; and Pacific—Alaska, California, Hawaii, Oregon, and Washington.

Table 6-15. Access to Paid Leave Benefits, March 2020

(Percent.)

Characteristic	Civilian[1]			Private industry			State and local government		
	Paid sick leave	Paid vacation	Paid holidays	Paid sick leave	Paid vacation	Paid holidays	Paid sick leave	Paid vacation	Paid holidays
ALL WORKERS	78	76	78	75	79	80	91	60	68
Worker Characteristics									
Management, professional, and related	92	79	82	92	90	91	93	46	56
Management, business, and financial	95	96	95	95	97	96	-	-	-
Professional and related	91	71	76	90	86	88	93	40	51
Teachers	89	18	34	-	-	-	93	14	31
Primary, secondary, and special education school teachers	98	15	28	-	-	-	99	11	26
Registered nurses	94	90	92	-	-	-	-	-	-
Service	62	60	60	59	58	57	85	75	79
Protective service	84	84	82	74	76	70	91	90	90
Sales and office	78	81	84	77	81	84	92	86	88
Sales and related	65	70	76	65	70	76	-	-	-
Office and administrative support	85	88	89	84	88	89	93	87	88
Natural resources, construction, and maintenance	70	81	81	68	80	80	96	96	95
Construction, extraction, farming, fishing, and forestry	60	71	72	57	69	70	-	-	-
Installation, maintenance, and repair	80	92	91	79	91	91	-	-	-
Production, transportation, and material moving	73	85	86	72	86	87	90	62	74
Production	72	90	92	72	90	92	-	-	-
Transportation and material moving	74	80	81	73	82	82	-	-	-
Full-time workers	88	87	88	86	91	90	99	67	73
Part-time workers	45	39	47	45	41	49	46	23	33
Union workers	93	75	81	88	91	91	98	58	69
Nonunion workers	75	76	78	74	78	79	86	63	66
Average Wage Within the Following Percentiles[2]									
Lowest 25 percent	52	55	59	49	54	58	79	58	65
Lowest 10 percent	33	40	43	31	40	43	67	45	54
Second 25 percent	82	83	83	80	83	83	96	86	89
Third 25 percent	89	91	91	87	91	92	97	62	70
Highest 25 percent	94	81	84	92	93	93	96	40	51
Highest 10 percent	95	83	85	94	94	94	94	38	49
Establishment Characteristics									
Goods-producing industries	74	89	89	74	89	89	-	-	-
Service-providing industries	78	74	76	76	77	78	91	60	67
Education and health services	87	69	74	84	82	84	93	44	55
Educational services	90	40	51	81	55	61	93	36	49
Elementary and secondary schools	93	27	39	-	-	-	93	25	38
Junior colleges, colleges, and universities	90	70	82	88	74	85	91	69	80
Health care and social assistance	85	87	87	84	86	87	92	93	92
Hospitals	95	94	94	-	-	-	92	92	92
Public administration	92	91	91	-	-	-	92	91	91
Number of Workers									
1 to 99 workers	69	70	72	67	71	73	90	55	62
1 to 49 workers	66	68	71	66	69	71	86	62	67
50 to 99 workers	76	74	76	74	78	79	93	47	56
100 workers or more	86	82	84	85	88	88	92	62	70
100 to 499 workers	83	82	83	82	86	86	90	60	68
500 workers or more	90	82	85	88	90	91	93	63	70
Geographic Areas[3]									
Northeast	81	75	78	80	78	81	90	56	64
New England	84	74	78	83	77	81	91	55	60
Middle Atlantic	80	75	78	79	78	81	90	57	65
South	72	75	77	68	77	78	92	61	68
South Atlantic	72	76	78	69	77	78	91	65	76
East South Central	68	76	80	64	79	82	90	61	72
West South Central	73	74	74	69	77	78	95	56	56
Midwest	73	76	77	71	79	79	89	55	66
East North Central	73	76	77	71	79	79	88	55	68
West North Central	74	77	77	72	80	79	92	57	62
West	88	79	81	88	81	82	94	67	72
Mountain	77	77	81	75	80	83	89	61	66
Pacific	93	80	81	93	81	82	96	70	74

[1]Includes workers in the private nonfarm economy except those in private households, and workers in the public sector, except the federal government.
[2]The percentile groupings are based on the average wage for each occupation surveyed, which may include workers both above and below the threshold.
[3]The states that comprise the Census divisions are: New England—Connecticut, Maine, Massachusetts, New Hampshire, Rhode Island, and Vermont; Middle Atlantic—New Jersey, New York, and Pennsylvania; South Atlantic—Delaware, District of Columbia, Florida, Georgia, Maryland, North Carolina, South Carolina, Virginia, and West Virginia; East South Central—Alabama, Kentucky, Mississippi, and Tennessee; West South Central—Arkansas, Louisiana, Oklahoma, and Texas; East North Central—Illinois, Indiana, Michigan, Ohio, and Wisconsin; West North Central—Iowa, Kansas, Minnesota, Missouri, Nebraska, North Dakota, and South Dakota; Mountain—Arizona, Colorado, Idaho, Montana, Nevada, New Mexico, Utah, and Wyoming; and Pacific—Alaska, California, Hawaii, Oregon, and Washington.
- = No workers in this area or data does not meet standards of reliability or precision.

Table 6-16. Quality of Life Benefits:[1] Access for Civilian Workers, March 2020

(Percent.)

Characteristic	Childcare[2]	Flexible workplace	Flexible work schedule	Subsidized commuting	Wellness programs	Employee assistance programs
ALL WORKERS	11	7	12	8	44	54
Worker Characteristics						
Management, professional, and related	18	15	21	14	60	70
Management, business, and financial	20	23	30	16	62	70
Professional and related	17	11	18	13	59	71
Teachers	14	3	8	7	55	68
Primary, secondary, and special education school teachers	11	2	4	3	54	68
Registered nurses	28	3	10	14	81	87
Service	10	2	9	6	27	36
Protective service	10	2	5	9	43	58
Sales and office	9	7	11	7	45	57
Sales and related	5	5	10	4	38	53
Office and administrative support	11	8	12	9	50	59
Natural resources, construction, and maintenance	6	2	4	4	29	37
Construction, extraction, farming, fishing, and forestry	5	1	3	4	24	29
Installation, maintenance, and repair	6	2	5	5	35	46
Production, transportation, and material moving	5	2	4	4	45	55
Production	8	3	5	3	48	54
Transportation and material moving	3	1	3	4	42	56
Full-time workers	13	9	13	10	50	61
Part-time workers	6	2	10	4	25	35
Union workers	15	3	6	12	58	78
Nonunion workers	11	8	13	8	42	51
Average Wage Within the Following Percentiles[3]						
Lowest 25 percent	5	2	7	3	27	35
Lowest 10 percent	5	1	8	3	17	25
Second 25 percent	8	5	9	7	41	51
Third 25 percent	13	7	12	11	52	63
Highest 25 percent	20	15	22	15	62	74
Highest 10 percent	23	20	27	19	66	79
Establishment Characteristics						
Goods-producing industries	9	6	9	5	46	52
Service-providing industries	12	7	13	9	44	55
Education and health services	17	4	11	10	52	64
Educational services	15	4	7	8	58	71
Elementary and secondary schools	10	2	2	3	53	67
Junior colleges, colleges, and universities	28	9	17	20	77	90
Health care and social assistance	18	4	13	11	49	60
Hospitals	36	2	7	18	83	95
Public administration	17	6	12	17	64	81
Number of Workers						
1 to 99 workers	6	6	11	5	26	33
1 to 49 workers	5	6	10	5	21	28
50 to 99 workers	7	7	12	6	39	4f
100 workers or more	17	8	14	11	63	7
100 to 499 workers	9	6	13	8	54	f
500 workers or more	25	10	15	15	73	
Geographic Areas[4]						
Northeast	14	7	15	11	43	
New England	15	7	18	13	48	
Middle Atlantic	14	6	15	10	41	
South	11	7	11	7	45	
South Atlantic	12	8	12	7	46	
East South Central	6	6	9	4	47	
West South Central	10	7	10	6	44	
Midwest	10	7	12	6	46	
East North Central	10	8	12	6	47	
West North Central	9	6	12	6	45	
West	11	6	12	12	42	
Mountain	11	8	12	8	45	
Pacific	11	5	12	13	41	

[1]Includes workers in the private nonfarm economy except those in private households, and workers in the public sector, except the federal government.
[2]A workplace program that provides for either the full or partial cost of caring for an employee's children in a nursery, day care center, or a baby sitter in facilities either on or off the employer's premises.
[3]The categories are based on the average wage for each occupation surveyed, which may include workers with earnings both above and below the threshold.
[4]The states that comprise the Census divisions are: New England—Connecticut, Maine, Massachusetts, New Hampshire, Rhode Island, and Vermont; Middle Atlantic—New Je and Pennsylvania; South Atlantic—Delaware, District of Columbia, Florida, Georgia, Maryland, North Carolina, South Carolina, Virginia, and West Virginia; East South Central Kentucky, Mississippi, and Tennessee; West South Central—Arkansas, Louisiana, Oklahoma, and Texas; East North Central—Illinois, Indiana, Michigan, Ohio, and Wiscons Central—Iowa, Kansas, Minnesota, Missouri, Nebraska, North Dakota, and South Dakota; Mountain—Arizona, Colorado, Idaho, Montana, Nevada, New Mexico, Utah, and \ Pacific—Alaska, California, Hawaii, Oregon, and Washington.

Table 6-17. Financial Benefits: Access for Civilian Workers, March 2020

(Percent.)

Characteristic	Health savings account	Section 125 cafeteria benefits			Savings plans with no employer contribution[1]	Financial planning	Student loan repayment
		Flexible benefits	Dependent care flexible spending account	Healthcare flexible spending account			
ALL WORKERS	33	16	43	46	21	22	4
Worker Characteristics							
Management, professional, and related	47	25	61	66	31	30	6
Management, business, and financial	54	23	67	69	24	34	7
Professional and related	44	26	59	65	34	28	6
Teachers	37	34	56	63	53	24	6
Primary, secondary, and special education school teachers	38	37	55	64	55	21	6
Registered nurses	46	34	75	78	35	32	10
Service	16	10	24	27	15	12	3
Protective service	24	23	43	54	41	20	1
Sales and office	36	13	42	45	17	24	2
Sales and related	31	6	31	33	9	23	2
Office and administrative support	40	17	48	52	21	24	3
Natural resources, construction, and maintenance	24	11	28	31	16	13	2
Construction, extraction, farming, fishing, and forestry	19	9	19	22	14	10	1
Installation, maintenance, and repair	30	13	37	41	19	17	3
Production, transportation, and material moving	26	14	43	45	21	21	2
Production	28	16	44	46	20	26	3
Transportation and material moving	24	11	42	43	21	16	1
Full-time workers	39	19	51	55	24	25	4
Part-time workers	12	4	18	18	11	13	2
Union workers	30	20	59	66	45	27	4
Nonunion workers	33	15	40	43	17	21	4
Average Wage Within Following Percentiles:[2]							
Lowest 25 percent	16	7	20	21	12	14	2
Lowest 10 percent	9	6	13	13	7	7	2
Second 25 percent	30	13	40	44	18	18	3
Third 25 percent	39	20	52	57	25	25	3
Highest 25 percent	49	25	65	70	33	32	7
Highest 10 percent	54	24	68	75	32	35	9
Establishment Characteristics							
...ds-producing industries	33	16	41	45	14	25	3
...ce-providing industries	32	16	43	47	23	21	4
...cation and health services	33	24	51	57	34	21	5
...ucational services	39	34	59	66	55	24	4
...ementary and secondary schools	35	36	54	62	54	21	7
...ior colleges, colleges, and universities	51	35	80	85	65	36	5
...care and social assistance	29	18	46	52	22	20	8
...als	48	35	80	86	33	39	4
...istration	35	35	65	70	65	30	
...rs							
	21	9	25	28	13	11	3
	19	7	21	23	10	9	2
	29	14	37	43	21	17	4
	44	23	61	64	29	32	5
	39	17	51	53	22	30	4
	48	29	71	77	38	35	6
	26	11	42	48	24	21	4
	30	12	50	53	24	25	5
	25	11	40	46	24	20	3
	32	20	41	44	20	23	4
	31	19	42	45	20	23	4
	31	22	39	40	23	24	6
	34	22	42	45	19	21	4
	36	17	45	48	21	23	3
	36	17	46	48	23	24	3
	37	16	45	47	17	22	3
	35	12	43	46	20	20	3
	37	15	45	47	21	21	3
	34	11	42	46	20	19	3

...t of the employee, but with no employer contribution. These are cash or deferred arrangement plans or individual retirement
...uthorized by section 401(k), 403(b), or 457 of the Internal Revenue Code. The employees' contributions can be pre- and post-tax.
...mployer to fund the established plan.
...s based on the average wage for the occupation, which may include workers with earnings both above and below the threshold.
...nerated using ECEC data for March 2016.
...gland—Connecticut, Maine, Massachusetts, New Hampshire, Rhode Island, and Vermont; Middle Atlantic—New Jersey, New York,
...mbia, Florida, Georgia, Maryland, North Carolina, South Carolina, Virginia, and West Virginia; East South Central—Alabama,
...Arkansas, Louisiana, Oklahoma, and Texas; East North Central—Illinois, Indiana, Michigan, Ohio, and Wisconsin; West North
...Dakota, and South Dakota; Mountain—Arizona, Colorado, Idaho, Montana, Nevada, New Mexico, Utah, and Wyoming; and

Table 6-18 Nonproduction Bonuses: Access for Civilian Workers,[1] March 2020

(Percent.)

Characteristic	All nonproduction bonuses[2]	Cash-profit sharing bonus	Employee recognition bonus	End-of-year bonus	Holiday bonus	Payment in lieu of benefits bonus	Longevity bonus	Referral bonus	Other bonus[3]
ALL WORKERS	40	6	3	10	5	6	2	5	10
Worker Characteristics									
Management, professional, and related	46	6	5	11	3	9	2	6	13
Management, business, and financial	58	9	7	17	4	7	2	9	17
Professional and related	41	5	4	9	3	10	3	5	12
Teachers	30	-	2	1	1	17	4	([4])	10
Primary, secondary, and special education school teachers	33	-	2	1	-	20	5	-	12
Registered nurses	42	-	6	3	-	9	2	11	15
Service	26	1	2	7	5	5	2	4	5
Protective service	42	1	5	4	2	15	9	-	12
Sales and office	42	9	3	9	7	5	2	6	8
Sales and related	35	13	1	7	6	2	1	5	5
Office and administrative support	46	7	4	11	7	7	2	6	10
Natural resources, construction, and maintenance	43	6	1	14	11	4	1	3	8
Construction, extraction, farming, fishing, and forestry	42	6	1	15	12	3	1	1	7
Installation, maintenance, and repair	44	6	2	13	10	5	1	6	10
Production, transportation, and material moving	41	7	1	9	6	4	1	5	15
Production	48	11	1	13	8	4	1	5	16
Transportation and material moving	35	4	1	6	5	5	1	5	14
Full-time workers	45	7	4	11	6	7	2	6	12
Part-time workers	22	4	1	5	4	2	1	3	3
Union workers	40	5	3	2	1	20	5	2	15
Nonunion workers	40	6	3	11	6	4	1	6	9
Average Wage Within the Following Percentiles[5]									
Lowest 25 percent	26	5	1	6	5	2	1	4	4
Lowest 10 percent	18	1	1	6	4	-	([4])	3	3
Second 25 percent	41	5	2	11	8	4	2	5	11
Third 25 percent	45	7	4	11	6	8	2	5	13
Highest 25 percent	50	8	6	12	3	11	2	7	14
Highest 10 percent	55	9	7	14	3	13	2	8	16
Establishment Characteristics									
Goods-producing industries	50	10	1	17	8	4	1	4	15
Service-providing industries	38	5	3	9	5	6	2	5	9
Education and health services	32	1	3	5	4	10	3	4	9
Educational services	28	-	2	1	1	16	4	([4])	8
Elementary and secondary schools	30	-	2	1	-	19	5	-	10
Junior colleges, colleges, and universities	26	-	5	-	-	13	4	1	4
Health care and social assistance	35	1	3	7	6	6	2	7	10
Hospitals	38	1	6	4	2	9	2	9	15
Public administration	46	-	6	2	1	23	10	-	14
Number of Workers									
1 to 99 workers	37	3	2	13	8	4	1	4	6
1 to 49 workers	36	3	2	14	8	4	1	3	6
50 to 99 workers	39	3	2	10	8	5	2	7	9
100 workers or more	42	9	4	7	3	8	2	6	14
100 to 499 workers	43	10	3	7	4	6	2	7	11
500 workers or more	42	7	5	7	1	10	3	6	16
Geographic Areas[6]									
Northeast	41	4	3	11	4	11	2	5	10
New England	41	3	-	14	4	8	2	5	8
Middle Atlantic	41	4	3	10	4	12	1	5	10
South	42	7	3	11	8	3	2	5	11
South Atlantic	44	6	4	11	9	4	2	6	12
East South Central	39	8	2	8	9	2	3	3	11
West South Central	39	7	2	12	6	2	2	3	9
Midwest	40	7	2	8	5	6	2	7	12
East North Central	41	7	3	8	5	7	2	7	13
West North Central	38	7	2	7	5	4	2	8	9
West	35	5	4	8	4	7	1	4	8
Mountain	35	6	3	9	6	2	1	4	10
Pacific	34	5	4	7	3	9	1	4	7

[1]Includes workers in the private nonfarm economy except those in private households, and workers in the public sector, except the federal government.
[2]The sum of the individual components may be greater than the total because some employees may have access to more than one type of stock option.
[3]Includes all other bonuses provided to employees and not published separately.
[4]Less than 0.5.
[5]The categories are based on the average wage for each occupation surveyed, which may include workers with earnings both above and below the threshold.
[6]The states that comprise the Census divisions are: New England—Connecticut, Maine, Massachusetts, New Hampshire, Rhode Island, and Vermont; Middle Atlantic—New Jersey, New York, and Pennsylvania; South Atlantic—Delaware, District of Columbia, Florida, Georgia, Maryland, North Carolina, South Carolina, Virginia, and West Virginia; East South Central—Alabama, Kentucky, Mississippi, and Tennessee; West South Central—Arkansas, Louisiana, Oklahoma, and Texas; East North Central—Illinois, Indiana, Michigan, Ohio, and Wisconsin; West North Central—Iowa, Kansas, Minnesota, Missouri, Nebraska, North Dakota, and South Dakota; Mountain—Arizona, Colorado, Idaho, Montana, Nevada, New Mexico, Utah, and Wyoming; and Pacific—Alaska, California, Hawaii, Oregon, and Washington.

Table 6-19 Unmarried Domestic Partner Benefits: Access[1] for Civilian Workers,[2] March 2020

(Percent.)

Characteristic	Defined benefit retirement survivor benefits		Healthcare benefits	
	Same sex	Opposite sex	Same sex	Opposite sex
ALL WORKERS	16	16	44	41
Worker Characteristics				
Management, professional, and related	27	26	58	54
Management, business, and financial	23	24	66	61
Professional and related	29	28	55	50
Teachers	48	47	46	42
Primary, secondary, and special education school teachers	56	55	48	45
Registered nurses	24	23	54	51
Service	10	9	26	26
Protective service	33	33	41	38
Sales and office	13	13	45	42
Sales and related	6	5	35	33
Office and administrative support	18	17	51	48
Natural resources, construction, and maintenance	12	11	39	36
Construction, extraction, farming, fishing, and forestry	11	10	36	35
Installation, maintenance, and repair	13	12	42	37
Production, transportation, and material moving	11	11	39	35
Production	8	5	36	32
Transportation and material moving	15	15	41	38
Full-time workers	19	19	51	47
Part-time workers	7	7	19	18
Union workers	48	44	66	59
Nonunion workers	11	11	40	38
Average Wage Within the Following Percentiles[3]				
Lowest 25 percent	5	5	21	21
Lowest 10 percent	2	2	14	14
Second 25 percent	12	11	42	40
Third 25 percent	19	19	51	47
Highest 25 percent	32	31	65	59
Highest 10 percent	33	31	74	66
Establishment Characteristics				
Goods-producing industries	10	8	42	40
Service-providing industries	17	17	44	41
Education and health services	27	26	46	44
Educational services	49	48	48	43
Elementary and secondary schools	56	55	46	42
Junior colleges, colleges, and universities	42	42	57	50
Health care and social assistance	13	12	45	44
Hospitals	28	27	61	56
Public administration	55	55	51	46
Number of Workers				
1 to 99 workers	7	7	31	30
1 to 49 workers	5	5	26	25
50 to 99 workers	14	13	43	43
100 workers or more	25	24	56	51
100 to 499 workers	17	16	50	47
500 workers or more	34	33	63	56
Geographic Areas[4]				
Northeast	21	21	50	47
New England	15	15	47	44
Middle Atlantic	23	23	51	48
South	15	15	34	32
South Atlantic	13	13	34	31
East South Central	15	14	31	29
West South Central	17	18	37	36
Midwest	11	10	36	31
East North Central	11	9	37	31
West North Central	12	11	32	31
West	20	20	61	59
Mountain	17	17	53	49
Pacific	21	21	64	63

[1]The percentage of workers with access to the benefit reflects both the availability of the benefit and the employer's policy on providing the benefit to unmarried domestic partners.
[2]Includes workers in the private nonfarm economy except those in private households, and workers in the public sector, except the federal government.
[3]The categories are based on the average wage for each occupation surveyed, which may include workers with earnings both above and below the threshold.
[4]The states that comprise the Census divisions are: New England—Connecticut, Maine, Massachusetts, New Hampshire, Rhode Island, and Vermont; Middle Atlantic—New Jersey, New York, and Pennsylvania; South Atlantic—Delaware, District of Columbia, Florida, Georgia, Maryland, North Carolina, South Carolina, Virginia, and West Virginia; East South Central—Alabama, Kentucky, Mississippi, and Tennessee; West South Central—Arkansas, Louisiana, Oklahoma, and Texas; East North Central—Illinois, Indiana, Michigan, Ohio, and Wisconsin; West North Central—Iowa, Kansas, Minnesota, Missouri, Nebraska, North Dakota, and South Dakota; Mountain—Arizona, Colorado, Idaho, Montana, Nevada, New Mexico, Utah, and Wyoming; and Pacific—Alaska, California, Hawaii, Oregon, and Washington.

CHAPTER 7: RECENT TRENDS IN THE LABOR MARKET

HIGHLIGHTS

This chapter contains information on local area unemployment statistics, movement of work, job openings, hires, and separations.

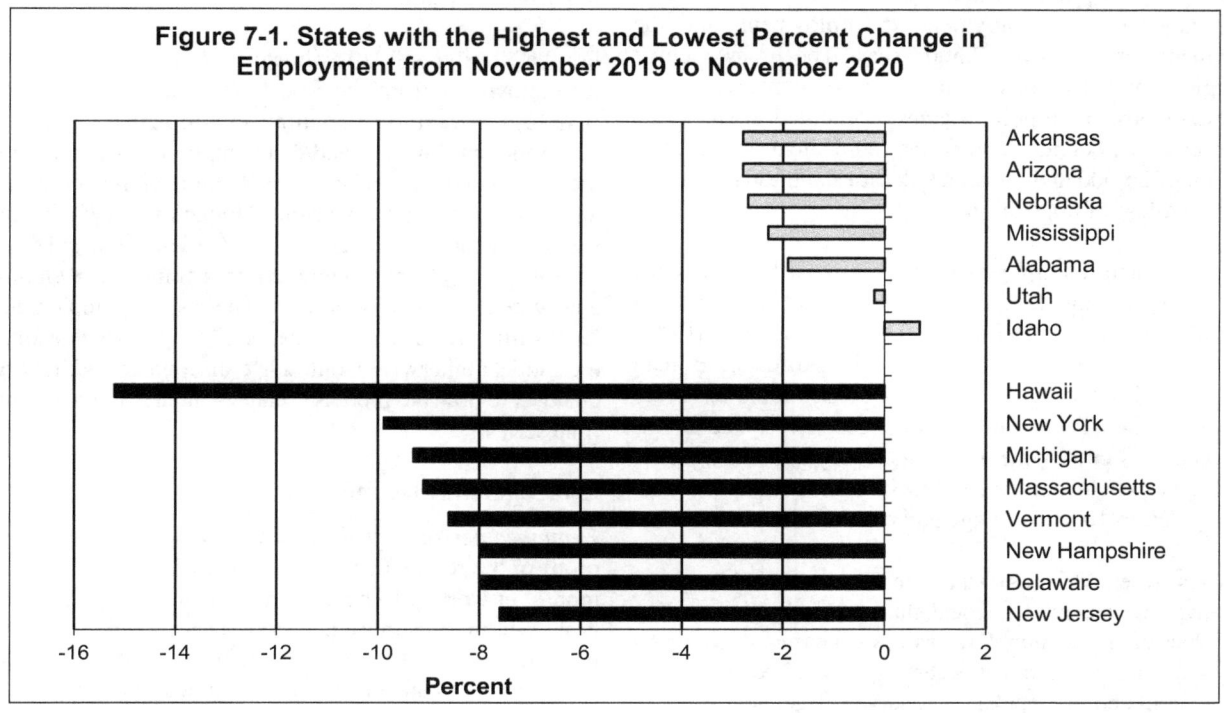

Figure 7-1. States with the Highest and Lowest Percent Change in Employment from November 2019 to November 2020

Employment declined in each state except Idaho from November 2019 to November 2020 as COVID-19 spread throughout the United States and many businesses were forced to close. Hawaii experienced the highest decrease in employment at 15.2 percent followed by New York at 9.9 percent and Michigan at 9.3 percent. At the metro level, unemployment rates were higher in 386 of the 389 metropolitan areas in November 2020 than they were in November 2019. (See Table 7-1.)

OTHER HIGHLIGHTS

- The unemployment rate in Las Vegas-Henderson-Paradise, NV experienced the highest increase in unemployment among all metropolitan areas with a census population of 1 million or more, rising from 3.6 percent to 11.5 percent. The leisure and hospitality industry was particularly impacted by the global pandemic. (See Table 7-3.)

- The number of job openings decreased to less the 5 million in April 2020, the lowest number since 2014. In contrast, just one year earlier, there were nearly 7.3 million job openings. Job openings began to rebound in the second half of 2020. (See Table 7-4.)

- In 2020, the number of layoffs increased from 1.8 million in February 2020 to nearly 11.5 million layoffs in March 2020 due in large part to stay-at-home orders and businesses being forced to close due to COVID-19. In April 2020, layoffs remained extremely high as an additional 7.7 jobs were lost. (See Table 7-8.)

NOTES AND DEFINITIONS

LOCAL AREA UNEMPLOYMENT STATISTICS

Collection and Coverage

The LAUS program provides monthly and annual average estimates for labor force, employment, unemployment, and the unemployment rate for over 7,500 areas. The areas include census regions and divisions, states, metropolitan areas, metropolitan divisions, micropolitan areas, combined areas, small labor market areas, counties and county equivalents, cities with a population of 25,000 and over, and all cities and towns in New England regardless of population.

The labor force and unemployment data are based on the same concepts and definitions as those used for the official national estimates obtained from the Current Population Survey (CPS), a sample survey of households that is conducted for the Bureau of Labor Statistics (BLS) by the U.S. Census Bureau. More information on the CPS can be found in Chapter 1. The LAUS program measures employment and unemployment on a place-of-residence basis. The universe for each is the civilian noninstitutional population 16 years of age and over.

The estimates presented in this chapter are based on sample surveys, administrative data, and modeling and, thus, are subject to sampling and other types of errors. *Sampling error* is a measure of sampling variability—that is, variation that occurs by chance because a sample rather than the entire population is surveyed. Survey data also are subject to *nonsampling errors*, such as those which can be introduced into the data collection and processing operations. Estimates not directly derived from sample surveys are subject to additional errors resulting from the specific estimation processes used.

Impact of Coronavirus (Covid-19) Pandemic on November 2020 and Household Data

BLS has continued to review all estimation and methodological procedures for the establishment survey, which included the review of data, estimation processes, the application of the birth-death model, and seasonal adjustment. Business births and deaths cannot be adequately captured by the establishment survey as they occur. Therefore, the Current Employment Statistics (CES) program uses a model to account for the relatively stable net employment change generated by business births and deaths. Due to the impact of COVID-19, the relationship between business births and deaths is no longer stable.

Typically, reports with zero employment are not included in estimation. For the October final and November preliminary estimates, CES included a portion of these reports in the estimates and made modifications to the birth-death model. In addition for both months, the establishment survey included a portion of the reports that returned to reporting positive employment from reporting zero employment.

For the November 2020 estimates of household employment and unemployment from the Local Area Unemployment Statistics (LAUS) program, BLS continued to implement level-shift outliers in the employment and/or unemployment inputs to the state models, based on statistical evaluation of movements in each area's inputs. Both the Current Population Survey inputs, which serve as the primary inputs to the LAUS models, and the nonfarm payroll employment and unemployment insurance claims covariates were examined for outliers. The resulting implementation of level shifts preserved movements in the published estimates that the models otherwise would have discounted, without requiring changes to how the models create estimates at other points in the time series.

Concepts and Definitions

Employed persons are those who did any work at all for pay or profit in the reference week (the week including the 12th of the month) or worked 15 hours or more without pay in a family business or farm, plus those not working who had a job from which they were temporarily absent, whether or not paid, for such reasons as labor management dispute, illness, or vacation.

The *employment-population ratio* is the proportion of the civilian noninstitutional population 16 years of age and over that is employed.

The *labor force* is the sum of employed and unemployed persons.

Unemployed persons are those who were not employed during the reference week (based on the definition above), had actively looked for a job sometime in the 4-week period ending with the reference week, and were currently available for work; persons on layoff expecting recall need not be looking for work to be counted as unemployed.

The *unemployment rate* is the number of unemployed expressed as a percent of the labor force.

Sources of Additional Information

For more extensive information on Local Area Unemployment Statistics, please see https://www.bls.gov/lau/ and BLS news release USDL 21-0001 "Metropolitan Area Employment and Unemployment—November 2020."

Table 7-1. Employees on Nonfarm Payrolls by State and Selected Metropolitan Areas, October 2019–November 2020

(Number in thousands, percent.)

State and area	October		November		Change from November 2019 to November 2020	
	2019	2020	2019	2020	Number	Percent
Alabama	2 085.7	2 035.1	2 093.1	2 052.3	-40.8	-1.9
Anniston-Oxford-Jacksonville	47.6	44.6	47.7	44.9	-2.8	-5.9
Auburn-Opelika	68.6	66.3	69.2	66.6	-2.6	-3.8
Birmingham-Hoover	548.4	529.2	551.0	532.9	-18.1	-3.3
Daphne-Fairhope-Foley	79.9	77.6	79.8	78.1	-1.7	-2.1
Decatur	57.5	55.9	57.9	56.0	-1.9	-3.3
Dothan	60.2	58.6	60.5	58.8	-1.7	-2.8
Florence-Muscle Shoals	57.9	56.3	58.2	56.4	-1.8	-3.1
Gadsden	37.4	34.7	37.8	35.4	-2.4	-6.3
Huntsville	246.4	240.5	247.3	242.2	-5.1	-2.1
Mobile	187.2	179.0	187.5	180.2	-7.3	-3.9
Montgomery	176.7	168.4	177.2	169.7	-7.5	-4.2
Tuscaloosa	114.9	110.0	115.4	110.6	-4.8	-4.2
Alaska	324.3	303.4	315.1	297.6	-17.5	-5.6
Anchorage	175.9	167.0	174.4	164.8	-9.6	-5.5
Fairbanks	38.0	36.0	37.0	35.0	-2.0	-5.4
Arizona	2 982.3	2 907.7	3 019.3	2 935.4	-83.9	-2.8
Flagstaff	70.0	58.2	69.4	57.7	-11.7	-16.9
Lake Havasu-City-Kingman	52.7	50.9	53.3	51.2	-2.1	-3.9
Phoenix-Mesa-Scottsdale	2 216.9	2 163.6	2 244.9	2 187.6	-57.3	-2.6
Prescott	66.4	66.8	67.0	66.7	-0.3	-0.4
Sierra Vista-Douglas	34.4	34.6	34.8	34.5	-0.3	-0.9
Tucson	392.8	378.7	397.9	383.1	-14.8	-3.7
Yuma	56.9	54.1	58.3	54.9	-3.4	-5.8
Arkansas	1 286.5	1 243.1	1 286.4	1 249.8	-36.6	-2.8
Fayetteville-Springdale-Rogers	268.2	265.2	268.7	267.5	-1.2	-0.4
Fort Smith	113.6	109.5	114.4	110.4	-4.0	-3.5
Hot Springs	39.3	38.6	39.3	38.8	-0.5	-1.3
Jonesboro	61.1	61.7	61.5	62.3	0.8	1.3
Little Rock-North Little Rock-Conway	365.8	348.5	366.1	348.9	-17.2	-4.7
Pine Bluff	32.9	31.4	32.9	31.6	-1.3	-4.0
California	17 593.6	16 235.7	17 697.6	16 357.2	-1 340.4	-7.6
Bakersfield	279.1	255.2	280.8	257.2	-23.6	-8.4
Chico	82.2	73.8	81.7	72.9	-8.8	-10.8
El Centro	53.4	49.4	54.0	49.4	-4.6	-8.5
Fresno	366.4	344.6	368.3	346.8	-21.5	-5.8
Hanford-Corcoran	41.1	38.2	41.4	38.1	-3.3	-8.0
Los Angeles-Long Beach-Anaheim	6 293.1	5 771.5	6 332.7	5 817.8	-514.9	-8.1
Madera	40.0	38.0	40.1	38.0	-2.1	-5.2
Merced	72.5	66.4	71.4	66.3	-5.1	-7.1
Modesto	183.4	168.1	183.9	168.0	-15.9	-8.6
Napa	77.0	69.6	76.2	69.2	-7.0	-9.2
Oxnard-Thousand Oaks-Ventura	314.6	291.3	316.9	294.3	-22.6	-7.1
Redding	69.5	65.0	69.4	65.3	-4.1	-5.9
Riverside-San Bernardino-Ontario	1 554.3	1 448.9	1 574.1	1 466.1	-108.0	-6.9
Sacramento—Roseville—Arden-Arcade	1 025.0	959.4	1 031.4	964.3	-67.1	-6.5
Salinas	146.6	132.6	147.5	133.2	-14.3	-9.7
San Diego-Carlsbad	1 514.6	1 412.0	1 524.0	1 426.3	-97.7	-6.4
San Francisco-Oakland-Hayward	2 502.2	2 258.9	2 512.8	2 278.0	-234.8	-9.3
San Jose-Sunnyvale-Santa Clara	1 153.9	1 081.7	1 160.3	1 091.8	-68.5	-5.9
San Luis Obispo-Paso Robles-Arroyo	121.8	106.3	122.2	107.2	-15.0	-12.3
Grande Santa Cruz-Watsonville	105.9	92.2	105.7	92.1	-13.6	-12.9
Santa Maria-Santa Barbara	189.5	175.6	190.7	176.8	-13.9	-7.3
Santa Rosa	213.9	194.5	213.1	193.9	-19.2	-9.0
Stockton-Lodi	250.2	231.6	251.4	234.7	-16.7	-6.6
Vallejo-Fairfield	145.5	131.8	145.8	132.4	-13.4	-9.2
Visalia-Porterville	130.3	121.8	130.6	123.5	-7.1	-5.4
Yuba City	48.6	42.3	49.3	42.1	-7.2	-14.6
Colorado	2 806.2	2 687.1	2 820.1	2 683.2	-136.9	-4.9
Boulder	200.1	188.0	202.2	187.7	-14.5	-7.2
Colorado Springs	302.3	295.0	304.1	296.0	-8.1	-2.7
Denver-Aurora-Lakewood	1 553.3	1 500.2	1 555.4	1 503.7	-51.7	-3.3
Fort Collins	178.3	168.1	179.3	166.8	-12.5	-7.0
Grand Junction	65.8	66.1	65.4	65.6	0.2	0.3
Greeley	115.8	109.0	115.5	109.3	-6.2	-5.4
Pueblo	64.1	62.1	64.7	62.3	-2.4	-3.7

Table 7-1. Employees on Nonfarm Payrolls by State and Selected Metropolitan Areas, October 2019–November 2020—*Continued*

(Number in thousands, percent.)

State and area	October 2019	October 2020	November 2019	November 2020	Change from November 2019 to November 2020 Number	Percent
Connecticut	1 700.1	1 608.9	1 710.1	1 613.8	-96.3	-5.6
Bridgeport-Stamford-Norwalk	406.1	368.7	408.7	370.0	-38.7	-9.5
Danbury	78.0	72.5	78.6	73.8	-4.8	-6.1
Hartford-West Hartford-East Hartford	588.5	561.0	591.0	565.1	-25.9	-4.4
New Haven	293.8	280.7	294.3	279.6	-14.7	-5.0
Norwich-New London-Westerly	129.4	117.0	129.7	116.1	-13.6	-10.5
Waterbury	68.6	61.9	69.2	62.2	-7.0	-10.1
Delaware	468.5	432.7	469.7	432.1	-37.6	-8.0
Dover	71.8	69.1	72.9	68.7	-4.2	-5.8
Salisbury	164.0	155.9	162.0	153.4	-8.6	-5.3
District of Columbia	804.2	755.3	807.0	756.4	-50.6	-6.3
Washington-Arlington-Alexandria	3 377.2	3 205.7	3 398.5	3 218.8	-179.7	-5.3
Florida	9 010.0	8 594.1	9 088.4	8 660.5	-427.9	-4.7
Cape Coral-Fort Myers	278.8	270.3	283.1	271.2	-11.9	-4.2
Crestview-Fort Walton Beach-Destin	118.6	113.7	118.0	113.0	-5.0	-4.2
Deltona-Daytona Beach-Ormond Beach	205.2	200.6	207.4	202.4	-5.0	-2.4
Gainesville	150.8	144.6	151.8	144.8	-7.0	-4.6
Homosassa Springs	33.3	31.5	33.6	31.7	-1.9	-5.7
Jacksonville	735.6	705.4	740.4	712.0	-28.4	-3.8
Lakeland-Winter Haven	236.7	230.4	240.3	232.8	-7.5	-3.1
Miami-Fort Lauderdale-West Palm Beach	2 729.5	2 552.3	2 749.9	2 573.9	-176.0	-6.4
Naples-Immokalee-Marco Island	154.5	149.8	158.8	153.9	-4.9	-3.1
North Port-Sarasota-Bradenton	312.5	301.0	317.3	303.8	-13.5	-4.3
Ocala	107.6	108.6	108.2	110.1	1.9	1.8
Orlando-Kissimmee-Sanford	1 337.4	1 215.1	1 347.7	1 222.6	-125.1	-9.3
Palm Bay-Melbourne-Titusville	233.9	227.8	236.0	229.3	-6.7	-2.8
Panama City	80.2	77.8	79.8	77.4	-2.4	-3.0
Pensacola-Ferry Pass-Brent	186.8	179.7	188.4	180.6	-7.8	-4.1
Port St Lucie	155.7	153.5	157.5	154.4	-3.1	-2.0
Punta Gorda	49.7	50.2	51.1	50.8	-0.3	-0.6
Sebastian-Vero Beach	54.1	52.6	55.1	53.7	-1.4	-2.5
Sebring	26.4	26.7	26.8	27.0	0.2	0.7
Tallahassee	189.6	175.7	190.8	176.2	-14.6	-7.7
Tampa-St Petersburg-Clearwater	1 399.2	1 339.7	1 409.0	1 352.6	-56.4	-4.0
The Villages	32.2	32.3	32.5	32.3	-0.2	-0.6
Georgia	4 651.0	4 521.6	4 674.7	4 561.7	-113.0	-2.4
Albany	63.1	60.4	63.6	60.4	-3.2	-5.0
Athens-Clarke County	98.0	94.8	98.3	95.1	-3.2	-3.3
Atlanta-Sandy Springs-Roswell	2 878.5	2 787.2	2 894.2	2 808.7	-85.5	-3.0
Augusta-Richmond County	243.4	231.8	244.2	232.0	-12.2	-5.0
Brunswick	44.7	39.0	44.9	39.2	-5.7	-12.7
Columbus	122.5	116.8	123.2	116.5	-6.7	-5.4
Dalton	66.2	63.6	66.1	63.8	-2.3	-3.5
Gainesville	94.5	92.0	94.9	92.4	-2.5	-2.6
Hinesville	21.5	21.6	21.7	22.0	0.3	1.4
Macon	102.9	100.2	103.9	101.4	-2.5	-2.4
Rome	42.5	42.4	42.7	42.6	-0.1	-0.2
Savannah	186.2	180.6	187.8	182.9	-4.9	-2.6
Valdosta	56.6	57.8	57.1	58.8	1.7	3.0
Warner Robins	77.4	73.6	78.0	74.5	-3.5	-4.5
Hawaii	658.0	545.0	662.5	562.0	-100.5	-15.2
Kahului-Wailuku-Lahaina	79.9	58.0	80.2	60.3	-19.9	-24.8
Urban Honolulu	474.2	401.6	477.3	413.9	-63.4	-13.3
Idaho	768.1	769.9	766.7	771.8	5.1	0.7
Boise City	348.2	348.5	349.8	348.9	-0.9	-0.3
Coeur d'Alene	68.3	66.0	67.6	65.3	-2.3	-3.4
Idaho Falls	70.9	74.1	71.4	74.4	3.0	4.2
Lewiston	29.0	27.0	29.0	26.8	-2.2	-7.6
Pocatello	37.9	35.7	38.0	35.8	-2.2	-5.8
Twin Falls	48.1	48.9	47.9	48.8	0.9	1.9
Illinois	6 178.9	5 775.5	6 169.3	5 752.3	-417.0	-6.8
Bloomington	94.1	88.0	94.2	88.3	-5.9	-6.3
Carbondale-Marion	58.8	56.7	59.2	57.3	-1.9	-3.2
Champaign-Urbana	118.7	115.4	119.6	114.8	-4.8	-4.0
Chicago-Naperville-Elgin	4 808.4	4 477.3	4 802.6	4 461.6	-341.0	-7.1

Table 7-1. Employees on Nonfarm Payrolls by State and Selected Metropolitan Areas, October 2019–November 2020—*Continued*

(Number in thousands, percent.)

State and area	October		November		Change from November 2019 to November 2020	
	2019	2020	2019	2020	Number	Percent
Illinois— *Continued*						
Danville	27.4	26.5	27.6	26.6	-1.0	-3.6
Davenport-Moline-Rock Island	189.0	177.4	188.0	177.3	-10.7	-5.7
Decatur	50.6	46.9	50.5	46.8	-3.7	-7.3
Kankakee	46.9	44.8	46.8	44.5	-2.3	-4.9
Peoria	171.6	155.0	170.1	153.8	-16.3	-9.6
Rockford	151.0	138.5	149.9	137.7	-12.2	-8.1
Springfield	110.4	104.2	110.0	104.1	-5.9	-5.4
Indiana	3 186.6	3 089.5	3 194.7	3 087.8	-106.9	-3.3
Bloomington	81.8	77.8	82.1	77.9	-4.2	-5.1
Columbus	53.3	51.3	53.6	51.4	-2.2	-4.1
Elkhart-Goshen	137.2	128.6	137.6	129.1	-8.5	-6.2
Evansville	163.6	161.8	164.6	162.4	-2.2	-1.3
Fort Wayne	228.5	221.8	230.4	222.0	-8.4	-3.6
Indianapolis-Carmel-Anderson	1 097.4	1 074.9	1 098.9	1 074.6	-24.3	-2.2
Kokomo	40.9	39.6	41.0	39.1	-1.9	-4.6
Lafayette-West Lafayette	110.6	103.7	111.8	104.2	-7.6	-6.8
Michigan City-La Porte	42.2	40.2	42.2	40.2	-2.0	-4.7
Muncie	51.8	48.6	52.2	48.6	-3.6	-6.9
South Bend-Mishawaka	145.2	132.3	145.9	132.8	-13.1	-9.0
Terre Haute	70.5	66.5	71.0	66.7	-4.3	-6.1
Iowa	1 604.1	1 529.6	1 604.0	1 522.0	-82.0	-5.1
Ames	55.5	56.4	55.6	55.1	-0.5	-0.9
Cedar Rapids	147.2	139.2	147.9	138.8	-9.1	-6.2
Des Moines-West Des Moines	377.9	356.9	377.3	356.8	-20.5	-5.4
Dubuque	61.3	57.8	61.6	58.1	-3.5	-5.7
Iowa City	102.3	98.6	102.5	98.1	-4.4	-4.3
Sioux City	88.9	87.3	89.4	88.4	-1.0	-1.1
Waterloo-Cedar Falls	91.4	88.0	91.2	88.0	-3.2	-3.5
Kansas	1 435.8	1 383.8	1 439.2	1 382.3	-56.9	-4.0
Lawrence	55.1	51.4	55.2	51.3	-3.9	-7.1
Manhattan	44.3	40.6	44.2	40.7	-3.5	-7.9
Topeka	112.3	108.8	111.6	108.7	-2.9	-2.6
Wichita	307.6	296.6	308.1	295.1	-13.0	-4.2
Kentucky	1 954.3	1 855.0	1 959.3	1 857.5	-101.8	-5.2
Bowling Green	77.3	70.2	78.4	72.1	-6.3	-8.0
Elizabethtown-Fort Knox	56.2	52.5	56.6	52.6	-4.0	-7.1
Lexington-Fayette	282.0	267.3	281.9	269.6	-12.3	-4.4
Louisville/Jefferson County	679.0	645.5	680.6	647.8	-32.8	-4.8
Owensboro	54.1	50.9	54.1	51.0	-3.1	-5.7
Louisiana	1 994.7	1 884.5	2 006.3	1 908.4	-97.9	-4.9
Alexandria	62.1	59.9	62.1	60.3	-1.8	-2.9
Baton Rouge	411.7	393.5	414.2	395.5	-18.7	-4.5
Hammond	46.7	44.5	47.0	44.7	-2.3	-4.9
Houma-Thibodaux	88.3	83.9	88.4	86.4	-2.0	-2.3
Lafayette	205.0	194.8	205.0	196.0	-9.0	-4.4
Lake Charles	113.4	93.1	112.7	98.0	-14.7	-13.0
Monroe	78.2	79.2	79.0	79.7	0.7	0.9
New Orleans-Metairie	585.4	529.5	590.1	539.8	-50.3	-8.5
Shreveport-Bossier City	180.9	172.1	182.1	174.7	-7.4	-4.1
Maine	645.6	597.6	635.1	590.6	-44.5	-7.0
Bangor	70.2	66.6	70.1	66.0	-4.1	-5.8
Lewiston-Auburn	52.4	48.9	52.4	48.9	-3.5	-6.7
Portland-South Portland	215.3	200.5	213.7	199.4	-14.3	-6.7
Maryland	2 777.9	2 647.9	2 795.6	2 671.7	-123.9	-4.4
Baltimore-Columbia-Towson	1 432.2	1 358.0	1 443.2	1 371.5	-71.7	-5.0
California-Lexington Park	47.8	44.3	48.0	44.2	-3.8	-7.9
Cumberland	39.6	36.4	39.6	36.5	-3.1	-7.8
Hagerstown-Martinsburg	107.7	98.7	110.1	99.4	-10.7	-9.7
Massachusetts	3 728.1	3 384.5	3 729.6	3 389.4	-340.2	-9.1
Barnstable Town	107.2	93.7	103.4	92.0	-11.4	-11.0
Boston-Cambridge-Nashua	2 837.1	2 577.2	2 840.3	2 582.0	-258.3	-9.1
Leominster-Gardner	53.9	48.5	54.2	48.6	-5.6	-10.3
New Bedford	67.2	62.0	67.6	62.4	-5.2	-7.7
Pittsfield	41.3	37.0	41.2	37.1	-4.1	-10.0
Springfield	343.8	303.5	345.0	304.9	-40.1	-11.6
Worcester	293.1	271.9	295.0	275.4	-19.6	-6.6

Table 7-1. Employees on Nonfarm Payrolls by State and Selected Metropolitan Areas, October 2019–November 2020—Continued

(Number in thousands, percent.)

State and area	October 2019	October 2020	November 2019	November 2020	Change from November 2019 to November 2020 Number	Change from November 2019 to November 2020 Percent
Michigan	4 457.4	4 072.9	4 480.1	4 062.6	-417.5	-9.3
Ann Arbor	233.3	221.7	235.0	221.3	-13.7	-5.8
Battle Creek	58.3	51.9	58.7	52.6	-6.1	-10.4
Bay City	35.3	31.3	35.4	30.9	-4.5	-12.7
Detroit-Warren-Dearborn	2 047.5	1 862.9	2 057.3	1 865.6	-191.7	-9.3
Flint	137.0	131.1	144.5	130.7	-13.8	-9.6
Grand Rapids-Wyoming	569.3	528.4	569.1	529.1	-40.0	-7.0
Jackson	58.1	53.6	58.5	53.8	-4.7	-8.0
Kalamazoo-Portage	152.7	143.1	153.0	141.9	-11.1	-7.3
Lansing-East Lansing	238.6	217.0	243.7	217.1	-26.6	-10.9
Midland	37.6	35.0	37.6	34.9	-2.7	-7.2
Monroe	41.7	36.0	41.9	35.4	-6.5	-15.5
Muskegon	64.7	57.4	64.9	57.8	-7.1	-10.9
Niles-Benton Harbor	63.2	58.4	62.6	58.2	-4.4	-7.0
Saginaw	86.4	79.3	88.5	79.7	-8.8	-9.9
Minnesota	3 008.7	2 822.9	2 994.6	2 802.7	-191.9	-6.4
Duluth	138.7	127.4	138.0	125.9	-12.1	-8.8
Mankato-North Mankato	60.9	57.8	60.6	58.0	-2.6	-4.3
Minneapolis-St Paul-Bloomington	2 050.9	1 923.8	2 044.6	1 912.0	-132.6	-6.5
Rochester	125.2	117.8	123.9	117.6	-6.3	-5.1
St. Cloud	112.7	108.6	112.4	108.1	-4.3	-3.8
Mississippi	1 166.9	1 139.0	1 171.2	1 144.1	-27.1	-2.3
Gulfport-Biloxi-Pascagoula	156.8	152.7	157.7	153.2	-4.5	-2.9
Hattiesburg	66.4	65.5	67.3	66.8	-0.5	-0.7
Jackson	282.6	270.4	282.8	271.2	-11.6	-4.1
Missouri	2 927.5	2 804.3	2 928.1	2 821.4	-106.7	-3.6
Cape Girardeau	45.7	41.4	45.7	41.6	-4.1	-9.0
Columbia	102.1	98.6	102.4	98.9	-3.5	-3.4
Jefferson City	77.9	75.9	78.0	76.0	-2.0	-2.6
Joplin	81.7	80.3	82.1	80.2	-1.9	-2.3
Kansas City	1 106.5	1 062.3	1 110.2	1 068.1	-42.1	-3.8
St. Joseph	62.9	61.3	63.0	61.5	-1.5	-2.4
St. Louis	1 407.4	1 333.6	1 407.1	1 339.4	-67.7	-4.8
Springfield	220.4	214.2	221.1	215.9	-5.2	-2.4
Montana	488.3	475.3	485.5	471.8	-13.7	-2.8
Billings	86.5	84.4	86.0	83.7	-2.3	-2.7
Great Falls	36.4	34.9	36.4	34.9	-1.5	-4.1
Missoula	64.4	63.3	63.5	62.9	-0.6	-0.9
Nebraska	1 036.5	1 011.9	1 037.6	1 009.3	-28.3	-2.7
Grand Island	42.1	40.7	42.0	40.6	-1.4	-3.3
Lincoln	194.9	195.0	197.2	194.5	-2.7	-1.4
Omaha-Council Bluffs	513.9	498.2	514.5	498.9	-15.6	-3.0
Nevada	1 431.7	1 320.5	1 438.1	1 329.5	-108.6	-7.6
Carson City	31.1	29.8	31.2	29.6	-1.6	-5.1
Las Vegas-Henderson-Paradise	1 044.7	935.2	1 050.9	944.4	-106.5	-10.1
Reno	251.7	237.8	254.0	240.8	-13.2	-5.2
New Hampshire	690.6	633.7	687.6	632.5	-55.1	-8.0
Dover-Durham	55.6	48.2	55.2	48.2	-7.0	-12.7
Manchester	118.0	108.0	118.7	108.9	-9.8	-8.3
Portsmouth	94.5	84.6	93.9	83.6	-10.3	-11.0
New Jersey	4 230.1	3 912.7	4 252.3	3 930.6	-321.7	-7.6
Atlantic City-Hammonton	132.8	115.4	132.1	116.3	-15.8	-12.0
Ocean City	41.5	38.5	39.2	36.5	-2.7	-6.9
Trenton	282.8	267.1	286.3	269.3	-17.0	-5.9
Vineland-Bridgeton	59.8	56.4	59.8	55.6	-4.2	-7.0
New Mexico	865.2	811.0	868.0	809.7	-58.3	-6.7
Albuquerque	402.4	392.1	403.7	391.4	-12.3	-3.0
Farmington	47.6	43.9	47.6	44.2	-3.4	-7.1
Las Cruces	75.4	69.9	75.6	69.9	-5.7	-7.5
Santa Fe	65.5	59.1	65.9	59.1	-6.8	-10.3
New York	9 878.7	8 892.3	9 918.8	8 940.0	-978.8	-9.9
Albany-Schenectady-Troy	478.4	437.4	482.4	438.6	-43.8	-9.1
Binghamton	104.6	97.8	104.3	97.7	-6.6	-6.3
Buffalo-Cheektowaga-Niagara Falls	569.2	531.2	571.7	531.0	-40.7	-7.1
Elmira	37.3	35.7	37.3	34.4	-2.9	-7.8
Glens Falls	55.3	50.3	54.3	49.6	-4.7	-8.7

Table 7-1. Employees on Nonfarm Payrolls by State and Selected Metropolitan Areas, October 2019–November 2020—Continued

(Number in thousands, percent.)

State and area	October 2019	October 2020	November 2019	November 2020	Change from November 2019 to November 2020 Number	Change from November 2019 to November 2020 Percent
New York—*Continued*						
Ithaca	65.2	62.7	65.5	62.7	-2.8	-4.3
Kingston	63.8	60.4	63.2	60.0	-3.2	-5.1
New York-Newark-Jersey City	10 052.5	9 049.5	10 115.7	9 116.1	-999.6	-9.9
Rochester	546.6	494.5	546.0	495.2	-50.8	-9.3
Syracuse	326.0	291.7	326.0	292.6	-33.4	-10.2
Utica-Rome	128.9	119.8	129.2	119.7	-9.5	-7.4
Watertown-Fort Drum	41.6	38.0	41.6	37.8	-3.8	-9.1
North Carolina	4 617.8	4 384.4	4 633.3	4 408.0	-225.3	-4.9
Asheville	201.1	180.6	201.3	181.6	-19.7	-9.8
Burlington	64.6	61.6	64.5	62.2	-2.3	-3.6
Charlotte-Concord-Gastonia	1 249.8	1 175.4	1 252.9	1 185.2	-67.7	-5.4
Durham-Chapel Hill	323.8	306.1	326.2	308.3	-17.9	-5.5
Fayetteville	131.5	121.5	132.7	122.7	-10.0	-7.5
Goldsboro	41.0	37.6	41.5	37.9	-3.6	-8.7
Greensboro-High Point	367.1	339.4	369.6	340.0	-29.6	-8.0
Greenville	81.8	76.2	82.5	76.4	-6.1	-7.4
Hickory-Lenoir-Morganton	156.3	143.2	157.1	143.6	-13.5	-8.6
Jacksonville	50.3	49.3	50.8	49.7	-1.1	-2.2
New Bern	45.3	42.7	45.5	42.4	-3.1	-6.8
Raleigh	658.3	617.1	659.4	623.5	-35.9	-5.4
Rocky Mount	57.0	52.9	57.4	53.0	-4.4	-7.7
Wilmington	134.5	124.1	135.5	124.9	-10.6	-7.8
Winston-Salem	273.5	256.7	272.4	256.8	-15.6	-5.7
North Dakota	445.6	416.4	443.4	412.4	-31.0	-7.0
Bismarck	73.8	70.3	73.7	70.2	-3.5	-4.7
Fargo	147.8	142.7	147.8	142.0	-5.8	-3.9
Grand Forks	55.9	53.7	56.3	53.5	-2.8	-5.0
Ohio	5 617.7	5 261.1	5 624.2	5 282.3	-341.9	-6.1
Akron	343.0	312.9	343.6	315.2	-28.4	-8.3
Canton-Massillon	174.4	162.4	174.2	162.0	-12.2	-7.0
Cincinnati	1 119.4	1 071.1	1 123.1	1 071.9	-51.2	-4.6
Cleveland-Elyria	1 079.3	990.5	1 085.5	995.7	-89.8	-8.3
Columbus	1 119.7	1 047.3	1 128.6	1 056.0	-72.6	-6.4
Dayton	395.3	374.3	395.3	375.8	-19.5	-4.9
Lima	52.7	49.2	53.0	49.5	-3.5	-6.6
Mansfield	51.5	49.7	51.9	50.1	-1.8	-3.5
Springfield	49.8	48.1	49.8	48.5	-1.3	-2.6
Toledo	313.8	293.0	314.5	292.6	-21.9	-7.0
Weirton-Steubenville	40.7	38.2	40.4	38.7	-1.7	-4.2
Youngstown-Warren-Boardman	216.6	194.1	216.1	194.4	-21.7	-10.0
Oklahoma	1 721.2	1 635.7	1 722.8	1 642.5	-80.3	-4.7
Enid	25.4	23.0	25.4	23.6	-1.8	-7.1
Lawton	45.6	43.3	46.0	44.1	-1.9	-4.1
Oklahoma City	670.4	646.2	670.3	650.6	-19.7	-2.9
Tulsa	466.8	441.4	466.9	442.4	-24.5	-5.2
Oregon	1 960.9	1 838.2	1 962.8	1 842.2	-120.6	-6.1
Albany	46.7	45.0	46.9	45.1	-1.8	-3.8
Bend-Redmond	87.6	81.4	86.6	81.1	-5.5	-6.4
Corvallis	45.0	40.9	45.3	41.0	-4.3	-9.5
Eugene	165.7	159.9	165.8	160.4	-5.4	-3.3
Grants Pass	27.6	25.6	27.5	25.3	-2.2	-8.0
Medford	90.4	85.8	90.4	86.2	-4.2	-4.6
Portland-Vancouver-Hillsboro	1 231.0	1 144.2	1 232.5	1 149.6	-82.9	-6.7
Salem	174.4	159.9	174.4	159.5	-14.9	-8.5
Pennsylvania	6 132.1	5 674.3	6 152.2	5 697.0	-455.2	-7.4
Allentown-Bethlehem-Easton	386.5	362.5	388.5	369.0	-19.5	-5.0
Altoona	61.3	57.7	61.2	57.7	-3.5	-5.7
Bloomsburg-Berwick	43.8	42.5	43.9	42.7	-1.2	-2.7
Chambersburg-Waynesboro	62.7	59.5	63.2	59.9	-3.3	-5.2
East Stroudsburg	59.5	52.6	59.8	52.3	-7.5	-12.5
Erie	128.6	116.8	128.7	117.2	-11.5	-8.9
Gettysburg	35.4	34.8	35.2	34.7	-0.5	-1.4
Harrisburg-Carlisle	355.2	342.1	357.7	344.1	-13.6	-3.8
Johnstown	54.8	51.0	54.8	51.3	-3.5	-6.4
Lancaster	262.3	255.9	263.6	255.9	-7.7	-2.9

Table 7-1. Employees on Nonfarm Payrolls by State and Selected Metropolitan Areas, October 2019–November 2020—Continued

(Number in thousands, percent.)

State and area	October		November		Change from November 2019 to November 2020	
	2019	2020	2019	2020	Number	Percent
Pennsylvania—Continued						
Lebanon	54.7	51.6	54.9	51.8	-3.1	-5.6
Philadelphia-Camden-Wilmington	3 005.2	2 800.2	3 013.1	2 809.0	-204.1	-6.8
Pittsburgh	1 206.7	1 121.0	1 208.2	1 122.3	-85.9	-7.1
Reading	184.2	183.4	185.1	184.1	-1.0	-0.5
Scranton—Wilkes-Barre—Hazleton	266.5	241.6	266.8	243.8	-23.0	-8.6
State College	82.3	75.3	83.0	75.2	-7.8	-9.4
Williamsport	53.8	47.2	53.9	47.9	-6.0	-11.1
York-Hanover	190.7	181.6	191.5	183.1	-8.4	-4.4
Rhode Island	511.3	473.3	510.3	472.8	-37.5	-7.3
Providence-Warwick	607.0	566.5	609.1	566.4	-42.7	-7.0
South Carolina	2 204.1	2 129.1	2 217.4	2 152.2	-65.2	-2.9
Charleston-North Charleston	375.8	354.6	379.0	359.0	-20.0	-5.3
Columbia	406.9	392.4	410.1	395.1	-15.0	-3.7
Florence	92.6	89.4	93.2	91.3	-1.9	-2.0
Greenville-Anderson-Mauldin	436.7	426.0	437.7	432.0	-5.7	-1.3
Hilton Head Island-Bluffton-Beaufort	85.3	83.5	85.0	84.2	-0.8	-0.9
Myrtle Beach-Conway-North Myrtle Beach	175.3	158.9	173.6	158.9	-14.7	-8.5
Spartanburg	164.7	154.4	164.7	154.7	-10.0	-6.1
Sumter	40.0	37.9	40.1	37.3	-2.8	-7.0
South Dakota	444.8	432.0	442.9	430.0	-12.9	-2.9
Rapid City	69.6	65.7	68.2	64.8	-3.4	-5.0
Sioux Falls	161.3	155.7	160.7	155.6	-5.1	-3.2
Tennessee	3 159.3	3 049.3	3 184.7	3 066.2	-118.5	-3.7
Chattanooga	269.2	266.8	270.8	267.8	-3.0	-1.1
Clarksville	94.1	92.0	94.9	93.0	-1.9	-2.0
Cleveland	50.0	48.6	51.5	49.2	-2.3	-4.5
Jackson	70.1	66.9	70.4	67.3	-3.1	-4.4
Johnson City	82.0	78.1	82.5	78.2	-4.3	-5.2
Kingsport-Bristol-Bristol	121.3	115.2	121.9	115.4	-6.5	-5.3
Knoxville	410.6	402.6	412.6	404.7	-7.9	-1.9
Memphis	658.3	634.9	666.0	638.0	-28.0	-4.2
Morristown	47.8	46.7	48.2	46.7	-1.5	-3.1
Nashville-Davidson—Murfreesboro—Franklin	1 063.3	1 010.3	1 073.7	1 019.3	-54.4	-5.1
Texas	12 938.7	12 436.4	13 017.7	12 528.4	-489.3	-3.8
Abilene	73.5	71.0	74.0	71.8	-2.2	-3.0
Amarillo	121.6	115.2	122.7	115.7	-7.0	-5.7
Austin-Round Rock	1 130.7	1 113.5	1 136.1	1 123.3	-12.8	-1.1
Beaumont-Port Arthur	166.4	154.5	167.1	156.1	-11.0	-6.6
Brownsville-Harlingen	144.8	136.6	145.8	137.5	-8.3	-5.7
College Station-Bryan	127.0	124.6	128.5	125.5	-3.0	-2.3
Corpus Christi	195.1	180.1	196.1	180.8	-15.3	-7.8
Dallas-Fort Worth-Arlington	3 825.0	3 732.2	3 861.3	3 765.2	-96.1	-2.5
El Paso	327.9	312.0	329.5	316.2	-13.3	-4.0
Houston-The Woodlands-Sugar Land	3 181.9	3 030.4	3 203.5	3 056.2	-147.3	-4.6
Killeen-Temple	146.6	141.5	147.9	142.7	-5.2	-3.5
Laredo	108.6	101.0	109.0	102.2	-6.8	-6.2
Longview	100.7	93.5	100.9	93.8	-7.1	-7.0
Lubbock	151.3	146.4	152.7	146.9	-5.8	-3.8
McAllen-Edinburg-Mission	274.5	259.3	275.5	262.2	-13.3	-4.8
Midland	115.1	101.4	115.5	102.2	-13.3	-11.5
Odessa	84.0	74.6	83.8	74.2	-9.6	-11.5
San Angelo	49.8	46.6	50.5	46.9	-3.6	-7.1
San Antonio-New Braunfels	1 093.3	1 049.7	1 097.2	1 054.1	-43.1	-3.9
Sherman-Denison	48.5	47.8	48.9	48.7	-0.2	-0.4
Texarkana	61.2	60.6	61.6	61.2	-0.4	-0.6
Tyler	106.8	104.6	107.9	105.8	-2.1	-1.9
Victoria	41.8	39.1	41.8	39.3	-2.5	-6.0
Waco	123.1	123.2	124.7	123.9	-0.8	-0.6
Wichita Falls	60.1	57.2	60.4	57.7	-2.7	-4.5
Utah	1 587.1	1 578.4	1 593.0	1 590.2	-2.8	-0.2
Logan	66.1	66.0	66.1	66.7	0.6	0.9
Ogden-Clearfield	272.9	274.9	272.4	276.1	3.7	1.4
Provo-Orem	278.0	275.6	278.8	278.1	-0.7	-0.3
St. George	72.4	72.1	72.4	72.6	0.2	0.3
Salt Lake City	766.3	752.2	770.3	756.5	-13.8	-1.8
Vermont	319.7	289.4	317.8	290.6	-27.2	-8.6
Burlington-South Burlington	128.6	114.8	127.3	115.6	-11.7	-9.2

Table 7-1. Employees on Nonfarm Payrolls by State and Selected Metropolitan Areas, October 2019–November 2020—Continued

(Number in thousands, percent.)

State and area	October		November		Change from November 2019 to November 2020	
	2019	2020	2019	2020	Number	Percent
Virginia	4 082.0	3 909.2	4 115.6	3 933.0	-182.6	-4.4
Blacksburg-Christiansburg-Radford	76.1	75.5	79.5	76.3	-3.2	-4.0
Charlottesville	122.2	119.1	123.2	120.1	-3.1	-2.5
Harrisonburg	70.9	67.0	71.1	66.9	-4.2	-5.9
Lynchburg	106.8	99.5	106.7	99.7	-7.0	-6.6
Richmond	689.8	658.4	697.9	665.5	-32.4	-4.6
Roanoke	162.8	156.2	164.0	157.9	-6.1	-3.7
Staunton-Waynesboro	52.1	52.9	52.4	53.3	0.9	1.7
Virginia Beach-Norfolk-Newport News	795.3	769.4	798.8	771.8	-27.0	-3.4
Winchester	66.7	61.5	67.0	61.7	-5.3	-7.9
Washington	3 501.8	3 302.7	3 510.9	3 318.5	-192.4	-5.5
Bellingham	96.8	93.4	96.7	93.7	-3.0	-3.1
Bremerton-Silverdale	96.3	94.5	97.0	94.5	-2.5	-2.6
Kennewick-Richland	120.2	119.8	120.4	119.7	-0.7	-0.6
Longview	41.3	39.7	41.4	39.9	-1.5	-3.6
Mount Vernon-Anacortes	52.5	49.1	52.6	49.4	-3.2	-6.1
Olympia-Tumwate	123.4	117.0	123.5	118.0	-5.5	-4.5
Seattle-Tacoma-Bellevue	2 106.5	1 963.8	2 115.4	1 973.2	-142.2	-6.7
Spokane-Spokane Valley	259.7	238.5	259.0	239.3	-19.7	-7.6
Walla Walla	29.2	28.1	29.0	27.8	-1.2	-4.1
Wenatchee	46.8	43.5	46.6	43.2	-3.4	-7.3
Yakima	88.6	84.9	88.9	84.8	-4.1	-4.6
West Virginia	726.9	680.6	723.8	679.8	-44.0	-6.1
Beckley	45.1	43.3	44.5	42.4	-2.1	-4.7
Charleston	108.8	102.2	108.7	103.0	-5.7	-5.2
Huntington-Ashland	135.6	130.9	136.1	130.5	-5.6	-4.1
Morgantown	72.3	69.7	72.5	70.1	-2.4	-3.3
Parkersburg-Vienna	38.8	37.7	38.9	37.8	-1.1	-2.8
Wheeling	66.5	57.7	66.6	58.3	-8.3	-12.5
Wisconsin	2 999.9	2 797.6	2 999.7	2 791.4	-208.3	-6.9
Appleton	127.1	117.7	127.3	117.7	-9.6	-7.5
Eau Claire	88.3	83.2	88.3	83.4	-4.9	-5.5
Fond du Lac	49.3	47.8	49.5	48.2	-1.3	-2.6
Green Bay	181.9	172.2	182.7	172.1	-10.6	-5.8
Janesville-Beloit	70.2	65.5	70.5	65.1	-5.4	-7.7
La Crosse-Onalaska	79.4	74.5	80.1	74.8	-5.3	-6.6
Madison	415.1	392.0	417.5	389.2	-28.3	-6.8
Milwaukee-Waukesha-West Allis	879.2	821.8	881.5	818.0	-63.5	-7.2
Oshkosh-Neenah	97.3	93.4	97.8	93.6	-4.2	-4.3
Racine	78.3	76.6	78.1	76.9	-1.2	-1.5
Sheboygan	62.9	59.9	62.5	60.1	-2.4	-3.8
Wausau	74.0	69.6	74.2	69.7	-4.5	-6.1
Wyoming	290.6	277.3	285.3	271.3	-14.0	-4.9
Casper	39.8	37.1	39.5	37.3	-2.2	-5.6
Cheyenne	47.7	46.1	47.5	45.6	-1.9	-4.0

Table 7-2. Civilian Labor Force by State and Selected Metropolitan Areas, October 2019–November 2020

(Number in thousands, percent.)

| State and area | October | | November | |
	2019	2020	2019	2020
Alabama	2 252 789	2 256 233	2 249 775	2 272 019
Anniston-Oxford-Jacksonville	46 508	44 797	46 408	44 769
Auburn-Opelika	77 850	76 044	78 204	76 343
Birmingham-Hoover	557 216	548 095	557 869	550 653
Daphne-Fairhope-Foley	97 213	95 828	96 603	96 167
Decatur	72 973	71 425	73 115	71 986
Dothan	64 373	63 835	64 230	64 065
Florence-Muscle Shoals	66 575	65 480	66 387	65 564
Gadsden	42 766	41 107	42 785	41 254
Huntsville	231 034	227 720	231 135	229 252
Mobile	190 090	189 142	189 712	188 454
Montgomery	172 879	171 126	172 696	170 961
Tuscaloosa	121 013	119 106	121 064	119 357
Alaska	344 605	351 295	343 483	353 452
Anchorage	192 732	200 537	195 228	202 679
Fairbanks	44 717	45 896	44 677	45 771
Arizona	3 601 094	3 591 571	3 615 186	3 596 047
Flagstaff	79 349	69 805	78 173	69 076
Lake Havasu-City-Kingman	88 263	87 146	88 701	86 633
Phoenix-Mesa-Scottsdale	2 535 869	2 545 839	2 548 538	2 550 954
Prescott	107 722	110 001	108 301	109 192
Sierra Vista-Douglas	51 646	52 130	51 708	51 985
Tucson	501 592	498 262	504 426	499 320
Yuma	102 978	96 981	102 376	97 533
Arkansas	1 367 199	1 330 991	1 361 974	1 323 556
Fayetteville-Springdale-Rogers	284 397	278 859	283 345	278 544
Fort Smith	118 838	116 214	119 034	116 095
Hot Springs	40 921	40 997	40 659	40 565
Jonesboro	66 775	66 986	66 690	66 715
Little Rock-North Little Rock-Conway	358 233	343 658	357 079	340 488
Pine Bluff	34 975	33 665	34 794	33 469
California	19 538 254	19 289 337	19 534 610	18 928 834
Bakersfield	399 408	378 798	395 137	370 897
Chico	100 659	96 203	99 254	92 998
El Centro	72 614	68 078	72 396	65 425
Fresno	448 769	449 041	448 416	440 003
Hanford-Corcoran	57 617	56 079	57 402	54 651
Los Angeles-Long Beach-Anaheim	6 789 821	6 698 362	6 807 214	6 578 840
Madera	61 525	61 648	60 686	59 964
Merced	118 481	116 060	115 475	112 012
Modesto	244 850	239 738	243 932	233 703
Napa	75 561	73 597	73 640	70 955
Oxnard-Thousand Oaks-Ventura	425 299	419 394	425 979	412 590
Redding	75 417	74 796	74 708	73 130
Riverside-San Bernardino-Ontario	2 084 065	2 103 030	2 095 092	2 071 914
Sacramento—Roseville—Arden-Arcade	1 104 810	1 110 741	1 105 018	1 089 342
Salinas	224 987	195 440	219 427	188 295
San Diego-Carlsbad	1 598 643	1 608 934	1 600 077	1 582 455
San Francisco-Oakland-Hayward	2 608 916	2 551 436	2 606 601	2 503 008
San Jose-Sunnyvale-Santa Clara	1 090 633	1 089 736	1 090 607	1 073 458
San Luis Obispo-Paso Robles-Arroyo	142 355	134 203	142 044	131 759
Grande Santa Cruz-Watsonville	143 704	131 294	141 792	128 086
Santa Maria-Santa Barbara	220 335	218 297	218 458	213 583
Santa Rosa	263 296	257 909	260 583	250 179
Stockton-Lodi	327 968	328 635	325 674	321 465
Vallejo-Fairfield	210 932	207 576	210 399	203 615
Visalia-Porterville	202 214	193 275	203 387	191 474
Yuba City	76 877	71 300	76 823	69 235
Colorado	3 183 835	3 148 728	3 178 357	3 135 429
Boulder	198 261	192 301	198 526	192 190
Colorado Springs	358 748	357 895	359 210	359 580
Denver-Aurora-Lakewood	1 695 627	1 692 196	1 690 044	1 697 382
Fort Collins	211 959	205 059	211 387	202 898
Grand Junction	77 377	78 970	76 804	78 770
Greeley	175 276	171 525	173 704	170 016
Pueblo	77 084	77 470	77 322	77 967

Table 7-2. Civilian Labor Force by State and Selected Metropolitan Areas, October 2019–November 2020—*Continued*

(Number in thousands, percent.)

State and area	October		November	
	2019	2020	2019	2020
Connecticut	1 925 483	1 851 420	1 927 932	1 888 211
Bridgeport-Stamford-Norwalk	467 659	442 180	469 897	452 023
Danbury	107 380	102 413	107 876	104 708
Hartford-West Hartford-East Hartford	634 415	619 053	634 432	632 201
New Haven	333 480	324 881	333 337	329 562
Norwich-New London-Westerly	142 565	135 723	142 720	137 488
Waterbury	112 374	106 930	112 691	109 660
Delaware	487 774	479 126	488 408	475 623
Dover	80 257	80 344	80 546	79 299
Salisbury	192 626	187 087	190 382	183 191
District of Columbia	409 726	396 355	412 346	397 448
Washington-Arlington-Alexandria	3 495 773	3 372 052	3 494 549	3 362 312
Florida	10 458 221	10 137 710	10 411 499	10 135 780
Cape Coral-Fort Myers	351 228	346 291	352 406	345 887
Crestview-Fort Walton Beach-Destin	129 537	125 136	127 755	124 296
Deltona-Daytona Beach-Ormond Beach	302 993	297 542	302 269	298 707
Gainesville	149 740	145 016	148 873	144 685
Homosassa Springs	47 560	45 466	47 355	45 748
Jacksonville	800 967	778 243	796 323	782 451
Lakeland-Winter Haven	309 933	307 848	309 867	309 538
Miami-Fort Lauderdale-West Palm Beach	3 190 930	3 063 603	3 165 667	3 037 858
Naples-Immokalee-Marco Island	180 325	175 894	183 572	179 699
North Port-Sarasota-Bradenton	370 079	360 063	371 219	361 795
Ocala	139 117	141 736	138 518	143 034
Orlando-Kissimmee-Sanford	1 380 096	1 315 501	1 373 242	1 312 239
Palm Bay-Melbourne-Titusville	288 618	284 489	287 508	285 158
Panama City	89 638	87 308	88 130	86 777
Pensacola-Ferry Pass-Brent	231 193	224 801	230 265	225 308
Port St Lucie	220 854	218 341	220 487	218 659
Punta Gorda	71 956	72 516	72 707	73 002
Sebastian-Vero Beach	65 470	64 320	66 003	65 351
Sebring	36 060	36 627	36 302	37 025
Tallahassee	199 012	187 801	197 548	187 482
Tampa-St Petersburg-Clearwater	1 577 390	1 536 930	1 570 918	1 546 512
The Villages	32 901	32 522	32 923	32 592
Georgia	5 140 986	5 087 994	5 135 208	5 162 384
Albany	66 804	65 279	66 811	66 394
Athens-Clarke County	99 897	97 837	99 617	98 955
Atlanta-Sandy Springs-Roswell	3 116 953	3 086 646	3 113 823	3 130 221
Augusta-Richmond County	267 736	260 743	266 860	258 751
Brunswick	52 637	47 455	52 488	48 053
Columbus	123 200	119 506	123 143	120 090
Dalton	59 069	56 827	58 378	57 582
Gainesville	102 981	100 965	102 867	102 033
Hinesville	34 380	34 592	34 422	35 376
Macon	102 708	102 061	102 965	103 987
Rome	44 467	44 641	44 454	45 135
Savannah	188 554	186 997	188 458	190 474
Valdosta	64 060	65 836	64 215	67 584
Warner Robins	86 157	83 240	86 159	84 682
Hawaii	663 747	639 224	667 857	659 148
Kahului-Wailuku-Lahaina	86 124	82 093	86 322	82 384
Urban Honolulu	450 270	434 382	452 986	450 466
Idaho	888 851	914 261	887 607	903 702
Boise City	375 535	385 603	379 480	383 511
Coeur d'Alene	79 673	79 264	80 122	78 854
Idaho Falls	73 189	77 095	73 553	76 482
Lewiston	31 744	30 846	32 050	29 892
Pocatello	43 005	41 775	43 372	41 319
Twin Falls	54 103	56 029	54 103	55 434
Illinois	6 443 336	6 303 579	6 416 333	6 136 270
Bloomington	97 093	97 063	96 687	92 253
Carbondale-Marion	60 810	62 458	61 081	60 114
Champaign-Urbana	128 412	132 985	128 542	125 202
Chicago-Naperville-Elgin	4 845 658	4 684 202	4 830 451	4 626 078

Table 7-2. Civilian Labor Force by State and Selected Metropolitan Areas, October 2019–November 2020—Continued

(Number in thousands, percent.)

State and area	October		November	
	2019	2020	2019	2020
Illinois— *Continued*				
Danville	33 480	34 588	33 357	32 521
Davenport-Moline-Rock Island	197 733	190 807	195 763	182 855
Decatur	48 737	49 143	48 435	46 482
Kankakee	56 899	57 741	56 735	54 747
Peoria	176 229	171 981	174 407	161 995
Rockford	165 994	164 205	165 336	155 573
Springfield	107 942	109 650	107 432	104 337
Indiana	3 392 188	3 370 613	3 385 064	3 325 870
Bloomington	81 761	80 463	81 883	79 406
Columbus	44 861	44 904	44 983	44 590
Elkhart-Goshen	111 645	108 742	111 351	107 810
Evansville	163 517	166 511	163 969	165 808
Fort Wayne	222 745	220 507	219 621	217 617
Indianapolis-Carmel-Anderson	1 073 393	1 099 491	1 072 507	1 083 734
Kokomo	37 042	37 464	36 993	36 438
Lafayette-West Lafayette	115 869	113 328	116 509	112 310
Michigan City-La Porte	47 828	48 273	47 785	47 874
Muncie	54 541	53 492	54 732	52 682
South Bend-Mishawaka	160 327	155 441	160 524	153 641
Terre Haute	75 830	74 265	76 256	73 334
Iowa	1 759 289	1 640 453	1 752 989	1 618 578
Ames	61 675	59 972	61 308	58 019
Cedar Rapids	150 289	139 664	150 091	136 593
Des Moines-West Des Moines	372 407	344 453	368 670	337 609
Dubuque	57 465	53 326	57 378	52 533
Iowa City	101 354	95 776	100 884	93 558
Sioux City	94 657	91 274	94 776	91 408
Waterloo-Cedar Falls	92 096	86 250	91 241	84 909
Kansas	1 493 923	1 516 391	1 497 273	1 533 375
Lawrence	66 705	65 834	67 073	66 356
Manhattan	48 965	46 876	49 129	47 703
Topeka	118 752	120 036	118 671	121 540
Wichita	314 612	322 597	316 287	324 695
Kentucky	2 075 032	1 953 500	2 078 031	1 995 581
Bowling Green	85 283	77 201	85 288	80 038
Elizabethtown-Fort Knox	67 067	62 886	67 158	64 025
Lexington-Fayette	275 928	264 269	275 843	270 683
Louisville/Jefferson County	675 402	649 148	674 579	657 184
Owensboro	55 884	52 696	55 664	53 748
Louisiana	2 108 448	2 116 818	2 109 627	2 094 476
Alexandria	63 580	63 905	63 388	62 879
Baton Rouge	419 704	426 441	421 252	420 133
Hammond	55 250	56 380	55 370	55 441
Houma-Thibodaux	89 386	90 202	88 875	90 409
Lafayette	213 448	215 783	212 311	212 320
Lake Charles	109 938	101 270	109 308	102 522
Monroe	79 295	83 856	79 709	82 684
New Orleans-Metairie	600 032	600 842	602 500	595 502
Shreveport-Bossier City	187 051	189 590	187 596	188 200
Maine	695 929	679 522	689 655	671 966
Bangor	72 575	70 727	72 158	69 543
Lewiston-Auburn	56 434	55 150	56 165	54 757
Portland-South Portland	211 155	203 443	209 148	203 066
Maryland	3 278 073	3 154 803	3 270 600	3 141 812
Baltimore-Columbia-Towson	1 528 235	1 464 763	1 525 470	1 464 152
California-Lexington Park	57 687	53 294	57 429	53 021
Cumberland	45 581	42 029	45 131	41 757
Hagerstown-Martinsburg	135 769	127 211	136 804	127 076
Massachusetts	3 819 962	3 612 815	3 825 517	3 569 886
Barnstable Town	126 240	116 090	122 235	111 976
Boston-Cambridge-Nashua	2 836 192	2 680 350	2 841 892	2 656 665
Leominster-Gardner	80 413	76 185	81 118	75 564
New Bedford	85 705	82 069	86 401	81 371
Pittsfield	42 316	39 951	42 396	39 436
Springfield	380 896	353 325	382 344	352 140
Worcester	363 777	349 007	365 861	349 706

Table 7-2. Civilian Labor Force by State and Selected Metropolitan Areas, October 2019–November 2020—*Continued*

(Number in thousands, percent.)

State and area	October		November	
	2019	2020	2019	2020
Michigan	4 943 286	4 903 046	4 931 109	4 912 353
Ann Arbor	199 449	201 857	202 006	200 785
Battle Creek	61 970	60 695	62 723	60 820
Bay City	49 540	47 708	49 855	47 214
Detroit-Warren-Dearborn	2 180 195	2 142 620	2 156 528	2 173 817
Flint	183 174	180 451	183 897	178 815
Grand Rapids-Wyoming	575 962	577 580	579 732	574 837
Jackson	73 197	73 211	74 151	72 964
Kalamazoo-Portage	168 752	170 149	169 991	167 752
Lansing-East Lansing	252 500	242 536	253 153	241 039
Midland	39 639	39 483	40 076	39 200
Monroe	74 841	72 563	75 770	71 483
Muskegon	76 240	75 692	77 174	75 442
Niles-Benton Harbor	72 591	72 903	72 846	72 165
Saginaw	85 380	83 936	86 708	83 882
Minnesota	3 125 946	3 019 072	3 123 662	3 034 412
Duluth	143 597	135 853	144 196	136 029
Mankato-North Mankato	63 954	61 748	63 516	62 452
Minneapolis-St Paul-Bloomington	2 036 557	1 957 120	2 041 061	1 968 687
Rochester	126 368	121 641	125 266	122 170
St. Cloud	114 567	112 381	114 227	113 136
Mississippi	1 276 407	1 289 502	1 279 839	1 280 512
Gulfport-Biloxi-Pascagoula	164 063	169 104	164 715	167 408
Hattiesburg	68 979	71 755	69 787	72 290
Jackson	269 741	272 621	269 642	270 322
Missouri	3 103 578	2 977 451	3 099 987	2 995 373
Cape Girardeau	48 788	44 538	48 890	44 651
Columbia	99 703	95 574	99 976	96 177
Jefferson City	74 904	72 454	74 810	72 441
Joplin	85 225	83 255	85 480	83 340
Kansas City	1 143 396	1 115 869	1 146 503	1 127 734
St. Joseph	63 738	61 676	63 502	61 939
St. Louis	1 484 448	1 431 232	1 484 554	1 421 814
Springfield	236 833	228 513	237 954	230 988
Montana	535 076	534 105	534 315	533 418
Billings	87 561	87 504	87 577	87 307
Great Falls	37 962	37 389	38 082	37 582
Missoula	64 444	64 940	64 012	65 013
Nebraska	1 038 851	1 029 456	1 037 741	1 031 599
Grand Island	44 175	43 256	43 662	43 509
Lincoln	187 420	190 798	187 817	189 941
Omaha-Council Bluffs	501 611	493 655	497 824	491 651
Nevada	1 555 164	1 547 904	1 554 598	1 514 131
Carson City	26 409	26 316	26 314	25 636
Las Vegas-Henderson-Paradise	1 138 969	1 138 873	1 139 511	1 111 714
Reno	261 178	255 419	262 162	253 539
New Hampshire	773 369	724 427	773 447	746 958
Dover-Durham	87 013	77 995	86 660	79 756
Manchester	123 065	116 006	123 988	120 335
Portsmouth	77 788	71 260	77 309	72 181
New Jersey	4 533 349	4 394 721	4 534 778	4 518 710
Atlantic City-Hammonton	121 075	115 350	120 041	120 174
Ocean City	43 924	42 304	43 106	42 572
Trenton	205 097	201 551	206 167	207 112
Vineland-Bridgeton	66 107	65 290	65 723	65 807
New Mexico	963 427	929 379	967 203	932 032
Albuquerque	441 248	432 240	443 346	433 270
Farmington	52 844	49 988	52 437	49 924
Las Cruces	98 847	91 917	99 237	92 309
Santa Fe	75 279	69 556	76 493	70 386
New York	9 543 205	9 055 222	9 487 235	9 093 641
Albany-Schenectady-Troy	451 813	431 570	451 668	432 476
Binghamton	106 473	103 632	105 698	103 504
Buffalo-Cheektowaga-Niagara Falls	543 054	530 377	539 888	529 122
Elmira	35 222	35 039	34 987	34 344
Glens Falls	58 882	55 947	58 333	55 598

Table 7-2. Civilian Labor Force by State and Selected Metropolitan Areas, October 2019–November 2020—*Continued*

(Number in thousands, percent.)

State and area	October 2019	October 2020	November 2019	November 2020
New York—*Continued*				
Ithaca	50 174	49 486	49 795	49 554
Kingston	88 786	86 760	87 788	86 566
New York-Newark-Jersey City	9 985 876	9 504 816	9 949 170	9 633 947
Rochester	524 666	497 276	520 672	498 071
Syracuse	308 525	289 346	306 415	290 180
Utica-Rome	128 614	124 518	128 183	124 726
Watertown-Fort Drum	43 558	41 013	43 582	41 094
North Carolina	5 123 098	4 953 747	5 100 768	4 967 029
Asheville	241 355	224 872	239 917	225 219
Burlington	83 405	81 141	82 915	81 357
Charlotte-Concord-Gastonia	1 386 509	1 343 528	1 378 324	1 342 107
Durham-Chapel Hill	308 753	297 267	307 990	298 592
Fayetteville	149 199	143 054	149 085	144 021
Goldsboro	51 591	49 564	52 152	49 671
Greensboro-High Point	375 966	359 207	375 109	358 818
Greenville	91 338	86 493	91 146	86 697
Hickory-Lenoir-Morganton	176 864	166 645	176 490	166 811
Jacksonville	65 817	65 448	65 882	65 766
New Bern	51 878	50 156	51 903	49 729
Raleigh	741 613	709 754	736 107	713 783
Rocky Mount	65 290	63 501	65 444	63 260
Wilmington	155 622	147 382	155 884	148 229
Winston-Salem	335 529	322 042	331 760	321 394
North Dakota	403 653	399 912	399 846	397 281
Bismarck	67 059	68 175	66 983	68 677
Fargo	139 371	141 995	139 290	142 370
Grand Forks	54 148	54 789	53 997	54 934
Ohio	5 828 726	5 851 499	5 808 659	5 668 884
Akron	361 987	356 319	361 052	346 640
Canton-Massillon	199 960	199 341	199 093	192 506
Cincinnati	1 132 089	1 143 481	1 129 263	1 117 875
Cleveland-Elyria	1 039 084	1 019 544	1 038 615	1 006 326
Columbus	1 108 550	1 117 941	1 110 232	1 087 759
Dayton	394 304	401 082	391 422	388 571
Lima	47 673	48 111	47 691	46 715
Mansfield	51 779	53 567	52 036	52 232
Springfield	64 014	65 373	63 271	63 445
Toledo	307 515	308 630	304 821	297 642
Weirton-Steubenville	51 340	50 466	50 846	49 735
Youngstown-Warren-Boardman	238 741	229 858	237 505	223 496
Oklahoma	1 854 653	1 879 243	1 852 252	1 872 610
Enid	26 944	26 139	26 875	26 418
Lawton	50 868	51 181	51 183	51 305
Oklahoma City	692 149	703 268	691 956	701 650
Tulsa	485 661	485 059	484 695	482 235
Oregon	2 109 185	2 144 159	2 103 774	2 111 864
Albany	58 943	60 396	58 829	59 416
Bend-Redmond	96 369	97 197	95 449	95 857
Corvallis	48 875	48 170	49 105	47 639
Eugene	181 792	188 913	181 668	186 563
Grants Pass	35 818	35 770	35 590	34 836
Medford	104 139	106 789	103 552	105 228
Portland-Vancouver-Hillsboro	1 331 691	1 357 442	1 334 229	1 325 854
Salem	202 380	201 794	201 777	197 900
Pennsylvania	6 545 629	6 362 288	6 536 425	6 312 563
Allentown-Bethlehem-Easton	448 697	434 481	449 086	437 360
Altoona	59 553	57 662	59 482	57 207
Bloomsburg-Berwick	43 285	42 830	43 148	42 531
Chambersburg-Waynesboro	78 205	76 987	78 498	76 301
East Stroudsburg	83 516	78 140	83 705	77 245
Erie	129 331	122 861	129 217	121 907
Gettysburg	55 545	55 675	55 091	55 078
Harrisburg-Carlisle	304 253	301 880	304 620	300 425
Johnstown	58 402	55 785	58 468	55 601
Lancaster	286 906	289 513	286 594	286 018

Table 7-2. Civilian Labor Force by State and Selected Metropolitan Areas, October 2019–November 2020—*Continued*

(Number in thousands, percent.)

State and area	October		November	
	2019	2020	2019	2020
Pennsylvania—*Continued*				
Lebanon	73 001	72 129	72 858	71 489
Philadelphia-Camden-Wilmington	3 157 453	3 072 488	3 152 069	3 067 586
Pittsburgh	1 222 465	1 176 925	1 220 951	1 166 695
Reading	217 403	222 527	217 344	220 360
Scranton—Wilkes-Barre—Hazleton	279 529	264 043	279 327	263 232
State College	82 034	76 643	82 187	76 055
Williamsport	57 148	52 391	57 158	52 524
York-Hanover	238 249	233 437	238 331	232 939
Rhode Island	557 600	542 488	560 489	543 568
Providence-Warwick	693 593	673 225	697 292	672 991
South Carolina	2 384 080	2 385 928	2 372 583	2 310 692
Charleston-North Charleston	394 987	391 493	394 746	380 444
Columbia	406 498	408 889	405 600	395 282
Florence	97 570	98 639	97 430	96 389
Greenville-Anderson-Mauldin	438 404	445 374	435 541	433 760
Hilton Head Island-Bluffton-Beaufort	91 025	92 516	90 169	89 789
Myrtle Beach-Conway-North Myrtle Beach	202 110	192 291	198 976	187 238
Spartanburg	166 512	165 030	165 181	159 020
Sumter	43 854	43 640	43 661	41 287
South Dakota	466 961	463 806	466 655	462 354
Rapid City	75 155	72 838	74 624	72 334
Sioux Falls	156 720	154 033	157 101	154 794
Tennessee	3 369 212	3 329 990	3 366 225	3 450 249
Chattanooga	278 238	280 084	277 686	287 682
Clarksville	118 366	117 490	118 072	121 741
Cleveland	61 336	61 224	62 326	63 856
Jackson	65 341	64 282	65 297	66 766
Johnson City	92 670	90 225	92 754	93 600
Kingsport-Bristol-Bristol	138 279	133 494	137 807	136 551
Knoxville	436 014	434 189	434 995	451 628
Memphis	645 219	658 162	648 047	665 684
Morristown	53 467	53 077	53 592	55 227
Nashville-Davidson—Murfreesboro—Franklin	1 105 919	1 072 705	1 102 956	1 116 010
Texas	14 161 315	14 082 369	14 209 425	14 204 927
Abilene	80 021	78 621	80 211	79 351
Amarillo	132 989	128 368	133 302	128 261
Austin-Round Rock	1 251 714	1 260 137	1 254 411	1 267 080
Beaumont-Port Arthur	174 624	170 749	174 868	173 825
Brownsville-Harlingen	166 663	164 646	167 329	166 918
College Station-Bryan	139 186	138 882	139 654	139 283
Corpus Christi	207 222	200 540	207 904	202 507
Dallas-Fort Worth-Arlington	4 012 036	4 023 581	4 035 848	4 058 826
El Paso	368 494	363 186	368 898	371 715
Houston-The Woodlands-Sugar Land	3 449 631	3 426 109	3 467 354	3 461 040
Killeen-Temple	178 647	176 680	179 709	178 372
Laredo	118 980	116 013	119 514	117 793
Longview	100 021	96 949	99 837	97 407
Lubbock	164 291	162 447	164 576	162 863
McAllen-Edinburg-Mission	354 494	352 867	356 747	359 711
Midland	111 009	104 558	111 123	105 407
Odessa	88 389	86 195	88 379	86 981
San Angelo	55 455	53 386	55 526	53 590
San Antonio-New Braunfels	1 219 723	1 209 099	1 220 539	1 214 391
Sherman-Denison	64 281	64 411	64 467	65 223
Texarkana	65 251	65 464	65 489	65 848
Tyler	107 593	107 985	108 146	109 010
Victoria	46 141	45 234	46 349	45 731
Waco	126 403	128 745	127 219	129 522
Wichita Falls	65 676	64 663	65 821	64 965
Utah	1 623 876	1 645 301	1 629 725	1 655 977
Logan	72 537	73 668	72 365	74 179
Ogden-Clearfield	335 063	343 417	335 639	345 943
Provo-Orem	318 960	322 553	320 261	325 971
St. George	77 355	79 263	77 464	79 611
Salt Lake City	674 617	682 408	679 128	686 541
Vermont	339 366	319 337	339 375	322 112
Burlington-South Burlington	125 594	116 416	125 115	117 854

Table 7-2. Civilian Labor Force by State and Selected Metropolitan Areas, October 2019–November 2020—*Continued*

(Number in thousands, percent.)

State and area	October		November	
	2019	2020	2019	2020
Virginia	4 440 231	4 267 127	4 431 196	4 267 895
Blacksburg-Christiansburg-Radford	89 507	87 447	92 132	87 964
Charlottesville	123 914	120 594	124 038	121 177
Harrisonburg	68 805	64 895	68 278	64 535
Lynchburg	125 006	116 441	123 964	116 170
Richmond	693 242	664 484	693 533	666 465
Roanoke	159 012	152 011	158 511	152 856
Staunton-Waynesboro	61 548	61 228	61 190	61 356
Virginia Beach-Norfolk-Newport News	861 868	837 550	856 143	834 079
Winchester	75 274	69 921	74 757	69 855
Washington	3 950 939	4 001 573	3 947 984	3 834 552
Bellingham	116 357	124 808	116 639	115 516
Bremerton-Silverdale	130 423	139 733	131 624	129 735
Kennewick-Richland	148 024	159 878	146 289	149 247
Longview	48 321	51 299	48 596	47 458
Mount Vernon-Anacortes	63 801	65 760	63 525	61 267
Olympia-Tumwate	145 859	152 978	146 356	142 323
Seattle-Tacoma-Bellevue	2 178 160	2 167 744	2 190 123	2 131 071
Spokane-Spokane Valley	283 290	288 224	283 967	267 429
Walla Walla	33 748	33 728	33 364	31 424
Wenatchee	68 206	67 775	65 148	62 709
Yakima	137 142	138 086	129 158	129 459
West Virginia	807 512	768 754	801 681	767 530
Beckley	47 430	46 866	46 610	45 826
Charleston	93 593	90 596	92 825	90 749
Huntington-Ashland	147 696	145 563	147 169	144 443
Morgantown	72 148	70 632	71 673	70 713
Parkersburg-Vienna	39 691	39 090	39 466	38 988
Wheeling	66 698	60 529	66 634	60 264
Wisconsin	3 104 233	3 132 672	3 099 895	3 111 323
Appleton	129 840	130 115	129 827	129 472
Eau Claire	92 288	92 919	92 113	93 221
Fond du Lac	57 161	58 916	57 087	59 441
Green Bay	173 327	176 508	173 484	175 339
Janesville-Beloit	84 938	85 824	85 334	84 782
La Crosse-Onalaska	77 108	76 968	77 359	77 019
Madison	391 475	397 327	392 185	393 256
Milwaukee-Waukesha-West Allis	818 355	837 044	818 281	824 966
Oshkosh-Neenah	91 238	93 119	91 241	92 857
Racine	97 840	102 537	97 594	101 613
Sheboygan	61 425	62 518	61 032	62 631
Wausau	73 343	73 673	73 448	73 695
Wyoming	293 310	295 966	292 723	293 696
Casper	39 482	39 629	39 651	39 950
Cheyenne	48 535	48 929	48 745	48 870

Table 7-3. Unemployment Number and Rate by State and Selected Metropolitan Area October 2019–November 2020

(Number, rate.)

State and area	October 2019	October 2020	November 2019	November 2020	October 2019	October 2020	November 2019	November 2020
Alabama	57 113	122 127	54 861	90 944	2.5	5.4	2.4	4.0
Anniston-Oxford-Jacksonville	1 381	2 908	1 332	2 134	3.0	6.5	2.9	4.8
Auburn-Opelika	1 747	3 453	1 706	2 587	2.2	4.5	2.2	3.4
Birmingham-Hoover	12 785	28 629	12 270	21 195	2.3	5.2	2.2	3.8
Daphne-Fairhope-Foley	2 246	4 683	2 198	3 442	2.3	4.9	2.3	3.6
Decatur	1 670	2 880	1 611	2 233	2.3	4.0	2.2	3.1
Dothan	1 612	3 183	1 582	2 448	2.5	5.0	2.5	3.8
Florence-Muscle Shoals	1 886	3 087	1 802	2 339	2.8	4.7	2.7	3.6
Gadsden	1 285	2 661	1 163	1 908	3.0	6.5	2.7	4.6
Huntsville	4 989	9 569	4 756	7 150	2.2	4.2	2.1	3.1
Mobile	5 943	14 917	5 690	10 919	3.1	7.9	3.0	5.8
Montgomery	4 459	12 261	4 256	8 967	2.6	7.2	2.5	5.2
Tuscaloosa	2 800	7 141	2 748	5 231	2.3	6.0	2.3	4.4
Alaska	19 701	19 029	20 910	28 661	5.7	5.4	6.1	8.1
Anchorage	9 924	10 708	10 368	15 840	5.1	5.3	5.3	7.8
Fairbanks	2 225	1 974	2 376	2 926	5.0	4.3	5.3	6.4
Arizona	161 137	281 359	154 572	273 365	4.5	7.8	4.3	7.6
Flagstaff	3 921	6 728	3 710	6 636	4.9	9.6	4.7	9.6
Lake Havasu-City-Kingman	4 788	7 835	4 689	7 505	5.4	9.0	5.3	8.7
Phoenix-Mesa-Scottsdale	97 704	189 550	94 318	184 712	3.9	7.4	3.7	7.2
Prescott	4 538	7 472	4 478	7 298	4.2	6.8	4.1	6.7
Sierra Vista-Douglas	2 732	3 385	2 710	3 335	5.3	6.5	5.2	6.4
Tucson	21 280	38 967	20 493	38 083	4.2	7.8	4.1	7.6
Yuma	17 092	15 075	15 592	13 672	16.6	15.5	15.2	14.0
Arkansas	42 231	75 789	41 816	75 624	3.1	5.7	3.1	5.7
Fayetteville-Springdale-Rogers	6 417	11 872	6 220	11 826	2.3	4.3	2.2	4.2
Fort Smith	4 058	6 828	3 947	6 734	3.4	5.9	3.3	5.8
Hot Springs	1 375	3 080	1 324	2 974	3.4	7.5	3.3	7.3
Jonesboro	1 646	3 186	1 596	3 110	2.5	4.8	2.4	4.7
Little Rock-North Little Rock-Conway	10 411	21 999	10 244	21 384	2.9	6.4	2.9	6.3
Pine Bluff	1 587	2 697	1 611	2 695	4.5	8.0	4.6	8.1
California	725 895	1 682 556	718 032	1 491 595	3.7	8.7	3.7	7.9
Bakersfield	25 064	38 520	25 238	35 031	6.3	10.2	6.4	9.4
Chico	4 180	6 869	4 172	6 345	4.2	7.1	4.2	6.8
El Centro	14 190	12 395	13 506	10 723	19.5	18.2	18.7	16.4
Fresno	27 444	40 134	29 945	37 764	6.1	8.9	6.7	8.6
Hanford-Corcoran	3 790	5 035	4 157	4 841	6.6	9.0	7.2	8.9
Los Angeles-Long Beach-Anaheim	264 634	718 302	255 515	629 073	3.9	10.7	3.8	9.6
Madera	3 458	5 043	3 757	4 843	5.6	8.2	6.2	8.1
Merced	7 121	10 422	7 734	10 118	6.0	9.0	6.7	9.0
Modesto	12 367	21 047	12 853	19 433	5.1	8.8	5.3	8.3
Napa	1 814	4 728	1 920	4 269	2.4	6.4	2.6	6.0
Oxnard-Thousand Oaks-Ventura	14 466	28 941	14 679	25 889	3.4	6.9	3.4	6.3
Redding	2 957	5 036	2 973	4 782	3.9	6.7	4.0	6.5
Riverside-San Bernardino-Ontario	80 663	183 229	77 264	163 309	3.9	8.7	3.7	7.9
Sacramento—Roseville—Arden-Arcade	36 192	81 359	35 800	73 068	3.3	7.3	3.2	6.7
Salinas	8 764	14 779	10 271	14 455	3.9	7.6	4.7	7.7
San Diego-Carlsbad	47 861	120 033	46 727	105 187	3.0	7.5	2.9	6.6
San Francisco-Oakland-Hayward	63 687	177 751	61 892	153 424	2.4	7.0	2.4	6.1
San Jose-Sunnyvale-Santa Clara	26 355	63 076	25 860	55 276	2.4	5.8	2.4	5.1
San Luis Obispo-Paso Robles-Arroyo	3 649	7 876	3 634	7 110	2.6	5.9	2.6	5.4
Grande Santa Cruz-Watsonville	4 999	9 114	5 643	8 586	3.5	6.9	4.0	6.7
Santa Maria-Santa Barbara	6 870	13 413	6 989	12 313	3.1	6.1	3.2	5.8
Santa Rosa	6 282	15 549	6 305	13 757	2.4	6.0	2.4	5.5
Stockton-Lodi	16 984	31 682	17 551	28 984	5.2	9.6	5.4	9.0
Vallejo-Fairfield	7 092	17 074	7 026	15 341	3.4	8.2	3.3	7.5
Visalia-Porterville	16 960	20 357	17 605	18 752	8.4	10.5	8.7	9.8
Yuba City	4 026	6 264	4 357	5 985	5.2	8.8	5.7	8.6
Colorado	75 314	192 251	74 970	193 219	2.4	6.1	2.4	6.2
Boulder	4 128	9 952	3 955	9 723	2.1	5.2	2.0	5.1
Colorado Springs	10 079	21 306	10 038	21 525	2.8	6.0	2.8	6.0
Denver-Aurora-Lakewood	39 124	109 153	38 272	107 992	2.3	6.5	2.3	6.4
Fort Collins	4 219	10 416	4 145	10 478	2.0	5.1	2.0	5.2
Grand Junction	2 151	4 477	2 161	4 725	2.8	5.7	2.8	6.0
Greeley	3 834	10 587	3 801	10 852	2.2	6.2	2.2	6.4
Pueblo	2 654	6 023	2 701	6 471	3.4	7.8	3.5	8.3

Table 7-3. Unemployment Number and Rate by State and Selected Metropolitan Area October 2019–November 2020—*Continued*

(Number, rate.)

State and area	October 2019	October 2020	November 2019	November 2020	October 2019	October 2020	November 2019	November 2020
Connecticut	66 634	107 228	62 775	145 249	3.5	5.8	3.3	7.7
Bridgeport-Stamford-Norwalk	16 492	27 098	15 571	36 085	3.5	6.1	3.3	8.0
Danbury	3 047	5 224	2 917	6 920	2.8	5.1	2.7	6.6
Hartford-West Hartford-East Hartford	22 142	34 620	20 730	47 271	3.5	5.6	3.3	7.5
New Haven	11 282	17 746	10 507	24 395	3.4	5.5	3.2	7.4
Norwich-New London-Westerly	4 719	9 156	4 600	11 956	3.3	6.7	3.2	8.7
Waterbury	4 806	7 368	4 549	10 035	4.3	6.9	4.0	9.2
Delaware	18 749	26 451	17 290	22 277	3.8	5.5	3.5	4.7
Dover	3 396	4 759	3 030	3 964	4.2	5.9	3.8	5.0
Salisbury	7 742	11 359	8 735	10 460	4.0	6.1	4.6	5.7
District of Columbia	21 517	32 658	20 781	29 023	5.3	8.2	5.0	7.3
Washington-Arlington-Alexandria	100 524	221 032	96 701	196 277	2.9	6.6	2.8	5.8
Florida	295 902	637 230	283 039	640 028	2.8	6.3	2.7	6.3
Cape Coral-Fort Myers	10 132	18 597	9 848	19 597	2.9	5.4	2.8	5.7
Crestview-Fort Walton Beach-Destin	3 086	4 760	3 150	5 391	2.4	3.8	2.5	4.3
Deltona-Daytona Beach-Ormond Beach	9 804	16 957	9 666	18 201	3.2	5.7	3.2	6.1
Gainesville	4 087	6 158	3 849	6 814	2.7	4.2	2.6	4.7
Homosassa Springs	2 030	2 884	2 044	3 178	4.3	6.3	4.3	6.9
Jacksonville	22 647	37 718	21 787	40 867	2.8	4.8	2.7	5.2
Lakeland-Winter Haven	10 618	21 903	10 145	22 797	3.4	7.1	3.3	7.4
Miami-Fort Lauderdale-West Palm Beach	80 710	232 203	74 470	214 159	2.5	7.6	2.4	7.0
Naples-Immokalee-Marco Island	5 401	8 766	5 133	8 871	3.0	5.0	2.8	4.9
North Port-Sarasota-Bradenton	10 540	17 561	10 405	18 726	2.8	4.9	2.8	5.2
Ocala	4 797	7 695	4 752	8 579	3.4	5.4	3.4	6.0
Orlando-Kissimmee-Sanford	38 327	102 973	36 726	101 310	2.8	7.8	2.7	7.7
Palm Bay-Melbourne-Titusville	8 434	14 135	8 218	15 077	2.9	5.0	2.9	5.3
Panama City	2 774	3 895	2 698	4 449	3.1	4.5	3.1	5.1
Pensacola-Ferry Pass-Brent	6 570	10 715	6 436	11 840	2.8	4.8	2.8	5.3
Port St Lucie	7 470	11 688	7 224	12 493	3.4	5.4	3.3	5.7
Punta Gorda	2 390	3 678	2 412	3 943	3.3	5.1	3.3	5.4
Sebastian-Vero Beach	2 323	3 547	2 241	3 786	3.5	5.5	3.4	5.8
Sebring	1 488	2 149	1 473	2 444	4.1	5.9	4.1	6.6
Tallahassee	5 831	9 415	5 465	10 567	2.9	5.0	2.8	5.6
Tampa-St Petersburg-Clearwater	45 757	83 508	44 485	88 812	2.9	5.4	2.8	5.7
The Villages	1 295	1 835	1 387	2 064	3.9	5.6	4.2	6.3
Georgia	159 171	224 757	141 518	276 684	3.1	4.4	2.8	5.4
Albany	2 564	3 641	2 361	4 447	3.8	5.6	3.5	6.7
Athens-Clarke County	2 936	3 580	2 523	4 329	2.9	3.7	2.5	4.4
Atlanta-Sandy Springs-Roswell	91 054	143 385	81 063	176 049	2.9	4.6	2.6	5.6
Augusta-Richmond County	8 495	10 331	7 731	12 315	3.2	4.0	2.9	4.8
Brunswick	1 663	2 067	1 435	2 600	3.2	4.4	2.7	5.4
Columbus	4 389	5 970	3 963	6 748	3.6	5.0	3.2	5.6
Dalton	2 738	2 384	2 214	3 007	4.6	4.2	3.8	5.2
Gainesville	2 558	2 901	2 247	3 583	2.5	2.9	2.2	3.5
Hinesville	1 174	1 355	1 051	1 711	3.4	3.9	3.1	4.8
Macon	3 485	4 998	3 087	6 092	3.4	4.9	3.0	5.9
Rome	1 488	1 611	1 404	1 993	3.3	3.6	3.2	4.4
Savannah	5 576	8 754	4 909	10 731	3.0	4.7	2.6	5.6
Valdosta	2 086	2 633	1 899	3 281	3.3	4.0	3.0	4.9
Warner Robins	2 806	3 304	2 357	3 896	3.3	4.0	2.7	4.6
Hawaii	17 540	90 464	17 344	66 466	2.6	14.2	2.6	10.1
Kahului-Wailuku-Lahaina	2 288	18 198	2 167	13 192	2.7	22.2	2.5	16.0
Urban Honolulu	11 110	53 667	11 123	39 631	2.5	12.4	2.5	8.8
Idaho	20 787	45 940	24 433	43 135	2.3	5.0	2.8	4.8
Boise City	8 805	20 691	10 084	18 889	2.3	5.4	2.7	4.9
Coeur d'Alene	2 204	5 118	2 683	4 965	2.8	6.5	3.3	6.3
Idaho Falls	1 432	2 934	1 639	2 717	2.0	3.8	2.2	3.6
Lewiston	845	1 334	958	1 321	2.7	4.3	3.0	4.4
Pocatello	1 011	2 103	1 122	1 932	2.4	5.0	2.6	4.7
Twin Falls	1 185	2 554	1 429	2 410	2.2	4.6	2.6	4.3
Illinois	224 741	452 588	215 173	398 829	3.5	7.2	3.4	6.5
Bloomington	3 279	4 395	3 112	4 248	3.4	4.5	3.2	4.6
Carbondale-Marion	2 261	3 196	2 166	3 063	3.7	5.1	3.5	5.1
Champaign-Urbana	4 337	5 975	4 072	5 649	3.4	4.5	3.2	4.5
Chicago-Naperville-Elgin	160 831	373 644	152 664	322 567	3.3	8.0	3.2	7.0

Table 7-3. Unemployment Number and Rate by State and Selected Metropolitan Area October 2019– November 2020—*Continued*

(Number, rate.)

State and area	October 2019	October 2020	November 2019	November 2020	October 2019	October 2020	November 2019	November 2020
Illinois— *Continued*								
Danville	1 571	2 129	1 565	1 979	4.7	6.2	4.7	6.1
Davenport-Moline-Rock Island	7 610	9 507	7 848	8 701	3.8	5.0	4.0	4.8
Decatur	2 369	3 620	2 336	3 576	4.9	7.4	4.8	7.7
Kankakee	2 413	3 305	2 739	3 300	4.2	5.7	4.8	6.0
Peoria	7 338	10 521	7 308	10 071	4.2	6.1	4.2	6.2
Rockford	8 290	11 523	8 832	10 989	5.0	7.0	5.3	7.1
Springfield	3 808	6 064	3 724	6 002	3.5	5.5	3.5	5.8
Indiana	102 208	178 035	104 202	162 527	3.0	5.3	3.1	4.9
Bloomington	2 500	3 574	2 511	3 025	3.1	4.4	3.1	3.8
Columbus	999	1 872	1 037	1 728	2.2	4.2	2.3	3.9
Elkhart-Goshen	3 235	5 078	3 233	4 793	2.9	4.7	2.9	4.4
Evansville	4 695	7 947	4 803	7 191	2.9	4.8	2.9	4.3
Fort Wayne	7 289	11 336	6 775	10 342	3.3	5.1	3.1	4.8
Indianapolis-Carmel-Anderson	29 436	59 195	30 094	53 159	2.7	5.4	2.8	4.9
Kokomo	1 215	2 266	1 239	2 039	3.3	6.0	3.3	5.6
Lafayette-West Lafayette	3 151	5 347	3 179	4 922	2.7	4.7	2.7	4.4
Michigan City-La Porte	1 679	3 371	1 789	3 288	3.5	7.0	3.7	6.9
Muncie	1 960	3 000	1 998	2 627	3.6	5.6	3.7	5.0
South Bend-Mishawaka	5 484	10 021	5 463	8 919	3.4	6.4	3.4	5.8
Terre Haute	2 778	4 098	2 937	3 837	3.7	5.5	3.9	5.2
Iowa	40 745	50 728	42 650	49 991	2.3	3.1	2.4	3.1
Ames	914	1 185	1 037	1 182	1.5	2.0	1.7	2.0
Cedar Rapids	3 857	5 321	4 112	5 179	2.6	3.8	2.7	3.8
Des Moines-West Des Moines	8 510	11 539	8 845	10 879	2.3	3.3	2.4	3.2
Dubuque	1 202	1 800	1 338	1 750	2.1	3.4	2.3	3.3
Iowa City	1 731	2 754	1 889	2 583	1.7	2.9	1.9	2.8
Sioux City	2 413	2 647	2 521	2 681	2.5	2.9	2.7	2.9
Waterloo-Cedar Falls	2 494	2 779	2 556	2 803	2.7	3.2	2.8	3.3
Kansas	42 395	71 481	43 110	82 019	2.8	4.7	2.9	5.3
Lawrence	1 747	3 190	1 779	3 549	2.6	4.8	2.7	5.3
Manhattan	1 192	1 799	1 229	2 253	2.4	3.8	2.5	4.7
Topeka	3 491	5 512	3 615	6 530	2.9	4.6	3.0	5.4
Wichita	9 712	21 391	9 935	23 429	3.1	6.6	3.1	7.2
Kentucky	79 834	133 602	78 739	102 101	3.8	6.8	3.8	5.1
Bowling Green	3 152	5 160	2 956	3 593	3.7	6.7	3.5	4.5
Elizabethtown-Fort Knox	2 557	4 245	2 524	3 233	3.8	6.8	3.8	5.0
Lexington-Fayette	8 388	16 077	8 270	12 037	3.0	6.1	3.0	4.4
Louisville/Jefferson County	22 540	41 982	22 302	32 815	3.3	6.5	3.3	5.0
Owensboro	1 913	3 211	1 879	2 557	3.4	6.1	3.4	4.8
Louisiana	105 844	195 730	104 716	169 348	5.0	9.2	5.0	8.1
Alexandria	3 338	4 313	3 374	3 697	5.3	6.7	5.3	5.9
Baton Rouge	19 430	33 956	19 099	29 771	4.6	8.0	4.5	7.1
Hammond	3 096	5 908	3 073	5 182	5.6	10.5	5.5	9.3
Houma-Thibodaux	4 210	7 045	4 129	6 100	4.7	7.8	4.6	6.7
Lafayette	10 553	17 675	10 427	15 354	4.9	8.2	4.9	7.2
Lake Charles	4 658	11 880	4 714	9 633	4.2	11.7	4.3	9.4
Monroe	4 469	6 416	4 483	5 570	5.6	7.7	5.6	6.7
New Orleans-Metairie	28 174	67 584	27 451	58 486	4.7	11.2	4.6	9.8
Shreveport-Bossier City	10 120	16 951	10 048	14 726	5.4	8.9	5.4	7.8
Maine	16 749	32 361	19 516	31 477	2.4	4.8	2.8	4.7
Bangor	1 743	3 044	1 964	2 872	2.4	4.3	2.7	4.1
Lewiston-Auburn	1 404	2 760	1 541	2 598	2.5	5.0	2.7	4.7
Portland-South Portland	4 374	9 578	4 909	8 970	2.1	4.7	2.3	4.4
Maryland	108 418	238 641	104 359	206 834	3.3	7.6	3.2	6.6
Baltimore-Columbia-Towson	51 640	104 166	48 978	89 343	3.4	7.1	3.2	6.1
California-Lexington Park	1 696	2 731	1 613	2 445	2.9	5.1	2.8	4.6
Cumberland	2 319	2 776	2 231	2 583	5.1	6.6	4.9	6.2
Hagerstown-Martinsburg	4 542	7 207	4 313	6 485	3.3	5.7	3.2	5.1
Massachusetts	90 037	248 787	87 801	222 745	2.4	6.9	2.3	6.2
Barnstable Town	3 243	7 969	3 654	7 402	2.6	6.9	3.0	6.6
Boston-Cambridge-Nashua	62 187	177 541	60 115	157 139	2.2	6.6	2.1	5.9
Leominster-Gardner	2 162	5 733	2 177	5 196	2.7	7.5	2.7	6.9
New Bedford	3 028	6 204	3 006	5 692	3.5	7.6	3.5	7.0
Pittsfield	1 180	2 946	1 237	2 721	2.8	7.4	2.9	6.9
Springfield	11 348	25 346	10 884	24 484	3.0	7.2	2.8	7.0
Worcester	9 572	22 734	9 262	21 646	2.6	6.5	2.5	6.2

Table 7-3. Unemployment Number and Rate by State and Selected Metropolitan Area October 2019– November 2020—*Continued*

(Number, rate.)

State and area	October 2019	October 2020	November 2019	November 2020	October 2019	October 2020	November 2019	November 2020
Michigan	173 524	280 991	159 361	309 645	3.5	5.7	3.2	6.3
Ann Arbor	4 698	8 009	4 384	6 764	2.4	4.0	2.2	3.4
Battle Creek	2 045	3 586	1 991	3 193	3.3	5.9	3.2	5.2
Bay City	1 895	2 458	1 797	2 298	3.8	5.2	3.6	4.9
Detroit-Warren-Dearborn	87 008	150 837	75 903	192 413	4.0	7.0	3.5	8.9
Flint	8 268	11 476	6 894	9 981	4.5	6.4	3.7	5.6
Grand Rapids-Wyoming	13 348	23 993	13 310	21 499	2.3	4.2	2.3	3.7
Jackson	2 250	3 813	2 195	3 373	3.1	5.2	3.0	4.6
Kalamazoo-Portage	4 872	7 713	4 731	6 857	2.9	4.5	2.8	4.1
Lansing-East Lansing	8 519	10 806	6 366	9 407	3.4	4.5	2.5	3.9
Midland	1 163	1 645	1 198	1 505	2.9	4.2	3.0	3.8
Monroe	2 068	3 810	2 155	3 006	2.8	5.3	2.8	4.2
Muskegon	2 612	5 376	2 768	4 797	3.4	7.1	3.6	6.4
Niles-Benton Harbor	2 131	3 775	2 265	3 382	2.9	5.2	3.1	4.7
Saginaw	3 833	4 920	3 311	4 505	4.5	5.9	3.8	5.4
Minnesota	81 756	118 189	88 135	117 017	2.6	3.9	2.8	3.9
Duluth	4 674	6 345	5 581	6 426	3.3	4.7	3.9	4.7
Mankato-North Mankato	1 316	1 824	1 279	1 896	2.1	3.0	2.0	3.0
Minneapolis-St Paul-Bloomington	52 771	82 970	53 457	77 165	2.6	4.2	2.6	3.9
Rochester	2 718	4 310	2 921	4 021	2.2	3.5	2.3	3.3
St. Cloud	2 769	4 052	3 125	4 509	2.4	3.6	2.7	4.0
Mississippi	65 083	90 003	65 909	76 512	5.1	7.0	5.1	6.0
Gulfport-Biloxi-Pascagoula	8 503	12 381	8 692	10 566	5.2	7.3	5.3	6.3
Hattiesburg	3 032	4 464	3 065	3 783	4.4	6.2	4.4	5.2
Jackson	12 087	17 312	12 188	14 702	4.5	6.4	4.5	5.4
Missouri	86 305	112 888	96 022	115 569	2.8	3.8	3.1	3.9
Cape Girardeau	1 332	1 532	1 556	1 591	2.7	3.4	3.2	3.6
Columbia	1 884	2 467	2 242	2 631	1.9	2.6	2.2	2.7
Jefferson City	1 564	1 826	1 912	1 993	2.1	2.5	2.6	2.8
Joplin	2 253	2 835	2 549	2 951	2.6	3.4	3.0	3.5
Kansas City	32 617	48 653	33 772	51 448	2.9	4.4	2.9	4.6
St. Joseph	1 592	1 879	1 698	2 012	2.5	3.0	2.7	3.2
St. Louis	43 061	62 857	45 468	61 532	2.9	4.4	3.1	4.3
Springfield	5 765	6 852	6 820	7 335	2.4	3.0	2.9	3.2
Montana	16 905	22 350	18 209	22 776	3.2	4.2	3.4	4.3
Billings	2 558	3 557	2 661	3 469	2.9	4.1	3.0	4.0
Great Falls	1 197	1 648	1 215	1 686	3.2	4.4	3.2	4.5
Missoula	1 841	2 710	1 984	2 661	2.9	4.2	3.1	4.1
Nebraska	29 226	27 870	27 173	27 864	2.8	2.7	2.6	2.7
Grand Island	1 839	1 479	1 202	1 741	4.2	3.4	2.8	4.0
Lincoln	4 775	5 060	4 636	5 189	2.5	2.7	2.5	2.7
Omaha-Council Bluffs	13 504	14 814	13 026	14 342	2.7	3.0	2.6	2.9
Nevada	55 450	181 521	52 974	149 589	3.6	11.7	3.4	9.9
Carson City	874	1 741	871	1 499	3.3	6.6	3.3	5.8
Las Vegas-Henderson-Paradise	42 928	156 207	40 777	127 969	3.8	13.7	3.6	11.5
Reno	7 357	16 118	7 108	13 737	2.8	6.3	2.7	5.4
New Hampshire	16 995	27 258	17 891	25 984	2.2	3.8	2.3	3.5
Dover-Durham	1 762	2 983	1 865	2 924	2.0	3.8	2.2	3.7
Manchester	2 583	4 460	2 741	4 208	2.1	3.8	2.2	3.5
Portsmouth	1 589	2 775	1 642	2 719	2.0	3.9	2.1	3.8
New Jersey	154 959	336 043	157 091	447 511	3.4	7.6	3.5	9.9
Atlantic City-Hammonton	5 818	13 812	6 004	18 212	4.8	12.0	5.0	15.2
Ocean City	2 457	3 722	3 763	5 814	5.6	8.8	8.7	13.7
Trenton	6 301	12 630	6 202	17 011	3.1	6.3	3.0	8.2
Vineland-Bridgeton	3 329	5 300	3 479	7 385	5.0	8.1	5.3	11.2
New Mexico	44 673	73 711	44 691	67 575	4.6	7.9	4.6	7.3
Albuquerque	19 692	32 496	19 219	29 439	4.5	7.5	4.3	6.8
Farmington	2 879	4 634	2 941	4 191	5.4	9.3	5.6	8.4
Las Cruces	5 051	6 817	5 267	6 564	5.1	7.4	5.3	7.1
Santa Fe	2 801	5 326	2 746	4 695	3.7	7.7	3.6	6.7
New York	354 358	814 901	341 376	737 748	3.7	9.0	3.6	8.1
Albany-Schenectady-Troy	15 559	23 934	15 278	20 982	3.4	5.5	3.4	4.9
Binghamton	4 463	6 210	4 475	5 570	4.2	6.0	4.2	5.4
Buffalo-Cheektowaga-Niagara Falls	22 017	35 636	22 591	31 373	4.1	6.7	4.2	5.9
Elmira	1 402	2 229	1 347	2 107	4.0	6.4	3.9	6.1
Glens Falls	2 135	3 008	2 475	2 802	3.6	5.4	4.2	5.0

Table 7-3. Unemployment Number and Rate by State and Selected Metropolitan Area October 2019– November 2020—Continued

(Number, rate.)

State and area	October 2019	October 2020	November 2019	November 2020	October 2019	October 2020	November 2019	November 2020
New York—*Continued*								
Ithaca	1 811	2 212	1 641	1 967	3.6	4.5	3.3	4.0
Kingston	3 084	4 922	3 047	4 288	3.5	5.7	3.5	5.0
New York-Newark-Jersey City	352 358	896 086	336 610	916 650	3.5	9.4	3.4	9.5
Rochester	20 288	31 103	20 539	28 041	3.9	6.3	3.9	5.6
Syracuse	12 148	17 973	12 183	16 112	3.9	6.2	4.0	5.6
Utica-Rome	5 080	7 529	5 294	6 948	3.9	6.0	4.1	5.6
Watertown-Fort Drum	2 134	2 347	2 565	2 182	4.9	5.7	5.9	5.3
North Carolina	180 081	297 061	177 831	301 765	3.5	6.0	3.5	6.1
Asheville	6 826	12 975	6 562	12 773	2.8	5.8	2.7	5.7
Burlington	2 850	4 764	2 766	4 831	3.4	5.9	3.3	5.9
Charlotte-Concord-Gastonia	44 535	79 352	44 615	79 463	3.2	5.9	3.2	5.9
Durham-Chapel Hill	9 598	15 354	9 253	15 592	3.1	5.2	3.0	5.2
Fayetteville	6 983	11 686	6 970	12 038	4.7	8.2	4.7	8.4
Goldsboro	1 985	2 867	1 938	3 044	3.8	5.8	3.7	6.1
Greensboro-High Point	13 906	24 608	13 662	24 869	3.7	6.9	3.6	6.9
Greenville	3 510	5 111	3 466	5 341	3.8	5.9	3.8	6.2
Hickory-Lenoir-Morganton	5 995	9 965	5 850	10 208	3.4	6.0	3.3	6.1
Jacksonville	2 810	3 815	2 702	3 997	4.3	5.8	4.1	6.1
New Bern	1 860	2 784	1 840	2 862	3.6	5.6	3.5	5.8
Raleigh	22 830	37 203	22 409	37 622	3.1	5.2	3.0	5.3
Rocky Mount	3 095	5 172	3 025	5 242	4.7	8.1	4.6	8.3
Wilmington	5 013	8 025	4 934	8 152	3.2	5.4	3.2	5.5
Winston-Salem	11 231	19 087	11 065	19 432	3.3	5.9	3.3	6.0
North Dakota	6 535	15 905	7 968	16 424	1.6	4.0	2.0	4.1
Bismarck	1 164	2 163	1 449	2 325	1.7	3.2	2.2	3.4
Fargo	2 194	4 098	2 545	4 263	1.6	2.9	1.8	3.0
Grand Forks	974	1 652	1 126	1 868	1.8	3.0	2.1	3.4
Ohio	220 052	336 924	214 762	297 258	3.8	5.8	3.7	5.2
Akron	14 090	21 220	13 843	18 715	3.9	6.0	3.8	5.4
Canton-Massillon	8 326	11 394	8 519	10 108	4.2	5.7	4.3	5.3
Cincinnati	39 612	63 724	37 845	53 795	3.5	5.6	3.4	4.8
Cleveland-Elyria	34 760	66 434	34 448	58 214	3.3	6.5	3.3	5.8
Columbus	37 429	61 074	36 112	53 190	3.4	5.5	3.3	4.9
Dayton	15 638	23 327	14 344	20 338	4.0	5.8	3.7	5.2
Lima	1 831	2 907	1 775	2 486	3.8	6.0	3.7	5.3
Mansfield	2 159	3 119	2 260	2 888	4.2	5.8	4.3	5.5
Springfield	3 099	3 654	2 657	3 228	4.8	5.6	4.2	5.1
Toledo	12 171	19 206	11 753	16 640	4.0	6.2	3.9	5.6
Weirton-Steubenville	2 823	3 579	2 722	3 308	5.5	7.1	5.4	6.7
Youngstown-Warren-Boardman	12 586	17 175	12 820	15 316	5.3	7.5	5.4	6.9
Oklahoma	62 648	114 673	59 724	108 454	3.4	6.1	3.2	5.8
Enid	798	1 551	808	1 482	3.0	5.9	3.0	5.6
Lawton	1 885	3 171	1 785	2 921	3.7	6.2	3.5	5.7
Oklahoma City	20 734	41 299	20 172	38 368	3.0	5.9	2.9	5.5
Tulsa	17 223	31 853	15 600	30 074	3.5	6.6	3.2	6.2
Oregon	63 668	135 573	61 282	115 365	3.0	6.3	2.9	5.5
Albany	2 056	3 803	1 993	3 243	3.5	6.3	3.4	5.5
Bend-Redmond	2 818	5 885	2 831	5 178	2.9	6.1	3.0	5.4
Corvallis	1 142	2 244	1 026	1 814	2.3	4.7	2.1	3.8
Eugene	5 982	11 752	5 730	9 729	3.3	6.2	3.2	5.2
Grants Pass	1 396	2 333	1 383	1 983	3.9	6.5	3.9	5.7
Medford	3 311	6 670	3 208	5 650	3.2	6.2	3.1	5.4
Portland-Vancouver-Hillsboro	40 298	88 955	38 933	77 952	3.0	6.6	2.9	5.9
Salem	6 471	11 895	6 149	10 210	3.2	5.9	3.0	5.2
Pennsylvania	289 032	443 538	284 629	382 770	4.4	7.0	4.4	6.1
Allentown-Bethlehem-Easton	19 561	29 963	18 902	27 545	4.4	6.9	4.2	6.3
Altoona	2 721	3 462	2 720	3 152	4.6	6.0	4.6	5.5
Bloomsburg-Berwick	1 797	2 269	1 786	2 006	4.2	5.3	4.1	4.7
Chambersburg-Waynesboro	3 046	4 469	2 965	3 603	3.9	5.8	3.8	4.7
East Stroudsburg	4 572	6 820	4 586	5 888	5.5	8.7	5.5	7.6
Erie	5 779	9 410	5 948	8 450	4.5	7.7	4.6	6.9
Gettysburg	1 828	2 491	1 756	2 121	3.3	4.5	3.2	3.9
Harrisburg-Carlisle	11 788	17 564	11 190	15 127	3.9	5.8	3.7	5.0
Johnstown	2 911	3 649	3 077	3 346	5.0	6.5	5.3	6.0
Lancaster	10 094	14 979	9 624	12 614	3.5	5.2	3.4	4.4

Table 7-3. Unemployment Number and Rate by State and Selected Metropolitan Area October 2019– November 2020—*Continued*

(Number, rate.)

State and area	October 2019	October 2020	November 2019	November 2020	October 2019	October 2020	November 2019	November 2020
Pennsylvania—*Continued*								
Lebanon	2 898	4 228	2 819	3 671	4.0	5.9	3.9	5.1
Philadelphia-Camden-Wilmington	133 014	228 675	127 987	217 114	4.2	7.4	4.1	7.1
Pittsburgh	52 756	81 747	52 783	71 263	4.3	6.9	4.3	6.1
Reading	9 638	15 148	9 413	12 954	4.4	6.8	4.3	5.9
Scranton—Wilkes-Barre—Hazleton	14 641	21 327	14 775	18 824	5.2	8.1	5.3	7.2
State College	2 815	3 189	2 685	2 801	3.4	4.2	3.3	3.7
Williamsport	2 653	3 683	2 714	3 273	4.6	7.0	4.7	6.2
York-Hanover	9 351	13 515	8 998	11 509	3.9	5.8	3.8	4.9
Rhode Island	16 402	35 139	18 234	37 810	2.9	6.5	3.3	7.0
Providence-Warwick	20 250	43 817	21 889	45 560	2.9	6.5	3.1	6.8
South Carolina	56 883	97 269	53 912	95 625	2.4	4.1	2.3	4.1
Charleston-North Charleston	7 837	15 767	7 436	15 118	2.0	4.0	1.9	4.0
Columbia	9 020	15 327	8 612	15 362	2.2	3.7	2.1	3.9
Florence	2 509	4 207	2 368	4 119	2.6	4.3	2.4	4.3
Greenville-Anderson-Mauldin	9 516	15 717	9 044	15 541	2.2	3.5	2.1	3.6
Hilton Head Island-Bluffton-Beaufort	1 971	3 014	1 815	2 974	2.2	3.3	2.0	3.3
Myrtle Beach-Conway-North Myrtle Beach	6 701	10 744	6 593	10 739	3.3	5.6	3.3	5.7
Spartanburg	3 638	7 198	3 491	6 887	2.2	4.4	2.1	4.3
Sumter	1 249	2 066	1 210	2 059	2.8	4.7	2.8	5.0
South Dakota	14 240	15 376	15 316	15 324	3.0	3.3	3.3	3.3
Rapid City	2 438	2 674	2 657	2 669	3.2	3.7	3.6	3.7
Sioux Falls	4 067	4 623	4 354	4 553	2.6	3.0	2.8	2.9
Tennessee	108 485	238 253	104 839	172 514	3.2	7.2	3.1	5.0
Chattanooga	8 517	15 796	8 207	12 365	3.1	5.6	3.0	4.3
Clarksville	5 012	8 797	4 536	6 543	4.2	7.5	3.8	5.4
Cleveland	1 935	4 089	1 923	3 003	3.2	6.7	3.1	4.7
Jackson	2 227	4 686	2 138	3 530	3.4	7.3	3.3	5.3
Johnson City	3 116	6 057	3 143	4 725	3.4	6.7	3.4	5.0
Kingsport-Bristol-Bristol	4 728	8 669	4 577	6 867	3.4	6.5	3.3	5.0
Knoxville	12 940	25 861	12 734	19 548	3.0	6.0	2.9	4.3
Memphis	25 024	63 387	25 064	44 486	3.9	9.6	3.9	6.7
Morristown	1 882	3 462	1 849	2 599	3.5	6.5	3.5	4.7
Nashville-Davidson—Murfreesboro—Franklin	28 627	65 182	26 697	46 670	2.6	6.1	2.4	4.2
Texas	474 329	938 545	480 312	1 129 593	3.3	6.7	3.4	8.0
Abilene	2 261	3 830	2 271	4 762	2.8	4.9	2.8	6.0
Amarillo	3 255	5 616	3 269	6 906	2.4	4.4	2.5	5.4
Austin-Round Rock	32 040	63 023	31 794	74 345	2.6	5.0	2.5	5.9
Beaumont-Port Arthur	8 866	16 930	9 192	20 592	5.1	9.9	5.3	11.8
Brownsville-Harlingen	8 543	15 346	8 968	18 707	5.1	9.3	5.4	11.2
College Station-Bryan	3 663	6 283	3 621	7 740	2.6	4.5	2.6	5.6
Corpus Christi	8 281	16 553	8 506	20 200	4.0	8.3	4.1	10.0
Dallas-Fort Worth-Arlington	126 006	241 480	124 584	289 682	3.1	6.0	3.1	7.1
El Paso	13 625	25 961	13 630	34 695	3.7	7.1	3.7	9.3
Houston-The Woodlands-Sugar Land	124 867	262 368	127 368	309 221	3.6	7.7	3.7	8.9
Killeen-Temple	6 443	10 687	6 497	13 120	3.6	6.0	3.6	7.4
Laredo	4 081	8 946	4 206	10 705	3.4	7.7	3.5	9.1
Longview	3 557	7 243	3 624	8 696	3.6	7.5	3.6	8.9
Lubbock	4 398	8 167	4 327	10 088	2.7	5.0	2.6	6.2
McAllen-Edinburg-Mission	20 055	36 437	22 062	44 984	5.7	10.3	6.2	12.5
Midland	2 309	8 344	2 364	9 789	2.1	8.0	2.1	9.3
Odessa	2 426	9 682	2 563	11 432	2.7	11.2	2.9	13.1
San Angelo	1 613	3 098	1 625	3 850	2.9	5.8	2.9	7.2
San Antonio-New Braunfels	36 236	74 741	36 267	89 224	3.0	6.2	3.0	7.3
Sherman-Denison	1 914	3 244	1 941	3 988	3.0	5.0	3.0	6.1
Texarkana	2 561	3 919	2 524	4 513	3.9	6.0	3.9	6.9
Tyler	3 444	6 404	3 493	7 732	3.2	5.9	3.2	7.1
Victoria	1 537	3 307	1 640	4 048	3.3	7.3	3.5	8.9
Waco	3 983	6 843	3 952	8 499	3.2	5.3	3.1	6.6
Wichita Falls	1 933	3 864	1 933	4 738	2.9	6.0	2.9	7.3
Utah	34 061	61 284	33 756	64 664	2.1	3.7	2.1	3.9
Logan	1 253	1 781	1 225	1 952	1.7	2.4	1.7	2.6
Ogden-Clearfield	6 900	11 558	6 829	12 356	2.1	3.4	2.0	3.6
Provo-Orem	6 174	9 893	5 997	10 647	1.9	3.1	1.9	3.3
St. George	1 839	3 280	1 831	3 404	2.4	4.1	2.4	4.3
Salt Lake City	14 097	27 713	13 869	28 617	2.1	4.1	2.0	4.2
Vermont	5 798	7 610	7 647	9 162	1.7	2.4	2.3	2.8
Burlington-South Burlington	1 809	2 513	2 347	3 004	1.4	2.2	1.9	2.5

Table 7-3. Unemployment Number and Rate by State and Selected Metropolitan Area October 2019–November 2020—*Continued*

(Number, rate.)

State and area	Number				Rate			
	October 2019	October 2020	November 2019	November 2020	October 2019	October 2020	November 2019	November 2020
Virginia	111 836	213 299	108 653	195 153	2.5	5.0	2.5	4.6
Blacksburg-Christiansburg-Radford	2 419	3 282	2 367	3 151	2.7	3.8	2.6	3.6
Charlottesville	2 742	5 026	2 708	4 615	2.2	4.2	2.2	3.8
Harrisonburg	1 555	2 307	1 521	2 181	2.3	3.6	2.2	3.4
Lynchburg	3 609	5 538	3 533	5 241	2.9	4.8	2.9	4.5
Richmond	18 686	36 766	17 983	33 055	2.7	5.5	2.6	5.0
Roanoke	4 079	7 011	3 996	6 514	2.6	4.6	2.5	4.3
Staunton-Waynesboro	1 449	2 309	1 375	2 192	2.4	3.8	2.2	3.6
Virginia Beach-Norfolk-Newport News	24 317	48 422	23 484	43 479	2.8	5.8	2.7	5.2
Winchester	1 781	2 590	1 747	2 423	2.4	3.7	2.3	3.5
Washington	143 866	221 082	152 256	225 136	3.6	5.5	3.9	5.9
Bellingham	5 029	7 814	5 365	8 133	4.3	6.3	4.6	7.0
Bremerton-Silverdale	5 062	7 447	5 233	7 804	3.9	5.3	4.0	6.0
Kennewick-Richland	6 334	8 406	7 285	9 644	4.3	5.3	5.0	6.5
Longview	2 489	3 423	2 618	3 534	5.2	6.7	5.4	7.4
Mount Vernon-Anacortes	2 939	4 248	3 219	4 632	4.6	6.5	5.1	7.6
Olympia-Tumwate	6 130	8 464	6 423	8 982	4.2	5.5	4.4	6.3
Seattle-Tacoma-Bellevue	66 178	113 336	66 544	107 862	3.0	5.2	3.0	5.1
Spokane-Spokane Valley	12 215	16 826	13 201	18 186	4.3	5.8	4.6	6.8
Walla Walla	1 322	1 560	1 393	1 800	3.9	4.6	4.2	5.7
Wenatchee	2 565	3 579	3 164	4 127	3.8	5.3	4.9	6.6
Yakima	6 350	8 428	8 299	10 033	4.6	6.1	6.4	7.7
West Virginia	36 871	44 290	38 187	44 072	4.6	5.8	4.8	5.7
Beckley	2 200	2 945	2 339	2 930	4.6	6.3	5.0	6.4
Charleston	4 190	5 994	4 312	5 823	4.5	6.6	4.6	6.4
Huntington-Ashland	6 675	8 663	6 608	7 944	4.5	6.0	4.5	5.5
Morgantown	2 509	2 952	2 521	2 950	3.5	4.2	3.5	4.2
Parkersburg-Vienna	1 940	2 305	2 004	2 311	4.9	5.9	5.1	5.9
Wheeling	3 521	3 869	3 670	3 775	5.3	6.4	5.5	6.3
Wisconsin	86 937	163 416	93 112	138 654	2.8	5.2	3.0	4.5
Appleton	3 149	5 480	3 317	4 582	2.4	4.2	2.6	3.5
Eau Claire	2 397	3 985	2 535	3 715	2.6	4.3	2.8	4.0
Fond du Lac	1 419	2 326	1 435	2 136	2.5	3.9	2.5	3.6
Green Bay	4 568	8 385	4 862	6 996	2.6	4.8	2.8	4.0
Janesville-Beloit	2 760	4 838	3 009	4 041	3.2	5.6	3.5	4.8
La Crosse-Onalaska	1 807	2 980	1 865	2 613	2.3	3.9	2.4	3.4
Madison	8 482	16 684	8 767	13 993	2.2	4.2	2.2	3.6
Milwaukee-Waukesha-West Allis	25 904	55 484	26 957	44 496	3.2	6.6	3.3	5.4
Oshkosh-Neenah	2 411	3 954	2 498	3 375	2.6	4.2	2.7	3.6
Racine	3 547	6 544	3 721	5 305	3.6	6.4	3.8	5.2
Sheboygan	1 513	2 631	1 635	2 299	2.5	4.2	2.7	3.7
Wausau	1 788	2 852	1 854	2 514	2.4	3.9	2.5	3.4
Wyoming	9 855	14 953	10 771	14 532	3.4	5.1	3.7	4.9
Casper	1 488	3 043	1 570	2 805	3.8	7.7	4.0	7.0
Cheyenne	1 632	2 189	1 659	2 059	3.4	4.5	3.4	4.2

Table 7-4. Job Openings Levels and Rates, by Industry, 2009–October 2020

(Seasonally adjusted, levels in thousands, rates per 100.)

Year and month	Level											
	Total nonfarm[1]	Total private[1]	Construction	Manufacturing	Trade, transportation, and utilities[2]	Retail trade	Professional and business services	Education and health services	Leisure and hospitality[3]	Accommodation and food services	Government[4]	State and local government
2009												
January	2 731	2 382	38	112	504	376	536	590	241	206	349	291
February	2 838	2 470	73	130	452	323	533	551	326	296	368	306
March	2 521	2 152	48	111	442	297	452	507	263	239	369	264
April	2 343	1 976	29	103	341	219	438	521	273	247	367	315
May	2 574	2 294	51	99	547	406	446	531	296	268	280	253
June	2 517	2 188	67	107	451	299	405	523	283	264	329	286
July	2 264	1 980	50	110	303	196	449	536	259	223	284	233
August	2 365	2 058	65	123	426	281	420	546	198	173	307	275
September	2 481	2 199	66	131	381	261	464	537	286	260	282	226
October	2 422	2 045	54	132	339	215	413	531	261	244	377	274
November	2 435	2 096	49	127	365	241	435	508	279	251	338	250
December	2 487	2 169	55	152	410	299	432	543	258	239	318	247
2010												
January	2 833	2 437	54	142	451	332	457	623	279	257	396	249
February	2 651	2 303	65	157	468	343	430	521	266	239	348	220
March	2 679	2 257	86	153	500	348	390	528	239	211	422	261
April	3 217	2 587	101	191	448	294	513	521	283	255	631	256
May	3 019	2 622	88	190	486	323	603	510	312	260	398	246
June	2 813	2 511	83	210	474	314	582	458	329	267	301	220
July	3 127	2 806	113	241	483	324	621	543	323	285	321	239
August	3 025	2 674	59	188	451	284	641	497	364	319	351	246
September	2 912	2 582	78	189	440	255	634	512	317	283	330	253
October	3 256	2 911	67	198	513	333	652	630	417	382	345	275
November	3 134	2 810	66	207	490	327	700	551	319	291	324	257
December	2 969	2 584	32	171	506	325	579	546	352	312	385	293
2011												
January	3 100	2 770	61	217	557	353	538	552	366	331	330	269
February	3 213	2 894	45	209	643	397	610	571	389	342	319	256
March	3 253	2 921	67	211	568	351	641	600	393	352	332	272
April	3 337	2 985	91	247	628	401	590	610	331	289	352	298
May	3 207	2 901	124	220	640	431	585	587	319	279	306	240
June	3 467	3 103	77	217	668	451	676	616	406	325	364	307
July	3 676	3 348	94	250	679	437	790	642	363	288	328	260
August	3 358	3 026	111	234	570	396	669	650	392	343	332	279
September	3 763	3 371	87	254	637	392	891	608	428	362	392	333
October	3 650	3 283	82	233	687	410	708	635	429	366	367	294
November	3 485	3 142	63	200	739	497	667	637	434	380	342	287
December	3 662	3 311	56	215	666	442	847	628	441	402	351	284
2012												
January	3 904	3 565	85	246	666	403	948	684	453	380	339	275
February	3 605	3 203	61	237	651	389	747	677	379	320	403	323
March	3 976	3 566	94	312	695	448	837	689	447	398	409	321
April	3 878	3 497	134	265	640	384	772	686	481	404	381	300
May	3 861	3 455	105	306	624	372	750	727	458	393	405	336
June	3 916	3 524	70	308	631	377	774	760	483	411	393	319
July	3 790	3 417	95	287	671	416	740	693	489	424	373	311
August	3 839	3 417	134	268	747	483	730	665	423	364	422	327
September	3 861	3 482	92	252	780	496	694	709	422	368	379	309
October	3 808	3 428	107	278	553	305	755	705	483	429	380	315
November	3 787	3 439	73	220	679	469	749	731	499	442	348	298
December	3 840	3 446	93	223	775	507	697	705	481	415	393	320
2013												
January	3 915	3 477	116	251	751	473	776	632	470	415	438	353
February	3 981	3 553	121	276	651	402	757	687	520	468	428	356
March	4 080	3 672	121	260	732	472	750	710	514	451	408	345
April	4 078	3 635	133	257	804	534	761	721	478	430	442	356
May	4 173	3 755	137	253	817	558	788	689	469	422	418	369
June	4 166	3 756	146	223	888	634	749	682	489	438	410	362
July	3 946	3 576	111	254	727	488	696	657	503	451	370	321
August	4 112	3 718	129	286	769	484	809	755	523	429	393	352
September	4 105	3 711	121	270	815	530	751	669	550	482	394	343
October	4 268	3 873	141	302	793	530	819	684	540	450	395	352
November	4 002	3 616	117	272	793	508	745	657	543	462	386	332
December	3 996	3 662	86	265	799	525	774	613	585	504	334	292
2014												
January	4 131	3 756	152	261	829	528	713	709	596	505	375	327
February	4 347	3 939	122	279	879	630	848	728	558	485	409	350
March	4 388	3 949	130	284	937	665	773	756	571	518	439	372
April	4 662	4 204	137	288	962	652	842	728	662	570	458	391
May	4 775	4 326	137	301	939	625	857	818	710	621	449	381
June	4 999	4 473	171	320	947	634	916	847	674	598	526	460
July	4 919	4 450	158	330	939	601	908	883	630	566	469	410
August	5 383	4 946	148	327	1 183	840	967	931	705	621	437	363
September	4 876	4 412	105	312	923	589	941	876	708	632	464	395
October	5 066	4 635	156	301	970	598	956	893	671	604	431	363
November	4 719	4 270	104	285	871	508	970	796	631	573	449	374
December	4 981	4 499	100	281	870	544	1 041	937	707	621	482	411

[1]Includes natural resources and mining, information, financial activities, and other services, not shown separately.
[2]Includes wholesale trade and transportation, warehousing, and utilities, not shown separately.
[3]Includes arts, entertainment, and recreation, not shown separately.
[4]Includes federal government, not shown separately.

Table 7-4. Job Openings Levels and Rates, by Industry, 2009–October 2020—*Continued*

(Seasonally adjusted, levels in thousands, rates per 100.)

Year and month	Rate											
	Total[1]	Total private[1]	Construction	Manufacturing	Trade, transportation, and utilities[2]	Retail trade	Professional and business services	Education and health services	Leisure and hospitality[3]	Accommodation and food services	Government[4]	State and local government
2009												
January	2.0	2.1	0.6	0.9	1.9	2.5	3.0	2.9	1.8	1.8	1.5	1.4
February	2.1	2.2	1.1	1.0	1.8	2.1	3.1	2.7	2.4	2.6	1.6	1.5
March	1.9	1.9	0.8	0.9	1.7	2.0	2.6	2.5	2.0	2.1	1.6	1.3
April	1.7	1.8	0.5	0.8	1.3	1.5	2.6	2.6	2.0	2.2	1.6	1.6
May	1.9	2.1	0.8	0.8	2.2	2.7	2.6	2.6	2.2	2.3	1.2	1.3
June	1.9	2.0	1.1	0.9	1.8	2.0	2.4	2.6	2.1	2.3	1.4	1.4
July	1.7	1.8	0.8	0.9	1.2	1.3	2.7	2.7	1.9	2.0	1.2	1.2
August	1.8	1.9	1.1	1.0	1.7	1.9	2.5	2.7	1.5	1.5	1.3	1.4
September	1.9	2.0	1.1	1.1	1.5	1.8	2.7	2.7	2.1	2.3	1.2	1.1
October	1.8	1.9	0.9	1.1	1.4	1.5	2.4	2.6	2.0	2.2	1.6	1.4
November	1.8	1.9	0.8	1.1	1.5	1.7	2.6	2.5	2.1	2.2	1.5	1.3
December	1.9	2.0	1.0	1.3	1.6	2.0	2.5	2.7	2.0	2.1	1.4	1.2
2010												
January	2.1	2.2	1.0	1.2	1.8	2.3	2.7	3.0	2.1	2.3	1.7	1.3
February	2.0	2.1	1.2	1.3	1.9	2.3	2.5	2.6	2.0	2.1	1.5	1.1
March	2.0	2.1	1.5	1.3	2.0	2.3	2.3	2.6	1.8	1.9	1.8	1.3
April	2.4	2.3	1.8	1.6	1.8	2.0	3.0	2.6	2.1	2.3	2.7	1.3
May	2.3	2.4	1.6	1.6	1.9	2.2	3.5	2.5	2.3	2.3	1.7	1.2
June	2.1	2.3	1.5	1.8	1.9	2.1	3.4	2.2	2.5	2.3	1.3	1.1
July	2.3	2.5	2.0	2.0	1.9	2.2	3.6	2.6	2.4	2.5	1.4	1.2
August	2.3	2.4	1.0	1.6	1.8	1.9	3.7	2.4	2.7	2.8	1.5	1.2
September	2.2	2.3	1.4	1.6	1.8	1.7	3.6	2.5	2.4	2.5	1.5	1.3
October	2.4	2.6	1.2	1.7	2.0	2.2	3.7	3.0	3.1	3.3	1.5	1.4
November	2.3	2.5	1.2	1.8	1.9	2.2	4.0	2.7	2.4	2.5	1.4	1.3
December	2.2	2.3	0.6	1.5	2.0	2.2	3.3	2.6	2.6	2.7	1.7	1.5
2011												
January	2.3	2.5	1.1	1.8	2.2	2.4	3.1	2.7	2.7	2.9	1.5	1.4
February	2.4	2.6	0.8	1.8	2.5	2.7	3.4	2.8	2.9	2.9	1.4	1.3
March	2.4	2.6	1.2	1.8	2.2	2.3	3.6	2.9	2.9	3.0	1.5	1.4
April	2.5	2.7	1.6	2.1	2.5	2.7	3.3	2.9	2.4	2.5	1.6	1.5
May	2.4	2.6	2.2	1.8	2.5	2.9	3.3	2.8	2.3	2.4	1.4	1.2
June	2.6	2.7	1.4	1.8	2.6	3.0	3.8	2.9	3.0	2.8	1.6	1.6
July	2.7	3.0	1.7	2.1	2.6	2.9	4.3	3.1	2.6	2.5	1.5	1.3
August	2.5	2.7	2.0	1.9	2.2	2.6	3.7	3.1	2.8	2.9	1.5	1.4
September	2.8	3.0	1.5	2.1	2.5	2.6	4.8	2.9	3.1	3.1	1.8	1.7
October	2.7	2.9	1.4	1.9	2.7	2.7	3.9	3.0	3.1	3.1	1.6	1.5
November	2.6	2.8	1.1	1.7	2.9	3.3	3.7	3.0	3.1	3.2	1.5	1.5
December	2.7	2.9	1.0	1.8	2.6	2.9	4.6	3.0	3.2	3.3	1.6	1.5
2012												
January	2.8	3.1	1.5	2.0	2.6	2.7	5.1	3.2	3.2	3.2	1.5	1.4
February	2.6	2.8	1.1	2.0	2.5	2.6	4.0	3.2	2.7	2.7	1.8	1.7
March	2.9	3.1	1.6	2.6	2.7	2.9	4.5	3.2	3.2	3.3	1.8	1.7
April	2.8	3.0	2.3	2.2	2.5	2.5	4.1	3.2	3.4	3.3	1.7	1.5
May	2.8	3.0	1.8	2.5	2.4	2.4	4.0	3.4	3.2	3.2	1.8	1.7
June	2.8	3.0	1.2	2.5	2.4	2.5	4.1	3.5	3.4	3.4	1.8	1.6
July	2.7	3.0	1.7	2.3	2.6	2.7	3.9	3.2	3.4	3.5	1.7	1.6
August	2.8	2.9	2.3	2.2	2.9	3.2	3.9	3.1	3.0	3.0	1.9	1.7
September	2.8	3.0	1.6	2.1	3.0	3.2	3.7	3.3	3.0	3.0	1.7	1.6
October	2.7	2.9	1.9	2.3	2.1	2.0	4.0	3.3	3.4	3.5	1.7	1.6
November	2.7	3.0	1.3	1.8	2.6	3.0	4.0	3.4	3.5	3.6	1.6	1.5
December	2.8	3.0	1.6	1.8	2.9	3.3	3.7	3.3	3.3	3.3	1.8	1.6
2013												
January	2.8	3.0	2.0	2.0	2.8	3.1	4.1	2.9	3.2	3.3	2.0	1.8
February	2.9	3.0	2.0	2.2	2.5	2.6	4.0	3.2	3.6	3.7	1.9	1.8
March	2.9	3.1	2.0	2.1	2.8	3.1	3.9	3.3	3.5	3.6	1.8	1.8
April	2.9	3.1	2.2	2.1	3.0	3.4	4.0	3.3	3.3	3.4	2.0	1.8
May	3.0	3.2	2.3	2.1	3.1	3.6	4.1	3.2	3.2	3.4	1.9	1.9
June	3.0	3.2	2.4	1.8	3.3	4.0	3.9	3.1	3.3	3.5	1.9	1.9
July	2.8	3.0	1.9	2.1	2.7	3.1	3.6	3.0	3.4	3.5	1.7	1.7
August	2.9	3.1	2.2	2.3	2.9	3.1	4.2	3.4	3.5	3.4	1.8	1.8
September	2.9	3.1	2.0	2.2	3.0	3.4	3.9	3.1	3.7	3.8	1.8	1.8
October	3.0	3.3	2.3	2.4	3.0	3.4	4.2	3.1	3.6	3.5	1.8	1.8
November	2.8	3.0	1.9	2.2	3.0	3.2	3.8	3.0	3.6	3.6	1.7	1.7
December	2.8	3.1	1.4	2.1	3.0	3.3	4.0	2.8	3.9	3.9	1.5	1.5
2014												
January	2.9	3.1	2.5	2.1	3.1	3.3	3.6	3.2	4.0	3.9	1.7	1.7
February	3.1	3.3	2.0	2.3	3.3	4.0	4.3	3.3	3.7	3.8	1.8	1.8
March	3.1	3.3	2.1	2.3	3.5	4.2	3.9	3.4	3.8	4.0	2.0	1.9
April	3.3	3.5	2.2	2.3	3.5	4.1	4.2	3.3	4.3	4.4	2.1	2.0
May	3.3	3.6	2.2	2.4	3.5	3.9	4.3	3.7	4.6	4.7	2.0	2.0
June	3.5	3.7	2.7	2.6	3.5	4.0	4.6	3.8	4.4	4.5	2.3	2.3
July	3.4	3.7	2.5	2.6	3.4	3.8	4.5	4.0	4.1	4.3	2.1	2.1
August	3.7	4.0	2.3	2.6	4.3	5.2	4.8	4.2	4.6	4.7	2.0	1.9
September	3.4	3.6	1.7	2.5	3.4	3.7	4.7	3.9	4.6	4.8	2.1	2.0
October	3.5	3.8	2.4	2.4	3.5	3.7	4.7	4.0	4.3	4.5	1.9	1.9
November	3.3	3.5	1.6	2.3	3.2	3.2	4.8	3.5	4.1	4.3	2.0	1.9
December	3.4	3.7	1.6	2.2	3.2	3.4	5.1	4.1	4.5	4.6	2.1	2.1

[1]Includes natural resources and mining, information, financial activities, and other services, not shown separately.
[2]Includes wholesale trade and transportation, warehousing, and utilities, not shown separately.
[3]Includes arts, entertainment, and recreation, not shown separately.
[4]Includes federal government, not shown separately.

Table 7-4. Job Openings Levels and Rates, by Industry, 2009–October 2020—*Continued*

(Seasonally adjusted, levels in thousands, rates per 100.)

Year and month	Level											
	Total nonfarm[1]	Total private[1]	Construction	Manufacturing	Trade, transportation, and utilities[2]	Retail trade	Professional and business services	Education and health services	Leisure and hospitality[3]	Accommodation and food services	Government[4]	State and local government
2015												
January	5 362	4 854	148	322	998	616	1 028	922	802	716	508	427
February	5 446	4 918	153	301	1 061	681	1 082	922	750	653	528	430
March	5 208	4 688	172	324	898	527	1 101	904	719	630	520	426
April	5 712	5 160	177	334	998	589	1 239	1 009	720	648	552	444
May	5 599	5 065	180	332	1 007	543	1 235	986	703	632	534	454
June	5 263	4 783	160	294	951	572	1 109	1 005	666	599	479	390
July	6 143	5 602	155	374	1 259	823	1 146	1 185	761	692	541	446
August	5 510	5 018	167	320	1 038	661	1 091	1 040	695	637	492	402
September	5 445	4 980	107	317	1 051	678	1 110	1 068	705	631	465	395
October	5 832	5 313	145	321	1 111	655	1 212	1 079	785	708	520	434
November	5 573	5 074	91	258	1 010	578	1 285	1 096	764	678	500	406
December	5 676	5 159	116	305	999	642	1 199	1 062	747	670	517	426
2016												
January	5 994	5 487	160	317	1 088	732	1 294	1 184	752	662	507	411
February	5 757	5 267	197	320	1 064	714	1 238	1 017	764	689	490	386
March	6 137	5 629	214	337	1 059	710	1 488	1 075	818	703	508	408
April	5 868	5 338	193	399	1 082	655	1 073	1 114	762	650	531	424
May	5 812	5 265	184	361	1 077	718	1 170	1 098	744	653	546	450
June	5 768	5 278	186	376	1 077	716	1 140	1 066	799	700	490	404
July	6 094	5 510	239	377	1 088	696	1 254	1 137	758	653	584	489
August	5 716	5 209	205	333	1 030	641	1 097	1 053	805	710	507	407
September	5 816	5 291	242	321	1 028	694	1 198	1 104	732	652	524	416
October	5 626	5 149	225	299	1 035	670	978	1 238	765	657	477	400
November	5 867	5 310	179	315	996	646	1 216	1 182	767	660	557	466
December	5 835	5 300	139	341	1 050	683	1 073	1 195	748	654	535	387
2017												
January	5 607	5 130	151	371	967	618	996	1 156	737	652	477	397
February	5 872	5 361	185	361	1 019	644	987	1 227	893	805	511	430
March	5 816	5 288	183	399	1 087	690	1 024	1 125	742	649	528	438
April	6 142	5 575	222	387	1 031	628	1 054	1 115	841	759	567	474
May	5 851	5 294	180	350	1 048	679	1 016	1 100	836	779	557	447
June	6 351	5 772	218	406	1 110	674	1 241	1 176	854	737	579	474
July	6 354	5 802	243	391	1 172	692	1 123	1 173	865	757	551	449
August	6 335	5 794	225	422	1 249	763	1 107	1 174	895	799	541	459
September	6 239	5 684	181	427	1 200	731	1 119	1 132	759	656	555	466
October	6 383	5 854	207	424	1 152	746	1 301	1 136	826	735	529	451
November	6 204	5 694	218	417	1 293	948	1 029	1 116	879	789	510	435
December	6 235	5 688	180	381	1 446	1 004	953	1 135	886	794	547	458
2018												
January	6 645	6 073	245	440	1 396	902	1 125	1 174	929	838	571	444
February	6 575	5 969	207	438	1 323	856	1 115	1 177	921	803	606	538
March	6 865	6 215	230	424	1 420	926	1 204	1 231	926	829	650	535
April	6 985	6 371	250	455	1 524	1 029	1 209	1 234	960	854	614	531
May	7 028	6 419	276	465	1 486	969	1 234	1 205	967	846	609	506
June	7 280	6 633	319	474	1 472	965	1 263	1 260	1 074	913	648	530
July	7 326	6 638	310	478	1 465	935	1 256	1 257	1 027	932	688	563
August	7 249	6 518	313	502	1 289	789	1 322	1 248	1 005	898	732	606
September	7 282	6 672	293	471	1 480	895	1 337	1 270	1 058	962	609	526
October	7 237	6 627	279	494	1 400	928	1 337	1 236	1 007	914	609	513
November	7 509	6 858	272	502	1 632	1 088	1 329	1 252	1 018	916	651	536
December	7 303	6 687	291	441	1 436	945	1 351	1 291	1 082	956	616	518
2019												
January	7 520	6 808	299	427	1 429	808	1 386	1 379	1 125	1 019	712	573
February	7 048	6 343	277	462	1 258	791	1 404	1 205	1 001	897	704	575
March	7 364	6 625	354	441	1 298	749	1 355	1 378	1 022	918	739	604
April	7 284	6 540	430	479	1 346	740	1 377	1 377	1 017	903	744	590
May	7 300	6 600	373	482	1 283	746	1 268	1 358	1 018	898	701	590
June	7 185	6 497	325	486	1 342	813	1 290	1 303	959	849	688	572
July	7 236	6 529	353	477	1 288	838	1 287	1 325	957	844	707	579
August	7 166	6 429	353	445	1 289	792	1 288	1 315	943	821	738	622
September	7 046	6 325	333	441	1 280	743	1 260	1 216	995	847	721	608
October	7 309	6 546	325	403	1 472	877	1 218	1 306	975	840	763	638
November	6 793	6 070	215	401	1 271	752	1 217	1 311	966	845	723	606
December	6 552	5 838	216	360	1 192	762	1 223	1 203	916	789	715	626
2020												
January	7 012	6 231	267	408	1 214	759	1 265	1 294	919	771	781	669
February	7 004	6 236	296	422	1 168	715	1 357	1 252	950	815	769	649
March	6 011	5 284	240	310	1 069	626	1 192	1 193	664	534	727	596
April	4 996	4 332	247	315	883	521	982	1 051	314	273	664	550
May	5 371	4 736	315	306	997	670	976	975	622	521	635	564
June	6 001	5 347	244	346	1 075	669	1 077	1 089	838	725	654	542
July	6 697	5 879	332	430	1 181	773	1 178	1 288	770	676	818	536
August	6 352	5 636	275	469	1 130	705	1 195	1 182	761	678	716	594
September	6 494	5 795	223	492	1 142	671	1 268	1 215	772	686	699	605
October	6 632	5 936	246	531	1 083	643	1 220	1 373	817	718	696	601

[1]Includes natural resources and mining, information, financial activities, and other services, not shown separately.
[2]Includes wholesale trade and transportation, warehousing, and utilities, not shown separately.
[3]Includes arts, entertainment, and recreation, not shown separately.
[4]Includes federal government, not shown separately.

Table 7-4. Job Openings Levels and Rates, by Industry, 2009–October 2020—*Continued*

(Seasonally adjusted, levels in thousands, rates per 100.)

Year and month	Total[1]	Total private[1]	Construction	Manufacturing	Trade, transportation, and utilities[2]	Retail trade	Professional and business services	Education and health services	Leisure and hospitality[3]	Accommodation and food services	Government[4]	State and local government
2015												
January	3.7	3.9	2.3	2.6	3.6	3.8	5.0	4.1	5.1	5.3	2.3	2.2
February	3.7	4.0	2.3	2.4	3.8	4.2	5.3	4.1	4.8	4.8	2.3	2.2
March	3.6	3.8	2.6	2.6	3.3	3.3	5.3	4.0	4.6	4.7	2.3	2.2
April	3.9	4.1	2.7	2.6	3.6	3.6	6.0	4.4	4.6	4.8	2.4	2.3
May	3.8	4.1	2.7	2.6	3.6	3.4	5.9	4.3	4.4	4.7	2.4	2.3
June	3.6	3.8	2.4	2.3	3.4	3.5	5.3	4.4	4.2	4.4	2.1	2.0
July	4.1	4.5	2.3	2.9	4.5	5.0	5.5	5.1	4.8	5.1	2.4	2.3
August	3.7	4.0	2.5	2.5	3.7	4.1	5.2	4.5	4.4	4.7	2.2	2.0
September	3.7	4.0	1.6	2.5	3.8	4.2	5.3	4.6	4.4	4.6	2.1	2.0
October	3.9	4.2	2.2	2.5	4.0	4.0	5.8	4.6	4.9	5.1	2.3	2.2
November	3.8	4.0	1.4	2.0	3.6	3.6	6.1	4.7	4.7	4.9	2.2	2.1
December	3.8	4.1	1.7	2.4	3.6	3.9	5.7	4.5	4.6	4.8	2.3	2.2
2016												
January	4.0	4.3	2.4	2.5	3.9	4.4	6.1	5.0	4.6	4.8	2.2	2.1
February	3.9	4.2	2.9	2.5	3.8	4.3	5.8	4.3	4.7	4.9	2.2	2.0
March	4.1	4.4	3.1	2.7	3.8	4.3	6.9	4.6	5.0	5.0	2.2	2.1
April	3.9	4.2	2.8	3.1	3.8	4.0	5.1	4.7	4.7	4.6	2.3	2.1
May	3.9	4.1	2.7	2.8	3.8	4.3	5.5	4.6	4.6	4.7	2.4	2.3
June	3.8	4.1	2.7	3.0	3.8	4.3	5.4	4.5	4.9	5.0	2.2	2.0
July	4.0	4.3	3.4	3.0	3.8	4.2	5.9	4.6	4.6	4.6	2.6	2.4
August	3.8	4.1	2.9	2.6	3.6	3.9	5.2	4.4	4.9	5.0	2.2	2.0
September	3.9	4.1	3.5	2.5	3.6	4.2	5.6	4.6	4.4	4.6	2.3	2.1
October	3.7	4.0	3.2	2.4	3.7	4.0	4.6	5.1	4.6	4.6	2.1	2.0
November	3.9	4.1	2.6	2.5	3.5	3.9	5.7	4.9	4.6	4.6	2.4	2.3
December	3.9	4.1	2.0	2.7	3.7	4.1	5.0	5.0	4.5	4.6	2.3	1.9
2017												
January	3.7	4.0	2.2	2.9	3.4	3.7	4.7	4.8	4.4	4.6	2.1	2.0
February	3.9	4.2	2.6	2.8	3.6	3.9	4.6	5.1	5.3	5.6	2.2	2.2
March	3.8	4.1	2.6	3.1	3.8	4.2	4.8	4.7	4.5	4.5	2.3	2.2
April	4.0	4.3	3.1	3.0	3.6	3.8	4.9	4.6	5.0	5.3	2.5	2.4
May	3.8	4.1	2.5	2.7	3.7	4.1	4.7	4.5	5.0	5.4	2.4	2.2
June	4.2	4.4	3.0	3.2	3.9	4.1	5.7	4.8	5.1	5.1	2.5	2.4
July	4.2	4.5	3.4	3.1	4.1	4.2	5.2	4.8	5.1	5.2	2.5	2.4
August	4.1	4.4	3.1	3.3	4.4	4.6	5.1	4.8	5.3	5.5	2.4	2.2
September	4.1	4.4	2.5	3.3	4.2	4.4	5.2	4.6	4.5	4.6	2.4	2.3
October	4.2	4.5	2.9	3.3	4.0	4.5	5.9	4.6	4.9	5.1	2.3	2.3
November	4.0	4.4	3.0	3.2	4.5	5.7	4.7	4.6	5.2	5.4	2.2	2.2
December	4.1	4.3	2.5	2.9	5.0	6.0	4.4	4.6	5.2	5.4	2.4	2.3
2018												
January	4.3	4.6	3.3	3.4	4.8	5.4	5.1	4.8	5.4	5.7	2.5	2.2
February	4.3	4.5	2.8	3.4	4.6	5.1	5.1	4.8	5.4	5.5	2.6	2.7
March	4.4	4.7	3.1	3.3	4.9	5.5	5.5	5.0	5.4	5.6	2.8	2.7
April	4.5	4.8	3.3	3.5	5.2	6.1	5.5	5.0	5.6	5.8	2.7	2.6
May	4.5	4.8	3.7	3.5	5.1	5.8	5.6	4.9	5.6	5.7	2.6	2.5
June	4.7	5.0	4.2	3.6	5.1	5.8	5.7	5.1	6.2	6.2	2.8	2.6
July	4.7	5.0	4.1	3.6	5.0	5.6	5.7	5.0	5.9	6.3	3.0	2.8
August	4.6	4.9	4.1	3.8	4.5	4.8	5.9	5.0	5.8	6.0	3.2	3.0
September	4.6	5.0	3.8	3.6	5.1	5.4	6.0	5.1	6.1	6.5	2.6	2.6
October	4.6	5.0	3.6	3.7	4.8	5.6	6.0	4.9	5.8	6.2	2.6	2.5
November	4.8	5.1	3.6	3.8	5.6	6.5	5.9	5.0	5.9	6.2	2.8	2.7
December	4.6	5.0	3.8	3.3	4.9	5.7	6.0	5.1	6.2	6.4	2.7	2.6
2019												
January	4.5	5.1	3.9	3.2	4.9	4.9	6.2	5.5	6.4	6.8	3.1	2.8
February	4.7	4.7	3.6	3.5	4.3	4.8	6.2	4.8	5.7	6.0	3.0	2.8
March	4.6	4.9	4.5	3.3	4.5	4.6	6.0	5.4	5.8	6.1	3.2	3.0
April	4.6	4.9	5.4	3.6	4.6	4.5	5.3	5.4	5.8	6.0	3.2	2.9
May	4.5	4.9	4.8	3.6	4.4	4.6	5.6	5.3	5.8	6.0	3.0	2.9
June	4.6	4.8	4.2	3.7	4.6	5.0	5.7	5.1	5.5	5.7	3.0	2.8
July	4.5	4.8	4.5	3.6	4.4	5.1	5.7	5.2	5.5	5.6	3.0	2.8
August	4.4	4.8	4.5	3.3	4.4	4.8	5.7	5.1	5.4	5.5	3.2	3.0
September	4.6	4.7	4.2	3.3	4.4	4.5	5.6	4.8	5.6	5.6	3.1	3.0
October	4.3	4.8	4.1	3.1	5.0	5.3	5.4	5.1	5.5	5.6	3.3	3.1
November	4.1	4.5	2.8	3.0	4.4	4.6	5.4	5.1	5.5	5.6	3.1	3.0
December	...	4.3	2.8	2.7	4.1	4.6	5.4	4.7	5.2	5.2	3.1	3.1
2020												
January	4.4	4.6	3.4	3.1	4.2	4.6	5.6	5.0	5.2	5.1	3.3	3.3
February	4.4	4.6	3.7	3.2	4.0	4.4	5.9	4.8	5.3	5.4	3.3	3.2
March	3.8	3.9	3.1	2.4	3.7	3.9	5.3	4.6	3.9	3.7	3.1	2.9
April	3.7	3.8	3.6	2.7	3.5	3.8	4.9	4.6	3.5	3.5	3.0	2.8
May	3.9	4.1	4.3	2.5	3.9	4.7	4.8	4.2	5.9	5.6	2.9	3.0
June	4.2	4.4	3.3	2.8	4.0	4.4	5.2	4.6	6.6	6.5	3.0	2.9
July	4.6	4.7	4.4	3.4	4.3	5.0	5.6	5.3	5.8	5.8	3.7	2.8
August	4.3	4.5	3.7	3.7	4.1	4.5	5.6	4.9	5.7	5.8	3.2	3.1
September	4.4	4.6	3.0	3.9	4.1	4.3	5.9	5.0	5.6	5.7	3.1	3.1
October	4.5	4.7	3.2	4.2	3.9	4.1	5.6	5.6	5.8	5.8	3.1	3.1

[1]Includes natural resources and mining, information, financial activities, and other services, not shown separately.
[2]Includes wholesale trade and transportation, warehousing, and utilities, not shown separately.
[3]Includes arts, entertainment, and recreation, not shown separately.
[4]Includes federal government, not shown separately.

Table 7-5. Hires Levels[1] and Rates,[2] by Industry, 2009–October 2020

(Seasonally adjusted, levels in thousands, rates per 100.)

Year and month	Total[4]	Total private[4]	Construction	Manufacturing	Trade, transportation, and utilities[5]	Retail trade	Professional and business services	Education and health services	Leisure and hospitality[6]	Accommodation and food services	Government[7]	State and local government
2009												
January	4 095	3 800	368	207	827	567	711	524	715	598	295	264
February	4 061	3 789	343	254	791	549	731	532	692	591	271	246
March	3 858	3 605	328	239	807	537	680	497	632	559	253	228
April	3 888	3 515	331	210	818	593	668	491	617	531	374	228
May	3 758	3 496	324	178	805	546	643	484	678	587	262	240
June	3 639	3 375	277	195	727	506	611	501	630	537	263	234
July	3 857	3 601	323	247	744	507	722	512	615	514	256	219
August	3 810	3 529	264	240	768	538	665	532	653	533	281	255
September	3 944	3 710	319	277	844	579	711	527	630	518	234	212
October	3 838	3 510	317	237	727	503	692	513	614	512	328	287
November	4 024	3 736	316	245	817	533	783	503	685	568	288	253
December	4 004	3 753	347	246	769	527	783	500	651	555	251	227
2010												
January	3 904	3 615	305	225	790	565	770	453	663	564	289	242
February	3 864	3 580	282	256	786	549	767	475	613	532	284	237
March	4 302	3 959	416	257	915	669	771	522	676	570	344	253
April	4 159	3 820	361	278	815	563	806	474	678	550	338	231
May	4 420	3 686	307	254	803	549	791	469	641	527	735	242
June	4 111	3 833	279	261	860	584	867	505	637	508	278	223
July	4 163	3 882	336	272	855	585	815	540	668	537	281	239
August	4 046	3 780	338	270	776	556	879	465	643	527	266	223
September	4 034	3 784	315	261	838	569	791	507	668	558	250	220
October	4 173	3 865	358	267	822	583	811	505	659	559	309	278
November	4 182	3 903	337	284	833	566	838	529	657	560	279	252
December	4 299	4 013	378	274	794	508	971	506	670	565	285	254
2011												
January	4 000	3 714	280	262	824	588	860	452	641	543	286	256
February	4 231	4 003	345	270	901	608	905	479	666	567	227	199
March	4 430	4 179	378	268	887	620	990	471	771	640	251	222
April	4 296	4 028	372	267	871	612	932	502	679	564	268	244
May	4 261	4 022	392	270	855	590	964	475	655	537	239	209
June	4 366	4 075	396	256	887	605	848	515	733	610	291	270
July	4 261	4 020	337	257	860	608	914	492	723	600	242	213
August	4 298	4 057	339	262	832	565	941	508	729	603	241	221
September	4 429	4 159	381	245	856	598	965	503	749	612	270	245
October	4 370	4 101	333	247	852	569	962	489	739	605	269	242
November	4 365	4 093	321	227	847	581	926	520	791	634	272	248
December	4 356	4 062	322	268	824	522	909	520	750	613	294	271
2012												
January	4 457	4 172	332	267	873	588	944	537	776	620	285	264
February	4 560	4 260	345	264	859	578	1 012	564	771	612	300	272
March	4 575	4 279	315	277	887	588	945	528	860	702	296	268
April	4 389	4 098	279	262	892	587	914	494	758	618	291	260
May	4 533	4 228	324	253	894	591	987	550	737	606	306	276
June	4 440	4 121	356	274	892	590	906	524	722	599	319	289
July	4 327	4 032	370	248	864	584	868	515	752	626	295	271
August	4 450	4 136	337	233	929	617	825	514	802	667	315	278
September	4 302	4 022	366	229	882	612	845	508	722	617	280	248
October	4 389	4 120	319	250	907	604	882	522	762	636	269	239
November	4 489	4 213	388	247	893	617	920	512	720	598	276	257
December	4 452	4 162	320	234	894	593	907	532	814	654	290	259
2013												
January	4 487	4 204	337	247	901	615	879	540	805	678	283	250
February	4 571	4 275	378	246	957	668	862	520	792	667	296	265
March	4 369	4 100	355	221	820	562	870	547	805	679	270	251
April	4 572	4 282	294	244	905	630	928	571	859	729	290	263
May	4 663	4 376	339	275	917	645	916	580	811	674	288	270
June	4 440	4 196	340	235	882	620	956	479	810	665	244	219
July	4 561	4 291	307	235	913	634	968	554	792	663	270	249
August	4 730	4 430	303	266	991	700	1 011	588	772	650	299	273
September	4 726	4 433	319	261	981	679	963	555	826	686	293	266
October	4 518	4 237	372	231	969	691	863	516	803	667	281	257
November	4 622	4 326	311	259	1 014	713	949	538	789	652	296	269
December	4 614	4 333	270	248	1 008	750	960	551	800	652	280	255
2014												
January	4 626	4 336	285	243	945	620	985	563	834	693	289	265
February	4 696	4 405	282	241	1 014	718	992	541	853	711	291	266
March	4 763	4 456	270	257	1 016	709	1 004	583	833	713	307	280
April	4 880	4 582	299	252	1 115	793	1 000	580	864	711	298	271
May	4 808	4 522	319	251	1 089	754	927	548	902	739	285	257
June	4 925	4 600	284	266	1 089	749	1 026	551	909	764	326	294
July	5 008	4 721	334	267	1 092	758	1 055	584	876	726	287	259
August	4 810	4 542	340	243	1 030	712	1 071	515	847	702	267	239
September	5 149	4 815	296	288	1 058	726	1 094	667	919	766	334	307
October	5 111	4 806	328	296	1 134	780	1 079	600	893	740	306	277
November	4 978	4 682	322	263	1 103	760	933	577	910	758	296	267
December	5 192	4 874	399	276	1 119	783	1 041	603	936	781	318	289

[1]Hires are the number of hires during the entire month.
[2]The hires rate is the number of hires during the entire month as a percent of total employment.
[3]Detail will not necessarily add to totals because of the independent seasonal adjustment of the various series.
[4]Includes natural resources and mining, information, financial activities, and other services, not shown separately.
[5]Includes wholesale trade and transportation, warehousing, and utilities, not shown separately.
[6]Includes arts, entertainment, and recreation, not shown separately.
[7]Includes federal government, not shown separately.
. . . = Not available.

Table 7-5. Hires Levels[1] and Rates,[2] by Industry, 2009–October 2020—*Continued*

(Seasonally adjusted, levels in thousands, rates per 100.)

Year and month	Rate											
	Total[4]	Total private[4]	Construction	Manufacturing	Trade, transportation, and utilities[5]	Retail trade	Professional and business services	Education and health services	Leisure and hospitality[6]	Accommodation and food services	Government[7]	State and local government
2009												
January	3.1	3.4	5.6	1.7	3.3	3.8	4.2	2.7	5.4	5.3	1.3	1.3
February	3.0	3.4	5.3	2.1	3.1	3.7	4.3	2.7	5.2	5.3	1.2	1.2
March	2.9	3.3	5.2	2.0	3.2	3.7	4.1	2.5	4.8	5.0	1.1	1.2
April	2.9	3.2	5.4	1.7	3.3	4.1	4.0	2.5	4.7	4.8	1.6	1.2
May	2.9	3.2	5.3	1.5	3.2	3.8	3.9	2.5	5.2	5.2	1.2	1.2
June	2.8	3.1	4.6	1.7	2.9	3.5	3.7	2.6	4.8	4.8	1.2	1.2
July	3.0	3.3	5.4	2.1	3.0	3.5	4.4	2.6	4.7	4.6	1.1	1.1
August	2.9	3.3	4.5	2.1	3.1	3.7	4.0	2.7	5.0	4.8	1.2	1.3
September	3.0	3.4	5.5	2.4	3.4	4.0	4.3	2.7	4.8	4.7	1.0	1.1
October	3.0	3.3	5.5	2.1	3.0	3.5	4.2	2.6	4.7	4.7	1.5	1.5
November	3.1	3.5	5.6	2.1	3.3	3.7	4.7	2.5	5.3	5.1	1.3	1.3
December	3.1	3.5	6.1	2.1	3.1	3.7	4.7	2.5	5.0	5.0	1.1	1.2
2010												
January	3.0	3.4	5.5	2.0	3.2	3.9	4.6	2.3	5.1	5.1	1.3	1.2
February	3.0	3.3	5.1	2.2	3.2	3.8	4.6	2.4	4.7	4.8	1.3	1.2
March	3.3	3.7	7.5	2.2	3.7	4.6	4.7	2.6	5.2	5.1	1.5	1.2
April	3.2	3.6	6.5	2.4	3.3	3.9	4.8	2.4	5.2	5.0	1.5	1.3
May	3.4	3.4	5.6	2.2	3.3	3.8	4.7	2.4	4.9	5.0	3.2	1.2
June	3.1	3.6	5.1	2.3	3.5	4.0	5.2	2.5	4.9	4.7	1.2	1.1
July	3.2	3.6	6.1	2.4	3.5	4.1	4.9	2.7	5.1	4.6	1.2	1.1
August	3.1	3.5	6.1	2.3	3.2	3.8	5.2	2.3	4.9	4.8	1.2	1.2
September	3.1	3.5	5.7	2.3	3.4	3.9	4.7	2.5	5.1	4.7	1.2	1.1
October	3.2	3.6	6.5	2.3	3.3	4.0	4.8	2.5	5.0	5.0	1.1	1.1
November	3.2	3.6	6.1	2.5	3.4	3.9	4.9	2.6	5.0	5.0	1.4	1.4
December	3.3	3.7	6.9	2.4	3.2	3.5	5.7	2.5	5.0	5.0	1.3	1.3
2011												
January	3.1	3.4	5.2	2.3	3.3	4.0	5.0	2.2	4.9	4.8	1.3	1.3
February	3.2	3.7	6.3	2.3	3.6	4.2	5.3	2.4	5.1	5.0	1.0	1.0
March	3.4	3.8	6.9	2.3	3.6	4.3	5.7	2.3	5.8	5.6	1.1	1.2
April	3.3	3.7	6.8	2.3	3.5	4.2	5.4	2.5	5.1	5.0	1.2	1.3
May	3.2	3.7	7.1	2.3	3.4	4.0	5.6	2.3	4.9	4.7	1.1	1.1
June	3.3	3.7	7.2	2.2	3.5	4.1	4.9	2.5	5.5	5.3	1.3	1.4
July	3.2	3.7	6.1	2.2	3.4	4.1	5.3	2.4	5.4	5.2	1.1	1.1
August	3.3	3.7	6.1	2.2	3.3	3.8	5.4	2.5	5.4	5.3	1.1	1.2
September	3.3	3.8	6.8	2.1	3.4	4.1	5.5	2.5	5.6	5.3	1.2	1.3
October	3.3	3.7	6.0	2.1	3.4	3.9	5.5	2.4	5.5	5.2	1.2	1.3
November	3.3	3.7	5.7	1.9	3.4	3.9	5.3	2.5	5.9	5.5	1.2	1.3
December	3.3	3.7	5.7	2.3	3.3	3.5	5.1	2.5	5.5	5.3	1.3	1.4
2012												
January	3.3	3.7	5.9	2.3	3.5	4.0	5.3	2.6	5.7	5.3	1.3	1.4
February	3.4	3.8	6.1	2.2	3.4	3.9	5.7	2.7	5.7	5.2	1.4	1.4
March	3.4	3.8	5.6	2.3	3.5	4.0	5.3	2.6	6.3	6.0	1.3	1.4
April	3.3	3.7	5.0	2.2	3.5	4.0	5.1	2.4	5.5	5.3	1.3	1.4
May	3.4	3.8	5.8	2.1	3.5	4.0	5.5	2.7	5.4	5.2	1.4	1.4
June	3.3	3.7	6.3	2.3	3.5	4.0	5.0	2.5	5.3	5.1	1.5	1.5
July	3.2	3.6	6.6	2.1	3.4	3.9	4.8	2.5	5.5	5.3	1.3	1.4
August	3.3	3.7	6.0	1.9	3.7	4.2	4.6	2.5	5.8	5.6	1.4	1.5
September	3.2	3.6	6.5	1.9	3.5	4.1	4.7	2.4	5.2	5.2	1.3	1.3
October	3.3	3.7	5.6	2.1	3.6	4.1	4.9	2.5	5.5	5.3	1.2	1.3
November	3.3	3.7	6.8	2.1	3.5	4.1	5.1	2.5	5.2	5.0	1.3	1.3
December	3.3	3.7	5.6	2.0	3.5	4.0	5.0	2.5	5.8	5.5	1.3	1.4
2013												
January	3.3	3.7	5.9	2.1	3.5	4.1	4.8	2.6	5.7	5.6	1.3	1.3
February	3.4	3.8	6.5	2.0	3.7	4.5	4.7	2.5	5.6	5.5	1.4	1.4
March	3.2	3.6	6.1	1.8	3.2	3.8	4.7	2.6	5.7	5.6	1.2	1.4
April	3.4	3.8	5.1	2.0	3.5	4.2	5.0	2.7	6.1	6.0	1.3	1.3
May	3.4	3.8	5.8	2.3	3.6	4.3	4.9	2.8	5.7	5.5	1.3	1.4
June	3.3	3.7	5.8	2.0	3.4	4.1	5.1	2.3	5.7	5.4	1.1	1.1
July	3.3	3.7	5.2	2.0	3.5	4.2	5.2	2.6	5.5	5.4	1.2	1.3
August	3.5	3.9	5.1	2.2	3.8	4.6	5.4	2.8	5.4	5.3	1.4	1.4
September	3.5	3.9	5.4	2.2	3.8	4.5	5.2	2.6	5.8	5.6	1.3	1.4
October	3.3	3.7	6.3	1.9	3.7	4.5	4.6	2.4	5.6	5.4	1.3	1.3
November	3.4	3.7	5.2	2.1	3.9	4.7	5.0	2.5	5.5	5.3	1.4	1.4
December	3.4	3.7	4.6	2.1	3.9	4.9	5.1	2.6	5.5	5.3	1.3	1.3
2014												
January	3.4	3.7	4.8	2.0	3.6	4.1	5.2	2.7	5.8	5.6	1.3	1.4
February	3.4	3.8	4.7	2.0	3.9	4.7	5.2	2.5	5.9	5.7	1.3	1.4
March	3.5	3.8	4.5	2.1	3.9	4.6	5.3	2.7	5.7	5.7	1.4	1.5
April	3.5	3.9	4.9	2.1	4.3	5.2	5.3	2.7	5.7	5.7	1.4	1.4
May	3.5	3.9	5.2	2.1	4.2	4.9	4.9	2.6	6.1	5.9	1.3	1.3
June	3.5	3.9	4.6	2.2	4.1	4.9	5.4	2.6	6.2	6.1	1.5	1.5
July	3.6	4.0	5.4	2.2	4.1	4.9	5.5	2.7	6.0	6.1	1.2	1.3
August	3.5	3.9	5.5	2.0	3.9	4.6	5.6	2.4	5.8	5.6	1.2	1.3
September	3.7	4.1	4.7	2.4	4.0	4.7	5.7	3.1	6.2	6.1	1.5	1.6
October	3.7	4.1	5.2	2.4	4.3	5.0	5.6	2.8	6.0	5.8	1.4	1.4
November	3.6	4.0	5.1	2.1	4.2	4.9	4.8	2.7	6.1	6.0	1.4	1.4
December	3.7	4.1	6.3	2.2	4.2	5.0	5.4	2.8	6.3	6.1	1.4	1.5

[1]Hires are the number of hires during the entire month.
[2]The hires rate is the number of hires during the entire month as a percent of total employment.
[3]Detail will not necessarily add to totals because of the independent seasonal adjustment of the various series.
[4]Includes natural resources and mining, information, financial activities, and other services, not shown separately.
[5]Includes wholesale trade and transportation, warehousing, and utilities, not shown separately.
[6]Includes arts, entertainment, and recreation, not shown separately.
[7]Includes federal government, not shown separately.
. . . = Not available.

Table 7-5. Hires Levels[1] and Rates,[2] by Industry, 2009–October 2020—*Continued*

(Seasonally adjusted, levels in thousands, rates per 100.)

Year and month	Level[3]											
	Total[4]	Total private[4]	Construc-tion	Manufac-turing	Trade, transpor-tation, and utilities[5]	Retail trade	Profes-sional and business services	Education and health services	Leisure and hospitality[6]	Accommo-dation and food services	Govern-ment[7]	State and local govern-ment
2015												
January	5 061	4 744	352	255	1 085	763	1 035	601	909	743	316	284
February	5 127	4 807	334	263	1 071	737	1 082	627	927	764	320	291
March	5 126	4 797	318	267	1 105	762	1 076	608	919	764	328	295
April	5 196	4 847	346	261	1 074	748	1 095	606	953	797	349	307
May	5 142	4 819	311	257	1 108	770	1 068	610	966	793	323	290
June	5 125	4 789	342	268	1 104	763	1 033	594	918	782	336	303
July	5 150	4 798	307	266	1 108	759	1 011	630	955	826	352	314
August	5 163	4 822	325	274	1 059	748	1 039	617	1 016	871	341	306
September	5 287	4 964	335	291	1 067	738	1 083	645	1 016	860	323	291
October	5 338	4 978	333	283	1 073	750	1 085	661	1 013	856	360	325
November	5 358	5 007	348	271	1 080	763	1 115	665	1 027	870	352	315
December	5 540	5 168	335	270	1 108	781	1 217	650	1 045	880	371	335
2016												
January	5 204	4 845	287	281	1 052	758	1 192	585	943	782	360	328
February	5 559	5 214	355	292	1 193	866	1 107	654	1 080	924	344	305
March	5 362	4 988	353	256	1 073	740	1 111	619	1 028	862	374	338
April	5 277	4 936	361	274	1 076	717	1 096	633	993	857	341	307
May	5 206	4 850	324	271	1 031	705	1 100	647	1 018	860	356	319
June	5 277	4 932	282	284	1 062	728	1 070	667	1 037	864	345	310
July	5 419	5 024	346	281	1 078	751	1 189	639	1 033	863	395	362
August	5 301	4 951	340	266	1 083	724	1 095	651	1 040	867	350	316
September	5 283	4 903	317	286	1 099	754	1 096	656	959	825	380	347
October	5 234	4 907	354	286	1 088	744	1 062	639	990	829	327	293
November	5 316	4 983	342	280	1 006	655	1 110	648	1 082	922	333	306
December	5 380	5 053	453	303	1 030	695	1 106	644	1 027	862	327	289
2017												
January	5 517	5 173	401	311	1 044	697	1 158	627	1 047	889	344	308
February	5 366	5 016	367	297	1 124	783	1 041	635	1 018	853	350	317
March	5 395	5 055	389	327	1 084	748	1 046	665	1 005	877	340	308
April	5 265	4 931	389	318	1 006	680	1 001	663	1 020	833	334	310
May	5 454	5 111	390	331	1 060	727	1 095	680	998	835	343	310
June	5 642	5 307	375	336	1 106	755	1 253	657	1 039	855	335	304
July	5 502	5 163	369	330	1 002	671	1 184	682	1 028	826	339	308
August	5 528	5 187	389	365	1 014	678	1 141	705	1 005	836	341	311
September	5 401	5 045	400	328	1 021	667	1 144	656	982	818	356	323
October	5 635	5 294	399	347	1 037	690	1 181	676	1 061	876	341	301
November	5 473	5 102	363	344	1 054	708	1 107	695	1 023	854	371	344
December	5 426	5 074	324	361	1 092	694	1 079	677	1 000	849	351	322
2018												
January	5 511	5 190	357	366	1 119	751	1 115	673	1 016	846	321	287
February	5 669	5 309	403	377	1 110	743	1 153	677	1 056	875	360	329
March	5 629	5 289	366	363	1 121	753	1 170	693	1 040	847	340	309
April	5 587	5 234	358	362	1 146	778	1 112	665	1 048	859	353	317
May	5 819	5 463	397	366	1 115	732	1 169	732	1 095	902	356	329
June	5 783	5 407	372	364	1 117	736	1 208	735	1 051	856	376	341
July	5 691	5 330	385	382	1 098	741	1 139	700	1 106	913	361	323
August	5 792	5 416	384	364	1 208	790	1 104	731	1 058	874	376	341
September	5 610	5 264	376	331	1 123	758	1 098	697	1 060	891	346	308
October	5 855	5 507	356	393	1 201	752	1 184	745	1 096	915	348	313
November	5 818	5 452	396	369	1 174	738	1 125	727	1 080	912	366	324
December	5 762	5 408	382	352	1 143	769	1 169	755	1 058	901	354	317
2019												
January	5 834	5 443	443	353	1 122	722	1 081	756	1 152	974	391	357
February	5 703	5 346	357	342	1 133	738	1 168	737	1 082	911	357	320
March	5 689	5 337	363	352	1 080	715	1 168	740	1 095	931	352	313
April	6 000	5 625	423	359	1 145	748	1 248	736	1 144	982	376	338
May	5 687	5 343	386	340	1 169	766	1 132	677	1 064	898	344	309
June	5 760	5 420	423	326	1 176	787	1 123	679	1 131	992	340	305
July	5 975	5 605	379	335	1 220	796	1 195	763	1 121	962	370	332
August	5 839	5 443	410	334	1 168	775	1 142	690	1 130	960	396	327
September	5 959	5 593	452	344	1 196	787	1 178	740	1 160	985	366	325
October	5 757	5 397	475	312	1 112	716	1 118	722	1 101	934	360	316
November	5 857	5 485	426	357	1 170	763	1 157	730	1 078	891	371	321
December	5 927	5 574	467	334	1 161	772	1 151	723	1 165	979	352	309
2020												
January	5 921	5 541	435	311	1 220	818	1 163	753	1 126	949	381	336
February	5 864	5 489	390	334	1 221	812	1 104	762	1 091	923	375	324
March	5 111	4 744	389	299	1 137	764	1 103	663	673	546	367	309
April	4 047	3 812	246	326	1 025	723	800	545	490	460	235	189
May	7 199	6 952	679	523	1 341	886	938	1 093	1 513	1 368	247	197
June	6 970	6 688	499	432	1 362	911	1 175	899	1 759	1 597	281	241
July	5 903	5 569	396	341	1 227	811	1 152	788	1 168	1 001	334	262
August	5 952	5 394	396	384	1 248	863	1 170	719	934	806	558	243
September	5 886	5 570	394	374	1 255	745	1 108	725	1 053	938	316	257
October	5 912	5 578	400	376	1 278	777	1 116	735	1 044	912	334	284

[1]Hires are the number of hires during the entire month.
[2]The hires rate is the number of hires during the entire month as a percent of total employment.
[3]Detail will not necessarily add to totals because of the independent seasonal adjustment of the various series.
[4]Includes natural resources and mining, information, financial activities, and other services, not shown separately.
[5]Includes wholesale trade and transportation, warehousing, and utilities, not shown separately.
[6]Includes arts, entertainment, and recreation, not shown separately.
[7]Includes federal government, not shown separately.
. . . = Not available.

Table 7-5. Hires Levels[1] and Rates,[2] by Industry, 2009–October 2020—*Continued*

(Seasonally adjusted, levels in thousands, rates per 100.)

Year and month	Total[4]	Total private[4]	Construction	Manufacturing	Trade, transportation, and utilities[5]	Retail trade	Professional and business services	Education and health services	Leisure and hospitality[6]	Accommodation and food services	Government[7]	State and local government
2015												
January	3.6	4.0	5.6	2.1	4.1	4.9	5.3	2.8	6.1	5.8	1.4	1.5
February	3.6	4.0	5.3	2.1	4.0	4.7	5.6	2.9	6.2	5.9	1.5	1.5
March	3.6	4.0	5.0	2.2	4.1	4.9	5.5	2.8	6.1	5.9	1.5	1.5
April	3.7	4.1	5.4	2.1	4.0	4.8	5.6	2.8	6.3	6.2	1.6	1.6
May	3.6	4.0	4.8	2.1	4.1	4.9	5.4	2.8	6.4	6.1	1.5	1.5
June	3.6	4.0	5.3	2.2	4.1	4.9	5.2	2.7	6.1	6.1	1.5	1.6
July	3.6	4.0	4.7	2.2	4.1	4.9	5.1	2.9	6.3	6.3	1.5	1.6
August	3.6	4.0	5.0	2.2	3.9	4.8	5.3	2.8	6.7	6.7	1.6	1.6
September	3.7	4.1	5.2	2.4	4.0	4.7	5.5	2.8	6.7	6.7	1.5	1.6
October	3.7	4.1	5.1	2.3	4.0	4.8	5.5	2.9	6.7	6.6	1.5	1.5
November	3.8	4.1	5.3	2.2	4.0	4.9	5.5	3.0	6.6	6.5	1.6	1.7
December	3.9	4.3	5.1	2.2	4.1	5.0	6.1	2.9	6.8	6.7	1.7	1.7
2016												
January	3.6	4.0	4.3	2.3	3.9	4.8	6.0	2.6	6.1	5.9	1.6	1.7
February	3.9	4.3	5.3	2.4	4.4	5.5	5.5	2.9	7.0	7.0	1.6	1.6
March	3.7	4.1	5.3	2.1	4.0	4.7	5.6	2.8	6.6	6.5	1.7	1.7
April	3.7	4.1	5.4	2.2	4.0	4.5	5.5	2.8	6.4	6.4	1.5	1.6
May	3.6	4.0	4.8	2.2	3.8	4.5	5.5	2.9	6.5	6.4	1.6	1.6
June	3.7	4.0	4.2	2.3	3.9	4.6	5.3	2.9	6.6	6.5	1.6	1.6
July	3.8	4.1	5.1	2.3	4.0	4.7	5.9	2.8	6.6	6.4	1.8	1.9
August	3.7	4.0	5.0	2.2	4.0	4.6	5.4	2.9	6.6	6.4	1.6	1.6
September	3.6	4.0	4.7	2.3	4.0	4.7	5.4	2.9	6.1	6.1	1.7	1.8
October	3.6	4.0	5.2	2.3	4.0	4.7	5.3	2.8	6.3	6.1	1.5	1.5
November	3.7	4.1	5.0	2.3	3.7	4.1	5.5	2.8	6.8	6.8	1.5	1.6
December	3.7	4.1	6.6	2.5	3.8	4.4	5.5	2.8	6.5	6.4	1.5	1.5
2017												
January	3.8	4.2	5.9	2.5	3.8	4.4	5.7	2.7	6.6	6.5	1.5	1.6
February	3.7	4.1	5.3	2.4	4.1	4.9	5.1	2.8	6.4	6.3	1.6	1.6
March	3.7	4.1	5.6	2.6	4.0	4.7	5.1	2.9	6.3	6.4	1.5	1.6
April	3.6	4.0	5.6	2.6	3.7	4.3	4.9	2.9	6.4	6.1	1.5	1.6
May	3.7	4.1	5.6	2.7	3.9	4.6	5.4	2.9	6.2	6.1	1.5	1.6
June	3.9	4.3	5.4	2.7	4.0	4.8	6.1	2.8	6.5	6.2	1.5	1.6
July	3.7	4.2	5.3	2.7	3.7	4.2	5.8	2.9	6.4	6.0	1.5	1.6
August	3.8	4.2	5.6	2.9	3.7	4.3	5.5	3.0	6.2	6.1	1.5	1.6
September	3.7	4.1	5.7	2.6	3.7	4.2	5.6	2.8	6.1	6.0	1.6	1.7
October	3.8	4.2	5.7	2.8	3.8	4.4	5.7	2.9	6.6	6.4	1.5	1.5
November	3.7	4.1	5.1	2.8	3.8	4.5	5.4	3.0	6.3	6.2	1.7	1.8
December	3.7	4.1	4.6	2.9	4.0	4.4	5.2	2.9	6.2	6.1	1.6	1.6
2018												
January	3.7	4.1	5.0	3.0	4.1	4.8	5.4	2.9	6.3	6.1	1.4	1.5
February	3.8	4.2	5.6	2.9	4.0	4.7	5.5	2.9	6.5	6.3	1.6	1.7
March	3.8	4.2	5.1	2.9	4.1	4.8	5.6	2.9	6.4	6.1	1.5	1.6
April	3.8	4.2	5.0	2.9	4.2	4.9	5.3	2.8	6.5	6.2	1.6	1.6
May	3.9	4.3	5.5	2.9	4.0	4.6	5.6	3.1	6.7	6.5	1.6	1.7
June	3.9	4.3	5.1	3.0	4.0	4.7	5.8	3.1	6.4	6.1	1.7	1.7
July	3.8	4.2	5.3	2.9	4.0	4.7	5.4	3.0	6.8	6.5	1.6	1.6
August	3.9	4.3	5.2	2.6	4.4	5.0	5.3	3.1	6.5	6.3	1.7	1.7
September	3.8	4.1	5.1	3.1	4.1	4.8	5.2	2.9	6.5	6.4	1.5	1.6
October	3.9	4.3	4.8	2.9	4.3	4.8	5.6	3.1	6.7	6.6	1.5	1.6
November	3.9	4.3	5.4	2.7	4.2	4.7	5.3	3.1	6.6	6.5	1.6	1.6
December	3.8	4.2	5.2	. . .	4.1	4.9	5.5	3.2	6.4	6.4	1.6	1.6
2019												
January	3.9	4.3	6.0	2.7	4.0	4.6	5.1	3.2	7.0	6.9	1.7	1.8
February	3.8	4.2	4.8	2.7	4.1	4.7	5.5	3.1	6.6	6.5	1.6	1.6
March	3.8	4.2	4.9	2.7	3.9	4.6	5.5	3.1	6.6	6.6	1.6	1.6
April	4.0	4.4	5.7	2.8	4.1	4.8	5.9	3.1	6.9	7.0	1.7	1.7
May	3.8	4.2	5.2	2.6	4.2	4.9	5.3	2.8	6.4	6.4	1.5	1.6
June	3.8	4.2	5.6	2.5	4.2	5.0	5.3	2.8	6.8	7.0	1.5	1.5
July	4.0	4.4	5.1	2.6	4.4	5.1	5.6	3.2	6.8	6.8	1.6	1.7
August	3.9	4.2	5.5	2.6	4.2	5.0	5.3	2.8	6.8	6.8	1.7	1.7
September	3.9	4.3	6.0	2.7	4.3	5.0	5.5	3.0	7.0	6.9	1.6	1.7
October	3.8	4.2	6.3	2.4	4.0	4.6	5.2	3.0	6.6	6.6	1.6	1.6
November	3.9	4.2	5.7	2.8	4.2	4.9	5.4	3.0	6.6	6.2	1.6	1.6
December	3.9	4.3	6.2	2.6	4.2	4.9	5.4	3.0	6.9	6.8	1.6	1.6
2020												
January	3.9	4.3	5.7	2.4	4.4	5.2	5.4	3.1	6.7	6.6	1.7	1.7
February	3.8	4.2	5.1	2.6	4.4	5.2	5.1	3.1	6.5	6.4	1.6	1.6
March	3.4	3.7	5.1	2.3	4.1	4.9	5.1	2.7	4.1	3.9	1.6	1.6
April	3.1	3.5	3.7	2.8	4.2	5.4	4.2	2.5	5.7	6.2	1.1	1.0
May	5.4	6.2	9.7	4.5	5.4	6.5	4.8	4.9	15.2	15.6	1.2	1.1
June	5.1	5.7	7.0	3.6	5.3	6.3	6.0	3.9	14.7	15.3	1.3	1.3
July	4.2	4.7	5.5	2.8	4.7	5.5	5.8	3.4	9.3	9.1	1.5	1.4
August	4.2	4.5	5.5	3.2	4.7	5.7	5.8	3.1	7.4	7.3	2.5	1.3
September	4.2	4.6	5.4	3.1	4.7	4.9	5.5	3.1	8.0	8.2	1.4	1.4
October	4.2	4.6	5.5	3.1	4.8	5.1	5.5	3.2	7.8	7.8	1.6	1.5

[1]Hires are the number of hires during the entire month.
[2]The hires rate is the number of hires during the entire month as a percent of total employment.
[3]Detail will not necessarily add to totals because of the independent seasonal adjustment of the various series.
[4]Includes natural resources and mining, information, financial activities, and other services, not shown separately.
[5]Includes wholesale trade and transportation, warehousing, and utilities, not shown separately.
[6]Includes arts, entertainment, and recreation, not shown separately.
[7]Includes federal government, not shown separately.
. . . = Not available.

Table 7-6. Separations Levels[1] and Rates,[2] by Industry, 2009–October 2020

(Seasonally adjusted, levels in thousands, rates per 100.)

Year and month	Level[3]											
	Total[4]	Total private[4]	Construc-tion	Manufac-turing	Trade, transpor-tation, and utilities[5]	Retail trade	Profes-sional and business services	Education and health services	Leisure and hospitality[6]	Accommo-dation and food services	Govern-ment[7]	State and local govern-ment
2009												
January	4 925	4 644	502	487	1 002	651	875	495	742	627	281	260
February	4 824	4 529	454	429	934	624	943	509	733	636	294	277
March	4 693	4 427	474	427	970	625	818	486	700	613	266	244
April	4 695	4 419	476	403	985	677	858	484	697	589	275	254
May	4 184	3 859	383	370	874	571	705	404	641	564	326	242
June	4 226	3 908	388	355	786	536	734	478	690	562	319	244
July	4 256	3 959	423	309	858	562	739	494	645	528	297	271
August	3 992	3 725	336	283	793	535	685	502	681	560	267	242
September	4 123	3 820	386	305	917	618	697	491	606	528	303	282
October	4 003	3 740	381	284	829	567	682	469	636	516	263	225
November	3 983	3 702	332	259	822	535	746	458	685	573	281	246
December	4 103	3 813	374	250	877	567	714	470	676	568	290	256
2010												
January	3 989	3 703	393	245	757	504	757	451	675	566	286	264
February	3 978	3 675	355	267	801	552	761	458	620	549	303	272
March	4 072	3 769	361	263	863	636	760	459	644	537	303	268
April	3 948	3 641	350	246	801	573	738	467	639	535	307	260
May	3 911	3 600	347	221	778	536	759	422	622	522	311	254
June	4 308	3 756	297	245	826	586	798	489	658	508	552	274
July	4 299	3 859	347	259	841	579	797	507	706	529	440	256
August	4 067	3 642	334	271	756	540	837	453	603	490	425	280
September	4 047	3 643	335	242	791	540	775	498	618	513	404	297
October	3 883	3 622	346	264	763	539	754	430	647	525	262	222
November	4 041	3 746	329	258	821	581	771	474	663	558	295	267
December	4 143	3 844	393	261	781	524	877	492	626	528	299	273
2011												
January	4 045	3 759	325	245	815	527	849	449	649	533	286	258
February	4 014	3 742	317	243	825	576	836	469	629	548	272	247
March	4 109	3 835	337	249	826	593	903	443	689	566	274	249
April	3 994	3 700	371	242	762	550	869	445	623	522	294	263
May	4 179	3 877	366	258	836	590	903	451	675	547	302	275
June	4 168	3 899	412	241	811	569	840	484	693	578	270	237
July	4 180	3 866	327	238	807	559	893	451	711	589	314	288
August	4 189	3 897	341	240	827	583	888	488	705	579	293	263
September	4 213	3 927	347	232	831	581	907	428	734	590	286	256
October	4 147	3 887	319	235	821	553	930	455	661	542	260	234
November	4 237	3 933	317	236	814	567	919	472	747	599	305	272
December	4 090	3 769	296	237	820	540	785	480	720	589	320	292
2012												
January	4 195	3 901	324	241	821	546	843	514	717	580	294	267
February	4 322	4 017	336	245	818	576	961	489	735	585	305	274
March	4 257	3 947	310	239	839	563	900	480	759	615	310	283
April	4 329	4 013	292	248	864	574	873	488	742	599	316	283
May	4 430	4 099	338	232	855	592	955	506	737	603	331	300
June	4 383	4 086	358	265	885	607	861	541	729	613	297	269
July	4 178	3 880	369	228	849	585	810	470	727	612	298	265
August	4 338	4 034	328	235	922	629	803	510	731	612	304	276
September	4 100	3 834	352	225	862	587	827	440	671	564	266	236
October	4 260	3 958	296	240	879	586	842	496	731	606	302	270
November	4 303	4 011	372	249	816	544	894	495	693	578	292	257
December	4 117	3 827	273	227	872	617	807	476	741	597	290	256
2013												
January	4 381	4 082	332	235	921	630	819	530	755	640	298	268
February	4 257	3 966	331	236	889	617	772	524	744	629	291	260
March	4 215	3 918	336	217	843	580	811	484	756	639	296	267
April	4 424	4 127	305	248	867	613	882	538	810	679	297	270
May	4 433	4 136	296	267	880	605	873	567	754	624	297	259
June	4 313	4 027	330	236	812	575	921	502	754	629	287	258
July	4 459	4 168	303	265	898	594	890	544	761	625	291	261
August	4 522	4 249	282	235	933	666	997	532	732	609	273	240
September	4 521	4 236	286	234	917	654	928	537	826	684	285	257
October	4 354	4 060	340	207	952	663	849	503	757	639	294	256
November	4 332	4 049	281	230	958	693	905	493	748	613	283	259
December	4 387	4 087	290	235	894	648	905	538	757	630	299	269
2014												
January	4 464	4 172	247	256	952	661	915	540	800	671	292	265
February	4 511	4 223	255	218	970	690	945	511	841	699	288	256
March	4 498	4 193	242	246	999	717	956	528	765	636	305	277
April	4 584	4 304	252	245	1 030	746	952	568	809	666	280	254
May	4 569	4 271	282	233	1 029	723	911	509	820	682	298	270
June	4 617	4 346	263	245	1 023	721	962	527	878	741	272	241
July	4 786	4 506	285	250	1 068	744	995	531	869	729	280	255
August	4 654	4 349	306	223	994	688	1 018	499	842	680	305	284
September	4 861	4 563	262	262	1 023	713	1 038	589	890	744	298	269
October	4 941	4 643	308	265	1 067	741	1 096	574	867	722	298	271
November	4 642	4 362	306	224	1 040	729	905	518	861	709	280	252
December	4 815	4 505	360	266	1 056	753	898	552	885	743	310	283

[1]Total separations are the number of separations during the entire month.
[2]The total separations rate is the number of total separations during the entire month as a percent of total employment.
[3]Detail will not necessarily add to totals because of the independent seasonal adjustment of the various series.
[4]Includes natural resources and mining, information, financial activities, and other services, not shown separately.
[5]Includes wholesale trade and transportation, warehousing, and utilities, not shown separately.
[6]Includes arts, entertainment, and recreation, not shown separately.
[7]Includes federal government, not shown separately.

Table 7-6. Separations Levels[1] and Rates,[2] by Industry, 2009–October 2020—*Continued*

(Seasonally adjusted, levels in thousands, rates per 100.)

Year and month	Rate											
	Total[4]	Total private[4]	Construction	Manufacturing	Trade, transportation, and utilities[5]	Retail trade	Professional and business services	Education and health services	Leisure and hospitality[6]	Accommodation and food services	Government[7]	State and local government
2009												
January	3.7	4.2	7.7	3.9	3.9	4.4	5.1	2.5	5.6	5.6	1.2	1.3
February	3.6	4.1	7.0	3.5	3.7	4.2	5.6	2.6	5.6	5.7	1.3	1.4
March	3.5	4.0	7.5	3.5	3.9	4.3	4.9	2.5	5.3	5.5	1.2	1.2
April	3.6	4.0	7.7	3.3	3.9	4.7	5.2	2.5	5.3	5.3	1.2	1.3
May	3.2	3.5	6.3	3.1	3.5	3.9	4.2	2.1	5.3	5.3	1.2	1.3
June	3.2	3.6	6.4	3.0	3.2	3.7	4.4	2.4	4.9	5.0	1.4	1.2
July	3.3	3.7	7.1	2.7	3.5	3.9	4.5	2.4	5.3	5.0	1.4	1.2
August	3.1	3.5	5.7	2.4	3.2	3.7	4.2	2.5	4.9	4.7	1.3	1.4
September	3.2	3.5	6.7	2.6	3.7	4.3	4.2	2.5	5.2	5.0	1.2	1.2
October	3.1	3.5	6.7	2.5	3.4	3.9	4.1	2.4	4.6	4.7	1.3	1.4
November	3.1	3.4	5.8	2.3	3.4	3.7	4.5	2.3	4.9	5.2	1.2	1.1
December	3.2	3.6	6.6	2.2	3.6	4.0	4.3	2.4	5.2	5.1	1.3	1.3
2010												
January	3.1	3.5	7.0	2.1	3.1	3.5	4.6	2.3	5.2	5.1	1.3	1.3
February	3.1	3.4	6.5	2.3	3.3	3.8	4.6	2.3	4.8	5.0	1.3	1.4
March	3.1	3.5	6.5	2.3	3.5	4.4	4.6	2.3	5.0	4.9	1.3	1.4
April	3.0	3.4	6.3	2.1	3.3	4.0	4.4	2.3	4.9	4.8	1.4	1.4
May	3.0	3.3	6.3	1.9	3.2	3.7	4.5	2.1	4.8	4.7	1.4	1.3
June	3.3	3.5	5.4	2.1	3.4	4.1	4.8	2.5	5.0	4.6	2.4	1.4
July	3.3	3.6	6.3	2.2	3.4	4.0	4.8	2.5	5.4	4.8	2.0	1.3
August	3.1	3.4	6.1	2.3	3.1	3.7	5.0	2.3	4.6	4.4	1.9	1.4
September	3.1	3.4	6.1	2.1	3.2	3.7	4.6	2.5	4.7	4.6	1.8	1.5
October	3.0	3.3	6.3	2.3	3.1	3.7	4.5	2.1	4.9	4.7	1.2	1.1
November	3.1	3.5	6.0	2.2	3.3	4.0	4.5	2.4	5.1	5.0	1.3	1.4
December	3.2	3.5	7.2	2.2	3.2	3.6	5.1	2.4	4.8	4.7	1.3	1.4
2011												
January	3.1	3.5	6.0	2.1	3.3	3.6	5.0	2.2	4.9	4.7	1.3	1.3
February	3.1	3.4	5.8	2.1	3.3	4.0	4.9	2.3	4.8	4.9	1.2	1.3
March	3.1	3.5	6.2	2.1	3.3	4.1	5.2	2.2	5.2	5.0	1.2	1.3
April	3.0	3.4	6.8	2.1	3.1	3.8	5.0	2.2	4.7	4.6	1.3	1.4
May	3.2	3.5	6.6	2.2	3.3	4.0	5.2	2.2	5.1	4.8	1.4	1.4
June	3.2	3.6	7.4	2.1	3.2	3.9	4.8	2.4	5.2	5.1	1.2	1.2
July	3.2	3.5	5.9	2.0	3.2	3.8	5.1	2.2	5.3	5.2	1.4	1.5
August	3.2	3.5	6.1	2.0	3.3	4.0	5.1	2.4	5.3	5.1	1.3	1.4
September	3.2	3.6	6.2	2.0	3.3	3.9	5.2	2.1	5.5	5.1	1.3	1.3
October	3.1	3.5	5.7	2.0	3.3	3.8	5.2	2.2	5.5	4.7	1.2	1.2
November	3.2	3.6	5.7	2.0	3.2	3.8	5.3	2.3	5.5	5.2	1.4	1.4
December	3.1	3.4	5.3	2.0	3.3	3.7	4.4	2.3	5.3	5.1	1.5	1.5
2012												
January	3.1	3.5	5.8	2.0	3.2	3.7	4.8	2.5	5.3	5.0	1.3	1.4
February	3.2	3.6	6.0	2.1	3.2	3.9	5.4	2.4	5.4	5.0	1.4	1.4
March	3.2	3.5	5.5	2.0	3.3	3.8	5.0	2.3	5.5	5.2	1.4	1.5
April	3.2	3.6	5.2	2.1	3.4	3.9	4.9	2.4	5.4	5.1	1.4	1.5
May	3.3	3.7	6.0	1.9	3.4	4.0	5.3	2.4	5.4	5.1	1.5	1.5
June	3.3	3.6	6.4	2.2	3.5	4.1	4.8	2.6	5.3	5.1	1.4	1.6
July	3.1	3.5	6.6	1.9	3.3	3.9	4.5	2.3	5.3	5.2	1.4	1.4
August	3.2	3.6	5.8	2.0	3.6	4.2	4.4	2.5	5.3	5.2	1.4	1.4
September	3.0	3.4	6.2	1.9	3.4	3.9	4.6	2.1	4.8	4.7	1.2	1.2
October	3.2	3.5	5.2	2.0	3.4	3.9	4.6	2.4	5.3	5.1	1.4	1.4
November	3.2	3.6	6.5	2.1	3.2	3.6	4.9	2.4	5.0	4.8	1.3	1.4
December	3.0	3.4	4.8	1.9	3.4	4.1	4.4	2.3	5.3	5.0	1.3	1.3
2013												
January	3.2	3.6	5.8	2.0	3.6	4.2	4.5	2.5	5.4	5.3	1.4	1.4
February	3.1	3.5	5.7	2.0	3.5	4.1	4.2	2.5	5.3	5.2	1.3	1.4
March	3.1	3.4	5.8	2.0	3.3	3.9	4.4	2.3	5.4	5.3	1.4	1.4
April	3.3	3.6	5.3	2.1	3.4	4.1	4.8	2.6	5.7	5.6	1.4	1.4
May	3.3	3.6	5.1	2.2	3.4	4.0	4.7	2.7	5.3	5.1	1.4	1.4
June	3.2	3.5	5.6	2.0	3.2	3.8	5.0	2.4	5.3	5.1	1.3	1.4
July	3.3	3.6	5.2	2.2	3.5	3.9	4.8	2.6	5.3	5.1	1.3	1.4
August	3.3	3.7	4.8	2.0	3.6	4.4	5.3	2.5	5.1	5.0	1.3	1.3
September	3.3	3.7	4.8	1.9	3.5	4.3	5.0	2.5	5.8	5.6	1.3	1.3
October	3.2	3.5	5.7	1.7	3.7	4.4	4.5	2.4	5.3	5.2	1.3	1.3
November	3.2	3.5	4.7	1.9	3.7	4.6	4.8	2.3	5.2	5.0	1.3	1.4
December	3.2	3.5	4.9	1.9	3.4	4.2	4.8	2.5	5.2	5.1	1.4	1.4
2014												
January	3.2	3.6	4.1	2.1	3.6	4.3	4.9	2.5	5.5	5.4	1.3	1.4
February	3.3	3.6	4.3	1.8	3.7	4.5	5.0	2.4	5.8	5.6	1.3	1.3
March	3.3	3.6	4.0	2.0	3.8	4.7	5.0	2.5	5.3	5.1	1.4	1.5
April	3.3	3.7	4.1	2.0	3.9	4.9	5.0	2.7	5.5	5.3	1.3	1.3
May	3.3	3.7	4.6	1.9	3.9	4.7	4.8	2.4	5.6	5.4	1.4	1.4
June	3.3	3.7	4.3	2.0	3.9	4.7	5.0	2.5	6.0	5.9	1.2	1.3
July	3.4	3.8	4.6	2.1	4.1	4.8	5.2	2.5	5.8	5.4	1.3	1.3
August	3.3	3.7	4.9	1.8	3.8	4.5	5.3	2.3	5.7	5.4	1.4	1.5
September	3.5	3.9	4.2	2.1	3.9	4.6	5.4	2.7	6.0	5.9	1.4	1.4
October	3.5	3.9	4.9	2.2	4.0	4.8	5.7	2.7	5.9	5.7	1.4	1.4
November	3.3	3.7	4.9	1.8	3.9	4.7	4.7	2.4	5.8	5.6	1.3	1.4
December	3.4	3.8	5.7	2.2	4.0	4.9	4.6	2.5	5.9	5.8	1.4	1.5

[1]Total separations are the number of separations during the entire month.
[2]The total separations rate is the number of total separations during the entire month as a percent of total employment.
[3]Detail will not necessarily add to totals because of the independent seasonal adjustment of the various series.
[4]Includes natural resources and mining, information, financial activities, and other services, not shown separately.
[5]Includes wholesale trade and transportation, warehousing, and utilities, not shown separately.
[6]Includes arts, entertainment, and recreation, not shown separately.
[7]Includes federal government, not shown separately.

Table 7-6. Separations Levels[1] and Rates,[2] by Industry, 2009–October 2020—*Continued*

(Seasonally adjusted, levels in thousands, rates per 100.)

Year and month	Total[4]	Total private[4]	Construction	Manufacturing	Trade, transportation, and utilities[5]	Retail trade	Professional and business services	Education and health services	Leisure and hospitality[6]	Accommodation and food services	Government[7]	State and local government
2015												
January	4 911	4 602	326	267	1 081	769	1 001	541	898	735	309	278
February	4 828	4 515	301	256	966	671	1 032	578	881	714	312	286
March	5 064	4 727	348	259	1 094	762	1 059	554	911	755	337	304
April	4 942	4 624	284	263	1 033	719	1 065	543	920	774	318	290
May	4 826	4 506	269	239	1 053	742	1 012	563	864	736	321	274
June	4 992	4 649	340	268	1 065	745	988	563	906	762	343	310
July	4 887	4 570	278	257	1 093	752	975	574	886	778	317	284
August	5 055	4 731	305	267	1 058	754	1 001	592	982	836	324	293
September	5 114	4 779	315	272	1 067	737	1 055	582	945	808	335	303
October	5 032	4 688	294	275	1 021	716	1 035	587	965	803	344	313
November	5 052	4 721	299	269	1 045	753	1 087	615	939	802	331	300
December	5 208	4 861	290	263	1 072	763	1 122	596	1 002	846	347	318
2016												
January	5 144	4 807	293	271	1 080	752	1 155	576	927	772	337	300
February	5 282	4 951	337	311	1 067	757	1 092	592	1 029	894	331	299
March	5 140	4 806	324	283	1 023	702	1 099	565	985	835	333	303
April	5 122	4 781	340	277	1 025	702	1 081	588	974	843	341	307
May	5 137	4 793	332	291	1 011	703	1 128	587	975	820	344	311
June	5 061	4 695	280	265	1 032	693	1 026	609	979	832	367	335
July	5 114	4 817	317	262	1 070	751	1 140	595	991	847	297	267
August	5 188	4 827	339	274	1 053	707	1 084	618	1 008	824	361	332
September	4 988	4 650	278	286	1 090	758	1 023	571	926	777	338	309
October	5 098	4 763	327	285	1 046	737	1 057	585	986	826	335	301
November	5 114	4 782	322	283	1 020	702	1 078	610	1 017	874	331	300
December	5 087	4 780	414	290	966	660	1 051	584	1 005	836	307	285
2017												
January	5 338	4 997	376	303	1 046	692	1 079	629	1 038	894	341	303
February	5 141	4 794	327	285	1 082	774	1 029	561	986	837	347	314
March	5 254	4 932	370	322	1 091	766	1 019	625	982	845	322	289
April	5 101	4 767	380	315	975	680	1 001	622	952	803	334	295
May	5 280	4 929	377	322	1 053	745	1 070	633	952	797	351	323
June	5 457	5 124	363	326	1 076	741	1 208	624	1 005	830	333	300
July	5 351	5 021	377	328	1 012	684	1 135	619	992	762	330	298
August	5 368	5 030	361	303	1 009	677	1 114	677	1 009	835	338	305
September	5 334	4 995	379	320	1 004	682	1 133	608	1 034	857	339	307
October	5 347	5 011	381	319	988	685	1 133	654	969	814	336	300
November	5 221	4 882	319	325	1 063	737	1 088	638	997	828	339	303
December	5 265	4 905	297	343	1 066	701	1 035	658	984	839	360	331
2018												
January	5 346	5 012	334	351	1 111	740	1 023	632	1 036	862	334	306
February	5 276	4 952	325	350	1 007	682	1 111	630	1 032	859	324	287
March	5 475	5 133	362	350	1 086	754	1 131	673	1 013	828	342	310
April	5 449	5 110	335	342	1 128	773	1 084	657	1 035	856	339	303
May	5 513	5 177	354	339	1 063	715	1 153	683	1 049	871	336	304
June	5 558	5 207	364	339	1 108	754	1 164	682	1 014	814	351	320
July	5 579	5 214	369	357	1 100	762	1 113	666	1 075	876	365	328
August	5 568	5 223	351	336	1 185	813	1 064	685	1 049	868	345	315
September	5 517	5 170	347	316	1 169	821	1 053	656	1 079	907	347	313
October	5 638	5 284	332	358	1 184	779	1 150	683	1 073	909	354	321
November	5 692	5 331	390	358	1 146	749	1 105	712	1 073	900	361	327
December	5 569	5 227	355	338	1 154	781	1 141	699	1 026	870	342	303
2019												
January	5 590	5 219	394	339	1 087	726	1 071	715	1 088	929	371	337
February	5 676	5 310	381	337	1 125	736	1 125	740	1 092	930	366	334
March	5 553	5 212	346	364	1 106	735	1 153	702	1 039	900	341	303
April	5 763	5 414	404	352	1 117	752	1 187	675	1 114	954	349	318
May	5 547	5 211	380	336	1 147	766	1 123	635	1 045	873	336	302
June	5 568	5 227	415	324	1 125	765	1 075	618	1 117	975	341	308
July	5 769	5 427	381	325	1 218	801	1 144	674	1 108	959	342	305
August	5 660	5 312	409	320	1 201	802	1 113	635	1 067	905	348	306
September	5 739	5 387	431	349	1 201	796	1 141	661	1 096	944	352	311
October	5 580	5 211	450	333	1 062	687	1 079	668	1 067	896	369	314
November	5 657	5 307	416	318	1 198	816	1 131	663	1 063	888	350	309
December	5 762	5 419	432	342	1 115	741	1 134	690	1 146	963	343	298
2020												
January	5 713	5 382	386	331	1 220	830	1 151	701	1 090	918	331	283
February	5 595	5 244	359	318	1 221	812	1 073	699	1 036	880	351	311
March	14 643	14 243	756	804	2 408	1 654	1 714	1 747	5 345	4 746	400	361
April	9 975	9 536	835	762	1 953	1 267	1 359	1 323	1 989	1 675	439	400
May	4 236	3 935	292	285	936	530	875	538	640	534	302	248
June	4 899	4 656	343	392	1 077	640	926	603	858	722	243	200
July	4 988	4 729	347	359	1 123	717	986	632	820	705	259	214
August	4 689	4 413	324	332	1 103	719	960	606	708	655	276	219
September	4 844	4 504	290	354	1 063	687	989	618	737	653	340	250
October	5 142	4 674	331	350	1 123	739	1 011	647	777	678	469	266

[1]Total separations are the number of separations during the entire month.
[2]The total separations rate is the number of total separations during the entire month as a percent of total employment.
[3]Detail will not necessarily add to totals because of the independent seasonal adjustment of the various series.
[4]Includes natural resources and mining, information, financial activities, and other services, not shown separately.
[5]Includes wholesale trade and transportation, warehousing, and utilities, not shown separately.
[6]Includes arts, entertainment, and recreation, not shown separately.
[7]Includes federal government, not shown separately.

Table 7-6. Separations Levels[1] and Rates,[2] by Industry, 2009–October 2020—*Continued*

(Seasonally adjusted, levels in thousands, rates per 100.)

Year and month	Rate											
	Total[4]	Total private[4]	Construction	Manufacturing	Trade, transportation, and utilities[5]	Retail trade	Professional and business services	Education and health services	Leisure and hospitality[6]	Accommodation and food services	Government[7]	State and local government
2015												
January	3.5	3.9	5.2	2.2	4.1	5.0	5.1	2.5	6.0	5.7	1.4	1.4
February	3.4	3.8	4.7	2.1	3.6	4.3	5.3	2.7	5.9	5.6	1.4	1.5
March	3.6	4.0	5.5	2.1	4.1	4.9	5.4	2.5	6.1	5.9	1.5	1.6
April	3.5	3.9	4.4	2.1	3.9	4.6	5.4	2.5	6.1	6.0	1.4	1.5
May	3.4	3.8	4.2	1.9	3.9	4.8	5.2	2.6	5.7	5.7	1.5	1.4
June	3.5	3.9	5.3	2.2	4.0	4.8	5.0	2.6	6.0	5.9	1.6	1.6
July	3.4	3.8	4.3	2.1	4.1	4.8	4.9	2.6	5.8	6.0	1.4	1.5
August	3.6	3.9	4.7	2.2	3.9	4.8	5.1	2.7	6.5	6.4	1.5	1.5
September	3.6	4.0	4.8	2.2	4.0	4.7	5.3	2.6	6.2	6.2	1.5	1.6
October	3.5	3.9	4.5	2.2	3.8	4.6	5.2	2.6	6.3	6.1	1.6	1.6
November	3.5	3.9	4.5	2.2	3.9	4.8	5.5	2.8	6.1	6.1	1.5	1.6
December	3.6	4.0	4.4	2.1	4.0	4.9	5.6	2.7	6.5	6.4	1.6	1.6
2016												
January	3.6	4.0	4.4	2.2	4.0	4.8	5.8	2.6	6.0	5.8	1.5	1.6
February	3.7	4.1	5.1	2.5	3.9	4.8	5.5	2.6	6.6	6.7	1.5	1.5
March	3.6	4.0	4.8	2.3	3.8	4.4	5.5	2.5	6.3	6.3	1.5	1.6
April	3.6	3.9	5.1	2.2	3.8	4.4	5.4	2.6	6.3	6.3	1.5	1.6
May	3.6	3.9	5.0	2.4	3.7	4.4	5.6	2.6	6.3	6.1	1.5	1.6
June	3.5	3.8	4.2	2.1	3.8	4.4	5.1	2.7	6.3	6.2	1.7	1.7
July	3.5	3.9	4.7	2.1	3.9	4.7	5.7	2.6	6.3	6.3	1.3	1.4
August	3.6	3.9	5.0	2.2	3.9	4.5	5.4	2.7	6.4	6.1	1.6	1.7
September	3.4	3.8	4.1	2.3	4.0	4.8	5.1	2.5	5.9	5.8	1.5	1.6
October	3.5	3.9	4.8	2.3	3.8	4.6	5.2	2.6	6.2	6.1	1.5	1.5
November	3.5	3.9	4.7	2.3	3.7	4.4	5.3	2.7	6.4	6.5	1.5	1.5
December	3.5	3.9	6.1	2.4	3.5	4.2	5.2	2.5	6.3	6.2	1.4	1.5
2017												
January	3.7	4.1	5.5	2.5	3.8	4.3	5.3	2.7	6.5	6.6	1.5	1.6
February	3.5	3.9	4.7	2.3	4.0	4.9	5.1	2.4	6.2	6.1	1.6	1.6
March	3.6	4.0	5.3	2.6	4.0	4.8	5.0	2.7	6.2	6.2	1.4	1.5
April	3.5	3.9	5.5	2.5	3.6	4.3	4.9	2.7	6.0	5.9	1.5	1.5
May	3.6	4.0	5.4	2.6	3.9	4.7	5.2	2.7	5.9	5.8	1.6	1.7
June	3.7	4.1	5.2	2.6	3.9	4.7	5.9	2.7	6.3	6.1	1.5	1.5
July	3.6	4.0	5.4	2.6	3.7	4.3	5.5	2.7	6.2	5.5	1.5	1.5
August	3.7	4.0	5.2	2.4	3.7	4.3	5.4	2.9	6.2	6.1	1.5	1.6
September	3.6	4.0	5.4	2.6	3.7	4.3	5.5	2.6	6.4	6.2	1.5	1.6
October	3.6	4.0	5.4	2.6	3.6	4.3	5.5	2.8	6.0	5.9	1.5	1.5
November	3.5	3.9	4.5	2.6	3.9	4.7	5.3	2.7	6.2	6.0	1.5	1.5
December	3.6	3.9	4.2	2.7	3.9	4.4	5.0	2.8	6.1	6.1	1.6	1.7
2018												
January	3.6	4.0	4.7	2.8	4.0	4.7	4.9	2.7	6.4	6.2	1.5	1.6
February	3.6	3.9	4.5	2.8	3.7	4.3	5.3	2.7	6.4	6.2	1.4	1.5
March	3.7	4.1	5.0	2.8	3.9	4.8	5.4	2.9	6.2	6.0	1.5	1.6
April	3.7	4.1	4.6	2.7	4.1	4.9	5.2	2.8	6.4	6.2	1.5	1.5
May	3.7	4.1	4.9	2.7	3.9	4.5	5.5	2.9	6.5	6.3	1.5	1.5
June	3.7	4.1	5.0	2.7	4.0	4.8	5.6	2.9	6.2	5.8	1.6	1.6
July	3.7	4.1	5.0	2.8	4.0	4.8	5.3	2.8	6.6	6.3	1.6	1.7
August	3.7	4.1	4.8	2.6	4.3	5.1	5.1	2.9	6.4	6.2	1.5	1.6
September	3.7	4.1	4.7	2.5	4.2	5.2	5.0	2.8	6.6	6.5	1.5	1.6
October	3.8	4.2	4.5	2.8	4.3	5.0	5.5	2.9	6.6	6.5	1.6	1.6
November	3.8	4.2	5.3	2.8	4.1	4.8	5.2	3.0	6.6	6.4	1.6	1.7
December	3.7	4.1	4.8	2.6	4.2	5.0	5.4	2.9	6.2	6.2	1.5	1.5
2019												
January	3.7	4.1	5.3	2.6	3.9	4.6	5.1	3.0	6.6	6.6	1.6	1.7
February	3.8	4.2	5.1	2.6	4.1	4.7	5.3	3.1	6.6	6.6	1.6	1.7
March	3.7	4.1	4.6	2.8	4.0	4.7	5.4	2.9	6.3	6.4	1.5	1.5
April	3.8	4.2	5.4	2.7	4.0	4.8	5.6	2.8	6.7	6.8	1.5	1.6
May	3.7	4.1	5.1	2.6	4.1	4.9	5.3	2.6	6.3	6.2	1.5	1.5
June	3.7	4.1	5.5	2.5	4.1	4.9	5.0	2.6	6.8	6.9	1.5	1.6
July	3.8	4.2	5.1	2.5	4.4	5.1	5.4	2.8	6.7	6.8	1.5	1.5
August	3.7	4.1	5.4	2.5	4.3	5.1	5.2	2.6	6.4	6.4	1.5	1.5
September	3.8	4.2	5.7	2.7	4.3	5.1	5.3	2.7	6.6	6.7	1.6	1.6
October	3.7	4.0	6.0	2.6	3.8	4.4	5.0	2.7	6.6	6.3	1.6	1.6
November	3.7	4.1	5.5	2.5	4.3	5.2	5.3	2.7	6.3	6.2	1.5	1.6
December	3.8	4.2	5.7	2.7	4.0	4.7	5.3	2.8	6.8	6.7	1.5	1.5
2020												
January	3.8	4.2	5.1	2.6	4.4	5.3	5.3	2.9	6.5	6.4	1.5	1.4
February	3.7	4.0	4.7	2.5	4.4	5.2	5.0	2.8	6.1	6.1	1.5	1.6
March	9.7	11.1	9.9	6.3	8.7	10.6	8.0	7.1	32.7	34.1	1.8	1.8
April	7.6	8.8	12.7	6.6	8.0	9.5	7.1	6.1	23.2	22.5	2.0	2.1
May	3.2	3.5	4.2	2.4	3.8	3.9	4.5	2.4	6.4	6.1	1.4	1.4
June	3.6	4.0	4.8	3.2	4.2	4.4	4.7	2.6	7.2	6.9	1.1	1.1
July	3.6	4.0	4.8	3.0	4.3	4.9	5.0	2.7	6.5	6.4	1.2	1.1
August	3.3	3.7	4.5	2.7	4.2	4.8	4.8	2.6	5.6	5.9	1.3	1.2
September	3.4	3.8	4.0	2.9	4.0	4.6	4.9	2.7	5.6	5.7	1.6	1.3
October	3.6	3.9	4.5	2.9	4.2	4.9	4.9	2.8	5.8	5.8	2.2	1.4

[1] Total separations are the number of separations during the entire month.
[2] The total separations rate is the number of total separations during the entire month as a percent of total employment.
[3] Detail will not necessarily add to totals because of the independent seasonal adjustment of the various series.
[4] Includes natural resources and mining, information, financial activities, and other services, not shown separately.
[5] Includes wholesale trade and transportation, warehousing, and utilities, not shown separately.
[6] Includes arts, entertainment, and recreation, not shown separately.
[7] Includes federal government, not shown separately.

NOTES AND DEFINITIONS

JOB OPENINGS AND LABOR TURNOVER SURVEY

Data from a sample of approximately 16,000 businesses for the Job Openings and Labor Turnover Survey (JOLTS) are collected and compiled monthly from a sample of business establishments by the Bureau of Labor Statistics (BLS). Each month, data are collected in a survey of business establishments for total employment, job openings, hires, quits, layoffs and discharges, and other separations. Data collection methods include computer-assisted telephone interviewing, touchtone data entry, fax, and mail.

Concepts and Definitions

The JOLTS program covers all private nonfarm establishments such as factories, offices, and stores, as well as federal, state, and local government entities in the 50 states and the District of Columbia.

Employment includes persons on the payroll who worked or received pay for the pay period that includes the 12th day of the reference month. Full-time, part-time, permanent, short-term, seasonal, salaried, and hourly employees are included, as are employees on paid vacations or other paid leave. Proprietors or partners of unincorporated businesses, unpaid family workers, or persons on leave without pay or on strike for the entire pay period, are not counted as employed. Employees of temporary help agencies, employee leasing companies, outside contractors, and consultants are counted by their employer of record, not by the establishment where they are working.

Job openings information is submitted by establishments for the last business day of the reference month. A job opening requires that: 1) a specific position exists and there is work available for that position, 2) work could start within 30 days regardless of whether a suitable candidate is found, and 3) the employer is actively recruiting from outside the establishment to fill the position. Included are full-time, part-time, permanent, short-term, and seasonal openings. Active recruiting means that the establishment is taking steps to fill a position by advertising in newspapers or on the Internet, posting help-wanted signs, accepting applications, or using other similar methods.

Jobs to be filled only by internal transfers, promotions, demotions, or recall from layoffs are excluded. Also excluded are jobs with start dates more than 30 days in the future, jobs for which employees have been hired but have not yet reported for work, and jobs to be filled by employees of temporary help agencies, employee leasing companies, outside contractors, or consultants. The job openings rate is computed by dividing the number of job openings by the sum of employment and job openings and multiplying that quotient by 100.

Hires are the total number of additions to the payroll occurring at any time during the reference month, including both new and rehired employees, full-time and part-time, permanent, short-term and seasonal employees, employees recalled to the location after a layoff lasting more than 7 days, on-call or intermittent employees who returned to work after having been formally separated, and transfers from other locations. The hires count does not include transfers or promotions within the reporting site, employees returning from strike, employees of temporary help agencies or employee leasing companies, outside contractors, or consultants. The hires rate is computed by dividing the number of hires by employment and multiplying that quotient by 100.

Separations are the total number of terminations of employment occurring at any time during the reference month, and are reported by type of separation—quits, layoffs and discharges, and other separations. Quits are voluntary separations by employees (except for retirements, which are reported as other separations). Layoffs and discharges are involuntary separations initiated by the employer and include layoffs with no intent to rehire, formal layoffs lasting or expected to last more than 7 days, discharges resulting from mergers, downsizing, or closings, firings or other discharges for cause, terminations of permanent or short-term employees, and terminations of seasonal employees. Other separations include retirements, transfers to other locations, deaths, and separations due to disability. Separations do not include transfers within the same location or employees on strike.

The separations rate is computed by dividing the number of separations by employment and multiplying that quotient by 100. The quits, layoffs and discharges, and other separations rates are computed similarly, dividing the number by employment and multiplying by 100.

The JOLTS annual level estimates for hires, quits, layoffs and discharges, other separations, and total separations are the sum of the 12 published monthly levels. The annual rate estimates are computed by dividing the annual level by the Current Employment Statistics (CES) annual average employment level, and multiplying that quotient by 100. This figure will be approximately equal to the sum of the 12 monthly rates.

Annual estimates are not calculated for job openings because job openings are a stock, or point-in-time, measurement for the last business day of each month. Only jobs still open on the last day of the month are counted. For the same reason job openings cannot be cumulated throughout each month, annual figures for job openings cannot be created by summing the monthly estimates. Hires and separations are flow measures and are cumulated over the month with a total reported for the month. Therefore, the annual figures can be created by summing the monthly estimates.

Sources of Additional Information

For more extensive information see the Job Openings and Labor Turnover Survey (JOLTS) page on the BLS Web site at <http://www.bls.gov/jlt/>.

Table 7-7. Quits Levels[1] and Rates,[2] by Industry, 2009–October 2020

(Seasonally adjusted, levels in thousands, rates per 100.)

Year and month	Level[3]											
	Total[4]	Total private[4]	Construction	Manufacturing	Trade, transportation, and utilities[5]	Retail trade	Professional and business services	Education and health services	Leisure and hospitality[6]	Accommodation and food services	Government[7]	State and local government
2009												
January	1 978	1 873	87	112	465	344	346	256	404	371	105	100
February	1 945	1 842	97	99	402	307	308	260	417	385	102	99
March	1 829	1 721	92	86	434	318	279	240	384	353	108	103
April	1 713	1 609	60	78	375	274	285	231	367	325	104	100
May	1 684	1 580	82	87	356	262	294	235	345	302	104	95
June	1 686	1 586	76	88	366	283	275	257	353	305	100	93
July	1 689	1 582	64	92	391	285	268	240	337	311	107	103
August	1 561	1 460	39	86	336	243	250	241	345	313	101	92
September	1 631	1 530	73	90	364	263	265	261	300	285	100	93
October	1 663	1 567	61	80	379	280	272	259	331	297	96	90
November	1 803	1 691	92	72	410	284	278	262	371	335	112	104
December	1 758	1 646	84	70	396	295	296	254	372	339	112	101
2010												
January	1 744	1 640	100	82	343	256	329	231	379	324	104	98
February	1 834	1 718	83	105	419	328	322	239	374	341	116	106
March	1 853	1 744	83	86	409	307	340	243	367	337	110	100
April	1 898	1 793	64	89	430	326	352	286	365	324	105	96
May	1 814	1 715	60	85	421	324	337	239	357	321	98	88
June	1 911	1 778	62	98	422	318	374	263	327	297	133	105
July	1 789	1 677	69	84	425	328	325	241	336	304	112	92
August	1 852	1 739	79	107	404	302	381	240	336	300	114	99
September	1 901	1 774	83	97	416	317	363	247	356	315	127	113
October	1 848	1 741	81	99	393	308	360	249	362	306	108	99
November	1 881	1 777	70	94	420	320	355	266	364	322	105	96
December	1 968	1 856	90	105	396	295	395	251	385	342	112	104
2011												
January	1 833	1 710	70	102	367	248	369	227	375	336	123	113
February	1 952	1 841	72	96	440	310	410	244	371	331	111	104
March	2 028	1 919	80	112	440	333	451	254	382	338	109	101
April	1 883	1 775	94	103	404	310	369	244	372	328	108	99
May	1 966	1 836	84	108	449	334	369	258	367	328	129	122
June	1 923	1 822	79	111	430	329	368	245	392	354	101	91
July	1 990	1 860	74	103	419	312	410	234	381	333	130	122
August	2 043	1 918	67	100	443	330	396	275	419	370	125	116
September	2 045	1 929	86	94	440	323	442	248	401	348	116	106
October	2 000	1 892	81	108	445	323	442	245	339	302	107	98
November	2 031	1 909	116	118	398	283	434	247	378	336	122	113
December	1 975	1 832	82	107	445	336	315	265	406	352	143	134
2012												
January	2 032	1 902	78	103	417	308	405	274	402	358	130	120
February	2 123	1 984	81	108	456	342	409	305	414	362	139	127
March	2 163	2 030	91	110	460	330	410	288	444	396	133	124
April	2 136	1 996	72	113	468	341	376	280	437	390	140	130
May	2 140	2 001	79	110	463	334	407	280	437	387	139	126
June	2 151	2 027	90	112	480	343	363	277	454	405	124	116
July	2 075	1 949	81	102	476	339	348	274	431	382	126	116
August	2 080	1 952	66	110	479	328	344	288	388	340	129	120
September	1 957	1 838	74	107	438	325	351	253	389	355	118	109
October	2 037	1 904	101	105	474	327	319	263	413	367	133	123
November	2 070	1 931	104	106	445	322	355	287	411	370	139	128
December	2 045	1 915	75	109	434	324	384	281	420	381	130	120
2013												
January	2 281	2 150	134	100	537	394	353	313	456	404	131	124
February	2 281	2 152	107	108	497	356	383	300	484	428	129	119
March	2 118	1 994	93	97	453	330	385	289	447	388	124	113
April	2 297	2 144	90	117	496	362	452	301	449	406	153	143
May	2 237	2 103	91	118	455	321	441	293	446	399	134	124
June	2 203	2 076	99	109	455	331	460	294	429	381	127	117
July	2 367	2 233	103	118	467	349	527	316	452	401	134	122
August	2 331	2 205	93	105	537	414	458	299	424	374	127	114
September	2 307	2 184	92	114	535	405	433	310	444	396	123	114
October	2 374	2 244	92	106	525	389	454	322	522	475	130	118
November	2 384	2 257	80	121	548	406	487	299	483	426	127	119
December	2 281	2 143	78	114	481	356	469	322	456	403	138	126
2014												
January	2 312	2 181	96	114	537	404	449	303	464	417	132	122
February	2 401	2 267	97	110	553	410	433	309	529	483	135	125
March	2 441	2 304	93	121	560	410	520	274	497	440	137	127
April	2 476	2 334	106	107	571	422	480	321	506	461	141	130
May	2 486	2 344	123	117	611	436	458	322	459	411	141	131
June	2 506	2 388	116	108	589	436	506	327	513	456	118	107
July	2 637	2 497	110	132	612	456	505	346	517	461	140	132
August	2 564	2 412	127	115	558	412	493	297	544	488	152	147
September	2 737	2 577	108	135	589	421	555	347	549	502	160	148
October	2 721	2 568	108	131	603	447	512	361	586	518	152	142
November	2 588	2 452	93	108	613	442	455	343	565	502	136	125
December	2 543	2 403	118	131	607	440	412	336	553	499	141	129

[1]Quits are the number of quits during the entire month.
[2]The quits rate is the number of quits during the entire month as a percent of total employment.
[3]Detail will not necessarily add to totals because of the independent seasonal adjustment of the various series.
[4]Includes natural resources and mining, information, financial activities, and other services, not shown separately.
[5]Includes wholesale trade and transportation, warehousing, and utilities, not shown separately.
[6]Includes arts, entertainment, and recreation, not shown separately.
[7]Includes federal government, not shown separately.

Table 7-7. Quits Levels[1] and Rates,[2] by Industry, 2009–October 2020—*Continued*

(Seasonally adjusted, levels in thousands, rates per 100.)

Year and month	Rate											
	Total[4]	Total private[4]	Construction	Manufacturing	Trade, transportation, and utilities[5]	Retail trade	Professional and business services	Education and health services	Leisure and hospitality[6]	Accommodation and food services	Government[7]	State and local government
2009												
January	1.5	1.7	1.3	0.9	1.8	2.3	2.0	1.3	3.1	3.3	0.5	0.5
February	1.5	1.7	1.5	0.8	1.6	2.1	1.8	1.3	3.2	3.4	0.5	0.5
March	1.4	1.6	1.5	0.7	1.7	2.2	1.7	1.2	2.9	3.2	0.5	0.5
April	1.3	1.5	1.0	0.6	1.5	1.9	1.7	1.2	2.8	2.9	0.5	0.5
May	1.3	1.5	1.3	0.7	1.4	1.8	1.8	1.2	2.6	2.7	0.5	0.5
June	1.3	1.5	1.3	0.7	1.5	1.9	1.7	1.3	2.7	2.7	0.4	0.5
July	1.3	1.5	1.1	0.8	1.6	2.0	1.6	1.2	2.6	2.8	0.5	0.5
August	1.2	1.4	0.7	0.7	1.4	1.7	1.5	1.2	2.6	2.8	0.4	0.5
September	1.3	1.4	1.3	0.8	1.5	1.8	1.6	1.3	2.3	2.6	0.4	0.5
October	1.3	1.5	1.1	0.7	1.5	1.9	1.6	1.3	2.5	2.7	0.4	0.5
November	1.4	1.6	1.6	0.6	1.7	2.0	1.7	1.3	2.9	3.0	0.5	0.5
December	1.4	1.5	1.5	0.6	1.6	2.1	1.8	1.3	2.9	3.1	0.5	0.5
2010												
January	1.3	1.5	1.8	0.7	1.4	1.8	2.0	1.2	2.9	2.9	0.5	0.5
February	1.4	1.6	1.5	0.9	1.7	2.3	1.9	1.2	2.9	3.1	0.5	0.5
March	1.4	1.6	1.5	0.8	1.7	2.1	2.1	1.2	2.8	3.1	0.5	0.5
April	1.5	1.7	1.1	0.8	1.8	2.3	2.1	1.4	2.8	2.9	0.4	0.4
May	1.4	1.6	1.1	0.7	1.7	2.2	2.0	1.2	2.7	2.9	0.4	0.4
June	1.5	1.6	1.1	0.8	1.7	2.2	2.2	1.3	2.5	2.7	0.6	0.5
July	1.4	1.6	1.3	0.7	1.7	2.3	1.9	1.2	2.6	2.7	0.5	0.5
August	1.4	1.6	1.4	0.9	1.6	2.1	2.3	1.2	2.6	2.7	0.5	0.5
September	1.5	1.6	1.5	0.8	1.7	2.2	2.2	1.2	2.7	2.8	0.6	0.6
October	1.4	1.6	1.5	0.9	1.6	2.1	2.1	1.2	2.8	2.7	0.5	0.5
November	1.4	1.6	1.3	0.8	1.7	2.2	2.1	1.3	2.8	2.9	0.5	0.5
December	1.5	1.7	1.6	0.9	1.6	2.0	2.3	1.2	2.9	3.0	0.5	0.5
2011												
January	1.4	1.6	1.3	0.9	1.5	1.7	2.2	1.1	2.9	3.0	0.6	0.6
February	1.5	1.7	1.3	0.8	1.8	2.1	2.4	1.2	2.8	2.9	0.5	0.5
March	1.5	1.8	1.5	1.0	1.8	2.3	2.6	1.3	2.9	3.0	0.5	0.5
April	1.4	1.6	1.7	0.9	1.6	2.1	2.1	1.2	2.8	2.9	0.5	0.5
May	1.5	1.7	1.5	0.9	1.8	2.3	2.1	1.3	2.8	2.9	0.6	0.6
June	1.5	1.7	1.4	0.9	1.7	2.2	2.1	1.2	2.9	3.1	0.5	0.5
July	1.5	1.7	1.3	0.9	1.7	2.1	2.4	1.2	2.8	2.9	0.6	0.6
August	1.5	1.7	1.2	0.9	1.8	2.2	2.3	1.4	3.1	3.2	0.6	0.6
September	1.5	1.7	1.5	0.8	1.8	2.2	2.5	1.2	3.0	3.0	0.5	0.6
October	1.5	1.7	1.5	0.9	1.8	2.2	2.5	1.2	2.5	2.6	0.5	0.5
November	1.5	1.7	2.1	1.0	1.6	1.9	2.5	1.2	2.8	2.9	0.6	0.6
December	1.5	1.7	1.5	0.9	1.8	2.3	1.8	1.3	3.0	3.0	0.7	0.7
2012												
January	1.5	1.7	1.4	0.9	1.6	2.1	2.3	1.3	3.0	3.1	0.6	0.6
February	1.6	1.8	1.4	0.9	1.8	2.3	2.3	1.5	3.0	3.1	0.6	0.7
March	1.6	1.8	1.6	0.9	1.8	2.2	2.3	1.4	3.2	3.4	0.6	0.6
April	1.6	1.8	1.3	0.9	1.8	2.3	2.1	1.4	3.2	3.3	0.6	0.7
May	1.6	1.8	1.4	0.9	1.8	2.2	2.3	1.4	3.2	3.3	0.6	0.7
June	1.6	1.8	1.6	0.9	1.9	2.3	2.0	1.3	3.3	3.4	0.6	0.6
July	1.5	1.7	1.4	0.9	1.9	2.3	1.9	1.3	3.1	3.2	0.6	0.6
August	1.5	1.7	1.2	0.9	1.9	2.2	1.9	1.4	2.8	2.9	0.6	0.6
September	1.5	1.6	1.3	0.9	1.7	2.2	1.9	1.2	2.8	3.0	0.5	0.6
October	1.5	1.7	1.8	0.9	1.9	2.2	1.8	1.3	3.0	3.1	0.6	0.6
November	1.5	1.7	1.8	0.9	1.7	2.2	2.0	1.4	3.0	3.1	0.6	0.7
December	1.5	1.7	1.3	0.9	1.7	2.2	2.1	1.3	3.0	3.2	0.6	0.6
2013												
January	1.7	1.9	2.3	0.8	2.1	2.6	1.9	1.5	3.3	3.4	0.6	0.6
February	1.7	1.9	1.8	0.9	1.9	2.4	2.1	1.4	3.4	3.5	0.6	0.6
March	1.6	1.8	1.6	0.8	1.8	2.2	2.1	1.4	3.2	3.2	0.6	0.6
April	1.7	1.9	1.6	1.0	1.9	2.4	2.4	1.4	3.2	3.3	0.7	0.8
May	1.6	1.8	1.6	1.0	1.8	2.1	2.4	1.4	3.1	3.3	0.6	0.6
June	1.6	1.8	1.7	0.9	1.8	2.2	2.5	1.4	3.0	3.1	0.6	0.6
July	1.7	1.9	1.8	1.0	1.8	2.3	2.8	1.5	3.2	3.3	0.6	0.6
August	1.7	1.9	1.6	0.9	2.1	2.7	2.5	1.4	3.0	3.0	0.6	0.6
September	1.7	1.9	1.6	1.0	2.1	2.7	2.3	1.5	3.1	3.2	0.6	0.6
October	1.7	1.9	1.6	0.9	2.0	2.6	2.4	1.5	3.6	3.9	0.6	0.6
November	1.7	2.0	1.3	1.0	2.1	2.7	2.6	1.4	3.4	3.4	0.6	0.6
December	1.7	1.9	1.3	0.9	1.8	2.3	2.5	1.5	3.2	3.3	0.6	0.7
2014												
January	1.7	1.9	1.6	0.9	2.1	2.6	2.4	1.4	3.2	3.4	0.6	0.6
February	1.7	2.0	1.6	0.9	2.1	2.7	2.3	1.5	3.6	3.9	0.6	0.7
March	1.8	2.0	1.5	1.0	2.1	2.7	2.7	1.3	3.4	3.5	0.6	0.7
April	1.8	2.0	1.7	0.9	2.2	2.8	2.5	1.5	3.5	3.7	0.6	0.7
May	1.8	2.0	2.0	1.0	2.3	2.8	2.4	1.5	3.1	3.3	0.6	0.7
June	1.8	2.0	1.9	0.9	2.2	2.8	2.6	1.5	3.5	3.6	0.5	0.6
July	1.9	2.1	1.8	1.1	2.3	3.0	2.6	1.6	3.5	3.7	0.6	0.7
August	1.8	2.1	2.0	0.9	2.1	2.7	2.6	1.4	3.7	3.9	0.7	0.8
September	2.0	2.2	1.7	1.1	2.2	2.7	2.9	1.6	3.7	4.0	0.7	0.8
October	1.9	2.2	1.7	1.1	2.3	2.9	2.7	1.7	4.0	4.1	0.7	0.7
November	1.8	2.1	1.5	0.9	2.3	2.9	2.4	1.6	3.8	3.9	0.6	0.7
December	1.8	2.0	1.9	1.1	2.3	2.8	2.1	1.5	3.7	3.9	0.6	0.7

[1]Quits are the number of quits during the entire month.
[2]The quits rate is the number of quits during the entire month as a percent of total employment.
[3]Detail will not necessarily add to totals because of the independent seasonal adjustment of the various series.
[4]Includes natural resources and mining, information, financial activities, and other services, not shown separately.
[5]Includes wholesale trade and transportation, warehousing, and utilities, not shown separately.
[6]Includes arts, entertainment, and recreation, not shown separately.
[7]Includes federal government, not shown separately.

Table 7-7. Quits Levels[1] and Rates,[2] by Industry, 2009–October 2020—*Continued*

(Seasonally adjusted, levels in thousands, rates per 100.)

Year and month	Level[3]											
	Total[4]	Total private[4]	Construction	Manufacturing	Trade, transportation, and utilities[5]	Retail trade	Professional and business services	Education and health services	Leisure and hospitality[6]	Accommodation and food services	Government[7]	State and local government
2015												
January	2 766	2 623	110	145	610	450	548	362	584	527	143	130
February	2 731	2 582	111	124	563	410	563	382	544	495	149	139
March	2 748	2 593	115	122	618	459	544	360	573	538	155	145
April	2 706	2 560	122	139	614	442	511	350	545	492	147	138
May	2 746	2 597	117	126	621	451	555	364	534	477	149	133
June	2 756	2 591	112	138	620	461	508	352	597	539	165	153
July	2 768	2 614	107	127	610	434	516	379	606	549	154	142
August	2 888	2 726	100	137	624	454	562	396	648	580	162	151
September	2 783	2 629	119	144	636	458	505	357	607	550	154	142
October	2 814	2 647	95	140	618	451	536	379	600	545	167	155
November	2 891	2 738	123	136	634	486	554	416	622	573	153	143
December	3 043	2 877	127	135	683	502	575	398	651	595	166	155
2016												
January	2 893	2 729	96	149	655	479	572	343	633	572	164	150
February	2 997	2 836	104	154	636	472	593	392	661	591	161	149
March	2 900	2 738	142	140	647	473	541	370	629	582	162	150
April	2 954	2 793	113	137	653	468	582	391	649	588	161	148
May	3 010	2 845	122	138	596	450	675	393	666	596	165	152
June	2 988	2 796	118	137	638	452	545	404	653	590	192	179
July	2 976	2 816	129	145	627	460	619	394	654	587	160	147
August	3 007	2 825	146	150	654	474	597	383	645	581	182	170
September	3 044	2 871	106	152	680	474	619	403	666	588	173	161
October	3 078	2 905	128	167	659	486	612	385	683	607	174	161
November	3 017	2 860	155	157	651	467	582	378	703	629	157	143
December	2 986	2 824	135	160	604	428	607	382	685	608	162	154
2017												
January	3 176	2 996	152	172	668	482	633	428	645	577	180	162
February	3 081	2 908	156	178	690	505	563	387	641	568	173	158
March	3 134	2 953	162	186	680	505	589	421	646	573	182	168
April	3 034	2 875	157	181	599	437	582	415	659	581	159	144
May	3 126	2 961	149	202	664	490	583	410	662	597	166	153
June	3 157	2 993	139	202	646	460	622	425	658	590	164	148
July	3 118	2 955	150	198	668	462	607	389	622	561	163	149
August	3 134	2 970	153	185	651	458	660	386	626	566	164	149
September	3 212	3 041	170	192	651	451	667	404	652	601	171	158
October	3 193	3 025	178	196	642	444	650	428	628	570	168	152
November	3 157	2 979	139	192	643	442	676	412	662	593	178	161
December	3 222	3 046	147	211	681	480	632	410	680	604	176	164
2018												
January	3 034	2 862	154	212	656	452	552	382	612	540	172	159
February	3 175	3 015	151	216	637	444	630	396	695	622	160	145
March	3 301	3 131	157	216	664	456	636	414	701	629	170	158
April	3 373	3 187	171	201	701	495	684	437	708	638	185	169
May	3 405	3 221	168	200	709	494	642	491	699	624	184	169
June	3 389	3 198	179	208	721	518	661	450	690	612	190	177
July	3 443	3 260	202	218	710	517	644	440	720	640	183	168
August	3 446	3 273	181	207	740	505	605	473	725	643	174	160
September	3 400	3 226	162	199	766	560	601	435	731	647	173	156
October	3 485	3 299	171	209	756	530	652	482	721	643	186	169
November	3 460	3 266	182	222	709	485	626	500	706	636	195	177
December	3 415	3 235	180	202	725	500	630	497	714	646	180	162
2019												
January	3 530	3 334	189	221	706	502	647	481	767	695	196	182
February	3 541	3 358	194	209	737	509	650	497	795	714	183	168
March	3 525	3 347	146	221	744	514	697	486	747	666	178	158
April	3 492	3 306	144	219	729	502	654	447	757	679	187	172
May	3 486	3 294	163	203	774	538	638	412	761	688	192	177
June	3 481	3 298	186	197	754	541	633	421	783	705	183	169
July	3 612	3 433	178	193	772	542	687	473	787	709	180	163
August	3 544	3 363	173	197	771	547	650	462	780	698	181	162
September	3 429	3 242	185	214	741	525	642	447	722	647	187	169
October	3 442	3 261	189	200	630	433	632	464	776	692	180	161
November	3 528	3 341	164	201	802	577	622	462	736	650	188	171
December	3 528	3 331	170	206	734	507	622	500	771	698	197	174
2019												
January	3 575	3 399	165	188	831	597	684	476	758	679	176	156
February	3 436	3 245	153	183	794	546	628	478	699	622	191	172
March	2 789	2 619	130	150	607	386	561	426	534	483	170	152
April	1 877	1 731	86	104	447	305	337	356	255	225	146	130
May	2 067	1 945	104	143	484	306	411	286	369	338	122	105
June	2 605	2 492	131	186	613	410	441	394	487	457	113	96
July	2 932	2 789	143	179	753	524	533	438	501	469	143	123
August	2 839	2 696	103	207	722	502	558	398	488	473	142	124
September	3 074	2 920	142	235	702	466	627	425	536	498	155	134
October	3 150	2 972	122	216	732	500	599	464	574	522	178	149

[1]Quits are the number of quits during the entire month.
[2]The quits rate is the number of quits during the entire month as a percent of total employment.
[3]Detail will not necessarily add to totals because of the independent seasonal adjustment of the various series.
[4]Includes natural resources and mining, information, financial activities, and other services, not shown separately.
[5]Includes wholesale trade and transportation, warehousing, and utilities, not shown separately.
[6]Includes arts, entertainment, and recreation, not shown separately.
[7]Includes federal government, not shown separately.

Table 7-7. Quits Levels[1] and Rates,[2] by Industry, 2009–October 2020—*Continued*

(Seasonally adjusted, levels in thousands, rates per 100.)

Year and month	Rate											
	Total[4]	Total private[4]	Construc-tion	Manufac-turing	Trade, transpor-tation, and utilities[5]	Retail trade	Profes-sional and business services	Education and health services	Leisure and hospitality[6]	Accommo-dation and food services	Govern-ment[7]	State and local govern-ment
2015												
January	2.0	2.2	1.7	1.2	2.3	2.9	2.8	1.7	3.9	4.1	0.6	0.7
February	1.9	2.2	1.7	1.0	2.1	2.6	2.9	1.8	3.6	3.9	0.7	0.7
March	2.0	2.2	1.8	1.0	2.3	3.0	2.8	1.6	3.8	4.2	0.7	0.8
April	1.9	2.1	1.9	1.1	2.3	2.8	2.6	1.6	3.6	3.8	0.7	0.7
May	1.9	2.2	1.8	1.0	2.3	2.9	2.8	1.7	3.5	3.7	0.7	0.7
June	1.9	2.2	1.7	1.1	2.3	3.0	2.6	1.6	4.0	4.2	0.7	0.8
July	1.9	2.2	1.7	1.0	2.3	2.8	2.6	1.7	4.0	4.2	0.7	0.7
August	2.0	2.3	1.5	1.1	2.3	2.9	2.8	1.8	4.3	4.5	0.7	0.8
September	2.0	2.2	1.8	1.2	2.4	2.9	2.6	1.6	4.0	4.2	0.7	0.7
October	2.0	2.2	1.5	1.1	2.3	2.9	2.7	1.7	3.9	4.2	0.8	0.8
November	2.0	2.3	1.9	1.1	2.4	3.1	2.8	1.9	4.0	4.3	0.7	0.7
December	2.1	2.4	1.9	1.1	2.5	3.2	2.9	1.8	4.2	4.5	0.8	0.8
2016												
January	2.0	2.3	1.4	1.2	2.4	3.0	2.9	1.5	4.1	4.3	0.7	0.8
February	2.1	2.3	1.6	1.2	2.4	3.0	3.0	1.8	4.3	4.4	0.7	0.8
March	2.0	2.3	2.1	1.1	2.4	3.0	2.7	1.6	4.0	4.4	0.7	0.8
April	2.1	2.3	1.7	1.1	2.4	3.0	2.9	1.7	4.2	4.4	0.7	0.8
May	2.1	2.3	1.8	1.1	2.2	2.8	3.4	1.7	4.3	4.5	0.7	0.8
June	2.1	2.3	1.8	1.1	2.3	2.9	2.7	1.8	4.2	4.4	0.9	0.9
July	2.1	2.3	1.9	1.2	2.3	2.9	3.1	1.7	4.2	4.4	0.7	0.8
August	2.1	2.3	2.2	1.2	2.4	3.0	3.0	1.7	4.1	4.3	0.8	0.9
September	2.1	2.3	1.6	1.2	2.5	3.0	3.1	1.8	4.2	4.4	0.8	0.8
October	2.1	2.4	1.9	1.4	2.4	3.1	3.0	1.7	4.3	4.5	0.8	0.8
November	2.1	2.3	2.3	1.3	2.4	2.9	2.9	1.7	4.4	4.6	0.7	0.7
December	2.1	2.3	2.0	1.3	2.2	2.7	3.0	1.7	4.3	4.5	0.7	0.8
2017												
January	2.2	2.4	2.2	1.4	2.4	3.0	3.1	1.9	4.1	4.2	0.8	0.8
February	2.1	2.4	2.3	1.4	2.5	3.2	2.8	1.7	4.0	4.2	0.8	0.8
March	2.1	2.4	2.4	1.5	2.5	3.2	2.9	1.8	4.1	4.2	0.8	0.9
April	2.1	2.3	2.3	1.5	2.2	2.8	2.9	1.8	4.1	4.3	0.7	0.7
May	2.1	2.4	2.1	1.6	2.4	3.1	2.8	1.8	4.1	4.4	0.7	0.8
June	2.2	2.4	2.0	1.6	2.4	2.9	3.0	1.8	4.1	4.3	0.7	0.8
July	2.1	2.4	2.2	1.6	2.4	2.9	3.0	1.7	3.9	4.1	0.7	0.8
August	2.1	2.4	2.2	1.5	2.4	2.9	3.2	1.7	3.9	4.1	0.7	0.8
September	2.2	2.4	2.4	1.5	2.4	2.9	3.2	1.7	4.1	4.4	0.8	0.8
October	2.2	2.4	2.5	1.6	2.3	2.8	3.2	1.8	3.9	4.1	0.7	0.8
November	2.1	2.4	2.0	1.5	2.3	2.8	3.3	1.8	4.1	4.3	0.8	0.8
December	2.2	2.4	2.1	1.7	2.5	3.0	3.1	1.8	4.2	4.4	0.8	0.8
2018												
January	2.1	2.3	2.2	1.7	2.4	2.9	2.7	1.6	3.8	3.9	0.8	0.8
February	2.1	2.4	2.1	1.7	2.3	2.8	3.0	1.7	4.3	4.5	0.7	0.7
March	2.2	2.5	2.2	1.7	2.4	2.9	3.1	1.8	4.3	4.5	0.8	0.8
April	2.3	2.5	2.4	1.6	2.5	3.1	3.3	1.9	4.4	4.6	0.8	0.9
May	2.3	2.6	2.3	1.6	2.6	3.1	3.1	2.1	4.3	4.5	0.8	0.9
June	2.3	2.5	2.5	1.6	2.6	3.3	3.2	1.9	4.2	4.4	0.8	0.9
July	2.3	2.6	2.8	1.7	2.6	3.3	3.1	1.9	4.4	4.6	0.8	0.9
August	2.3	2.6	2.5	1.6	2.7	3.2	2.9	2.0	4.4	4.6	0.8	0.8
September	2.3	2.5	2.2	1.6	2.8	3.6	2.9	1.8	4.5	4.6	0.8	0.8
October	2.3	2.6	2.3	1.6	2.7	3.4	3.1	2.0	4.4	4.6	0.8	0.9
November	2.3	2.6	2.5	1.7	2.6	3.1	3.0	2.1	4.3	4.6	0.9	0.9
December	2.3	2.5	2.4	1.6	2.6	3.2	3.0	2.1	4.4	4.6	0.8	0.8
2019												
January	2.4	2.6	2.5	1.7	2.5	3.2	3.1	2.0	4.7	4.9	0.9	0.9
February	2.4	2.6	2.6	1.6	2.7	3.2	3.1	2.1	4.8	5.1	0.8	0.9
March	2.3	2.6	2.0	1.7	2.7	3.3	3.3	2.0	4.5	4.7	0.8	0.8
April	2.3	2.6	1.9	1.7	2.6	3.2	3.1	1.9	4.6	4.8	0.8	0.9
May	2.3	2.6	2.2	1.6	2.8	3.4	3.0	1.7	4.6	4.9	0.9	0.9
June	2.3	2.6	2.5	1.5	2.7	3.5	3.0	1.7	4.7	5.0	0.8	0.9
July	2.4	2.7	2.4	1.5	2.8	3.5	3.2	2.0	4.8	5.0	0.8	0.8
August	2.3	2.6	2.3	1.5	2.8	3.5	3.0	1.9	4.7	4.9	0.8	0.8
September	2.3	2.5	2.5	1.7	2.7	3.4	3.0	1.8	4.3	4.6	0.8	0.9
October	2.3	2.5	2.5	1.6	2.3	2.8	2.9	1.9	4.6	4.9	0.8	0.9
November	2.3	2.6	2.2	1.6	2.9	3.7	3.0	1.9	4.4	4.6	0.8	0.9
December	2.3	2.6	2.2	1.6	2.6	3.2	2.9	2.0	4.6	4.9	0.9	0.9
2019												
January	2.3	2.6	2.2	1.5	3.0	3.8	3.2	1.9	4.5	4.7	0.8	0.8
February	2.3	2.5	2.0	1.4	2.9	3.5	2.9	1.9	4.2	4.3	0.8	0.9
March	1.8	2.0	1.7	1.2	2.2	2.5	2.6	1.7	3.3	3.5	0.7	0.8
April	1.4	1.6	1.3	0.9	1.8	2.3	1.7	1.6	3.0	3.0	0.7	0.7
May	1.6	1.7	1.5	1.2	1.9	2.2	2.1	1.3	3.7	3.9	0.6	0.6
June	1.9	2.1	1.8	1.5	2.4	2.8	2.2	1.7	4.1	4.4	0.5	0.5
July	2.1	2.4	2.0	1.5	2.9	3.5	2.7	1.9	4.0	4.3	0.7	0.7
August	2.0	2.3	1.4	1.7	2.7	3.3	2.8	1.7	3.8	4.3	0.6	0.7
September	2.2	2.4	2.0	1.9	2.6	3.1	3.1	1.8	4.1	4.4	0.7	0.7
October	2.2	2.5	1.7	1.8	2.7	3.3	2.9	2.0	4.3	4.5	0.8	0.8

[1]Quits are the number of quits during the entire month.
[2]The quits rate is the number of quits during the entire month as a percent of total employment.
[3]Detail will not necessarily add to totals because of the independent seasonal adjustment of the various series.
[4]Includes natural resources and mining, information, financial activities, and other services, not shown separately.
[5]Includes wholesale trade and transportation, warehousing, and utilities, not shown separately.
[6]Includes arts, entertainment, and recreation, not shown separately.
[7]Includes federal government, not shown separately.

Table 7-8. Layoffs and Discharges Levels[1] and Rates,[2] by Industry, 2009–October 2020

(Annual data not seasonally adjusted, monthly data seasonally adjusted, levels in thousands, rates per 100.)

Year and month	Level												
	Total	Total private	Mining and logging	Construction	Manufacturing	Durable goods	Non-durable goods	Trade, transportation, and utilities	Wholesale trade	Retail trade	Transportation, warehousing, and utilities	Information	Financial activities
2011	22 134	20 794	83	2 893	1 393	768	622	3 830	632	2 517	679	280	656
2012	22 023	20 747	148	2 812	1 332	802	529	3 827	678	2 438	709	288	690
2013	20 959	19 783	150	2 426	1 243	776	466	3 810	554	2 504	755	405	748
2014	21 147	20 074	141	1 986	1 213	716	497	4 061	615	2 629	814	454	666
2015	21 779	20 440	241	2 134	1 277	790	487	4 020	570	2 583	867	344	702
2016	21 239	19 901	173	2 237	1 294	801	493	3 687	493	2 306	890	307	705
2017	21 608	20 263	128	2 245	1 253	702	549	3 741	490	2 302	890	307	705
2018	21 803	20 544	129	2 002	1 371	753	620	4 171	502	2 658	951	396	683
2019	21 739	20 492	152	2 571	1 305	747	559	4 022	604	2 400	1 012	409	634
											1 019	449	644
2009													
January	2 614	2 482	16	392	354	252	102	456	130	256	70	37	139
February	2 590	2 439	19	349	310	209	101	477	94	280	103	38	132
March	2 560	2 446	23	373	314	218	96	451	83	257	112	39	128
April	2 651	2 523	17	398	303	220	83	526	92	345	89	47	111
May	2 228	2 050	22	296	258	171	87	445	88	260	97	41	118
June	2 242	2 067	18	304	235	155	79	367	70	212	84	37	116
July	2 274	2 140	20	348	199	112	88	396	82	230	84	46	119
August	2 113	1 994	11	291	175	95	80	391	81	240	70	34	95
September	2 195	2 045	16	306	187	106	81	479	68	306	105	28	76
October	2 028	1 930	16	314	186	110	76	362	64	234	64	40	91
November	1 911	1 796	11	232	172	99	72	362	67	214	81	33	53
December	2 045	1 926	13	270	158	96	63	417	80	228	109	45	87
2010													
January	1 902	1 770	9	267	140	93	47	338	83	211	45	36	60
February	1 817	1 694	8	256	147	83	64	300	67	173	60	23	66
March	1 916	1 781	8	259	153	83	71	401	52	303	47	24	70
April	1 744	1 610	7	262	135	71	64	315	57	208	50	23	65
May	1 761	1 611	9	278	115	70	45	292	66	167	59	34	84
June	2 061	1 708	7	225	130	63	68	334	47	222	64	24	49
July	2 173	1 910	7	263	153	85	68	347	83	212	52	27	74
August	1 886	1 646	8	249	144	77	66	264	50	174	40	26	50
September	1 834	1 627	9	238	130	72	58	304	69	185	50	29	52
October	1 746	1 647	8	240	141	79	63	309	56	188	65	22	76
November	1 848	1 712	10	246	146	77	68	335	59	222	54	23	64
December	1 865	1 737	9	300	130	73	58	322	65	191	66	30	67
2011													
January	1 846	1 743	8	244	124	64	60	371	72	236	63	24	66
February	1 748	1 639	3	238	126	71	55	317	46	227	44	21	66
March	1 787	1 679	3	243	116	62	55	322	48	226	48	29	42
April	1 787	1 660	8	260	119	58	61	286	39	201	46	20	38
May	1 903	1 795	7	270	131	72	59	309	63	209	36	26	44
June	1 926	1 818	8	323	109	65	43	307	64	195	48	25	63
July	1 850	1 728	6	236	111	64	46	301	49	197	55	24	44
August	1 842	1 728	9	264	119	66	53	313	34	222	57	20	49
September	1 875	1 755	8	247	119	67	53	319	50	218	51	21	66
October	1 796	1 704	5	222	102	56	46	298	50	181	67	21	52
November	1 911	1 798	8	191	104	62	42	344	47	241	57	22	64
December	1 811	1 700	8	204	111	60	52	315	70	170	76	26	61
2012													
January	1 817	1 713	10	228	114	63	51	329	89	187	53	24	42
February	1 896	1 788	11	248	109	62	47	290	38	194	58	29	72
March	1 775	1 660	13	210	104	57	46	299	58	183	57	28	52
April	1 868	1 755	12	206	111	63	48	314	60	187	67	26	70
May	1 968	1 831	15	252	100	55	45	322	47	215	60	26	68
June	1 883	1 772	14	257	138	91	48	322	39	215	68	20	63
July	1 729	1 623	8	273	106	62	44	296	44	196	56	20	52
August	1 889	1 775	15	247	101	64	38	372	52	255	65	38	55
September	1 808	1 720	13	269	102	68	34	348	68	209	71	24	39
October	1 897	1 793	13	193	119	78	41	332	66	216	51	18	62
November	1 920	1 827	13	259	125	72	53	290	55	177	58	20	82
December	1 708	1 614	13	191	99	65	34	346	62	219	65	20	54
2013													
January	1 690	1 593	13	185	108	71	37	306	56	192	57	22	69
February	1 655	1 559	13	216	108	66	42	303	38	200	65	24	56
March	1 780	1 657	9	239	102	71	31	306	37	207	62	12	50
April	1 786	1 699	12	203	109	74	35	305	31	202	72	26	45
May	1 833	1 730	10	191	121	80	41	356	50	236	70	29	66
June	1 755	1 661	10	222	103	66	37	287	36	199	52	42	52
July	1 731	1 634	17	191	114	66	47	348	81	195	73	45	68
August	1 814	1 725	10	170	109	64	45	309	40	192	77	58	63
September	1 892	1 781	14	179	99	60	38	306	47	198	61	44	91
October	1 681	1 573	16	242	85	55	30	343	52	223	68	43	61
November	1 630	1 538	11	194	91	49	43	328	40	223	65	23	60
December	1 774	1 679	13	204	99	58	41	344	46	238	60	43	63
2014													
January	1 815	1 722	10	144	114	76	38	353	50	222	81	40	65
February	1 758	1 668	9	144	79	52	27	330	37	219	73	55	65
March	1 697	1 594	13	144	94	43	51	329	30	223	75	47	64
April	1 752	1 670	8	141	117	76	42	363	46	252	65	39	62
May	1 706	1 620	17	148	94	55	39	317	39	216	62	30	66
June	1 753	1 653	10	135	112	61	51	328	57	214	58	28	57
July	1 801	1 718	11	169	89	57	32	366	78	220	67	47	46
August	1 698	1 615	10	156	83	43	40	344	72	214	58	26	47
September	1 716	1 636	14	147	107	62	45	325	45	212	68	33	39
October	1 844	1 763	13	183	108	62	45	349	57	212	80	40	42
November	1 727	1 636	14	204	101	64	37	333	53	214	67	39	55
December	1 860	1 749	15	229	114	68	46	326	51	213	61	32	64

[1] Layoffs and discharges are the number of layoffs and discharges during the entire month.
[2] The layoffs and discharges rate is the number of layoffs and discharges during the entire month as a percent of total employment.

Table 7-8. Layoffs and Discharges Levels[1] and Rates,[2] by Industry, 2009–October 2020
—Continued

(Annual data not seasonally adjusted, monthly data seasonally adjusted, levels in thousands, rates per 100.)

Year and month	Level												
	Finance and insurance	Real estate and rental and leasing	Profes-sional and business services	Education and health services	Educa-tional services	Health care and social assistance	Leisure and hospitality	Arts, enter-tainment, and recreation	Accommo-dation and food services	Other services	Govern-ment	Federal	State and local govern-ment
2011	364	295	5 144	1 988	410	1 576	3 442	949	2 492	1 085	1 340	117	1 221
2012	375	313	5 214	2 067	445	1 624	3 367	961	2 407	1 007	1 275	125	1 150
2013	427	321	4 751	2 036	465	1 571	3 326	895	2 429	893	1 177	118	1 058
2014	423	243	5 216	2 039	424	1 617	3 535	1 044	2 489	762	1 072	92	979
2015	417	288	5 210	1 824	399	1 425	3 715	1 067	2 648	970	1 340	130	1 210
2016	420	285	5 201	1 977	397	1 579	3 472	989	2 482	848	1 337	119	1 219
2017	383	303	4 891	2 064	427	1 638	3 847	1 153	2 695	1 012	1 342	120	1 223
2018	417	218	4 989	2 101	480	1 622	3 800	1 146	2 654	938	1 257	89	1 168
2019	323	319	5 012	2 008	399	1 611	3 560	965	2 594	763	1 248	120	1 127
2009													
January	89	50	476	191	32	159	319	77	243	102	132	10	121
February	84	47	563	199	42	157	291	64	226	62	150	10	141
March	75	53	511	195	36	159	297	52	244	117	114	11	103
April	68	44	496	215	44	171	317	65	251	95	127	13	115
May	80	37	365	141	44	98	271	34	237	93	177	68	109
June	69	47	412	165	33	133	306	78	228	107	175	63	113
July	74	45	419	222	51	171	284	86	198	87	134	12	122
August	41	54	392	205	46	160	308	85	223	92	119	7	113
September	34	42	394	191	41	150	276	60	216	93	150	7	143
October	42	49	369	185	36	149	286	82	204	81	98	8	91
November	31	22	396	175	25	150	297	72	226	64	115	20	95
December	46	41	377	176	29	146	288	75	213	94	120	10	110
2010													
January	34	26	383	179	29	150	274	50	223	83	132	9	124
February	36	30	388	188	25	162	226	35	191	92	123	11	112
March	39	31	363	176	36	140	260	76	184	66	135	16	119
April	38	28	344	154	27	127	251	62	190	54	134	24	110
May	43	41	329	156	29	127	240	61	179	73	151	40	111
June	29	20	373	181	37	144	312	117	195	73	354	242	112
July	38	36	428	224	36	189	326	141	186	59	263	154	109
August	34	15	411	178	43	135	237	72	164	79	240	122	118
September	43	9	364	220	47	173	232	62	170	49	208	84	124
October	53	24	361	150	22	128	261	63	198	78	99	21	77
November	39	25	366	178	36	142	265	62	203	79	136	11	124
December	43	24	432	192	37	156	218	52	166	36	127	10	118
2011													
January	36	30	431	149	33	116	247	72	175	78	103	7	95
February	38	29	376	168	50	119	234	39	195	89	108	8	101
March	27	15	408	148	35	113	296	77	219	72	108	9	99
April	14	24	448	155	30	125	226	55	171	101	126	12	114
May	28	16	481	156	34	121	289	86	203	84	108	10	97
June	33	30	428	190	35	156	284	76	208	81	108	11	97
July	26	18	436	171	38	134	295	72	223	104	123	9	114
August	24	25	439	175	27	148	261	75	186	78	114	12	101
September	43	23	413	149	34	116	311	89	221	101	120	11	109
October	23	29	418	167	35	132	304	81	223	114	92	9	84
November	41	23	436	196	42	154	341	104	237	92	113	10	102
December	33	28	430	160	30	130	298	76	222	87	112	5	106
2012													
January	23	19	377	201	59	142	302	92	210	86	104	10	94
February	25	47	512	143	27	116	299	96	203	74	108	9	99
March	20	32	431	153	27	126	300	96	204	71	115	8	107
April	49	21	444	180	41	139	279	94	186	113	113	10	104
May	39	29	488	187	43	144	273	82	190	100	137	9	128
June	34	29	437	217	40	177	244	65	178	59	111	9	102
July	24	27	392	163	36	127	258	65	193	54	106	12	94
August	30	25	413	157	26	131	311	69	242	67	114	13	102
September	26	13	426	142	23	119	257	70	187	99	88	11	77
October	34	28	464	197	55	142	289	76	213	106	103	11	92
November	55	26	493	167	34	132	269	73	196	110	93	10	83
December	25	29	372	150	38	112	297	104	193	73	93	10	83
2013													
January	38	31	421	156	32	125	259	61	199	54	97	8	89
February	38	18	351	193	46	147	244	57	187	50	97	9	88
March	26	25	379	154	39	115	283	56	228	122	123	8	115
April	27	18	386	175	41	134	329	86	243	109	87	9	78
May	34	32	398	199	32	167	272	80	193	89	103	14	89
June	23	29	415	158	35	123	287	74	212	86	95	10	85
July	42	27	325	167	35	131	279	81	198	79	97	8	89
August	36	26	480	181	50	132	281	68	212	65	88	9	79
September	53	38	454	179	48	131	354	89	265	64	111	10	101
October	33	28	361	152	31	121	211	67	144	60	108	15	93
November	38	22	375	164	42	122	235	75	159	57	91	7	84
December	37	26	387	170	45	126	277	71	206	77	96	9	87
2014													
January	47	17	420	194	49	145	314	81	234	68	93	8	85
February	37	27	457	162	34	128	291	95	196	75	90	9	82
March	44	20	401	205	49	156	246	71	176	52	103	6	97
April	38	25	431	192	29	163	276	96	180	40	83	6	77
May	20	46	401	155	33	122	334	88	245	60	87	8	79
June	36	20	417	160	32	127	337	74	264	68	101	10	90
July	25	21	440	151	35	116	318	80	239	81	83	9	75
August	31	17	472	155	35	120	258	102	156	64	83	8	76
September	25	14	421	190	43	147	305	94	211	54	80	9	71
October	31	11	531	178	32	146	257	75	182	63	80	8	73
November	33	22	396	143	27	116	277	84	193	74	91	8	84
December	51	14	436	168	32	136	304	84	220	61	111	6	105

[1]Layoffs and discharges are the number of layoffs and discharges during the entire month.
[2]The layoffs and discharges rate is the number of layoffs and discharges during the entire month as a percent of total employment.

Table 7-8. Layoffs and Discharges Levels[1] and Rates,[2] by Industry, 2009–October 2020 —Continued

(Annual data not seasonally adjusted, monthly data seasonally adjusted, levels in thousands, rates per 100.)

Year and month	Rate												
	Total	Total private	Mining and logging	Construction	Manufacturing	Durable goods	Non-durable goods	Trade, transportation, and utilities	Wholesale trade	Retail trade	Transportation, warehousing, and utilities	Information	Financial activities
2011	16.8	18.9	10.5	52.3	11.9	10.6	14.0	15.3	11.5	17.2	14.0	10.5	8.5
2012	16.4	18.5	17.5	49.8	11.2	10.7	11.9	15.1	12.1	16.4	14.3	10.8	8.9
2013	15.4	17.3	17.4	41.4	10.3	10.3	10.4	14.8	9.8	16.6	14.9	15.0	9.5
2014	15.2	17.1	15.8	32.3	10.0	9.3	11.0	15.4	10.7	17.1	15.6	16.7	8.3
2015	15.4	17.1	29.6	33.0	10.3	10.2	10.6	15.0	9.9	16.5	16.0	12.5	8.6
2016	14.7	16.3	25.9	33.2	10.5	10.4	10.6	13.6	8.5	14.6	16.0	11.0	8.5
2017	14.7	16.3	18.9	32.2	10.1	9.1	11.7	13.6	8.4	14.5	16.5	14.1	8.1
2018	14.6	16.2	17.7	27.5	10.8	9.5	13.1	15.1	8.6	16.8	16.9	14.4	7.4
2019	14.4	16.0	20.7	34.3	10.2	9.3	11.7	14.5	10.2	15.3	16.5	15.7	7.4
2009													
January	1.9	2.2	2.1	6.0	2.8	3.2	2.2	1.8	2.3	1.7	1.4	1.3	1.7
February	1.9	2.2	2.5	5.4	2.5	2.7	2.2	1.9	1.7	1.9	2.1	1.3	1.7
March	1.9	2.2	3.2	5.9	2.6	2.9	2.1	1.8	1.5	1.8	2.3	1.4	1.6
April	2.0	2.3	2.3	6.5	2.5	3.0	1.8	2.1	1.7	2.4	1.8	1.7	1.4
May	1.7	1.9	3.2	4.8	2.2	2.3	1.9	1.8	1.6	1.8	2.0	1.5	1.5
June	1.7	1.9	2.6	5.1	2.0	2.2	1.7	1.5	1.3	1.5	1.8	1.3	1.5
July	1.7	2.0	2.9	5.9	1.7	1.6	1.9	1.6	1.5	1.6	1.8	1.6	1.5
August	1.6	1.8	1.7	5.0	1.5	1.3	1.8	1.6	1.5	1.7	1.8	1.2	1.2
September	1.7	1.9	2.4	5.3	1.6	1.5	1.8	1.9	1.3	2.1	2.2	1.0	1.0
October	1.6	1.8	2.5	5.5	1.6	1.6	1.7	1.5	1.2	1.6	1.4	1.5	1.2
November	1.5	1.7	1.7	4.1	1.5	1.4	1.6	1.5	1.2	1.5	1.7	1.2	0.7
December	1.6	1.8	2.0	4.8	1.4	1.4	1.4	1.7	1.5	1.6	2.3	1.6	1.1
2010													
January	1.5	1.6	1.4	4.8	1.2	1.3	1.0	1.4	1.5	1.5	0.9	1.3	0.8
February	1.4	1.6	1.2	4.6	1.3	1.2	1.4	1.2	1.3	1.2	1.3	0.8	0.9
March	1.5	1.7	1.2	4.7	1.3	1.2	1.6	1.6	1.0	2.1	1.0	0.9	0.9
April	1.3	1.5	1.1	4.7	1.2	1.0	1.4	1.3	1.1	1.4	1.1	0.8	0.8
May	1.3	1.5	1.3	5.0	1.0	1.0	1.0	1.2	1.2	1.2	1.3	1.3	1.1
June	1.6	1.6	1.0	4.1	1.1	0.9	1.5	1.4	0.9	1.5	1.4	0.9	0.6
July	1.7	1.8	1.0	4.8	1.3	1.2	1.5	1.4	1.5	1.5	1.1	1.0	1.0
August	1.4	1.5	1.2	4.5	1.2	1.1	1.5	1.1	0.9	1.2	0.8	0.9	0.6
September	1.4	1.5	1.2	4.3	1.1	1.0	1.3	1.2	1.3	1.3	1.0	0.9	0.6
October	1.3	1.5	1.1	4.4	1.2	1.1	1.4	1.3	1.0	1.3	1.0	1.1	0.7
November	1.4	1.6	1.3	4.5	1.3	1.1	1.5	1.4	1.0	1.3	1.4	0.8	1.0
December	1.4	1.6	1.3	5.5	1.1	1.0	1.3	1.3	1.2	1.5	1.1	0.8	0.8
2011													
January	1.4	1.6	1.2	4.5	1.1	0.9	1.3	1.5	1.3	1.6	1.3	0.9	0.9
February	1.3	1.5	0.4	4.4	1.1	1.0	1.2	1.3	0.8	1.6	0.9	0.8	0.9
March	1.4	1.5	0.4	4.4	1.0	0.9	1.2	1.3	0.9	1.5	1.0	1.1	0.5
April	1.4	1.5	1.1	4.7	1.0	0.8	1.4	1.1	0.7	1.4	1.0	0.7	0.5
May	1.4	1.6	0.9	4.9	1.1	1.0	1.3	1.2	1.2	1.4	0.7	1.0	0.6
June	1.5	1.7	1.1	5.8	0.9	0.9	1.0	1.2	1.2	1.3	1.0	0.9	0.8
July	1.4	1.6	0.8	4.2	0.9	0.9	1.0	1.2	0.9	1.3	1.1	0.9	0.6
August	1.4	1.6	1.1	4.8	1.0	0.9	1.2	1.2	0.6	1.5	1.2	0.7	0.6
September	1.4	1.6	1.0	4.4	1.0	0.9	1.2	1.3	0.9	1.5	1.0	0.8	0.9
October	1.4	1.5	0.7	4.0	0.9	0.8	1.0	1.2	0.9	1.2	1.4	0.8	0.7
November	1.4	1.6	1.0	3.4	0.9	0.8	1.0	1.4	0.9	1.6	1.2	0.8	0.8
December	1.4	1.5	0.9	3.6	0.9	0.8	1.2	1.2	1.3	1.1	1.5	1.0	0.8
2012													
January	1.4	1.5	1.2	4.1	1.0	0.8	1.2	1.3	1.6	1.3	1.1	0.9	0.5
February	1.4	1.6	1.3	4.4	0.9	0.8	1.1	1.1	0.7	1.2	1.2	1.1	0.9
March	1.3	1.5	1.5	3.7	0.9	0.8	1.0	1.2	1.0	1.2	1.2	1.0	0.7
April	1.4	1.6	1.4	3.7	0.9	0.8	1.1	1.2	1.1	1.3	1.4	1.0	0.9
May	1.5	1.6	1.7	4.5	0.8	0.7	1.0	1.3	0.8	1.5	1.2	1.0	0.9
June	1.4	1.6	1.7	4.6	1.2	1.2	1.1	1.3	0.7	1.5	1.4	0.7	0.8
July	1.3	1.4	1.0	4.9	0.9	0.8	1.0	1.2	0.8	1.3	1.1	0.8	0.7
August	1.4	1.6	1.7	4.4	0.8	0.9	0.8	1.5	0.9	1.7	1.3	1.4	0.7
September	1.3	1.5	1.5	4.8	0.9	0.9	0.8	1.4	1.2	1.4	1.4	0.9	0.5
October	1.4	1.6	1.6	3.4	1.0	1.0	0.9	1.3	1.2	1.4	1.0	0.7	0.8
November	1.4	1.6	1.5	4.6	1.0	1.0	1.2	1.1	1.0	1.2	1.2	0.7	1.0
December	1.3	1.4	1.5	3.3	0.8	0.9	0.8	1.4	1.1	1.5	1.3	0.7	0.7
2013													
January	1.2	1.4	1.6	3.2	0.9	0.9	0.8	1.2	1.0	1.3	1.1	0.8	0.9
February	1.2	1.4	1.6	3.7	0.9	0.9	0.9	1.2	0.7	1.3	1.3	0.9	0.7
March	1.3	1.5	1.1	4.1	0.9	0.9	0.7	1.2	0.7	1.4	1.2	0.4	0.6
April	1.3	1.5	1.4	3.5	0.9	1.0	0.8	1.2	0.5	1.4	1.4	0.9	0.6
May	1.3	1.5	1.1	3.3	1.0	1.1	0.9	1.4	0.9	1.6	1.4	1.1	0.8
June	1.3	1.5	1.1	3.8	0.9	0.9	0.8	1.1	0.6	1.3	1.4	1.5	0.7
July	1.3	1.4	1.9	3.3	0.9	0.9	1.1	1.4	1.4	1.3	1.4	1.7	0.9
August	1.3	1.5	1.1	2.9	0.9	0.8	1.0	1.2	0.7	1.3	1.5	2.2	0.8
September	1.4	1.5	1.6	3.0	0.8	0.8	0.9	1.2	0.8	1.3	1.2	1.6	1.1
October	1.2	1.4	1.8	4.1	0.7	0.7	0.7	1.3	0.9	1.5	1.3	1.6	0.8
November	1.2	1.3	1.3	3.3	0.8	0.6	0.9	1.3	0.7	1.5	1.3	0.8	0.8
December	1.3	1.5	1.5	3.4	0.8	0.8	0.9	1.3	0.8	1.6	1.2	1.6	0.8
2014													
January	1.3	1.5	1.1	2.4	0.9	1.0	0.8	1.4	0.9	1.5	1.6	1.5	0.8
February	1.3	1.4	1.1	2.4	0.7	0.7	0.6	1.3	0.7	1.4	1.4	2.0	0.8
March	1.2	1.4	1.4	2.4	0.8	0.6	1.1	1.3	0.5	1.5	1.5	1.7	0.8
April	1.3	1.4	0.9	2.3	1.0	1.0	0.9	1.4	0.8	1.6	1.3	1.4	0.8
May	1.2	1.4	1.9	2.4	0.8	0.7	0.9	1.2	0.7	1.4	1.2	1.1	0.8
June	1.3	1.4	1.1	2.2	0.9	0.8	1.1	1.2	1.0	1.4	1.1	1.0	0.7
July	1.3	1.5	1.2	2.7	0.7	0.7	0.7	1.4	1.4	1.4	1.3	1.7	0.6
August	1.2	1.4	1.1	2.5	0.7	0.6	0.9	1.3	1.3	1.4	1.1	1.0	0.6
September	1.2	1.4	1.5	2.4	0.9	0.8	1.0	1.2	0.8	1.4	1.3	1.0	0.6
October	1.3	1.5	1.4	2.9	0.9	0.8	1.0	1.3	1.0	1.4	1.3	1.2	0.5
November	1.2	1.4	1.6	3.2	0.8	0.8	0.8	1.3	0.9	1.4	1.5	1.5	0.5
December	1.3	1.5	1.7	3.6	0.9	0.9	1.0	1.2	0.9	1.4	1.1	1.2	0.8

[1] Layoffs and discharges are the number of layoffs and discharges during the entire month.
[2] The layoffs and discharges rate is the number of layoffs and discharges during the entire month as a percent of total employment.

Table 7-8. Layoffs and Discharges Levels[1] and Rates,[2] by Industry, 2009–October 2020
—*Continued*

(Annual data not seasonally adjusted, monthly data seasonally adjusted, levels in thousands, rates per 100.)

Year and month	\[Rate\] Finance and insurance	Real estate and rental and leasing	Professional and business services	Education and health services	Educational services	Health care and social assistance	Leisure and hospitality	Arts, entertainment, and recreation	Accommodation and food services	Other services	Government	Federal	State and local government
2011	6.3	15.3	29.6	9.8	12.6	9.2	25.8	49.5	21.8	20.2	6.1	4.1	6.3
2012	6.4	16.0	29.0	10.0	13.3	9.3	24.5	48.8	20.4	18.5	5.8	4.4	6.0
2013	7.3	16.1	25.6	9.7	13.9	8.9	23.3	44.1	19.9	16.3	5.4	4.3	5.5
2014	7.1	11.9	27.3	9.5	12.4	9.0	24.1	49.6	19.8	13.7	4.9	3.4	5.1
2015	6.9	13.8	26.5	8.3	11.5	7.7	24.5	49.3	20.4	17.3	6.1	4.7	6.3
2016	6.8	13.3	25.9	8.7	11.1	8.3	22.2	43.9	18.5	14.9	6.0	4.3	6.3
2017	6.1	13.8	23.8	8.9	11.6	8.4	24.0	49.4	19.6	17.5	6.0	4.3	6.3
2018	6.6	9.7	23.8	8.9	12.9	8.1	23.3	48.1	19.1	16.1	5.6	3.2	5.9
2019	5.0	13.7	23.5	8.3	10.6	7.9	21.5	39.7	18.3	12.9	5.5	4.2	5.7
2009													
January	1.5	2.4	2.8	1.0	1.0	1.0	2.4	3.9	2.2	1.9	0.6	0.4	0.6
February	1.4	2.3	3.3	1.0	1.4	1.0	2.2	3.3	2.0	1.1	0.7	0.3	0.7
March	1.3	2.6	3.0	1.0	1.2	1.0	2.3	2.7	2.2	2.2	0.5	0.4	0.5
April	1.2	2.2	3.0	1.1	1.4	1.0	2.4	3.4	2.3	1.8	0.6	0.4	0.6
May	1.4	1.9	2.2	0.7	1.4	0.6	2.1	1.8	2.1	1.7	0.8	2.4	0.6
June	1.2	2.4	2.5	0.8	1.1	0.8	2.3	4.1	2.0	2.0	0.8	2.2	0.6
July	1.3	2.3	2.5	1.1	1.7	1.0	2.2	4.5	1.8	1.6	0.6	0.4	0.6
August	0.7	2.7	2.4	1.0	1.5	1.0	2.4	4.5	2.0	1.7	0.5	0.2	0.6
September	0.6	2.1	2.4	1.0	1.3	0.9	2.1	3.1	1.9	1.7	0.7	0.2	0.7
October	0.7	2.5	2.2	0.9	1.2	0.9	2.2	4.3	1.8	1.5	0.4	0.3	0.5
November	0.5	1.1	2.4	0.9	0.8	0.9	2.3	3.8	2.0	1.2	0.5	0.7	0.5
December	0.8	2.1	2.3	0.9	0.9	0.9	2.2	4.0	1.9	1.8	0.5	0.4	0.6
2010													
January	0.6	1.3	2.3	0.9	0.9	0.9	2.1	2.7	2.0	1.6	0.6	0.3	0.6
February	0.6	1.5	2.3	0.9	0.8	1.0	1.7	1.8	1.7	1.7	0.5	0.4	0.6
March	0.7	1.6	2.2	0.9	1.1	0.8	2.0	4.0	1.7	1.2	0.6	0.6	0.6
April	0.7	1.4	2.1	0.8	0.9	0.8	1.9	3.2	1.7	1.0	0.6	0.8	0.6
May	0.7	2.1	2.0	0.8	0.9	0.8	1.8	3.2	1.6	1.4	0.7	1.2	0.6
June	0.5	1.0	2.2	0.9	1.2	0.9	2.4	6.1	1.8	1.4	1.6	7.6	0.6
July	0.7	1.9	2.6	1.1	1.1	1.1	2.5	7.3	1.7	1.1	1.2	5.1	0.6
August	0.6	0.8	2.4	0.9	1.4	0.8	1.8	3.8	1.5	1.5	1.1	4.1	0.6
September	0.7	0.5	2.2	1.1	1.5	1.0	1.8	3.2	1.5	0.9	0.9	2.9	0.6
October	0.9	1.2	2.1	0.7	0.7	0.8	2.0	3.3	1.8	1.5	0.4	0.7	0.4
November	0.7	1.3	2.2	0.9	1.1	0.8	2.0	3.3	1.8	1.5	0.6	0.4	0.6
December	0.7	1.2	2.5	1.0	1.1	0.9	1.7	2.7	1.5	0.7	0.6	0.3	0.6
2011													
January	0.6	1.6	2.5	0.7	1.0	0.7	1.9	3.8	1.6	1.5	0.5	0.3	0.5
February	0.7	1.5	2.2	0.8	1.5	0.7	1.8	2.0	1.7	1.7	0.5	0.3	0.5
March	0.5	0.8	2.4	0.7	1.1	0.7	2.2	4.0	1.9	1.3	0.5	0.3	0.5
April	0.2	1.3	2.6	0.8	0.9	0.7	1.7	2.9	1.5	1.9	0.6	0.4	0.6
May	0.5	0.8	2.8	0.8	1.1	0.7	2.2	4.5	1.8	1.6	0.5	0.4	0.5
June	0.6	1.5	2.5	0.9	1.1	0.9	2.1	3.9	1.8	1.5	0.5	0.4	0.5
July	0.5	0.9	2.5	0.8	1.2	0.8	2.2	3.7	1.9	1.9	0.6	0.3	0.6
August	0.4	1.3	2.5	0.9	0.8	0.9	1.9	3.9	1.6	1.5	0.5	0.4	0.5
September	0.7	1.2	2.4	0.7	1.0	0.7	2.3	4.6	1.9	1.9	0.5	0.4	0.6
October	0.4	1.5	2.4	0.8	1.1	0.8	2.3	4.2	1.9	2.1	0.4	0.3	0.4
November	0.7	1.2	2.5	1.0	1.3	0.9	2.5	5.4	2.0	1.7	0.5	0.4	0.5
December	0.6	1.5	2.4	0.8	0.9	0.8	2.2	3.9	1.9	1.6	0.5	0.2	0.6
2012													
January	0.4	1.0	2.1	1.0	1.8	0.8	2.2	4.7	1.8	1.6	0.5	0.4	0.5
February	0.4	2.4	2.9	0.7	0.8	0.7	2.2	4.9	1.7	1.4	0.5	0.3	0.5
March	0.3	1.6	2.4	0.7	0.8	0.7	2.2	4.8	1.7	1.3	0.5	0.3	0.6
April	0.8	1.1	2.5	0.9	1.2	0.8	2.0	4.8	1.6	2.1	0.5	0.3	0.5
May	0.7	1.5	2.7	0.9	1.3	0.8	2.0	4.2	1.6	1.9	0.6	0.3	0.7
June	0.6	1.5	2.4	1.0	1.2	1.0	1.8	3.3	1.5	1.1	0.5	0.3	0.5
July	0.4	1.4	2.2	0.8	1.1	0.7	1.9	3.3	1.6	1.0	0.5	0.4	0.5
August	0.5	1.3	2.3	0.8	0.8	0.8	2.3	3.5	2.0	1.2	0.5	0.4	0.5
September	0.4	0.7	2.4	0.7	0.7	0.7	1.9	3.5	1.6	1.8	0.4	0.4	0.4
October	0.6	1.4	2.6	0.9	1.7	0.8	2.1	3.8	1.8	1.9	0.5	0.4	0.5
November	0.9	1.3	2.7	0.8	1.0	0.8	1.9	3.7	1.6	2.0	0.4	0.4	0.4
December	0.4	1.5	2.0	0.7	1.1	0.6	2.1	5.2	1.6	1.3	0.4	0.4	0.4
2013													
January	0.6	1.6	2.3	0.7	1.0	0.7	1.8	3.0	1.7	1.0	0.4	0.3	0.5
February	0.7	0.9	1.9	0.9	1.4	0.8	1.7	2.8	1.5	0.9	0.4	0.3	0.5
March	0.4	1.3	2.1	0.7	1.2	0.7	2.0	2.8	1.9	2.2	0.6	0.3	0.6
April	0.5	0.9	2.1	0.8	1.2	0.8	2.3	4.3	2.0	2.0	0.4	0.3	0.4
May	0.6	1.6	2.1	0.9	1.0	0.9	1.9	3.9	1.6	1.6	0.5	0.5	0.5
June	0.4	1.4	2.2	0.7	1.0	0.7	2.0	3.7	1.7	1.6	0.4	0.3	0.4
July	0.7	1.3	1.7	0.8	1.1	0.7	2.0	4.0	1.6	1.4	0.4	0.3	0.5
August	0.6	1.3	2.6	0.9	1.5	0.7	2.0	3.4	1.7	1.2	0.4	0.3	0.4
September	0.9	1.9	2.4	0.8	1.4	0.7	2.5	4.4	2.2	1.2	0.5	0.4	0.5
October	0.6	1.4	1.9	0.7	0.9	0.7	1.5	3.3	1.2	1.1	0.5	0.6	0.5
November	0.6	1.1	2.0	0.8	1.2	0.7	1.6	3.7	1.3	1.0	0.4	0.3	0.4
December	0.6	1.3	2.1	0.8	1.3	0.7	1.9	3.5	1.7	1.4	0.4	0.3	0.5
2014													
January	0.8	0.9	2.2	0.9	1.4	0.8	2.2	3.9	1.9	1.2	0.4	0.3	0.4
February	0.6	1.3	2.4	0.8	1.0	0.7	2.0	4.5	1.6	1.4	0.4	0.3	0.4
March	0.7	1.0	2.1	1.0	1.4	0.9	1.7	3.4	1.4	0.9	0.5	0.2	0.5
April	0.6	1.2	2.3	0.9	0.9	0.9	1.9	4.6	1.4	0.7	0.4	0.2	0.4
May	0.3	2.2	2.1	0.7	1.0	0.7	2.3	4.2	2.0	1.1	0.4	0.3	0.4
June	0.6	1.0	2.2	0.7	0.9	0.7	2.3	3.5	2.1	1.2	0.5	0.4	0.5
July	0.4	1.0	2.3	0.7	1.0	0.6	2.2	3.8	1.9	1.5	0.4	0.3	0.4
August	0.5	0.8	2.5	0.7	1.0	0.7	1.8	4.9	1.2	1.1	0.4	0.3	0.4
September	0.4	0.7	2.2	0.9	1.3	0.8	2.1	4.5	1.7	1.0	0.4	0.3	0.4
October	0.5	0.6	2.8	0.8	0.9	0.8	1.7	3.5	1.4	1.1	0.4	0.3	0.4
November	0.5	1.1	2.0	0.7	0.8	0.6	1.9	3.9	1.5	1.3	0.4	0.3	0.4
December	0.8	0.7	2.2	0.8	0.9	0.7	2.0	3.9	1.7	1.1	0.5	0.2	0.5

[1] Layoffs and discharges are the number of layoffs and discharges during the entire month.
[2] The layoffs and discharges rate is the number of layoffs and discharges during the entire month as a percent of total employment.

Table 7-8. Layoffs and Discharges Levels[1] and Rates,[2] by Industry, 2009–October 2020 —Continued

(Annual data not seasonally adjusted, monthly data seasonally adjusted, levels in thousands, rates per 100.)

Year and month	Total	Total private	Mining and logging	Construction	Manufacturing	Durable goods	Non-durable goods	Trade, transportation, and utilities	Wholesale trade	Retail trade	Transportation, warehousing, and utilities	Information	Financial activities
2015													
January	1 800	1 690	21	210	101	57	44	373	64	237	72	31	50
February	1 746	1 644	21	182	109	71	38	307	48	190	68	27	39
March	1 960	1 840	22	213	113	69	44	379	64	228	87	30	67
April	1 848	1 734	26	143	99	63	36	330	30	222	78	36	71
May	1 708	1 599	20	138	89	52	38	333	25	225	82	27	59
June	1 813	1 692	10	216	106	62	45	353	73	216	64	30	55
July	1 721	1 619	23	153	108	72	36	372	67	235	70	26	66
August	1 773	1 671	23	184	109	68	41	321	42	214	64	26	71
September	1 963	1 846	20	188	110	69	41	317	26	200	91	25	67
October	1 852	1 734	18	189	114	69	44	323	49	208	65	30	45
November	1 779	1 659	17	165	111	71	40	309	44	189	76	31	58
December	1 804	1 680	19	154	104	67	37	304	38	201	65	22	58
2016													
January	1 831	1 713	16	186	100	63	37	331	52	207	72	27	52
February	1 926	1 809	21	221	131	92	39	319	45	196	78	30	60
March	1 877	1 759	26	165	112	71	40	279	47	161	71	24	71
April	1 774	1 649	17	214	112	67	45	279	46	169	63	31	60
May	1 792	1 668	16	197	131	88	43	331	58	193	80	33	54
June	1 733	1 631	16	152	106	66	39	319	39	188	92	26	47
July	1 786	1 698	9	168	92	59	33	362	36	238	88	30	46
August	1 827	1 705	14	177	106	66	40	307	47	175	86	25	46
September	1 596	1 484	10	154	107	61	46	322	31	236	56	14	56
October	1 636	1 536	11	183	95	57	39	272	34	172	67	19	56
November	1 767	1 645	8	148	105	61	44	289	29	188	72	28	81
December	1 718	1 625	5	256	102	57	45	272	29	172	71	20	65
2017													
January	1 765	1 664	12	188	108	60	48	314	48	169	98	29	46
February	1 698	1 586	11	149	81	50	31	315	50	217	48	23	68
March	1 749	1 663	9	196	111	68	43	325	54	204	67	30	67
April	1 704	1 591	9	212	111	53	58	286	35	178	73	27	48
May	1 796	1 670	16	214	99	56	43	299	44	187	68	41	51
June	1 958	1 845	10	210	101	64	37	342	40	219	82	37	58
July	1 900	1 787	10	219	109	59	50	271	43	169	60	27	66
August	1 866	1 749	9	197	96	63	34	301	44	183	75	32	65
September	1 807	1 704	7	203	105	58	46	278	32	175	71	42	42
October	1 819	1 707	11	184	104	53	51	278	34	190	54	40	77
November	1 732	1 633	12	170	114	57	57	350	32	245	73	26	49
December	1 736	1 606	11	133	107	59	48	328	34	187	107	43	49
2018													
January	1 957	1 853	8	172	111	65	46	376	53	233	90	40	67
February	1 781	1 675	7	170	115	60	55	305	43	192	70	37	46
March	1 794	1 683	9	184	111	54	56	315	28	217	70	36	43
April	1 729	1 639	9	154	120	67	52	350	42	228	80	35	63
May	1 776	1 684	11	168	117	65	52	284	23	175	85	33	60
June	1 807	1 711	15	172	111	61	50	313	36	198	79	36	57
July	1 791	1 671	14	156	117	62	55	318	36	206	76	29	39
August	1 796	1 683	14	160	113	61	52	387	39	268	81	36	43
September	1 780	1 664	14	175	99	59	41	350	43	223	84	36	53
October	1 830	1 719	10	145	132	81	51	369	60	215	94	23	44
November	1 910	1 805	11	193	111	61	50	373	51	225	96	28	61
December	1 832	1 730	9	155	119	57	62	370	48	239	83	37	56
2019													
January	1 734	1 612	13	183	97	47	50	316	54	182	81	35	54
February	1 791	1 668	13	176	111	60	51	325	43	191	92	37	59
March	1 698	1 596	13	179	123	76	47	310	33	189	88	36	35
April	1 950	1 844	12	240	113	65	49	347	36	227	84	38	49
May	1 764	1 678	10	207	114	61	53	316	45	196	76	37	56
June	1 763	1 664	8	220	108	53	55	311	55	180	75	27	64
July	1 812	1 714	12	187	113	63	50	370	69	212	89	57	67
August	1 792	1 689	10	220	104	59	46	361	52	219	90	39	62
September	1 962	1 860	12	223	113	66	47	386	70	228	89	35	60
October	1 778	1 657	12	244	114	73	41	365	66	211	88	40	42
November	1 769	1 672	14	233	95	62	33	311	46	185	81	33	44
December	1 893	1 815	17	243	110	67	43	323	35	197	90	37	48
2020													
January	1 749	1 659	9	194	115	64	51	325	47	193	85	24	40
February	1 846	1 752	6	202	113	63	49	363	47	224	91	32	67
March	11 489	11 316	32	604	632	374	257	1 730	154	1 226	350	64	228
April	7 708	7 481	59	709	635	447	188	1 458	220	940	297	97	208
May	1 903	1 780	22	177	121	85	37	419	97	221	101	29	56
June	1 995	1 913	17	197	184	127	57	419	80	203	135	21	67
July	1 745	1 690	15	192	154	102	52	317	53	171	92	21	83
August	1 533	1 464	11	206	102	60	42	340	61	194	85	25	52
September	1 437	1 311	11	135	97	65	32	302	21	191	90	17	60
October	1 676	1 454	11	197	111	67	44	323	33	198	92	21	49

[1]Layoffs and discharges are the number of layoffs and discharges during the entire month.
[2]The layoffs and discharges rate is the number of layoffs and discharges during the entire month as a percent of total employment.

Table 7-8. Layoffs and Discharges Levels[1] and Rates,[2] by Industry, 2009–October 2020
—Continued

(Annual data not seasonally adjusted, monthly data seasonally adjusted, levels in thousands, rates per 100.)

Year and month	Level												
	Finance and insurance	Real estate and rental and leasing	Professional and business services	Education and health services	Educational services	Health care and social assistance	Leisure and hospitality	Arts, entertainment, and recreation	Accommodation and food services	Other services	Government	Federal	State and local government
2015													
January	24	26	408	131	32	99	291	102	188	76	110	10	101
February	17	22	408	156	31	125	318	116	201	77	102	9	93
March	45	23	462	154	30	124	319	119	200	81	120	13	107
April	43	28	467	142	30	112	359	91	267	62	114	11	102
May	37	22	403	155	32	123	312	68	245	62	109	18	91
June	33	22	399	151	38	112	274	81	193	98	121	11	110
July	48	18	409	144	25	119	237	46	190	81	102	10	92
August	42	29	370	147	38	109	314	75	239	105	102	8	95
September	37	30	493	179	37	141	315	78	237	133	117	11	106
October	25	20	445	157	46	111	334	102	232	78	118	11	108
November	30	28	457	160	39	122	300	84	216	48	121	12	109
December	37	20	473	155	19	136	324	98	225	68	124	11	114
2016													
January	31	21	515	165	35	130	259	91	168	63	118	11	107
February	38	22	449	168	54	114	340	63	277	70	117	11	105
March	49	22	502	167	38	129	327	101	226	86	118	11	108
April	33	27	432	150	39	111	286	68	219	67	125	12	113
May	36	18	389	163	37	126	277	83	195	77	124	12	112
June	27	21	431	167	37	130	300	82	218	68	102	11	91
July	26	20	464	157	35	123	309	76	233	61	89	9	79
August	37	19	431	196	28	169	328	115	213	65	122	10	112
September	31	25	351	130	19	111	238	68	170	101	111	9	102
October	46	35	392	162	24	138	272	83	190	47	100	11	89
November	33	23	453	199	26	173	281	68	214	78	121	10	111
December	32	33	395	154	26	128	289	89	200	66	93	5	88
2017													
January	27	19	384	129	30	98	369	70	298	86	101	10	92
February	43	25	399	144	15	129	316	73	244	79	113	11	101
March	32	35	373	157	32	125	308	63	245	88	86	10	75
April	22	26	366	170	39	131	263	70	193	99	112	14	98
May	26	24	432	188	40	148	259	86	173	72	126	8	117
June	41	17	533	160	38	122	332	106	226	63	113	9	104
July	32	34	473	174	31	143	351	169	181	86	114	11	103
August	33	32	390	232	32	200	349	107	242	79	117	10	107
September	18	24	433	159	33	127	355	121	234	80	103	9	94
October	50	27	414	175	47	128	320	95	225	105	111	10	102
November	32	17	339	180	38	142	314	95	220	78	99	11	87
December	27	21	369	195	48	148	274	66	208	98	130	8	122
2018													
January	46	21	412	187	44	143	402	101	302	77	105	8	96
February	29	17	431	176	40	137	319	97	222	68	106	12	95
March	25	19	427	222	40	181	292	107	185	45	111	9	102
April	42	21	342	173	33	140	308	106	202	85	90	7	83
May	37	23	427	156	36	120	332	99	233	96	93	7	86
June	36	21	444	187	34	153	298	119	179	78	96	6	90
July	26	14	395	183	49	134	332	118	214	87	120	12	108
August	28	15	407	157	47	110	292	93	199	73	113	6	107
September	40	13	386	163	37	126	313	82	231	74	116	6	110
October	29	16	430	163	30	133	324	84	240	77	111	7	104
November	39	22	438	179	47	132	327	97	230	85	105	5	100
December	39	17	448	156	39	117	291	86	204	90	102	7	95
2019													
January	30	24	375	184	43	141	296	83	213	58	122	9	113
February	28	32	401	193	46	147	280	81	199	71	123	6	118
March	22	13	399	167	36	131	275	56	220	58	102	6	96
April	30	18	477	181	41	140	329	79	250	59	106	6	99
May	23	33	441	178	40	138	255	96	159	65	86	7	78
June	31	33	378	162	28	135	307	63	244	79	99	8	91
July	32	35	397	162	22	140	299	69	231	49	98	7	91
August	35	27	405	137	35	101	266	77	189	86	104	11	93
September	25	35	441	178	32	145	345	74	272	66	103	10	93
October	18	24	390	167	29	137	247	81	165	36	121	26	96
November	20	23	434	165	31	134	298	84	214	44	98	12	86
December	24	24	454	150	26	124	342	108	234	91	78	9	69
2020													
January	31	9	413	160	22	139	295	90	205	84	90	16	74
February	42	25	392	167	30	136	318	77	240	93	95	8	86
March	77	151	1 086	1 274	272	1 001	4 783	545	4 238	884	173	9	164
April	53	156	904	918	227	691	1 722	281	1 441	770	227	12	215
May	23	33	405	215	30	185	257	74	183	80	123	24	100
June	41	25	423	155	30	126	351	103	248	81	81	14	67
July	50	33	390	165	31	134	293	81	213	61	55	12	43
August	21	31	352	164	21	143	188	35	154	23	69	23	46
September	26	34	305	155	28	127	166	44	122	63	127	60	67
October	20	29	358	154	35	119	177	46	130	54	222	152	70

[1]Layoffs and discharges are the number of layoffs and discharges during the entire month.
[2]The layoffs and discharges rate is the number of layoffs and discharges during the entire month as a percent of total employment.

Table 7-8. Layoffs and Discharges Levels[1] and Rates,[2] by Industry, 2009–October 2020 —Continued

(Annual data not seasonally adjusted, monthly data seasonally adjusted, levels in thousands, rates per 100.)

Year and month	Rate												
	Total	Total private	Mining and logging	Construc-tion	Manufac-turing	Durable goods	Non-durable goods	Trade, transpor-tation, and utilities	Whole-sale trade	Retail trade	Transpor-tation, ware-housing, and utilities	Infor-mation	Financial activities
2015													
January	1.3	1.4	2.3	3.3	0.8	0.7	1.0	1.4	1.1	1.5	1.3	1.1	0.6
February	1.2	1.4	2.4	2.9	0.9	0.9	0.8	1.2	0.8	1.2	1.3	1.0	0.5
March	1.4	1.5	2.5	3.4	0.9	0.9	1.0	1.4	1.1	1.5	1.6	1.1	0.8
April	1.3	1.5	3.1	2.2	0.8	0.8	0.8	1.2	0.5	1.4	1.4	1.3	0.9
May	1.2	1.3	2.5	2.1	0.7	0.7	0.8	1.2	0.4	1.4	1.5	1.0	0.7
June	1.3	1.4	1.3	3.4	0.9	0.8	1.0	1.3	1.3	1.4	1.2	1.1	0.7
July	1.2	1.3	2.8	2.4	0.9	0.9	0.8	1.4	1.1	1.5	1.3	0.9	0.8
August	1.2	1.4	2.9	2.8	0.9	0.9	0.9	1.2	0.7	1.4	1.2	1.0	0.9
September	1.4	1.5	2.5	2.9	0.9	0.9	0.9	1.2	0.4	1.3	1.7	0.9	0.8
October	1.3	1.4	2.4	2.9	0.9	0.9	1.0	1.2	0.9	1.3	1.2	1.1	0.5
November	1.2	1.4	2.2	2.5	0.9	0.9	0.9	1.2	0.8	1.2	1.4	1.2	0.7
December	1.3	1.4	2.6	2.3	0.8	0.9	0.8	1.1	0.7	1.3	1.2	0.7	0.7
2016													
January	1.3	1.4	2.2	2.8	0.8	0.8	0.8	1.2	0.9	1.3	1.3	1.0	0.7
February	1.3	1.5	2.9	3.3	1.1	1.2	0.9	1.2	0.8	1.2	1.5	1.0	0.7
March	1.3	1.4	3.7	2.5	0.9	0.9	0.9	1.0	0.8	1.0	1.3	0.8	0.8
April	1.2	1.4	2.5	3.2	0.9	0.9	1.0	1.0	0.8	1.1	1.1	1.1	0.7
May	1.2	1.4	2.4	2.9	1.1	1.1	0.9	1.2	1.0	1.2	1.4	1.2	0.6
June	1.2	1.3	2.4	2.3	0.9	0.9	0.9	1.2	0.7	1.2	1.6	1.0	0.6
July	1.2	1.4	1.4	2.5	0.7	0.8	0.8	1.3	0.6	1.5	1.6	1.0	0.6
August	1.3	1.4	2.1	2.6	0.9	0.8	0.9	1.1	0.8	1.1	1.5	0.9	0.7
September	1.1	1.2	1.5	2.3	0.9	0.8	1.0	1.2	0.5	1.5	1.0	0.5	0.7
October	1.1	1.3	1.8	2.7	0.8	0.7	0.8	1.0	0.6	1.1	1.2	0.7	0.9
November	1.2	1.3	1.3	2.2	0.8	0.8	0.9	1.1	0.5	1.2	1.3	1.0	0.7
December	1.2	1.3	0.8	3.7	0.8	0.7	1.0	1.0	0.5	1.1	1.3	0.7	0.8
2017													
January	1.2	1.3	1.8	2.8	0.9	0.8	1.0	1.1	0.8	1.0	1.7	1.0	0.6
February	1.2	1.3	1.7	2.2	0.7	0.6	0.7	1.1	0.8	1.3	0.9	0.8	0.9
March	1.2	1.3	1.3	2.8	0.9	0.9	0.9	1.2	0.9	1.3	1.2	1.1	0.8
April	1.2	1.3	1.3	3.1	0.9	0.7	1.2	1.1	0.6	1.2	1.3	1.0	0.6
May	1.2	1.3	2.3	3.1	0.8	0.7	0.9	1.1	0.8	1.2	1.1	1.5	0.6
June	1.3	1.5	1.5	3.0	0.8	0.8	0.8	1.2	0.7	1.4	1.4	1.4	0.6
July	1.3	1.4	1.4	3.1	0.9	0.8	1.2	1.0	0.7	1.1	1.0	0.9	0.7
August	1.3	1.4	1.3	2.8	0.8	0.8	0.7	1.1	0.8	1.1	1.3	1.1	0.8
September	1.2	1.4	1.0	2.9	0.8	0.8	1.0	1.0	0.6	1.2	1.3	1.1	0.8
October	1.2	1.4	1.6	2.6	0.8	0.7	1.1	1.0	0.6	1.1	1.2	1.5	0.5
November	1.2	1.3	1.8	2.4	0.9	0.7	1.2	1.3	0.5	1.5	1.0	1.4	0.9
December	1.2	1.3	1.6	1.9	0.9	0.8	1.0	1.2	0.6	1.2	1.8	1.5	0.6
2018													
January	1.3	1.5	1.1	2.4	0.9	0.8	1.0	1.4	0.9	1.5	1.5	1.4	0.8
February	1.2	1.3	1.0	2.4	0.9	0.8	1.2	1.1	0.7	1.2	1.2	1.3	0.5
March	1.2	1.3	1.2	2.5	0.9	0.7	1.2	1.1	0.5	1.4	1.2	1.3	0.5
April	1.2	1.3	1.3	2.1	0.9	0.9	1.1	1.3	0.7	1.4	1.4	1.2	0.7
May	1.2	1.3	1.5	2.3	0.9	0.8	1.1	1.0	0.4	1.1	1.4	1.2	0.7
June	1.2	1.4	2.0	2.4	0.9	0.8	1.0	1.1	0.6	1.3	1.3	1.3	0.7
July	1.2	1.3	1.9	2.1	0.9	0.8	1.2	1.2	0.6	1.3	1.3	1.0	0.5
August	1.2	1.3	1.9	2.2	0.9	0.8	1.1	1.4	0.7	1.7	1.3	1.3	0.5
September	1.2	1.4	1.3	2.4	0.8	0.7	0.9	1.3	0.7	1.4	1.4	1.3	0.6
October	1.2	1.4	1.3	2.0	1.0	1.0	1.1	1.3	1.0	1.4	1.6	0.8	0.5
November	1.3	1.4	1.6	2.6	0.9	0.8	1.1	1.3	0.9	1.4	1.6	1.0	0.7
December	1.2	1.4	1.3	2.1	0.9	0.7	1.3	1.3	0.8	1.5	1.4	1.3	0.6
2019													
January	1.2	1.3	1.7	2.5	0.8	0.6	1.0	1.1	0.9	1.2	1.3	1.2	0.6
February	1.2	1.3	1.8	2.4	0.9	0.7	1.1	1.2	0.7	1.2	1.5	1.3	0.7
March	1.1	1.2	1.8	2.4	1.0	0.9	1.0	1.1	0.6	1.2	1.4	1.3	0.4
April	1.3	1.4	1.6	3.2	0.9	0.8	1.0	1.3	0.6	1.5	1.4	1.3	0.6
May	1.2	1.3	1.4	2.8	0.9	0.8	1.1	1.1	0.8	1.3	1.2	1.3	0.6
June	1.2	1.3	1.1	2.9	0.8	0.7	1.1	1.1	0.9	1.2	1.2	0.9	0.7
July	1.2	1.3	1.6	2.5	0.9	0.8	1.0	1.3	1.2	1.4	1.4	2.0	0.8
August	1.2	1.3	1.4	2.9	0.8	0.7	1.0	1.3	0.9	1.4	1.5	1.4	0.7
September	1.3	1.4	1.7	3.0	0.9	0.8	1.0	1.4	1.2	1.5	1.4	1.2	0.7
October	1.2	1.3	1.7	3.2	0.9	0.9	0.9	1.3	1.1	1.4	1.4	1.4	0.5
November	1.2	1.3	1.9	3.1	0.7	0.8	0.7	1.1	0.8	1.2	1.3	1.2	0.5
December	1.2	1.4	2.3	3.2	0.9	0.8	0.9	1.2	0.6	1.3	1.5	1.3	0.5
2020													
January	1.1	1.3	1.2	2.6	0.9	0.8	1.1	1.2	0.8	1.2	1.4	0.8	0.5
February	1.2	1.4	0.8	2.6	0.9	0.8	1.0	1.3	0.8	1.4	1.5	1.1	0.8
March	7.6	8.8	4.5	7.9	4.9	4.7	5.4	6.2	2.6	7.8	5.6	2.2	2.6
April	5.9	6.9	9.1	10.8	5.5	6.3	4.3	6.0	4.0	7.1	5.3	3.7	2.4
May	1.4	1.6	3.4	2.5	1.0	1.2	0.8	1.7	1.7	1.6	1.8	1.1	0.7
June	1.4	1.6	2.6	2.7	1.5	1.7	1.3	1.6	1.4	1.4	2.4	0.8	0.8
July	1.3	1.4	2.4	2.7	1.3	1.4	1.1	1.2	1.0	1.2	1.6	0.8	1.0
August	1.1	1.2	1.7	2.9	0.8	0.8	0.9	1.3	1.1	1.3	1.5	1.0	0.6
September	1.0	1.1	1.8	1.9	0.8	0.8	0.7	1.1	0.4	1.3	1.5	0.7	0.7
October	1.2	1.2	1.8	2.7	0.9	0.9	1.0	1.2	0.6	1.3	1.5	0.8	0.6

[1] Layoffs and discharges are the number of layoffs and discharges during the entire month.
[2] The layoffs and discharges rate is the number of layoffs and discharges during the entire month as a percent of total employment.

Table 7-8. Layoffs and Discharges Levels[1] and Rates,[2] by Industry, 2009–October 2020 —Continued

(Annual data not seasonally adjusted, monthly data seasonally adjusted, levels in thousands, rates per 100.)

Year and month	Finance and insurance	Real estate and rental and leasing	Professional and business services	Education and health services	Educational services	Health care and social assistance	Leisure and hospitality	Arts, entertainment, and recreation	Accommodation and food services	Other services	Government	Federal	State and local government
2015													
January	0.4	1.3	2.1	0.6	0.9	0.5	1.9	4.8	1.4	1.3	0.5	0.3	0.5
February	0.3	1.1	2.1	0.7	0.9	0.7	2.1	5.4	1.6	1.4	0.5	0.3	0.5
March	0.7	1.1	2.3	0.7	0.9	0.7	2.1	5.5	1.6	1.5	0.5	0.5	0.6
April	0.7	1.3	2.4	0.7	0.9	0.6	2.4	4.3	2.1	1.1	0.5	0.4	0.5
May	0.6	1.1	2.1	0.7	0.9	0.7	2.0	3.1	1.9	1.1	0.5	0.7	0.5
June	0.6	1.1	2.0	0.7	1.1	0.6	1.8	3.8	1.5	1.7	0.6	0.4	0.6
July	0.8	0.9	2.0	0.6	0.7	0.6	1.6	2.1	1.5	1.4	0.5	0.4	0.5
August	0.7	1.4	1.9	0.6	1.1	0.6	2.1	3.4	1.8	1.7	0.5	0.3	0.5
September	0.6	1.3	2.5	0.8	1.1	0.8	2.1	3.5	1.8	2.1	0.5	0.4	0.5
October	0.4	0.9	2.2	0.7	1.3	0.6	2.2	4.6	1.8	1.4	0.5	0.4	0.6
November	0.5	1.3	2.3	0.7	1.1	0.7	2.0	3.9	1.6	0.9	0.5	0.4	0.6
December	0.6	1.0	2.4	0.7	0.6	0.7	2.2	5.0	1.7	1.4	0.5	0.4	0.6
2016													
January	0.5	1.0	2.5	0.7	1.0	0.7	1.7	4.2	1.2	1.0	0.5	0.4	0.5
February	0.6	1.0	2.2	0.8	1.6	0.6	2.2	2.8	2.1	1.2	0.5	0.4	0.6
March	0.8	1.0	2.5	0.7	1.1	0.7	2.1	4.4	1.7	1.6	0.5	0.4	0.6
April	0.6	1.2	2.2	0.7	1.1	0.6	1.9	3.0	1.7	1.2	0.6	0.4	0.6
May	0.5	0.8	2.0	0.7	1.1	0.7	1.7	3.6	1.4	1.4	0.6	0.4	0.6
June	0.4	1.0	2.1	0.7	1.0	0.7	1.9	3.5	1.7	1.2	0.4	0.4	0.5
July	0.4	1.0	2.2	0.7	1.0	0.6	2.0	3.2	1.7	1.1	0.4	0.3	0.4
August	0.6	0.9	2.2	0.8	0.8	0.8	2.1	5.0	1.6	1.2	0.6	0.4	0.6
September	0.5	1.1	1.7	0.6	0.5	0.6	1.5	3.0	1.3	1.6	0.5	0.3	0.5
October	0.7	1.6	1.9	0.7	0.6	0.7	1.7	3.7	1.4	0.9	0.4	0.4	0.5
November	0.5	1.0	2.2	0.9	0.7	0.9	1.8	3.0	1.6	1.4	0.6	0.4	0.6
December	0.5	1.6	2.0	0.7	0.7	0.7	2.0	4.6	1.5	1.4	0.4	0.2	0.4
2017													
January	0.5	0.9	1.9	0.6	0.8	0.5	2.2	3.0	2.1	1.5	0.4	0.3	0.5
February	0.7	1.2	1.9	0.6	0.4	0.7	1.9	3.0	1.8	1.4	0.5	0.4	0.6
March	0.5	1.8	1.8	0.7	0.9	0.7	1.9	2.6	1.8	1.6	0.4	0.4	0.4
April	0.4	1.2	1.8	0.7	1.1	0.7	1.7	2.8	1.5	1.7	0.5	0.5	0.5
May	0.4	1.2	2.1	0.8	1.1	0.8	1.6	3.6	1.2	1.2	0.6	0.3	0.6
June	0.7	0.9	2.6	0.7	1.0	0.6	2.1	4.3	1.7	1.1	0.5	0.3	0.5
July	0.5	1.6	2.2	0.8	0.8	0.7	2.2	6.9	1.3	1.4	0.5	0.4	0.5
August	0.5	1.4	1.9	0.9	0.9	0.9	2.1	4.5	1.7	1.3	0.5	0.4	0.5
September	0.3	1.1	2.1	0.7	0.9	0.7	2.2	5.1	1.7	1.3	0.5	0.3	0.5
October	0.8	1.2	2.0	0.7	1.2	0.7	2.0	4.1	1.6	1.8	0.5	0.3	0.5
November	0.5	0.7	1.6	0.8	1.1	0.8	2.0	4.1	1.6	1.4	0.5	0.4	0.5
December	0.5	0.9	1.8	0.8	1.2	0.7	1.8	3.4	1.6	2.1	0.6	0.3	0.6
2018													
January	0.7	1.0	2.0	0.8	1.2	0.7	2.5	4.3	2.2	1.3	0.5	0.3	0.5
February	0.5	0.7	2.1	0.8	1.1	0.7	2.0	4.1	1.6	1.2	0.5	0.4	0.5
March	0.4	0.8	2.1	0.9	1.1	0.9	1.8	4.6	1.3	0.8	0.5	0.3	0.5
April	0.7	0.9	1.6	0.7	0.9	0.7	1.9	4.5	1.5	1.5	0.4	0.3	0.4
May	0.6	1.0	2.0	0.7	1.0	0.6	2.0	4.2	1.7	1.6	0.4	0.2	0.4
June	0.6	0.9	2.1	0.8	0.9	0.8	1.8	5.0	1.3	1.3	0.4	0.2	0.5
July	0.4	0.6	1.9	0.8	1.3	0.7	2.0	4.9	1.5	1.5	0.5	0.4	0.6
August	0.4	0.7	1.9	0.7	1.3	0.6	1.8	3.9	1.4	1.3	0.5	0.2	0.5
September	0.6	0.6	1.8	0.7	1.0	0.6	1.9	3.4	1.7	1.3	0.5	0.2	0.6
October	0.5	0.7	2.0	0.7	0.8	0.7	2.0	3.5	1.7	1.3	0.5	0.2	0.5
November	0.6	1.0	2.1	0.8	1.3	0.7	2.0	4.0	1.6	1.5	0.5	0.2	0.5
December	0.6	0.7	2.1	0.7	1.1	0.6	1.8	3.6	1.5	1.5	0.5	0.3	0.5
2019													
January	0.5	1.1	1.8	0.8	1.1	0.7	1.8	3.4	1.5	1.0	0.5	0.3	0.6
February	0.4	1.4	1.9	0.8	1.2	0.7	1.7	3.3	1.4	1.2	0.5	0.2	0.6
March	0.3	0.6	1.9	0.7	1.0	0.6	1.7	2.3	1.6	1.0	0.5	0.2	0.5
April	0.5	0.8	2.2	0.8	1.1	0.7	2.0	3.3	1.8	1.0	0.5	0.2	0.5
May	0.4	1.4	2.1	0.7	1.1	0.7	1.5	4.0	1.1	1.1	0.4	0.3	0.4
June	0.5	1.4	1.8	0.7	0.7	0.7	1.9	2.6	1.7	1.3	0.4	0.3	0.5
July	0.5	1.5	1.9	0.7	0.6	0.7	1.8	2.8	1.6	0.8	0.4	0.2	0.5
August	0.5	1.2	1.9	0.6	0.9	0.5	1.6	3.2	1.3	1.4	0.5	0.4	0.5
September	0.4	1.5	2.1	0.7	0.9	0.7	2.1	3.0	1.9	1.1	0.5	0.3	0.5
October	0.3	1.0	1.8	0.7	0.8	0.7	1.5	3.3	1.2	0.6	0.5	0.9	0.5
November	0.3	1.0	2.0	0.7	0.8	0.6	1.8	3.4	1.5	0.7	0.4	0.4	0.4
December	0.4	1.0	2.1	0.6	0.7	0.6	2.0	4.3	1.6	1.5	0.3	0.3	0.3
2020													
January	0.5	0.4	1.9	0.7	0.6	0.7	1.8	3.6	1.4	1.4	0.4	0.6	0.4
February	0.7	1.0	1.8	0.7	0.8	0.7	1.9	3.1	1.7	1.6	0.4	0.3	0.4
March	1.2	6.4	5.1	5.2	7.2	4.8	29.2	22.3	30.4	15.0	0.8	0.3	0.8
April	0.8	7.3	4.7	4.2	6.8	3.7	20.1	24.3	19.4	16.8	1.0	0.4	1.1
May	0.4	1.5	2.1	1.0	0.9	1.0	2.6	6.1	2.1	1.7	0.6	0.8	0.5
June	0.6	1.2	2.1	0.7	0.9	0.7	2.9	7.0	2.4	1.6	0.4	0.5	0.4
July	0.8	1.5	2.0	0.7	0.9	0.7	2.3	5.1	1.9	1.1	0.3	0.4	0.2
August	0.3	1.4	1.8	0.7	0.6	0.7	1.5	2.1	1.4	0.4	0.3	0.7	0.2
September	0.4	1.5	1.5	0.7	0.8	0.6	1.3	2.6	1.1	1.1	0.6	1.9	0.4
October	0.3	1.3	1.8	0.7	1.0	0.6	1.3	2.6	1.1	1.0	1.0	5.1	0.4

[1]Layoffs and discharges are the number of layoffs and discharges during the entire month.
[2]The layoffs and discharges rate is the number of layoffs and discharges during the entire month as a percent of total employment.

CHAPTER 8: LABOR-MANAGEMENT RELATIONS

HIGHLIGHTS

This chapter contains information on historical trends in union membership, earnings, and work stoppages.

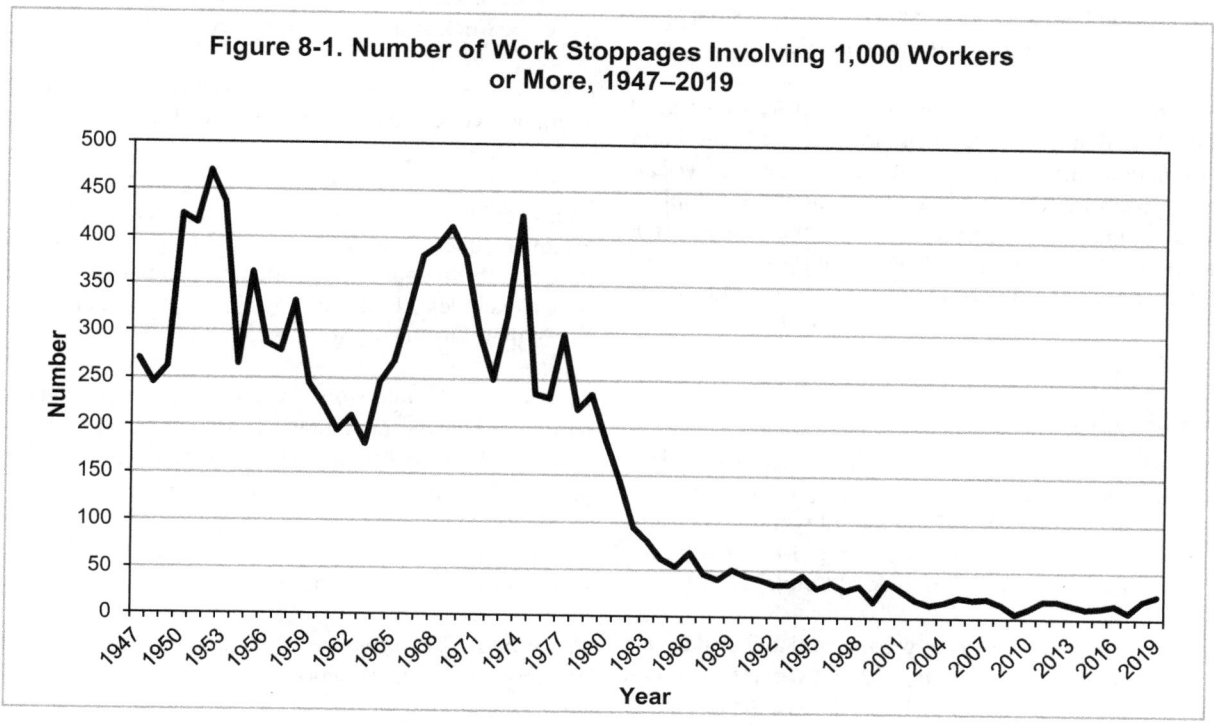

Figure 8-1. Number of Work Stoppages Involving 1,000 Workers or More, 1947–2019

In 2019, the number of work stoppages involving 1,000 employees or more increased for the second straight year to 25—the highest level since 2001 but still far lower than the high of 470 in 1952. The number of workers involved (425,000) was lower than last year but the second highest number since 1989. In comparison, in 2017, only 25,000 workers were involved in a work stoppage. (See Table 8-1)

OTHER HIGHLIGHTS

- Union membership continued to be higher for men (10.8 percent) than for women (9.7 percent) in 2019. According to race, Blacks had the highest rate of union membership at 11.2 percent, followed by Whites at 10.3 percent, Asians at 8.8 percent, and Hispanics at 8.9 percent. (See Table 8-2.)

- The number of workers in a union or employee association declined again in 2019 to 14.5 million after increasing in 2017. This number has been gradually declining since 1983 when a high of 17.7 million workers were involved in a union or employee association. The percentage of workers belonging to a union decreased again from 10.5 percent in 2018 to 10.3 percent in 2019. (Table 8-5.)

- Workers in the public sector were far more likely to be members of a union than those in the private sector (33.6 percent compared with 6.2 percent). In the private sector, workers in utilities had the highest unionization rate at 23.4 percent while those in finance had the lowest rate at 1.1 percent. (See Table 8-3.)

- Hawaii had the highest rate of union membership at 23.5 percent surpassing New York at 21.0 percent and Washington at 18.8 percent. The South continued to have low rates of union membership. South Carolina (2.2 percent), North Carolina (2.3 percent), and Texas (4.0 percent) had the lowest rates of union membership in the country. (See Table 8-6.)

NOTES AND DEFINITIONS

WORK STOPPAGES

Collection and Coverage

Data on work stoppages measure the number and duration of major strikes or lockouts (involving 1,000 workers or more) during the year, the number of workers involved in these stoppages, and the amount of time lost due to these stoppages.

Information on work stoppages is obtained from reports issued by the Federal Mediation and Conciliation Service, state labor market information offices, Bureau of Labor Statistics (BLS) Strike Reports from the Office of Employment and Unemployment Statistics, and media sources such as the Daily Labor Report and the Wall Street Journal. One or both parties involved in the work stoppage (employer and/or union) is contacted to verify the duration of the stoppage and number of workers idled by the stoppage.

Concepts and Definitions

Days of idleness is calculated by taking the number of workers involved in the strike or lockout and multiplying it by the number of days workers are off the job. The number of working days lost for every major work stoppage is based on a 5-day workweek (Monday through Friday), excluding federal holidays.

Major work stoppage includes both worker-initiated strikes and employer-initiated lockouts involving 1,000 workers or more. BLS does not distinguish between lockouts and strikes in its statistics.

Workers involved consists of workers directly involved in the stoppage. This category does not measure the indirect or secondary effect of stoppages on other establishments whose employees are idle from material shortages or lack of service.

Sources of Additional Information

Additional information is available in BLS news release USDL 20-0244, "Major Work Stoppages in 2019". More information on measures and methods used to calculate the information in this chapter can be found on the BLS Web site at https://www.bls.gov/opub/hom/home.htm.

UNION MEMBERSHIP

Collection and Coverage

The estimates of union membership are obtained from the Current Population Survey (CPS), which provides basic information on the labor force, employment, and unemployment. The survey is conducted monthly for the Bureau of Labor Statistics by the U.S. Census Bureau from a scientifically selected national sample of about 60,000 households. The union membership and earnings data are tabulated from one-quarter of the CPS monthly sample and are limited to wage and salary workers. All self-employed workers are excluded. The data in these tables are annual averages.

Beginning in January of each year, data reflect revised population controls used in the CPS.

Concepts and Definitions

Full-time workers are workers who usually work 35 hours or more per week at their sole or principal job.

Part-time workers are workers who usually work fewer than 35 hours per week at their sole or principal job.

Wage and salary workers are workers who receive wages, salaries, commissions, tips, payment in kind, or piece rates. The group includes employees in both the private and public sectors, but, for the purposes of the union membership and earnings series, excludes all self-employed persons, regardless of whether or not their businesses are incorporated.

Hispanic or Latino ethnicity refers to persons who identified themselves in the enumeration process as being Spanish, Hispanic, or Latino. Persons whose ethnicity is identified as Hispanic or Latino may be of any race.

Union members are members of a labor union or an employee association similar to a union.

Represented by unions refers to union members, as well as to workers who have no union affiliation but whose jobs are covered by a union contract.

Median earnings is the amount which divides a given earnings distribution into two equal groups, one having earnings above the median and the other having earnings below the median. The estimating procedure places each reported or calculated weekly earnings value into $50-wide intervals which are centered around multiples of $50. The actual value is estimated through the linear interpolation of the interval in which the median lies.

Usual weekly earnings represent earnings before taxes and other deductions and include any overtime pay, commissions, or tips usually received (at the main job in the case of multiple jobholders). Prior to 1994, respondents were asked how much they usually earned per week. Since January 1994, respondents have been asked to identify the easiest way for them to report earnings (hourly, weekly, biweekly, twice monthly, monthly, annually, other) and how much they usually earn in the reported time period. Earnings reported on a basis other than weekly are converted to a weekly equivalent. The term "usual" is as perceived by the respondent. If the respondent asks for a definition of "usual," interviewers are instructed to define the term as more than half of the weeks worked during the past 4 or 5 months.

Sources of Additional Information

For additional information see BLS news release USDL 20-0108 "Union Members–2019."

Table 8-1. Work Stoppages Involving 1,000 Workers or More, 1947–2019

(Number, percent.)

Year	Stoppages beginning during the year		Days idle during the year[1]	
	Number	Workers involved (thousands)[2]	Number (thousands)	Percent of estimated total working time[3]
1947	270	1 629	25 720	. . .
1948	245	1 435	26 127	0.22
1949	262	2 537	43 420	0.38
1950	424	1 698	30 390	0.26
1951	415	1 462	15 070	0.12
1952	470	2 746	48 820	0.38
1953	437	1 623	18 130	0.14
1954	265	1 075	16 630	0.13
1955	363	2 055	21 180	0.16
1956	287	1 370	26 840	0.20
1957	279	887	10 340	0.07
1958	332	1 587	17 900	0.13
1959	245	1 381	60 850	0.43
1960	222	896	13 260	0.09
1961	195	1 031	10 140	0.07
1962	211	793	11 760	0.08
1963	181	512	10 020	0.07
1964	246	1 183	16 220	0.11
1965	268	999	15 140	0.10
1966	321	1 300	16 000	0.10
1967	381	2 192	31 320	0.18
1968	392	1 855	35 367	0.20
1969	412	1 576	29 397	0.16
1970	381	2 468	52 761	0.29
1971	298	2 516	35 538	0.19
1972	250	975	16 764	0.09
1973	317	1 400	16 260	0.08
1974	424	1 796	31 809	0.16
1975	235	965	17 563	0.09
1976	231	1 519	23 962	0.12
1977	298	1 212	21 258	0.10
1978	219	1 006	23 774	0.11
1979	235	1 021	20 409	0.09
1980	187	795	20 844	0.09
1981	145	729	16 908	0.07
1982	96	656	9 061	0.04
1983	81	909	17 461	0.08
1984	62	376	8 499	0.04
1985	54	324	7 079	0.03
1986	69	533	11 861	0.05
1987	46	174	4 481	0.02
1988	40	118	4 381	0.02
1989	51	452	16 996	0.07
1990	44	185	5 926	0.02
1991	40	392	4 584	0.02
1992	35	364	3 989	0.01
1993	35	182	3 981	0.01
1994	45	322	5 021	0.02
1995	31	192	5 771	0.02
1996	37	273	4 889	0.02
1997	29	339	4 497	0.01
1998	34	387	5 116	0.02
1999	17	73	1 996	0.01
2000	39	394	20 419	0.06
2001	29	99	1 151	(4)
2002	19	46	660	(4)
2003	14	129	4 091	0.01
2004	17	171	3 344	0.01
2005	22	100	1 736	0.01
2006	20	70	2 688	0.01
2007	21	189	1 265	(4)
2008	15	72	1 954	0.01
2009	5	13	124	(4)
2010	11	45	302	(4)
2011	19	113	1 020	(4)
2012	19	148	1 131	(4)
2013	15	55	290	(4)
2014	11	34	200	(4)
2015	12	47	740	(4)
2016	15	99	1 543	(4)
2017	7	25	439	(4)
2018	20	485	2 815	0.01
2019	25	425	3 244	. . .

[1]Days idle include all stoppages in effect during the reference period. For work stoppages that are still ongoing at the end of the calendar year, only those days of idleness during the calendar year are counted.
[2]Workers are counted more than once if involved in more than one stoppage during the reference period.
[3]Agricultural and government workers are included in the calculation of estimated working time; private household, forestry, and fishery workers are excluded.
[4]Less than 0.005 percent.
. . . = Not available.

Table 8-2. Union Affiliation of Employed Wage and Salary Workers, by Selected Characteristics, 2014–2019

(Numbers in thousands, percent.)

Characteristic	2014					2015					2016				
	Total employed	Member of union[1]		Represented by union[2]		Total employed	Member of union[1]		Represented by union[2]		Total employed	Member of union[1]		Represented by union[2]	
		Total	Percent of employed	Total	Percent of employed		Total	Percent of employed	Total	Percent of employed		Total	Percent of employed	Total	Percent of employed
SEX AND AGE															
Both Sexes, 16 Years and Over	131 431	14 576	11.1	16 152	12.3	133 743	14 795	11.1	16 441	12.3	136 101	14 555	10.7	16 271	12.0
16 to 24 years	18 019	804	4.5	956	5.3	18 311	800	4.4	967	5.3	18 556	816	4.4	988	5.3
25 years and over	113 412	13 772	12.1	15 196	13.4	115 431	13 995	12.1	15 474	13.4	117 545	13 739	11.7	15 283	13.0
25 to 34 years	30 158	2 879	9.5	3 205	10.6	30 870	2 985	9.7	3 363	10.9	31 750	2 924	9.2	3 296	10.4
35 to 44 years	27 948	3 460	12.4	3 823	13.7	28 101	3 457	12.3	3 785	13.5	28 515	3 423	12.0	3 782	13.3
45 to 54 years	28 540	3 927	13.8	4 286	15.0	28 764	3 909	13.6	4 306	15.0	28 807	3 846	13.3	4 269	14.8
55 to 64 years	20 781	2 924	14.1	3 229	15.5	21 288	3 035	14.3	3 329	15.6	21 778	2 903	13.3	3 209	14.7
65 years and over	5 985	582	9.7	653	10.9	6 408	610	9.5	691	10.8	6 696	643	9.6	726	10.8
Men, 16 Years and Over	68 048	7 939	11.7	8 717	12.8	69 298	7 963	11.5	8 760	12.6	70 589	7 888	11.2	8 704	12.3
16 to 24 years	9 141	462	5.1	540	5.9	9 250	485	5.2	563	6.1	9 412	484	5.1	568	6.0
25 years and over	58 907	7 476	12.7	8 177	13.9	60 048	7 478	12.5	8 197	13.7	61 177	7 404	12.1	8 136	13.3
25 to 34 years	16 172	1 611	10.0	1 773	11.0	16 550	1 639	9.9	1 825	11.0	16 930	1 640	9.7	1 833	10.8
35 to 44 years	14 769	1 913	13.0	2 108	14.3	14 844	1 857	12.5	2 023	13.6	15 102	1 881	12.5	2 051	13.6
45 to 54 years	14 508	2 085	14.4	2 256	15.6	14 696	2 079	14.1	2 281	15.5	14 775	2 048	13.9	2 253	15.3
55 to 64 years	10 419	1 553	14.9	1 689	16.2	10 698	1 588	14.8	1 717	16.0	10 957	1 511	13.8	1 633	14.9
65 years and over	3 040	315	10.4	351	11.5	3 259	315	9.7	352	10.8	3 412	323	9.5	365	10.7
Women, 16 Years and Over	63 383	6 638	10.5	7 434	11.7	64 445	6 833	10.6	7 681	11.9	65 512	6 667	10.2	7 567	11.6
16 to 24 years	8 879	342	3.8	416	4.7	9 061	315	3.5	405	4.5	9 143	332	3.6	420	4.6
25 years and over	54 505	6 296	11.6	7 019	12.9	55 384	6 518	11.8	7 277	13.1	56 368	6 335	11.2	7 147	12.7
25 to 34 years	13 985	1 268	9.1	1 431	10.2	14 320	1 346	9.4	1 538	10.7	14 820	1 284	8.7	1 463	9.9
35 to 44 years	13 180	1 548	11.7	1 715	13.0	13 257	1 600	12.1	1 762	13.3	13 412	1 542	11.5	1 731	12.9
45 to 54 years	14 032	1 842	13.1	2 030	14.5	14 068	1 830	13.0	2 025	14.4	14 032	1 797	12.8	2 016	14.4
55 to 64 years	10 362	1 371	13.2	1 541	14.9	10 590	1 447	13.7	1 613	15.2	10 820	1 392	12.9	1 576	14.6
65 years and over	2 946	267	9.1	302	10.2	3 149	294	9.3	339	10.8	3 283	320	9.8	361	11.0
RACE, HISPANIC ORIGIN, AND SEX															
White, 16 Years and Over[3]	104 065	11 274	10.8	12 503	12.0	104 991	11 301	10.8	12 627	12.0	106 160	11 120	10.5	12 436	11.7
Men	54 747	6 295	11.5	6 900	12.6	55 402	6 222	11.2	6 875	12.4	56 007	6 153	11.0	6 769	12.1
Women	49 318	4 979	10.1	5 602	11.4	49 590	5 079	10.2	5 752	11.6	50 153	4 967	9.9	5 667	11.3
Black, 16 Years and Over[3]	15 830	2 097	13.2	2 303	14.6	16 552	2 246	13.6	2 427	14.7	17 014	2 209	13.0	2 475	14.5
Men	7 243	1 047	14.5	1 147	15.8	7 558	1 097	14.5	1 174	15.5	7 852	1 104	14.1	1 229	15.7
Women	8 586	1 050	12.2	1 156	13.5	8 995	1 149	12.8	1 253	13.9	9 163	1 105	12.1	1 245	13.6
Asian, 16 Years and Over[3]	7 476	779	10.4	866	11.6	7 883	770	9.8	860	10.9	8 340	752	9.0	839	10.1
Men	3 921	361	9.2	416	10.6	4 113	367	8.9	416	10.1	4 368	355	8.1	404	9.3
Women	3 555	418	11.8	450	12.6	3 770	403	10.7	444	11.8	3 972	397	10.0	435	10.9
Hispanic, 16 Years and Over[4]	21 571	1 978	9.2	2 220	10.3	22 351	2 104	9.4	2 365	10.6	23 085	2 032	8.8	2 308	10.0
Men	12 339	1 155	9.4	1 286	10.4	12 670	1 211	9.6	1 346	10.6	13 125	1 209	9.2	1 348	10.3
Women	9 232	823	8.9	933	10.1	9 681	892	9.2	1 019	10.5	9 960	823	8.0	960	9.6
FULL- OR PART-TIME STATUS[5]															
Full-time workers	106 526	13 132	12.3	14 491	13.6	109 080	13 340	12.2	14 768	13.5	111 091	13 119	12.0	14 593	13.1
Part-time workers	24 707	1 424	5.8	1 636	6.6	24 445	1 431	5.9	1 646	6.7	24 832	1 415	6.0	1 655	6.7

[1]Data refer to members of a labor union or to an employee association similar to a union.

[2]Data refer to members of a labor union or to an employee association similar to a union, as well as to workers who report no union affiliation but whose jobs are covered by a union or an employee association contract.

[3]Beginning in 2003, persons who selected this race group only; persons who selected more than one race group are not included. Prior to 2003, persons who reported more than one race group were included in the group they identified as their main race. Additionally, estimates for the above race groups (White, Black, and Asian) do not sum to totals because data are not presented for all races.

[4]May be of any race.

[5]The distinction between full- and part-time workers is based on hours usually worked. Data will not sum to totals because full- or part-time status on the principal job is not identifiable for a small number of multiple job holders.

Table 8-2. Union Affiliation of Employed Wage and Salary Workers, by Selected Characteristics, 2014–2019
—Continued

(Numbers in thousands, percent.)

Characteristic	2017					2018					2019				
	Total employed	Member of union[1]		Represented by union[2]		Total employed	Member of union[1]		Represented by union[2]		Total employed	Member of union[1]		Represented by union[2]	
		Total	Percent of employed	Total	Percent of employed		Total	Percent of employed	Total	Percent of employed		Total	Percent of employed	Total	Percent of employed
SEX AND AGE															
Both Sexes, 16 Years and Over	137 890	14 817	10.7	16 444	11.9	140 099	14 744	10.5	16 380	11.7	141 737	14 574	10.3	16 383	11.6
16 to 24 years	18 757	877	4.7	1 014	5.4	18 698	823	4.4	966	5.2	18 869	827	4.4	977	5.2
25 years and over	119 133	13 940	11.7	15 430	13.0	121 401	13 921	11.5	15 415	12.7	122 868	13 747	11.2	15 406	12.5
25 to 34 years	32 407	3 061	9.4	3 426	10.6	33 232	3 084	9.3	3 452	10.4	33 718	2 973	8.8	3 464	10.3
35 to 44 years	28 729	3 421	11.9	3 806	13.2	29 433	3 445	11.7	3 802	12.9	29 898	3 515	11.8	3 906	13.1
45 to 54 years	28 655	3 771	13.2	4 145	14.5	28 525	3 664	12.8	4 029	14.1	28 191	3 543	12.6	3 918	13.9
55 to 64 years	22 382	3 032	13.5	3 329	14.9	22 839	3 041	13.3	3 355	14.7	23 207	2 952	12.7	3 266	14.1
65 years and over	6 960	655	9.4	723	10.4	7 372	687	9.3	777	10.5	7 854	764	9.7	852	10.9
Men, 16 Years and Over	71 469	8 166	11.4	8 930	12.5	72 632	8 082	11.1	8 868	12.2	73 349	7 950	10.8	8 845	12.1
16 to 24 years	9 486	529	5.6	609	6.4	9 366	513	5.5	587	6.3	9 449	495	5.2	574	6.1
25 years and over	61 983	7 637	12.3	8 321	13.4	63 266	7 569	12.0	8 281	13.1	63 899	7 455	11.7	8 271	12.9
25 to 34 years	17 199	1 755	10.2	1 940	11.3	17 710	1 781	10.1	1 957	11.0	17 892	1 648	9.2	1 922	10.7
35 to 44 years	15 220	1 900	12.5	2 088	13.7	15 617	1 884	12.1	2 057	13.2	15 811	1 958	12.4	2 136	13.5
45 to 54 years	14 693	2 040	13.9	2 189	14.9	14 593	1 934	13.3	2 109	14.5	14 363	1 923	13.4	2 088	14.5
55 to 64 years	11 318	1 617	14.3	1 745	15.4	11 575	1 611	13.9	1 752	15.1	11 777	1 520	12.9	1 674	14.2
65 years and over	3 554	324	9.1	359	10.1	3 771	360	9.5	405	10.8	4 056	406	10.0	451	11.1
Women, 16 Years and Over	66 421	6 651	10.0	7 514	11.3	67 467	6 662	9.9	7 512	11.1	68 388	6 624	9.7	7 538	11.0
16 to 24 years	9 271	348	3.8	405	4.4	9 332	310	3.3	379	4.1	9 420	332	3.5	403	4.3
25 years and over	57 150	6 303	11.0	7 109	12.4	58 135	6 352	10.9	7 134	12.3	58 969	6 292	10.7	7 135	12.1
25 to 34 years	15 208	1 306	8.6	1 486	9.8	15 521	1 303	8.4	1 495	9.6	15 826	1 326	8.4	1 541	9.7
35 to 44 years	13 509	1 521	11.3	1 718	12.7	13 817	1 561	11.3	1 744	12.6	14 086	1 557	11.1	1 770	12.6
45 to 54 years	13 962	1 731	12.4	1 956	14.0	13 932	1 730	12.4	1 920	13.8	13 828	1 620	11.7	1 830	13.2
55 to 64 years	11 065	1 415	12.8	1 584	14.3	11 264	1 430	12.7	1 603	14.2	11 430	1 431	12.5	1 592	13.9
65 years and over	3 406	330	9.7	364	10.7	3 601	327	9.1	372	10.3	3 797	357	9.4	401	10.6
RACE, HISPANIC ORIGIN, AND SEX															
White, 16 Years and Over[3]	107 121	11 358	10.6	12 589	11.8	108 164	11 215	10.4	12 471	11.5	109 132	11 208	10.3	12 583	11.5
Men	56 545	6 432	11.4	7 025	12.4	57 132	6 311	11.0	6 920	12.1	57 537	6 280	10.9	6 965	12.1
Women	50 576	4 926	9.7	5 564	11.0	51 032	4 904	9.6	5 551	10.9	51 594	4 928	9.6	5 618	10.9
Black, 16 Years and Over[3]	17 498	2 210	12.6	2 459	14.1	17 994	2 258	12.5	2 487	13.8	18 231	2 043	11.2	2 310	12.7
Men	8 042	1 101	13.7	1 205	15.0	8 330	1 111	13.3	1 221	14.7	8 440	1 002	11.9	1 132	13.4
Women	9 456	1 109	11.7	1 254	13.3	9 664	1 147	11.9	1 266	13.1	9 791	1 042	10.6	1 178	12.0
Asian, 16 Years and Over[3]	8 561	763	8.9	843	9.8	8 973	758	8.4	855	9.5	9 291	817	8.8	932	10.0
Men	4 457	365	8.2	402	9.0	4 652	375	8.1	416	8.9	4 795	384	8.0	438	9.1
Women	4 105	398	9.7	441	10.7	4 321	383	8.9	439	10.2	4 496	433	9.6	494	11.0
Hispanic, 16 Years and Over[4]	23 656	2 201	9.3	2 476	10.5	24 591	2 239	9.1	2 482	10.1	25 417	2 258	8.9	2 590	10.2
Men	13 342	1 261	9.5	1 410	10.6	13 775	1 304	9.5	1 443	10.5	14 100	1 312	9.3	1 490	10.6
Women	10 315	940	9.1	1 067	10.3	10 815	934	8.6	1 039	9.6	11 317	947	8.4	1 099	9.7
FULL- OR PART-TIME STATUS[5]															
Full-time workers	113 272	13 396	11.8	14 812	13.1	115 567	13 415	11.6	14 844	12.8	117 584	13 224	11.2	14 822	12.6
Part-time workers	24 433	1 403	5.7	1 611	6.6	24 346	1 313	5.4	1 518	6.2	23 946	1 329	5.5	1 540	6.4

[1]Data refer to members of a labor union or to an employee association similar to a union.

[2]Data refer to members of a labor union or to an employee association similar to a union, as well as to workers who report no union affiliation but whose jobs are covered by a union or an employee association contract.

[3]Beginning in 2003, persons who selected this race group only; persons who selected more than one race group are not included. Prior to 2003, persons who reported more than one race group were included in the group they identified as their main race. Additionally, estimates for the above race groups (White, Black, and Asian) do not sum to totals because data are not presented for all races.

[4]May be of any race.

[5]The distinction between full- and part-time workers is based on hours usually worked. Data will not sum to totals because full- or part-time status on the principal job is not identifiable for a small number of multiple job holders.

Table 8-3. Union Affiliation of Wage and Salary Workers, by Occupation and Industry, 2018–2019

(Thousands of people, percent.)

Occupation and industry	2018					2019				
	Total employed	Member of union[1]		Represented by union[2]		Total employed	Member of union[1]		Represented by union[2]	
		Total	Percent of employed	Total	Percent of employed		Total	Percent of employed	Total	Percent of employed
OCCUPATION										
Management, professional, and related	55 258	6 183	11.2	7 069	12.8	56 495	6 277	11.1	7 211	12.8
Management, business, and financial operations	21 196	916	4.3	1 130	5.3	21 991	957	4.4	1 183	5.4
Management	14 299	607	4.2	750	5.2	14 753	614	4.2	748	5.1
Business and financial operations	6 897	309	4.5	379	5.5	7 238	343	4.7	435	6.0
Professional and related	34 062	5 267	15.5	5 939	17.4	34 504	5 319	15.4	6 028	17.5
Computer and mathematical	4 937	181	3.7	227	4.6	5 145	196	3.8	254	4.9
Architecture and engineering	3 124	232	7.4	263	8.4	3 137	220	7.0	264	8.4
Life, physical, and social science	1 436	141	9.8	160	11.1	1 392	120	8.6	138	9.9
Community and social service	2 614	360	13.8	395	15.1	2 617	408	15.6	454	17.4
Legal	1 585	94	6.0	121	7.6	1 598	78	4.9	110	6.9
Education, training, and library	9 140	3 089	33.8	3 435	37.6	9 233	3 057	33.1	3 381	36.6
Arts, design, entertainment, sports, and media	2 417	161	6.6	187	7.7	2 259	165	7.3	180	8.0
Health care practitioner and technical	8 810	1 008	11.4	1 152	13.1	9 123	1 076	11.8	1 247	13.7
Services	24 320	2 389	9.8	2 613	10.7	24 547	2 294	9.3	2 539	10.3
Health care support	3 507	284	8.1	314	8.9	3 605	265	7.4	298	8.3
Protective service	3 193	1 081	33.9	1 135	35.5	3 073	1 038	33.8	1 100	35.8
Food preparation and serving related	8 052	314	3.9	373	4.6	8 306	294	3.5	351	4.2
Building and grounds cleaning and maintenance	4 990	453	9.1	510	10.2	4 962	433	8.7	483	9.7
Personal care and service	4 577	256	5.6	282	6.2	4 600	264	5.7	307	6.7
Sales and office	30 767	1 993	6.5	2 223	7.2	30 700	1 879	6.1	2 155	7.0
Sales and related	13 694	455	3.3	538	3.9	13 371	374	2.8	467	3.5
Office and administrative support	17 073	1 538	9.0	1 685	9.9	17 329	1 505	8.7	1 688	9.7
Natural resources, construction, and maintenance	12 319	1 865	15.1	1 978	16.1	12 427	1 854	14.9	1 991	16.0
Farming, fishing, and forestry	1 024	24	2.4	31	3.0	1 060	22	2.1	36	3.4
Construction and extraction	6 776	1 158	17.1	1 217	18.0	6 859	1 192	17.4	1 269	18.5
Installation, maintenance, and repair	4 518	682	15.1	730	16.2	4 508	640	14.2	686	15.2
Production, transportation, and material moving	17 435	2 315	13.3	2 497	14.3	17 567	2 269	12.9	2 487	14.2
Production	8 272	985	11.9	1 062	12.8	8 304	976	11.8	1 067	12.8
Transportation and material moving	9 163	1 330	14.5	1 435	15.7	9 263	1 294	14.0	1 420	15.3
INDUSTRY										
Private sector	118 968	7 578	6.4	8 512	7.2	120 714	7 508	6.2	8 562	7.1
Agriculture and related industries	1 344	29	2.2	35	2.6	1 352	23	1.7	38	2.8
Nonagricultural industries	117 624	7 548	6.4	8 477	7.2	119 362	7 485	6.3	8 524	7.1
Mining	721	34	4.7	38	5.3	710	28	4.0	33	4.7
Construction	8 169	1 048	12.8	1 125	13.8	8 352	1 055	12.6	1 133	13.6
Manufacturing	14 861	1 340	9.0	1 444	9.7	15 070	1 291	8.6	1 423	9.4
Durable goods	9 401	850	9.0	917	9.8	9 502	835	8.8	912	9.6
Nondurable goods	5 460	490	9.0	527	9.6	5 568	455	8.2	510	9.2
Wholesale and retail trade	18 736	805	4.3	928	5.0	18 113	741	4.1	863	4.8
Wholesale trade	3 351	137	4.1	158	4.7	3 186	143	4.5	160	5.0
Retail trade	15 385	669	4.3	769	5.0	14 927	598	4.0	704	4.7
Transportation and utilities	6 467	1 116	17.3	1 185	18.3	6 745	1 166	17.3	1 259	18.7
Transportation and warehousing	5 410	904	16.7	968	17.9	5 659	912	16.1	997	17.6
Utilities	1 057	212	20.1	217	20.5	1 086	254	23.4	261	24.0
Information[3]	2 536	244	9.6	260	10.3	2 352	242	10.3	263	11.2
Publishing, except Internet	437	17	3.9	18	4.2	355	12	3.3	13	3.8
Motion pictures and sound recording	395	49	12.5	50	12.6	386	53	13.6	57	14.7
Broadcasting, except Internet	526	41	7.7	45	8.6	482	53	11.0	57	11.9
Telecommunications	851	131	15.4	138	16.2	821	115	14.1	125	15.3
Financial activities	9 148	192	2.1	253	2.8	9 364	182	1.9	237	2.5
Finance and insurance	6 770	99	1.5	137	2.0	6 982	87	1.2	125	1.8
Finance	4 244	55	1.3	81	1.9	4 390	49	1.1	74	1.7
Insurance	2 526	43	1.7	56	2.2	2 592	37	1.4	51	2.0
Real estate and rental and leasing	2 379	94	3.9	115	4.8	2 382	95	4.0	112	4.7
Professional and business services	15 228	390	2.6	481	3.2	15 720	339	2.2	471	3.0
Professional and technical services	9 718	148	1.5	203	2.1	10 280	143	1.4	227	2.2
Management, administrative, and waste services	5 510	242	4.4	278	5.0	5 440	197	3.6	244	4.5
Education and health services	22 982	1 853	8.1	2 144	9.3	23 690	1 885	8.0	2 182	9.2
Education services	4 828	632	13.1	748	15.5	4 922	608	12.3	693	14.1
Health care and social assistance	18 154	1 221	6.7	1 396	7.7	18 768	1 278	6.8	1 489	7.9
Leisure and hospitality	12 582	367	2.9	436	3.5	13 097	384	2.9	457	3.5
Arts, entertainment, and recreation	2 390	136	5.7	159	6.6	2 498	164	6.6	184	7.4
Accommodation and food services	10 193	231	2.3	277	2.7	10 599	220	2.1	274	2.6
Accommodation	1 369	113	8.3	127	9.3	1 427	93	6.5	100	7.0
Food services and drinking places	8 823	118	1.3	150	1.7	9 172	128	1.4	173	1.9
Other services[3]	6 192	159	2.6	184	3.0	6 150	172	2.8	202	3.3
Other services, except private households	5 431	155	2.9	179	3.3	5 327	163	3.1	193	3.6
Public sector	21 131	7 167	33.9	7 868	37.2	21 023	7 066	33.6	7 821	37.2
Federal government	3 707	977	26.4	1 128	30.4	3 798	974	25.6	1 158	30.5
State government	7 109	2 035	28.6	2 259	31.8	6 958	2 043	29.4	2 249	32.3
Local government	10 315	4 155	40.3	4 481	43.4	10 267	4 050	39.4	4 414	43.0

Note: Updated population controls are introduced annually with the release of January data. Data refer to the sole or principal job of full- and part-time workers. Excluded are all self-employed workers, regardless of whether or not their businesses are incorporated.

[1]Data refer to members of a labor union or an employee association similar to a union.
[2]Data refer to members of a labor union or an employee association similar to a union, as well as to workers who report no union affiliation but whose jobs are covered by a union or an employee association contract.
[3]Includes other industries, not shown separately.

Table 8-4. Median Weekly Earnings of Full-Time Wage and Salary Workers, by Union Affiliation, Occupation, and Industry, 2018–2019

(Dollars.)

Occupation and industry	2018				2019			
	Total	Member of union[1]	Represented by union[2]	Non-union	Total	Member of union[1]	Represented by union[2]	Non-union
OCCUPATION								
Management, professional, and related	1 246	1 229	1 222	1 250	1 309	1 254	1 246	1 327
Management, business, and financial operations	1 355	1 318	1 334	1 356	1 415	1 365	1 366	1 420
Management	1 429	1 401	1 425	1 430	1 478	1 446	1 430	1 481
Business and financial operations	1 216	1 159	1 164	1 221	1 285	1 217	1 247	1 290
Professional and related	1 176	1 210	1 193	1 173	1 237	1 239	1 227	1 240
Computer and mathematical	1 539	1 458	1 460	1 543	1 579	1 392	1 394	1 592
Architecture and engineering	1 484	1 516	1 529	1 479	1 550	1 492	1 490	1 557
Life, physical, and social science	1 270	1 331	1 323	1 262	1 334	1 538	1 552	1 286
Community and social service	913	1 076	1 083	880	968	1 178	1 159	928
Legal	1 467	1 593	1 503	1 464	1 562	1 569	1 566	1 561
Education, training, and library	1 002	1 151	1 136	909	1 057	1 173	1 157	972
Arts, design, entertainment, sports, and media	1 086	1 277	1 205	1 074	1 151	1 389	1 356	1 139
Health care practitioner and technical	1 140	1 292	1 288	1 122	1 180	1 275	1 272	1 162
Services	569	802	781	541	592	874	848	573
Health care support	561	618	618	552	591	684	680	584
Protective service	848	1 137	1 132	715	900	1 243	1 234	739
Food preparation and serving related	501	609	598	496	522	624	604	519
Building and grounds cleaning and maintenance	551	679	670	533	580	706	692	567
Personal care and service	544	590	587	541	565	620	620	559
Sales and office	742	835	828	735	758	867	854	750
Sales and related	798	774	766	800	830	798	783	833
Office and administrative support	717	850	843	703	732	885	875	717
Natural resources, construction, and maintenance	824	1 181	1 176	782	869	1 207	1 185	810
Farming, fishing, and forestry	581	(3)	(3)	581	574	(3)	(3)	572
Construction and extraction	808	1 178	1 172	759	866	1 201	1 183	801
Installation, maintenance, and repair	934	1 208	1 204	891	939	1 236	1 215	902
Production, transportation, and material moving	707	924	913	680	727	924	918	705
Production	723	935	923	699	745	910	907	722
Transportation and material moving	689	913	902	657	711	943	926	685
INDUSTRY								
Private sector	861	999	989	848	893	1 025	1 013	881
Agriculture and related industries	619	(3)	(3)	619	611	(3)	(3)	610
Nonagricultural industries	865	1 001	991	853	897	1 027	1 015	886
Mining	1 291	(3)	(3)	1 269	1 423	(3)	(3)	1 410
Construction	868	1 220	1 210	819	909	1 257	1 240	868
Manufacturing	917	992	992	908	936	962	962	933
Durable goods	951	1 025	1 023	941	973	982	983	972
Nondurable goods	858	923	931	843	883	914	912	879
Wholesale and retail trade	722	759	743	721	748	790	779	746
Wholesale trade	917	896	917	917	963	937	944	964
Retail trade	671	719	700	669	701	744	730	699
Transportation and utilities	901	1 106	1 091	864	906	1 184	1 151	862
Transportation and warehousing	838	1 024	1 014	808	840	1 103	1 066	799
Utilities	1 292	1 329	1 327	1 271	1 329	1 461	1 449	1 273
Information[4]	1 169	1 355	1 336	1 157	1 182	1 265	1 214	1 174
Publishing, except Internet	1 153	(3)	(3)	1 151	1 159	(3)	(3)	1 168
Motion pictures and sound recording	1 114	(3)	(3)	1 027	1 042	1 453	1 398	1 018
Broadcasting, except Internet	1 056	(3)	(3)	1 051	1 061	1 371	1 345	1 019
Telecommunications	1 170	1 331	1 325	1 150	1 213	1 257	1 206	1 217
Financial activities	1 047	937	940	1 052	1 125	950	980	1 128
Finance and insurance	1 130	909	948	1 134	1 167	1 033	1 062	1 169
Finance	1 155	(3)	940	1 159	1 225	(3)	1 030	1 227
Insurance	1 071	(3)	953	1 078	1 124	(3)	(3)	1 123
Real estate and rental and leasing	897	979	921	896	948	941	937	949
Professional and business services	1 094	888	906	1 105	1 149	903	918	1 155
Professional and technical services	1 364	1 264	1 205	1 367	1 452	1 179	1 230	1 455
Management, administrative, and waste services	664	711	711	661	698	770	769	694
Education and health services	860	984	978	845	896	1 059	1 051	879
Education services	985	1 068	1 053	968	1 015	1 129	1 116	994
Health care and social assistance	822	920	921	813	864	1 008	1 006	851
Leisure and hospitality	584	700	695	579	601	722	698	597
Arts, entertainment, and recreation	732	772	791	726	759	819	823	752
Accommodation and food services	551	666	655	546	574	656	615	571
Accommodation	615	715	702	604	621	704	685	616
Food services and drinking places	536	621	619	535	562	611	595	560
Other services[4]	735	1 165	1 186	725	762	1 091	1 098	752
Other services, except private households	764	1 171	1 195	754	796	1 114	1 117	785
Public sector	999	1 099	1 094	936	1 043	1 147	1 141	973
Federal government	1 166	1 076	1 112	1 228	1 222	1 151	1 183	1 241
State government	967	1 074	1 058	916	1 015	1 138	1 126	959
Local government	969	1 114	1 106	859	999	1 150	1 136	888

Note: Updated population controls are introduced annually with the release of January data. Data refer to the sole or principal job of full- and part-time workers. Excluded are all self-employed workers, regardless of whether or not their businesses are incorporated.

[1]Data refer to members of a labor union or an employee association similar to a union.
[2]Data refer to members of a labor union or an employee association similar to a union, as well as to workers who report no union affiliation but whose jobs are covered by a union or an employee association contract.
[3]Data not shown where base is less than 50,000.
[4]Includes other industries, not shown separately.

Table 8-5. Union or Employee Association Members Among Wage and Salary Employees, 1977–2019

(Numbers in thousands, percent.)

Year	Total wage and salary employment	Union or employee association member	Union or association members as a percent of total wage and salary employment
1977	81 334	19 335	23.8
1978	84 968	19 548	23.0
1979	87 117	20 986	24.1
1980	87 480	20 095	23.0
1983[1]	88 290	17 717	20.1
1984	92 194	17 340	18.8
1985	94 521	16 996	18.0
1986	96 903	16 975	17.5
1987	99 303	16 913	17.0
1988	101 407	17 002	16.8
1989	103 480	16 980	16.4
1990	103 905	16 740	16.1
1991	102 786	16 568	16.1
1992	103 688	16 390	15.8
1993	105 087	16 598	15.8
1994[2]	107 989	16 748	15.5
1995	110 038	16 360	14.9
1996	111 960	16 269	14.5
1997	114 533	16 110	14.1
1998	116 730	16 211	13.9
1999	118 963	16 477	13.9
2000	120 786	16 258	13.5
2001	122 482	16 387	13.4
2002	121 826	16 145	13.3
2003	122 358	15 776	12.9
2004	123 554	15 472	12.5
2005	125 889	15 685	12.5
2006	128 237	15 359	12.0
2007	129 767	15 670	12.1
2008	129 377	16 098	12.4
2009	124 490	15 327	12.3
2010	124 073	14 715	11.9
2011	125 187	14 764	13.0
2012	127 577	14 366	11.3
2013	129 110	14 528	11.3
2014	131 431	14 576	11.1
2015	133 743	14 795	11.1
2016	136 101	14 555	10.7
2017	137 890	14 817	10.7
2018	140 099	14 744	10.5
2019	141 737	14 574	10.3

[1]Annual average data beginning in 1983 are not directly comparable with the data for 1977–1980.
[2]Data beginning in 1994 are not strictly comparable with data for 1993 and earlier years because of the introduction of a major redesign of the Current Population Survey questionnaire and collection methodology and the introduction of 1990 census–based population controls.
. . . = Not available.

Table 8-6. Union Affiliation of Employed Wage and Salary Workers, by State, 2018–2019

(Numbers in thousands, percent.)

State	2018					2019				
	Total employed	Member of union[1]		Represented by union[2]		Total employed	Member of union[1]		Represented by union[2]	
		Total	Percent of employed	Total	Percent of employed		Total	Percent of employed	Total	Percent of employed
UNITED STATES	140 099	14 744	10.5	16 380	11.7	141 737	14 574	10.3	16 383	11.6
Alabama	1 950	180	9.2	196	10.1	2 041	173	8.5	199	9.8
Alaska	299	55	18.5	60	20.0	282	48	17.1	53	18.7
Arizona	2 943	156	5.3	191	6.5	3 028	174	5.7	214	7.1
Arkansas	1 176	56	4.8	62	5.3	1 200	62	5.2	71	5.9
California	16 399	2 405	14.7	2 587	15.8	16 485	2 504	15.2	2 726	16.5
Colorado	2 564	281	11.0	307	12.0	2 631	237	9.0	259	9.8
Connecticut	1 677	268	16.0	280	16.7	1 680	244	14.5	269	16.0
Delaware	434	45	10.3	47	10.8	432	38	8.7	43	9.9
District of Columbia	354	35	9.9	41	11.6	361	34	9.3	37	10.2
Florida	8 702	484	5.6	588	6.8	8 827	551	6.2	667	7.6
Georgia	4 466	201	4.5	249	5.6	4 422	180	4.1	223	5.0
Hawaii	601	139	23.1	146	24.3	574	135	23.5	147	25.5
Idaho	733	34	4.7	41	5.6	764	37	4.9	46	6.0
Illinois	5 694	786	13.8	839	14.7	5 658	771	13.6	832	14.7
Indiana	3 049	269	8.8	283	9.3	3 007	249	8.3	296	9.8
Iowa	1 461	113	7.7	129	8.8	1 543	97	6.3	122	7.9
Kansas	1 283	90	7.0	129	10.1	1 280	112	8.7	130	10.1
Kentucky	1 812	161	8.9	207	11.4	1 786	144	8.0	169	9.5
Louisiana	1 785	89	5.0	104	5.8	1 784	94	5.3	108	6.1
Maine	573	74	12.9	85	14.8	588	69	11.8	81	13.7
Maryland	2 784	307	11.0	336	12.1	2 912	330	11.3	371	12.8
Massachusetts	3 397	464	13.7	493	14.5	3 397	406	12.0	449	13.2
Michigan	4 320	625	14.5	663	15.4	4 323	589	13.6	648	15.0
Minnesota	2 634	395	15.0	421	16.0	2 662	364	13.7	381	14.3
Mississippi	1 121	58	5.1	80	7.1	1 105	70	6.3	93	8.4
Missouri	2 675	251	9.4	283	10.6	2 661	297	11.1	333	12.5
Montana	427	50	11.8	60	14.0	437	46	10.5	52	12.0
Nebraska	882	59	6.6	71	8.0	894	75	8.4	86	9.6
Nevada	1 376	191	13.9	216	15.7	1 379	201	14.6	222	16.1
New Hampshire	664	68	10.2	77	11.6	677	69	10.3	79	11.6
New Jersey	3 935	587	14.9	639	16.2	4 094	642	15.7	712	17.4
New Mexico	812	56	6.8	67	8.2	813	58	7.1	72	8.8
New York	8 404	1 872	22.3	2 027	24.1	8 253	1 732	21.0	1 877	22.7
North Carolina	4 331	118	2.7	174	4.0	4 396	102	2.3	150	3.4
North Dakota	343	18	5.2	23	6.7	356	21	6.0	27	7.5
Ohio	5 054	639	12.6	722	14.3	5 127	610	11.9	673	13.1
Oklahoma	1 583	90	5.7	117	7.4	1 554	96	6.2	123	7.9
Oregon	1 738	242	13.9	256	14.7	1 772	255	14.4	277	15.7
Pennsylvania	5 575	701	12.6	748	13.4	5 642	676	12.0	740	13.1
Rhode Island	479	83	17.4	89	18.5	475	83	17.4	90	19.0
South Carolina	2 016	55	2.7	72	3.6	2 140	47	2.2	59	2.7
South Dakota	387	22	5.6	28	7.1	395	22	5.6	26	6.7
Tennessee	2 816	155	5.5	179	6.4	2 947	135	4.6	162	5.5
Texas	11 989	512	4.3	653	5.4	12 334	497	4.0	642	5.2
Utah	1 343	56	4.1	76	5.7	1 409	62	4.4	83	5.9
Vermont	291	31	10.5	34	11.6	290	33	11.2	35	12.0
Virginia	3 875	168	4.3	213	5.5	3 881	156	4.0	201	5.2
Washington	3 270	649	19.8	671	20.5	3 393	638	18.8	684	20.2
West Virginia	684	68	10.0	74	10.8	704	72	10.2	78	11.1
Wisconsin	2 700	219	8.1	233	8.6	2 698	218	8.1	245	9.1
Wyoming	235	15	6.5	18	7.7	243	18	7.3	21	8.7

Note: Updated population controls are introduced annually with the release of January data. Data refer to the sole or principal job of full- and part-time workers. Excluded are all self-employed workers, regardless of whether or not their businesses are incorporated.

[1] Data refer to members of a labor union or an employee association similar to a union.
[2] Data refer to members of a labor union or an employee association similar to a union, as well as to workers who report no union affiliation but whose jobs are covered by a union or an employee association contract.

CHAPTER 9: THE IMPACT OF CORONAVIRUS (COVID-19) ON THE LABOR MARKET

HIGHLIGHTS

This chapter examines the impact that Coronavirus (COVID-19) had on the labor market throughout 2020. The chapter addresses the sharp decline in employment, the increase in unemployment, and the rise of telework. In addition, it provides information on how Americans planned to use their stimulus payments.

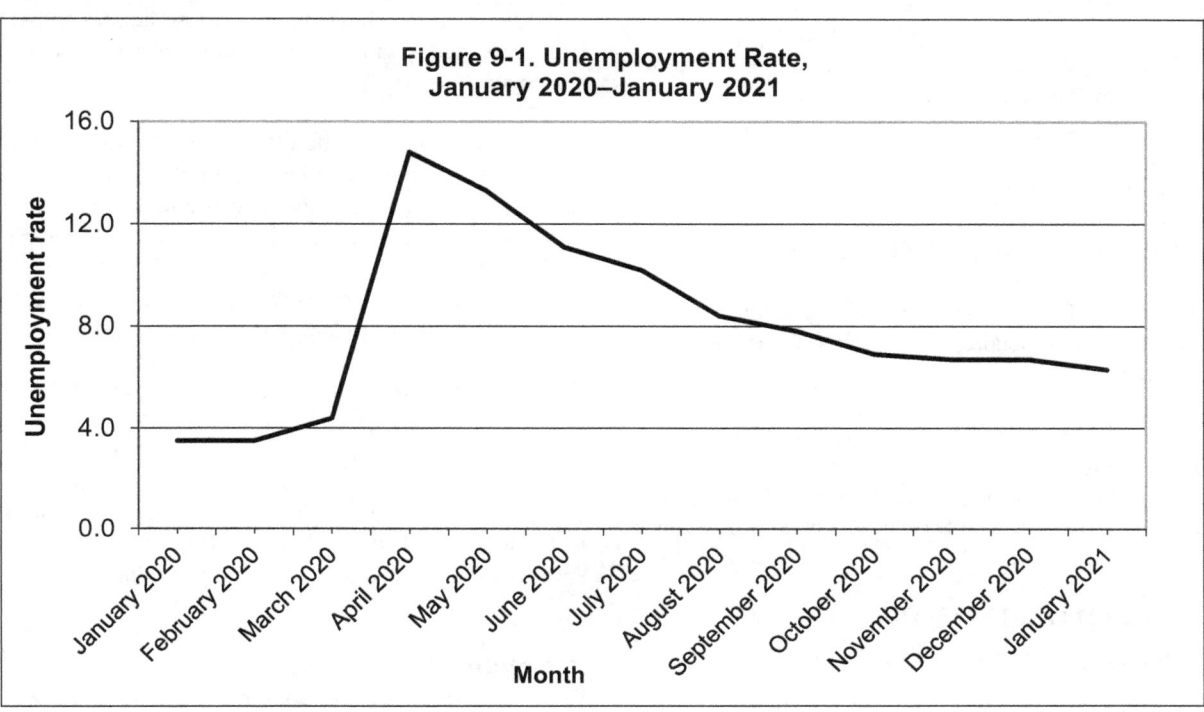

The unemployment rose sharply from 3.5 percent in February 2020, to 4.4 percent in March 2020 to 14.8 percent in April 2020. Although the unemployment rate declined in the second half of 2020, it remained much higher than before the pandemic. (See Table 9-1.)

OTHER HIGHLIGHTS

• In June 2020, approximately 31.3 percent of total employed people teleworked because of the pandemic. By December 2020, the number of those teleworking declined to 23.7 percent. (See Table 9-4.)

• Women were more likely than men to telework (36.0 percent compared with 27.2 percent). By race, Asians were far more likely to work at home than any other race. Nearly half (48.5 percent) of all Asians teleworked while only 30.8 percent of Whites and 25.7 percent of Blacks teleworked. (See Table 9-4.)

• Those with higher levels of educational attainment were more likely to work at home than those with less education. In June 2020, 63.3 percent of those with an advanced degree teleworked while only 4.8 percent of those with less than a high school diploma did. (See Table 9-4.)

• Among those unable to work because their employer closed or lost business due to COVID-19, nearly 20 percent received pay while 80.4 percent did not receive pay. However, in education, library and training occupation, 54.2 of workers who were unable to work at some point during the pandemic did receive pay. (See Table 9-7.)

NOTES AND DEFINITIONS

Collection and Coverage

The Bureau of Labor Statistics (BLS) added questions to the Current Population Survey (CPS) to help gauge the effects of the coronavirus (COVID-19) pandemic on the labor market. The data in Tables 9-4 through 9-8 pertain to June 2020.

BLS asked whether people teleworked or worked from home because of the pandemic; whether people were unable to work because their employers closed or lost business due to the pandemic; whether they were paid for that missed work; and whether the pandemic prevented job-seeking activities. All of these supplemental questions refer to activities at any time during the "last 4 weeks" and follow the monthly labor force questions.

The Current Population Survey (CPS), also referred to as the household survey, is a monthly sample survey of 60,000 eligible households conducted by the U.S. Census Bureau for the Bureau of Labor Statistics. More detailed information on the CPS can be found in Chapter 1.

COVID-19 also had an impact on the Current Expenditure Survey (CES), or the establishment survey. In the establishment survey, more data continued to be collected by web than in months prior to the pandemic. More information on the CES can be found in Chapter 2.

CONCEPTS AND DEFINITIONS

Telework Because of the Pandemic

Whether a person teleworked was determined through answers to the question: "At any time in the last 4 weeks, did you telework or work at home for pay because of the coronavirus pandemic?" (The question was asked of people 16 years or older who were employed at the time of the survey.)

These data refer to employed people who teleworked or worked at home for pay at some point in the last 4 weeks specifically because of the coronavirus pandemic. People did not have to telework for the entire time that they worked to be counted among those who telework. By design, people whose telework was unrelated to the pandemic, such as employed people who worked entirely from home before the pandemic, should not be included in this measure.

Unable to Work Because of the Pandemic

Whether people were unable to work was determined through answers to the question: "At any time in the last 4 weeks, were you unable to work because your employer closed or lost business due to the coronavirus pandemic?" (The question was asked of all people 16 years or older.)

This question was designed to capture information on both those who were unable to work because their business closed entirely due to the pandemic, as well as those who were unable to work or worked reduced hours because of partial cutbacks in business operations. This includes people whose hours had been reduced because of the pandemic but continued to work for the same employer.

These data do not include all people who were unable to work because of the pandemic. For example, it may exclude people who are unable to work now because of the pandemic but were unemployed before it started. It may exclude people who are unable to work because of health concerns or fear of getting ill. It may exclude people who were not working before but might want to work now, like a student who planned to get a summer job.

The fact that someone is employed at the time of the survey does not necessarily mean they are working for the same employer that closed or lost business. For example, someone who worked two jobs before the pandemic, but lost one because that business closed, would still be employed on the other job. Someone who lost a job at a business that closed but then began working at another job may also be counted in this measure.

Pay Status of those Unable to Work

People who reported that they were unable to work (as defined above) were asked: "Did you receive any pay from your employer for the hours you did not work in the last 4 weeks?" No information was collected about how much pay they received, such as whether they were paid for all of the time not worked. Also, no information was collected about the source of the pay from the employer, such as whether or not it was tied to the Paycheck Protection Program (PPP) or other program participation.

Did Not Look for Work Because of the Pandemic

Whether the pandemic kept people from looking for work was determined through answers to the question: "Did the coronavirus pandemic prevent you from looking for work in the last 4 weeks?" (The question was asked of people 16 years or older who were not in the labor force at the time of the survey—that is, they were neither employed nor unemployed. To be counted as unemployed, by definition, people must either be actively looking for work or on temporary layoff.)

Table 9-1. Unemployment Rate by Selected Characteristics, January 2016–January 2021

(Rate.)

Month and year	Total	Men, 20 years and over	Women, 20 years and over	16 to 19 years old	White	Black or African American	Asian	Hispanic or Latino
January 2016	4.8	4.3	4.5	15.9	4.2	8.5	3.6	5.9
February 2016	4.9	4.4	4.5	15.4	4.2	8.6	3.8	5.5
March 2016	5.0	4.5	4.7	16.0	4.3	8.9	3.9	5.6
April 2016	5.1	4.7	4.6	16.1	4.4	8.8	3.8	6.2
May 2016	4.8	4.4	4.3	15.9	4.2	8.2	4.1	5.7
June 2016	4.9	4.5	4.4	16.0	4.3	8.7	3.6	6.0
July 2016	4.8	4.7	4.1	15.2	4.2	8.2	3.8	5.4
August 2016	4.9	4.5	4.4	15.7	4.4	8.0	4.1	5.6
September 2016	5.0	4.7	4.4	16.1	4.4	8.5	3.8	6.2
October 2016	4.9	4.6	4.4	15.8	4.4	8.5	3.4	5.7
November 2016	4.7	4.4	4.3	15.5	4.2	8.2	3.1	5.6
December 2016	4.7	4.4	4.3	14.9	4.2	8.0	2.7	5.8
January 2017	4.7	4.2	4.3	14.9	4.2	7.4	3.7	5.8
February 2017	4.6	4.2	4.2	14.7	4.0	8.0	3.4	5.6
March 2017	4.4	4.2	4.0	13.7	3.9	7.9	3.3	5.0
April 2017	4.5	4.0	4.2	14.9	3.9	7.8	3.3	5.2
May 2017	4.4	3.9	4.1	13.9	3.8	7.6	3.6	5.2
June 2017	4.3	4.0	4.0	12.4	3.8	7.1	3.7	5.0
July 2017	4.3	4.0	3.9	12.1	3.7	7.2	3.8	5.1
August 2017	4.4	4.1	3.9	13.8	3.9	7.5	3.9	5.1
September 2017	4.2	3.9	3.9	13.2	3.7	7.2	3.6	5.1
October 2017	4.1	3.8	3.7	14.2	3.6	7.6	3.0	5.0
November 2017	4.2	3.8	3.7	16.5	3.7	7.5	3.0	4.9
December 2017	4.1	3.8	3.8	14.1	3.7	6.9	2.5	5.0
January 2018	4.0	3.7	3.6	14.0	3.5	7.5	3.0	4.9
February 2018	4.1	3.6	3.8	14.5	3.6	6.8	2.9	4.9
March 2018	4.0	3.6	3.7	13.4	3.5	6.6	3.1	4.9
April 2018	4.0	3.8	3.6	13.3	3.6	6.5	2.9	4.8
May 2018	3.8	3.6	3.4	12.5	3.5	5.8	2.2	4.8
June 2018	4.0	3.7	3.7	11.2	3.5	6.5	3.3	4.6
July 2018	3.8	3.4	3.5	12.0	3.3	6.4	3.1	4.5
August 2018	3.8	3.5	3.5	12.6	3.4	6.2	2.9	4.7
September 2018	3.7	3.5	3.3	12.7	3.3	6.2	3.5	4.6
October 2018	3.8	3.5	3.4	12.5	3.3	6.4	3.1	4.4
November 2018	3.8	3.4	3.5	12.9	3.4	6.2	2.8	4.6
December 2018	3.9	3.6	3.5	13.1	3.4	6.8	3.3	4.5
January 2019	4.0	3.6	3.6	13.2	3.5	6.9	3.0	4.8
February 2019	3.8	3.4	3.4	13.9	3.2	7.0	3.1	4.3
March 2019	3.8	3.6	3.4	12.7	3.3	6.5	3.1	4.5
April 2019	3.7	3.5	3.2	13.4	3.2	6.6	2.3	4.1
May 2019	3.7	3.4	3.3	12.3	3.3	6.1	2.5	4.1
June 2019	3.6	3.3	3.3	11.4	3.3	6.0	2.2	4.3
July 2019	3.6	3.4	3.3	12.0	3.3	5.6	2.8	4.4
August 2019	3.7	3.4	3.3	12.4	3.4	5.2	2.8	4.2
September 2019	3.5	3.3	3.0	12.5	3.2	5.4	2.5	4.0
October 2019	3.6	3.3	3.2	12.6	3.3	5.6	2.9	4.2
November 2019	3.6	3.2	3.3	12.5	3.3	5.7	2.6	4.3
December 2019	3.6	3.1	3.3	13.0	3.1	6.2	2.6	4.3
January 2020	3.5	3.1	3.2	12.6	3.0	6.1	3.1	4.3
February 2020	3.5	3.2	3.1	11.5	3.0	6.0	2.4	4.4
March 2020	4.4	4.1	4.0	14.1	3.9	6.8	4.1	6.0
April 2020	14.8	13.1	15.5	32.1	14.1	16.7	14.5	18.9
May 2020	13.3	11.6	13.9	29.6	12.3	16.7	14.9	17.6
June 2020	11.1	10.2	11.3	22.6	10.1	15.3	13.9	14.5
July 2020	10.2	9.4	10.4	19.1	9.2	14.4	11.9	12.7
August 2020	8.4	8.0	8.3	16.4	7.4	12.8	10.6	10.5
September 2020	7.8	7.3	7.7	16.3	7.0	12.0	8.8	10.3
October 2020	6.9	6.7	6.5	14.0	6.0	10.8	7.6	8.8
November 2020	6.7	6.6	6.2	13.9	5.9	10.3	6.7	8.4
December 2020	6.7	6.4	6.3	16.0	6.0	9.9	5.9	9.3
January 2021	6.3	6.0	6.0	14.8	5.7	9.2	6.6	8.6

Table 9-2. Unemployment Rate by State by Month, January 2020–December 2020

(Rate.)

State	January 2020	February 2020	March 2020	April 2020	May 2020	June 2020	July 2020	August 2020	September 2020	October 2020	November 2020	December 2020
Alabama	2.7	2.7	3.0	13.8	9.6	7.6	7.9	5.6	6.7	5.7	4.4	3.9
Alaska	6.0	5.8	5.2	13.5	12.7	12.4	11.6	7.4	7.2	5.9	6.3	5.8
Arizona	4.5	4.5	6.1	13.4	9.0	10.0	10.7	5.9	6.5	7.9	8.0	7.5
Arkansas	3.5	3.5	5.0	10.8	9.6	8.1	7.1	7.4	7.2	6.2	6.3	4.2
California	3.9	3.9	5.5	16.4	16.4	14.9	13.5	11.2	11.1	9.0	8.1	9.0
Colorado	2.5	2.5	5.2	12.2	10.2	10.6	7.4	6.7	6.4	6.4	6.4	8.4
Connecticut	3.7	3.8	3.4	8.3	9.6	10.1	10.2	8.1	7.7	6.1	8.2	8.0
Delaware	4.0	3.9	5.0	14.9	15.9	12.6	10.5	8.9	8.3	5.6	5.1	5.3
District of Columbia	5.2	5.1	6.0	11.7	8.8	8.7	8.5	8.6	9.0	8.3	7.5	7.9
Florida	2.8	2.8	4.4	13.8	13.7	10.3	11.4	7.3	7.2	6.4	6.3	6.1
Georgia	3.1	3.1	4.6	12.6	9.4	7.6	7.6	5.7	6.3	4.5	5.7	5.6
Hawaii	2.7	2.7	2.4	23.8	23.5	13.4	13.5	13.0	15.0	14.2	10.4	9.3
Idaho	2.8	2.7	2.5	11.8	9.0	5.8	5.1	4.2	6.1	5.5	4.9	4.4
Illinois	3.5	3.4	4.2	17.2	15.3	14.5	11.5	11.0	10.4	7.4	6.9	7.6
Indiana	3.1	3.1	3.0	17.5	12.3	11.1	7.9	6.4	6.3	5.5	5.1	4.3
Iowa	2.8	2.8	3.3	11.0	10.2	8.4	6.8	6.3	4.8	3.7	3.8	3.1
Kansas	3.1	3.1	2.8	11.9	10.0	7.5	7.2	6.9	5.9	5.0	5.1	3.8
Kentucky	4.3	4.2	5.2	16.6	10.9	4.4	4.5	7.5	5.6	7.3	5.7	6.0
Louisiana	5.3	5.2	6.7	15.1	14.2	9.5	9.4	7.7	8.0	9.4	8.5	7.2
Maine	3.1	3.2	3.0	10.4	9.4	6.7	9.9	7.0	6.1	5.4	4.9	4.9
Maryland	3.3	3.3	3.3	10.1	10.0	8.3	7.8	7.0	7.6	7.7	6.8	6.3
Massachusetts	2.8	2.8	2.8	16.2	16.6	17.7	16.2	11.4	9.8	7.4	6.7	7.4
Michigan	3.8	3.6	4.3	24.0	21.3	14.9	8.7	8.7	8.6	6.1	7.0	7.5
Minnesota	3.2	3.1	2.9	8.7	9.9	8.6	7.6	7.4	5.9	4.6	4.5	4.4
Mississippi	5.5	5.4	5.1	16.3	10.5	8.8	9.4	7.8	7.2	7.4	6.3	6.2
Missouri	3.5	3.5	3.9	10.2	10.1	7.8	6.9	7.0	4.8	4.6	4.5	5.8
Montana	3.5	3.5	3.6	11.9	9.0	7.2	6.5	5.8	5.4	5.0	4.6	4.4
Nebraska	2.9	2.9	4.0	8.7	5.3	5.5	4.9	4.0	3.6	3.0	3.0	3.0
Nevada	3.6	3.6	6.9	30.1	25.3	15.2	14.2	13.3	12.5	11.9	10.4	9.2
New Hampshire	2.6	2.6	2.4	17.1	15.4	9.2	8.0	6.6	5.8	4.2	3.9	4.0
New Jersey	3.8	3.8	3.7	16.3	15.4	16.8	14.2	11.1	6.7	8.0	10.2	7.6
New Mexico	4.8	4.8	6.3	11.9	9.1	8.4	12.7	11.4	9.9	8.1	7.2	8.2
New York	3.8	3.7	4.1	15.3	14.5	15.6	15.9	12.5	9.7	9.2	8.4	8.2
North Carolina	3.6	3.6	4.3	12.9	12.8	7.5	8.5	6.5	7.2	6.2	6.2	6.2
North Dakota	2.3	2.2	2.0	9.1	9.1	7.4	6.6	5.0	4.4	4.7	4.5	4.1
Ohio	4.1	4.1	5.8	17.6	13.9	11.0	9.0	8.9	8.3	6.1	5.7	5.5
Oklahoma	3.3	3.2	2.9	14.7	12.6	6.4	7.1	5.7	5.4	6.2	6.1	5.3
Oregon	3.3	3.3	3.5	14.9	14.3	11.6	10.4	8.5	7.9	6.8	6.0	6.4
Pennsylvania	4.7	4.7	5.8	16.1	13.4	13.2	12.5	10.4	8.3	7.4	6.8	6.7
Rhode Island	3.4	3.4	4.7	18.1	16.4	12.6	11.3	12.9	10.5	7.1	7.3	8.1
South Carolina	2.4	2.5	3.2	12.8	12.4	8.7	8.7	6.4	5.2	4.2	4.4	4.6
South Dakota	3.4	3.3	3.1	10.9	9.4	7.2	6.4	4.8	4.1	3.7	3.5	3.0
Tennessee	3.3	3.4	3.3	15.5	11.0	9.6	9.7	8.6	6.5	7.3	5.2	6.4
Texas	3.5	3.5	5.1	13.5	13.0	8.4	8.0	6.8	8.3	6.9	8.1	7.2
Utah	2.5	2.5	3.8	10.4	8.6	5.3	4.5	4.1	5.0	4.1	4.3	3.6
Vermont	2.4	2.4	3.1	16.5	12.8	9.5	8.3	4.8	4.3	3.2	3.0	3.1
Virginia	2.7	2.6	3.3	11.2	9.0	8.1	7.9	6.1	6.2	5.2	4.8	4.9
Washington	3.9	3.8	5.1	16.3	15.1	10.0	10.2	8.4	8.3	6.0	5.7	7.1
West Virginia	5.0	4.9	6.0	15.9	12.9	10.5	10.0	8.9	8.6	6.4	6.3	6.3
Wisconsin	3.5	3.5	3.1	13.6	12.1	8.6	7.1	6.3	5.4	6.0	5.3	5.5
Wyoming	3.7	3.7	3.8	9.6	8.8	7.6	7.1	6.6	6.1	5.5	5.1	4.8

Table 9-3. Percent Change in Unemployment in Each State Since February 2020

(Percent.)

State	Percent change in unemployment
Alabama	-1.7
Alaska	-7.5
Arizona	-3.1
Arkansas	-2.8
California	-9.0
Colorado	-5.7
Connecticut	-6.8
Delaware	-10.0
District of Columbia	-7.2
Florida	-5.3
Georgia	-2.0
Hawaii	-15.7
Idaho	0.2
Illinois	-7.5
Indiana	-3.4
Iowa	-4.3
Kansas	-4.9
Kentucky	-6.2
Louisiana	-4.9
Maine	-8.2
Maryland	-5.2
Massachusetts	-10.4
Michigan	-12.6
Minnesota	-9.1
Mississippi	-1.9
Missouri	-3.7
Montana	-3.5
Nebraska	-2.7
Nevada	-7.4
New Hampshire	-10.4
New Jersey	-9.0
New Mexico	-9.0
New York	-12.0
North Carolina	-4.7
North Dakota	-7.4
Ohio	-6.8
Oklahoma	-4.6
Oregon	-8.5
Pennsylvania	-9.0
Rhode Island	-10.1
South Carolina	-2.8
South Dakota	-3.3
Tennessee	-3.7
Texas	-4.0
Utah	0.3
Vermont	-9.6
Virginia	-4.9
Washington	-6.7
West Virginia	-6.4
Wisconsin	-7.7
Wyoming	-4.4

Table 9-4. Employed Persons who Teleworked or Worked at Home for Pay at Any Time in the Last Four Weeks due to the Coronavirus Pandemic, June 2020

(Number in thousands, percent.)

Characteristic	Total employed	Persons who teleworked because of the coronavirus pandemic[1]		Percent distribution	
		Total	Percent of total employed	Total employed	People who teleworked because of the coronavirus pandemic[1]
Total, 16 Years and Over	142 811	44 644	31.3	100.0	100.0
16 to 24 years	16 553	2 490	15.0	11.6	5.6
16 to 19 years	4 884	322	6.6	3.4	0.7
20 to 24 years	11 669	2 168	18.6	8.2	4.9
25 to 54 years	92 407	32 147	34.8	64.7	72.0
25 to 34 years	32 009	11 391	35.6	22.4	25.5
35 to 44 years	30 909	11 012	35.6	21.6	24.7
45 to 54 years	29 489	9 744	33.0	20.6	21.8
55 years and over	33 851	10 008	29.6	23.7	22.4
55 to 64 years	24 673	7 527	30.5	17.3	16.9
65 years and over	9 178	2 481	27.0	6.4	5.6
Men, 16 Years and Over	76 425	20 772	27.2	53.5	46.5
16 to 24 years	8 420	1 034	12.3	5.9	2.3
25 to 54 years	49 575	14 929	30.1	34.7	33.4
55 years and over	18 430	4 810	26.1	12.9	10.8
Women, 16 Years and Over	66 386	23 872	36.0	46.5	53.5
16 to 24 years	8 132	1 456	17.9	5.7	3.3
25 to 54 years	42 832	17 218	40.2	30.0	38.6
55 years and over	15 421	5 198	33.7	10.8	11.6
White	112 020	34 489	30.8	78.4	77.3
Black or African American	17 019	4 379	25.7	11.9	9.8
Asian	8 786	4 265	48.5	6.2	9.6
Hispanic or Latino ethnicity	24 794	5 240	21.1	17.4	11.7
Married, spouse present	77 620	27 148	35.0	54.4	60.8
Widowed, divorced, or separated[2]	20 705	5 776	27.9	14.5	12.9
Never married	44 486	11 720	26.3	31.2	26.3
With own children under 18	46 521	16 161	34.7	32.6	36.2
With no own children under 18	96 290	28 484	29.6	67.4	63.8
Total, 25 years and over	126 259	42 154	33.4	100.0	100.0
Less than a high school diploma	7 218	346	4.8	5.7	0.8
High school graduates, no college[3]	29 355	3 690	12.6	23.2	8.8
Some college or associate degree	32 643	7 274	22.3	25.9	17.3
Bachelor's degree and higher[4]	57 043	30 843	54.1	45.2	73.2
Bachelor's degree only	34 353	16 488	48.0	27.2	39.1
Advanced degree	22 690	14 356	63.3	18.0	34.1

. . . = Not available.
[1]Data refer to those who teleworked or worked at home for pay specifically because of the coronavirus pandemic.
[2]Separated includes persons who are married, spouse absent.
[3]Includes persons with a high school diploma or equivalent.
[4]Includes persons with bachelor's, master's, professional, and doctoral degrees.

Table 9-5. Employed Persons who Teleworked or Worked at Home for Pay at Any Time in the Last Four Weeks Due to the Coronavirus Pandemic by Usual Full- or Part-Time Status, Occupation, Industry, and Class of Worker, June 2020

(Number in thousands.)

Characteristic	Total employed	Persons who teleworked because of the coronavirus pandemic[1]		Percent distribution	
		Total	Percent of total employed	Total employed	People who teleworked because of the coronavirus pandemic[1]
Usual Full- or Part-Time Status					
Total, 16 years and over	142 811	44 644	31.3	100.0	100.0
Full-time workers	120 169	40 252	33.5	84.1	90.2
Part-time workers	22 642	4 393	19.4	15.9	9.8
Occupation					
Management, professional, and related	63 336	33 001	52.1	44.3	73.9
Management, business, and financial operations	26 928	13 337	49.5	18.9	29.9
Management	18 950	8 362	44.1	13.3	18.7
Business and financial operations	7 978	4 974	62.3	5.6	11.1
Professional and related	36 408	19 665	54.0	25.5	44.0
Computer and mathematical	5 990	4 353	72.7	4.2	9.8
Architecture and engineering	3 007	1 637	54.4	2.1	3.7
Life, physical, and social science	1 767	1 165	65.9	1.2	2.6
Community and social services	2 794	1 744	62.4	2.0	3.9
Legal	1 919	1 277	66.5	1.3	2.9
Education, training, and library	8 495	5 903	69.5	5.9	13.2
Arts, design, entertainment, sports, and media	2 932	1 506	51.4	2.1	3.4
Healthcare practitioners and technical	9 503	2 080	21.9	6.7	4.7
Service	21 164	1 421	6.7	14.8	3.2
Healthcare support	4 525	325	7.2	3.2	0.7
Protective service	3 041	287	9.5	2.1	0.6
Food preparation and serving related	5 606	242	4.3	3.9	0.5
Building and grounds cleaning and maintenance	4 934	182	3.7	3.5	0.4
Personal care and service	3 058	385	12.6	2.1	0.9
Sales and office	28 458	8 731	30.7	19.9	19.6
Sales and related	13 463	3 436	25.5	9.4	7.7
Office and administrative support	14 995	5 294	35.3	10.5	11.9
Natural resources, construction, and maintenance	12 779	717	5.6	8.9	1.6
Farming, fishing, and forestry	948	13	1.4	0.7	0.0
Construction and extraction	7 371	384	5.2	5.2	0.9
Installation, maintenance, and repair	4 460	319	7.2	3.1	0.7
Production, transportation, and material moving	17 074	775	4.5	12.0	1.7
Production	7 187	446	6.2	5.0	1.0
Transportation and material moving	9 887	329	3.3	6.9	0.7
Industry[1]					
Agriculture and related industries	2 353	145	6.2	1.6	0.3
Nonagricultural industries	140 458	44 499	31.7	98.4	99.7
Mining, quarrying, and oil and gas extraction	679	225	33.2	0.5	0.5
Construction	10 571	1 240	11.7	7.4	2.8
Manufacturing	14 203	3 732	26.3	9.9	8.4
Durable goods manufacturing	8 866	2 440	27.5	6.2	5.5
Nondurable goods manufacturing	5 337	1 292	24.2	3.7	2.9
Wholesale and retail trade	17 783	2 855	16.1	12.5	6.4
Wholesale trade	3 151	817	25.9	2.2	1.8
Retail trade	14 632	2 038	13.9	10.2	4.6
Transportation and utilities	7 949	1 130	14.2	5.6	2.5
Transportation and warehousing	6 557	638	9.7	4.6	1.4
Utilities	1 392	492	35.3	1.0	1.1
Information	2 469	1 381	55.9	1.7	3.1
Financial activities	10 611	5 853	55.2	7.4	13.1
Finance and insurance	7 557	4 702	62.2	5.3	10.5
Real estate and rental and leasing	3 054	1 151	37.7	2.1	2.6
Professional and business services	18 826	8 802	46.8	13.2	19.7
Professional and technical services	12 687	7 609	60.0	8.9	17.0
Management, administrative, and waste services	6 139	1 193	19.4	4.3	2.7
Education and health services	33 196	13 434	40.5	23.2	30.1
Educational services	12 876	8 502	66.0	9.0	19.0
Health care and social assistance	20 320	4 932	24.3	14.2	11.0
Hospitals	7 158	1 417	19.8	5.0	3.2
Health services, except hospitals	10 037	2 363	23.5	7.0	5.3
Social assistance	3 125	1 152	36.9	2.2	2.6
Leisure and hospitality	10 189	1 308	12.8	7.1	2.9
Arts, entertainment, and recreation	2 454	741	30.2	1.7	1.7
Accommodation and food services	7 735	567	7.3	5.4	1.3
Other services	6 400	1 428	22.3	4.5	3.2
Other services, except private households	5 837	1 385	23.7	4.1	3.1
Private households	564	43	7.7	0.4	0.1
Public administration	7 581	3 112	41.0	5.3	7.0
Class of Worker[2]					
Wage and salary workers	127 284	41 065	32.3	89.1	92.0
Private industries	106 786	30 956	29.0	74.8	69.3
Government	20 498	10 109	49.3	14.4	22.6
Federal	3 863	1 796	46.5	2.7	4.0
State	7 040	3 824	54.3	4.9	8.6
Local	9 595	4 489	46.8	6.7	10.1
Self-employed workers	15 426	3 578	23.2	10.8	8.0
Self-employed workers, incorporated	6 208	1 768	28.5	4.3	4.0
Self-employed workers, unincorporated	9 218	1 809	19.6	6.5	4.1

[1]Data refer to those who teleworked or worked at home for pay specifically because of the coronavirus pandemic.
[2] Unpaid family workers are included in the total but not shown separately.

Table 9-6. Persons Unable to Work at Some Point in the Last Four Weeks because Their Employer Closed or Lost Business due to the Coronavirus Pandemic by Receipt of Pay from Their Employer For Hours Not Worked and Selected Characteristics, June 2020

(Number in thousands, percent.)

Characteristic	Total civilian noninstitutional population	Unable to work because employer closed or lost business due to the coronavirus pandemic						
		Number	Percent of total	Employees who received pay	Employees who did not receive pay	Total, percent of persons unable to work	Percent who received pay	Percent who did not receive pay
Total, 16 Years and Over	260 204	40 368	15.5	6 223	34 146	100.0	15.4	84.6
16 to 24 Years	37 479	6 796	18.1	591	6 205	100.0	8.7	91.3
16 to 19 years	16 557	2 139	12.9	178	1 960	100.0	8.3	91.7
20 to 24 years	20 922	4 658	22.3	413	4 245	100.0	8.9	91.1
25 to 54 years	126 061	23 871	18.9	4 040	19 831	100.0	16.9	83.1
25 to 34 years	44 851	8 626	19.2	1 398	7 228	100.0	16.2	83.8
35 to 44 years	41 294	7 686	18.6	1 296	6 391	100.0	16.9	83.1
45 to 54 years	39 916	7 558	18.9	1 346	6 213	100.0	17.8	82.2
55 years and over	96 664	9 701	10.0	1 592	8 109	100.0	16.4	83.6
55 to 64 years	42 204	6 352	15.1	1 147	5 205	100.0	18.1	81.9
65 years and over	54 460	3 349	6.1	445	2 904	100.0	13.3	86.7
Men, 16 Years and Over	125 860	19 802	15.7	2 783	17 019	100.0	14.1	85.9
16 to 24 years	18 818	3 085	16.4	247	2 838	100.0	8.0	92.0
25 to 54 years	62 226	11 957	19.2	1 860	10 097	100.0	15.6	84.4
55 years and over	44 816	4 760	10.6	676	4 084	100.0	14.2	85.8
Women, 16 Years and Over	134 344	20 566	15.3	3 440	17 127	100.0	16.7	83.3
16 to 24 years	18 661	3 711	19.9	344	3 367	100.0	9.3	90.7
25 to 54 years	63 835	11 914	18.7	2 180	9 734	100.0	18.3	81.7
55 years and over	51 848	4 941	9.5	916	4 025	100.0	18.5	81.5
White	201 233	30 003	14.9	4 618	25 385	100.0	15.4	84.6
Black or African American	33 323	5 883	17.7	1 083	4 799	100.0	18.4	81.6
Asian	16 471	2 761	16.8	293	2 468	100.0	10.6	89.4
Hispanic or Latino ethnicity	44 132	9 091	20.6	1 152	7 938	100.0	12.7	87.3
Married, spouse present	131 397	18 138	13.8	3 146	14 992	100.0	17.3	82.7
Widowed, divorced, or separated[1]	47 324	6 395	13.5	1 099	5 296	100.0	17.2	82.8
Never married	81 483	15 835	19.4	1 977	13 858	100.0	12.5	87.5
With own children under 18	62 968	11 659	18.5	1 939	9 720	100.0	16.6	83.4
With no own children under 18	197 236	28 710	14.6	4 284	24 426	100.0	14.9	85.1
Total, 25 years and over	222 725	33 572	15.1	5 631	27 941	100.0	16.8	83.2
Less than a high school diploma	19 463	3 130	16.1	298	2 832	100.0	9.5	90.5
High school graduates, no college[2]	60 795	9 387	15.4	1 352	8 036	100.0	14.4	85.6
Some college or associate degree	57 417	9 811	17.1	1 468	8 343	100.0	15.0	85.0
Bachelor's degree and higher[3]	85 050	11 243	13.2	2 513	8 730	100.0	22.4	77.6
Bachelor's degree only	52 330	7 513	14.4	1 511	6 001	100.0	20.1	79.9
Advanced degree	32 720	3 731	11.4	1 002	2 729	100.0	26.9	73.1

[1]Separated includes persons who are married, spouse absent.
[2] Includes persons with a high school diploma or equivalent.
[3]Includes persons with bachelor's, master's, professional, and doctoral degrees.

Table 9-7. Employed Persons Unable to Work at Some Point in the Last Four Weeks because Their Employer Closed or Lost Business Due to the Coronavirus, June 2020

(Number, percent.)

Characteristic	Total civilian noninstitutional population	Unable to work because employer closed or lost business due to the coronavirus pandemic						
		Number	Percent of total	Employees who received pay	Employees who did not receive pay	Total, percent of persons unable to work	Percent who received pay	Percent who did not receive pay
Usual Full- or Part-Time Status								
Total, 16 years and over	142 811	23 307	16.3	4 573	18 734	100.0	19.6	80.4
Full-time workers	120 169	17 003	14.1	3 820	13 183	100.0	22.5	77.5
Part-time workers	22 642	6 304	27.8	753	5 551	100.0	12.0	88.0
Occupation								
Management, professional, and related occupations	63 336	8 046	12.7	2 282	5 764	100.0	28.4	71.6
Management, business, and financial operations occupations	26 928	3 186	11.8	699	2 487	100.0	21.9	78.1
Management occupations	18 950	2 495	13.2	510	1 985	100.0	20.5	79.5
Business and financial operations occupations	7 978	691	8.7	188	502	100.0	27.3	72.7
Professional and related occupations	36 408	4 860	13.3	1 583	3 277	100.0	32.6	67.4
Computer and mathematical occupations	5 990	462	7.7	149	313	100.0	32.3	67.7
Architecture and engineering occupations	3 007	268	8.9	63	205	100.0	23.6	76.4
Life, physical, and social science occupations	1 767	156	8.8	48	108	100.0	30.5	69.5
Community and social services occupations	2 794	306	10.9	80	226	100.0	26.3	73.7
Legal occupations	1 919	209	10.9	64	144	100.0	30.8	69.2
Education, training, and library occupations	8 495	1 348	15.9	731	617	100.0	54.2	45.8
Arts, design, entertainment, sports, and media occupations	2 932	844	28.8	137	707	100.0	16.2	83.8
Healthcare practitioners and technical occupations	9 503	1 268	13.3	311	957	100.0	24.5	75.5
Service occupations	21 164	5 797	27.4	811	4 986	100.0	14.0	86.0
Healthcare support occupations	4 525	768	17.0	141	627	100.0	18.3	81.7
Protective service occupations	3 041	316	10.4	64	252	100.0	20.2	79.8
Food preparation and serving related occupations	5 606	1 961	35.0	304	1 657	100.0	15.5	84.5
Building and grounds cleaning and maintenance occupations	4 934	1 336	27.1	175	1 161	100.0	13.1	86.9
Personal care and service occupations	3 058	1 416	46.3	127	1 288	100.0	9.0	91.0
Sales and office occupations	28 458	4 486	15.8	733	3 753	100.0	16.3	83.7
Sales and related occupations	13 463	2 489	18.5	290	2 199	100.0	11.7	88.3
Office and administrative support occupations	14 995	1 997	13.3	443	1 554	100.0	22.2	77.8
Natural resources, construction, and maintenance occupations	12 779	2 273	17.8	293	1 980	100.0	12.9	87.1
Farming, fishing, and forestry occupations	948	62	6.5	7	55	100.0	. . .	. . .
Construction and extraction occupations	7 371	1 504	20.4	189	1 315	100.0	12.6	87.4
Installation, maintenance, and repair occupations	4 460	707	15.9	97	610	100.0	13.7	86.3
Production, transportation, and material moving occupations	17 074	2 705	15.8	453	2 252	100.0	16.8	83.2
Production occupations	7 187	1 115	15.5	223	892	100.0	20.0	80.0
Transportation and material moving occupations	9 887	1 590	16.1	230	1 359	100.0	14.5	85.5
Industry								
Agriculture and related industries	2 353	188	8.0	30	158	100.0	16.1	83.9
Nonagricultural industries	140 458	23 118	16.5	4 543	18 576	100.0	19.7	80.3
Mining, quarrying, and oil and gas extraction	679	76	11.2	21	55	100.0	27.6	72.4
Construction	10 571	2 018	19.1	254	1 764	100.0	12.6	87.4
Manufacturing	14 203	1 886	13.3	406	1 480	100.0	21.5	78.5
Durable goods manufacturing	8 866	1 214	13.7	280	935	100.0	23.0	77.0
Nondurable goods manufacturing	5 337	671	12.6	126	545	100.0	18.8	81.2
Wholesale and retail trade	17 783	2 813	15.8	409	2 404	100.0	14.5	85.5
Wholesale trade	3 151	434	13.8	69	365	100.0	15.9	84.1
Retail trade	14 632	2 379	16.3	339	2 039	100.0	14.3	85.7
Transportation and utilities	7 949	1 192	15.0	195	997	100.0	16.3	83.7
Transportation and warehousing	6 557	1 081	16.5	159	921	100.0	14.7	85.3
Utilities	1 392	111	8.0	35	76	100.0	31.9	68.1
Information	2 469	343	13.9	62	281	100.0	18.1	81.9
Financial activities	10 611	1 059	10.0	156	903	100.0	14.7	85.3
Finance and insurance	7 557	481	6.4	107	373	100.0	22.3	77.7
Real estate and rental and leasing	3 054	578	18.9	49	530	100.0	8.4	91.6
Professional and business services	18 826	2 794	14.8	366	2 428	100.0	13.1	86.9
Professional and technical services	12 687	1 489	11.7	244	1 244	100.0	16.4	83.6
Management, administrative, and waste services	6 139	1 305	21.3	122	1 183	100.0	9.3	90.7
Education and health services	33 196	4 942	14.9	1 697	3 244	100.0	34.3	65.7
Educational services	12 876	1 875	14.6	1 043	832	100.0	55.6	44.4
Health care and social assistance	20 320	3 067	15.1	654	2 413	100.0	21.3	78.7
Hospitals	7 158	704	9.8	244	460	100.0	34.6	65.4
Health services, except hospitals	10 037	1 697	16.9	300	1 397	100.0	17.7	82.3
Social assistance	3 125	666	21.3	110	556	100.0	16.5	83.5
Leisure and hospitality	10 189	3 537	34.7	517	3 020	100.0	14.6	85.4
Arts, entertainment, and recreation	2 454	937	38.2	176	761	100.0	18.8	81.2
Accommodation and food services	7 735	2 600	33.6	341	2 259	100.0	13.1	86.9
Other services	6 400	1 872	29.2	203	1 668	100.0	10.9	89.1
Other services, except private households	5 837	1 727	29.6	199	1 528	100.0	11.5	88.5
Private households	564	144	25.6	4	140	100.0	3.0	97.0
Public administration	7 581	589	7.8	257	332	100.0	43.7	56.3

[1]Unpaid family workers are included in the total but not shown separately.

Table 9-7. Employed Persons Unable to Work at Some Point in the Last Four Weeks because Their Employer Closed or Lost Business Due to the Coronavirus, June 2020—*Continued*

(Number, percent.)

Characteristic	Total civilian noninstitutional population	Unable to work because employer closed or lost business due to the coronavirus pandemic						
		Number	Percent of total	Employees who received pay	Employees who did not receive pay	Total, percent of persons unable to work	Percent who received pay	Percent who did not receive pay
Class of Worker[1]								
Wage and salary workers	127 284	18 001	14.1	4 199	13 802	100.0	23.3	76.7
Private industries	106 786	15 861	14.9	3 013	12 848	100.0	19.0	81.0
Government	20 498	2 140	10.4	1 186	954	100.0	55.4	44.6
Federal	3 863	239	6.2	133	106	100.0	55.7	44.3
State	7 040	701	10.0	386	315	100.0	55.0	45.0
Local	9 595	1 199	12.5	667	532	100.0	55.6	44.4
Self-employed workers	15 426	5 293	34.3	374	4 919	100.0	7.1	92.9
Self-employed workers, incorporated	6 208	1 974	31.8	205	1 769	100.0	10.4	89.6
Self-employed workers, unincorporated	9 218	3 319	36.0	169	3 150	100.0	5.1	94.9

[1]Unpaid family workers are included in the total but not shown separately.

Table 9-8. Persons Not in the Labor Force who Did Not Look for Work in the Last Four Weeks because of the Coronavirus Pandemic by Selected Characteristics, June 2020

(Number, percent.)

Characteristic	Total not in the labor force	Did not look for work in the last 4 weeks because of the coronavirus pandemic		Other persons not in the labor force	
		Total	Percent of total in the labor force	Total	Percent of total not in the labor force
TOTAL					
Total, 16 Years and Over	99 321	7 043	7.1	92 278	92.9
16 to 24 years	16 410	1 953	11.9	14 456	88.1
16 to 19 years	10 092	907	9.0	9 184	91.0
20 to 24 years	6 318	1 046	16.6	5 272	83.4
25 to 54 years	23 718	3 412	14.4	20 306	85.6
25 to 34 years	8 611	1 422	16.5	7 189	83.5
35 to 44 years	7 351	1 058	14.4	6 293	85.6
45 to 54 years	7 757	933	12.0	6 824	88.0
55 years and over	59 193	1 677	2.8	57 516	97.2
55 to 64 years	15 022	963	6.4	14 059	93.6
65 Years and over	44 171	714	1.6	43 457	98.4
Men, 16 Years and Over	40 431	3 100	7.7	37 331	92.3
16 to 24 years	8 175	935	11.4	7 241	88.6
25 to 54 years	7 623	1 474	19.3	6 149	80.7
55 years and over	24 632	691	2.8	23 941	97.2
Women, 16 Years and Over	58 890	3 943	6.7	54 948	93.3
16 to 24 years	8 235	1 019	12.4	7 216	87.6
25 to 54 years	16 095	1 938	12.0	14 157	88.0
55 years and over	34 561	986	2.9	33 575	97.1
White	76 488	4 709	6.2	71 779	93.8
Black or African American	13 189	1 508	11.4	11 681	88.6
Asian	6 269	500	8.0	5 769	92.0
Hispanic or Latino ethnicity	15 126	1 799	11.9	13 326	88.1
Married, spouse present	47 188	2 234	4.7	44 954	95.3
Widowed, divorced, or separated[1]	24 064	1 227	5.1	22 837	94.9
Never married	28 069	3 582	12.8	24 487	87.2
With own children under 18	11 967	1 429	11.9	10 538	88.1
With no own children under 18	87 354	5 614	6.4	81 740	93.6
Total, 25 Years and Over	82 911	5 089	6.1	77 822	93.9
Less than a high school diploma	10 926	659	6.0	10 267	94.0
High school graduates, no college[2]	27 472	1 617	5.9	25 854	94.1
Some college or associate degree	20 803	1 417	6.8	19 386	93.2
Bachelor's degree and higher[3]	23 711	1 396	5.9	22 315	94.1
Bachelor's degree only	14 932	947	6.3	13 985	93.7
Advanced degree	8 780	449	5.1	8 331	94.9
WANT A JOB					
Total, 16 Years and Over	8 633	3 735	43.3	4 898	56.7
16 to 24 years	2 640	1 030	39.0	1 610	61.0
25 to 54 years	3 907	1 832	46.9	2 075	53.1
55 years and over	2 087	873	41.8	1 213	58.2
Men	4 301	1 764	41.0	2 537	59.0
Women	4 332	1 971	45.5	2 361	54.5
White	5 855	2 490	42.5	3 366	57.5
Black or African American	1 676	772	46.0	905	54.0
Asian	617	277	44.9	340	55.1
Hispanic or Latino ethnicity	1 906	947	49.7	959	50.3
Total, 25 years and over	5 993	2 705	45.1	3 288	54.9
Less than a high school diploma	804	327	40.7	476	59.3
High school graduates, no college[2]	1 787	837	46.8	950	53.2
Some college or associate degree	1 664	839	50.4	825	49.6
Bachelor's degree and higher[3]	1 738	702	40.4	1 036	59.6
DO NOT WANT A JOB					
Total, 16 Years and Over	90 688	3 308	3.6	87 381	96.4
16 to 24 years	13 770	923	6.7	12 847	93.3
25 to 54 years	19 812	1 581	8.0	18 231	92.0
55 years and over	57 106	804	1.4	56 303	98.6
Men	36 129	1 336	3.7	34 793	96.3
Women	54 559	1 972	3.6	52 587	96.4
White	70 633	2 219	3.1	68 414	96.9
Black or African American	11 512	736	6.4	10 776	93.6
Asian	5 652	223	3.9	5 429	96.1
Hispanic or Latino ethnicity	13 220	853	6.4	12 367	93.6
Total, 25 years and over	76 918	2 384	3.1	74 534	96.9
Less than a high school diploma	10 122	332	3.3	9 790	96.7
High school graduates, no college[2]	25 684	781	3.0	24 904	97.0
Some college or associate degree	19 139	578	3.0	18 561	97.0
Bachelor's degree and higher[3]	21 973	694	3.2	21 279	96.8

[1] Separated includes persons who are married, spouse absent.
[2] Includes persons with a high school diploma or equivalent.
[3] Includes persons with a high school diploma or equivalent.

Table 9-9. Household Data, January 2020 to January 2021

(Number in thousands, rate.)

Characteristic	January 2020	November 2020	December 2020	January 2021
Employment Status				
Civilian noninstitutional population	259 502	261 085	261 230	260 851
Civilian labor force	164 455	160 536	160 567	160 161
Participation rate	63.4	61.5	61.5	61.4
Employed	158 659	149 809	149 830	150 031
Employment-population ratio	61.1	57.4	57.4	57.5
Unemployed	5 796	10 728	10 736	10 130
Unemployment rate	3.5	6.7	6.7	6.3
Not in labor force	95 047	100 548	100 663	100 690
Unemployment Rates				
Total, 16 years and over	3.5	6.7	6.7	6.3
Adult men (20 years and over)	3.1	6.6	6.4	6.0
Adult women (20 years and over)	3.2	6.2	6.3	6.0
Teenagers (16 to 19 years)	12.6	13.9	16.0	14.8
White	3.0	5.9	6.0	5.7
Black or African American	6.1	10.3	9.9	9.2
Asian	3.1	6.7	5.9	6.6
Hispanic or Latino ethnicity	4.3	8.4	9.3	8.6
Total, 25 years and over	2.9	6.0	5.8	5.7
Less than a high school diploma	5.7	9.2	9.8	9.1
High school graduates, no college	3.7	7.8	7.8	7.1
Some college or associate's degree	2.7	6.3	6.3	6.2
Bachelor's degree and higher	2.0	4.2	3.8	4.0
Reason for Unemployment				
Job losers and persons who completed temporary jobs	2 575	7 468	7 210	6 997
Job leavers	828	698	743	653
Reentrants	1 831	1 968	2 250	1 963
New entrants	560	551	509	542
Duration of Unemployment				
Less than 5 weeks	2 071	2 455	2 904	2 278
5 to 14 weeks	1 752	2 404	2 222	2 528
15 to 26 weeks	881	1 875	1 572	1 346
27 weeks and over	1 163	3 929	3 956	4 023
Employed Persons at Work Part-Time				
Part-time for economic reasons	4 269	6 641	6 170	5 954
Slack work or business conditions	2 627	5 223	4 891	4 756
Could only find part-time work	1 336	1 167	1 045	986
Part-time for noneconomic reasons	22 027	18 580	18 237	18 519
Persons Not in the Labor Force				
Marginally attached to the labor force	1 323	2 083	2 186	1 917
Discouraged workers	335	657	663	624

Table 9-10. Employed Persons with a Job but Not at Work by Reason, January 2017– January 2021

(Number in thousands.)

Year	January 2017	January 2018	January 2019	January 2020	January 2021
Total Not at Work	4,903	5,269	4,929	4,392	5,545
Vacation	1,757	1,839	1,894	1,651	909
Own illness, injury, or medical problems	1,075	1,283	1,063	1,071	1,955
Childcare problems	29	41	37	30	59
Other family or personal obligations	276	304	262	224	331
Labor dispute	6	7	23	4	5
Bad weather	476	544	302	275	197
Maternity or paternity leave	361	375	327	237	330
School or training	136	117	101	121	95
Civic or military duty	8	4	5	5	11
Other reasons	781	755	914	773	1,654

Table 9-11. How Respondents Used or Planned to Use Their Stimulus Payments, June 11–June 16, 2020

(Percent.)

Expenditure category	Percent
Mostly pay for expenses	59.0
Mostly pay off debt	13.0
Mostly add to savings	12.0
Did not/Do not expect to receive	14.0
Did not respond	1.0

Table 9-12. Stimulus Payment Use, by Household Gross Income, June 11–June 16, 2020

(Percent.)

Income	Mostly pay for expenses	Mostly pay off debt	Mostly add to saving	Did not expect or do not expect to receive
Less than $25,000	77	8	3	12
$25,000–$34,999	73	12	6	9
$35,000–$49,999	71	14	9	6
$50,000–$74,999	65	16	14	6
$75,000–$99,999	58	17	18	8
$100,000–$149,999	48	18	22	13
$150,000–$199,999	39	16	20	25
$200,000 and above	15	5	10	70
Did not report	58	13	10	19

CHAPTER 10: THE WORKING POOR

HIGHLIGHTS

This chapter includes information on the working poor which was collected in the Annual Social and Economic Supplement (ASEC) to the Current Population Survey (CPS). For more information about the CPS, please see Chapter 1.

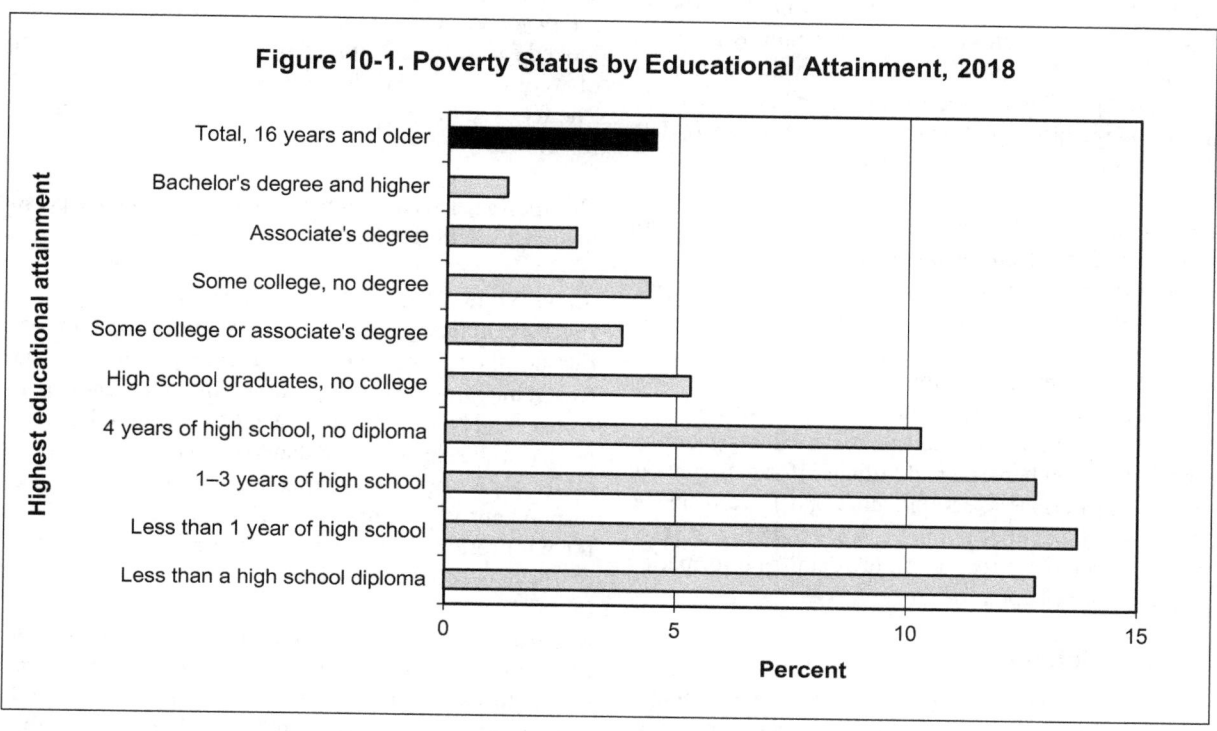

Figure 10-1. Poverty Status by Educational Attainment, 2018

Poverty rates declined as educational attainment levels increased. In 2018, the poverty rate of those with less than a high school diploma was 13.5 percent. For high school graduates, the poverty rates declined to 6.4 percent. Those with a bachelor's degree or higher had the lowest poverty rate at 1.4 percent. (See Table 10-3.)

OTHER HIGHLIGHTS

• Over 3.6 million families lived in poverty in 2018 despite having at least one member of the family in the labor force for a half the year or more. (See Table 10-1.)

• Full-time workers continued to be much less likely to be among the working poor than were part-time workers. Among persons in the labor force for 27 weeks or more, 2.8 percent of those usually employed full-time were classified as working poor, compared with 11.1 percent of part-time workers. (See Table 10-2.)

• Women were more likely than men to be among the working poor. In 2018, 5.3 percent of women who were in the labor force for 27 weeks or more were in poverty compared with 3.7 percent of men. Blacks and Hispanics continued to be far more likely than Whites and Asians to be among the working poor. (See Table 10-3.)

• Younger people in the labor force had a much higher rate of poverty than older workers. In 2018, 37.5 percent of unrelated individuals aged 16 to 19 in the labor force for 27 weeks or more were in poverty compared with 6.1 percent of those aged 25 to 64 years. (See Table 10-6.)

NOTES AND DEFINITIONS

Collection and Coverage

The data presented in this chapter were collected in the Annual Social and Economic Supplement (ASEC) to the Current Population Survey (CPS). Conducted by the U.S. Census Bureau for the Bureau of Labor Statistics, the CPS is a monthly sample survey of about 60,000 eligible households. Data from the CPS are used to obtain monthly estimates of the nation's employment and unemployment levels. The ASEC, conducted in the months of February through April, includes questions about work activity and income during the previous calendar year. For instance, data collected in 2019 are for the 2018 calendar year.

The estimates presented in this report are based on a sample and, consequently, may differ from estimates that would have been obtained from a complete count using the same questionnaire and procedures. Sampling variability may be relatively large in cases where the numbers are small. Thus, both small estimates and small differences between estimates should be interpreted with caution. For a detailed explanation of the ASEC supplement to the CPS, its sampling variability, more extensive definitions than those provided here, and additional information about income and poverty measures, see "Income and Poverty in the United States: 2017 *Current Population Reports*, p60-263 (U.S. Census Bureau, September 2018). For more detailed information on the CPS, please see Chapter 1.

Concepts and Definitions

Family. A family is defined as a group of two or more people residing together who are related by birth, marriage, or adoption. The count of families used in this report includes only primary families. A primary family consists of the reference person (the householder) and all people living in the household who are related to the reference person. Families are classified either as married-couple families or as those maintained by men or women without spouses present. Family status is determined at the time of the survey interview and, thus, may be different from that of the previous year.

Income. Data on income are limited to money income—before personal income taxes and payroll deductions—received in the calendar year preceding the CPS supplement. Data on income do not include the value of noncash benefits, such as food stamps, Medicare, Medicaid, public housing, and employer-provided benefits.

Hispanic or Latino ethnicity. This term refers to people who identified themselves in the CPS enumeration process as being of Hispanic, Latino, or Spanish ethnicity. People whose ethnicity is identified as Hispanic or Latino may be of any race.

Involuntary part-time workers. These are people who, during at least 1 week of the year, worked fewer than 35 hours because of slack work or unfavorable business conditions or because they could not find full-time work. The number of weeks of involuntary part-time work is accumulated over the year.

Labor force. People in the labor force are those who worked or looked for work sometime during the calendar year. The number of weeks in the labor force is accumulated over the entire year. The focus in this report is on people who were in the labor force for 27 weeks or more.

Occupation. This term refers to the job in which a person worked the most weeks during the calendar year.

Race. White, Black or African American, and Asian are categories used to describe the race of people. People in these categories are those who selected that race group only. Data for the two remaining race categories—American Indian and Alaska Native, and Native Hawaiian and Other Pacific Islander—and for people who selected more than one race category are included in totals, but are not shown separately because the number of survey respondents is too small to develop estimates of sufficient quality for publication. In the enumeration process, race is determined by the household respondent.

Related children. Related children are children under age 18 (including sons, daughters, stepchildren, and adopted children) of the husband, wife, or person maintaining the family, as well as other children related to the householder by birth, marriage, or adoption.

Unrelated individuals. These are people who are not living with anyone related to them by birth, marriage, or adoption. Such individuals may live alone, reside in a nonrelated family household, or live in group quarters with other unrelated individuals.

Unemployed. Unemployed people are those who looked for work while not employed or those who were on layoff from a job and were expecting to be recalled to that job. The number of weeks unemployed is accumulated over the entire year.

Unemployed. Unemployed people are those who looked for work while not employed or those who were on layoff from a job and were expecting to be recalled to that job. The number of weeks unemployed is accumulated over the entire year.

Unrelated individuals. These are people who are not living with anyone related to them by birth, marriage, or adoption. Such individuals may live alone, reside in a nonrelated family household, or live in group quarters with other unrelated individuals.

Working poor. The working poor are people who spent at least 27 weeks in the labor force (that is, working or looking for work) but whose incomes still fell below the official poverty level.

Working-poor rate. This rate is the number of individuals in the labor force for at least 27 weeks whose incomes still fell below the official poverty level, as a percentage of all people who were in the labor force for at least 27 weeks during the calendar year.

Sources of Additional Information

Additional information on the working poor can be found in BLS Report 1087 "A Profile of the Working Poor."

Table 10-1. Poverty Status of People and Primary Families in the Labor Force for 27 Weeks or More, 2008–2018

(Number in thousands, percent.)

Characteristic	2008	2009	2010	2011	2012	2013	2014	2015	2016	2017	2018
Total in the Labor Force[1]	147 838	147 902	146 859	147 475	148 735	149 483	150 319	152 230	153 364	154 762	156 454
In poverty	8 883	10 391	10 512	10 382	10 612	10 450	9 487	8 560	7 572	6 946	6 964
Working-poor rate	6.0	7.0	7.2	7.0	7.1	7.0	6.3	5.6	4.9	4.5	4.5
Unrelated individuals	32 785	33 798	34 099	33 731	34 810	35 061	35 018	35 953	35 789	36 959	37 082
In poverty	3 275	3 947	3 947	3 621	3 851	4 141	3 395	3 137	2 792	2 524	2 684
Working-poor rate	10.0	11.7	11.6	10.7	11.1	11.8	9.7	8.7	7.8	6.8	7.2
Primary families[2]	65 907	65 467	64 931	66 225	66 541	66 462	66 732	67 193	67 628	67 588	68 099
In poverty	4 538	5 193	5 269	5 469	5 478	5 137	5 108	4 607	4 082	3 854	3 628
Working-poor rate	6.9	7.9	8.1	8.3	8.2	7.7	7.7	6.9	6.0	5.7	5.3

[1]Includes individuals in families, not shown separately.
[2]Primary families with at least one member in the labor force for more than half the year.

Table 10-2. People in the Labor Force: Poverty Status and Work Experience, by Weeks in the Labor Force, 2018

(Number in thousands, percent.)

Characteristic	Total in labor force	27 weeks or more in the labor force	
		Total	50 to 52 weeks
Total			
Total in the labor force	168 617	156 454	142 870
Did not work during the year	2 215	1 053	881
Worked during the year	166 402	155 401	141 990
Usual full-time workers	134 458	130 045	122 333
Usual part-time workers	31 944	25 356	19 657
Involuntary part-time workers	5 709	4 875	3 971
Voluntary part-time workers	26 236	20 481	15 686
At or Above Poverty Level			
Total in the labor force	159 557	149 490	137 067
Did not work during the year	1 359	595	498
Worked during the year	158 198	148 896	136 569
Usual full-time workers	130 059	126 342	119 079
Usual part-time workers	28 140	22 554	17 489
Involuntary part-time workers	4 570	3 949	3 184
Voluntary part-time workers	23 569	18 605	14 305
Below Poverty Level			
Total in the labor force	9 060	6 964	5 804
Did not work during the year	857	458	383
Worked during the year	8 204	6 505	5 421
Usual full-time workers	4 399	3 703	3 253
Usual part-time workers	3 804	2 802	2 168
Involuntary part-time workers	1 138	926	786
Voluntary part-time workers	2 666	1 876	1 381
Rate[1]			
Total in the labor force	5.4	4.5	4.1
Did not work during the year	38.7	43.5	43.5
Worked during the year	4.9	4.2	3.8
Usual full-time workers	3.3	2.8	2.7
Usual part-time workers	11.9	11.1	11.0
Involuntary part-time workers	19.9	19.0	19.8
Voluntary part-time workers	10.2	9.2	8.8

[1]Number below the poverty level as a percentage of the total in the labor force.

Table 10-3. People in the Labor Force for 27 Weeks or More: Poverty Status by Educational Attainment, Race, Hispanic or Latino Ethnicity, and Gender, 2018

(Number in thousands, rate.)

Characteristic	Total	Men	Women	Below poverty level			Rate[1]		
				Total	Men	Women	Total	Men	Women
Total, 16 Years and Older	156 454	83 072	73 382	6 964	3 099	3 865	4.5	3.7	5.3
Less than a high school diploma	11 858	7 402	4 456	1 598	866	731	13.5	11.7	16.4
Less than 1 year of high school	3 711	2 497	1 215	508	299	209	13.7	12.0	17.2
1–3 years of high school	6 347	3 794	2 552	899	453	446	14.2	11.9	17.5
4 years of high school, no diploma	1 800	1 111	689	191	115	76	10.6	10.3	11.1
High school graduates, no college[2]	40 705	24 034	16 671	2 604	1 164	1 440	6.4	4.8	8.6
Some college or associate's degree	43 303	21 673	21 631	1 888	680	1 208	4.4	3.1	5.6
Some college, no degree	26 627	13 786	12 841	1 336	460	877	5.0	3.3	6.8
Associate's degree	16 677	7 887	8 790	552	220	331	3.3	2.8	3.8
Bachelor's degree and higher[3]	60 588	29 964	30 624	874	388	486	1.4	1.3	1.6
White, 16 Years and Older	121 723	65 970	55 752	4 758	2 250	2 508	3.9	3.4	4.5
Less than a high school diploma	9 292	5 999	3 293	1 185	676	509	12.8	11.3	15.5
Less than 1 year of high school	3 087	2 131	956	422	249	174	13.7	11.7	18.2
1–3 years of high school	4 876	3 022	1 854	626	342	284	12.8	11.3	15.3
4 years of high school, no diploma	1 329	846	483	137	85	51	10.3	10.1	10.6
High school graduates, no college[2]	31 615	19 074	12 542	1 673	801	872	5.3	4.2	7.0
Some college or associate's degree	33 663	17 258	16 405	1 269	482	787	3.8	2.8	4.8
Some college, no degree	20 411	10 908	9 503	892	328	563	4.4	3.0	5.9
Associate's degree	13 252	6 350	6 902	377	154	224	2.8	2.4	3.2
Bachelor's degree and higher[3]	47 153	23 640	23 513	631	291	340	1.3	1.2	1.4
Black or African American, 16 Years and Older	19 521	9 097	10 423	1 531	519	1 012	7.8	5.7	9.7
Less than a high school diploma	1 455	749	706	258	110	148	17.7	14.7	20.9
Less than 1 year of high school	254	127	127	29	17	12	11.5	13.4	9.6
1–3 years of high school	890	455	435	186	72	114	20.9	15.9	26.2
4 years of high school, no diploma	311	167	144	43	21	21	13.7	12.7	14.9
High school graduates, no college[2]	6 028	3 224	2 804	736	267	469	12.2	8.3	16.7
Some college or associate's degree	6 238	2 709	3 529	425	109	317	6.8	4.0	9.0
Some college, no degree	4 054	1 753	2 301	287	64	222	7.1	3.7	9.7
Associate's degree	2 184	956	1 228	139	44	94	6.4	4.7	7.7
Bachelor's degree and higher[3]	5 800	2 415	3 385	111	33	78	1.9	1.4	2.3
Asian, 16 Years and Older	10 003	5 350	4 653	321	179	143	3.2	3.3	3.1
Less than a high school diploma	527	284	243	57	31	26	10.8	11.0	10.6
Less than 1 year of high school	215	119	96	33	18	15	15.2	14.8	15.7
1–3 years of high school	234	114	121	17	8	9	7.1	6.9	7.2
4 years of high school, no diploma	78	51	27	8	6	2	10.2	. . .	. . .
High school graduates, no college[2]	1 524	835	688	82	42	40	5.4	5.0	5.9
Some college or associate's degree	1 698	912	786	78	52	26	4.6	5.7	3.4
Some college, no degree	1 032	585	447	65	42	23	6.3	7.1	5.3
Associate's degree	667	327	339	13	10	3	2.0	3.2	0.9
Bachelor's degree and higher[3]	6 255	3 319	2 936	104	54	50	1.7	1.6	1.7
Hispanic or Latino Ethnicity, 16 Years and Older	27 278	15 514	11 764	2 147	1 119	1 028	7.9	7.2	8.7
Less than a high school diploma	6 111	4 054	2 056	885	513	372	14.5	12.7	18.1
Less than 1 year of high school	2 830	1 973	858	408	250	158	14.4	12.7	18.5
1–3 years of high school	2 589	1 642	947	396	214	183	15.3	13.0	19.3
4 years of high school, no diploma	692	440	251	80	50	31	11.6	11.3	12.2
High school graduates, no college	8 774	5 445	3 329	717	380	337	8.2	7.0	10.1
Some college or associate's degree	7 017	3 498	3 519	379	147	233	5.4	4.2	6.6
Some college, no degree	4 656	2 406	2 250	275	105	170	5.9	4.4	7.5
Associate's degree	2 361	1 092	1 269	105	42	63	4.4	3.8	5.0
Bachelor's degree and higher	5 376	2 517	2 859	166	79	86	3.1	3.2	3.0

[1]Number below the poverty level as a percentage of the total in the labor force for 27 weeks or more.
[2]Includes people with a high school diploma or equivalent.
[3]Includes people with bachelor's, master's, professional, and doctoral degrees.
. . . = Not available.

Table 10-4. Primary Families: Poverty Status, Presence of Related Children, and Work Experience of Family Members in the Labor Force for 27 Weeks or More, 2018

(Number in thousands.)

Year	Total families	At or above poverty level	Below poverty level	Rate[1]
Total Primary Families	68 099	64 472	3 628	5.3
With related children under 18 years	34 531	31 469	3 062	8.9
Without children	33 568	33 003	565	1.7
With one member in the labor force	28 658	25 527	3 131	10.9
With two or more members in the labor force	39 442	38 944	497	1.3
With two members	32 803	32 363	440	1.3
With three or more members	6 639	6 581	57	0.9
Married-Couple Families[2]	50 523	49 116	1 407	2.8
With related children under 18 years	24 317	23 183	1 133	4.7
Without children	26 206	25 932	274	1.0
With one member in the labor force	17 187	16 077	1 110	6.5
Husband	11 931	11 090	841	7.0
Wife	4 504	4 277	227	5.0
Relative	752	709	42	5.6
With two or more members in the labor force	33 336	33 039	297	0.9
With two members	28 215	27 951	264	0.9
With three or more members	5 121	5 088	33	0.6
Families Maintained by Women[3]	11 940	10 126	1 814	15.2
With related children under 18 years	7 368	5 747	1 621	22.0
Without children	4 572	4 379	193	4.2
With one member in the labor force	8 088	6 427	1 660	20.5
Householder	6 415	4 961	1 454	22.7
Relative	1 673	1 466	207	12.3
With two or more members in the labor force	3 852	3 698	154	4.0
Families Maintained by Men[3]	5 636	5 230	406	7.2
With related children under 18 years	2 847	2 539	308	10.8
Without children	2 790	2 691	98	3.5
With one member in the labor force	3 383	3 023	360	10.6
Householder	2 704	2 421	283	10.5
Relative	680	603	77	11.3
With two or more members in the labor force	2 253	2 207	46	2.1

[1]Number below the poverty level as a percentage of the total in the labor force for 27 weeks or more who worked during the year.
[2]Refers to opposite-sex married-couple families only.
[3]No opposite-sex spouse present.

Table 10-5. People in Families and Unrelated Individuals: Poverty Status and Work Experience, 2018

(Numbers in thousands, rate.)

Poverty status and work experience	Total people	In married-couple families[1]				In families maintained by women[2]			In families maintained by men[2]			Unrelated individuals
		Husbands	Wives	Related children under 18 years	Other relatives	Householder	Related children under 18 years	Other relatives	Householder	Related children under 18 years	Other relatives	
Total												
All people	258 527	61 168	62 021	5 692	22 439	15 039	2 145	14 540	6 461	690	7 058	61 276
With labor force activity	168 617	45 715	38 247	1 335	14 108	10 409	465	9 043	4 991	194	4 693	39 416
1 to 26 weeks	12 163	1 514	2 471	714	2 422	634	264	1 056	257	87	411	2 334
27 weeks or more	156 454	44 202	35 777	621	11 686	9 775	201	7 987	4 734	108	4 281	37 082
With no labor force activity	89 910	15 453	23 773	4 357	8 331	4 631	1 680	5 497	1 469	495	2 365	21 860
At or Above the Poverty Level												
All people	231 065	58 265	59 074	5 370	21 618	11 298	1 507	12 455	5 639	585	6 409	48 844
With labor force activity	159 557	44 446	37 595	1 301	13 881	8 493	381	8 416	4 592	180	4 514	35 758
1 to 26 weeks	10 067	1 354	2 308	702	2 337	302	217	863	179	78	367	1 360
27 weeks or more	149 490	43 092	35 287	599	11 544	8 191	164	7 553	4 414	102	4 147	34 398
With no labor force activity	71 508	13 820	21 480	4 069	7 737	2 806	1 126	4 039	1 047	405	1 895	13 086
Below Poverty Line												
All people	27 462	2 903	2 946	322	821	3 741	638	2 086	821	104	649	12 432
With labor force activity	9 060	1 269	653	34	227	1 916	84	627	399	14	179	3 658
1 to 26 weeks	2 097	160	163	13	85	331	47	193	78	8	44	975
27 weeks or more	6 964	1 110	490	22	142	1 584	37	434	321	6	135	2 684
With no labor force activity	18 402	1 633	2 294	288	594	1 825	553	1 459	422	90	470	8 774
Rate[3]												
All people	10.6	4.7	4.8	5.7	3.7	24.9	29.7	14.3	12.7	15.1	9.2	20.3
With labor force activity	5.4	2.8	1.7	2.6	1.6	18.4	18.1	6.9	8.0	7.3	3.8	9.3
1 to 26 weeks	17.2	10.5	6.6	1.8	3.5	52.3	17.8	18.3	30.4	9.6	10.7	41.8
27 weeks or more	4.5	2.5	1.4	3.5	1.2	16.2	18.4	5.4	6.8	5.5	3.2	7.2
With no labor force activity	20.5	10.6	9.6	6.6	7.1	39.4	33.0	26.5	28.7	18.2	19.9	40.1

[1]Refers to opposite-sex married-couple families only.
[2]No opposite-sex spouse present.
[3]Number below the poverty level as a percentage of the total.
- = Represents zero, rounds to zero, or indicates that base is less than 80,000.

Table 10-6. Unrelated Individuals in the Labor Force for 27 Weeks or More: Poverty Status by Age, Gender, Race, Hispanic or Latino Ethnicity and Living Arrangement, 2018

(Number in thousands, percent.)

Characteristic	Total	At or Above the Poverty Level	Below the Poverty Level	Rate[1]
AGE AND GENDER				
Total Unrelated Individuals	37 082	34 398	2 684	7.2
16 to 19 years	336	210	126	37.5
20 to 24 years	4 381	3 747	634	14.5
25 to 64 years	29 348	27 551	1 797	6.1
65 Years and Older	3 017	2 890	127	4.2
Men	20 187	18 910	1 277	6.3
Women	16 896	15 489	1 407	8.3
Race and Hispanic or Latino Ethnicity				
White	28 146	26 276	1 870	6.6
Men	15 518	14 611	908	5.8
Women	12 628	11 666	962	7.6
Black or African American	5 765	5 178	587	10.2
Men	2 881	2 612	269	9.3
Women	2 883	2 566	317	11.0
Asian	1 822	1 715	106	5.8
Men	1 020	955	65	6.4
Women	802	761	42	5.2
Hispanic or Latino, ethnicity	5 263	4 716	546	10.4
Men	3 177	2 915	262	8.3
Women	2 085	1 801	284	13.6
Living Arrangement				
Living alone	18 879	17 861	1 018	5.4
Living with others	18 203	16 537	1 666	9.2

[1]Number below the poverty level as a percentage of the total in the labor force for 27 weeks or more.

Table 10-7. People in the Labor Force for 27 Weeks or More: Poverty Status and Labor Market Problems of Full-Time Wage and Salary Workers, 2018

(Number in thousands, percent.)

Characteristic	Total	At or above the poverty level	Below poverty level	Rate[1]
Total, Full-Time Wage and Salary Workers	124 053	120 790	3 264	2.6
No unemployment, involuntary part-time employment, or low earnings[2]	107 667	106 954	714	0.7
Workers Experiencing One Labor Market Problem				
Unemployment only	4 727	4 465	262	5.5
Involuntary part-time employment only	2 472	2 429	43	1.7
Low earnings only	6 850	5 280	1 570	22.9
Workers Experiencing Multiple Labor Market Problems				
Unemployment and involuntary part-time employment	716	632	84	11.8
Unemployment and low earnings	847	536	311	36.8
Involuntary part-time employment and low earnings	500	337	162	32.5
Unemployment, involuntary part-time employment, and low earnings	273	157	117	42.7
Workers Experiencing Each Labor Market Problem				
Unemployment (alone or with other problems)	6 564	5 790	774	11.8
Involuntary part-time employment (alone or with other problems)	3 962	3 555	406	10.3
Low earnings (alone or with other problems)	8 470	6 309	2 161	25.5

[1]Number below the poverty level as a percentage of the total in the labor force for 27 weeks or more.
[2]The low-earnings threshold in 2016 was $353.25 per week.

CHAPTER 11: CONSUMER EXPENDITURES

HIGHLIGHTS

The principal objective of the Consumer Expenditure (CE) Survey is to collect information about the buying habits of American households. The survey breaks down expenditures for different demographic categories, such as income, age, family size, and geographic location. These data are used in a variety of government, business, and academic research projects and provide important weights for the periodic revisions of the Consumer Price Index (CPI).

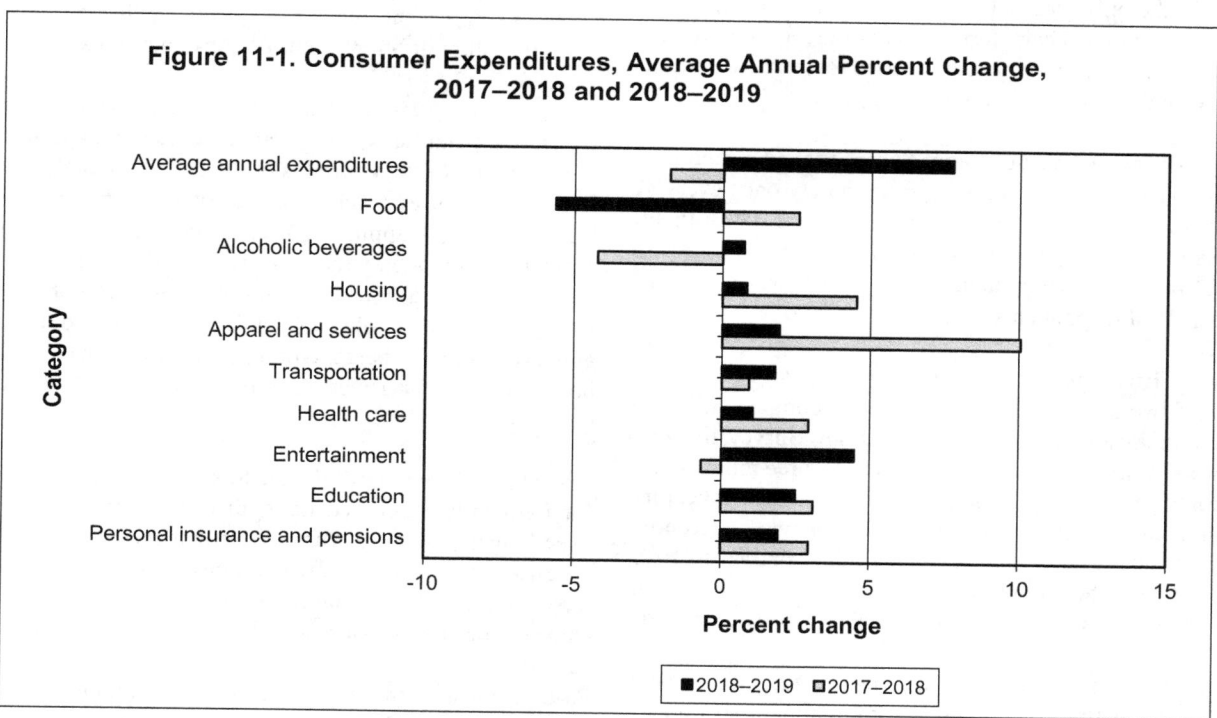

Figure 11-1. Consumer Expenditures, Average Annual Percent Change, 2017–2018 and 2018–2019

In 2019, average annual expenditures increased 3.0 percent after increasing 1.9 percent the previous year. They increased for most major categories; exceptions include reading, entertainment, and miscellaneous expenditures. (See Table 11-1.)

OTHER HIGHLIGHTS

- Average annual consumer expenditures varied substantially by age group. Older age groups typically spend more in health care while those in younger age groups spent more on education. In 2019, persons 65 years and older had $6,833 in annual expenditures for healthcare while those under 30 years of age had only $2,175 in annual expenditures. (See Table 11-10.)

- As educational attainment increased, so did average annual expenditures. Those with less than a high school diploma had average annual expenditures of $30,276 while those with a master's, professional, or doctoral degree had average annual expenditures of $97,588. (See Table 11-13.)

- Cities in the South and the Midwest typically had lower average annual expenditures than those in the North or the West. Among the selected cities list in Table 11-15, Miami had the lowest average annual expenditures at $57,472 followed by Detroit at $65,163. Meanwhile, Seattle had the highest average annual expenditures at $81,266. (See Table 11-15.)

NOTES AND DEFINITIONS

Purpose, Collection, and Coverage

The buying habits of American consumers change over time because of changes in relative prices, real income, family size and composition, and other determinants of tastes and preferences. The introduction of new products into the marketplace and the emergence of new concepts in retailing also influence consumer buying habits. Data from the Consumer Expenditure Survey (CE), the only national survey that relates family expenditures to demographic characteristics, are of great importance to researchers. The survey data are also used to revise the Consumer Price Index market baskets and item samples.

Until the 1970s, the Bureau of Labor Statistics (BLS) conducted surveys of consumer expenditures approximately once every 10 years. The last such survey was conducted in 1972–1973. In late 1979, in a significant departure from previous methodology, BLS initiated a survey to be conducted on a continuous basis with rotating panels of respondents.

The current CE is similar to its 1972–1973 predecessor in that it consists of two separate components. Each component has its own questionnaire and sample: (1) the Interview Survey, in which an interviewer visits each consumer unit every three months for a twelve-month period; and (2) the Diary Survey, a record-keeping survey completed by other consumer units for two consecutive one-week periods. The Census Bureau, under contract to BLS, collects the data for both components of the survey. Beginning in 1999, the sample was increased from 5,000 to 7,500 households.

In 2003, the survey modified the questions on race and Hispanic origin to comply with the new standards for maintaining, collecting, and presenting federal data on race and ethnicity for federal statistical agencies. Beginning with the data collected in 2003, the CE tables use data collected from the new race and ethnicity questions. A number of new classifications were made with publication of the 2003 data.

Beginning with the publication of the 2004 tables, the CE has been implementing multiple imputations of income data. Prior to 2004, the CE only published income data collected from complete income reporters. The introduction of multiply imputed income data affects the published CE tables in several ways, because income data are now published for all consumer units (instead of for complete reporters only). The most obvious result of this change is seen on the tables showing expenditures categorized by income before taxes, including income by quintile. Starting with the 2004 data, columns describing income, expenditures, and characteristics for "total complete reporting" and "incomplete reporting of income" no longer appear in these tables, and the column entitled "all consumer units" appears on all income tables. Due to the implementation of income imputation, data for 2004 are not strictly comparable to those of prior years, especially for the income tables. Averages for demographic

characteristics and annual expenditures will change due to differences between the incomplete and complete income reporters in these categories. Furthermore, certain expenditures (such as personal insurance and pensions) are computed using income data. As a result of imputation, average annual values for these expenditures may be substantially different in the 2004 CE tables than in tables for previous years. The regular flow of data resulting from this design substantially enhances the usefulness of the survey by providing more timely information on consumption patterns within different kinds of consumer units.

The Quarterly *Interview Survey* is designed to collect data on the types of expenditures that respondents can be expected to recall after a period of three months or longer. These include relatively large expenditures (such as those for property, travel, automobiles, and major appliances) and expenditures that occur on a regular basis (such as those for rent, utilities, insurance premiums, and clothing). The interview also obtains "global estimates" for food and other selected items. The survey collects data for approximately 95 percent of total expenditures. Each sample household is interviewed once per quarter, for five consecutive quarters.

The *Diary Survey* is designed to collect data on expenditures for frequently purchased items that are more difficult to recall over longer periods of time. Respondents complete a diary of expenses for two consecutive 1-week periods. Expenditures for tobacco, drugs (including nonprescription drugs), and personal care supplies and services are also collected in the Diary Survey.

Participants in both surveys record dollar amounts for goods and services purchased during the reporting period, regardless of whether payment was made at the time of purchase. Excluded from both surveys are business-related expenditures and expenditures for which the family is reimbursed. Information is collected on demographic and family characteristics at the initial interview for each survey.

The tables in this chapter present integrated data from the Diary Survey and the Interview Survey and provide a complete accounting of consumer expenditures and income, which neither survey component is designed to do alone. Data for some expenditure items are only collected in one of the surveys. For example, the Diary Survey does not collect data for expenditures on overnight travel or information on reimbursements, while the Interview Survey records these purchases. Examples of expenditures for which reimbursements are netted out include those for medical care, auto repair, and construction, repairs, alterations, and maintenance of property.

For items unique to one survey or the other, the choice of which survey to use as the source of data is obvious. However, there is considerable overlap in coverage between the two surveys. Integrating the data thus presents the problem of determining the appropriate survey component. When data are available from both survey sources, the more reliable of the two (as determined by statistical methods) is selected. As a result, some items are selected from the Interview Survey and others are selected from the Diary Survey.

Data Included in This Edition

Data for single characteristics are for calendar year 2019 and data for two cross-classified characteristics are for an average of calendar years 2018 and 2019. Income values from the survey are derived from "complete income reporters" only. Complete income reporters are defined as consumer units that provide values for at least one of the major sources of their income: wages and salaries, self-employment income, retirement income, dividends and interest, and welfare benefits. Some consumer units are defined as complete income reporters, even though they may not have provided a full accounting of all income from all sources.

Consumer units are classified by quintiles of income before taxes, age of reference person, size of consumer unit, region, composition of consumer unit, number of earners in consumer unit, housing tenure, race, type of area (urban or rural), and occupation.

Concepts and Definitions

A *consumer unit* comprises either (1) all members of a particular household related by blood, marriage, adoption, or other legal arrangements; (2) a person living alone, sharing a household with others, living as a roomer in a private home or lodging house or in permanent living quarters in a hotel or motel, but who is financially independent; or (3) two or more persons living together who pool their income to make joint expenditure decisions. Financial independence is determined by the three major expense categories: housing, food, and other living expenses. To be considered financially independent, at least two of the three major expense categories have to be provided by the respondent. The terms "family," "household," and "consumer unit" are used interchangeably in descriptions of the CE.

An *earner* is a consumer unit member, 14 years of age or older, who reported having worked at least 1 week during the 12 months prior to the interview date.

The *education of reference person* refers to the number of years of formal education of the reference person, on the basis of the highest grade completed. If enrolled at time of the interview, the interviewer records the grade currently attended. Persons not reporting the extent of their education are classified under no school or not reported.

The *householder* or *reference person* is the first member of the consumer unit mentioned by the respondent as owner or renter of the premises at the time of the initial interview.

Housing tenure refers to the family's principal place of residence during the survey. "Owner" includes families living in their own homes, cooperatives or condominium apartments, or townhouses. "Renter" includes families paying rent, as well as families living rent-free in lieu of wages.

Quintiles of income before taxes refers to the ranking of complete income reporters in ascending order, according to the level of total before-tax income reported by the consumer unit. The ranking is then divided into five equal groups. Incomplete income reporters are not ranked and are shown separately.

Total expenditures include the transaction costs, including excise and sales taxes of goods and services acquired during the interview period. Estimates include expenditures for gifts and contributions and payments for pensions and personal insurance.

Sources of Additional Information

More extensive descriptions and tables can be found in an updated version of *BLS Handbook of Methods* and in an anthology of articles relating to consumer expenditures. These resources can be found on the BLS Web site at <https://www.bls.gov>.

Table 11-1. Consumer Expenditures, Annual Average of All Consumer Units, 2005–2019

(Number, dollar, percent.)

Item	2005	2006	2007	2008	2009	2010	2011	2012	2013	2014	2015	2016	2017	2018	2019
NUMBER OF CONSUMER UNITS (THOUSANDS)	117 356	118 843	120 171	120 770	120 847	121 107	122 287	124 416	125 670	127 006	128 437	129 549	130 001	131 439	132 242
CONSUMER UNIT CHARACTERISTICS															
Income Before Taxes	58 712	60 533	63 091	63 563	62 857	62 481	63 685	65 596	63 784	66 877	69 627	74 664	73 573	78 635	82 852
Age of Reference Person	48.6	48.7	48.8	49.1	49.4	49.4	49.7	50.0	50.1	50.3	50.5	50.9	50.9	51.1	51.6
Average Number in Consumer Unit															
All persons	2.5	2.5	2.5	2.5	2.5	2.5	2.5	2.5	2.5	2.5	2.5	2.5	2.5	2.5	2.5
Children under 18 years	0.6	0.6	0.6	0.6	0.6	0.6	0.6	0.6	0.6	0.6	0.6	0.6	0.6	0.6	0.6
Persons 65 years and over	0.3	0.3	0.3	0.3	0.3	0.3	0.3	0.3	0.3	0.4	0.4	0.4	0.4	0.4	0.4
Earners	1.3	1.3	1.3	1.3	1.3	1.3	1.3	1.3	1.3	1.3	1.3	1.3	1.3	1.3	1.3
Vehicles	2.0	1.9	1.9	2.0	2.0	1.9	1.9	1.9	1.9	1.9	1.9	1.9	1.9	1.9	1.9
Percent Homeowner	67	67	67	66	66	66	65	64	64	63	62	62	63	63	64
With mortgage	43	43	43	42	41	41	40	39	37	37	35	36	36	37	37
Without mortgage	25	24	23	24	25	25	25	26	26	26	27	27	27	26	27
AVERAGE ANNUAL EXPENDITURES	46 409	48 398	49 638	50 486	49 067	48 109	49 705	51 442	51 100	53 495	55 978	57 311	60 060	61 224	63 036
Food	5 931	6 111	6 133	6 443	6 372	6 129	6 458	6 599	6 602	6 759	7 023	7 203	7 729	7 923	8 169
Food at home	3 297	3 417	3 465	3 744	3 753	3 624	3 838	3 921	3 977	3 971	4 015	4 049	4 363	4 464	4 643
Cereals and bakery products	445	446	460	507	506	502	531	538	544	519	518	524	564	569	583
Meats, poultry, fish, and eggs	764	797	777	846	841	784	832	852	856	892	896	890	944	961	980
Dairy products	378	368	387	430	406	380	407	419	414	423	413	410	450	449	455
Fruits and vegetables	552	592	600	657	656	679	715	731	751	756	769	783	837	858	876
Other food at home	1 158	1 212	1 241	1 305	1 343	1 278	1 353	1 380	1 412	1 382	1 419	1 442	1 568	1 627	1 749
Food away from home	2 634	2 694	2 668	2 698	2 619	2 505	2 620	2 678	2 625	2 787	3 008	3 154	3 365	3 459	3 526
Alcoholic Beverages	426	497	457	444	435	412	456	451	445	463	515	484	558	583	579
Housing	15 167	16 366	16 920	17 109	16 895	16 557	16 803	16 887	17 148	17 798	18 409	18 886	19 884	20 091	20 679
Shelter	8 805	9 673	10 023	10 183	10 075	9 812	9 825	9 891	10 080	10 491	10 742	11 128	11 895	11 747	12 190
Owned dwellings	5 958	6 516	6 730	6 760	6 543	6 277	6 148	6 056	6 108	6 149	6 210	6 295	6 947	6 678	6 797
Rented dwellings	2 345	2 590	2 602	2 724	2 860	2 900	3 029	3 186	3 324	3 631	3 802	4 035	4 167	4 249	4 432
Other lodging	502	567	691	698	672	635	648	649	649	710	730	798	782	821	961
Utilities, fuels, and public services	3 183	3 397	3 477	3 649	3 645	3 660	3 727	3 648	3 737	3 921	3 885	3 884	3 836	4 049	4 055
Household operations	801	948	984	998	1 011	1 007	1 122	1 159	1 144	1 174	1 309	1 384	1 412	1 522	1 570
Housekeeping supplies	611	640	639	654	659	612	615	610	645	632	655	660	755	747	766
Household furnishings and equipment	1 767	1 708	1 797	1 624	1 506	1 467	1 514	1 580	1 542	1 581	1 818	1 829	1 987	2 025	2 098
Apparel and Services	1 886	1 874	1 881	1 801	1 725	1 700	1 740	1 736	1 604	1 786	1 846	1 803	1 833	1 866	1 883
Transportation	8 344	8 508	8 758	8 604	7 658	7 677	8 293	8 998	9 004	9 073	9 503	9 049	9 576	9 761	10 742
Vehicle purchases (net outlay)	3 544	3 421	3 244	2 755	2 657	2 588	2 669	3 210	3 271	3 301	3 997	3 634	4 054	3 975	4 394
Gasoline and motor oil	2 013	2 227	2 384	2 715	1 986	2 132	2 655	2 756	2 611	2 468	2 090	1 909	1 968	2 109	2 094
Other vehicle expenses	2 339	2 355	2 592	2 621	2 536	2 464	2 454	2 490	2 584	2 723	2 756	2 884	2 842	2 859	3 474
Public and other transportation	448	505	538	513	479	493	516	542	537	581	661	623	712	818	781
Health Care	2 664	2 766	2 853	2 976	3 126	3 157	3 313	3 556	3 631	4 290	4 342	4 612	4 928	4 968	5 193
Health insurance	1 361	1 465	1 545	1 653	1 785	1 831	1 922	2 061	2 229	2 868	2 977	3 160	3 414	3 405	3 529
Medical services	677	670	709	727	736	722	768	839	796	790	791	838	872	909	984
Drugs	521	514	481	482	486	485	489	515	470	486	425	463	486	483	486
Medical supplies	105	117	118	114	119	119	134	142	135	146	149	151	156	172	194
Entertainment	2 388	2 376	2 698	2 835	2 693	2 504	2 572	2 605	2 482	2 728	2 842	2 913	3 203	3 226	3 090
Personal Care Products and Services	541	585	588	616	596	582	634	628	608	645	683	707	762	768	786
Reading	126	117	118	116	110	100	115	109	102	103	114	118	110	108	92
Education	940	888	945	1 046	1 068	1 074	1 051	1 207	1 138	1 236	1 315	1 329	1 491	1 407	1 443
Tobacco Products and Smoking Supplies	319	327	323	317	380	362	351	332	330	319	349	337	332	347	320
Miscellaneous	808	846	808	840	816	849	775	829	645	782	871	959	1 010	993	899
Cash Contributions	1 663	1 869	1 821	1 737	1 723	1 633	1 721	1 913	1 834	1 788	1 819	2 081	1 873	1 888	1 995
Personal Insurance and Pensions	5 204	5 270	5 336	5 605	5 471	5 373	5 424	5 591	5 528	5 726	6 349	6 831	6 771	7 296	7 165
Life and other personal insurance	381	322	309	317	309	318	317	353	319	327	333	322	418	465	520
Pensions and Social Security	4 823	4 948	5 027	5 288	5 162	5 054	5 106	5 238	5 209	5 399	6 016	6 509	6 353	6 831	6 645

Table 11-2. Consumer Expenditures, Deciles of Income, 2019

(Number, dollar, percent.)

Item	All consumer units	Lowest 10 percent	Second 10 percent	Third 10 percent	Fourth 10 percent	Fifth 10 percent	Sixth 10 percent	Seventh 10 percent	Eighth 10 percent	Ninth 10 percent	Highest 10 percent
NUMBER OF CONSUMER UNITS (THOUSANDS) ..	132 242	13 221	13 146	13 216	13 171	13 293	13 285	13 240	13 135	13 192	13 344
CONSUMER UNIT CHARACTERISTICS											
Income Before Taxes	82 852	6 268	17 823	27 642	37 910	49 578	63 972	81 821	105 052	141 980	294 483
Income After Taxes	71 487	6 386	18 120	28 230	37 675	46 829	59 421	74 234	93 571	122 353	226 602
Age of Reference Person	51.6	51.7	61.4	57.4	52.5	50.5	48.3	47.9	47.5	48.7	49.8
Average Number in Consumer Unit											
All persons	2.5	1.5	1.7	2.0	2.3	2.4	2.6	2.8	2.9	3.1	3.2
Children under 18 years	0.6	0.3	0.3	0.4	0.6	0.5	0.6	0.7	0.7	0.8	0.8
Persons 65 years and over	0.4	0.3	0.6	0.6	0.5	0.5	0.4	0.3	0.3	0.2	0.2
Earners	1.3	0.4	0.5	0.7	1.0	1.2	1.5	1.7	1.9	2.1	2.1
Vehicles	1.9	0.9	1.1	1.5	1.7	1.8	2.1	2.2	2.4	2.8	2.9
Percent Distribution											
Male	48	38	36	40	45	49	48	54	55	56	58
Female	52	62	64	60	55	51	52	46	45	44	42
Percent Homeowner	64	35	51	56	54	60	64	71	74	82	89
With mortgage	37	12	14	19	23	31	38	50	54	63	68
Without mortgage	27	23	37	37	32	28	26	22	20	19	22
Food	8 169	3 938	4 861	5 169	6 550	7 100	7 909	8 733	9 428	12 080	15 881
Food at home	4 643	2 513	3 065	3 261	4 084	4 255	4 588	4 961	5 435	6 627	7 628
Cereals and bakery products	583	342	405	400	532	485	612	609	712	810	924
Meats, poultry, fish, and eggs	980	535	650	748	884	931	973	1 107	1 094	1 390	1 490
Dairy products	455	251	299	319	385	408	462	468	529	662	764
Fruits and vegetables	876	458	567	622	782	833	849	900	1 041	1 235	1 475
Other food at home	1 749	927	1 145	1 172	1 501	1 598	1 692	1 877	2 059	2 531	2 976
Food away from home	3 526	1 424	1 795	1 909	2 466	2 845	3 321	3 772	3 992	5 453	8 253
Alcoholic Beverages	579	189	228	258	404	420	462	646	671	1 014	1 495
Housing	20 679	10 587	12 478	14 043	15 569	17 165	18 985	21 613	23 617	29 271	43 257
Shelter	12 190	6 661	7 366	8 347	9 053	10 051	11 040	12 553	13 621	17 223	25 855
Owned dwellings	6 797	2 069	2 829	3 361	3 543	4 531	5 327	7 270	8 193	11 949	18 792
Rented dwellings	4 432	4 155	4 293	4 621	5 058	4 983	5 133	4 517	4 440	3 836	3 284
Other lodging	961	438	244	365	453	537	580	765	987	1 438	3 779
Utilities, fuels, and public services	4 055	2 277	2 747	3 295	3 552	3 747	4 033	4 447	4 781	5 420	6 231
Household operations	1 570	519	750	832	1 044	1 161	1 232	1 577	1 767	2 431	4 358
Housekeeping supplies	766	408	452	563	611	666	732	853	848	1 093	1 426
Household furnishings and equipment	2 098	723	1 162	1 006	1 309	1 540	1 948	2 183	2 601	3 103	5 386
Apparel and Services	1 883	846	791	1 101	1 390	1 355	1 705	1 976	2 513	2 759	4 376
Transportation	10 742	4 195	4 970	6 169	8 155	9 318	10 381	11 741	14 089	16 920	21 386
Vehicle purchases (net outlay)	4 394	1 525	1 969	2 262	3 123	3 983	4 030	4 866	5 810	7 355	8 971
Gasoline and motor oil	2 094	983	1 012	1 403	1 800	1 900	2 259	2 481	2 706	3 138	3 246
Other vehicle expenses	3 474	1 335	1 687	2 157	2 817	2 975	3 535	3 761	4 600	5 303	6 542
Public and other transportation	781	351	303	347	416	460	558	633	972	1 123	2 627
Health Care	5 193	2 163	3 551	3 789	4 110	4 514	4 874	5 902	6 173	7 131	9 684
Health insurance	3 529	1 496	2 446	2 661	2 769	3 152	3 358	3 972	4 177	4 865	6 371
Medical services	984	343	560	521	705	763	871	1 191	1 274	1 359	2 244
Drugs	486	263	352	442	485	442	487	503	518	648	718
Medical supplies	194	62	194	166	151	157	157	236	204	259	351
Entertainment	3 090	1 046	1 172	1 848	1 842	2 011	2 524	3 127	3 651	4 934	8 706
Personal Care Products and Services	786	333	393	517	587	653	761	891	903	1 189	1 630
Reading	92	54	67	75	49	91	90	106	81	142	165
Education	1 443	825	709	575	407	625	749	1 022	1 357	2 583	5 543
Tobacco Products and Smoking Supplies	320	290	308	313	342	346	390	394	400	267	152
Miscellaneous	899	341	482	624	740	703	1 035	848	843	1 359	2 003
Cash Contributions	1 995	542	756	1 086	1 228	1 157	1 499	1 982	2 370	3 000	6 294
Personal Insurance and Pensions	7 165	507	731	1 564	2 448	3 910	5 356	7 453	9 851	14 264	25 394
Life and other personal insurance	520	108	187	267	291	342	388	555	538	880	1 629
Pensions and Social Security	6 645	399	544	1 297	2 157	3 569	4 968	6 898	9 313	13 384	23 765

Table 11-3. Consumer Expenditures, Averages by Income Before Taxes, 2019

(Number, dollar, percent.)

Item	All consumer units	Less than $15,000	$15,000 to $29,999	$30,000 to $39,999	$40,000 to $49,999	$50,000 to $69,999	$70,000 to $99,999	$100,000 to $149,999	$150,000 to $199,999	$200,000 and over
NUMBER OF CONSUMER UNITS (THOUSANDS)	132 242	15 848	19 856	12 991	11 208	17 470	19 119	18 225	8 266	9 260
CONSUMER UNIT CHARACTERISTICS										
Income Before Taxes	82 852	7 574	22 189	34 772	44 831	59 328	83 558	121 433	171 061	343 498
Income After Taxes	71 487	7 743	22 672	34 981	42 723	55 500	75 811	106 439	144 046	258 975
Age of Reference Person	51.6	53.0	60.1	53.9	51.1	48.9	47.8	47.9	48.8	50.2
Average Number in Consumer Unit										
All persons	2.5	1.5	1.9	2.2	2.4	2.5	2.8	3.0	3.2	3.2
Children under 18 years	0.6	0.3	0.4	0.5	0.5	0.6	0.7	0.7	0.8	0.8
Persons 65 years and over	0.4	0.4	0.6	0.6	0.5	0.4	0.3	0.2	0.2	0.3
Earners	1.3	0.4	0.6	0.9	1.1	1.4	1.7	2.0	2.1	2.1
Vehicles	1.9	0.9	1.3	1.6	1.7	2.0	2.2	2.6	2.8	3.0
Percent Distribution										
Male	48	36	38	45	48	49	54	55	57	59
Female	52	64	62	55	52	51	46	45	43	41
Percent Homeowner	64	36	54	57	55	63	71	77	86	91
With mortgage	37	12	16	22	27	37	50	58	66	68
Without mortgage	27	24	38	35	28	27	21	19	19	23
AVERAGE ANNUAL EXPENDITURES	63 036	26 194	34 201	40 942	47 299	54 212	66 801	84 994	109 020	160 318
Food	8 169	3 917	4 992	5 791	7 193	7 369	8 672	10 633	12 764	17 102
Food at home	4 643	2 528	3 185	3 636	4 329	4 318	4 983	5 908	6 917	7 954
Cereals and bakery products	583	346	409	438	545	547	621	746	885	937
Meats, poultry, fish, and eggs	980	542	682	858	919	933	1 071	1 215	1 400	1 558
Dairy products	455	255	307	346	419	421	490	580	676	798
Fruits and vegetables	876	458	603	668	859	818	903	1 118	1 312	1 552
Other food at home	1 749	927	1 184	1 326	1 586	1 599	1 897	2 250	2 645	3 110
Food away from home	3 526	1 389	1 806	2 155	2 865	3 051	3 689	4 725	5 847	9 148
Alcoholic Beverages	579	184	229	372	410	427	616	872	1 042	1 618
Housing	20 679	10 685	13 372	14 851	16 752	18 274	21 619	26 123	32 596	47 329
Shelter	12 190	6 671	7 942	8 637	9 794	10 649	12 549	15 256	19 126	28 574
Owned dwellings	6 797	2 120	3 130	3 451	3 961	5 192	7 208	9 841	13 786	20 747
Rented dwellings	4 432	4 155	4 512	4 764	5 336	4 864	4 584	4 263	3 435	3 259
Other lodging	961	396	300	422	496	592	757	1 152	1 906	4 567
Utilities, fuels, and public services	4 055	2 313	3 007	3 500	3 666	3 954	4 475	5 047	5 656	6 478
Household operations	1 570	527	827	923	1 158	1 213	1 627	1 981	2 799	4 998
Housekeeping supplies	766	410	507	568	687	697	794	982	1 283	1 381
Household furnishings and equipment	2 098	764	1 090	1 224	1 447	1 761	2 173	2 858	3 732	5 899
Apparel and Services	1 883	862	912	1 193	1 400	1 586	1 899	2 565	3 437	4 806
Transportation	10 742	4 239	5 500	7 459	8 359	10 377	12 252	15 050	19 055	22 255
Vehicle purchases (net outlay)	4 394	1 607	2 091	2 728	3 088	4 379	5 176	6 191	8 761	8 996
Gasoline and motor oil	2 094	970	1 170	1 699	1 864	2 153	2 496	2 927	3 181	3 283
Other vehicle expenses	3 474	1 319	1 905	2 697	2 904	3 333	3 898	4 910	5 691	6 876
Public and other transportation	781	344	334	335	503	512	682	1 023	1 421	3 101
Health Care	5 193	2 318	3 689	4 038	4 518	4 673	5 791	6 685	7 592	10 414
Health insurance	3 529	1 598	2 576	2 807	3 016	3 221	3 927	4 576	5 167	6 754
Medical services	984	376	546	575	882	832	1 131	1 328	1 467	2 538
Drugs	486	273	372	516	444	473	505	557	706	725
Medical supplies	194	70	196	140	176	146	228	224	252	397
Entertainment	3 090	1 047	1 494	1 783	1 945	2 401	3 121	4 150	5 639	9 852
Personal Care Products and Services	786	340	428	584	647	718	841	1 052	1 234	1 796
Reading	92	53	78	54	96	77	94	118	117	181
Education	1 443	822	578	567	552	671	1 010	1 862	3 212	6 614
Tobacco Products and Smoking Supplies	320	291	308	338	344	376	409	320	201	155
Miscellaneous	899	353	597	614	813	877	855	991	1 542	2 335
Cash Contributions	1 995	577	904	1 195	1 124	1 389	2 033	2 657	3 208	7 618
Personal Insurance and Pensions	7 165	507	1 120	2 102	3 144	4 998	7 588	11 913	17 381	28 241
Life and other personal insurance	520	118	237	271	294	396	530	673	986	1 928
Pensions and Social Security	6 645	389	883	1 831	2 850	4 602	7 058	11 240	16 395	26 313

Table 11-4. Consumer Expenditures, Generation of Reference Person, 2019

(Number, dollar, percent.)

Item	All consumer units	Birth year of 1997 and later	Birth year from 1981 to 1996	Birth year from 1965 to 1980	Birth year from 1946 to 1964	Birth year of 1945 or earlier
NUMBER OF CONSUMER UNITS (THOUSANDS)	132 242	3 698	33 033	35 498	43 148	16 865
CONSUMER UNIT CHARACTERISTICS						
Income Before Taxes	82 852	27 779	79 514	106 173	86 251	43 680
Income After Taxes	71 487	26 565	70 565	90 964	72 201	40 323
Age of Reference Person	51.6	20.2	30.7	46.2	63.1	80.8
Average Number in Consumer Unit						
All persons	2.5	1.8	2.8	3.1	2.1	1.6
Children under 18 years	0.6	0.3	1.0	1.0	0.2	(^{1})
Persons 65 years and over	0.4	(^{1})	(^{1})	(^{1})	0.6	1.4
Earners	1.3	1.2	1.6	1.8	1.1	0.3
Vehicles	1.9	1.0	1.7	2.2	2.1	1.5
Percent Distribution						
Male	48	45	52	48	49	41
Female	52	55	48	52	51	59
Percent Homeowner	64	12	43	66	76	81
With mortgage	37	5	35	52	38	17
Without mortgage	27	7	8	14	38	64
AVERAGE ANNUAL EXPENDITURES	63 036	34 092	59 866	76 788	63 956	44 412
Food	8 169	5 288	7 740	10 073	8 180	5 625
Food at home	4 643	2 516	4 114	5 616	4 862	3 591
Cereals and bakery products	583	313	499	719	606	471
Meats, poultry, fish, and eggs	980	562	891	1 177	1 024	731
Dairy products	455	249	383	556	476	382
Fruits and vegetables	876	508	781	1 041	909	723
Other food at home	1 749	884	1 560	2 123	1 848	1 285
Food away from home	3 526	2 772	3 626	4 457	3 318	2 034
Alcoholic Beverages	579	201	528	641	688	360
Housing	20 679	10 040	20 958	24 353	20 185	16 041
Shelter	12 190	6 493	13 027	14 456	11 450	8 926
Owned dwellings	6 797	682	5 036	8 837	7 550	5 370
Rented dwellings	4 432	5 144	7 392	4 538	2 653	2 803
Other lodging	961	666	599	1 081	1 248	752
Utilities, fuels, and public services	4 055	1 772	3 538	4 751	4 264	3 570
Household operations	1 570	355	1 883	1 798	1 267	1 518
Housekeeping supplies	766	308	546	887	897	729
Household furnishings and equipment	2 098	1 114	1 965	2 462	2 307	1 298
Apparel and Services	1 883	1 048	2 030	2 437	1 723	1 015
Transportation	10 742	8 106	11 052	13 346	10 363	6 205
Vehicle purchases (net outlay)	4 394	4 378	4 669	5 509	4 038	2 419
Gasoline and motor oil	2 094	1 307	2 196	2 664	2 010	1 082
Other vehicle expenses	3 474	1 793	3 459	4 285	3 454	2 219
Public and other transportation	781	628	728	888	861	485
Health Care	5 193	1 078	3 428	5 133	6 273	6 932
Health insurance	3 529	595	2 364	3 498	4 235	4 717
Medical services	984	335	735	1 007	1 185	1 054
Drugs	486	102	239	429	637	800
Medical supplies	194	45	91	199	217	362
Entertainment	3 090	1 141	2 556	3 856	3 469	2 000
Personal Care Products and Services	786	433	666	971	804	675
Reading	92	39	55	87	105	160
Education	1 443	3 636	1 282	2 164	1 248	263
Tobacco Products and Smoking Supplies	320	144	343	360	355	140
Miscellaneous	899	284	678	1 056	1 035	790
Cash Contributions	1 995	302	1 059	2 247	2 442	2 528
Personal Insurance and Pensions	7 165	2 351	7 492	10 065	7 085	1 680
Life and other personal insurance	520	89	252	617	727	402
Pensions and Social Security	6 645	2 262	7 240	9 447	6 358	1 277

^{1}Value is too small to display.

Table 11-5. Consumer Expenditures, Averages by Quintiles of Income Before Taxes, 2019

(Number, dollar, percent.)

Item	All consumer units	Lowest 20 percent	Second 20 percent	Third 20 percent	Fourth 20 percent	Highest 20 percent
NUMBER OF CONSUMER UNITS (THOUSANDS)	132 242	26 367	26 387	26 578	26 375	26 536
CONSUMER UNIT CHARACTERISTICS						
Income Before Taxes	82 852	12 029	32 768	56 773	93 390	218 670
Income After Taxes	71 487	12 236	32 945	53 123	83 864	174 777
Age of Reference Person	51.6	56.5	54.9	49.4	47.7	49.2
Average Number in Consumer Unit						
All persons	2.5	1.6	2.2	2.5	2.8	3.2
Children under 18 years	0.6	0.3	0.5	0.6	0.7	0.8
Persons 65 years and over	0.4	0.5	0.6	0.4	0.3	0.2
Earners	1.3	0.4	0.9	1.3	1.8	2.1
Vehicles	1.9	1.0	1.6	1.9	2.3	2.8
Percent Distribution						
Male	48	37	43	49	55	57
Female	52	63	57	51	45	43
Percent Homeowner	64	43	55	62	73	86
With mortgage	37	13	21	35	52	66
Without mortgage	27	30	35	27	21	20
AVERAGE ANNUAL EXPENDITURES	63 036	28 672	40 472	53 045	71 173	121 571
Food	8 169	4 400	5 859	7 505	9 080	13 987
Food at home	4 643	2 790	3 672	4 422	5 198	7 129
Cereals and bakery products	583	373	466	549	660	867
Meats, poultry, fish, and eggs	980	592	816	952	1 100	1 440
Dairy products	455	275	352	435	499	713
Fruits and vegetables	876	513	702	841	970	1 355
Other food at home	1 749	1 036	1 336	1 645	1 968	2 754
Food away from home	3 526	1 610	2 187	3 084	3 882	6 858
Alcoholic Beverages	579	209	331	441	658	1 255
Housing	20 679	11 531	14 805	18 075	22 611	36 302
Shelter	12 190	7 013	8 699	10 546	13 085	21 564
Owned dwellings	6 797	2 448	3 452	4 929	7 730	15 390
Rented dwellings	4 432	4 224	4 839	5 058	4 479	3 558
Other lodging	961	341	409	558	876	2 615
Utilities, fuels, and public services	4 055	2 511	3 423	3 890	4 613	5 828
Household operations	1 570	634	938	1 196	1 672	3 400
Housekeeping supplies	766	430	587	699	850	1 260
Household furnishings and equipment	2 098	942	1 157	1 744	2 391	4 250
Apparel and Services	1 883	818	1 246	1 530	2 245	3 571
Transportation	10 742	4 581	7 160	9 850	12 910	19 166
Vehicle purchases (net outlay)	4 394	1 746	2 692	4 006	5 336	8 168
Gasoline and motor oil	2 094	998	1 601	2 079	2 593	3 193
Other vehicle expenses	3 474	1 511	2 486	3 255	4 179	5 926
Public and other transportation	781	327	381	509	802	1 879
Health Care	5 193	2 855	3 950	4 694	6 036	8 415
Health insurance	3 529	1 970	2 715	3 255	4 074	5 622
Medical services	984	451	613	817	1 232	1 804
Drugs	486	307	463	465	511	683
Medical supplies	194	128	159	157	220	305
Entertainment	3 090	1 109	1 845	2 268	3 388	6 828
Personal Care Products and Services	786	363	552	707	897	1 411
Reading	92	61	62	90	94	153
Education	1 443	767	491	687	1 189	4 072
Tobacco Products and Smoking Supplies	320	299	327	368	397	209
Miscellaneous	899	411	682	869	846	1 683
Cash Contributions	1 995	649	1 157	1 328	2 175	4 657
Personal Insurance and Pensions	7 165	619	2 006	4 633	8 647	19 861
Life and other personal insurance	520	147	279	365	546	1 257
Pensions and Social Security	6 645	471	1 727	4 268	8 101	18 604

Table 11-6. Consumer Expenditures, Averages by Occupation of Reference Person, 2019

(Number, dollar, percent.)

Item	All consumer units	Self-employed workers	Wage and salary earners						Retired	All others, including those not reporting
			Total wage and salary earners	Managers and professional workers	Technical sales and clerical workers	Service workers	Construction workers and mechanics	Operators, fabricators, and laborers		
NUMBER OF CONSUMER UNITS (THOUSANDS)	132 242	8 326	80 630	33 153	20 641	15 896	4 024	6 915	27 917	15 370
CONSUMER UNIT CHARACTERISTICS										
Income Before Taxes	82 852	134 345	98 796	137 660	75 394	65 516	76 247	71 950	42 252	45 060
Income After Taxes	71 487	110 448	84 254	112 402	67 267	59 681	68 234	65 820	39 591	41 344
Age of Reference Person	51.6	50.8	44.3	45.2	42.9	44.7	41.6	45.6	74.3	48.5
Average Number in Consumer Unit										
All persons	2.5	2.8	2.6	2.6	2.5	2.7	2.7	2.9	1.7	3.0
Children under 18 years	0.6	0.7	0.7	0.7	0.7	0.7	0.8	0.8	0.1	1.0
Persons 65 years and over	0.4	0.3	0.2	0.1	0.2	0.2	0.1	0.2	1.3	0.0
Earners	1.3	1.8	1.8	1.8	1.7	1.7	1.7	1.9	0.2	1.0
Vehicles	1.9	2.2	2.0	2.2	1.9	1.7	2.1	2.3	1.7	2.0
Percent Distribution										
Male	48	58	52	50	45	47	92	77	43	31
Female	52	42	48	50	55	53	8	23	57	69
Percent Homeowner										
With mortgage	64	71	61	70	54	50	57	63	80	46
With mortgage	37	43	44	54	39	32	36	42	23	25
Without mortgage	27	28	17	16	15	17	21	21	57	22
AVERAGE ANNUAL EXPENDITURES	63 036	86 662	69 099	86 702	60 179	53 462	57 906	54 107	47 259	46 939
Food	8 169	11 015	8 693	10 032	8 111	7 447	8 591	6 938	6 492	6 827
Food at home	4 643	5 589	4 802	5 297	4 500	4 370	5 096	4 127	4 057	4 315
Cereals and bakery products	583	688	594	650	549	556	612	536	526	569
Meats, poultry, fish, and eggs	980	1 278	996	1 027	951	956	1 130	974	867	931
Dairy products	455	520	463	533	437	391	462	371	416	444
Fruits and vegetables	876	1 108	903	1 005	847	822	952	736	774	790
Other food at home	1 749	1 995	1 847	2 082	1 717	1 645	1 941	1 511	1 474	1 581
Food away from home	3 526	5 426	3 890	4 735	3 611	3 077	3 494	2 810	2 435	2 513
Alcoholic Beverages	579	877	647	877	550	423	586	393	480	249
Housing	20 679	26 116	22 304	27 325	19 427	18 638	18 497	17 560	16 635	16 536
Shelter	12 190	15 396	13 376	16 512	11 749	11 186	10 664	9 810	9 149	9 757
Owned dwellings	6 797	9 141	7 398	10 157	5 697	5 081	5 496	5 676	5 791	4 206
Rented dwellings	4 432	4 388	5 001	4 838	5 370	5 474	4 792	3 716	2 523	4 937
Other lodging	961	1 867	978	1 518	682	631	376	418	835	614
Utilities, fuels, and public services ...	4 055	4 872	4 159	4 566	3 811	3 832	3 881	4 158	3 766	3 593
Household operations	1 570	2 006	1 719	2 454	1 316	1 136	1 317	979	1 401	855
Housekeeping supplies	766	1 078	744	896	691	634	652	501	777	686
Household furnishings and equipment ...	2 098	2 764	2 306	2 897	1 861	1 849	1 983	2 112	1 542	1 646
Apparel and Services	1 883	2 578	2 050	2 478	1 967	1 651	1 589	1 502	1 342	1 590
Transportation	10 742	12 022	12 367	14 726	11 262	9 767	10 790	11 270	7 255	7 860
Vehicle purchases (net outlay)	4 394	3 923	5 236	6 483	4 699	3 779	4 302	4 755	2 779	3 161
Gasoline and motor oil	2 094	2 502	2 379	2 491	2 227	2 148	2 768	2 600	1 359	1 714
Other vehicle expenses	3 474	4 306	3 917	4 523	3 676	3 225	3 478	3 587	2 496	2 474
Public and other transportation	781	1 291	835	1 229	660	615	243	328	621	510
Health Care	5 193	6 858	4 795	6 099	4 180	3 604	3 569	3 844	6 670	3 699
Health insurance	3 529	4 660	3 261	3 981	2 957	2 521	2 515	2 846	4 648	2 295
Medical services	984	1 402	966	1 371	720	682	665	581	1 015	797
Drugs	486	576	402	520	356	294	305	287	710	473
Medical supplies	194	220	167	227	146	106	85	130	297	134
Entertainment	3 090	4 868	3 321	4 547	2 780	2 213	2 485	2 159	2 297	2 333
Personal Care Products and Services ...	786	1 008	836	1 062	744	663	655	541	700	563
Reading	92	123	80	108	70	55	56	50	139	57
Education	1 443	2 477	1 667	2 329	1 423	1 213	904	724	371	1 653
Tobacco Products and Smoking Supplies ...	320	283	336	216	370	376	633	539	200	474
Miscellaneous	899	1 501	937	1 249	826	541	770	800	740	663
Cash Contributions	1 995	3 046	1 921	2 783	1 407	1 083	1 803	1 321	2 341	1 186
Personal Insurance and Pensions ...	7 165	13 889	9 145	12 872	7 064	5 789	6 978	6 466	1 597	3 247
Life and other personal insurance ...	520	874	520	757	411	331	251	298	500	364
Pensions and Social Security	6 645	13 015	8 625	12 114	6 653	5 459	6 727	6 168	1 097	2 884

Table 11-7. Consumer Expenditures, Averages by Number of Earners, 2019

(Number, dollar, percent.)

Item	All consumer units	Single consumer		Consumer units of two or more persons			
		No earner	One earner	No earner	One earner	Two earners	Three or more earners
NUMBER OF CONSUMER UNITS (THOUSANDS)	132 242	17 458	22 433	12 973	24 489	43 078	11 812
CONSUMER UNIT CHARACTERISTICS							
Income Before Taxes	82 852	21 207	54 023	36 677	78 107	124 323	138 024
Income After Taxes	71 487	19 883	45 528	35 661	68 542	104 703	121 379
Age of Reference Person	51.6	69.9	44.6	68.1	50.3	44.3	48.7
Average Number in Consumer Unit							
All persons	2.5	1.0	1.0	2.2	3.0	3.0	4.4
Children under 18 years	0.6	X	X	0.2	1.0	0.9	1.0
Persons 65 years and over	0.4	0.7	0.1	1.4	0.4	0.2	0.2
Earners	1.3	X	1.0	X	1.0	2.0	3.3
Vehicles	1.9	1.0	1.2	2.0	1.9	2.4	3.0
Percent Distribution							
Male	48	36	54	49	44	51	50
Female	52	64	46	51	56	49	50
Percent Homeowner	64	58	43	78	63	69	77
With mortgage	37	15	26	20	37	52	59
Without mortgage	27	43	17	58	27	18	18
AVERAGE ANNUAL EXPENDITURES	63 036	30 451	44 220	49 557	63 867	81 662	92 029
Food	8 169	3 971	5 141	7 150	8 775	10 311	12 137
Food at home	4 643	2 544	2 627	4 507	5 255	5 591	6 971
Cereals and bakery products	583	334	307	599	673	685	896
Meats, poultry, fish, and eggs	980	512	508	973	1 124	1 186	1 524
Dairy products	455	261	247	460	508	550	674
Fruits and vegetables	876	480	500	863	1 010	1 040	1 305
Other food at home	1 749	957	1 064	1 612	1 939	2 130	2 572
Food away from home	3 526	1 427	2 514	2 643	3 521	4 720	5 166
Alcoholic Beverages	579	246	558	549	444	777	713
Housing	20 679	12 793	16 017	17 216	21 209	25 471	26 370
Shelter	12 190	7 930	10 565	9 123	12 185	14 944	14 908
Owned dwellings	6 797	3 622	3 987	5 746	6 698	8 965	10 281
Rented dwellings	4 432	3 870	5 979	2 317	4 551	4 668	3 535
Other lodging	961	438	600	1 060	936	1 311	1 092
Utilities, fuels, and public services	4 055	2 596	2 586	4 052	4 331	4 760	5 862
Household operations	1 570	1 025	771	1 295	1 583	2 273	1 602
Housekeeping supplies	766	463	418	877	898	869	1 088
Household furnishings and equipment	2 098	778	1 677	1 870	2 212	2 625	2 910
Apparel and Services	1 883	798	1 255	1 377	2 095	2 541	2 364
Transportation	10 742	3 735	7 195	8 179	10 572	14 280	18 097
Vehicle purchases (net outlay)	4 394	1 326	2 699	3 163	4 093	6 113	7 852
Gasoline and motor oil	2 094	678	1 439	1 607	2 149	2 714	3 591
Other vehicle expenses	3 474	1 375	2 509	2 738	3 444	4 490	5 571
Public and other transportation	781	356	548	672	885	963	1 083
Health Care	5 193	4 078	2 775	7 251	5 344	5 821	6 576
Health insurance	3 529	2 624	1 775	5 186	3 592	3 972	4 636
Medical services	984	778	644	971	1 034	1 161	1 205
Drugs	486	463	240	780	544	493	519
Medical supplies	194	213	116	313	175	195	215
Entertainment	3 090	1 439	1 883	2 403	3 132	4 274	4 227
Personal Care Products and Services	786	426	528	741	825	978	1 078
Reading	92	94	66	150	88	90	94
Education	1 443	352	958	453	1 319	1 959	3 442
Tobacco Products and Smoking Supplies	320	203	247	301	364	356	430
Miscellaneous	899	599	787	733	965	1 030	1 119
Cash Contributions	1 995	1 410	1 510	2 185	2 528	2 064	2 220
Personal Insurance and Pensions	7 165	307	5 300	869	6 205	11 712	13 161
Life and other personal insurance	520	186	216	532	610	696	746
Pensions and Social Security	6 645	121	5 084	338	5 596	11 016	12 416

X = Not applicable.

Table 11-8. Consumer Expenditures, Averages by Size of Consumer Unit, 2019

(Number, dollar, percent.)

Item	All consumer units	One person	Two or more persons				
			Total	Two persons	Three persons	Four persons	Five or more persons
NUMBER OF CONSUMER UNITS (THOUSANDS)	132 242	39 892	92 351	43 558	19 224	17 011	12 557
CONSUMER UNIT CHARACTERISTICS							
Income Before Taxes	82 852	39 661	101 508	89 202	110 152	117 916	108 736
Income After Taxes	71 487	34 305	87 549	75 819	93 129	102 982	98 784
Age of Reference Person	51.6	55.7	49.8	55.5	46.6	43.9	42.8
Average Number in Consumer Unit							
All persons	2.5	1.0	3.1	2.0	3.0	4.0	5.7
Children under 18 years	0.6	X	0.8	0.1	0.7	1.5	2.7
Persons 65 years and over	0.4	0.4	0.4	0.7	0.2	0.1	0.2
Earners	1.3	0.6	1.6	1.2	1.8	2.0	2.3
Vehicles	1.9	1.1	2.3	2.2	2.3	2.5	2.5
Percent Distribution							
Male	48	46	49	51	46	50	44
Female	52	54	51	49	54	50	56
Percent Homeowner	64	49	70	72	66	73	65
With mortgage	37	21	44	37	45	57	50
Without mortgage	27	28	26	35	21	16	15
AVERAGE ANNUAL EXPENDITURES	63 036	38 266	73 707	66 861	74 134	85 139	81 361
Food	8 169	4 659	9 668	8 422	9 754	11 108	11 953
Food at home	4 643	2 593	5 518	4 691	5 477	6 449	7 230
Cereals and bakery products	583	318	696	563	685	861	956
Meats, poultry, fish, and eggs	980	510	1 181	976	1 130	1 356	1 754
Dairy products	455	253	541	456	534	643	711
Fruits and vegetables	876	492	1 040	888	1 030	1 244	1 311
Other food at home	1 749	1 020	2 059	1 807	2 098	2 344	2 499
Food away from home	3 526	2 066	4 150	3 731	4 277	4 659	4 722
Alcoholic Beverages	579	430	643	799	504	560	421
Housing	20 679	14 622	23 292	21 338	23 486	26 281	25 732
Shelter	12 190	9 412	13 390	12 481	13 614	14 684	14 448
Owned dwellings	6 797	3 827	8 080	7 270	8 014	9 750	8 730
Rented dwellings	4 432	5 056	4 162	3 837	4 620	3 886	4 961
Other lodging	961	529	1 148	1 374	980	1 048	758
Utilities, fuels, and public services	4 055	2 590	4 688	4 248	4 653	5 174	5 606
Household operations	1 570	883	1 867	1 375	2 088	2 782	1 995
Housekeeping supplies	766	437	906	886	803	924	1 118
Household furnishings and equipment	2 098	1 301	2 441	2 348	2 328	2 718	2 564
Apparel and Services	1 883	1 066	2 232	1 741	2 223	3 018	2 887
Transportation	10 742	5 683	12 928	11 095	13 091	16 202	14 600
Vehicle purchases (net outlay)	4 394	2 098	5 385	4 397	5 306	7 528	6 033
Gasoline and motor oil	2 094	1 106	2 521	2 090	2 540	3 065	3 249
Other vehicle expenses	3 474	2 014	4 105	3 670	4 292	4 702	4 521
Public and other transportation	781	466	917	938	954	908	797
Health Care	5 193	3 343	5 992	6 324	5 594	6 030	5 397
Health insurance	3 529	2 146	4 127	4 293	3 873	4 170	3 879
Medical services	984	702	1 106	1 128	1 025	1 243	968
Drugs	486	336	550	650	519	433	411
Medical supplies	194	159	209	252	178	184	139
Entertainment	3 090	1 693	3 690	3 681	3 402	3 944	3 815
Personal Care Products and Services	786	484	916	883	840	1 035	988
Reading	92	77	99	120	72	90	78
Education	1 443	693	1 767	1 276	2 485	2 148	1 859
Tobacco Products and Smoking Supplies	320	228	360	339	378	364	399
Miscellaneous	899	706	982	954	1 045	982	984
Cash Contributions	1 995	1 466	2 224	2 412	1 695	2 114	2 528
Personal Insurance and Pensions	7 165	3 115	8 914	7 477	9 562	11 265	9 722
Life and other personal insurance	520	203	656	671	706	664	519
Pensions and Social Security	6 645	2 912	8 258	6 806	8 857	10 600	9 203

X = Not applicable.

Table 11-9. Consumer Expenditures, Averages by Composition of Consumer Unit, 2019

(Number, dollar, percent.)

Item	All consumer unit	Married couple consumer units						Other married couple consumer units	One parent, at least one child under 18 years	Single person and other consumer units
		Total	Married couple only	Married couple with children						
				Total	Oldest child under 6 years	Oldest child 6 to 17 years	Oldest child 18 years or over			
NUMBER OF CONSUMER UNITS (THOUSANDS)	132 242	64 640	28 814	30 392	5 572	14 930	9 890	5 434	6 423	61 179
CONSUMER UNIT CHARACTERISTICS										
Income Before Taxes	82 852	117 048	102 290	132 212	151 081	125 624	131 527	110 485	46 173	50 573
Income After Taxes	71 487	99 478	85 769	112 219	121 405	108 289	112 977	100 915	44 625	44 733
Age of Reference Person	51.6	51.4	59.1	44.2	33.5	41.4	54.4	50.8	39.8	53.0
Average Number in Consumer Unit										
All persons	2.5	3.2	2.0	4.0	3.4	4.2	3.9	5.1	3.0	1.6
Children under 18 years	0.6	0.8	([1])	1.5	1.4	2.2	0.6	1.4	1.7	0.2
Persons 65 years and over	0.4	0.5	0.8	0.1	([1])	([2])	0.3	0.7	([2])	0.4
Earners	1.3	1.7	1.2	2.0	1.7	1.8	2.5	2.4	1.1	0.9
Vehicles	1.9	2.5	2.4	2.6	2.0	2.4	3.0	2.8	1.2	1.4
Percent Distribution										
Male	48	55	57	53	60	51	53	47	20	44
Female	52	45	43	47	40	49	47	53	80	56
Percent Homeowner	64	79	83	76	68	73	85	78	35	51
With mortgage	37	51	42	58	58	60	57	57	28	24
Without mortgage	27	28	41	17	10	13	28	21	7	27
AVERAGE ANNUAL EXPENDITURES	63 036	81 898	74 353	89 900	80 311	91 267	93 206	77 802	48 615	44 564
Food	8 169	10 547	9 117	11 957	9 549	12 395	12 638	10 821	7 239	5 719
Food at home	4 643	6 054	5 156	6 857	5 431	7 033	7 385	6 696	4 208	3 174
Cereals and bakery products	583	760	618	878	659	926	926	904	583	393
Meats, poultry, fish, and eggs	980	1 284	1 066	1 459	1 049	1 489	1 642	1 549	889	664
Dairy products	455	599	503	691	559	726	712	635	384	307
Fruits and vegetables	876	1 158	998	1 307	1 060	1 370	1 348	1 238	708	593
Other food at home	1 749	2 253	1 970	2 522	2 104	2 521	2 757	2 371	1 645	1 217
Food away from home	3 526	4 493	3 962	5 101	4 119	5 362	5 253	4 124	3 031	2 545
Alcoholic Beverages	579	697	837	610	455	588	730	401	323	482
Housing	20 679	25 431	23 066	27 599	29 899	27 943	25 784	25 835	17 340	16 002
Shelter	12 190	14 479	13 275	15 668	16 509	16 341	14 180	14 204	10 332	9 968
Owned dwellings	6 797	9 709	8 781	10 565	10 234	10 796	10 402	9 841	3 448	4 072
Rented dwellings	4 432	3 339	2 698	3 913	5 386	4 346	2 428	3 532	6 469	5 372
Other lodging	961	1 430	1 796	1 191	888	1 198	1 349	830	414	523
Utilities, fuels, and public services	4 055	4 979	4 566	5 213	4 010	5 236	5 855	5 859	3 613	3 125
Household operations	1 570	2 159	1 527	2 852	5 825	2 577	1 594	1 634	1 358	969
Housekeeping supplies	766	1 023	1 012	1 017	759	1 002	1 184	1 116	615	506
Household furnishings and equipment	2 098	2 791	2 686	2 848	2 796	2 786	2 971	3 023	1 423	1 434
Apparel and Services	1 883	2 377	1 789	2 952	2 409	3 253	2 795	2 460	2 143	1 324
Transportation	10 742	14 107	12 164	16 126	12 800	15 384	19 119	13 124	8 491	7 424
Vehicle purchases (net outlay)	4 394	5 857	4 827	7 132	5 362	6 690	8 797	4 191	3 378	2 954
Gasoline and motor oil	2 094	2 727	2 241	3 081	2 504	3 039	3 469	3 328	1 848	1 451
Other vehicle expenses	3 474	4 473	4 017	4 845	3 904	4 684	5 619	4 816	2 834	2 485
Public and other transportation	781	1 049	1 080	1 067	1 030	971	1 233	788	430	534
Health Care	5 193	6 985	7 605	6 375	5 727	6 189	7 022	7 081	2 634	3 567
Health insurance	3 529	4 796	5 154	4 429	3 937	4 306	4 893	4 948	1 694	2 384
Medical services	984	1 299	1 343	1 280	1 339	1 293	1 227	1 171	598	692
Drugs	486	646	803	486	312	419	684	680	229	343
Medical supplies	194	244	304	180	139	171	218	282	113	149
Entertainment	3 090	4 222	4 265	4 385	3 321	5 097	3 903	3 049	2 087	1 995
Personal Care Products and Services	786	989	950	1 029	742	1 053	1 156	984	771	571
Reading	92	114	138	89	64	105	78	120	42	74
Education	1 443	2 004	1 433	2 650	1 055	2 974	3 060	1 426	1 019	895
Tobacco Products and Smoking Supplies	320	316	298	305	174	332	337	478	249	331
Miscellaneous	899	1 046	1 055	1 053	641	1 084	1 239	943	1 341	697
Cash Contributions	1 995	2 740	3 100	2 564	1 715	2 791	2 700	1 808	856	1 328
Personal Insurance and Pensions	7 165	10 323	8 535	12 206	11 760	12 080	12 648	9 271	4 079	4 152
Life and other personal insurance	520	802	851	788	569	719	1 015	617	225	252
Pensions and Social Security	6 645	9 521	7 683	11 418	11 191	11 361	11 633	8 654	3 854	3 900

[1] No data reported.
[2] Value is too small to display.

Table 11-10. Consumer Expenditures, Averages by Selected Age of Reference Person, 2019

(Number, dollar, percent.)

Item	All consumer units	Under 30 years	30 years and older	Under 50	50 years and older	Under 55 years	55 years and older	Under 65 years	65 years and older
NUMBER OF CONSUMER UNITS (THOUSANDS)	132 242	16 876	115 366	61 246	70 996	73 172	59 070	97 737	34 505
CONSUMER UNIT CHARACTERISTICS									
Income Before Taxes	82 852	53 655	87 123	86 546	79 665	90 051	73 933	92 453	55 656
Income After Taxes	71 487	48 832	74 801	75 795	67 771	78 398	62 927	79 269	49 445
Age of Reference Person	51.6	24.8	55.5	35.3	65.6	38.0	68.3	43.4	74.6
Average Number in Consumer Unit									
All persons	2.5	2.1	2.5	2.9	2.1	2.9	1.9	2.7	1.7
Children under 18 years	0.6	0.5	0.6	1.0	0.2	0.9	0.1	0.8	0.1
Persons 65 years and over	0.4	(1)	0.5	(1)	0.7	(1)	0.9	0.1	1.4
Earners	1.3	1.4	1.3	1.6	1.0	1.6	0.9	1.6	0.5
Vehicles	1.9	1.4	2.0	1.8	2.0	1.9	1.9	2.0	1.7
Percent Distribution									
Male	48	50	48	50	46	49	47	49	45
Female	52	50	52	50	54	51	53	51	55
Percent Homeowner	64	26	69	50	76	53	77	58	79
With mortgage	37	20	40	40	35	42	32	42	24
Without mortgage	27	6	29	10	41	11	45	17	55
AVERAGE ANNUAL EXPENDITURES	63 036	47 609	65 347	64 615	61 670	66 860	58 277	67 519	50 220
Food	8 169	6 251	8 476	8 645	7 737	8 737	7 440	8 698	6 599
Food at home	4 643	3 068	4 897	4 644	4 643	4 753	4 502	4 837	4 063
Cereals and bakery products	583	385	615	583	583	594	569	606	516
Meats, poultry, fish, and eggs	980	674	1 030	988	974	1 010	942	1 023	852
Dairy products	455	284	483	449	460	459	449	469	414
Fruits and vegetables	876	581	924	874	878	891	857	899	809
Other food at home	1 749	1 144	1 846	1 750	1 747	1 798	1 685	1 841	1 472
Food away from home	3 526	3 183	3 579	4 002	3 094	3 985	2 938	3 861	2 536
Alcoholic Beverages	579	431	603	542	614	570	592	606	501
Housing	20 679	16 616	21 283	21 635	19 867	22 019	19 026	21 810	17 472
Shelter	12 190	10 803	12 393	13 232	11 291	13 369	10 730	13 048	9 760
Owned dwellings	6 797	2 619	7 409	6 278	7 245	6 692	6 928	6 996	6 235
Rented dwellings	4 432	7 713	3 952	6 202	2 905	5 837	2 691	5 089	2 571
Other lodging	961	470	1 033	752	1 142	840	1 111	964	954
Utilities, fuels, and public services	4 055	2 725	4 250	3 894	4 194	4 055	4 055	4 141	3 810
Household operations	1 570	1 009	1 652	1 819	1 355	1 755	1 341	1 623	1 418
Housekeeping supplies	766	397	825	650	871	695	857	747	821
Household furnishings and equipment	2 098	1 682	2 164	2 040	2 156	2 146	2 043	2 249	1 663
Apparel and Services	1 883	1 682	1 915	2 126	1 666	2 163	1 526	2 079	1 305
Transportation	10 742	9 407	10 938	11 527	10 065	12 061	9 109	11 890	7 492
Vehicle purchases (net outlay)	4 394	4 078	4 440	4 784	4 057	5 097	3 523	4 959	2 792
Gasoline and motor oil	2 094	1 825	2 134	2 334	1 887	2 381	1 739	2 345	1 383
Other vehicle expenses	3 474	2 843	3 567	3 635	3 335	3 780	3 095	3 765	2 649
Public and other transportation	781	661	797	774	786	803	752	820	668
Health Care	5 193	2 175	5 637	3 920	6 295	4 166	6 469	4 616	6 833
Health insurance	3 529	1 480	3 829	2 672	4 269	2 842	4 380	3 099	4 748
Medical services	984	466	1 060	821	1 125	853	1 146	960	1 054
Drugs	486	151	537	302	647	329	683	399	737
Medical supplies	194	78	211	125	253	141	259	159	293
Entertainment	3 090	1 827	3 282	3 010	3 162	3 118	3 057	3 333	2 381
Personal Care Products and Services	786	529	826	772	799	803	765	811	715
Reading	92	47	99	66	116	70	120	77	138
Education	1 443	2 277	1 321	1 583	1 323	1 845	945	1 829	349
Tobacco Products and Smoking Supplies	320	262	328	338	305	341	294	356	219
Miscellaneous	899	571	947	825	964	848	963	930	811
Cash Contributions	1 995	531	2 209	1 449	2 466	1 600	2 484	1 794	2 564
Personal Insurance and Pensions	7 165	5 004	7 481	8 176	6 292	8 518	5 488	8 690	2 843
Life and other personal insurance	520	149	574	384	636	425	636	518	523
Pensions and Social Security	6 645	4 855	6 907	7 792	5 656	8 093	4 852	8 172	2 320

[1]Value is too small to display.

Table 11-11. Consumer Expenditures, Averages by Race of Reference Person, 2019

(Number, dollar, percent.)

Item	All consumer units	White, Asian, and other races			Black
		Total	White and other races	Asian	
NUMBER OF CONSUMER UNITS (THOUSANDS)	132 242	114 554	108 246	6 308	17 688
CONSUMER UNIT CHARACTERISTICS					
Income Before Taxes	82 852	86 743	85 417	109 492	57 649
Income After Taxes	71 487	74 436	73 341	93 221	52 389
Age of Reference Person	51.6	52.1	52.4	45.8	48.3
Average Number in Consumer Unit					
All persons	2.5	2.5	2.4	2.8	2.4
Children under 18 years	0.6	0.6	0.6	0.7	0.7
Persons 65 years and over	0.4	0.4	0.4	0.3	0.3
Earners	1.3	1.3	1.3	1.6	1.2
Vehicles	1.9	2.0	2.0	1.6	1.4
Percent Distribution					
Male	48	50	49	57	39
Female	52	50	51	43	61
Percent Homeowner	64	67	68	54	43
With mortgage	37	39	39	35	29
Without mortgage	27	28	29	19	14
Food	8 169	8 492	8 425	9 620	5 983
Food at home	4 643	4 803	4 789	5 040	3 553
Cereals and bakery products	583	605	602	648	435
Meats, poultry, fish, and eggs	980	987	980	1 109	935
Dairy products	455	481	485	412	275
Fruits and vegetables	876	905	885	1 242	678
Other food at home	1 749	1 825	1 836	1 629	1 230
Food away from home	3 526	3 689	3 636	4 581	2 429
Alcoholic Beverages	579	633	647	400	213
Housing	20 679	21 215	21 012	24 694	17 176
Shelter	12 190	12 468	12 225	16 637	10 390
Owned dwellings	6 797	7 217	7 132	8 682	4 079
Rented dwellings	4 432	4 207	4 053	6 837	5 889
Other lodging	961	1 045	1 040	1 118	422
Utilities, fuels, and public services	4 055	4 101	4 126	3 664	3 760
Household operations	1 570	1 638	1 616	2 019	1 128
Housekeeping supplies	766	797	808	602	553
Household furnishings and equipment	2 098	2 211	2 237	1 772	1 345
Apparel and Services	1 883	1 870	1 864	1 968	1 971
Transportation	10 742	11 087	11 070	11 378	8 509
Vehicle purchases (net outlay)	4 394	4 593	4 625	4 059	3 100
Gasoline and motor oil	2 094	2 141	2 146	2 042	1 794
Other vehicle expenses	3 474	3 536	3 544	3 400	3 070
Public and other transportation	781	817	755	1 877	546
Health Care	5 193	5 476	5 521	4 700	3 354
Health insurance	3 529	3 661	3 673	3 462	2 674
Medical services	984	1 082	1 100	769	352
Drugs	486	522	534	319	247
Medical supplies	194	211	214	150	81
Entertainment	3 090	3 322	3 335	3 101	1 548
Personal Care Products and Services	786	795	798	738	727
Reading	92	98	99	77	52
Education	1 443	1 533	1 442	3 085	862
Tobacco Products and Smoking Supplies	320	333	345	133	232
Miscellaneous	899	950	951	924	568
Cash Contributions	1 995	2 127	2 123	2 207	1 139
Personal Insurance and Pensions	7 165	7 515	7 347	10 407	4 894
Life and other personal insurance	520	529	521	666	461
Pensions and Social Security	6 645	6 987	6 826	9 740	4 433

Table 11-12. Consumer Expenditures, Averages by Hispanic Origin of Reference Person, 2019

(Number, dollar, percent.)

Item	All consumer units	Hispanic[1]	Not Hispanic		
			Total	White, Asian, and other races	Black
NUMBER OF CONSUMER UNITS (THOUSANDS)	132 242	17 921	114 321	96 992	17 328
CONSUMER UNIT CHARACTERISTICS					
Income Before Taxes	82 852	64 577	85 717	90 734	57 632
Income After Taxes	71 487	60 235	73 251	76 983	52 366
Age of Reference Person	51.6	45.4	52.5	53.3	48.2
Average Number in Consumer Unit					
All persons	2.5	3.2	2.3	2.3	2.4
Children under 18 years	0.6	1.0	0.5	0.5	0.7
Persons 65 years and over	0.4	0.2	0.4	0.5	0.3
Earners	1.3	1.6	1.3	1.3	1.2
Vehicles	1.9	1.7	2.0	2.1	1.4
Percent Distribution					
Male	48	48	48	50	39
Female	52	52	52	50	61
Percent Homeowner	64	48	66	70	43
With mortgage	37	33	38	40	29
Without mortgage	27	16	28	31	14
AVERAGE ANNUAL EXPENDITURES	63 036	54 734	64 350	67 370	47 213
Food	8 169	8 136	8 172	8 547	5 969
Food at home	4 643	4 818	4 614	4 801	3 504
Cereals and bakery products	583	604	580	605	431
Meats, poultry, fish, and eggs	980	1 118	957	962	928
Dairy products	455	470	452	483	270
Fruits and vegetables	876	988	857	889	672
Other food at home	1 749	1 637	1 767	1 862	1 204
Food away from home	3 526	3 318	3 559	3 746	2 465
Alcoholic Beverages	579	360	616	684	212
Housing	20 679	19 202	20 915	21 591	17 088
Shelter	12 190	11 734	12 262	12 611	10 308
Owned dwellings	6 797	5 051	7 071	7 606	4 079
Rented dwellings	4 432	6 338	4 133	3 834	5 802
Other lodging	961	345	1 058	1 170	428
Utilities, fuels, and public services	4 055	4 052	4 055	4 108	3 762
Household operations	1 570	1 108	1 642	1 734	1 128
Housekeeping supplies	766	634	788	827	552
Household furnishings and equipment	2 098	1 673	2 168	2 312	1 337
Apparel and Services	1 883	1 938	1 874	1 851	2 006
Transportation	10 742	10 721	10 746	11 144	8 517
Vehicle purchases (net outlay)	4 394	4 267	4 414	4 646	3 111
Gasoline and motor oil	2 094	2 438	2 040	2 083	1 798
Other vehicle expenses	3 474	3 407	3 485	3 558	3 073
Public and other transportation	781	609	807	856	534
Health Care	5 193	3 485	5 462	5 837	3 349
Health insurance	3 529	2 429	3 702	3 886	2 672
Medical services	984	659	1 035	1 158	346
Drugs	486	294	517	563	251
Medical supplies	194	103	208	231	80
Entertainment	3 090	1 937	3 278	3 576	1 554
Personal Care Products and Services	786	752	791	801	734
Reading	92	46	100	108	51
Education	1 443	826	1 540	1 660	870
Tobacco Products and Smoking Supplies	320	167	344	364	234
Miscellaneous	899	656	937	1 001	577
Cash Contributions	1 995	907	2 166	2 348	1 146
Personal Insurance and Pensions	7 165	5 600	7 410	7 857	4 906
Life and other personal insurance	520	280	557	574	465
Pensions and Social Security	6 645	5 320	6 853	7 284	4 441

[1]May be of any race.

Table 11-13. Consumer Expenditures, Averages by Education of Reference Person, 2019

(Number, dollar, percent.)

Item	All consumer units	Less than a college graduate					College graduate or more		
		Total	Less than a high school graduate	High school graduate	High school graduate with some college	Associate's degree	Total	Bachelor's degree	Master's, professional, or doctoral degree
NUMBER OF CONSUMER UNITS (THOUSANDS)	132 242	73 574	7 558	25 129	26 041	14 845	58 668	33 841	24 828
CONSUMER UNIT CHARACTERISTICS									
Income Before Taxes	82 852	52 027	31 970	42 599	56 109	71 039	121 507	104 922	144 112
Income After Taxes	71 487	47 890	31 079	39 729	51 414	64 082	101 080	88 400	118 363
Age of Reference Person	51.6	52.4	56.3	54.6	50.1	50.8	50.5	49.3	52.1
Average Number in Consumer Unit									
All persons	2.5	2.4	2.3	2.2	2.4	2.6	2.6	2.5	2.6
Children under 18 years	0.6	0.6	0.7	0.5	0.6	0.6	0.6	0.6	0.6
Persons 65 years and over	0.4	0.4	0.4	0.5	0.4	0.4	0.4	0.3	0.4
Earners	1.3	1.1	0.8	1.0	1.3	1.4	1.5	1.5	1.5
Vehicles	1.9	1.8	1.1	1.6	1.8	2.2	2.1	2.1	2.2
Percent Distribution									
Male	48	45	43	44	45	46	52	53	52
Female	52	55	57	56	55	54	48	47	48
Percent Homeowner	64	56	45	56	55	65	73	69	79
With mortgage	37	28	15	24	29	40	49	46	52
Without mortgage	27	28	30	32	26	25	24	23	26
AVERAGE ANNUAL EXPENDITURES	63 036	46 344	30 276	40 029	49 559	59 579	83 856	73 832	97 588
Food	8 169	6 553	4 879	5 762	7 005	7 946	10 143	9 517	11 021
Food at home	4 643	3 981	3 721	3 534	4 131	4 599	5 448	5 067	5 988
Cereals and bakery products	583	507	492	471	515	563	675	631	738
Meats, poultry, fish, and eggs	980	897	837	849	903	997	1 082	987	1 218
Dairy products	455	376	329	339	392	436	550	510	607
Fruits and vegetables	876	714	697	642	730	816	1 073	972	1 216
Other food at home	1 749	1 487	1 366	1 234	1 590	1 787	2 068	1 967	2 209
Food away from home	3 526	2 572	1 158	2 227	2 874	3 347	4 695	4 450	5 032
Alcoholic Beverages	579	338	169	284	367	466	874	808	966
Housing	20 679	15 625	11 618	14 214	16 306	18 864	27 003	23 683	31 536
Shelter	12 190	8 872	6 992	8 109	9 311	10 350	16 352	14 307	19 140
Owned dwellings	6 797	4 083	2 223	3 540	4 281	5 599	10 201	8 453	12 584
Rented dwellings	4 432	4 375	4 637	4 209	4 577	4 169	4 502	4 727	4 197
Other lodging	961	414	132	359	452	582	1 648	1 127	2 358
Utilities, fuels, and public services	4 055	3 646	2 817	3 446	3 747	4 229	4 568	4 252	5 000
Household operations	1 570	936	550	853	981	1 195	2 364	1 825	3 100
Housekeeping supplies	766	622	471	509	629	880	939	842	1 077
Household furnishings and equipment	2 098	1 549	788	1 298	1 638	2 211	2 779	2 458	3 219
Apparel and Services	1 883	1 362	999	1 163	1 366	1 882	2 521	2 324	2 794
Transportation	10 742	8 905	4 909	7 557	9 431	12 301	13 044	12 315	14 039
Vehicle purchases (net outlay)	4 394	3 781	1 703	3 117	3 896	5 761	5 162	5 043	5 326
Gasoline and motor oil	2 094	1 894	1 333	1 689	1 992	2 355	2 345	2 320	2 380
Other vehicle expenses	3 474	2 873	1 659	2 454	3 153	3 710	4 226	3 970	4 577
Public and other transportation	781	358	213	298	390	475	1 310	983	1 757
Health Care	5 193	3 971	2 533	3 785	4 044	4 892	6 724	6 001	7 711
Health insurance	3 529	2 777	1 773	2 665	2 805	3 429	4 473	4 059	5 037
Medical services	984	621	391	543	664	796	1 439	1 259	1 686
Drugs	486	425	292	408	432	508	561	491	659
Medical supplies	194	148	78	169	143	158	250	193	328
Entertainment	3 090	2 118	1 147	1 639	2 430	2 868	4 295	3 442	5 480
Personal Care Products and Services	786	591	323	462	613	911	1 028	917	1 182
Reading	92	67	35	75	66	72	123	104	150
Education	1 443	563	303	259	912	599	2 546	1 839	3 512
Tobacco Products and Smoking Supplies	320	433	341	496	423	392	178	212	131
Miscellaneous	899	675	387	448	700	1 161	1 179	961	1 477
Cash Contributions	1 995	1 045	508	854	1 207	1 358	3 187	2 406	4 252
Personal Insurance and Pensions	7 165	4 098	2 124	3 031	4 690	5 868	11 011	9 304	13 337
Life and other personal insurance	520	318	168	269	313	486	772	570	1 049
Pensions and Social Security	6 645	3 780	1 955	2 763	4 377	5 382	10 239	8 735	12 289

Table 11-14. Consumer Expenditures, Averages by Housing Tenure and Type of Area, 2019

(Number, dollar, percent.)

Item	All consumer units	Housing tenure				Type of area			
		Homeowner			Renter	Urban			Rural
		Total	Homeowner with mortgage	Homeowner without mortgage		Total	Central city	Other urban	
NUMBER OF CONSUMER UNITS (THOUSANDS)	132 242	84 291	49 241	35 049	47 951	121 604	48 030	73 574	10 639
Income After Taxes	71 487	85 251	100 526	63 791	47 293	72 889	65 487	77 721	55 465
Age of Reference Person	51.6	55.9	50.1	64.1	43.8	51.2	49.3	52.5	55.0
Average Number in Consumer Unit									
All persons	2.5	2.6	2.9	2.1	2.2	2.4	2.3	2.5	2.5
Children under 18 years	0.6	0.6	0.8	0.3	0.6	0.6	0.5	0.6	0.6
Persons 65 years and over	0.4	0.5	0.3	0.8	0.2	0.4	0.3	0.4	0.5
Earners	1.3	1.4	1.7	0.9	1.2	1.3	1.3	1.4	1.1
Vehicles	1.9	2.3	2.4	2.2	1.2	1.9	1.6	2.1	2.5
Percent Distribution									
Male	48	50	52	47	46	48	48	49	45
Female	52	50	48	53	54	52	52	51	55
Percent Homeowner	64	100	100	100	X	62	50	70	78
With mortgage	37	58	100	X	X	38	30	43	32
Without mortgage	27	42	X	100	X	25	20	28	46
Food	8 169	9 180	9 937	7 915	6 399	8 279	7 543	8 768	6 908
Food at home	4 643	5 216	5 468	4 783	3 641	4 672	4 182	4 997	4 319
Cereals and bakery products	583	654	684	601	459	588	523	631	527
Meats, poultry, fish, and eggs	980	1 100	1 133	1 044	771	982	886	1 047	958
Dairy products	455	517	546	468	346	456	400	494	437
Fruits and vegetables	876	979	1 020	907	697	891	819	939	705
Other food at home	1 749	1 966	2 085	1 763	1 368	1 754	1 554	1 886	1 691
Food away from home	3 526	3 964	4 469	3 133	2 759	3 607	3 361	3 771	2 589
Alcoholic Beverages	579	683	775	528	398	598	575	614	359
Housing	20 679	22 314	26 418	16 522	17 809	21 283	19 768	22 277	13 772
Shelter	12 190	11 999	15 186	7 520	12 527	12 703	12 322	12 951	6 334
Owned dwellings	6 797	10 587	13 736	6 163	136	7 021	5 366	8 102	4 238
Rented dwellings	4 432	138	134	143	11 979	4 701	6 153	3 754	1 348
Other lodging	961	1 274	1 316	1 214	412	980	804	1 095	748
Utilities, fuels, and public services	4 055	4 805	5 152	4 319	2 736	4 067	3 661	4 332	3 916
Household operations	1 570	1 939	2 220	1 544	921	1 617	1 420	1 745	1 035
Housekeeping supplies	766	945	955	928	451	758	623	847	852
Household furnishings and equipment	2 098	2 625	2 905	2 211	1 174	2 139	1 741	2 401	1 635
Apparel and Services	1 883	2 052	2 290	1 675	1 587	1 951	1 817	2 041	1 099
Transportation	10 742	12 581	14 414	10 002	7 510	10 679	9 405	11 510	11 468
Vehicle purchases (net outlay)	4 394	5 340	6 082	4 298	2 730	4 284	3 748	4 634	5 646
Gasoline and motor oil	2 094	2 368	2 714	1 881	1 613	2 072	1 725	2 299	2 344
Other vehicle expenses	3 474	3 976	4 672	2 993	2 592	3 510	3 075	3 795	3 057
Public and other transportation	781	898	945	830	575	812	856	783	420
Health Care	5 193	6 450	6 404	6 525	2 983	5 179	4 384	5 698	5 358
Health insurance	3 529	4 396	4 393	4 400	2 006	3 515	3 015	3 841	3 697
Medical services	984	1 218	1 249	1 177	573	1 000	833	1 109	806
Drugs	486	603	541	696	281	466	382	522	711
Medical supplies	194	234	221	252	124	198	155	227	143
Entertainment	3 090	3 873	4 379	3 081	1 715	3 125	2 715	3 396	2 686
Personal Care Products and Services	786	909	1 006	760	572	815	750	858	463
Reading	92	113	108	125	55	93	87	97	83
Education	1 443	1 549	1 959	970	1 257	1 519	1 506	1 527	579
Tobacco Products and Smoking Supplies	320	300	317	277	355	299	252	330	554
Miscellaneous	899	1 023	1 174	802	682	918	796	999	678
Cash Contributions	1 995	2 598	2 292	3 029	935	2 008	1 801	2 143	1 847
Personal Insurance and Pensions	7 165	8 762	10 949	5 689	4 358	7 346	6 633	7 811	5 098
Life and other personal insurance	520	707	816	554	190	523	431	583	478
Pensions and Social Security	6 645	8 055	10 133	5 135	4 167	6 822	6 202	7 228	4 620

X = Not applicable.

Table 11-15. Consumer Expenditures, Averages by Selected Cities, 2018–2019

(Number, dollar, percent.)

Item	Washington, D.C.	Miami	Dallas-Fort Worth	New York	Philadelphia	Boston	Chicago	Detroit	Minneapolis-St. Paul	Los Angeles	Seattle	Anchorage
NUMBER OF CONSUMER UNITS (THOUSANDS)	2 424	2 341	2 942	7 308	1 895	1 918	3 375	1 959	1 687	6 769	1 891	234
CONSUMER UNIT CHARACTERISTICS												
Income Before Taxes	128 871	73 793	89 438	103 011	98 206	104 623	86 575	87 214	108 799	90 037	115 137	94 235
Age of Reference Person	50.6	52.3	46.5	52.1	53.3	52.3	50.3	52.6	49.4	49.9	46.6	50.1
Average Number in Consumer Unit												
All persons	2.7	2.5	2.5	2.5	2.5	2.3	2.6	2.5	2.3	3.0	2.0	2.3
Children under 18 years	0.7	0.5	0.7	0.5	0.6	0.4	0.7	0.6	0.5	1.0	1.0	0.5
Persons 65 years and over	0.3	0.4	0.2	0.4	0.4	0.4	0.3	0.4	0.3	0.0	0.0	0.3
Earners	1.6	1.3	1.4	1.3	1.4	1.4	1.5	1.4	1.4	2.0	1.0	1.4
Vehicles	1.9	1.5	1.7	1.2	1.6	1.6	1.7	1.9	2.3	2.0	2.0	2.4
Percent Homeowner	68.0	56.0	57.0	49.0	65.0	56.0	63.0	74.0	65.0	50.0	58.0	65.0
AVERAGE ANNUAL EXPENDITURES	95 441	57 472	66 966	73 806	72 460	83 297	64 804	65 163	84 006	69 824	81 266	76 784
Food	11 608	6 304	7 651	9 843	8 813	9 979	8 891	8 277	9 769	9 177	10 291	10 323
Food at home	5 927	3 954	4 087	5 352	4 786	5 858	5 068	4 590	5 497	4 584	5 543	6 636
Cereals and bakery products	700	426	527	710	679	841	653	600	617	576	657	913
Meats, poultry, fish, and eggs ...	1 225	1 011	845	1 323	996	1 086	1 079	1 023	1 129	989	1 056	1 377
Dairy products	603	393	366	539	483	552	489	422	567	449	528	628
Fruits and vegetables	1 291	848	798	1 145	928	1 231	1 071	908	1 059	944	1 183	1 164
Other food at home	2 108	1 276	1 551	1 635	1 701	2 148	1 777	1 636	2 126	1 625	2 121	2 556
Food away from home	5 681	2 350	3 564	4 491	4 026	4 121	3 822	3 687	4 271	4 593	4 748	3 686
Alcoholic Beverages	1 203	510	615	670	756	925	653	716	1 112	599	837	666
Housing	31 694	20 479	25 150	28 040	25 569	30 043	23 677	19 730	26 654	24 613	29 234	23 436
Shelter	19 936	13 557	15 485	19 344	15 015	19 188	15 162	10 866	16 027	16 703	18 778	14 072
Owned dwellings	12 677	6 104	8 304	9 868	8 482	10 081	9 342	7 036	9 788	7 501	10 016	8 530
Rented dwellings	5 533	6 657	6 220	8 443	4 925	7 967	4 785	2 980	4 335	8 478	7 073	4 525
Other lodging	1 726	797	961	1 033	1 608	1 140	1 036	850	1 904	724	1 689	1 017
Utilities, fuels, and public services	4 639	3 968	4 813	4 110	4 392	4 480	4 066	4 112	3 924	3 848	3 963	4 672
Household operations	3 122	1 081	1 799	1 771	2 324	2 399	1 511	1 628	2 401	1 647	2 552	1 281
Housekeeping supplies	1 069	660	761	776	1 010	905	807	922	951	673	765	967
Household furnishings and equipment	2 929	1 214	2 292	2 039	2 829	3 070	2 131	2 202	3 351	1 743	3 175	2 444
Apparel and Services	3 159	1 381	1 831	2 801	2 908	2 128	1 873	2 908	2 999	2 080	2 915	2 653
Transportation	13 646	10 915	10 472	9 255	11 136	11 779	9 084	11 260	11 049	10 959	11 506	13 313
Vehicle purchases (net outlay)	5 712	3 108	3 601	2 219	4 037	4 941	3 188	3 507	3 705	3 435	3 902	5 539
Gasoline and motor oil	2 107	2 421	2 277	1 521	1 908	1 857	1 882	2 111	2 216	2 890	2 290	2 363
Other vehicle expenses	3 837	4 626	3 748	3 641	3 911	3 584	2 955	4 939	3 664	3 723	3 689	3 816
Public and other transportation	1 990	759	846	1 874	1 280	1 398	1 059	703	1 465	910	1 625	1 594
Health Care	6 813	4 807	5 734	4 728	5 609	6 470	5 504	5 042	6 448	4 158	5 140	5 179
Entertainment	4 211	1 752	2 729	3 005	3 403	3 768	2 796	4 227	4 962	2 901	4 725	5 311
Personal Care Products and Services	1 232	870	818	913	1 014	911	871	805	950	872	963	743
Reading	142	47	86	86	97	227	110	99	291	91	119	129
Education	2 371	1 442	1 606	2 711	1 618	4 681	1 711	1 044	2 932	1 854	2 098	1 218
Tobacco Products and Smoking Supplies	134	174	202	213	248	218	258	437	437	201	367	435
Miscellaneous	1 705	583	841	1 200	1 098	1 404	609	1 596	1 325	1 172	981	1 328
Cash Contributions	3 428	848	1 491	1 685	2 025	2 057	1 246	1 420	5 498	1 910	1 772	1 810
Personal Insurance and Pensions	14 095	7 358	7 739	8 658	8 168	8 707	7 520	7 604	9 581	9 238	10 317	10 241
Life and other personal insurance	673	333	374	635	610	487	480	410	597	444	454	507
Pensions and Social Security	13 422	7 025	7 365	8 023	7 558	8 220	7 040	7 194	8 984	8 794	9 864	9 734

Table 11-16. Consumer Expenditures, Averages by Region of Residence, 2019

(Number, dollar, percent.)

Item	All consumer units	Region[1]			
		Northeast	South	Midwest	West
NUMBER OF CONSUMER UNITS (THOUSANDS)	132 242	23 243	28 140	50 977	29 882
CONSUMER UNIT CHARACTERISTICS					
Income Before Taxes	82 852	88 486	78 586	79 348	88 463
Income After Taxes	71 487	76 169	68 547	68 669	75 424
Age of Reference Person	51.6	53.1	52.0	51.0	50.9
Average Number in Consumer Unit					
All persons	2.5	2.4	2.4	2.4	2.6
Children under 18 years	0.6	0.5	0.6	0.6	0.6
Persons 65 years and over	0.4	0.4	0.4	0.4	0.4
Earners	1.3	1.3	1.3	1.3	1.4
Vehicles	1.9	1.6	2.1	1.9	2.0
Percent Distribution					
Male	48	48	48	47	51
Female	52	52	52	53	49
Percent Homeowner	64	61	69	65	59
With mortgage	37	37	39	36	38
Without mortgage	27	24	30	28	22
AVERAGE ANNUAL EXPENDITURES	63 036	68 795	59 909	58 622	69 029
Food	8 169	8 966	7 682	7 616	8 947
Food at home	4 643	5 192	4 478	4 316	4 930
Cereals and bakery products	583	700	555	534	602
Meats, poultry, fish, and eggs	980	1 153	960	924	963
Dairy products	455	522	435	405	505
Fruits and vegetables	876	1 007	804	798	975
Other food at home	1 749	1 809	1 723	1 655	1 883
Food away from home	3 526	3 774	3 204	3 300	4 017
Alcoholic Beverages	579	660	575	512	634
Housing	20 679	23 525	18 678	18 781	23 590
Shelter	12 190	14 643	10 457	10 466	14 857
Owned dwellings	6 797	8 093	6 418	6 004	7 500
Rented dwellings	4 432	5 467	2 990	3 611	6 383
Other lodging	961	1 083	1 048	851	974
Utilities, fuels, and public services	4 055	4 239	3 950	4 115	3 909
Household operations	1 570	1 612	1 518	1 440	1 808
Housekeeping supplies	766	781	803	767	715
Household furnishings and equipment	2 098	2 250	1 951	1 993	2 299
Apparel and Services	1 883	2 282	1 756	1 722	1 968
Transportation	10 742	10 495	10 512	10 665	11 284
Vehicle purchases (net outlay)	4 394	4 079	4 545	4 579	4 180
Gasoline and motor oil	2 094	1 779	1 980	2 100	2 437
Other vehicle expenses	3 474	3 607	3 354	3 368	3 665
Public and other transportation	781	1 029	634	618	1 003
Health Care	5 193	5 209	5 643	4 982	5 116
Health insurance	3 529	3 559	3 834	3 479	3 305
Medical services	984	998	1 030	858	1 146
Drugs	486	419	570	481	466
Medical supplies	194	233	208	165	199
Entertainment	3 090	3 176	3 115	2 845	3 416
Personal Care Products and Services	786	871	717	752	845
Reading	92	90	110	79	100
Education	1 443	2 637	1 024	1 111	1 476
Tobacco Products and Smoking Supplies	320	309	372	353	223
Miscellaneous	899	1 127	790	790	1 011
Cash Contributions	1 995	1 638	1 776	1 852	2 724
Personal Insurance and Pensions	7 165	7 809	7 158	6 563	7 697
Life and other personal insurance	520	614	524	511	458
Pensions and Social Security	6 645	7 196	6 634	6 052	7 239

[1]The states that comprise the Census regions are: Northeast—Connecticut, Maine, Massachusetts, New Hampshire, New Jersey, New York, Pennsylvania, Rhode Island, and Vermont; South—Alabama, Arkansas, Delaware, District of Columbia, Florida, Georgia, Kentucky, Louisiana, Maryland, Mississippi, North Carolina, Oklahoma, South Carolina, Tennessee, Texas, Virginia, and West Virginia; Midwest—Illinois, Indiana, Iowa, Kansas, Michigan, Minnesota, Missouri, Nebraska, North Dakota, Ohio, South Dakota, and Wisconsin; and West—Alaska, Arizona, California, Colorado, Hawaii, Idaho, Montana, Nevada, New Mexico, Oregon, Utah, Washington, and Wyoming.

Table 11-17. Consumer Expenditures, Averages for Single Men by Income Before Taxes, 2018–2019

Item	All single men	Complete reporting of income						
		Less than $15,000	$15,000 to $29,999	$30,000 to $39,999	$40,000 to $49,999	$50,000 to $69,999	$70,000 to $99,999	$100,000 and over
NUMBER OF CONSUMER UNITS (THOUSANDS)	18,028	4,324	4,213	2,029	1,538	2,316	1,987	1,622
Income After Taxes	38,600	7,157	20,848	31,535	39,771	50,490	67,597	123,801
Age of Reference Person	50.2	48.2	59.3	48.2	47.1	45.3	46.8	48.9
Average Number in Consumer Unit								
All persons	1.0	1.0	1.0	1.0	1.0	1.0	1.0	1.0
Persons 65 years and over	0.3	0.3	0.5	0.3	0.2	0.1	0.1	0.2
Earners	0.7	0.4	0.4	0.8	0.9	0.9	0.9	1.0
Vehicles	1.2	0.7	1.3	1.3	1.4	1.4	1.6	1.5
Percent Homeowner	43	25	47	40	43	51	56	59
With mortgage	21	8	13	16	22	31	40	44
Without mortgage	22	17	34	24	20	20	16	16
Food	4,871	3,194	4,000	4,232	5,104	5,742	6,573	8,572
Food at home	2,447	1,880	2,177	2,350	2,586	2,836	2,955	3,373
Cereals and bakery products	288	237	256	306	288	315	335	374
Meats, poultry, fish, and eggs	528	391	468	502	611	602	598	782
Dairy products	232	183	208	249	205	248	285	325
Fruits and vegetables	425	295	406	360	458	494	523	622
Other food at home	975	774	839	934	1,024	1,176	1,214	1,269
Food away from home	2,424	1,314	1,822	1,882	2,519	2,906	3,618	5,199
Alcoholic Beverages	577	230	255	658	584	756	910	1,500
Housing	14,313	8,600	11,446	13,199	14,479	16,750	19,981	27,747
Shelter	9,560	5,776	7,636	8,451	9,600	10,721	13,832	19,104
Owned dwellings	3,540	1,326	2,441	2,536	3,205	4,426	6,587	8,877
Rented dwellings	5,583	4,375	4,896	5,666	6,007	5,832	6,665	8,402
Other lodging	437	76	299	249	388	464	580	1,825
Utilities, fuels, and public services	2,449	1,597	2,356	2,431	2,547	2,814	3,133	3,539
Household operations	738	303	574	904	878	781	1,078	1,498
Housekeeping supplies	418	445	282	356	410	419	467	727
Household furnishings and equipment	1,149	479	598	1,057	1,044	2,015	1,471	2,880
Apparel and Services	977	474	506	644	973	1,658	1,438	2,375
Transportation	6,214	3,042	4,425	7,137	6,373	8,757	8,866	11,130
Vehicle purchases (net outlay)	2,322	1,079	1,548	3,425	1,904	3,575	3,372	3,586
Gasoline and motor oil	1,322	761	1,063	1,396	1,505	1,833	1,770	1,950
Other vehicle expenses	2,111	984	1,578	2,106	2,579	2,760	3,113	3,912
Public and other transportation	459	218	237	210	384	589	610	1,682
Health Care	2,738	1,347	2,975	2,441	2,877	2,809	3,520	5,004
Health insurance	1,796	963	1,906	1,636	1,724	1,950	2,329	3,127
Medical services	552	173	541	444	876	548	644	1,309
Drugs	264	182	281	307	177	231	321	444
Medical supplies	126	29	246	54	100	80	227	124
Entertainment	1,703	873	1,205	1,650	1,768	2,115	2,227	3,927
Personal Care Products and Services	270	145	214	252	243	265	519	486
Reading	67	66	62	48	55	70	107	74
Education	596	609	434	645	569	388	729	1,081
Tobacco Products and Smoking Supplies	325	319	367	356	326	317	282	261
Miscellaneous	725	377	612	502	728	717	1,475	1,312
Cash Contributions	1,511	389	1,014	963	1,341	1,580	2,659	5,141
Personal Insurance and Pensions	3,859	392	1,021	2,595	3,725	5,429	7,788	15,129
Life and other personal insurance	186	81	155	109	141	220	268	537
Pensions and Social Security	3,673	311	865	2,486	3,584	5,209	7,521	14,592

Table 11-18. Consumer Expenditures, Averages for Single Women by Income Before Taxes, 2018–2019

Item	All single women	Less than $15,000	$15,000 to $29,999	$30,000 to $39,999	$40,000 to $49,999	$50,000 to $69,999	$70,000 or more
NUMBER OF CONSUMER UNITS (THOUSANDS)	21 282	6 787	6 488	2 141	1 562	2 002	2 302
CONSUMER UNIT CHARACTERISTICS							
Income Before Taxes	33 057	7 941	21 265	34 431	44 400	58 805	108 988
Income After Taxes	29 206	7 958	20 603	32 048	39 456	51 211	87 377
Age of Reference Person	58.7	56.1	67.6	56.6	52.9	51.0	54.0
Average Number in Consumer Unit							
All persons	1.0	1.0	1.0	1.0	1.0	1.0	1.0
Persons 65 years and over	0.5	0.4	0.7	0.4	0.3	0.3	0.2
Earners	0.5	0.3	0.3	0.7	0.8	0.8	0.9
Vehicles	0.9	0.6	1.0	1.1	1.1	1.1	1.2
Percent Homeowner	53	35	62	56	56	58	69
With mortgage	21	9	17	19	35	32	45
Without mortgage	32	26	45	37	20	26	24
AVERAGE ANNUAL EXPENDITURES	36 061	21 919	30 046	37 283	43 953	48 207	75 548
Food	4 299	3 115	3 788	4 352	5 215	5 126	6 997
Food at home	2 557	2 049	2 421	2 703	2 776	2 804	3 588
Cereals and bakery products	322	265	322	348	355	332	396
Meats, poultry, fish, and eggs	468	388	461	483	518	507	583
Dairy products	270	211	266	303	279	309	347
Fruits and vegetables	515	405	480	553	581	571	723
Other food at home	983	779	892	1 016	1 043	1 085	1 540
Food away from home	1 741	1 067	1 367	1 649	2 439	2 322	3 409
Alcoholic Beverages	284	122	179	281	294	485	773
Housing	14 131	9 056	12 435	14 873	16 582	18 561	27 360
Shelter	8 883	5 749	7 499	9 554	10 492	12 059	17 548
Owned dwellings	3 833	1 713	3 384	3 784	4 492	5 158	9 793
Rented dwellings	4 562	3 745	3 845	5 257	5 535	6 281	6 196
Other lodging	488	291	270	513	465	620	1 559
Utilities, fuels, and public services	2 604	1 832	2 742	2 854	2 984	2 982	3 675
Household operations	930	482	917	872	1 021	1 265	1 984
Housekeeping supplies	519	344	480	501	600	593	920
Household furnishings and equipment	1 195	649	797	1 092	1 484	1 663	3 233
Apparel and Services	1 062	558	844	912	1 391	1 377	2 451
Transportation	4 676	2 635	3 903	5 049	6 927	6 110	9 700
Vehicle purchases (net outlay)	1 518	746	1 160	1 280	2 696	1 659	4 105
Gasoline and motor oil	903	607	767	1 128	1 222	1 369	1 325
Other vehicle expenses	1 782	1 001	1 674	2 187	2 478	2 515	2 879
Public and other transportation	473	281	303	454	531	568	1 390
Health Care	3 520	2 310	3 874	3 803	3 805	4 112	5 068
Health insurance	2 287	1 567	2 668	2 457	2 358	2 368	3 060
Medical services	695	392	625	665	919	1 192	1 229
Drugs	398	285	434	527	378	371	515
Medical supplies	139	66	146	154	149	181	263
Entertainment	1 801	1 050	1 361	1 690	1 928	2 394	4 555
Personal Care Products and Services	663	377	519	742	763	1 011	1 358
Reading	100	60	116	99	112	134	134
Education	832	1 292	299	977	712	875	879
Tobacco Products and Smoking Supplies	167	204	150	134	133	175	163
Miscellaneous	713	286	585	875	1 043	1 235	1 422
Cash Contributions	1 268	514	1 104	1 373	1 181	1 374	3 821
Personal Insurance and Pensions	2 545	340	888	2 123	3 867	5 240	10 868
Life and other personal insurance	236	129	202	229	241	269	623
Pensions and Social Security	2 309	212	686	1 894	3 626	4 971	10 245

Table 11-19. Consumer Expenditures, Averages for Age Groups by Income Before Taxes: Reference Person Under 25 Years of Age, 2018–2019

(Number, dollar, percent.)

Item	Total under 25 years	Complete reporting of income					
		Less than $15,000	$15,000 to $29,999	$30,000 to $39,999	$40,000 to $49,999	$50,000 to $69,999	$70,000 or more
NUMBER OF CONSUMER UNITS (THOUSANDS)	7 458	2 755	1 309	806	629	855	1 105
CONSUMER UNIT CHARACTERISTICS							
Income Before Taxes	35 143	6 011	21 991	34 825	44 561	58 928	99 833
Income After Taxes	32 770	5 974	22 242	33 582	42 514	54 205	89 335
Age of Reference Person	21.5	20.5	21.7	21.8	22.4	22.4	22.6
Average Number in Consumer Unit							
All persons	1.9	1.2	1.9	2.0	2.3	2.3	3.0
Children under 18 years	0.3	0.1	0.4	0.3	0.4	0.3	0.5
Earners	1.3	0.8	1.2	1.3	1.6	1.8	2.3
Vehicles	1.1	0.5	1.0	1.2	1.7	1.7	2.1
Percent Distribution							
Male	48	42	44	54	48	59	53
Female	52	58	56	46	52	41	47
Percent Homeowner	15	3	11	13	27	27	34
With mortgage	9	1	3	4	18	20	25
Without mortgage	6	2	8	9	8	8	9
AVERAGE ANNUAL EXPENDITURES	35 739	18 213	28 645	38 553	43 058	49 301	67 238
Food	5 272	2 938	4 196	4 679	6 111	6 601	8 897
Food at home	2 571	1 097	2 110	2 386	3 492	3 512	4 208
Cereals and bakery products	342	136	267	313	504	442	585
Meats, poultry, fish, and eggs	531	199	443	455	715	773	894
Dairy products	257	117	194	280	392	379	360
Fruits and vegetables	493	181	419	369	692	664	875
Other food at home	948	463	786	968	1 189	1 253	1 494
Food away from home	2 700	1 841	2 086	2 293	2 619	3 089	4 689
Alcoholic Beverages	298	147	148	321	273	496	565
Housing	12 064	5 898	11 090	13 012	15 438	17 048	21 820
Shelter	8 065	4 245	7 659	8 571	10 322	11 412	13 826
Owned dwellings	1 114	284	545	598	1 845	2 044	3 096
Rented dwellings	6 564	3 481	6 774	7 789	8 219	9 060	10 237
Other lodging	387	479	[1]339	[1]184	[1]258	308	494
Utilities, fuels, and public services	2 062	746	1 907	2 504	2 932	3 233	3 801
Household operations	559	163	503	530	757	784	1 338
Housekeeping supplies	314	185	204	262	362	373	579
Household furnishings and equipment	1 066	559	818	1 145	1 064	1 246	2 275
Apparel and Services	1 272	581	974	1 129	1 426	2 031	2 196
Transportation	7 031	2 793	5 003	8 494	8 907	11 756	14 152
Vehicle purchases (net outlay)	2 899	843	1 623	[1]3661	[1]3694	5 876	6 229
Gasoline and motor oil	1 496	756	1 223	1 578	1 997	2 250	2 737
Other vehicle expenses	2 095	753	1 568	2 888	2 660	3 090	4 376
Public and other transportation	541	442	590	367	555	540	810
Health Care	1 355	389	722	1 297	1 343	2 015	3 982
Health insurance	840	253	441	913	1 000	1 324	2 260
Medical services	321	60	151	276	190	367	1 244
Drugs	141	57	83	61	[1]81	248	375
Medical supplies	53	[1]19	[1]48	[1]46	[1]72	[1]76	103
Entertainment	1 399	709	1 096	2 008	1 741	1 674	2 410
Personal Care Products and Services	477	323	341	413	588	545	875
Reading	40	22	47	[1]63	[1]45	[1]54	46
Education	2 626	3 693	2 779	3 228	1 960	791	1 154
Tobacco Products and Smoking Supplies	208	94	186	279	278	387	277
Miscellaneous	311	145	226	536	668	389	333
Cash Contributions	390	154	241	312	598	471	1 031
Personal Insurance and Pensions	2 997	328	1 594	2 783	3 681	5 044	9 500
Life and other personal insurance	71	[1]1	[1]26	[1]56	[1]70	55	325
Pensions and Social Security	2 926	326	1 568	2 727	3 610	4 988	9 174

[1]Data are likely to have large sampling errors.

Table 11-20. Consumer Expenditures, Averages for Age Groups by Income Before Taxes: Reference Person 25 to 34 Years of Age, 2018–2019

(Number, dollar, percent.)

Item	Complete reporting of income							
	Total 25-34 years	Less than $15,000	$15,000 to $29,999	$30,000 to $39,999	$40,000 to $49,999	$50,000 to $69,999	$70,000 to $99,999	$100,000 or more
NUMBER OF CONSUMER UNITS (THOUSANDS)	21 265	1 899	2 202	2 075	2 147	3 681	3 979	5 282
CONSUMER UNIT CHARACTERISTICS								
Income Before Taxes	75 133	7 361	22 921	34 806	44 512	59 428	83 156	154 455
Income After Taxes	66 574	8 055	25 647	35 390	42 842	54 890	74 853	128 479
Age of Reference Person	29.8	29.5	29.5	29.2	29.4	29.5	29.7	30.7
Average Number in Consumer Unit								
All persons	2.7	2.2	2.7	2.5	2.6	2.6	2.9	2.9
Children under 18 years	0.9	0.9	1.2	1.0	0.9	0.9	0.9	0.8
Earners	1.5	0.8	1.1	1.2	1.4	1.6	1.8	2.0
Vehicles	1.7	0.9	1.2	1.4	1.5	1.7	2.0	2.1
Percent Distribution								
Male	51	40	37	46	48	49	58	58
Female	49	60	63	54	52	51	42	42
Percent Homeowner	41	15	17	23	32	38	54	63
With mortgage	33	8	7	16	24	30	46	56
Without mortgage	8	7	9	7	8	8	8	7
AVERAGE ANNUAL EXPENDITURES	57 095	26 715	32 239	39 037	45 183	51 664	62 008	91 454
Food	7 357	4 703	4 882	5 201	7 019	6 812	8 356	10 474
Food at home	3 864	2 951	2 847	2 967	3 853	3 578	4 400	5 010
Cereals and bakery products	462	400	334	336	469	414	541	592
Meats, poultry, fish, and eggs	826	658	626	720	855	746	904	1 045
Dairy products	366	232	256	278	339	331	460	482
Fruits and vegetables	754	556	603	566	843	656	848	973
Other food at home	1 455	1 105	1 028	1 067	1 346	1 431	1 647	1 918
Food away from home	3 493	1 752	2 036	2 234	3 166	3 234	3 956	5 464
Alcoholic Beverages	577	228	131	299	382	524	602	1 179
Housing	20 063	11 474	12 990	14 983	16 371	17 979	21 193	30 363
Shelter	12 558	7 517	8 471	9 642	10 324	11 441	13 026	18 553
Owned dwellings	4 467	987	827	1 527	2 378	3 242	5 336	9 441
Rented dwellings	7 612	6 414	7 519	7 911	7 693	7 863	7 216	8 056
Other lodging	478	117	126	205	253	337	474	1 056
Utilities, fuels, and public services	3 394	2 219	2 564	2 997	3 095	3 256	3 760	4 259
Household operations	1 699	646	783	870	1 139	1 236	1 811	3 256
Housekeeping supplies	527	359	307	355	469	468	526	871
Household furnishings and equipment	1 885	733	864	1 118	1 344	1 578	2 069	3 424
Apparel and Services	2 010	1 216	1 284	1 512	1 687	1 713	1 897	3 371
Transportation	10 599	4 461	6 323	8 123	8 579	10 355	11 575	15 821
Vehicle purchases (net outlay)	4 491	1 502	2 434	3 283	3 432	4 551	4 765	7 082
Gasoline and motor oil	2 143	1 254	1 447	1 848	1 847	2 141	2 462	2 749
Other vehicle expenses	3 246	1 483	2 112	2 568	2 869	3 165	3 665	4 519
Public and other transportation	718	222	330	423	432	497	683	1 471
Health Care	3 117	826	1 072	1 840	2 274	2 936	3 934	5 160
Health insurance	2 189	554	708	1 271	1 541	2 061	2 848	3 609
Medical services	630	136	214	338	523	576	736	1 099
Drugs	207	109	114	164	146	196	248	312
Medical supplies	90	28	36	66	64	103	101	140
Entertainment	2 470	926	1 294	1 607	1 817	2 085	2 709	4 302
Personal Care Products and Services	641	380	371	428	470	607	709	996
Reading	55	19	52	40	47	46	70	74
Education	1 146	1 127	980	731	721	929	960	1 851
Tobacco Products and Smoking Supplies	339	405	361	264	350	303	438	282
Miscellaneous	679	128	330	372	784	918	636	964
Cash Contributions	854	378	392	717	621	826	876	1 370
Personal Insurance and Pensions	7 188	445	1 776	2 922	4 060	5 634	8 054	15 246
Life and other personal insurance	211	33	56	109	123	213	209	415
Pensions and Social Security	6 977	411	1 720	2 813	3 937	5 421	7 845	14 831

Table 11-21. Consumer Expenditures, Averages for Age Groups by Income Before Taxes: Reference Person 35 to 44 Years of Age, 2018–2019

(Number, dollar, percent.)

Item	Complete reporting of income							
	Total 25-34 years	Less than $15,000	$15,000 to $29,999	$30,000 to $39,999	$40,000 to $49,999	$50,000 to $69,999	$70,000 to $99,999	$100,000 or more
NUMBER OF CONSUMER UNITS (THOUSANDS)	22 165	1 407	1 870	1 878	1 683	3 226	4 092	8 009
CONSUMER UNIT CHARACTERISTICS								
Income Before Taxes	99 951	6 950	22 769	34 747	44 835	59 602	83 636	185 776
Income After Taxes	86 482	7 592	25 630	36 956	44 247	55 952	76 507	152 437
Age of Reference Person	39.5	39.3	39.2	39.4	39.4	39.5	39.4	39.6
Average Number in Consumer Unit								
All persons	3.4	2.5	2.8	3.2	3.2	3.1	3.5	3.7
Children under 18 years	1.4	1.1	1.2	1.4	1.4	1.2	1.5	1.6
Earners	1.7	0.7	1.2	1.4	1.5	1.6	1.8	2.0
Vehicles	2.0	1.0	1.3	1.5	1.6	1.8	2.1	2.5
Percent Distribution								
Male	49	36	42	37	44	49	52	54
Female	51	64	58	63	56	51	48	46
Percent Homeowner	59	28	33	38	36	55	62	80
With mortgage	48	14	15	22	25	44	54	72
Without mortgage	11	14	18	16	10	10	8	9
AVERAGE ANNUAL EXPENDITURES	73 326	31 620	33 674	41 382	46 235	54 945	72 160	110 748
Food	9 790	5 598	5 195	7 394	7 043	8 145	9 585	13 350
Food at home	5 442	3 793	3 409	4 505	4 131	4 664	5 489	6 924
Cereals and bakery products	695	461	436	586	505	551	729	896
Meats, poultry, fish, and eggs	1 178	884	782	993	1 005	1 021	1 295	1 398
Dairy products	553	394	353	402	363	457	553	731
Fruits and vegetables	997	614	611	819	786	903	947	1 289
Other food at home	2 018	1 441	1 226	1 705	1 473	1 733	1 965	2 611
Food away from home	4 348	1 805	1 786	2 888	2 912	3 480	4 095	6 426
Alcoholic Beverages	634	296	166	205	296	370	500	1 116
Housing	24 211	12 904	13 457	15 469	17 668	18 488	22 487	35 258
Shelter	14 373	7 707	7 886	9 169	10 541	11 239	13 227	20 932
Owned dwellings	7 998	2 250	1 563	2 101	2 660	4 902	6 724	14 914
Rented dwellings	5 563	5 317	6 246	6 862	7 518	5 943	5 899	4 407
Other lodging	811	141	77	206	363	393	604	1 611
Utilities, fuels, and public services	4 482	2 923	3 295	3 714	3 922	4 201	4 578	5 394
Household operations	2 309	652	703	774	973	1 161	1 744	4 365
Housekeeping supplies	810	602	470	546	713	648	770	1 072
Household furnishings and equipment	2 237	1 019	1 103	1 266	1 518	1 240	2 168	3 495
Apparel and Services	2 467	1 223	1 130	1 901	1 336	1 759	2 535	3 602
Transportation	13 025	6 240	6 992	7 742	7 922	9 925	15 310	18 012
Vehicle purchases (net outlay)	5 627	2 991	3 007	2 682	2 308	3 449	7 680	7 920
Gasoline and motor oil	2 601	1 431	1 810	2 045	2 308	2 377	2 762	3 192
Other vehicle expenses	3 953	1 575	1 992	2 730	2 899	3 562	4 147	5 394
Public and other transportation	843	243	184	286	408	537	721	1 506
Health Care	4 571	1 527	1 505	1 958	2 650	3 610	4 908	7 049
Health insurance	3 084	895	999	1 261	1 670	2 480	3 373	4 776
Medical services	990	290	287	390	605	745	1 004	1 591
Drugs	361	300	151	252	298	287	390	472
Medical supplies	136	42	68	56	77	98	141	210
Entertainment	3 616	1 552	1 115	1 343	1 855	2 524	3 411	5 954
Personal Care Products and Services	892	395	356	614	584	670	894	1 319
Reading	99	[1]73	19	[1]64	37	70	97	156
Education	1 183	415	260	411	744	805	977	2 064
Tobacco Products and Smoking Supplies	384	483	384	500	417	487	422	269
Miscellaneous	1 005	283	870	327	902	1 047	874	1 388
Cash Contributions	1 915	195	490	613	816	1 156	1 598	3 554
Personal Insurance and Pensions	9 534	437	1 736	2 841	3 965	5 889	8 562	17 658
Life and other personal insurance	459	[1]74	114	129	191	237	388	868
Pensions and Social Security	9 075	363	1 623	2 711	3 774	5 652	8 174	16 790

[1]Data are likely to have large sampling errors.

Table 11-22. Consumer Expenditures, Averages for Age Groups by Income Before Taxes: Reference Person 45 to 54 Years of Age, 2018–2019

(Number, dollar, percent.)

Item	Complete reporting of income							
	Total 45-54 years	Less than $15,000	$15,000 to $29,999	$30,000 to $39,999	$40,000 to $49,999	$50,000 to $69,999	$70,000 to $99,999	$100,000 or more
NUMBER OF CONSUMER UNITS (THOUSANDS)	22 666	2 007	1 933	1 437	1 498	2 721	3 706	9 365
CONSUMER UNIT CHARACTERISTICS								
Income Before Taxes	108 249	6 425	22 507	34 830	44 634	59 513	83 623	193 106
Income After Taxes	91 293	6 689	23 398	34 725	43 142	55 203	75 459	156 565
Age of Reference Person	49.6	49.7	49.7	49.7	49.5	49.5	49.7	49.6
Average Number in Consumer Unit								
All persons	2.9	1.9	2.3	2.4	2.6	2.7	2.9	3.3
Children under 18 years	0.7	0.4	0.6	0.7	0.6	0.7	0.7	0.8
Persons 65 years and over	0.1	(1)	0.1	(1)	0.1	(1)	0.1	(1)
Earners	1.8	0.5	1.0	1.3	1.5	1.7	1.9	2.3
Vehicles	2.2	0.9	1.2	1.5	1.8	2.0	2.3	3.0
Percent Distribution								
Male	47	35	38	39	44	47	48	52
Female	53	65	62	61	56	53	52	48
Percent Homeowner	69	33	37	48	49	60	74	89
With mortgage	52	18	15	30	35	42	61	73
Without mortgage	16	16	22	19	14	18	13	16
AVERAGE ANNUAL EXPENDITURES	76 724	26 688	31 791	39 440	43 953	53 062	68 238	117 702
Food	9 800	4 555	5 164	5 286	6 059	7 054	8 588	14 338
Food at home	5 394	3 086	3 294	3 335	3 812	4 215	4 909	7 371
Cereals and bakery products	690	447	432	389	459	546	599	951
Meats, poultry, fish, and eggs	1 153	644	703	794	929	912	992	1 566
Dairy products	532	305	289	359	375	407	494	728
Fruits and vegetables	1 019	546	659	560	695	858	885	1 406
Other food at home	1 999	1 144	1 211	1 233	1 355	1 491	1 940	2 720
Food away from home	4 406	1 469	1 870	1 951	2 246	2 839	3 679	6 967
Alcoholic Beverages	688	259	227	373	364	383	565	1 104
Housing	23 719	11 822	12 627	14 526	15 471	18 127	21 478	33 793
Shelter	13 927	6 967	7 812	8 526	9 248	10 782	12 575	19 707
Owned dwellings	8 943	1 889	2 148	3 239	3 430	4 944	7 889	15 192
Rented dwellings	3 819	4 909	5 520	5 090	5 640	5 280	4 101	2 212
Other lodging	1 166	169	144	197	178	559	585	2 303
Utilities, fuels, and public services	4 838	2 657	3 027	3 614	3 817	4 177	4 946	6 180
Household operations	1 535	499	659	740	758	986	1 096	2 515
Housekeeping supplies	920	832	402	524	597	649	857	1 269
Household furnishings and equipment	2 499	867	727	1 122	1 051	1 532	2 003	4 122
Apparel and Services	2 357	825	1 105	1 377	1 272	1 617	1 985	3 591
Transportation	12 783	3 991	4 832	7 369	8 004	9 659	12 785	18 809
Vehicle purchases (net outlay)	4 792	(2)990	1 240	2 736	2 719	3 350	5 155	7 261
Gasoline and motor oil	2 649	1 114	1 461	1 810	2 026	2 275	2 690	3 545
Other vehicle expenses	4 335	1 499	1 867	2 411	2 974	3 430	4 286	6 248
Public and other transportation	1 007	388	264	412	286	603	654	1 755
Health Care	5 240	1 494	2 238	2 806	3 494	3 779	5 589	7 596
Health insurance	3 557	971	1 378	1 861	2 299	2 595	3 964	5 140
Medical services	1 002	223	473	528	711	690	890	1 533
Drugs	480	254	280	336	392	375	493	628
Medical supplies	201	45	107	82	92	119	242	296
Entertainment	3 905	1 143	1 298	1 741	2 141	2 284	3 209	6 369
Personal Care Products and Services	976	291	418	521	619	731	907	1 451
Reading	92	(2)34	(2)40	(2)37	63	57	84	141
Education	2 754	225	226	437	521	1 219	1 533	5 459
Tobacco Products and Smoking Supplies	406	410	593	565	584	520	436	269
Miscellaneous	1 139	668	701	674	521	834	1 134	1 590
Cash Contributions	2 174	473	772	805	856	1 191	1 603	3 760
Personal Insurance and Pensions	10 691	500	1 549	2 924	3 984	5 608	8 341	19 433
Life and other personal insurance	639	130	168	169	249	340	469	1 133
Pensions and Social Security	10 053	370	1 381	2 755	3 734	5 268	7 873	18 300

[1]Value too small to display.
[2]Data are likely to have large sampling errors.

Table 11-23. Consumer Expenditures, Averages for Age Groups by Income Before Taxes: Reference Person 55 to 64 Years of Age, 2018–2019

(Number, dollar, percent.)

Item		Complete reporting of income						
	Total	Less than $15,000	$15,000 to $29,999	$30,000 to $39,999	$40,000 to $49,999	$50,000 to $69,999	$70,000 to $99,999	$100,000 or more
NUMBER OF CONSUMER UNITS (THOUSANDS)	24 523	3 451	3 207	1 896	1 778	2 836	3 422	7 932
CONSUMER UNIT CHARACTERISTICS								
Income Before Taxes	93 983	7 034	22 556	34 527	44 943	59 154	83 976	202 668
Income After Taxes	77 984	7 166	22 202	33 468	42 251	54 066	74 245	160 163
Age of Reference Person	59.5	59.8	60.0	59.9	59.8	59.6	59.4	59.0
Average Number in Consumer Unit								
All persons	2.2	1.5	1.8	2.0	2.0	2.1	2.3	2.7
Children under 18 years	0.2	0.1	0.2	0.2	0.2	0.2	0.2	0.2
Persons 65 years and over	0.1	0.1	0.1	0.1	0.2	0.1	0.1	0.1
Earners	1.4	0.3	0.7	1.0	1.2	1.4	1.7	2.1
Vehicles	2.2	1.1	1.5	1.8	1.9	2.2	2.5	3.1
Percent Distribution								
Male	49	42	42	44	43	47	51	57
Female	51	58	58	56	57	53	49	43
Percent Homeowner	75	48	56	67	67	81	87	92
With mortgage	43	17	24	27	40	44	55	61
Without mortgage	32	31	32	40	27	38	32	31
AVERAGE ANNUAL EXPENDITURES	68 214	28 308	34 574	41 059	46 340	53 986	65 454	116 746
Food	8 300	4 282	5 279	6 050	6 286	7 194	8 493	12 474
Food at home	4 923	3 058	3 729	4 048	3 913	4 535	5 126	6 644
Cereals and bakery products	611	406	516	480	478	608	603	802
Meats, poultry, fish, and eggs	1 058	703	825	966	895	965	1 133	1 349
Dairy products	475	310	337	384	348	449	489	651
Fruits and vegetables	920	504	608	769	688	866	958	1 302
Other food at home	1 859	1 136	1 443	1 450	1 505	1 646	1 943	2 541
Food away from home	3 376	1 224	1 549	2 002	2 373	2 660	3 366	5 829
Alcoholic Beverages	672	175	297	394	503	378	542	1 304
Housing	21 047	11 050	13 113	14 143	15 725	18 277	20 030	32 858
Shelter	11 980	6 405	7 449	7 413	8 910	9 149	11 155	19 385
Owned dwellings	8 151	2 854	3 425	3 777	4 459	6 176	8 209	14 920
Rented dwellings	2 631	3 209	3 751	3 232	4 026	2 359	2 093	1 799
Other lodging	1 198	342	273	403	425	615	854	2 666
Utilities, fuels, and public services	4 448	2 721	3 270	3 740	3 756	4 215	4 674	5 986
Household operations	1 248	516	633	770	709	888	1 178	2 210
Housekeeping supplies	857	489	649	677	717	651	893	1 224
Household furnishings and equipment	2 514	919	1 112	1 543	1 631	3 374	2 130	4 053
Apparel and Services	1 845	949	860	1 172	1 390	1 370	1 515	3 217
Transportation	11 266	4 544	6 258	7 460	8 965	9 362	10 510	18 644
Vehicle purchases (net outlay)	4 447	1 651	2 406	2 684	3 394	3 586	3 382	7 915
Gasoline and motor oil	2 241	1 095	1 258	1 736	1 961	2 197	2 519	3 216
Other vehicle expenses	3 710	1 580	2 232	2 781	2 939	3 165	3 862	5 756
Public and other transportation	867	219	361	258	670	415	748	1 758
Health Care	5 850	2 633	3 125	4 133	3 936	5 218	6 400	9 178
Health insurance	3 856	1 640	2 090	2 747	2 695	3 495	4 217	6 033
Medical services	1 210	555	543	780	740	960	1 301	2 024
Drugs	584	353	369	482	402	614	647	796
Medical supplies	200	85	123	124	98	148	235	325
Entertainment	3 865	1 659	1 602	1 994	2 265	2 644	4 038	6 912
Personal Care Products and Services	811	352	328	552	622	732	789	1 341
Reading	99	58	67	65	50	90	97	153
Education	1 757	160	230	350	266	374	989	4 569
Tobacco Products and Smoking Supplies	426	427	528	612	456	438	510	296
Miscellaneous	1 175	569	685	765	1 061	878	948	1 973
Cash Contributions	2 268	640	701	730	1 152	1 503	1 954	4 636
Personal Insurance and Pensions	8 832	809	1 500	2 638	3 664	5 528	8 639	19 191
Life and other personal insurance	724	183	400	444	367	476	679	1 345
Pensions and Social Security	8 108	625	1 100	2 194	3 297	5 053	7 959	17 846

Table 11-24. Consumer Expenditures, Averages for Age Groups by Income Before Taxes: Reference Person 65 Years of Age and Over, 2018–2019

(Number, dollar, percent.)

Item	Complete reporting of income							
	Total	Less than $15,000	$15,000 to $29,999	$30,000 to $39,999	$40,000 to $49,999	$50,000 to $69,999	$70,000 to $99,999	$100,000 or more
NUMBER OF CONSUMER UNITS (THOUSANDS)	33 764	4 983	9 694	4 915	3 211	3 918	3 215	3 828
CONSUMER UNIT CHARACTERISTICS								
Income Before Taxes	53 684	9 583	21 887	34 778	45 012	59 061	83 225	192 843
Income After Taxes	48 233	9 627	21 659	34 588	42 857	56 429	76 158	155 963
Age of Reference Person	74.5	76.4	76.5	74.3	73.4	73.2	72.4	71.2
Average Number in Consumer Unit								
All persons	1.8	1.3	1.4	1.8	1.9	2.1	2.2	2.4
Children under 18 years	0.1	(^{1})	(^{1})	0.1	(^{1})	0.1	0.1	0.1
Persons 65 years and over	1.4	1.1	1.2	1.5	1.6	1.6	1.6	1.6
Earners	0.5	0.1	0.2	0.3	0.5	0.8	1.1	1.4
Vehicles	1.7	0.9	1.3	1.9	2.0	2.2	2.3	2.6
Percent Distribution								
Male	45	32	37	48	48	51	56	63
Female	55	68	63	52	52	49	44	37
Percent Homeowner	80	55	75	86	87	88	90	92
With mortgage	24	12	17	23	28	28	39	41
Without mortgage	55	43	58	63	60	60	50	51
AVERAGE ANNUAL EXPENDITURES	50 637	25 941	34 169	45 709	52 525	56 833	66 707	106 249
Food	6 602	3 453	4 559	6 282	7 189	7 421	8 661	11 651
Food at home	4 036	2 402	3 010	4 007	4 278	4 682	5 015	6 257
Cereals and bakery products	524	308	393	539	534	640	671	756
Meats, poultry, fish, and eggs	841	493	617	816	850	989	1 004	1 398
Dairy products	416	241	316	415	438	482	531	630
Fruits and vegetables	800	494	604	769	845	882	977	1 288
Other food at home	1 455	866	1 079	1 468	1 611	1 689	1 832	2 186
Food away from home	2 566	1 051	1 550	2 275	2 911	2 738	3 645	5 394
Alcoholic Beverages	474	159	218	394	457	608	749	1 090
Housing	17 212	10 659	13 276	15 138	17 634	18 783	22 152	31 766
Shelter	9 562	6 461	7 680	7 983	9 174	10 005	12 181	18 068
Owned dwellings	6 077	2 721	4 167	5 221	6 382	6 890	8 867	12 946
Rented dwellings	2 578	3 442	3 170	2 034	1 820	2 097	1 979	2 283
Other lodging	908	299	343	728	972	1 019	1 335	2 839
Utilities, fuels, and public services	3 808	2 436	3 107	3 799	4 172	4 324	4 826	5 695
Household operations	1 390	641	945	1 202	1 545	1 509	1 834	3 099
Housekeeping supplies	790	412	545	806	940	983	1 012	1 182
Household furnishings and equipment	1 661	709	1 000	1 347	1 804	1 962	2 298	3 722
Apparel and Services	1 259	530	756	878	1 182	1 250	1 849	3 091
Transportation	7 486	3 180	4 819	7 449	7 281	10 079	9 721	15 493
Vehicle purchases (net outlay)	2 731	1 042	1 742	2 871	2 155	4 282	3 134	5 810
Gasoline and motor oil	1 412	675	939	1 505	1 584	1 837	1 986	2 388
Other vehicle expenses	2 654	1 175	1 782	2 617	3 061	3 290	3 688	4 946
Public and other transportation	689	289	357	457	482	671	913	2 348
Health Care	6 818	3 968	5 337	6 905	8 117	8 123	8 437	10 327
Health insurance	4 762	2 967	3 825	4 950	5 472	5 602	5 802	6 899
Medical services	1 027	521	689	810	1 399	1 243	1 354	2 014
Drugs	752	378	567	935	891	950	876	1 009
Medical supplies	277	103	256	210	355	329	405	404
Entertainment	2 663	1 172	1 603	3 249	2 895	2 659	3 345	5 529
Personal Care Products and Services	698	325	468	705	764	777	938	1 348
Reading	151	90	128	144	171	155	197	230
Education	362	258	186	127	367	258	474	1 237
Tobacco Products and Smoking Supplies	208	186	190	172	249	239	228	242
Miscellaneous	919	375	592	1 010	1 217	951	1 184	1 841
Cash Contributions	2 594	879	1 379	1 953	2 012	2 322	4 024	8 289
Personal Insurance and Pensions	3 192	705	658	1 303	2 990	3 208	4 749	14 115
Life and other personal insurance	518	232	296	458	560	584	857	1 141
Pensions and Social Security	2 674	473	362	845	2 430	2 624	3 892	12 973

^{1}Value too small to display.

CHAPTER 12: AMERICAN TIME USE SURVEY

HIGHLIGHTS

This chapter presents data from the American Time Use Survey (ATUS). The survey was introduced in the sixth edition of the *Handbook of U.S. Labor Statistics*. Its purpose is to collect data on the activities people do during the day and the amount of time they spend on each one.

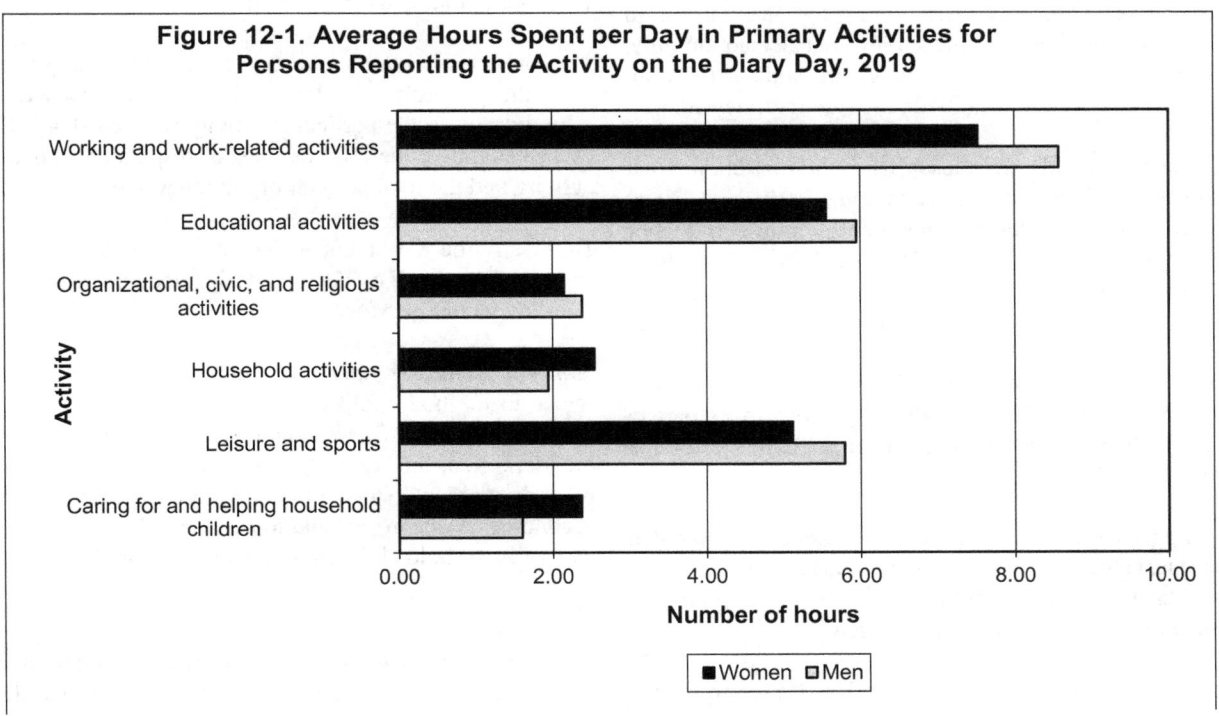

Figure 12-1. Average Hours Spent per Day in Primary Activities for Persons Reporting the Activity on the Diary Day, 2019

In 2019, on days that they worked, employed men worked 48 minutes more than employed women. Men also spent more time on leisure and sports; educational activities; and organizational, civic and religious activities. In contrast, women spent more time caring for and helping household members, purchasing goods and services, and household activities. (See Table 12-1.)

OTHER HIGHLIGHTS

- On an average day, 22 percent of men did housework—such as cleaning or laundry—compared with 46 percent of women. Over 48 percent of men did food preparation or cleanup, compared with 70 percent of women. Men were slightly more likely to engage in lawn and garden care than were women—10.3 percent, compared with 7.2 percent. (Table 12-1.)

- Hours spent in primary activities varied greatly by age. Persons aged 35 to 44 spent 3.99 hours in leisure activities compared with 7.67 hours for those 75 years and over. Specifically, individuals age 75 and over averaged about 44 minutes of reading per day whereas individuals age 20 to 24 years only read on average 6 minutes per day. (Table 12-2.)

- In 2019, on the days they worked, nearly 82 percent of employed persons did some or all of their work at their workplace and 24 percent did some or all of their work at home. Employed persons spent more time working at the workplace than at home—7.9 hours compared with 3.3 hours. Starting in March 2020, many employees began to work at home a due to stay-at-home orders instituted by states because of the global pandemic. (Table 12-5.)

- Multiple jobholders were nearly twice as likely to work on an average weekend day or holiday as were single jobholders—58 percent, compared with 31 percent. (Table 12-3.)

NOTES AND DEFINITIONS

Survey Methodology

While the Bureau of Labor Statistics (BLS) has long produced statistics about the labor market, including information about employment, hours, and earnings, the American Time Use Survey (ATUS) marks the first time that a federal statistical agency has produced estimates on how Americans spend another critical resource—their time. Data collection for the ATUS began in January 2003. Sample cases for the survey are selected monthly, and interviews are conducted continuously throughout the year. In 2019, approximately 9,400 individuals were interviewed.

ATUS sample households are chosen from the households that have completed their eighth (final) interview for the Current Population Survey (CPS), the nation's monthly household labor force survey. (See Chapter 1 of this *Handbook* for a description of the CPS.) ATUS sample households are selected to ensure that estimates will be representative of the nation.

An individual age 15 years or older is randomly chosen from each sample household. This "designated person" takes part in a one-time telephone interview about his or her activities on the previous day (the "diary day").

All ATUS interviews are conducted using Computer Assisted Telephone Interviewing. Procedures are in place to collect information from the small number of households that did not provide a telephone number during the CPS interview.

ATUS designated persons are preassigned a day of the week about which to report. Pre-assignment is designed to reduce variability in response rates across the week and to allow oversampling of weekend days so that accurate weekend day measures can be developed. Interviews occur on the day following the assigned day. For example, a person assigned to report about a Monday would be contacted on the following Tuesday. Ten percent of designated persons are assigned to report about each of the five weekdays. Twenty five percent are assigned to report about each weekend day. Households are called for up to 8 consecutive weeks (for example, 8 Tuesdays) in order to secure an interview.

Concepts and Definitions

Average day reflects an average distribution across all persons in the reference population and all days of the week. Average day measures for the entire population provide a mechanism for seeing the overall distribution of time allocation for society as a whole. The ATUS collects data about daily activities from all segments of the population age 15 and over, including persons who are employed and not employed. Many activities are not typically done on a daily basis, and some activities are only done by a subset of the population.

Average hours per day refers to time spent in a 24-hour day (between 4 a.m. on the diary day and 4 a.m. on the interview day) doing a specified activity.

Average hours per day, persons reporting the activity on the diary day is computed using responses only from those engaged in the particular activity on the diary day.

Average hours per day, population is computed using all responses from the sample population, including those from respondents who did not do the particular activity on their diary day. These estimates reflect the total number of respondents engaged in an activity and the total amount of time they spent on the activity.

Diary day the day about which the designated person reports. For example, the diary day of a designated person interviewed on Tuesday would be Monday.

Household children refers to children under 18 years of age who reside in the household of the ATUS respondent. The children may be related to the respondent (such as their own children, grandchildren, nieces, nephews, brothers, or sisters) or not related (such as foster children or children of roommates). For secondary childcare calculations, respondents are asked about care of household children under 13 years of age.

Earnings

Usual weekly earnings represent the earnings of full-time wage and salary workers before taxes and other deductions and include any overtime pay, commissions, or tips usually received (at the main job in the case of multiple jobholders). Usual weekly earnings are only updated in ATUS for about a third of employed respondents—if the respondent changed jobs or employment status or if the CPS weekly earnings value was imputed. This means that the earnings information could be out of date because the CPS interview was done 2 to 5 months prior to the ATUS interview. Respondents are asked to identify the easiest way for them to report earnings (hourly, weekly, biweekly, twice monthly, annually, or other) and how much they usually earn in the reported time period. Earnings reported on a basis other than weekly are converted to a weekly equivalent. The term "usual" is as perceived by the respondent. If the respondent asks for a definition of usual, interviewers are instructed to define the term as more than half the weeks worked during the past 4 or 5 months.

Weekly earnings ranges refers to The ranges used represent approximately 25 percent of full-time wage and salary workers. For example, 25 percent of full-time wage and salary workers with one job only had weekly earnings of $500 or less. These dollar values vary from year to year.

Employment Status

Employed persons are those who, at any time during the seven days prior to the interview: 1) did any work at all as paid employees, worked in their own business professions, or on their own farms, or usually worked 15 hours or more an unpaid workers in family-operated enterprises; and 2) all those who were not working but had jobs or businesses from which they were temporarily absent due to illness, bad weather, vacation, childcare problems, labor-management disputes, maternity or paternity leave, job training, or other family or personal reasons, whether or not they were paid for the time off or were seeking other jobs.

Employed full time workers are those who usually work 35 hours or more per week at all jobs combined.

Employed part time workers are those who usually work fewer than 35 hours per week at all jobs combined.

Not employed includes persons are not employed if they do not meet the conditions for employment. Not employed workers include those classified as unemployed as well as those classified as not in the labor force (using CPS definitions).

The numbers of employed and not employed persons in this report do not correspond to published totals from the CPS. While the information on employment from the ATUS is useful for assessing work in the context of other daily activities, the employment data are not intended for analysis of current employment trends. Compared to the CPS and other estimates of employment, the ATUS estimates are based on a much smaller sample and are only available with a substantial lag.

Major Activity Category Definitions

Caring for and helping household members refers to time spent doing activities to care for or help any child (under age 18) or adult in the household, regardless of relationship to the respondent or the physical or mental health status of the person being helped, is classified here. Caring for and helping activities for household children and adults are coded separately in subcategories.

Caring for and helping non-household members includes time spent caring for and helping any child or adult who is not part of the respondent's household, regardless of the relationship to the respondent or the physical or mental health status of the person being helped, is classified in this category.

Eating and drinking includes all time spent eating or drinking (except when identified by the respondent as part of a work or volunteer activity), whether alone, with others, at home, at a place of purchase, in transit, or somewhere else, is classified in this category.

Educational activities include taking classes (including Internet and other distance-learning courses), doing research and homework, and taking care of administrative tasks, such as registering for classes or obtaining a school ID. For high school students, before- and after-school extracurricular activities (except sports) also are classified as educational activities.

Household activities are those done by respondents to maintain their households. These include housework, cooking, yard care, pet care, vehicle maintenance and repair, and home maintenance, repair, decoration, and renovation. Food preparation is always classified as a household activity.

Leisure and sports includes sports, exercise, and recreation; socializing and communicating; and other leisure activities, such as watching television, reading or attending entertainment events.

Organizational, civic, and religious activities captures time spent volunteering for or through an organization, performing civic obligations, and participating in religious and spiritual activities.

Other activities, not elsewhere classified includes security procedures related to traveling, traveling not associated with a specific activity category, ambiguous activities that could not be coded, or missing activities that were considered too private to report.

Personal care activities consist of sleeping, bathing, dressing, health-related self-care, and personal or private activities. Receiving unpaid personal care from others (for example, "my sister put polish on my nails") is also captured in this category.

Primary activity is the main activity of a respondent at a specified time.

Purchasing goods and service includes the purchase of consumer goods as well as the purchase or use of professional and personal care services, household services, and government services. Most purchases and rentals of consumer goods, regardless of mode or place of purchase or rental are classified in this category.

Secondary activity is an activity done at the same time as a primary activity. With the exception of the care of children under age 13, information on secondary activities is not systematically collected in the ATUS.

Telephone calls, mail, and email captures telephone communication and handling household or personal mail and email. Telephone and Internet purchases are classified in purchasing goods and services.

Working and work-related activities refers to time spent working, doing activities as part of one's job, engaging in income-generating activities (not as part of one's job), and job search activities. "Working" includes hours spent doing the specific tasks required of one's main or other job, regardless of location or time of day. Travel time related to working and work-related activities includes time spent commuting to and from one's job, as well as time spent traveling for work-related activities, generating income, and job searching.

Sources of Additional Information

Additional information, including expanded definitions and estimation methodology, is available from BLS news release USDL 20-1275 "American Time Use Survey—2019 Results" which is available on the BLS Web site at <https://www.bls.gov/tus/>.

Table 12-1. Average Hours Per Day Spent in Primary Activities[1] for the Total Population and for Persons Reporting the Activity on the Diary Day, by Activity Category and Sex, 2018 and 2019 Annual Averages

(Hours, percent.)

Activity	Hours per day, total population			Percent of population reporting the activity on the diary day			Hours per day for persons reporting the activity on the diary day		
	Both sexes	Men	Women	Both sexes	Men	Women	Both sexes	Men	Women
2018									
All Activities[2]	24.00	24.00	24.00	X	X	X	X	X	X
Personal care activities	9.58	9.35	9.78	100.0	100.0	100.0	9.58	9.36	9.78
Sleeping	8.82	8.75	8.87	99.9	99.9	99.9	8.82	8.76	8.88
Eating and drinking	1.19	1.23	1.15	95.6	95.6	95.6	1.24	1.28	1.21
Household activities	1.78	1.36	2.17	76.7	68.5	84.4	2.32	1.99	2.57
Housework	0.55	0.24	0.83	34.8	20.2	48.5	1.57	1.20	1.71
Food preparation and cleanup	0.59	0.37	0.80	57.6	45.9	68.6	1.02	0.80	1.17
Lawn and garden care	0.18	0.25	0.11	8.8	11.0	6.8	2.02	2.28	1.61
Household management	0.14	0.12	0.16	19.1	15.6	22.4	0.73	0.75	0.71
Purchasing goods and services	0.72	0.61	0.82	43.6	40.2	46.9	1.65	1.52	1.76
Consumer goods purchases	0.33	0.25	0.41	39.7	36.6	42.7	0.84	0.69	0.96
Professional and personal care services	0.09	0.08	0.10	7.4	5.8	9.0	1.24	1.40	1.15
Caring for and helping household members	0.51	0.32	0.70	24.1	19.2	28.7	2.14	1.67	2.43
Caring for and helping household children	0.39	0.22	0.54	19.1	14.9	23.0	2.02	1.51	2.34
Caring for and helping non-household members	0.21	0.19	0.24	11.4	9.7	12.9	1.89	1.97	1.83
Caring for and helping non-household adults	0.07	0.08	0.07	7.2	6.4	8.0	1.00	1.24	0.82
Working and work-related activities	3.57	4.16	3.02	44.1	49.7	38.9	8.09	8.37	7.75
Working	3.23	3.75	2.75	42.5	47.6	37.6	7.61	7.87	7.30
Educational activities	0.46	0.49	0.43	7.9	7.9	7.8	5.83	6.20	5.47
Attending class	0.25	0.28	0.22	4.9	5.2	4.6	5.08	5.28	4.86
Homework and research	0.17	0.18	0.17	5.9	5.8	6.1	2.95	3.06	2.84
Organizational, civic, and religious activities	0.30	0.26	0.35	14.1	11.4	16.7	2.16	2.30	2.07
Religious and spiritual activities	0.14	0.11	0.17	9.8	7.5	11.9	1.44	1.47	1.42
Volunteering (organizational and civic activities)	0.13	0.12	0.14	5.7	5.1	6.3	2.25	2.29	2.21
Leisure and sports	5.27	5.69	4.87	95.6	96.2	94.9	5.51	5.91	5.13
Socializing and communicating	0.64	0.59	0.69	35.0	32.3	37.6	1.83	1.83	1.82
Watching television	2.84	3.09	2.61	78.4	79.1	77.7	3.63	3.91	3.36
Participating in sports, exercise, and recreation	0.29	0.36	0.23	19.1	21.1	17.2	1.51	1.68	1.31
Telephone calls, mail, and e-mail	0.15	0.09	0.20	19.2	14.8	23.4	0.76	0.62	0.84
Other activities n.e.c.	0.26	0.24	0.28	21.0	19.6	22.3	1.24	1.24	1.24
2019									
All Activities[2]	24.00	24.00	24.00	X	X	X	X	X	X
Personal care activities	9.62	9.41	9.83	100.0	100.0	100.0	9.62	9.41	9.83
Sleeping	8.84	8.76	8.91	100.0	100.0	99.9	8.84	8.76	8.92
Eating and drinking	1.18	1.19	1.17	95.8	96.2	95.5	1.23	1.24	1.23
Household activities	1.78	1.39	2.16	78.3	71.4	84.9	2.28	1.94	2.54
Housework	0.53	0.27	0.78	34.6	22.2	46.2	1.54	1.20	1.69
Food preparation and cleanup	0.60	0.39	0.79	59.7	48.3	70.3	1.00	0.81	1.13
Lawn and garden care	0.17	0.24	0.11	8.7	10.3	7.2	2.00	2.35	1.53
Household management	0.15	0.11	0.19	19.1	15.5	22.4	0.78	0.70	0.83
Purchasing goods and services	0.75	0.61	0.87	43.5	38.0	48.6	1.71	1.60	1.80
Consumer goods purchases	0.35	0.28	0.42	39.8	34.9	44.4	0.88	0.79	0.94
Professional and personal care services	0.09	0.06	0.12	7.8	5.9	9.7	1.14	0.96	1.24
Caring for and helping household members	0.49	0.32	0.65	23.7	19.9	27.3	2.06	1.60	2.37
Caring for and helping household children	0.37	0.23	0.49	19.0	15.4	22.5	1.92	1.49	2.20
Caring for and helping non-household members	0.19	0.16	0.21	10.5	8.7	12.3	1.78	1.83	1.74
Caring for and helping non-household adults	0.06	0.06	0.07	7.2	6.4	7.9	0.90	0.93	0.87
Working and work-related activities	3.61	4.36	2.91	44.6	50.8	38.7	8.11	8.58	7.53
Working	3.26	3.92	2.64	43.0	49.3	37.0	7.60	7.96	7.15
Educational activities	0.46	0.43	0.49	8.0	7.2	8.8	5.73	5.95	5.56
Attending class	0.24	0.23	0.24	4.4	4.0	4.7	5.39	5.61	5.21
Homework and research	0.19	0.17	0.21	6.1	5.0	7.2	3.13	3.51	2.88
Organizational, civic, and religious activities	0.30	0.25	0.35	13.4	10.4	16.3	2.24	2.38	2.15
Religious and spiritual activities	0.14	0.10	0.17	9.2	6.6	11.8	1.47	1.56	1.42
Volunteering (organizational and civic activities)	0.13	0.11	0.14	5.5	4.5	6.5	2.29	2.51	2.15
Leisure and sports	5.19	5.53	4.86	95.2	95.6	94.9	5.45	5.79	5.12
Socializing and communicating	0.64	0.62	0.66	34.8	32.5	37.0	1.83	1.90	1.78
Watching television	2.81	3.00	2.64	77.9	78.7	77.2	3.61	3.81	3.42
Participating in sports, exercise, and recreation	0.31	0.39	0.23	19.3	20.7	18.0	1.59	1.91	1.26
Telephone calls, mail, and e-mail	0.16	0.12	0.19	20.7	16.1	25.0	0.76	0.77	0.75
Other activities n.e.c.	0.28	0.23	0.31	20.4	17.3	23.3	1.35	1.35	1.34

Note: Data refer to respondents age 15 years and over, unless otherwise specified.

n.e.c. = Not elsewhere classified.

[1]A primary activity is designated by a respondent as his or her main activity. Other activities done simultaneously are not included.
[2]All major activity categories include related travel time.
X = Not applicable.

Table 12-2. Average Hours Per Day Spent in Primary Activities[1] for the Total Population, by Age, Sex, Race, Hispanic Origin, and Educational Attainment, 2019 Annual Averages

(Hours.)

Characteristic	Hours per day spent in primary activities[2]											
	Personal care activities	Eating and drinking	Household activities	Purchasing goods and services	Caring for and helping household members	Caring for and helping non-household members	Working and work-related activities	Educational activities	Organizational, civic, and religious activities	Leisure activities	Telephone calls, mail, and e-mail	Other activities n.e.c.
Both Sexes, 15 Years and Over	9.62	1.18	1.78	0.75	0.49	0.19	3.61	0.46	0.30	5.19	0.16	0.28
15 to 19 years	10.60	1.06	0.84	0.49	0.06	0.08	1.24	3.48	0.21	5.34	0.26	0.34
20 to 24 years	10.08	1.13	1.02	0.72	0.17	0.15	4.16	1.24	0.09	4.91	0.10	0.22
25 to 34 years	9.61	1.14	1.52	0.59	1.00	0.11	4.85	0.36	0.19	4.28	0.10	0.25
35 to 44 years	9.27	1.12	1.85	0.74	1.14	0.12	5.04	0.08	0.25	3.99	0.12	0.28
45 to 54 years	9.39	1.19	1.76	0.83	0.43	0.13	5.21	0.04	0.27	4.38	0.12	0.26
55 to 64 years	9.42	1.20	2.12	0.75	0.18	0.34	3.80	0.01	0.35	5.45	0.15	0.24
65 to 74 years	9.54	1.28	2.38	0.98	0.15	0.35	1.10	0.01	0.57	7.10	0.24	0.28
75 years and over	9.88	1.35	2.40	0.85	0.10	0.21	0.37	*	0.50	7.67	0.26	0.40
Men, 15 Years and Over	9.41	1.19	1.39	0.61	0.32	0.16	4.36	0.43	0.25	5.53	0.12	0.23
15 to 19 years	10.44	0.99	0.66	0.21	0.04	0.09	1.87	3.06	0.17	5.87	*	*
20 to 24 years	9.91	1.22	0.91	0.56	0.05	0.08	4.18	1.09	*	5.75	0.04	0.17
25 to 34 years	9.29	1.12	1.11	0.45	0.53	0.10	5.76	0.39	0.18	4.77	0.09	0.21
35 to 44 years	8.98	1.12	1.31	0.58	0.75	0.14	6.31	0.07	0.21	4.24	0.08	0.20
45 to 54 years	9.22	1.20	1.40	0.71	0.38	0.10	5.91	*	0.24	4.51	0.09	0.23
55 to 64 years	9.14	1.24	1.80	0.68	0.16	0.25	4.52	*	0.28	5.62	0.11	0.21
65 to 74 years	9.42	1.29	1.83	0.81	0.07	0.33	1.53	*	0.52	7.73	0.18	0.28
75 years and over	9.84	1.42	1.99	0.88	0.11	0.15	0.53	*	0.37	8.15	0.20	0.36
Women, 15 Years and Over	9.83	1.17	2.16	0.87	0.65	0.21	2.91	0.49	0.35	4.86	0.19	0.31
15 to 19 years	10.77	1.14	1.03	0.78	0.07	0.07	0.60	3.90	0.25	4.79	0.19	0.39
20 to 24 years	10.25	1.04	1.12	0.89	0.30	*	4.15	1.38	0.14	4.07	0.17	0.27
25 to 34 years	9.94	1.16	1.93	0.73	1.47	0.11	3.94	0.34	0.20	3.78	0.11	0.28
35 to 44 years	9.55	1.11	2.36	0.89	1.53	0.10	3.82	0.09	0.29	3.75	0.16	0.35
45 to 54 years	9.55	1.18	2.12	0.94	0.47	0.15	4.53	0.07	0.30	4.26	0.15	0.28
55 to 64 years	9.68	1.16	2.41	0.81	0.20	0.42	3.14	*	0.41	5.29	0.19	0.27
65 to 74 years	9.65	1.28	2.86	1.13	0.23	0.36	0.72	*	0.62	6.56	0.30	0.28
75 years and over	9.91	1.30	2.70	0.83	0.08	0.26	0.26	*	0.60	7.32	0.31	0.43
White, 15 Years and Over	9.56	1.22	1.87	0.76	0.48	0.19	3.62	0.38	0.30	5.20	0.14	0.28
Men	9.36	1.23	1.45	0.63	0.32	0.16	4.40	0.35	0.24	5.51	0.11	0.24
Women	9.76	1.21	2.26	0.88	0.64	0.22	2.88	0.42	0.35	4.91	0.17	0.31
Black, 15 Years and Over	9.98	0.88	1.33	0.69	0.45	0.18	3.56	0.61	0.37	5.49	0.22	0.23
Men	9.68	0.91	1.03	0.57	0.24	0.16	3.93	0.77	0.32	6.03	0.15	0.20
Women	10.24	0.86	1.60	0.79	0.63	0.20	3.24	0.47	0.41	5.02	0.28	0.26
Asian, 15 Years and Over	9.64	1.38	1.54	0.75	0.71	0.12	3.79	1.31	0.20	3.99	0.25	0.33
Men	9.69	1.33	1.09	0.56	0.52	0.13	4.63	1.07	0.09	4.36	*	0.19
Women	9.59	1.43	1.98	0.93	0.90	0.11	2.95	*	0.31	3.63	0.17	*
Hispanic,[3] 15 Years and Over	9.94	1.16	1.74	0.75	0.56	0.11	3.90	0.51	0.35	4.59	0.11	0.27
Men	9.69	1.16	1.08	0.71	0.31	0.08	4.94	0.47	0.30	4.94	0.09	0.22
Women	10.19	1.16	2.41	0.80	0.81	0.13	2.86	0.55	0.39	4.25	0.13	0.32
Marital Status and Sex												
Married, spouse present	9.37	1.27	2.07	0.80	0.74	0.19	3.91	0.06	0.37	4.81	0.12	0.28
Men	9.10	1.29	1.62	0.70	0.51	0.17	4.79	0.06	0.34	5.12	0.09	0.22
Women	9.64	1.25	2.55	0.90	0.98	0.21	3.00	0.07	0.40	4.49	0.16	0.34
Other marital statuses	9.88	1.09	1.49	0.69	0.23	0.18	3.31	0.86	0.23	5.57	0.19	0.27
Men	9.75	1.07	1.13	0.51	0.11	0.14	3.87	0.85	0.15	6.00	0.16	0.25
Women	10.00	1.10	1.79	0.85	0.33	0.21	2.83	0.88	0.30	5.21	0.22	0.29
Educational Attainment, 25 Years and Over												
Less than a high school diploma	10.05	1.07	1.99	0.60	0.42	0.15	2.98	*	0.39	5.98	0.11	0.24
High school graduate, no college[4]	9.62	1.13	2.03	0.71	0.47	0.24	3.38	*	0.29	5.73	0.13	0.24
Some college or associate degree	9.47	1.15	1.97	0.72	0.57	0.21	3.72	0.18	0.30	5.29	0.14	0.28
Bachelor's degree and higher[5]	9.27	1.31	1.86	0.89	0.65	0.17	4.31	0.12	0.36	4.56	0.19	0.31
Some college or associate degree	9.33	1.24	1.90	0.91	0.61	0.19	4.27	0.14	0.30	4.63	0.19	0.28
Bachelor's degree and higher	9.18	1.40	1.81	0.86	0.71	0.16	4.38	0.10	0.44	4.44	0.19	0.34

Note: 0.00 = Estimates are approximately zero.

[1]A primary activity is designated by a respondent as his or her main activity. Other activities done simultaneously are not included.
[2]All major activity categories include related travel time.
[3]May be of any race.
[4]Includes persons with a high school diploma or equivalent.
[5]Includes persons with bachelor's, master's, professional, and doctoral degrees.
* = Figure does not meet standards of reliability or quality.

Table 12-3. Average Hours Worked Per Day by Employed Persons on Weekdays and Weekends, by Selected Characteristics, 2019 Annual Averages

(Number, percent.)

Characteristic	Total employed (thousands)	Employed persons who worked on an average day			Employed persons who worked on an average weekday			Employed persons who worked on an average Saturday, Sunday, or holiday[1]		
		Number (thousands)	Percent of employed	Hours per day[2]	Number[3] (thousands)	Percent of employed	Hours per day[2]	Number[4] (thousands)	Percent of employed	Hours per day[2]
Both Sexes[5]	166 302	112 700	67.8	7.62	137 205	82.5	8.00	55 476	33.4	5.42
Full-time worker	129 758	92 422	71.2	8.08	113 286	87.3	8.50	43 569	33.6	5.53
Part-time worker	36 544	20 278	55.5	5.48	23 896	65.4	5.58	11 910	32.6	5.01
Men[5]	88 481	62 714	70.9	7.97	75 678	85.5	8.36	31 628	35.7	5.74
Full-time worker	75 124	55 194	73.5	8.32	66 654	88.7	8.74	27 368	36.4	5.87
Part-time worker	13 357	7 520	56.3	5.38	8 964	67.1	5.48	4 289	32.1	4.96
Women[5]	77 821	49 987	64.2	7.17	61 482	79.0	7.54	23 929	30.7	5.00
Full-time worker	54 634	37 228	68.1	7.73	46 605	85.3	8.16	16 325	29.9	4.99
Part-time worker	23 187	12 759	55.0	5.54	14 936	64.4	5.65	7 623	32.9	5.04
Multiple Job Holding Status										
Single job holder	149 821	99 423	66.4	7.59	122 459	81.7	7.94	46 392	31.0	5.42
Multiple job holder	16 481	13 277	80.6	7.84	14 698	89.2	8.43	9 483	57.5	5.38
Educational Attainment, 25 Years and Over										
Less than a high school diploma	10 339	6 832	66.1	8.07	8 503	82.2	8.12	2 950	28.5	7.74
High school graduate, no college[6]	36 458	24 095	66.1	8.11	29 360	80.5	8.43	11 370	31.2	6.12
Some college or associate degree	34 223	22 597	66.0	7.82	27 625	80.7	8.14	10 555	30.8	5.79
Bachelor's degree or higher[7]	63 210	45 069	71.3	7.36	55 153	87.3	7.91	21 501	34.0	4.04

Note: Data refer to persons age 15 years and over, unless otherwise specified.

[1]Holidays are New Year's Day, Easter, Memorial Day, the Fourth of July, Labor Day, Thanksgiving Day, and Christmas Day.
[2]Includes work at main and other job(s) and excludes travel related to work.
[3]Number was derived by multiplying the "total employed" by the percentage of employed persons who worked on an average weekday.
[4]Number was derived by multiplying the "total employed" by the percentage of employed persons who worked on an average Saturday, Sunday, or holiday.
[5]Includes workers whose hours vary.
[6]Includes persons with a high school diploma or equivalent.
[7]Includes persons with bachelor's, master's, professional, and doctoral degrees.

Table 12-4. Average Hours Worked Per Day at Main Job Only by Employed Persons on Weekdays and Weekend Days, by Selected Characteristics, 2019 Annual Averages

(Number, percent.)

Characteristic	Total employed (thousands)	Worked on an average day			Worked on an average weekday			Worked on an average Saturday, Sunday, or holiday[1]		
		Number (thousands)	Percent	Hours per day[2]	Number[3] (thousands)	Percent	Hours per day[2]	Number[4] (thousands)	Percent	Hours per day[2]
Class of Worker										
Wage and salary workers	155 419	103 942	66.9	7.61	128 023	82.4	7.96	47 890	30.8	5.37
Self-employed workers[5]	10 785	7 022	65.1	6.57	8 161	75.7	6.89	4 147	38.5	4.98
Occupation										
Management, business, and financial operations	28 036	20 329	72.5	7.80	25 974	92.6	8.35	7 734	27.6	3.69
Professional and related	43 322	29 382	67.8	7.14	36 418	84.1	7.63	12 601	29.1	3.75
Services	27 886	17 143	61.5	7.48	19 825	71.1	7.65	10 866	39.0	6.74
Sales and related	13 725	9 244	67.4	7.14	10 758	78.4	7.44	5 904	43.0	5.93
Office and administrative support	18 566	12 209	65.8	7.25	15 584	83.9	7.46	4 207	22.7	5.45
Farming, fishing, and forestry	1 485	*	*	7.90	*	*	8.64	*	*	6.54
Construction and extraction	9 234	6 139	66.5	7.89	7 755	84.0	8.17	2 499	27.1	5.91
Installation, maintenance, and repair	5 229	*	*	8.57	*	*	8.66	*	*	7.92
Production	8 790	5 845	66.5	8.33	7 266	82.7	8.62	2 390	27.2	6.18
Transportation and material moving	10 029	6 560	65.4	8.15	7 999	79.8	8.35	3 246	32.4	7.00
Earnings of Full-Time Wage and Salary Earners[6]										
$0 to $630	26 965	18 168	67.4	7.85	21 995	81.6	8.04	9 739	36.1	6.93
$631 to $960	26 993	18 656	69.1	8.25	23 710	87.8	8.53	7 392	27.4	6.29
$961 to $1,530	26 595	17 768	66.8	8.09	23 080	86.8	8.56	6 512	24.5	4.56
$1,531 and higher	26 498	19 545	73.8	8.11	23 883	90.1	8.75	8 234	31.1	3.26

Note: Data refer to persons age 15 years and over, unless otherwise specified.

[1]Holidays are New Year's Day, Easter, Memorial Day, the Fourth of July, Labor Day, Thanksgiving Day, and Christmas Day.
[2]Includes work at main job only and excludes travel related to work.
[3]Number was derived by multiplying the "total employed" by the percentage of employed persons who worked on an average weekday.
[4]Number was derived by multiplying the "total employed" by the percentage of employed persons who worked on an average Saturday, Sunday, or holiday.
[5]Includes self-employed workers whose businesses are unincorporated. Self-employed workers whose businesses are incorporated are classified as wage and salary workers.
[6]These values are based on usual weekly earnings. Each earnings range represents approximately 25 percent of full-time wage and salary workers who held only one job.
* = Figure does not meet standards for reliability or quality.

Table 12-5. Average Hours Worked Per Day at All Jobs by Employed Persons at Workplaces or at Home, by Selected Characteristics, 2019 Annual Averages

(Number, percent.)

Characteristic	Total employed (thousands)	Employed persons who reported working on an average day[1]								
		Number (thousands)	Percent	Average hours of work	Location of work[2]					
					Persons who reported working at their workplaces on an average day			Persons who reported working at home on an average day[3]		
					Number (thousands)	Percent	Average hours of work at workplace	Number (thousands)	Percent	Average hours of work at home
Full- and Part-Time Status and Sex										
Both sexes[4]	166 302	112 700	67.8	7.62	92 274	81.9	7.86	26 730	23.7	3.27
Full-time worker	129 758	92 422	71.2	8.08	76 840	83.1	8.28	21 996	23.8	3.40
Part-time worker	36 544	20 278	55.5	5.48	15 434	76.1	5.80	4 734	23.3	2.64
Men[4]	88 481	62 714	70.9	7.97	53 215	84.9	8.20	13 657	21.8	3.01
Full-time worker	75 124	55 194	73.5	8.32	47 265	85.6	8.50	12 120	22.0	3.08
Part-time worker	13 357	7 520	56.3	5.38	5 950	79.1	5.80	1 537	20.4	2.51
Women[4]	77 821	49 987	64.2	7.17	39 058	78.1	7.40	13 073	26.2	3.53
Full-time worker	54 634	37 228	68.1	7.73	29 575	79.4	7.92	9 876	26.5	3.80
Part-time worker	23 187	12 759	55.0	5.54	9 483	74.3	5.80	3 197	25.1	2.70
Multiple Job Holding Status										
Single job holder	149 821	99 423	66.4	7.59	82 444	82.9	7.89	21 753	21.9	3.30
Multiple job holder	16 481	13 277	80.6	7.84	9 829	74.0	7.64	4 976	37.5	3.14
Educational Attainment, 25 Years and Over										
Less than a high school diploma	10 339	6 832	66.1	8.07	6 105	89.4	8.04	687	10.1	*
High school graduate, no college[5]	36 458	24 095	66.1	8.11	21 490	89.2	8.18	3 744	15.5	2.65
Some college or associate degree	34 223	22 597	66.0	7.82	18 481	81.8	8.14	4 393	19.4	3.90
Bachelor's degree or higher[6]	63 210	45 069	71.3	7.36	33 249	73.8	7.82	16 761	37.2	3.29
Bachelor's degree only	36 985	25 713	69.5	7.57	19 507	75.9	7.95	8 728	33.9	3.52
Advanced degree	26 225	19 357	73.8	7.08	13 742	71.0	7.64	8 033	41.5	3.04

Note: Data refer to persons age 15 years and over, unless otherwise specified.

[1]Includes work at main and other job(s) and excludes travel related to work.
[2]Respondents may have worked at more than one location.
[3]"Working at home" includes any time the respondent reported doing activities that were identified as "part of one's job"; this category is not restricted to persons whose usual workplace is their home.
[4]Includes workers whose hours vary.
[5]Includes persons with a high school diploma or equivalent.
[6]Includes persons with bachelor's, master's, professional, and doctoral degrees.
* = Figure does not meet standards for reliability or quality.

Table 12-6. Average Hours Worked Per Day at Main Job Only by Employed Persons at Workplaces or at Home, by Selected Characteristics, 2019 Annual Averages

(Number, percent.)

Characteristic	Total employed (thousands)	Employed persons who reported working on an average day[1]			Location of work[2]					
		Number (thousands)	Percent	Hours of work	Persons who reported working at their workplaces on an average day			Persons who reported working at home on an average day[3]		
					Number (thousands)	Percent	Hours of work at workplace	Number (thousands)	Percent	Hours of work at home
Class of Worker										
Wage and salary worker	155 419	103 942	66.9	7.61	87 517	84.2	7.85	21 343	20.5	3.21
Self-employed worker[3]	10 785	7 022	65.1	6.57	3 483	49.6	7.20	3 698	52.7	4.06
Occupation[4]										
Management, business, and financial operations	28 036	20 329	72.5	7.80	14 964	73.6	8.19	7 455	36.7	4.13
Professional and related	43 322	29 382	67.8	7.14	21 954	74.7	7.63	9 612	32.7	3.11
Services	27 886	17 143	61.5	7.48	14 747	86.0	7.60	2 706	15.8	2.16
Sales and related	13 725	9 244	67.4	7.14	7 537	81.5	7.25	2 208	23.9	3.77
Office and administrative support	18 566	12 209	65.8	7.25	10 775	88.3	7.50	1 607	13.2	3.38
Farming, fishing, and forestry	1 485	*	*	7.90	*	*	8.10	*	*	*
Construction and extraction	9 234	6 139	66.5	7.89	5 653	92.1	8.11	699	11.4	2.43
Installation, maintenance, and repair	5 229	*	*	*	3 133	95.6	8.86	114	3.5	*
Production	8 790	5 845	66.5	8.33	5 521	94.5	8.37	401	6.9	2.61
Transportation and material moving	10 029	6 560	65.4	8.15	5 889	89.8	8.07	231	3.5	*
Earnings of Full-Time Wage and Salary Earners[5]										
$0 to $650	26 965	18 168	67.4	7.85	16 832	92.6	7.94	1 727	9.5	2.60
$651 to $1,000	26 993	18 656	69.1	8.25	16 702	89.5	8.52	2 236	12.0	2.98
1,001 to $1,620	26 595	17 768	66.8	8.09	15 124	85.1	8.44	3 716	20.9	2.67
$1,621 and higher	26 498	19 545	73.8	8.11	15 247	78.0	8.47	6 733	34.4	3.62

Note: Data refer to persons age 15 years and over, unless otherwise specified.

[1]Individuals may have worked at more than one location.
[2]Working at home includes any time persons did work at home and is not restricted to persons whose usual workplace is their home.
[3]Includes self-employed workers whose businesses are unincorporated. Self-employed workers whose businesses are incorporated are classified as wage and salary workers.
[4]These values were generated using the 2010 Census occupational classification system which was introduced with the 2011 estimates. Estimates are not strictly comparable to those from earlier years.
[5]These values are based on usual weekly earnings. Each earnings range covers approximately 25 percent of full-time wage and salary workers.
* = Figure does not meet standards for reliability or quality.

Table 12-7. Average Hours Per Day Spent by Persons Age 18 Years and Over Caring for Household Children Under 18 Years, by Sex of Respondent, Age of Youngest Household Child, and Day, 2015–2019 Combined Annual Averages

(Number.)

Activity	Hours per day caring for household children								
	Total			Weekdays			Weekends and holidays		
	Both sexes	Men	Women	Both sexes	Men	Women	Both sexes	Men	Women
Persons in Households with Children Under 18 Years									
Caring for household children as a primary activity	1.38	0.90	1.78	1.44	0.87	1.92	1.23	0.96	1.45
Physical care	0.44	0.24	0.60	0.45	0.23	0.64	0.39	0.24	0.52
Education-related activities	0.10	0.06	0.14	0.13	0.07	0.17	0.04	0.03	0.05
Reading to/with children	0.04	0.03	0.05	0.04	0.03	0.05	0.03	0.02	0.04
Talking to/with children	0.05	0.03	0.07	0.06	0.04	0.08	0.03	0.02	0.04
Playing/doing hobbies with children	0.29	0.25	0.31	0.25	0.21	0.29	0.37	0.35	0.38
Looking after children	0.09	0.06	0.11	0.08	0.04	0.10	0.12	0.09	0.15
Attending children's events	0.06	0.05	0.07	0.05	0.04	0.06	0.09	0.08	0.09
Travel related to care of household children	0.19	0.12	0.24	0.23	0.14	0.30	0.09	0.08	0.10
Other childcare activities	0.13	0.06	0.18	0.15	0.07	0.22	0.06	0.05	0.07
Persons in Households with Youngest Child 6 to 17 Years									
Caring for household children as a primary activity	0.80	0.53	1.03	0.87	0.54	1.16	0.64	0.52	0.73
Physical care	0.15	0.08	0.21	0.17	0.09	0.24	0.11	0.07	0.15
Education-related activities	0.11	0.06	0.15	0.13	0.07	0.19	0.05	0.04	0.06
Reading to/with children	0.02	0.01	0.02	0.02	0.01	0.02	0.01	0.01	0.02
Talking to/with children	0.06	0.04	0.08	0.07	0.04	0.09	0.04	0.02	0.06
Playing/doing hobbies with children	0.06	0.07	0.06	0.05	0.05	0.05	0.09	0.11	0.08
Looking after children	0.05	0.03	0.06	0.05	0.03	0.06	0.06	0.04	0.08
Attending children's events	0.08	0.07	0.09	0.06	0.05	0.07	0.12	0.12	0.12
Travel related to care of household children	0.17	0.11	0.22	0.20	0.13	0.26	0.09	0.07	0.11
Other childcare activities	0.10	0.05	0.15	0.13	0.06	0.18	0.05	0.04	0.07
Persons in Households with Youngest Child Under 6 Years									
Caring for household children as a primary activity	2.16	1.42	2.74	2.23	1.37	2.90	1.99	1.54	2.36
Physical care	0.82	0.45	1.11	0.85	0.45	1.16	0.75	0.46	1.00
Education-related activities	0.09	0.05	0.12	0.12	0.06	0.16	0.03	0.02	0.03
Reading to/with children	0.07	0.05	0.09	0.08	0.05	0.09	0.06	0.05	0.07
Talking to/with children	0.04	0.03	0.05	0.04	0.03	0.05	0.03	0.02	0.03
Playing/doing hobbies with children	0.59	0.52	0.65	0.53	0.44	0.60	0.72	0.67	0.76
Looking after children	0.14	0.09	0.18	0.12	0.07	0.16	0.19	0.14	0.23
Attending children's events	0.04	0.03	0.05	0.04	0.03	0.05	0.04	0.04	0.05
Travel related to care of household children	0.21	0.13	0.28	0.27	0.15	0.36	0.09	0.09	0.10
Other childcare activities	0.16	0.08	0.22	0.19	0.09	0.27	0.07	0.05	0.08

Note: Universe includes respondents age 18 years and over living in households with children under 18 years of age, whether or not they provided childcare.

CHAPTER 13: INCOME IN THE UNITED STATES (CENSUS BUREAU)

This chapter presents data on income and earnings in the United States collected by the Census Bureau. Income, as distinguished from earnings, includes income from pensions, investments, and other sources and is measured as real income in 2019 dollars.

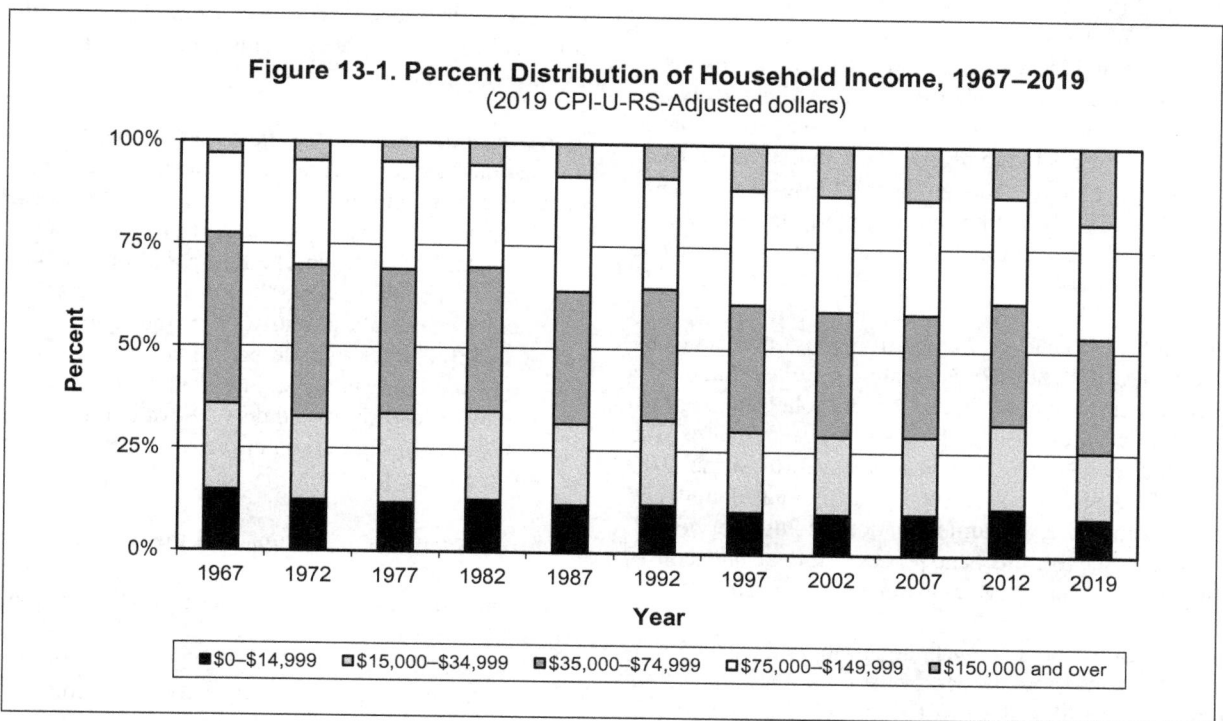

Figure 13-1. Percent Distribution of Household Income, 1967–2019
(2019 CPI-U-RS-Adjusted dollars)

In 2019, 18.6 percent of households had an income above $150,000 and 10.3 had an income over $200,000—the highest it has ever been and an increase from 8.8 percent in 2019. Meanwhile, the number of households making $25,000 or less decreased from 18.9 percent to 17.1 percent. (See Table 13-2.)

OTHER HIGHLIGHTS:

- Median income varied by race and ethnic origin. In 2019, Asians had the highest median income at $98,174 followed non-Hispanic Whites ($76,057), Hispanics ($56,113), and Blacks ($45,438). (See Table 13-1.)

- Real median income increased in all four regions listed on Table 13-1. The West experienced the highest increase at 7.0 percent, followed by the Northeast at 6.8 percent, the South at 6.1 percent and the Midwest at 4.8 percent. (See Table 13-1.)

- Median household income increased in 2019 to $68,703. It has increased each year since 2015 after decreasing every year from 2008 to 2012. It varied significantly by state. Median household income was the highest in Maryland ($95,572) followed by the District of Columbia ($93,111) and Hawaii ($88,006). (See Table 13-5.)

- Mississippi continued to have the lowest family income at $58,503 in 2019 followed by West Virginia at $60,920. The District of Columbia had the highest median family income at $130,291 followed by Massachusetts ($108,348) and New Jersey ($105,705). (See Table 13-7.)

NOTES AND DEFINITIONS

Collection and Coverage

The data in Tables 13-1 through 13-5 are from the Annual Social and Economic Supplement (ASEC) to the Current Population Survey (CPS). The CPS ASEC provides timely estimates of household income and individual earnings, as well as the distribution of that income. The population represented is the civilian noninstitutionalized population living in the United States. Members of the Armed Forces living off post or with their families on post are included if at least one civilian adult lives in the household, hence, the CPS ASEC universe is slightly larger than the CPS universe which does not include persons who are on active duty in the armed forces.

The data in Tables 13-6 and 13-7 come from the American Community Survey (ACS). The ACS is an annual survey that covers the same type of information that had been collected every 10 years from the decennial census long form questionnaire. The ACS eliminated the need for a separate long form in the 2010 Census. The CPS ASEC and ACS surveys differ in the length and detail of its questionnaire, the number of households interviewed, the methodology used to collect and process the data, and, consequently, in the income and poverty estimates produced.

The sample size of the ACS is much larger (approximately 3 million compared with the sample size of the CPS ASEC 100,000). Although it is smaller, the CPS ASEC is a high quality source of information due to its detailed questionnaire and experienced interviewing staff. Another notable difference between the two surveys is that the ACS is a mandatory whereas the CPS ASEC is voluntary.

Concepts and Definitions

The *Gini index of income inequality* (also known as the Gini ratio, Gini coefficient, or index of income concentration) is a statistical measure that summarizes the dispersion of income across an entire income distribution. Values range from 0 to 1. A Gini value of 1 indicates "perfect" inequality; that is, one household has all the income and the rest have none. A value of zero indicates "perfect" equality, a situation in which all households have equal income.

Equivalence-adjusted income inequality is another way to measure income inequality. Equivalence adjusted income takes into consideration the number of people living in the household and how these people share resources and take advantage of economies of scale. For example, the household-income-based distribution treats income of $30,000 for a single-person household and a family household similarly, while the equivalence-adjusted income of $30,000 for a single-person household would be more than twice the equivalence-adjusted income of $30,000 for a family household with two adults and two children. The equivalence adjustment used here is based on a three-parameter scale that reflects:

1. On average, children consume less than adults.

2. As family size increases, expenses do not increase at the same rate

3. The increase in expenses is larger for a first child of a single-parent family than the first child of a two-adult family.

Additional Information

Additional information is available in the Census publication "Income and Poverty in the United States: 2019 *Current Population Reports*, p60-270 (U.S. Census Bureau, September 2019)

Table 13-1. Income and Earnings Summary Measures, by Selected Characteristics, 2018 and 2019

(Numbers in thousands, dollars, percent; income in 2019 dollars.)

Characteristic	2018			2019			Percent change in real median income (2019 less 2018)	
	Number	Median income (dollars)		Number	Median income (dollars)		Estimate	Margin of error [1] (+/-)
		Estimate	Margin of error [1] (+/-)		Estimate	Margin of error [1] (+/-)		
ALL HOUSEHOLDS	128 579	64 324	704	128 451	68 703	904	6.8	1.55
Type of Households								
Family households	83 482	82 124	676	83 677	88 149	1 113	7.3	1.47
Married-couple	61 959	95 351	1 145	62 342	102 308	1 022	7.3	1.53
Female householder, no husband present	15 043	45 946	1 136	14 832	48 098	985	4.7	2.92
Male householder, no wife present	6 480	62 632	1 269	6 503	69 244	2 988	10.6	5.05
Nonfamily households	45 096	38 813	840	44 774	41 232	466	6.2	2.28
Female householder	23 515	32 587	679	23 470	34 612	851	6.2	3.05
Male householder	21 582	46 583	884	21 304	48 496	1 252	4.1	3.13
Race[2]and Hispanic Origin of Householder								
White	100 528	68 156	657	100 568	72 204	800	5.9	1.25
White, not Hispanic	84 727	71 922	664	84 868	76 057	876	5.7	1.25
Black	17 167	42 110	922	17 054	45 438	1 212	7.9	3.51
Asian	6 981	88 774	2 856	6 853	98 174	3 068	10.6	5.24
Hispanic (any race)	17 758	52 382	748	17 667	56 113	1 173	7.1	2.30
Age of Householder								
Under 65 years	94 423	72 958	584	93 524	77 873	1 151	6.7	1.58
15 to 24 years	6 199	44 320	2 738	5 406	47 934	2 132	8.2	8.15
25 to 34 years	20 611	67 084	1 095	20 424	70 283	1 406	4.8	2.42
35 to 44 years	21 370	82 206	1 090	21 432	88 858	2 531	8.1	3.01
45 to 54 years	22 071	85 994	1 878	21 659	92 221	1 983	7.2	3.17
55 to 64 years	24 172	70 200	1 470	24 603	75 686	1 482	7.8	2.71
65 years and older	34 156	44 487	831	34 927	47 357	911	6.5	2.57
Nativity of Householder								
Native born	108 560	65 407	725	108 851	69 474	960	6.2	1.57
Foreign born	20 019	59 841	1 616	19 600	64 900	1 930	8.5	4.19
Naturalized citizen	11 043	66 707	2 292	11 208	71 538	2 040	7.2	4.69
Not a citizen	8 976	52 885	1 072	8 392	57 668	2 598	9.0	4.94
Region								
Northeast	22 054	71 383	1 920	22 031	76 221	1 952	6.8	3.00
Midwest	27 686	65 230	1 471	27 757	68 354	1 824	4.8	3.10
South	49 743	58 337	836	49 486	61 884	766	6.1	1.82
West	29 096	70 779	1 624	29 177	75 769	1 244	7.0	2.58
Residence								
Inside metropolitan statistical areas	110 789	67 363	620	110 679	71 961	699	6.8	1.29
Inside principal cites	42 983	60 434	1 245	42 992	63 745	1 586	5.5	3.01
Outside principal cites	67 806	72 213	771	67 687	77 170	1 021	6.9	1.57
Outside metropolitan statistical areas	17 790	50 771	1 659	17 772	52 100	1 150	2.6	2.80

[1]A margin of error is a measure of an estimate's variability. The larger the margin of error in relation to the size of the estimate, the less reliable the estimate.
[2]Federal surveys now give respondents the option of reporting more than one race. Therefore, there are two basic ways of defining a race group. A group such as Asian may be
   defined as those who reported Asian and no other race (the race-alone or single-race concept) or as those who reported Asian regardless of whether they also reported another race
   (the race-alone-or-in-combination concept). This table shows data using the race-alone concept. The use of the single-race population does not imply that it is the preferred method
   of presenting or analyzing data; the Census Bureau uses a variety of approaches. Information on people who reported more than one race, such as White and American Indian and Alaska
   Native or Asian and Black or African American, is available from Census 2010 through American FactFinder. About 2.9 percent of respondents reported more than one race in Census 2010.
X = Not applicable.
N = Represents or rounds to zero.

Table 13-2. Households, by Total Money Income, Race, and Hispanic Origin of Householder, 1967–2019

(Numbers in thousands, percent, dollars; income in 2019 CPI-U-RS adjusted dollars.)

Race and Hispanic origin of householder and year	Number	Percent distribution										Median income (dollars)		Mean income (dollars)	
		Total	Under $15,000	$15,000 to $24,999	$25,000 to $34,999	$35,000 to $49,999	$50,000 to $74,999	$75,000 to $99,999	$100,000 to $149,999	$150,000 to $199,000	$200,000 and over	Value	Standard error	Value	Standard error
All Races															
1967[1]	60 813	100.0	14.8	10.2	10.9	16.8	24.8	11.9	7.7	1.7	1.2	47 938	287	53 616	287
1968	62 214	100.0	13.4	10.1	10.4	16.5	24.8	13.7	8.2	1.8	1.1	50 004	297	56 572	297
1969	63 401	100.0	13.2	9.9	9.4	16.0	24.3	14.2	9.4	2.2	1.3	51 863	315	59 004	305
1970	64 778	100.0	13.3	10.1	9.7	15.7	24.1	13.7	9.9	2.2	1.4	51 461	310	58 926	310
1971[2]	66 676	100.0	13.3	10.2	10.6	15.2	23.5	13.9	9.7	2.2	1.4	50 960	325	58 609	306
1972[3]	68 251	100.0	12.4	10.3	10.0	14.7	22.4	14.7	10.9	2.7	1.8	53 143	334	61 851	316
1973	69 859	100.0	11.6	10.8	9.5	14.3	22.2	14.9	11.8	3.0	1.9	54 216	339	62 700	314
1974[4,5]	71 163	100.0	11.8	10.7	10.0	15.3	22.0	14.9	10.9	2.7	1.6	52 499	332	61 393	316
1975[5]	72 867	100.0	12.4	11.4	10.7	14.7	22.1	14.3	10.5	2.4	1.5	51 124	342	59 698	306
1976[6]	74 142	100.0	12.0	11.3	10.3	14.8	21.8	14.5	11.2	2.5	1.7	51 973	317	61 133	310
1977	76 030	100.0	11.9	11.2	10.5	14.2	21.3	14.7	11.6	2.9	1.8	52 302	323	62 044	311
1978	77 330	100.0	11.6	10.5	10.1	14.2	21.0	14.9	12.4	3.2	2.0	54 326	362	63 940	403
1979[7]	80 776	100.0	11.8	10.2	10.2	14.4	20.5	15.1	12.2	3.4	2.1	54 222	423	64 410	401
1980	82 368	100.0	12.2	10.7	10.3	14.6	21.2	14.0	12.0	3.2	1.8	52 461	443	62 394	375
1981	83 527	100.0	12.5	10.9	11.0	14.3	20.6	14.0	11.8	3.1	1.8	51 627	445	61 677	370
1982	83 918	100.0	12.7	10.8	10.9	14.5	20.8	13.4	11.6	3.3	2.1	51 487	382	62 050	378
1983	85 407	100.0	12.7	10.9	10.6	14.8	20.1	13.3	11.9	3.4	2.2	51 126	383	62 181	383
1984[8]	86 789	100.0	12.2	10.8	10.1	14.7	19.7	13.7	12.6	3.7	2.4	52 679	394	64 546	390
1985[9]	88 458	100.0	12.1	10.6	10.1	14.3	19.8	13.6	13.1	3.9	2.6	53 664	478	66 043	430
1986	89 479	100.0	12.0	10.0	9.9	13.6	19.4	13.9	13.6	4.4	3.1	55 597	474	68 688	459
1987[10]	91 124	100.0	11.6	10.0	9.9	13.6	18.9	14.2	13.9	4.6	3.3	56 261	437	69 968	472
1988	92 830	100.0	11.4	9.7	9.9	13.1	19.4	14.0	14.3	4.8	3.5	56 725	456	70 877	521
1989	93 347	100.0	10.8	10.0	9.6	13.4	19.2	13.9	14.3	5.0	3.9	57 705	522	72 904	522
1990	94 312	100.0	11.1	10.1	9.5	13.9	19.5	13.7	13.8	4.8	3.7	56 966	479	71 158	494
1991	95 669	100.0	11.6	10.3	9.8	14.0	19.1	13.5	13.7	4.8	3.3	55 302	438	69 613	471
1992[11]	96 426	100.0	11.8	10.6	10.1	13.5	18.8	13.5	13.5	4.8	3.4	54 874	427	69 568	480
1993[12]	97 107	100.0	11.8	10.6	10.1	13.7	18.4	13.1	13.5	4.9	3.9	54 581	420	72 379	644
1994[13]	98 990	100.0	11.3	10.8	10.1	13.5	18.4	12.7	13.9	5.1	4.2	55 215	414	73 816	653
1995[14]	99 627	100.0	10.5	10.4	10.2	13.1	18.8	13.3	14.2	5.1	4.3	56 945	542	75 096	676
1996	101 018	100.0	10.6	10.5	9.6	13.5	17.9	13.5	14.3	5.4	4.6	57 772	479	76 705	707
1997	102 528	100.0	10.3	10.3	9.4	13.2	18.0	13.3	14.7	5.8	5.1	58 961	448	79 175	729
1998	103 874	100.0	9.8	9.8	9.2	12.9	17.5	13.7	15.3	6.2	5.5	61 128	595	81 517	724
1999[15]	106 434	100.0	9.0	9.7	9.1	13.0	17.5	13.3	15.6	6.6	6.3	62 641	481	84 254	719
2000[16]	108 209	100.0	9.3	9.3	8.9	13.1	17.7	13.2	15.4	6.8	6.2	62 512	323	85 059	551
2001	109 297	100.0	9.7	9.6	9.1	12.9	17.7	12.8	15.6	6.3	6.2	61 126	307	84 257	552
2002	111 278	100.0	9.9	9.8	9.2	13.3	17.4	12.7	15.6	6.3	5.9	60 435	326	82 442	509
2003	112 000	100.0	10.2	9.7	9.7	12.4	17.4	12.7	15.3	6.3	6.2	60 360	431	82 305	495
2004[17]	113 343	100.0	10.3	9.7	9.8	12.8	17.4	12.6	15.0	6.3	6.1	60 150	437	82 038	509
2005	114 384	100.0	10.1	9.8	9.5	12.7	17.6	12.9	14.7	6.5	6.2	60 794	335	83 127	516
2006	116 011	100.0	9.6	9.5	9.4	13.0	17.5	12.7	15.0	6.7	6.5	61 268	433	84 617	537
2007	116 783	100.0	10.0	10.0	9.0	12.8	17.3	12.6	15.3	6.7	6.4	62 090	285	83 568	480
2008	117 181	100.0	10.4	10.0	9.4	13.4	17.0	12.5	15.0	6.3	6.0	59 877	268	81 447	474
2009[18]	117 538	100.0	10.4	10.0	9.7	13.2	17.4	12.4	14.5	6.3	6.0	59 458	419	81 196	477
2010[19]	119 927	100.0	11.2	10.7	9.4	13.3	16.8	12.4	14.1	6.3	5.9	57 904	628	79 192	696
2011	121 084	100.0	11.6	10.2	10.2	13.1	17.2	11.9	13.8	6.2	5.8	57 021	470	79 375	690
2012	122 459	100.0	11.4	10.6	10.1	12.5	17.4	12.0	13.9	6.3	5.9	56 912	384	79 510	773
2013[20]	123 931	100.0	11.4	10.3	9.5	12.5	16.8	12.0	13.9	6.7	6.9	58 904	1 183	82 660	1 201
2014	124 587	100.0	11.4	10.5	9.6	12.6	16.4	12.1	14.0	6.6	6.8	58 001	697	81 870	793
2015	125 819	100.0	10.6	10.0	9.6	12.1	16.1	12.4	14.9	7.1	7.2	60 987	570	85 533	715
2016	126 224	100.0	10.4	9.0	9.2	12.3	16.7	12.2	15.0	7.2	8.0	62 898	764	88 578	822
2017	127 669	100.0	10.0	9.1	9.2	12.0	16.4	12.4	14.7	7.3	8.9	63 761	552	91 406	979
2018	128 579	100.0	10.1	8.8	8.7	12.0	17.0	12.5	15.0	7.2	8.8	64 324	704	91 652	914
2019	128 451	100.0	9.1	8.0	8.3	11.7	16.5	12.3	15.5	8.3	10.3	68 703	904	98 088	1 042

[1]Implementation of a new Curent Population Survey (CPS) Annual Social and Economic Supplements (ASEC) processing system.
[2]Introduction of 1970 census sample design and population controls.
[3]Full implementation of 1970 census–based sample design.
[4]Implementation of a new CPS ASEC processing system. Questionnaire expanded to ask 11 income questions.
[5]Some of these estimates were derived using Pareto interpolation and may differ from published data that were derived using linear interpolation.
[6]First-year medians were derived using both Pareto and linear interpolation. Before this year, all medians were derived using linear interpolation.
[7]Implementation of 1980 census population controls. Questionnaire expanded to show 27 possible values from a list of 51 possible sources of income.
[8]Implementation of Hispanic population weighting controls and introduction of 1980 census–based sample design.
[9]Recording of amounts for earnings from longest job increased to $299,999. Full implementation of 1980 census–based sample design.
[10]Implementation of a new CPS ASEC processing system.
[11]Implementation of 1990 census population controls.
[12]Data collection method changed from paper and pencil to computer-assisted interviewing. In addition, the 1994 ASEC was revised to allow for the coding of different income amounts on selected questionnaire items. Limits either increased or decreased in the following categories: earnings limits increased to $999,999, Social Security limits increased to $49,999, Supplemental Security Income and public assistance limits increased to $24,999, veterans' benefits limits increased to $99,999, and child support and alimony limits decreased to $49,999.
[13]Introduction of 1990 census sample design.
[14]Full implementation of 1990 census–based sample design and metropolitan definitions, 7,000 household sample reduction, and revised editing of responses on race.
[15]Implementation of the 2000 census–based population controls.
[16]Implementation of a 28,000 household sample expansion.
[17]Data revised to reflect a correction to the weights in the 2005 ASEC.
[18]Median income is calculated using $2,500 intervals. Beginning with 2009 income data, the Census Bureau expanded the upper income intervals used to calculate medians to $250,000 or more.
[19]Implementation of 2010 census-based population controls.
[20]Data are based on the CPS ASEC sample of 68,000 addresses. The 2014 CPS ASEC included redesigned questions for income and health insurance coverage.

Table 13-2. Households, by Total Money Income, Race, and Hispanic Origin of Householder, 1967–2019 —Continued

(Numbers in thousands, percent, dollars; income in 2019 CPI-U-RS adjusted dollars.)

Race and Hispanic origin of householder and year	Number	Percent distribution										Median income (dollars)		Mean income (dollars)	
		Total	Under $15,000	$15,000 to $24,999	$25,000 to $34,999	$35,000 to $49,999	$50,000 to $74,999	$75,000 to $99,999	$100,000 to $149,999	$150,000 to $199,999	$200,000 and over	Value	Standard error	Value	Standard error
White[21]															
1967	54 188	100.0	13.5	9.4	10.4	16.9	25.8	12.6	8.2	1.8	1.3	49 992	298	55 576	309
1968	55 394	100.0	12.3	9.3	9.8	16.5	25.7	14.5	8.8	1.9	1.2	52 064	319	58 606	319
1969	56 248	100.0	12.0	9.3	8.9	15.8	25.2	15.0	10.0	2.4	1.5	54 126	325	61 192	336
1970	57 575	100.0	12.1	9.4	9.3	15.5	24.9	14.3	10.5	2.3	1.6	53 600	339	60 988	330
1971[2]	59 463	100.0	12.1	9.5	10.2	15.0	24.4	14.5	10.4	2.4	1.5	53 303	334	60 731	325
1972[3]	60 618	100.0	11.2	9.6	9.5	14.6	23.2	15.4	11.7	2.9	2.0	55 752	352	64 257	343
1973	61 965	100.0	10.5	10.0	9.1	14.0	22.8	15.6	12.6	3.2	2.1	56 821	356	65 124	343
1974[4,5]	62 984	100.0	10.6	10.0	9.7	15.2	22.7	15.6	11.6	2.9	1.8	54 904	339	63 667	339
1975[5]	64 392	100.0	11.0	10.8	10.5	14.6	22.7	14.9	11.2	2.6	1.6	53 464	321	61 904	335
1976[6]	65 353	100.0	10.7	10.5	10.0	14.8	22.3	15.2	11.9	2.8	1.9	54 443	371	63 485	337
1977	66 934	100.0	10.5	10.5	10.2	14.1	21.9	15.5	12.3	3.1	2.0	54 999	380	64 467	342
1978	68 028	100.0	10.2	9.9	9.9	14.2	21.4	15.7	13.0	3.4	2.2	56 475	409	66 309	439
1979[7]	70 766	100.0	10.4	9.5	9.9	14.3	21.0	15.8	13.0	3.6	2.3	56 851	444	66 950	439
1980	71 872	100.0	10.6	10.1	10.0	14.6	21.8	14.7	12.7	3.5	2.0	55 346	468	64 911	409
1981	72 845	100.0	10.8	10.2	10.7	14.4	21.2	14.7	12.6	3.4	2.0	54 548	414	64 262	401
1982	73 182	100.0	11.0	10.2	10.5	14.7	21.3	14.0	12.5	3.6	2.3	53 902	403	64 607	416
1983	74 376	100.0	10.9	10.3	10.4	15.0	20.8	13.9	12.7	3.6	2.4	53 616	399	64 761	415
1984[8]	75 328	100.0	10.5	10.2	9.9	14.7	20.4	14.4	13.3	4.0	2.7	55 575	460	67 208	429
1985[9]	76 576	100.0	10.5	10.0	9.8	14.2	20.3	14.2	13.8	4.2	2.9	56 595	497	68 754	475
1986	77 284	100.0	10.3	9.5	9.7	13.6	19.9	14.5	14.5	4.7	3.4	58 451	467	71 548	503
1987[10]	78 519	100.0	9.7	9.5	9.7	13.5	19.5	15.0	14.8	4.9	3.5	59 277	490	72 958	518
1988	79 734	100.0	9.6	9.0	9.8	13.0	20.0	14.6	15.1	5.1	3.8	59 967	583	73 900	572
1989	80 163	100.0	9.0	9.6	9.4	13.3	19.6	14.5	15.0	5.4	4.2	60 699	486	75 941	578
1990	80 968	100.0	9.2	9.7	9.4	14.0	19.9	14.2	14.6	5.0	3.9	59 416	448	74 029	545
1991	81 675	100.0	9.7	9.9	9.6	14.0	19.5	14.0	14.5	5.1	3.6	57 951	462	72 552	519
1992[11]	81 795	100.0	9.8	10.1	10.0	13.6	19.2	14.2	14.3	5.1	3.7	57 691	460	72 710	533
1993[12]	82 387	100.0	9.9	10.1	9.8	13.7	19.0	13.7	14.2	5.2	4.2	57 584	552	75 623	718
1994[13]	83 737	100.0	9.6	10.3	9.9	13.4	18.9	13.2	14.7	5.4	4.6	58 234	538	77 070	738
1995[14]	84 511	100.0	9.0	10.0	10.0	13.0	19.1	13.8	14.9	5.5	4.7	59 769	514	78 089	745
1996	85 059	100.0	9.0	10.1	9.4	13.5	18.2	14.0	15.1	5.7	5.0	60 489	514	79 750	777
1997	86 106	100.0	8.8	9.8	9.2	13.0	18.2	13.8	15.5	6.1	5.6	62 095	647	82 696	828
1998	87 212	100.0	8.2	9.3	9.0	12.9	17.7	14.2	16.0	6.6	6.0	64 315	530	85 215	825
1999[15]	88 893	100.0	7.6	9.3	9.0	12.9	17.7	13.6	16.4	6.9	6.7	65 149	542	87 315	813
2000[16]	90 030	100.0	8.0	9.0	8.6	13.0	17.7	13.6	16.2	7.2	6.6	65 379	475	88 213	622
2001	90 682	100.0	8.3	9.4	8.9	12.7	17.9	13.2	16.3	6.7	6.8	64 439	498	87 592	619
White Alone[22]															
2002	91 645	100.0	8.6	9.4	8.9	13.0	17.5	13.1	16.5	6.6	6.3	64 250	429	85 740	574
2003	91 962	100.0	8.7	9.3	9.5	12.5	17.5	13.0	16.1	6.7	6.6	63 583	410	85 816	566
2004[17]	92 880	100.0	8.8	9.4	9.6	12.6	17.6	13.0	15.8	6.7	6.5	63 304	408	85 352	578
2005	93 588	100.0	8.6	9.3	9.3	12.7	17.7	13.4	15.4	6.9	6.6	63 718	458	86 562	589
2006	94 705	100.0	8.1	9.1	9.2	12.9	17.7	13.2	15.8	7.0	7.0	64 410	307	87 842	602
2007	95 112	100.0	8.4	9.6	8.9	12.6	17.5	13.0	16.1	7.1	6.9	64 417	313	86 932	545
2008	95 297	100.0	9.0	9.7	9.1	13.2	17.2	13.0	15.8	6.6	6.4	62 268	298	84 740	537
2009[18]	95 489	100.0	8.9	9.6	9.5	13.1	17.8	12.9	15.2	6.7	6.4	61 947	303	84 263	534
2010[19]	96 306	100.0	9.4	10.4	9.2	13.2	17.1	12.8	15.0	6.6	6.3	60 763	489	82 741	783
2011	96 964	100.0	9.8	9.6	10.1	13.1	17.6	12.4	14.5	6.6	6.2	59 481	422	82 946	791
2012	97 705	100.0	9.6	10.2	10.0	12.5	17.6	12.6	14.6	6.7	6.3	59 912	705	83 015	851
2013[20]	98 807	100.0	9.8	10.0	9.2	12.4	17.0	12.7	14.5	7.1	7.3	62 378	935	85 551	1 371
2014[20]	98 679	100.0	9.9	10.1	9.3	12.5	16.8	12.7	14.7	6.9	7.3	61 470	631	85 277	930
2015[20]	99 313	100.0	8.9	9.5	9.4	12.2	16.3	12.9	15.8	7.4	7.6	64 864	676	88 731	834
2016[20]	99 400	100.0	8.9	8.6	8.9	12.3	16.8	12.5	15.9	7.5	8.5	65 901	585	91 988	936
2017[20]	100 113	100.0	8.5	8.6	8.9	11.9	16.6	12.8	15.5	7.7	9.4	67 617	878	95 448	1 101
2018[20]	100 528	100.0	8.5	8.3	8.4	11.8	17.3	13.1	15.7	7.6	9.3	68 156	657	95 650	1 052
2019[20]	100 568	100.0	7.8	7.5	8.0	11.5	16.7	12.7	16.3	8.7	10.8	72 204	800	101 732	1 192

[1]Implementation of a new Curent Population Survey (CPS) Annual Social and Economic Supplements (ASEC) processing system.
[2]Introduction of 1970 census sample design and population controls.
[3]Full implementation of 1970 census–based sample design.
[4]Implementation of a new CPS ASEC processing system. Questionnaire expanded to ask 11 income questions.
[5]Some of these estimates were derived using Pareto interpolation and may differ from published data that were derived using linear interpolation.
[6]First-year medians were derived using both Pareto and linear interpolation. Before this year, all medians were derived using linear interpolation.
[7]Implementation of 1980 census population controls. Questionnaire expanded to show 27 possible values from a list of 51 possible sources of income.
[8]Implementation of Hispanic population weighting controls and introduction of 1980 census–based sample design.
[9]Recording of amounts for earnings from longest job increased to $299,999. Full implementation of 1980 census–based sample design.
[10]Implementation of a new CPS ASEC processing system.
[11]Implementation of 1990 census population controls.
[12]Data collection method changed from paper and pencil to computer-assisted interviewing. In addition, the 1994 ASEC was revised to allow for the coding of different income amounts on selected questionnaire items. Limits either increased or decreased in the following categories: earnings limits increased to $999,999, Social Security limits increased to $49,999, Supplemental Security Income and public assistance limits increased to $24,999, veterans' benefits limits increased to $99,999, and child support and alimony limits decreased to $49,999.
[13]Introduction of 1990 census sample design.
[14]Full implementation of 1990 census–based sample design and metropolitan definitions, 7,000 household sample reduction, and revised editing of responses on race.
[15]Implementation of the 2000 census–based population controls.
[16]Implementation of a 28,000 household sample expansion.
[17]Data revised to reflect a correction to the weights in the 2005 ASEC.
[18]Median income is calculated using $2,500 intervals. Beginning with 2009 income data, the Census Bureau expanded the upper income intervals used to calculate medians to $250,000 or more.
[19]Implementation of 2010 census-based population controls.
[20]Data are based on the CPS ASEC sample of 68,000 addresses. The 2014 CPS ASEC included redesigned questions for income and health insurance coverage.
[21]For 2001 and earlier years, the CPS allowed respondents to report only one race group.
[22]Beginning with the 2003 CPS, respondents were allowed to choose one or more races. White alone refers to people who reported White and did not report any other race category. The use of this single-race population does not imply that it is the preferred method of presenting or analyzing the data; the Census Bureau uses a variety of approaches. Information on people who reported more than one race, such as White and American Indian and Alaska Native or Asian and Black or African American, is available from Census 2010 through American FactFinder. About 2.9 percent of respondents reported more than one race in Census 2010.

Table 13-2. Households, by Total Money Income, Race, and Hispanic Origin of Householder, 1967–2019
—Continued

(Numbers in thousands, percent, dollars; income in 2019 CPI-U-RS adjusted dollars.)

Race and Hispanic origin of householder and year	Number	Percent distribution										Median income (dollars)		Mean income (dollars)	
		Total	Under $15,000	$15,000 to $24,999	$25,000 to $34,999	$35,000 to $49,999	$50,000 to $74,999	$75,000 to $99,999	$100,000 to $149,999	$150,000 to $199,000	$200,000 and over	Value	Standard error	Value	Standard error
White, Not Hispanic[21]															
1972[3]	58 005	100.0	11.1	9.3	9.3	14.3	23.2	15.6	12.0	3.0	2.0	56 546	442	65 002	478
1973	59 236	100.0	10.4	9.9	8.9	13.8	22.8	15.8	12.9	3.3	2.2	57 321	441	65 851	458
1974[4,5]	60 164	100.0	10.5	9.8	9.5	15.0	22.7	15.9	11.9	3.0	1.8	55 373	447	64 385	463
1975[5]	61 533	100.0	10.8	10.6	10.3	14.5	22.7	15.2	11.6	2.7	1.7	53 867	470	62 662	499
1976[6]	62 365	100.0	10.4	10.3	9.9	14.6	22.4	15.4	12.2	2.8	1.9	55 553	532	64 300	472
1977	63 721	100.0	10.4	10.3	10.0	13.9	21.9	15.7	12.6	3.2	2.1	56 090	520	65 265	507
1978	64 836	100.0	10.0	9.8	9.7	14.0	21.5	15.9	13.4	3.5	2.3	57 539	498	67 092	475
1979[7]	67 203	100.0	10.2	9.4	9.8	14.2	21.0	16.1	13.2	3.8	2.4	57 651	526	67 724	488
1980	68 106	100.0	10.3	9.9	9.8	14.5	21.9	14.9	13.0	3.6	2.0	56 327	526	65 765	487
1981	68 996	100.0	10.5	10.0	10.6	14.3	21.2	15.0	12.8	3.5	2.1	55 335	463	65 071	445
1982	69 214	100.0	10.7	9.9	10.4	14.6	21.4	14.3	12.8	3.7	2.3	54 806	453	65 557	462
1983	69 648	100.0	10.4	10.0	10.2	14.9	21.0	14.2	13.0	3.8	2.6	54 994	455	66 463	467
1984[8]	70 586	100.0	10.0	9.9	9.7	14.7	20.4	14.7	13.7	4.2	2.8	56 729	518	68 376	503
1985[9]	71 540	100.0	10.1	9.6	9.7	14.1	20.4	14.5	14.2	4.4	3.0	57 868	486	70 092	523
1986	72 067	100.0	9.9	9.2	9.4	13.5	20.0	14.8	14.9	4.9	3.6	59 780	507	72 969	551
1987[10]	73 120	100.0	9.2	9.1	9.5	13.3	19.6	15.2	15.2	5.1	3.7	60 907	558	74 385	568
1988	74 067	100.0	9.1	8.7	9.5	12.9	20.1	14.8	15.6	5.3	4.0	61 619	596	75 408	583
1989	74 495	100.0	8.5	9.4	9.2	13.1	19.6	14.7	15.4	5.6	4.4	62 005	499	77 462	624
1990	75 035	100.0	8.8	9.2	9.2	13.8	20.0	14.5	15.1	5.3	4.1	60 775	466	75 669	563
1991	75 625	100.0	9.2	9.6	9.4	13.9	19.6	14.3	15.0	5.4	3.7	59 335	480	74 109	544
1992[11]	75 107	100.0	9.2	9.8	9.7	13.3	19.3	14.5	14.9	5.3	4.0	59 627	607	74 557	566
1993[12]	75 697	100.0	9.4	9.7	9.5	13.5	19.1	14.1	14.8	5.5	4.5	59 704	575	77 617	762
1994[13]	77 004	100.0	8.9	10.0	9.7	13.2	19.0	13.5	15.2	5.7	4.8	60 113	524	79 032	771
1995[14]	76 932	100.0	8.1	9.5	9.6	12.8	19.3	14.2	15.6	5.9	5.0	62 128	533	80 636	794
1996	77 240	100.0	8.4	9.6	9.1	13.3	18.2	14.4	15.8	6.1	5.3	63 136	712	82 163	...
1997	77 936	100.0	8.1	9.4	8.9	12.7	18.1	14.1	16.2	6.5	6.0	64 652	556	85 346	...
1998	78 577	100.0	7.6	8.8	8.6	12.5	17.7	14.6	16.8	7.0	6.4	66 715	631	87 944	884
1999[15]	79 819	100.0	7.2	8.9	8.7	12.4	17.5	13.9	17.0	7.3	7.2	67 969	706	90 178	879
2000[16]	80 527	100.0	7.7	8.7	8.3	12.7	17.5	13.7	16.8	7.6	0.0	67 920	448	90 897	671
2001	80 818	100.0	7.9	9.0	8.6	12.3	17.7	13.4	16.9	7.1	7.2	67 027	457	90 389	674
White Alone, Not Hispanic[22]															
2002	81 166	100.0	8.1	9.1	8.5	12.4	17.5	13.3	17.2	7.0	6.8	66 835	431	88 517	619
2003	81 148	100.0	8.3	9.0	9.0	12.0	17.3	13.3	16.8	7.2	7.2	66 573	529	89 021	621
2004[17]	81 628	100.0	8.3	9.1	9.1	12.2	17.3	13.3	16.6	7.1	7.1	66 359	500	88 539	634
2005	82 003	100.0	8.1	9.0	8.9	12.2	17.5	13.7	16.1	7.3	7.2	66 644	371	90 028	654
2006	82 675	100.0	7.6	8.8	8.8	12.4	17.4	13.4	16.5	7.4	7.6	66 635	393	91 195	663
2007	82 765	100.0	7.9	9.2	8.5	12.0	17.3	13.2	16.9	7.6	7.5	67 884	502	90 456	600
2008	82 884	100.0	8.3	9.2	8.8	12.5	17.1	13.4	16.6	7.1	7.0	66 099	441	88 206	593
2009[18]	83 158	100.0	8.2	9.0	9.1	12.8	17.7	13.1	15.9	7.1	6.9	65 053	548	87 484	588
2010[19]	83 314	100.0	8.7	10.0	8.7	12.8	17.0	13.0	15.8	7.0	7.0	63 996	862	86 173	889
2011	83 573	100.0	9.0	9.3	9.5	12.7	17.5	12.7	15.3	7.1	6.9	63 124	615	86 650	896
2012	83 792	100.0	8.8	9.8	9.4	12.1	17.5	13.0	15.4	7.2	6.9	63 597	659	86 838	945
2013[20]	84 432	100.0	9.2	9.4	8.6	11.7	17.2	13.2	15.2	7.6	8.0	66 318	964	89 292	1 533
2014	84 228	100.0	9.3	9.5	8.8	12.0	16.6	12.8	15.4	7.5	8.0	65 135	654	89 142	1 030
2015	84 445	100.0	8.2	9.1	8.9	11.7	16.1	13.0	16.7	8.0	8.3	67 930	962	92 355	943
2016	84 387	100.0	8.4	8.2	8.5	11.8	16.6	12.6	16.5	8.0	9.4	69 292	894	95 624	1 067
2017	84 706	100.0	8.0	8.3	8.4	11.4	16.2	13.0	16.1	8.3	10.4	71 117	1 156	99 871	1 211
2018	84 727	100.0	8.0	7.8	7.9	11.2	17.0	13.2	16.5	8.1	10.3	71 922	664	100 041	1 191
2019	84 868	100.0	7.3	7.3	7.5	11.0	16.2	12.8	16.8	9.3	11.8	76 057	876	106 659	1 359

[3]Full implementation of 1970 census–based sample design.
[4]Implementation of a new CPS ASEC processing system. Questionnaire expanded to ask 11 income questions.
[5]Some of these estimates were derived using Pareto interpolation and may differ from published data that were derived using linear interpolation.
[6]First-year medians were derived using both Pareto and linear interpolation. Before this year, all medians were derived using linear interpolation.
[7]Implementation of 1980 census population controls. Questionnaire expanded to show 27 possible values from a list of 51 possible sources of income.
[8]Implementation of Hispanic population weighting controls and introduction of 1980 census–based sample design.
[9]Recording of amounts for earnings from longest job increased to $299,999. Full implementation of 1980 census–based sample design.
[10]Implementation of a new CPS ASEC processing system.
[11]Implementation of 1990 census population controls.
[12]Data collection method changed from paper and pencil to computer-assisted interviewing. In addition, the 1994 ASEC was revised to allow for the coding of different income amounts on selected questionnaire items. Limits either increased or decreased in the following categories: earnings limits increased to $999,999, Social Security limits increased to $49,999, Supplemental Security Income and public assistance limits increased to $24,999, veterans' benefits limits increased to $99,999, and child support and alimony limits decreased to $49,999.
[13]Introduction of 1990 census sample design.
[14]Full implementation of 1990 census–based sample design and metropolitan definitions, 7,000 household sample reduction, and revised editing of responses on race.
[15]Implementation of the 2000 census–based population controls.
[16]Implementation of a 28,000 household sample expansion.
[17]Data revised to reflect a correction to the weights in the 2005 ASEC.
[18]Median income is calculated using $2,500 intervals. Beginning with 2009 income data, the Census Bureau expanded the upper income intervals used to calculate medians to $250,000 or more.
[19]Implementation of 2010 census-based population controls.
[20]Data are based on the CPS ASEC sample of 68,000 addresses. The 2014 CPS ASEC included redesigned questions for income and health insurance coverage.
[21]For 2001 and earlier years, the CPS allowed respondents to report only one race group.
[22]Beginning with the 2003 CPS, respondents were allowed to choose one or more races. White alone refers to people who reported White and did not report any other race category. The use of this single-race population does not imply that it is the preferred method of presenting or analyzing the data; the Census Bureau uses a variety of approaches. Information on people who reported more than one race, such as White and American Indian and Alaska Native or Asian and Black or African American, is available from Census 2010 through American FactFinder. About 2.9 percent of respondents reported more than one race in Census 2010.
. . . = Not available.

Table 13-2. Households, by Total Money Income, Race, and Hispanic Origin of Householder, 1967–2019
—Continued

(Numbers in thousands, percent, dollars; income in 2019 CPI-U-RS adjusted dollars.)

Race and Hispanic origin of householder and year	Number	Percent distribution										Median income (dollars)		Mean income (dollars)	
		Total	Under $15,000	$15,000 to $24,999	$25,000 to $34,999	$35,000 to $49,999	$50,000 to $74,999	$75,000 to $99,999	$100,000 to $149,999	$150,000 to $199,999	$200,000 and over	Value	Standard error	Value	Standard error
Black[21]															
1967[1]	5 728	100.0	26.8	17.7	15.2	16.4	14.8	5.5	2.7	0.6	0.3	29 026	795	34 878	640
1968	5 870	100.0	24.4	17.0	15.5	16.2	16.6	6.5	3.2	0.4	0.1	30 701	733	37 392	648
1969	6 053	100.0	24.0	16.1	14.1	17.7	16.9	6.7	3.8	0.5	0.1	32 717	793	38 948	681
1970	6 180	100.0	24.1	15.8	13.7	17.1	16.7	7.4	4.4	0.6	0.2	32 624	737	39 836	708
1971[2]	6 578	100.0	24.7	16.2	14.2	16.3	16.7	7.3	3.8	0.6	0.2	31 486	771	39 016	659
1972[3]	6 809	100.0	23.1	16.5	13.8	15.9	16.0	9.2	4.3	0.8	0.4	32 542	802	41 108	721
1973	7 040	100.0	21.4	16.9	12.9	16.2	17.9	8.6	4.7	0.9	0.4	33 447	857	41 534	679
1974[4,5]	7 263	100.0	23.0	16.4	13.8	16.2	16.5	8.7	4.6	0.6	0.2	32 652	648	40 609	594
1975[5]	7 489	100.0	24.3	16.9	12.9	15.7	16.8	8.3	4.3	0.7	0.1	32 096	777	40 063	584
1976[6]	7 776	100.0	23.1	17.6	12.7	14.8	17.3	8.7	4.8	0.6	0.3	32 373	660	41 362	607
1977	7 977	100.0	22.9	17.5	13.4	14.9	16.4	8.4	5.3	0.7	0.4	32 455	716	41 585	609
1978	8 066	100.0	23.4	15.4	12.6	14.5	17.5	8.6	6.7	1.1	0.2	33 939	1 181	43 373	931
1979[7]	8 586	100.0	23.7	15.8	13.0	14.7	16.3	9.2	6.1	1.0	0.3	33 378	1 002	42 828	867
1980	8 847	100.0	24.9	16.3	12.6	14.7	16.6	8.2	5.6	0.9	0.3	31 885	989	41 382	838
1981	8 961	100.0	26.6	16.0	13.1	13.8	15.5	8.4	5.6	0.9	0.1	30 610	846	40 211	801
1982	8 916	100.0	26.3	15.6	13.7	13.2	16.9	8.4	4.4	1.0	0.3	30 549	806	40 195	827
1983	9 236	100.0	27.2	15.9	12.5	14.3	15.0	8.1	5.7	1.1	0.2	30 426	938	40 468	821
1984[8]	9 480	100.0	25.5	16.1	12.4	15.0	15.1	7.7	6.4	1.3	0.4	31 659	1 001	42 223	854
1985[9]	9 797	100.0	25.0	15.2	11.9	14.8	15.8	8.6	6.9	1.2	0.6	33 671	1 076	43 933	938
1986	9 922	100.0	25.7	14.2	11.8	13.9	16.0	9.3	6.4	1.9	0.7	33 675	1 087	45 180	1 010
1987[10]	10 192	100.0	25.7	14.2	11.6	15.1	14.7	9.0	6.9	1.6	1.1	33 833	1 065	45 683	1 033
1988	10 561	100.0	25.3	14.2	11.3	13.8	15.3	9.2	8.0	2.0	1.0	34 185	1 172	46 832	1 124
1989	10 486	100.0	24.7	13.4	11.0	14.3	16.4	9.1	8.2	2.2	0.8	36 099	1 208	47 901	1 071
1990	10 671	100.0	24.9	13.9	10.9	14.1	16.5	9.4	7.3	2.1	0.9	35 531	1 333	47 208	1 048
1991	11 083	100.0	26.0	13.3	11.3	13.9	16.4	9.2	7.1	1.9	0.8	34 524	1 193	45 971	987
1992[11]	11 269	100.0	26.2	14.1	11.3	13.9	15.9	8.9	6.8	2.1	0.9	33 593	1 128	45 585	1 017
1993[12]	11 281	100.0	25.2	14.4	12.0	14.1	14.8	8.7	7.5	2.2	1.2	34 126	1 109	47 572	1 299
1994[13]	11 655	100.0	23.3	14.0	11.9	14.1	14.7	9.7	8.4	2.5	1.4	35 985	1 101	50 073	1 182
1995[14]	11 577	100.0	21.5	14.0	12.0	14.2	17.0	9.3	8.9	1.9	1.2	37 421	1 050	50 802	1 429
1996	12 109	100.0	21.3	14.3	11.5	14.0	16.5	10.6	8.0	2.3	1.5	38 223	1 237	52 837	1 698
1997	12 474	100.0	20.3	13.6	11.1	15.1	16.9	10.2	8.7	2.7	1.4	39 913	1 130	52 520	1 240
1998	12 579	100.0	20.7	13.5	11.4	13.8	16.4	10.2	9.3	2.9	1.8	39 852	1 027	53 667	1 179
1999[15]	12 838	100.0	18.0	12.8	10.9	14.6	16.2	11.1	9.9	4.0	2.5	42 960	1 317	59 203	1 398
2000[16]	13 174	100.0	17.6	11.9	11.5	14.5	18.1	11.1	9.5	3.9	2.0	44 166	962	58 325	972
2001	13 315	100.0	18.8	12.3	10.9	14.8	17.3	10.5	10.4	3.0	1.8	42 658	826	56 812	986
Black Alone[23]															
2002	13 465	100.0	19.0	13.0	11.1	15.8	16.1	9.8	9.6	3.2	2.3	41 364	917	57 018	1 083
2003	13 629	100.0	19.6	12.8	12.0	13.7	16.9	10.2	9.7	3.1	2.1	41 308	885	55 919	986
2004[17]	13 809	100.0	20.3	12.1	12.3	14.7	16.3	10.1	9.1	3.0	2.0	40 832	699	55 129	982
2005	14 002	100.0	19.8	13.7	11.4	13.8	16.9	9.8	9.2	3.3	2.1	40 495	650	55 713	995
2006	14 354	100.0	19.1	12.9	11.5	14.9	16.8	9.6	9.7	3.3	2.3	40 636	504	57 361	1 167
2007	14 551	100.0	19.6	13.1	10.5	14.7	16.7	9.8	10.0	3.4	2.1	41 922	966	57 638	1 057
2008	14 595	100.0	19.5	13.0	11.6	15.6	16.6	9.3	9.2	3.1	2.0	40 731	864	55 389	975
2009[18]	14 730	100.0	19.7	13.6	11.8	14.8	16.2	9.8	9.1	2.9	2.0	38 921	774	55 001	1 032
2010[19]	15 265	100.0	22.1	13.5	11.3	14.7	15.3	10.1	8.1	3.0	1.9	37 749	965	52 829	1 210
2011	15 583	100.0	22.6	14.0	11.7	13.5	15.5	9.0	8.4	3.2	2.1	36 715	954	53 832	1 505
2012	15 872	100.0	21.7	14.3	11.7	13.3	16.5	8.9	8.6	3.0	2.1	37 171	1 450	53 253	1 382
2013[20]	16 009	100.0	20.9	13.5	12.0	14.6	16.1	7.7	9.2	3.5	2.4	38 831	1 550	55 463	2 143
2014[20]	16 437	100.0	20.8	14.0	12.0	14.4	15.4	8.9	8.7	3.3	2.6	38 264	820	55 378	1 229
2015[20]	16 539	100.0	20.3	13.6	11.7	13.0	15.6	10.0	9.3	3.6	2.8	39 817	911	58 652	1 528
2016[20]	16 733	100.0	19.6	12.4	11.4	13.6	16.7	9.7	9.7	3.8	3.1	42 071	1 264	61 200	1 633
2017[20]	17 019	100.0	18.9	12.6	12.2	13.8	15.7	9.6	10.0	3.6	3.5	41 055	1 455	60 521	1 409
2018[20]	17 167	100.0	19.1	12.6	11.3	13.9	16.3	9.7	9.6	4.2	3.3	42 110	922	59 728	1 370
2019[20]	17 054	100.0	17.2	11.5	11.4	13.7	16.8	9.8	10.8	4.2	4.6	45 438	1 212	66 553	1 882

[1]Implementation of a new Current Population Survey (CPS) Annual Social and Economic Supplements (ASEC) processing system.
[2]Introduction of 1970 census sample design and population controls.
[3]Full implementation of 1970 census–based sample design.
[4]Implementation of a new CPS ASEC processing system. Questionnaire expanded to ask 11 income questions.
[5]Some of these estimates were derived using Pareto interpolation and may differ from published data that were derived using linear interpolation.
[6]First-year medians were derived using both Pareto and linear interpolation. Before this year, all medians were derived using linear interpolation.
[7]Implementation of 1980 census population controls. Questionnaire expanded to show 27 possible values from a list of 51 possible sources of income.
[8]Implementation of Hispanic population weighting controls and introduction of 1980 census–based sample design.
[9]Recording of amounts for earnings from longest job increased to $299,999. Full implementation of 1980 census–based sample design.
[10]Implementation of a new CPS ASEC processing system.
[11]Implementation of 1990 census population controls.
[12]Data collection method changed from paper and pencil to computer-assisted interviewing. In addition, the 1994 ASEC was revised to allow for the coding of different income amounts on selected questionnaire items. Limits either increased or decreased in the following categories: earnings limits increased to $999,999, Social Security limits increased to $49,999, Supplemental Security Income and public assistance limits increased to $24,999, veterans' benefits limits increased to $99,999, and child support and alimony limits decreased to $49,999.
[13]Introduction of 1990 census sample design.
[14]Full implementation of 1990 census–based sample design and metropolitan definitions, 7,000 household sample reduction, and revised editing of responses on race.
[15]Implementation of the 2000 census–based population controls.
[16]Implementation of a 28,000 household sample expansion.
[17]Data revised to reflect a correction to the weights in the 2005 ASEC.
[18]Median income is calculated using $2,500 intervals. Beginning with 2009 income data, the Census Bureau expanded the upper income intervals used to calculate medians to $250,000 or more.
[19]Implementation of 2010 census-based population controls.
[20]Data are based on the CPS ASEC sample of 68,000 addresses. The 2014 CPS ASEC included redesigned questions for income and health insurance coverage.
[21]For 2001 and earlier years, the CPS allowed respondents to report only one race group.
[23]Black alone refers to persons who reported Black and did not report any other race category.

Table 13-2. Households, by Total Money Income, Race, and Hispanic Origin of Householder, 1967–2019
—Continued

(Numbers in thousands, percent, dollars; income in 2019 CPI-U-RS adjusted dollars.)

Race and Hispanic origin of householder and year	Number	Percent distribution										Median income (dollars)		Mean income (dollars)	
		Total	Under $15,000	$15,000 to $24,999	$25,000 to $34,999	$35,000 to $49,999	$50,000 to $74,999	$75,000 to $99,999	$100,000 to $149,999	$150,000 to $199,000	$200,000 and over	Value	Standard error	Value	Standard error
Black Alone or in Combination															
2002	13 778	100.0	19.0	13.0	11.1	15.8	16.2	9.8	9.6	3.3	2.3	41 579	900	57 478	1 102
2003	13 969	100.0	19.5	12.8	12.0	13.6	16.9	10.3	9.7	3.1	2.1	41 369	855	56 177	979
2004[17]	14 151	100.0	20.2	12.1	12.2	14.6	16.5	10.1	9.2	3.1	2.0	41 022	618	55 300	966
2005	14 399	100.0	19.7	13.7	11.4	13.8	16.9	9.8	9.3	3.3	2.1	40 621	637	56 071	1 004
2006	14 709	100.0	18.9	12.9	11.4	14.9	16.9	9.6	9.8	3.3	2.4	40 843	498	57 826	1 167
2007	14 976	100.0	19.5	13.1	10.5	14.7	16.6	9.8	10.2	3.4	2.2	42 138	945	57 885	1 041
2008	15 056	100.0	19.4	12.9	11.7	15.6	16.7	9.3	9.3	3.1	2.1	40 882	860	55 563	956
2009[18]	15 212	100.0	19.7	13.5	11.8	14.8	16.3	9.8	9.1	2.9	2.1	39 119	821	55 281	1 014
2010[19]	15 909	100.0	21.9	13.6	11.3	14.7	15.2	10.0	8.2	3.1	2.0	37 786	909	53 466	1 212
2011	16 165	100.0	22.5	14.0	11.7	13.5	15.5	9.0	8.5	3.2	2.2	36 871	1 036	54 118	1 449
2012	16 559	100.0	21.6	14.2	11.7	13.3	16.4	8.9	8.8	3.1	2.2	37 614	1 464	53 725	1 354
2013[20]	16 723	100.0	20.4	13.3	12.2	14.7	16.3	7.6	9.4	3.6	2.5	39 314	1 407	56 804	2 392
2014	17 198	100.0	20.7	13.9	11.9	14.4	15.3	9.0	8.8	3.4	2.7	38 540	839	55 800	1 232
2015	17 322	100.0	20.1	13.5	11.7	12.9	15.7	10.1	9.4	3.6	2.9	40 155	969	59 140	1 539
2016	17 505	100.0	19.2	12.3	11.4	13.7	16.9	9.8	9.8	3.8	3.2	42 684	1 022	61 921	1 640
2017	17 813	100.0	18.6	12.5	12.2	13.8	15.9	9.6	10.0	3.7	3.6	41 705	1 179	60 883	1 360
2018	18 095	100.0	18.7	12.6	11.4	13.9	16.4	9.7	9.7	4.2	3.4	42 447	933	60 439	1 358
2019	18 055	100.0	16.8	11.5	11.3	13.5	16.9	9.8	10.9	4.3	4.9	46 073	1 148	67 924	1 919
Asian and Pacific Islander[21]															
1987[10]	. . .	100.0	10.0	9.0	8.8	10.0	15.9	14.7	18.5	7.9	5.2	69 570	4 254	. . .	. . .
1988	1 913	100.0	8.1	8.7	9.0	10.9	17.7	14.8	16.9	7.8	6.1	67 230	4 545	84 053	4 130
1989	1 988	100.0	7.6	7.9	7.2	10.6	19.2	14.9	17.9	8.1	6.7	72 070	3 205	89 593	4 289
1990	1 958	100.0	8.3	7.5	8.0	10.1	17.5	16.3	17.5	8.0	6.8	73 150	3 565	88 298	4 112
1991	2 094	100.0	10.0	7.4	8.1	12.8	17.5	13.5	17.1	7.8	5.9	66 909	3 551	84 952	4 119
1992[11]	2 262	100.0	9.7	8.1	8.7	10.3	18.9	13.5	17.5	7.3	6.0	67 707	3 215	83 915	3 795
1993[12]	2 233	100.0	11.6	8.6	8.4	10.9	15.2	13.1	19.0	7.2	6.1	66 996	5 420	87 781	5 814
1994[13]	2 040	100.0	9.6	8.9	7.1	10.6	17.3	13.3	18.3	7.6	7.3	69 279	4 319	89 953	5 273
1995[14]	2 777	100.0	9.7	8.5	8.1	9.5	18.5	14.4	17.2	7.1	7.1	67 870	2 801	92 292	6 125
1996	2 998	100.0	10.4	7.4	6.7	10.9	17.8	12.2	18.7	9.6	6.4	70 443	4 153	92 045	5 430
1997	3 125	100.0	9.3	7.9	6.5	10.1	18.3	13.9	17.3	9.0	7.7	72 096	3 297	93 830	4 783
1998	3 308	100.0	8.7	7.5	6.7	11.3	17.0	12.4	19.9	8.8	7.9	73 315	3 357	94 648	4 497
1999[15]	3 742	100.0	8.5	7.0	5.8	10.4	16.7	12.6	17.4	9.3	12.3	78 440	4 548	103 725	4 325
2000[16]	3 963	100.0	7.7	6.0	6.1	10.4	15.9	13.4	19.3	10.3	10.9	83 007	2 329	108 375	3 700
2001	4 071	100.0	8.6	6.5	6.7	10.2	16.4	13.5	18.2	9.7	10.3	77 638	3 048	105 899	4 112
Asian Alone[24]															
2002	3 917	100.0	8.4	6.6	7.2	11.5	16.3	12.5	18.8	8.8	9.8	74 995	2 159	99 821	3 202
2003	4 040	100.0	11.6	7.4	6.2	7.8	15.6	13.1	18.6	9.3	10.3	77 612	2 508	97 501	2 840
2004[17]	4 123	100.0	8.4	6.6	7.0	9.3	17.0	13.3	18.3	9.4	10.6	78 019	2 727	103 815	3 303
2005	4 273	100.0	9.2	6.9	6.6	8.5	15.8	13.4	18.7	9.2	11.7	80 174	1 537	105 110	3 050
2006	4 454	100.0	7.9	6.1	7.1	9.3	15.5	13.1	18.0	11.7	11.4	81 653	3 500	112 229	3 973
2007	4 494	100.0	8.6	6.7	6.5	9.5	15.5	12.5	19.5	10.6	10.6	81 706	2 816	105 086	3 050
2008	4 573	100.0	9.9	6.9	6.7	10.8	14.4	11.8	18.5	10.1	10.8	78 129	2 714	102 588	2 943
2009[18]	4 687	100.0	10.3	6.4	6.9	10.2	15.0	11.9	17.5	10.0	11.9	78 201	2 490	108 472	3 625
2010[19]	5 212	100.0	9.8	7.6	6.8	9.5	15.8	12.4	17.1	10.4	10.7	75 510	3 045	99 394	3 278
2011	5 374	100.0	9.1	8.0	7.7	10.1	15.9	13.4	17.8	8.6	9.5	74 194	2 936	97 564	3 885
2012	5 560	100.0	9.8	6.4	7.3	9.0	16.9	12.4	17.4	9.9	10.9	76 567	3 468	101 962	3 369
2013[20]	5 818	100.0	9.7	7.3	5.0	9.6	15.6	12.8	17.9	8.8	13.3	79 568	6 080	111 256	8 076
2014	6 040	100.0	9.6	6.5	7.5	9.2	14.1	12.5	17.6	11.4	11.6	80 312	3 747	105 461	3 414
2015	6 328	100.0	9.1	6.4	6.0	9.1	14.8	12.2	16.9	11.1	14.4	83 270	3 012	113 756	3 953
2016	6 392	100.0	8.7	6.0	6.2	7.7	14.7	13.4	16.9	12.1	14.4	86 754	2 042	115 051	3 190
2017	6 750	100.0	7.8	6.4	5.9	9.3	14.7	12.6	16.4	11.4	15.4	84 887	1 855	119 325	4 517
2018	6 981	100.0	8.3	6.2	5.9	8.5	14.0	12.0	18.1	10.3	16.7	88 774	2 856	121 987	3 787
2019	6 853	100.0	6.5	5.0	5.2	8.7	12.9	12.5	17.9	12.5	18.9	98 174	3 068	133 111	4 440
Asian Alone or in Combination															
2002	4 079	100.0	8.6	6.6	7.3	11.3	16.7	12.4	18.8	8.8	9.6	74 509	1 854	99 007	3 097
2003	4 235	100.0	11.4	7.4	6.4	7.9	15.9	13.0	18.7	9.2	10.0	77 003	2 824	96 720	2 737
2004[17]	4 346	100.0	8.5	6.6	6.9	9.4	17.1	13.5	18.1	9.4	10.4	77 944	2 584	103 291	3 207
2005	4 500	100.0	9.1	6.6	6.7	8.7	15.9	13.3	18.8	9.2	11.7	80 114	1 574	104 980	3 014
2006	4 664	100.0	7.9	6.0	7.0	9.4	15.8	13.1	18.1	11.7	11.0	81 223	3 381	111 257	3 831
2007	4 715	100.0	8.6	6.6	6.6	9.7	15.4	12.8	19.1	10.7	10.5	81 426	2 818	104 521	2 940
2008	4 805	100.0	9.8	6.9	6.7	11.0	14.5	11.8	18.6	10.0	10.8	78 046	2 767	102 752	2 912
2009[18]	4 940	100.0	10.3	6.4	6.9	10.5	15.0	11.8	17.5	9.8	11.8	77 728	2 820	107 635	3 478
2010[19]	5 550	100.0	9.5	7.7	6.9	9.9	16.0	12.5	17.0	10.2	10.4	74 650	2 832	98 371	3 108
2011	5 705	100.0	9.2	8.1	7.5	10.3	15.8	13.3	17.6	8.5	9.7	74 041	2 931	97 725	3 847
2012	5 872	100.0	9.7	6.3	7.4	9.1	17.1	12.4	17.2	9.8	11.0	76 061	3 188	102 300	3 476
2013[20]	6 160	100.0	9.7	7.2	5.3	9.9	15.1	13.2	17.6	8.9	13.1	79 666	5 772	111 112	7 638

[10]Implementation of a new CPS ASEC processing system.
[11]Implementation of 1990 census population controls.
[12]Data collection method changed from paper and pencil to computer-assisted interviewing. In addition, the 1994 ASEC was revised to allow for the coding of different income amounts on selected questionnaire items. Limits either increased or decreased in the following categories: earnings limits increased to $999,999, Social Security limits increased to $49,999, Supplemental Security Income and public assistance limits increased to $24,999, veterans' benefits limits increased to $99,999, and child support and alimony limits decreased to $49,999.
[13]Introduction of 1990 census sample design.
[14]Full implementation of 1990 census–based sample design and metropolitan definitions, 7,000 household sample reduction, and revised editing of responses on race.
[15]Implementation of the 2000 census–based population controls.
[16]Implementation of a 28,000 household sample expansion.
[17]Data revised to reflect a correction to the weights in the 2005 ASEC.
[18]Median income is calculated using $2,500 intervals. Beginning with 2009 income data, the Census Bureau expanded the upper income intervals used to calculate medians to $250,000 or more.
[19]Implementation of 2010 census-based population controls.
[20]Data are based on the CPS ASEC sample of 68,000 addresses. The 2014 CPS ASEC included redesigned questions for income and health insurance coverage.
[21]For 2001 and earlier years, the CPS allowed respondents to report only one race group.
[24]Asian alone refers to persons who reported Asian and did not report any other race category.
. . . = Not available.

Table 13-2. Households, by Total Money Income, Race, and Hispanic Origin of Householder, 1967–2019 —*Continued*

(Numbers in thousands, percent, dollars; income in 2019 CPI-U-RS adjusted dollars.)

Race and Hispanic origin of householder and year	Number	Percent distribution										Median income (dollars)		Mean income (dollars)	
		Total	Under $15,000	$15,000 to $24,999	$25,000 to $34,999	$35,000 to $49,999	$50,000 to $74,999	$75,000 to $99,999	$100,000 to $149,999	$150,000 to $199,000	$200,000 and over	Value	Standard error	Value	Standard error
Asian Alone or in Combination—*Continued*															
2014[20]	6 333	100.0	9.3	6.5	7.4	9.2	14.3	12.9	17.6	11.3	11.5	80 888	3 523	106 088	3 427
2015[20]	6 640	100.0	9.3	6.5	6.0	9.1	15.0	12.0	16.9	11.1	14.1	82 833	2 483	113 449	3 904
2016[20]	6 750	100.0	8.7	6.1	6.2	7.8	14.9	13.3	16.9	12.0	14.0	86 105	1 982	113 870	3 105
2017[20]	7 124	100.0	7.9	6.4	6.2	9.4	14.8	12.5	16.4	11.1	15.4	84 485	1 889	118 800	4 373
2018[20]	7 416	100.0	8.2	6.3	5.9	8.6	14.1	12.2	18.1	10.1	16.6	88 388	2 475	121 066	3 592
2019[20]	7 334	100.0	6.3	5.1	5.1	8.6	13.6	12.5	17.9	12.5	18.3	97 150	2 746	131 643	4 343
Hispanic[25]															
1972[3]	2 655	100.0	11.9	16.0	13.5	20.6	22.1	9.5	4.8	0.9	0.6	42 073	1 352	48 359	1 352
1973	2 722	100.0	12.2	14.2	14.0	18.8	22.3	11.4	5.8	0.9	0.4	42 003	1 570	48 801	1 307
1974[4,5]	2 897	100.0	13.0	15.4	13.8	18.0	22.1	10.4	5.7	1.1	0.5	41 757	1 504	48 373	1 296
1975[5]	2 948	100.0	16.4	14.7	15.0	17.5	21.5	8.9	4.7	0.8	0.5	38 408	1 397	45 596	1 333
1976[6]	3 081	100.0	16.2	15.3	13.6	18.1	20.0	10.3	5.1	1.1	0.3	39 203	1 375	46 327	1 240
1977	3 304	100.0	13.7	14.8	14.1	18.2	20.8	10.6	6.0	1.4	0.4	41 030	1 185	48 421	1 230
1978	3 291	100.0	13.9	13.3	12.9	18.6	20.7	12.0	6.7	1.4	0.6	42 565	1 697	50 279	1 673
1979[7]	3 684	100.0	14.4	12.9	13.2	16.8	21.4	10.9	7.8	1.6	0.9	42 960	2 037	51 979	1 718
1980	3 906	100.0	15.9	14.0	13.4	17.0	19.6	11.2	6.6	1.4	0.7	40 437	1 803	49 392	1 618
1981	3 980	100.0	15.3	13.8	13.4	17.1	20.3	10.5	7.6	1.3	0.7	41 412	1 866	49 730	1 563
1982	4 085	100.0	17.2	15.2	13.3	16.6	18.8	9.9	6.9	1.1	0.9	38 742	1 684	47 814	1 596
1983	4 326	100.0	18.4	14.8	12.7	16.4	19.0	9.5	7.2	1.4	0.5	38 938	1 623	47 415	1 498
1984[8]	4 883	100.0	17.8	14.3	12.3	15.3	19.8	10.7	7.3	1.8	0.8	39 934	1 647	49 657	1 593
1985[9]	5 213	100.0	17.0	15.7	12.1	15.8	18.8	10.1	8.1	1.6	0.8	39 684	1 525	49 586	1 327
1986	5 418	100.0	16.4	14.3	13.0	15.4	18.5	10.7	8.7	2.2	0.9	40 982	1 756	51 748	1 400
1987[10]	5 642	100.0	16.7	14.0	12.6	15.9	17.4	11.2	8.3	2.3	1.5	41 743	1 492	53 509	1 630
1988	5 910	100.0	16.5	12.4	13.4	15.0	18.8	11.8	8.1	2.3	1.6	42 419	1 769	54 158	1 889
1989	5 933	100.0	15.7	12.4	12.0	16.0	18.6	11.7	9.4	2.6	1.6	43 761	1 396	55 880	1 580
1990	6 220	100.0	15.5	15.0	11.8	15.8	19.5	10.6	8.1	2.1	1.5	42 482	1 433	53 216	1 443
1991	6 379	100.0	16.0	13.8	12.8	16.0	18.7	10.6	8.3	2.2	1.5	41 654	1 425	53 000	1 395
1992[11]	7 153	100.0	16.6	14.0	13.4	16.1	18.4	10.2	7.8	2.4	1.1	40 475	1 376	51 625	1 335
1993[12]	7 362	100.0	16.3	14.8	13.6	16.2	18.2	9.2	8.5	1.9	1.4	39 984	1 322	52 921	1 831
1994[13]	7 735	100.0	17.7	14.4	12.4	15.8	17.6	9.4	8.5	2.3	1.8	40 082	1 225	54 048	2 218
1995[14]	7 939	100.0	17.4	14.6	14.1	15.4	17.1	9.9	7.7	2.2	1.4	38 201	1 369	52 140	1 924
1996	8 225	100.0	15.7	15.1	13.1	15.9	17.6	10.1	8.3	2.4	1.8	40 541	1 293	55 352	2 107
1997	8 590	100.0	15.7	13.9	12.2	16.1	18.5	10.2	8.6	2.7	2.1	42 427	1 245	57 173	1 898
1998	9 060	100.0	14.2	13.7	11.9	16.2	18.1	11.3	9.3	3.2	2.2	44 535	1 412	60 177	2 105
1999[15]	9 579	100.0	11.5	13.4	11.3	16.9	18.9	11.2	11.1	3.1	2.5	47 326	1 132	62 170	1 815
2000[16]	10 034	100.0	11.3	11.9	11.6	15.9	20.0	12.3	11.1	3.3	2.7	49 378	1 171	65 471	1 550
2001	10 499	100.0	11.4	12.6	11.5	16.0	19.4	11.6	11.2	3.6	2.7	48 586	1 014	64 245	1 336
2002	11 339	100.0	12.0	11.8	11.9	17.3	18.4	11.8	10.7	3.4	2.7	47 174	1 130	63 967	1 407
2003	11 693	100.0	12.3	12.0	13.3	16.0	18.7	11.2	10.5	3.2	2.8	45 978	1 052	61 962	1 128
2004[17]	12 178	100.0	12.7	12.0	13.2	15.7	19.5	10.5	10.4	3.4	2.6	46 497	1 071	62 244	1 252
2005	12 519	100.0	12.4	12.0	12.3	16.5	19.2	11.5	9.9	3.5	2.6	47 200	771	61 859	1 023
2006	12 973	100.0	12.1	11.5	12.2	15.8	19.5	11.5	10.8	4.0	2.7	48 023	1 056	64 286	1 213
2007	13 339	100.0	12.5	12.3	11.5	16.6	18.6	11.9	10.5	3.5	2.6	47 809	1 057	62 826	1 088
2008	13 425	100.0	13.8	13.0	11.1	17.6	17.5	10.3	10.6	3.7	2.5	45 129	952	61 387	1 046
2009[18]	13 298	100.0	13.5	12.9	12.1	15.8	18.0	10.8	10.6	3.5	2.9	45 437	986	62 386	1 126
2010[19]	14 435	100.0	14.6	12.8	12.3	15.7	17.7	11.0	9.6	3.8	2.3	44 220	1 125	60 393	1 276
2011	14 939	100.0	14.7	12.1	13.5	15.8	18.4	9.7	9.7	3.7	2.5	44 000	1 025	59 639	1 113
2012	15 589	100.0	15.1	13.0	13.2	14.8	18.2	10.2	9.7	3.4	2.5	43 512	980	59 595	1 281
2013[20]	16 088	100.0	13.7	13.4	13.2	16.1	16.2	9.9	9.7	4.0	3.6	43 627	2 148	63 337	3 078
2014[20]	16 239	100.0	13.5	13.2	11.9	15.0	17.9	11.6	10.7	3.5	2.7	45 931	918	62 192	1 166
2015[20]	16 667	100.0	12.6	11.9	12.4	14.6	17.5	11.9	10.7	4.4	3.8	48 719	1 092	68 644	1 486
2016[20]	16 915	100.0	11.9	10.8	11.3	15.4	18.0	12.3	12.0	4.6	3.9	50 791	1 185	71 182	1 416
2017[20]	17 336	100.0	11.8	10.4	11.4	14.3	19.0	12.0	12.2	4.5	4.3	52 321	791	70 568	1 577
2018[20]	17 758	100.0	11.2	10.9	10.7	15.0	18.6	12.8	11.6	4.8	4.4	52 382	748	72 230	1 648
2019[20]	17 667	100.0	10.7	8.8	10.5	14.1	19.5	12.2	13.0	5.9	5.3	56 113	1 173	75 058	1 621

[3]Full implementation of 1970 census–based sample design.
[4]Implementation of a new CPS ASEC processing system. Questionnaire expanded to ask 11 income questions.
[5]Some of these estimates were derived using Pareto interpolation and may differ from published data that were derived using linear interpolation.
[6]First-year medians were derived using both Pareto and linear interpolation. Before this year, all medians were derived using linear interpolation.
[7]Implementation of 1980 census population controls. Questionnaire expanded to show 27 possible values from a list of 51 possible sources of income.
[8]Implementation of Hispanic population weighting controls and introduction of 1980 census–based sample design.
[9]Recording of amounts for earnings from longest job increased to $299,999. Full implementation of 1980 census–based sample design.
[10]Implementation of a new CPS ASEC processing system.
[11]Implementation of 1990 census population controls.
[12]Data collection method changed from paper and pencil to computer-assisted interviewing. In addition, the 1994 ASEC was revised to allow for the coding of different income amounts on selected questionnaire items. Limits either increased or decreased in the following categories: earnings limits increased to $999,999, Social Security limits increased to $49,999, Supplemental Security Income and public assistance limits increased to $24,999, veterans' benefits limits increased to $99,999, and child support and alimony limits decreased to $49,999.
[13]Introduction of 1990 census sample design.
[14]Full implementation of 1990 census–based sample design and metropolitan definitions, 7,000 household sample reduction, and revised editing of responses on race.
[15]Implementation of the 2000 census–based population controls.
[16]Implementation of a 28,000 household sample expansion.
[17]Data revised to reflect a correction to the weights in the 2005 ASEC.
[18]Median income is calculated using $2,500 intervals. Beginning with 2009 income data, the Census Bureau expanded the upper income intervals used to calculate medians to $250,000 or more.
[19]Implementation of 2010 census-based population controls.
[20]Data are based on the CPS ASEC sample of 68,000 addresses. The 2014 CPS ASEC included redesigned questions for income and health insurance coverage.
[25]Because Hispanics may be of any race, data in this report was collected by 15.0 percent of White householders who reported only one race, 4.3 percent of Black householders who reported only one race, and 2.4 percent of Asian householders who reported only one race. Data users should exercise caution when interpreting aggregate results for the Hispanic population and for race groups, because these populations consist of many distinct groups that differ in socioeconomic characteristics, culture, and recentness of immigration. Data were first collected for Hispanics in 1972.

Table 13-3. Income Deficit or Surplus of Families and Unrelated Individuals by Poverty Status, 2019

(Numbers of families and unrelated individuals in thousands, deficits and surpluses in dollars.)

Characteristic	Total	Size of deficit or surplus								Average deficit or surplus (dollars)		Deficit or surplus per capita (dollars)	
		Under $1,000	$1,000 to $2,499	$2,500 to $4,999	$5,000 to $7,499	$7,500 to $9,999	$10,000 to $12,499	$12,500 to $14,499	$15,000 or more	Estimate	90 percent confidence interval[1] (+/-)	Estimate	90 percent confidence interval[1] (+/-)
Below Poverty Threshold, Deficit													
All families	6 554	468	514	899	805	760	589	528	1 991	10 668	265	3 117	86
Married-couple families	2 507	223	236	332	351	272	246	181	665	9 858	359	2 735	121
Families with a female householder, no husband present	3 300	193	223	465	352	379	298	293	1 095	11 367	392	3 331	117
Families with a male householder, no wife present	746	51	55	101	101	109	45	54	231	10 294	721	3 601	309
Unrelated individuals	11 300	1 019	1 681	2 150	929	887	1 529	3 104	0	7 375	117	7 375	117
Male	4 858	399	739	861	402	390	626	1 441	0	7 542	209	7 542	209
Female	6 441	620	942	1 288	528	497	904	1 663	0	7 249	155	7 249	155
Above Poverty Threshold, Surplus													
All families	77 145	438	694	1 242	1 256	1 335	1 324	1 474	69 382	104 450	1 461	33 398	492
Married-couple families	59 848	201	302	623	619	741	694	923	55 745	118 114	1 746	37 311	572
Families with a female householder, no husband present	11 538	183	305	470	504	455	480	415	8 726	51 693	1 655	17 044	585
Families with a male householder, no wife present	5 759	55	87	149	133	138	149	136	4 912	68 155	2 949	23 347	1 114
Unrelated individuals	48 817	878	1 666	2 653	2 613	2 118	2 442	2 202	34 245	43 768	885	43 768	885
Male	24 459	331	713	1 080	1 076	860	1 214	1 062	18 125	48 431	1 342	48 431	1 342
Female	24 358	548	953	1 573	1 537	1 258	1 229	1 140	16 120	39 086	1 291	39 086	1 291

[1]A 90 percent confidence interval is a measure of an estimate's variability. The larger the confidence interval in relation to the size of the estimate, the less reliable the estimate.
– = Quantity represents or rounds to zero.

Table 13-4. Income Distribution Measures Using Money Income and Equivalence-Adjusted Income, 2018 and 2019

(Percent distribution.)

Measure	2018				2019				Percent change (2018–2019)			
	Money income		Equivalence-adjusted income		Money income		Equivalence-adjusted income		Money income		Equivalence-adjusted income	
	Estimate	90 percent confidence interval[1] (+/-)	Estimate	90 percent confidence interval[1] (+/-)	Estimate	90 percent confidence interval[1] (+/-)	Estimate	90 percent confidence interval[1] (+/-)	Estimate	90 percent confidence interval[1] (+/-)	Estimate	90 percent confidence interval[1] (+/-)
Shares of Aggregate Income by Percentile												
Lowest quintile	3.1	0.05	3.5	0.06	3.1	0.05	3.6	0.06	1.8	2.19	2.4	2.13
Second quintile	8.3	0.08	9.1	0.08	8.3	0.09	9.0	0.10	–	1.46	-0.4	1.25
Middle quintile	14.1	0.11	14.7	0.11	14.1	0.12	14.6	0.12	-0.5	1.14	-0.8	1.14
Fourth quintile	22.6	0.16	22.4	0.15	22.7	0.16	22.3	0.16	0.4	0.97	-0.4	0.98
Highest quintile	52.0	0.34	50.3	0.33	51.9	0.35	50.5	0.36	-0.2	0.90	0.3	0.94
Top 5 percent	23.1	0.42	22.5	0.40	23.0	0.44	22.7	0.44	-0.6	2.59	0.7	2.56
Summary Measures												
Gini index of income inequality	0.486	0.004	0.464	0.003	0.484	0.004	0.465	0.004	-0.20	0.99	0.10	1.03
Mean logrithmic deviation of income	0.616	0.014	0.628	0.012	0.590	0.011	0.597	0.012	-4.200	2.600	-4.900	2.320

[1]A 90-percent confidence interval is a measure of an estimate's variability. The larger the confidence interval in relation to the size of the estimate, the less reliable the estimate.
– = Quantity represents or rounds to zero.

Table 13-5.   Median Household Income by State, 2005 to 2019

(Income in 2019 CPI-U-RS adjusted dollars.)

State	2005	2006	2007	2008	2009	2010	2011	2012	2013	2014	2015	2016	2017	2018	2019
UNITED STATES	60 794	61 268	62 090	59 877	59 458	57 904	57 021	56 912	58 904	58 001	60 987	62 898	63 761	64 324	68 703
Alabama	48 752	48 241	52 176	52 941	47 755	48 100	48 518	48 487	52 017	45 701	48 030	50 308	53 049	50 841	56 200
Alaska	73 346	71 713	77 862	76 168	73 585	67 977	65 424	71 003	79 666	73 105	81 054	80 673	81 335	69 979	78 394
Arizona	59 375	59 306	58 360	55 843	54 634	55 107	55 388	52 480	57 834	53 242	56 381	60 832	62 263	63 411	70 674
Arkansas	48 106	47 103	50 425	47 120	43 644	45 343	47 051	43 527	43 285	48 559	46 184	48 908	51 887	50 683	54 539
California	67 918	70 316	68 890	67 865	67 051	63 788	60 795	63 609	66 829	65 384	68 670	70 993	73 045	71 766	78 105
Colorado	66 204	70 796	75 573	72 542	66 807	70 779	66 789	63 871	74 654	65 874	71 864	75 179	78 204	74 357	72 499
Connecticut	74 585	79 322	79 281	76 993	77 463	77 554	74 520	71 671	76 170	75 842	78 655	80 886	77 494	74 131	87 291
Delaware	67 236	66 654	67 475	60 352	62 249	64 882	62 268	54 631	59 461	62 179	62 325	61 840	67 750	66 190	74 194
District of Columbia	59 044	61 619	62 770	66 170	63 476	66 896	62 941	72 786	66 019	73 805	75 614	75 622	84 772	87 304	93 111
Florida	56 416	58 059	56 604	53 394	54 505	51 782	51 383	51 395	53 350	49 876	52 687	54 521	55 365	55 634	58 368
Georgia	60 269	62 721	60 123	55 025	51 769	51 842	52 372	53 682	51 657	53 567	54 784	57 026	60 475	56 832	56 628
Hawaii	78 195	76 863	79 134	73 230	66 472	69 964	67 265	62 765	70 612	76 990	69 617	76 848	76 759	81 559	88 006
Idaho	57 972	58 741	60 794	56 445	55 875	55 288	54 064	53 460	53 278	57 765	55 708	60 261	62 052	59 792	65 988
Illinois	63 513	61 866	64 900	63 390	63 152	59 610	57 685	57 717	59 291	59 362	65 192	65 398	68 801	71 416	74 399
Indiana	55 690	57 717	58 654	55 374	52 921	54 218	50 631	51 492	54 364	51 951	56 095	59 761	61 290	60 977	66 693
Iowa	61 022	61 173	60 453	59 685	60 585	57 598	57 209	59 618	66 128	62 491	65 669	62 957	66 192	69 963	66 054
Kansas	55 152	57 901	59 945	56 989	53 414	54 118	52 570	55 781	52 567	57 771	59 205	60 523	59 343	65 096	73 151
Kentucky	48 160	50 189	48 765	48 980	50 961	48 301	45 403	45 834	49 334	46 250	45 740	48 335	51 805	55 543	55 662
Louisiana	48 865	46 380	51 065	47 093	54 269	46 181	46 317	43 601	51 034	45 839	49 555	44 954	45 436	50 878	51 707
Maine	57 640	58 016	59 199	56 217	56 740	56 323	56 609	54 838	60 413	55 897	54 771	54 180	55 605	59 726	66 546
Maryland	79 410	80 928	81 122	75 837	76 669	75 442	78 462	80 137	76 238	82 332	79 416	78 581	85 618	87 785	95 572
Massachusetts	73 511	70 330	72 263	71 800	70 920	71 603	72 125	71 012	68 736	68 264	73 229	76 990	79 517	87 909	87 707
Michigan	60 278	61 835	61 024	59 264	54 939	54 379	55 682	55 795	62 182	56 216	58 491	60 823	58 827	61 544	64 119
Minnesota	71 147	71 450	71 762	65 379	66 998	61 482	65 868	68 936	70 709	72 688	74 167	74 808	72 979	73 118	81 426
Mississippi	43 142	44 149	46 079	43 383	41 900	44 842	46 809	40 875	35 548	38 397	43 204	43 785	45 139	43 556	44 787
Missouri	56 411	56 664	56 864	54 800	58 254	53 839	52 145	55 515	50 900	61 215	63 879	58 612	58 957	62 844	60 597
Montana	48 966	52 249	53 960	51 065	48 301	48 508	45 883	50 298	47 490	55 239	55 461	60 806	59 872	58 724	60 195
Nebraska	62 890	61 197	60 781	60 383	59 240	60 697	63 357	58 228	63 343	61 474	65 258	63 255	62 141	68 799	73 071
Nevada	63 265	66 456	66 818	65 163	61 437	60 165	53 591	52 803	56 993	53 913	56 122	59 054	60 533	62 985	70 906
New Hampshire	74 780	78 770	83 527	78 771	76 603	78 300	75 049	75 656	75 958	79 340	81 661	81 245	78 877	82 820	86 900
New Jersey	83 158	86 510	74 791	77 735	77 375	73 993	71 014	74 399	70 083	70 525	73 764	72 943	74 299	75 520	87 726
New Mexico	51 110	50 880	54 826	50 115	52 010	53 037	47 825	48 442	44 153	50 466	48 688	51 618	47 559	49 158	53 113
New York	61 909	61 295	60 497	60 065	59 982	58 497	57 684	53 190	54 926	58 707	62 594	65 453	64 185	68 493	71 855
North Carolina	55 190	50 586	53 784	51 101	50 056	51 504	51 498	46 355	50 937	50 572	54 815	57 278	51 674	54 336	61 159
North Dakota	55 369	52 175	58 348	59 077	59 814	59 937	64 205	62 210	65 024	65 647	61 957	64 118	62 750	67 710	70 031
Ohio	58 008	58 344	60 689	55 867	54 802	53 920	50 862	49 503	55 786	53 663	57 517	57 514	63 294	62 750	64 663
Oklahoma	49 402	49 367	53 417	54 887	54 800	50 650	55 199	54 001	50 745	51 020	50 801	54 273	54 110	55 420	59 397
Oregon	57 950	59 857	62 094	61 572	58 647	59 462	58 698	57 758	53 863	63 642	65 646	63 000	65 181	70 418	74 413
Pennsylvania	60 760	61 619	59 870	61 185	57 540	56 773	56 837	57 902	60 631	59 640	65 166	64 965	63 916	65 693	70 582
Rhode Island	64 938	68 304	67 006	63 374	61 676	60 662	55 858	62 544	61 914	63 380	60 107	65 550	68 209	63 394	70 151
South Carolina	52 794	50 357	54 649	50 178	49 094	48 999	45 663	49 532	47 888	48 567	50 027	57 888	56 879	58 485	62 028
South Dakota	56 627	57 742	57 375	61 421	54 738	53 293	53 796	55 125	58 715	57 348	59 421	61 205	59 358	60 540	64 255
Tennessee	51 713	51 725	50 919	47 258	48 397	45 348	48 164	47 963	47 665	47 255	51 074	54 700	57 681	57 076	56 627
Texas	54 358	55 048	56 924	55 338	56 708	55 542	55 874	57 926	56 509	58 237	60 940	61 947	62 672	60 868	67 444
Utah	71 931	69 438	66 164	74 439	69 866	66 629	63 217	65 083	67 107	68 515	71 499	71 892	72 785	78 463	84 523
Vermont	66 539	66 073	58 576	60 357	62 493	65 721	59 080	62 005	72 016	65 623	64 200	64 814	66 416	71 335	74 305
Virginia	68 127	72 604	73 126	73 782	72 267	70 937	71 331	72 101	72 450	71 511	66 350	70 795	73 851	78 549	81 313
Washington	66 463	69 558	71 790	67 409	72 137	65 997	64 763	69 373	70 268	63 850	72 562	74 906	74 612	81 170	82 454
West Virginia	47 827	48 834	52 026	45 225	48 364	50 267	47 642	48 586	47 344	42 754	46 212	47 253	48 973	51 489	53 706
Wisconsin	58 594	65 706	63 381	60 945	61 202	59 167	59 304	59 213	56 861	62 782	59 809	63 727	66 208	63 764	67 355
Wyoming	58 684	59 794	60 250	63 488	62 674	61 341	62 096	64 158	74 136	60 199	65 745	61 609	62 092	63 672	65 134

Table 13-6. Median Family Income in the Past Twelve Months, by the Number of Earners and State, 2019

(Income in 2019 inflation-adjusted dollars.)

State	Total	No earners	1 earner	2 earners	3 or more earners
UNITED STATES	80 944	44 184	55 937	102 225	125 744
Alabama	66 171	37 972	49 191	90 456	115 834
Alaska	91 971	58 268	63 223	113 614	156 265
Arizona	74 468	48 956	55 159	93 799	113 351
Arkansas	62 387	33 103	46 120	83 460	100 973
California	91 377	45 417	62 171	114 555	129 636
Colorado	95 164	56 871	66 942	112 177	133 870
Connecticut	101 272	49 785	68 400	129 566	144 678
Delaware	87 148	58 796	61 395	104 294	140 946
District of Columbia	130 291	26 273	70 070	183 611	146 200
Florida	71 348	48 662	52 534	90 059	108 943
Georgia	74 833	39 684	52 458	96 422	120 564
Hawaii	96 462	50 405	71 514	109 161	149 539
Idaho	72 365	51 682	51 837	86 441	111 475
Illinois	87 771	47 155	57 983	110 996	129 615
Indiana	73 876	42 918	51 689	92 533	119 234
Iowa	78 152	47 140	51 095	96 142	118 461
Kansas	79 006	47 493	51 957	94 688	119 687
Kentucky	66 183	33 922	49 041	87 811	116 620
Louisiana	65 105	29 458	46 909	95 162	118 385
Maine	76 316	43 156	54 679	94 710	120 589
Maryland	105 679	55 164	70 964	129 951	153 302
Massachusetts	108 348	45 337	70 834	133 420	157 639
Michigan	75 703	46 545	53 159	96 651	122 558
Minnesota	93 584	54 995	61 811	111 657	138 424
Mississippi	58 503	29 365	44 765	81 304	103 801
Missouri	73 457	42 743	50 521	92 873	117 610
Montana	73 014	48 164	54 201	87 469	115 352
Nebraska	80 062	48 255	50 847	95 938	114 630
Nevada	76 124	48 385	53 731	93 628	112 105
New Hampshire	97 112	50 707	71 169	115 981	141 494
New Jersey	105 705	51 720	71 064	131 145	154 942
New Mexico	61 826	35 875	46 945	82 793	106 418
New York	89 475	38 828	59 956	114 750	143 609
North Carolina	72 049	41 558	50 653	93 000	113 440
North Dakota	87 055	47 102	55 022	101 126	133 871
Ohio	74 911	42 442	51 776	96 702	121 974
Oklahoma	68 358	37 144	48 528	90 008	111 604
Oregon	82 540	51 553	61 303	104 260	122 234
Pennsylvania	81 075	42 624	57 213	102 700	128 538
Rhode Island	89 373	45 467	63 724	109 961	142 094
South Carolina	70 537	44 019	49 390	93 275	115 971
South Dakota	76 826	48 145	51 723	92 028	120 946
Tennessee	69 993	37 586	50 182	90 608	112 627
Texas	76 727	38 341	52 308	98 766	114 533
Utah	86 152	55 055	66 445	91 089	123 044
Vermont	83 458	47 909	55 409	103 965	126 733
Virginia	93 497	52 356	64 079	115 916	136 540
Washington	94 709	54 338	70 194	116 620	137 132
West Virginia	60 920	34 941	50 235	86 041	111 613
Wisconsin	81 829	50 505	54 660	100 210	124 839
Wyoming	79 946	59 698	57 091	95 545	125 307

Table 13-7. Median Family Income in the Past Twelve Months, by Size of Family and State, 2019

(Income in 2019 inflation-adjusted dollars.)

State	Total	2-person families	3-person families	4-person families	5-person families	6-person families	7-or-more-person families
UNITED STATES	80 944	71 805	82 677	99 048	91 850	88 019	92 188
Alabama	66 171	59 818	66 280	80 845	82 751	68 579	72 891
Alaska	91 971	85 572	101 965	101 575	97 738	107 693	85 854
Arizona	74 468	69 122	74 639	84 669	78 221	75 728	89 229
Arkansas	62 387	57 753	66 203	67 349	73 462	62 588	73 346
California	91 377	82 418	91 605	105 232	93 599	91 290	103 663
Colorado	95 164	87 103	95 050	114 066	99 808	95 538	98 967
Connecticut	101 272	89 186	102 282	129 379	122 257	105 569	110 212
Delaware	87 148	77 853	91 369	107 204	89 704	92 029	94 706
District of Columbia	130 291	130 524	119 439	171 779	101 688	101 430	132 818
Florida	71 348	65 935	70 815	84 165	83 987	79 653	85 231
Georgia	74 833	67 463	75 460	91 161	83 538	75 947	80 298
Hawaii	96 462	83 198	94 851	118 223	114 056	124 654	159 184
Idaho	72 365	64 929	72 304	89 661	83 750	77 911	83 324
Illinois	87 771	76 602	91 581	107 226	101 397	96 209	104 700
Indiana	73 876	65 577	77 161	90 654	86 511	82 051	89 777
Iowa	78 152	70 892	80 912	95 199	90 621	81 905	73 350
Kansas	79 006	71 559	83 375	92 890	85 338	88 311	89 678
Kentucky	66 183	58 298	67 461	81 619	80 588	78 362	78 523
Louisiana	65 105	57 592	67 337	82 529	77 115	78 977	80 109
Maine	76 316	68 863	82 132	91 651	90 576	102 368	66 944
Maryland	105 679	93 255	107 552	130 252	123 729	109 374	114 890
Massachusetts	108 348	90 912	110 779	140 309	136 558	123 756	118 427
Michigan	75 703	66 198	79 484	97 970	90 349	88 409	79 118
Minnesota	93 584	81 478	100 430	118 646	111 100	98 284	93 641
Mississippi	58 503	53 919	57 747	70 656	65 680	72 054	51 228
Missouri	73 457	65 680	75 500	89 418	89 820	85 509	86 044
Montana	73 014	67 777	75 151	81 958	96 821	87 931	80 221
Nebraska	80 062	71 440	85 929	96 749	91 073	98 499	78 422
Nevada	76 124	68 953	76 591	83 731	85 351	90 484	101 189
New Hampshire	97 112	82 328	106 627	128 157	118 282	111 284	114 210
New Jersey	105 705	87 432	111 046	132 708	121 129	120 528	129 381
New Mexico	61 826	57 296	62 443	66 343	69 830	79 265	70 218
New York	89 475	76 219	91 381	111 054	106 785	101 285	106 289
North Carolina	72 049	66 044	72 069	88 942	81 350	78 973	75 935
North Dakota	87 055	77 965	89 584	103 996	108 050	108 815	56 769
Ohio	74 911	66 242	78 059	95 003	91 001	83 297	79 527
Oklahoma	68 358	63 012	67 362	78 458	78 319	66 027	71 958
Oregon	82 540	73 378	88 474	100 533	91 814	89 536	94 583
Pennsylvania	81 075	70 577	87 217	103 857	95 586	93 690	79 116
Rhode Island	89 373	79 791	95 390	108 105	100 194	83 981	119 212
South Carolina	70 537	64 083	70 883	85 227	81 003	72 771	77 344
South Dakota	76 826	70 592	82 532	90 951	89 748	79 431	76 827
Tennessee	69 993	63 203	71 133	85 923	76 965	79 656	83 473
Texas	76 727	70 418	76 170	88 109	81 948	77 396	81 685
Utah	86 152	72 855	85 507	95 430	102 955	102 724	102 263
Vermont	83 458	73 601	87 394	111 095	102 299	112 542	105 548
Virginia	93 497	81 900	97 056	114 910	102 513	107 096	110 945
Washington	94 709	85 189	98 730	112 182	100 851	100 914	97 296
West Virginia	60 920	54 841	67 702	73 600	82 769	62 751	81 240
Wisconsin	81 829	72 171	87 353	103 708	97 066	86 649	84 311
Wyoming	79 946	71 840	83 878	100 012	82 634	92 855	119 973

CHAPTER 14: OCCUPATIONAL SAFETY AND HEALTH

HIGHLIGHTS

This chapter includes data on work-related illnesses and injuries and fatal work injuries from the Injuries, Illnesses, and Fatalities (IIF) program. Data are classified by industry and selected worker characteristics.

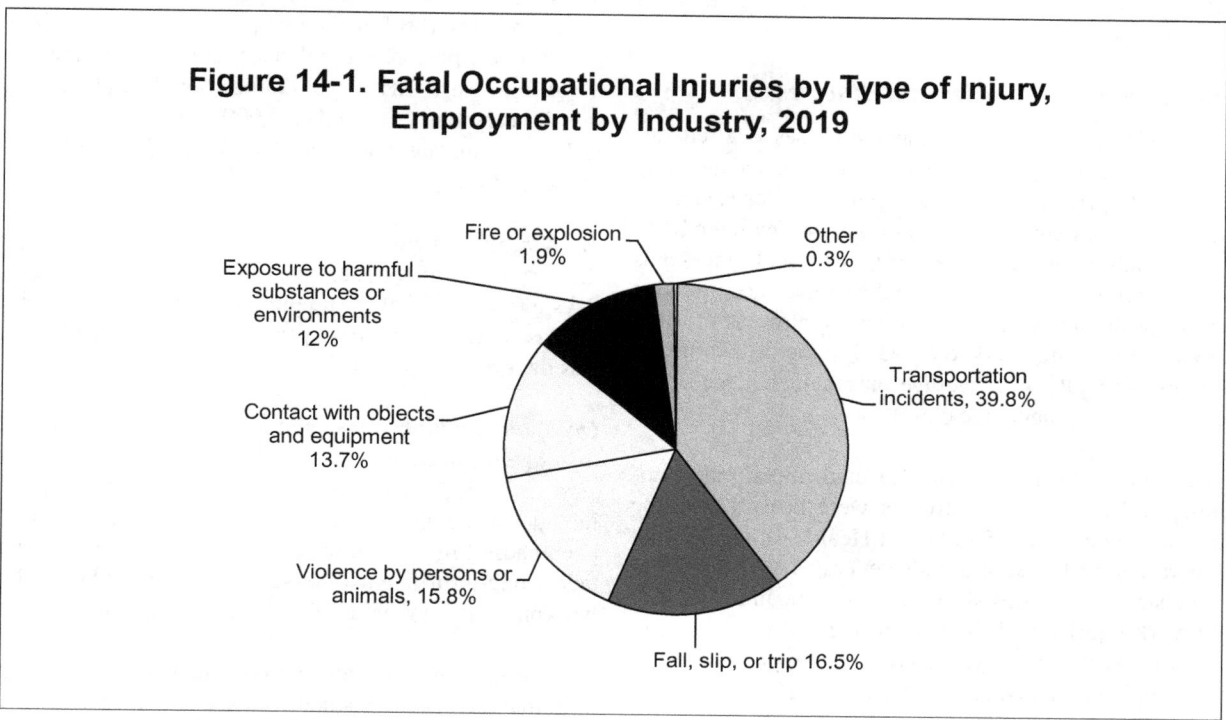

Figure 14-1. Fatal Occupational Injuries by Type of Injury, Employment by Industry, 2019

Transportation incidents remained the most frequent fatal event in 2019 accounting for approximately 40 percent of all fatal occupational injuries. More than 2,100 people died in transportation incidents—the highest level since the series began in 2011. In 2019, there were a total of 5,333 fatal occupational injuries which is the highest amount since 2007. The number of suicides and homicides increased for the second consecutive year after decreasing in 2017. (See Table 14-9.)

OTHER HIGHLIGHTS

• Unintentional overdoses due to nonmedical use of drugs or alcohol while at work increased from 305 to 313. This is the seventh consecutive annual increase. (See Table 14-9.)

• In 2019, there were over 3.3 million nonfatal workplace injuries in the United States including private industry and state and local governments. The incidence rate of total recordable cases in all industries was 2.8 cases per 100 full-time equivalent workers, the same as in 2017 and 2018. (Table 14-1.)

• Men accounted for approximately 93 percent of workplace fatalities in 2019. (Table 14-8.)

• Skin disorders accounted for nearly 25,000 nonfatal occupational injuries and illnesses in 2019 while hearing loss accounted for nearly 17,000 and respiratory conditions accounted for over 15,000 nonfatal occupational injuries and illnesses. (See Table 14-6.)

NOTES AND DEFINITIONS

Collection and Coverage

The Injuries, Illnesses, and Fatalities (IIF) program at the Bureau of Labor Statistics (BLS) provides annual reports on the number of workplace injuries, illnesses, and fatalities. BLS has reported annually on the number of work-related injuries, illnesses, and fatalities since 1972 after the Occupational Safety and Health Act of 1970 was passed.

Nonfatal Occupational Injuries and Illnesses

The Survey of Occupational Injuries and Illnesses is a federal-state program in which employer's reports are collected annually from over 200,000 private industry and public sector establishments and processed by state agencies cooperating with the BLS. Summary information on the number of injuries and illnesses is copied by these employers directly from their recordkeeping logs to the survey questionnaire. The questionnaire also asks for the number of employee hours worked (needed in the calculation of incidence rates) as well as its average employment (needed to verify the unit's employment-size class).

Occupational injury and illness data for coal, metal, and non-metal mining and for railroad activities were provided by the Department of Labor's Mine Safety and Health Administration and the Department of Transportation's Federal Railroad Administration. The survey excludes all work-related fatalities as well as nonfatal work injuries and illnesses to the self employed; to workers on farms with 10 or fewer employees; to private household workers; and, nationally, to federal, state, and local government workers.

Injuries and illnesses logged by employers conform with definitions and recordkeeping guidelines set by the Occupational Safety and Health Administration, U.S. Department of Labor. Under those guidelines, nonfatal cases are recordable if they are occupational illnesses or if they are occupational injuries which involve lost worktime, medical treatment other than first aid, restriction of work or motion, loss of consciousness, or transfer to another job. Employers keep counts of injuries separate from illnesses and also identify for each whether a case involved any days away from work or days of restricted work activity, or both, beyond the day of injury or onset of illness.

Occupational injuries, such as sprains, cuts, and fractures, account for the vast majority of all cases that employers log and report to the BLS survey. Occupational illnesses are new cases recognized, diagnosed, and reported during the year. Overwhelmingly, those reported are easier to directly relate to workplace activity (e.g., contact dermatitis or carpal tunnel syndrome) than are long-term latent illnesses, such as cancers. The latter illnesses are believed to be under recorded and, thus, understated in the BLS survey.

Concepts and Definitions

Days away from work are cases that involve days away from work, days of restricted work activity, or both.

The data are presented in the form of *incidence rates*, defined as the number of injuries and illnesses or cases of days away from work per 100 full-time employees. The formula is (N/EH) x 200,000, where N = number of injuries and illnesses or days away from work, EH = total hours worked by all employees during the calendar year, and 200,000 represents the base for 100 full-time equivalent workers (working 40 hours per week, 50 weeks per year).

Median days away from work is a measure used to summarize the varying lengths of absences from work among the cases with days away from work. The median is the point at which half of the cases involved more days away from work and half involved less days away from work.

Occupational illness is an abnormal condition or disorder (other than one resulting from an occupational injury) caused by exposure to environmental factors associated with employment. It includes acute and chronic illnesses and diseases that may have been caused by inhalation, absorption, ingestion, or direct contact. Long-term latent illnesses can be difficult to relate to the workplace and are believed to be understated in this survey.

Occupational injury is any injury—such as a cut, fracture, sprain, or amputation—that results from a work accident or from exposure to an incident in the work environment.

Fatal Occupational Injuries

The Bureau of Labor Statistics (BLS) Census of Fatal Occupational Injuries (CFOI) produces comprehensive, accurate, and timely counts of fatal work injuries. CFOI is a federal-state cooperative program that has been implemented in all 50 states and the District of Columbia since 1992. To compile counts that are as complete as possible, the census uses multiple sources to identify, verify, and profile fatal worker injuries. Information about each workplace fatality—occupation and other worker characteristics, equipment involved, and circumstances of the event—is obtained by cross referencing the source records, such as death certificates, workers' compensation reports, and federal and state agency administrative reports. To ensure that fatalities are work-related, cases are substantiated with two or more independent source documents, or a source document and a follow-up questionnaire.

Data compiled by the CFOI program are issued annually for the preceding calendar year. These data are used by safety and health policy analysts and researchers to help prevent fatal work injuries by:

- Informing workers of life threatening hazards associated with various jobs;
- Promoting safer work practices through enhanced job safety training;
- Assessing and improving workplace safety standards; and
- Identifying new areas of safety research.

The National Safety Council has adopted the Census of Fatal Occupational Injuries figure, beginning with the 1992 data year, as the authoritative count for work related deaths in the United States.

Sources of Additional Information

For more extensive definitions and description of collection methods see the *BLS Handbook of Methods* and BLS news release USDL 20-2030, "Employer-Reported Workplace Injuries and Illnesses, 2019" and USDL 20-2265 "National Census of Fatal Occupational Injuries in 2019" available on the BLS Web site at <https://www.bls.gov/iif/>.

Table 14-1. Incidence Rate[1] and Number of Nonfatal Occupational Injuries by Industry and Ownership, 2019

(Number, rate.)

Industry[2]	Incidence rate	Number of cases (thousands)	Percent relative standard cases	
			Incidence rate[2]	Number of cases (housands)
All Industries Including Private, State and Local Government[3]	2.8	3 326	0.5	0.5
Private industry[3]	2.6	2 687	0.6	0.5
Goods-producing[3]	3.0	641	1.3	1.0
Natural resources and mining[3,4]	3.2	57	4.2	3.4
Agriculture, forestry, fishing and hunting[3]	4.9	48	3.9	3.9
Mining, quarrying, and oil and gas extraction[4]	1.2	9	5.7	5.1
Construction	2.7	195	3.2	2.4
Manufacturing	3.0	388	1.0	0.9
Service-providing	2.5	2 046	0.7	0.6
Trade, transportation, and utilities[5]	3.3	766	0.9	0.9
Wholesale trade	2.6	150	2.7	2.7
Retail trade	3.3	386	1.2	1.2
Transportation and warehousing[5]	4.3	219	1.5	1.4
Information	1.1	30	6.8	6.5
Finance, insurance, and real estate	0.9	69	4.8	4.6
Finance and insurance	0.4	25	5.9	5.8
Real estate and rental and leasing	2.2	44	6.5	6.5
Professional and business services	1.3	207	2.8	2.5
Professional, scientific, and technical services	0.8	70	5.6	4.9
Management of companies and enterprises	0.7	16	7.2	7.0
Educational and health services	3.4	579	1.1	0.9
Educational services	1.7	24	2.9	3.0
Health care and social assistance	6.9	39	3.2	2.0
Leisure, entertainment, and hospitality	3.2	333	1.5	1.5
Arts, entertainment, and recreation	3.7	53	3.5	3.3
Accommodation and food services	3.1	280	1.7	1.7
Other services (except public administration)	1.9	62	5.4	5.1
State and local government[3]	4.3	639	1.3	1.3
State government[3]	3.3	128	2.4	2.1
Local government[3]	4.7	511	1.5	1.5

[1]The incidence rates represent the number of injuries and illnesses per 100 full-time workers and were calculated as: (N/EH) x 200,000 (where N = number of injuries and illnesses; EH = total hours worked by all employees during the calendar year; 200,000 = base for 100 equivalent full-time workers working 40 hours per week, 50 weeks per year).
[2]Totals include data for industries not shown separately.
[3]Excludes farms with fewer than 11 employees.
[4]Data for Mining include establishments not governed by the Mine Safety and Health Administration rules and reporting, such as those in Oil and Gas Extraction and related support activities.
[5]Data for employers in railroad transportation are provided to BLS by the Federal Railroad Administration, U.S. Department of Transportation.

Table 14-2.   Highest Incidence Rates[1] of Total Nonfatal Occupational Injury and Illness Cases, 2019

(Rate per 100 full-time workers.)

Industry sector[2]	NAICS Code[3]	Incidence rate
All Industries Including State and Local Government		3.0
Prefabricated wood building manufacturing	321 992	13.8
Nursing and residential care facilities	623	11.5
Veterinary services	54 194	10.7
Steel foundries (except investment)	331 513	9.7
Couriers and express delivery services	4 921	8.8
Armored car services	561 613	8.8
Skiing facilities	71 392	8.5
Hospitals	622	8.1
Ambulance services	62 191	7.9
Truss manufacturing	321 214	7.7
Truck trailer manufacturing	336 212	7.6
Nursing and residential care facilities	623	7.6
Hog and pig farming	1 122	7.5
Dried and dehydrated food manufacturing	311 423	7.5
Aluminum foundries (except die-casting)	331 524	7.4
Light truck and utility vehicle manufacturing	336 112	7.4
Psychiatric and substance abuse hospitals	6 222	7.2
Performing arts companies	7 111	7.2
Travel trailer and camper manufacturing	336 214	7.1
Scheduled passenger air transportation	481 111	7.1
Framing contractors	23 813	7.0
Seafood product preparation and packaging	3 117	6.9
Manufactured home (mobile home) manufacturing	321 991	6.8
Pet and pet supplies stores	45 391	6.8
Correctional institutions	92 214	6.8

[1]The incidence rates represent the number of injuries and illnesses per 100 full-time workers and were calculated as: (N/EH) x 200,000 (where N = number of injuries and illnesses; EH = total hours worked by all employees during the calendar year; 200,000 = base for 100 equivalent full-time workers working 40 hours per week, 50 weeks per year).
[2]High rate industries were those having the highest incidence rate of total recordable cases of injuries and illnesses and at least 500 total recordable cases at the most detailed level of publication based on the North American Industry Classification System—United States, 2017.
[3]North American Industry Classification, United States 2017
[4]Excludes farms with fewer than 11 employees.

Table 14-3. Highest Incidence Rate[1] of Nonfatal Occupational Injuries and Illness Cases With Days Away From Work, Restricted Job Activity, or Job Transfer, 2019

(Number, rate per 100 full-time workers.)

Industry[2]	NAICS Code[3]	Incidence rate
All Industries Including State and Local Government[4]		1.6
Prefabricated wood building manufacturing	321 992	7.8
Nursing and residential care facilities	623	7.3
Couriers and express delivery services	4 921	6.5
Scheduled passenger air transportation	481 111	5.9
Steel foundries (except investment)	331 513	5.7
Skiing facilities	71 392	5.2
Amusement and theme parks	71 311	5.0
Elevator and moving stairway manufacturing	333 921	4.9
Rendering and meat byproduct processing	311 613	4.8
Seafood product preparation and packaging	3 117	4.8
Soft drink manufacturing	312 111	4.8
Urban transit systems	4 851	4.7
Hospitals	622	4.7
Dried and dehydrated food manufacturing	311 423	4.6
Truss manufacturing	321 214	4.6
Nursing and residential care facilities	623	4.6
Framing contractors	23 813	4.5
Refrigerated warehousing and storage	49 312	4.5
Ambulance services	62 191	4.5
Solid waste collection	562 111	4.4
Aluminum foundries	331 524	4.3
Light truck and utility vehicle manufacturing	336 112	4.3
Industrial launderers	812 332	4.3
Correctional institutions	92 214	4.3
Manufactured home (mobile home) manufacturing	321 991	4.2
Automobile manufacturing	336 111	4.2

[1]The incidence rates represent the number of injuries and illnesses per 100 full-time workers and were calculated as: (N/EH) x 200,000 (where N = number of injuries and illnesses; EH = total hours worked by all employees during the calendar year; 200,000 = base for 100 equivalent full-time workers working 40 hours per week, 50 weeks per year).
[2]High rate industries were those having the highest incidence rate of injury and illness cases with days away from work, restricted work activity or job transfer and at least 500 total recordable cases at the most detailed level of publication, based on the *North American Industry Classification System*—United States, 2017.
[3]*North American Industry Classification System*—United States, 2017.
[4]Excludes farms with fewer than 11 employees.

Table 14-4.   Highest Incidence Rate[1] of Nonfatal Occupational Injuries and Illnesses With Cases Away From Work, 2019[2]

(Incidence rate per 100 full-time workers.)

Industry[3]	NAICS code[4]	Incidence rate
All Industries Including State and Local Government		0.9
Nursing and residential care facilities	623	6.0
Prefabricated wood building manufacturing	321 992	5.1
Scheduled passenger air transportation	481 111	4.2
Elevator and moving stairway manufacturing	333 921	3.8
Correctional institutions	92 214	3.7
Hospitals	622	3.5
Couriers and express delivery services	4 921	3.4
Urban transit systems	4 851	3.2
Other support activities for transportation	4 889	3.2
Seafood product preparation and packaging	3 117	3.1
Marine cargo handling	48 832	3.1
Bituminous coal underground mining	212 112	3.0
Solid waste collection	562 111	3.0
Ambulance services	62 191	3.0
Siding contractors	23 817	2.8
Steel foundries	331 513	2.7
Interurban and rural bus transportation	4 852	2.7
Framing contractors	23 813	2.6
Reconstituted wood product manufacturing	321 219	2.5
Psychiatric and substance abuse hospitals	6 222	2.5
Nursing and residential care facilities	623	2.5
Dairy cattle and milk production	11 212	2.4
Water supply and irrigation systems	22 131	2.4
Skiing facilities	71 392	2.4
Truss manufacturing	321 214	2.3
Concrete block and brick manufacturing	327 331	2.3

[1] The incidence rates represent the number of injuries and illnesses per 100 full-time workers and were calculated as: (N/EH) x 200,000 (where N = number of injuries and illnesses; EH = total hours worked by all employees during the calendar year; 200,000 = base for 100 equivalent full-time workers working 40 hours per week, 50 weeks per year).
[2] Days-away-from-work cases include those that result in days away from work with or without job transfer or restriction.
[3] High rate industries were those having the highest incidence rate of injury and illness cases with days away from work and at least 500 total recordable cases at the most detailed level of publication based on the North American Industry Classification System —United States, 2017.
[4] North American Industry Classification System —United States, 2017.
[5] Data for mining operators in this industry are provided to BLS by the Mine Safety and Health Administration U.S. Department of Labor. Independent mining contractors are excluded. These data do not reflect the changes the Occupational Safety and Health Administration made to its recordkeeping requirements effective January 1, 2002; therefore, estimates for these industries are not comparable to estimates in other industries.

Table 14-5.   Highest Incidence Rate[1] of Nonfatal Injury and Illness Cases With Job Transfer or Restriction, 2019

(Rate per 100 full-time workers.)

Industry[2]	NAICS code[3]	Incidence rate
All Industries Including State and Local Government[4]		0.7
Amusement and theme parks	71 311	3.7
Soft drink manufacturing	312 111	3.3
Dried and dehydrated food manufacturing	311 423	3.2
Rendering and meat byproduct processing	311 613	3.1
Couriers and express delivery services	4 921	3.1
Steel foundries (except investment)	331 513	3.0
Aluminum foundries (except die-casting)	331 524	3.0
Light truck and utility vehicle manufacturing	336 112	3.0
Manufactured home (mobile home) manufacturing	321 991	2.9
Motor home manufacturing	336 213	2.8
Skiing facilities	71 392	2.8
Prefabricated wood building manufacturing	321 992	2.7
Refrigerated warehousing and storage	49 312	2.7
Animal (except poultry) slaughtering	311 611	2.6
Industrial launderers	812 332	2.6
Secondary smelting, refining, and alloying of nonferrous metal (except copper and aluminum	331 492	2.5
Iron foundries	331 511	2.5
Automobile manufacturing	336 111	2.5

[1]The incidence rates represent the number of injuries and illnesses per 100 full-time workers and were calculated as: (N/EH) x 200,000 (where N = number of injuries and illnesses; EH = total hours worked by all employees during the calendar year; 200,000 = base for 100 equivalent full-time workers working 40 hours per week, 50 weeks per year).
[2]High rate industries were those having the highest incidence rate of injury and illness cases with days away from work and at least 500 total recordable cases at the most detailed level of publication based on the North American Industry Classification System —United States, 2012.
[3]North American Industry Classification System —United States, 2012.
[4] Excludes farms with fewer than 11 employees.

Table 14-6.   Nonfatal Occupational Illnesses by Major Industry Sector and Category of Illness, 2019

(Number, rate.)

Characteristic	Total cases		Skin diseases or disorders		Respiratory conditions		Poisionings		Hearing loss		All other illnesses	
	Number of cases (000s)	Incidence rate[1]	Number of cases (000s)	Incidence rate[1]	Number of cases (000s)	Incidence rate[1]	Number of cases (000s)	Incidence rate[1]	Number of cases (000s)	Incidence rate[1]	Number of cases (000s)	Incidence rate[1]
All Industries Including Private, State and Local Government[2]	170.9	14.6	24.9	2.1	15.1	1.3	2.4	0.2	16.9	1.4	111.6	9.5
Private Industry[2]	127.2	12.4	18.2	1.8	10.8	1.1	1.7	0.2	14.5	1.4	82.0	8.0
Goods-Producing[2]	41.2	19.0	5.6	2.6	2.2	1.0	0.6	0.3	11.6	5.3	21.2	9.8
Natural resources and mining[2,3]	3.0	17.1	0.9	4.9	0.3	1.4	0.1	0.4	0.2	1.8	1.6	9.3
Construction	5.2	7.3	1.3	1.8	0.6	0.9	0.4	0.6	0.4	0.2	2.5	3.5
Manufacturing	33.0	25.8	3.5	2.7	1.3	1.0	0.1	0.1	11.0	8.4	17.1	13.4
Service-Providing	86.0	10.7	12.6	1.6	8.6	1.1	1.2	0.1	2.9	0.4	60.7	7.5
Trade, transportation, and utilities[4]	23.0	10.0	3.0	1.3	2.0	0.9	0.3	0.1	2.2	0.9	15.5	6.7
Information	1.5	5.6	0.2	0.8	...	0.1	0.1	0.3	0.1	0.4	1.1	4.1
Finance, insurance, and real estate	...	...	0.4	0.5	0.9	1.2	(5)	(5)	...	...	2.2	2.8
Professional and business services	9.1	5.5	1.6	1.0	0.9	0.6	0.2	0.1	0.3	0.2	6.0	3.6
Educational and health services	34.8	20.6	4.4	2.6	3.6	2.1	0.2	0.1	0.1	0.1	26.6	15.7
Leisure, entertainment, and hospitality	12.0	11.5	2.5	2.4	0.7	0.7	0.4	0.4	0.1	0.1	8.3	8.0
Other services (except public administration)	2.1	6.4	0.6	1.7	0.4	1.1	...	...	0.1	0.3	1.1	3.3
State and Local Government[2]	43.7	29.7	6.7	4.6	4.3	2.9	0.6	0.4	2.4	1.3	29.7	20.2
State government[2]	10.3	26.3	1.0	2.5	1.0	2.6	0.1	0.2	0.5	1.5	7.7	19.6
Local government[2]	33.3	30.9	5.8	5.3	3.2	3.0	0.5	0.5	1.9	1.2	21.9	20.4

[1]The incidence rates represent the number of injuries and illnesses per 100 full-time workers and were calculated as: (N/EH) x 200,000 (where N = number of injuries and illnesses; EH = total hours worked by all employees during the calendar year; 200,000 = base for 100 equivalent full-time workers working 40 hours per week, 50 weeks per year).
[2]Excludes farms with fewer than 11 employees.
[3]Data for Mining (Sector 21 in the North American Industry Classification System—United States, 2012) include establishments not governed by the Mine Safety and Health Administration rules and reporting, such as those in Oil and Gas Extraction and related support activities. Data for mining operators in coal, metal, and nonmetal mining are provided to BLS by the Mine Safety and Health Administration, U.S. Department of Labor.
[4] Data for employers in railroad transportation are provided to BLS by the Federal Railroad Administration, U.S. Department of Transportation.
[5] Data too small to be displayed.
... = Figure does not meet standards of reliability or quality.

Table 14-7. Number of Fatal Work Injuries by Employee Status, 2003–2019

(Number.)

Year	Total	Wage and salary workers	Self-employed workers
2003	5 575	4 405	1 170
2004	5 764	4 587	1 177
2005	5 734	4 592	1 142
2006	5 840	4 808	1 032
2007	5 657	4 613	1 044
2008	5 214	4 183	1 031
2009	4 551	3 488	1 063
2010	4 690	3 651	1 039
2011	4 693	3 642	1 051
2012	4 628	3 571	1 057
2013	4 585	3 535	1 050
2014	4 821	3 728	1 093
2015	4 836	3 751	1 085
2016	5 190	4 098	1 092
2017	5 147	4 069	1 078
2018	5 250	4 178	1 072
2019	5 333	4 240	1 093

Table 14-8. Fatal Occupational Injuries Counts and Rates by Selected Demographic Characteristics 2015–2019

(Number, rate.)

Characteristic	2015	2016	2017	2018	2019
TOTAL[1]	4 836	5 190	5 147	5 250	5 333
Employee Status					
Wage and salary workers[2]	3 751	4 098	4 069	4 178	4 240
Self-employed[3]	1 085	1 092	1 078	1 072	1 093
Sex					
Men	4 492	4 803	4 761	4 837	4 896
Women	344	387	386	413	437
Age					
Under 16 years	12	13	15	13	17
16 to 17 years	12	17	7	9	17
18 to 19 years	50	43	62	56	50
20 to 24 years	329	310	293	282	325
25 to 34 years	758	834	872	946	866
35 to 44 years	864	979	907	966	967
45 to 54 years	1 130	1 145	1 059	1 114	1 082
55 to 64 years	1 031	1 160	1 155	1 104	1 212
65 years and over	650	688	775	759	793
Race and Hispanic Origin					
White	3 241	3 481	3 449	3 405	3 297
Black	495	587	530	615	634
Hispanic[4]	903	879	903	961	1 088
American Indian or Alaskan Native	36	38	38	42	30
Asian	114	160	144	153	181
Native Hawaiian or Pacific Islander	9	7	17	10	14
Multiple races	12	15	9	14	22
Other or not reported	26	23	57	50	67

[1]The Census of Fatal Occupational Injuries (CFOI) has published data on fatal occupational injuries for the United States since 1992. During this time, the classification systems and definitions of many data elements have changed.
[2]May include volunteers and other workers receiving compensation.
[3]Includes self-employed workers, owners of unincorporated businesses and farms, paid and unpaid family workers, and members of partnerships; may also include owners of incorporated businesses.
[4]May be of any race. The race categories shown exclude data for Hispanics and Latinos.
[5]May be of any race.

Table 14-9. Fatal Occupational Injuries for Selected Events or Exposures, 2015–2019

(Number.)

Characteristic	2015	2016	2017	2018	2019
TOTAL	4 836	5 190	5 147	5 250	5 333
Violence and Other Injuries by Persons or Animals	703	866	807	828	841
Intentional injury by person	646	792	733	757	761
Homicides	417	500	458	453	454
Shooting by other person—intentional	354	394	351	351	363
Stabbing, cutting, slashing, piercing	28	38	47	44	42
Suicides	229	291	275	304	307
Transportation Incidents	2 054	2 083	2 077	2 080	2 122
Aircraft incidents	139	130	126	133	152
Rail vehicle incidents	50	50	48	48	47
Pedestrian vehicular incident	289	342	313	325	341
Pedestrian struck by vehicle in work zone	44	58	56	58	56
Water vehicle incident	44	48	68	58	63
Roadway incident involving motorized land vehicle	1 264	1 252	1 299	1 276	1 270
Roadway collision with other vehicle	660	628	663	677	729
Roadway collision moving in same direction	166	168	189	183	194
Roadway collision moving in opposite directions, oncoming	224	199	214	243	258
Roadway collision moving perpendicularly	154	150	149	141	153
Roadway collision with object other than vehicle	360	342	377	373	325
Vehicle struck object or animal on side of roadway	335	321	348	345	301
Roadway noncollision incident	240	278	252	222	212
Jack-knifed or overturned, roadway	201	238	197	170	164
Nonroadway incident involving motorized land vehicle	253	245	209	225	236
Nonroadway noncollision incident	182	182	166	164	193
Jack-knifed or overturned, nonroadway	131	120	111	105	128
Fire or Explosion	121	88	123	115	99
Fall, Slip, Trip	800	849	887	791	880
Fall on same level	125	134	151	154	146
Fall to lower level	648	697	713	615	711
Fall from collapsing structure or equipment	55	65	48	50	37
Fall through surface or existing opening	87	87	85	83	95
Exposure to Harmful Substances or Environments	424	518	531	621	642
Exposure to electricity	134	154	136	160	166
Exposure to temperature extremes	40	48	38	60	53
Exposure to other harmful substances	215	268	317	355	379
Inhalation of harmful substance	45	39	43	42	59
Contact with Objects and Equipment	722	761	695	786	732
Struck by object or equipment	519	553	503	566	518
Struck by powered vehicle nontransport	216	232	197	215	205
Struck by falling object or equipment	247	255	237	278	241
Struck by discharged or flying equipment	22	15	28	32	26
Caught in or compressed by equipment or objects	99	117	108	137	120
Caught in running equipment or machinery	74	103	76	106	93
Struck, caught, or crushed in collapsing structure, equipment, or material	90	82	70	73	83

Table 14-10. Fatal Occupational Injuries Counts and Rates for Selected Occupations, 2015–2019

(Number, rate.)

Occupation	2015	2016	2017	2018	2019
TOTAL[1]	4 836	5 190	5147.0	5250.0	5 333
OCCUPATION (SOC)[2]					
Management	379	377	396.0	387.0	380
Business and Financial Operations	31	27	29.0	38.0	29
Computer and Mathematical	8	16	11.0	12.0	15
Architecture and Engineering	37	41	23.0	30.0	43
Life, Physical, and Social Science	11	15	13.0	18.0	15
Community and Social Services	28	27	37.0	23.0	31
Legal	12	13	11.0	15.0	11
Education, Training, and Library	19	32	30.0	27.0	24
Arts, Design, Entertainment, Sports, and Media	65	64	47.0	71.0	40
Health Care Practitioners and Technical	74	60	57.0	65.0	56
Health Care Support	23	30	28.0	32.0	38
Protective Service	213	281	266.0	270.0	231
Fire Fighting and Prevention Workers	30	35	35.0	33.0	24
Law enforcement workers	102	127	117.0	127.0	97
Food Preparation and Serving Related	56	92	89.0	100.0	99
Building and Grounds Cleaning and Maintenance	289	329	326.0	350.0	333
Building cleaning and pest control workers	59	74	68.0	66.0	63
Grounds maintenance workers	183	217	191.0	225.0	229
Personal Care and Service	51	55	69.0	63.0	61
Sales and Related	228	254	232.0	241.0	240
Supervisors, sales workers	101	104	98.0	102.0	99
Retail sales workers	82	102	89.0	99.0	96
Office and Administrative Support	86	78	101.0	69.0	92
Farming, Fishing, and Forestry	284	290	264.0	262.0	291
Agricultural workers	180	157	155.0	158.0	183
Fishing and hunting workers	25	26	41.0	31.0	44
Forest, conservation, and logging workers	69	95	57.0	57.0	49
Construction and Extraction	924	970	965.0	1003.0	1 066
Supervisors, construction and extraction workers	123	134	121.0	144.0	136
Construction trades workers	694	736	747.0	731.0	809
Extraction workers	45	41	41.0	64.0	50
Installation, Maintenance, and Repair	392	470	414.0	420.0	438
Vehicle and mobile equipment mechanics, installers, and repairers	129	154	143.0	152.0	155
Production	250	216	221.0	225.0	245
Transportation and Material Moving	1 301	1 388	1443.0	1443.0	1 481
Air transportation workers	57	75	59.0	71.0	85
Motor vehicle operators	978	1 012	1084.0	1044.0	1 091
Material moving	206	228	235.0	255.0	238
Military	73	62	72.0	82.0	65

Note: Data for all years are final. Totals for major categories may include subcategories not shown separately.

[1]The Census of Fatal Occupational Injuries (CFOI) has published data on fatal occupational injuries for the United States since 1992. During this time, the classification systems and definitions of many data elements have changed.
[2]CFOI has used several versions of the Standard Occupation Classification (SOC) system since 2003 to define occupation.

Table 14-11. Fatal Occupational Counts and Rates by Selected Industries, 2015–2019

(Number, rate.)

Occupation	2015	2016	2017	2018	2019
TOTAL	4 836	5 190	5 147.0	5 250.0	5 333.0
NAICS INDUSTRY					
Private Industry	4 379	4 693	4 674.0	4 779.0	4 907.0
Goods-Producing	1 980	1 991	1 967.0	2 055.0	...
Agriculture, Forestry, Fishing and Hunting	570	593	581.0	574.0	573.0
Crop production	230	261	263.0	250.0	221.0
Animal production and aquaculture	171	151	152.0	161.0	189.0
Forestry and logging	81	106	76.0	84.0	59.0
Mining, Quarrying, and Oil and Gas Extraction	120	89	112.0	130.0	127.0
Mining (except oil and gas)	28	22	31.0	34.0	23.0
Support activities for mining	86	56	73.0	83.0	82.0
Construction	937	991	971.0	1 008.0	1 061.0
Construction of buildings	175	182	196.0	200.0	...
Heavy and civil engineering construction	148	159	152.0	180.0	156.0
Specialty trade contractors	595	631	610.0	609.0	...
Manufacturing	353	318	303.0	343.0	...
Food manufacturing	44	40	51.0	41.0	...
Fabricated metal product manufacturing	66	41	50.0	56.0	...
Service-Providing	2 399	2 702	2 707.0	2 724.0	...
Wholesale Trade	175	179	174.0	202.0	178.0
Retail Trade	269	282	287.0	274.0	291.0
Motor vehicle and parts dealers	62	42	54.0	68.0	58.0
Food and beverage stores	58	71	60.0	42.0	54.0
Transportation and Warehousing	765	825	882.0	874.0	913.0
Truck transportation	546	570	599.0	607.0	617.0
Utilities	22	30	28.0	29.0	22.0
Information	42	46	43.0	31.0	...
Finance and Insurance	19	26	32.0	30.0	21.0
Real Estate and Rental and Leasing	64	91	69.0	78.0	87.0
Professional, Scientific, and Technical Services	76	100	69.0	87.0	86.0
Administrative and Support and Waste Management and Remediation Services	401	439	460.0	497.0	498.0
Educational Services	30	42	43.0	30.0	45.0
Health Care and Social Assistance	109	117	146.0	138.0	152.0
Arts, Entertainment, and Recreation	82	96	91.0	78.0	83.0
Accommodation and Food Services	143	202	171.0	175.0	188.0
Other Services, Except Public Administration	202	223	205.0	195.0	210.0
Government	457	497	473.0	471.0	426.0
Federal Government	118	107	116.0	124.0	111.0
State Government	81	97	91.0	69.0	75.0
Local Government	257	291	265.0	276.0	240.0

... = Data not available.

Table 14-12. Fatal Occupational Injury Counts and Rates by State of Incident, 2015–2019

(Number, rate.)

State	2015	2016	2017	2018	2019
Total[1]	4 836	5 190	5147.0	5250.0	5 333
Alabama	70	100	83.0	89.0	89
Alaska	14	35	33.0	32.0	51
Arizona	69	77	90.0	82.0	94
Arkansas	74	68	76.0	76.0	62
California	388	376	376.0	422.0	451
Colorado	75	81	77.0	72.0	84
Connecticut	44	28	35.0	48.0	26
Delaware	8	12	10.0	7.0	18
District of Columbia	8	5	13.0	10.0	10
Florida	272	309	299.0	332.0	306
Georgia	180	171	194.0	186.0	207
Hawaii	18	29	20.0	22.0	26
Idaho	36	30	37.0	45.0	36
Illinois	172	171	163.0	184.0	158
Indiana	115	137	138.0	173.0	146
Iowa	60	76	72.0	77.0	76
Kansas	60	74	72.0	61.0	83
Kentucky	99	92	70.0	83.0	78
Louisiana	112	95	117.0	98.0	119
Maine	15	18	18.0	17.0	20
Maryland	69	92	87.0	97.0	78
Massachusetts	69	109	108.0	97.0	86
Michigan	134	162	153.0	155.0	164
Minnesota	74	92	101.0	75.0	80
Mississippi	77	71	90.0	78.0	59
Missouri	117	124	125.0	145.0	106
Montana	36	38	32.0	28.0	38
Nebraska	50	60	35.0	44.0	53
Nevada	44	54	32.0	39.0	40
New Hampshire	18	22	11.0	20.0	11
New Jersey	97	101	69.0	83.0	74
New Mexico	35	41	44.0	43.0	55
New York (including NYC)	236	272	313.0	271.0	273
New York City	74	56	87.0	73.0	91
North Carolina	150	174	183.0	178.0	186
North Dakota	47	28	38.0	35.0	37
Ohio	202	164	174.0	158.0	166
Oklahoma	91	92	91.0	91.0	73
Oregon	44	72	60.0	62.0	69
Pennsylvania	173	163	172.0	177.0	154
Rhode Island	6	9	8.0	9.0	10
South Carolina	117	96	88.0	98.0	108
South Dakota	21	31	30.0	32.0	20
Tennessee	112	122	128.0	122.0	124
Texas	527	545	534.0	488.0	608
Utah	42	44	43.0	49.0	51
Vermont	9	10	22.0	11.0	10
Virginia	106	153	118.0	157.0	180
Washington	70	78	84.0	86.0	84
West Virginia	35	47	51.0	57.0	46
Wisconsin	104	105	106.0	114.0	113
Wyoming	34	34	20.0	31.0	32

[1]The Census of Fatal Occupational Injuries (CFOI) has published data on fatal occupational injuries for the United States since 1992. During this time, the classification systems and definitions of many data elements have changed..

INDEX